HISTORY OF THE CHRISTIAN CHURCH

This volume constitutes the second part of

THE HISTORY OF THE REFORMATION

by Philip Schaff

It is included as Volume VIII in the 8-volume

HISTORY OF THE CHRISTIAN CHURCH

Volume VII in this series, on the German
Reformation, constitutes the first part of
this 2-volume unit on The History of the
Reformation

HISTORY

OF

THE CHRISTIAN CHURCH

BY

PHILIP SCHAFF

PROFESSOR OF CHURCH HISTORY IN THE UNION THEOLOGICAL SEMINARY
NEW YORK

𝔒𝔥𝔯𝔦𝔰𝔱𝔦𝔞𝔫𝔲𝔰 𝔰𝔲𝔪 : 𝔒𝔥𝔯𝔦𝔰𝔱𝔦𝔞𝔫𝔦 𝔫𝔦𝔥𝔦𝔩 𝔞 𝔪𝔢 𝔞𝔩𝔦𝔢𝔫𝔲𝔪 𝔭𝔲𝔱𝔬

Volume VIII

MODERN CHRISTIANITY

THE SWISS REFORMATION

WM. B. EERDMANS PUBLISHING COMPANY

GRAND RAPIDS   MICHIGAN

This is a reproduction of the Third Edition, Revised

PHOTOLITHOPRINTED BY EERDMANS PRINTING COMPANY
GRAND RAPIDS, MICHIGAN, UNITED STATES OF AMERICA

PREFACE

THIS volume concludes the history of the productive period of the Reformation, in which Luther, Zwingli, and Calvin were the chief actors. It follows the Protestant movement in German, Italian, and French Switzerland, to the close of the sixteenth century. During the last year, the sixth centenary of the oldest surviving Republic was celebrated with great patriotic enthusiasm. On the first day of August, in the year 1291, the freemen of Uri, Schwyz, and Unterwalden formed "in the name of the Lord" a perpetual alliance for the mutual protection of their persons, property, and liberty, against internal and external foes. On the same day, in 1891, the great event was commemorated in every village of Switzerland by the ringing of bells and the illumination of the mountains, while on the following day — a Sunday — thanksgiving services were held in every church, Catholic and Protestant. The chief festivities took place, from July 31 to Aug. 2, in the towns of Schwyz and Brunnen, and were attended by the Federal and Cantonal dignitaries, civil and military, and a vast assembly of spectators. The most interesting feature was a dramatic representation of the leading events in Swiss history — the sacred oaths of Schwyz, Brunnen, and Grütli, the poetic legend of William Tell, the heroic battles for liberty and independence against Austria, Burgundy, and France, the venerable figure of Nicolas von der Flue appearing as a peacemaker in the Diet at Stans, and the chief scenes of the Reformation, the Revolution, and the modern reconstruction. The drama, enacted in the open field in view of mountains and meadows and the lake of Luzern, is said to have equalled in interest and skill of execution the famous Passion Play of Oberammergau. Similar celebrations took place, not only in every city and village of Switzerland, but also in the Swiss colonies in foreign lands, notably in New York, on the 5th, 6th, and 7th of September.[1]

---

[1] The celebration has elicited some valuable contributions to the authentic history of Switzerland, which may be added to the literature on p. 3. I mention Dr. W. OECHSLI: *Die Anfänge der schweizerischen Eidgenossenschaft.* Zürich, 1891. — JOS. IG. VON AH: *Die Bundesbriefe der alten Eidgenossen von 1291 bis 1513.* Einsiedeln, 1891. — PIERRE VAUCHER: *Les Commencements de la Confédération suisse.* Lausanne, 1891. — Prof. GEORG VON WYSS: *Rede bei der Bundesfeier der Eidgenössischen polytechn. Schule, und der Hochschule Zürich am 25 Juli 1891.* Zürich, 1891. — *Denkschrift der historischen u. antiquarischen Gesellschaft zu Basel. Zur Erinnerung an den Bund der Eidgenossen vom 1. Aug. 1291.* Basel, 1891. — The second volume of DIERAUER'S *Geschichte der Schweizerischen Eidgenossenschaft* appeared at Gotha, 1892, but goes only to the year 1516, when the history of the Reformation began.

Between Switzerland and the United States there has always been a natural sympathy and friendship. Both aim to realize the idea of a government of freedom without license, and of authority without despotism; a government of law and order without a standing army; a government of the people, by the people, and for the people, under the sole headship of Almighty God.

At the time of the Reformation, Switzerland numbered as many Cantons (13) as our country originally numbered States, and the Swiss Diet was then a loose confederation representing only the Cantons and not the people, just as was our Continental Congress. But by the revision of the Constitution in 1848 and 1874, the Swiss Republic, following the example of our Constitution, was consolidated from a loose, aristocratic Confederacy of independent Cantons into a centralized federal State,[1] with a popular as well as a cantonal representation. In one respect the modern Swiss Constitution is even more democratic than that of the United States; for, by the *Initiative* and the *Referendum*, it gives to the people the right of proposing or rejecting national legislation.

But there is a still stronger bond of union between the two countries than that which rests on the affinity of political institutions. Zwingli and Calvin directed and determined the westward movement of the Reformation to France, Holland, England, and Scotland, and exerted, indirectly, a moulding influence upon the leading Evangelical Churches of America. George Bancroft, the American historian, who himself was not a Calvinist, derives the republican institutions of the United States from Calvinism through the medium of English Puritanism. A more recent writer, Douglas Campbell, of Scotch descent, derives them from Holland, which was still more under the influence of the Geneva Reformer than England. Calvinism breeds manly, independent, and earnest characters who fear God and nothing else, and favors political and religious freedom. The earliest and most influential settlers of the United States — the Puritans of England, the Presbyterians of Scotland and Ireland, the Huguenots of France, the Reformed from Holland and the Palatinate, — were Calvinists, and brought with them the Bible and the Reformed Confessions of Faith. Calvinism was the ruling theology of New England during the whole Colonial Period, and it still rules in great measure the theology of the Presbyterian, Congregational, and Baptist Churches.

In the study of the sources I have derived much benefit from the libraries of Switzerland, especially the *Stadtbibliothek* of Zürich, which contains the invaluable Simler collection and every important work relating to the Reformation in Switzerland. I take great pleasure in expressing my obligation to Dr. G. von Wyss, president, and Dr. Escher, librarian, for their courtesy and kindness on repeated visits to that library.

The sources on the Reformation in French Switzerland are now made fully accessible by the new critical edition of Calvin's works, by Herminjard's collection of the correspondence of the French-speaking Reformers (not yet completed), and by the publications of the documentary history of Geneva during the period of Calvin's labors, including the registers of the Council and of the Consistory.

---

[1] A *Bundesstaat*, as distinct from a *Staatenbund*.

I have freely quoted from Calvin's works and letters, which give us the best insight into his mind and heart. I have consulted also his chief biographers, — French, German, and English: his enthusiastic admirers, — Beza, Henry, Stähelin, Bungener, and Merle D'Aubigné; his virulent detractors, — Bolsec, Galiffe, and Audin; and his impartial critics, — Dyer, and Kampschulte. Dr. Henry's work (1844) was the first adequate biography of the great Reformer, and is still unsurpassed as a rich collection of authentic materials, although not well arranged and digested.[1] Dr. Merle D'Aubigné's "History of the Reformation" comes down only to 1542. Thomas H. Dyer, LL.D., the author of the "History of Modern Europe," from the fall of Constantinople to 1871, and other historical works, has written the first able and readable "Life of Calvin" in the English language, which is drawn chiefly from Calvin's correspondence, from Ruchat, Henry, and, in the Servetus chapter, from Mosheim and Trechsel, and is, on the whole, accurate and fair, but cold and unsympathetic. The admirable work of Professor Kampschulte is based on a thorough mastery of the sources, but it is unfortunately incomplete, and goes only as far as 1542. The materials for a second and third volume were placed after his death (December, 1872) into the hands of Professor Cornelius of Munich, who, however, has so far only written a few sections. His admiration for Calvin's genius and pure character (see p. 205) presents an interesting parallel to Döllinger's eloquent tribute to Luther (quoted in vol. VI. 741), and is all the more valuable as he dissented from Calvin's theology and church polity; for he was an Old Catholic and intimate friend of Reusch and Döllinger.[2]

The sole aim of the historian ought to be the truth, the whole truth, and nothing but the truth.

I have dedicated this volume to my countrymen and oldest surviving friends in Switzerland, Dr. GEORG VON WYSS of Zürich and Dr. FRÉDÉRIC GODET of Neuchâtel. The one represents German, the other French Switzerland. Both are well known; the one for his historical, the other for his exegetical works. They have followed the preparation of this book with sympathetic interest, and done me the favor of revising the proof-sheets.[3]

---

[1] The first and second volumes of Dr. Henry's larger biography are sometimes quoted from the English translation of Dr. Stebbing; but the third volume always from the original, as Dr. Stebbing omits the appendices and nearly all the original documents.

[2] Professor Reusch of Bonn kindly informed me by letter (Sept. 8, 1891) that Kampschulte first studied for the priesthood and was an orthodox and pious Catholic, but opposed the Vatican decree of papal infallibility in 1870, and may therefore be considered as having been virtually excommunicated. He administered to him the last sacrament (which the ultramontane priest was prohibited from doing by the Archbishop of Cologne). The first volume of Kampschulte's work was fully and favorably reviewed in Reusch's *Literaturblatt* for 1869, No. 662, by Dr. Hefele of Tübingen, shortly before he became bishop of Rottenburg. Hefele, as a member of the Vatican council, was one of the most learned opponents of papal infallibility, but afterwards submitted for the sake of peace. A biographical notice of Kampschulte by Cornelius is to be found in the fifteenth volume of the *Allgemeine Deutsche Biographie.*

[3] I take the liberty of quoting a few passages from recent letters of these Swiss scholars which will interest the reader. Dr. von Wyss writes: "*Ihr Vaterland in Amerika und die englische Sprache geben dem Werke ein Gepräge, welches dasselbe von deutschen ähnlichen*

I feel much encouraged by the kind reception of my Church History at home and abroad. The first three volumes have been freely translated into Chinese by the Rev. D. Z. Sheffield (a missionary of the American Board), and into Hindostani by the Rev. Robert Stewart (of the Presbyterian Mission of Sialkot).

I have made considerable progress in the fifth volume, which will complete the history of the Middle Ages. It was delayed till I could make another visit to Rome and Florence, and study more fully the *Renaissance*, which preceded the Reformation. Two or three more volumes will be necessary to bring the history down to the present time, according to the original plan. But how many works remain unfinished in this world! *Ars longa, vita brevis.*

JUNE, 1892.

POSTSCRIPT.

The above Preface was ready for the printer, and the book nearly finished, when, on the 15th of July last, I was suddenly interrupted by a stroke of paralysis at Lake Mohonk (where I spent the summer); but, in the good providence of God, my health has been nearly restored. My experience is recorded in the 103d Psalm of thanksgiving and praise.

I regret that I could not elaborate chs. XVII. and XVIII., especially the influence of Calvin upon the Reformed Churches of Europe and America (§§ 162 and 163), as fully as I wished. My friend, the Rev. Samuel Macauley Jackson, who happened to be with me when I was taken sick, aided me in

Schriften eindrücklich unterscheidet — es liegt ein so unmittelbares Auffassen und Erfassen der Hauptsache, auf die es ankömmt, ein so bestimmtes Losgehen auf das Leben, das Praktische, darin — dass mich dieser charakteristische Zug Ihrer gewaltigen Arbeit ungemein anzieht. Wie verschieden sind doch die Anlagen und die Bedürfnisse der Völker! Wer wollte deutsches, französisches, englisches, amerikanisches Blut und Wesen (ich nenne sie nach der historischen Reihenfolge) zusammenschmelzen können! Ueberall ein eigenthümlicher Zug! Jeder werthvoll und lieb, wenn er nicht übertrieben wird! Wer soll die Einheit bilden? Darüber sind wir, mein hochverehrter Freund (ich bin glücklich, so sagen zu dürfen), einig. Aber was wird es einst sein, wenn wir diese Einigung in ihrer vollen Verwirklichung, über dieser Erde, erblicken werden!" — "Ich lese die Probebogen allezeit mit dem grössten Vergnügen. Die Klarheit, Bestimmtheit und Genauigkeit Ihrer Darstellung (bis in's Einzelnste) und der Geist von dem sie getragen ist, gewähren mir die grösste Befriedigung. . . . Was Zwingli in seiner Expositio Fidei an König Franz I. über die Welt jenseits des Grabes sagt, ist mir von allen seinen Aeusserungen stets das Liebste, und in nichts fühle ich mich ihm mehr verwandt als gerade darin, — sowie in der Liebe, die ihn zu Bullinger zog." —Dr. Godet (Dec. 3, 1891): *"Du scheinst zu fürchten, dass die Druckbogen mir eine Last seien. Im Gegentheil, sie sind mir eine Freude und Belehrung gewesen. Ich habe nie etwas so Befriedigendes über den Gegenstand gelesen. Calvin tritt hervor mit seinem wahren Gesicht und in seiner hehren Gestalt. Ich danke Dir herzlich für diese Mittheilung."* The same, in a more recent letter: . . . *"Qu'il nous soit donné à tous deux avant de quitter cette vie de pouvoir terminer nos travaux commencés, — toi, ton Histoire . . . moi, mon Introduction au Nouveau Testament. . . . Le premier volume, les épitres de Paul, sera, j'espère, terminé et imprimé avec la fin de l'année (1892) si . . ."* The venerable author is now in his eightieth year.

the last chapter, on Beza, for which he was well prepared by previous studies. I had at first intended to add a history of the French Reformation, but this would make the volume too large and delay the publication. I have added, however, in an appendix, a list of literature which I prepared some time ago in the Library of the Society of the History of French Protestantism at Paris, and brought down to date. Most of the books are in my possession.

I may congratulate myself that, notwithstanding this serious interruption, I am enabled to publish the history of the Reformation of my native land before the close of the fiftieth anniversary of my academic teaching, which I began in December, 1842, in the University of Berlin, when my beloved teacher, Neander, was in the prime of his usefulness. A year afterwards, I received, at his and Tholuck's recommendation, a call to a theological professorship from the Synod of the German Reformed Church in the United States, and I have never regretted accepting it. For it is a great privilege to labor, however humbly, for the kingdom of Christ in America, which celebrates in this month, with the whole civilized world, the fourth centennial of its discovery.

Thankful for the past, I look hopefully to the future.

PHILIP SCHAFF.

Union Theological Seminary,
New York, October 12, 1892.

PREFACE TO THE SECOND EDITION.

The first edition (of 1500 copies) being exhausted, I have examined the volume and corrected a number of typographical errors, mostly in the French words of the last chapters. There was no occasion for other improvements.

P. S.

August 9, 1893.

CONTENTS

HISTORY OF THE REFORMATION

SECOND BOOK

THE SWISS REFORMATION

CHAPTER I.

INTRODUCTION.

CHAPTER II.

ZWINGLI'S TRAINING. A.D. 1484–1519.

CHAPTER III.

THE REFORMATION IN ZÜRICH. 1519–1526.

CHAPTER IV.

SPREAD OF THE REFORMATION IN GERMAN SWITZERLAND AND THE GRISONS.

CHAPTER V.

THE CIVIL AND RELIGIOUS WAR BETWEEN THE ROMAN CATHOLIC AND REFORMED CANTONS.

CHAPTER VI.

THE PERIOD OF CONSOLIDATION.

THIRD BOOK.

THE REFORMATION IN FRENCH SWITZERLAND, OR THE CALVINISTIC MOVEMENT.

CHAPTER VII.

THE PREPARATORY WORK. FROM 1526 TO 1536.

CHAPTER VIII.

JOHN CALVIN AND HIS WORK. FROM 1536 TO 1564.

CHAPTER IX.

FROM FRANCE TO SWITZERLAND. 1509–1536.

CHAPTER X.

CALVIN'S FIRST SOJOURN AND LABORS IN GENEVA. 1536–1538.

CHAPTER XI.

CALVIN IN GERMANY. FROM 1538 TO 1541.

CHAPTER XII.

CALVIN'S SECOND SOJOURN AND LABORS AT GENEVA. 1541–1564.

xvi   CONTENTS.

CHAPTER XVIII.

CLOSING SCENES IN THE LIFE OF CALVIN.

CHAPTER XIX.

THEODORE BEZA.

APPENDIX.

ILLUSTRATIONS

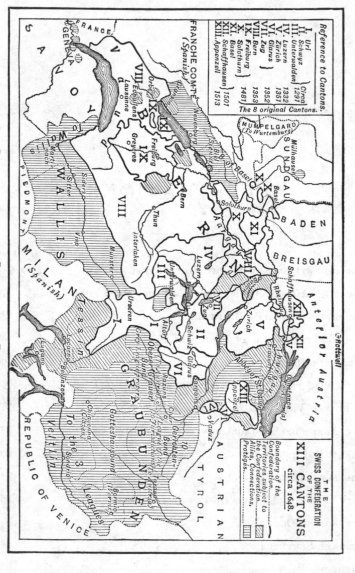

SWITZERLAND IN THE PERIOD OF THE REFORMATION.

Reference to Cantons.

I. Uri
II. Schwyz   } 1291
III. Unterwalden

IV. Luzern   1332
V. Zürich   1351
VI. Glarus   1352
VII. Zug   1352
VIII. Bern   1353
IX. Freiburg   } 1481
X. Solothurn

XI. Basel   1501
XII. Schaffhausen 1501
XIII. Appenzell   1513

The 8 original Cantons.

THE
SWISS CONFEDERATION
OF THE
XIII CANTONS
circa 1648.

Boundary of the
Confederation. ——
Territories subject to
the Confederation. ——
Allies, Connections. ——
Proteges. ——

HISTORY

OF

THE REFORMATION

SECOND BOOK.

THE SWISS REFORMATION.

CHAPTER I.

INTRODUCTION.

§ 1. *Switzerland before the Reformation.*

SWITZERLAND belongs to those countries whose historic significance stands in inverse proportion to their size. God often elects small things for great purposes. Palestine gave to the world the Christian religion. From little Greece proceeded philosophy and art. Switzerland is the cradle of the Reformed churches. The land of the snow-capped Alps is the source of mighty rivers, and of the Reformed faith, as Germany is the home of the Lutheran faith; and the principles of the Swiss Reformation, like the waters of the Rhine and the Rhone, travelled westward with the course of the sun to France, Holland, England, Scotland, and to a new continent, which Zwingli and Calvin knew only by name. Compared with intellectual and moral achievements, the conquests of the sword dwindle into insignificance. Ideas rule the world; ideas are immortal.

Before the sixteenth century, Switzerland exerted no influence in the affairs of Europe except by the bravery of its inhabitants in self-defence of their liberty and in foreign wars. But in the sixteenth century she stands next to Germany in that great religious renovation which has affected all modern history.[1]

The Republic of Switzerland, which has maintained itself in the midst of monarchies down to this day, was founded by "the eternal covenant" of the three "forest cantons," Uri, Schwyz, and Unterwalden, August 1, 1291, and grew from time to time by conquest, purchase, and free association. Lucerne (the fourth forest canton) joined the confederacy in 1332, Zurich in 1351, Glarus and Zug in 1352, Berne in 1353, Freiburg and Solothurn (Soleur) in 1481, Basle and Schaffhausen in 1501, Appenzell in 1513, — making in all thirteen cantons at the time of the Reformation. With them were connected by purchase, or conquest, or free consent, as common territories or free bailiwicks,[2] the adjoining lands of Aargau, Thurgau, Wallis, Geneva, Graubündten (Grisons, Rhätia), the princedom of Neuchatel and Valangin, and several cities (Biel, Mühlhausen, Rotweil, Locarno, etc.). Since 1798 the number of cantons has increased to twenty-two, with a population of nearly three millions (in 1890). The Republic of the United States started with thirteen States, and has grown likewise by purchase or conquest and the organization and incorporation of new territories, but more rapidly, and on a much larger scale.

The romantic story of William Tell, so charmingly told by Ægidius Tschudi, the Swiss Herodotus,[3] and by Johannes

---

[1] "The affairs of Switzerland," says Hallam (*Middle Ages*, II. 108, Am. ed.), "occupy a very small space in the great chart of European history; but in some respects they are more interesting than the revolutions of mighty kingdoms. Nowhere besides do we find so many titles to our sympathy, or the union of so much virtue with so complete success. . . . Other nations displayed an insuperable resolution in the defence of walled towns; but the steadiness of the Swiss in the field of battle was without a parallel, unless we recall the memory of Lacedæmon."

[2] They were called *gemeine Herrschaften* or *Vogteien* and *zugewandte Orte*.

[3] Or the father of Swiss historiography, as he is also called. His *Chronicon Helveticum* or *Eidgenössische Chronik* (1000–1470) was first edited by Professor

von Müller, the Swiss Tacitus, and embellished by the poetic genius of Friedrich Schiller, must be abandoned to the realm of popular fiction, like the cognate stories of Scandinavian and German mythology, but contains, nevertheless, an abiding element of truth as setting forth the spirit of those bold mountaineers who loved liberty and independence more than their lives, and expelled the foreign invaders from their soil. The glory of an individual belongs to the Swiss people. The sacred oath of the men of Grütli on the Lake of Lucerne, at the foot of Seelisberg (1306 or 1308?), and the more certain confederation of Dec. 9, 1315, at Brunnen, were renewals of the previous covenant of 1291.[1]

The Swiss successfully vindicated their independence against the attacks of the House of Habsburg in the memorable battles of Morgarten ("the Marathon of Switzerland," 1315), Sempach (1386), and Näfels (1388), against King Louis XI. of France at St. Jacob near Basle (the Thermopylæ of Switzerland, 1444), and against Duke Charles the Bold of Burgundy at Granson, Murten (Morat), and Nancy (1476 and 1477).

Nature and history made Switzerland a federative republic.

Iselin, Basle, 1734 and '36, in 2 vols. Ægidius Tschudi of Glarus (1505–1572) derived the Tell legend from the *Weisse Buch* of Sarnen, and Etterlin of Lucerne, and adorned it with his fancy and masterly power of narration. He was a pupil of Zwingli, but remained in the old church. In a letter to Zwingli, February, 1517, he says, *"Non cum aliquo docto libentius esse velim, quam tecum."* Zw., *Opera*, VII. 21. The MS. of his *Chronik* is preserved in the city library of Zürich. It is carefully described, with a facsimile in the *Neujahrsblatt* of the *Stadtbibliothek in Zürich auf das Jahr 1889* (Zürich, Orell Füssli & Co.).

[1] On the origin of the Swiss Confederation and the Tell and Grütli legends, see the critical researches of Kopp, *Urkunden zur Geschichte der eidgenössischen Bünde*, Luzern, 1835, and Wien, 1851, 2 vols. Hisely, *Recherches critiques sur Guillaume Tell*, Lausanne, 1843. Kopp, *Zur Tell-Sage*, Luzern, 1854 and '56. Karl Hagen, *Die Politik der Kaiser Rudolf von Habsburg und Albrecht I. und die Entstehung der schweizerischen Eidgenossenschaft*, Bern, 1857. G. von Wyss, *Die Gesch. der drei Länder Uri, Schwyz und Unterwalden, 1212–1315*, Zürich, 1858; *Zürich am Ausgange des dreizehnten Jahrh.*, Zürich, 1876. A. Rilliet, *Les origines de la confédération suisse, histoire et légende*, 2d ed., Genève, 1869. Dierauer, *Gesch. der Schweiz. Eidgenossenschaft*, Gotha, 1887, vol. I. 81–151.

This republic was originally a loose, aristocratic confederacy of independent cantons, ruled by a diet of one house where each canton had the same number of deputies and votes, so that a majority of the Diet could defeat a majority of the people. This state of things continued till 1848, when (after the defeat of the *Sonderbund* of the Roman Catholic cantons) the constitution was remodelled on democratic principles, after the American example, and the legislative power vested in two houses, one (the *Ständerath* or Senate) consisting of forty-four deputies of the twenty-two sovereign cantons (as in the old Diet), the other (the *Nationalrath* or House of Representatives) representing the people in proportion to their number (one to every twenty thousand souls); while the executive power was given to a council of seven members (the *Bundesrath*) elected for three years by both branches of the legislature. Thus the confederacy of cantons was changed into a federal state, with a central government elected by the people and acting directly on the people.[1]

This difference in the constitution of the central authority must be kept in mind in order to understand why the Reformation triumphed in the most populous cantons, and yet was defeated in the Diet.[2] The small forest cantons had each as many votes as the much larger cantons of Zurich and Berne, and kept out Protestantism from their borders till the year 1848. The loose character of the German Diet and the absence of centralization account in like manner for the victory of Protestantism in Saxony, Hesse, and other states

---

[1] The *Staatenbund* became a *Bundesstaat*. The same difference exists between the American Confederacy during the Revolutionary War and the United States after the war, as also between the old German *Bund* and the new German *Empire*.

[2] The numerical strength of Protestantism at the death of Zwingli was probably not far from two-thirds of the population. The relation of the two confessions has undergone no material change in Switzerland. In 1888 the Protestants numbered 1,724,257; the Roman Catholics, 1,190,008; the Jews, 8,386.

and imperial cities, notwithstanding the hostile resolutions of the majority of the Diet, which again and again demanded the execution of the Edict of Worms.

The Christianization of Switzerland began in the fourth or third century under the Roman rule, and proceeded from France and Italy. Geneva, on the border of France and Savoy, is the seat of the oldest church and bishopric founded by two bishops of Vienne in Southern Gaul. The bishopric of Coire, in the south-eastern extremity, appears first in the acts of a Synod of Milan, 452. The northern and interior sections were Christianized in the seventh century by Irish missionaries, Columban and Gallus. The last founded the abbey of St. Gall, which became a famous centre of civilization for Alamannia. The first, and for a long time the only, university of Switzerland was that of Basle (1460), where one of the three reformatory councils was held (1430). During the Middle Ages the whole country, like the rest of Europe, was subject to the Roman see, and no religion was tolerated but the Roman Catholic. It was divided into six episcopal dioceses, — Geneva, Coire, Constance, Basle, Lausanne, and Sion (Sitten). The Pope had several legates in Switzerland who acted as political and military agents, and treated the little republic like a great power. The most influential bishop, Schinner of Sion, who did substantial service to the warlike Julius II. and Leo X., attained even a cardinal's hat. Zwingli, who knew him well, might have acquired the same dignity if he had followed his example.

§ 2. *The Swiss Reformation.*

The Church in Switzerland was corrupt and as much in need of reform as in Germany. The inhabitants of the old cantons around the Lake of Lucerne were, and are to this day, among the most honest and pious Catholics; but the clergy were ignorant, superstitious, and immoral, and set a bad example to the laity. The convents were in a state of decay, and could not furnish a single champion able to cope with the Reformers in learning and moral influence. Celibacy made concubinage a common and pardonable offence. The bishop of Constance (Hugo von Hohenlandenberg) absolved guilty priests on the payment of a fine of four guilders for every child born to them, and is said to have derived from this source seventy-five hundred guilders in a single year (1522). In a pastoral letter, shortly before the Reformation, he complained of the immorality of many priests who openly kept concubines or bad women in their houses, who refuse to dismiss them, or bring them back secretly, who gamble, sit with laymen in taverns, drink to excess, and utter blasphemies.[1]

The people were corrupted by the foreign military service (called *Reislaufen*), which perpetuated the fame of the Swiss for bravery and faithfulness, but at the expense of independence and good morals.[2] Kings and popes vied with each other in tempting offers to secure Swiss soldiers, who often fought against each other on foreign battle-fields, and returned with rich pensions and dissolute habits. Zwingli knew this evil from personal experience as chaplain in the Italian campaigns, attacked it before he thought of reforming the Church, continued to oppose it when called to Zurich, and found his death at the hands of a foreign mercenary.

On the other hand, there were some hopeful signs of progress. The reformatory councils of Constance and Basle were not yet entirely forgotten among the educated classes. The revival of letters stimulated freedom of thought, and opened the eyes to abuses. The University of Basle became

---

[1] Schuler, *Huldreich Zwingli*, p. 196 ; Mörikofer, *Ulrich Zwingli*, vol. I. 67. Zwingli was reported to have said, that of a thousand priests and monks, scarcely one was chaste. Egli, *Actensammlung*, p. 62.

[2] *Reislaufen* means running to war (from *Reis = Kriegszug, war*). The heroic devotion of Swiss soldiers in defence of foreign masters is immortalized by the Thorwaldsen statue of the wounded lion in Luzern.

a centre of literary activity and illuminating influences. There Thomas Wyttenbach of Biel taught theology between 1505 and 1508, and attacked indulgences, the mass, and the celibacy of the priesthood. He, with seven other priests, married in 1524, and was deposed as preacher, but not excommunicated. He combined several high offices, but died in great poverty, 1526. Zwingli attended his lectures in 1505, and learned much from him. In Basle, Erasmus, the great luminary of liberal learning, spent several of the most active years of his life (1514–1516 and 1521–1529), and published, through the press of his friend Frobenius, most of his books, including his editions of the Greek Testament. In Basle several works of Luther were reprinted, to be scattered through Switzerland. Capito, Hedio, Pellican, and Œcolampadius likewise studied, taught, and preached in that city.

But the Reformation proceeded from Zurich, not from Basle, and was guided by Zwingli, who combined the humanistic culture of Erasmus with the ability of a popular preacher and the practical energy of an ecclesiastical reformer.

The Swiss Reformation may be divided into three acts and periods, —

I. The Zwinglian Reformation in the German cantons from 1516 to Zwingli's death and the peace of Cappel, 1531.

II. The Calvinistic Reformation in French Switzerland from 1531 to the death of Calvin, 1564.

III. The labors of Bullinger in Zurich (d. 1575), and Beza in Geneva (d. 1605) for the consolidation of the work of their older friends and predecessors.

The Zwinglian movement was nearly simultaneous with the German Reformation, and came to an agreement with it at Marburg in fourteen out of fifteen articles of faith, the only serious difference being the mode of Christ's presence in the eucharist. Although Zwingli died in the prime of life, he already set forth most of the characteristic features of the Reformed Churches, at least in rough outline.

But Calvin is the great theologian, organizer, and disciplinarian of the Reformed Church. He brought it nearer the Lutheran Church in the doctrine of the Lord's Supper, but he widened the breach in the doctrine of predestination.

Zwingli and Bullinger connect the Swiss Reformation with that of Germany, Hungary, and Bohemia; Calvin and Beza, with that of France, Holland, England, and Scotland.

§ 3. *The Genius of the Swiss Reformation compared with the German.*

On the difference between the Lutheran and the Reformed Confessions see GÖBEL, HUNDESHAGEN, SCHNEKENBURGER, SCHWEIZER, etc., quoted in SCHAFF, *Creeds of Christendom,* vol. I. 211.

Protestantism gives larger scope to individual and national freedom and variety of development than Romanism, which demands uniformity in doctrine, discipline, and worship. It has no visible centre or headship, and consists of a number of separate and independent organizations under the invisible headship of Christ. It is one flock, but in many folds. Variety in unity and unity in variety are the law of God in nature and history. Protestantism so far has fully developed variety, but not yet realized unity.

The two original branches of evangelical Christendom are the Lutheran and the Reformed Confessions. They are as much alike and as much distinct as the Greek and the Roman branches of Catholicism, which rest on the national bases of philosophical Greece and political Rome. They are equally evangelical, and admit of an organic union, which has actually been effected in Prussia and other parts of Germany since the third anniversary of the Reformation in 1817. Their differences are theological rather than religious; they affect the intellectual conception, but not the heart and soul of piety. The only serious doctrinal difference which divided Luther and Zwingli at Marburg was the mode of the real presence in the eucharist; as the double procession of the

Holy Spirit was for centuries the only doctrinal difference between the Greek and Roman Churches. But other differences of government, discipline, worship, and practice developed themselves in the course of time, and overshadowed the theological lines of separation.

The Lutheran family embraces the churches which bear the name of Luther and accept the Augsburg Confession; the Reformed family (using the term *Reformed* in its historic and general sense) comprehends the churches which trace their origin directly or indirectly to the labors of Zwingli and Calvin.[1] In England the second or Puritan Reformation gave birth to a number of new denominations, which, after the Toleration Act of 1689, were organized into distinct Churches. In the eighteenth century arose the Wesleyan revival movement, which grew into one of the largest and most active churches in the English-speaking world.

Thus the Reformation of the sixteenth century is the mother or grandmother of at least half a dozen families of evangelical denominations, not counting the sub-divisions. Lutheranism has its strength in Germany and Scandinavia; the Reformed Church, in Great Britain and North America.

The Reformed Confession has developed different types. Travelling westward with the course of Christianity and civilization, it became more powerful in Holland, England, and Scotland than in Switzerland; but the chief characteristics which distinguish it from the Lutheran Confession were already developed by Zwingli and Calvin.

[1] On the Continent and in works of church history the designation *Reformed* includes Presbyterians, Episcopalians, Congregationalists, and other non-Lutheran Protestants. Calvinism and Puritanism are not church terms, but denote schools and parties within the Reformed churches. The Anglican Reformed Church stands by itself as a communion which was reformed under Lutheran and Calvinistic influences, but occupies a position between Catholicism and Protestantism. In modern English and American usage, the term *Reformed* has assumed a restricted sectional sense in connection with other terms, as Reformed Dutch, Reformed German, Reformed Presbyterian, Reformed Episcopalian.

The Swiss and the German Reformers agreed in opposition to Romanism, but the Swiss departed further from it. The former were zealous for the sovereign glory of God, and, in strict interpretation of the first and second commandments, abolished the heathen elements of creature worship; while Luther, in the interest of free grace and the peace of conscience, aimed his strongest blows at the Jewish element of monkish legalism and self-righteousness. The Swiss theology proceeds from God's grace to man's needs; the Lutheran, from man's needs to God's grace.

Both agree in the three fundamental principles of Protestantism: the absolute supremacy of the Divine Scriptures as a rule of faith and practice; justification by free grace through faith; the general priesthood of the laity. But as regards the first principle, the Reformed Church is more radical in carrying it out against human traditions, abolishing all those which have no root in the Bible; while Luther retained those which are not contrary to the Bible. As regards justification by faith, Luther made it the article of the standing or falling Church; while Zwingli and Calvin subordinated it to the ulterior truth of eternal foreordination by free grace, and laid greater stress on good works and strict discipline. Both opposed the idea of a special priesthood and hierarchical rule; but the Swiss Reformers gave larger scope to the popular lay element, and set in motion the principle of congregational and synodical self-government and self-support.

Both brought the new Church into close contact with the State; but the Swiss Reformers controlled the State in the spirit of republican independence, which ultimately led to a separation of the secular and spiritual powers, or to a free Church in a free State (as in the free churches of French Switzerland, and in all the churches of the United States); while Luther and Melanchthon, with their native reverence for monarchical institutions and the German Empire, taught passive obedience in politics, and brought the Church under bondage to the civil authority.

All the evangelical divines and rulers of the sixteenth and seventeenth centuries were inconsistently intolerant in theory and practice; but the Reformation, which was a revolt against papal tyranny and a mighty act of emancipation, led ultimately to the triumph of religious freedom as its legitimate fruit.

The Reformed Church does not bear the name of any man, and is not controlled by a towering personality, but assumed different types under the moulding influence of Zwingli and Bullinger in Zurich, of Œcolampadius in Basle, of Haller in Berne, of Calvin and Beza in Geneva, of Ursinus and Olevianus in the Palatinate, of Cranmer, Latimer, and Ridley in England, of Knox in Scotland. The Lutheran Church, as the very name indicates, has the stamp of Luther indelibly impressed upon it; although the milder and more liberal Melanchthonian tendency has in it a legitimate place of honor and power, and manifests itself in all progressive and unionistic movements as those of Calixtus, of Spener, and of the moderate Lutheran schools of our age.

Calvinism has made a stronger impression on the Latin and Anglo-Saxon races than on the German; while Lutheranism is essentially German, and undergoes more or less change in other countries.

Calvin aimed at a reformation of discipline as well as theology, and established a model theocracy in Geneva, which lasted for several generations. Luther contented himself with a reformation of faith and doctrine, leaving the practical consequences to time, but bitterly lamented the Antinomian disorder and abuse which for a time threatened to neutralize his labors in Saxony.

The Swiss Reformers reduced worship to the utmost simplicity and naked spirituality, and made its effect for kindling or chilling devotion to depend upon the personal piety and intellectual effort of the minister and the merits of his sermons and prayers. Luther, who was a poet and a musician, left larger scope for the æsthetic and artistic element; and his Church developed a rich liturgical and hymnological literature. Congregational singing, however, flourishes in both denominations; and the Anglican Church produced the best liturgy, which has kept its place to this day, with increasing popularity.

The Reformed Church excels in self-discipline, liberality, energy, and enterprise; it carries the gospel to all heathen lands and new colonies; it builds up a God-fearing, manly, independent, heroic type of character, such as we find among the French Huguenots, the English Puritans, the Scotch Covenanters, the Waldenses in Piedmont; and sent in times of persecution a noble army of martyrs to the prison and the stake. The Lutheran Church cultivates a hearty, trustful, inward, mystic style of piety, the science of theology, biblical and historical research, and wrestles with the deepest problems of philosophy and religion.

God has wisely distributed his gifts, with abundant opportunities for their exercise in the building up of his kingdom.

§ 4. *Literature on the Swiss Reformation.*

Compare the literature on the Reformation in general, vol. VI. 89–93, and the German Reformation, pp. 94–97. The literature on the Reformation in French Switzerland will be given in a later chapter (pp. 223 sqq.).

The largest collection of the Reformation literature of German Switzerland is in the *Stadtbibliothek* (in the *Wasserkirche*) and in the *Cantonalbibliothek* of Zürich. The former includes the 200 vols. of the valuable MSS. collection of SIMLER (d. 1788), and the *Thesaurus Hottingerianus*. I examined these libraries in August, 1886, with the kind aid of Profs. O. F. Fritsche, Alex. Schweizer, Georg von Wyss, and Dr. Escher, and again in July, 1890.

For lists of books on Swiss history in general consult the following works: GOTTLIEB EMANUEL VON HALLER: *Bibliothek der Schweizer-Geschichte und aller Theile, so dahin Bezug haben* (Bern, 1785–'88, 7 vols.); with the continuations of GEROLD MEYER VON KNONAU (from 1840–'45, Zür., 1850) and LUDWIG VON SINNER (from 1786–1851, Bern and Zürich, 1851). The *Catalog der Stadtbibliothek in Zürich* (Zürich, 1864–'67, 4 Bde, much enlarged in the written catalogues). E. Fr. von Mülinen: *Prodromus einer Schweizer. Historiographie* (Bern, 1874). The author promises a complete Lexicon of Swiss chroniclers, etc., annalists and historians in about 4 vols.

I. Sources: The works of Zwingli, Œcolampadius, Leo Judæ, Bullinger, Watt (Vadianus), and other Reformers of the Swiss cantons.

Herminjard: *Correspondance des Réformateurs.* Genève, 1866–'86. 7 vols.

Bullinger (Heinrich, Zwingli's successor, d. 1575): *Reformationsgeschichte, nach den Autographen herausgeg. von J. J. Hottinger und H. H. Vögeli.* Frauenfeld, 1838–'40, 3 vols. 8°. From 1519 to 1532. In the Swiss-German dialect.

Kessler (Johannes, Reformer of St. Gallen): *Sabbata. Chronik der Jahre 1523–'39.* Ed. by *E. Götzinger.* St. Gallen, 1866–'68. 2 parts. Kessler was the student whom Luther met at Jena on his return to Wittenberg (*see* vol. VI. 385).

Simler (Joh. Jac.) : *Sammlung alter und neuer Urkunden zur Beleuchtung der Kirchengeschichte, vornehmlich des Schweizerlandes.* Zürich, 1757–'63. 2 Bde in 6 Theilen. 8°. Also the first 30 vols. of his above-mentioned collection of MSS., which includes many printed pamphlets and documents.

Die Eidgenössischen Abschiede. Bd. III. Abth. 2: *Abschiede von 1500–'20, bearbeitet von Segesser* (Luzern, 1869) ; Bd. IV. 1 a: *A.D. 1521–'28, bearbeitet von Strickler* (Brugg, 1873) ; Bd. IV. 1 b: *A.D. 1529–'32* (Zürich, 1876) ; Bd. IV. 1 c: *A.D. 1533–'40, bearbeitet von Deschwanden* (Luzern, 1878) ; Bd. IV. 1 d: *A.D. 1541–'48, bearbeitet von Deschwanden* (Luzern, 1882). The publication of these official acts of the Swiss Diet was begun at the expense of the Confederacy, a.d. 1839, and embraces the period from 1245 to 1848.

Strickler (Joh.) : *Actensammlung zur Schweizerischen Reformationsgeschichte in den Jahren 1521–'32.* Zürich, 1878–'84. 5 vols. 8°. Mostly in Swiss-German, partly in Latin. The fifth vol. contains Addenda, Registers, and a list of books on the history of the Reformation to 1533.

Egli (Emil) : *Actensammlung zur Geschichte der Zürcher Reformation von 1519–'33.* Zürich, 1879. (Pages vii. and 947.)

Stürler (M. v.) : *Urkunden der Bernischen Kirchenreform.* Bern, 1862. Goes only to 1528.

On the Roman Catholic side: *Archiv für die Schweizer. Reformations-Geschichte, herausgeg. auf Veranstaltung des Schweizer. Piusvereins.* Solothurn, 1868–'76. 3 large vols. This includes in vol. I. the *Chronik der Schweizerischen Reformation* (till 1534), by Hans Salat of Luzern (d. after 1543), a historian and poet, whose life and writings were edited by Baechtold, Basel, 1876. Vol. II. contains the papal addresses to the Swiss Diet, etc. Vol. III. 7–82 gives a very full bibliography bearing upon the Reformation and the history of the Swiss Cantons down to 1871. This work is overlooked by most Protestant historians. Bullinger wrote against Salat a book entitled *Salz zum Salat.*

II. LATER HISTORICAL WORKS:

HOTTINGER (JOH. HEINRICH, an eminent Orientalist, 1620–'67): *Historiæ Ecclesiasticæ Novi Test.* Tiguri [Turici], 1651–'67. 9 vols. 8°. The last four volumes of this very learned but very tedious work treat of the Reformation. The seventh volume has a chapter of nearly 600 pages (24–618) *de Indulgentiis in specie!*

HOTTINGER (JOH. JACOB, 1652–1735, third son of the former): *Helvetische Kirchengeschichten*, etc. Zür., 1698–1729. 4 vols. 4°. Newly ed. by Wirz and Kirchhofer. *See* below.

MISCELLANEA TIGURINA *edita, inedita, vetera, nova, theologica, historica*, etc., ed. by J. J. ULRICH. Zür., 1722–'24. 3 vols. 8°. They contain small biographies of Swiss Reformers and important documents of Bullinger, Leo Judæ, Breitinger, Simler, etc.

FÜSSLIN (or FÜSSLI, JOH. CONR. F., 1704–1775): *Beiträge zur Erläuterung der Kirchenreformationsgeschichten des Schweizerlands.* Zür., 1740–'53. 5 vols. 8°. Contains important original documents and letters.

RUCHAT (ABRAH., 1680–1750): *Histoire de la Réformation de la Suisse, 1516–1556.* Genève, 1727, '28. 6 vols. 8°. New edition with Appendixes by L. VULLIEMIN. Paris and Lausanne, 1835–'38. 7 vols. 8°. Chiefly important for the French cantons. An English abridgment of the first four vols. in one vol. by J. COLLINSON (Canon of Durham), London, 1845, goes to the end of A.D. 1536.

WIRZ (LUDW.) and KIRCHHOFER (MELCH.): *Helvet. Kirchengeschichte. Aus Joh. Jac. Hottinger's älterem Werke und anderen Quellen neu bearbeitet.* Zürich, 1808–'19. 5 vols. The modern history is contained in vols. IV. and V. The fifth vol. is by KIRCHHOFER.

MERLE D'AUBIGNÉ (professor of Church history at Geneva, d. 1872): *Histoire de la Réformation du 16 siècle.* Paris, 1838 sqq. *Histoire de la Réformation au temps du Calvin.* Paris, 1863–'78. Both works were translated and published in England and America, in various editions.

TRECHSEL (FRIEDR., 1805–1885): *Beiträge zur Geschichte der Schweiz. Reformirten Kirche, zunächst derjenigen des Cantons Bern.* Bern, 1841, '42, 4 Hefte.

GIESELER (d. 1854): *Ch. History.* Germ. ed. III. A. 128 sqq.; 277 sqq. Am. ed. vol. IV. 75–99, 209–217. His account is very valuable for the extracts from the sources.

BAUR (d. at Tübingen, 1860): *Kirchengeschichte.* Bd. IV. 80–96. Posthumous, Tübingen, 1863.

HAGENBACH (KARL RUD., professor of Church history at Basel, d. 1874): *Geschichte der Reformation, 1517–1555.* Leipzig, 1834, 4th ed. 1870 (vol. III. of his general *Kirchengeschichte*). Fifth ed., with a literary and critical appendix, by Dr. F. NIPPOLD, Leipzig, 1887. English translation by Miss E. MOORE, Edinburgh and New York, 1878, '79, 2 vols.

CHASTEL (ÉTIENNE, professor of Church history in the University of Geneva, d. 1885) : *Histoire du Christianisme, Tom. IV.: Age Moderne* (p. 66 sqq.). Paris, 1882.

BERNER BEITRÄGE *zur Geschichte der Schweizerischen Reformationskirchen. Von* BILLETER, FLÜCKIGER, HUBLER, KASSER, MARTHALER, STRASSER. *Mit weiteren Beiträgen vermehrt und herausgegeben von* FR. NIPPOLD. Bern, 1884. (Pages 454.)

On the Confessions of the Swiss Reformation see SCHAFF: *Creeds of Christendom,* New York, 4th ed. 1884, vol. I. 354 sqq.

Biographies of ZWINGLI, ŒCOLAMPADIUS, LEO JUDÆ, BULLINGER, HALLER, etc., will be noticed in the appropriate sections.

III. GENERAL HISTORIES OF SWITZERLAND.

MÜLLER (JOH. VON, the classical historian of Switzerland, d. 1809) : *Geschichte der Schweizerischen Eidgenossenschaft, fortgesetzt von* GLUTZ-BLOTZHEIM (d. 1818) *und* JOH. JAC. HOTTINGER. Vols. V. and VII. of the whole work. A masterpiece of genius and learning, but superseded in its earlier part, where he follows Tschudi, and accepts the legendary tales of Tell and Grütli. The Reformation history is by HOTTINGER (b. 1783, d. 1860), and was published also under the title *Gesch. der Eidgenossen während der Zeit der Kirchentrennung.* Zürich, 1825 and '29, 2 vols. It was continued by VULLIEMIN in his *Histoire de la confédération suisse dans les XVIᵉ et XVIIᵉ siècles.* Paris and Lausanne, 1841 and '42. 3 vols. The first of these three volumes relates to the Reformation in *French* Switzerland, which was omitted in the German work of Hottinger, but was afterwards translated into German by others, and incorporated into the German edition (Zürich, 1786–1853, 15 vols.; the Reformation period in vols. VI.–X.). There is also a complete French edition of the entire History of Switzerland by JOH. VON MÜLLER, GLUTZ-BLOTZHEIM, HOTTINGER, VULLIEMIN, and MONNARD (Paris et Genève, 1837–'51, 18 vols. Three vols. from Vulliemin, five from Monnard, and the rest translated).

Other general Histories of Switzerland by ZSCHOKKE (1822, 8th ed. 1849; Engl. transl. by Shaw, 1848, new ed. 1875), MEYER VON KNONAU (2 vols.), VÖGELIN (6 vols.), MORIN, ZELLWEGER, VULLIEMIN (German ed. 1882), DÄNDLIKER (Zürich, 1883 sqq., 3 vols., illustr.), Mrs. HUG and RICH. STEAD (London, 1890), and DIERAUER (Gotha, 1887 sqq.; second vol., 1892).

BLUNTSCHLI (J. C., a native of Zürich, professor of jurisprudence and international law at Heidelberg, d. 1881) : *Geschichte des Schweizerischen Bundesrechts von den ersten ewigen Bünden bis auf die Gegenwart.* Stuttgart, 2d ed. 1875. 2 vols. Important for the relation of Church and State in the period of the Reformation (vol. I. 292 sqq.). L. R. VON SALIS: *Schweizerisches Bundesrecht seit dem 29. Mai 1874.* Bern, 1892. 3 vols. (also in French and Italian).

E. EGLI : *Kirchengeschichte der Schweiz bis auf Karl d. Gr.* Zürich, 1892.

Comp. RUD. STÄHELIN on the literature of the Swiss Reformation, from 1875–1882, in Brieger's " Zeitschrift für Kirchengeschichte," vols. III. and VI.

HVLDRYCHVS ZVINGLIVS.

DVM PATRIÆ QVÆRO PER DOGMATA SANCTA SALVTEM
INGRATO PATRIÆ CÆSVS AB ENSE CADO

OBIIT AÑO DÑI M D XXXI OCDOB
ÆTATIS SVÆ XLVIII

H. ZWINGLI. From the original oil-painting of Hans Asper, in the City
Library of Zurich. Reproduced from a photograph of J. Ganz.

CHAPTER II.

ZWINGLI'S TRAINING.

§ 5. *The Zwingli Literature.*

The general literature in § 4, especially Bullinger's History and Egli's Collection. The public libraries and archives in Zürich contain the various editions of Zwingli's works, and the remains of his own library with marginal notes, which were exhibited in connection with the Zwingli celebration in 1884. See *Zwingli-Ausstellung veranstaltet von der Stadtbibliothek in Zürich in Verbindung mit dem Staatsarchiv und der Cantonalbibliothek.* Zürich, 1884. A pamphlet of 24 pages, with a descriptive catalogue of Zwingli's books and remains. The annotations furnish fragmentary material for a knowledge of his theological growth. *See* Usteri's *Initia Zwingli,* quoted below.

I. SOURCES:

HULDREICH ZWINGLI: *Opera omnia,* ed. MELCHIOR SCHULER (d. 1859) and JOH. SCHULTHESS (d. 1836). Tiguri, 1828–'42. 8 vols. Vols. I. and II., the German writings; III.–VI., Scripta Latina; VII. and VIII., Epistolæ. A supplement of 75 pages was ed. by G. SCHULTHESS (d. 1866) and MARTHALER in 1861, and contains letters of Zwingli to Rhenanus and others. A new critical edition is much needed and contemplated for the "Corpus Reformatorum" by a commission of Swiss scholars. Zwingli's Correspond. in HERMINJARD, vols. I. and II.

The first edition of Zwingli's Works appeared at Zürich, 1545, in 4 vols. USTERI and VÖGELIN: *M. H. Zwingli's Schriften im Auszuge,* Zürich, 1819 and '20, 2 vols. (A systematic exhibition of Zwingli's teaching in modern German.) Another translation of select works into modern German by R. CHRISTOFFEL, Zür., 1843, 9 small vols.

Comp. also PAUL SCHWEIZER (Staatsarchivar in Zürich, son of Dr. Alexander Schweizer): *Zwingli-Autographen im Staats-Archiv zu Zürich.* 1885. (23 pages; separately publ. from the "Theol. Zeitschrift aus der Schweiz.")

JOANNIS ŒCOLAMPADII *et* HULDRICHI ZWINGLII *Epistolarum libri IV.* Basil. 1536.

HERMINJARD (A. L.): *Correspondance des Réformateurs.* Genève, 1866 sqq. Letters of Zwingli in vol. I. Nos. 82 and 146 (and eight letters to him, Nos. 17, 19, 32, etc.), and in vol. II. No. 191 (and nine letters to him).

Briefwechsel des BEATUS RHENANUS. *Gesammelt u. herausgeg. von Dr.* ADELBERT HORAWITZ *und Dr.* KARL HARTFELDER. Leipzig, 1886. Contains also the correspondence between Rhenanus and Zwingli. *See* Index, p. 700.

II. Biographies of Zwingli, including Short Sketches:

Oswald Myconius: *De Vita et Obitu Zw.*, 1536. Republ. in *Vitæ quatuor Reformatorum*, with Preface by Neander, 1840. Nüscheler, Zürich, 1776. J. Caspar Hess: *Vie d'Ulrich Zwingle*, Geneva, 1810; German ed. more than doubled by a literary appendix of 372 pages, by Leonh. Usteri, Zürich, 1811, 2 vols. (Engl. transl. from the French by Aiken, Lond., 1812). Rotermund, Bremen, 1818. J. M. Schuler: *H. Zw. Gesch. seiner Bildung zum Reformator seines Vaterlandes.* Zür., 1818, 2d ed. 1819. Horner, Zür., 1818. L. Usteri, in the Appendix to his ed. of Zwingli's German works, Zür., 1819. Several sketches of Zwingli appeared in connection with the celebration of the Zürich Reformation in 1819, especially in the festal oration of J. J. Hess: *Emendationis sacrorum beneficium*, Turici, 1819. J. J. Hottinger, Zür., 1842 (translation by Th. C. Porter: *Life and Times of U. Z.*, Harrisburg, Penn., 1857, 421 pages). Robbins, in "Bibliotheca Sacra," Andover, Mass., 1851. L. Mayer, in his "History of the German Ref. Church," vol. I., Philadelphia, 1851. Dan. Wise, Boston, 1850 and 1882. Roeder, St. Gallen and Bern, 1855. R. Christoffel, Elberfeld, 1857 (Engl. transl. by John Cochran, Edinb., 1858). Salomon Vögelin: *Erinnerungen an Zw.* Zür., 1865. W. M. Blackburn, Philad., 1868. * J. C. Mörikofer, Leipzig, 1867 and '69, 2 vols. The best biography from the sources. Dr. Volkmar: *Vortrag,* Zür., 1870 (30 pages). G. Finsler: *U. Zw.,* 3 *Vorträge,* Zür., 1873. G. A. Hoff: *Vie d'Ulr. Zw.,* Paris, 1882 (pp. 305). Jean Grob, Milwaukee, Wis., 1883, 190 pages (Engl. transl., N. York, 1884). Ch. Alphonse Witz: *Ulrich Zwingli, Vorträge,* Gotha, 1884 (pp. 144). Güder, in "Herzog's Encycl.," XVIII. 701–706; revised by R. Stähelin in second ed., XVII., 584–635. E. Combe: *U. Z.; le réformateur suisse.* Lausanne, 1884 (pp. 40). H. Rörich: *U. Z. Notice biographique,* Genève, 1884 (pp. 40). J. G. Hardy: *U. Zwingli, or Zurich and its Reformer.* Edinb., 1888.

III. On Zwingli's Wife:

Salomon Hess: *Anna Reinhard, Gattin und Wittwe von U. Zwingli.* Zürich, 2d ed. 1820. (Some truth and much fiction.) Gerold Meyer von Knonau: *Züge aus dem Leben der Anna Reinhard.* Erlangen, 1835. (Reliable.)

IV. Commemorative Addresses of 1884 at the Fourth Centennial of Zwingli's Birth:

Comp. the list in the *Züricher Taschenbuch auf das Jahr 1885,* pp. 265–268; and Flaigg, in *Theol. Zeitschrift aus der Schweiz,* 1885, pp. 219 sqq. Some of the biographies mentioned sub II. are commemorative addresses.

* Alex. Schweizer (d. 1888): *Zwingli's Bedeutung neben Luther. Festrede in der Universitätsaula, Jan. 6, 1884, weiter ausgeführt.* Zur., 1884 (pp. 89). Also a series of articles of Schweizer in the "Protestant. Kirchenzeitung," Berlin, 1883, Nos. 16, 17, 18, 23, 24, 26, 27, in defence of Zwingli against the charges of Janssen. Joh. Martin Usteri (pastor at Affoltern, then Prof. at Erlangen, d. 1889): *Ulrich Zwingli, ein Martin Luther ebenbürtiger* [?]

Zeuge des evang. Glaubens. Festschrift mit Vorrede von H. v. der Goltz.
Zürich, 1883 (144 pp.); *Zwingli und Erasmus,* Zürich, 1885 (39 pp.);
Initia Zwinglii, in the "Studien und Kritiken" for 1885 (pp.
607–672), 1886 (pp. 673–737), and 1889 (pp. 140 and 141). Rud. Stähelin: *Huldreich Zwingli und sein Reformationswerk. Zum vierhundertjährigen Geburtstag Z.'s dargestellt.* Halle, 1883 (pages 81). Ernst Stähelin: *H. Z.'s Predigt an unser Schweizervolk und unsere Zeit.* Basel, 1884. Ernst Müller: *Ulrich Zw. Ein Bernischer Beitrag zur Zwinglifeier.* Bern, 1884.
E. Dietz: *Vie d'U. Z. à l'occasion du 400° anniversaire de sa naissance.*
Paris and Strasbourg, 1884 (pp. 48). Herm. Spörri: *Durch Gottes Gnade allein. Zur Feier des 400 jähr. Geb. tages Zw.'s.* Hamburg, 1884. Joh. G.
Dreydorff: *U. Zw. Festpredigt.* Leipzig, 1884. Sal. Vögelin: *U. Z.*
Zür., 1884. G. Finsler (Zwingli's twenty-second successor as Antistes
in Zürich): *Ulrich Zw. Festschrift zur Feier seines 400 jähr. Geburtstags.*
Zür., 3d ed. 1884 (transl. into Romansch by Darms, Coire, 1884). Finsler
and Meyer von Knonau: *Festvorträge bei der Feier des 400 jähr. Geburtstags U. Z.* Zür., 1884 (pp. 24). Finsler delivered also the chief address
at the unveiling of Zwingli's monument, Aug. 25, 1885. Œchsli: *Zur Zwingli-Feier.* Zür., 1884. *Die Zwinglifeier in Bern,* Jan. 6, 1884. Several
addresses, 80 pages. Alfred Krauss (professor in Strassburg): *Zwingli.*
Strassb., 1884 (pp. 19). Aug. Bouvier: *Foi, Culture et Patriotisme.
Deux discours à l'occasion du quatrième centenaire de Ulrich Zwingli.* Genève
and Paris, 1884. (In "Nouvelles Paroles de Foi et de Liberté," and
separately.) W. Gamper (Reform. minister at Dresden): *U. Z. Festpredigt zur 400 jähr. Gedenkfeier seines Geburtstages.* Dresden, 1884.
G. K. von Toggenburg (pseudonymous R. Cath.): *Die wahre Union und
die Zwinglifeier.* St. Gallen and Leipzig, 1884 (pp. 190). *Zwingliana,* in
the "Theol. Zeitschrift aus der Schweiz." Zür., 1884, No. II. Kappeler,
Grob und Egg: *Zur Erinnerung. Drei Reden gehalten in Kappel, Jan. 6,
1884.* Affoltern a. A. 1884 (pp. 27). — In America also several addresses
were delivered and published in connection with the Zwingli commemoration in 1883 and '84. Besides, some books of Zwingli's were republished; e.g. the *Hirt* (Shepherd) by Riggenbach (Basel, 1884); the
Lehrbüchlein, Latin and German, by E. Egli (Zür., 1884).

V. On the Theology of Zwingli:

Edw. Zeller (professor of philosophy in Berlin): *Das theologische System
Zwingli's.* Tübingen, 1853.

Ch. Sigwart: *Ulrich Zwingli. Der Charakter seiner Theologie mit besonderer
Rücksicht auf Picus von Mirandola dargestellt.* Stuttg. und Hamb., 1855.

Herm. Spörri (Ref. pastor in Hamburg): *Zwingli-Studien.* Leipzig, 1886
(pp. 131). Discussions on Zwingli's doctrine of the Church, the Bible,
his relation to humanism and Christian art.

* August Baur (D.D., a Würtemberg pastor in Weilimdorf near Stuttgart):
Zwingli's Theologie, ihr Werden und ihr System. Halle, vol. I. 1885 (pp.
543); vol. II. P. I., 1888 (pp. 400), P. II., 1889. This work does for Zwingli
what Jul. Köstlin did for Luther and A. Herrlinger for Melanchthon.

ALEX. SCHWEIZER, in his *Festrede*, treats more briefly, but very ably, of Zwingli's theological opinions (pp. 60–88).

VI. RELATION OF ZWINGLI TO LUTHER AND CALVIN:

MERLE D'AUBIGNÉ: *Le Lutheranisme et la Réforme.* Paris, 1844. Engl. translation: *Luther and Calvin.* N. York, 1845.

HUNDESHAGEN: *Charakteristik U. Zwingli's und seines Reformationswerks unter Vergleichung mit Luther und Calvin*, in the "Studien und Kritiken," 1862. Compare also his *Beiträge zur Kirchenverfassungsgeschichte und Kirchenpolitik*, Bd. I. Wiesbaden, 1864, pp. 136–297. (Important for Zwingli's church polity.)

G. PLITT (Lutheran): *Gesch. der ev. Kirche bis zum Augsburger Reichstage.* Erlangen, 1867, pp. 417–488.

A. F. C. VILMAR (Luth.): *Luther, Melanchthon, Zwingli.* Frankf.-a.-M., 1869.

G. UHLHORN (Luth.): *Luther and the Swiss*, translated by G. F. KROTEL, Philadelphia, 1876.

ZWINGLI WIRTH (Reformed): *Luther und Zwingli.* St. Gallen, 1884 (pp. 37).

VII. SPECIAL POINTS IN ZWINGLI'S HISTORY AND THEOLOGY:

KRADOLFER: *Zwingli in Marburg.* Berlin, 1870.

EMIL EGLI: *Die Schlacht von Cappel 1531. Mit 2 Plänen und einem Anhang ungedruckter Quellen.* Zür., 1873 (pp. 88). By the same: *Das Religionsgespräch zu Marburg.* Zür., 1884. In the "Theol. Zeitschrift aus der Schweiz."

MARTIN LENZ: *Zwingli und Landgraf Philipp*, in Brieger's "Zeitschrift für Kirchengeschichte" for 1879 (Bd. III.).

H. BAVINCK: *De ethick van U. Zwingli.* Kampen, 1880.

JUL. WERDER: *Zwingli als politischer Reformator*, in the "Basler Beiträge zur vaterländ. Geschichte," Basel, 1882, pp. 263–290.

HERM. ESCHER: *Die Glaubensparteien in der Schweiz. Eidgenossenschaft und ihre Beziehungen zum Auslande von 1527-'31.* Frauenfeld, 1882. (pp. 326.) Important for Zwingli's Swiss and foreign policy, and his views on the relation of Church and State.

W. OECHSLI: *Die Anfänge des Glaubenskonfliktes zwischen Zürich und den Eidgenossen.* Winterthur, 1883 (pp. 42).

MARTHALER: *Zw.'s Lehre vom Glauben.* Zür., 1884.

AUG. BAUR: *Die erste Züricher Disputation.* Halle, 1883 (pp. 32).

A. ERICHSON: *Zwingli's Tod und dessen Beurtheilung durch Zeitgenossen*, Strassb., 1883 (pp. 43); *U. Zw. und die elsässischen Reformatoren*, Strassb., 1884 (pp. 40).

FLÜCKIGER: *Zwingli's Beziehungen zu Bern*, in the "Berner Beiträge." Bern, 1884.

J. MART. USTERI: *Initia Zwinglii*, and *Zw. and Erasmus.* See above, p. 18.

H. FENNER: *Zw. als Patriot und Politiker.* Frauenfeld, 1884 (pp. 38).

G. Heer: *U. Zw. als Pfarrer von Glarus.* Zürich, 1884 (pp. 42).

Gust. Weber (musical director and organist of the Grossmünster in Zürich):
H. Zwingli. Seine Stellung zur Musik und seine Lieder. Zürich and Leipzig,
1884 (pp. 68).

A. Zahn: *Zwingli's Verdienste um die biblische Abendmahlslehre.* Stuttgart, 1884.

G. Wunderli: *Zürich in der Periode 1519-'31.* Zürich, 1888.

On Zwingli and the Anabaptists, see the literature in § 24.

VIII. In part also the biographies of Œcolampadius, Bullinger, Leo
Judæ, Haller, etc.

The best books on Zwingli are Mörikofer's biography, Usteri on the education of Zwingli, Baur on his theology, Escher and Oechsli on his state and
church polity, and Schweizer and R. Stähelin on his general character and
position in history.

§ 6. *Zwingli's Birth and Education.*

Franz: *Zwingli's Geburtsort. Beitrag zur reformator. Jubelfeier 1819.* (The
author was pastor of Wildhaus.) St. Gallen, 1818. Schuler: *Huldreich
Zwingli. Geschichte seiner Bildung zum Reformator des Vaterlandes.* Zürich,
1819. (404 pp. Very full, but somewhat too partial, and needing correction.)

Huldreich or Ulrich Zwingli[1] was born January 1,
1484, seven weeks after Luther, in a lowly shepherd's cot-
tage at Wildhaus in the county of Toggenburg, now belonging to the Canton St. Gall.

He was descended from the leading family in this retired
village. His father, like his grandfather, was the chief
magistrate (*Ammann*); his mother, the sister of a priest
(John Meili, afterwards abbot of Fischingen, in Thurgau,
1510–1523); his uncle, on the father's side, dean of the
chapter at Wesen on the wild lake of Wallenstadt. He had
seven brothers (he being the third son) and two sisters.

The village of Wildhaus is the highest in the valley, surrounded by Alpine meadows and the lofty mountain scenery
of Northeastern Switzerland, in full view of the seven Chur-
firsten and the snow-capped Sentis. The principal industry
of the inhabitants was raising flocks. They are described as

---

[1] The name is often misspelled *Zwingel* (by Luther), or *Zwingle* (by English
and American writers).

a cheerful, fresh and energetic people; and these traits we find in Zwingli.[1] The Reformation was introduced there in 1523. Not very far distant are the places where Zwingli spent his public life, — Glarus, Einsiedeln, and Zurich.

THE HOUSE WHERE ZWINGLI WAS BORN AT WILDHAUS IN TOGGENBURG.
(From Schuler's *H. Zwingli*.)

Zwingli was educated in the Catholic religion by his God-fearing parents, and by his uncle, the dean of Wesen, who favored the new humanistic learning. He grew up a healthy, vigorous boy. He had at a very early age a tender sense of veracity as "the mother of all virtues," and, like young Washington, he would never tell a lie.

When ten years of age he was sent from Wesen to a Latin school at Basle, and soon excelled in the three chief branches taught there, — Latin grammar, music and dialectics.

[1] Mörikofer (I. 4): "*Zwingli erinnert in seinem Wesen immer wieder an seine hohe, helle Heimath; wir haben stets den in frischer Bergluft gestärkten und gestählten Alpensohn vor uns.*"

In 1498 he entered a college at Berne under the charge of Heinrich Wölflin (Lupulus), who was reputed to be the best classical scholar and Latin poet in Switzerland, and followed the reform movement in 1522.[1]

From 1500 to 1502 he studied in the University of Vienna, which had become a centre of classical learning by the labors of distinguished humanists, Corvinus, Celtes, and Cuspinian, under the patronage of the Emperor Maximilian I.[2] He studied scholastic philosophy, astronomy, and physics, but chiefly the ancient classics. He became an enthusiast for the humanities. He also cultivated his talent for music. He played on several instruments — the lute, harp, violin, flute, dulcimer, and hunting-horn — with considerable skill. His papal opponents sneeringly called him afterwards "the evangelical lute-player, piper, and whistler." He regarded this innocent amusement as a means to refresh the mind and to soften the temper. In his poetical and musical taste he resembles Luther, without reaching his eminence.

In 1502 he returned to Basle, taught Latin in the school of St. Martin, pursued his classical studies, and acquired the degree of master of arts in 1506; hence he was usually called Master Ulrich. He never became a doctor of divinity, like Luther. In Basle he made the acquaintance of Leo Jud (Judæ, also called Master Leu), who was graduated with him and became his chief co-laborer in Zurich. Both attended with much benefit the lectures of Thomas Wyttenbach, professor of theology since 1505. Zwingli calls him his beloved and faithful teacher, who opened his eyes to several abuses of the Church, especially the indulgences, and taught

[1] Lupulus was deposed from his canonry for marrying in 1524, but reinstated after the introduction of the Reformation. "*Dass Lupulus eine uneheliche Tochter hatte* (before his marriage), *wurde ihm leicht verziehen.*" Mörikofer, I. 7. He lamented Zwingli's early death in a Latin epitaph in verse.

[2] There is no evidence that he became acquainted in Vienna with Eck and Faber, the famous champions of popery, nor with his friends Glareanus and Vadianus. See Horawitz, *Der Humanismus in Wien*, 1883.

him "not to rely on the keys of the Church, but to seek the remission of sins alone in the death of Christ, and to open access to it by the key of faith." [1]

§ 7. *Zwingli in Glarus.*

G. HEER: *Ulrich Zwingli als Pfarrer in Glarus.* Zürich, 1884.

Zwingli was ordained to the priesthood by the bishop of Constance, and appointed pastor of Glarus, the capital of the canton of the same name.[2] He had to pay over one hundred guilders to buy off a rival candidate (Göldli of Zurich) who was favored by the Pope, and compensated by a papal pension. He preached his first sermon in Rapperschwyl, and read his first mass at Wildhaus. He labored at Glarus ten years, from 1506 to 1516. His time was occupied by preaching, teaching, pastoral duties, and systematic study. He began to learn the Greek language "without a teacher,"[3] that he might study the New Testament in the original.[4] He acquired considerable facility in Greek. The Hebrew language he studied at a later period in Zurich, but with less zeal and success. He read with great enthusiasm the ancient Greek and Roman philosophers, poets, orators, and historians. He speaks in terms of admiration of Homer, Pindar, Demosthenes, Cicero, Livy, Cæsar, Seneca, Pliny, Tacitus, Plutarch. He committed Valerius Maximus to memory for the historical examples. He wrote comments

[1] *Werke*, I. A. 254; *Opera*, III. 544. Leo Judæ, in the preface to Zwingli's Annotations to the N. T., reports that Zwingli and he derived from Wyttenbach's lectures in 1505 "*quidquid nobis fuit solidæ eruditionis.*"

[2] The church in which he preached is jointly occupied by the Roman Catholics and the Protestants, the community being divided. The old church burnt down in 1861, but a new and better one was built on the same spot.

[3] "*Absque duce*," says Myconius, in a letter to Zwingli, Oct. 28, 1518. *Opera*, VII. 51, 52.

[4] Zwingli wrote to Joachim Watt from Glarus, Feb. 23, 1513 (*Opera*, VII. 9): "*Ita enim Græcis studere destinavi ut qui me præter Deum amoveat, nesciam, on gloriæ (quam nullis in rebus quærere honeste possem), sed sacratissimarum terarum ergo.*"

on Lucian. He perceived, like Justin Martyr, the Alexandrian Fathers, and Erasmus, in the lofty ideas of the heathen philosophers and poets, the working of the Holy Spirit, which he thought extended beyond Palestine throughout the world. He also studied the writings of Picus della Mirandola (d. 1494), which influenced his views on providence and predestination.

During his residence in Glarus he was brought into correspondence with Erasmus through his friend Loreti of Glarus, called Glareanus, a learned humanist and poet-laureate, who at that time resided in Basle, and belonged to the court of admirers of the famous scholar. He paid him also a visit in the spring of 1515, and found him a man in the prime of life, small and delicate, but amiable and very polite. He addressed him as " the greatest philosopher and theologian; " he praises his " boundless learning," and says that he read his books every night before going to sleep. Erasmus returned the compliments with more moderation, and speaks of Zwingli's previous letter as being " full of wit and learned acumen." In 1522 Zwingli invited him to settle in Zurich; but Erasmus declined it, preferring to be a cosmopolite. We have only one letter of Zwingli to Erasmus, but six of Erasmus to Zwingli.[1] The influence of the great scholar on Zwingli was emancipating and illuminating. Zwingli, although not exactly his pupil, was no doubt confirmed by him in his high estimate of the heathen classics, his opposition to ecclesiastical abuses, his devotion to the study of the Scriptures, and may have derived from him his moderate view of hereditary sin and guilt, and the first suggestion of the figurative interpretation of the words of institution of the Lord's Supper.[2] But he dissented from the semi-Pela-

---

[1] *Opera*, vol. VII., pp. 10, 12, 221, 222, 251, 307, 310.

[2] Melanchthon wrote, Oct. 12, 1529: *"Cinglius mihi confessus est, se ex Erasmi scriptis primum hausisse opinionem suam de cœna Domini."* *Corp. Reform.* IV. 970.

gianism of Erasmus, and was a firm believer in predestination. During the progress of the Reformation they were
gradually alienated, although they did not get into a personal controversy. In a letter of Sept. 3, 1522, Erasmus
gently warns Zwingli to fight not only bravely, but also
prudently, and Christ would give him the victory.[1] He did
not regret his early death. Glareanus also turned from him,
and remained in the old Church. But Zwingli never lost
respect for Erasmus, and treated even Hutten with generous
kindness after Erasmus had cast him off.[2]

On his visit to Basle he became acquainted with his biographer, Oswald Myconius, the successor of Œcolampadius
(not to be confounded with Frederick Myconius, Luther's
friend).

Zwingli took a lively interest in public affairs. Three
times he accompanied, according to Swiss custom, the re-
cruits of his congregation as chaplain to Italy, in the service
of Popes Julius II. and Leo X., against France. He witnessed the storming of Pavia (1512),[3] probably also the
victory at Novara (1513), and the defeat at Marignano
(1515). He was filled with admiration for the bravery of
his countrymen, but with indignation and grief at the demoralizing effect of the foreign military service. He openly
attacked this custom, and made himself many enemies among
the French party.

His first book, "The Labyrinth," is a German poem against
the corruptions of the times, written about 1510.[4] It represents the fight of Theseus with the Minotaur and the wild
beasts in the labyrinth of the world, — the one-eyed lion

---

[1] "*Tu pugna, mi Zwingli, non modo fortiter, verum etiam prudenter. Dabit
Christus, ut pugnes feliciter.*" *Opera*, VII. 221.

[2] See vol. VI. 202, 427. On Zwingli's relation to Erasmus, see Mörikofer,
I. 23 sqq., 176 sqq., and the monograph of Usteri quoted above, p. 19.

[3] He gave a lively Latin narrative of the battle of the Swiss against the
French in Pavia to his friend Vadianus.

[4] *Opera* (*Deutsche Schriften*), Tom. II. B. pp. 243–247.

(Spain), the crowned eagle (the emperor), the winged lion (Venice), the cock (France), the ox (Switzerland), the bear (Savoy). The Minotaur, half man, half bull, represents, he says, "the sins, the vices, the irreligion, the foreign service of the Swiss, which devour the sons of the nation." His second poetic work of that time, "The Fable of the Ox," [1] is likewise a figurative attack upon the military service by which Switzerland became a slave of foreign powers, especially of France.

He superintended the education of two of his brothers and several of the noblest young men of Glarus, as Ægidius Tschudi (the famous historian), Valentine Tschudi, Heer, Nesen, Elmer, Brunner, who were devotedly and gratefully attached to him, and sought his advice and comfort, as their letters show.

Zwingli became one of the most prominent and influential public men in Switzerland before he left Glarus; but he was then a humanist and a patriot rather than a theologian and a religious teacher. He was zealous for intellectual culture and political reform, but shows no special interest in the spiritual welfare of the Church. He did not pass through a severe struggle and violent crisis, like Luther, but by diligent seeking and searching he attained to the knowledge of the truth. His conversion was a gradual intellectual process, rather than a sudden breach with the world; but, after he once had chosen the Scriptures for his guide, he easily shook off the traditions of Rome, which never had a very strong hold upon him. That process began at Glarus, and was completed at Zurich.

His moral character at Glarus and at Einsiedeln was, unfortunately, not free from blemish. He lacked the grace of continence, and fell with apparent ease into a sin which

---

[1] *Fabelgedicht vom Ochsen und etlichen Thieren, Op.*, II. B. 257–269. The ox is again the symbol of Switzerland. See the comments of the editors, pp. 262 sqq.

was so common among priests, and so easily overlooked if only proper caution was observed, according to the wretched maxim, "*Si non caste, saltem caute.*" The fact rests on his own honest confession, and was known to his friends, but did not injure his standing and influence; for he was in high repute as a priest, and even enjoyed a papal pension. He resolved to reform in Glarus, but relapsed in Einsiedeln under the influence of bad examples, to his deep humiliation. After his marriage in Zurich, his life was pure and honorable and above the reproach of his enemies.

NOTES ON ZWINGLI'S MORAL CHARACTER.

Recent discussions have given undue prominence to the blot which rests on Zwingli's earlier life, while yet a priest in the Roman Church. Janssen, the ultramontane historian, has not one word of praise for Zwingli, and violates truth and charity by charging him with habitual, promiscuous, and continuous licentiousness, not reflecting that he thereby casts upon the Roman Church the reproach of inexcusable laxity in discipline. Zwingli was no doubt guilty of occasional transgressions, but probably less guilty than the majority of Swiss priests who lived in open or secret concubinage at that time (see § 2, p. 6); yea, he stood so high in public estimation at Einsiedeln and Zurich, that Pope Hadrian VI., through his Swiss agent, offered him every honor except the papal chair. But we will not excuse him, nor compare his case (as some have done) with that of St. Augustin; for Augustin, when he lived in concubinage, was not a priest and not even baptized, and he confessed his sin before the whole world with deeper repentance than Zwingli, who rather made light of it. The facts are these : —

1) Bullinger remarks (*Reformationsgesch.* I. 8) that Zwingli was suspected in Glarus of improper connection with several women ("*weil er wegen einiger Weiber verargwohnt war*"). Bullinger was his friend and successor, and would not slander him; but he judged mildly of a vice which was so general among priests on account of celibacy. He himself was the son of a priest, as was also Leo Judæ.

2) Zwingli, in a confidential letter to Canon Utinger at Zurich, dated Einsiedeln, Dec. 3, 1518 (*Opera*, VII. 54–57), contradicts the rumor that he had seduced the daughter of an influential citizen in Einsiedeln, but admits his unchastity. This letter is a very strange apology, and, as he says himself, a *blateratio* rather than a *satisfactio*. He protests, on the one hand (what Janssen omits to state), that he never dishonored a married woman or a virgin or a nun ("*ea ratio nobis perpetuo fuit, nec alienum thorum conscendere, nec virginem vitiare, nec Deo dicatam profanare*"); but, on the other hand, he speaks lightly, we may say frivolously, of his intercourse with the impure daughter of a barber who was already dishonored, and apologizes for similar offences com-

mitted in Glarus. This is the worst feature in the letter, and casts a dark shade on his character at that time. He also refers (p. 57) to the saying of Æneas Sylvius (Pope Pius II.): *"Non est qui vigesimum annum excessit, nec virginem tetigerit."* His own superiors set him a bad example. Nevertheless he expresses regret, and applies to himself the word, 2 Pet. 2 : 22, and says, *"Christus per nos blasphematur."*

3) Zwingli, with ten other priests, petitioned the bishop of Constance in Latin (Einsiedeln, July 2, 1522), and the Swiss Diet in German (Zurich, July 13, 1522), to permit the free preaching of the gospel and the marriage of the clergy. He enforces the petition by an incidental confession of the scandalous life of the clergy, including himself (*Werke*, I. 39): *"Euer ehrsam Wysheit hat bisher gesehen das unehrbar schandlich Leben, welches wir leider bisher geführt haben (wir wollen allein von uns selbst geredet haben) mit Frauen, damit wir männiglich übel verärgert und verbösert haben."* But this document with eleven signatures (Zwingli's is the last) is a *general* confession of clerical immorality in the past, and does not justify Janssen's inference that Zwingli continued such life at that time. Janssen (*Ein zweites Wort an meine Kritiker*, p. 47), moreover, mistakes in this petition the Swiss word *rüw* (*Ruhe*, rest) for *rüwen* (*Reue*, repentance), and makes the petitioners say that they felt "no repentance," instead of "no rest." The document, on the contrary, shows a decided advance of moral sentiment as compared with the lame apology in the letter to Utinger, and deeply deplores the state of clerical immorality. It is rather creditable to the petitioners than otherwise; certainly very honest.

4) In a letter to his five brothers, Sept. 17, 1522, to whom he dedicated a sermon on "the ever pure Virgin Mary, mother of God," Zwingli confesses that he was subject to *Hoffahrt, Fressen, Unlauterkeit*, and other sins of the flesh (*Werke*, I. 86). This is his latest confession; but if we read it in connection with the whole letter, it makes the impression that he must have undergone a favorable change about that time, and concluded a regular, though secret, connection with his wife. As to temperance, Bullinger (I. 305) gives him the testimony that he was "very temperate in eating and drinking."

5) Zwingli was openly married in April, 1524, to Anna Reinhart, a respectable widow, and mother of several children, after having lived with her about two years before in secret marriage. But this fact, which Janssen construes into a charge of "unchaste intercourse," was known to his intimate friends; for Myconius, in a letter of July 22, 1522, sends greetings to Zwingli and his wife ("*Vale cum uxore quam felicissime et tuis omnibus,*" Opera, VII. 210; and again: "*Vale cum uxore in Christo,*" p. 253). The same is implied in a letter of Bucer, April 14, 1524 (p. 335; comp. the note of the editors). "The cases," says Mörikofer (I. 211), "were very frequent at that time, even with persons of high position, that secret marriages were not ratified by a religious ceremony till weeks and months afterwards." Before the Council of Trent secret marriages were legitimate and valid. (*Can. et Decr. Conc. Trid.*, Sess. XXIV., *Decr. de reform. matrimonii.*)

Zwingli's character was unmercifully attacked by Janssen in his *Geschichte des deutschen Volkes*, III. 83 sq.; *An meine Kritiker* (1883), 127–140; *Ein zweites Wort an meine Kritiker* (1883), 45–48; defended as far as truth permits

by Ebrard, *Janssen und die Reformation* (1882) ; Usteri, *Ulrich Zwingli* (1883),
34–47 ; Alex. Schweizer, articles in the "Protest. Kirchenzeitung," Berlin,
1883, Nos. 23–27. Janssen answered Ebrard, but not Usteri and Schweizer.
The main facts were correctly stated before this controversy by Mörikofer, I.
49–53 and 128), and briefly also by Hagenbach, and Merle (bk. VIII. ch. 6).

§ 8. *Zwingli in Einsiedeln.*

In 1516 Zwingli left Glarus on account of the intrigues
of the French political party, which came into power after
the victory of the French at Marignano (1515), and accepted
a call to Einsiedeln, but kept his charge and expected to
return ; for the congregation was much attached to him, and
promised to build him a new parsonage.   He supplied the
charge by a vicar, and drew his salary for two years, until
he was called to Zurich, when he resigned.

Einsiedeln [1] is a village with a Benedictine convent in the
Catholic canton Schwyz.   It was then, and is to this day,
a very famous resort of pilgrims to the shrine of a wonder-
working black image of the Virgin Mary, which is supposed
to have fallen from heaven.   The number of annual pilgrims
from Switzerland, Germany, France, and Italy exceeds a
hundred thousand.

Here, then, was a large field of usefulness for a preacher.
The convent library afforded special facilities for study.

Zwingli made considerable progress in his knowledge of
the Scriptures and the Fathers.   He read the annotations of
Erasmus and the commentaries of Origen, Ambrose, Jerome,
and Chrysostom.   He made extracts on the margin of his
copies of their works which are preserved in the libraries at
Zurich.   He seems to have esteemed Origen, Jerome, and
Chrysostom more, and Augustin less, than Luther did ; but
he also refers frequently to Augustin in his writings.[2]

[1] Maria-Einsiedeln, Deiparæ Virginis Eremus, Eremitarum Cœnobium in
Helvetiis, Notre-Dame-des-Eremites.

[2] Usteri has examined the marginal annotations in Zwingli's patristic
library, and gives the scanty results in his *Initia Zwinglii*, in "Studien und
Kritiken," 1886, p. 681 sq.   The Zwingli library was on exhibition at Zurich,
Jan. 4–13, 1884, and a catalogue printed.

We have an interesting proof of his devotion to the Greek
Testament in a MS. preserved in the city library at Zurich.
In 1517 he copied with his own hand very neatly the Epistles
of Paul and the Hebrews in a little book for constant and
convenient use. The text is taken from the first edition of
Erasmus, which appeared in March, 1516, and corrects some
typographical errors. It is very legible and uniform, and
betrays an experienced hand; the marginal notes, in Latin,
from Erasmus and patristic commentators, are very small
and almost illegible. On the last page he added the following note in Greek :—

"These Epistles were written at Einsiedeln of the blessed
Mother of God by Huldreich Zwingli, a Swiss of Toggenburg, in the year one thousand five hundred and seventeen
of the Incarnation, in the month of June.[1] Happily ended."[2]

At the same time he began at Einsiedeln to attack from
the pulpit certain abuses and the sale of indulgences, when
Samson crossed the Alps in August, 1518. He says that he
began to preach the gospel before Luther's name was known
in Switzerland, adding, however, that at that time he de-

---

[1] Skirophorion, *i.e.* the 12th Attic month, answering to the latter part of
June and the first part of July. Σκιροφόρια was the festival of Athena Σκιράς,
celebrated in that month. The year (1517) refutes the error of several biographers, who date the MS. back to the period of Glarus. Besides, there was
no printed copy of the Greek Testament before 1516.

[2] The subscription (as I copied it, with its slight errors, in the Wasserkirche,
Aug. 14, 1886) reads as follows : —

Ταῦται αἱ Ἐπῖστολαῖ[αὶ] γραφεῖσαι
Ἐρήμου τῆς μακαρῖας θεο-
τόκου, παρὰ τῷ Ὑλδε-
ρύχῳ Ζυγγλῖῳ Δωγ-
γίῳ ἐλβετίῳ, χϊλῖο-
στῳ πεντακοσιόστῳ
ἑπτὰ καὶ δεκάτῳ
ἀπὸ τῆς θεογο-
νίας, μηνὸς
σκιῤῥοφορι-
ωνος
Ευτιχῶς [εὐτυχῶς].

pended too much on Jerome and other Fathers instead of
the Scriptures. He told Cardinal Schinner in 1517 that
popery had poor foundation in the Scriptures. Myconius,
Bullinger, and Capito report, in substantial agreement, that
Zwingli preached in Einsiedeln against abuses, and taught
the people to worship Christ, and not the Virgin Mary.
The inscription on the entrance gate of the convent, promising complete remission of sins, was taken down at his
instance.[1] Beatus Rhenanus, in a letter of Dec. 6, 1518,
applauds his attack upon Samson, the restorer of indulgences, and says that Zwingli preached to the people the
purest philosophy of Christ from the fountain.[2]

On the strength of these testimonies, many historians
date the Swiss Reformation from 1516, one year before
that of Luther, which began Oct. 31, 1517. But Zwingli's preaching at Einsiedeln had no such consequences as
Luther's Theses. He was not yet ripe for his task, nor
placed on the proper field of action. He was at that
time simply an Erasmian or advanced liberal in the
Roman Church, laboring for higher education rather than
religious renovation, and had no idea of a separation. He
enjoyed the full confidence of the abbot, the bishop of Constance, Cardinal Schinner, and even the Pope. At Schinner's recommendation, he was offered an annual pension of
fifty guilders from Rome as an encouragement in the pursuit

---

[1] The inscription was, "*Hic est plena remissio omnium peccatorum a culpa et a
pœna.*" But the sermon against the worship of saints, pilgrimages and vows,
of which Bullinger speaks (I. 81), was preached later, in 1522, at the Feast
of Angels, during a visit of Zwingli to Einsiedeln. See Pestalozzi, *Leo Judœ*,
p. 16, and Gieseler, III. i. p. 138.

[2] *Opera*, VII. A. 57 : "*Risimus abunde veniarum institorem* [Bernh. Samson],
quem in litteris tuis graphice depinxisti. . . ." Then he complains that most of
the priests teach heathen and Jewish doctrines, but that Zwingli and his like
"*purissimam Christi philosophiam ex ipsis fontibus populo proponere, non Scoticis
et Gabrielicis interpretationibus depravatam; sed ab Augustino, Ambrosio, Cypriano,
Hieronymo, germane et sincere expositam.*" Rhenanus contrasts the Fathers
with the Scholastics, Duns Scotus, and Gabriel Biel.

of his studies, and he actually received it for about five
years (from 1515 to 1520). Pucci, the papal nuncio at
Zurich, in a letter dated Aug. 24, 1518, appointed him papal
chaplain (Accolitus Capellanus), with all the privileges and
honors of that position, assigning as the reason "his splendid
virtues and merits," and promising even higher dignities.[1]
He also offered to double his pension, and to give him in
addition a canonry in Basle or Coire, on condition that he
should promote the papal cause. Zwingli very properly declined the chaplaincy and the increase of salary, and declared
frankly that he would never sacrifice a syllable of the truth
for love of money; but he continued to receive the former
pension of fifty guilders, which was urged upon him without
condition, for the purchase of books. In 1520 he declined
it altogether, — what he ought to have done long before.[2]
Francis Zink, the papal chaplain at Einsiedeln, who paid
the pension, was present at Zwingli's interview with Pucci,
and says, in a letter to the magistracy at Zurich (1521), that
Zwingli could not well have lived without the pension, but
felt very badly about it, and thought of returning to Einsiedeln.[3] Even as late as Jan. 23, 1523, Pope Adrian VI.,
unacquainted with the true state of things, wrote to Zwingli
a kind and respectful letter, hoping to secure through him
the influence of Zurich for the holy see.[4]

[1] See the letter of Anthonius Puccius to Zwingli in *Opera*, VII. A. 48 sq.
The document of the appointment, with the signature and seal of the papal
legate, dated Sept. 1, 1518, is kept in the city library at Zurich.

[2] Zwingli speaks of this pension very frankly and with deep regret in a
letter to his brothers (1522), and in his Exposition of the Conclusions (1523).
Werke, I. A. 86 and 354.

[3] *Opera*, VII. A. 179: *"Ipse arbiter interfui, quum Domino Legato Pucci ingenue
fassus est, ipsum pecuniæ causa rebus Papæ agendis non inserviturum,"* etc.

[4] *Opera*, VII. A. 266. The Pope addresses Zwingli *"Dilecte fili,"* praises
his *"egregia virtus,"* assures him of his special confidence in him and his best
wishes for him. At the same time the Pope wrote to Francis Zink to spare
no effort to secure Zwingli for the papal interest; and Zink replied to Myconius, when asked what the Pope offered in return, *"Omnia usque ad thronum
papalem."* Zwingli despised it all. *Ibid.* p. 266, note.

§ 9. *Zwingli and Luther.*

Comp. Vol. VI. 620–651, and the portrait of Luther, p. 107.

The training of Zwingli for his life-work differs considerably from that of Luther. This difference affected their future work, and accounts in part for their collision when they met as antagonists in writing, and on one occasion (at Marburg) face to face, in a debate on the real presence. Comparisons are odious when partisan or sectarian feeling is involved, but necessary and useful if impartial.

Both Reformers were of humble origin, but with this difference: Luther descended from the peasantry, and had a hard and rough schooling, which left its impress upon his style of polemics, and enhanced his power over the common people; while Zwingli was the son of a magistrate, the nephew of a dean and an abbot, and educated under the influence of the humanists, who favored urbanity of manners. Both were brought up by pious parents and teachers in the Catholic faith; but Luther was far more deeply rooted in it than Zwingli, and adhered to some of its doctrines, especially on the sacraments, with great tenacity to the end. He also retained a goodly portion of Romish exclusivism and intolerance. He refused to acknowledge Zwingli as a brother, and abhorred his view of the salvation of unbaptized children and pious heathen.

Zwingli was trained in the school of Erasmus, and passed from the heathen classics directly to the New Testament. He represents more than any other Reformer, except Melanchthon, the spirit of the Renaissance in harmony with the Reformation.[1] He was a forerunner of modern liberal

[1] Martin, in his *Histoire de France*, VIII. 156, makes a similar remark, "*On peut considérer l'œuvre de Zwingli comme le plus puissant effort qui ait été fuit pour sanctifier la Renaissance et l'unir à la Réforme en Jésus-Christ.*" He calls Zwingli (p. 168) the man of the largest thought and greatest heart of the Reformation ("*qui porte en lui la plus large pensée et le plus grand cœur de la Réformation*").

theology. Luther struggled through the mystic school of
Tauler and Staupitz, and the severe moral discipline of monasticism, till he found peace and comfort in the doctrine
of justification by faith. Both loved poetry and music next
to theology, but Luther made better use of them for public
worship, and composed hymns and tunes which are sung to
this day.

Both were men of providence, and became, innocently,
reformers of the Church by the irresistible logic of events.
Both drew their strength and authority from the Word of
God. Both labored independently for the same cause of
evangelical truth, the one on a smaller, the other on a much
larger field. Luther owed nothing to Zwingli, and Zwingli
owed little or nothing to Luther. Both were good scholars,
great divines, popular preachers, heroic characters.

Zwingli broke easily and rapidly with the papal system,
but Luther only step by step, and after a severe struggle
of conscience. Zwingli was more radical than Luther, but
always within the limits of law and order, and without a
taint of fanaticism; Luther was more conservative, and yet
the chief champion of freedom in Christ. Zwingli leaned
to rationalism, Luther to mysticism; yet both bowed to the
supreme authority of the Scriptures. Zwingli had better
manners and more self-control in controversy; Luther surpassed him in richness and congeniality of nature. Zwingli
was a republican, and aimed at a political and social, as well
as an ecclesiastical reformation; Luther was a monarchist,
kept aloof from politics and war, and concentrated his force
upon the reformation of faith and doctrine. Zwingli was
equal to Luther in clearness and acuteness of intellect and
courage of conviction, superior in courtesy, moderation,
and tolerance, but inferior in originality, depth, and force.
Zwingli's work and fame were provincial; Luther's, world-
wide. Luther is the creator of the modern high-German
book language, and gave to his people a vernacular Bible

of enduring vitality. Zwingli had to use the Latin, or to struggle with an uncouth dialect; and the Swiss Version of the Bible by his faithful friend Leo Judæ remained confined to German Switzerland, but is more accurate, and kept pace in subsequent revisions with the progress of exegesis. Zwingli can never inspire, even among his own countrymen, the same enthusiasm as Luther among the Germans. Luther is the chief hero of the Reformation, standing in the front of the battle-field before the Church and the world, defying the papal bull and imperial ban, and leading the people of God out of the Babylonian captivity under the gospel banner of freedom.

Each was the right man in the right place; neither could have done the work of the other. Luther was foreordained for Germany, Zwingli for Switzerland. Zwingli was cut down in the prime of life, fifteen years before Luther; but, even if he had outlived him, he could not have reached the eminence which belongs to Luther alone. The Lutheran Church in Germany and the Reformed Church of Switzerland stand to this day the best vindication of their distinct, yet equally evangelical Christian work and character.

NOTES.

I add the comparative estimates of the two Reformers by two eminent and equally unbiassed scholars, the one of German Lutheran, the other of Swiss Reformed, descent.

Dr. Baur (the founder of the Tübingen school of critical historians) says: [1] " When the two men met, as at Marburg, Zwingli appears more free, more unprejudiced, more fresh, and also more mild and conciliatory; while Luther shows himself harsh and intolerant, and repels Zwingli with the proud word: 'We have another spirit than you.' [2] A comparison of their controversial writings can only result to the advantage of Zwingli. But there can be no doubt that, judged by the merits and effects of their reformatory labors, Luther stands much higher than Zwingli. It is true, even in this respect, both stand quite independent of each other. Zwingli has by no means received his impulse from Luther; but Luther alone stands on the proper field

[1] *Kirchengeschichte*, IV. 87 sq.

[2] Martin, another impartial and dogmatically unbiassed writer, likewise gives, with reference to the Marburg conference, " the honors of the debate, for logic and for moderation and brotherly charity," to Zwingli. *Hist. de France*, VIII. 114, note. So does Dean Stanley.

of battle where the cause of the Reformation had to be fought out. He is the path-breaking Reformer, and without his labors Zwingli could never have reached the historic significance which properly belongs to him alongside of Luther." [1]

Dr. Alexander Schweizer (of Zurich), in his commemorative oration of 1884, does equal justice to both: "Luther and Zwingli founded, each according to his individuality, the Reformation in the degenerated Church, both strengthening and supplementing each other, but in many respects also going different ways. How shall we estimate them, elevating the one, lowering the other, as is the case with Goethe and Schiller? Let us rather rejoice, according to Goethe's advice, in the possession of two such men. May those Lutherans who wish to check the growing union with the Reformed, continue to represent Luther as the only Reformer, and, in ignorance of Zwingli's deep evangelical piety, depreciate him as a mere humanistic illuminator: this shall not hinder us from doing homage at the outset to Luther's full greatness, contented with the independent position of our Zwingli alongside of this first hero of the Reformation; yea, we deem it our noblest task in this Zwingli festival at Zurich, which took cheerful part in the preceding Luther festival, to acknowledge Luther as the chief hero of the battle of the Reformation, and to put his world-historical and personal greatness in the front rank; and this all the more since Zwingli himself, and afterwards Calvin, have preceded us in this high estimate of Luther." [2]

Phillips Brooks (Bishop of Massachusetts, the greatest preacher of the Protestant Episcopal Church in the United States, d. 1893): "Of all the Reformers, in this respect [*tolerance*], Zwingli, who so often in the days of darkness is the man of light, is the noblest and clearest. At the conference in Marburg he contrasts most favorably with Luther in his willingness to be reconciled for the good of the common cause, and he was one of the very few who in those days believed that the good and earnest heathen could be saved." (*Lectures on Tolerance,* New York, 1887, p. 34.)

Of secular historians, J. Michelet (*Histoire de France,* X. 310 sq.) shows a just appreciation of Zwingli, and his last noble confession addressed to the King of France. He says of him: "*Grand docteur, meilleur patriote, nature forte et simple, il a montré le type même, le vrai génie de la Suisse, dans sa fière indépendance de l'Italie, de l'Allemagne. . . . Son langage à François 1er, digne de la Renaissance, établissait la question de l'Église dans sa grandeur.*" He then quotes the passage of the final salvation of all true and noble men, which no man with a heart can ever forget.

[1] "*Neben Luther.*" This is the proper expression, which also Schweizer has chosen. Usteri places Zwingli too high when he calls him "*ein Martin Luther ebenbürtiger Zeuge des evangelischen Glaubens.*" He is independent, but not equal.

[2] *Zwingli's Bedeutung neben Luther. Festrede zu Zwingli's 400 jährigem Geburtstag 1 Jan., 1484, gehalten in der Universitätsaula zu Zürich 7 Jan., 1884* (Zürich, 1884), p. 8.

CHAPTER III.

THE REFORMATION IN ZURICH. 1519-1526.

§ 10. *Zwingli called to Zurich.*

THE fame of Zwingli as a preacher and patriot secured him a call to the position of chief pastor of the Great Minster (Grossmünster), the principal church in Zurich, which was to become the Wittenberg of Switzerland. Many of the Zurichers had heard him preach on their pilgrimages to Einsiedeln. His enemies objected to his love of music and pleasure, and charged him with impurity, adding slander to truth. His friend Myconius, the teacher of the school connected with the church, exerted all his influence in his favor. He was elected by seventeen votes out of twenty-four, Dec. 10, 1518.

He arrived in Zurich on the 27th of the month, and received a hearty welcome. He promised to fulfil his duties faithfully, and to begin with the continuous exposition of the Gospel of Matthew, so as to bring the whole life of Christ before the mind of the people. This was a departure from the custom of following the prescribed Gospel and Epistle lessons, but justified by the example of the ancient Fathers, as Chrysostom and Augustin, who preached on whole books. The Reformed Churches reasserted the freedom of selecting texts; while Luther retained the Catholic system of pericopes.

Zurich, the most flourishing city in German Switzerland, beautifully situated in an amphitheatre of fertile hills, on the lake of the same name and the banks of the Limmat, dates its existence from the middle of the ninth century

38

when King Louis the German founded there the abbey of Frauenmünster (853). The spot was known in old Roman times as a custom station (*Turicum*). It became a free imperial city of considerable commerce between Germany and Italy, and was often visited by kings and emperors.

The Great Minster was built in the twelfth century, and passed into the Reformed communion, like the minsters of Basle, Berne, and Lausanne, which are the finest churches in Switzerland.

In the year 1315 Zurich joined the Swiss confederacy by an eternal covenant with Lucerne, Uri, Schwyz, and Unterwalden. This led to a conflict with Austria, which ended favorably for the confederacy.[1]

In the beginning of the sixteenth century Zurich numbered seven

THE GREAT MINSTER IN ZURICH IN THE YEAR 1519. (After the copperplate of Hegi.)

thousand inhabitants. It was the centre of the international relations of Switzerland, and the residence of the embassadors of foreign powers which rivalled with each other in securing the support of Swiss soldiers. This fact brought wealth and luxury, and fostered party spirit and the

---

[1] On the early history of Zurich, see Bluntschli, *Geschichte der Republik Zürich*, 2d ed. 1856; G. v. Wyss, *Zürich am Ausgange des 13ten Jahrh.*, 1876; Dierauer, *Geschichte der Schweiz. Eidgenossenschaft*, vol. I. (1887), 171–217.

lust of gain and power among the citizens. Bullinger says,
" Before the preaching of the gospel [the Reformation],
Zurich was in Switzerland what Corinth was in Greece." [1]

§ 11. *Zwingli's Public Labors and Private Studies.*

Zwingli began his duties in Zurich on his thirty-sixth
birthday (Jan. 1, 1519) by a sermon on the genealogy of
Christ, and announced that on the next day (which was a
Sunday) he would begin a series of expository discourses on
the first Gospel. From Matthew he proceeded to the Acts,
the Pauline and Catholic Epistles; so that in four years he
completed the homiletical exposition of the whole New
Testament except the Apocalypse (which he did not regard
as an apostolic book). In the services during the week he
preached on the Psalms. He prepared himself carefully
from the original text. He probably used for his first course
Chrysostom's famous Homilies on Matthew. With the Greek
he was already familiar since his sojourn in Glarus. The
Hebrew he learned from a pupil of Reuchlin who had come
to Zurich. His copy of Reuchlin's *Rudimenta Hebraica* is
marked with many notes from his hand.[2]

His sermons, as far as published, are characterized, as
Hagenbach says, " by spiritual sobriety and manly solidity."
They are plain, practical, and impressive, and more ethical
than doctrinal.

He made it his chief object " to preach Christ from the
fountain," and " to insert the pure Christ into the hearts." [3]
He would preach nothing but what he could prove from the
Scriptures, as the only rule of Christian faith and practice.

---

[1] Mörikofer (I. 430 sqq.) gives a disgusting example of the rudeness and
licentiousness of the Zurichers of that time.

[2] He wrote to Myconius in 1522: "*Statui proximis diebus in manus resumere
literas Hebraicas; nam futuro Decembri . . . Psalmos prælegam.*" *Opera*, VII. 145.

[3] *Christum ex fontibus prædicare, purum Christum animis inserere.* Comp. his
letter to Myconius (1520), *Opera*, VII. 142 sqq.

This is a reformatory idea; for the aim of the Reformation
was to reopen the fountain of the New Testament to the
whole people, and to renew the life of the Church by the
power of the primitive gospel. By his method of preaching
on entire books he could give his congregation a more complete idea of the life of Christ and the way of salvation than
by confining himself to detached sections. He did not at
first attack the Roman Church, but only the sins of the
human heart; he refuted errors by the statement of truth.[1]

His sermons gained him great popularity in Zurich. The
people said, "Such preaching was never heard before." Two
prominent citizens, who were disgusted with the insipid
legendary discourses of priests and monks, declared after
hearing his first sermon, "This is a genuine preacher of the
truth, a Moses who will deliver the people from bondage."
They became his constant hearers and devoted friends.

Zwingli was also a devoted pastor, cheerful, kind, hospitable and benevolent. He took great interest in young men,
and helped them to an education. He was, as Bullinger
says, a fine-looking man, of more than middle size, with a
florid complexion, and an agreeable, melodious voice, which,
though not strong, went to the heart. We have no portrait
from his lifetime; he had no Lucas Kranach near him, like
Luther; all his pictures are copies of the large oil painting
of Hans Asper in the city library at Zurich, which was made
after his death, and is rather hard and wooden.[2]

Zwingli continued his studies in Zurich and enlarged his
library, with the help of his friends Glareanus and Beatus
Rhenanus, who sent him books from Basle, the Swiss headquarters of literature. He did not neglect his favorite
classics, and read, as Bullinger says, Aristotle, Plato, Thu-

[1] He did not elaborate his discourses on Matthew for publication, but we have
fragmentary reports from the year 1525. See the extracts in Mörikofer, I. 57–63.

[2] See Asper's portrait on p. 16, and the description of the Zwingli pictures
in Mörikofer, I. 345, and in the pamphlet, *Zwingli-Ausstellung*, Zurich, January, 1884.

cydides, Homer, Horace, Sallust, and Seneca. But his chief attention was now given to the Scriptures and the patristic commentaries.

In the meantime Luther's reform was shaking the whole Church, and strengthened and deepened his evangelical convictions in a general way, although he had formed them independently. Some of Luther's books were reprinted in Basle in 1519, and sent to Zwingli by Rhenanus. Lutheran ideas were in the air, and found attentive ears in Switzerland. He could not escape their influence. The eucharistic controversy produced an alienation; but he never lost his great respect for Luther and his extraordinary services to the Church.[1]

§ 12. *Zwingli and the Sale of Indulgences.*

Bernhardin Samson, a Franciscan monk of Milan, crossed the St. Gotthard to Switzerland in August, 1518, as apostolic general commissioner for the sale of indulgences. He is the Tetzel of Switzerland, and equalled him in the audacious profanation of holy things by turning the forgiveness of sins and the release from purgatorial punishment into merchandise. He gave the preference to the rich who were willing to buy letters of indulgence on parchment for a crown. To the poor he sold the same article on common paper for a few coppers. In Berne he absolved the souls of all the departed Bernese of the pains of purgatory. In Bremgarten he excommunicated Dean Bullinger (the father of Henry) for opposing his traffic. But in Zurich he was stopped in his career.

Zwingli had long before been convinced of the error of indulgences by Wyttenbach when he studied in Basle. He had warned the people against Samson at Einsiedeln. He exerted

[1] In Zwingli's library are few works of Luther, and they have no annotations. (Usteri, *l.c.*, p. 716.) His noble tribute to Luther is quoted in this *History,* vol. VI. 668.

his influence against him in Zurich; and the magistracy, and even the bishop of Constance (who preferred to sell indulgences himself) supported the opposition. Samson was obliged to return to Italy with his " heavy, three-horse wagon of gold." Rome had learned a lesson of wisdom from Luther's Theses, and behaved in the case of Samson with more prudence and deference to the sentiment of the enlightened class of Catholics. Leo X., in a brief of April, 1519, expressed his willingness to recall and to punish him if he had transgressed his authority.[1]

The opposition to the sale of indulgences is the opening chapter in the history of the German Reformation, but a mere episode in the Swiss Reformation. That battle had been fought out victoriously by Luther. Zwingli came in no conflict with Rome on this question, and was even approved for his conduct by Dr. Faber, the general vicar of the diocese of Constance, who was then his friend, but became afterwards his enemy.

§ 13. *Zwingli during the Pestilence.*

In the summer of 1519 Zwingli went to the famous bath of Pfäffers at Ragatz to gather strength for his prospectively onerous duties at Zurich, in view of the danger of the approach of the plague from Basle. As soon as he learned, in August, that the plague had broken out in Zurich, he hastened back without stopping to visit his relations on the way. For several weeks he devoted himself, like a faithful shepherd, day after day, to the care of the sick, until he fell sick himself at the end of September. His life was in great danger, as he had worn himself out. The papal legate sent his own physician to his aid. The pestilence destroyed twenty-five hundred lives; that is, more than one-third of the population of Zurich. Zwingli recovered, but felt the effects on his brain and memory, and a lassitude in all his

[1] Mörikofer, I. 65 sqq.

limbs till the end of the year. His friends at home and abroad, including Faber, Pirkheimer, and Dürer at Nürnberg, congratulated him on his recovery.

The experience during this season of public distress and private affliction must have exerted a good influence upon his spiritual life.[1] We may gather this from the three poems, which he composed and set to music soon afterwards, on his sickness and recovery. They consist each of twenty-six rhymed iambic verses, and betray great skill in versification. They breathe a spirit of pious resignation to the will of God, and give us an insight into his religious life at that time.[2] He wrote another poem in 1529, and versified the Sixty-ninth Psalm.[3]

ZWINGLI'S POEMS DURING THE PESTILENCE, WITH A FREE CONDENSED TRANSLATION.

I. *Im Anfang der Krankheit.*

Hilf, Herr Gott, hilf
In dieser Noth;
Ich mein', der Tod
Syg[4] an der Thür.
Stand, Christe, für;
Denn du ihn überwunden hast!
Zu dir ich gilf:[5]
Ist es din Will,
Zuch us den Pfyl,[6]

Der mich verwundt,
Nit lass ein Stund
Mich haben weder Rüw[7] noch Rast!
Willt du dann glych[8]
Todt haben mich
Inmitts der Tagen min,
So soll es willig syn.
Thu, wie du willt,
Mich nüt befilt.[9]

[1] Merle d'Aubigné overrates the influence of this sickness by dating from it Zwingli's conversion and entire consecration to God. There was no sudden change in his life, as in Paul or Luther: he developed gradually.

[2] The original is given in *Werke*, II. 269–274, with a good modern reproduction by Fulda; also by Mörikofer, I. 72–74; and Hagenbach, 218 (5th ed. by Nippold). Abridged translations in the English editions of Merle d'Aubigné's *History of the Reformation*, Bk. VIII. ch. 8 ("Lo! at my door gaunt death I spy," etc.), and in Miss Moore's translation of Hagenbach's *History of the Reformation* (Edinb., 1878, vol. I. 274). The structure of the poems is very artificial and difficult to reproduce.

[3] These poems passed into the oldest Zurich hymn and tune books of 1560 and 1570, and are printed together by Wackernagel, *Das Deutsche Kirchenlied*, vol. III. 500–503.

[4] Sei.   [5] flehe, schreie.   [6] Pfeil.   [7] Ruh.   [8] doch.   [9] fehlt.

Din Haf[1] bin ich,
Mach ganz ald[2] brich.
Dann nimmst du hin
Den Geiste min

Von dieser Erd,
Thust du's, dass er nit böser werd,
Ald[2] andern nit
Befleck ihr Leben fromm und Sitt.

II. *Mitten in der Krankheit.*

Tröst, Herr Gott, tröst!
Die Krankheit wachst,[3]
Weh und Angst fasst
Min Seel und Lyb.[4]
Darum dich schyb[5]
Gen mir, einiger Trost, mit Gnad!
Die gwüss erlöst
Ein jeden, der
Sin herzlich B'ger
Und Hoffnung setzt
In dich, verschätzt.
Darzu diss Zyt all Nutz und Schad.
Nun ist es um;

Min Zung ist stumm,
Mag sprechen nit ein Wort;
Min Sinn' sind all verdorrt,
Darum ist Zyt,[6]
Dass du min Stryt[7]
Führist fürhin;
So ich nit bin
So stark, dass ich
Mög tapferlich
Thun Widerstand
Des Tüfels Facht[8] und frefner Hand.
Doch wird min Gmüth
Stät bliben dir, wie er auch wüth.

III. *Zur Genesung.*

G'sund, Herr Gott, g'sund!
Ich mein', ich kehr
Schon wiedrum her.
Ja, wenn dich dunkt,
Der Sünden Funk'
Werd nit mehr bherrschen mich uf
    Erd,
So muss min Mund
Din Lob und Lehr
Ussprechen mehr
Denn vormals je,
Wie es auch geh'
Einfältiglich ohn' alle G'fährd.
Wiewohl ich muss

Des Todes buss
Erliden zwar einmal
Villicht mit gröss'rer Qual,
Denn jezund wär'
Geschehen, Herr!
So ich sunst bin
Nach[9] gfahren hin,
So will ich doch
Den Trutz und Poch[10]
In dieser Welt
Tragen fröhlich um Widergelt,[11]
Mit Hülfe din,
Ohn' den nüt[12] mag vollkommen syn.

I. *In the Beginning of his Sickness.*

Help me, O Lord,
    My strength and rock;
Lo, at the door
    I hear death's knock.

Uplift thine arm,
    Once pierced for me,
That conquered death,
    And set me free.

[1] Gefäss.	[4] Leib.	[7] Streit.	[10] Ungestüm.
[2] oder.	[5] wende.	[8] Anfechtung.	[11] Vergeltung.
[3] wächst.	[6] Zeit.	[9] beinahe.	[12] nichts.

Yet, if thy voice,
In life's mid-day,
Recalls my soul,
Then I obey.

In faith and hope
Earth I resign,
Secure of heaven,
For I am Thine.

II. *In the Midst of his Sickness.*

My pains increase;
Haste to console;
For fear and woe
Seize body and soul.

Lo! Satan strains
To snatch his prey;
I feel his grasp;
Must I give way?

Death is at hand,
My senses fail,
My tongue is dumb;
Now, Christ, prevail.

He harms me not,
I fear no loss,
For here I lie
Beneath Thy cross.

III. *On recovering from his Sickness.*

My God! my Lord!
Healed by Thy hand,
Upon the earth
Once more I stand.

Though now delayed,
My hour will come,
Involved, perchance,
In deeper gloom.

Let sin no more
Rule over me;
My mouth shall sing
Alone of Thee.

But, let it come;
With joy I'll rise,
And bear my yoke
Straight to the skies.

§ 14. *The Open Breach. Controversy about Fasts.* 1522.

Zwingli was permitted to labor in Zurich for two years without serious opposition, although he had not a few enemies, both religious and political. The magistracy of Zurich took at first a neutral position, and ordered the priests of the city and country to preach the Scriptures, and to be *silent* about human inventions (1520). This is the first instance of an episcopal interference of the civil authority in matters of religion. It afterwards became a settled custom in Protestant Switzerland with the full consent of Zwingli. He was appointed canon of the Grossmünster, April 29, 1521, with an additional salary of seventy guilders, after he had given up the papal pension. With this moderate income he was contented for the rest of his life.

During Lent, 1522, Zwingli preached a sermon in which he showed that the prohibition of meat in Lent had no foundation in Scripture. Several of his friends, including his publisher, Froschauer, made practical use of their liberty. This brought on an open rupture. The bishop of Constance sent a strong deputation to Zurich, and urged the observance of the customary fasts. The magistracy prohibited the violation, and threatened to punish the offenders (April 9, 1522).[1] Zwingli defended himself in a tract on the free use of meats (April 16).[2] It is his first printed book. He essentially takes the position of Paul, that, in things indifferent, Christians have liberty to use or to abstain, and that the Church authorities have no right to forbid this liberty. He appeals to such passages as 1 Cor. 8:8; 10:25; Col. 2:16; 1 Tim. 4:1; Rom. 14:1–3; 15:1, 2.

The bishop of Constance issued a mandate to the civil authorities (May 24), exhorting them to protect the ordinances of the Holy Church.[3] He admonished the canons, without naming Zwingli, to prevent the spread of heretical doctrines. He also sought and obtained the aid of the Swiss Diet, then sitting at Lucerne.

Zwingli was in a dangerous position. He was repeatedly threatened with assassination. But he kept his courage, and

---

[1] Egli, *Actensammlung*, p. 77 (No. 237). Mörikofer (I. 97) gives a wrong date (March 19, 1521); but Egli's printer made an error in correcting him by quoting vol. II. instead of I.

[2] *Von Erkiesen und Fryheit der Spysen* (*De delectu et libero ciborum usu*). *Werke*, I. B. 1–30; a Latin version by Gwalter in *Opera Lat.* I. 324–339.

[3] Egli, p. 85; Strickler, I. 428. I give it here as a fair specimen of the semi-barbarous German of Swiss documents of that period. "*Dass unser vätterlicher getrüwer rat und früntlich ernstlich pitt ist, ir wöllen die ärgenuss und widerwärtigkeit by üch selbs, den üwern und andern fürkommen und üch obgemeldten der hailigen kirchen ordnungen und guoten gewonhaiten in cristenlicher geainter gehorsami verglychen, die vollziechen und solichs by den üwern zuo gesche(h)en, sovil an üch, verschaffen. Das halten wir dem Evangelio, der leer Pauli und dem hailigen unserm cristenlichen glouben glychmässig. Ir tuond ouch daran üch und den üwern wolfart, von uns gnädigklich und früntlich zuo erkennen und zuo verdienen.*"

felt sure of ultimate victory. He replied in the *Archeteles* ("the Beginning and the End"), hoping that this first answer would be the last.[1] He protested that he had done no wrong, but endeavored to lead men to God and to his Son Jesus Christ in plain language, such as the common people could understand. He warned the hierarchy of the approaching collapse of the Romish ceremonies, and advised them to follow the example of Julius Cæsar, who folded his garments around him that he might fall with dignity. The significance of this book consists in the strong statement of the authority of the Scriptures against the authority of the Church. Erasmus was much displeased with it.

§ 15. *Petition for the Abolition of Clerical Celibacy. Zwingli's Marriage.*

In July of the same year (1522), Zwingli, with ten other priests, sent a Latin petition to the bishop, and a German petition to the Swiss Diet, to permit the free preaching of the gospel and the marriage of the clergy as the only remedy against the evils of enforced celibacy. He quotes the Scriptures for the divine institution and right of marriage, and begs the confederates to permit what God himself has sanctioned. He sent both petitions to Myconius in Lucerne for signatures. Some priests approved, but were afraid to sign; others said the petition was useless, and could only be granted by the pope or a council.[2]

The petition was not granted. Several priests openly disobeyed. One married even a nun of the convent of Oetenbach (1523); Reubli of Wyticon married, April 28, 1523; Leo Judæ, Sept. 19, 1523.

Zwingli himself entered into the marriage relation in 1522,[3]

---

[1] *Opera*, III. 26–76.

[2] *Werke*, I. A. 30–51; III. 16–25.

[3] See the letters of Myconius from 1522, where he sends salutations to Zwingli's wife, quoted in § 7, p. 28.

but from prudential reasons he did not make it public till April 5, 1524 (more than a year before Luther's marriage, which took place June 13, 1525). Such cases of secret marriage were not unfrequent; but it would have been better for his fame if, as a minister and reformer, he had exercised self-restraint till public opinion was ripe for the change.

His wife, Anna Reinhart,[1] was the widow of Hans Meyer von Knonau,[2] the mother of three children, and lived near Zwingli. She was two years older than he. His enemies spread the report that he married for beauty and wealth; but she possessed only four hundred guilders besides her wardrobe and jewelry. She ceased to wear her jewelry after marrying the Reformer.

We have only one letter of Zwingli to his wife, written from Berne, Jan. 11, 1528, in which he addresses her as his dearest house-wife.[3] From occasional expressions of respect and affection for his wife, and from salutations of friends to her, we must infer that his family life was happy; but it lacked the poetic charm of Luther's home. She was a useful helpmate in his work.[4] She contributed her share towards

---

[1] His letter to her bears the inscription, "*Der Frauen Anna Reinhartin in Zürich, seiner lieben Hausfrau.*" *Opera*, VIII. 134. Others spell the name *Reinhard*.

[2] A soldier of wild habits, who belonged to one of the oldest and richest families of Zurich, and died 1517.

[3] It is as follows (VIII. 134): "*Gnad und Fried von Gott. Liebste Hausfrau, ich sage Gott Dank, dass er dir eine fröhliche Geburt verliehen hat; der wolle uns die nach seinem Willen zu erziehen verleihen. Schicke meiner Base ein oder zwei Tüchli [Tüchlein], solcher Mass und Weise, als du sie trägst. Sie kommt ziemlich [sittsam], doch nicht beginlich [i.e., wie eine Nonne, eine Beghine], ist eine Frau von 40 Jahren in alle Weis und Mass, wie sie Meister Jörgen Frau beschrieben hat. Thut mir und uns Allen über die Mass gütlich. Bis [Sei] hiemit Gott befohlen. Grüsse mir Gevatter Schaffnerin, Ulmann Trinkler, Schulthess Effingerin und wer dir lieb sei. Bitt Gott für mich und uns Alle. Gegeben zu Bern 11. Tag Jänners. Grüsse mir alle deine Kinder. Besonders Margreth tröste in meinem Namen. Huldreich Zwingli, dein Hauswirth.*"

[4] One of his friends calls her "*eine Mitarbeiterin am Wort, welche dir, dem Apostel, behülflich ist.*" Finsler, *U. Zwingli*, p. 52 sq.

the creation of pastoral family life, with its innumerable happy homes.[1]

In Zwingli's beautiful copy of the Greek Bible (from the press of Aldus in Venice, 1518), which is still preserved and called "Zwingli's Bible," he entered with his own hand a domestic chronicle, which records the names, birthdays, and sponsors of his four children, as follows: "Regula Zwingli, born July 13, 1524;[2] Wilhelm Zwingli, born January 29, 1526;[3] Huldreich Zwingli, born Jan. 6, 1528;[4] Anna Zwingli, born May 4, 1530."[5] His last male descendant was his grandson, Ulrich, professor of theology, born 1556, died 1601. The last female descendant was his great-granddaughter, Anna Zwingli, who presented his MS. copy of the Greek Epistles of Paul to the city library of Zurich in 1634.

Zwingli lived in great simplicity, and left no property. His little study (the "Zwingli-Stübli"), in the official dwelling of the deacon of the Great Minster, is carefully preserved in its original condition.

§ 16. *Zwingli and Lambert of Avignon.*

In July, 1522, there appeared in Zurich a Franciscan monk, Lambert of Avignon, in his monastic dress, riding on a donkey. He had left his convent in the south of France, and was in search of evangelical religion. Haller of Berne recommended him to Zwingli. Lambert preached some Latin sermons against the abuses of the Roman Church, but still advocated the worship of saints and of the Virgin Mary.

[1] Comp. vol. VI. § 79, p. 473 sqq.

[2] She married Rudolf Gwalter, Bullinger's adopted son and successor, and first editor of Zwingli's collected works.

[3] He studied at Strassburg with Capito, and died with him of the pestilence, 1541.

[4] He became pastor of the Prediger-Kirche, and married Bullinger's oldest daughter, Anna.

[5] Anna died very young, and her death is recorded in the same book.

Zwingli interrupted him with the remark, "You err," and convinced him of his error in a disputation.

The Franciscan thanked God and proceeded to Wittenberg, where Luther received him kindly. At the Synod of Homberg (1526) he advocated a scheme of Presbyterian church government, and at the conference at Marburg he professed to be converted to Zwingli's view of the Lord's Supper.[1]

§ 17. *The Sixty-seven Conclusions.*

On the Sixty-seven Conclusions and the Three Disputations see ZWINGLI: *Werke,* I. A. 105 sqq.; BULLINGER: I. 97 sqq.; EGLI: 111, 114, 173 sqq.; MÖRIKOFER: I. 138 sqq., 191 sqq. The text of the Sixty-seven Articles in Swiss-German, *Werke,* I. A. 153–157; in modern German and Latin, in SCHAFF: *Creeds of Christendom,* III. 197–207.

Zwingli's views, in connection with the Lutheran Reformation in Germany, created a great commotion, not only in the city and canton of Zurich, but in all Switzerland. At his suggestion, the government — that is, the burgomaster and the small and large Council (called The Two Hundred) — ordered a public disputation which should settle the controversy on the sole basis of the Scriptures.

For this purpose Zwingli published Sixty-seven Articles or Conclusions (*Schlussreden*). They are the first public statement of the Reformed faith, but they never attained symbolical authority, and were superseded by maturer confessions. They resemble the Ninety-five Theses of Luther against indulgences, which six years before had opened the drama of the German Reformation; but they mark a great advance in Protestant sentiment, and cover a larger number of topics. They are full of Christ as the only Saviour and Mediator, and clearly teach the supremacy of the Word of God as the only rule of faith; they reject and attack the primacy of the Pope, the Mass, the invocation of saints,

---

[1] See vol. VI. 582 sqq., 586 sq., 649. Comp. Bullinger, I. 76 sqq.; Haller's letter to Zwingli, July 8, 1522 (*Opera,* VII. 206 sq.).

the meritoriousness of human works, the fasts, pilgrimages, celibacy, purgatory, etc., as unscriptural commandments of men.

The following are the most important of these theses: —

1. All who say that the gospel is nothing without the approbation of the Church, err and cast reproach upon God.

2. The sum of the gospel is that our Lord Jesus Christ, the true Son of God, has made known to us the will of his heavenly Father, and redeemed us by his innocence from eternal death, and reconciled us to God.

3. Therefore Christ is the only way to salvation to all who were, who are, who shall be.

4. Whosoever seeks or shows another door, errs — yea, is a murderer of souls and a robber.

7. Christ is the head of all believers who are his body; but without him the body is dead.

8. All who live in this Head are his members and children of God. And this is the Church, the communion of saints, the bride of Christ, the *Ecclesia catholica.*

15. Who believes the gospel shall be saved; who believes not, shall be damned. For in the gospel the whole truth is clearly contained.

16. From the gospel we learn that the doctrines and traditions of men are of no use to salvation.

17. Christ is the one eternal high-priest. Those who pretend to be high-priests resist, yea, set aside, the honor and dignity of Christ.

18. Christ, who offered himself once on the cross, is the sufficient and perpetual sacrifice for the sins of all believers. Therefore the mass is no sacrifice, but a commemoration of the one sacrifice of the cross, and a seal of the redemption through Christ.

19. Christ is the only Mediator between God and us.

22. Christ is our righteousness. From this it follows that our works are good so far as they are Christ's, but not good so far as they are our own.

24. Christians are not bound to any works which Christ has not commanded. They may eat at all times all kinds of food.

26. Nothing is more displeasing to God than hypocrisy.

27. All Christians are brethren.

28. Whatsoever God permits and has not forbidden, is right. Therefore marriage is becoming to all men.

34. The spiritual [hierarchical] power, so called, has no foundation in the Holy Scriptures and the teaching of Christ.[1]

35. But the secular power [of the state] is confirmed by the teaching and example of Christ.[2]

---

[1] Zwingli means the worldly power and splendor of the pope and the bishops, and quotes against it the lessons of humility, Matt. 18: 1; 1 Pet. 5:1-3: "*Die Höhe nach der die päpst und bishof strytend, hat keinen Grund.*" See his *Uslegung* or defence of the Articles, *Werke*, I. 346 sq.

[2] For this he quotes Luke 2 : 5 and Matt. 22 : 21.

37, 38. All Christians owe obedience to the magistracy, provided it does not command what is against God.[1]

49. I know of no greater scandal than the prohibition of lawful marriage to priests, while they are permitted for money to have concubines. Shame![2]

50. God alone forgives sins, through Jesus Christ our Lord alone.

57. The Holy Scripture knows nothing of a purgatory after this life.

58, 59. God alone knows the condition of the departed, and the less he has made known to us, the less we should pretend to know.

66. All spiritual superiors should repent without delay, and set up the cross of Christ alone, or they will perish. The axe is laid at the root.

§ 18. *The Public Disputations.* 1523.

The first disputation was held in the city hall on Thursday, Jan. 29, 1523, in the German language, before about six hundred persons, including all the clergy and members of the small and large councils of Zurich. St. Gall was represented by Vadian; Berne, by Sebastian Meyer; Schaffhausen, by Sebastian Hofmeister. Œcolampadius from Basle expected no good from disputations, and declined to come. He agreed with Melanchthon's opinion about the Leipzig disputation of Eck with Carlstadt and Luther. Nevertheless, he attended, three years afterwards, the Disputation at Baden. The bishop of Constance sent his general vicar, Dr. Faber, hitherto a friend of Zwingli, and a man of respectable learning and an able debater, with three others as counsellors and judges. Faber declined to enter into a detailed discussion of theological questions which, he thought, belong to the tribunal of councils or of renowned universities, as

[1] In the *Uslegung* (I. 352 sq.) he explains Rom. 13:1: "Let every soul be subject unto the higher powers." "Every soul," he says, "means every living man, and includes popes, bishops, priests, monks and nuns. Every power is from God; consequently, also, a bad magistracy, with which God punishes our sins (Isa. 3:4). Then we must also obey the pope, even a bad one, because he is set over us by God for punishment. This I believe firmly, but I believe also that God will lead us out of this captivity, as he led Israel out of Egypt through his servant Moses."

[2] "*Pfui der Schande,*" is added in the German text. In the Swiss dialect, "*Pfuch der Schand!*" (I. A. 156). In the defence of this article (I. 378 sq.), Zwingli strongly illustrates the evil effects of the lewd life of the unmarried clergy upon the morals of the laity. "It is easy," he says, "to command chastity; but no one is able to keep it without the grace of God." Concerning his own case, see § 7, p. 27.

Paris, Cologne and Louvain. Zwingli answered his objections, and convinced the audience.[1]

On the same day the magistracy passed judgment in favor of Zwingli, and directed him "to continue to preach the holy gospel as heretofore, and to proclaim the true, divine Scriptures until he was better informed." All other preachers and pastors in the city and country were warned "not to preach anything which they could not establish by the holy Gospel and other divine Scriptures," and to avoid personal controversy and bitter names.[2]

Zwingli prepared a lengthy and able defence of his Articles against the charges of Faber, July, 1523.[3]

The disputation soon produced its natural effects. Ministers took regular wives; the nunnery of Oetenbach was emptied; baptism was administered in the vernacular, and without exorcism; the mass and worship of images were neglected and despised. A band of citizens, under the lead of a shoemaker, Klaus Hottinger, overthrew the great wooden crucifix in Stadelhofen, near the city, and committed other lawless acts.[4]

Zwingli was radical in his opposition to idolatrous and superstitious ceremonies, but disapproved disorderly methods, and wished the magistracy to authorize the necessary changes.

Consequently, a second disputation was arranged for October 26, 1523, to settle the question of images and of the

---

[1] An unofficial report of the disputation was published by Hegenwald, March 3, 1523 (*Werke*, I. A. 105–168). Faber issued, March 10, a counter-report. Seven Zurichers replied to him in "*Das Gyrenrupfen*" (*Geyerrupfen*), 1523, and charged him with lying and claiming the speeches of others. Salat's *Historische Nachricht* of the deputation is a "*parteiische Verstümmelung und Entstellung*" of Hegenwald's report, and hence of no historical value (Schuler and Schulthess, in their ed. of Zw. I. 109). Comp. Aug. Baur, *Die erste Zürcher Disputation*, Halle, 1883.

[2] Egli, 114 sq.; Bullinger, I. 103.

[3] *Werke*, I. A. 169–425.

[4] Füssli, II. 33–39; Egli, 176, 178.

mass. All the ministers of the city and canton were ordered to attend; the twelve other cantons, the bishops of Constance, Coire and Basle, and the University of Basle were urgently requested to send learned delegates. The bishop of Constance replied (Oct. 16) that he must obey the Pope and the Emperor, and advised the magistracy to wait for a general council. The bishop of Basle excused himself on account of age and sickness, but likewise referred to a council and warned against separation. The bishop of Coire made no answer. Most of the cantons declined to send delegates, except Schaffhausen and St. Gall. Unterwalden honestly replied that they had no learned men among them, but pious priests who faithfully adhered to the old faith of Christendom, which they preferred to all innovations.

The second disputation was held in the city hall, and lasted three days. There were present about nine hundred persons, including three hundred and fifty clergymen and ten doctors. Dr. Vadian of St. Gall, Dr. Hofmeister of Schaffhausen, and Dr. Schappeler of St. Gall presided. Zwingli and Leo Judæ defended the Protestant cause, and had the advantage of superior Scripture learning and argument. The Roman party betrayed much ignorance; but Martin Steinli of Schaffhausen ably advocated the mass. Konrad Schmid of Küssnacht took a moderate position, and produced great effect upon the audience by his eloquence. His judgment was, first to take the idolatry out of the heart before abolishing the outward images, and to leave the staff to the weak until they are able to walk without it and to rely solely on Christ.[1]

---

[1] The only German report of the second disputation, in *Werke*, I. A. 459–540 (comp. Bullinger, I. 131 sqq.), is from the pen of Ludwig Hetzer, chaplain at Wädenschweil, then priest at Zurich, an ardent friend of the Reformation, who afterwards joined the Anabaptists, and was beheaded at Constance. Gwalter made an abridged Latin translation in *Zw. Opera*, II. 623–646. Zwingli took the ground that a truly Christian congregation was a better church than all the bishops and popes, and had as good a right to settle religious contro-

The Council was not prepared to order the immediate abolition of the mass and the images. It punished Hottinger and other "idol-stormers" by banishment, and appointed a commission of ministers and laymen, including Zwingli, Schmidt and Judæ, who should enlighten the people on the subject by preaching and writing. Zwingli prepared his "Short and Christian Introduction," which was sent by the Council of Two Hundred to all the ministers of the canton, the bishops of Constance, Basle, and Coire, the University of Basle, and to the twelve other cantons (Nov. 17, 1523).[1] It may be compared to the instruction of Melanchthon for the visitation of the churches of Saxony (1528).

A third disputation, of a more private character, was held Jan. 20, 1524. The advocates of the mass were refuted and ordered not to resist any longer the decisions of the magistracy, though they might adhere to their faith.

During the last disputation, Zwingli preached a sermon on the corrupt state of the clergy, which he published by request in March, 1524, under the title "The Shepherd."[2] He represents Christ as the good Shepherd in contrast with the selfish hirelings, according to the parable in the tenth chapter of the Gospel of John. Among the false shepherds he counts the bishops who do not preach at all; those priests who teach their own dreams instead of the Word of God; those who preach the Word but for the glorification of popery; those who deny their preaching by their conduct; those who preach for filthy lucre; and, finally, all who mislead men away from the Creator to the creature. Zwingli

---

versies as a council, where the Word of God was not allowed to decide. "*Ja, Höngg und Küssnacht ist ein gewüssere Kilch denn all züsammen gerottet bishof und päpst.*" *Werke,* I. 472.

[1] *Ein kurz christenliche ynleitung, die ein eersamer rat der statt Zürich den sœlsorgern und prädicanten . . . zugesandt habend,* etc. *Werke,* I. A. 541–565. Gwalter gives a Latin version, *Op.* I. 264–268.

[2] *Der Hirt, wie man die waren christenlichen hirten und widerum die falschen erkennen . . . sölle. Werke,* I. A. 631–668.

treats the papists as refined idolaters, and repeatedly denounces idolatry as the root of the errors and abuses of the Church.

During the summer of 1524 the answers of the bishops and the Diet appeared, both in opposition to any innovations. The bishop of Constance, in a letter to Zurich, said that he had consulted several universities; that the mass and the images were sufficiently warranted by the Scriptures, and had always been in use. The canton appointed a commission of clergymen and laymen to answer the episcopal document.[1] The Swiss Diet, by a deputation, March 21, 1524, expressed regret that Zurich sympathized with the new, unchristian Lutheran religion, and prayed the canton to remain faithful to old treaties and customs, in which case the confederates would cheerfully aid in rooting out real abuses, such as the shameful trade in benefices, the selling of indulgences, and the scandalous lives of the clergy.

Thus forsaken by the highest ecclesiastical and civil authorities, the canton of Zurich acted on its own responsibility, and carried out the contemplated reforms.

The three disputations mark an advance beyond the usual academic disputations in the Latin language. They were held before laymen as well as clergymen, and in the vernacular. They brought religious questions before the tribunal of the people according to the genius of republican institutions. They had, therefore, more practical effect than the disputation at Leipzig. The German Reformation was decided by the will of the princes; the Swiss Reformation, by the will of the people: but in both cases there was a sympathy between the rulers and the majority of the population.

---

[1] The answer was written by Zwingli, and printed Aug. 18, 1524. *Werke*, I. A. 584–630.

§ 19. *The Abolition of the Roman Worship.* 1524.

BULLINGER, I. 173 sqq.   FÜSSLI, I. 142 sqq.   EGLI, 234 sqq.

By these preparatory measures, public opinion was prepared for the practical application of the new ideas. The
old order of worship had to be abolished before the new
order could be introduced. The destruction was radical, but
orderly. It was effected by the co-operation of the preachers
and the civil magistracy, with the consent of the people. It
began at Pentecost, and was completed June 20, 1524.

In the presence of a deputation from the authorities of
Church and State, accompanied by architects, masons and
carpenters, the churches of the city were purged of pictures,.
relics, crucifixes, altars, candles, and all ornaments, the frescoes effaced, and the walls whitewashed, so that nothing
remained but the bare building to be filled by a worshiping
congregation. The pictures were broken and burnt, some
given to those who had a claim, a few preserved as antiqui-
ties. The bones of the saints were buried. Even the organs
were removed, and the Latin singing of the choir abolished,
but fortunately afterwards replaced by congregational singing of psalms and hymns in the vernacular (in Basle as
early as 1526, in St. Gall 1527, in Zurich in 1598). "Within
thirteen days," says Bullinger, "all the churches of the city
were cleared; costly works of painting and sculpture, especially a beautiful table in the Waterchurch, were destroyed.
The superstitious lamented; but the true believers rejoiced
in it as a great and joyous worship of God." [1]

In the following year the magistracy melted, sold, or gave
away the rich treasures of the Great Minster and the Frauen-
minster, — chalices, crucifixes, and crosses of gold and silver,

[1] I. 175. Bullinger justifies the abolition of church music (which took place
in the Grossmünster, Dec. 9, 1527) with St. Paul's objection to the unintelligible glossolalia without interpretation (1 Cor. 14 : 6–9). He must, of course,
mean the chanting of a choir in Latin. The Swiss Reformed churches excel
in congregational singing.

precious relics, clerical robes, tapestry, and other ornaments.[1] In 1533 not a copper's worth was left in the sacristy of the Great Minster.[2] Zwingli justified this vandalism by the practice of a conquering army to spike the guns and to destroy the forts and provisions of the enemy, lest he might be tempted to return.

The same work of destruction took place in the village churches in a less orderly way. Nothing was left but the bare buildings, empty, cold and forbidding.

The Swiss Reformers proceeded on a strict construction of the second commandment as understood by Jews and Moslems. They regarded all kinds of worship paid to images and relics as a species of idolatry. They opposed chiefly the paganism of popery; while Luther attacked its legalistic Judaism, and allowed the pictures to remain as works of art and helps to devotion. For the classical literature of Greece and Rome, however, Zwingli had more respect than Luther. It should be remarked also that he was not opposed to images as such any more than to poetry and music, but only to their idolatrous use in churches. In his reply to Valentin Compar of Uri (1525), he says, "The controversy is not about images which do not offend the faith and the honor of God, but about idols to which divine honors are paid. Where there is no danger of idolatry, the images may remain; but idols should not be tolerated. All the papists tell us that images are the books for the unlearned. But where has God commanded us to learn from such books?" He thought that the absence of images in churches would tend to increase the hunger for the Word of God.[3]

[1] Egli, p. 269 (No. 614, Jan. 9, 1525); Mörikofer, I. 315 sq. Janssen (III. 84 sq.) dwells with circumstantial minuteness on the confiscation and robbery of these church treasures, some of which dated from the time of Charlemagne.

[2] Egli, p. 893 (No. 2004, c. 1533). Uetinger declared that between 1524 and 1532 all the treasury of the sacristy was squandered, and nobody knew what had become of it. "*Prorsus nihil supererat.*"

[3] *Werke*, II. A. 17–59. Comp. Mörikofer, I. 269–274.

The Swiss iconoclasm passed into the Reformed Churches of France, Holland, Scotland, and North America. In recent times a reaction has taken place, not in favor of image worship, which is dead and gone, but in favor of Christian art; and more respect is paid to the decency and beauty of the house of God and the comfort of worshipers.

§ 20. *The Reformed Celebration of the Lord's Supper.*

ZWINGLI, *Werke*, II. B. 233. BULLINGER, I. 263. FÜSSLI, IV. 64.

The mass was gone. The preaching of the gospel and the celebration of the Lord's Supper by the whole congregation, in connection with a kind of Agape, took its place.

The first celebration of the communion after the Reformed usage was held in the Holy Week of April, 1525, in the Great Minster. There were three services, — first for the youth on Maundy-Thursday, then for the middle-aged on Good Friday, and last for the old people on Easter. The celebration was plain, sober, solemn. The communicants were seated around long tables, which took the place of the altar, the men on the right, the women on the left. They listened reverently to the prayers, the words of institution, the Scripture lessons, taken from the eleventh chapter of the first Corinthians and the mysterious discourse in the sixth chapter of John on the spiritual eating and drinking of Christ's flesh and blood, and to an earnest exhortation of the minister. They then received in a kneeling posture the sacred emblems in wooden plates and wooden cups. The whole service was a commemoration of Christ's atoning death and a spiritual communion with him, according to the theory of Zwingli.

In the liturgical part he retained more from the Catholic service than we might expect; namely, the Introit, the Gloria in Excelsis, the Creed, and several responses; but all were translated from Latin into the Swiss dialect, and with curious modifications. Thus the Gloria in Excelsis, the Creed, and the One Hundred and Third Psalm were said alternately by the men and the women, instead of the minister and the deacon, as in the Catholic service, or the minister and the congregation, as in the Lutheran and Episcopal services.[1] In most of the Reformed churches (except the Anglican) the responses passed out of use, and the kneeling posture in receiving the communion gave way to the standing or sitting posture.

The communion service was to be held four times in the year, — at Easter, Whitsunday, autumn, and Christmas. It was preceded by preparatory devotions, and made a season of special solemnity. The mass was prohibited at first only in the city, afterwards also in the country.

Zwingli furnished also in 1525 an abridged baptismal service in the vernacular language, omitting the formula of exorcism and all those elements for which he found no Scripture warrant.[2]

The Zwinglian and Calvinistic worship depends for its effect too much upon the intellectual and spiritual power of the minister, who can make it either very solemn and impressive, or very cold and barren. The Anglican Church has the advantage of an admirable liturgy.

---

[1] *Werke*, II. B. 237 sqq. I give a specimen from the *Gloria in Excelsis*: —

DER PFARRER: *Eer sye gott in den höhinnen!*
DIE MANN: *Und frid uf erden!*
DIE WYBER: *Den menschen ein recht gmüt!*
DIE MANN: *Wir lobend dich, wir prysend dich.*
DIE WYBER: *Wir betend dich an, wir verehrend dich*, etc.

Shorter responses, however, occur between the minister or deacon and the congregation.

[2] The first German baptismal service by Zwingli and Leo Judæ appeared in the summer of 1523, the second in May, 1525. *Werke*, II. B. 224 sqq.; 230 sq.

§ 21. *Other Changes.   A Theological School.   The Caro-linum.   A System of Theology.*

Other changes completed the Reformation.   The Corpus
Christi festival was abolished, and the Christian year reduced
to the observance of Christmas, Good Friday, Easter, and
Pentecost.   Processions and pilgrimages ceased.   The property of convents was confiscated and devoted to schools and
hospitals.   The matrimonial legislation was reconstructed,
and the care of the poor organized.   In 1528 a synod
assembled for the first time, to which each congregation
sent its minister and two lay delegates.

A theological college, called Carolinum, was established
from the funds of the Great Minster, and opened June 19,
1525.   It consisted of the collegium humanitatis, for the
study of the ancient languages, philosophy and mathematics,
and the Carolinum proper, for the study of the Holy Scriptures, which were explained in daily lectures, and popular-
ized by the pastors for the benefit of the congregation.   This
was called prophesying (1 Cor. 14:1).[1]   Zwingli wrote a
tract on Christian education (1526).[2]   He organized this
school of the prophets, and explained in it several books
of the Old Testament, according to the Septuagint.   He
recommended eminent scholars to professorships.   Among
the earliest teachers were Ceporin, Pellican, Myconius, Collin,
Megander, and Bibliander.   To Zwingli Zurich owes its theological and literary reputation.   The Carolinum secured an
educated ministry, and occupied an influential position in
the development of theological science and literature till the

[1] Comp. Pestalozzi, *Leo Judæ*, p. 76, and Güder on " Prophezei," in Herzog[2],
XII. 288.

[2] Republished by Emil Egli, *U. Zwingli's Lehrubchlein, oder wie man die
Jugend in guten Sitten und christlicher Zucht auferziehen und lehren solle.*   Zurich,
1884.   With an appendix of documents relating to the school at Zurich in
Zwingli's time.

ZÜRICH IN THE SIXTEENTH CENTURY.

LEO IUDAE THEOLOGUS,
INTER TIGURINÆ ECCLESIÆ PASTORES ET
MINISTROS NON POSTREMUS ANNOS XIX. ET AMPLIUS:
Veteris Testamenti libros Hebraicos, simplici et purâ dicti
one, è sacra Hebræorum lingua, in Latinam et Germanicam
transtulit, fide et religione summâ:

Obijt Tiguri iam senex, mole grandis huius operis
oppressus ANNO M·D·XLII. Ætatis LX.

Con: Meyer fecit A6 75.

nineteenth century, when it was superseded by the organization of a full university.[1]

Zwingli wrote in the course of three months and a half an important work on the true, evangelical, as opposed to the false, popish faith, and dedicated it to Francis I., king of France, in the vain hope of gaining him to the cause of the Reformation.[2] It completes his theological opposition to the papacy. It is the first systematic exposition of the Reformed faith, as Melanchthon's *Loci* was the first system of Lutheran theology; but it was afterwards eclipsed by Calvin's *Institutes*, which were addressed to the same king with no better effect. Francis probably never read either; but the dedication remains as a connecting link between the Swiss and the French Reformation. The latter is a child of the former.

§ 22. *The Translation of the Bible. Leo Judæ.*

METZGER (Antistes in Schaffhausen): *Geschichte der deutschen Bibelübersetzung der schweizerischen reformirten Kirche.* Basel, 1876. PESTALOZZI: *Leo Judæ.* Elberfeld, 1860.

A most important part of the Reformation was a vernacular translation of the Bible. Luther's New Testament (1522) was reprinted at Basel with a glossary. In Zurich it was adapted to the Swiss dialect in 1524, and revised and improved in subsequent editions. The whole Bible was published in German by Froschauer at Zurich in 1530, four

---

[1] Prof. Dr. Georg von Wyss, in his festive discourse on the University of Zurich (*Die Hochschule Zürich in d. Jahren 1833–1883*, Zürich, 1883), gives a brief sketch of the development of the Carolinum. The first theological faculty of the university consisted of three Zurichers, Hirzel, Schulthess and Salomon Hess, who had been professors of the Carolinum, and two Germans, Rettig and Hitzig. Besides there were five Privatdocenten, ministers of Zurich. See also Prof. Steiner's *Festrede zur 50 jährigen Stiftungsfeier der Züricher Universität*, 1883.

[2] *Commentarius de vera et falsa religione*, March, 1525. *Opera*, III. 145–325. Leo Judæ published a German translation, 1526. When Erasmus received the book, he said, "*O bone Zwingli, quid scribis, quod ipse prius non scripserim?*" So Zwingli reports in a letter to Vadian, *Opera*, VII. 399.

years before Luther completed his version (1534).[1] The translation of the Prophets and the Apocrypha was prepared by Conrad Pellican, Leo Judæ, Theodor Bibliander, and other Zurich divines. The beautiful edition of 1531 contained also a new version of the Poetical books, with an introduction (probably by Zwingli), summaries, and parallel passages.

The Swiss translation cannot compare with Luther's in force, beauty, and popularity; but it is more literal, and in subsequent revisions it has kept pace with the progress of exegesis. It brought the Word of God nearer to the heart and mind of the Swiss people, and is in use to this day alongside of the Lutheran version.[2]

The chief merit in this important service belongs to Leo Jud or Judæ.[3] He was born in 1482, the son of a priest in Alsass, studied with Zwingli at Basle, and became his successor as priest at Einsiedeln, 1519, and his colleague and faithful assistant as minister of St. Peter's in Zurich since 1523. He married in the first year of his pastorate at Zurich. His relation to Zwingli has been compared with the relation of Melanchthon to Luther. He aided Zwingli in the second disputation, in the controversy with the Anabaptists, and with Luther, edited and translated several of his writings, and taught Hebrew in the Carolinum. Zwingli called him his "dear brother and faithful co-worker in the gospel of Jesus Christ." He was called to succeed the Reformer after the catastrophe of Cappel; but he declined on account of his unfitness for administrative work, and

---

[1] Five complete editions of the Bible were printed in Zurich before 1534. Pestalozzi, *Leo Judæ*, p. 77.

[2] On the different editions see Metzger, *l.c.* 109 sqq., and Fritzsche, in Herzog[2], XII. 555 sq. The versicular division was first introduced in the edition of 1589. The first thorough revision was prepared by Antistes Breitinger, 1629. Other revisions followed in 1665, 1724, 1755, 1772, 1817, 1860, and 1868. The last is pronounced by Fritzsche one of the best translations, based upon a conscientious use of the latest exegetical labors.

[3] He avoided his family name Jud (Jew); and the Zurichers called him "Master Leu" (Leo). In all his Latin writings he uses the Latin form.

recommended Bullinger, who was twenty years younger. He continued to preach and to teach till his death, and declined several calls to Wurtemberg and Basle. He advocated strict discipline and a separation of religion from politics. He had a melodious voice, and was a singer, musician, and poet, but excelled chiefly as a translator into German and Latin.[1] He wrote a Latin and two German catechisms, and translated Thomas à Kempis' *Imitatio Christi*, Augustin's *De Spiritu et Litera*, the first Helvetic Confession, and other useful books into German, besides portions of the Bible. He prepared also a much esteemed Latin version of the Old Testament, which is considered his best work. He often consulted in it his colleagues and Michael Adam, a converted Jew. He did not live to see the completion, and left this to Bibliander and Pellican. It appeared in a handsome folio edition, 1543, with a preface by Pellican, and was several times reprinted.[2] He lived on a miserable salary with a large family, and yet helped to support the poor and entertained strangers, aided by his industrious and pious wife, known in Zurich as "Mutter Leuin." Four days before his death, June 19, 1542, he summoned his colleagues to his chamber, spoke of his career with great humility and gratitude to God, and recommended to them the care of the church and the completion of his Latin Bible. His death was lamented as a great loss by Bullinger and Calvin and the people of Zurich.[3]

§ 23. *Church and State.*

The Reformation of Zurich was substantially completed in 1525. It was brought about by the co-operation of the

[1] Pellican says of him, "*Utilissima transtulit admodum feliciter.*"

[2] On his Latin Bible see Pestalozzi, 76 sqq., 165, and Fritzsche in Herzog[2] VIII. 463.

[3] On his works see Pestalozzi, pp. 96–106. His hymns and versified Psalms are printed in Wackernagel, *Das Deutsche Kirchenlied*, vol. III. p. 722 sqq. (Nos. 832–837).

secular and spiritual powers. Zwingli aimed at a reformation of the whole religious, political, and social life of the people, on the basis and by the power of the Scriptures.[1]

The patriot, the good citizen, and the Christian were to him one and the same. He occupied the theocratic standpoint of the Old Testament. The preacher is a prophet: his duty is to instruct, to exhort, to comfort, to rebuke sin in high and low places, and to build up the kingdom of God; his weapon is the Word of God. The duty of the magistracy is to obey the gospel, to protect religion, to punish wickedness. Calvin took the same position in Geneva, and carried it out much more fully than Zwingli.

The bishop of Constance, to whose diocese Zurich belonged, opposed the Reformation; and so did the other bishops of Switzerland. Hence the civil magistracy assumed the episcopal rights and jurisdiction, under the spiritual guidance of the Reformers. It first was impartial, and commanded the preachers of the canton to teach the Word of God, and to be silent about the traditions of men (1520). Then it prohibited the violation of the Church fasts (1522), and punished the image-breakers, in the interest of law and order (1523). But soon afterwards it openly espoused the cause of reform in the disputation of 1523, and authorized the abolition of the old worship and the introduction of the new (1524 and 1525). It confiscated the property of the churches and convents, and took under its control the regulation of marriage, the care of the poor, and the education of the clergy. The Church was reduced legally to a state of

---

[1] Bluntschli (*Geschichte des schweizerischen Bundesrechtes*, Stuttgart, 1875, 2d ed. I. 293 sq.): "*Zwingli wur von Anfang an und durch sein ganzes Leben hindurch kaum viel weniger darauf bedacht, politisch einzugreifen als die Kirche zu reformiren. Während Luther mit ganzer Seele die Wiederbelebung und Reinigung des christlichen Glaubens anstrebte und sich ausschliesslich dieser Aufgabe widmete, wollte Zwingli nicht bloss Kirchen-, sondern zugleich auch Staatsmann sein. Indem sich Zwingli der kirchlichen Reformation in der Schweiz bemächtigte und diese von Zürich aus über die ganze Schweiz zu verbreiten trachtete, ging er zugleich mit Planen um, die Schweiz politisch umzugestalten.*"

dependence, though she was really the moving and inspiring power of the State, and was supported by public sentiment. In a republic the majority of the people rule, and the minority must submit. The only dissenters in Zurich were a small number of Romanists and Anabaptists, who were treated with the same disregard of the rights of conscience as the Protestants in Roman Catholic countries, only with a lesser degree of severity. The Reformers refused to others the right of protest which they claimed and exercised for themselves, and the civil magistracy visited the poor Anabaptists with capital punishment.

The example of Zurich was followed by the other cantons in which the Reformation triumphed. Each has its own ecclesiastical establishment, which claims spiritual jurisdiction over all the citizens of its territory. There is no national Reformed Church of Switzerland, with a centre of unity.

This state of things is the same as that in Protestant Germany, but differs from it as a republic differs from a monarchy. In both countries the bishops, under the command of the Pope, condemned Protestantism, and lost the control over their flock. The Reformers, who were mere presbyters, looked to the civil rulers for the maintenance of law and order. In Germany, after the Diet of Speier in 1526, the princes assumed the episcopal supervision, and regulated the Church in their own territories for good or evil. The people were passive, and could not even elect their own pastors. In Switzerland, we have instead a sort of democratic episcopate or republican Cæsaropapacy, where the people hold the balance of power, and make and unmake their government.

In the sixteenth and seventeenth centuries Church and State, professing the same religion, had common interests, and worked in essential harmony; but in modern times the mixed character, the religious indifferentism, the hostility and the despotism of the State, have loosened the connection, and provoked the organization of free churches in several cantons (Geneva, Vaud, Neuchatel), on the basis of self-support and self-government. The State must first and last be just, and either support all the religions of its citizens alike, or none. It owes the protection of law to all, within the limits of order and peace. But the Church has the right of self-government, and ought to be free of the control of politicians.[1]

Among the ministers of the Reformation period, Zwingli, and, after his death, Bullinger, exercised a sort of episcopate in fact, though not in form; and their successors in the Great Minster stood at the head of the clergy of the canton. A similar position is occupied by the Antistes of Basle and the Antistes of Schaffhausen. They correspond to the Superintendents of the Lutheran churches in Germany.

Zwingli was the first among the Reformers who organized a regular synodical Church government. He provided for a synod composed of all ministers of the city and canton, two lay delegates of every parish, four members of the small and four members of the great council. This mixed body represented alike Church and State, the clergy and the laity. It was to meet twice a year, in spring and fall, in the city hall of Zurich, with power to superintend the doctrine and morals of the clergy, and to legislate on the internal affairs of the Church. The first meeting was held at Easter, 1528. Zwingli presided, and at his side was Leo Judæ. The second meeting took place May 19, 1528. The proceedings show that the synod exercised strict discipline over the morals of

---

[1] The government of the Protestant cantons of Switzerland tolerates and supports now, in the pulpit and the chair, all sorts of errors and heresies far worse than those for which the Anabaptists were drowned in the sixteenth century. In 1839 the magistracy of Zurich called the infidel Dr. Strauss to the chair of dogmatic theology in the university; but on that occasion the country people asserted their sovereignty, upset the rule of the radical party, and defeated its aim.

the clergy and people, and censured intemperance, extravagance in dress, neglect of Church ordinances, etc.[1]

But German Switzerland never went to such rigors of discipline as Geneva under the influence of Calvin.

§ 24. *Zwingli's Conflict with Radicalism.*

Comp. Literature in vol. VI., § 102, p. 606 sq.

I. SOURCES:

In the Staatsarchiv of Zurich there are preserved about two hundred and fifty documents under the title, *Wiedertäuferacten*, — * EGLI : *Actensammlung zur Gesch. der Zürcher Reformation*, Zürich, 1879 (see the Alph. Index, p. 920, sub *Wiedertäufer*). The official reports are from their opponents. The books of the Anabaptists are scarce. A large collection of them is in the Baptist Theological Seminary at Rochester, N.Y. The principal ones are the tracts of Dr. Hübmaier (see vol. VI. 606); a few letters of Grebel, Hut, Reubli, etc., and other documents mentioned and used by Cornelius (*Gesch. des Münsterschen Aufruhrs*) ; the Moravian, Austrian, and other Anabaptist chronicles (see Beck, below) ; and the Anabaptist hymns reprinted in Wackernagel's *Deutsche Kirchenlied*, vols. III. and V. (see below).

ZWINGLI : *Wer Ursach gebe zu Aufruhr, wer die wahren Aufrührer seien*, etc., Dec. 7, 1524. A defence of Christian unity and peace against sedition. (*Werke*, II. A. 376–425.) *Vom Touff, vom Wiedertouff, und vom Kindertouff*, May 27, 1525 (in *Werke*, II. A. 280–303. Republished in modern German by Christoffel, Zürich, 1843. The book treats in three parts of baptism, rebaptism, and infant baptism). Answer to Balthasar Hübmaier, Nov. 5, 1525 (*Werke*, II. A. 337 sqq.). *Elenchus contra Catabaptistas*, 1527 (*Opera*, III. 357 sqq.). His answer to Schwenkfeld's 64 Theses concerning baptism (in *Op*. III. 563–583; comp. A. Baur, II. 245–267). ŒCOLAMPADIUS : *Ein gesprech etlicher predicanten zu Basel gehalten mit etlichen Bekennern des Wiedertouffs*, Basel, 1525. BULLINGER (HEINRICH) : *Der Wiedertäufferen ursprung, fürgang, Sekten*, etc. Zürich, 1560. (A Latin translation by J. SIMLER.) See also his *Reformationsgeschichte*, vol. I.

II. LATER DISCUSSIONS :

OTT (J. H.) : *Annales Anabaptistici*. Basel, 1672.

ERBKAM (H. W.) : *Geschichte der protestantischen Secten im Zeitalter der Reformation*. Hamburg und Gotha, 1848. pp. 519–583.

HEBERLE : *Die Anfänge des Anabaptismus in der Schweiz*, in the "Jahrbücher fur deutsche Theologie," 1858.

* CORNELIUS (C. A., a liberal Roman Catholic): *Geschichte des Münsterschen Aufruhrs*. Leipzig, 1855. *Zweites Buch : Die Wiedertaufe*. 1860. He treats of the Swiss Anabaptists (p. 15 sqq.), and adds historical documents from many archives (p. 240 sqq.). A very important work.

[1] *Opera*, III. B. 19 sqq.; Mörikofer, II. 121 sq.

MÖRIKOFER: *U. Zwingli.* Zürich, 1867. I. 279-313; II. 69-76. Very unfavorable to the Anabaptists.

R. VON LILIENKRON: *Zur Liederdichtung der Wiedertäufer.* München, 1877.

*EGLI (EMIL): *Die Züricher Wiedertäufer zur Reformationszeit. Nach den Quellen des Staatsarchivs.* Zürich, 1878 (104 pp.). By the same: *Die St. Galler Täufer.* Zürich, 1887. Important for the documents and the external history.

*BURRAGE (HENRY S., American Baptist): *The Anabaptists in Switzerland.* Philadelphia, 1882, 231 pp. An account from the Baptist point of view. Comp. his *Baptist Hymn Writers,* Portland, 1888, pp. 1-25.

USTERI (J. M.): *Darstellung der Tauflehre Zwingli's,* in the "Studien und Kritiken" for 1882, pp. 205-284.

*BECK (JOSEPH): *Die Geschichtsbücher der Wiedertäufer in Oestreich-Ungarn . . . von 1526 bis 1785.* Wien, 1883. Publ. by the Imperial Academy of Sciences in Vienna.

STRASSER (G.): *Der schweizerische Anabaptismus zur Zeit der Reformation,* in the "Berner Beiträge," 1884.

NITSCHE (RICHARD, Roman Catholic): *Geschichte der Wiedertäufer in der Schweiz zur Reformationszeit.* Einsiedeln, New York, Cincinnati and St. Louis (Benziger), 1885 (107 pp.). He gives a list of literature on pp. vi.-viii.

KELLER (LUDWIG): *Die Reformation und die ältern Reformparteien.* Leipzig, 1885, pp. 364-435. He is favorable to the Anabaptists, and connects them with the Waldensian Brethren and other mediæval sects by novel, but arbitrary combinations and conjectures. He mistakes coincidences for historical connections.

BAUR (AUG.): *Zwingli's Theologie,* vol. II. (1888), 1-267. An elaborate discussion and defence of Zwingli's conduct towards the radicals, with full extracts from his writings, but unjust to the Baptists.

The monographs of SCHREIBER on *Hübmaier* (1839 and 1840, unfinished), KEIM on *Ludwig Hätzer* (1856), and KELLER on *Hans Denck (Ein Apostel der Wiedertäufer,* 1882), touch also on the Anabaptist movement in Switzerland. KURTZ, in the tenth ed. of his *Kirchengeschichte* (1887), II. 150-164, gives a good general survey of the Anabaptist movement in Germany, Switzerland, and Holland, including the Mennonites.

Having considered Zwingli's controversy with Romanism, we must now review his conflict with Radicalism, which ran parallel with the former, and exhibits the conservative and churchly side of his reformation. Radicalism was identical with the Anabaptist movement, but the baptismal question was secondary. It involved an entire reconstruction of the Church and of the social order. It meant revolution. The Romanists pointed triumphantly to revolution as the legitimate and inevitable result of the Reformation; but history has proved the difference. Liberty is possible without license, and differs as widely from it as from despotism.

The Swiss Reformation, like the German, was disturbed and checked by the radical excesses. It was placed between the two fires of Romanism and Ultraprotestantism. It was attacked in the front and rear, from without and within, — by the Romanists on the ground of tradition, by the Radicals on the ground of the Bible. In some respects the danger from the latter was greater. Liberty has more to fear from the abuses of its friends than from the opposition of its foes. The Reformation would have failed if it had identified itself with the revolution. Zwingli applied to the Radicals the words of St. John to the antichristian teachers: "They went out from us, but they were not of us" (1 John 2:19). He considered the controversy with the Papists as mere child's play when compared to that with the Ultraprotestants.[1]

The Reformers aimed to reform the old Church by the Bible; the Radicals attempted to build a new Church from the Bible. The former maintained the historic continuity; the latter went directly to the apostolic age, and ignored the intervening centuries as an apostasy. The Reformers founded a popular state-church, including all citizens with their families; the Anabaptists organized on the voluntary principle select congregations of baptized believers, separated from the world and from the State. Nothing is more characteristic of radicalism and sectarianism than an utter want of historical sense and respect for the past. In its extreme form it rejects even the Bible as an external authority, and relies on inward inspiration. This was the case with the Zwickau Prophets who threatened to break up Luther's work at Wittenberg.

---

[1] He wrote to Vadian, May 28, 1525 (*Opera*, VII. 398): "*omnes pugnæ priores lusus fuerunt præ ista.*"

The Radicals made use of the right of protest against the Reformation, which the Reformers so effectually exercised against popery. They raised a protest against Protestantism. They charged the Reformers with inconsistency and semi-popery; yea, with the worst kind of popery. They denounced the state-church as worldly and corrupt, and its ministers as mercenaries. They were charged in turn with pharisaical pride, with revolutionary and socialistic tendencies. They were cruelly persecuted by imprisonment, exile, torture, fire and sword, and almost totally suppressed in Protestant as well as in Roman Catholic countries. The age was not ripe for unlimited religious liberty and congregational self-government. The Anabaptists perished bravely as martyrs of conscience.[1]

Zwingli took essentially, but quite independently, the same position towards the Radicals as Luther did in his controversy with Carlstadt, Münzer, and Hübmaier.[2] Luther, on the contrary, radically misunderstood Zwingli by confounding him with Carlstadt and the Radicals. Zwingli was in his way just as conservative and churchly as the Saxon Reformer. He defended and preserved the state-church, or the people's church, against a small fraction of sectaries and separatists who threatened its dissolution. But his position was more difficult. He was much less influenced by tradition, and further removed from Romanism. He himself aimed from the start at a thorough, practical purification of church life, and so far agreed with the Radicals. Moreover, he doubted for a while the expediency (not the right) of infant baptism, and deemed it better to put off the sac-

---

[1] Luther called them martyrs of the devil; but Leonhard Käser, to whom he wrote a letter of comfort, and whom he held up as a model martyr to the heretical martyrs (see *Letters*, ed. De Wette, III. 179), was not a Lutheran, as he thought, but the pastor of an Anabaptist congregation at Scherding. He was burnt Aug. 18, 1527, by order of the bishop of Passau. See Cornelius, II. 56.

[2] On Luther and the Radicals see vol. VI. 375 sqq. and 606 sqq.

rament to years of discretion.[1] He rejected the Roman doctrine of the necessity of baptism for salvation and the damnation of unbaptized infants dying in infancy. He understood the passage, Mark 16 : 16, "He that believeth and is baptized shall be saved," as applying only to adults who have heard the gospel and can believe, but not to children. On maturer reflection he modified his views. He learned from experience that it was impossible to realize an ideal church of believers, and stopped with what was attainable. As to infant baptism, he became convinced of its expediency in Christian families. He defended it with the analogy of circumcision in the Old Testament (Col. 2 : 11), with the comprehensiveness of the New Covenant, which embraces whole families and nations, and with the command of Christ, "Suffer little children to come unto Me," from which he inferred that he who refuses children to be baptized prevents them from coming to Christ. He also appealed to 1 Cor. 7 : 14, which implies the church-membership of the children of Christian parents, and to the examples of family baptisms in Acts 16 : 33, 18 : 8, and 1 Cor. 1 : 16.

The Radical movement began in Zurich in 1523, and lasted till 1532. The leaders were Conrad Grebel, from one of the first families of Zurich, a layman, educated in the universities of Vienna and Paris, whom Zwingli calls the corypheus of the Anabaptists; Felix Manz, the illegitimate son of a canon of the Great Minster, a good Hebrew scholar; Georg Blaurock, a monk of Coire, called on account of his eloquence "the mighty Jörg," or "the second Paul"; and Ludwig Hätzer of Thurgau, chaplain at Wädenschwyl, who,

---

[1] Hagenbach (p. 357), on the strength of Hottinger, states that the Council of Zurich, at the advice of Zwingli, by a mandate of Jan. 17, 1525, allowed a delay of eight *years* for the baptism of children. But this must be an error; for on the eighteenth of January, 1525, the Council, after a disputation with the Anabaptists, commanded the baptism of all unbaptized children within eight *days*, on pain of the banishment of the parents. Egli, *Actensammlung*, p. 276.

with Hans Denck, prepared the first Protestant translation of the Hebrew Prophets,[1] and acted as secretary of the second Zurich disputation, and edited its proceedings. With them were associated a number of ex-priests and ex-monks, as William Reubli, minister at Wyticon, Johann Brödli (Paniculus) at Zollicon, and Simon Stumpf at Höng. They took an active part in the early stages of the Reformation, prematurely broke the fasts, and stood in the front rank of the image-stormers. They went ahead of public opinion and the orderly method of Zwingli. They opposed the tithe, usury, military service, and the oath. They denied the right of the civil magistracy to interfere in matters of religion. They met as "brethren" for prayer and Scripture-reading in the house of "Mother Manz," and in the neighborhood of Zurich, especially at Zollicon.

The German Radicals, Carlstadt and Münzer, were for a short time in Switzerland and on the Rhine, but did not re-baptize and had no influence upon the Swiss Radicals, who opposed rebellion to the civil authority. Carlstadt gradually sobered down; Münzer stirred up the Peasants' War, seized the sword and perished by the sword. Dr. Hübmaier of Bavaria, the most learned among the Anabaptists, and their chief advocate, took part in the October disputation at Zurich in 1523, but afterwards wrote books against Zwingli (on the baptism of believers, 1525, and a dialogue with Zwingli, 1526), was expelled from Switzerland, and organized flourishing congregations in Moravia.

The Radical opinions spread with great rapidity, or rose simultaneously, in Berne, Basle, St. Gall, Appenzell, all along the Upper Rhine, in South Germany, and Austria. The Anabaptists were driven from place to place, and travelled as fugitive evangelists. They preached repentance

---

[1] Their translation of the Prophets appeared at Worms in 1527 (and often), and preceded that of the Zurich Bible (in 1529), and that of Luther, which was not completed till 1532.

and faith, baptized converts, organized congregations, and exercised rigid discipline. They called themselves simply "brethren" or "Christians." They were earnest and zealous, self-denying and heroic, but restless and impatient. They accepted the New Testament as their only rule of faith and practice, and so far agreed with the Reformers, but utterly broke with the Catholic tradition, and rejected Luther's theory of forensic, solifidian justification, and the real presence. They emphasized the necessity of good works, and deemed it possible to keep the law and to reach perfection. They were orthodox in most articles of the common Christian faith, except Hätzer and Denck, who doubted the doctrine of the Trinity and the divinity of Christ.

The first and chief aim of the Radicals was not (as is usually stated) the opposition to infant baptism, still less to sprinkling or pouring, but the establishment of a pure church of converts in opposition to the mixed church of the world. The rejection of infant baptism followed as a necessary consequence. They were not satisfied with separation from popery; they wanted a separation from all the ungodly. They appealed to the example of the disciples in Jerusalem, who left the synagogue and the world, gathered in an upper room, sold their goods, and held all things in common. They hoped at first to carry Zwingli with them, but in vain; and then they charged him with treason to the truth, and hated him worse than the pope.

Zwingli could not follow the Anabaptists without bringing the Reformation into discredit with the lovers of order, and rousing the opposition of the government and the great mass of the people. He opposed them, as Augustin opposed the schismatical Donatists. He urged moderation and patience. The Apostles, he said, separated only from the open enemies of the gospel, and from the works of darkness, but bore with the weak brethren. Separation would not cure the evils of the Church. There are many honest people

who, though weak and sick, belong to the sheepfold of
Christ, and would be offended at a separation. He appealed
to the word of Christ, "He that is not against me, is for me,"
and to the parable of the tares and the wheat. If all the
tares were to be rooted up now, there would be nothing left
for the angels to do on the day of final separation.

§ 25. *The Baptismal Controversy.*

The opposition to the mixed state-church or popular
church, which embraced all the baptized, legitimately led to
the rejection of infant baptism. A new church required a
new baptism.

This became now the burning question. The Radicals
could find no trace of infant baptism in the Bible, and
denounced it as an invention of the pope[1] and the devil.
Baptism, they reasoned, presupposes instruction, faith, and
conversion, which is impossible in the case of infants.[2]
Voluntary baptism of adult and responsible converts is,
therefore, the only valid baptism. They denied that baptism
is necessary for salvation, and maintained that infants are or
may be saved by the blood of Christ without water-baptism.[3]
But baptism is necessary for church membership as a sign
and seal of conversion.

From this conception of baptism followed as a further
consequence the rebaptism of those converts who wished to
unite with the new church. Hence the name *Anabaptists*
or *Rebaptizers* (*Wiedertäufer*), which originated with the

---

[1] They derived it from Pope Nicolas II. (A.D. 1059–'61), whose pontificate
was entirely under the control of Hildebrand, afterwards Gregory VII. The
reference shows the prevailing ignorance of Church history. Pedobaptism is
much older than the papacy.

[2] Hübmaier, when in Waldshut, substituted first a simple benediction of
children, in place of baptism, but baptized when the parents wished it. See
Gieseler, III. A. p. 210, note.

[3] The Augsburg Confession (Art. IX.) condemns the Anabaptists for
teaching "*pueros sine baptismo salvos fieri.*"

Pedobaptists, but which they themselves rejected, because they knew no other kind of baptism except that of converts. The demand of rebaptism virtually unbaptized and unchristianized the entire Christian world, and completed the rupture with the historic Church. It cut the last cord of union of the present with the past.

The first case was the rebaptism of Blaurock by Grebel in February, 1525, soon after the disputation with Zwingli. At a private religious meeting, Blaurock asked Grebel to give him the true Christian baptism on confession of his faith, fell on his knees and was baptized. Then he baptized all others who were present, and partook with them of the Lord's Supper, or, as they called it, the breaking of bread.[1] Reubli introduced rebaptism in Waldshut at Easter, 1525, convinced Hübmaier of its necessity, and rebaptized him with about sixty persons. Hübmaier himself rebaptized about three hundred.[2]

---

[1] Füssli, II. 338. The report of a Moravian Baptist chronicle, quoted by Cornelius (II. 26 sq.), is as follows: " *Und es hat sich begeben, dass sie bei einander gewesen sind, bis die Angst auf sie kam und sie in ihren Herzen gedrungen wurden; da haben sie angefangen ihre Kniee zu beugen vor dem höchsten Gott im Himmel, und ihn angerufen, dass er ihnen geben wolle, seinen göttlichen Willen zu vollbringen. Darauf hat Jürg [Blaurock] sich erhoben und um Gottes willen gebeten, dass Conrad [Grebel] ihn taufe mit der rechten wahren christlichen Taufe auf seinen Glauben und seine Erkenntniss; ist wieder auf die Kniee gefallen und von Conrad getauft worden; und alle übrigen Anwesenden haben sich dann von Jürg taufen lassen. Hiernächst hat derselbe, seinem eigenen Bericht zufolge, damit die Brüder des Todes Christi allweg eingedenk wären und sein vergossen Blut nicht vergässen, ihnen den Brauch Christi angezeigt, den er in seinem Nachtmal gehalten hat, und zugleich mit ihnen das Brot gebrochen und den Trank getrunken, damit sie sich erinnerten, dass sie alle durch den einigen Leib Christi erlöst und durch sein einiges Blut abgewaschen seien, auf dass sie alle eins und je einer des anderen Bruder und Schwester in Christo ihrem Herrn wären.*"
Cornelius adds to this report: "*Diese Dinge haben sich wenige Tage nach der Disputation des 18. Januar zugetragen, und rasch, noch ehe die Verbannten ihren Abschied genommen hatten, ist, zum Theil mit ihrer Hülfe, der Gebrauch der Taufe und des Herrn Brodes nach Zollikon und über die ganze Genossenschaft verbreitet worden.*"

[2] So Hübmaier testified before the magistrate at Zurich (Egli, *Actensammlung*, p. 431): "*Da käme Wilhelm (Reubli) und toufte ihn (Hübmaier), und liessend sich uf dasselb mal mit ihm bi 60 personen toufen. Darnach habe er die*

Baptism was not bound to any particular form or time or place or person; any one could administer the ordinance upon penitent believers who desired it. It was first done mostly in houses, by sprinkling or pouring, occasionally by partial or total immersion in rivers.[1]

The *mode* of baptism was no point of dispute between Anabaptists and Pedobaptists in the sixteenth century. The Roman Church provides for immersion and pouring as equally valid. Luther preferred immersion, and prescribed it in his baptismal service.[2] In England immersion was the *normal* mode down to the middle of the seventeenth century.[3] It was adopted by the English and American Baptists as the *only* mode; while the early Anabaptists, on the other hand, baptized by sprinkling and pouring as well. We learn this from the reports in the suits against them at Zurich. Blaurock baptized by sprinkling,[4] Manz by pouring.[5] The first

Osterfirtag für und für und ob 300 menschen getouft." Nothing is said about the mode. Soon afterwards (July 5, 1525), Hübmaier published his book, *Von dem Christlichen Touff der Gläubigen* against Zwingli, but without naming him. Zwingli replied November, 1525. See A. Baur, *Zwingli's Theol.*, II. 137 sq., 141 sqq.

[1] Nitsche, p. 30: "*Wenn über jemand der Geist Gottes kam, beklagte und beweinte er seine Sünden und bat den ersten besten, ihn zu taufen; dieser bespritzte oder überschüttete ihn unter Nennung der drei göttlichen Personen mit Wasser. Einem förmlichen Untertauchen, wie es später wohl vorkommt, begegnen wir zunächst nicht. . . . Meistens wurde die Taufe in irgend einem Hause vollzogen; aber auch im Freien wurde getauft: so Rudolph Breitinger bei Gelegenheit eines Spazierganges am Neppelbach, ein anderer beim Brunnen zu Hirslanden.*" Egli, p. 23 sq.: "*Wie es scheint, war Blaurock der eigentlich populäre Täufer und wandte den Gebrauch allgemeiner an auf den ersten Besten, der weinend zu ihm kam.*"

[2] See vol. VI. 608, note, and my book on the *Didache*, p. 41 sqq.

[3] Edward VI. and Queen Elizabeth were immersed, according to the rubric of the English Prayer Book. Erasmus says, "With us" (on the Continent) "infants have the water poured on them; in England they are dipped."

[4] In the trial of fourteen Anabaptists, Feb. 7, 1525, Marx Bosshard testified that Hans Bruggbach of Zumikon, after the reading of a portion of the New Testament in a meeting, confessed and deplored his sins, and requested, as a sign of his conversion, to be sprinkled in the name of the Father, the Son, and the Holy Ghost; whereupon Blaurock sprinkled him. "*Darauf habe ihn Blaurock bespritzt.*" Egli, *Actensammlung*, p. 282.

[5] In the same suit Jörg Schad said, "*er habe sich lassen begüssen mit Wasser, und syg* [sei] *Felix Manz töifer gesin* [*Täufer gewesen*]." *Ibid.*, p. 283.

clear case of immersion among the Swiss Anabaptists is that of Wolfgang Uliman (an ex-monk of Coire, and for a while assistant of Kessler in St. Gall). He was converted by Grebel on a journey to Schaffhausen, and, not satisfied with being "sprinkled merely out of a dish," was "drawn under and covered over in the Rhine."[1] On Palm Sunday, April 9, 1525, Grebel baptized a large number in the Sitter, a river a few miles from St. Gall, which descends from the Säntis and flows into the Thur, and is deep enough for immersion.[2]

The Lord's Supper was administered by the Baptists in the simplest manner, after a plain supper (in imitation of the original institution and the Agape), by the recital of the words of institution, and the distribution of bread and wine. They reduced it to a mere commemoration.

The two ideas of a pure church of believers and of the baptism of believers were the fundamental articles of the Anabaptist creed. On other points there was a great variety and confusion of opinions. Some believed in the sleep of the soul between death and resurrection, a millennial reign of Christ, and final restoration; some entertained communistic and socialistic opinions which led to the catastrophe of Münster (1534). Wild excesses of immorality occurred here and there.[3]

But it is unjust to charge the extravagant dreams and practices of individuals upon the whole body. The Swiss Anabaptists had no connection with the Peasants' War, which barely touched the border of Switzerland, and were upon the whole, like the Moravian Anabaptists, distinguished for simple piety and strict morality. Bullinger, who was

---

[1] Kessler, *Sabbata*, I. 266 ("*in dem Rhin von dem Grebel under getrückt und bedeckt*"). Comp. Burrage, 105.

[2] Burrage, p. 117. I was informed by Mr. Steiger of Herisau (Appenzell) that the modern Baptists in St. Gall and Appenzell baptize by immersion in the Sitter; but their number has greatly diminished since the death of Schlatter.

[3] As in St. Gall and Appenzell; see Cornelius, II. 64 sq.

opposed to them, gives the Zurich Radicals the credit that they denounced luxury, intemperance in eating and drinking, and all vices, and led a serious, spiritual life. Kessler of St. Gall, likewise an opponent, reports their cheerful martyrdom, and exclaims, "Alas! what shall I say of the people? They move my sincere pity; for many of them are zealous for God, but without knowledge." And Salat, a Roman Catholic contemporary, writes that with "cheerful, smiling faces, they desired and asked death, and went into it singing German psalms and other prayers." [1]

The Anabaptists produced some of the earliest Protestant hymns in the German language, which deserve the attention of the historian. Some of them passed into orthodox collections in ignorance of the real authors. Blaurock, Manz, Hut, Hätzer, Koch, Wagner, Langmantel, Sattler, Schiemer, Glait, Steinmetz, Büchel, and many others contributed to this interesting branch of the great body of Christian song. The Anabaptist psalms and hymns resemble those of Schwenkfeld and his followers. They dwell on the inner life of the Christian, the mysteries of regeneration, sanctification, and personal union with Christ. They breathe throughout a spirit of piety, devotion, and cheerful resignation under suffering, and readiness for martyrdom. They are hymns of the cross, to comfort and encourage the scattered sheep of Christ ready for the slaughter, in imitation of their divine Shepherd.

NOTES.

The Anabaptist hymns appeared in a collection under the title "*Aussbund Etlicher schöner Christlicher Geseng wie die in der Gefengniss zu Passau im Schloss von den Schweitzern und auch von anderen rechtgläubigen Christen hin und her gedicht worden,*" 1583, and often. Also in other collections of the sixteenth century. They are reprinted in Wacknernagel, *Das Deutsche Kirchenlied*, vol. III. (1870), pp. 440–491, and vol. V. (1877), pp. 677–887. He embodies them in this monumental corpus hymnologicum, as he does the Schwenkfeld-

---

[1] A. Baur, who sides altogether with Zwingli, must nevertheless admit (II. 187) that "the majority of the Swiss Anabaptists were quiet and honorable people of earnest character and unblemished reputation as citizens."

ian and the Roman Catholic hymns of the fifteenth century, but under express reservation of his high-Lutheran orthodoxy. He refuses to acknowledge the Anabaptists as martyrs any longer (as he had done in his former work on German hymnology), because they stand, he says (III. 439), "*ausserhalb der Wahrheit, ausserhalb der heiligen lutherischen Kirche!*" Hymnology is the last place for sectarian exclusiveness. It furnishes one of the strongest evidences of Christian union in the sanctuary of worship, where theological quarrels are forgotten in the adoration of a common Lord and Saviour. Luther himself, as Wackernagel informs us, received unwittingly in his hymn book of 1545 a hymn of the Anabaptist Grünwald, and another of the Schwenkfeldian Reusner. Wackernagel is happily inconsistent when he admits (p. 440) that much may be learned from the Anabaptist hymns, and that a noble heart will not easily condemn those victims of Rome and of the house of Habsburg. He gives first the hymns of Thomas Münzer, who can hardly be called an Anabaptist and was disowned by the better portion.

Burrage, in *Baptist Hymn Writers*, Portland, 1888, p. 1 sqq., gives some extracts of Anabaptist hymns. The following stanza, from a hymn of Schiemer or Schöner, characterizes the condition and spirit of this persecuted people: —

> " We are, alas, like scattered sheep,
> The shepherd not in sight,
> Each far away from home and hearth,
> And, like the birds of night
> That hide away in rocky clefts,
> We have our rocky hold,
> Yet near at hand, as for the birds,
> There waits the hunter bold."

§ 26. *Persecution of the Anabaptists.*

We pass now to the measures taken against the separatists. At first Zwingli tried to persuade them in private conferences, but in vain. Then followed a public disputation, which took place by order of the magistracy in the council hall, Jan. 17, 1525. Grebel was opposed to it, but appeared, together with Manz and Reubli. They urged the usual arguments against infant baptism, that infants cannot understand the gospel, cannot repent and exercise faith. Zwingli answered them, and appealed chiefly to circumcision and 1 Cor. 7:14, where Paul speaks of the children of Christian parents as "holy." He afterwards published his views in a book, " On Baptism, Rebaptism, and Infant Baptism " (May 27, 1525). Bullinger, who was present at the disputation, reports that the Anabaptists were unable to refute

Zwingli's arguments and to maintain their ground. Another disputation was held in March, and a third in November, but with no better result. The magistracy decided against them, and issued an order that infants should be baptized as heretofore, and that parents who refuse to have their children baptized should leave the city and canton with their families and goods.

The Anabaptists refused to obey, and ventured on bold demonstrations. They arranged processions, and passed as preachers of repentance, in sackcloth and girdled, through the streets of Zurich, singing, praying, exhorting, abusing the old dragon (Zwingli) and his horns, and exclaiming, " Woe, woe unto Zurich!" [1]

The leaders were arrested and shut up in a room in the Augustinian convent. A commission of ministers and magistrates were sent to them to convert them. Twenty-four professed conversion, and were set free. Fourteen men and seven women were retained and shut up in the Witch Tower, but they made their escape April 5.

Grebel, Manz, and Blaurock were rearrested, and charged with communistic and revolutionary teaching. After some other excesses, the magistracy proceeded to threaten those who stubbornly persisted in their error, with death by drowning. He who dips, shall be dipped, — a cruel irony.

It is not known whether Zwingli really consented to the death sentence, but he certainly did not openly oppose it.[2]

---

[1] Zwingli, *Opera*, III. 364.

[2] Egli (*Die Zürcher Wiedertäufer*, p. 93) thinks that if he consented, he did it with reluctant heart, not, like Calvin in the case of Servetus, with a strong sense of duty. Keller (*Die Reformation*, p. 407, note) asserts, on the strength of Hübmaier, that Zwingli preached in 1525 that Anabaptists should be beheaded "according to the imperial laws," but there is no proof of this, and Baur (II. 180) denies it. Comp. the correspondence of Capito with Zwingli on the case of Manz, *Opera*, VIII. 16, 30, 44. Capito of Strassburg was disturbed by the execution of Manz, who had died so heroically, as reported (*mortem obiise magnifice*, p. 16); but Zwingli assured him that the magistracy condemned him to death reluctantly and from necessity (*quam coacte Senatus*

Six executions in all took place in Zurich between 1527 and 1532. Manz was the first victim. He was bound, carried to a boat, and thrown into the river Limmat near the lake, Jan. 5, 1527. He praised God that he was about to die for the truth, and prayed with a loud voice, " Into thy hands, O Lord, I commend my spirit ! " Bullinger describes his heroic death. Grebel had escaped the same fate by previous death in 1526. The last executions took place March 23, 1532, when Heinrich Karpfis and Hans Herzog were drowned. The foreigners were punished by exile, and met death in Roman Catholic countries. Blaurock was scourged, expelled, and burnt, 1529, at Clausen in the Tyrol. Hätzer, who fell into carnal sins, was beheaded for adultery and bigamy at Constance, Feb. 24, 1529. John Zwick, a Zwinglian, says that " a nobler and more manful death was never seen in Constance." Thomas Blaurer bears a similar testimony.[1] Hübmaier, who had fled from Waldshut to Zurich, December, 1525, was tried before the magistracy, recanted, and was sent out of the country to recant his re-cantation.[2] He labored successfully in Moravia, and was burnt at the stake in Vienna, March 10, 1528. Three days afterwards his faithful wife, whom he had married in Waldshut, was drowned in the Danube.

Other Swiss cantons took the same measures against the Anabaptists as Zurich. In Zug, Lorenz Fürst was drowned, Aug. 17, 1529. In Appenzell, Uliman and others were beheaded, and some women drowned. At Basle, Œcolampadius held several disputations with the Anabaptists, but without effect; whereupon the Council banished them, with the threat that they should be drowned if they returned

---

judicis partem tandem usurpavit).   This is, of course, unsatisfactory.   Banishment in this case, as in that of Servetus, would have been severe enough.

[1] Burrage defends Hätzer against the charges of immorality (p. 200 sqq.) ; but Keim and Cornelius (II. 59) sustain them.

[2] Baur, II. 173 sq.   Zwingli's letter to Capito, Jan. 1, 1526, published by Rud. Stähelin, *Briefe aus der Reformationszeit* (Basel, 1887), p. 20.

(Nov. 13, 1530). The Council of Berne adopted the same course.

In Germany and in Austria the Anabaptists fared still worse. The Diet of Speier, in April, 1529, decreed that "every Anabaptist and rebaptized person of either sex be put to death by sword, or fire, or otherwise." The decree was severely carried out, except in Strassburg and the domain of Philip of Hesse, where the heretics were treated more leniently. The most blood was shed in Roman Catholic countries. In Görz the house in which the Anabaptists were assembled for worship was set on fire. " In Tyrol and Görz," says Cornelius,[1] " the number of executions in the year 1531 reached already one thousand; in Ensisheim, six hundred. At Linz seventy-three were killed in six weeks. Duke William of Bavaria, surpassing all others, issued the fearful decree to behead those who recanted, to burn those who refused to recant. . . . Throughout the greater part of Upper Germany the persecution raged like a wild chase. . . . The blood of these poor people flowed like water so that they cried to the Lord for help. . . . But hundreds of them of all ages and both sexes suffered the pangs of torture without a murmur, despised to buy their lives by recantation, and went to the place of execution joyfully and singing psalms."

The blood of martyrs is never shed in vain. The Anabaptist movement was defeated, but not destroyed; it revived among the Mennonites, the Baptists in England and America, and more recently in isolated congregations on the Continent. The questions of the subjects and mode of baptism still divide Baptist and Pedobaptist churches, but the doctrine of the salvation of unbaptized infants is no longer condemned as a heresy; and the principle of religious liberty and separation of Church and State, for which the Swiss and German Anabaptists suffered and died, is making steady progress.

[1] *l. c.* II. 57 sq.

Germany and Switzerland have changed their policy, and allow to Baptists, Methodists, and other Dissenters from the state-church that liberty of public worship which was formerly denied them; and the state-churches reap the benefit of being stirred up by them to greater vitality. In England the Baptists are one of the leading bodies of Dissenters, and in the United States the largest denomination next to the Methodists and Roman Catholics.

§ 27. *The Eucharistic Controversy. Zwingli and Luther.*

ZWINGLI's eucharistic writings: On the Canon of the Mass (1523); On the same, against Emser (1524); Letter to Matthew Alber at Reutlingen (1524); The 17th ch. of his Com. on the True and False Religion (in Latin and German, March 23, 1525); Answer to Bugenhagen (1525); Letter to Billicanus and Urbanus Rhegius (1526); Address to Osiander of Nürnberg (1527); *Friendly Exegesis,* addressed to Luther (Feb. 20, 1527); Reply to Luther on the true sense of the words of institution of the Lord's Supper (1527); The report on the Marburg Colloquy (1529). In *Opera,* vol. II. B., III., IV. 173 sqq.

For an exposition of Zwingli's doctrine on the Lord's Supper and his controversy with Luther, see vol. VI. 520–550 and 669–682; and A. BAUR, *Zwingli's Theol.* II. 268 sqq. (very full and fair).

The eucharistic controversy between Zwingli and Luther has been already considered in connection with the German Reformation, and requires only a brief notice here. It lasted from 1524 to 1529, and culminated in the Colloquy at Marburg, where the two views came into closer contact and collision than ever before or since, and where every argument for or against the literal interpretation of the words of institution and the corporal presence was set forth with the clearness and force of the two champions.

Zwingli and Luther agreed in the principle of a state-church or people's church (*Volks-Kirche*), as opposed to individualism, separatism, and schism. Both defended the historic continuity of the Church, and put down the revolutionary radicalism which constructed a new church on the voluntary principle. Both retained infant baptism as a part of Christian family religion, against the Anabaptists, who introduced a new baptism with their new church of converts. Luther never appreciated this agreement in the general standpoint, and made at the outset the radical mistake of confounding Zwingli with Carlstadt and the Radicals.[1]

But there was a characteristic difference between the two Reformers in the general theory of the sacraments, and especially the Lord's Supper. Zwingli stood midway between Luther and the Anabaptists. He regarded the sacraments as signs and seals of a grace already received rather than as means of a grace to be received. They set forth and confirm, but do not create, the thing signified. He rejected the doctrine of baptismal regeneration and of the corporal presence; while Luther adhered to both with intense earnestness and treated a departure as damnable heresy. Zwingli's theory reveals the spiritualizing and rationalizing tendency of his mind; while Luther's theory reveals his realistic and mystical tendency. Yet both were equally earnest in their devotion to the Scriptures as the Word of God and the supreme rule of faith and practice.

When they met face to face at Marburg,—once, and only once, in this life,—they came to agree in fourteen out of fifteen articles, and even in the fifteenth article they agreed in the principal part, namely, the spiritual presence and fruition of Christ's body and blood, differing only in regard to the corporal presence and oral manducation, which the one denied, the other asserted. Zwingli showed on that occasion marked ability as a debater, and superior courtesy

---

[1] A. Baur (*Zw. Theol.*, II. 811) says on this misunderstanding: "*Luther warf von Anfang an Zwingli mit Münzer und Karlstadt zusammen. Kein Vorwurf und Vorurtheil gegen Zwingli ist ungerechter, aber auch kein Vorwurf glänzender widerlegt, als dieser, und zwar eben durch die Klarheit und Bestimmtheit, mit welcher Zwingli seine Principien gegen die Wiedertäufer entfaltet. Im Gegentheil; die maasslose Subjectivität die bei Münzer, Karlstadt, bei den Wiedertäufern zum Ausbruch kommt, und die solche Willkühr bleibt, auch wenn sie sich auf den Buchstaben der Schrift beruft, ist das vollständige Gegentheil der Principien Zwingli's.*"

and liberality as a gentleman. Luther received the impression that Zwingli was a "very good man,"[1] yet of a "different spirit," and hence refused to accept his hand of fellowship offered to him with tears. The two men were differently constituted, differently educated, differently situated and equipped, each for his own people and country; and yet the results of their labors, as history has proved, are substantially the same.

§ 28. *The Works of Zwingli.*

A list of Zwingli's works in the edition of Schuler and Schulthess, vol. VIII. 696–704; of his theological works, in Baur, *Zwingli's Theol.*, II. 834–837.

During the twelve short years of his public labors as a reformer, from 1519 to 1531, Zwingli developed an extraordinary literary activity. He attacked the Papists and the Radicals, and had to reply in self-defence. His advice was sought from the friends of reform in all parts of Switzerland, and involved him in a vast correspondence. He wrote partly in Latin, partly in the Swiss-German dialect. Several of his books were translated by Leo Judæ. He handled the German with more skill than his countrymen; but it falls far short of the exceptional force and beauty of Luther's German, and could make no impression outside of Switzerland. The editors of his complete works (Schuler and Schulthess) give, in eight large octavo volumes, eighty German and fifty-nine Latin books and tracts, besides two volumes of epistles by Zwingli and to Zwingli.

His works may be divided into seven classes, as follows:—

1. Reformatory and Polemical Works: (*a*) against popery and the papists (on Fasts; on Images; on the Mass; Against Faber; Against Eck; Against Compar; Against Emser, etc.); (*b*) on the controversy with the Anabaptists; (*c*) on the

---

[1] He called Zwingli "*optimus vir,*" in a letter to Bullinger, written nine years later (1538).

Lord's Supper, against Luther's doctrine of the corporal real presence.

2. Reformatory and Doctrinal: The Exposition of his 67 Conclusions (1524); A Commentary on the False and True Religion, addressed to King Francis I. of France (1525); A Treatise on Divine Providence (1530); A Confession of Faith addressed to the Emperor Charles V. and the Augsburg Diet (1530); and his last confession, written shortly before his death (1531), and published by Bullinger.

3. Practical and Liturgical: The Shepherd; Forms of Baptism and the Celebration of the Lord's Supper; Sermons, etc.

4. Exegetical: Extracts from lectures on Genesis, Exodus, Psalms, Isaiah, and Jeremiah, the four Gospels, and most of the Epistles, edited by Leo Judæ, Megander, and others.

5. Patriotic and Political: Against foreign pensions and military service; addresses to the Confederates, and the Council of Zurich; on Christian education; on peace and war, etc.

6. Poetical: The Labyrinth and The Fable (his earliest productions); three German poems written during the pestilence; one written in 1529, and a versified Psalm (69th).

7. Epistles. They show the extent of his influence, and include letters to Zwingli from Erasmus, Pucci, Pope Adrian VI., Faber, Vadianus, Glareanus, Myconius, Œcolampadius, Haller, Megander, Beatus Rhenanus, Urbanus Rhegius, Bucer, Hedio, Capito, Blaurer, Farel, Comander, Bullinger, Fagius, Pirkheimer, Zasius, Frobenius, Ulrich von Hutten, Philip of Hesse, Duke Ulrich of Württemberg, and other distinguished persons.

§ 29. *The Theology of Zwingli.*

I. ZWINGLI: *Commentarius de Vera et Falsa Religione*, 1525 (German translation by Leo Judæ); *Fidei Ratio ad Carolum V.*, 1530; *Christianæ Fidei
brevis et clara Expositio*, 1531; *De Providentia*, 1530 (expansion of a sermon preached at Marburg and dedicated to Philip of Hesse).

II. The theology of Zwingli is discussed by ZELLER, SIGWART, SPÖRRI,
SCHWEIZER, and most fully and exhaustively by A. BAUR. See lit. § 5,
p. 18. Comp. SCHAFF, *Creeds of Christendom*, I. 369 sqq., and *Church History*, VI. 721 sqq.

The dogmatic works of Zwingli contain the germs of
the evangelical Reformed theology, in distinction from the
Roman and the Lutheran, and at the same time several
original features which separate it from the Calvinistic system. He accepted with all the Reformers the œcumenical
creeds and the orthodox doctrines of the Trinity, and the
divine-human personality of Christ. He rejected with Luther
the scholastic additions of the middle ages, but removed
further from the traditional theology in the doctrine of the
sacraments and the real presence. He was less logical and
severe than Calvin, who surpassed him in constructive
genius, classical diction and rhetorical finish. He drew his
theology from the New Testament and the humanistic culture of the Erasmian type. His love for the classics accounts
for his liberal views on the extent of salvation by which he
differs from the other Reformers. It might have brought
him nearer to Melanchthon; but Melanchthon was under
the overawing influence of Luther, and was strongly preju-
diced against Zwingli. He was free from traditional bondage,
and in several respects in advance of his age.

Zwingli's theology is a system of rational supernaturalism,
more clear than profound, devoid of mysticism, but simple,
sober, and practical. It is prevailingly soteriological, that
is, a doctrine of the way of salvation, and rested on these
fundamental principles: The Bible is the only sure directory
of salvation (which excludes or subordinates human tradi-

tions); Christ is the only Saviour and Mediator between God and men (which excludes human mediators and the worship of saints); Christ is the only head of the Church visible and invisible (against the claims of the pope); the operation of the Holy Spirit and saving grace are not confined to the visible Church (which breaks with the principle of exclusiveness).

1. Zwingli emphasizes the Word of God contained in the Bible, especially in the New Testament, as the only rule of Christian faith and practice. This is the objective principle of Protestantism which controls his whole theology. Zwingli first clearly and strongly proclaimed it in his Conclusions (1523), and assigned to it the first place in his system; while Luther put his doctrine of justification by faith or the subjective principle in the foreground, and made it the article of the standing or falling church. But with both Reformers the two principles so-called resolve themselves into the one principle of Christ, as the only and sufficient source of saving truth and saving grace, against the traditions of men and the works of men. Christ is before the Bible, and is the beginning and end of the Bible. Evangelical Christians believe in the Bible because they believe in Christ, and not *vice versa*. Roman Catholics believe in the Bible because they believe in the Church, as the custodian and infallible interpreter of the Bible.

As to the extent of the Bible, or the number of inspired books, Zwingli accepted the Catholic Canon, with the exception of the Apocalypse, which he did not regard as an apostolic work, and hence never used for doctrinal purposes.[1] Calvin doubted the genuineness of the Second Epistle of Peter and the Pauline origin of the Epistle to the Hebrews. Both accepted the canon on the internal testimony of the

---

[1] He missed in it both the style and the genius of St. John. *"Non sapit os et ingenium Joannis."* Zwingli and Luther were both wrong in their unfavorable judgment of the Revelation of " the Son of Thunder."

Holy Spirit, rather than the external authority of the Church. Luther, on the one hand, insisted in the eucharistic controversy on the most literal interpretation of the words of institution against all arguments of grammar and reason; and yet, on the other hand, he exercised the boldest subjective criticism on several books of the Old and New Testaments, especially the Epistle of James and the Epistle to the Hebrews, because he could not harmonize them with his understanding of Paul's doctrine of justification. He thus became the forerunner of the higher or literary criticism which claims the Protestant right of the fullest investigation of all that pertains to the origin, history, and value of the Scriptures. The Reformed Churches, especially those of the English tongue, while claiming the same right, are more cautious and conservative in the exercise of it; they lay greater stress on the objective revelation of God than the subjective experience of man, and on historic evidence than on critical conjectures.

2. The doctrine of eternal election and providence. Zwingli gives prominence to God's sovereign election as the primary source of salvation. He developed his view in a Latin sermon, or theological discourse, on Divine Providence, at the Conference of Marburg, in October, 1529, and enlarged and published it afterwards at Zurich (Aug. 20, 1530), at the special request of Philip of Hesse.[1] Luther heard the discourse, and had no objection to it, except that he disliked the Greek and Hebrew quotations, as being out of place in the pulpit. Calvin, in a familiar letter to Bullinger, justly called the essay paradoxical and immoderate. It is certainly more paradoxical than orthodox, and contains some unguarded expressions and questionable illustrations; yet it does not go beyond Luther's book on the "Slavery of the

---

[1] *Ad illustrissimum Cattorum Principem Philippum Sermonis de Providentia Dei anamnema.* In *Opera*, vol. IV. 79–144. Leo Judæ published a German translation in 1531.

Human Will," and the first edition of Melanchthon's *Loci*, or Calvin's more mature and careful statements. All the Reformers were originally strong Augustinian predestinarians and denied the liberty of the human will. Augustin and Luther proceeded from anthropological premises, namely, the total depravity of man, and came to the doctrine of predestination as a logical consequence, but laid greater stress on sacramental grace. Zwingli, anticipating Calvin, started from the theological principle of the absolute sovereignty of God and the identity of foreknowledge and foreordination. His Scripture argument is chiefly drawn from the ninth chapter of Romans, which, indeed, strongly teaches the freedom of election,[1] but should never be divorced from the tenth chapter, which teaches with equal clearness human responsibility, and from the eleventh chapter, which prophesies the future conversion of the Gentile nations and the people of Israel.

Zwingli does not shrink from the abyss of supralapsarianism. God, he teaches, is the supreme and only good, and the omnipotent cause of all things. He rules and administers the world by his perpetual and immutable providence, which leaves no room for accidents. Even the fall of Adam, with its consequences, is included in his eternal will as well as his eternal knowledge. So far sin is necessary, but only as a means to redemption. God's agency in respect to sin is free from sin, since he is not bound by law, and has no bad motive or affection.[2] Election is free and independent;

---

[1] P. 114: "*Nos cum Paulo in hac sententia sumus, ut prædestinatio libera sit, citra omnem respectum bene aut male factorum.*" He refers especially to what Paul says about God hardening Pharaoh's heart, and hating Esau and loving Jacob before they were born. But this has reference to their position in history, and not to their eternal salvation or perdition.

[2] *De Providentia Dei* (p. 113): "*Impulit Deus [latronem] ut occideret; sed æque impellit judicem, ut percussorem justitiæ mactet. Et qui impellit, agit sine omni criminis suspicione; non enim est sub lege. Qui vero impellitur, tam abest ut sit alienus a crimine, ut nullam fere rem gerat sine aliqua labis aspergine, quia sub lege est.*" Zwingli defends this view by the illustration of the magistracy

it is not conditioned by faith, but includes faith.[1] Salvation is possible without baptism, but not without Christ. We are elected in order that we may believe in Christ and bring forth the fruits of holiness. Only those who hear and reject the gospel in unbelief are foreordained to eternal punishment. All children of Christian parents who die in infancy are included among the elect, whether baptized or not, and their early death before they have committed any actual sin is a sure proof of their election.[2] Of those outside the Church we cannot judge, but may entertain a charitable hope, as God's grace is not bound. In this direction Zwingli was more liberal than any Reformer and opened a new path. St. Augustin moderated the rigor of the doctrine of predestination by the doctrine of baptismal regeneration and the hypothesis of future purification. Zwingli moderated it by extending the divine revelation and the working of the Holy Spirit beyond the boundaries of the visible Church and the ordinary means of grace.

It is very easy to caricature the doctrine of predestination, and to dispose of it by the plausible objections that it teaches the necessity of sin, that it leads to fatalism and pantheism, that it supersedes the necessity of personal effort for growth in grace, and encourages carnal security. But every one who knows history at all knows also that the

taking a man's life. So a soldier may kill an enemy in battle, without committing murder. Melanchthon traced (1521) the adultery and murder of David and the treason of Judas to the Divine impulse; but he abandoned afterwards (1535) this "Stoic figment of fatalism."

[1] P. 121: "*Fides iis datur, qui ad vitam eternam electi et ordinati sunt; sic tamen ut electio antecedat, et fides velut symbolum electionem sequatur. Sic enim habet Paulus, Rom. 8 : 29.*"

[2] He reasons thus: Nothing separates us from God but sin; children have not committed actual sin; Christ has expiated for original sin; consequently children of Christian parents, about whom we have an express promise, are certainly among the elect if they are taken away in infancy. "*Defungi in illis electionis signum est perinde ac fides in adultis. Et qui reprobi sunt et a Deo repudiati, in hoc statu innocentiæ non moriuntur, sed divina providentia servantur ut repudiatio illorum criminosa vita notetur.*" (P. 127.)

strongest predestinarians were among the most earnest and active Christians. It will be difficult to find purer and holier men than St. Augustin and Calvin, the chief champions of this very system which bears their name. The personal assurance of election fortified the Reformers, the Huguenots, the Puritans, and the Covenanters against doubt and despondency in times of trial and temptation. In this personal application the Reformed doctrine of predestination is in advance of that of Augustin. Moreover, every one who has some perception of the metaphysical difficulties of reconciling the fact of sin with the wisdom and holiness of God, and harmonizing the demands of logic and of conscience, will judge mildly of any earnest attempt at the solution of the apparent conflict of divine sovereignty and human responsibility.

And yet we must say that the Reformers, following the lead of the great saint of Hippo, went to a one-sided extreme. Melanchthon felt this, and proposed the system of synergism, which is akin to the semi-Pelagian and Arminian theories. Œcolampadius kept within the limits of Christian experience and expressed it in the sound sentence, "*Salus nostra ex Deo, perditio nostra ex nobis.*" We must always keep in mind both the divine and the human, the speculative and the practical aspects of this problem of ages; in other words, we must combine divine sovereignty and human responsibility as complemental truths. There is a moral as well as an intellectual logic, — a logic of the heart and conscience as well as a logic of the head. The former must keep the latter in check and save it from running into supralapsarianism and at last into fatalism and pantheism, which is just as bad as Pelagianism.

3. Original sin and guilt. Here Zwingli departed from the Augustinian and Catholic system, and prepared the way for Arminian and Socinian opinions. He was far from denying the terrible curse of the fall and the fact of original

sin; but he regarded original sin as a calamity, a disease, a natural defect, which involves no personal guilt, and is not punishable until it reveals itself in actual transgression. It is, however, the fruitful germ of actual sin, as the inborn rapacity of the wolf will in due time prompt him to tear the sheep.[1]

4. The doctrine of the sacraments, and especially of the Lord's Supper, is the most characteristic feature of the Zwinglian, as distinct from the Lutheran, theology. Calvin's theory stands between the two, and tries to combine the Lutheran realism with the Zwinglian spiritualism. This subject has been sufficiently handled in previous chapters.[2]

5. Eschatology. Here again Zwingli departed further from Augustin and the mediæval theology than any other Reformer, and anticipated modern opinions. He believed (with the Anabaptists) in the salvation of infants dying in infancy, whether baptized or not. He believed also in the salvation of those heathen who loved truth and righteousness in this life, and were, so to say, unconscious Christians, or pre-Christian Christians. This is closely connected with his humanistic liberalism and enthusiasm for the ancient classics. He admired the wisdom and the virtue of the Greeks and Romans, and expected to meet in heaven, not only the saints of the Old Testament from Adam down to John the Baptist, but also such men as Socrates, Plato, Pindar, Aristides, Numa, Cato, Scipio, Seneca; yea, even such mythical characters as Hercules and Theseus. There is, he says, no good and holy man, no faithful soul, from the beginning to the end of the world, that shall not see God in his glory.[3]

---

[1] He describes original sin in Latin as *defectus naturalis* and *conditio misera*, in German as a *Brest* or *Gebrechen*, *i.e.* disease. He compares it to the misfortune of one born in slavery. He explains his view more fully in his tract, *De peccato originali ad Urbanum Rhegium*, 1526 (*Opera*, III. 627–645), and in his Confession to Charles V.

[2] § 27, p. 85 sq.; vol. VI. 620 sqq., and *Creeds of Christendom*, I. 372–377.

[3] He often speaks on this subject in his epistles, commentaries, the tract

Zwingli traced salvation exclusively to the sovereign grace of God, who can save whom, where, and how he pleases, and who is not bound to any visible means. But he had no idea of teaching salvation without Christ and his atonement, as he is often misunderstood and misrepresented. "Christ," he says (in the third of his Conclusions), "is the only wisdom, righteousness, redemption, and satisfaction for the sins of the whole world. Hence it is a denial of Christ when we confess another ground of salvation and satisfaction." He does not say (and did not know) where, when, and how Christ is revealed to the unbaptized subjects of his saving grace: this is hidden from mortal eyes; but we have no right to set boundaries to the infinite wisdom and love of God.

The Roman Catholic Church teaches the necessity of baptism for salvation, and assigns all heathen to hell and all unbaptized children to the *limbus infantum* (a border region of hell, alike removed from burning pain and heavenly bliss). Lutheran divines, who accept the same baptismal theory, must consistently exclude the unbaptized from beatitude, or leave them to the uncovenanted mercy of God. Zwingli and Calvin made salvation depend on eternal election, which may be indefinitely extended beyond the visible Church and sacraments. The Scotch Presbyterian Confession condemns the "horrible dogma" of the papacy concerning the damnation of unbaptized infants. The Westminster Confession teaches that "elect infants dying in infancy," and "all other elect persons, who are incapable of being outwardly called by the ministry of the word, are saved by

on Providence, and most confidently at the close of his Exposition of the Christian Faith, addressed to the king of France. See the passages in Schaff, *Creeds of Christendom*, I, 382, and A. Baur, *l.c.* II. 772. Comp. also Zeller, *l.c.* p. 163; Alex. Schweizer, *Die Prot. Centraldogmen*, I. 94 sqq., and *Reform. Glaubenslehre*, II. 10 sq.; Dorner, *Gesch. der protest. Theol.*, p. 284 (who with his usual fairness vindicates Zwingli against misrepresentations).

Christ through the Spirit, who worketh when, and where, and how he pleaseth." [1]

The old Protestant eschatology is deficient. It rejects the papal dogma of purgatory, and gives nothing better in its place. It confounds Hades with Hell (in the authorized translations of the Bible [2]), and obliterates the distinction between the middle state before, and the final state after, the resurrection. The Roman purgatory gives relief in regard to the fate of imperfect Christians, but none in regard to the infinitely greater number of unbaptized infants and adults who never hear of Christ in this life. Zwingli boldly ventured on a solution of the mysterious problem which is more charitable and hopeful and more in accordance with the impartial justice and boundless mercy of God.

His charitable hope of the salvation of infants dying in infancy and of an indefinite number of heathen is a renewal and enlargement of the view held by the ancient Greek Fathers (Justin Martyr, Clement of Alexandria, Origen, Gregory of Nyssa). It was adopted by the Baptists, Armenians, Quakers, and Methodists, and is now held by the great majority of Protestant divines of all denominations.

[1] Chapter X. 3. " Elect" infants, however, implies, in the strict Calvinistic system, " reprobate " infants who are lost. This negative feature has died out. See on this subject Schaff, *Creeds of Christendom*, I. 378–384, and his *Creed Revision in the Presbyterian Churches*, New York, 1890, p. 17 sqq.

[2] This serious error is corrected in the Revised English Version of 1881. It is an anachronism when a scholar of the nineteenth century denies the distinction between Hades or Sheol (*i.e.* the spirit-world or realm of the dead) and Gehenna (*i.e.* hell, or the place and state of the lost).

CHAPTER IV.

SPREAD OF THE REFORMATION IN SWITZERLAND.

§ 30. *The Swiss Diet and the Conference at Baden,* 1526.

THOMAS MURNER: *Die Disputacion vor den XII Orten einer löblichen Eidgenos-senschaft . . . zu Baden gehalten.* Luzern, 1527. This is the official Catholic report, which agrees with four other protocols preserved in Zurich. (Müller-Hottinger, VII. 84.) Murner published also a Latin edition, *Causa Helvetica orthodoxæ fidei,* etc. Lucernæ, 1528. BULLINGER, I. 331 sqq. The writings of ZWINGLI, occasioned by the Disputation in Baden, in his *Opera,* vol. II. B. 396–522.

HOTTINGER: *Geschichte der Eidgenossen während der Zeit der Kirchentrennung,* pp. 77–96. MÖRIKOFER: *Zw.,* II. 34–43. MERLE: *Reform.,* Bk. XI. ch. 13. HERZOG: *Oekolampad,* vol. II. ch. 1. HAGENBACH: *Oekolampad,* pp. 90–98. A. BAUR: *Zw.'s Theol.,* I. 501–518.

THE Diet of Switzerland took the same stand against the Zwinglian Reformation as the Diet of the German Empire against the Lutheran movement. Both Diets consisted only of one house, and this was composed of the hereditary nobility and aristocracy. The people were not directly represented by delegates of their own choice. The majority of voters were conservative, and in favor of the old faith; but the majority of the people in the larger and most prosperous cantons and in the free imperial cities favored progress and reform, and succeeded in the end.

The question of the Reformation was repeatedly brought before the Swiss Diet, and not a few liberal voices were heard in favor of abolishing certain crying abuses; but the majority of the cantons, especially the old forest-cantons around the lake of Lucerne, resisted every innovation. Berne was anxious to retain her political supremacy, and vacillated. Zwingli had made many enemies by his opposi-

98

tion to the foreign military service and pensions of his countrymen. Dr. Faber, the general vicar of the diocese of
Constance, after a visit to Rome, openly turned against his
former friend, and made every effort to unite the interests
of the aristocracy with those of the hierarchy. "Now," he
said, "the priests are attacked, the nobles will come next." [1]

At last the Diet resolved to settle the difficulty by a public
disputation. Dr. Eck, well known to us from the disputation at Leipzig for his learning, ability, vanity and conceit,[2]
offered his services to the Diet in a flattering letter of Aug.
13, 1524. He had then just returned from a third visit to
Rome, and felt confident that he could crush the Protestant
heresy in Switzerland as easily as in Germany. He spoke
contemptuously of Zwingli, as one who "had no doubt
milked more cows than he had read books." About the
same time the Roman counter-reformation had begun to be
organized at the convent of Regensburg (June, 1524), under
the lead of Bavaria and Austria.

The disputation was opened in the Catholic city of Baden,
in Aargau, May 21, 1526, and lasted eighteen days, till the
8th of June. The cantons and four bishops sent deputies,
and many foreign divines were present. The Protestants
were a mere handful, and despised as "a beggarly, miserable
rabble." Zwingli, who foresaw the political aim and result
of the disputation, was prevented by the Council of Zurich
from leaving home, because his life was threatened; but he
influenced the proceedings by daily correspondence and
secret messengers. No one could doubt his courage, which
he showed more than once in the face of greater danger,
as when he went to Marburg through hostile territory, and
to the battlefield at Cappel. But several of his friends were
sadly disappointed at his absence. He would have equalled
Eck in debate and excelled him in biblical learning. Eras-

[1] "*Jetzst geht's über die Geistlichen, dann kommt es an die Junker.*"
[2] Comp. vol. VI. § 37, p. 178 sqq.

mus was invited, but politely declined on account of sickness.

The arrangements for the disputation and the local sympathies were in favor of the papal party. Mass was said every morning at five, and a sermon preached; the pomp of ritualism was displayed in solemn processions. The presiding officers and leading secretaries were Romanists; nobody besides them was permitted to take notes.[1] The disputation turned on the real presence, the sacrifice of the mass, the invocation of the Virgin Mary and of saints, on images, purgatory, and original sin. Dr. Eck was the champion of the Roman faith, and behaved with the same polemical dexterity and overbearing and insolent manner as at Leipzig: robed in damask and silk, decorated with a golden ring, chain and cross; surrounded by patristic and scholastic folios, abounding in quotations and arguments, treating his opponents with proud contempt, and silencing them with his stentorian voice and final appeals to the authority of Rome. Occasionally he uttered an oath, *"Potz Marter."* A contemporary poet, Nicolas Manuel, thus described his conduct: —

> "Eck stamps with his feet, and claps his hands,
>   He raves, he swears, he scolds;
> 'I do,' cries he, 'what the Pope commands,
>   And teach whatever he holds.'"[2]

Œcolampadius of Basle and Haller of Berne, both plain and modest, but able, learned and earnest men, defended the Reformed opinions. Œcolampadius declared at the outset that he recognized no other rule of judgment than the Word of God. He was a match for Eck in patristic

---

[1] Nevertheless, two young friends of the Reformation published reports from memory.

[2] In *Eck's und Faber's Badenfahrt:*

> "*Eck zappelt mit Füssen und Händen,*
> *Fing an zu schelten und schänden.*
> *Er sprach: Ich blib by dem Verstand,*
> *Den Papst, Cardinal, und Bishof hand.*"

learning, and in solid arguments. His friends said, " Œcolampadius is vanquished, not by argument, but by vociferation." [1] Even one of the Romanists remarked, "If only
this pale man were on our side!" His host judged that he
must be a very pious heretic, because he saw him constantly
engaged in study and prayer; while Eck was enjoying rich
dinners and good wines, which occasioned the remark, "Eck
is bathing in Baden, but in wine." [2]

The papal party boasted of a complete victory. All innovations were forbidden; Zwingli was excommunicated; and
Basle was called upon to depose Œcolampadius from the
pastoral office. Faber, not satisfied with the burning of
heretical books, advocated even the burning of the Protestant versions of the Bible. Thomas Murner, a Franciscan
monk and satirical poet, who was present at Baden, heaped
upon Zwingli and his adherents such epithets as tyrants,
liars, adulterers, church robbers, fit only for the gallows!
He had formerly (1512) chastised the vices of priests and
monks, but turned violently against the Saxon Reformer, and
earned the name of " Luther-Scourge " (*Lutheromastix*). He
was now made lecturer in the Franciscan convent at Lucerne,
and authorized to edit the acts of the Baden disputation.[3]

[1] "*Nicht überdisputirt, aber überschrieen ist er.*"

[2] In another witty poem, quoted by Bullinger (I. 357 sq.), the two disputants
are thus contrasted : —

> "*Also fing an die Disputaz :*
> *Hans Eck empfing da manchen Kratz,*
> *Das that ihn übel schmerzen,*
> *Denn alles, was er fürherbracht,*
> *That ihm Hans Husschyn* [*Œkolampadius*] *kürzen.*

> *Herr Doctor Husschyn hochgelehrt*
> *Hat sich gen Ecken tapfer gwehrt,*
> *Oft gnommen Schwert und Stangen.*
> *Eck floh dann zu dem röm'schen Stuhl*
> *Und auch all sin Anhangen.*"

[3] He also issued, in 1527, an almanac with satirical caricatures of heretics,
where Zwingli is represented hanging on the gallows, and is called "*Kirchen-
dieb,*" "*Feigenfresser,*" "*Geiger des heil. Evangeliums und Lautenschläger des Alten
und Neuen Testaments,*" etc. Kessler's *Sabbata*, Schaffhausen, 1865, and Hagenbach, p. 372.

The result of the Baden disputation was a temporary triumph for Rome, but turned out in the end, like the Leipzig disputation of 1519, to the furtherance of the Reformation. Impartial judges decided that the Protestants had been silenced by vociferation, intrigue and despotic measures, rather than refuted by sound and solid arguments from the Scriptures. After a temporary reaction, several cantons which had hitherto been vacillating between the old and the new faith, came out in favor of reform.

§ 31. *The Reformation in Berne.*

I. The acts of the disputation of Berne were published in 1528 at Zurich and Strassburg, afterwards repeatedly at Berne, and are contained, together with two sermons of Zwingli, in ZWINGLI's *Werke*, II. A. 63–229.— VALERIUS ANSHELM: *Berner Chronik*, new ed. by *Stierlin* and *Wyss*. Bern, 1884, '86, 2 vols. STÜRLER: *Urkunden der Bernischen Kirchenreform.* Bern, 1862. STRICKLER: *Aktensammlung*, etc. Zurich, 1878 (I. 1).

II. KUHN: *Die Reformatoren Berns.* Bern, 1828. SAM. FISCHER: *Geschichte der Disputation zu Bern.* Zürich, 1828. MELCH. KIRCHHOFER: *Berthold Haller oder die Reformation zu Bern.* Zürich, 1828. C. PESTALOZZI: *B. Haller, nach handschriftl. und gleichzeitigen Quellen.* Elberfeld, 1861. The monographs on *Niclaus Manuel* by GRÜNEISEN, Stuttgart, 1837, and by BÄCHTHOLD, Frauenfeld, 1878. HUNDESHAGEN: *Die Conflicte des Zwinglianismus, Lutherthums und Calvinismus in der Bernischen Landeskirche von 1532-'58.* Bern, 1842. F. TRECHSEL: articles *Berner Disputation* and *Berner Synodus*, and *Haller*, in Herzog[2], II. 313–324, and V 556–561. *Berner Beiträge*, etc., 1884, quoted on p. 15. See also the lit. by NIPPOLD in his Append. to Hagenbach's *Reform. Gesch.*, p. 695 sq.

III. KARL LUDWIG VON HALLER (a distinguished Bernese and convert to Romanism, expelled from the Protestant Council of Berne, 1820; d. 1854): *Geschichte der kirchlichen Revolution oder protestantischen Reform des Kantons Bern und umliegender Gegenden.* Luzern, 1836 (346 pages). French translation, *Histoire de la revolution religieuse dans la Swiss occidentale.* Paris, 1839. This is a reactionary account professedly drawn from Protestant sources and represents the Swiss Reformation as the mother of the Revolution of 1789. To the French version of this book Archbishop Spalding of Baltimore (he does not mention the original) confesses to be "indebted for most of the facts" in his chapter on the Swiss Reformation which he calls a work established " by intrigue, chicanery, persecution, and open violence!" *Hist. of the Prot. Ref. in Germany and Switzerland*, I. 181, 186 (8th ed., Baltimore, 1875).

Berne, the largest, most conservative and aristocratic of the Swiss cantons, which contains the political capital of the Confederacy, was the first to follow Zurich, after considerable hesitation. This was an event of decisive importance.

The Reformation was prepared in the city and throughout the canton by three ministers, Sebastian Meyer, Berthold Haller, and Francis Kolb, and by a gifted layman, Niclaus Manuel, — all friends of Zwingli. Meyer, a Franciscan monk, explained in the convent the Epistles of Paul, and in the pulpit, the Apostles' Creed. Haller, a native of Würtemberg, a friend and fellow-student of Melanchthon, an instructive preacher and cautious reformer, of a mild and modest disposition, settled in Berne as teacher in 1518, was elected chief pastor at the cathedral 1521, and labored there faithfully till his death (1536). He was often in danger, and wished to retire; but Zwingli encouraged him to remain at the post of duty. Without brilliant talents or great learning, he proved eminently useful by his gentle piety and faithful devotion to duty. Manuel, a poet, painter, warrior and statesman, helped the cause of reform by his satirical dramas, which were played in the streets, his exposure of Eck and Faber after the Baden disputation, and his influence in the council of the city (d. 1530). His services to Zwingli resemble the services of Hutten to Luther. The Great Council of the Two Hundred protected the ministers in preaching the pure gospel.

The Peasants' War in Germany and the excesses of the Radicals in Switzerland produced a temporary reaction in favor of Romanism. The government prohibited religious controversy, banished Meyer, and ordered Haller, on his return from the Baden disputation, to read Romish mass again; but he declined, and declared that he would rather give up his position, as he preferred the Word of God to his daily bread. The elections in 1527 turned out in favor of the party of progress. The Romish measures were revoked, and a disputation ordered to take place Jan. 6, 1528, in Berne.

The disputation at Berne lasted nineteen days (from Jan. 6 to 26). It was the Protestant counterpart of the disputation at Baden in composition, arrangements and result. It had the same effect for Berne as the disputations of 1523 had for Zurich. The invitations were general; but the Roman Catholic cantons and the four bishops who were invited refused, with the exception of the bishop of Lausanne, to send delegates, deeming the disputation of Baden final. Dr. Eck, afraid to lose his fresh laurels, was unwilling, as he said, "to follow the heretics into their nooks and corners"; but he severely attacked the proceedings. The Reformed party was strongly represented by delegates from Zurich, Basel, and St. Gall, and several cities of South Germany. Zurich sent about one hundred ministers and laymen, with a strong protection. The chief speakers on the Reformed side were Zwingli, Haller, Kolb, Œcolampadius, Capito, and Bucer from Strassburg; on the Roman side, Grab, Huter, Treger, Christen, and Burgauer. Joachim von Watt of St. Gall presided. Popular sermons were preached during the disputation by Blaurer of Constance, Zwingli, Bucer, Œcolampadius, Megander, and others.

The Reformers carried an easy and complete victory, and reversed the decision of Baden. The ten Theses or Conclusions, drawn up by Haller and revised by Zwingli, were fully discussed, and adopted as a sort of confession of faith for the Reformed Church of Berne. They are as follows : —

1. The holy Christian Church, whose only Head is Christ, is born of the Word of God, and abides in the same, and listens not to the voice of a stranger.

2. The Church of Christ makes no laws and commandments without the Word of God. Hence human traditions are no more binding on us than as far as they are founded in the Word of God.

3. Christ is the only wisdom, righteousness, redemption, and satisfaction for the sins of the whole world. Hence it is a denial of Christ when we confess another ground of salvation and satisfaction.

4. The essential and corporal presence of the body and blood of Christ cannot be demonstrated from the Holy Scripture.

5. The mass as now in use, in which Christ is offered to God the Father for the sins of the living and the dead, is contrary to the Scripture, a blasphemy against the most holy sacrifice, passion, and death of Christ, and on account of its abuses an abomination before God.

6. As Christ alone died for us, so he is also to be adored as the only Mediator and Advocate between God the Father and the believers. Therefore it is contrary to the Word of God to propose and invoke other mediators.

7. Scripture knows nothing of a purgatory after this life. Hence all masses and other offices for the dead [1] are useless.

8. The worship of images is contrary to Scripture. Therefore images should be abolished when they are set up as objects of adoration.

9. Matrimony is not forbidden in the Scripture to any class of men; but fornication and unchastity are forbidden to all.

10. Since, according to the Scripture, an open fornicator must be excommunicated, it follows that unchastity and impure celibacy are more pernicious to the clergy than to any other class.

All to the glory of God and his holy Word.

Zwingli preached twice during the disputation.[2] He was in excellent spirits, and at the height of his fame and public usefulness. In the first sermon he explained the Apostles' Creed, mixing in some Greek and Hebrew words for his theological hearers. In the second, he exhorted the Bernese to persevere after the example of Moses and the heroes of faith. Perseverance alone can complete the triumph. (*Ferendo vincitur fortuna.*) Behold these idols conquered, mute, and scattered before you. The gold you spent upon them must henceforth be devoted to the good of the living images of God in their poverty. "Hold fast," he said in conclusion, "to the liberty wherewith Christ has set us free (Gal. 5:1). You know how much we have suffered in our conscience, how we were directed from one false comfort to another, from one commandment to another which only burdened our conscience and gave us no rest. But now ye have found freedom and peace in the knowledge and faith of Jesus Christ. From this freedom let nothing separate you. To

---

[1] "*All todtendienst, als vigil, seelmess, seelgrät, sibend, dryssgest, jarzyt, kerzen, und derglychen.*"

[2] The sermons are printed in *Werke*, II. B. 203-229.

hold it fast requires great fortitude. You know how our ancestors, thanks to God, have fought for our bodily liberty; let us still more zealously guard our spiritual liberty; not doubting that God, who has enlightened and drawn you, will in due time also draw our dear neighbors and fellow-confederates to him, so that we may live together in true friendship. May God, who created and redeemed us all, grant this to us and to them. Amen."

By a reformation edict of the Council, dated Feb. 7, 1528, the ten Theses were legalized, the jurisdiction of the bishops abolished, and the necessary changes in worship and discipline provisionally ordered, subject to fuller light from the Word of God. The parishes of the city and canton were separately consulted by delegates sent to them Feb. 13 and afterwards, and the great majority adopted the reformation by popular vote, except in the highlands where the movement was delayed.

After the catastrophe of Cappel the reformation was consolidated by the so-called "Berner Synodus," which met Jan. 9–14, 1532. All the ministers of the canton, two hundred and twenty in all, were invited to attend. Capito, the reformer of Strassburg, exerted a strong influence by his addresses. The Synod adopted a book of church polity and discipline; the Great Council confirmed it, and ordered annual synods. Hundeshagen pronounces this constitution a "true masterpiece even for our times," and Trechsel characterizes it as excelling in apostolic unction, warmth, simplicity and practical wisdom.[1]

Since that time Berne has remained faithful to the Reformed Church. In 1828 the Canton by order of the government celebrated the third centenary of the Reformation.

---

[1] The constitution was printed at Basle in the same year, and repeatedly since. Trechsel gives an epitome of it in Herzog², II. 320 sqq.

§ 32.   *The Reformation in Basel.   Œcolampadius.*

I. The sources are chiefly in the *Bibliotheca Antistitii* and the University Library of Basel, and in the City Library of Zürich; letters of ŒCOLAMPADIUS to Zwingli, in Bibliander's *Epistolæ Joh. Œcolampadii et Huldr. Zwinglii* (Basel, 1536, fol.); in Zwingli's *Opera*, vols. VII. and VIII.; and in HERMINJARD, *Correspondance des Réformateurs*, passim. Several letters of ERASMUS, and his *Consilium Senatui Basiliensi in negotio Lutherano anno 1525 exhibitum. Antiquitates Gernlerianæ*, Tom. I. and II. An important collection of letters and documents prepared by direction of Antistes LUKAS GERNLER of Basel (1625–1675), who took part in the Helvetic Consensus Formula. The *Athenæ Rauricæ sive Catalogus Professorum Academiæ Basiliensis*, by Herzog, Basel, 1778. The *Basler Chroniken*, publ. by the Hist. Soc. of Basel, ed. with comments by W. VISCHER (son), Leipz. 1872.

II. PET. OCHS: *Geschichte der Stadt und Landschaft Basel.* Berlin and Leipzig, 1786–1822. 8 vols. The Reformation is treated in vols. V. and VI., but without sympathy. JAK. BURCKHARDT: *Kurze Geschichte der Reformation in Basel.* Basel, 1819. K. R. HAGENBACH: *Kirchliche Denkwürdigkeiten zur Geschichte Basels seit der Reformation.* Basel, 1827 (pp. 268). The first part also under the special title: *Kritische Geschichte und Schicksale der ersten Basler Confession.* By the same: *Die Theologische Schule Basels und ihrer Lehrer von Stiftung der Hochschule 1460 bis zu De Wette's Tod 1849* (pp. 75). JARKE (R. Cath.): *Studien und Skizzen zur Geschichte der Reformation.* Schaffhausen (Hurter), 1846 (pp. 576). FRIED. FISCHER: *Der Bildersturm in der Schweiz und in Basel insbesondere.* In the "Basler Jahrbuch" for 1850. W. VISCHER: *Actenstücke zur Geschichte der Reformation in Basel.* In the "Basler Beiträge zur vaterländischen Geschichte," for 1854. By the same: *Geschichte der Universität Basel von der Gründung 1460 bis zur Reformation 1529.* Basel, 1860. BOOS: *Geschichte der Stadt Basel.* Basel, 1877 sqq. The first volume goes to 1501; the second has not yet appeared.

III. Biographical. S. HESS: *Lebensgeschichte Joh. Oekolampads.* Zürich, 1793 (chiefly from Zürich sources, contained in the *Simler* collection). J. J. HERZOG (editor of the well-known " Encyclopædia," d. 1882): *Das Leben Joh. Oekolampads und die Reformation der Kirche zu Basel.* Basel, 1843. 2 vols. Comp. his article in Herzog [2], vol. X. 708–724. K. R. HAGENBACH: *Johann Oekolampad und Oswald Myconius, die Reformatoren Basels. Leben und ausgewählte Schriften.* Elberfeld, 1859. His *Reformationsgesch.*, 5th ed., by *Nippold*, Leipzig, 1887, p. 386 sqq. On Œcolampadius' connection with the Eucharistic Controversy and part in the Marburg Colloquy, see SCHAFF, vol. VI. 620, 637, and 642.

The example of Berne was followed by Basel, the wealthiest and most literary city in Switzerland, an episcopal see since the middle of the eighth century, the scene of the reformatory Council of 1430–1448, the seat of a University since 1460, the centre of the Swiss book trade, favorably situated for commerce on the banks of the Rhine and on the borders of Germany and France. The soil was prepared for the Reformation by scholars like Wyttenbach and Erasmus, and by evangelical preachers like Capito and Hedio. Had Erasmus been as zealous for religion as he was for letters, he would have taken the lead, but he withdrew more and more from the Reformation, although he continued to reside in Basel till 1529 and returned there to die (1536).[1]

The chief share in the work fell to the lot of Œcolampadius (1482–1531). He is the second in rank and importance among the Reformers in German Switzerland. His relation to Zwingli is similar to that sustained by Melanchthon to Luther, and by Beza to Calvin, — a relation in part subordinate, in part supplemental. He was inferior to Zwingli in originality, force, and popular talent, but surpassed him in scholastic erudition and had a more gentle disposition. He was, like Melanchthon, a man of thought rather than of action, but circumstances forced him out of his quiet study to the public arena.

Johann Œcolampadius[2] was born at Weinsberg in the present kingdom of Würtemberg in 1482, studied law in Bologna, philology, scholastic philosophy, and theology in Heidelberg and Tübingen with unusual success. He was a precocious genius, like Melanchthon. In his twelfth year he composed (according to Capito) Latin poems. In 1501 he became Baccalaureus, and soon afterwards Master of Arts. He devoted himself chiefly to the study of the Greek and

---

[1] On Erasmus and his relation to the Reformation, see above, p. 24 sq., and especially vol. VI. 399–434.

[2] A Greek name given him for *Hausschein* or *Husschyn* (*Houselamp*); but in the university register of Heidelberg he is entered under the family name of *Hussgen* or *Heussgen*, i.e. *Little House*. His mother was descended of the old Basel family of *Pfister*. Hence he says in the Preface to his Commentary on Isaiah: "*Basilea mihi ab avo patria.*" See Hagenbach, *Oekol.*, p. 3 sq.

Hebrew Scriptures. Erasmus gave him the testimony of being the best Hebraist (after Reuchlin). At Tübingen he formed a friendship with Melanchthon, his junior by fifteen years, and continued on good terms with him notwithstanding their difference of opinion on the Eucharist. He delivered at Weinsberg a series of sermons on the Seven Words of Christ on the Cross, which were published by Zasius in 1512, and gained for him the reputation of an eminent preacher of the gospel.

In 1515 he received a call, at Capito's suggestion, from Christoph von Utenheim, bishop of Basel (since 1502), to the pulpit of the cathedral in that city. In the year following he acquired the degree of licentiate, and later that of doctor of divinity. Christoph von Utenheim belonged to the better class of prelates, who desired a reformation within the Church, but drew back after the Diet of Worms, and died at Delsberg in 1522. His motto was: " The cross of Christ is my hope ; I seek mercy, not works." [1]

Œcolampadius entered into intimate relations with Erasmus, who at that time took up his permanent abode in Basel. He rendered him important service in his Annotations to the New Testament, and in the second edition of the Greek Testament (concerning the quotations from the Septuagint and Hebrew). The friendship afterwards cooled down in consequence of their different attitude to the question of reform.

In 1518 Œcolampadius showed his moral severity and zeal for a reform of the pulpit by an attack on the prevailing custom of entertaining the people in the Easter season with all kinds of jokes. " What has," he asks, "a preacher of repentance to do with fun and laughter? Is it necessary for us to yield to the impulse of nature? If we can crush our sins by laughter, what is the use of repenting in sackcloth

---

[1] " *Spes mea crux Christi ; gratiam, non opera quæro.*" The motto of Gerson and many mystics.

and ashes? What is the use of tears and cries of sorrow? . . . No one knows that Jesus laughed, but every one knows that he wept. The Apostles sowed the seed weeping. Many as are the symbolic acts of the prophets, no one of them lowers himself to become an actor. Laughter and song were repugnant to them. They lived righteously before the Lord, rejoicing and yet trembling, and saw as clear as the sun at noonday that all is vanity under the sun. They saw the net being drawn everywhere and the near approach of the judge of the world."[1]

After a short residence at Weinsberg and Augsburg, Œcolampadius surprised his friends by entering a convent in 1520, but left it in 1522 and acted a short time as chaplain for Franz von Sickingen at Ebernburg, near Creuznach, where he introduced the use of the German language in the mass.

By the reading of Luther's writings, he became more and more fixed in evangelical convictions. He cautiously attacked transubstantiation, Mariolatry, and the abuses of the confessional, and thereby attracted the favorable attention of Luther, who wrote to Spalatin (June 10, 1521): "I am surprised at his spirit, not because he fell upon the same theme as I, but because he has shown himself so liberal, prudent, and Christian. God grant him growth." In June, 1523, Luther expressed to Œcolampadius much satisfaction at his lectures on Isaiah, notwithstanding the displeasure of Erasmus, who would probably, like Moses, die in the land of Moab. " He has done his part," he says, "by exposing the bad; to show the good and to lead into the land of promise, is beyond his power." Luther and Œcolampadius met personally at Marburg in 1529, but as antagonists on the doctrine of the Lord's Supper, in which the latter stood on the side of Zwingli.

In Nov. 17, 1522, Œcolampadius settled permanently in Basel and labored there as preacher of the Church of St. Martin and professor of theology in the University till his

---

[1] *De Risu Paschali*, printed by Frobenius at Basel, 1518.

death. Now began his work as reformer of the church of Basel, which followed the model of Zürich. He sought the friendship of Zwingli in a letter full of admiration, dated Dec. 10, 1522.[1] They continued to co-operate in fraternal harmony to the close of their lives.

Œcolampadius preached on Sundays and week days, explaining whole books of the Bible after the example of Zwingli, and attracted crowds of people. With the consent of the Council, he gradually abolished crying abuses, distributed the Lord's Supper under both kinds, and published in 1526 a German liturgy, which retained in the first editions several distinctively Catholic features such as priestly absolution and the use of lights on the altar.

In 1525 he began to take an active part in the unfortunate Eucharistic controversy by defending the figurative interpretation of the words of institution: "This is (the figure of) my body," chiefly from the writings of the fathers, with which he was very familiar.[2] He agreed in substance with Zwingli, but differed from him by placing the metaphor in the predicate rather than the verb, which simply denotes a connection of the subject with the predicate whether real or figurative, and which was not even used by our Lord in Aramaic. He found the key for the interpretation in John 6 : 63, and held fast to the truth that Christ himself is and remains the true bread of the *soul* to be partaken of by *faith*. At the conference in Marburg (1529) he was, next to Zwingli, the chief debater on the Reformed side. By this course he alienated his old friends, Brentius, Pirkheimer, Billican, and Luther. Even Melanchthon, in a letter to him (1529), regretted that the "*horribilis dissensio de Cœna Domini*" interfered with the enjoyment of their friendship,

---

[1] *Opera Zwinglii*, VII. 251, and Zwingli's reply, p. 261. Hagenbach gives a German translation of the letters, p. 26 sq. and 38.

[2] *De genuina verborum Domini "hoc est corpus meum" juxta vetustissimos auctores expositione.* (Strassburg), September, 1525. Comp. vol. VI. 612 sqq.

though it did not shake his good will towards him ("*benevo-
lentiam erga te meam*"). He concluded to be hereafter "a
spectator rather than an actor in this tragedy."

Œcolampadius had also much trouble with the Anabaptists,
and took the same conservative and intolerant stand against
them as Luther at Wittenberg, and Zwingli at Zürich. He
made several fruitless attempts in public disputations to convince them of their error.[1]

The civil government of Basel occupied for a while middle
ground, but the disputation of Baden, at which Œcolampadius
was the champion of the Reformed doctrines,[2] brought on
the crisis. He now took stronger ground against Rome and
attacked what he regarded as the idolatry of the mass. The
triumph of the Reformation in Berne in 1528 gave the final
impetus.

On the 9th of February, 1529, an unbloody revolution
broke out. Aroused by the intrigues of the Roman party,
the Protestant citizens to the number of two thousand came
together, broke to pieces the images still left, and compelled
the reactionary Council to introduce everywhere the form of
religious service practised in Zürich.

Erasmus, who had advised moderation and quiet waiting
for a general Council, was disgusted with these violent measures, which he describes in a letter to Pirkheimer of Nürnberg, May 9, 1529. "The smiths and workmen," he says,
"removed the pictures from the churches, and heaped such
insults on the images of the saints and the crucifix itself,
that it is quite surprising there was no miracle, seeing how
many there always used to occur whenever the saints were
even slightly offended. Not a statue was left either in the
churches, or the vestibules, or the porches, or the monasteries.
The frescoes were obliterated by means of a coating of lime;

---

[1] See above, p. 69 sqq., and the extracts of his disputations with the
Anabaptists in Hagenbach, p. 108 sqq.; Herzog, I. 299 sqq., and II. 75 sqq.

[2] See above, p. 100.

whatever would burn was thrown into the fire, and the rest pounded into fragments. Nothing was spared for either love or money. Before long the mass was totally abolished, so that it was forbidden either to celebrate it in one's own house or to attend it in the neighboring villages." [1]

The great scholar who had done so much preparatory work for the Reformation, stopped half-way and refused to identify himself with either party. He reluctantly left Basel (April 13, 1529) with the best wishes for her prosperity, and resided six years at Freiburg in Baden, a sickly, sensitive, and discontented old man. He was enrolled among the professors of the University, but did not lecture. He returned to Basel in August, 1535, and died in his seventieth year, July 12, 1536, without priest or sacrament, but invoking the mercy of Christ, repeating again and again, " O Lord Jesus, have mercy on me ! " He was buried in the Minster of Basel.

Glareanus and Beatus Rhenanus, humanists, and friends of Zwingli and Erasmus, likewise withdrew from Basel at this critical moment. Nearly all the professors of the University emigrated. They feared that science and learning would suffer from theological quarrels and a rupture with the hierarchy.

The abolition of the mass and the breaking of images, the destruction of the papal authority and monastic institutions, would have been a great calamity had they not been followed by the constructive work of the evangelical faith which was the moving power, and which alone could build up a new Church on the ruins of the old. The Word of God was preached from the fountain. Christ and the Gospel were put in the place of the Church and tradition. German service with congregational singing and communion was substituted

---

[1] The modern revival of archæological and artistic taste in Switzerland has brought about a restoration of the old frescoes and sculptures of the beautiful Minster and Cloister of Basel, and of the chamber where the great Council was held.

for the Latin mass. The theological faculty was renewed by the appointment of Simon Grynäus, Sebastian Münster, Oswald Myconius, and other able and pious scholars to professorships.

Œcolampadius became the chief preacher of the Minster and Antistes, or superintendent, of the clergy of Basel.

On the 1st of April, 1529, an order of liturgical service and church discipline was published by the Council, which gave a solid foundation to the Reformed Church of the city of Basel and the surrounding villages.[1] This document breathes the spirit of enthusiasm for the revival of apostolic Christianity, and aims at a reformation of faith and morals. It contains the chief articles which were afterwards formulated in the Confession of Basel (1534), and rules for a corresponding discipline. It retains a number of Catholic customs such as daily morning and evening worship, weekly communion in one of the city churches, the observance of the great festivals, including those of the Virgin Mary, the Apostles, and the Saints.

To give force to these institutions, the ban was introduced in 1530, and confided to a council of three pious, honest, and brave laymen for each of the four parishes of the city; two to be selected by the Council, and one by the congregation, who, in connection with the clergy, were to watch over the morals, and to discipline the offenders, if necessary, by excommunication. In accordance with the theocratic idea of the relation of Church and State, dangerous heresies which denied any of the twelve articles of the Apostles' Creed, and blasphemy of God and the sacrament, were made punishable with civil penalties such as confiscation of property, banishment, and even death. Those, it is said, " shall be punished according to the measure of their guilt in body, life, and property, who despise, spurn, or contemn the eternal, pure, elect queen, the blessed Virgin Mary, or other beloved

---

[1] In Ochs, *l.c.* V. 686 sq.; Bullinger, II. 82 sqq.

saints of God who now live with Christ in eternal blessedness, so as to say that the mother of God is only a woman like other women, that she had more children than Christ, the Son of God, that she was not a virgin before or after his birth," etc. Such severe measures have long since passed away. The mixing of civil and ecclesiastical punishments caused a good deal of trouble. Œcolampadius opposed the supremacy of the State over the Church. He presided over the first synods.

After the victory of the Reformation, Œcolampadius continued unto the end of his life to be indefatigable in preaching, teaching, and editing valuable commentaries (chiefly on the Prophets). He took a lively interest in French Protestant refugees, and brought the Waldenses, who sent a deputation to him, into closer affinity with the Reformed churches.[1] He was a modest and humble man, of a delicate constitution and ascetic habits, and looked like a church father. He lived with his mother; but after her death, in 1528, he married, at the age of forty-five, Wilibrandis Rosenblatt, the widow of Cellarius (Keller), who afterwards married in succession two other Reformers (Capito and Bucer), and survived four husbands. This tempted Erasmus to make the frivolous joke (in a letter of March 21, 1528), that his friend had lately married a good-looking girl to crucify his flesh, and that the Lutheran Reformation was a comedy rather than a tragedy, since the tumult always ended in a wedding. He afterwards apologized to him, and disclaimed any motive of unkindness. Œcolampadius had three children, whom he named Eusebius, Alitheia, and Irene (Godliness, Truth, Peace), to indicate what were the pillars of his theology and his household. His last days were made sad by the news of Zwingli's death, and the conclusion of a peace unfavorable to the Reformed churches. The call from Zürich to become Zwingli's successor he declined. A few weeks

[1] See Herzog, II. 239 sqq.; Hagenbach, 150 sqq.

later, on the 24th of November, 1531, he passed away in peace
and full of faith, after having partaken of the holy communion with his family, and admonished his colleagues to
continue faithful to the cause of the Reformation. He was
buried behind the Minster.[1]

His works have never been collected, and have only historical interest. They consist of commentaries, sermons,
exegetical and polemical tracts, letters, and translations from
Chrysostom, Theodoret, and Cyril of Alexandria.[2]

Basel became one of the strongholds of the Reformed
Church of Switzerland, together with Zürich, Geneva, and
Berne. The Church passed through the changes of German
Protestantism, and the revival of the nineteenth century.
She educates evangelical ministers, contributes liberally from
her great wealth to institutions of Christian benevolence and
the spread of the Gospel, and is (since 1816) the seat of the
largest Protestant missionary institute on the Continent,
which at the annual festivals forms a centre for the friends
of missions in Switzerland, Würtemberg, and Baden. The
neighboring Chrischona is a training school of German ministers for emigrants to America.

§ 33. *The Reformation in Glarus. Tschudi. Glarean.*

VALENTIN TSCHUDI: *Chronik der Reformationsjahre 1521–1533. Mit Glossar
und Commentar von Dr. Joh. Strickler.* Glarus, 1888 (pp. 258). Publ. in
the "Jahrbuch des historischen Vereins des Kantons Glarus," Heft XXIV.,
also separately issued. The first edition of Tschudi's *Chronik (Beschryb
oder Erzellung,* etc.) was published by *Dr. J. J. Blumer,* in vol. IX. of the
"Archiv für schweizerische Geschichte," 1853, pp. 332–447, but not in
the original spelling and without comments.

---

[1] Malignant enemies spread the rumor that he committed suicide or was
fetched by the devil. See Hagenbach, p. 181. A similar rumor was started
about Luther's death, and revived in our days by Majunke in *Luther's Lebens-
ende,* 4th ed. Mainz, 1890, but refuted by Kolde and Kawerau.

[2] Hess (pp. 413–430) gives a chronological list of his works, which is sup-
plemented by Herzog (II. 255 sqq.). Hagenbach's biography, p. 191 sqq.,
gives extracts from his sermons and catechetical writings.

BLUMER and HEER: *Der Kanton Glarus, historisch, geographisch und topographisch beschrieben.* St. Gallen, 1846. DR. J. J. BLUMER: *Die Reformation im Lande Glarus.* In the "Jahrbuch des historischen Vereins des Kantons Glarus." Zürich and Glarus, 1873 and 1875 (Heft IX. 9–48; XI. 3–26). H. G. SULZBERGER: *Die Reformation des Kant. Glarus und des St. Gallischen Bezirks Werdenberg.* Heiden, 1875 (pp. 44).

HEINRICH SCHREIBER: *Heinrich Loriti Glareanus, gekrönter Dichter, Philolog und Mathematiker aus dem 16ten Jahrhundert.* Freiburg, 1837. OTTO FRIDOLIN FRITZSCHE (Prof. of Church hist. in Zürich): *Glarean, sein Leben und seine Schriften.* Frauenfeld, 1890 (pp. 136). Comp. also GEIGER: *Renaissance und Humanismus* (1882), pp. 420–423, for a good estimate of Glarean as a humanist.

The canton Glarus with the capital of the same name occupies the narrow Linththal surrounded by high mountains, and borders on the territory of Protestant Zürich and of Catholic Schwyz. It wavered for a good while between the two opposing parties and tried to act as peacemaker. Landammann Hans Aebli of Glarus, a friend of Zwingli and an enemy of the foreign military service, prevented a bloody collision of the Confederates in the first war of Cappel. This is characteristic of the position of that canton.

Glarus was the scene of the first public labors of Zwingli from 1506 to 1516.[1] He gained great influence as a classical scholar, popular preacher, and zealous patriot, but made also enemies among the friends of the foreign military service, the evils of which he had seen in the Italian campaigns. He established a Latin school and educated the sons of the best families, including the Tschudis, who traced their ancestry back to the ninth century. Three of them are connected with the Reformation, — Ægidius and Peter, and their cousin Valentin.

Ægidius (Gilg) Tschudi, the most famous of this family, the Herodotus of Switzerland (1505–1572), studied first with Zwingli, then with Glarean at Basel and Paris, and occupied important public positions, as delegate to the Diet at Einsiedeln (1529), as governor of Sargans, as Landammann of

----

[1] See above, p. 23 sqq.

Glarus (1558), and as delegate of Switzerland to the Diet of Augsburg (1559). He also served a short time as officer in the French army. He remained true to the old faith, but enjoyed the confidence of both parties by his moderation. He expressed the highest esteem for Zwingli in a letter of February, 1517.[1] His History of Switzerland extends from A.D. 1000 to 1470, and is the chief source of the period before the Reformation. He did not invent, but he embellished the romantic story of Tell and of Grütli, which has been relegated by modern criticism to the realm of innocent poetic fiction.[2] He wrote also an impartial account of the Cappeler War of 1531.[3]

His elder brother, Peter, was a faithful follower of Zwingli, but died early, at Coire, 1532.[4]

Valentin Tschudi also joined the Reformation, but showed the same moderation to the Catholics as his cousin Ægidius

---

[1] In Zwingli's *Opera*, VII. 20 sq. See above, p. 3.

[2] The full title of his history is: ÆGIDII TSCHUDII *gewesenen Landammanns zu Glarus Chronicon Helveticum oder gründliche Beschreibung der merkwürdigsten Begegnussen löblicher Eidgenossenschaft*, first printed in Basel, 1734, '36, in 2 large fol. vols. The continuation from 1470–1564 is preserved in Ms. in the monastic library at Engelberg. His graphic narrative of Tell, reproduced by John von Müller and dramatized by Schiller, though disproved by modern criticism, will live in story and song. We may apply to it Schiller's lines: —

> "*Alles wiederholt sich nur im Leben,*
> *Ewig jung ist nur die Phantasie :*
> *Was sich nie und nirgends hat begeben,*
> *Das allein veraltet nie.*"

See Jakob Vogel: *Egid. Tschudi als Staatsmann und Geschichtschreiber. Mit dessen Bildniss.* Zürich, 1856. Blumer: *Tschudi als Geschichtschreiber*, 1874 ("Jahrbuch des hist. Vereins des Kant. Glarus," pp. 81–100). Georg von Wyss: *Die eigenhändige Handschrift der eidgenöss. Chronik des Aeg. Tschudi in der Stadt-Bibl. in Zürich* ("Neujahrblatt" of the City Library of Zürich for 1889). Blumer and Von Wyss give the best estimate of Tschudi. Goethe says that Tschudi's Swiss History and Aventin's Bavarian History are sufficient to educate a useful public man without any other book.

[3] Published from MS. in the "Helvetica," ed. by Jos. Ant. Balthasar. vol. II. Aarau and Berne, 1826 (pp. 165 sqq.).

[4] See his letters to Zwingli of Dec. 27, 1529, and Dec. 15, 1530, from Coire. In Zwingli's *Opera*, VIII. 386 and 562.

showed to the Protestants. After studying several years under Zwingli, he went, in 1516, with his two cousins to the classical school of Glarean at Basel, and followed him to Paris. From that city he wrote a Greek letter to Zwingli, Nov. 15, 1520, which is still extant and shows his progress in learning.[1] On Zwingli's recommendation, he was elected his successor as pastor at Glarus, and was installed by him, Oct. 12, 1522. Zwingli told the congregation that he had formerly taught them many Roman traditions, but begged them now to adhere exclusively to the Word of God.

Valentin Tschudi adopted a middle way, and was supported by his deacon, Jacob Heer. He pleased both parties by reading mass early in the morning for the old believers, and afterwards preaching an evangelical sermon for the Protestants. He is the first example of a latitudinarian or comprehensive broad-churchman. In 1530 he married, and ceased to read mass, but continued to preach to both parties, and retained the respect of Catholics by his culture and conciliatory manner till his death, in 1555. He defended his moderation and reserve in a long Latin letter to Zwingli, March 15, 1530.[2] He says that the controversy arose from external ceremonies, and did not touch the rock of faith, which Catholics and Protestants professed alike, and that he deemed it his duty to enjoin on his flock the advice of Paul to the Romans (ch. 14), to exercise mutual forbearance, since each stands or falls to the same Lord. The unity of the Spirit is the best guide. He feared that by extreme measures, more harm was done than good, and that the liberty gained may degenerate into license, impiety, and contempt of authority. He begs Zwingli to use his influence for the restoration of order and peace, and signs himself "forever yours" (*semper futurus tuus*). The same spirit of moderation characterizes his

---

[1] There are nine of his letters in Zwingli's *Opera*, VII. and VIII.

[2] In Strickler's edition of his *Chronik*, pp. 241–244, and in Zwingli's *Opera*, VIII. 433–436.

Chronicle of the Reformation period, and it is difficult to find out from this colorless and unimportant narrative, to which of the two parties he belonged.

It is a remarkable fact that the influence of Tschudi's example is felt to this day in the peaceful joint occupation of the church at Glarus, where the sacrifice of the mass is offered by a priest at the altar, and a sermon preached from the pulpit by a Reformed pastor in the same morning.[1]

Another distinguished man of Glarus and friend of Zwingli in the earlier part of his career, is Heinrich Loriti, or Loreti, better known as Glareanus, after the humanistic fashion of that age.[2] He was born at Mollis, a small village of that canton, in 1488, studied at Cologne and Basel, sided with Reuchlin in the quarrel with the Dominican obscurantists,[3] travelled extensively, was crowned as poet-laureate by the Emperor Maximilian (1512), taught school and lectured successively at Basel (1514), Paris (1517), again at Basel (1522), and Freiburg (since 1529). He acquired great fame as a philologist, poet, geographer, mathematician, musician, and successful teacher. Erasmus called him, in a letter to Zwingli (1514),[4] the prince and champion of the Swiss humanists, and in other letters he praised him as a man pure and chaste in morals, amiable in society, well versed in history, mathematics, and music, less in Greek, averse to the subtleties of the schoolmen, bent upon learning Christ from the fountain, and of extraordinary working power. He was full of wit and quaint humor, but conceited, sanguine, irritable, suspicious, and sarcastic. Glarean became acquainted

---

[1] The old church of Glarus in which Zwingli and Tschudi preached, burned down in 1861; but the same custom is continued in the new Romanesque church, to the satisfaction of both parties. So I was informed by the present pastor, Dr. Buss, in 1890.

[2] From his native canton, Glarus (*Glareana*, also *Glarona* or *Clarona*; for the natives: *Glareanus* or *Glaronensis*). For another derivation see Fritzsche, *l.c.* p. 8.

[3] He figures in the *Epistolæ Virorum Obscurorum* as a terrible heretic.

[4] Zwingli's *Opera*, VII. 10.

with Zwingli in 1510, and continued to correspond with him till 1523.[1] He bought books for him at Basel (*e.g.* the Aldine editions of Lactantius and Tertullian) and sought a place as canon in Zürich. In his last letter to him he called him "the truly Christian theologian, the bishop of the Church of Zürich, his very great friend."[2] He read Luther's book on the Babylonian Captivity three times with enthusiasm. But when Erasmus broke both with Zwingli and Luther, he withdrew from the Reformation, and even bitterly opposed Zwingli and Œcolampadius.

He left Basel, Feb. 20, 1529, for Catholic Freiburg, and was soon followed by Erasmus and Amerbach. Here he labored as an esteemed professor of poetry and fruitful author, until his death (1563). He was surrounded by Swiss and German students. He corresponded, now, as confidentially with Ægidius Tschudi as he had formerly corresponded with Zwingli, and co-operated with him in saving a portion of his countrymen for the Catholic faith.[3] He gave free vent to his disgust with Protestantism, and yet lamented the evils of the Roman Church, the veniality and immorality of priests who cared more for Venus than for Christ.[4] A fearful charge. He received a Protestant student from Zürich with the rude words: "You are one of those who carry the gospel in the mouth and the devil in the heart"; but when reminded that he did not show the graces of the muses, he excused himself by his old age, and

---

[1] We have from him twenty-eight letters to Zwingli from July 13, 1510, to Feb. 16, 1523, printed in Zwingli's *Opera*, VII. and VIII., from the originals in the State Archives of Zürich. Zwingli's letters to Glarean are lost, and were probably destroyed after his rupture with the Reformer.

[2] "*Theologo vere Christiano, Ecclesiæ Tigurinæ episcopo, amico nostro summo.*" Zwingli's *Opera*, VII. 274.

[3] There are thirty-eight MS. letters of Glarean to Tschudi, from 1533 to 1561, in the City Library of Zürich; another copy in the cantonal library of Glarus.

[4] Nov. 21, 1556: "*Omnes clerici ad Venerem magis quam ad Christum inclinant.*"

treated the young man with the greatest civility. He became a pessimist, and expected the speedy collapse of the world. His friendship with Erasmus was continued with interruptions, and at last suffered shipwreck. He charged him once with plagiarism, and Erasmus ignored him in his testament.[1] It was a misfortune for both that they could not understand the times, which had left them behind. The thirty works of Glarean (twenty-two of them written in Freiburg) are chiefly philological and musical, and have no bearing on theology.[2] They were nevertheless put on the Index by Pope Paul IV., in 1559. He bitterly complained of this injustice, caused by ignorance or intrigue, and did all he could, with the aid of Tschudi, to have his name removed, which was done after the seven Catholic cantons had testified that Glarean was a good Christian.[3]

The Reformation progressed in Glarus at first without much opposition. Fridolin Brunner, pastor at Mollis, wrote to Zwingli, Jan. 15, 1527, that the Gospel was gaining ground in all the churches of the canton. Johann Schindler preached in Schwanden with great effect. The congregations decided for the Reformed preachers, except in Näfels. The reverses at Cappel in 1531 produced a reaction, and

---

[1] But Dr. Bonifacius Amerbach, the chief heir, sent Glarean a silver cup of Erasmus. See the *Inventarium über die Hinterlassenschaft des Erasmus vom 22 Juli, 1536*, p. 13. This curious document of nineteen pages was published in 1889 by Dr. Ludwig Sieber, librarian of the University of Basel. He also published *Das Testament des Erasmus vom 22 Jan. 1527*, Basel, 1890.

[2] The most important is his *Dodekachordon* (Basel, 1547), which makes an epoch in the history of music. "His theory of the twelve church modes as parallel to the ancient Greek modes, will assure for Glareanus a lasting place among writers on the science of music." (Glover's *Dictionary of Music and Musicians*, 1889, vol. I. 598.) Music was to him a sacred art. His editions of Greek and Latin classics with critical notes, especially on Livy, are esteemed and used by modern philologists. Fritzsche gives a full account of his works, pp. 83–127.

[3] His name was left out of the Indexes of the sixteenth century after that of 1559, but strangely reappears again in the Index Matriti, 1667, p. 485. Fritzsche, p. 74.

caused some losses, but the Reformed Church retained the majority of the population to this day, and with it the preponderance of intelligence, enterprise, wealth, and prosperity, although the numerical relation has recently changed in favor of the Catholics, in consequence of the emigration of Protestants to America, and the immigration of Roman-Catholic laborers, who are attracted by the busy industries (as is the case also in Zürich, Basel, and Geneva).[1]

§ 34. *The Reformation in St. Gall, Toggenburg, and Appenzell. Watt and Kessler.*

The sources and literature in the City Library of St. Gall which bears the name of Vadian (Watt) and contains his MSS. and printed works.

I. The historical works of VADIANUS, especially his *Chronicle of the Abbots of St. Gall* from 1200–1540, and his *Diary* from 1529–'33, edited by *Dr. E. Goetzinger*, St. Gallen, 1875–'79, 3 vols. — *Joachimi Vadiani Vita per Joannem Kesslerum conscripta.* Edited from the MS. by *Dr. Goetzinger* for the Historical Society of St. Gall, 1865. — JOHANNES KESSLER'S *Sabbata. Chronik der Jahre 1523–1539. Herausgegeben von Dr. Ernst Goetzinger.* St. Gallen, 1866. In "Mittheilungen zur vaterländischen Geschichte" of the Historical Society of St. Gall, vols. V. and VI. The MS. of 532 pages, written in the Swiss dialect by Kessler's own hand, is preserved in the Vadian library.

II. J. V. ARX (Rom. Cath., d. 1833): *Geschichte des Kant. St. Gallen.* St. Gallen, 1810–'13, 3 vols. — J. M. FELS: *Denkmal Schweizerischer Reformatoren.* St. Gallen, 1819. — JOH. FR. FRANZ: *Die schwärmerischen Gräuelscenen der St. Galler Wiedertäufer zu Anfang der Reformation.* Ebnat in Toggenberg, 1824. — JOH. JAKOB BERNET: *Johann Kessler, genannt Ahenarius, Bürger und Reformator zu Sankt Gallen.* St. Gallen, 1826. — K. WEGELIN: *Geschichte der Grafschaft Toggenburg.* St. Gallen, 1830–'33, 2 Parts. — FR. WEIDMANN: *Geschichte der Stiftsbibliothek St. Gallens.* 1841. — A. NÄF: *Chronik oder Denkwürdigkeiten der Stadt und Landschaft St. Gallen.* Zürich, 1851. — J. K. BÜCHLER: *Die Reformation im Lande Appenzell.* Trogen, 1860. In the "Appenzellische Jahrbücher." — G. JAK. BAUMGARTNER: *Geschichte des Schweizerischen Freistaates und Kantons St. Gallen.* Zürich, 1868, 2 vols. — H. G. SULZBERGER: *Geschichte der Reformation in Toggenburg; in St. Gallen; im Rheinthal; in den eidgenössischen Herrschaften Sargans und Gaster, sowie in Rapperschwil; in Hohensax-Forsteck; in Appenzell.* Several pamphlets reprinted from the "Appenzeller Sonntagsblatt," 1872 sqq.

---

[1] In 1850 the Protestant population of Glarus numbered 26,281; the Catholic, 3,932. In 1888 the proportion was 25,935 to 7,790. See Fritzsche, p. 53.

III. Theod. Pressel: *Joachim Vadian.* In the ninth volume of the "Leber und ausgewählte Schriften der Väter und Begründer der reformirten Kirche." Elberfeld, 1861 (pp. 103). — Rud. Stähelin: *Die reformatorische Wirksamkeit des St. Galler Humanisten Vadian,* in "Beiträge zur vaterländischen Geschichte," Basel, 1882, pp. 193–262; and his art. "Watt" in Herzog[2], XVI. (1885), pp. 663–668.   Comp. also Meyer von Knonau, "St. Gallen," in Herzog[2], IV. 725–735.

The Reformation in the northeastern parts of Switzerland — St. Gall, Toggenburg, Schaffhausen, Appenzell, Thurgau, Aargau — followed the course of Zürich, Berne, and Basel. It is a variation of the same theme, on the one hand, in its negative aspects: the destruction of the papal and episcopal authority, the abolition of the mass and superstitious rites and ceremonies, the breaking of images and relics as symbols of idolatry, the dissolution of convents and confiscation of Church property, the marriage of priests, monks, and nuns; on the other hand, in its positive aspects: the introduction of a simpler and more spiritual worship with abundant preaching and instruction from the open Bible in the vernacular, the restoration of the holy communion under both kinds, as celebrated by the congregation, the direct approach to Christ without priestly mediation, the raising of the laity to the privileges of the general priesthood of believers, care for lower and higher education. These changes were made by the civil magistracy, which assumed the episcopal authority and function, but acted on the initiative of the clergy and with the consent of the majority of the people, which in democratic Switzerland was after all the sovereign power. An Antistes was placed at the head of the ministers as a sort of bishop or general superintendent. Synods attended to legislation and administration. The congregations called and supported their own pastors.

St. Gall — so-called from St. Gallus (Gilian), an Irish missionary and pupil of Columban, who with several hermits settled in the wild forest on the Steinach about 613 — was a centre of Christianization and civilization in Alemannia and Eastern Switzerland. A monastery was founded about 720 by St. Othmar and became a royal abbey exempt from episcopal jurisdiction, and very rich in revenues from landed possessions in Switzerland, Swabia, and Lombardy, as well as in manuscripts of classical and ecclesiastical learning. Church poetry, music, architecture, sculpture, and painting flourished there in the ninth and tenth centuries. Notker Balbulus, a monk of St. Gall (d. c. 912), is the author of the sequences or hymns in rhythmical prose (*prosæ*), and credited with the mournful meditation on death ("*Media vita in morte sumus*"), which is still in use, but of later and uncertain origin. With the increasing wealth of the abbey the discipline declined and worldliness set in. The missionary and literary zeal died out. The bishop of Constance was jealous of the independence and powers of the abbot. The city of St. Gall grew in prosperity and longed for emancipation from monastic control. The clergy needed as much reformation as the monks. Many of them lived in open concubinage, and few were able to make a sermon. The high festivals were profaned by scurrilous popular amusements. The sale of indulgences was carried on with impunity.

The Reformation was introduced in the city and district of St. Gall by Joachim von Watt, a layman (1484-1551), and John Kessler, a minister (1502-1574). The co-operation of the laity and clergy is congenial to the spirit of Protestantism which emancipated the Church from hierarchical control.

Joachim von Watt, better known by his Latin name Vadianus, excelled in his day as a humanist, poet, historian, physician, statesman, and reformer. He was descended from an old noble family, the son of a wealthy merchant, and studied the humanities in the University of Vienna (1502),[1]

[1] He arrived at Vienna in the autumn of 1502, shortly after Zwingli had left the University. See Stähelin, *l.c.*, who refers for confirmation to Egli, Aschbach, and Horawitz. The usual opinion is that Vadian and Zwingli (and Glareanus) studied together and formed their friendship at Vienna. So also Pressel, *l.c.*, p. 11.

which was then at the height of its prosperity under the teaching of Celtes and Cuspinian, two famous humanists and Latin poets. He acquired also a good knowledge of philosophy, theology, law, and medicine. After travelling through Poland, Hungary, and Italy, he returned to Vienna and taught classical literature and rhetoric. He was crowned poet and orator by Maximilian (March 12, 1514), and elected rector of the University in 1516. He published several classical authors and Latin poems, orations, and essays. He stood in friendly correspondence with Reuchlin, Hutten, Hesse, Erasmus, and other leaders of the new learning, and especially also with Zwingli.[1]

In 1518 Watt returned to St. Gall and practised as physician till his death, but took at the same time an active part in all public affairs of Church and State. He was repeatedly elected burgomaster. He was a faithful co-worker of Zwingli in the cause of reform. Zwingli called him "a physician of body and soul of the city of St. Gall and the whole confederacy," and said, "I know no Swiss that equals him." Calvin and Beza recognized in him "a man of rare piety and equally rare learning." He called evangelical ministers and teachers to St. Gall. He took a leading part in the religious disputations at Zürich (1523–1525), and presided over the disputation at Berne (1528).

St. Gall was the first city to follow the example of Zürich under his lead. The images were removed from the churches and publicly burnt in 1526 and 1528; only the organ and the bones of St. Othmar (the first abbot) and Notker were saved. An evangelical church order was introduced in 1527. At the same time the Anabaptists endangered the Reformation by strange excesses of fanaticism. Watt had no serious objection to their doctrines, and was a friend and brother-in-

[1] His published correspondence with Zwingli begins with a letter from Vienna, April 9, 1511, and embraces four letters of Vadian, and thirty-eight letters of Zwingli, in Zwingli's *Opera*, vols. VII. and VIII.

law of Grebel, their leader, but he opposed them in the interest of peace and order.

The death of the abbot, March 21, 1529, furnished the desired opportunity, at the advice of Zürich and Zwingli, to abolish the abbey and to confiscate its rich domain, with the consent of the majority of the citizens, but in utter disregard of legal rights. This was a great mistake, and an act of injustice.

The disaster of Cappel produced a reaction, and a portion of the canton returned to the old church. A new abbot was elected, Diethelm Blaurer; he demanded the property of the convent and sixty thousand guilders damages for what had been destroyed and sold. The city had to yield. He held a solemn entry. He attended the last session of the Council of Trent and took a leading part in the counter-Reformation.

Watt showed, during this critical period, courage and moderation. He retained the confidence of his fellow-citizens, who elected him nine times to the highest civil office. He did what he could, in co-operation with Kessler and Bullinger, to save and consolidate the Reformed Church during the remaining years of his life. He was a portly, handsome, and dignified man, and wrote a number of geographical, historical, and theological works.[1]

John Kessler (Chessellius or Ahenarius), the son of a day-laborer of St. Gall, studied theology at Basel, and Wittenberg. He was one of the two students who had an interesting interview with Dr. Luther in the hotel of the Black Bear at Jena in March, 1522, on his return as Knight George from the Wartburg.[2] It was the only friendly meeting of Luther with the Swiss. Had he shown the same kindly feeling to Zwingli

---

[1] Pressel, pp. 100–103, gives the titles of twenty-seven of his writings, mostly Latin, published between 1510 and 1548.

[2] Reported by him in the Swiss dialect with charming naiveté in *Sabbata*, pp. 145–151: "*Wie mir M. Luther uff der strass [Reise] gen Wittenberg begegnet ist.*" Kessler's companion was John Spengler. See an account of the interview, in vol. VI. p. 385.

at Marburg, the cause of the Reformation would have been the gainer.

Kessler supported himself by the trade of a saddler, and preached in the city and surrounding villages. He was also chief teacher of the Latin school. In 1571, a year before his death, he was elected Antistes or head of the clergy of St. Gall. He had a wife and eleven children, nine of whom survived him. He was a pure, amiable, unselfish, and useful man and promoter of evangelical religion. His portrait in oil adorns the City Library of St. Gall.

The county of Toggenburg, the home of Zwingli, was subject to the abbot of St. Gall since 1468, but gladly received the Reformed preachers under the influence of Zwingli, his relatives and friends. In 1524 the council of the community enjoined upon the ministers to teach nothing but what they could prove from the sacred Scriptures. The people resisted the interference of the abbot, the bishop of Constance, and the canton Schwyz. In 1528 the Reformation was generally introduced in the towns of the district. With the help of Zürich and Glarus, the Toggenburgers bought their freedom from the abbot of St. Gall for fifteen hundred guilders, in 1530; but were again subjected to his authority in 1536. The county was incorporated in the canton St. Gall in 1803. The majority of the people are Protestants.

The canton Appenzell received its first Protestant preachers — John Schurtanner of Teufen, John Dorig of Herisau, and Walter Klarer of Hundwil — from the neighboring St. Gall, through the influence of Watt. The Reformation was legally ratified by a majority vote of the people, Aug. 26, 1523. The congregations emancipated themselves from the jurisdiction of the abbot of St. Gall, and elected their own pastors. The Anabaptist disturbances promoted the Roman-Catholic reaction. The population is nearly equally divided, — Innerrhoden, with the town of Appenzell, remained Catholic; Ausserrhoden, with Herisau, Trogen, and Gais, is Reformed, and more industrious and prosperous.

The Reformation in Thurgau and Aargau presents no features of special interest.[1]

§ 35. Reformation in Schaffhausen. Hofmeister.

MELCHIOR KIRCHOFER: *Schaffhauserische Jahrbücher von 1519–1539, oder Geschichte der Reformation der Stadt und Landschaft Schaffhausen.* Schaffhausen, 1819; 2d ed. Frauenfeld, 1838 (pp. 152). By the same: *Sebastian Wagner, genannt Hofmeister.* Zürich, 1808. — EDW. IM-THURM und HANS W. HARDER: *Chronik der Stadt Schaffhausen* (till 1790). Schaffhausen, 1844. — H. G. SULZBERGER: *Geschichte der Reformation des Kant. Schaffhausen.* Schaffhausen, 1876 (pp. 47).

Schaffhausen on the Rhine and the borders of Württemberg and Baden followed the example of the neighboring canton Zürich, under the lead of Sebastian Hofmeister (1476–1533), a Franciscan monk and doctor and professor of theology at Constance, where the bishop resided. He addressed Zwingli, in 1520, as "the firm preacher of the truth," and wished to become his helper in healing the diseases of the Church of Switzerland.[2] He preached in his native city of Schaffhausen against the errors and abuses of Rome, and attended as delegate the religious disputations at Zürich (January and October, 1523), which resulted in favor of the Reformation.

He was aided by Sebastian Meyer, a Franciscan brother who came from Berne, and by Ritter, a priest who had formerly opposed him.

The Anabaptists appeared from Zürich with their radical views. The community was thrown into disorder. The

---

[1] Comp. Oelhafen, *Chronik der Stadt Aarau,* 1840; Sulzberger, *Reformation im Kanton Aargau,* 1881; Pupikofer, *Geschichte des Thurgau's,* 1828–'30, 2 vols.; second ed. 1889–'90; Sulzberger, *Die Reformation im Kanton Thurgau,* 1872.

[2] Hofmeister's letters in Zwingli's *Opera,* VII. 146, 289; II. 166, 348. He subscribes himself Sebastianus Œconomus seu Hofmeister. His last letter is dated from Zofingen (1529), and very severe against Luther's writings on the sacramental controversy.

magistracy held Hofmeister and Myer responsible, and banished them from the canton. A reaction followed, but the Reformation triumphed in 1529. The villages followed the city. Some noble families remained true to the old faith, and emigrated.

Schaffhausen was favored by a succession of able and devoted ministers, and gave birth to some distinguished historians.[1]

§ 36. *The Grisons* (*Graubünden*).

Colonel Landammann Theofil Sprecher a Bernegg at Maienfeld, Graubünden, has a complete library of the history of the Grisons, including some of the manuscripts of Campell and De Porta. I was permitted to use it for this and the following two sections under his hospitable roof in June, 1890. I have also examined the *Kantons-Bibliothek* of Graubünden in the "Rætische Museum" at Coire, which is rich in the (Romanic) literature of the Grisons.

I. Ulrici Campelli *Rætiæ Alpestris Topographica Descriptio*, edited by Chr. J. Kind, Basel (Schneider), 1884, pp. 448, and *Historia Rætica*, edited by Plac. Plattner, Basel, tom. I., 1877, pp. 724, and tom. II., 1890, pp. 781. These two works form vols. VII., VIII., and IX. of *Quellen zur Schweizer-Geschichte*, published by the General Historical Society of Switzerland. They are the foundation for the topography and history of the Grisons in the sixteenth century. Campell was Reformed pastor at Süs in the Lower Engadin, and is called "the father of the historians of Rätia." De Porta says that all historians of Rätia have ploughed with his team. An abridged German translation from the Latin manuscripts was published by *Conradin von Mohr:* Ulr. Campell's *Zwei Bücher rätischer Geschichte*, Chur (Hitz), 1849 and 1851, 2 vols., pp. 236 and 566.

R. Ambrosius Eichhorn (Presbyter Congregationis S. Blasii, in the Black Forest): *Episcopatus Curiensis in Rhœtia sub metropoli Moguntina chronologice et diplomatice illustratus.* Typis San-Blasianis, 1797 (pp. 368, 4°). To which is added *Codex Probationum ad Episcopatum Curiensem ex præcipuis documentis omnibus ferme ineditis collectus*, 204 pp. The Reformation

---

[1] Johannes von Müller, called the German Tacitus (1752–1809); Melchior Kirchhofer (1775–1853), who wrote valuable biographies of the minor Reformers (Hofmeister, Haller, Myconius, and Farel), and the fifth volume of Wirz's *Helvetische Kirchengeschichte;* and Friedrich von Hurter (1787–1865), the author of the best history of Pope Innocent III. (1834–'42, 4 vols.). Hurter was formerly Antistes of the Reformed Church of Schaffhausen, but became (partly by the study of the palmy period of the mediæval hierarchy) a Roman Catholic in 1844, and was appointed imperial counsellor and historiographer of Austria, 1845.

period is described pp. 139 sqq. Eichhorn was a Roman Catholic priest, and gives the documents relating to the episcopal see of Coire from A.D. 766–1787. On "Zwinglianisms in Rætia," see pp. 142, 146, 248. (I examined a copy in the Episcopal Library at Coire.)

II. General works on the history of the Grisons by JOH. GULER (d. 1637), FORTUNATUS SPRECHER A BERNEGG (d. 1647), FORTUNATUS JUVALTA (d. 1654). TH. VON MOHR AND CONRADIN VON MOHR (or MOOR): *Archiv für die Geschichte der Republik Graubünden*. Chur, 1848–'86. 9 vols. A collection of historical works on Graubünden, including the *Codex diplomaticus, Sammlung der Urkunden zur Geschichte Chur-Rhätiens und der Republik Graübunden*. The Codex was continued by JECKLIN, 1883–'86. — CONRADIN VON MOOR : *Bündnerische Geschichtschreiber und Chronisten*. Chur, 1862–'77. 10 parts. By the same: *Geschichte von Currätien und der Republ. Graubünden*. Chur, 1869. — JOH. ANDR. VON SPRECHER: *Geschichte der Republik der drei Bünde im 18ten Jahrh*. Chur, 1873–'75. 2 vols. — A good popular summary: *Graubündnerische Geschichten erzählt für die reformirten Volksschulen* (by P. KAISER). Chur, 1852 (pp. 281). — Also J. K. VON TSCHARNER: *Der Kanton Graubünden, historisch, statistisch, geographisch dargestellt*. Chur, 1842.

The Reformation literature see in § 37.

III. On the history of Valtellina, Chiavenna, and Bormio, which until 1797 were under the jurisdiction of the Grisons, the chief writers are : —

FR. SAV. QUADRIO: *Dissertazioni critico-storiche intorno alla Rezia di qua dalle Alpi, oggi detta Valtellina*. Milano, 1755. 2 vols., especially the second vol., which treats *la storia ecclesiastica*. — ULYSSES VON SALIS: *Staats-Gesch. des Thals Veltlin und der Graftschaften Clefen und Worms*. 1792. 4 vols. — LAVIZARI: *Storia della Valtellina*. Capolago, 1838. 2 vols. — ROMEGIALLI: *Storia della Valtellina e delle già contee di Bormio e Chiavenna*. Sondrio, 1834–'39. 4 vols. — WIEZEL: *Veltliner Krieg*, edited by Hartmann. Strassburg, 1887.

The canton of the Grisons or Graubünden[1] was at the time of the Reformation an independent democratic republic in friendly alliance with the Swiss Confederacy, and continued independent till 1803, when it was incorporated as a canton. Its history had little influence upon other countries, but reflects the larger conflicts of Switzerland with some original features. Among these are the Romanic and Italian conquests of Protestantism, and the early recognition of the principle of religious liberty. Each congregation was allowed to choose between the two contending churches according to

---

[1] *Respublica Grisonum ; I Grigioni ; Les Grisons.*

the will of the majority, and thus civil and religious war was prevented, at least during the sixteenth century.[1]

Graubünden is, in nature as well as in history, a Switzerland in miniature. It is situated in the extreme south-east of the republic, between Austria and Italy, and covers the principal part of the old Roman province of Rätia.[2] It forms a wall between the north and the south, and yet combines both with a network of mountains and valleys from the regions of the eternal snow to the sunny plains of the vine, the fig, and the lemon. In territorial extent it is the largest canton, and equal to any in variety and beauty of scenery and healthy climate. It is the fatherland of the Rhine and the Inn. The Engadin is the highest inhabited valley of Switzerland, and unsurpassed for a combination of attractions for admirers of nature and seekers of health. It boasts of the healthiest climate with nine months of dry, bracing cold and three months of delightfully cool weather.

The inhabitants are descended from three nationalities, speak three languages, — German, Italian, and Romansh (Romanic), — and preserve many peculiarities of earlier ages. The German language prevails in Coire, along the Rhine, and in the Prättigau, and is purer than in the other cantons. The Italian is spoken to the south of the Alps in the valleys of Poschiavo and Bregaglia (as also in the neighboring canton Ticino). The Romansh language is a

---

[1] The Grisons are ignored or neglected in general Church histories. Even Hagenbach, who was a Swiss, devotes less than two pages to them (*Geschichte der Reformation*, p. 366, 5th ed. by Nippold, 1887). A fuller account (the only good one in English) is given by Dr. McCrie, a Scotch Presbyterian, in his *History of the Reformation in Italy*, ch. VI. The increasing travel of English and American tourists to that country, especially to the Engadin, gives wider interest to its history, and may justify the space here given to it.

[2] *Rœtia* or *Rhœtia*, a net, is derived from *Rhœtus*, the mythical chief of the oldest immigrants from Etruria, or from the Celtic *rhin*, Rhine, river, and survives in the names *Realta*, *Rhäzüns*, and *Reambs*, *i.e. Rœtia alta, una*, and *ampla*. It was conquered under Augustus by Drusus, 14 B.C., and ruled by a governor at Coire or *Curia Rhœtorum* till *c.* 400. The ivy-clad tower of the episcopal palace of Coire is of Roman origin, and is called *Marsœl*, *i.e. Mars in oculis*.

remarkable relic of prehistoric times, an independent sister
of the Italian, and is spoken in the Upper and Lower Engadin, the Münster valley, and the Oberland. It has a considerable literature, mostly religious, which attracts the
attention of comparative philologists.[1]

The Grisonians (Graubündtner) are a sober, industrious,
and heroic race, and have maintained their independence
against the armies of Spain, Austria, and France. They
have a natural need and inclination to emigrate to richer
countries in pursuit of fortune, and to return again to their
mountain homes. They are found in all the capitals of
Europe and America as merchants, hotel keepers, confec-
tioners, teachers, and soldiers.

The institutions of the canton are thoroughly democratic
and exemplify the good and evil effects of popular sov·
ereignty.[2] "Next to God and the sun," says an old Engadin proverb, "the poorest inhabitant is the chief magistrate."
There are indeed to this day in the Grisons many noble
families, descended in part from mediæval robber-chiefs and
despots whose ruined castles still look down from rocks and
cliffs, and in greater part from distinguished officers and
diplomatists in foreign service; but they have no more influence than their personal merits and prestige warrant. In
official relations and transactions the titles of nobility are
forbidden.[3]

[1] The Romansh language (to distinguish it from other Romanic languages)
has two dialects, the Ladin of the Engadin, the Albula, and Münster valleys,
and the Romansh of the Oberland, Ilanz, Disentis, Oberhalbstein, etc. It is
spoken by about 37,000 inhabitants. The whole population of the canton in
1890 was 94,879, — 53,168 Protestants and 41,711 Roman Catholics. The
largest number of Romansh books is in the Cantonal Library at Coire, and
the Böhmer collection in the University Library of Strassburg. Colonel von
Sprecher at Maienfeld also has about four hundred volumes.

[2] "In no nation, ancient or modern," says Dr. McCrie (p. 293), "have
the principles of democracy been carried to such extent as in the Grison
Republic."

[3] The best known and most respectable noble families are the Salis (one
of them a distinguished lyric poet), Planta, Bavier, Sprecher, Albertini,

Let us briefly survey the secular history before we proceed to the Reformation.

The Grisons were formed of three loosely connected confederacies or leagues, that is, voluntary associations of freemen, who, during the fifteenth century, after the example of their Swiss neighbors, associated for mutual protection and defence against domestic and foreign tyrants.[1] These three leagues united in 1471 at Vatzerol in an eternal covenant, which was renewed in 1524, promising to each other by an oath mutual assistance in peace and war. The three confederacies sent delegates to the Diet which met alternately at Coire, Ilanz, and Davos.

At the close of the fifteenth century two leagues of the Grisons entered into a defensive alliance with the seven old cantons of Switzerland. The third league followed the example.[2]

In the beginning of the sixteenth century the Grisonians

Tscharner, Juvalta, Mohr, Buol. See *Sammlung rhätischer Geschlechter*. Chur, 1847.

[1] The three confederacies or *Bünde* (whence the canton has its name *Graubünden*) are : —

1) The *Gotteshausbund* (*Lia de Ca Dé*), *the League of the House of God*. It dates from 1396, and had its centre since 1419 at Coire, the capital of the canton.

2) The *Obere Bund* or *Graue Bund* (*Lia Grischa*), *the Gray League* (hence the term *Graue*, Grisons, *Grays*). It was founded under an elm tree at Truns in 1424, and gathered around the abbey of Disentis.

3) The *Zehngerichtenbund* (*Lia dellas desch dretturas*), *the League of the Ten Jurisdictions*. It originated in 1436 at Davos and in the valley of Prättigau.

After the middle of the fifteenth century these leagues appear in the documents under the name of the *Gemeine drei Bünde* or *Freistaat der drei Bünde in Hohenrhätien*. A modern historian says: "*Frei und selbstherrlich sind viele Völker geworden, aber wenige auf so rechtliche und ruhige Weise als das Bündner Volk.*" See the documents in Tschudi, I. 593; II. 153; and compare Müller, *Schweizergeschichte*, III. 283, 394, and Bluntschli, *Geschichte des schweizerischen Bundesrechts*, I. 196 sqq. (2d ed. Stuttgart, 1875).

[2] The alliance was formed with the two older leagues separately in 1497 and 1498. The league of the Ten Jurisdictions was not admitted by the seven cantons because the house of Austria had possessions there; but in 1590 it concluded an eternal agreement with Zürich and Glarus, in 1600 with Wallis, and in 1602 with Bern. See Bluntschli, *l.c.* I. 198 sq. and the documents from the Archives of Zürich in vol. II. 99–107.

acquired by conquest from the duchy of Milan several beautiful and fertile districts south of the Alps adjoining the Milanese and Venetian territories, namely, the Valtellina and the counties of Bormio (Worms) and Chiavenna (Cleven), and annexed them as dependencies ruled by bailiffs. It would have been wiser to have received them as a fourth league with equal rights and privileges. These Italian possessions involved the Grisons in the conflict between Austria and Spain on the one hand, which desired to keep them an open pass, and between France and Venice on the other, which wanted them closed against their political rivals. Hence the Valtellina has been called the Helena of a new Trojan War. Graubünden was invaded during the Thirty Years' War by Austro-Spanish and French armies. After varied fortunes, the Italian provinces were lost to Graubünden through Napoleon, who, by a stroke of the pen, Oct. 10, 1797, annexed the Valtellina, Bormio, and Chiavenna to the new Cisalpine Republic. The Congress of Vienna transferred them to Austria in 1814, and since 1859 they belong to the united Kingdom of Italy.

§ 37. *The Reformation in the Grisons. Comander. Gallicius. Campell.*

The work of CAMPELL quoted in § 36.

BARTHOLOMÄUS ANHORN: *Heilige Wiedergeburt der evang. Kirche in den gemeinen drei Bündten der freien hohen Rhätien, oder Beschreibung ihrer Reformation und Religionsverbesserung,* etc. Brugg, 1680 (pp. 246). A new ed. St. Gallen, 1860 (pp. 144, 8°). By the same: *Püntner Aufruhr im Jahr 1607,* ed. from MSS. by *Conradin von Mohr,* Chur, 1862; and his *Graw-Püntner [Graubündner]-Krieg,* 1603–1629, ed. by *Conr. von Mohr,* Chur, 1873.

* PETRUS DOMINICUS ROSIUS DE PORTA (Reformed minister at Scamff, or Scanfs, in the Upper Engadin): *Historia Reformationis Ecclesiarum Ræticarum, ex genuinis fontibus et adhuc maximam partem numquam impressis sine partium studio deducta,* etc. Curiæ Rætorum. Tom. I., 1771 (pp. 658, 4°); Tom. II., 1777 (pp. 668); Tom. III., Como, 1786. Comes down to 1642. Next to Campell, the standard authority and chief source of later works.

LEONHARD TRUOG (Reformed pastor at Thusis): *Reformations-Geschichte von Graubünden aus zuverlässigen Quellen sorgfältig geschöpft. Denkmal der drit-*

ten Sekular-Jubelfeier der Bündnerischen Reformation. Chur (Otto), 1819
(pp. 132). — *Reformationsbüchlein. Ein Denkmal des im Jahr 1819 in der
Stadt Chur gefeierten Jubelfestes.* Chur (Otto), 1819 (pp. 304).

* CHRISTIAN IMMANUEL KIND (Pfarrer und Cancellarius der evang. rhätischen
Synode, afterward Staats-Archivarius of the Grisons, d. May 23, 1884):
*Die Reformation in den Bisthümern Chur und Como. Dargestellt nach den
besten älteren und neueren Hülfsmitteln.* Chur, 1858 (Grubenmann), pp. 310,
8°. A popular account based on a careful study of the sources. By the
same: *Die Stadt Chur in ihrer ältesten Geschichte,* Chur, 1859; *Philipp Gallicius,* 1868; *Georg Jenatsch,* in "Allg. Deutsche Biogr.," Bd. XIII. —
GEORG LEONHARDI (pastor in Brusio, Poschiavo): *Philipp Gallicius, Reformator Graubündens.* Bern, 1865 (pp. 103). The same also in Romansch.
— H. G. SULZBERGER (in Sevelen, St. Gallen, d. 1888): *Geschichte der
Reformation im Kanton Graubünden.* Chur, 1880. pp. 90 (revised by Kind).
— FLORIAN PEER: *L'église de Rhétie au XVIme et XVIIme siècles.* Genève,
1888. — HEROLD: *J. Komander,* in Meili's *Zeitschrift,* Zurich, 1891.

The Christianization of the Grisons is traced back by tradition to St. Lucius, a royal prince of Britain, and Emerita,
his sister, in the latter part of the second century.[1] A chapel
on the mountain above Coire perpetuates his memory. A
bishop of Coire (Asimo) appears first in the year 452, as sign-
ing by proxy the creed of Chalcedon.[2] The bishops of Coire
acquired great possessions and became temporal princes.[3]
The whole country of the Grisons stood under the jurisdiction of the bishops of Coire and Como.

The state of religion and the need of a reformation were
the same as in the other cantons of Switzerland.

The first impulse to the Reformation came from Zürich

---

[1] He is identified, in the tradition of Wales, with King Lucius who introduced Christianity into Britain and built the first church at Llandaff in
180. See Alois Lütolf, *Die Glaubensboten der Schweiz vor St. Gallus,* Luzern,
1871, pp. 95–125. He gives from MSS. the oldest *Vita S. Lucii Confessoris*
(pp. 115–121).

[2] S. Asimo was not himself at Chalcedon, 450, but authorized Abundantius, bishop of Como, to give his assent to the Chalcedon Christology at a
council held at Milan in 452, as appears from the following document: "*Ego
Abundantius episcopus ecclesiæ Comensis in omnia supra scripta pro me ac* PRO
ABSENTE SANCTO FRATRE MEO, ASIMONE, EPISCOPO ECCLESIÆ CURIENSIS PRI-
MÆ RHÆTIÆ, *subscripsi, anathema dicens his qui de incarnationis Dominicæ
sacramento impie senserunt.*" Quoted by Eichhorn, *l.c.* pp. 1 and 2.

[3] Frederick Barbarossa gave to the bishop the title *princeps,* about 1170.

with which Coire had close connections. Zwingli sent an
address to the "three confederacies in Rhätia," expressing
a special interest in them as a former subject of the bishop
of Coire, exhorting them to reform the Church in alliance
with Zürich, and recommending to them his friend Comander (Jan. 16, 1525).[1] Several of his pupils preached in
Fläsch, Malans, Maienfeld, Coire, and other places as early
as 1524. After his death Bullinger showed the same interest in the Grisons. The Reformation passed through the
usual difficulties first with the Church of Rome, then with
Anabaptists, Unitarians, and the followers of the mystical
Schwenkfeld, all of whom found their way into that remote
corner of the world. One of the leading Anabaptists of
Zürich, Georg Blaurock, was an ex-monk of Coire, and on
account of his eloquence called "the mighty Jörg," or "the
second Paul." He was expelled from Zürich, and burnt by
the Catholics in the Tyrol (1529).

The Reformers abolished the indulgences, the sacrifice of
the mass, the worship of images, sacerdotal celibacy and concubinage, and a number of unscriptural and superstitious
ceremonies, and introduced instead the Bible and Bible
preaching in church and school, the holy communion in
both kinds, clerical family life, and a simple evangelical
piety, animated by an active faith in Christ as the only
Saviour and Mediator. Where that faith is wanting the service in the barren churches is jejune and chilly.

The chief Reformers of the Grisons were Comander, Gallicius, Campell, and Vergerius, and next to them Alexander
Salandronius (Salzmann), Blasius, and John Travers. The
last was a learned and influential layman of the Engadin.
Comander labored in the German, Gallicius and Campell
in the Romansh, Vergerius in the Italian sections of the

---

[1] The MS. of this exhortation is in the Archives of Zürich and was first
printed in Joh. Jak. Simler's *Sammlung alter und neuer Urkunden zur Beleuchtung der Kirchengeschichte* (1759), vol. I. 108–114.

Grisons. They were Zwinglians in theology,[1] and introduced the changes of Zürich and Basel. Though occupy-
ing only a second or third rank among the Reformers, they
were the right men in the right places, faithful, self-denying
workers in a poor country, among an honest, industrious,
liberty-loving but parsimonious people. With small means
they accomplished great and permanent results.

JOHN COMANDER (DORFMANN), formerly a Roman priest,
of unknown antecedents, preached the Reformed doctrines in
the church of St. Martin at Coire from 1524. He learned
Hebrew in later years, to the injury of his eyes, that he
might read the Old Testament in the original. Zwingli
sent him Bibles and commentaries. The citizens protected
him against violence and accompanied him to and from
church. The bishop of Coire arraigned him for heresy
before the Diet of the three confederacies in 1525.

The Diet, in spite of the remonstrance of the bishop,
ordered a public disputation at Ilanz, the first town on the
Rhine. The disputation was begun on Sunday after Epiph-
any, Jan. 7, 1526, under the presidency of the civil authorities, and lasted several days. It resembled the disputations
of Zürich, and ended in a substantial victory of the Reformation. The conservative party was represented by the
Episcopal Vicar, the abbot of St. Lucius, the deans, and a
few priests and monks; the progressive party, by several
young preachers, Comander, Gallicius, Blasius, Pontisella,
Fabricius, and Hartmann. Sebastian Hofmeister of Schaffhausen was present as a listener, and wrote an account of
the speeches.[2]

Comander composed for the occasion eighteen theses, — an

---

[1] With the exception of Vergerius, who vacillated between Calvinism and
Lutheranism. See below, p. 154 (§ 38).

[2] His report and Comander's conclusions are printed in Füsslin's *Beiträge
zur Kirchen- und Reformationsgesch. des Schweitzerlandes*, 1741, vol. I. 337–382.
A fuller account is given by Campell in his *Rätische Geschichte*, II. 287–308
(Mohr's German ed.).

abridgment of the sixty-seven conclusions of Zwingli. The first thesis was : " The Christian Church is born of the Word of God and should abide in it, and not listen to the voice of a stranger" (John 10 : 4, 5). He defended this proposition with a wealth of biblical arguments which the champions of Rome were not able to refute. There was also some debate about the rock-passage in Matt. 16 : 18, the mass, purgatory, and sacerdotal celibacy. The Catholics brought the disputation to an abrupt close.

In the summer of the same year (June 26, 1526), the Diet of Ilanz proclaimed religious freedom, or the right of all persons in the Grisons, of both sexes, and of whatever condition or rank, to choose between the Catholic and the Reformed religion. Heretics, who after due admonition adhered to their error, were excluded and subjected to banishment (but not to death). This remarkable statute was in advance of the intolerance of the times, and forms the charter of religious freedom in the Grisons.[1]

The Diet of Ilanz ordered the ministers to preach nothing

---

[1] Campell, II. 309 : " *Die Disputation* [of Ilanz] *blieb nicht ohne alle Frucht. Sie hatte wenigstens die Folge, dass ein Gesetz erlassen wurde, wonach es in den drei Bünden Jedermann, wess Standes oder Geschlechts er auch war, freigestellt wurde, nach Gutdünken zu einer der beiden Confessionem, der katholischen oder evangelischen, sich zu bekennen und an ihr festzuhalten. Hiebei wurde, unter Androhung einer angemessenen Strafe, Jedem streng untersagt, irgend Jemanden um seines Glaubens willen zu schmähen oder, sei es öffentlich oder heimlich, zu verfolgen, wie diess von der andern Partei schon oft genug geschehen war. Bei dieser Gelegenheit wurde ein altes Landesgesetz den Geistlichen aufs Neue eingeschärft, wonach selbe durchaus keine andere, als die in der h. Schrift enthaltene Lehre dem Volke vortragen sollten.*" [Then follows a list of the leading statesmen, John Travers, John Guler, etc., who contributed to this result.] " *Mit dem nämlichen Gesetz über freie Ausübung des evangelischen Glaubens wurde die ganze Kezerei der Wiedertaufe streng untersagt und alle ihre Anhänger mit Verbannung bedroht. Die strenge Ueberwachung der erstern dieser zwei Verordnungen hatte in Bezug auf öffentliche Ruhe und Frieden zwischen beiden Confessionen äusserst wohlthätige Folgen, indem beide Theile sich lange Zeit hindurch der grössten Mässigung beflissen, bis erst in den letzten Jahren bei den katholischen Geistlichen sich abermals eine feindselige Stimmung gegen die evangelischen Prediger in Schmähungen aller Art kund gab, worüber mannigfache Klagen vor dem Beitag laut wurden.*" — Comp. Bullinger, I. 315; De Porta, I. 146.

but what they could prove from the Scriptures, and to give themselves diligently to the study of the same. The political authority of the bishop of Coire was curtailed, appeals to him from the civil jurisdiction were forbidden, and the parishes were empowered to elect and to dismiss their own priests or pastors.[1]

Thus the episcopal monarchy was abolished and congregational independency introduced, but without the distinction made by the English and American Congregationalists between the church proper, or the body of converted believers, and the congregation of hearers or mere nominal Christians.

This legislation was brought about by the aid of liberal Catholic laymen, such as John Travers and John Guler, who at that time had not yet joined the Reformed party. The strict Catholics were dissatisfied, but had to submit. In 1553 the Pope sent a delegate to Coire and demanded the introduction of the Inquisition; but Comander, Bullinger, and the French ambassador defeated the attempt.

Comander, aided by his younger colleague, Blasius, and afterwards by Gallicius, continued to maintain the Reformed faith against Papists, Anabaptists, and also against foreign pensioners who had their headquarters at Coire, and who punished him for his opposition by a reduction of his scanty salary of one hundred and twenty guilders. He was at times tempted to resign, but Bullinger urged him to hold on.[2] He stood at the head of the Reformed synod till his death in 1557.

He was succeeded by Fabricius, who died of the pestilence in 1566.

PHILIP GALLICIUS (SALUZ) developed a more extensive activity. He is the Reformer of the Engadin, but labored also

---

[1] Campell, II. 310 sqq., gives the principal of the Twenty Articles of the Diet of Ilanz.

[2] See his letters to Bullinger and Vadian in De Porta, I. 67, 179 sqq.; II. 278.

as pastor and evangelist in Domleschg, Langwies, and Coire. He was born on the eastern frontier of Graubünden in 1504, and began to preach already in 1520. He had an irresistible eloquence and power of persuasion. When he spoke in Romansh, the people flocked from every direction to hear him. He was the chief speaker at two disputations in Süs, a town of the Lower Engadin, against the Papists (1537), and against the Anabaptists (1544).[1] He also introduced the Reformation in Zuz in the Lower Engadin, 1554, with the aid of JOHN TRAVERS, a distinguished patriot, states-man, soldier, and lay-preacher, who was called "the steel-clad knight in the service of the Lord."

Gallicius suffered much persecution and poverty, but remained gentle, patient, and faithful to the end. When preaching in the Domleschg he had not even bread to feed his large family, and lived for weeks on vegetables and salt. And yet he educated a son for the ministry at Basel, and dissuaded him from accepting a lucrative offer in another calling. He also did as much as he could for the Italian refugees. He died of the pestilence with his wife and three sons at Coire, 1566.

He translated the Lord's Prayer, the Apostles' Creed, and the Ten Commandments, and several chapters of the Bible, into the Romansh language, and thus laid the foundation of the Romansh literature. He also wrote a catechism and a Latin grammar, which were printed at Coire. He prepared the Confession of Rætia, in 1552, which was afterwards superseded by the Confession of Bullinger in 1566.

ULRICH CAMPELL (b. c. 1510, d. 1582) was pastor at Coire and at Süs, and, next to Gallicius, the chief reformer of the Engadin. He is also the first historian of Rætia and one of the founders of the religious literature in Romanic Rætia. His history is written in good Latin, and based upon personal observation, the accounts of the ancient Romans,

---

[1] A full account of the first disputation in Campell, II. 342–366.

the researches of Tschudi, and communications of Bullinger and Vadian. It begins A.D. 100 and ends about 1582.

The Romansh literature was first cultivated during the Reformation.[1] Gallicius, Campell, and Biveroni (Bifrun) are the founders of it. Campell prepared a metrical translation of the Psalter, with original hymns and a catechism (1562). Jacob Biveroni, a lawyer of Samaden, published a translation of Comander's Catechism, which was printed at Poschiavo, 1552, and (with the aid of Gallicius and Campell) the entire New Testament, which appeared first in 1560 at Basel, and became the chief agency in promoting the evangelical faith in those regions. The people, who knew only the Romansh language, says a contemporary, "were amazed like the Israelites of old at the sight of the manna."

The result of the labors of the Reformers and their successors in Graubünden was the firm establishment of an evangelical church which numbered nearly two-thirds of the population; while one-third remained Roman Catholic. This numerical relation has substantially remained to this day with some change in favor of Rome, though not by conversion, but by emigration and immigration. The two churches live peacefully together. The question of religion was decided in each community by a majority vote, like any political or local question. The principle of economy often gave the decision either for the retention of the Roman priest, or the choice of a Reformed preacher.[2] Some stingy congregations remained vacant to get rid of all obligations, or hired now a priest, now a preacher for a short season. Gallicius complained to Bullinger about this independence which favored

---

[1] "*Erst die Reformation,*" says Leonhardi (*Philipp Gallicius,* p. 87), "*hat eine rhäto-romanische Literatur geschaffen. Die Mönche und Priester behaupteten, der Engadiner Dialect sei so verdorben, dass er keines schriftlichen Ausdruckes fähig sei.*"

[2] The same regard for economy inclines at this day some Roman Catholic congregations to prefer a Capuchin monk to a secular priest. So I was informed by the Archivarius of the bishop of Coire in June, 1890.

license under the name of liberty. Not unfrequently congregations are deceived by foreign adventurers who impose
themselves upon them as pastors.

The democratic autonomy explains the curious phenome-
non of the mixture of religion in the Grisons. The traveller
may pass in a few hours through a succession of villages and
churches of different creeds. At Coire the city itself is
Reformed, and the Catholics with their bishop form a separate town on a hill, called the Court (of the bishop).

There is in Graubünden neither a State church nor a free
church, but a people's church.[1] Every citizen is baptized,
confirmed, and a church member. Every congregation is
sovereign, and elects and supports its own pastor. In 1537
a synod was constituted, which meets annually in the month
of June. It consists of all the ministers and three representatives of the government, and attends to the examination and ordination of candidates, and the usual business
of administration. The civil government watches over the
preservation of the church property, and prevents a collision
of ecclesiastical and civil legislation, but the administration
of church property is in the hands of the local congregations
or parishes. The Second Helvetic Confession of Bullinger
was formally accepted as the creed of the Church in 1566,
but has latterly gone out of use. Ministers are only required
to teach the doctrines of the Bible in general conformity
to the teaching of the Reformed Church. Pastors are at
liberty to use any catechism they please. The cultus is very
simple, and the churches are devoid of all ornament. Many
pious customs prevail among the people. A Protestant college was opened at Coire in the year 1542 with Pontisella, a native of Bregaglia, as first rector, who had been
gratuitously educated at Zürich by the aid of Bullinger.
With the college was connected a theological seminary for

---

[1] A *Volkskirche* or *Gemeindekirche*, which embraces the whole civil community.

the training of ministers. This was abolished in 1843,[1] and its funds were converted into scholarships for candidates, who now pursue their studies at Basel and Zürich or in German universities. In 1850 the Reformed college at Coire and the Catholic college of St. Lucius have been consolidated into one institution (*Cantonsschule*) located on a hill above Coire, near the episcopal palace.

During the sixteenth and seventeenth centuries the Reformed clergy were orthodox in the sense of moderate Calvinism; in the eighteenth century Pietism and the Moravian community exerted a wholesome influence on the revival of spiritual life.[2] In the present century about one-half of the clergy have been brought up under the influence of German Rationalism, and preach Christian morality without supernatural dogmas and miracles.

The Protestant movement in the Italian valleys of the Grisons began in the middle of the sixteenth century, but may as well be anticipated here.

§ 38. *The Reformation in the Italian Valleys of the Grisons. Vergerio.*

I. P. DOM. ROSIUS DE PORTA: *Dissertatio historico-ecclesiastica qua ecclesiarum colloquio Vallis Prægalliæ et Comitatiis Clavennæ olim comprehensarum Reformatio et status . . . exponitur.* Curiæ, 1787 (pp. 56, 4°). His *Historia Reformationis Eccles. Rhæticarum*, Bk. II. ch. v. pp. 139–179 (on Vergerio).— DAN. GERDES (a learned Reformed historian, 1698–1765): *Specimen Italiæ Reformatæ.* L. Batav. 1765.—*THOMAS MCCRIE (1772–1835, author of the *Life of John Knox*, etc.): *History of the Progress and Suppression of the Reformation in Italy.* Edinburgh, 1827. 2d ed. 1833. Republished by the Presbyterian Board of Publication, Philadelphia, 1842. Ch. VI., pp. 291 sqq., treats of the foreign Italian churches and the Reformation in the Grisons. —F. TRECHSEL: *Die protest. Antitrinitarier*, Heidelberg, 1844, vol. II. 64

---

[1] The last professors of theology were Antistes Kind (my pastor), and Dr. Schirks, both able and pious men.

[2] On this movement see Munz, *Die Brüdergemeinde in Bünden*, in "Der Kirchenfreund," Basel, Nos. 19–21, 1886. Johann Baptist von Albertini (d. 1831), one of the bishops and hymnists of the Moravians, and a friend of Schleiermacher, descended from a Bünden family.

sqq.) — G. Leonhardi : *Ritter Johannes Guler von Weineck, Lebensbild eines Rhätiers aus dem 17ᵗᵉⁿ Jahrh.* Bern, 1863. By the same : *Puschlaver Mord. Veltiner Mord. Die Ausrottung des Protestantismus im Misoxerthal.* In the Zeitschrift " der Wahre Protestant," Basel, 1852–'54. — B. Reber : *Georg Jenatsch, Graubündens Pfarrer und Held während des dreissigjährigen Kriegs.* In the "Beitäge zur vaterländischen Geschichte," Basel, 1860. — E. Lech-ner : *Das Thal Bergell (Bregaglia) in Graubünden, Natur, Sagen, Geschichte, Volk, Sprache, etc.* Leipzig, 1865 (pp. 140). — Y. F. Fetz (Rom. Cath.) : *Geschichte der kirchenpolitischen Wirren im Freistaat der drei Bünde vom Anfang des 17ᵗᵉⁿ Jahrh. bis auf die Gegenwart.* Chur, 1875 (pp. 367). — *Karl Benrath : *Bernardino Ochino von Siena.* Leipzig, 1875 (English translation with preface by William Arthur, London, 1876). Comp. his *Ueber die Quellen der italienischen Reformationsgeschichte.* Bonn, 1876. — *Joh. Kaspar Mörikofer : *Geschichte der evangelischen Flüchtlinge in der Schweiz.* Zürich, 1876. — John Stoughton : *Footprints of Italian Re-formers.* London, 1881 (pp. 235, 267 sqq.). — Em. Comba (professor of church history in the Waldensian Theological College at Florence) : *Storia della Riforma in Italia.* Firenze, 1881 (only 1 vol. so far). *Biblioteca della Riforma Italiana Sec. XVI.* Firenze, 1883–'86. 6 vols. *Visita ai Grigioni Riformati Italiani.* Firenze, 1885. *Vera Narrazione del Massacro di Valtellina.* Zürich, 1621. Republished in Florence, 1886. Comp. literature on p. 131.

II. The Vergerius literature. The works of Vergerius, Latin and Italian, are very rare. Niceron gives a list of fifty-five, Sixt (pp. 595–601) of eighty-nine. He began a collection of his *Opera adversus Papatum,* of which only the first volume has appeared, at Tübingen, 1563. Recently Emil Comba has edited his *Trattacelli e sua storia di Francesco Spiera* in the first two volumes of his " Biblioteca della Riforma Italiana," Firenze, 1883, and the *Parafrasi sopra l' Epistola ai Romani,* 1886. Sixt has pub-lished, from the Archives of Königsberg, forty-four letters of Vergerius to Albert, Duke of Prussia (pp. 533 sqq.), and Kausler and Schott (librarian at Stuttgart), his correspondence with Christopher, Duke of Würtemberg (*Briefwechsel zwischen Christoph Herzog von Würt. und P. P. Vergerius,* Tübingen, 1875). — Walter Friedensburg : *Die Nunciaturen des Vergerio, 1533–'36.* Gotha, 1892 (615 pp.). From the papal archives.

*Chr. H. Sixt : *Petrus Paulus Vergerius, päpstlicher Nuntius, katholischer Bischof und Vorkämpfer des Evangeliums.* Braunschweig, 1855 (pp. 601). With a picture of Vergerius. 2d (title) ed. 1871. The labors in the Grisons are described in ch. III. 181 sqq. — Scattered notices of Vergerius are found in Sleidan, Seckendorf, De Porta, Sarpi, Pallavicini, Raynal-dus, Maimburg, Bayle, Niceron, Schelhorn, Salig, and Meyer (in his monograph on Locarno, I. 36, 51; II. 236–255). A good article by Schott in Herzog², XVI. 351–357. (Less eulogistic than Sixt.)

The evangelical Reformation spread in the Italian portions of the Grisons; namely, the valleys of Pregell or Bregaglia,[1]

---

[1] This is the Italian name; in Latin, *Prægallia;* in German, *Bergell.*

and Poschiavo (Puschlav), which still belong to the Canton, and in the dependencies of the Valtellina (Veltlin), Bormio (Worms), and Chiavenna (Cleven), which were ruled by governors (like the Territories of the United States), but were lost to the Grisons in 1797. The Valtellina is famous for its luxuriant vegetation, fiery wine, and culture of silk. A Protestant congregation was also organized at Locarno in the Canton Ticino (Tessin), which then was a dependency of the Swiss Confederacy. This Italian chapter of the history of Swiss Protestantism is closely connected with the rise and suppression of the Reformation in Italy and the emigration of many Protestant confessors, who, like the French Huguenots of a later period, were driven from their native land, to enrich with their industry and virtue foreign countries where they found a hospitable home.

The first impulse to the Reformation in the Italian Grisons came from Gallicius and Campell, who labored in the neighboring Engadin, and knew Italian as well as Romansh. The chief agents were Protestant refugees who fled from the Inquisition to Northern Italy and found protection under the government of the Grisons. Many of them settled there permanently; others went to Zürich, Basel, and Geneva. In the year 1550 the number of Italian refugees was about two hundred. Before 1559 the number had increased to eight hundred. One fourth or fifth of them were educated men. Some inclined to Unitarian and Anabaptist opinions, and prepared the way for Socinianism. Among the latter may be mentioned Francesco Calabrese (in the Engadin); Tiriano (at Coire); Camillo Renato, a forerunner of Socinianism (at Tirano in the Valtellina); Ochino, the famous Capuchin pulpit orator (who afterwards went to Geneva, England, and Zürich); Lelio Sozini (who died at Zürich, 1562); and his more famous nephew, Fausto Sozini (1539–1604), the proper founder of Socinianism, who ended his life in Poland.

The most distinguished of the Italian evangelists in the

Grisons, is Petrus Paulus Vergerius (1498–1565).[1] He labored there four years (1549–1553), and left some permanent traces of his influence. He ranks among the secondary Reformers, and is an interesting but somewhat ambiguous and unsatisfactory character, with a changeful career. He held one of the highest positions at the papal court, and became one of its most decided opponents.

PETRUS PAULUS VERGERIUS.

Vergerio was at first a prominent lawyer at Venice. After the death of his wife (Diana Contarini), he entered the service of the Church, and soon rose by his talents and attain-

---

[1] PIERPAOLO VERGERIO, also called the younger, to distinguish him from an older member of his illustrious family. De Porta thus introduces his account, *l.c.*: "*Inter exsules, qui ob Evangelii confessionem Italiæ profugi in Rhætia consederunt, haud ullus sive generis nobilitatem, sive dignitatem, sive vitæ actæ rationem spectes, majorem meretur attentionem quam P. P. Vergerius.*"

ments to influential positions. He was sent by Clement VII., together with Campeggi and Pimpinelli, to the Diet of Augsburg, 1530, where he associated with Faber, Eck, and Cochlæus, and displayed great zeal and skill in attempting to suppress the Protestant heresy. He was made papal secretary and domestic chaplain, 1532. He was again sent by Paul III. to Germany, in 1535, to negotiate with the German princes about the proposed General Council at Mantua. He had a personal interview with Luther in Wittenberg (Nov. 7), and took offence at his bad Latin, blunt speech, and plebeian manner. He could not decide, he said in his official report to the papal secretary (Nov. 12), whether this German "beast" was possessed by an evil demon or not, but he certainly was the embodiment of arrogance, malice, and unwisdom.[1] He afterwards spoke of Luther as "a man of sacred memory," and "a great instrument of God," and lauded him in verses which he composed on a visit to Eisleben in 1559. On his return to Italy, he received as reward for his mission the archbishopric of Capo d' Istria, his native place (not far from Trieste). He aspired even to the cardinal's hat. He attended — we do not know precisely in what capacity, whether in the name of the Pope, or of Francis I. of France — the Colloquies at Worms and Regensburg, in 1540 and 1541, where he met Melanchthon and Calvin. Melanchthon presented him on that occasion with a copy of the Augsburg Confession and the Apology.[2] At that time he was, according to his confession, still as blind and impious as Saul. In the address De Unitate et Pace Ecclesiæ, which he delivered at Worms, Jan. 1, 1541, and which is diplomatic rather than theological,[3] he urged a General Council as a means to

---

[1] Sixt gives (pp. 35–45), from Seckendorf, Sarpi, and Pallavicini, a full account of this characteristic interview, which belongs to the history of the Lutheran and Roman Catholic churches. The official report is published by Friedensburg.

[2] With a letter printed in his Opera, Corp. Reform. IV. 22, and in Sixt, 94.

[3] Translated from the Latin in Sixt, 75–94. The address was printed and distributed immediately after the delivery, but has become very rare.

restore the unity and peace of the Church on the traditional basis.

His conversion was gradually brought about by a combination of several causes, — the reading of Protestant books which he undertook with the purpose to refute them, his personal intercourse with Lutheran divines and princes in Germany, the intolerance of his Roman opponents, and the fearful death of Spiera. He acquired an experimental knowledge of the evangelical doctrine of justification by faith, which at that time commended itself even to some Roman divines of high standing, as Cardinal Contarini and Reginald Pole, and which was advocated by Paleario of Siena, and by a pupil of Valdés in an anonymous Italian tract on "The Benefit of Christ's Death."[1] He began to preach evangelical doctrines and to reform abuses. His brother, bishop of Pola, fully sympathized with him. He roused the suspicion of the Curia and the Inquisition. He went to Trent in February, 1546, to justify himself before the Council, but was refused admittance, and forbidden to return to his dio-

---

[1] *Trattato utilissimo del beneficio di Giesù Christo crucifisso, verso i Christiani.* Venet. 1540. It was circulated in more than forty thousand copies within six years, translated into several languages, and republished from an English version (made from the French), 4th ed., London, 1638, by the Religious Tract Society of London, with an introduction by John Ayer, and again in Boston, 1860 (Gould & Lincoln, pp. 160, with facsimile of the title-page). The Italian original was recovered at Cambridge, 1855. Vergerius wrote in 1558 that there appeared no book in his age, at least in Italian, "so sweet, so pious, so simple, and so well adapted to instruct the weak on the article of justification" (Sixt, p. 103). The tract was formerly (by Tiraboschi, Gerdes, McCrie, Jules Bonnet, Mrs. Young, and others) ascribed to Aonio Paleario, professor of classical literature at Siena; but it was written by a pupil of the Spanish nobleman, Juan de Valdés, at Naples, and revised by Flaminio. Ranke found in the Acts of the Inquisition the notice, "*Quel libro del beneficio di Christo fu il suo autore un monaco di Sanseverino in Napoli discepolo del Valdés, fu revisore di detto libro il Flaminio, fu stampato molte volte,*" etc. *Die Römischen Päpste,* vol. I. pp. 90–92 (8th ed. 1883). Benrath found the name of the author, Don Benedetto de Mantova, "Zeitschrift für Kirchengesch.," I. 575–596 (1877). Comp. his article *Paleario,* in Herzog[2], XI. 165, note, and E. Böhmer on Valdés, *ibid.* XVI. 276 sqq. Böhmer says that there are two Italian copies of the tract in the imperial library at Vienna.

cese. He retired to Riva on the Lago di Garda, not far from Trent.

In 1548 he paid a visit to Padua to take some of his nephews to college. He found the city excited by the fearful tragedy of Francesco Spiera, a lawyer and convert from Romanism, who had abjured the evangelical faith from fear of the Inquisition, and fell into a hell of tortures of conscience under the conviction that he had committed the unpardonable sin by rejecting the truth. He was for several weeks a daily witness, with many others, of the agonies of this most unfortunate of apostates, and tried in vain to comfort him. He thought that we must not despair of any sinner, though he had committed the crimes of Cain and Judas. He prepared himself for his visits by prayer and the study of the comforting promises of the Scriptures. But Spiera had lost all faith, all hope, all comfort; he insisted that he had committed the sin against the Holy Spirit which cannot be forgiven in this world nor in the world to come; he was tormented by the remembrance of the sins of his youth, the guilt of apostasy, the prospect of eternal punishment which he felt already, and died in utter despair with a heart full of hatred and blasphemy. His death was regarded as a signal judgment of God, a warning example, and an argument for the truth of the evangelical doctrines.[1]

Vergerio was overwhelmed by this experience, and brought to a final decision. He wrote an apology in which he gives

---

[1] I have given a full account of this tragedy in an appendix to my (German) book on the *Sin against the Holy Ghost* (Halle, 1841), pp. 173–210, from a rare publication of 191 pages (then in possession of Dr. Hengstenberg in Berlin): *Francisci Spierœ, qui, quod susceptam semel evangelicœ veritatis professionem abnegasset damnassetque, in horrendam incidit desperationem, Historia, a quatuor summis viris summa fide conscripta, cum clariss. virorum prœfationibus, Cölii S. C. et Io. Calvini et Petri Pauli Vergerii Apologia: in quibus multa hoc tempore scitu digna gravissime tractantur.* . . . Basil. 1550. It was reprinted at Tübingen, 1558. Vergerio first published an account in his *Apologia*, 1548 (not 1549), which is contained in that book, and informed Calvin of it in a letter. Sixt gives large extracts, pp. 125–160. See Comba, *Francesco Spiera*, Firenze, 1833.

an account of the sad story, and renounces his connection
with Rome at the risk of persecution, torture, and death.
He sent it to the suffragan bishop of Padua, Dec. 13, 1548.

He was deposed and excommunicated by the pope, July 3,
1549, and fled over Bergamo to the Grisons. He remained
there till 1553, with occasional journeys to the Valtellina,
Chiavenna, Zürich, Bern, and Basel. He was hospitably
received, and developed great activity in preaching and
writing. People of all classes gathered around him, and
were impressed by his commanding presence and eloquence.
He founded a printing-press in Poschiavo in 1549, and issued
from it his thunderbolts against popery. He preached at
Pontresina and Samaden in the Upper Engadin, and effected
the abolition of the mass and the images. He labored as
pastor three years (1550–53) at Vicosoprano in Bregaglia.
He travelled through the greater part of Switzerland, and
made the acquaintance of Bullinger, Calvin, and Beza.

But the humble condition of the Grisons did not satisfy his
ambition. He felt isolated, and complained of the inhospitable valleys. He disliked the democratic institutions.
He quarrelled with the older Reformers, Comander and Gallicius. He tried to get the whole Synod of the Grisons under
his control, and, failing in this, to organize a separate synod
of the Italian congregations. Then he aspired to a more
prominent position at Zürich or Geneva or Bern, but Bullinger and Calvin did not trust him.

In November, 1553, he gladly accepted a call to Würtemberg as counsellor of Duke Christopher, one of the best
princes of the sixteenth century, and spent his remaining
twelve years in the Duke's service. He resided in Tübingen,
but had no official connection with the University. He continued to write with his rapid pen inflammatory tracts against
popery, promoted the translation and distribution of the
Bible in the South Slavonic dialect, maintained an extensive
correspondence, and was used in various diplomatic and

evangelical missions to the Emperor Maximilian at Vienna, to the kings of Bohemia, and Poland. On his first journey to Poland he made the personal acquaintance of Albert, Duke of Prussia, who esteemed him highly and supplied him with funds. He entered into correspondence with Queen Elizabeth, in the vain hope of an invitation to England. He desired to be sent as delegate to the religious conference at Poissy in France, 1561, but was again disappointed. He paid four visits to the Grisons (November, 1561; March, 1562; May, 1563; and April, 1564), to counteract the intrigues of the Spanish and papal party, and to promote the harmony of the Swiss Church with that of Würtemberg. On his second visit he went as far as the Valtellina. He received an informal invitation to attend the Council of Trent in 1561 from Delfino, the papal nuncio, in the hope that he might be induced to recant; he was willing to go at the risk of meeting the fate of Hus at Constance, but on condition of a safe conduct, which was declined.[1] At last he wished to unite with the Bohemian Brethren, whom he admired for their strict discipline combined with pure doctrine; he translated and published their Confession of Faith. He was in constant need of money, and his many begging letters to the Dukes of Würtemberg and of Prussia make a painful impression; but we must take into account the printing expenses of his many books, his frequent journeys, and the support of three nephews and a niece. In his fifty-ninth year he conceived the plan of contracting a marriage, and asked the Duke to double his allowance of two hundred guilders, but the request was declined and the marriage given up.[2]

He died Oct. 4, 1565, at Tübingen, and was buried there. Dr. Andreae, the chief author of the Lutheran Formula of Concord, preached the funeral sermon, which the learned

---

[1] See his letters to Duke Albert of Prussia, and the report of Pallavicini, XV. 10; and Sixt, 485 sqq., 490 sqq.

[2] Sixt, 510 sqq.

Crusius took down in Greek. Duke Christopher erected a monument to his memory with a eulogistic inscription.[1]

The very numerous Latin and Italian books and fugitive tracts of Vergerio are chiefly polemical against the Roman hierarchy of which he had so long been a conspicuous member.[2] He exposed, with the intemperate zeal of a proselyte, the *chronique scandaleuse* of the papacy, including the mythical woman-pope, Johanna (John VIII.), who was then generally believed to have really existed.[3] He agreed with Luther that the papacy was an invention of the Devil; that the pope was the very Antichrist seated in the temple of God as predicted by Daniel (11:36) and Paul (2 Thess. 2: 3 sq.), and the beast of the Apocalypse; and that he would soon be destroyed by a divine judgment. He attacked all the contemporary popes, except Adrian VI., to whom he gives credit for honesty and earnestness. He is especially severe on "Saul IV." (Paul IV.), who as Cardinal Caraffa had made some wise and bold utterances on the corruption of the clergy, but since his elevation to the "apostate chair, which corrupts every one who ascends it," had become the leader of the Counter-Reformation with its measures of violence and blood. Such monsters, he says, are the popes. One contradicts the other, and yet they are all infallible, and demand absolute submission. Rather die a thousand times than have any communion with popery and fall away from Christ, the

---

[1] The epitaphium, in eighteen hexameters, plays ingeniously on his name, — *Peter*, who denied the Lord, and, after his conversion, fed his sheep; *Paul*, who first persecuted and then built up the Church; and *Vergerius*, "*vergens ad orcum* and *vergens ad astra poli.*" The monument in the Georgenkirche was destroyed by the Jesuits in 1636 and restored 1672, but has disappeared since, according to Schott (Herzog², XVI. 357), whose statement (againt Sixt, 527) is confirmed by Dr. Weizsäcker (in a private letter of Jan. 5, 1891).

[2] Many of them appeared anonymously or under such false names as Athanasius, Fra Giovanni, Lambertus de Nigromonte, Valerius Philarchus, etc.

[3] This mediæval fiction was probably a Roman satire on the monstrous regiment of bad women who controlled the papacy in the tenth century. It was first disproved by David Blondel. See vol. IV. 265 sq.

Son of God, who was crucified for us and rose from the dead. Popery and the gospel are as incompatible as darkness and light, as Belial and Christ. No compromise is possible between them. Vergerio was hardly less severe on the cardinals and bishops, although he allowed some honorable exceptions. He attacked and ridiculed the Council of Trent, then in session, and tried to show that it was neither general, nor free, nor Christian. He used the same arguments against it as the Old Catholics used against the Vatican Council of 1870. He repelled the charge of heresy and turned it against his former co-religionists. The Protestants who follow the Word of God are orthodox, the Romanists who follow the traditions of men are the heretics.

His anti-popery writings were read with great avidity by his contemporaries, but are now forgotten. Bullinger was unfavorably impressed, and found in them no solid substance, but only frivolous mockery and abuse.

As regards the differences among Protestants, Vergerio was inconsistent. He first held the Calvinistic theory of the Lord's Supper, and expressed it in his own Catechism,[1] in a letter to Bullinger of Jan. 16, 1554, and even later, in June, 1556, at Wittenberg, where he met Melanchthon and Eber. But in Würtemberg he had to subscribe the Augsburg Confession, and in a letter to the Duke of Würtemberg, Oct. 23, 1557, he confessed the ubiquitarian theory of Luther. He also translated the Catechism of Brenz and the Würtemberg Confession into Italian, and thereby offended the Swiss Zwinglians, but told them that he was merely the translator. He never attributed much importance to the difference, and kept aloof from the eucharistic controversy.[2] He was not a profound theologian, but an ecclesiastical politician and diplomatist, after as well as before his conversion.

Vergerio left the Roman Church rather too late, when the

[1] *Fondamento della religione christiana per uso della Valtellina.* 1553.
[2] His views on the Eucharist are discussed by Sixt, 208, 214, and 497 sqq.

Counter-Reformation had already begun to crush Protestantism in Italy. He was a man of imposing personality, considerable learning and eloquence, wit and irony, polemic
dexterity, and diplomatic experience, but restless, vain, and
ambitious. He had an extravagant idea of his own importance. He could not forget his former episcopal authority
and pretensions, nor his commanding position as the representative of the pope. He aspired to the dignity and influence of a sort of Protestant internuncio at all the courts
of Europe, and of a mediator between the Lutheran and
Reformed Churches. Pallavicino, the Jesuit historian of
the Council of Trent, characterizes him as a lively and bold
man who could not live without business, and imagined that
business could not get along without him. Calvin found in
him much that is laudable, but feared that he was a restless
busybody. Gallicius wrote to Bullinger: "I wish that Vergerio would be more quiet, and persuade himself that the
heavens will not fall even if he, as another Atlas, should
withdraw his support." Nevertheless, Vergerio filled an
important place in the history of his times. He retained
the esteem of the Lutheran princes and theologians, and he
is gratefully remembered for his missionary services in the
two Italian valleys of the Grisons, which have remained
faithful to the evangelical faith to this day.

§ 39. *Protestantism in Chiavenna and the Valtellina, and its
Suppression. The Valtellina Massacre. George Jenatsch.*

See literature in §§ 36 and 38, pp. 131 and 144 sq.

We pass now to the Italian dependencies of the Grisons,
where Protestantism has had only a transient existence.

At Chiavenna the Reformed worship was introduced in
1544 by Agostino Mainardi, a former monk of Piedmont,
under the protection of Hercules von Salis, governor of the
province. He was succeeded by Jerome Zanchi (1516–

1590), an Augustinian monk who had been converted by reading the works of the Reformers under the direction of Vermigli at Lucca, and became one of the most learned and acute champions of the Calvinistic system. He fled to the Grisons in 1551, and preached at Chiavenna. Two years later he accepted a call to a Hebrew professorship at Strassburg. There he got into a controversy with Marbach on the doctrine of predestination, which he defended with logical rigor.[1] In 1563 he returned to Chiavenna as pastor. He had much trouble with restless Italian refugees and with the incipient heresy of Socinianism. In 1568 he left for Heidelberg, as professor of theology on the basis of the Palatinate Catechism, which in 1563 had been introduced under the pious Elector Frederick III. He prepared the way for Calvinistic scholasticism. A complete edition of his works appeared at Geneva, 1619, in three folio volumes.

Chiavenna had several other able pastors, — Simone Florillo, Scipione Lentulo of Naples, Ottaviano Meio of Lucca.

Small Protestant congregations were founded in the Valtellina, at Caspan (1546), Sondrio (the seat of government), Teglio, Tirano, and other towns. Dr. McCrie says: " Upon the whole, the number of Protestant churches to the south of the Alps appears to have exceeded twenty, which were all served, and continued till the end of the sixteenth century to be for the most part served, by exiles from Italy."

But Protestantism in Chiavenna, Bormio, and the Valtellina was at last swept out of existence. We must here anticipate a bloody page of the history of the seventeenth century.

Several causes combined for the destruction of Protestantism in Upper Italy. The Catholic natives were never friendly to the heretical refugees who settled among them, and called them *banditi*, which has the double meaning of exile and outlaw. They reproached the Grisons for receiving them

---

[1] Schweizer, *Centraldogmen der Ref. Kirche*, I. 422 sqq.

after they had been expelled from other Christian countries. They were kept in a state of political vassalage, instead of being admitted to equal rights with the three leagues. The provincial governors were often oppressive, sold the subordinate offices to partisans, and enriched themselves at the expense of the inhabitants. The Protestants were distracted by internal feuds. The Roman Counter-Reformation was begun with great zeal and energy in Upper Italy and Switzerland by the saintly Cardinal Charles Borromeo, archbishop of Milan. Jesuits and Capuchins stirred up the hatred of the ignorant and superstitious people against the Protestant heretics. In the Grisons themselves the Roman Catholic party under the lead of the family of Planta, and the Protestants, headed by the family of Salis, strove for the mastery. The former aimed at the suppression of the Reformation in the leagues as well as the dependencies, and were suspected of treasonable conspiracy with Spain and Austria. The Protestant party held a court (*Strafgericht*, a sort of tribunal of inquisition) at Thusis in 1618, which included nine preachers, and condemned the conspirators. The aged Zambra, who in the torture confessed complicity with Spain, was beheaded; Nicolaus Rusca, an esteemed priest, leader of the Spanish Catholic interests in the Valtellina, called the hammer of the heretics, was cruelly tortured to death; Bishop John Flugi was deposed and outlawed; the brothers Rudolf and Pompeius Planta, the knight Jacob Robustelli, and other influential Catholics were banished, and the property of the Plantas was confiscated.

These unrighteous measures created general indignation. The exiles fostered revenge, and were assured of Spanish aid. Robustelli returned, after his banishment, to the Valtellina, and organized a band of about three hundred desperate bandits from the Venetian and Milanese territories for the overthrow of the government of the Grisons and the extermination of Protestantism.

This is the infamous "Valtellina Massacre" (*Veltliner Mord*) of July, 1620. It may be called an imitation of the Sicilian Vespers, and of the Massacre of St. Bartholomew. It was the fiendish work of religious fanaticism combined with political discontent. The tragedy began in the silence of the night, from July 18th to 19th, by the murder of sixty defenceless adult Protestants of Tirano; the Podesta Enderlin was shot down in the street, mutilated, and thrown into the Adda; Anton von Salis took refuge in the house of a Catholic friend, but was sought out and killed; the head of the Protestant minister, Anton Bassa of Poschiavo, was posted on the pulpit of the church. The murderers proceeded to Teglio, and shot down about the same number of persons in the church, together with the minister, who was wounded in the pulpit, and exhorted the hearers to persevere; a number of women and children, who had taken refuge in the tower of the church, were burnt. The priest of Teglio took part in the bloody business, carrying the cross in the left, and the sword in the right hand. At Sondrio, the massacre raged for three days. Seventy-one Protestants, by their determined stand, were permitted to escape to the Engadin, but one hundred and forty fell victims to the bandits; a butcher boasted of having murdered eighteen persons. Not even the dead were spared; their bodies were exhumed, burnt, thrown into the water, or exposed to wild beasts. Paula Baretta, a noble Venetian lady of eighty years, who had left a nunnery for her religious conviction, was shamefully maltreated and delivered to the Inquisition at Milan, where a year afterward she suffered death at the stake. Anna of Libo fled with a child of two years in her arms; she was overtaken and promised release on condition of abjuring her faith. She refused, saying, "You may kill the body, but not the soul"; she pressed her child to her bosom, and received the death-blow. When the people saw the stream of blood on the market-place before the chief

church, they exclaimed: "This is the revenge for our murdered arch-priest Rusca!" He was henceforth revered as
a holy martyr. At Morbegno the Catholics behaved well,
and aided the Protestants in making their escape. The
fugitives were kindly received in the Grisons and other parts
of Switzerland. From the Valtellina Robustelli proceeded
to Poschiavo, burnt the town of Brusio, and continued there
the butchery of Protestants till he was checked.[1]

The Valtellina declared itself independent and elected the
knight Robustelli military chief. The canons of the Council
of Trent were proclaimed, papal indulgences introduced, the
evangelical churches and cemeteries reconsecrated for Catholic use, the corpses of Protestants dug up, burnt, and cast into
the river. Addresses were sent to the Pope and the kings
of Spain and France, explaining and excusing the foul deeds
by which the rebels claimed to have saved the Roman religion and achieved political freedom from intolerable tyranny.

Now began the long and bloody conflicts for the recovery
of the lost province, in which several foreign powers took
part. The question of the Valtellina (like the Eastern
question in modern times) became a European question, and
was involved in the Thirty Years' War. Spain, in possession
of Milan, wished to join hands with Austria across the Alpine
passes of the Grisons; while France and Venice had a political motive to keep them closed. Austrian and Spanish
troops conquered and occupied the Valtellina and the three
leagues, expelled the Protestant preachers, and inflicted un-

---

[1] Moderate Catholic historians dare not defend this massacre, any more
than that of St. Bartholomew, but explain it as a terrible Nemesis and desperate self-vindication against the oppressions of the commissioners of the
Grisons. So Fetz, who says (*l.c.* p. 113): "*Die besonnenen Katholiken haben
diese schauerliche Selbsthülfe, wodurch viele Unschuldige als Opfer der Rache gefallen, niemals gebilligt; andererseits konnten und können billig denkende Protestanten
das arge Treiben der Prädicanten und reformirten Machthaber im Veltlin und Um-
gebung ebensowenig gutheissen, denn dieses arge Treiben war die erste und letzte
Ursache der verzweifelten Selbsthülfe.*" But Italian Catholic writers (as Cantù)
call it *sacro macello, a sacred slaughter!*

speakable misery upon the people. France, no less Catholic under the lead of Cardinal Richelieu, but jealous of the house of Habsburg, came to the support of the Protestants in the Grisons, as well as the Swedes in the north, and sent an army under the command of the noble Huguenot Duke Henri de Rohan, who defeated the Austrians and Spaniards, and conquered the Valtellina (1635).

The Grisons with French aid recovered the Valtellina by the stipulation of Chiavenna, 1636, which guaranteed to the three leagues all the rights of sovereignty, but on condition of tolerating no other religion in that province but the Roman Catholic. Rohan, who had the best intentions for the Grisons, desired to save Protestant interests, but Catholic France would not agree. He died in 1638, and was buried at Geneva.

The Valtellina continued to be governed by bailiffs till 1797. It is now a part of the kingdom of Italy, and enjoys the religious freedom guaranteed by the constitution of 1848.[1]

In this wild episode of the Thirty Years' War, a Protestant preacher, Colonel Georg Jenatsch, plays a prominent figure as a romantic hero. He was born at Samaden in the Upper Engadin, 1590, studied for the Protestant ministry at Zürich, successively served the congregations at Scharans and at Berbenno in the Valtellina, and narrowly escaped the massacre at Sondrio by making his flight through dangerous mountain passes. He was an eloquent speaker, an ardent patriot, a shrewd politician, and a brave soldier, but ambitious, violent, unscrupulous, extravagant, and unprincipled. He took part in the cruel decision of the court of Thusis (1618), and killed Pompeius Planta with an axe (1621). He served as guide and counsellor of the Duke de Rohan, and by his knowledge, pluck, and energy, materially aided him in the

---

[1] The *statuto fondamentale* of Sardinia, which in 1870 was extended over all Italy, declares the Roman Catholic Church to be the state religion, but grants toleration to all other forms of worship. The Waldenses have recently established preaching stations at Chiavenna and other places of Upper Italy.

defeat of Austria. Being disappointed in his ambition, he turned traitor to France, joined the Austrian party and the Roman Church (1635), but educated his children in the Protestant religion. He was murdered at a banquet in Coire (1639) by an unknown person in revenge for the murder of Pompeius Planta. He is buried in the Catholic church, near the bishop's palace. A Capuchin monk delivered the funeral oration.[1]

§ 40. *The Congregation of Locarno.*

FERDINAND MEYER: *Die evangelische Gemeinde von Locarno, ihre Auswanderung nach Zürich und ihre weiteren Schicksale.* Zürich, 1836. 2 vols. An exhaustive monograph carefully drawn from MS. sources, and bearing more particularly on the Italian congregation at Zürich, to which the leading Protestant families of Locarno emigrated.

Locarno, a beautiful town on the northern end of the Lago Maggiore, was subject to the Swiss Confederacy and ruled by bailiffs.[2] It had in the middle of the sixteenth century a Protestant congregation of nearly two hundred members.[3] Chief among them were Beccaria, Taddeo Duno, Lodovico Ronco, and Martino Muralto. A religious disputation was held there in 1549, about the authority of the pope, the merit of good works, justification, auricular confession, and purgatory.[4] It ended in a tumult. Wirz, the presiding bailiff, who knew neither Latin nor Italian, gave a decision in favor of the Roman party. Beccaria refused to submit, escaped, and went to Zürich, where he was kindly received

---

[1] He is the hero of a drama by Arnold von Salis, and of a classical novel by the Swiss poet, Conrad Ferdinand Meyer (*Jürg Jenatsch.* Leipzig. 3d ed. 1882). A full biography of Jenatsch by Dr. E. Haffter is announced.

[2] It originally belonged to the Duchy of Milan, and was ceded to Switzerland in 1512, together with Lugano and Domo d'Ossola. In 1803 it became, with Lugano and Bellinzona, one of the three capitals of the Italian canton Ticino. In 1878 Bellinzona was declared the only capital.

[3] Meyer gives a complete list of members from the Archives of Zürich, and two lists of those who emigrated to Zürich, vol. I. 511–515 and 521–525.

[4] An account of it by Duno in a letter to Bullinger, and in the book *De persecutione.* See Meyer, I. 190 sqq.

by Bullinger. He became afterwards a member of the Synod of Graubünden, and was sent as an evangelist to Misocco, but returned to Zürich.

The faithful Protestants of Locarno, who preferred emigration to submission, wandered with wives and children on foot and on horseback over snow and ice to Graubünden and Zürich, in 1556. Half of them remained in the Grisons, and mingled with the evangelical congregations. The rest organized an Italian congregation in Zürich under the fostering care of Bullinger. It was served for a short time by Vergerio, who came from Tübingen for the purpose, and then by Bernardino Ochino, who had fled from England to Basel after the accession of Queen Mary. Ochino was a brilliant genius and an eloquent preacher, then already sixty-eight years old, but gave offence by his Arian and other heretical opinions, and was required to leave in 1563. He went to Basel, Strassburg, Nürnberg, Krakau; was expelled from Poland, Aug. 6, 1564; and died in poverty in Moravia, 1565, a victim of his subtle speculations and the intolerance of his times. He wrote an Italian catechism for the Locarno congregation in the form of a dialogue (1561).

The most important accession to the exiles was Pietro Martire Vermigli, who had likewise fled from England, first to Strassburg (1553), then to Zürich (1555). He was received as a member into the council of the Locarno congregation, presented with the citizenship of Zürich, and elected professor of Hebrew in place of Conrad Pellican (who died in 1556). He labored there till his death, in 1562, in intimate friendship and harmony with Bullinger, generally esteemed and beloved. He was one of the most distinguished and useful Italian converts, and, like Zanchi, an orthodox Calvinist.

The Italian congregation was enlarged by new fugitives from Locarno and continued to the end of the sixteenth century. The principal families of Duno, Muralto, Orelli, Pestalozzi, and others were received into citizenship, took a prominent position in the history of Zürich, and promoted its industry and prosperity, like the exiled Huguenots in Brandenburg, Holland, England, and North America.[1]

§ 41. *Zwinglianism in Germany.*

The principles of the Helvetic Reformation spread also to some extent in Germany, but in a modified form, and prepared the way for the mediating (Melanchthonian) character of the German Reformed Church. Although Luther overshadowed every other personality in Germany, Zwingli had also his friends and admirers, especially the Landgrave, Philip of Hesse, who labored very zealously, though unsuccessfully, for a union of the Lutherans and the Reformed. Bucer and Capito at Strassburg, Cellarius at Augsburg, Blaurer at Constance, Hermann at Reutlingen, and Somius at Ulm, strongly sympathized with the genius and tendency of the Zürich Reformer.[2] His influence was especially felt in those free cities of Southern Germany where the democratic element prevailed.

Four of these cities, Strassburg, Constance, Memmingen, and Lindau, handed to the Diet of Augsburg, 11th July, 1530, a special confession (*Confessio Tetrapolitana*) drawn up by Bucer, with the assistance of Hedio, and answered by the Roman divines, Faber, Eck, and Cochlæus. It is the first symbolical book of the German Reformed Church (Zwingli's writings having never acquired symbolical authority), but was superseded by the Heidelberg Catechism (1563) and the Second Helvetic Confession (1566). It strikes a middle course between the Augsburg Confession of Melanchthon and the private Confession sent in by Zwingli during the same Diet, and anticipates Calvin's view on the Lord's Supper by teaching a real fruition of the true body and blood of Christ,

---

[1] On the industry of the Italians in Zürich, see Meyer, II. 375–391.
[2] See the correspondence of Zwingli, in his *Opera*, vols. VII. and VIII.

not through the mouth, but tnrough faith, for the nourishment of the soul into eternal life.[1]

The Zwinglian Reformation was checked and almost destroyed in Germany by the combined opposition of Romanism and Lutheranism. The four cities could not maintain their isolated position, and signed the Augsburg Confession for political reasons, to join the Smalcaldian League. The Reformed Church took a new start in the Palatinate under the combined influence of Zwingli, Melanchthon, and Calvin (1563), gained strength by the accession of the reigning dynasty of Prussia (since 1614), and was ultimately admitted to equal rights with the Roman Catholic and Lutheran Churches in the German Empire by the Treaty of Westphalia (1648).

[1] See VI. 718–721.

CHAPTER V.

THE CIVIL WAR BETWEEN THE ROMAN CATHOLIC AND REFORMED CANTONS.

See the works of ESCHER, OECHSLI, and FENNER, quoted on p. 19; MÖRIKO-
FER, *Zwingli*, II. 346–452; and BLUNTSCHLI, *Geschichte des schweizerischen
Bundesrechtes von den ewigen Bünden bis auf die Gegenwart.* Stuttgart.
2d ed. 1875, 2 vols.

§ 42. *The First War of Cappel.* 1529.

THE year 1530 marks the height of the Zwinglian Reformation. It was firmly established in the leading cities and
cantons of Zürich, Bern, and Basel. It had gained a strong
majority of the people in Northern and Eastern Switzerland,
and in the Grisons. It had fair prospects of ultimate success
in the whole confederacy, when its further progress was suddenly arrested by the catastrophe of Cappel and the death of
Zwingli.

The two parties had no conception of toleration (except in
Glarus and the Grisons), but aimed at supremacy and excluded each other wherever they had the power. They
came into open conflict in the common territories or free
bailiwicks, by the forcible attempts made there to introduce
the new religion, or to prevent its introduction. The Protestants, under the lead of Zwingli, were the aggressors, especially in the confiscation of the rich abbey of St. Gall. They
had in their favor the right of progress and the majority of
the population. But the Roman Catholics had on their side
the tradition of the past, the letter of the law, and a majority
of Cantons and of votes in the Diet, in which the people
were not directly represented. They strictly prohibited
Protestant preaching within their own jurisdiction, and even

began bloody persecution. Jacob Kaiser (or Schlosser), a
Zürich minister, was seized on a preaching expedition, and
publicly burnt at the stake in the town of Schwyz (May,
1529).[1] His martyrdom was the signal of war. The Protestants feared, not without good reason, that this case was
the beginning of a general persecution.

With the religious question was closely connected the
political and social question of the foreign military service,[2]
which Zwingli consistently opposed in the interest of patriotism, and which the Roman Catholics defended in the interest
of wealth and fame.   This was a very serious matter, as may
be estimated from the fact that, according to a statement of
the French ambassador, his king had sent, from 1512 to 1531,
no less than 1,133,547 gold crowns to Switzerland, a sum
equal to four times the amount at present valuation.   The
pensions were the Judas price paid by foreign sovereigns to
influential Swiss for treason to their country.   In his opposition to this abuse, Zwingli was undoubtedly right, and his
view ultimately succeeded, though long after his death.[3]

Both parties organized for war, which broke out in 1529,
and ended in a disastrous defeat of the Protestants in 1531.
Sixteen years later, the Lutheran princes suffered a similar
defeat in the Smalcaldian War against the Emperor (1547).
The five Forest Cantons — Uri, Schwyz, Unterwalden, Luzern,
and Zug — formed a defensive and offensive league (November, 1528; the preparations began in 1527), and even entered,
first secretly, then openly, into an alliance with Ferdinand
Duke of Austria and King of Bohemia and Hungary (April,
1529).   This alliance with the old hereditary enemy of
Switzerland, whom their ancestors had defeated in glorious

[1] For the particulars of this case see Mörikofer, II. 146 sqq., and Christoffel, I. 376 sq.

[2] The *Reislaufen*, or running to war; *reisig*, in old German, means ready
for war (*kriegsrüstig*).

[3] Christoffel, I. 382.   Comp. § 7, p. 24.

battles, was treasonable and a step towards the split of the confederacy in two hostile camps (which was repeated in 1846). King Ferdinand had a political and religious interest in the division of Switzerland and fostered it. Freiburg, Wallis, and Solothurn sided with the Catholic Cantons, and promised aid in case of war. The Protestant Cantons, led by Zürich (which made the first step in this direction) formed a Protestant league under the name of the Christian co-burghery (*Burgrecht*) with the cities of Constance (Dec. 25, 1527), Biel and Mühlhausen (1529), and Strassburg (Jan. 9, 1530).[1]

Zwingli, provoked by the burning of Kaiser, and seeing the war clouds gathering all around, favored prompt action, which usually secures a great advantage in critical moments. He believed in the necessity of war; while Luther put his sole trust in the Word of God, although he stirred up the passions of war by his writings, and had himself the martyr's courage to go to the stake. Zwingli was a free republican; while Luther was a loyal monarchist. He belonged to the Cromwellian type of men who "trust in God and keep their powder dry." In him the reformer, the statesman, and the patriot were one. He appealed to the examples of Joshua and Gideon, forgetting the difference between the Old and the New dispensation. "Let us be firm," he wrote to his peace-loving friends in Bern (May 30, 1529), "and fear not to take up arms. This peace, which some desire so much, is not peace, but war; while the war that we call for, is not war, but peace. We thirst for no man's blood, but we will cut the nerves of the oligarchy. If we shun it, the truth of the gospel and the ministers' lives will never be secure among us."[2]

---

[1] The documents of these leagues are given by Bullinger, Hottinger, and by Bluntschli, *l.c.* I. 303–305, 318 sq.; II. 238–255.

[2] "*Quod hactenus ad vos scripsi, iterum atque iterum facio, ut constantes sitis, neque bellum metuatis. Nam ista pax, quam quidam tantopere urgent, bellum est, non pax; et bellum, cui nos instamus, pax est, non bellum. Non enim sitimus*

Zürich was first ready for the conflict and sent four thousand well-equipped soldiers to Cappel, a village with a Cistercian convent, in the territory of Zürich on the frontier of the Canton Zug.[1] Smaller detachments were located at Bremgarten, and on the frontier of Schwyz, Basel, St. Gall. Mühlhausen furnished auxiliary troops. Bern sent five thousand men, but with orders to act only in self-defence.

Zwingli accompanied the main force to Cappel. "When my brethren expose their lives," he said to the burgomaster, who wished to keep him back, "I will not remain quiet at home. The army requires a watchful eye." He put the halberd which he had worn as chaplain at Marignano, over his shoulder, and mounted his horse, ready to conquer or to die for God and the fatherland.[2]

He prepared excellent instructions for the soldiers, and a plan of a campaign that should be short, sharp, decisive, and, if possible, unbloody.

Zürich declared war June 9, 1529. But before the forces crossed the frontier of the Forest Cantons, Landammann Aebli of Glarus, where the Catholics and Protestants wor-

---

cujusquam sanguinem, neque etiam per tumultum hauriemus, sed in hoc sumus, ut oligarchiæ nervi succidantur. Id nisi fiat, neque Evangelii veritas, neque illius ministri apud nos in tuto erunt. Nihil crudele cogitamus: sed quicquid agimus, amicum et paternum est." Opera, VIII. 294.

[1] Cappel has become famous by the battle of 1531 and the death of Zwingli. It lies six miles from the town of Zug. The battle-field and the monument of Zwingli are about ten minutes' walk from Cappel. The old church is well preserved, and has recently been repaired. See Annales Cœnobii Capelloni per H. Bullingerum et P. Simlerum, in Simler's (printed) Sammlung alter und neuer Urkunden (Zürich, 1760), II. 397; and Pestalozzi's Bullinger, p. 20.

[2] It is stated by Bullinger, and usually supposed, that he only went in the capacity of chaplain, like Konrad Schmid and Franz Zingg, who likewise preached in the army. The armor seems to indicate the warrior, as Hagenbach thinks (p. 405), but not necessarily. There is no evidence that Zwingli actually fought in any battle. A. Baur (Zwingli's Theologie, II. 759) says that he went to war simply as patriot and chaplain, not as politician and captain. It is difficult, however, to separate these characters in him. The weapons of Zwingli — a harness, a helmet, and a sword — were kept in the arsenal at Luzern till 1848 in the Sonderbundskrieg, when they were carried to Zürich.

ship in one church, appeared from a visit to the hostile army as peacemaker, and prevented a bloody collision. He was a friend of Zwingli, an enemy of the mercenary service, and generally esteemed as a true patriot. With tears in his eyes, says Bullinger, he entreated the Zürichers to put off the attack even for a few hours, in the hope of bringing about an honorable peace. "Dear lords of Zürich, for God's sake, prevent the division and destruction of the confederacy." Zwingli opposed him, and said: "My dear friend,[1] you will answer to God for this counsel. As long as the enemies are in our power, they use good words; but as soon as they are well prepared, they will not spare us." He foresaw what actually happened after his death. Aebli replied: "I trust in God that all will go well. Let each of us do his best." And he departed.

Zwingli himself was not unwilling to make peace, but only on four conditions which he sent a day after Aebli's appeal, in a memorandum to the Council of Zürich (June 11): 1) That the Word of God be preached freely in the entire confederacy, but that no one be forced to abolish the mass, the images, and other ceremonies which will fall of themselves under the influence of scriptural preaching; 2) that all foreign military pensions be abolished; 3) that the originators and the dispensers of foreign pensions be punished while the armies are still in the field; 4) that the Forest Cantons pay the cost of war preparations, and that Schwyz pay one thousand guilders for the support of the orphans of Kaiser (Schlosser) who had recently been burnt there as a heretic.

An admirable discipline prevailed in the camp of Zürich, that reminds one of the Puritan army of Cromwell. Zwingli or one of his colleagues preached daily; prayers were

---

[1] They addressed each other " *Gevatter*," "*gossip*," which denotes a baptismal relationship. When Zwingli was pastor at Glarus, he stood sponsor to Aebli's children in baptism.

offered before each meal; psalms, hymns, and national songs resounded in the tents; no oath was heard; gambling and swearing were prohibited, and disreputable women excluded; the only exercises were wrestling, casting stones, and military drill. There can be little doubt that if the Zürichers had made a timely attack upon the Catholics and carried out the plan of Zwingli, they would have gained a complete victory and dictated the terms of peace. How long the peace would have lasted is a different question; for behind the Forest Cantons stood Austria, which might at any time have changed the situation.

But counsels of peace prevailed. Bern was opposed to the offensive, and declared that if the Zürichers began the attack, they should be left to finish it alone. The Zürichers themselves were divided, and their military leaders (Berger and Escher) inclined to peace.

The Catholics, being assured that they need not fear an attack from Bern, mustered courage and were enforced by troops from Wallis and the Italian bailiwicks. They now numbered nearly twelve thousand armed men.

The hostile armies faced each other from Cappel and Baar, but hesitated to advance. Catholic guards would cross over the border to be taken prisoners by the Zürichers, who had an abundance of provision, and sent them back well fed and clothed. Or they would place a large bucket of milk on the border line and asked the Zürichers for bread, who supplied them richly; whereupon both parties peacefully enjoyed a common meal, and when one took a morsel on the enemy's side, he was reminded not to cross the frontier. The soldiers remembered that they were Swiss confederates, and that many of them had fought side by side on foreign battle-fields.[1] " We shall not fight," they said; "and pray God that the storm may pass away without doing us any harm." Jacob Sturm,

---

[1] Similar episodes of kindly intercourse occurred between the Confederate and Union soldiers during the civil war in the United States.

the burgomaster of Strassburg, who was present as a mediator, was struck with the manifestation of personal harmony and friendship in the midst of organized hostility. "You are a singular people," he said; "though disunited, you are united."

§ 43. The First Peace of Cappel. June, 1529.

After several negotiations, a treaty of Peace was concluded June 25, 1529, between Zürich, Bern, Basel, St. Gall, and the cities of Mühlhausen and Biel on the one hand, and the five Catholic Cantons on the other. The deputies of Glarus, Solothurn, Schaffhausen, Appenzell, Graubünden, Sargans, Strassburg, and Constanz acted as mediators.

The treaty was not all that Zwingli desired, especially as regards the abolition of the pensions and the punishment of the dispensers of pensions (wherein he was not supported by Bern), but upon the whole it was favorable to the cause of the Reformation.

The first and most important of the Eighteen Articles of the treaty recognizes, for the first time in Europe, the principle of parity or legal equality of the Roman Catholic and Protestant Churches, — a principle which twenty-six years afterwards was recognized also in Germany (by the *Augsburger Religionsfriede* of 1555), but which was not finally settled there till after the bloody baptism of the Thirty Years' War, in the Treaty of Westphalia (1648), against which the Pope of Rome still protests in vain. That article guarantees to the Reformed and Roman Catholic Cantons religious freedom in the form of mutual toleration, and to the common bailiwicks the right to decide by majority the question whether they would remain Catholics or become Protestants.[1] The

---

[1] The Swiss German text of the first Article of the first *Landsfriede* of Cappel is as follows (Bluntschli, II. 257) : " *Des ersten von wägen des Göttlichen worts, diewyl und nieman zum glouben bezwungen sol werden, das dann die fünff vrt und die iren, des selben ouch nitt genötiget. Aber die zügewandten und vogthien, wo man mitt einandern zü beherschen hat, belangend, wo die selben die mess abge-*

treaty also provided for the payment of the expenses of the war by the five cantons, and for an indemnity to the family of the martyred Kaiser. The abolition of the foreign pensions was not demanded, but recommended to the Roman Catholic Cantons. The alliance with Austria was broken. The document which contained the treasonable treaty was cut to pieces by Aebli in the presence of Zwingli and the army of Zürich.[1]

The Catholics returned to their homes discontented. The Zürichers had reason to be thankful; still more the Berners, who had triumphed with their policy of moderation.

Zwingli wavered between hopes and fears for the future, but his trust was in God. He wrote (June 30) to Conrad Som, minister at Ulm: "We have brought peace with us, which for us, I hope, is quite honorable; for we did not go

stellt und die bilder verbränt oder abgethan, das die selben an lib eer und güt, nitt gestraaft söllind werden. Wo aber die mess und ander ceremonien noch vorhanden, die söllend nitt gezwungen, ouch inen keine predicanten, so es nitt durch den meer-theyl erkendt wirt, geschickt, uffgestellt oder gegäben werden, sunder was under inen den kylchgenossen die uff oder abzüthünd, dessglychen mitt der Spys, die Gott nitt verbotten zü essen, gemeret wird, daby sol es biss uff der kylchgenossen gefallen blyben: und dhein teyl dem andern sinen glouben, weder smehen noch straafen."

Bluntschli (a great authority in Swiss as well as international law) thus explains this article (I. 324): "In ihm ist bereits das Princip der Parität, d. h. der staatlichen Gleichberechtigung, beider christlichen Confessionen enthalten. Es ist anerkannt, dass kein Ort [Canton] den andern, dass auch die Eidgenossen-schaft nicht einzelne Orte zur Beibehaltung oder zur Abänderung ihres christlichen Glaubens zwingen dürfe. Die katholischen Stände verzichteten somit hierin den reformirten gegenüber ausdrücklich auf die Festhaltung des alten Rechtes des Mittel-alters, wornach jede energische Abweichung von dem katholischen Glauben als ein Verbrechen behandelt und der Krieg gegen die Ketzer als Pflicht angesehen ward. Sie erkannten das Princip der Glaubensfreiheit, welches von den Reformirten zuerst verkündigt worden war, nun den Reformirten Orten gegenüber an, nahmen es aber gleichzeitig auch für sich selber in Anspruch. Und hinwieder gestanden die Refor-mirten Stände die Folgerichtigkeit dieses Schlusses zu, und verzichteten darauf, die Orte zur Annahme der Reformation zu nöthigen." Comp. the treaty of Ilanz, p. 139.

[1] The treaty of peace is given by Bullinger, II. 185 sqq. and 212; by Escher and Hottinger, in the "Archiv für schweizerische Geschichte und Landeskunde," Zürich, 1827, vol. I.; and by Bluntschli, l.c. II. 255–269 (comp. I. 323–331).

forth to shed blood.[1] We have sent back our foes with a wet blanket. Their compact with Austria was cut to pieces before mine eyes in the camp by the Landammann of Glarus, June 26, at 11 A.M. . . . God has shown again to the mighty ones that they cannot prevail against him, and that we may gain victory without a stroke if we hold to him."[2]

He gave vent to his conflicting feelings in a poem which he composed in the camp (during the peace negotiations), together with the music, and which became almost as popular in Switzerland as Luther's contemporaneous, but more powerful and more famous "*Ein feste Burg*," is to this day in Germany. It breathes the same spirit of trust in God.[3]

> "Do thou direct thy chariot, Lord,
>   And guide it at thy will;
> Without thy aid our strength is vain,
>   And useless all our skill.
> Look down upon thy saints brought low,
> And grant them victory o'er the foe.
>
> "Beloved Pastor, who hast saved
>   Our souls from death and sin,
> Uplift thy voice, awake thy sheep
>   That slumbering lie within
> Thy fold, and curb with thy right hand
> The rage of Satan's furious band.
>
> "Send down thy peace, and banish strife,
>   Let bitterness depart;
> Revive the spirit of the past
>   In every Switzer's heart:
> Then shall thy church forever sing
> The praises of her heavenly King."[4]

[1] " *Denn wir uff blutvergiessen nit uszogen.*"

[2] *Opera*, VIII. 310 sq.

[3] Bullinger reports: " *Dieses Lied wurde hernach weit und breit, auch an der Fürsten Höfen und in den Städten von Musicis gesungen und geblasen.*" On the other poems of Zwingli, see above, p. 44 sq.

[4] This is a free version of H. White (from Merle D'Aubigné), with some necessary changes. The original, in the Swiss German, was sung at the Zwingli festivals in 1884, and, with great effect, at the unveiling of the Zwingli statue in Zürich, August, 1885. It is as follows : —

§ 44. *Between the Wars. Political Plains of Zwingli.*

The effect of the first Peace of Cappel was favorable to the cause of the Reformation. It had now full legal recognition, and made progress in the Cantons and in the common territories. But the peace did not last long. The progress emboldened the Protestants, and embittered the Catholics.

The last two years of Zwingli were full of anxiety, but also full of important labors. He contemplated a political reconstruction of Switzerland, and a vast European league for the protection and promotion of Protestant interests.

He attended the theological Colloquy at Marburg (Sept. 29 to Oct. 3, 1529) in the hope of bringing about a union with the German Lutherans against the common foe at Rome. But Luther refused his hand of fellowship, and would not tolerate a theory of the Lord's Supper which he regarded as a dangerous heresy.[1]

While at Marburg, Zwingli made the personal acquaintance of the Landgraf, Philip of Hesse, and the fugitive Duke Ulrich of Würtemberg, who admired him, and sympathized with his theology as far as they understood it, but cared still more for their personal and political interests. He conceived with them the bold idea of a politico-ecclesiastical alliance of Protestant states and cities for the protection of religious liberty against the combined forces of the papacy and the empire which threatened that liberty. Charles V. had made peace with Clement VII., June 29, 1529, and crossed the

" Herr, nun heb den Wagen selb'!
Schelb [schief] wird sust [sonst]
All unser Fahrt.
Das brächt Lust
Der Widerpart,
Die dich
Veracht so freventlich.

Gott, erhöch den Namen dyn
In der Straf
Der bösen Böck!
Dyne Schaaf

Wiedrum erweck,
Die dich
Lieb haben inniglich!

Hilf, dass alle Bitterkeit
Scheide feer [fern],
Und alte Treu
Wiederkeer
Unde werde neu:
Dass wir
Ewig lobsingen Dir."

[1] See vol. VI. 629–653.

Alps in May, 1530, on his way to the Diet of Augsburg, offering to the Protestants bread with one hand, but concealing a stone in the other. Zwingli carried on a secret correspondence with Philip of Hesse from April 22, 1529, till Sept. 10, 1531.[1] He saw in the Roman empire the natural ally of the Roman papacy, and would not have lamented its overthrow.[2] Being a republican Swiss, he did not share in the loyal reverence of the monarchical Germans for their emperor. But all he could reasonably aim at was to curb the dangerous power of the emperor by strengthening the Protestant alliance. Further he did not go.[3]

He tried to draw into this alliance the republic of Venice and the kingdom of France, but failed. These powers were jealous of the grasping ambition of the house of Habsburg, but had no sympathy with evangelical reform. Francis I. was persecuting the Protestants at that very time in his own country.

It is dangerous to involve religion in entangling political alliances. Christ and the Apostles kept aloof from secular complications, and confined themselves to preaching the *ethics* of politics. Zwingli, with the best intentions, overstepped the line of his proper calling, and was doomed to bitter disappointment. Even Philip of Hesse, who pushed him into this net, grew cool, and joined the Lutheran League of Smalcald (1530), which would have nothing to do with the Protestants of Switzerland.

---

[1] See vol. VI. 633 sq., and Max Lenz, *Zwingli und Landgraf Philipp*, — three articles in Brieger's " Zeitschrift für Kirchengeschichte," 1879.

[2] " *Quid Germaniæ cum Roma ?* " he wrote to Conrad Som of Ulm in 1529 (*Opera*, VIII. 388). He reminded him of the German verse : —

" *Papstthum und Kaiserthum
Die sind beide von Rom.*"

[3] " *Von irgend einem Anschlag gegen den Kaiser,*" says Mörikofer, II. 299, " *war auch gar nie und von keiner Seite die Rede.*" Janssen, *Geschichte des deutschen Volkes*, III. 218 sq., unjustly charges Zwingli and Zürich with preaching open rebellion against the emperor, and attempting to replace him by the ambitious Landgraf of Hesse.

§ 45. *Zwingli's Last Theological Labors. His Confessions of Faith.*

During these fruitless political negotiations Zwingli never lost sight of his spiritual vocation. He preached and wrote incessantly; he helped the reform movement in every direction; he attended synods at Frauenfeld (May, 1530), at St. Gall (December, 1530), and Toggenburg (April, 1531); he promoted the organization and discipline of the Reformed churches, and developed great activity as an author. Some of his most important theological works — a commentary on the prophecies of Isaiah and Jeremiah, his treatise on Divine Providence, and two Confessions of Faith — belong to the last two years of his life.

He embraced the opportunity offered by the Diet of Augsburg to send a printed Confession of Faith to Charles V., July 8, 1530.[1] But it was treated with contempt, and not even laid before the Diet. Dr. Eck wrote a hasty reply, and denounced Zwingli as a man who did his best to destroy religion in Switzerland, and to incite the people to rebellion.[2] The Lutherans were anxious to conciliate the emperor, and repudiated all contact with Zwinglians and Anabaptists.[3]

A few months before his death (July, 1531) he wrote, at the request of his friend Maigret, the French ambassador at Zürich, a similar Confession addressed to King Francis I., to whom he had previously dedicated his "Commentary on the True and False Religion" (1524).[4] In this Confession he

---

[1] *Ratio Fidei*, etc., printed in *Opera*, vol. IV. 3–18, and in Niemeyer's *Collectio Confessionum* (1840), pp. 16–35. For an analysis see Schaff, *Ch. Hist.*, vol. VI. 721–723, and A. Baur, *Zwingli's Theologie*, II. 643 sqq.

[2] Zwingli sent an answer to the German princes assembled at Augsburg, dated Aug. 27, 1530. *Opera*, IV. 19–41.

[3] The Anabaptists are condemned (*damnant*) in Art. IX., the Zwinglians are disapproved (*improbant*) in Art. X., of the Augsburg Confession. See Melanchthon's *Judicium de Zwinglii doctrina*, written at Augsburg, July 25, 1530, in "Corpus Reform," II. 222 sq.

[4] *Christianæ Fidei brevis et clara Expositio*, in Zwingli's *Opera*, vol. IV. 42–78, and in Niemeyer's *Collectio*, pp. 36–77. For a summary, see Schaff, *Creeds of Christendom*, I. 368 sq., and Baur, *l.c.* II. 754–776.

discusses some of the chief points of controversy, — God and his Worship, the Person of Christ, Purgatory, the Real Presence, the Virtue of the Sacraments, the Civil Power, Remission of Sin, Faith and Good Works, Eternal Life, — and added an Appendix on the Eucharist and the Mass. He explains apologetically and polemically his doctrinal position in distinction from the Romanists, Lutherans, and Anabaptists. He begins with God as the ultimate ground of faith and only object of worship, and closes with an exhortation to the king to give the gospel free course in his kingdom. In the section on Eternal Life he expresses more strongly than ever his confident hope of meeting in heaven not only the saints of the Old and the New Dispensation from Adam down to the Apostles, but also the good and true and noble men of all nations and generations.[1]

This liberal extension of Christ's kingdom and Christ's salvation beyond the limits of the visible Church, although directly opposed to the traditional belief of the necessity of water baptism for salvation, was not altogether new. Justin Martyr, Origen, and other Greek fathers saw in the scattered

[1] " *Deinde sperandum est fore ut videas sanctorum, prudentium, fidelium, constantium, fortium virtuosorum omnium, quicunque a condito mundo fuerunt, sodalitatem, cœtum et contubernium. Hic duos Adamos, redemptum ac redemptorem: hic Abelum, Enochum, Noachum, Abrahamum, Isaacum, Judam, Mosen, Iosuam, Gedeonem, Samuelem, Pineam, Eliam, Eliscum, Iesaiam ac deiparam Virginem de qua ille præcinuit, Davidem, Ezekiam, Josiam, Baptistam, Petrum, Paulum : hic Herculem, Theseum, Socratem, Aristidem, Antigonum, Numam, Camillum, Catones, Scipiones : hic Ludovicum pium antecessoresque tuos, Ludovicos, Philippos, Pipinos, et quotquot in fide hinc migrarunt maiores tuos videbis. Denique non fuit vir bonus, non erit mens sancta, non est fidelis anima, ab ipso mundi exordio usque ad eius consummationem, quem non sis isthic cum deo visurus. Quo spectaculo quid lœtius, quid amoenius, quid denique honorificentius vel cogitari poterit ? Aut quo iustius omnes animi vires intendimus quam ad huiuscemodi vitœ lucrum ? " (Opera, IV. 65.)* The selection of examples might have been more judicious, or better be omitted altogether. It was this passage that so shocked Luther's churchly feelings that he called Zwingli a heathen. *Werke*, XXXII. 399 sq. " Bossuet," says Michelet (X. 311), " *cite ce passage pour en rire. Mais qui a un cœur le retiendra à jamais.*" There are few Protestant divines who would not agree with Zwingli as regards the salvation of unbaptized infants and pious heathen.

truths of the heathen poets and philosophers the traces of
the pre-Christian revelation of the Logos, and in the philosophy of the Greeks a schoolmaster to lead them to Christ.
The humanists of the school of Erasmus recognized a secondary inspiration in the classical writings, and felt tempted to
pray : " *Sancte Socrates, ora pro nobis.*" Zwingli was a humanist, but he had no sympathy with Pelagianism. On the
contrary, as we have shown previously, he traced salvation
to God's sovereign grace, which is independent of ordinary
means, and he first made a clear distinction between the
visible and the invisible Church. He did not intend, as he
has been often misunderstood, to assert the possibility of
salvation without Christ. " Let no one think," he wrote to
Urbanus Rhegius (a preacher at Augsburg), "that I lower
Christ; for whoever comes to God comes to him through
Christ. . . . The word, ' He who believeth not will be condemned,' applies only to those who can hear the gospel, but
not to children and heathen. . . . I openly confess that all
infants are saved by Christ, since grace extends as far as
sin. Whoever is born is saved by Christ from the curse of
original sin. If he comes to the knowledge of the law and
does the works of the law (Rom. 2 : 14, 26), he gives evidence
of his election. As Christians we have great advantages by
the knowledge of the gospel." He refers to the case of
Cornelius, who was pious before his baptism; and to the
teaching of Paul, who made the circumcision of the heart,
and not the circumcision of the flesh, the criterion of the
true Israelite (Rom. 2 : 28, 29).[1]

The Confession to Francis I. was the last work of Zwingli.
It was written three months before his death, and published
five years later (1536) by Bullinger, who calls it his "swan
song." The manuscript is preserved in the National Library
of Paris, but it is doubtful whether the king of France ever

---

[1] Comp. the remarks on pp. 95 sqq., and Schweizer's *Centraldogmen,* I.
94 sqq. and p. 131 sq.

saw it. Calvin dedicated to him his *Institutes*, with a most eloquent preface, but with no better success. Charles V. and Francis I. were as deaf to such appeals as the emperors of heathen Rome were to the Apologies of Justin Martyr and Tertullian. Had Francis listened to the Swiss Reformers, the history of France might have taken a different course.

§ 46. *The Second War of Cappel.* 1531.

EGLI: *Die Schlacht von Cappel, 1531.* Zürich, 1873. Comp. the lit. quoted § 42.

The political situation of Switzerland grew more and more critical. The treaty of peace was differently understood. The Forest Cantons did not mean to tolerate Protestantism in their own territory, and insulted the Reformed preachers ; nor would they concede to the local communities in the bailiwicks (St. Gall, Toggenburg, Thurgau, the Rheinthal) the right to introduce the Reformation by a majority vote ; while the Zürichers insisted upon both, and yet they prohibited the celebration of the mass in their own city and district. The Roman Catholic Cantons made new disloyal approaches to Austria, and sent a deputation to Charles V. at Augsburg which was very honorably received. The fugitive abbot of St. Gall also appeared with an appeal for aid to his restoration. The Zürichers were no less to blame for seeking the foreign aid of Hesse, Venice, and France. Bitter charges and counter-charges were made at the meetings of the Swiss Diet.[1]

[1] Bluntschli (who was a Protestant of Zürich) thinks that Zwingli and Zürich were upon the whole more to blame. He says, *l.c.* I. 334: "*Zwar hatte darin Zwingli ein richtiges politisches Princip ausgesprochen, dass im wirklichen ernsten Conflict zwischen der innern Berechtigung und dem äussern, formellen Recht am Ende dieses jener weichen müsse. Aber er hatte dieses Princip weder richtig angewendet ; denn ein solcher Widerspruch lag in dem eidgenössischen Bundesrecht denn doch nicht oder lange nicht in dem angegebenen Masse vor, noch waren die Mittel, welche er vorschlug, um ein vermeintlich besseres, weil natürlicheres Recht herzustellen, zu rechtfertigen. Und musste ein gerechter Mann zugeben, dass die Fünf Orte auch ihre Stellung nicht rein erhielten von Missbrauch, so war doch nicht zu läugnen, dass damals auf Seite der Städte und insbesondere Zürichs der Miss-*

The crisis was aggravated by an international difficulty. Graubünden sent deputies to the Diet with an appeal for aid against the Chatelan of Musso and the invasion of the Valtellina by Spanish troops. The Reformed Cantons favored co-operation, the Roman Catholic Cantons refused it. The expedition succeeded, the castle of Musso was demolished, and the Grisons took possession of the Valtellina (1530–32).

Zwingli saw no solution of the problem except in an honest, open war, or a division of the bailiwicks among the Cantons according to population, claiming two-thirds for Zürich and Bern. These bailiwicks were, as already remarked, the chief bone of contention. But Bern advocated, instead of war, a blockade of the Forest Cantons. This was apparently a milder though actually a more cruel course. The Waldstätters in their mountain homes were to be cut off from all supplies of grain, wine, salt, iron, and steel, for which they depended on their richer Protestant neighbors.[1] Zwingli protested. "If you have a right," he said in the pulpit, "to starve the Five Cantons to death, you have a right to attack them in open war. They will now attack you with the courage of desperation." He foresaw the disastrous result. But his protest was in vain. Zürich yielded to the counsel of Bern, which was adopted by the Protestant deputies, May 15, 1531.

The decision of the blockade was communicated to the Forest Cantons, and vigorously executed, Zürich taking the

brauch ihrer Stellung in eidgenössischen Dingen grösser war, dass somit die Städte sich durchaus nicht eigneten, als Vertreter der ' göttlichen Gerechtigkeit und Strafe' die Fünf Orte von ihren hergebrachten Rechten zu entsetzen. Auch in der auswärtigen Politik verliess Zwingli nun die Grundsätze des eidgenössischen Rechtes, die er selber vorher mit Nachdruck vertheidigt hatte. Er ging in reformatorischem Eifer Verbindungen ein und nahm an politischen Planen Theil, welche den Frieden und selbst die Existenz der Eidgenossenschaft gefährden mussten."

[1] Zürich was charged by Bern with an excess of passion, Bern by Zürich with an excess of prudence. In the language of Zwingli: —

" Bern klagt : Zürich ist zu hitzig,
Zürich klagt : Bern ist zu witzig."

lead. All supplies of provision from Zürich and Bern and even from the bailiwicks of St. Gall, Toggenburg, Sargans, and the Rheinthal were withheld. The previous year had been a year of famine and of a wasting epidemic (the sweating sickness). This year was to become one of actual starvation. Old men, innocent women and children were to suffer with the guilty. The cattle was deprived of salt. The Waldstätters were driven to desperation. Their own confederates refused them the daily bread, forgetful of the Christian precept, "If thine enemy hunger, feed him; if he thirst, give him to drink; for in so doing thou shalt heap coals of fire upon his head. Be not overcome with evil, but overcome evil with good" (Rom. 12: 20, 21).

Zwingli spent the last months before his death in anxiety and fear. His counsel had been rejected, and yet he was blamed for all these troubles. He had not a few enemies in Zürich, who undermined his influence, and inclined more and more to the passive policy of Bern. Under these circumstances, he resolved to withdraw from the public service. On the 26th of July he appeared before the Great Council, and declared, "Eleven years have I preached to you the gospel, and faithfully warned you against the dangers which threaten the confederacy if the Five Cantons — that is, those who hate the gospel and live on foreign pensions — are allowed to gain the mastery. But you do not heed my voice, and continue to elect members who sympathize with the enemies of the gospel. And yet ye make me responsible for all this misfortune. Well, I herewith resign, and shall elsewhere seek my support."

He left the hall with tears. His resignation was rejected and withdrawn. After three days he appeared again before the Great Council, and declared that in view of their promise of improvement he would stand by them till death, and do his best, with God's help. He tried to persuade the Bernese delegates at a meeting in Bremgarten in the house of his friend, Henry Bullinger, to energetic action, but in vain. " May God protect you, dear Henry; remain faithful to the Lord Jesus Christ and his Church."

These were the last words he spoke to his worthy successor. As he left, a mysterious personage, clothed in a snow-white robe, suddenly appeared, and after frightening the guards at the gate plunged into the water, and vanished. He had a strong foreboding of an approaching calamity, and did not expect to survive it. Halley's comet, which returns every seventy-six years, appeared in the skies from the middle of August to the 3d of September, burning like the fire of a furnace, and pointing southward with its immense tail of pale yellow color. Zwingli saw in it the sign of war and of his own death. He said to a friend in the graveyard of the minster (Aug. 10), as he gazed at the ominous star, " It will cost the life of many an honorable man and my own. The truth and the Church will suffer, but Christ will never forsake us." [1] Vadian of St. Gall likewise regarded the comet as a messenger of God's wrath; and the famous Theophrastus, who was at that time in St. Gall, declared that it foreboded great bloodshed and the death of illustrious men. It was then the universal opinion, shared also by Luther and Melanchthon, that comets, meteors, and eclipses were fireballs of an angry God. A frantic woman near Zürich saw blood springing from the earth all around her, and rushed into the street with the cry, "Murder, murder!" The atmosphere was filled with apprehensions of war and bloodshed. The blockade was continued, and all attempts at a compromise failed.

The Forest Cantons had only one course to pursue. The

[1] Bullinger, III. 46 (comp. 137): " *Min Jörg* [the Abbot Georg Müller of Wettingen], *mich und mengen eeren man* [*manchen Ehrenmann*] *wirt es kosten, und wirt die wahrheit und Kylch* [*Kirche*] *nodt lyden ; doch von Christus werdent wir nit verlassen.*" Another contemporary gives an account of a conversation of Dr. Joachim von Watt with some friends about the meaning of the comet's appearance. It was published in the " Schweizerische Museum," II. 335.

law of self-preservation drove them to open war. It was forced upon them as a duty. Fired by indignation against the starvation policy of their enemies, and inspired by love for their own families, the Waldstätters promptly organized an army of eight thousand men, and marched to the frontier of Zürich between Zug and Cappel, Oct. 9, 1531.

The news brought consternation and terror to the Zürichers, The best opportunity had passed. Discontent and dissension paralyzed vigorous action. Frightful omens demoralized the people. Zürich, which two years before might easily have equipped an army of five thousand, could now hardly collect fifteen hundred men against the triple force of the enemy, who had the additional advantage of fighting for life and home.

Zwingli would not forsake his flock in this extreme danger. He mounted his horse to accompany the little army to the battle-field with the presentiment that he would never return. The horse started back, like the horse of Napoleon when he was about to cross the Niemen. Many regarded this as a bad omen; but Zwingli mastered the animal, applied the spur, and rode to Cappel, determined to live or to die with the cause of the Reformation.

The battle raged several hours in the afternoon of the eleventh of October, and was conducted by weapons and stones, after the manner of the Swiss, and with much bravery on both sides. After a stubborn resistance, the Zürichers were routed, and lost the flower of their citizens, over five hundred men, including seven members of the Small Council, nineteen members of the Great Council of the Two Hundred, and several pastors who had marched at the head of their flocks.[1]

---

[1] Bullinger, III. 130, gives the names. The total number of the slain and mortally wounded Zürichers was five hundred and fourteen, while the Five Cantons lost only about eighty. The leaders of the army, Georg Göldli and Lavater, escaped, and were charged, the first with treason, the other with incompetency.

§ 47. *The Death of Zwingli.*

MÖRIKOFER, II. 414–420. — EGLI, quoted on p. 179. — A. ERICHSON: *Zwingli's Tod und dessen Beurtheilung durch Zeitgenosen.* Strassburg, 1883.

Zwingli himself died on the battle-field, in the prime of manhood, aged forty-seven years, nine months, and eleven days, and with him his brother-in-law, his step-son, his son-in-law, and his best friends. He made no use of his weapons, but contented himself with cheering the soldiers.[1] "Brave men," he said (according to Bullinger), "fear not! Though we must suffer, our cause is good. Commend your souls to God: he can take care of us and ours. His will be done."

Soon after the battle had begun, he stooped down to console a dying soldier, when a stone was hurled against his head by one of the Waldstätters and prostrated him to the ground. Rising again, he received several other blows, and a thrust from a lance. Once more he uplifted his head, and, looking at the blood trickling from his wounds, he exclaimed: "What matters this misfortune? They may kill the body, but they cannot kill the soul." These were his last words.[2]

He lay for some time on his back under a pear-tree (called the *Zwingli-Baum*) in a meadow, his hands folded as in prayer, and his eyes steadfastly turned to heaven.[3]

The stragglers of the victorious army pounced like hungry vultures upon the wounded and dying. Two of them asked Zwingli to confess to a priest, or to call upon the dear saints

---

[1] "*Zwingli blieb in nächster Nähe bei den Kämpfenden stehen, machte aber nach dem Zeugniss von Freund und Feind von seinen Waffen keinen Gebrauch.*" Mörikofer, II. 417.

[2] According to Osw. Myconius (*Vita H. Zwingli*, ch. 12), who gives the report of an eye-witness: "*Prostratum, ajebat, prementium multitudine jam tertio, sed in pedes semper restitisse: quarto fixum cuspide sub mento et in genua prolapsum dixisse: ' Ecquid hoc infortunii? Age, corpus quidem occidere possunt, animam non possunt.' Atque his dictis mox obdormivisse in Domino.*"

[3] Bullinger, III. 136: "*und verharret mitt sinem Gesicht zu stunen am hymel.*" According to Tschudi, he lay on his face. Salat also says ("Archiv," etc., I. 310): "*Zwingli ward funden ligend uf sim angsicht.*" But this is not necessarily a contradiction, as the dying man may have changed his position.

for their intercession. He shook his head twice, and kept his eyes still fixed on the heavens above. Then Captain Vokinger of Unterwalden, one of the foreign mercenaries, against whom the Reformer had so often lifted his voice, recognized him by the torch-light, and killed him with the sword, exclaiming, " Die, obstinate heretic." [1]

There he lay during the night. On the next morning the people gathered around the dead, and began to realize the extent of the victory. Everybody wanted to see Zwingli. Chaplain Stocker of Zug, who knew him well, made the remark that his face had the same fresh and vigorous expression as when he kindled his hearers with the fire of eloquence from the pulpit. Hans Schönbrunner, an ex-canon of Fraumünster in Zürich, as he passed the corpse of the Reformer, with Chaplain Stocker, burst into tears, and said, " Whatever may have been thy faith, thou hast been an honest patriot. May God forgive thy sins." [2] He voiced the sentiment of the better class of Catholics.

But the fanatics and foreign mercenaries would not even spare the dead. They decreed that his body should be quartered for treason and then burnt for heresy, according to the Roman and imperial law. The sheriff of Luzern executed the barbarous sentence. Zwingli's ashes were mingled with the ashes of swine, and scattered to the four winds of heaven. [3]

---

[1] Salat says that the man who did this cowardly act, was " *ein redlicher altcr Christ*," but does not name Vokinger (also spelt Fuckinger, or Fugginger).

[2] Mörikofer, II. 418.

[3] According to an uncertain and improbable tradition, the heart was, as it were, miraculously saved, and brought to Zürich, but thrown into the river to prevent idolatry. Myconius (*Vita Zw.*, c. 12) reports: " *Hostibus digressis, post diem tertium accedunt amantes Zwinglii, si quid reliquiarum eius offenderent, et ecce cor (mirabile dictu) se offert e mediis cineribus integrum et illæsum . . . Venit non multo postea vir mihi notissimus, sed et familiarissimus [Thomas Plater ?], rogans an portionem cordis cupiam videre Zwingliani, quod secum ferat in loculo : quia propter sermonem hunc inopinatum horror quidam totum corpus pervaserat, negaram, alioquin et huius rei possem esse testis oculatus.*"

The news of the disaster at Cappel spread terror among the citizens of Zürich. "Then," says Bullinger, "arose a loud and horrible cry of lamentation and tears, bewailing and groaning."

On no one fell the sudden stroke with heavier weight than on the innocent widow of Zwingli: she had lost, on the same day, her husband, a son, a brother, a son-in-law, a brother-in-law, and her most intimate friends. She remained alone with her weeping little children, and submitted in pious resignation to the mysterious will of God. History is silent about her grief; but it has been vividly and touchingly described in the Zürich dialect by Martin Usteri in a poem for the tercentenary Reformation festival in Zürich (1819).[1]

Bullinger, Zwingli's successor, took the afflicted widow into his house, and treated her as a member of his family. She survived her husband seven years, and died in peace.

---

[1] *Der armen Frow Zwinglin Klag*, published in the "Alpenrosen," Bern, 1820, p. 273; in Zwingli's *Werke*, II. B. 281; also in Christoffel, I. 413, and Mörikofer, II. 517. After giving vent to her woe, Anna Zwingli resorts to the Bible, which was her husband's comfort, and was to be hers. I select the first and the last of the fourteen stanzas of this poem, which Mörikofer numbers among "the imperishable monuments of the great man."

> 1. " *O Herre Gott, wie heftig shluog*
>   *Mich dynes Zornes Ruthen!*
>   *Du armes Herz, ist's nit genuog,*
>   *Kannst du noch nicht verbluoten?*
>   *Ich ring die Händ:*
>   *Käm' doch myn End!*
>   *Wer mag myn Elend fassen?*
>   *Wer misst die Not?*
>   *Myn Gott, Myn Gott,*
>   *Hast du mich gar verlassen?*
>
> . . . .
>
> 14. " *Komm du, o Buoch! du warst syn Hort,*
>   *Syn Trost in allem Uebel.*
>   *Ward er verfolgt mit That und Wort,*
>   *So griff er nach der Bibel,*
>   *Fand Hilf bei ihr.*
>   *Herr, zeige mir*
>   *Die Hilf in Jesu Namen!*
>   *Gib Muoth und Stärk*
>   *Zum schweren Werk*
>   *Dem schwachen Wybe! Amen.*"

A few steps from the pear-tree where Zwingli breathed his last, on a slight elevation, in view of the old church and abbey of Cappel, of the Rigi, Pilatus, and the more distant snow-capped Alps, there arises a plain granite monument, erected in 1838, mainly by the exertions of Pastor Esslinger, with suitable Latin and German inscriptions.[1]

A few weeks after Zwingli, his friend Œcolampadius died peacefully in his home at Basel (Nov. 24, 1531). The enemies spread the rumor that he had committed suicide. They deemed it impossible that an arch-heretic could die a natural death.[2]

§ 48. *Reflections on the Disaster at Cappel.*

We need not wonder that the religious and political enemies of Zwingli interpreted the catastrophe at Cappel as a signal judgment of God and a punishment for heresy. It is the tendency of superstition in all ages to connect misfortune with a particular sin. Such an uncharitable interpretation of Providence is condemned by the example of Job, the fate of prophets, apostles, and martyrs, and the express rebuke of the disciples by our Saviour in the case of the man born blind (John 9:31). But it is found only too often among Christians. It is painful to record that Luther, the great champion of the liberty of conscience, under the influence of his mediæval training, and unmindful of the adage, *De mortuis nihil nisi bonum*, surpassed even the most virulent Catholics in the abuse of Zwingli after his death. It is a sad com-

---

[1] Mrs. Meta Heusser (d. 1876), the most gifted Swiss poetess, who lived a few miles from Cappel, wrote two beautiful poems for the dedication of the monument, Oct. 11, 1838, which are printed in the first series of her *Lieder*, pp. 189 sqq. I quote the first stanza of the second poem: —

> " *Die Stätte, wo ein Heldenauge brach*
> *Ist theuer noch den spätEn Enkelsöhnen;*
> *Es schweigt der Todtenklage banges Ach,*
> *Verschlungen von des Sieges Jubeltönen.*"

[2] See above, § 31, pp. 115 sq., and the note on p. 188.

mentary on the narrowness and intolerance of the Re-former.[1]

The faithful friends of evangelical freedom and progress in Switzerland revered Zwingli as a martyr, and regarded the defeat at Cappel as a wholesome discipline or a blessing in disguise. Bullinger voiced their sentiments. "The victory of truth," he wrote after the death of his teacher and friend, "stands alone in God's power and will, and is not bound to person or time. Christ was crucified, and his enemies imagined they had conquered; but forty years afterwards Christ's victory became manifest in the destruction of Jerusalem. The truth conquers through tribulation and trial. The strength of the Christians is shown in weakness. Therefore, beloved brethren in Germany, take no offence at our defeat,

---

[1] In his letter to Albrecht of Prussia, April, 1532 (in De Wette, IV. 348–355), Luther expresses a doubt about Zwingli's salvation (on account of his denial of the corporal presence). He scorns the idea that he was a martyr; he regrets that the Catholic Cantons did not complete their victory by suppressing the Zwinglian heresy, and he warns the Duke of Prussia not to tolerate it in his dominion. In his furious polemic tract, *Short Confession of the Holy Sacrament*, written in 1545, a year before his death (*Werke*, Erlangen ed., vol. XXXII. 399–401, 410), Luther says that "Zwingel" (he always misspells his name) and Œcolampadius "perished in their sins"; that Zwingli died "in great and many sins and blasphemy" (*in grossen und vielen Sünden und Gotteslästerung*), having expressed a hope for the salvation of such "*gottlose Heiden*" as Socrates, Aristides, and the "*greuliche Numa*"; that he became a heathen; and that he perished by the sword because he took up the sword. He adds that he, Martin Luther, "would rather a hundred times be torn to pieces and burned than make common cause with Stenkefeld [Stinkfeld for Schwenkfeld], Zwingel, Carlstadt, and Œcolampadius!" *O sancta simplicitas!* How different is the conduct and judgment of Zwingli, who, at Marburg, with tears in his eyes, offered the hand of brotherhood to his great antagonist, and who said of him in the very heat of the eucharistic controversy: "Luther is so excellent a warrior of God, and searches the Scriptures with such great earnestness as no one on earth for these thousand years has done; and no one has ever equalled him in manly, unshaken spirit with which he has attacked the pope of Rome. He was the true David whom the Lord himself appointed to slay Goliath. He hurled the stones taken from the heavenly brook so skilfully that the giant fell prostrate on the ground. Saul has slain thousands, but David tens of thousands. He was the Hercules who rushed always to the post of danger in battle.... Therefore we should justly thank God for having raised such an instrument for his honor; and this we do with pleasure."

but persevere in the Word of God, which has always won the victory, though in its defence the holy prophets, apostles, and martyrs suffered persecution and death. Blessed are those who die in the Lord. Victory will follow in time. A thousand years before the eyes of the Lord are but as one day. He, too, is victorious who suffers and dies for the sake of truth."[1]

It is vain to speculate on mere possibilities. But it is more than probable that a victory of the Protestants at that time would have been in the end more injurious to their cause than defeat. The Zürichers would have forced the Reformation upon the Forest Cantons and all the bailiwicks, and would thereby have provoked a reaction which, with the aid of Austria and Spain and the counter-Reformation of the papacy, might have ended in the destruction of Protestantism, as it actually did in the Italian dependencies of Switzerland and the Grisons, in Italy, Spain, and Bohemia.

It was evidently the will of Providence that in Switzerland, as well as in Germany, both Churches, the Roman Catholic and the Evangelical, should co-exist, and live in mutual toleration and useful rivalry for a long time to come.

We must judge past events in the light of subsequent events and final results. " By their fruits ye shall know them."

The death of Zwingli is a heroic tragedy. He died for God and his country. He was a martyr of religious liberty and of the independence of Switzerland. He was right in his aim to secure the freedom of preaching in all the Cantons and bailiwicks, and to abolish the military pensions which made the Swiss tributary to foreign masters. But he had no right to coërce the Catholics, and to appeal to the sword. He was mistaken in the means, and he anticipated the proper time. It took nearly three centuries before these reforms could be executed.

---

[1] Christoffel, I. 409. Comp. also the beautiful preface of Zwingli to the history of the passion, in which he shows his readiness to die for Christ, quoted by Mörikofer, II. 415.

In 1847 the civil war in Switzerland was renewed in a different shape and under different conditions. The same Forest Cantons which had combined against the Reformation and for the foreign pensions, and had appealed to the aid of Austria, formed a confederacy within the confederacy (*Sonderbund*) against modern political liberalism, and again entered into an alliance with Austria; but at this time they were defeated by the federal troops under the wise leadership of General Dufour of Geneva, with very little bloodshed.[1] In the year 1848 while the revolution raged in other countries, the Swiss Diet quickly remodelled the constitution, and transformed the loose confederacy of independent Cantons into a federal union, after the model of the United States, with a representation of the people (in the *Nationalrath*) and a central government, acting directly upon the people. The federal constitution of 1848 guaranteed "the free exercise of public worship to the recognized Confessions" (*i.e.* the Roman Catholic and Reformed); the Revised Constitution of 1874 extended this freedom, within the limits of morality and public safety, to all other denominations; only the order of the Jesuits was excluded, for political reasons.

This liberty goes much further than Zwingli's plan, who would have excluded heretical sects. There are now, on the one hand, Protestant churches at Luzern, Baar, Brunnen, in the very heart of the Five Cantons (besides the numerous Anglican Episcopal, Scotch Presbyterian, and other services in all the Swiss summer resorts); and on the other hand, Roman Catholic churches in Zürich, Bern,

---

[1] The Swiss *Sonderbunds-Krieg* was an anticipation, on a small scale, of the Civil War in the United States, though the causes were different. In both cases the confederates rebelled against the federal government, and sought the aid of their hereditary enemy; the Swiss of the Catholic Forest Cantons that of Austria, the Americans of the slave-holding Southern States that of England. For a clear sketch of the *Sonderbunds-Krieg*, see Vuillemin, *Geschichte der Schweizerischen Eidgenossenschaft* (1882), pp. 517–537.

Basel, Geneva, where the mass was formerly rigidly prohibited.

As regards the foreign military service which had a tendency to denationalize the Swiss, Zwingli's theory has completely triumphed. The only relic of that service is the hundred Swiss guards, who, with their picturesque mediæval uniform, guard the pope and the Vatican. They are mostly natives of the Five Forest Cantons.

Thus history explains and rectifies itself, and fulfils its promises.

NOTES.

There is a striking correspondence between the constitution of the old Swiss Diet and the constitution of the old American Confederacy, as also between the modern Swiss constitution and that of the United States. The Swiss Diet seems to have furnished an example to the American Confederacy, and the Congress of the United States was a model to the Swiss Diet in 1848. The legislative power of Switzerland is vested in the Assembly of the Confederacy (*Bundesversammlung*) or Congress, which consists of the National Council (*Nationalrath*) or House of Representatives, elected by the people, — one out of twenty thousand, — and the Council of Cantons (*Ständerath*) or Senate, composed of forty-four delegates of the twenty-two Cantons (two from each) and corresponding to the old Diet. The executive power is exercised by the Council of the Confederacy (*Bundesrath*), which consists of seven members, and is elected every three years by the two branches of the legislature, one of them acting as President (*Bundespräsident*) for the term of one year (while the President of the United States is chosen by the people for four years, and selects his own cabinet. Hence the head of the Swiss Confederacy has very little power for good or evil, and is scarcely known). To the Supreme Court of the United States corresponds the *Bundesgericht*, which consists of eleven judges elected by the legislature for three years, and decides controversies between the Cantons. Comp. Bluntschli's *Geschichte des Schweizerischen Bundesrechts*, 1875; Rüttimann, *Das nordamerikanische Bundesstaatsrecht verglichen mit den politischen Einrichtungen der Schweiz*, Zürich, 1867–72, 2 vols.; and Sir Francis O. Adams and C. D. Cunningham, *The Swiss Confederation*, French translation with notes and additions by Henry G. Loumyer, and preface by L. Ruchonnet, Geneva, 1890.

The provisions of the Federal Constitution of Switzerland, May 29, 1874, in regard to religion, are as follows : —

Abschnitt I. Art. 49. " *Die Glaubens- und Gewissensfreiheit ist unverletzlich.*

Niemand darf zur Theilnahme an einer Religionsgenossenschaft, oder an einem religiösen Unterricht, oder zur Vornahme einer religiösen Handlung gezwungen, oder wegen Glaubensansichten mit Strafen irgend welcher Art belegt werden. . . .

Art. 50. *Die freie Ausübung gottesdienstlicher Handlungen ist innerhalb der Schranken der Sittlichkeit und der öffentlichen Ordnung gewährleistet.* . . .

Art. 51. *Der Orden der Jesuiten und die ihm affiliirten Gesellschaften dürfen in keinem Theile der Schweiz Aufnahme finden, und es ist ihren Gliedern jede Wirksamkeit in Kirche und Schule untersagt.*"

The same Constitution forbids the civil and military officers of the Confederation to receive pensions or titles or decorations from any foreign government.

I. Art. 12. "*Die Mitglieder der Bundesbehörden, die eidgenössischen Civil- und Militärbeamten und die eidgenössischen Repräsentanten oder Kommissarien dürfen von auswärtigen Regierungen weder Pensionen oder Gehalte, noch Titel, Geschenke oder Orden annehmen.*"

§ 49. *The Second Peace of Cappel.* November, 1531.

Besides the works already quoted, see WERNER BIEL's account of the immediate consequences of the war of Cappel in the "Archiv für Schweizerische Reformationsgeschichte" (Rom. Cath.), vol. III. 641–680. He was at that time the secretary of the city of Zürich. The articles of the Peace in HOTTINGER, *Schweizergeschichte*, VII. 497 sqq., and in BLUNTSCHLI, *l.c.* II. 269–276 (comp. I. 332 sqq.).

Few great battles have had so much effect upon the course of history as the little battle of Cappel. It arrested forever the progress of the Reformation in German Switzerland, and helped to check the progress of Protestantism in Germany. It encouraged the Roman Catholic reaction, which soon afterwards assumed the character of a formidable Counter-Reformation. But, while the march of Protestantism was arrested in its original homes, it made new progress in French Switzerland, in France, Holland, and the British Isles.

King Ferdinand of Austria gave the messenger of the Five Cantons who brought him the news of their victory at Cappel, fifty guilders, and forthwith informed his brother Charles V. at Brussels of the fall of "the great heretic Zwingli," which he thought was the first favorable event for the faith of the Catholic Church. The Emperor lost no time to congratulate the Forest Cantons on their victory, and to promise them his own aid and the aid of the pope, of his brother, and the Catholic princes, in case the Protestants should persevere in their opposition. The pope had already sent men and means for the support of his party.

The disaster of Cappel was a prelude to the disaster of Mühlberg on the Elbe, where Charles V. defeated the Smal-caldian League of the Lutheran princes, April 24, 1547. Luther was spared the humiliation. The victorious emperor stood on his grave at Wittenberg, but declined to make war upon the dead by digging up and burning his bones, as he was advised to do by his Spanish generals.

The war of Cappel was continued for a few weeks. Zürich rallied her forces as best she could. Bern, Basel, and Schaff-hausen sent troops, but rather reluctantly, and under the demoralizing effect of defeat. There was a want of har-mony and able leadership in the Protestant camp. The Forest Cantons achieved another victory on the Gubel (Oct. 24), and plundered and wasted the territory of Zürich; but as the winter approached, and as they did not receive the promised aid from Austria, they were inclined to peace. Bern acted as mediator.

The second religious Peace (the so-called *Zweite Lands-friede*) was signed Nov. 20, 1531,[1] between the Five Forest Cantons and the Zürichers, on the meadows of Teynikon, near Baar, in the territory of Zug, and confirmed Nov. 24 at Aarau by the consent of Bern, Glarus, Freiburg, and Appen-zell. It secured mutual toleration, but with a decided advan-tage to the Roman Catholics.

The chief provisions of the eight articles as regards relig-ion were these: —

1. The Five Cantons and their associates are to be left undisturbed in their "true, undoubted, Christian faith"; the Zürichers and their associates may likewise retain their "faith," but with the exception of Bremgarten, Mellingen, Rapperschwil, Toggenburg, Gaster, and Wesen. Legal tol-eration or parity was thus recognized, but in a manner which implies a slight reproach of the Reformed creed as a depar-

---

[1] It was concluded Nov. 16, but dated Nov. 20.

ture from the truth. Mutual recrimination was again prohibited, as in 1529.[1]

2. Both parties retain their rights and liberties in the

[1] The following is the Swiss-German text of the first article (Bluntschli, II. 271), which may be compared with the first article of the Peace of 1529 (see above, p. 171 sq.) : *"Zum ersten sollent und wollent Wir, die von Zürich, unsre getrüwe liebe Eydgenossen von den V Orten* [*i.e.* the Five Forest Cantons of the old confederacy], *dessglichen auch ihr lieb Mitbürger und Landlüt von Wallis und alle ihre Mithaften, si syegent geistlich oder weltlich, by ihrem waaren ungezwyffleten, christenlichen Glauben jetzt und hernach in ihren eignen Städten, Landen, Gebieten und Herrlichkeiten gänzlich ungearguirt und ungedisputirt blyben lassen, all böss Fünd, Uszüg, Gefährd und Arglist vermieden und hintangesetzt. — Hinwiderum so wöllent Wir, von den V Orten, unser Eydgnossen von Zürich und ihre eigne Mitverwandten by ihrem Glauben auch blyben lassen. Wir von den V Orten behaltend uns in diesem Frieden luter vor alle, die uns sampt und sonders mit Burg und Landrecht, auch in ander Wäg verwandt sind, auch all die, so uns Hilf, Rath, Bystand und Zuzug bewiesen und gethan, also dass die harin luter mit uns begriffen und verfaszt syn söllent. — Hinwiederum so behaltet Wir von Zürich uns vor, das die, so uns Hilf, Rath, Bystand und Zuzug gethan vor und in disem Krieg es sye in Abschlagung der Profiant oder in ander Weg, dass die auch in diesem Frieden vergriffen syn söllent. — Wyter so behaltend Wir, von den V Orten uns vor und durgent luter us, die us den fryen Aemptern im Ergöuw, Bremgarten, und Mellingen, so sich denen von Bern anhängig gemacht, ihnen zuzogen, und, uns zu überziehen, Vorschub gethan, dessglychen sie die Berner noch ufenthaltend, desshalben ihnen viellichter der Frieden nit annehmlich syn, zudem unsser Nothdurft zu Usführung des Kriegs gegen den Berneren will erforderen, dass man dasselbst Durchzug haben möcht, desshalb wir sie jetzmalen zu diesem Frieden nit begriffen lassent. Dessglychen behaltend Wir auch luter vor, die von Rapperschwyl, Toggenburg, Gastern und die von Wesen, so unsser Eydgnossen von Zürich nutzit angahnt noch verwandt sind, dass die in disem Frieden auch usgeschlossen und nit begriffen syn söllent, doch dass nach Gnaden und in Ziemlichkeit mit ihnen gehandlet werd, mit Straf oder mit Recht."* Bluntschli (I. 337) thus comments on this article : *"Auch jetzt wieder musste zunächst das Princip, dass beide Confessionen Geltung haben, das Princip der Parität, den verschiedenen eidgenössischen Ständen gegenüber anerkannt werden. Aber die Form, wie das geschah, war verletzend für die Reformirten. Es lag darin offenbar ein Hohn gegen diese, dass sie zu einem Vertrage ihre Zustimmung geben mussten, in welchem der katholische Glaube als der 'reine, unbezweifelte, christliche Glaube,' die Confession der Reformirten dagegen nur als 'ein Glaube,' schlechthin bezeichnet ward ; ein Spott, der immerhin von ungleicher Würdigung der beiden Confessionen ausging und insofern dem wahren Geiste des paritätischen Staatsprincips widersprach. Diese Herabsetzung und Demüthigung der Reformirten lag zwar nur in dem Ausdruck, nicht in dem Inhalt dieser Bestimmung. Aber gerade darum war sie um so weniger zu rechtfertigen. Sie reizte und erbitterte bloss den einen Theil, und kitzelte nur den Hochmuth des andern Theils. Wollte man ernstlich und auf die Dauer Frieden, so durfte man nicht solcher Gehässigkeit den Lauf lassen."*

common bailiwicks : those who had accepted the new faith
might retain it; but those who preferred the old faith should
be free to return to it, and to restore the mass, and the
images. In mixed congregations the church property is to
be divided according to population.

Zürich was required to give up her league with foreign
cities, as the Five Cantons had been compelled in 1529 to
break their alliance with Austria. Thus all leagues with
foreign powers, whether papal or Protestant, were forbidden
in Switzerland as unpatriotic. Zürich had to refund the
damages of two hundred and fifty crowns for war expenses,
and one hundred crowns for the family of Kaiser, which had
been imposed upon the Forest Cantons in 1529. Bern agreed
in addition to pay three thousand crowns for injury to property in the territory of Zug.

The two treaties of peace agree in the principle of toleration (as far as it was understood in those days, and forced
upon the two parties by circumstances), but with the opposite application to the neutral territory of the bailiwicks,
where the Catholic minority was protected against further
aggression. The treaty of 1529 meant a toleration chiefly
in the interest and to the advantage of Protestantism; the
treaty of 1531, a toleration in the interest of Romanism.

§ 50. *The Roman Catholic Reaction.*

The Romanists reaped now the full benefit of their victory.
They were no longer disturbed by the aggressive movements
of Protestant preachers, and they regained much of the lost
ground in the bailiwicks.

Romanism was restored in Rapperschwil and Gaster. The
abbot of St. Gall regained his convent and heavy damages
from the city; Toggenburg had to acknowledge his authority,
but a portion of the people remained Reformed. Thurgau
and the Rheinthal had to restore the convents. Bremgarten

and Mellingen had to pledge themselves to re-introduce the mass and the images. In Glarus, the Roman Catholic minority acquired several churches and preponderating influence in the public affairs of the Canton. In Solothurn, the Reformation was suppressed, in spite of the majority of the population, and about seventy families were compelled to emigrate. In the Diet, the Roman Cantons retained a plurality of votes.

The inhabitants of the Forest Cantons, full of gratitude, made a devout pilgrimage to St. Mary of Einsiedeln, where Zwingli had copied the Epistles of St. Paul from the first printed edition of the Greek Testament in 1516, and where he, Leo Judæ, and Myconius had labored in succession for a reformation of abuses, with the consent of Diepold von Geroldseck. That convent has remained ever since a stronghold of Roman Catholic piety and superstition in Switzerland, and attracts as many devout pilgrims as ever to the shrine of the "Black Madonna." It has one of the largest printing establishments, which sends prayer-books, missals, breviaries, diurnals, rituals, pictures, crosses, and crucifixes all over the German-speaking Catholic world.[1]

Bullinger, who succeeded Zwingli, closes his "History of the Reformation" mournfully, yet not without resignation and hope. "All manner of tyranny and overbearance," he says, "is restored and strengthened, and an insolent *régime* is working the ruin of the confederacy. Wonderful are the counsels of the Lord. But he doeth all things well. To him be glory and praise! Amen."

NOTE ON THE CONVENT OF EINSIEDELN.

(Comp. § 8, pp. 29 sqq.)

On a visit to Einsiedeln, June 12, 1890, I saw in the church a number of pilgrims kneeling before the wonder-working statue of the Black Madonna. The statue is kept in a special chapel, is coal-black, clothed in a silver gar-

---

[1] The firm of "Benziger Brothers, Printers to the Holy Apostolic See," Einsiedeln, New York, Cincinnati, and Chicago. The various illustrated catalogues of this establishment give an idea of the immense extent of its operations.

ment, crowned with a golden crown, surrounded by gilt ornaments, and holding the Christ-Child in her arms. The black color is derived by some from the smoke of fire which repeatedly consumed the church, while the statue is believed to have miraculously escaped; but the librarian (Mr. Meier) told me that it was from the smoke of candles, and that the face of the Virgin is now painted with oil.

The library of the abbey numbers 40,000 volumes (including 900 incunabula), among them several copies of the first print of Zwingli's *Commentary on the true and false Religion*, and other books of his. In the picture-gallery are life-size portraits of King Frederick William IV. of Prussia, his brother, the Prince of Prussia (afterwards Emperor William I. of Germany), of Napoleon III. and Eugenie, of the Emperor Francis Joseph of Austria and his wife, and their unfortunate son who committed suicide in 1889, and of Pope Pius IX. These portraits were presented to the convent on its tenth centenary

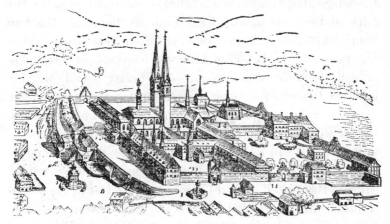

THE ABBEY OF EINSIEDELN IN THE 15TH AND 16TH CENTURIES.

in 1861. The convent was founded by St. Meinhard, a hermit, in the ninth century, or rather by St. Benno, who died there in 940. The abbey has now nearly 100 Benedictine monks, a gymnasium with 260 pupils of twelve to twenty years, a theological seminary, and two filial institutions in Indiana and Arkansas. The church is an imposing structure, after the model of St. Peter's in Rome, surrounded by colonnades. The costly chandelier is a present of Napoleon III. (1865).

The modern revival of Romanism, and the railroad from Wädensweil, opened 1877, have greatly increased the number of pilgrims. Goethe says of Einsiedeln: " *Es muss ernste Betrachtungen erregen, dass ein einzelner Funke von Sittlichkeit und Gottesfurcht hier ein immerbrennendes und leuchtendes Flämmchen angezündet, zu welchem glaübige Seelen mit grosser Beschwerlichkeit heranpilgern, um an dieser heiligen Flamme auch ihr Kerzlein anzuzünden. Wie dem auch sei, so deutet es auf ein grenzenloses Bedürfniss der Menschheit nach gleichem Lichte, gleicher Wärme, wie es jener Erste im tiefsten Gefühle und sicherster Ueberzengung gehegt und genossen.* "

For a history of Einsiedeln, see *Beschreibung des Klosters und der Wallfahrt Maria-Einsiedeln.* Einsiedeln. Benziger & Co. 122 pp.

The wood-cut on p. 197 represents the abbey as it was before and at the time of Zwingli, and is a fair specimen of a rich mediæval abbey, with church, dwellings for the brethren, library, school, and gardens. Einsiedeln lies in a dreary and sterile district, and derives its sole interest from this remarkable abbey.

§ 51. *The Relative Strength of the Confessions in Switzerland.*

We may briefly sum up the result of the Reformation in Switzerland as follows : —

Seven Cantons — Luzern, Uri, Schwyz, Unterwalden, Zug, Freiburg, and Soluthurn (Soleur) — remained firm to the faith of their ancestors. Four Cantons, including the two strongest — Zürich, Bern, Basel, and Schaffhausen — adopted the Reformed faith. Five Cantons — Glarus, St. Gall, Appenzell, Thurgau, and Aargau — are nearly equally divided between the two Confessions. Of the twenty-three subject towns and districts, only Morat and Granson became wholly Protestant, sixteen retained their former religion, and five were divided. In the Grisons nearly two-thirds of the population adopted the Zwinglian Reformation; but the Protestant gains in the Valtellina and Chiavenna were lost in the seventeenth century. Ticino and Wallis are Roman Catholic. In the French Cantons — Geneva, Canton de Vaud, and Neuchatel — the Reformation achieved a complete victory, chiefly through the labors of Calvin.

Since the middle of the sixteenth century the numerical relation of the two Churches has undergone no material change. Protestantism has still a majority of about half a million in a population of less than three millions. The Roman Catholic Church has considerably increased by immigration from Savoy and France, but has suffered some loss by the Old Catholic secession in 1870 under the lead of Bishop Herzog. The Methodists and Baptists are making progress chiefly in those parts where infidelity and indifferentism reign.

Each Canton still retains its connection with one or the other of the two Churches, and has its own church establishment; but the bond of union has been gradually relaxed, and religious liberty extended to dissenting communions, as Methodists, Baptists, Irvingites, and Old Catholics. The former exclusiveness is abolished, and the principle of parity or equality before the law is acknowledged in all the Cantons.

An impartial comparison between the Roman Catholic and the Reformed Cantons reveals the same difference as exists between Southern and Northern Ireland, Eastern and Western Canada, and other parts of the world where the two Churches meet in close proximity. The Roman Catholic Cantons have preserved more historical faith and superstition, churchly habits and customs; the Protestant Cantons surpass them in general education and intelligence, wealth and temporal prosperity; while in point of morality both are nearly equal.

§ 52. *Zwingli Redivivus.*

The last words of the dying Zwingli, "They may kill the body, but cannot kill the soul," have been verified in his case. His body was buried with his errors and defects, but his spirit still lives; and his liberal views on infant salvation, and the extent of God's saving grace beyond the limits of the visible Church, which gave so much offence in his age, even to the Reformers, have become almost articles of faith in evangelical Christendom.

Ulrich Zwingli is, next to Martin Luther and John Knox, the most popular among the Reformers.[1] He moved in sympathy with the common people; he spoke and wrote their language; he took part in their public affairs; he was a faithful pastor of the old and young, and imbedded himself in their affections; while Erasmus, Melanchthon, Œcolam-

---

[1] The German *volksthümlich* expresses the idea better than *popular*.

padius, Calvin, Beza, and Cranmer stood aloof from the masses. He was a man of the people and for the people, — a typical Swiss; as Luther was a typical German. Both fairly represented the virtues and faults of their nation. Both were the best hated as well as the best loved men of their age, according to the faith which divided, and still divides, their countrymen.

Martin Luther and Ulrich Zwingli have been honored by a fourth centennial commemoration of their birth, — the one in 1883, the other in 1884. Such honor is almost without a precedent, at least in the history of theology.[1]

The Zwingli festival was not merely an echo of the Luther festival, but was observed throughout the Reformed churches of Europe and America with genuine enthusiasm, and gave rise to an extensive Zwingli literature. It is in keeping with the generous Christian spirit which the Swiss Reformer showed towards the German Reformer at Marburg, that many Reformed churches in Switzerland, as well as else-where, heartily united in the preceding jubilee of Luther, forgetting the bitter controversies of the sixteenth century, and remembering gratefully his great services to the cause of truth and liberty.[2]

In the following year (Aug. 25, 1885), a bronze statue was erected to Zwingli at Zürich in front of the Wasserkirche and City Library, beneath the minster where he preached. It represents the Reformer as a manly figure, looking trust-fully up to heaven, with the Bible in one hand and the sword in the other, — a combination true to history. Dr. Alexander

---

[1] I say "almost." In 1880, five hundred years after the completion of Wiclif's English Bible, his memory was celebrated throughout the English-speaking Protestant world in five continents. The sixth centenary of Dante's birth was celebrated in 1865 in Florence and all Italy. The last divine whose centennial birthday was observed is Neander, the Church historian. An eloquent commemorative oration was delivered on that occasion by Dr. Har-nack, his successor, in the Aula of the University of Berlin, Jan. 17, 1889.

[2] See the literature on the Zwingli centennial in § 5, pp. 17 sq. and the literature of the Luther celebration in vol. VI. 104 sq. and 730.

Schweizer, one of the ablest Swiss divines (d. July 3, 1888), whose last public service was the Zwingli oration in the University, Jan. 7, 1884, protested against the sword, and left the committee on the monument. Dr. Konrad Ferdinand Meyer, the poet of the occasion, changed the sword of Zwingli, with poetic ingenuity, into the sword of Vokinger, by which he was slain.[1] Antistes Finsler, in his oration, gave the sword a double meaning, as in the case of Paul, who is likewise represented with the sword, namely, the sword by which he was slain, and the sword of the spirit with which he still is fighting; while at the same time it distinguishes Zwingli from Luther, and shows him as the patriot and statesman.

The whole celebration — the orderly enthusiasm of the people, the festive addresses of representative men of Church and State, the illumination of the city and the villages around the beautiful lake — bore eloquent witness to the fact that Zwingli has impressed his image indelibly upon the memory of German Switzerland. Although his descendants are at present about equally divided between orthodox conservatives and rationalistic " reformers " (as they call themselves), they forgot their quarrels on that day, and cordially united in tributes to the abiding merits of him who, whatever were his faults, has emancipated the greater part of Switzerland from the tyranny of popery, and led them to the fresh fountain of the teaching and example of Christ.[2]

[1] " *Hier das Schwert in meiner Hand*
   Ist das Schwert, das mich erschlug."

[2] See an account of that memorable celebration (which I witnessed myself) in *Erinnerungsblätter zur Einweihung des Zwingli-Denkmals in Zürich. Herausgegeben vom Denkmal-Komite.* In 2 parts, Zürich, 1885. The chief address was made by Antistes Finsler, the twenty-second successor of Zwingli. A part of the celebration was a dramatic representation of Zwingli's death (a historic tragedy by Charlotte Birch-Pfeiffer), and a banquet in the Tonhalle-Pavilion, where addresses were delivered by delegates from different Cantons. Zwingli's poem, " *Herr, nun heb den Wagen selbst,*" was sung with great spirit by the Concordia. The Swiss poet, Dr. Meyer, wrote the *Festcantate.* The statue was made by Natter, a Roman Catholic sculptor of Vienna, who attended the unveiling. A significant fact.

M. HEINRICUS BULINGERUS
PASTOR TIGURINUS,
SUCCESSOR ZUINGLIſ. A˙1531.
Obijt a˙ 1574. die 17 Sept. Ætatis. 71.
Sic vixi, vivoq meis nunc denique libris :
Vt nunquam videar mortuus eſſe bonis.

CHAPTER VI.

THE PERIOD OF CONSOLIDATION.

§ 53. *Literature.*

Supplementary to the literature in § 4, pp. 12 sqq.

I. Manuscript sources preserved in the City Library of Zürich, which was founded 1629, and contains c. 132,000 printed vols. and 3,500 MSS. See Salomon Vögelin: *Geschichte der Wasserkirche und der Stadtbibliothek in Zürich.* Zürich, 1848 (pp. 110 and 123). The Wasserkirche (*capella aquatica*) is traced back to Charles the Great. It contains also the remains of the lake dwellings. The bronze statue of Zwingli stands in front of it. The THESAURUS HOTTINGERIANUS, a collection of correspondence made by the theologian, *J. H. Hottinger*, 55 vols., embraces the whole Bullinger correspondence, which has been much used, but never published in full. — The SIMLER COLLECTION of 196 vols. fol., with double index of 62 vols. fol., contains correspondence, proclamations, pamphlets, official mandates, and other documents, chronologically arranged, very legible, on good paper. Johann Jacob Simler (1716–1788), professor and inspector of the theological college, spent the leisure hours of his whole life in the collection of papers and documents relating to the history of Switzerland, especially of the Reformation. This unique collection was acquired by the government, and presented to the City Library in 1792. It has often been used, and, though partly depreciated by more recent discoveries, is still a treasure-house of information. The Bullinger correspondence is found in the volumes from A.D. 1531–1575. — ACTA ECCLESIASTICA *intermixtis politicis et politico-ecclesiasticis* MANUSCRIPTA *ex ipsis fontibus hausta in variis fol. Tomis chronologice pro administratione* ANTISTITII TURICENSIS *in ordinem redacta.* 33 vols. fol. Beautifully written. Comes down to the administration of Antistes Joh. Jak. Hess (1795–1798). Tom I. extends from 1519–1531; tom. II. contains a biography of Bullinger, with his likeness, and the acts during his administration. — The State Archives of the City and Canton Zürich.

II. Printed works. JOH. CONR. FÜSSLIN: *Beyträge zur Erläuterung der Kirchen-Reformationsgeschichten des Schweitzerlandes.* Zürich, 1741–1753. 5 Parts. Contains important documents relating to the Reformation in Zürich and the Anabaptists, the disputation at Ilanz, etc. — SIMLER'S *Sammlung alter und neuer Urkunden.* Zürich, 1760. 2 vols. — JOH. JAK. HOTTINGER (Prof. of Theol. and Canon of the Great Minster): *Helvetische Kirchengeschichten vorstellend der Helvetiern ehemaliges Heidenthum, und durch die Gnade Gottes*

203

gefolgtes Christenthum, etc. Zürich, 1698–1729. 4 Theile 4°. 2d ed. 1737. A work of immense industry, in opposition to a Roman Catholic work of Caspar Lang (Einsiedeln, 1692). The third volume goes from 1516 to 1700, the fourth to 1728. Superseded by Wirz. — LUDWIG WIRZ : *Helvetische Kirchengeschichte. Aus Joh. Jak. Hottingers älterem Werke und anderen Quellen neu bearbeitet.* Zürich, 1808–1819. 5 vols. The fifth volume is by MELCHIOR KIRCHHOFER, who gives the later history of Zwingli from 1525, and the Reformation in the other Cantons. — JOH. JAK. HOTTINGER: *Geschichte der Eidgenossen während der Zeiten der Kirchentrennung.* Zürich, 1825 and 1829. 2 vols. This work forms vols. VI. and VII. of Joh. von Müller's and Robert Glutz Blotzheim's *Geschichten Schweizerischer Eidgenossenschaft.* The second volume (p. 446 sqq.) treats of the period of Bullinger, and is drawn in part from the Simler Collection and the Archives of Zürich. French translation by L. VULLIEMIN : *Histoire des Suisses à l'époque de la Réformation.* Paris et Zurich, 1833. 2 vols. — G. R. ZIMMERMANN (Pastor of the Fraumünster and Decan): *Die Zürcher Kirche von der Reformation bis zum dritten Reformationsjubiläum (1519– 1819) nach der Reihenfolge der Zürcherischen Antistes.* Zürich, 1878 (pp. 414). On Bullinger, see pp. 36–73. Based upon the *Acta Ecclesiastica* quoted above. — JOH. STRICKLER'S *Actensammlung*, previously noticed (p. 13), extends only to 1532.

On the Roman Catholic side comp. *Archiv für die Schweiz. Reformationsgesch.*, noticed above, p. 13. The first volume (1868) contains Salat's *Chronik* down to 1534; the second (1872), 135 papal addresses to the Swiss Diet, mostly of the sixteenth century (from Martin V. to Clement VIII.), documents referring to 1531, Roman and Venetian sources on the Swiss Reformation, etc.; vol. III. (1876), a catalogue of books on Swiss history (7–98), and a number of documents from the Archives of Luzern and other cities, including three letters of King Francis I. to the Catholic Cantons, and an account of the immediate consequences of the War of Cappel by Werner Beyel, at that time secretary of the city of Zürich (pp. 641–680).

§ 54. *Heinrich Bullinger.* 1504–1575.

I. Sources. BULLINGER'S printed works (stated to be 150 by Scheuchzer in "Bibliotheca Helvetica," Zürich, 1733). His manuscript letters (mostly Latin) in the "Thesaurus Hottingerianus" and the "Simler Collection" of the City Library at Zürich. — The second volume of the *Acta Ecclesiastica*, quoted in § 53. — *The Zürich Letters or the Correspondence of several English Bishops and others with some of the Helvetian Reformers, chiefly from the Archives of Zurich*, translated and edited for the "Parker Society" by Dr. H. Robinson, Cambridge (University Press), 2d ed. 1846 (pp. 576).

II. SALOMON HESS: *Leben Bullinger's.* Zürich, 1828–'29, 2 vols. Not very accurate. — *CARL PESTALOZZI : *Heinrich Bullinger. Leben und ausgewählte Schriften. Nach handschriftlichen und gleichzeitigen Quellen.* Elberfeld, 1858. Extracts from his writings, pp. 505–622. Pestalozzi has faithfully used the written and printed sources in the Stadtbibliothek and Archives of Zürich. — R. CHRISTOFFEL: *H. Bullinger und seine Gattin.* 1875. — JUSTUS HEER: *Bullinger,* in Herzog [2], II. 779–794. A good summary.

Older biographical sketches by LUDWIG LAVATER (1576), JOSIAS SIMLER (1575), W. STUCKI (1575), etc. Incidental information about Bullinger in Hagenbach and other works on the Swiss Reformation, and in MEYER's *Die Gemeinde von Locarno,* 1836, especially I. 198–216.

After the productive period of the Zwinglian Reformation, which embraced fifteen years, from 1516 to 1531, followed the period of preservation and consolidation under difficult circumstances. It required a man of firm faith, courage, moderation, patience, and endurance. Such a man was providentially equipped in the person of Heinrich Bullinger, the pupil, friend, and successor of Zwingli, and second Antistes of Zürich. He proved that the Reformation was a work of God, and, therefore, survived the apparent defeat at Cappel.

He was born July 18, 1504, at Bremgarten in Aargau, the youngest of five sons of Dean Bullinger, who lived, like many priests of those days, in illegitimate, yet tolerated, wedlock.[1] The father resisted the sale of indulgences by Samson in 1518, and confessed, in his advanced age, from the pulpit, the doctrines of the Reformation (1529). In consequence of this act he lost his place. Young Henry was educated in the school of the Brethren of the Common Life at Emmerich, and in the University of Cologne. He studied scholastic and patristic theology. Luther's writings and Melanchthon's *Loci* led him to the study of the Bible and prepared him for a change.

He returned to Switzerland as Master of Arts, taught a school in the Cistercian Convent at Cappel from 1523 to 1529, and reformed the convent in agreement with the abbot, Wolfgang Joner. During that time he became acquainted

---

[1] The bishop of Constance allowed priests to keep concubines for an annual tribute of four Rhenish guilders, called the *Hurensold.* See Christoffel, *Zwingli,* II. 337, and Pestalozzi, p. 5.

with Zwingli, attended the Conference with the Anabaptists at Zürich, 1525, and the disputation at Bern, 1528. He married Anna Adlischweiler, a former nun, in 1529, who proved to be an excellent wife and helpmate. He accepted a call to Bremgarten as successor of his father.

After the disaster at Cappel, he removed to Zürich, and was unanimously elected by the Council and the citizens preacher of the Great Minster, Dec. 9, 1531. It was rumored that Zwingli himself, in the presentiment of his death, had designated him as his successor. No better man could have been selected. It was of vital importance for the Swiss churches that the place of the Reformer should be filled by a man of the same spirit, but of greater moderation and self-restraint.[1]

Bullinger now assumed the task of saving, purifying, and consolidating the life-work of Zwingli; and faithfully and successfully did he carry out this task. When he ascended the pulpit of the Great Minster in Dec. 23, 1531, many hearers thought that Zwingli had risen from the grave.[2] He took a firm stand for the Reformation, which was in danger of being abandoned by timid men in the Council. He kept free from interference with politics, which had proved ruinous to Zwingli. He established a more independent, though friendly relation between Church and State. He confined himself to his proper vocation as preacher and teacher.

In the first years he preached six or seven times a week; after 1542 only twice, on Sundays and Fridays. He followed the plan of Zwingli in explaining whole books of the Scrip-

---

[1] Pestalozzi, p. 25 : "*Zwingli und Bullinger — welche Verschiedenheit! Zwingli's rasches, feuriges Temperament, Bullinger's Ruhe und Gelassenheit; Zwingli's schneidender, stechender Witz, Bullinger's einlässliche Gründlichkeit; daher auch Zwingli's Kürze, Bullinger's Ausführlichkeit in den meisten seiner Arbeiten. Wie geeignet zur gegenseitigen Ergänzung!*"

[2] "*Talem concionem detonavit,*" wrote Myconius to Schenck, "*ut multi putarent Zwinglium non defunctum, sed ad Phœnicis modum renatum esse.*" Hottinger, *Helv. K. Gesch.* III. 28.

tures from the pulpit. His sermons were simple, clear, and practical, and served as models for young preachers.

He was a most devoted pastor, dispensing counsel and comfort in every direction, and exposing even his life during the pestilence which several times visited Zürich. His house was open from morning till night to all who desired his help. He freely dispensed food, clothing, and money from his scanty income and contributions of friends, to widows and orphans, to strangers and exiles, not excluding persons of other creeds. He secured a decent pension for the widow of Zwingli, and educated two of his children with his own. He entertained persecuted brethren for weeks and months in his own house, or procured them places and means of travel.[1]

He paid great attention to education, as superintendent of the schools in Zürich. He filled the professorships in the Carolinum with able theologians, as Pellican, Bibliander, Peter Martyr. He secured a well-educated ministry. He prepared, in connection with Leo Judæ, a book of church order, which was adopted by the Synod, Oct. 22, 1532, issued by authority of the burgomaster, the Small and the Great Council, and continued in force for nearly three hundred years. It provides the necessary rules for the examination, election, and duties of ministers (*Predicanten*) and deans (*Decani*), for semi-annual meetings of synods with clerical and lay representatives, and the power of discipline. The charges were divided into eight districts or chapters.[2]

Bullinger's activity extended far beyond the limits of Zürich. He had a truly Catholic spirit, and stood in correspondence with all the Reformed Churches. Beza calls him "the common shepherd of all Christian Churches"; Pellican, "a man of God, endowed with the richest gifts of heaven

---

[1] See the beautiful description of Pestalozzi, pp. 153 sqq.

[2] There are copies of several editions of this book in the City Library at Zürich, of 1532, 1535, 1563, etc. It is also printed in Simler's *Sammlung alter und neuer Urkunden*, I. 25–73.

for God's honor and the salvation of souls." He received
fugitive Protestants from Italy, France, England, and Germany with open arms, and made Zürich an asylum of religious liberty. He thus protected Celio Secondo Curione,
Bernardino Occhino, and Peter Martyr, and the immigrants
from Locarno, and aided in the organization of an Italian
congregation in Zürich.[1] Following the example of Zwingli
and Calvin, he appealed twice to the king of France for
toleration in behalf of the Huguenots. He dedicated to
Henry II. his book on Christian Perfection (1551), and to
Francis II. his Instruction in the Christian Religion (1559).
He sent deputations to the French court for the protection
of the Waldenses, and the Reformed congregation in Paris.

The extent of Bullinger's correspondence is astonishing.
It embraces letters to and from all the distinguished Protes-
tant divines of his age, as Calvin, Melanchthon, Bucer, Beza,
Laski, Cranmer, Hooper, Jewel, and crowned heads who
consulted him, as Henry VIII., Edward VI., of England,
Queen Elizabeth, Henry II. of France, King Christian of
Denmark, Philip of Hesse, and the Elector Frederick of the
Palatinate.

Bullinger came into contact with the English Reformation
from the time of Henry VIII. to the reign of Elizabeth,
especially during the bloody reign of Mary, when many
prominent exiles fled to Zürich, and found a fraternal reception under his hospitable roof. The correspondence of
Hooper, Jewel, Sandys, Grindal, Parkhurst, Foxe, Cox, and
other church dignitaries with Bullinger, Gwalter, Gessner,
Simler, and Peter Martyr, is a noble monument of the spiritual
harmony between the Reformed Churches of Switzerland and
England in the Edwardian and Elizabethan era. Archbishop
Cranmer invited Bullinger, together with Melanchthon, Calvin, and Bucer, to a conference in London, for the purpose

---

[1] See above, p. 155, and the works of Meyer and Mörikofer quoted there.

of framing an evangelical union creed; and Calvin answered that for such a cause he would be willing to cross ten seas. Lady Jane Grey, who was beheaded in 1554, read Bullinger's works, translated his book on marriage into Greek, consulted him about Hebrew, and addressed him with filial affection and gratitude. Her three letters to him are still preserved in Zürich. Bishop Hooper of Gloucester, who had enjoyed his hospitality in 1547, addressed him shortly before his martyrdom in 1554, as his "revered father and guide," and the best friend he ever had, and recommended his wife and two children to his care. Bishop Jewel, in a letter of May 22, 1559, calls him his "father and much esteemed master in Christ," thanks him for his "courtesy and kindness," which he and his friends experienced during the whole period of their exile, and informs him that the restoration of the Reformed religion under Elizabeth was largely due to his own "letters and recommendations"; adding that the queen refused to be addressed as the head of the Church of England, feeling that such honor belongs to Christ alone, and not to any human being. Bullinger's death was lamented in England as a public calamity.[1]

Bullinger faithfully maintained the doctrine and discipline of the Reformed Church against the Roman Catholics and Lutherans with moderation and dignity. He never returned the abuse of fanatics, and when, in 1548, the Interim drove the Lutheran preachers from the Swabian cities, he received them hospitably, even those who had denounced the Reformed doctrines from the pulpit. He represents the German-Swiss type of the Reformed faith in substantial agreement with a moderate Calvinism. He gave a full exposition of his theological views in the Second Helvetic Confession.

His theory of the sacrament was higher than that of Zwingli. He laid more stress on the objective value of the

---

[1] See the letters of Barlow to Simler (Bullinger's son-in-law), and Bishop Cox to Gwalter, in *Zurich Letters*, pp. 494 and 496.

institution. We recognize, he wrote to Faber, a mystery in the Lord's Supper; the bread is not common bread, but venerable, sacred, sacramental bread, the pledge of the spiritual real presence of Christ to those who believe. As the sun is in heaven, and yet virtually present on earth with his light and heat, so Christ sits in heaven, and yet efficaciously works in the hearts of all believers. When Luther, after Zwingli's death, warned Duke Albert of Prussia and the people of Frankfort not to tolerate the Zwinglians, Bullinger replied by sending to the duke a translation of Ratramnus' tract, *De corpore et sanguine Domini*, with a preface. He rejected the Wittenberg Concordia of 1536, because it concealed the Lutheran doctrine. He answered Luther's atrocious attack on the Zwinglians (1545) by a clear, strong, and temperate statement; but Luther died soon afterwards (1546) without retracting his charges. When Westphal renewed the unfortunate controversy (1552), Bullinger supported Calvin in defending the Reformed doctrine, but counselled moderation.[1] He and Calvin brought about a complete agreement on the sacramental question in the *Consensus Tigurinus*, which was adopted in 1549 at Zürich, in the presence of some members of the Council, and afterwards received the approval of the other Swiss Reformed churches.[2]

On the doctrine of Predestination, Bullinger did not go quite as far as Zwingli and Calvin, and kept within the infralapsarian scheme. He avoided to speak of the predestination of Adam's fall, because it seemed irreconcilable with the justice of the punishment of sin.[3] The *Consensus Genevensis* (1552), which contains Calvin's rigorous view, was not

---

[1] *Apologetica Defensio*, etc., February, 1556.

[2] Schaff, *Creeds of Christendom*, I. 471 sqq., and the literature there quoted.

[3] In the Second Helvetic Confession, ch. VIII., he dismisses the curious questions, "whether God would have Adam fall, or whether he forced him to fall, or why he did not hinder his fall, and such like," and says that it is sufficient to know that God did forbid our first parents to eat of the fruit, and punished them for disobedience.

signed by the pastors of Zürich. Theodor Bibliander, the father of biblical exegesis in Switzerland, and a forerunner of Arminianism, opposed it. He adhered to the semi-Pelagian theory of Erasmus, and was involved in a controversy with Peter Martyr, who was a strict Calvinist, and taught in Zürich since 1556. Bibliander was finally removed from his theological professorship (Feb. 8, 1560), but his salary was continued till his death (Nov. 26, 1564).[1]

On the subject of toleration and the punishment of heretics, Bullinger agreed with the prevailing theory, but favorably differed from the prevailing practice. He opposed the Anabaptists in his writings, as much as Zwingli, and, like Melanchthon, he approved of the unfortunate execution of Servetus, but he himself did not persecute. He tolerated Laelio Sozini, who quietly died at Zürich (1562), and Bernardino Occhino, who preached for some time to the Italian congregation in that city, but was deposed, without further punishment, for teaching Unitarian opinions and defending polygamy. In a book against the Roman Catholic Faber, Bullinger expresses the Christian and humane sentiment that no violence should be done to dissenters, and that faith is a free gift of God, which cannot be commanded or forbidden. He agreed with Zwingli's extension of salvation to all infants dying in infancy and to elect heathen; at all events, he nowhere dissents from these advanced views, and published with approbation Zwingli's last work, where they are most strongly expressed.[2]

Bullinger's house was a happy Christian home. He liked to play with his numerous children and grandchildren, and to write little verses for them at Christmas, like Luther.[3]

When his son Henry, in 1553, went to Strassburg, Wit-

---

[1] A fuller statement in Schaff, *Creeds*, I. 474 sqq., and especially Schweizer, *Central-dogmen*, I. 139, 258–292.

[2] See above, p. 177 sq.

[3] Some of these verses are still remembered in Switzerland. Specimens in Pestalozzi, 315 sqq.

tenberg, and Vienna to prosecute his theological studies, he wrote down for him wise rules of conduct, of which the following are the most important: 1) Fear God at all times, and remember that the fear of God is the beginning of wisdom.   2) Humble yourself before God, and pray to him alone through Christ, our only Mediator and Advocate. 3) Believe firmly that God has done all for our salvation through his Son.   4) Pray above all things for strong faith active in love.   5) Pray that God may protect your good name and keep thee from sin, sickness, and bad company. 6) Pray for the fatherland, for your dear parents, benefactors, friends, and all men, for the spread of the Word of God; conclude always with the Lord's Prayer, and use also the beautiful hymn, *Te Deum laudamus* [which he ascribes to Ambrose and Augustin].   7) Be reticent, be always more willing to hear than to speak, and do not meddle with things which you do not understand.   8) Study diligently Hebrew and Greek as well as Latin, history, philosophy, and the sciences, but especially the New Testament, and read daily three chapters in the Bible, beginning with Genesis. 9) Keep your body clean and unspotted, be neat in your dress, and avoid above all things intemperance in eating and drinking.   10) Let your conversation be decent, cheerful, moderate, and free from all uncharitableness.[1]   He recommended him to Melanchthon, and followed his studies with letters full of fatherly care and affection.[2]   He kept his parents with him till their death, the widow of Zwingli (d. 1538), and two of her children, whom he educated with his own. Notwithstanding his scanty income, he declined all presents, or sent them to the hospitals.   The whole people revered the venerable minister of noble features and white patriarchal beard.

[1] Pestalozzi, 588 sqq.

[2] The letters, pp. 595–617, are quite interesting.   Henry became pastor at Zollikon, and afterwards of St. Peter at Zürich.   He married a daughter of Gwalter, who was a granddaughter of Zwingli.

His last days were clouded, like those of many faithful servants of God. The excess of work and care undermined his health. In 1562 he wrote to Fabricius at Coire: "I almost sink under the load of business and care, and feel so tired that I would ask the Lord to give me rest if it were not against his will." The pestilence of 1564 and 1565 brought him to the brink of the grave, and deprived him of his wife, three daughters, and his brother-in-law. He bore these heavy strokes with Christian resignation. In the same two fatal years he lost his dearest friends, Calvin, Blaurer, Gessner, Froschauer, Bibliander, Fabricius, Farel. He recovered, and was allowed to spend several more years in the service of Christ. His youngest daughter, Dorothea, took faithful and tender care of his health. He felt lonely and homesick, but continued to preach and to write with the aid of pastor Lavater, his colleague and son-in-law. He preached his last sermon on Pentecost, 1575. He assembled, Aug. 26, all the pastors of the city and professors of theology around his sick-bed, assured them of his perseverance in the true apostolic and orthodox doctrine, recited the Apostles' Creed, and exhorted them to purity of life, harmony among themselves, and obedience to the magistrates. He warned them against intemperance, envy, and hatred, thanked them for their kindness, assured them of his love, and closed with a prayer of thanksgiving and some verses of the hymns of Prudentius. Then he took each by the hand and took leave of them with tears, as Paul did from the elders at Ephesus. A few weeks afterwards he died, after reciting several Psalms (51, 16, and 42), the Lord's Prayer, and other prayers, peacefully, in the presence of his family, Sept. 17, 1575. He was buried in the Great Minster, at the side of his beloved wife and his dear friend, Peter Martyr. According to his wish, Rudolph Gwalter, Zwingli's son-in-law and his adopted son, was unanimously elected his successor. Four of his successors were trained under his care and labored in his spirit.

The writings of Bullinger are very numerous, mostly doctrinal and practical, adapted to the times, but of little permanent value. Scheuchzer numbers one hundred and fifty printed books of his. The Zürich City Library contains about one hundred, exclusive of translations and new editions. Many are extant only in manuscript. He wrote Latin commentaries on the New Testament (except the Apocalypse), numerous sermons on Isaiah, Jeremiah, Daniel, the Apocalypse. His *Decades* (five series of ten sermons each on the Decalogue, the Apostles' Creed, and the Sacraments) were much esteemed and used in Holland and England. His work on the justifying grace of God was highly prized by Melanchthon. His History of the Swiss Reformation, written by his own hand, in two folio volumes, has been published in 1838–'40, in three volumes. His most important doctrinal work is the Second Helvetic Confession, which acquired symbolical authority.[1]

§ 55. *Antistes Breitinger* (1575–1645).

In the same year in which Bullinger died (1575), Johann Jakob Breitinger was born, who became his worthy successor as Antistes of Zürich (1613–1645).[2] He called him a saint, and followed his example. He was one of the most eminent Reformed divines of his age. Thoroughly trained in the universities of Herborn, Marburg, Franeker, Heidelberg, and Basel, he gained the esteem and affection of his fellow-citizens as teacher, preacher, and devoted pastor. During the fearful pestilence of 1611 he visited the sick from morning till night at the risk of his life.

He attended as one of the Swiss delegates the Synod of

---

[1] Extracts from Bullinger's Works are given by Pestalozzi, 505–622.

[2] The immediate successors of Bullinger were Gwalter, Zwingli's son-in-law (1575–1586), **Lavater** (1585–1586), **Stumpf** (1582–1592), **Leemann** (1592–1613).

Dort (1618 and 1619). He was deeply impressed with the learning, wisdom, and piety of that body, and fully agreed with its unjust and intolerant treatment of the Arminians.[1] On his return (May 21, 1619) he was welcomed by sixty-four Zürichers, who rode to the borders of the Rhine to meet him. Yet, with all his firmness of conviction, he was opposed to confessional polemics in an intensely polemic age, and admired the good traits in other churches and sects, even the Jesuits. He combined with strict orthodoxy a cheerful temper, a generous heart, and active piety. He had an open ear for appeals from the poor and the numerous sufferers in the murder of the Valtellina (1620) and during the Thirty Years' War. At his request, hospitals and orphan houses were founded and collections raised, which in the Minster alone, during eight years (1618–1628), exceeded fifty thousand pounds. He was in every way a model pastor, model churchman, and model statesman. Although he towered high above his colleagues, he disarmed envy and jealousy by his kindliness and Christian humility. Altogether he shines next to Zwingli and Bullinger as the most influential and useful Antistes of the Reformed Church of Zürich.[2]

§ 56. *Oswald Myconius, Antistes of Basel.*

I. Correspondence between MYCONIUS and ZWINGLI in Zwingli's *Opera*, vols. VII. and VIII. (28 letters of the former and 20 of the latter). — Correspondence with Bullinger in the Simler Collection. — *Antiqu. Gernl.*, I. — The *Chronicle* of FRIDOLIN RYFF, ed. by W. Vischer (son), in the *Basler Chroniken* (vol. 1, Leipzig, 1872), extends from 1514 to 1541.

II. MELCHIOR KIRCHOFER (of Schaffhausen): *Oswald Myconius, Antistes der Baslerischen Kirche.* Zürich, 1813 (pp. 387). Still very serviceable. — R. HAGENBACH: *Joh. Oecolampad und Oswald Myconius, die Reformatoren Basels.* Elberfeld, 1859 (pp. 309–462). Also his *Geschichte der ersten Basler Confession.* Basel, 1828. — B. RIGGENBACH, in Herzog[2], X. 403–405.

---

[1] Comp. Schweizer, *Centraldogmen*, II. 26, 116 sq., 140 sq., 143.

[2] J. C. Mörikofer (author of the *Life of Zwingli*), *Johann Jakob Breitinger* Leipzig, 1873. Karl Meyer, in Herzog[2], II. 597.

Oswald Myconius (1488–1552),[1] a native of Luzern, an intimate friend of Zwingli, and successor of Œcolampadius, was to the Church of Basel what Bullinger was to the Church of Zürich, — a faithful preserver of the Reformed religion, — but in a less difficult position and more limited sphere of usefulness. He spent his earlier life as classical teacher in Basel, Zürich, Luzern, Einsiedeln, and again in Zürich. His pupil, Thomas Plater, speaks highly of his teaching ability and success. Erasmus honored him with his friendship before he fell out with the Reformation.[2]

After the death of Zwingli and Œcolampadius, he moved to Basel as pastor of St. Alban (Dec. 22, 1531), and was elected Antistes or chief pastor of the Church of that city, and professor of New Testament exegesis in the university (August, 1532). He was not ordained, and had no academic degree, and refused to take one because Christ had forbidden his disciples to be called Rabbi (Matt. 23 : 8).[3] He carried out the views of Œcolampadius on discipline, and maintained the independence of the Church in its relation to the State and the university. He had to suffer much opposition from Carlstadt, who, by his recommendation, became professor of theology in Basel (1534), and ended there his restless life

---

[1] His proper name was Geisshüssler. He is to be distinguished from Friedrich Myconius (Mecum), who was a friend of Luther and superintendent of Gotha (d. 1546).

[2] In a letter of Oct. 5, 1532, Erasmus called Myconius a "*homo ineptus et quondam ludimagister frigidus.*" Epist. 1233. See Hagenbach. *Oekol. und Mycon.*, p. 329 sq. and 339, where he remarks: "*Und doch hatte Erasmus diesen Einfaltspinsel von Schulmeister früher seines Umgangs gewürdigt und ihn vor Vielen ausgezeichnet! Aber der grämliche Mann war jetzt gegen alles erbittert, was mit der von ihm verkannten und gehassten Reformation in Verbindung stand und glaubte sich, vom alten Ruhme seines Namens zehrend, berechtigt, seinem Unwillen jeden beliebigen Ausdruck zu geben.*"

[3] Hagenbach (341) : "*Myconius hatte keine kirchliche Ordination erhalten, noch viel weniger etwas von dem was man einen akademischen Grad nennt. Er war weder Baccalaureus, noch Licentiat, noch Magister, noch Doctor geworden.*" Luther was proud to be a doctor of divinity; but Melanchthon and Zwingli were satisfied with their M.A. Calvin, like Myconius, was never ordained, as far as we know, although he was intended for the priesthood.

(1541). He took special interest in the higher and lower schools. He showed hospitality to the numerous Protestants from France who, like Farel and Calvin, sought a temporary refuge in Basel. The English martyrologist, John Foxe, fled from the Marian persecution to Basel, finished and published there the first edition of his *Book of Martyrs* (1554).

On the doctrine of the Eucharist, Myconius, like Calvin after him, occupied a middle ground between Zwingli and Luther. He aided Bucer in his union movement which resulted in the adoption of the Wittenberg Concordia and a temporary conciliation of Luther with the Swiss (1536). He was suspected by the Zürichers of leaning too much to the Lutheran side, but he never admitted the corporal presence and oral manducation; he simply emphasized more than Zwingli the spiritual real presence and fruition of the body and blood of Christ. He thought that Luther and Zwingli had misunderstood each other.[1]

Myconius matured, on the basis of a draft of Œcolampadius, the First Basel Confession of Faith, which was adopted by the magistracy, Jan. 21, 1534, and also by the neighboring city of Mühlhausen.[2] It is very simple, and consists of twelve Articles, on God (the trinity), man, providence, Christ, the Church and sacraments, the Lord's Supper, the ban, the civil government, faith and good works, the last judgment, feasts, fasts, and celibacy, and the Anabaptists (condemning their

---

[1] Hagenbach (359): "*Was Zwingli verneint hatte, das verneinte auch er [Myconius] fortwährend. Nie hätte er zugegeben, dass Leib und Blut Christi ihrer leiblichen Substanz nach in den Elementen des Abendmahls vorhanden seien; nie zugegeben, dass sie auch von den Ungläubigen genossen werden. Was dagegen Zwingli mehr zugegeben, als in den Vordergrund gestellt hatte, den geistlichen Genuss durch den Glauben, das hob er mit Nachdruck hervor. Mit gutem Gewissen glaubte er in den Fusstapfen seines Meisters fortzuwandeln, der so redlich und tapfer in Marburg die Hand zum Frieden geboten hatte.*"

[2] *Bekanthnuss unseres heyl. christenlichen Gloubens, wie es die Kylch von Basel haldt;* also called *Confessio Mühlhusana.* In Niemeyer's *Collectio Confess.*, 78–84; and in Hagenbach's biography at the end, pp. 465–476. Comp. also his *History* of that Confession, and Schaff, *Creeds*, I. 387 sq.

views on infant baptism, the oath, and civil government).
It is written in Swiss-German, with marginal Scripture references and notes. It claims no infallibility or binding authority, and concludes with the words : "We submit this our
confession to the judgment of the divine Scriptures, and are
always ready, if we can be better informed from them, very
thankfully to obey God and his holy Word."

This Confession was superseded by maturer statements of
the Reformed faith, but retained a semi-symbolical authority
in the Church of Basel, as a venerable historical document.

Myconius wrote the first biography of Zwingli in twelve
short chapters (1532).[1] His other writings are not important.[2]

One of his most influential successors was Lukas Gernler,
who presided as Antistes over the Church of Basel from 1656
to 1675. He formulated the scholastic system of Calvinism,
with many subtle definitions and distinctions, in a Syllabus
of 588 Theses. In connection with John Henry Heidegger
of Zürich and the elder Turretin of Geneva, he prepared the
Helvetic Consensus Formula, the last and the most rigid of
Calvinistic symbols (1675). He was the last representative
of strict Calvinistic orthodoxy in Basel. He combined with
an intolerant creed a benevolent heart, and induced the
magistracy of Basel to found an orphan asylum. The famous
Hebrew and Talmudic scholars, John Buxtorf (1564–1629),
his son, John (1599–1664), and his grandson, John Jacob
(1645–1704), who adorned the university of Basel in the
seventeenth century, fully agreed with the doctrinal position
of Gernler, and defended even the rabbinical tradition of the
literal inspiration of the Masoretic text against Louis Cappel,
who attacked it with great learning (1650).[3]

---

[1] It was reprinted at Berlin, 1841, in *Vitæ Quatuor Reformatorum*, with a
Preface of Neander.

[2] See extracts in Hagenbach's biography, pp. 387–462.

[3] See Schaff, *Creeds of Christendom*, I. 477 sqq.

§ 57. *The Helvetic Confessions of Faith.*

NIEMEYER: *Collectio Confess.* (Hall. 1840), pp. 105–122 (Conf. Helv. prior, German and Latin), and 462–536 (Conf. Helv. posterior). — SCHAFF: *Creeds of Christendom* (New York, 6th ed. 1890), vol. I. 388–420 (history); III. 211–307 (First and Second Helv. Conf.), 831–909 (Second Helv. Conf. in English). Other literature quoted by Schaff, I. 385 and 399.

Bullinger and Myconius authoritatively formulated the doctrines of the Reformed Churches in Switzerland, and impressed upon them a strongly evangelical character, without the scholastic subtleties of a later period.

The Sixty-seven Conclusions and the two private Confessions of Zwingli (to Charles V., and Francis I.) were not intended to be used as public creeds, and never received the sanction of the Church. The Ten Theses of Bern (1528), the First Confession of Basel (1534), the Zürich Consensus (1549), and the Geneva Consensus (1552) were official documents, but had only local authority in the cities where they originated. But the First and Second Helvetic Confessions were adopted by the Swiss and other Churches, and kept their place as symbolical books for nearly three hundred years. They represent the Zwinglian type of doctrine modified and matured. They approach the Calvinistic system, without its logical rigor.

I. THE FIRST HELVETIC CONFESSION, 1536. It is also called the *Second Basel Confession*, to distinguish it from the First Basel Confession of 1534. It was made in Basel, but not for Basel alone. It owes its origin partly to the renewed efforts of the Strassburg Reformers, Bucer and Capito, to bring about a union between the Lutherans and the Zwinglians, and partly to the papal promise of convening a General Council. A number of Swiss divines were delegated by the magistrates of Zürich, Bern, Basel, Schaffhausen, St. Gall, Mühlhausen, and Biel, to a conference in the Augustinian convent at Basel, Jan. 30, 1536. Bucer and Capito also appeared on behalf of Strassburg. Bullinger, Myconius,

Grynæus, Leo Judæ, and Megander were selected as a commission to draw up a Confession of the faith of the Helvetic Churches, which might be used at the proposed General Council. It was examined and signed by all the clerical and lay delegates, February, 1536, and first published in Latin. Leo Judæ prepared the German translation, which is fuller than the Latin text, and of equal authority.

Luther, to whom a copy was sent through Bucer, unexpectedly expressed, in two remarkable letters,[1] his satisfaction with the earnest Christian character of this document, and promised to do all he could to promote union and harmony with the Swiss. He was then under the hopeful impressions of the "Wittenberg Concordia," which Bucer had brought about by his elastic diplomacy, May, 1536, but which proved, after all, a hollow peace, and could not be honestly signed by the Swiss. Luther himself made a new and most intemperate attack on the Zwinglians (1545), a year before his death.

The First Helvetic Confession is the earliest Reformed Creed that has acquired a national authority. It consists of 27 articles, is fuller than the First Confession of Basel, but not so full as the Second Helvetic Confession, by which it was afterwards superseded. The doctrine of the sacraments and of the Lord's Supper is essentially Zwinglian, yet emphasizes the significance of the sacramental signs and the real spiritual presence of Christ, who gives his body and blood — that is, himself — to believers, so that he more and more lives in them, and they in him.

Bullinger and Leo Judæ wished to add a caution against the binding authority of this or any other confession that might interfere with the supreme authority of the Word of God and with Christian liberty. They had a correct feeling of a difference between a confession of doctrine which may

---

[1] One to Jacob Meyer, burgomaster of Basel, Feb. 17, 1537, one to the Swiss Reformed Cantons, Dec. 1, 1537, in De Wette's ed., vol. V. 54 sqq. and 83 sqq.

be improved from time to time with the progress of religious knowledge, and a rule of faith which remains unchanged. A confession of the Church has relative authority as *norma normata*, and depends upon its agreement with the Holy Scriptures, which have absolute authority as *norma normans*.

II. THE SECOND HELVETIC CONFESSION, 1566.   This is far more important than the first, and obtained authority beyond the limits of Switzerland.   In the intervening thirty years Calvin had developed his theological system, and the Council of Trent had formulated the modern Roman creed. Bullinger prepared this Confession in 1562 for his private use, as a testimony of the faith in which he had lived and wished to die.   Two years afterwards, during the raging of the pestilence, he elaborated it more fully, in the daily expectation of death, and added it to his last will and testament, which was to be delivered to the magistracy of Zürich after his decease.

But events in Germany gave to this private creed a public character.   The pious elector of the Palatinate, Frederick III., being threatened by the Lutherans with exclusion from the treaty of peace on account of his secession to the Reformed Church and the publication of the Heidelberg Catechism (1563), requested Bullinger in 1565 to prepare a full and clear exposition of the Reformed faith, that he might answer the charges of heresy and dissension so constantly brought against the same.   Bullinger sent him a manuscript copy of his confession.   The Elector was so much pleased with it that he desired to have it translated and published in Latin and German before the Imperial Diet, which was to assemble at Augsburg in 1566 and to act on his alleged apostasy.

In the meantime the Swiss felt the need of such a Confession as a closer bond of union.   The First Helvetic Confession was deemed too short, and the Zürich Consensus of 1549 and the Geneva Consensus of 1552 treated only two articles, namely, the Lord's Supper and predestination.   Conferences were held, and Beza came in person to Zürich to take part in the work. Bullinger freely consented to a few changes, and prepared also the German version. Geneva, Bern, Schaffhausen, Biel, the Grisons, St. Gall, and Mühlhausen expressed their agreement. Basel alone, which had its own confession, declined for a long time, but ultimately acceded.

The new Confession was published at Zürich, March 12, 1566, in both languages, at public expense, and was forwarded to the Elector of the Palatinate and to Philip of Hesse. A French translation appeared soon afterwards in Geneva under the care of Beza.

In the same year the Elector Frederick made such a manly and noble defence of his faith before the Diet at Augsburg, that even his Lutheran opponents were filled with admiration for his piety, and thought no longer of impeaching him for heresy.

The Helvetic Confession is the most widely adopted, and hence the most authoritative of all the Continental Reformed symbols, with the exception of the Heidelberg Catechism. It was sanctioned in Zürich and the Palatinate (1566), Neuchâtel (1568), by the Reformed Churches of France (at the Synod of La Rochelle, 1571), Hungary (at the Synod of Debreczin, 1567), and Poland (1571 and 1578). It was well received also in Holland, England, and Scotland as a sound statement of the Reformed faith. It was translated not only into German, French, and English, but also into Dutch, Magyar, Polish, Italian, Arabic, and Turkish. In Austria and Bohemia the Reformed or Calvinists are officially called "the Church of the Helvetic Confession," the Lutherans, "the Church of the Augsburg Confession."

THIRD BOOK.

THE REFORMATION IN FRENCH SWITZERLAND,

OR

THE CALVINISTIC MOVEMENT.

CHAPTER VII.

THE PREPARATORY WORK.   FROM 1526 TO 1536.

§ 58. *Literature on Calvin and the Reformation in French Switzerland.*

Important documents relating to the Reformation in French Switzerland are contained in the Archives of Geneva and Bern. Many documents have been recently published by learned Genevese archæologists, as Galiffe, father and son, Grénus, Revilliod, E. Mallet, Chaponnière, Fick, and the Society of History and Archæology of Geneva.

The best Calvin libraries are in the University of Geneva, where his MSS. are preserved in excellent order, and in the St. Thomasstift at Strassburg. The latter was collected by Profs. Baum, Cunitz, and Reuss, the editors of Calvin's Works, during half a century, and embraces 274 publications of the Reformer (among them 36 Latin and 18 French editions of the *Institutio*), many rare contemporary works, and 700 modern books bearing upon Calvin and his Reformation. The Society of the History of French Protestantism in Paris (54 rue des saints pères) has a large collection of printed works.

I. CORRESPONDENCE OF THE SWISS REFORMERS AND THEIR FRIENDS.
Letters took to a large extent the place of modern newspapers and pamphlets; hence their large number and importance.

* A. S. HERMINJARD: *Correspondance des réformateurs dans les pays de langue française,* etc. Genève et Paris (Fischbacher, 33 rue de Seine), 1866–'86, 7 vols. To be continued. The most complete collection of letters of the Reformers of French Switzerland and their friends, with historical and biographical notes. The editor shows an extraordinary familiarity with the history of the French and Swiss Reformation. The first three volumes embrace the period from 1512 to 1536; vols. IV.–VII. extend from 1536 to 1542, or from the publication of Calvin's Institutes to the acceptance

of the ecclesiastical ordinances at Geneva. For the following years to
the death of Calvin (1564) we have the correspondence in the Strassburg-
Brunswick edition of Calvin's works, vols. X.-XX. See below.

II. The History of Geneva before, during, and after the Refor-
    mation:

Jac. Spon: *Histoire de la ville et de l'état de Genève.* Lyon, 1680, 2 vols.:
revised and enlarged by J. A. Gautier, Genève, 1730, 2 vols.

J. P. Bérenger: *Histoire de Genève jusqu'en 1761.* Genève. 1772, 6 vols.

(Grénus) *Fragments biographiques et historiques extraits des registres de Genève.*
Genève, 1815.

Mémoires *et* documents *publiés par la Société d'histoire et d'archéologie de
Genève.* 1840 sqq., vol. I.-XIV.

Francois Bonivard: *Les chroniques de Genève.* *Publiés par G. Revilliod.*
Genève, 1867, 2 vols.

* Amédée Roget (Professor at the University of Geneva, d. Sept. 29, 1883):
Histoire du peuple de Genève depuis la réforme jusqu'à l'escalade. Genève,
1870-'83. 7 vols. From 1536 to 1567. The work was to extend to
1602, but was interrupted by the death of the author. Impartial. The
best history of Geneva during the Reformation period. The author was
neither a eulogist nor a detractor of Calvin. — By the same: *L'église et
l'état à Genève du vivant de Calvin.* Genève, 1867 (pp. 91).

Jacq. Aug. Galiffe: *Matériaux pour l'histoire de Genève.* Genève, 1829 and '30,
2 vols. 8°; *Notices généalogiques sur les familles genevoises,* Genève, 1829,
4 vols. — J. B. G. Galiffe (son of the former, and Professor of the
Academy of Geneva): *Besançon Hugues, libérateur de Genève. Historique
de la fondation de l'independance Genevoise,* Genève, 1859 (pp. 330); *Genève
historique et archéol.,* Genève, 1869; *Quelques pages d'histoire exacte, soit les
procès criminels intentés à Genève en 1547, pour haute trahison contre noble
Ami Perrin, ancien syndic, conseiller et capitaine-général de la republique, et
contre son accusateur noble Laurent Meigret dit le Magnifique,* Genève, 1862
(135 pp. 4°); *Nouvelles pages d'histoire exacte soit le procès de Pierre Ameaux,*
Genève, 1863 (116 pp. 4°). The Galiffes, father and son, descended from
an old Genevese family, are Protestants, but very hostile to Calvin and
his institutions, chiefly from the political point of view. They maintain,
on the ground of family papers and the acts of criminal processes, that
Geneva was independent and free before Calvin, and that he introduced
a system of despotism. "*La plupart des faits racontés par le medecin Lyon-
nais*" (*Bolsec*), says the elder Galiffe (*Notices généalogiques,* III. 547),
"*sont parfaitement vrais.*" He judges Calvin by the modern theory of
toleration which Calvin and Beza with their whole age detested. "*Les
véritable protestants genevois,*" he says, "*étaient ceux qui voulaient que chacun
fût libre de penser ce que sa raison lui inspirait, et de ne faire que ce qu'elle
approuvait ; mais que personne ne se permit d'attaquer la religion de son pro-
chain, de se moquer de sa croyance, ou de le scandaliser par des démonstrations
malicieuses et par des fanfaronnades de supériorité qui ne prouvent que la
fatuité ridicule de ceux qui se nomment les élus.*" The Galiffes sympathize

with Ami Perrin, François Favre, Jean Philippe, Jean Lullin, Pierre Vandel, Michael Servet, and all others who were opposed to Calvin. For a fair criticism of the works of the Galiffes, see *La France Protestante*, II. 767 sqq., 2d ed.

III. THE REFORMERS BEFORE CALVIN:

* *Le Chroniqueur. Recueil historique, et journal de l'Helvetie romande, en l'an 1535 et en l'an 1536.* Edited by L. Vulliemin, 1835. Lausanne (Marc Duclos), 326 pp. 4°. Descriptions and reprints of documents relating to the religious condition in those two years, in the form of a contemporary journal.

MELCHIOR KIRCHHOFER (of Schaffhausen, 1773–1853): *Das Leben Wilhelm Farels aus den Quellen bearbeitet.* Zürich, 1831 and '33, 2 vols. (pp. 251 and 190, no index). Very good for that time. He also wrote biographies of Haller, Hofmeister, Myconius.

CH. CHENEVIÈRE: *Farel, Froment, Viret, réformateurs relig.* Genève, 1835.

H. JAQUEMOT: *Viret, réformateur de Lausanne.* Strassburg, 1856.

F. GODET (Professor and Pastor in Neuchatel): *Histoire de la réformation et du refuge dans le pays de Neuchatel.* Neuchatel, 1859 (209 pp.). Chiefly devoted to the labors of Farel, but carries the history down to the immigration of French refugees after the Revocation of the Edict of Nantes.

C. SCHMIDT (of Strassburg): *Wilhelm Farel und Peter Viret. Nach handschriftlichen und gleichzeitigen Quellen.* Elberfeld, 1860. (In vol. IX. of the "Leben und ausgewählte Schriften der Väter der reform. Kirche.")

T. CART: *Pierre Viret, le réformateur vaudois.* Lausanne, 1864.

C. JUNOD: *Farel, réformateur de la Swisse romande et réformateur de l'église de Neuchatel.* Neuchatel et Paris, 1865.

IV. WORKS AND CORRESPONDENCE OF JOHN CALVIN:

JOH. CALVINI: *Opera quœ supersunt omnia,* ed. G. Baum, E. Cunitz, E. Reuss, *theologi Argentoratenses.* Brunsvigæ, 1863 sqq. (in the *Corp. Reform.*). So far (1892) 48 vols. 4°. The most complete and most critical edition. The three editors died before the completion of their work, but left material for the remaining volumes (vols. 45 sqq.) which are edited by *Alf. Erichson.*

Older Latin edd., Geneva, 1617, 7 vols. folio, and Amstelod., 1667–'71, in 9 vols. folio. Separate Latin editions of the *Institutes,* by Tholuck (Berlin, 1834 and '46), and of the *Commentaries* on Genesis by Hengstenberg (Berlin, 1838), on the Psalms (Berlin, 1830–'34), and the New Testament, except the Apocalypse (1833–'38, in 7 vols.), by Tholuck. The same books have also been separately republished in French.

An English edition of Calvin's Works, by the "Calvin Translation Society," Edinburgh, 1843–'53, in 52 vols. The *Institutes* have been translated by Allen (London, 1813, often reprinted by the Presbyterian Board of Publication in Philadelphia), and by Henry Beveridge (Edinburgh, 1846). German translations of his *Institutes* by Fr. Ad. Krummacher (1834) and by B. Spiess (the first edition of 1536, Wiesbaden, 1887), and of parts of his *Comment.,* by C. F. L. Matthieu (1859 sqq.).

The extensive correspondence of Calvin was first edited in part by BEZA and JONVILLIERS (Calvin's secretary), Genevæ, 1575, and other editions; then by BRETSCHNEIDER (the Gotha Letters), Lips. 1835; by A. CROTTET, Genève, 1850; much more completely by JULES BONNET, *Lettres Françaises*, Paris, 1854, 2 vols.; an English translation (from the French and Latin) by D. CONSTABLE and M. R. GILCHRIST, Edinburgh and Philadelphia (Presbyterian Board of Publication), 1855 sqq., in 4 vols. (the fourth with an index), giving the letters in chronological order (till 1558). The last and best edition is by the Strassburg Professors in *Calvini Opera*, vol. X. Part II. to vol. XX., with ample *Prolegomena* on the various editions of Calvin's Letters and the manuscript sources. His letters down to 1542 are also given by HERMINJARD, vols. VI. and VII., quoted above.

V. BIOGRAPHIES OF CALVIN:

* THEODOR BEZA (d. 1605): *Johannis Calvini Vita.* First published with Calvin's posthumous Commentary on Joshua, in the year of his death. It is reprinted in all editions of Calvin's works, and in Tholuck's edition of Calvin's Commentary on the Gospels. In the same year Beza published a French edition under the title, *L'Histoire de la vie et mort de Maistre Jean Calvin avec le testament et derniere volonté dudit Calvin: et le catalogue des livres par luy composez.* Genève, 1564; second French edition, enlarged and improved by his friend and colleague, NIC. COLLADON, 1565; best edition, Geneva, 1657 (very rare, 204 pp.), which has been carefully republished from a copy in the Mazarin library, with an introduction and notes by ALFRED FRANKLIN, Paris, 1869 (pp. lxi and 294). This edition should be consulted. The three biographies of Beza (two French and one Latin) are reprinted in the Brunswick edition of Calvin's *Opera* with a *notice littéraire*, Tom. XXI. pp. 6–172, to which are added the *Epitaphia in Io. Calvinum scripta* (Hebrew, Greek, Latin, and French). There are also German, English, and Italian translations of this biography. An English translation by Francis Sibson of Trinity College, Dublin, reprinted in Philadelphia, 1836; another by Beveridge, Edinburgh, 1843.
The biography of Beza as enlarged by Colladon, though somewhat eulogistic, and especially Calvin's letters and works, and the letters of his friends who knew him best, furnish the chief material for an authentic biography.

HIEROSME HERMES BOLSEC: *Histoire de la vie, mœurs, actes, doctrine, constance et mort de Jean Calvin, jadis ministre de Genève, dédié au Reverendissime archeuesque, conte de l'Église de Lyon, et Primat de France,* Lyon, 1577 (26 chs. and 143 pp.); republished at Paris, 1582; and with an introduction and notes by L. Fr. Chastel, Lyon, 1875 (pp. xxxi and 328). I have used Chastel's edition. A Latin translation, *De J. Calvini magni quondam Genevensium ministri vita, moribus, rebus gestis, studiis ac denique morte,* appeared in Paris, 1577, also at Cologne, 1580; a German translation at Cologne, 1581. Bolsec was a Carmelite monk, then physician at Geneva, expelled on account of Pelagian views and opposition to Calvin, 1551; returned to the Roman Church; d. at Annecy about 1584. His book is a mean and unscrupulous libel, inspired by feelings of hatred and revenge;

but some of his facts are true, and have been confirmed by the documents published by Galiffe. Bolsec wrote a similar biography of Beza: *Histoire de la vie, mœurs, doctrine et déportments de Th. de Bèze dit le Spectable*, 1582. A French writer says, " *Ces biographies sont un tissu de calomnies qu' aucun historien sérieux, pas même le P. Maimbourg, n'a osé admettre et dont plus récemment M. Mignet a fait bonne justice.*" (A. Réville in Lichtenberger's "Encycl.," II. 343.) Comp. the article "Bolsec" in *La France Protestante*, 2d ed. (1879), II. 745–776.

Antibolseccus. Cleve, 1622. Of this book I find only the title.

JACQUES LE VASSEUR (canon and dean of the Church of Noyon): *Annales de l'église cathédrale de Noyon.* Paris, 1633, 2 vols. 4°. Contains some notices on the birth and relations of Calvin.

JACQUES DESMAY (R. C.): *Remarques sur la vie de J. Calvin hérésiarque tirées des Registres de Noyon.* Rouen, 1621 and 1657.

CHARLES DRELINCOURT (pastor at Charenton): *La défense de Calvin contre l'outrage fait à sa mémoire.* Genève, 1667; in German, Hanau, 1671. A refutation of the slanders of Bolsec and a posthumous book of Cardinal Richelieu on the easiest and surest method of conversion of those who separated themselves from the Roman Church. Bayle gives an epitome in his *Dictionnaire.*

MELCHIOR ADAM: *Vita Calvini*, in his *Vitæ Theologorum*, etc. 3d ed. Francof., 1705 (Part II., *Decades duæ*, etc., pp. 32–55). Chiefly from Beza.

ELIJAH WATERMAN (pastor of the Presbyterian Church in Bridgeport, Conn.): *Memoirs of the Life and Writings of John Calvin: together with a selection of Letters written by him and other distinguished Reformers.* Hartford, 1813.

VINCENT AUDIN (R. C., 1793–1851): *Histoire de la vie, des ouvrages et des doctrines de Calvin.* Paris, 1841, 2 vols.; 5th ed. 1851; 6th ed. 1873. English translation by John McGill; German translation, 1843. Written like a novel, with a deceptive mixture of truth and falsehood. It is a Bolsec redivivus. Audin says that he first cast away the book of Bolsec "as a shameful libel. All testimony was against Bolsec: Catholics and Protestants equally accused him. But, after a patient study of the reformer, we are now compelled to admit, in part, the recital of the physician of Lyon. Time has declared for Bolsec; each day gives the lie to the apologists of Calvin." He boasts of having consulted more than a thousand volumes on Calvin, but betrays his polemical bias by confessing that he "*desired to prove* that the refugee of Noyon was fatal to civilization, to the arts, and to civil and religious liberty." Audin wrote in the same spirit the history of Luther (1839, 3 vols.), Henry VIII. (1847), and Leo X. (1851). His work is disowned and virtually refuted by fair-minded Catholics like Kampschulte, Cornelius, and Funk.

*PAUL HENRY, D.D. (pastor of a French Reformed Church in Berlin): *Das Leben Johann Calvins des grossen Reformators*, etc. (dedicated to Neander). Hamburg, 1835–44, 3 vols. English translation (but without the notes and appendices, and differing from the author on the case of Servetus) by HENRY STEBBING, London and New York, 1851, in 2 vols. This large work marks an epoch as an industrious collection of valuable material, but is ill digested, and written with unbounded admiration for Calvin. Henry wrote also, in opposition to Audin and Galiffe, an abridged *Leben Johann Calvin's. Ein Zeugniss für die Wahrheit.* Hamburg and Gotha, 1846 (pp. 498).

THOMAS SMYTH, D.D.: *Calvin and his Enemies.* 1843; new ed. Philadelphia (Presbyterian Board of Publication), 1856, and again 1881. Apologetic.

THOMAS H. DYER: *The Life of John Calvin.* London (John Murray), 1850, pp. 560 (republished, New York, 1851). Graphic and impartial, founded upon Calvin's correspondence, Henry, and Trechsel (*Antitrinitarier*).

FELIX BUNGENER: *Calvin, sa vie, son œuvre, et ses écrits.* Paris, 2d ed. 1863 (pp. 468). English translation, Edinburgh, 1863.

* E. STÄHELIN (Reformed minister at Basel): *Johannes Calvin; Leben und ausgewählte Schriften.* Elberfeld, 1863, 2 vols. (in " Väter und Begründer der reform. Kirche," vol. IV. in two parts). One of the best biographies, though not as complete as Henry's, and in need of modification and additions from more recent researches.

PAUL PRESSEL (Luth.): *Johann Calvin. Ein evangelisches Lebensbild.* Elberfeld, 1864 (pp. 263). For the tercentenary of Calvin's death (May 27, 1864). Based upon Stähelin, Henry, Mignet, and Bonnet's edition of Calvin's letters.

ALBERT RILLIET: *Bibliographie de la vie de Calvin.* " Correspond. litteraire." Paris, 1864. *La premier séjour de Calvin à Genève.* Gen. 1878.

* GUIZOT (the great historian and statesman, a descendant of the Huguenots, d. at Val Richer, Sept. 12, 1874): *St. Louis and Calvin.* London, 1868. Comp. also his sketch in the *Musée des protestants célèbres.*

* F. W. KAMPSCHULTE (a liberal Roman Catholic, Professor of History at Bonn, died an Old Catholic, 1872): *Joh. Calvin, seine Kirche und sein Staat in Genf.* Leipzig, 1869, vol. I. (vols. II. and III. have not appeared). A most able, critical, and, for a Catholic, remarkably fair and liberal work, drawn in part from unpublished sources. — In the same spirit of fairness, Prof. FUNK of Tübingen wrote an article on Calvin in the 2d ed. of Wetzer and Welte's Catholic *Kirchenlexicon,* II. 1727–1744.

THOMAS M'CRIE, D.D.: *The Early Years of John Calvin. A Fragment, 1509–1536.* A posthumous work, edited by William Ferguson. Edinburgh, 1880 (pp. 199). Valuable as far as it goes.

Art. "Calvin" in *La France Protestante,* Paris, 2d ed. vol. III. (1881), 508–639.

ABEL LEFRANC: *La jeunesse de Calvin.* Paris, 1888 (pp. 229). The author brings to light new facts on the extent of the Protestant movement at Noyon. — Comp. his *Histoire de la Ville de Noyon et de ses institutions.* Paris, 1888.

Annales Calviniani by the editors of the Brunswick edition of Calvin's *Opera.* Tom. XXI. 183–818. From 1509 to 1572. Invaluable for reference.

VI. BIOGRAPHICAL SKETCHES AND ESSAYS ON SPECIAL POINTS CONNECTED
    WITH CALVIN:

FR. AUG. ALEX. MIGNET (eminent French historian and academician, 1796–
    1884): *Mémoire sur l'établissement de la réforme et sur la constitution du*
    Calvinisme à Genève. Paris, 1834. The same in German, Leipzig, 1843.

G. WEBER: *Geschichtliche Darstellung des Calvinismus im Verhältniss zum Staat*
    in Genf und Frankreich bis zur Aufhebung des Edikts von Nantes. Heidel-
    berg, 1836 (pp. 372).

* J. J. HERZOG: *Joh. Calvin*, Basel, 1843; and in his *Real-Encyklop.*[2] vol. III.
    77–106.

* JULES BONNET: *Lettres de Jean Calvin*, 1854; *Calvin au val d'Aoste*, 1861;
    Idelette de Bure, femme de Calvin (in "Bulletin de la société de l'histoire
    du Protest. français, 1856, Nos. 11 and 12); *Récits du seizième siècle*, Paris,
    1864; *Nouveaux récits*, 1870; *Derniers récits*, 1876.

E. RENAN: *Jean Calvin*, in *Études d'histoire religieuse*, 5th ed. Paris, 1862;
    English translation by O. B. Frothingham (*Studies of Religious History*
    and Criticism, New York, 1864, pp. 285–297).

J. H. ALBERT RILLIET: *Lettre à M. Merle d'Aubigné sur deux points obscurs de*
    la vie de Calvin, Genève, 1864. *Le premier sejour de Calvin à Genève*, in
    his and Dufour's edition of Calvin's French Catechism, Genève, 1878.

MÖNKEBERG: *Joachim Westphal and Joh. Calvin.* Hamburg, 1865.

J. KÖSTLIN: *Calvin's Institutio nach Form und Inhalt*, in the "Studien und
    Kritiken," 1868.

EDMOND STERN: *La théorie du culte d'après Calvin.* Strassburg, 1869.

JAMES ANTHONY FROUDE: *Calvinism, an Address delivered to the Students of*
    St. Andrews, March 17, 1871 (in his *Short Studies on Great Subjects*, Second
    Series, New York, 1873, pp. 9–53).

Principal WILLIAM CUNNINGHAM (Free Church of Scotland, d. 1861): *The*
    Reformers and the Theology of the Reformers. Edinburgh, 1862.

Principal JOHN TULLOCH (of the Established Church of Scotland, d. 1885):
    Leaders of the Reformation. Edinburgh, 1859; 3d ed. 1883.

PHILIP SCHAFF: *John Calvin*, in the "Bibliotheca Sacra," Andover, 1857, pp.
    125–146, and in *Creeds of Christendom* (New York, 1877), I. 421–471.

A. A. HODGE (d. at Princeton, 1885): *Calvinism*, in Johnson's "Universal
    Cyclopædia" (New York, 1875 sqq.), vol. I. pp. 727–734; new ed. 1886,
    vol. I. 676–683.

LYMAN H. ATWATER: *Calvinism in Doctrine and Life*, in the "Presbyterian
    Quarterly and Princeton Review," New York, January, 1875, pp. 73–106.

DARDIER and JUNDT: *Calvin*, in Lichtenberger's "Encyclopédie des sciences
    religieuses," Tom. II. 529–557. (Paris, 1877.)

P. LOBSTEIN: *Die Ethik Calvins in ihren Grundzügen.* Strassburg, 1877.

W. LINDSAY ALEXANDER: *Calvin*, in "Encycl. Brit.," 9th ed. vol. IV. 714 sqq

PIERRE VAUCHER: *Calvin et les Genevois.* Gen. 1880.

A. Pierson : *Studien over Joh. Kalvijn.* Haarlem, 1881–'83.

J. M. Usteri : *Calvin's Sacraments- und Tauflehre.* 1884.

B. Fontana : *Documenti dell' archivio Vaticano e dell' Estense, circa il soggiorno di Calv. a Ferrara.* Rom. 1885. E. Comba in "Revisita christ.," 1885, IV.–VII.

C. A. Cornelius (liberal Catholic) : *Die Verbannung Calvins aus Genf. im J. 1536.* München, 1886. *Die Rückkehr Calvins nach Genf. I. Die Guillermins* (pp. 62); *II. Die Artichauds ; III. Die Berufung* (pp. 102). München, 1888 and 1889. Separate print from the " Abhandlungen der K. bayer. Akademie der Wissenschaften," XIX. Bd. II. Abth. Cornelius, a friend of Döllinger, agrees in his high estimate of Calvin with Kampschulte, but dwells chiefly on the political troubles of Geneva during Calvin's absence (with large quotations from Herminjard's collection of letters), and stops with Calvin's return, September, 1540.

Charles W. Shields : *Calvin's Doctrine on Infant Salvation,* in the "Presb. and Ref. Review," New York, 1890, pp. 634–651. Tries to show that Calvin taught universal infant salvation (?).

Ed. Stricker : *Johann Calvin als erster Pfarrer der reformirten Gemeinde zu Strassburg. Nach urkundlichen Quellen.* Strassburg, 1890 (vi and 66 pp.). — In connection with Calvin's sojourn at Strassburg may also be consulted, R. Reuss : *Histoire de l'église de Strassbourg,* 1880 ; and A. Erichson : *L'église française de Strassbourg au XVIme siècle,* 1886.

E. Doumergue (Professor of Church History at Montauban) : *Essai sur l'histoire du culte réformé principalement au XVIe et au XIXe siècle.* Paris, 1890. The first part, pp. 1–116, treats of Calvin's Liturgies and labors for church poetry and music.

The literature on Servetus will be given below, in the section on Calvin and Servetus.

VII. Histories of the Reformation in French Switzerland :

* Abr. Ruchat (Professor of Theology in the Academy of Lausanne, d. 1750) : *Histoire de la réformation de la Suisse.* Genève, 1727 sq., 6 vols.; new ed. with appendices, by Prof. L. Vulliemin, Nyon, 1835–'38, 7 vols. Comes down to 1566. Strongly anti-Romish and devoted to Bern, diffuse and inelegant in style, but full of matter, " *un recueil de savantes dissertations, un extrait de documents* " (Dardier, in Lichtenberger's "Encyclop.," XI. 345). — An English abridgment in one volume by J. Collinson : *History of the Reformation in Switzerland by Ruchat.* London, 1845. Goes to 1537.

Dan. Gerdes (1698–1767) : *Introductio in Historiam Evangelii seculo XVI. passim per Europam renovati doctrinæque Reformatæ ; accedunt varia monumenta pietatis atque rei literariæ.* Groningæ, 1744–'52, 4 vols. Contains pictures of the Reformers and interesting documents. Parts of vols. I., II., and IV. treat of the Swiss Reformation.

C. B. Hundeshagen (Professor in Bern, afterwards in Heidelberg and Bonn; d. 1872) : *Die Conflicte des Zwinglianismus, Lutherthums und Calvinismus in der Bernischen Landeskirche von 1532–1558. Nach meist ungedruckten Quellen.* Bern, 1842.

* J. GABEREL (ancien pasteur): *Histoire de l'église de Genève depuis le commencement de la réforme jusqu'en 1815.* Genève, 1855–63, 3 vols.

P. CHARPENNE: *Histoire de la réformation et des réformateurs de Genève.* Paris, 1861.

FLEURY: *Histoire de l'église de Genève.* Genève, 1880. 2 vols.

The works of AMAD. ROGET, quoted sub II.

* MERLE D'AUBIGNÉ (Professor of Church History in the Free Church Theological Seminary at Geneva): *Histoire de la réformation en Europe au temps du Calvin.* Paris, 1863–'78. English translation in several editions, the best by Longmans, Green & Co., London, 1863–'78, 8 vols.; American edition by Carter, New York, 1870–'79, 8 vols. The second division of Merle's work on the Reformation. The last three volumes were edited after his death (Oct. 21, 1872) by Duchemin and Binder, and translated by William L. R. Cates. The work gives the history of the Reformation in Geneva down to 1542, and of the other Reformed Churches to the middle of the sixteenth century. It is, therefore, incomplete, but, as far as it goes, the most extensive, eloquent, and dramatic history of the Reformation by an enthusiastic partisan of the Reformers, especially Calvin, in full sympathy with their position and faith, except on the union of Church and State and the persecution of heretics. The first division, which is devoted to the Lutheran Reformation till 1530, had an extraordinary circulation in England and America. Ranke, with his calm, judicial temperament, wondered that such a book could be written in the nineteenth century. (See Preface to vol. VII. p. vi, note.)

ÉTIENNE CHASTEL (Professor of Church History in the University of Geneva, d. 1882): *Histoire du Christianisme.* Paris, 1882, 5 vols. Tom. IV. 66 sqq. treats of the Swiss Reformation.

G. P. FISHER: *The Reformation.* New York, 1873, ch. VII. pp. 192–241.

PHILIPPE GODET (son of Frederic, the commentator): *Histoire littéraire de la Suisse française.* Neuchâtel and Paris, 1890. Ch. II. 51–112 treats of the Reformers (Farel, Viret, Froment, Calvin, and Beza).

VIRGILE ROSSEL: *Histoire littéraire de la Suisse romande.* Genève (H. Georg), 1890, 2 vols. The first vol. *Des origines jusqu'au XVIIIme siècle.*

The Histories of the Reformation in France usually give also an account of the labors of Farel, Calvin, and Beza; *e.g.* the first volume of GOTTLOB VON POLENZ: *Geschichte des französischen Calvinismus* (Gotha, 1857 sqq.).

§ 59. *The Condition of French Switzerland before the Reformation.*

The losses of the Reformation in German Switzerland were more than made up by the gains in French Switzerland; that is, in the three Cantons, Vaud, Neuchâtel, and

Geneva.[1] Protestantism moved westward. Calvin continued, improved, and completed the work of Zwingli, and gave it a wider significance. Geneva took the place of Zürich, and surpassed in influence the city of Zwingli and the city of Luther. It became "the Protestant Rome," from which proceeded the ideas and impulses for the Reformed Churches of France, Holland, England, and Scotland. The city of Calvin has long since departed from his rigorous creed and theocratic discipline, and will never return to them; but the evangelical faith still lives there in renewed vigor; and among cities of the same size there is none that occupies a more important and influential position in theological and religious activity as well as literary and social culture, and as a convenient centre for the settlement of international questions, than Geneva.

The Reformation of French Switzerland cannot be separated from that of France. The inhabitants of the two countries are of the same Celtic or Gallic stock mixed with Germanic (Frank and Burgundian) blood. The first evangelists of Western Switzerland were Frenchmen who had to flee from their native soil. They became in turn, through their pupils, the founders of the Reformed Church of France. The Reformed Churches of the two countries are one in spirit. After the Revocation of the Edict of Nantes, many Huguenots found an asylum in Geneva, Vaud, and Neuchâtel. The French Swiss combine the best traits of the French character with Swiss solidity and love of freedom. They are ever ready to lend a helping hand to their brethren across the frontier, and they form at the same time a connecting link between them and the Protestants of the German tongue. Their excellent educational institutions attract students from abroad and train teachers for other countries.

---

[1] *La Suisse française* or *la Suisse romande*. Vaud has 1244 square miles; Neuchâtel, 312; Geneva, 109. The first numbered, in 1889, 251,000 inhabitants; the second, 109,000; the third, 107,000.

The territory of the French Cantons, which embraces 1665 square miles, was in the sixteenth century under the protection of the Swiss Confederacy.

Vaud was conquered by Bern from the Duke of Savoy, and ruled by bailiffs till 1798.[1]

The principality of Neuchâtel and Valangin concluded a co-burghery with Freiburg, 1290, with Bern, 1307, and with Solothurn, 1324. In 1707 the principality passed to King Frederick I. of Prussia, who confirmed the rights and liberties of the country and its old alliance with Switzerland. The connection with Prussia continued till 1857, when it was dissolved by free consent.[2]

Geneva was originally governed by a bishop and a count, who divided the spiritual and secular government between them. Duke Charles III. of Savoy tried to subdue the city with the aid of an unworthy and servile bishop, Pierre de la Baume, whom he had appointed from his own family with the consent of Pope Leo X.[3] But a patriotic party, under the lead of Philibert Berthelier, Besançon Hugues, and François Bonivard (Byron's " Prisoner of Chillon ") opposed the attempt and began a struggle for independence, which lasted several years, and resembles on a small scale the heroic struggle of Switzerland against foreign oppression. The patriots, on account of their alliance with the Swiss, were called *Eidgenossen*, — a German word for (Swiss) *Confed-*

---

[1] See Vulliemin, *Le canton de Vaud*, Lausanne, 3d ed., 1885. Verdeil, *Histoire du canton de Vaud*, Lausanne, 1854–'57, 4 vols.

[2] See the historical works on Neuchâtel by Chambrier, Matile, Boyve, Majer, Benoît.

[3] Pierre de la Baume was bishop of Geneva from 1523 to 1536, became bishop of Besançon 1542, and died 1544. Bonivard (as quoted by Audin, who praises the bishops of Geneva) says of him : " He was a great dissipator of goods, in all things superfluous, esteeming it a sovereign virtue in a prelate to have his table loaded with large dishes of meat and all sorts of wines ; and when there he gave himself up so completely as to exceed thirty-one courses." Audin adds (p. 116) : " This shaft would have been much more pointed, had not Bonivard often seated himself at this table and drank far otherwise than became the prior of St. Victor."

erates, which degenerated by mispronunciation into *Eignots* and *Huguenots*, and passed afterwards from Geneva to France as a nickname for Protestants.[1] The party of the Duke of Savoy and the bishop were nicknamed *Mamelukes* or slaves. The patriots gained the victory with the aid of the German Swiss. On Feb. 20, 1526, Bern and Freiburg concluded an alliance with Geneva, and pledged their armed aid for the protection of her independence. The citizens of Geneva ratified the Swiss alliance by an overwhelming majority, who shouted, "The Swiss and liberty!" The bishop appealed in vain to the pope and the emperor, and left Geneva for St. Claude. But he had to accept the situation, and continued to rule ten years longer (till 1536).[2]

This political movement, of which Berthelier is the chief hero, had no connection with the Reformation, but prepared the way for it, and was followed by the evangelical labors of Farel and Viret, and the organization of the Reformed Church under Calvin. During the war of emancipation there grew up an opposition to the Roman Church and the clergy of Geneva, which sided with Savoy and was very corrupt, even according to the testimonies of Roman Catholic writers, such as Bishop Antoine Champion, Bonivard, the Sœur de Jussie, and Francis of Sales. Reports of the Lutheran and Zwinglian reformation nursed the opposition. Freiburg (Fribourg) remained Roman Catholic,[3] and broke

---

[1] Merle D'Aubigné, I. 119: "Until after the Reformation, this sobriquet had a purely political meaning, in no respect religious, and designated simply the friends of independence. Many years after, the enemies of the Protestants of France called them by this name, wishing to stigmatize them and impute to them a foreign, republican, and heretical origin. Such is the true etymology of the term." There are, however, two other etymologies, — one from Hugh Capet, from whom descended Henry IV., the political and military leader of the Huguenots.

[2] For the details of these political struggles, which have little interest for Church history, see Merle D'Aubigné, I. 1–425; the Histories of Geneva, and Am. Roget, *Les Suisses et Genève, ou l'emancipation de la communauté genevoise au XVIᵉ siècle*, Genève, 1864, 2 vols. Also Kampschulte, *l.c.* I. 3–90.

[3] It is famous for the organ in the Church of St. Nicolas, for a suspension

the alliance with Geneva; but Bern strengthened the alliance and secured for Geneva political freedom from Savoy and religious freedom from Rome.

NOTES.

For the understanding of the geography and history of the Swiss Confederacy, the following facts should be considered in connection with the map facing p. 1.

1. The original Confederacy of the THREE FOREST CANTONS (*Urcantone, Waldstätte*), Uri, Schwyz, and Unterwalden, from Aug. 1, 1291 (the date of the renewal of an older covenant of 1244) to 1332. Victory at Morgarten over Duke Leopold of Austria, Nov. 15, 1315. (After 1352 the number of Forest Cantons was *five*, including Luzern and Zug.)

2. The Confederacy of the EIGHT CANTONS (*Orte*) from 1353 to 1481.

Luzern joined the Forest Cantons in 1332 (thenceforward the Confederacy was called the *Bund der Vier Waldstätte*, to which in 1352 was added Zug as the *Fifth Forest Canton;* hence the *Fünf Orte* or *Five Cantons*).

Zürich joined 1351.   Glarus joined 1352.
Zug   "   1352.   Bern   "   1353.

Victories over the Austrians at Sempach, July 9, 1386 (Arnold von Winkelried), and Näfels, April 9, 1388. Battle against the Dauphin of France (Louis XI.) Aug. 26, 1444, at St. Jacob near Basel (the Thermopylæ of the Swiss), and victories over Charles the Bold of Burgundy, at Grandson, June 22, 1476, and Nancy, Jan. 5, 1477.

3. The Confederacy of the THIRTEEN CANTONS, 1513–1798.

Freiburg joined 1481.   Schaffhausen joined 1501.
Solothurn   "   1481.   Appenzell   "   1513.
Basel   "   1501.

4. The Confederation under the French Directory, 1798–1802. Vaud, with the help of France, made herself independent of Bern, 1798. Valtellina Chiavenna, and Bormio were lost to the Grisons and attached to the Cisalpine Republic by Napoleon, 1797. Neuchâtel separated from Switzerland.

5. The Confederation of NINETEEN CANTONS from 1803–1813, under the influence of Napoleon as "Mediator."

6. Modern Switzerland of TWENTY-TWO CANTONS from the Congress of Vienna, 1815, to date.

The new Cantons are: Ticino, Valais, St. Gall, Aargau, Thurgau, Grisons, Geneva, Vaud, Neuchâtel. They were formerly dependent on, and protected by, or freely associated with, the Thirteen Cantons.

---

bridge, and a Catholic university. It is the seat of the bishop of Lausanne, and must not be confounded with Freiburg-im-Breisgau in the Grand Duchy of Baden, which is also a stronghold of Romanism.

§ 60. *William Farel* (1489–1565).

Letters of Farel and to Farel in HERMINJARD, beginning with vol. I. 193, and in the Strassburg edition of Calvin's correspondence, *Opera*, X.–XX.

Biographies by BEZA (*Icones*, 1580, with a picture); MELCHIOR ADAM (*Decades duæ*, 57–61); *KIRCHHOFER (1833, 2 vols.); VERHEIDEN (*Imagines et Elogia*, 1725, p. 86 sq., with picture); CHENEVIÈRE (1835); JUNOD (1865). MERLE D'AUBIGNÉ gives a very minute but broken account of Farel's earlier labors, especially in Geneva (vols. III., IV., V., books 5, 6, and 9). See also RUCHAT, F. GODET, and other works mentioned in § 58, and art. "Farel" in *La France Protestante*, tome VI. 386–415 (1888).

GUILLAUME FAREL.
(From Beza's *Icones*.)

Two years after the political emancipation of Geneva from the yoke of Savoy, Bern embraced the Protestant Reformation (1528), and at once exerted her political and moral influence for the introduction of the new religion into the neighboring French territory over which she had acquired control. She found three evangelists ready for this work, — one a native of Vaud, and two fugitive Frenchmen. The city of Freiburg, the Duke of Savoy, Charles V., and the pope endeavored to prevent the progress of heresy, but in vain.

The pioneer of Protestantism in Western Switzerland is William Farel. He was a travelling evangelist, always in motion, incessant in labors, a man full of faith and fire, as bold and fearless as Luther and far more radical, but without his genius. He is called the Elijah of the French Reformation, and "the scourge of the priests." Once an ardent papist, he became as ardent a Protestant, and looked hereafter only at the dark side, the prevailing corruptions and abuses of Romanism. He hated the pope as the veritable Antichrist, the mass as idolatry, pictures and relics as heathen idols which must be destroyed like the idols of the Canaanites. Without a regular ordination, he felt himself divinely called, like a prophet of old, to break down idolatry and to clear the way for the spiritual worship of God according to his own revealed word. He was a born fighter; he came, not to bring peace, but the sword. He had to deal with priests who carried firearms and clubs under their frocks, and he fought them with the sword of the word and the spirit. Once he was fired at, but the gun burst, and, turning round, he said, "I am not afraid of your shots." He never used violence himself, except in language. He had an indomitable will and power of endurance. Persecution and violence only stimulated him to greater exertions. His outward appearance was not prepossessing: he was small and feeble, with a pale but sunburnt face, narrow forehead, red and ill-combed beard, fiery eyes, and an expressive mouth.

Farel had some of the best qualities of an orator: a sonorous and stentorian voice, appropriate gesture, fluency of speech, and intense earnestness, which always commands attention and often produces conviction. His contemporaries speak of the thunders of his eloquence and of his transporting prayers. "*Tua illa fulgura,*" writes Calvin. "*Nemo tonuit fortius,*" says Beza. His sermons were extemporized, and have not come down to us. Their power lay in the oral delivery. We may compare him to Whitefield, who was likewise a travelling evangelist, endowed with the magnetism of living oratory. In Beza's opinion, Calvin was the most learned, Farel the most forcible, Viret the most gentle preacher of that age.[1]

The chief defect of Farel was his want of moderation and discretion. He was an iconoclast. His violence provoked unnecessary opposition, and often did more harm than good. Œcolampadius praised his zeal, but besought him to be also moderate and gentle. "Your mission," he wrote to him, "is to evangelize, not to curse. Prove yourself to be an evangelist, not a tyrannical legislator. Men want to be led, not driven." Zwingli, shortly before his death, exhorted him not to expose himself rashly, but to reserve himself for the further service of the Lord.

Farel's work was destructive rather than constructive. He could pull down, but not build up. He was a conqueror,

---

[1] Beza, in his *Icones,* thus describes Farel's best qualities : "*Hic enim ille est qui nullis difficultatibus fractus, nullis minis, convitiis, verberibus denique inflictis territus, Mombelgardenses, Neocomenses, Lausanenses, Aquileienses, Genevenses denique Christo lucrifecit. Fuit enim in hoc homine præter pietatem, doctrinam, vitæ innocentiam, eximiamque modestiam, singularis quædam animi præsentia, ingenium acre, sermo vehementiæ plenus, ut tonare potius quam loqui videretur : ardorque denique tantus in precando, ut audientes quasi in cœlum usque subveheret.*" And he compares Calvin, Farel, and Viret in these verses (in 1568) : —

> "*Gallica mirata est Calvinum ecclesia nuper,*
>   *Quo nemo docuit doctius.*
> *Est quoque te nuper mirata, Farelle, tonantem,*
>   *Quo nemo tonuit fortius.*
> *Et miratur adhuc fundentem mella Viretum,*
>   *Quo nemo fatur dulcius.*
> *Scilicet aut tribus his servavere testibus olim,*
>   *Aut interibis Gallia.*"

but not an organizer of his conquests; a man of action, not a man of letters; an intrepid preacher, not a theologian. He felt his defects, and handed his work over to the mighty genius of his younger friend Calvin. In the spirit of genuine humility and self-denial, he was willing to decrease that Calvin might increase. This is the finest trait in his character.[1]

Guillaume Farel, the oldest of seven children of a poor but noble family, was born in the year 1489 (five years after Luther and Zwingli, twenty years before Calvin) at Gap, a small town in the alps of Dauphiné in the south-east of France, where the religious views of the Waldenses were once widely spread. He inherited the blind faith of his parents, and doubted nothing. He made with them, as he remembered in his old age, a pilgrimage to a wonder-working cross which was believed to be taken from the cross of our Lord. He shared in the superstitious veneration of pictures and relics, and bowed before the authority of monks and priests. He was, as he said, more popish than popery.

At the same time he had a great thirst for knowledge, and was sent to school at Paris. Here he studied the ancient languages (even Hebrew), philosophy, and theology. His principal teacher, Jacques Le Fèvre d'Étaples (Faber Stapulensis, 1455–1536), the pioneer of the Reformation in France and translator of the Scriptures, introduced him into the knowledge of Paul's Epistles and the doctrine of justification by faith, and prophetically told him, already in 1512: "My son, God will renew the world, and you will witness it."[2] Farel acquired the degree of Master of Arts (January,

---

[1] "*L'homme du midi* [*Farel*] *était fait pour conquérir; l'homme du nord* [*Calvin*] *pour conserver et discipliner la conquête. Farel en eut le sentiment si distinct, qu'il s'effaça spontanément devant Calvin le jour où il le contraignit par les 'tonnerres' de sa parole de demeurer à Genève, qui avait besoin de son génie.*" Philippe Godet, *Hist. littér. de la Suisse française*, p. 51.

[2] "*Mon fils, Dieu renouvellera le monde et tu en seras le témoin.*" Herminjard, I. 5, note. Compare the passage there quoted from Le Fèvre's work on St. Paul.

1517), and was appointed teacher at the college of Cardinal Le Moine.

The influence of Le Fèvre and the study of the Bible brought him gradually to the conviction that salvation can be found only in Christ, that the word of God is the only rule of faith, and that the Roman traditions and rites are inventions of man. He was amazed that he could find in the New Testament no trace of the pope, of the hierarchy, of indulgences, of purgatory, of the mass, of seven sacraments, of sacerdotal celibacy, of the worship of Mary and the saints. Le Fèvre, being charged with heresy by the Sorbonne, retired in 1521 to his friend William Briçonnet, bishop of Meaux, who was convinced of the necessity of a reformation within the Catholic Church, without separation from Rome.[1] There he translated the New Testament into French, which was published in 1523 without his name (almost simultaneously with Luther's German New Testament). Several of his pupils, Farel, Gérard, Roussel, Michel d'Arande, followed him to Meaux, and were authorized by Briçonnet to preach in his diocese. Margaret of Valois, sister of King Francis I. (then Duchess of Alençon, afterwards Queen of Navarre), patronized the reformers and also the freethinkers. But Farel was too radical for the mild bishop, and forbidden to preach, April 12, 1523. He went to Gap and made some converts, including four of his brothers; but the people found his doctrine " very strange," and drove him away. There was no safety for him anywhere in France, which then began seriously to persecute the Protestants.

Farel fled to Basel, and was hospitably received by Œcolampadius. At his suggestion he held a public disputation in Latin on thirteen theses, in which he asserted the perfec-

---

[1] Herminjard (I. 3) begins his *Correspondance des Réf.* with a letter of Le Fèvre to Briçonnet, Dec. 15, 1512, in which he dedicated to him his Commentary on the Epistles of Paul.

tion of the Scriptures, Christian liberty, the duty of pastors
to preach the Gospel, the doctrine of justification by faith,
and denounced images, fasting, celibacy, and Jewish ceremonies (Feb. 23, 1524).[1] The disputation was successful,
and led to the conversion of the Franciscan monk Pellican,
a distinguished Greek and Hebrew scholar, who afterwards
became professor at Zürich. He also delivered public lectures and sermons. Œcolampadius wrote to Luther that
Farel was a match for the Sorbonne.[2] Erasmus, whom Farel
imprudently charged with cowardice and called a Balaam,
regarded him as a dangerous disturber of the peace,[3] and the
Council (probably at the advice of Erasmus) expelled him
from the city.

Farel now spent about a year in Strassburg with Bucer
and Capito. Before he went there he made a brief visit to
Zürich, Schaffhausen, and Constance, and became acquainted
with Zwingli, Myconius, and Grebel. He had a letter of
commendation to Luther from Œcolampadius, but it is not
likely that he went to Wittenberg, since there is no allusion
to it either in his or in Luther's letters. At the request of
Ulrich, Duke of Würtemberg, he preached in Mömpelgard
(Montbéliard), and roused a fierce opposition, which forced
him soon to return to Strassburg. Here he found Le Fèvre
and other friends from Meaux, whom the persecution had
forced to flee.

In 1526 Farel was again in Switzerland, and settled for a
while, at the advice of Haller, as school teacher under the

---

[1] Herminjard (I. 193–195) gives the theses from the Archives of Zürich.
The first is the most characteristic: "*Absolutissimam nobis præscripsit Christus
vivendi regulam, cui nec addere licet, nec detrahere.*" Œcolampadius served as
interpreter, since Farel's French pronunciation of Latin made it difficult to
understand him.

[2] "*Nimirum instructus ad totam Sorbonicam affligendam, si non et perdendam.*"
Letter of May 15, 1524, in Herminjard, I. 215.

[3] He described him in a letter to the official of Besançon, 1524: "*Nihil
vidi unquam mendacius, virulentius aut seditiosius.*" Quite natural from his
standpoint. The two characters had no points of contact.

name of Guillaume Ursinus (with reference to Bern, the city
of bears), at Aigle (Ælen)[1] in the Pays de Vaud on the
borders of Valais, subject to Bern.

He attended the Synod in Bern, January, 1528, which
decided the victory of the Reformation, and received a commission from that city to preach in all the districts under
its control (March 8, 1528). He accordingly labored as a
sort of missionary bishop at Murat (Murten), Lausanne,
Neuchâtel, Valangin, Yverdun, Biel (Bienne), in the Münster valley, at Orbe, Avenche, St. Blaise, Grandson, and
other places. He turned every stump and stone into a pulpit, every house, street, and market-place into a church;
provoked the wrath of monks, priests, and bigoted women;
was abused, called "heretic" and "devil," insulted, spit upon,
and more than once threatened with death. An attempt
to poison him failed. Wherever he went he stirred up all
the forces of the people, and made them take sides for or
against the new gospel.

His arrival in Neuchâtel (December, 1529) marks an epoch
in its history. In spite of violent opposition, he succeeded
in introducing the Reformation in the city and neighboring
villages. He afterwards returned to Neuchâtel, where he
finished his course.[2] Robert Olivetan, Calvin's cousin, published the first edition of his French translation of the Bible
at Neuchâtel in 1535. Farel had urged him to do this work.
It is the basis of the numerous French translations made
since that time.

In 1532 Farel with his friend Saunier visited the Waldenses in Piedmont at the request of Georg Morel and Peter
Masson, two Waldensian preachers, who were returning from
a visit to Strassburg and the Reformed Churches of Switzer-

[1] In August, 1526, Bucer addressed him, "*Ursinus, Ælœ episcopus.*" Herminjard, I. 461.

[2] For a graphic account of his labors in Neuchâtel, see Vuillemin's *Le
Chroniqueur*, pp. 86 sqq., and F. Godet, *Histoire de la réformation et du refuge
dans le pays de Neuchâtel* (1859), pp. 69–190.

land. He attended the Synod which met at Chanforans in the valley of Angrogne, Sept. 12, 1532, and resolved to adopt the doctrines of the Reformation. He advised them to establish schools. He afterwards collected money for them and sent them four teachers, one of whom was Robert Olivetan, who was at that time private tutor at Geneva. This is the beginning of the fraternal relations between the Waldenses and the Reformed Churches which continue to this day.

§ 61. *Farel at Geneva. First Act of the Reformation* (1535).

On their return from Piedmont, Farel and Saunier stopped at Geneva, Oct. 2, 1532. Zwingli had previously directed the attention of Farel to that city as an important field for the Reformation. Olivetan was there to receive them.

The day after their arrival the evangelists were visited by a number of distinguished citizens of the Huguenot party, among whom was Ami Perrin, one of the most ardent promoters of the Reformation, and afterwards one of the chief opponents of Calvin. They explained to them from the open Bible the Protestant doctrines, which would complete and consolidate the political freedom recently achieved. They stirred up a great commotion. The Council was alarmed, and ordered them to leave the city. Farel declared that he was no trumpet of sedition, but a preacher of the truth, for which he was ready to die. He showed credentials from Bern, which made an impression. He was also summoned to the Episcopal Council in the house of the Abbé de Beaumont, the vicar-general of the diocese. He was treated with insolence. "Come thou, filthy devil," said one of the canons, "art thou baptized? Who invited you hither? Who gave you authority to preach?" Farel replied with dignity: "I have been baptized in the name of the Father, the Son, and the Holy Ghost, and am not a devil. I go about preaching Christ, who died for our sins and rose for our justification.

Whoever believes in him will be saved; unbelievers will be lost. I am sent by God as a messenger of Christ, and am bound to preach him to all who will hear me. I am ready to dispute with you, and to give an account of my faith and ministry. Elijah said to King Ahab, 'It is thou, and not I, who disturbest Israel.' So I say, it is you and yours, who trouble the world by your traditions, your human inventions, and your dissolute lives." The priests had no intention to enter into a discussion; they knew and confessed, " If we argue, our trade is gone." One of the canons exclaimed: " He has blasphemed; we need no further evidence; he deserves to die." Farel replied: " Speak the words of God, and not of Caiaphas." Hereupon the whole assembly shouted: "Away with him to the Rhone! Kill the Lutheran dog!" He was reviled, beaten, and shot at. One of the syndics interposed for his protection. He was ordered by the Episcopal Council to leave Geneva within three hours.

He escaped with difficulty the fury of the priests, who pursued him with clubs. He was covered with spittle and bruises. Some Huguenots came to his defence, and accompanied him and Saunier in a boat across the lake to a place between Morges and Lausanne. At Orbe, Farel found Antoine Froment, a native of Dauphiné, and prevailed on him to go to Geneva as evangelist and a teacher of children (November, 1532); but he was also obliged to flee.

In this critical condition the Roman party, supported by Freiburg, called to their aid Guy Furbity, a learned Dominican doctor of the Sorbonne. He preached during advent, 1533, against the Protestant heresy with unmeasured violence. In Jan. 1, 1534, the bishop forbade all preaching without his permission.

Farel returned under the protection of Bern, and held a public disputation with Furbity, Jan. 29, 1534, in the presence of the Great and Small Councils and the delegates of Bern. He could not answer all his objections, but he denied the right of the Church to impose ordinances which were not authorized by the Scriptures, and defended the position that Christ was the only head of the Church. He used the occasion to explain the Protestant doctrines, and to attack the Roman hierarchy. Christ and the Holy Spirit, he said, are not with the pope, but with those whom he persecutes. The disputation lasted several days, and ended in a partial victory for Farel. Unable to argue from the Scriptures, Furbity confessed: "What I preached I cannot prove from the Bible; I have learned it from the *Summa* of St. Thomas"; but he repeated in the pulpit of St. Peter's his charges against the heretics, Feb. 15, and was put in prison for several years.

Farel continued to preach in private houses. On March 1, when a monk, Francis Coutelier, attacked the Reformation, he ascended the pulpit to refute him. This was his first public sermon in Geneva. The Freiburgers protested against these proceedings, and withdrew from the coburghery (April 12). The bishop pronounced the ban over the city (April 30); the Duke of Savoy threatened war. But Bern stood by Geneva, and under her powerful protection, Farel, Viret, and Froment vigorously pushed the Reformation, though not without much violence.

The priests, monks, and nuns gradually left the city, and the bishop transferred his see to Annecy, an asylum prepared by the Duke of Savoy. Sister Jeanne de Jussie, one of the nuns of St. Claire, has left us a lively and naive account of their departure to Annecy. "It was a piteous thing," she says, "to see this holy company in such a plight, so overcome with fatigue and grief that several swooned by the way. It was rainy weather, and all were obliged to walk through muddy roads, except four poor invalids who were in a carriage. There were six poor old women who had taken their vows more than sixteen years before. Two of these, who were past sixty-six, and had never seen anything of the world, fainted away repeatedly. They could not bear the wind; and when they saw the cattle in the fields, they took the cows for bears, and the long-wooled sheep for ravaging wolves. They who met them were so overcome with compassion that they could not speak a word. And though our mother, the vicaress, had supplied them all with good shoes to save their feet, the greater number could not walk in them, but hung them at their waists. And so they walked from five o'clock in the morning, when they left Geneva, till near midnight, when they got to St. Julien, which is only a little league off." It took the nuns fifteen hours to go a short league. The next day (Aug. 29) they reached Annecy under the ringing of all the bells of the city, and found rest in the monastery of the Holy Cross. The good sister Jussie saw in the Reformation a just punishment of the unfaithful clergy. "Ah," she said, "the prelates and churchmen did not observe their vows at this time, but squandered dissolutely the ecclesiastical property, keeping women in adultery and lubricity, and awakening the anger of God, which brought divine judgment on them."[1]

In Aug. 27, 1535, the Great Council of Two Hundred issued an edict of the Reformation, which was followed by another, May 21, 1536. The mass was abolished and forbidden, images and relics were removed from the churches. The citizens pledged themselves by an oath to live according to the precepts of the Gospel. A school was established for the elementary religious education of the young at the Convent de Rive, under the direction of Saunier. Out of it grew, afterwards, the college and academy of Calvin. A

[1] *Le commencement de l'hérésie en Génève.* Grénus, *Fragments historiques,* pp. 199–208; *Le Chroniqueur,* 147–150. Ruchat (III. 383, ed. Vulliemin) doubts the simplicity of these good sisters, and suspects them of occasional communication with the Franciscans through subterranean passages: "*Il y a pourtant quelque lieu de douter si ces religieuses étaient aussi simples que la sœur de Jussi voudrait nous le faire accroire. Les chemins souterrains qu'on découvrit après leur départ sous leur couvent (et qui conduissaient à celui des Cordeliers qui était à quelques pas de là), donnent tout lieu de soupçonner qu'elles recevaient de temps en temps des visites de ces bons frères, et qu'ainsi elles n'étaient pas tant novices dans les affaires du monde.*"

general hospital was founded at St. Claire, and endowed with the revenues of old Catholic hospitals. The bishop's palace was converted into a prison. Four ministers and two deacons were appointed with fixed salaries payable out of the ecclesiastical revenues. Daily sermons were introduced at St. Pierre and St. Gervais; the communion after the simple solemn fashion of Zürich was to be celebrated four times a year; baptism might be administered on any day, but only in the church, and by a minister. All shops were to be closed on Sunday. A strict discipline, which extended even to the headdress of brides, began to be introduced.

This was the first act in the history of the Reformation of Geneva. It was the work of Farel, but only preparatory to the more important work of Calvin. The people were anxious to get rid of the rule of Savoy and the bishop, but had no conception of evangelical religion, and would not submit to discipline. They mistook freedom for license. They were in danger of falling into the opposite extreme of disorder and confusion.

This was the state of things when Calvin arrived at Geneva in the summer of 1536, and was urged by Farel to assume the great task of building a new Church on the ruins of the old. Although twenty years older, he assumed willingly a subordinate position. He labored for a while as Calvin's colleague, and was banished with him from Geneva, because they demanded submission to a confession of faith and a rigorous discipline. Calvin went to Strassburg. Farel accepted a call as pastor to Neuchâtel (July, 1538), the city where he had labored before.

§ 62. *The Last Labors of Farel.*

For the remaining twenty-seven years of his life, Farel remained chief pastor at Neuchâtel, and built up the Protestant Church in connection with Fabri, his colleague. He tried to introduce a severe discipline, by which he offended many of the new converts, and even his friends in Bern; but Fabri favored a milder course.

From Neuchâtel Farel, following his missionary impulse, made preaching excursions to Geneva, Strassburg, and Metz, in Lorraine. At Metz he preached in the cemetery of the Dominicans, while the monks sounded all the bells to drown his voice. He accompanied Calvin to Zürich to bring about the Consensus Tigurinus with the Zwinglians (1549). He followed Servetus to the stake (Oct. 27, 1553), and exhorted him in vain to renounce his errors. He collected money for the refugees of Locarno, and sent letters of comfort to his persecuted brethren in France. He made two visits to Germany (1557) to urge upon the German princes an active intercession in behalf of the Waldenses and French Protestants, but without effect. In December, 1558, when already sixty-nine years of age, he married, against the advice of his friends, a poor maiden, who had fled with her widowed mother from France to Neuchâtel.[1] Calvin was much annoyed by this indiscretion, but besought the preachers of that city to bear with patience the folly of the old bachelor.

The marriage did not cool Farel's zeal. In 1559 he visited the French refugees in Alsace and Lorraine. In November, 1561, he accepted an invitation to Gap, his birthplace, and ventured to preach in public, notwithstanding the royal prohibition, to the large number of his fellow-citizens who had become Protestants.

Shortly before his death Calvin informed him of his illness, May 2, 1564, in the last letter from his pen: "Farewell, my best and truest brother! And since it is God's will that you

---

[1] Six years afterwards he became the father of a son, his only child, who survived him three years. John Knox surpassed him in matrimonial enterprise: he married, as a widower of fifty-eight, a Scotch lass of sixteen, of royal name and blood (Margaret Stuart), who bore him three daughters, and two years after his death (1572) contracted a second marriage. If Erasmus had lived, he might have pointed to these examples in confirmation of his witticisms on the marriages of Luther and Œcolampadius.

remain behind me in the world, live mindful of our friendship, which as it was useful to the Church of God, so the fruit of it awaits us in heaven. Pray do not fatigue yourself on my account. It is with difficulty that I draw my breath, and I expect that every moment will be the last. It is enough that I live and die for Christ, who is the reward of his followers both in life and in death. Again, farewell with the brethren." [1] Farel, notwithstanding the infirmity of old age, travelled to Geneva, and paid his friend a touching farewell visit, but returned home before his death. He wrote to Fabri: "Would I could die for him! What a beautiful course has he happily finished! God grant that we may thus finish our course according to the grace that he has given us."

His last journey was a farewell visit to the Protestants at Metz, who received him with open arms, and were exceedingly comforted by his presence (May, 1565). He preached with the fire of his youth. Soon after his return to Neuchâtel, he died peacefully, Sept. 13, 1565, seventy-six years old. The friends who visited him in his last days were deeply impressed with his heroic steadfastness and hopefulness. He was poor and disinterested, like all the Reformers.[2] A monument was erected to him at Neuchâtel, May 4, 1876.

The writings of Farel are polemical and practical tracts for the times, mostly in French.

---

[1] Calvin, *Opera*, XX. 302, where this epistola is called "*ultima omnium et valedictoria.*"

[2] *La France Prot.*, VI. 409: "*Toute sa succession se monta à 120 livres, preuve de son entière désintéressement.*" Godet, *l.c.*, p. 185: "*Calvin mourant ne laissa que 125 écus de fortune à ses héritiers. Le petit trésor de Farel trouvé après sa mort se montait à 120 livres du pays.*"

[3] See a list of 18 in Schmidt, *l.c.*, p. 38; a more complete one (24) in *La France Protest.*, VI. 410–414. Herminjard, in the 7 vols. of his *Correspond. des Réf.*, gives 107 of his letters, and 242 letters addressed to him.

§ 63. *Peter Viret and the Reformation in Lausanne.*

Biographies of Viret in BEZA's *Icones*, in VERHEIDEN's *Imagines et Elogia* (with a list of his works, pp. 88–90), by CHENEVIÈRE (1835), JAQUEMOT (1856), C. SCHMIDT (1860). References to him in RUCHAT, LE CHRONIQUEUR, GABEREL, MERLE D'AUBIGNÉ, etc.

Farel was aided in his evangelistic efforts chiefly by Viret and Froment, who agreed with his views, but differed from his violent method.

Peter Viret, the Reformer of Lausanne, was the only native Swiss among the pioneers of Protestantism in Western Switzerland; all others were fugitive Frenchmen. He was born, 1511, at Orbe, in the Pays de Vaud, and educated for the priesthood at Paris. He acquired a considerable amount of classical and theological learning, as is evident from his writings. He passed, like Luther and Farel, through a severe mental and moral struggle for truth and peace of conscience. He renounced Romanism before he was ordained, and returned to Switzerland. He was induced by Farel in 1531 to preach at Orbe. He met with considerable success, but also with great difficulty and opposition from priests and people. He converted his parents and about two hundred persons in Orbe, to whom he administered the holy communion in 1532. He shared the labors and trials of Farel and Froment in Geneva. An attempt was made to poison them; he alone ate of the poisoned dish, but recovered, yet with a permanent injury to his health.

His chief work was done at Lausanne, where he labored as pastor, teacher, and author for twenty-two years. By order of the government of Bern a public disputation was held Oct. 1 to 10, 1536.[1] Viret, Farel, Calvin, Fabri, Marcourt, and Caroli were called to defend the Reformed doctrines. Several priests and monks were present, as Drogy, Mimard, Michod, Loys, Berilly, and a French physician,

---

[1] The acts of this disputation are printed in Vullieniin's *Chroniqueur en l'an 1536*, No. 17, pp. 315–326. The chapter of Lausanne protested, pp. 316, 325.

Claude Blancherose. A deputy of Bern presided. The discussion was conducted in French. Farel prepared ten Theses in which he asserts the supremacy of the Bible, justification by faith alone, the high-priesthood and mediatorship of Christ, spiritual worship without ceremonies and images, the sacredness of marriage, Christian freedom in the observance or non-observance of things indifferent, such as fasts and feasts. Farel and Viret were the chief speakers. The result was the introduction of the Reformation, November 1 of the same year. Viret and Pierre Caroli were appointed preachers. Viret taught at the same time in the academy founded by Bern in 1540.

Caroli stayed only a short time. He was a native of France and a doctor of the Sorbonne, who had become nominally a Protestant, but envied Viret for his popularity, took offence at his sermons, and wantonly charged him, Farel, and Calvin, with Arianism. He was deposed as a slanderer, and at length returned to the Roman Church.[1]

In 1549 Beza was appointed second professor of theology at the academy, and greatly strengthened Viret's hands. Five young Frenchmen who were trained by them for the ministry, and had returned to their native land to preach the gospel, were seized at Lyons and burned, May 16, 1553, notwithstanding the intercession of the Reformed Cantons with King Henry II.

Viret attempted to introduce a strict discipline with the ban, but found as much opposition as Calvin at Geneva and Farel at Neuchâtel. Bern disapproved the ban and also the preaching of the rigorous doctrine of predestination. Beza was discouraged, and accepted a call to Geneva (September, 1558). Viret was deposed (Jan. 20, 1559). The professors of the academy and a number of preachers resigned. Viret went to Geneva and was appointed preacher of the city

[1] See his letter of submission to Pope Paul III., June, 1537, in Herminjard, IV. 248 sqq.

(March 2, 1559). His sermons were more popular and impressive than those of Calvin, and better attended.

With the permission of Geneva, he labored for a while as an evangelist, with great success, at Nismes, Montpellier, and Lyons. He presided as Moderator over the fourth national Synod of the Huguenots, August, 1563. He accepted a call from Jeanne d'Albret to an academy at Orthez, in Bearn, which she founded in 1566. There, in 1571, he died, the last of the triumvirate of the founders of the Reformed Church in French Switzerland. He was twice married, first to a lady of Orbe (1538); a second time, to a lady of Geneva (1546). He was small, sickly, and emaciated, but fervent in spirit, and untiring in labor.

Viret was an able and fruitful author, and shows an uncommon familiarity with classical and theological literature. He wrote, mostly in the form of dialogues, expositions of the Apostles' Creed, the Ten Commandments, the Lord's Prayer, a summary of Christian doctrine, polemical books against the Council of Trent, against the mass and other doctrines of Romanism, and tracts on Providence, the Sacraments, and practical religion. The most important is *The Christian Instruction in the Doctrine of the Gospel and the Law, and in the true Philosophy and Theology both Natural and Supernatural* (Geneva, 1564, 3 vols. fol.). His writings are exceedingly rare.[1]

§ 64. *Antoine Froment.*

A. FROMENT: *Les actes et gestes merveilleux de la cité de Genève, nouvellement convertie à l'Evangile.* Edited by G. Revilliod, Genève, 1854. A chronicle from 1532 to 1536, fresh and lively, but partial and often inaccurate. Much used by Merle d'Aubigné. Letters in HERMINJARD, Tom. IV.

There is no special monograph of Froment, and he is omitted in Beza's *Icones* and also in Verheiden's *Imagines et Elogia* (Hagæ, 1725), probably on account of his spotted character. Sketches in *La France Protest.*, VI. 723–733, and notices in Roget, Merle d'Aubigné, Gaberel, Polenz. A

[1] C. Schmidt, in his monograph on Viret, pp. 56–71, gives a list of them with extracts. Comp. Phil. Godet, *l.c.* 70 sqq.

good article by TH. SCHOTT in Herzog², IV. 677–699, and by ROGET in Lichtenberger's "Encycl.," V. 342–344. On his literary merits see PHIL. GODET, *Histoire litteraire de la Suisse Romande*, 82 sqq.

Antoine Froment was born in 1509 in Mens, in Dauphiné, and was one of the earliest disciples of Farel, his country-man. He accompanied him in his evangelistic tours through Switzerland, and shared in his troubles, persecutions, and successes. In 1532 he went for the first time to Geneva, and opened an elementary school in which he taught religion. He advertised it by placards in these words: " A man has arrived, who in the space of one month will teach anybody, great or small, male or female, to read and write French; who does not learn it in that time need not pay anything. He will also heal many diseases without charge." The peo-ple flocked to him; he was an able teacher, and turned his lessons into addresses and sermons.

On new year's day, in 1533, he preached his first sermon on the public place, Molard, attacked the pope, priests, and monks as false prophets (Matt. 7 : 15 sq.), but was inter-rupted by armed priests, and forced by the police to flee to a retreat. He left the city by night, in February, but returned again and again, and aided Farel, Viret, and Calvin.

Unfortunately he did not remain faithful to his calling, and fell into disgrace. He neglected his pastoral duties, kept a shop, and at last gave up the ministry. His colleagues, especially Calvin, complained bitterly of him.[1] In Decem-ber, 1549, he was engaged by Bonivard, the official historian of the Republic, to assist him in his Chronicle, which was completed in 1552. Then he became a public notary of Geneva (1553). He got into domestic troubles. Soon after the death of his first wife, formerly abbess of a convent, he married a second time (1561), but committed adultery with a servant, was deposed, imprisoned, and banished, 1562.

His misfortune seems to have wrought in him a beneficial

---

[1] " *Froment*," says Farel, " *a dégénéré en ivraie (ivresse).*"

change. In 1572 he was permitted on application to return to Geneva in view of his past services, and in 1574 he was reinstated as notary. He died in 1581 (?) The Genevese honored his memory as one, though the least important, and the least worthy, of the four Reformers of their city. His chief work is the Chronicle mentioned above, which supplements the Chronicles of Bonivard, and Sister Jeanne de Jussie.[1]

[1] Michelet (*Hist. de France*, XI. 91): "*Nul livre plus amusant que la chronique de Froment, hardi colporteur de la grâce, naif et mordant satirique que les dévotes génevoises, plaisamment dévoilées par lui, essayèrent de jeter au Rhône.*"

IEAN CALVIN

From the original oil painting in the University Library of Geneva. This picture represents the Reformer as teaching or preaching, and is considered the best.

CHAPTER VIII.

JOHN CALVIN AND HIS WORK.

The literature in § 58, pp. 225–231.

§ 65. *John Calvin compared with the Older Reformers.*

WE now approach the life and work of John Calvin, who labored more than Farel, Viret, and Froment. He was the chief founder and consolidator of the Reformed Church of France and French Switzerland, and left the impress of his mind upon all other Reformed Churches in Europe and America.

Revolution is followed by reconstruction and consolidation. For this task Calvin was providentially foreordained and equipped by genius, education, and circumstances.

Calvin could not have done the work of Farel; for he was not a missionary, or a popular preacher. Still less could Farel have done the work of Calvin; for he was neither a theologian, nor a statesman. Calvin, the Frenchman, would have been as much out of place in Zürich or Wittenberg, as the Swiss Zwingli and the German Luther would have been out of place and without a popular constituency in French-speaking Geneva. Each stands first and unrivalled in his particular mission and field of labor.

Luther's public career as a reformer embraced twenty-nine years, from 1517 to 1546; that of Zwingli, only twelve years, from 1519 to 1531 (unless we date it from his preaching at Einsiedeln in 1516); that of Calvin, twenty-eight years, from 1536 to 1564. The first reached an age of sixty-two: the second, of forty-seven; the third, of fifty-four. Calvin was twenty-five years younger than Luther and Zwingli, and had the great advantage of building on their foundation. He had less genius, but more talent. He was inferior to them as a man of action, but superior as a thinker and organizer. They cut the stones in the quarries, he polished them in the workshop. They produced the new ideas, he constructed them into a system. His was the work of Apollos rather than of Paul: to water rather than to plant, God giving the increase.

Calvin's character is less attractive, and his life less dramatic than Luther's or Zwingli's, but he left his Church in a much better condition. He lacked the genial element of humor and pleasantry; he was a Christian stoic: stern, severe, unbending, yet with fires of passion and affection glowing beneath the marble surface. His name will never rouse popular enthusiasm, as Luther's and Zwingli's did at the celebration of the fourth centennial of their birth; no statues of marble or bronze have been erected to his memory; even the spot of his grave in the cemetery at Geneva is unknown.[1] But he surpassed them in consistency and self-discipline, and by his exegetical, doctrinal, and polemical writings, he has exerted and still exerts more influence than any other Reformer upon the Protestant Churches of the Latin and Anglo-Saxon races. He made little Geneva for a hundred years the Protestant Rome and the best-disciplined Church in Christendom. History furnishes no more striking example of a man of so little personal popularity, and yet such great influence upon the people; of such natural timidity and bashfulness combined with such strength of intellect and character, and such control over his and future generations. He was by nature and taste a retir-

---

[1] A plain stone, with the letters "J. C.," is pointed out to the stranger as marking his resting-place in the cemetery of Plein Palais outside of the city, but it is not known on what authority. He himself especially enjoined that no monument should mark his grave.

ing scholar, but Providence made him an organizer and ruler of churches.

The three leading Reformers were of different nationality and education. Luther, the son of a German peasant, was trained in the school of monasticism and mysticism, under the influence of St. Augustin, Tauler, and Staupitz, and retained strong churchly convictions and prejudices. Zwingli, the son of a Swiss country magistrate, a republican patriot, an admiring student of the ancient classics and of Erasmus, passed through the door of the Renaissance to the Reformation, and broke more completely away from mediævalism. Calvin, a native Frenchman, a patrician by education and taste, studied law as well as theology, and by his legal and judicial mind was admirably qualified to build up a new Christian commonwealth.

Zwingli and Luther met once face to face at Marburg, but did not understand each other. The Swiss extended to the German the hand of fellowship, notwithstanding their difference of opinion on the mode of Christ's presence in the Eucharist; but Luther refused it, under the restraint of a narrower dogmatic conscience. Calvin saw neither, but was intimate with Melanchthon, whom he met at the Colloquies of Worms and Regensburg, and with whom he kept up a correspondence till his death. He rightly placed the German Reformer, as to genius and power, above the Swiss, and generously declared that, even if Luther should call him a devil, he would still esteem Luther as a most eminent servant of God. Luther saw, probably, only two books of Calvin, — his reply to Sadolet and his tract on the Lord's Supper; the former he read, as he says, with singular delight ("*cum singulari voluptate*"). How much more would he have been delighted with his Institutes or Commentaries! He sent respectful greetings to Calvin through Melanchthon, who informed him that he was in high favor with the Wittenberg doctor.

Calvin, in his theology, mediated between Zwingli and Luther. Melanchthon mediated between Luther and Calvin; he was a friend of both, though unlike either in disposition and temper, standing as a man of peace between two men of war. The correspondence between Calvin and Melanchthon, considering their disagreement on the deep questions of pre-destination and free-will, is highly creditable to their head and heart, and proves that theological differences of opinion need not disturb religious harmony and personal friendship.

The co-operative friendships between Luther and Melanch-thon, between Zwingli and Œcolampadius, between Farel and Calvin, between Calvin, Beza, and Bullinger, are among the finest chapters in the history of the Reformation, and reveal the hand of God in that movement.

Widely as these Reformers differed in talent, temperament, and sundry points of doctrine and discipline, they were great and good men, equally honest and earnest, unselfish and unworldly, brave and fearless, ready at any moment to go to the stake for their conviction. They labored for the same end: the renovation of the Catholic Church by leading it back to the pure and perennial fountain of the perfect teach-ing and example of Christ.

§ 66. *Calvin's Place in History.*

1. Calvin was, first of all, a theologian. He easily takes the lead among the systematic expounders of the Reformed system of Christian doctrine. He is scarcely inferior to Augustin among the fathers, or Thomas Aquinas among the schoolmen, and more methodical and symmetrical than either. Melanchthon, himself the prince of Lutheran divines and "the Preceptor of Germany," called him emphatically "the Theologian." [1]

---

[1] With this judgment the Strassburg editors of his works agree, by calling Calvin "*theologorum principem et antesignanum*" (*Opera*, I. IX.). Scaliger says: "Calvin is alone among theologians; there is no ancient to compare with

Calvin's theology is based upon a thorough knowledge of the Scriptures. He was the ablest exegete among the Reformers, and his commentaries rank among the very best of ancient and modern times. His theology, therefore, is biblical rather than scholastic, and has all the freshness of enthusiastic devotion to the truths of God's Word. At the same time he was a consummate logician and dialectician. He had a rare power of clear, strong, convincing statement. He built up a body of doctrines which is called after him, and which obtained symbolical authority through some of the leading Reformed Confessions of Faith.

Calvinism is one of the great dogmatic systems of the Church. It is more logical than Lutheranism and Arminianism, and as logical as Romanism. And yet neither Calvinism nor Romanism is absolutely logical. Both are happily illogical or inconsistent, at least in one crucial point: the former by denying that God is the author of sin — which limits Divine sovereignty; the latter by conceding that baptismal (*i.e.* regenerating or saving) grace is found outside of the Roman Church — which breaks the claim of exclusiveness.[1]

The Calvinistic system is popularly (though not quite correctly) identified with the Augustinian system, and shares its merit as a profound exposition of the Pauline doctrines of sin and grace, but also its fundamental defect of confining the saving grace of God and the atoning work of Christ to a small circle of the elect, and ignoring the general love of God to all mankind (John 3 : 16). It is a theology of Divine sovereignty rather than of Divine love; and yet the love of

him." The term ὁ θεολόγος, as a title of special distinction, was first given to the Apostle John, and afterwards to Gregory Nazianzen; in both cases with special reference to the advocacy of the divinity of Christ (the θεότης τοῦ λόγου). Calvin earned the title in a more comprehensive sense, as covering the whole field of exegetical, dogmatic, and polemic theology.

[1] Expressed in the formula of Cyprian: "*extra ecclesiam* [*Romanam*] *nulla salus.*" Cyprian was logically right, but theologically wrong, when, in his controversy with the Roman bishop, he denied the validity of heretical and schismatical baptism.

God in Christ is the true key to his character and works, and offers the only satisfactory solution of the dark mystery of sin. Arminianism is a reaction against scholastic Calvinism, as Rationalism is a more radical reaction against scholastic Lutheranism.[1]

Calvin did not grow before the public, like Luther and Melanchthon, who passed through many doctrinal changes and contradictions. He adhered to the religious views of his youth unto the end of his life.[2] His *Institutes* came like Minerva in full panoply out of the head of Jupiter. The book was greatly enlarged and improved in form, but remained the same in substance through the several editions (the last revision is that of 1559). It threw into the shade the earlier Protestant theologies, — as Melanchthon's *Loci*, and Zwingli's *Commentary on the True and False Religion*, — and it has hardly been surpassed since. As a classical production of theological genius it stands on a level with Origen's *De Principiis*, Augustin's *De Civitate Dei*, Thomas Aquinas' *Summa Theologiæ*, and Schleiermacher's *Der Christliche Glaube*.

2. Calvin is, in the next place, a legislator and disciplinarian. He is the founder of a new order of Church polity, which consolidated the dissipating forces of Protestantism, and fortified it against the powerful organization of Romanism on the one hand, and the destructive tendencies of sectarianism and infidelity on the other.

In this respect we may compare him to Pope Hildebrand, but with this great difference, that Hildebrand, the man of iron, reformed the papacy of his day on ascetic principles,

---

[1] Harnack excludes Calvinism and Arminianism from his *Dogmengeschichte*, while he devotes to Socinianism, which is not nearly as important, no less than thirty-eight pages (III. 653–691). A strange omission in this important work, completed in 1890. He explains this omission (in a private letter to me, dated March 3, 1891) on the ground that he includes Calvinism and Arminianism in the *Entwicklungsgeschichte des Protestantismus*, which he did not intend to treat in his *Dogmengeschichte*.

[2] Beza says: "In the doctrine which he delivered at first, Calvin persisted steadily to the last, scarcely making any change."

and developed the mediæval theocracy on the hierarchical basis of an exclusive and unmarried priesthood; while Calvin reformed the Church on social principles, and founded a theocracy on the democratic basis of the general priesthood of believers. The former asserted the supremacy of the Church over the State; the latter, the supremacy of Christ over both Church and State. Calvin united the spiritual and secular powers as the two arms of God, on the assumption of the obedience of the State to the law of Christ. The last form of this kind of theocracy or Christocracy was established by the Puritans in New England in 1620, and continued for several generations. In the nineteenth century, when the State has assumed a mixed religious and non-religious character, and is emancipating itself more and more from the rule of any church organization or creed, Calvin would, like his modern adherents in French Switzerland, Scotland, and America, undoubtedly be a champion of the freedom and independence of the Church and its separation from the State.

Calvin found the commonwealth of Geneva in a condition of license bordering on anarchy: he left it a well-regulated community, which John Knox, the Reformer of Scotland, from personal observation, declared to be "the most perfect school of Christ that ever was in the earth since the days of the Apostles," and which Valentin Andreæ, a shining light of the Lutheran Church, likewise from personal observation, half a century after Calvin's death, held up to the churches of Germany as a model for imitation.[1]

The moral discipline which Calvin introduced reflects the severity of his theology, and savors more of the spirit of the Old Testament than the spirit of the New. As a system, it has long since disappeared, but its best results remain in the pure, vigorous, and high-toned morality which distinguishes Calvinistic and Presbyterian communities.

[1] See these and other remarkable judgments quoted more fully in § 110.

It is by the combination of a severe creed with severe self-discipline that Calvin became the father of the heroic races of French Huguenots, Dutch Burghers, English Puritans, Scotch Covenanters, and New England Pilgrims, who sacrificed the world for the liberty of conscience. "A little bit of the world's history," says the German historian Häusser,[1] "was enacted in Geneva, which forms the proudest portion of the sixteenth and seventeenth centuries. A number of the most distinguished men in France, the Netherlands, and Great Britain professed her creed; they were sturdy, gloomy souls, iron characters cast in one mould, in which there was an interfusion of Romanic, Germanic, mediæval, and modern elements; and the national and political consequences of the new faith were carried out by them with the utmost rigor and consistency." A distinguished Scotch divine (Principal Tulloch) echoes this judgment when he says:[2] "It was the spirit bred by Calvin's discipline which, spreading into France and Holland and Scotland, maintained by its single strength the cause of a free Protestantism in all these lands. It was the same spirit which inspired the early and lived on in the later Puritans; which animated such men as Milton and Owen and Baxter; which armed the Parliament of England with strength against Charles I., and stirred the great soul of Cromwell in its proudest triumphs; and which, while it thus fed every source of political liberty in the Old World, burned undimned in the gallant crew of the 'Mayflower,' — the Pilgrim Fathers, — who first planted the seeds of civilization in the great continent of the West."[3]

[1] *The Period of the Reformation*, ed. by Oncken, transl. by Mrs. Sturgis (New York, 1874), p. 255.

[2] *Luther and Other Leaders of the Reformation*, p. 264 sq. (3d ed. 1883).

[3] George Bancroft, the historian of the United States, derives the free institutions of America chiefly from Calvinism through the medium of Puritanism. It is certain that, in the colonial period, Calvinism was the most powerful factor in the theology and religious life of America; but since the close of the eighteenth century, Arminian Methodism fairly divides the field

Calvin was intolerant of any dissent, either papal or heretical, and his early followers in Europe and America abhorred religious toleration (in the sense of indifference) as a pestiferous error; nevertheless, in their conflict with reactionary Romanism and political despotism, they became the chief promoters of civil and religious liberty based upon respect for God's law and authority. The solution of the apparent inconsistency lies in the fact that Calvinists fear God and nothing else. In their eyes, God alone is great, man is but a shadow. The fear of God makes them fearless of earthly despots. It humbles man before God, it exalts him before his fellow-men. The fear of God is the basis of moral self-government, and self-government is the basis of true freedom.[1]

3. Calvin's influence is not confined to the religious and moral sphere ; it extends to the intellectual and literary development of France. He occupies a prominent position in the history of the French language, as Luther, to a still higher degree, figures in the history of the German language. Luther gave to the Germans, in their own vernacular, a version of the Bible, a catechism, and a hymn-book. Calvin did not translate the Scriptures (although from his commentaries a tolerably complete version might be constructed), and his catechism and a few versified psalms never became

---

with it and is numerically the strongest denomination in the United States at the present day. The Baptists, who come next in numerical strength, the Presbyterians, the Congregationalists, and the Dutch and German Reformed rank on the Calvinistic, but the Protestant Episcopalians and Lutherans, predominantly on the Arminian side. The Episcopal Church, however, leaves room for the moderate Calvinism of the Thirty-nine Articles (Art. 17), the high Calvinism of the Lambeth Articles and Irish Articles, and the semi-Catholic tendency of the Prayer-Book. The Lutheran Formula of Concord is Calvinistic in the doctrine of unconditional election of believers and the slavery of the human will, but Arminian in the doctrine of universal atonement and universal vocation, and semi-Catholic in the doctrine of the sacraments (baptismal regeneration and the eucharistic presence).

[1] Goethe gives classic expression to this truth in the lines : —

"In der Beschränkung erst zeigt sich der Meister,
Und das Gesetz nur kann uns Freiheit geben."

popular; but he wrote classical French as well as classical Latin, and excelled his contemporaries in both. He was schooled in the Renaissance, but, instead of running into the pedantic Ciceronianism of Bembo, he made the old Roman tongue subservient to Christian thought, and raised the French language to the dignity of one of the chief organs of modern civilization, distinguished for directness, clearness, precision, vivacity, and elegance.

The modern French language and literature date from Calvin and his contemporary, François Rabelais (1483–1553). These two men, so totally different, reflect the opposite extremes of French character. Calvin was the most religious, Rabelais the most witty man, of his generation; the one the greatest divine, the other the greatest humorist, of France; the one a Christian stoic, the other a heathen Epicurean; the one represented discipline bordering on tyranny, the other liberty running into license. Calvin created the theological and polemical French style, — a style which suits serious discussion, and aims at instruction and conviction. Rabelais created the secular style, which aims to entertain and to please.[1]

Calvin sharpened the weapons with which Bossuet and the great Roman Catholic divines of the seventeenth century attacked Protestantism, with which Rousseau and the philosophers of the eighteenth century attacked Christianity, and with which Adolf Monod and Eugène Bersier of the nineteenth century preached the simple gospel of the New Testament.[2]

---

[1] Calvin alludes once (in a letter of 1553) to the *Pantagruel* of Rabelais, which was condemned as an obscene book.

[2] Bossuet (in his *Histoire des Variations*) says: "*Rien ne flattait davantage Calvin que la gloire de bien écrire. Donnons lui donc, puisqu'il le veut tant cette gloire, d'avoir aussi bien écrit qu'homme de son siècle. . . . Sa plume était plus correcte, surtout en latin, que celle de Luther; et son style, qui était plus triste, était aussi plus suivi et plus châtié. Ils excellaient l'un et l'autre à parler la langue de leur pays.*" Martin, in his *Histoire de France* (Tom. VIII. 185 sq.), discusses at some length the merits of Calvin for French prose, and calls him the first

§ 67. *Calvin's Literary Labors.*

The best edition of Calvin's *Opera* by the Strassburg professors, BAUM, CUNITZ, and REUSS (now all dead), embraces so far 48 quarto vols. (1863–1892); the remaining volumes were prepared for publication by Dr. Reuss before his death (1891). He wrote to me from Neuhof, near Strassburg, July 11, 1887 : "*Alles ist zum Druck vorbereitet und ganz fertig mit Prolegomenis, etc. Es bleibt nichts mehr zu thun übrig als die Correctur und die Fortsetzung des immer à jour gehaltenen Index rerum et nominum, et locorum S. S., was ein anderer nach meinem Tode besorgen kann. Denn ich werde die Vollendung nicht erleben. Für den Schluss habe ich sogar noch ein Supplement ausgearbeitet, nämlich eine französische Bibel, extrahirt aus den französischen Commentaren und Predigten, nebst allen Varianten der zu Calvin's Zeiten in Genf gedruckten Bibeln.*" Vol. 45 sqq. are edited by Erichson.

Older editions appeared at Geneva, 1617, in 7 vols., in 15 fol., and at Amsterdam, 1667–1671, in 9 vols. fol. The English translation, Edinburgh, 1843–1854, has 52 vols. 8°. Several works have been separately published in Latin, French, German, Dutch, English, and other languages. See a chronological list in HENRY: *Das Leben Joh. Calvins*, vol. III. Beilagen, 175–252, and in *La France Prot.* III. 545–636 (2d ed.).

The literary activity of Calvin, whether we look at the number or at the importance of works, is not surpassed by any ecclesiastical writer, ancient or modern, and excites double astonishment when we take into consideration the shortness of his life, the frailty of his health, and the multiplicity of his other labors as a teacher, preacher, church ruler, and correspondent. Augustin among the Fathers, Thomas Aquinas among the Schoolmen, Luther and Melanchthon among the Reformers, were equally fruitful; but they lived longer, with the exception of Thomas Aquinas. Calvin, moreover, wrote in two languages with equal clearness, force, and elegance ; while Augustin and Thomas Aquinas wrote only in Latin ; Luther was a master of German ; and Melanchthon, a master of Latin and Greek, but his German is as indifferent as Luther's Latin.

Calvin's works may be divided into ten classes.

writer of the sixteenth century "*par la durée et l'influence de sa langue, de son style.*" Pierre Larousse, in his *Grand Dictionnaire* (Tom. III. 186), calls Calvin "*fondateur de la Réforme en France et un des pères de notre langue.*" Equally favorable are the judgments of Sayous, Lacroix, Nisard, and Marc-Monnier.

1. EXEGETICAL WRITINGS. Commentaries on the Pentateuch and Joshua, on the Psalms, on the Larger and Minor
Prophets; Homilies on First Samuel and Job; Commentaries
on all the books of the New Testament, except the Apocalypse. They form the great body of his writings.[1]

2. DOCTRINAL. The *Institutes* (Latin and French), first
published at Basel, 1536; 2d ed., Strassburg, 1539; 5th Latin
ed., Geneva, 1559.[2]

Minor doctrinal works: Three Catechisms, 1537, 1542,
and 1545; On the Lord's Supper (Latin and French), 1541;
the Consensus Tigurinus, 1549 and 1551 (in both languages);
the Consensus Genevensis (Latin and French), 1552; the
Gallican Confession (Latin and French), 1559 and 1562.[3]

3. POLEMICAL and APOLOGETIC.[4]

(*a*) Against the Roman Church: Response to Cardinal
Sadoletus, 1539; Against Pighius, on Free-will, 1543; On
the Worship of Relics, 1543; Against the Faculty of the
Sorbonne, 1544; On the Necessity of a Reformation, 1544;
Against the Council of Trent, 1547.

(*b*) Against the Anabaptists: On the Sleep of the Soul
(Psychopannychia), 1534; Brief Instruction against the
Errors of the Sect of the Anabaptists, 1544.

(*c*) Against the Libertines: *Adversus fanaticam et furio-
sam sectam Libertinorum qui se Spirituales vocant* (also in
French), 1545.

(*d*) Against the Anti-Trinitarians: *Defensio orthodoxæ fidei
S. Trinitatis adversus prodigiosos errores Serveti*, 1554; *Re-*

---

[1] *Opera*, vols. XXIII.–XLIV., contain the Old Testament Commentaries.
Those on the New Testament have been separately edited in Latin by Tholuck, 1833–'38, 7 vols. 8°.

[2] *Ibid.* vols. I.–IV. (1863–'66). Latin and French. There are three English translations of the *Institutes*, one by Thomas Norton (London, 1561, etc.),
another by John Allen (London, 1813, 3d ed. 1844, in 2 vols.), a third by
Henry Beveridge (Edinburgh, 1845–'46, 3 vols.). The work was also translated into Italian, Spanish, Dutch, German, Hungarian, Greek, and other
languages. A new French ed. by Fr. Baumgartner, Gen. 1888.

[3] *Tractatus theologici minores*, in *Opera*, vol. V., etc.   [4] Vols. V.–IX.

sponsum ad Quæstiones G. Blandatræ, 1558; *Adversus Valentinum Gentilem,* 1561; *Responsum ad nobiles Fratres Polonos* (Socinians) *de controversia Mediatoris,* 1561; *Brevis admonitio ad Fratres Polonos ne triplicem in Deo essentiam pro tribus personis imaginando tres sibi Deos fabricent,* 1563.

(*e*) Defence of the Doctrine of Predestination against Bolsec and Castellio, 1554 and 1557.

(*f*) Defence of the Doctrine of the Lord's Supper against the Calumnies of Joachim Westphal, a Lutheran fanatic (two *Defensiones* and an *Admonitio ultima*), 1555, 1556, 1557, and a tract on the same subject against Hesshus (*ad discutiendas Heshusii nebulas*), 1561.

4. ECCLESIASTICAL and LITURGICAL. Ordinances of the Church of Geneva, 1537; Project of Ecclesiastical Ordinances, 1541; Formula of Oath prescribed to Ministers, 1542; Order of Marriage, 1545; Visitation of the Churches in the Country, 1546; Order of Baptism, 1551; Academic Laws, 1559; Ecclesiastical Ordinances, and Academic Laws, 1561; Liturgical Prayers.[1]

5. SERMONS and HOMILIES. They are very numerous, and were mostly taken down by auditors.[2]

6. MINOR TREATISES. His academic oration, for Cop in Paris, 1533; Against Astrology, 1549; On Certain Scandals, 1550, etc.

7. CONSILIA on various doctrinal and polemical subjects.

8. LETTERS. Calvin's correspondence was enormous, and fills ten volumes in the last edition of his works.[3]

---

[1] Vol. X. Pars I. (1871), pp. 5–146, and vol. VI. 161–210.

[2] Henry (II. 198) says that the Geneva library contains forty-four manuscript volumes of sermons of Calvin; but the librarian Diodati informed him afterwards (III. Preface, p. viii.) that there are only nine volumes left, namely, the sermons between the years 1549–'51, 1555–'56, 1560–'61. The sermons on the Decalogue, on Deuteronomy, on Job, on the Sacrifice of Abraham, and many others were published during his life-time.

[3] Vols. X.–XX. The Strassburg editors give in all 4271 letters of Calvin and to Calvin. Herminjard has published so far his correspondence down to 1542 (the seventh volume appeared in 1886).

9. POETICAL. A hymn to Christ, free metrical versions of several psalms, and an epic (*Epinicion Christo cantatum*, 1541).[1]

10. Calvin edited Seneca, *De Clementia*, with notes, 1532; a French translation of Melanchthon's *Loci*, with preface, 1546; and wrote preface to Olivetan's French Bible, 1535, etc.

The Adieus to the Little Council, and to the ministers of Geneva, delivered on his death-bed in 1564, form a worthy conclusion of the literary labors of this extraordinary teacher.

§ 68. *Tributes to the Memory of Calvin.*

Comp. the large collection of *Opinions and Testimonies respecting the Writings of Calvin*, in the last volume of the English edition of his works published by the Calvin Translation Society, Edinburgh, 1854, pp. 376–464. I have borrowed from it several older testimonies.

No name in church history — not even Hildebrand's or Luther's or Loyola's — has been so much loved and hated, admired and abhorred, praised and blamed, blessed and cursed, as that of John Calvin. Living in a fiercely polemic age, and standing on the watch-tower of the reform movement in Western Europe, he was the observed of all observers, and exposed to attacks from every quarter. Religious and sectarian passions are the deepest and strongest. Melanchthon prayed for deliverance from "the fury of theologians." Roman Catholics feared Calvin as their most dangerous enemy, though not a few of them honorably admitted his virtues. Protestants were divided according to creed and prejudice: some regarding him as the first among the Reformers and the nearest to Paul; others detesting his favorite doctrine of predestination. Even his share in the burning of Servetus was defended as just during the sixteenth and

---

[1] Vols. V. 423–428, and VI. 212–224. A French metrical translation of the *Epinicion* appeared in Paris, 1555, under the title, *Chant de Victoire chanté a Jesus Christ*, etc.

seventeenth centuries, but is now universally deplored or condemned.[1]

Upon the whole, the verdict of history is growingly in his favor. He improves upon acquaintance. Those who know him best esteem him most. The fruits of his labors are abundant, especially in the English-speaking world, and constitute his noblest monument. The slanderous charges of Bolsec, though feebly re-echoed by Audin, are no longer believed. All impartial writers admit the purity and integrity, if not the sanctity, of his character, and his absolute freedom from love of gain and notoriety. One of the most eminent skeptical historians of France goes so far as to pronounce him "the most Christian man" of his age. Few of the great luminaries of the Church of God have called forth such tributes of admiration and praise from able and competent judges.

The following selection of testimonies may be regarded as a fair index of the influence which this extraordinary man has exerted from his humble study in "the little corner" on the south-western border of Switzerland upon men of different ages, nationalities, and creeds, down to the present time.

[1] *La France Protestante par MM. Eugène et Émile Haag*, Paris, 2d ed. Tom. III. (1881), p. 508: "*Trois partis religieux, divisés par des animosités que le temps n'a pas encore assoupies, nous ont transmis des documents sur la vie de cet homme illustre. Les uns, depuis l'apostat Bolsec jusqu'au néo-catholique romantique Audin, depuis le luthérien fanatique Westphal jusqu'aux ' vieux genevois' Galiffe père et fils, n'écoutant que la voix d'une haine implacable ou d'une jalousie furieuse, nous le peignent comme une espèce de scélérat souillé des vices les plus honteux, comme un despote altéré de sang, tandis que les autres, depuis Théodore de Bèze, son collègue, jusqu'au pasteur Paul Henry, de Berlin, son zélé disciple, cédant à l'entraînement d'une amitié trop indulgente ou d'une admiration un peu exaltée, nous le présentent comme un parfait type de la vertu.*

"*D'autres, dans ces derniers temps surtout, s'élevant au-dessus d'étroits préjugés dogmatiques, moins hommes de parti que philosophes, ont entrepris de juger cette grande figure historique avec l'impartialité que commande l'histoire; ils ont vu en Calvin, non pas le fondateur d'une secte, mais une de ces hautes intelligences qui apparaissent de loin en loin pour dominer une époque, ' et répandent sur les plus grandes choses l'éclat de leur propre grandeur.'*"

TRIBUTES OF CONTEMPORARIES (*Sixteenth Century*).

MARTIN LUTHER (1483-1546).

From a letter to Bucer, Oct. 14, 1539.

"Present my respectful greetings to Sturm and Calvin [then at Strassburg], whose books I have perused with singular pleasure (*quorum libellos singulari cum voluptate legi*)."

MARTIN BUCER (1491-1551).

"Calvin is a truly learned and singularly eloquent man (*vere doctus mireque facundus vir*), an illustrious restorer of a purer Christianity (*purioris Christianismi instaurator eximius*)."

THEODORE BEZA (1519-1605).

From his *Vita Calvini* (Latin) at the close (*Opera*, XXI. 172).

"I have been a witness of Calvin's life for sixteen years, and I think I am fully entitled to say that in this man there was exhibited to all a most beautiful example of the life and death of the Christian (*longe pulcherrimum vere christianæ tum vitæ tum mortis exemplum*), which it will be as easy to calumniate as it will be difficult to emulate."

Compare also the concluding remarks of his French biography, vol. XXI. 46 (Aug. 19, 1564).

JOHN STURM of Strassburg (1507-1589).

"John Calvin was endued with a most acute judgment, the highest learning, and a prodigious memory, and was distinguished as a writer by variety, copiousness, and purity, as may be seen for instance from his *Institutes of the Christian Religion*. . . . I know of no work which is better adapted to teach religion, to correct morals, and to remove errors."

JEROME ZANCHI (1516-1590).

An Italian convert to Protestantism. Professor at Strassburg and Heidelberg.

From a letter to the Landgrave of Hesse.

"Calvin, whose memory is honored, as all Europe knows, was held in the highest estimation, not only for eminent piety and the highest learning (*præstanti pietate et maxima eruditione*), but likewise for singular judgment on every subject (*singulari in rebus omnibus judicio clarissimus*)."

Bishop JEWEL (1522-1571).

"Calvin, a reverend father, and worthy ornament of the Church of God."

JOSEPH SCALIGER (1540-1609).

"Calvin is an instructive and learned theologian, with a higher purity and elegance of style than is expected from a theologian. The two most eminent theologians of our times are John Calvin and Peter Martyr; the former of whom has treated sound learning as it ought to be treated, with truth and purity and simplicity, without any of the scholastic subtleties. Endued with a divine genius, he penetrated into many things which lie beyond the reach of all who are not deeply skilled in the Hebrew language, though he did not himself belong to that class."

"O how well Calvin apprehends the meaning of the Prophets! No one better. . . . O what a good book is the *Institutes!* . . . Calvin stands alone among theologians (*Solus inter theologos Calvinus*)."

This judgment of the greatest scholar of his age, who knew thirteen languages, and was master of philology, history, chronology, philosophy, and theology, is all the more weighty as he was one of the severest of critics.

FLORIMOND DE RÆMOND (1540–1602).

Counseiller du Roy au Parlement de Bordeaux.   Roman Catholic.

From his *L'histoire de la naissanse, progrez, et décadence de l'hérésie de ce siècle, divisé en huit livres, dedié à nôtre saint Père le Pape Paul cinquième.* Paris, 1605. Bk. VII. ch. 10.

"Calvin had morals better regulated and settled than N., and shewed from early youth that he did not allow himself to be carried away by the pleasures of sense (*plaisirs de la chair et du ventre*). . . . With a dry and attenuated body, he always possessed a fresh and vigorous intellect, ready in reply, bold in attack; even in his youth a great faster, either on account of his health, and to allay the headaches with which he was continually afflicted, or in order to have his mind more disencumbered for the purposes of writing, studying, and improving his memory. Calvin spoke little; what he said were serious and impressive words (*ce n'estoit que propos serieux et qui portoyent coup*); he never appeared in company, and always led a retired life. He had scarcely his equal; for during twenty-three years that he retained possession of the bishopric (*l'evesché*) of Geneva, he preached every day, and often twice on Sundays. He lectured on theology three times a week; and every Friday he entered into a conference which he called the Congregation. His remaining hours were employed in composition, and answering the letters which came to him as to a sovereign pontiff from all parts of heretical Christendom (*qui arrivoyent à luy de toute la Chrétienté hérétique, comme au Souveraine Pontife*). . . .

"Calvin had a brilliancy of spirit, a subtlety of judgment, a grand memory, an eminent erudition, and the power of graceful diction. . . . No man of all those who preceded him has surpassed him in style, and few since have attained that beauty and facility of language which he possessed."

ETIENNE PASQUIER (1528–1615).

Roman Catholic.   Conseiller et Avocat Général du Roy en la Chambre des Comptes de Paris.

From *Les Recherches de la France*, p. 769 (Paris, 1633).

. . . "He [Calvin] wrote equally well in Latin and French, the latter of which languages is greatly indebted to him for having enriched it with an infinite number of fine expressions (*enrichie d'une infinité de beaux traits*), though I could have wished that they had been written on a better subject. In short, a man wonderfully conversant with and attached to the books of the Holy Scriptures, and such, that if he had turned his mind in the proper direction, he might have been ranked with the most distinguished doctors of the Church."

JACQUES AUGUSTE DE THOU (THUANUS, 1553–1617).

President of the Parliament of Paris.   A liberal Roman Catholic and one of the framers of the Edict of Nantes.

From the 36th book of his *Historia sui Temporis* (from 1543–1607).

"John Calvin, of Noyon in Picardy, a person of lively spirit and great eloquence (*d'un esprit vif et d'une grande eloquence*),[1] and a theologian of high reputation among the Protestants, died of asthma, May 20 [27], 1564, at Geneva, where he had taught for twenty-three years, being nearly fifty-six years of age.   Though he had labored under various diseases for seven years, this did not render him less diligent in his office, and never hindered him from writing."

De Thou has nothing unfavorable to say of Calvin.

TESTIMONIES OF LATER FRENCH WRITERS.

CHARLES DRELINCOURT (1595–1669).

"In that prodigious multitude of books which were composed by Calvin, you see no words thrown away; and since the prophets and apostles, there never perhaps was a man who conveyed so many distinct statements in so few words, and in such appropriate and well-chosen terms (*en des mots si propres et si bien choisis*). . . .   Never did Calvin's life appear to me more pure or more innocent than after carefully examining the diabolical calumnies with which some have endeavored to defame his character, and after considering all the praises which his greatest enemies are constrained to bestow on his memory."

MOSES AMYRAUT (1596–1645).

"That incomparable Calvin, to whom mainly, next to God, the Church owes its Reformation, not only in France, but in many other parts of Europe."

Bishop JACQUES BÉNIGNE BOSSUET (1627–1704).

From his *Histoire des Variations des Eglises Protestantes* (1688), the greatest polemical work in French against the Reformation.

"I do not know if the genius of Calvin would be found as fitted to excite the imagination and stir up the populace as was that of Luther, but after the

---

[1] Or, as quoted from another edition by the Strassburg editors (XXI. 11): "*personnage d'un grand esprit et merveilleusement éloquent (admirabili facundia præditus).*"   A French translation of the *Historia* appeared in 1734.

movement had commenced, he rose in many countries, more especially in France, above Luther himself, and made himself head of a party which hardly yields to that of the Lutherans. By his searching intellect and his bold decisions, he improved upon all those who had sought in this century to establish a new church, and gave a new turn to the pretended reformation.

"It is a weak feeling which makes us desirous to find anything extraordinary in the death-beds of these people. God does not always bestow these examples. Since he permits heresy for the trial of his people, it is not to be wondered at that to complete this trial he allows the spirit of seduction to prevail in them even to the end, with all the fair appearances by which it is covered; and, without learning more of the life and death of Calvin, it is enough to know that he has kindled in his country a flame which not all the blood shed on its account has been able to extinguish, and that he has gone to appear before the judgment of God without feeling any remorse for a great crime. . . .

"Let us grant him then, since he wishes it so much, the glory of having written as well as any man of his age; let us even place him, if desired, above Luther; for whilst the latter was in some respects more original and lively, Calvin, his inferior in genius, appears to have surpassed him in learning. Luther triumphed as a speaker, but the pen of Calvin was more correct, especially in Latin, and his style, though severe, was much more consecutive and chaste. They equally excelled in speaking the language of their country, and both possessed an extraordinary vehemence. Each by his talents has gained many disciples and admirers. Each, elated by success, has fancied to raise himself above the Fathers; neither could bear contradiction, and their eloquence abounds in nothing more largely than virulent invective."

RICHARD SIMON (1638–1712).

One of the greatest critical and biblical scholars of the Roman Catholic Church.

From his *Critical History of the Old Testament* (Latin and French).

"As Calvin was endued with a lofty genius, we are constantly meeting with something in his commentaries which delights the mind (*quo animus rapitur*); and in consequence of his intimate and perfect acquaintance with human nature, his ethics are truly charming, while he does his utmost to maintain their accordance with the sacred text. Had he been less under the influence of prejudice, and had he not been solicitous to become the leader and standard-bearer of heresy, he might have produced a work of the greatest usefulness to the Catholic Church."

The same passage, with additions, occurs in French. Simon says that no author "had a better knowledge of the utter inability of the human heart," but that "he gives too much prominence to this inability," and "lets no opportunity pass of slandering the Roman Church," so that part of his commentaries is "useless declamations" (*déclamations inutiles*). "Calvin displays more genius and judgment in his works than Luther; he is more cautious, and takes care not to make use of weak proofs, of which his adversaries might take advantage. He is subtle to excess in his reasoning, and his commentaries are filled with references skilfully drawn from the text — which are capable of prepossessing the minds of those readers who are not profoundly acquainted with religion."

Simon greatly underrates Calvin's knowledge of Hebrew when he says that he knew not much more than the Hebrew letters. Dr. Diestel (*Geschichte des Alten Test. in der christl. Kirche*, 1869, p. 267) justly pronounces this a slander which is refuted by every page of Calvin's commentaries. He ascribes to him a very good knowledge of Hebrew: "*ausgewählt mit einer sehr tüchtigen hebräischen Sprachkenntniss.*"

PIERRE BAYLE (1647-1706).

Son of a Reformed minister, educated by the Jesuits of Toulouse, converted to Romanism, returned to Protestantism, skeptical, the author of a *Dictionnaire historique et critique.*

"That a man who had acquired so great a reputation and so great an authority should have had only a hundred crowns of salary, and have desired no more, and that after having lived fifty-five years with every sort of frugality, he left to his heirs only the value of three hundred crowns, including his library, is a circumstance so heroical, that one must be devoid of feeling not to admire it, and one of the most singular victories which virtue and greatness of soul have been able to achieve over nature, even among ministers of the gospel. Calvin has left imitators in so far as regards activity of life, zeal and affection for the interest of his party; they employ their eloquence, their pens, their endeavors, their solicitations in the advancement of the kingdom of God; but they do not forget themselves, and they are, generally speaking, an exemplification of the maxim that the Church is a good mother, in whose service nothing is lost.

"The Catholics have been at last obliged to dismiss to the region of fable the atrocious calumnies (*les calomnies atroces*) which they had uttered against the moral character of Calvin; their best authors now restrict themselves to stating that if he was exempt from the vices of the body, he has not been so from those of the mind, such as pride, passion, and slander. I know that the Cardinal de Richelieu, or that dexterous writer who has published under his name '*The Method of Conversation*,' had adopted the absurdities of Bolsec. But in general, eminent authors speak no more of that. The mob of authors will never renounce it. These calumnies are to be found in the '*Systema decretorum dogmaticorum*,' published at Avignon in 1693, by Francis Porter. Thus the work of Bolsec will always be cited as long as the Calvinists have adversaries, but it will be sufficient to brand it eternally with calumny that there is among Catholics a certain number of serious authors who will not adopt its fables."

JEAN ALPHONSE TURRETIN (1617-1737).

Professor of theology of Geneva and representative of a moderate Calvinism. The most distinguished theologian of his name, also called Turretin the younger, to distinguish him from his father François.

"John Calvin was a man whose memory will be blessed to the latest age (*vir benedictæ in omne ævum memoriæ*). . . . . He has by his immense labors instructed and adorned not only the Church of Geneva, but the whole Reformed world, so that not unfrequently all the Reformed Churches are in the gross called after his name."

MONTESQUIEU (1689–1755).

Author of *De l'esprit des lois* (the oracle of the friends of moderate freedom).

"The Genevese should bless the birthday of Calvin."

VOLTAIRE (1694–1778).

" Essai sur les mœurs et l'esprit des nations."

"The famous Calvin, whom we regard as the Apostle of Geneva, raised himself up to the rank of Pope of the Protestants (*s'érigea en pape des Protestants*). He was acquainted with Latin and Greek, and the bad philosophy of his time. He wrote better than Luther, and spoke worse; both were laborious and austere, but hard and violent (*durs et emportés*). . . . Calvinism conforms to the republican spirit, and yet Calvin had a tyrannical spirit. . . . He demanded the toleration which he needed for himself in France, and he armed himself with intolerance at Geneva. . . . The severity of Calvin was united with the greatest disinterestedness (*au plus grand désintéressement*)."

JEAN JAQUES ROUSSEAU (1712–1778).

A native of Geneva. The apostle of the French Revolution, as Calvin was the apostle of the French Reformation.

From *Lettres écrites de la montagne.*

" *Quel homme fut jamais plus tranchant, plus impérieux, plus décisif, plus divinement infaillible à son gré que Calvin, pour qui la moindre opposition . . . était toujours une œuvre de Satan, un crime digne du feu !* "

D'ALEMBERT (1717–1783).

"Calvin justly enjoyed a great reputation — a literary man of the first rank (*homme de lettre du premier ordre*) — writing in Latin as well as one could do in a dead language, and in French with singular purity for his time (*avec une pureté singulière pour son temps*). This purity, which our able grammarians admire even at this day, renders his writings far superior to almost all those of the same age, as the works of the Port-Royalists are distinguished even at the present day, for the same reason, from the barbarous rhapsodies of their opponents and contemporaries.

FREDERIC ANCILLON (1767–1837).

Tableau des Révolutions du Système Politique de l'Europe.

"Calvin was not only a profound theologian, but likewise an able legislator; the share which he had in the framing of the civil and religious laws which have produced for several centuries the happiness of the Genevan republic, is perhaps a fairer title to renown than his theological works; and this republic, celebrated notwithstanding its small size, and which knew how to unite morals with intellect, riches with simplicity, simplicity with taste, liberty with order, and which has been a focus of talents and virtues, has proved that Calvin knew men, and knew how to govern them."

Fr. Pierre Guillaume Guizot (1787–1874).

Celebrated French historian and statesman, of Huguenot descent.

From St. Louis et Calvin, pp. 361 sqq.

"Calvin is great by reason of his marvellous powers, his lasting labors, and the moral height and purity of his character. . . . Earnest in faith, pure in motive, austere in his life, and mighty in his works, Calvin is one of those who deserve their great fame. Three centuries separate us from him, but it is impossible to examine his character and history without feeling, if not affection and sympathy, at least profound respect and admiration for one of the great Reformers of Europe and of the great Christians of France."

By the same (1787–1874).

From Musée des protestants célèbres.

"*Luther vint pour détruire, Calvin pour fonder, par des nécessités égales, mais différentes. . . . Calvin fut l'homme de cette seconde époque de toutes les grandes révolutions sociales, où, après avoir conquis par la guerre le terrain qui doit leur appartenir, elles travaillent à s'y établir par la paix, selon des principes et sous les formes qui conviennent à leur nature. . . . L'idée générale selon laquelle Calvin agit en brûlant Servet était de son siècle, et on a tort de la lui imputer.*"

François Aug. Marie Mignet (1796–1884).

Celebrated French historian and academician.

From his Mémoire sur l'établissement de la Réforme à Genève.

"*Calvin fut, dans le protestantisme, après Luther, ce qu'est la conséquance après le principe; dans la Suisse, ce qu'est la règle après une révolution. . . . Calvin, s'il n'avait ni le génie de l'invention ni celui de la conquète; s'il n'était ni un révolutionnaire comme Luther ni un missionaire comme Farel, il avait une force de logique qui devait pousser plus loin la réforme du premier, et une faculté d'organisation qui devait achever l'œuvre du second. C'est par là qu'il renouvela la face du protestantisme et qu'il constitua Genève.*"

Jules Michelet (1798–1874).

Histoire de France, vol. XI. (Les Guerres de Religion), Paris, 1884, pp. 88, 89, 92.

"*C'était un travailleur terrible, avec un air souffrant, une constitution misérable et débile, veillant, s'usant, se consumant, ne distinguant ni nuit ni jour. . . .*

"*C'était une langue inouïe* [Calvin's French style], *la nouvelle langue française. Vingte ans après Commines, trente ans avant Montaigne, dejà la langue de Rousseau. . . . Son plus redoutable attribut, c'est sa pénétrante clarté, son extrême lumière d'argent, plutôt d'acier, d'une lame qui brille, mais qui tranche. On sent que cette lumière vient du dedans, du fond de la conscience, d'un cœur âprement convaincu, dont la logique est l'aliment. . . .*

"*Le fond de ce grand et puissant théologien était d'être un légiste. Il l'était de culture, d'esprit, de caractère. Il en avait les deux tendances: l'appel au juste, au vrai, un âpre besoin de justice; mais, d'autre part aussi, l'esprit dur, absolu, des tribunaux d'alors, et il le porta dans la théologie. . . . La prédestination de Calvin se trouva, en pratique, une machine a faire des martyrs.*"

Bon Louis Henri Martin (1810–1883).

Histoire de France depuis les temps les plus reculés jusqu'en 1789, Tom. VIII. p. 325, of the fourth edition, Paris, 1860. Crowned by the French Academy.

Martin, in his standard work, thus describes the influence of Calvin upon the city of Geneva: "*Calvin ne la sauve pas seulement, mais conquiert à cette petite ville une grandeur, une puissance morale immense. Il en fait la capitale de la Réforme, autant que la Réforme peut avoir une capitale, pour la moitié du monde protestant, avec une vaste influence, acceptée ou subie, sur l'autre moitié. Genève n'est rien par la population, par les armes, par le territoire: elle est tout par l'esprit. Un seul avantage matériel lui garantit tous ses avantages moraux: son admirable position, qui fait d'elle une petite France républicaine et protestante, indépendante de la monarchie catholique de France et à l'abri de l'absorption monarchique et catholique; la Suisse protestante, alliée nécessaire de la royauté française contre l'empereur, couvre Genève par la politique vis-à-vis du roi et par l'épée contre les maisons d'Autriche et de Savoie.*"

Ernest Renan (1823–1892).

Renan, a member of the French Academy, a brilliant genius, and one of the first historians of France, was educated for the Roman Catholic priesthood, but became a skeptic. This makes his striking tribute all the more significant.

From his article on John Calvin in his *Études d'histoire religieuse*, 7th ed. Paris, 1880, pp. 337–357.

"Calvin was one of those absolute men, cast complete in one mould, who is taken in wholly at a single glance: one letter, one action suffices for a judgment of him. There were no folds in that inflexible soul, which never knew doubt or hesitation. . . . Careless of wealth, of titles, of honors, indifferent to pomp, modest in his life, apparently humble, sacrificing everything to the desire of making others like himself, I hardly know of a man, save Ignatius Loyola, who could match him in those terrible transports. . . . It is surprising that a man who appears to us in his life and writings so unsympathetic should have been the centre of an immense movement in his generation, and that this harsh and severe tone should have exerted so great an influence on the minds of his contemporaries. How was it, for example, that one of the most distinguished women of her time, Renée of France, in her court at Ferrara, surrounded by the flower of European wits, was captivated by that stern master, and by him drawn into a course that must have been so thickly strewn with thorns? This kind of austere seduction is exercised by

those only who work with real conviction. Lacking that vivid, deep, sympathetic ardor which was one of the secrets of Luther's success, lacking the
charm, the perilous, languishing tenderness of Francis of Sales, Calvin succeeded more than all, in an age and in a country which called for a reaction
towards Christianity, simply because he was the most Christian man of his
century (*l'homme le plus chrétien de son siècle*, p. 342)."

FELIX BUNGENER (1814–1874).

Pastor of the national Church of Geneva, and author of several historical works.

From *Calvin, sa vie, son œuvre et ses écrits*, Paris, 1862; English translation
(Edinburgh, 1863), pp. 338, 349.

" Let us not give him praise which he would not have accepted. God alone
creates; a man is great only because God thinks fit to accomplish great things
by his instrumentality. Never did any great man understand this better than
Calvin. It cost him no effort to refer all the glory to God; nothing indicates
that he was ever tempted to appropriate to himself the smallest portion of it.
Luther, in many a passage, complacently dwells on the thought that a petty
monk, as he says, has so well made the Pope to tremble, and so well stirred
the whole world. Calvin will never say any such thing; he never even seems
to say it, even in the deepest recesses of his heart; everywhere you perceive
the man, who applies to all things — to the smallest as to the greatest — the
idea that it is God who does all and is all. Read again, from this point of
view, the very pages in which he appeared to you the haughtiest and most
despotic, and see if, even there, he is anything other than the workman referring all, and in all sincerity, to his master. . . . But the man, in spite of all
his faults, has not the less remained one of the fairest types of faith, of earnest
piety, of devotedness, and of courage. Amid modern laxity, there is no
character of whom the contemplation is more instructive; for there is no man
of whom it has been said with greater justice, in the words of an apostle,
'he endured as seeing him who is invisible.' "

FROM DUTCH SCHOLARS.

JAMES ARMINIUS (1560–1609).

The founder of Arminianism.

"Next to the study of the Scriptures which I earnestly inculcate, I exhort
my pupils to peruse Calvin's *Commentaries*, which I extol in loftier terms than
Helmich himself [a Dutch divine, 1551–1608]; for I affirm that he excels
beyond comparison (*incomparabilem esse*) in the interpretation of Scripture,
and that his commentaries ought to be more highly valued than all that is
handed down to us by the library of the fathers; so that I acknowledge him
to have possessed above most others, or rather above all other men, what may
be called an eminent spirit of prophecy (*spiritum aliquem prophetiæ eximium*).
His *Institutes* ought to be studied after the [Heidelberg] Catechism, as containing a fuller explanation, but with discrimination (*cum delectu*), like the
writings of all men."

DAN. GERDES (1698-1767).

Historia Evangelii Renovati, IV. 41 sq. (Groningæ, 1752).

"Calvin's labors were so highly useful to the Church of Christ, that there is hardly any department of the Christian world to be found that is not full of them, — hardly any heresy that has arisen which he has not successfully encountered with that two-edged sword, the Word of God, or a portion of Christian doctrine which he has not illustrated in a remarkable manner. Certainly his commentaries on the Old and New Testaments are all that could be desired; every one of his sermons is full of unction; his *Institutes* bear the most complete and finished execution; his doctrinal treatises are distinguished by solidity; his critical works by warmth and fervor; his practical writings by virtue and piety; and his letters by mildness, prudence, gravity, and wisdom."

JUDGMENTS OF GERMAN SCHOLARS.

JOHN LAWRENCE MOSHEIM (1695-1755).

From the English translation of his *Institutes of Ecclesiastical History*, by JAMES MURDOCK, D.D., New York, 1854, vol. III. 163, 167, 192.

"Calvin was venerated, even by his enemies, for his genius, learning, eloquence, and other endowments, and moreover was the friend of Melanchthon.

"Few persons of his age will bear any comparison with Calvin for patient industry, resolution, hatred of the Roman superstition, eloquence, and genius. Possessing a most capacious mind, he endeavored not only to establish and bless his beloved Geneva with the best regulations and institutions, but also to make it the mother and the focus of light and influence to the whole Reformed Church, just as Wittenberg was to the Lutheran community.

"The first rank among the interpreters of the age is deservedly assigned to John Calvin, who endeavored to expound nearly the whole of the sacred volume.

"His *Institutes* are written in a perspicuous and elegant style, and have nothing abstruse and difficult to be comprehended in the arguments or mode of reasoning."

JOHANNES VON MÜLLER (1752-1809).

The great historian of Switzerland, called "the German Tacitus."

Allgemeine Geschichte, Bk. III.

"John Calvin had the spirit of an ancient lawgiver, a genius and characteristic which gave him in part unmistakable advantages, and failings which were only the excess of virtues, by the assistance of which he carried through his objects. He had also, like other Reformers, an indefatigable industry, with a fixed regard to a certain end, an invincible perseverance in principles and duty during his life, and at his death the courage and dignity of an ancient Roman censor. He contributed greatly to the development and advance of the human intellect, and more, indeed, than he himself foresaw. For among the Genevese and in France, the principle of free inquiry, on which he was obliged at first to found his system, and to curb which he afterwards strove in vain, became more fruitful in consequences than among nations which are less inquisitive than the Genevese, and less daring than the French. From this source were developed gradually philosophical ideas, which, though they are not yet purified sufficiently from the passions and views of their founders, have yet banished a great number of gloomy and pernicious prejudices, and have opened us prospects of a pure practical wisdom and better success for the future."

Fr. AUGUST THOLUCK (1799–1877).

Commentary on the Epistle to the Romans, 3d ed. 1831, p. 19.

"In his [Calvin's] Exposition on the Epistle to the Romans are united pure Latinity, a solid method of unfolding and interpreting, founded on the principles of grammatical science and historical knowledge, a deeply penetrating faculty of mind, and vital piety."

Dr. TWESTEN (1789–1876).

The successor of Schleiermacher in the chair of systematic theology at Berlin, and an orthodox Lutheran in the United Evangelical Church of Prussia.

From his *Dogmatik der evangelisch Lutherischen Kirche*, I. 216 (4th ed. Hamburg, 1838).

After speaking very highly and justly of Melanchthon and John Gerhard, Twesten thus characterizes Calvin's *Institutes :* —

"*Mehr aus einem Gusz, als Melanchthon's Loci, die reife Frucht eines tief religiösen und ächt wissenschaftlichen Geistes, mit groszer Klarheit, Kraft und Schönheit der Darstellung geschrieben, einfach in der Anlage, reich und gründlich in der Ausführung, verdient es neben jenen auch in unserer Kirche als eins der vorzüglichsten Werke auf dem Gebiete der dogmatischen Literatur überhaupt studirt zu werden.*"

PAUL HENRY.

Doctor of theology and pastor of a French Reformed Church in Berlin, author of two learned biographies of Calvin: a large one, in 3 vols. (1833–1844), which is chiefly valuable as a collection of documents, and a popular one in 1 vol.

From *Das Leben Johann Calvins* (Hamburg and Gotha, 1846), pp. 443 sqq.

"The whole tendency of Calvin was practical; learning was subordinate; the salvation of the world, the truth was to him the main thing. His spiritual tendency was not philosophical, but his dialectical bent ran principles to their utmost consequences. He had an eye to the minutest details. His former study of law had trained him for business. . . . He was a watchman over the whole Church. . . . All his theological writings excel in acuteness, dialectics, and warmth of conviction. He had great eloquence at command, but despised the art of rhetoric. . . . Day and night he was occupied with the work of the Lord. He disliked the daily entreaties of his colleagues to grant himself some rest. He continued to labor through his last sicknesses, and only stopped dictating a week before his death, when his voice gave out. . . . All sought his counsel; for God endowed him with such a happy spirit of wisdom that no one regretted to have followed his advice. How great was his erudition! How marvellous his judgment! How peculiar his kindness, which came to the aid even of the smallest and lowliest, if necessary, and his meekness and patient forbearance with the imperfections of others!"

Dr. L. Stähelin.

Johannes Calvin. Leben und ausgewählte Schriften. Elberfeld, 1863. Vol. II. pp. 365–393.

This description of Calvin's character as a man and as a Christian is faithful in praise and censure, but too profuse to be inserted. Dr. Stähelin emphasizes the logic of his intellect and conscience, his firm assurance of eternal election, his constant sense of the nearness of God, "the majesty" of his character, the predominance of the Old Testament feature, his resemblance to Moses and the Hebrew Prophets, his irritability, anger, and contemptuousness, relieved by genuine humility before God, his faithfulness to friends, his life of unceasing prayer, his absolute disinterestedness and consecration to God. He also quotes the remarkable testimony of Renan, that Calvin was "the most Christian man in Christendom."

Dr. Friedrich Trechsel (1805–1885).

Die Protestantischen Antitrinitarier. Heidelberg, 1839–1844 (I. 177).

"People have often supposed that they were insulting Calvin's memory by calling him the Pope of Protestantism! He was so, but in the noblest sense of the expression, through the spiritual and moral superiority with which the Lord of the Church had endowed him for its deliverance; through his unwearied, universal zeal for God's honor; through his wise care for the edifying of the kingdom of Christ; in a word, through all which can be comprehended in the idea of the papacy, of truth and honor."

Ludwig Häusser (1818–1867).

Professor of history at Heidelberg.

The Period of the Reformation, edited by Oncken (1868, 2d ed. 1880), translated by Mrs. Sturge, New York, 1874 (pp. 241 and 244).

"As the German Reformation is connected with Martin Luther, and the Swiss with Ulrich Zwingli, that of the Romanic and Western European nations is connected with John Calvin, the most remarkable personage of the time. He was not equal either to Luther or Zwingli in general talent, mental vigor, or tranquility of soul; but in logical acuteness and talent for organization he was at least equal, if not superior, to either. He settled the basis for the development of many states and churches. He stamped the form of the Reformation in countries to which he was a stranger. The French date the beginnings of their literary development from him, and his influence was not restricted to the sphere of religion, but embraced their intellectual life in general; no one else has so permanently influenced the spirit and form of their written language as he.

"At a time when Europe had no solid results of reform to show, this little State of Geneva stood up as a great power; year by year it sent forth apostles ꓳ the world, who preached its doctrines everywhere, and it became the most dreaded counterpoise to Rome, when Rome no longer had any bulwark to defend her. The missionaries from this little community displayed the lofty and dauntless spirit which results from stoical education and training; they bore the stamp of a self-renouncing heroism which was elsewhere swallowed up in theological narrowness. They were a race with vigorous bones and sinews, for whom nothing was too daring, and who gave a new direction to Protestantism by causing it to separate itself from the old traditional monarchical authority, and to adopt the gospel of democracy as part of its creed. It formed a weighty counterpoise to the desperate efforts which the ancient Church and monarchical power were making to crush the spirit of the Reformation.

"It was impossible to oppose Caraffa, Philip II., and the Stuarts, with Luther's passive resistance; men were wanted who were ready to wage war to the knife, and such was the Calvinistic school. It everywhere accepted the challenge; throughout all the conflicts for political and religious liberty, up to the time of the first emigration to America, in France, the Netherlands, England, and Scotland, we recognize the Genevan school."

Dr. KARL RUDOLF HAGENBACH (1801–1874).

Swiss Reformed, of Basel.

Geschichte des Reformation, 5th ed. edited by Nippold, Leipzig, 1887, p. 605.

" *Calvin hatte so zu sagen kein irdisches Vaterland, dessen Freiheit er, wie Zwingli, zu wahren sich bewogen fand. Das himmlische Vaterland, die Stadt Gottes war es, in welche er alle zu sammeln sich berufen sah. Ihm galt nicht Grieche, nicht Skythe, nicht Franzose, nicht Deutscher, nicht Eidgenosz, sondern einzig und allein die neue Kreatur in Christo. Es wäre thöricht, ihm solches zum Vorwurf zu machen. Es ist vielmehr richtig bemerkt worden, wie Calvin, obgleich er nicht die Grösze Genfs als solche gesucht, dennoch dieser Stadt zu einer weltgeschichtlichen Grösze verholfen, die sie ohne ihn niemals erreicht haben würde. Aber so viel ist richtig, dasz das Reinmenschliche, das im Familien- und Volksleben seine Wurzel hat, und das durch das Christenthum nicht verdrängt, aber wohl veredelt werden soll, bei Calvin weniger zur Entwickelung kam. Männer des strengen Gedankens und einer rigiden Gesetzlichkeit werden geneigt sein, Calvin über Luther und Zwingli zu erheben. Und er hat auch seine unbestreitbaren Vorzüge. Poetisch angelegte Gemütsmenschen aber werden anfänglich Calvin und seiner vom Naturboden losgelösten, abstrakten Frömmigkeit gegenüber sich eines gewissen Fröstelns nicht erwehren können und einige Zeit brauchen, bis sie es überwunden haben; während sie sich zu dem herzgewinnenden Luther sogleich und auch dann noch hingezogen fühlen, wenn er schäumt und vor Zorn nbersprudelt.*"

Dr. IS. DORNER (1809–1884).

Geschichte der Protestantischen Theologie. München, 1867, pp. 374, 376.

"Calvin was equally great in intellect and character, lovely in social life, full of tender sympathy and faithfulness to friends, yielding and forgiving towards personal offences, but inexorably severe when he saw the honor of God obstinately and malignantly attacked. He combined French fire and practical good sense with German depth and soberness. He moved as freely in the world of ideas as in the business of Church government. He was an architectonic genius in science and practical life, always with an eye to the holiness and majesty of God." (Condensed translation.)

Dr. KAHNIS (Lutheran, 1814–1888).

Die Lutherische Dogmatik. Leipzig, 1861, vol. II. p. 490 sq.

"The fear of God was the soul of his piety, the rock-like certainty of his election before the foundation of the world was his power, and the doing of the will of God his single aim, which he pursued with trembling and fear. . . . No other Reformer has so well demonstrated the truth of Christ's word that, in the kingdom of God, dominion is service. No other had such an energy of self-sacrifice, such an irrefragable conscientiousness in the greatest as well as the smallest things, such a disciplined power. This man, whose dying body was only held together by the will flaming from his eyes, had a majesty of character which commanded the veneration of his contemporaries."

F. W. KAMPSCHULTE (1831–1872).

Catholic Professor of History in the University of Bonn from 1860 to 1872, and author of an able and impartial work on Calvin, which was interrupted by his death. Vols. II. and III. were never published. He protested against the Vatican decrees of 1870.

Johann Calvin. Seine Kirche und sein Staat in Genf. Erster Band, Leipzig, 1869, p. 274 sq.

"*Calvin's Lehrbuch der christlichen Religion ist ohne Frage das hervorragendste und bedeutendste Erzeugniss, welches die reformatorische Literatur des sechszehnten Jahrhunderts auf dem Gebiete der Dogmatik aufzuweisen hat. Schon ein ober-flächlicher Vergleich lässt uns den gewaltigen Fortschritt erkennen, den es gegenüber den bisherigen Leistungen auf diesem Gebiete bezeichnet. Statt der unvollkommenen, nach der einen oder andern Seite unzulänglichen Versuche Melanchthon's, Zwingli's, Farel's erhalten wir aus Calvin's Hand das Kunstwerk eines, wenn auch nicht harmonisch in sich abgeschlossenen, so doch wohlgegliederten, durchgebildeten Sys-tems, das in allen seinen Theilen die leitenden Grundgedanken widerspiegelt und von vollständiger Beherrschung des Stoffes zeugt. Es hatte eine unverkennbare Berechtigung, wenn man den Verfasser der Institution als den Aristoteles der Refor-mation bezeichnete. Die ausserordentliche Belesenheit in der biblischen und patris-tischen Literatur, wie sie schon in den früheren Ausgaben des Werkes hervortritt, setzt in Erstaunen. Die Methode ist lichtvoll und klar, der Gedankengang streng logisch, überall durchsichtig, die Eintheilung und Ordnung des Stoffes dem leitenden Grundgedanken entsprechend; die Darstellung schreitet ernst und gemessen vor und nimmt, obschon in den späteren Ausgaben mehr gelehrt als anziehend, mehr auf den Verstand als auf das Gemüth berechnet, doch zuweilen einen höheren Schwung an. Calvin's Institution enthält Abschnitte, die dem Schönsten, was von Pascal und Bossuet geschrieben worden ist, an die Seite gestellt werden können: Stellen, wie jene über die Erhabenheit der heiligen Schrift, über das Elend des gefallenen Men-schen, über die Bedeutung des Gebetes, werden nie verfehlen, auf den Leser einen tiefen Eindruck zu machen. Auch von den katholischen Gegnern Calvin's sind diese Vorzüge anerkannt und manche Abschnitte seines Werkes sogar benutzt worden.*

Man begreift es vollkommen, wenn er selbst mit dem Gefühl der Befriedigung und des Stolzes auf sein Werk blickt und in seinen übrigen Schriften gern auf das 'Lehrbuch' zurückverweist."

" Und doch beschleicht uns, trotz aller Bewunderung, zu der uns der Verfasser nöthigt, bei dem Durchlesen seines Werkes ein unheimliches Gefühl. Ein System, das von dem furchtbaren Gedanken der doppelten Prædestination ausgeht, welches die Menschen ohne jede Rücksicht auf das eigene Verhalten in Erwählte und Verworfene scheidet und die Einen wie die Anderen zu blossen Werkzeugen zur Verherrlichung der göttlichen Majestät macht . . . ein solches System kann unmöglich dem deukenden, Belehrung und Trost suchenden Menschengeist innere Ruhe und Befriedigung gewähren."

BAUM, CUNITZ, and REUSS.

JOH. CALVINI *Opera*, vol. I. p. ix.

The Strassburg editors of Calvin's Works belong to the modern liberal school of theology.

" Si Lutherum virum maximum, si Zwinglium civem Christianum nulli secundum, si Melanthonem præceptorem doctissimum merito appellaris, Calvinum jure vocaris THEOLOGORUM PRINCIPEM ET ANTESIGNANUM. *In hoc enim quis linguarum et literarum præsidia, quis disciplinarum fere omnium non miretur orbem? De cujus copia doctrinæ, rerumque dispositione aptissime concinnata, et argumentorum vi ac validitate in dogmaticis; de ingenii acumine et subtilitate, atque nunc festiva nunc mordaci salsedine in polemicis, de felicissima perspicuitate, sobrietate ac sagacitate in exegeticis, de nervosa eloquentia et libertate in paræneticis; de prudentia sapientiaque legislatoria in ecclesiis constituendis, ordinandis ac regendis incomparabile, inter omnes viros doctos et de rebus evangelicis libere sentientes jam abunde constat. Imo inter ipsos adversarios romanos nullus hodie est, vel mediocri harum rerum cognitione imbutus vel tantilla judicii præditus æquitate, qui argumentorum et sententiarum ubertatem, proprietatem verborum sermonemque castigatum, stili denique, tam latini quam gallici, gravitatem et luciditatem non admiretur. Quæ cuncta quum in singulis fere scriptis, tum præcipue relucent in immortali illa Institutione religionis Christianæ, quæ omnes ejusdem generis expositiones inde ab apostolorum temporibus conscriptas, adeoque ipsos Melanthonis Locos theologicos, absque omni controversia longe antecellit atque eruditum et ingenuum lectorem, etiamsi alicubi secus senserit, hodieque quasi vinctum trahit et vel invitum rapit in admirationem."*

TRIBUTES FROM ENGLISH WRITERS (MOSTLY EPISCOPAL).

RICHARD HOOKER (1553–1600).

From his Preface to the *Ecclesiastical Polity* (Keble's ed. vol. I. p. 158).

" Whom [Calvin], for my own part, I think incomparably the wisest man that ever the French Church did enjoy since the hour it enjoyed him. His bringing up was in the study of the civil law. Divine knowledge he gathered not by hearing or reading so much as by teaching others. For, though thousands were debtors to him, as touching knowledge of this kind, yet he to none, but only to God, the Author of that most blessed fountain, the Book of Life, and of the admirable dexterity of wit, together with the helps of other learning, which were his guides. — We should be injurious unto virtue itself, if we did derogate from them whom their industry hath made great. Two things of principal moment there are, which have deservedly procured him honor throughout the world: the one, his exceeding pains in composing the *Institutions of the Christian Religion;* the other, his no less industrious travails for exposition of Holy Scripture, according unto the same Institutions. . . .

"Of what account the Master of Sentences [Peter Lombard] was in the Church of Rome; the same and more, among the preachers of Reformed Churches, Calvin had purchased; so that the perfectest divines were judged they which were skilfullest in Calvin's writings; his books almost the very canon to judge both doctrine and discipline by."

Bishop LANCELOT ANDREWES (1555–1626).

"Calvin was an illustrious person, and never to be mentioned without a preface of the highest honor."

Dr. JOHN DONNE (1573–1631).

Royal Chaplain and Dean of St. Paul's, London; distinguished as a poet and divine.

"St. Augustin, for sharp insight and conclusive judgment in exposition of places of Scripture, which he always makes so liquid and pervious, hath scarce been equalled therein by any of all the writers in the Church of God, except Calvin may have that honor, for whom (when it concerns not points of controversy) I see the Jesuits themselves, though they dare not name him, have a high degree of reverence."

Bishop HALL (1574–1656).

Works, III. 516.

"Reverend Calvin, whose judgment I so much honor, that I reckon him among the best interpreters of Scripture since the Apostles left the earth."

Bishop SANDERSON (1587–1663).

"When I began to set myself to the study of Divinity as my proper business, Calvin's *Institutions* were recommended to me, as they generally were to all young scholars in those times, as the best and most perfect system of Divinity, and the fittest to be laid as a groundwork in the study of the profession. And, indeed, my expectation was not at all ill-deemed in the study of those *Institutions*."

RICHARD BAXTER (1615–1691).

"I know no man, since the Apostles' days, whom I value and honor more than Calvin, and whose judgment in all things, one with another, I more esteem and come nearer to."

Bishop WILSON of Calcutta.

From Sermon preached on the death of the Rev. Basil Wood.

"Calvin's *Commentaries* remain, after three centuries, unparalleled for force of mind, justness of exposition, and practical views of Christianity."

Archbishop LAWRENCE.

From his *Bampton Lectures.*

"Calvin was both a wise and a good man, inferior to none of his contemporaries in general ability, and superior to almost all in the art, as well as elegance, of composition, in the perspicuity and arrangement of his ideas, the structure of his periods, and the Latinity of his diction."

Archdeacon JULIUS CHARLES HARE (1795–1855).

He had, of all Englishmen, the best knowledge and highest appreciation of Luther.

From his *Mission of the Comforter*, II. 449.

"Calvin's *Commentaries*, although they too are almost entirely doctrinal and practical, taking little note of critical and philosophical questions, keep much closer to the text [than Luther's], and make it their one business to bring out the meaning of the words of Scripture with fulness and precision. This they do with the excellence of a master richly endowed with the word of wisdom and with the word of knowledge, and from the exemplary union of a severe masculine understanding with a profound insight into the spiritual depths of the Scriptures, they are especially calculated to be useful in counteracting the erroneous tendencies of an age, when we seem about to be inundated with all that was fantastical and irrational in the exegetical mysticism of the Fathers, and are bid to see divine power in all allegorical cobwebs, and heavenly life in artificial flowers. I do not mean to imply an adoption or approval of all Calvin's views, whether on doctrinal or other questions. But we may happily owe much gratitude and love, and the deepest intellectual obligations, to those whom at the same time we may deem to be mistaken on certain points."

THOMAS H. DYER.

The Life of John Calvin.   London, 1850, p. 533 sq.

"That Calvin was in some respects a really great man, and that the eloquent panegyric of his friend and disciple Beza contains much that is true, will hardly be denied. In any circumstances his wonderful abilities and extensive learning would have made him a shining light among the doctors of the Reformation; an accidental, or, as his friends and followers would say, a providential and predestinated visit to Geneva, made him the head of a numerous and powerful sect. Naturally deficient in that courage which forms so prominent a trait in Luther's character, and which prompted him to beard kings and emperors face to face, Calvin arrived at Geneva at a time when the rough and initiatory work of Reform had already been accomplished by his bolder and more active friend Farel. Some peculiar circumstances in the political condition of that place favored the views which he seems to have formed very shortly after his arrival. . . .

"The preceding narrative has already shown how, from that time to the hour of his death, his care and labor were constantly directed to the consolidation of his power, and to the development of his scheme of ecclesiastical polity. In these objects he was so successful that it may be safely affirmed that none of the Reformers, not even Luther himself, attained to so absolute and extensive an influence."

Archdeacon FREDERIC W. FARRAR, D.D., F.R.S.

History of Interpretation. London, 1886, pp. 342–344.

"The greatest exegete and theologian of the Reformation was undoubtedly CALVIN. He is not an attractive figure in the history of that great movement. The mass of mankind revolt against the ruthless logical rigidity of his 'horrible decree.' They fling it from their belief with the eternal 'God forbid!' of an inspired natural horror. They dislike the tyranny of theocratic sacerdotalism [?] which he established at Geneva. Nevertheless his Commentaries, almost alone among those of his epoch, are still a living force. They are far more profound than those of Zwingli, more thorough and scientific, if less original and less spiritual, than those of Luther. In spite of his many defects — the inequality of his works, his masterful arrogance of tone, his inconsequent and in part retrogressive view of inspiration, the manner in which he explains away every passage which runs counter to his dogmatic prepossessions — in spite, too, of his 'hard expressions and injurious declamations' — he is one of the greatest interpreters of Scripture who ever lived. He owes that position to a combination of merits. He had a vigorous intellect, a dauntless spirit, a logical mind, a quick insight, a thorough knowledge of the human heart, quickened by rich and strange experience; above all, a manly and glowing sense of the grandeur of the Divine. The neatness, precision, and lucidity of his style, his classic training and wide knowledge, his methodical accuracy of procedure, his manly independence, his avoidance of needless and commonplace homiletics, his deep religious feeling, his careful attention to the entire scope and context of every passage, and the fact that he has commented on almost the whole of the Bible, make him tower above the great majority of those who have written on Holy Scripture. Nothing can furnish a greater contrast to many helpless commentaries, with their congeries of vacillating *variorum* annotations heaped together in aimless multiplicity, than the terse and decisive notes of the great Genevan theologian. . . . A characteristic feature of Calvin's exegesis is its abhorrence of hollow orthodoxy. He regarded it as a disgraceful offering to a God of truth. He did not hold the theory of verbal dictation. He will never defend or harmonize what he regards as an oversight or mistake in the sacred writers. He scorns to support a good cause by bad reasoning. . . . But the most characteristic and original feature of his Commentaries is his anticipation of modern criticism in his views about the Messianic prophecies. He saw that the words of psalmists and prophets, while they not only admit of but demand 'germinant and springing developments,' were yet primarily applicable to the events and circumstances of their own days."

SCOTCH TRIBUTES.

In Scotland, the land of John Knox, who studied at the feet of Calvin, his principles were most highly appreciated and most fully carried out.

Sir WILLIAM HAMILTON (1788–1856).

"Looking merely to his learning and ability, Calvin was superior to all modern, perhaps to all ancient, divines. Succeeding ages have certainly not exhibited his equal. To find his peer we must ascend at least to Aquinas or Augustin."

Dr. WILLIAM CUNNINGHAM (1805–1861).

Principal of the New College and Professor of Church History in Edinburgh. Presbyterian of the Free Church.

Reformers, and the Theology of the Reformation. Edinburgh, 1866, pp. 292, 294, 299.

"John Calvin was by far the greatest of the Reformers with respect to the talents he possessed, the influence he exerted, and the service he rendered to the establishment and diffusion of important truth. . . .

"The systematizing of divine truth, and the full organization of the Christian Church according to the word of God, are the great peculiar achievements of Calvin. For this work God eminently qualified him, by bestowing upon him the highest gifts both of nature and of grace; and this work he was enabled to accomplish in such a way as to confer the greatest and most lasting benefits upon the Church of Christ, and to entitle him to the commendation and the gratitude of all succeeding ages. . . .

"Calvin certainly was not free from the infirmities which are always found in some form or degree even in the best men; and in particular, he occasionally exhibited an angry impatience of contradiction and opposition, and sometimes assailed and treated the opponents of the truth and cause of God with a violence and invective which cannot be defended, and should certainly not be imitated. He was not free from error, and is not to be implicitly followed in his interpretation of Scripture, or in his exposition of doctrine. But whether we look to the powers and capacities with which God endowed him, the manner in which he employed them, and the results by which his labors have been followed, — or to the Christian wisdom, magnanimity, and devotedness which marked his character and generally regulated his conduct, there is probably not one among the sons of men, beyond the range of those whom God miraculously inspired by his Spirit, who has stronger claims upon our veneration and gratitude."

In another place which I cannot refer to, Cunningham, the successor of Chalmers, says: "Calvin is the man who, next to St. Paul, has done most good to mankind."

Dr. John Tulloch (1823–1886).

Principal of St. Mary's College in the University of St. Andrews, of the Established Church of Scotland.

Luther and other Leaders of the Reformation. Edinburgh and London, 3d ed. 1883, pp. 234–237, 243, 245.

"Thus lived and died Calvin, a great, intense, and energetic character, who, more than any other of that great age, has left his impress upon the history of Protestantism. Nothing, perhaps, more strikes us than the contrast between the single naked energy which his character presents and of which his name has become symbolical, and the grand issues which have gone forth from it. Scarcely anywhere else can we trace such an impervious potency of intellectual and moral influence emanating from so narrow a centre.

"There is in almost every respect a singular dissimilarity between the Genevan and the Wittenberg reformer. In personal, moral, and intellectual features, they stand contrasted — Luther with his massive frame and full, big face and deep melancholy eyes; Calvin, of moderate stature, pale and dark complexion, and sparkling eyes, that burned nearly to the moment of his death (Beza: *Vita Calv.*). Luther, fond and jovial, relishing his beer and hearty family repasts with his wife and children; Calvin, spare and frugal, for many years taking only one meal a day, and scarcely needing sleep. In the one, we see a rich and complex and buoyant and affectionate nature touching humanity at every point, in the other, a stern and grave unity of moral character. Both were naturally of a somewhat proud and imperious temper, but the violence of Luther is warm and boisterous, that of Calvin is keen and zealous. It might have been a very uncomfortable thing, as Melanchthon felt, to be exposed to Luther's occasional storms; but after the storm was over, it was pleasant to be folded once more to the great heart that was sorry for its excesses. To be the object of Calvin's dislike and anger was something to fill one with dread, not only for the moment, but long afterwards, and at a distance, as poor Castellio felt when he gathered the pieces of driftwood on the banks of the Rhine at Basel.

"In intellect, as in personal features, the one was grand, massive, and powerful, through depth and comprehension of feeling, a profound but exaggerated insight, and a soaring eloquence; the other was no less grand and powerful, through clearness and correctness of judgment, vigor and consistency of reasoning, and weightiness of expression. Both are alike memorable in the service which they rendered to their native tongue — in the increased compass, flexibility, and felicitous mastery which they imparted to it. The Latin works of Calvin are greatly superior in elegance of style, symmetry of method, and proportionate vigor of argument. He maintains an academic elevation of tone, even when keenly agitated in temper; while Luther, as Mr. Hallam has it, sometimes descends to mere 'bellowing in bad Latin.' Yet there is a coldness in the elevation of Calvin, and in his correct and well-balanced sentences, for which we should like ill to exchange the kindling though rugged paradoxes of Luther. The German had the more rich and teeming — the Genevan the harder, more serviceable, and enduring mind. When interrupted in dictating for several hours, Beza tells us that he could return and commence where he had left off; and that amidst all the multiplicity of his engagements, he never forgot what he required to know for the performance of any duty.

"As preachers, Calvin seems to have commanded a scarcely less powerful success than Luther, although of a different character — the one stimulating and rousing, 'boiling over in every direction' — the other instructive, argumentative, and calm in the midst of his vehemence (Beza: *Vita Calv.*). Luther flashed forth his feelings at the moment, never being able to compose what might be called a regular sermon, but seizing the principal subject, and turning all his attention to that alone. Calvin was elaborate and careful in his sermons as in everything else. The one thundered and lightened, filling the souls of his hearers now with shadowy awe, and now with an intense glow of spiritual excitement; the other, like the broad daylight, filled them with a more diffusive though less exhilarating clearness. . . .

"An impression of majesty and yet of sadness must ever linger around the name of Calvin. He was great and we admire him. The world needed him and we honor him; but we cannot love him. He repels our affections while he extorts our admiration; and while we recognize the worth, and the divine necessity, of his life and work, we are thankful to survey them at a distance, and to believe that there are also other modes of divinely governing the world, and advancing the kingdom of righteousness and truth.

"Limited, as compared with Luther, in his personal influence, apparently less the man of the hour in a great crisis of human progress, Calvin towers far above Luther in the general influence over the world of thought and the course of history, which a mighty intellect, inflexible in its convictions and constructive in its genius, never fails to exercise."

WILLIAM LINDSAY ALEXANDER, D.D., F.R.S.E. (1808–1884).

Professor of Theology and one of the Bible Revisers.   Congregationalist.

From *Encyclopædia Britannica*, 9th ed. vol. IV. (1878) p. 721.

"Calvin was of middle stature; his complexion was somewhat pallid and dark; his eyes, to the latest clear and lustrous, bespoke the acumen of his genius. He was sparing in his food and simple in his dress; he took but little sleep, and was capable of extraordinary efforts of intellectual toil. His memory was prodigious, but he used it only as the servant of his higher faculties. As a reasoner he has seldom been equalled, and the soundness and penetration of his judgment were such as to give to his conclusions in practical questions almost the appearance of predictions, and inspire in all his friends the utmost confidence in the wisdom of his counsels. As a theologian he stands on an eminence which only Augustin has surpassed; whilst in his skill as an expounder of Scripture, and his terse and elegant style, he possessed advantages to which Augustin was a stranger. His private character was in harmony with his public reputation and position. If somewhat severe and irritable, he was at the same time scrupulously just, truthful, and stead-

fast; he never deserted a friend or took an unfair advantage of an antagonist; and on befitting occasions he could be cheerful and even facetious
among his intimates."

TESTIMONIES OF AMERICAN DIVINES.

Dr. Henry B. Smith (1815–1877).

Professor of Theology in the Union Theological Seminary, New York.   Presbyterian.

From his Address before the General Assembly of the Presbyterian Church,
St. Louis, 1855, delivered by request of the Presbyterian Historical Society.
See *Faith and Philosophy*, pp. 98 and 99.

"Though the Reformation, under God, began with Luther in the power
of faith, it was carried on by Calvin with greater energy, and with a more
constructive genius, both in theology and in church polity, as he also had a
more open field.   The Lutheran movement affected chiefly the centre and
the north of Europe; the Reformed Churches were planted in the west of
Europe, all around the ocean, in the British Isles, and by their very geographical site were prepared to act the most efficient part, and to leap the walls of
the old world, and colonize our shores.

"Nothing is more striking in a general view of the history of the Reformed
Churches than the variety of countries into which we find their characteristic
spirit, both in doctrine and polity, penetrating.   Throughout Switzerland it
was a grand popular movement.   There is first of all, Zwingli, the hero of
Zurich, already in 1516 preaching against the idolatrous veneration of Mary,
a man of generous culture and intrepid spirit, who at last laid down his life
upon the field of battle.   In Basle we find Œcolampadius, and also Bullinger
[in Zurich], the chronicler of the Swiss reform.   Farel aroused Geneva to
iconoclasm by his inspiring eloquence.

"Thither comes in 1536, from the France which disowned him, Calvin, the
mighty law-giver, great as a preacher, an expositor, a teacher and a ruler;
cold in exterior, but burning with internal fire; who produced at twenty-six
years of age his unmatched *Institutes*, and at thirty-five had made Geneva,
under an almost theocratic government, the model city of Europe, with its
inspiring motto, '*post tenebras lux*.'   He was feared and opposed by the libertines of his day, as he is in our own.   His errors were those of his own times:
his greatness is of all times.   Hooker calls him 'incomparably the wisest
man of the French Church;' he compares him to the 'Master of Sentences,'
and says, 'that though thousands were debtors to him as touching divine
knowledge, yet he was to none, only to God.'   Montesquieu declares that
'the Genevese should ever bless the day of his birth.'   Jewel terms him 'a
reverend Father, and worthy ornament of the Church of God.'   'He that will
not honor the memory of Calvin,' says Mr. Bancroft, 'knows but little of the
origin of American liberty.'   Under his influence Geneva became the 'fertile
seed-plot' of reform for all Europe; with Zurich and Strassburg, it was the
refuge of the oppressed from the British Isles, and thus indoctrinated England
and ourselves with its own spirit."

From Dr. Smith's article "Calvin" in Appleton's *American Cyclopædia*.

"Calvin's system of doctrine and polity has shaped more minds and entered into more nations than that of any other Reformer. In every land it made men strong against the attempted interference of the secular power with the rights of Christians. It gave courage to the Huguenots; it shaped the theology of the Palatinate; it prepared the Dutch for the heroic defence of their national rights; it has controlled Scotland to the present hour; it formed the Puritanism of England; it has been the basis of the New England character; and everywhere it has led the way in practical reforms. His theology assumed different types in the various countries into which it penetrated, while retaining its fundamental traits."

Dr. George P. Fisher (b. 1827).

Professor of Church History in Yale Divinity School, New Haven.   Congregationalist.

From his *History of the Reformation*.   New York, 1873, pp. 206 and 238.

"When we look at his extraordinary intellect, at his culture — which opponents, like Bossuet, have been forced to commend — at the invincible energy which made him endure with more than stoical fortitude infirmities of body under which most men would have sunk, and to perform, in the midst of them, an incredible amount of mental labor; when we see him, a scholar naturally fond of seclusion, physically timid, and recoiling from notoriety and strife, abjuring the career that was most to his taste, and plunging, with a single-hearted, disinterested zeal and an indomitable will, into a hard, protracted contest; and when we follow his steps, and see what things he effected, we cannot deny him the attributes of greatness. . . .

"His last days were of a piece with his life.   His whole course has been compared by Vinet to the growth of one rind of a tree from another, or to a chain of logical sequences.   He was endued with a marvellous power of understanding, although the imagination and sentiments were less roundly developed.   His systematic spirit fitted him to be the founder of an enduring school of thought.   In this characteristic he may be compared with Aquinas. He has been appropriately styled the Aristotle of the Reformation.   He was a perfectly honest man.   He subjected his will to the eternal rule of right, as far as he could discover it.   His motives were pure.   He felt that God was near him, and sacrificed everything to obey the direction of Providence.   The fear of God ruled in his soul; not a slavish fear, but a principle such as animated the prophets of the Old Covenant.   The combination of his qualities was such that he could not fail to attract profound admiration and reverence from one class of minds, and excite intense antipathy in another.   There is no one of the Reformers who is spoken of, at this late day, with so much personal feeling, either of regard or aversion.   But whoever studies his life and writings, especially the few passages in which he lets us into his confidence and appears to invite our sympathy, will acquire a growing sense of his intellectual and moral greatness, and a tender consideration for his errors.'

G. G. HERRICK, D.D.

Congregational Minister of Mount Vernon Church, Boston.

From *Some Heretics of Yesterday*.   Boston, 1890, pp. 210 sqq.

"Calvin gathered up the spiritual and intellectual forces that had been started by the Reformation movement, and marshalled and systematized them, and bound them into unity by the mastery of his logical thought, as the river gathers cloud and rill, and snow-drift and dew-fall, and constrains them through its own channel into the unity and directness of a powerful current. The action of Luther was impulsive, magnetic, popular, appealing to sentiment and feeling, that of Calvin was logical and constructive, appealing to understanding and reason.   He was the systematizer of the Reformation. . . .

"Calvin's work was national, and more; he gave to the Reformation a universality like that of the gigantic system with which they [the Reformers] all were at war.   Calvin, more than any other man that has ever lived, deserves to be called the Pope of Protestantism.   While he was still living his opinions were deferred to by kings and prelates, and even after he was dead his power was confessed by his enemies.   The papists called his *Institutes* The Heretics' Koran. . . .   He set up authority against authority, and maintained and perpetuated what he set up by the inherent clearness and energy and vigor of his own mental conceptions.   The authority of the Romish Pope was based upon the venerable tradition of the past that had grown up by the accretion of ages; the authority of the Protestant Pope rested upon a logical structure which he himself built up, out of blocks hewn from alleged Scripture assertion and legitimate inferences therefrom. . . .

"The man himself is one of the wonders of all time, and his work was admirable, beyond any words of appreciation that it is possible for me to utter.   For while he himself tolerated no differences of theological opinion, and would have bound all thought by his own logical chain, this nineteenth century is as much indebted to his work as it is to that of Luther.   That work constituted the world's largest step towards democratic freedom.   It set the individual man in the presence of the living God, and made the solitary soul, whether of prince or pauper, to feel its responsibility to, and dependence upon, Him alone who from eternity has decreed the sparrow's flight or fall. Out of this logical conception of the equality of all men in the presence of Jehovah, he deduced the true republican character of the Church; a theory to which all Americans, and especially we of New England, owe our rich inheritance.   He gave to the world, what it had not before, a majestic and consistent conception of a kingdom of God ruling in the affairs of men; of the beauty and the blessedness of a true Christian state; of the possibility of the city of God being one day realized in the universal subordination of human souls to divine authority. . . ."

For testimonies bearing upon Calvin's system of discipline, see below, § 110.

CHAPTER IX.

FROM FRANCE TO SWITZERLAND.

§ 69. *Calvin's Youth and Training.*

CALVINI *Opera*, vol. XXI. (1879). — On Noyon and the family of Calvin, JACQUES LE VASSEUR (Dr. of theology, canon and dean of the cathedral of Noyon): *Annales de l'église cathédrale de Noyon.* Paris, 1633, 2 vols. 4°. — JACQUES DESMAY (Dr. of the Sorbonne and vicar-general of the diocese of Rouen): *Remarques sur la vie de Jean Calvin tirées des Registres de Noyon, lieu de sa naissance.* Rouen, 1621.

THOMAS M'CRIE (d. 1835): *The Early Years of Calvin. A Fragment.* 1509–1536. *Ed. by William Ferguson.* Edinburgh, 1880 (199 pp.). A posthumous work of the learned biographer of Knox and Melville.

ABEL LEFRANC: *La Jeunesse de Calvin.* Paris (33 rue de Seine), 228 pp.

Comp. the biographies of Calvin by HENRY, large work, vol. I. chs. I.–VIII. (small ed. 1846, pp. 12–29); DYER (1850), pp. 4–10; STÄHELIN (1862) I. 3–12; *KAMPSCHULTE (1869), I. 221–225.

"As David was taken from the sheepfold and elevated to the rank of supreme authority; so God having taken me from my originally obscure and humble condition, has reckoned me worthy of being invested with the honorable office of a preacher and minister of the gospel. When I was yet a very little boy, my father had destined me for the study of theology. But afterwards, when he considered that the legal profession commonly raised those who follow it, to wealth, this prospect induced him suddenly to change his purpose. Thus it came to pass, that I was withdrawn from the study of philosophy and was put to the study of law. To this pursuit I endeavored faithfully to apply myself, in obedience to the will of my father; but God, by the secret guidance of his providence, at length gave a different direction to my course. And first, since I was too obstinately devoted to the superstitions of popery to be easily extricated from so profound an abyss of mire, God by a sudden conversion subdued and brought my mind to a teachable frame, which was more burdened in such matters than might have been expected from one at my early period of life. Having thus received some taste and knowledge of true godliness, I was immediately inflamed with so intense a desire to make progress therein, that though I did not altogether leave off other studies, I yet pursued them with less ardor." [1]

This is the meagre account which Calvin himself incidentally gives of his youth and conversion, in the Preface to his Commentary on the Psalms, when speaking of the life of David, in which he read his own spiritual experience. Only once more he alludes, very briefly, to his change of religion. In his Answer to Cardinal Sadoletus, he assures him that he did not consult his temporal interest when he left the papal party. "I might," he said, "have reached without difficulty the summit of my wishes, namely, the enjoyment of literary ease, with something of a free and honorable station." [2]

Luther indulged much more freely in reminiscences of his hard youth, his early monastic life, and his discovery of the doctrine of justification by faith alone, which gave peace and rest to his troubled conscience.

John Calvin [3] was born July 10, 1509, — twenty-five years after Luther and Zwingli, — at Noyon, an ancient cathedral city, called *Noyon-la-Sainte*, on account of its many churches, convents, priests, and monks, in the northern province of Picardy, which has given birth to the crusading monk, Peter of Amiens, to the leaders of the French Reformation and

---

[1] *Opera*, XXXI. 21 (Latin and French).   [2] *Opera*, V. 388 sqq.

[3] The Latinized form of *Cauvin* or *Chauvin*. *Alcuin*, one of his assumed names, is an anagram of *Calvin*. See *La France Protest.*, III. 518, note. He assumed the name *Calvinus* in his book on Seneca, 1532.

counter-Reformation (the Ligue), and to many revolutionary as well as reactionary characters.[1]

His father, Gérard Cauvin, a man of hard and severe character, occupied a prominent position as apostolic secretary to
the bishop of Noyon, proctor in the Chapter of the diocese,
and fiscal procurator of the county, and lived on intimate
terms with the best families of the neighborhood.[2] His
mother, Jeanne Lefranc, of Cambrai, was noted for her
beauty and piety, but died in his early youth, and is not
mentioned in his letters. The father married a second time.
He became involved in financial embarrassment, and was
excommunicated, perhaps on suspicion of heresy. He died
May 26 (or 25), 1531, after a long sickness, and would have
been buried in unconsecrated soil but for the intercession of
his son, Charles, who gave security for the discharge of his
father's obligations.[3]

Calvin had four brothers and two sisters.[4] Two of his
brothers died young, the other two received a clerical education, and were early provided with benefices through the
influence of the father.

Charles, his elder brother, was made chaplain of the cathedral in 1518, and curé of Roupy, but became a heretic or

---

[1] Michelet (*Histoire de France*, XI. 88) calls Picardy "*un pays fécond en
révolutionnaires, en brouillants amis de l'humanité.*" Lefranc (p. 24) : "*Les deux
mouvements contraires, la Réforme française et ce qui la combattit avec le plus
d'acharnement, la Ligue, sont nés dans le même pays.*" Noyon lies 67 miles
N.N.E. of Paris, is enclosed with gardens, has a large old cathedral, a bishop's
palace, a hospital, a seminary, several public fountains, manufactures of fine
linens, tulle, oil, leather, and a brisk trade, with a population of about 6000.
From Lippincott's *Gazetteer*, p. 1620.

[2] "*De notaire apostolique, la première charge qu'il obtint, il devint successivement
notaire du chapitre, greffier de l'officialité, procureur fiscal du comté et promoteur
du chapitre. C'est à Noyon, en quelque sorte, le fac-totum du clergé.*" Lefranc,
p. 2.

[3] Lefranc, pp. 17 and 199. Herminjard, II. 394. Bolsec, in his *Histoire
de Calvin*, calls Gérard Cauvin "*un très-exécrable blasphémateur de Dieu.*" Perhaps he confounded him with his eldest son, Charles.

[4] See the genealogical table in Henry, vol. III. ; Beilage, 16, p. 174.

infidel, was excommunicated in 1531, and died Oct. 1, 1537, having refused the sacrament on his death-bed. He was buried by night between the four pillars of a gibbet.[1]

His younger brother, Antoine, was chaplain at Tournerolle, near Traversy, but embraced the evangelical faith, and, with his sister, Marie, followed the Reformer to Geneva in 1536. Antoine kept there a bookstore, received the citizenship gratuitously, on account of the merits of his brother (1546), was elected a member of the Council of Two Hundred (1558), and of the Council of the Sixty (1570), also one of the directors of the hospital, and died in 1573. He was married three times, and divorced from his second wife, the daughter of a refugee, on account of her proved adultery (1557). Calvin had innocently to suffer for this scandal, but made him and his five children chief heirs of his little property.[2]

The other sister of Calvin was married at Noyon, and seems to have remained in the Roman Catholic Church.

A relative and townsman of Calvin, Pierre Robert, called Olivetan, embraced Protestantism some years before him, and studied Greek and Hebrew with Bucer at Strassburg in 1528.[3] He joined Farel in Neuchâtel, and published there his French translation of the Bible in 1535.

More than a hundred years after Calvin's death, another member of the family, Eloi Cauvin, a Benedictine monk, removed from Noyon to Geneva, and embraced the Reformed religion (June 13, 1667).[4]

These and other facts show the extent of the anti-papal

---

[1] " *Carolus ejus frater et presbyter Novioduni mortuus noctu et clam sepultus est inter quatuor columnas furcæ publicæ quia Eucharistiam sumere noluerat.*" Papire Masson, *Vita Calv.;* Lefranc, pp. 18–21 and 210.

[2] Beza, at the close of his Latin *Vita Calv.* (in Calvin's *Opera*, XXI. 171), and Lefranc, *l.c.*, p. 184.

[3] Letter of Bucer to Farel, May 1, 1528, in Herminjard, II. no. 232, and *Opera*, X. Pt. I. p. 1. The "*juvenis Noviodunensis*" there mentioned was not Calvin, as Kampschulte (I. 231) conjectures, but probably Olivetan. There is no trace of such an early visit of Calvin to Strassburg.

[4] *La France Prot.* III. 639.

sentiment in the family of Cauvin. In 1561 a large number of prominent persons of Noyon were suspected of heresy, and in 1562 the Chapter of Noyon issued a profession of faith against the doctrines of Calvin.[1]

After the death of Calvin, Protestantism was completely crushed out in his native town.

Calvin received his first education with the children of the noble family de Mommor (not Montmor), to which he remained gratefully attached. He made rapid progress in learning, and acquired a refinement of manners and a certain aristocratic air, which distinguished him from Luther and Zwingli. A son of de Mommor accompanied him to Paris, and followed him afterwards to Geneva.

His ambitious father destined him first for the clerical profession. He secured for him even in his twelfth year (1521) a part of the revenue of a chaplaincy in the cathedral of Noyon.[2] In his eighteenth year Calvin received, in addition, the charge of S. Martin de Marteville (Sept. 27, 1527), although he had not yet the canonical age, and had only received the tonsure.

Such shocking irregularities were not uncommon in those days. Pluralism and absenteeism, though often prohibited

---

[1] See the list and the profession in Lefranc, 216 sqq. He goes, however, too far when he says (p. x. sq.): "*Ce qui ressort d'une étude attentive des faits, c'est que Calvin est sorti déja protestant de sa ville natale. C'est dans ce centre qu'il puisa ses idées. Il y trouva tout d'abord l'appui le plus ferme, ses amis les plus chauds et ses lieutenants les plus dévoués. A un moment donné, la moitié de la population se déclara pour lui. Chose remarquable, un nombre considérable des ses compatriots, et parmi eux les personnages les plus en vue, le suivirent jusqu'à Genève. Durant toute sa vie, Calvin conserva d'actifs rapports avec sa ville natale et ceux de ses fidèles qui y étaient restés.*" Calvin was not converted before 1532. See § 72.

[2] Desmay (quoting from the Registres of Noyon, see *Op.* XXI. 189): "*Jean Calvin obtient une portion du revenue de la chapelle de la Gésine de la Vierge fondée dans la cathédrale de Noyon.*" There were four chaplains at Noyon. The first two had to say mass alternately every morning. John Calvin, not being ordained, had to pay a priest to take his place. Lefranc, p. 10. Zwingli received a papal pension even after he had begun his work of reform. See above, § 8, p. 31 sq. This is all wrong, but was not so considered at that time.

by councils, were among the crying abuses of the Church.
Charles de Hangest, bishop of Noyon, obtained at fifteen
years of age a dispensation from the pope "to hold all kinds
of offices, compatible and incompatible, secular and regular,
etiam tria curata"; and his nephew and successor, Jean
de Hangest, was elected bishop at nineteen years of age.
Odet de Châtillon, brother of the famous Coligny, was
created cardinal in his sixteenth year. Pope Leo X. received the tonsure as a boy of seven, was made archbishop in
his eighth, and cardinal-deacon in his thirteenth year (with
the reservation that he should not put on the insignia of his
dignity nor discharge the duties of his office till he was
sixteen), besides being canon in three cathedrals, rector in
six parishes, prior in three convents, abbot in thirteen additional abbeys, and bishop of Amalfi, deriving revenues from
them all!

Calvin resigned the chaplaincy in favor of his younger
brother, April 30, 1529. He exchanged the charge of S.
Martin for that of the village Pont-l'Evêque (the birthplace
of his father), July 5, 1529, but he resigned it, May 4, 1534,
before he left France. In the latter parish he preached
sometimes, but never administered the sacraments, not being
ordained to the priesthood.[1]

The income from the chaplaincy enabled him to prosecute
his studies at Paris, together with his noble companions.
He entered the College de la Marche in August, 1523, in
his fourteenth year.[2] He studied grammar and rhetoric with

---

[1] Beza says: "*Quo loco [Pons Episcopi] constat Calvinum, antequam Gallia
excederet, nullis alioqui pontificiis ordinibus (unquam) initiatum, aliquot ad popu-
lum conciones habuisse.*" *Op.* XXI. 121. "*Unquam*" is omitted in the text, but
added in the notes. The French biography of Colladon reads: "*En laquelle
cure il a depuis presché par fois, avans qu'il se retirast de France.*" *Ibid.* 54.

[2] This is the date given by Kampschulte (I. 223), Lefranc (p. 14), and
others. According to *Opera*, XXI. 189, Calvin was "*Corderii discipulus in
Collegio de la Marche Lutetiæ,*" in the year 1529; but in that year he was a
student of the university. There is some confusion in the dates referring to
the period of his studies in Paris.

an experienced and famous teacher, Marthurin Cordier (Cordatus). He learned from him to think and to write Latin, and dedicated to him in grateful memory his Commentary on the First Epistle to the Thessalonians (1550). Cordier became afterwards a Protestant and director of the College of Geneva, where he died at the age of eighty-five in the same year with Calvin (1564).[1]

From the College de la Marche Calvin was transferred to the strictly ecclesiastical College de Montague, in which philosophy and theology were taught under the direction of a learned Spaniard. In February, 1528, Ignatius Loyola, the founder of the order of the Jesuits, entered the same college and studied under the same teacher. The leaders of the two opposite currents in the religious movement of the sixteenth century came very near living under the same roof and sitting at the same table.

Calvin showed during this early period already the prominent traits of his character: he was conscientious, studious, silent, retired, animated by a strict sense of duty, and exceedingly religious.[2] An uncertain tradition says that his fellow-students called him "the Accusative," on account of his censoriousness.[3]

NOTES. SLANDEROUS REPORTS ON CALVIN'S YOUTH.

Thirteen years after Calvin's death, Bolsec, his bitter enemy, once a Romanist, then a Protestant, then a Romanist again, wrote a calumnious

[1] Cordier was called "*linguæ, morum vitæque magister.*" He was the Rollin of the sixteenth century. He wrote *Rudimenta grammaticæ; le miroir de la jeunesse; commentarius puerorum*, etc. See Lefranc, p. 62, and "Bulletin de la Soc. de l'hist. du Protest. français," XVII. 449.

[2] Beza-Colladon (XXI. 54): "*Quant à ses mœurs, il estoit sur tout fort consciencieux, ennemi des vices, et fort adonné au service de Dieu qu'on appeloit pour lors: tellement que son cœur tendoit entierement à la Theologie, et son père pretendoit de l'y faire employer.*" In the Latin *Vita*, Beza says that he was "*tenera ætate mirum in modum religiosus.*" With this agrees the testimony of the Roman Catholic, Florimond de Ræmond, previously quoted, p. 273.

[3] Le Vasseur, p. 1158. Beza gives some probability to this report by the notice that Calvin was "*severus omnium in suis sodalibus censor.*"

history of his life (*Histoire de la vie, mœurs, actes, doctrine, constance, et mort de Jean Calvin*, Lyon, 1577, republished by Louis-François Chastel, Magistrat, Lyon, 1875, pp. 323, with an introduction of xxxi. pp.). He represents Calvin as "a man, above all others who lived in the world, ambitious, impudent, arrogant, cruel, malicious, vindictive, and ignorant" (!) (p. 12).

Among other incredible stories he reports that Calvin in his youth was stigmatized (*fleur-de-lysé*, branded with the national flower of France) at Noyon in punishment of a heinous crime, and then fled from France in disgrace. "*Calvin*," he says (p. 28 sq.), "*pourveu d'une cure et d'une chapelle, fut surprins ou (et) convaincu du peché de Sodomie, pour lequel il fut en danger de mort par feu, comment est la commune peine de tel peché: mais que l'Evesque de laditte ville* [*Noyon*] *par compassion feit moderer laditte peine en une marque de fleur de lys chaude sur l'espaule. Iceluy Calvin confuz de telle vergongne et vitupère, se defit de ses deux bénéfices es mains du curé de Noyon, duquel ayant receu quelque somme d'argent s'en alla vers Allemaigne et Itallie: cherchant son adventure, et passa par la ville de Ferrare, ou il receut quelque aumone de Madame la Duchesse.*" Bolsec gives as his authority a Mr. Bertelier, secretary of the Council of Geneva, who, he says, was sent to Noyon to make inquiries about the early life of Calvin, and saw the document of his disgrace. But nobody else has seen such a document, and if it had existed at all, it would have been used against him by his enemies. The story is contradicted by all that is authentically known of Calvin, and has been abundantly refuted by Drelincourt, and recently again by Lefranc (p. 48 sqq., 176–182). Kampschulte (I. 224, note 2) declares it unworthy of serious refutation. Nevertheless it has been often repeated by Roman controversialists down to Audin.

The story is either a malignant slander, or it arose from confounding the Reformer with a younger person of the same name (*Jean Cauvin*), and chaplain of the same church at Noyon, who it appears was punished for some immorality of a different kind ("*pour avoir retenue en sa maison une femme du mauvais gouvernement*") in the year 1550, that is, about twenty years later, and who was no heretic, but died a "*bon Catholic*" (as Le Vasseur reports in *Annales de Noyon*, p. 1170, quoted by Lefranc, p. 182). B. C. Galiffe, who is unfriendly to Calvin, adopts the latter suggestion (*Quelques pages d'histoire exacte*, p. 118).

Several other myths were circulated about the Reformer; e.g., that he was the son of a concubine of a priest; that he was an intemperate eater; that he stole a silver goblet at Orleans, etc. See Lefranc, pp. 52 sqq.

Similar perversions and inventions attach to many a great name. The Sanhedrin who crucified the Lord circulated the story that the disciples stole his body and cheated the world. The heretical Ebionites derived the conversion of Paul from disappointed ambition and revenge for an alleged offence of the high-priest, who had refused to give him his daughter in marriage. The long-forgotten myth of Luther's suicide has been seriously revived in our own age (1890) by Roman Catholic priests (Majunke and Honef) in the interest of revived Ultramontanism, and is believed by thousands in spite of repeated refutation.

§ 70. *Calvin as a Student in the French Universities.*
A.D. 1528–1533.

The letters of CALVIN from 1530 to 1532, chiefly addressed to his fellow-student, François Daniel of Orleans, edited by JULES BONNET, in the Edinburgh ed. of CALVIN's *Letters*, I. 3 sqq.; HERMINJARD, II. 278 sqq.; *Opera*, X. Part II. 3 sqq. His first letter to Daniel is dated "*Melliani, 8 Idus Septembr.*," and is put by Herminjard and Reuss in the year 1530 (not 1529). *Mellianum* is Meillant, south of Bourges (and not to be confounded with Meaux, as is done in the Edinburgh edition).

Comp. BEZA–COLLADON, in *Op.* XXI. 54 sqq., 121 sqq. L. BONNET: *Études sur Calvin*, in the "Revue Chrétienne" for 1855. — KAMPSCHULTE, I. 226–240; M'CRIE, 12–28; LEFRANC, 72–108.

Calvin received the best education — in the humanities, law, philosophy, and theology — which France at that time could give. He studied successively in the three leading universities of Orleans, Bourges, and Paris, from 1528 to 1533, first for the priesthood, then, at the wish of his father, for the legal profession, which promised a more prosperous career. After his father's death, he turned again with double zeal to the study of the humanities, and at last to theology.

He made such progress in learning that he occasionally supplied the place of the professors. He was considered a doctor rather than an auditor.[1] Years afterwards, the memory of his prolonged night studies survived in Orleans and Bourges. By his excessive industry he stored his memory with valuable information, but undermined his health, and became a victim to headache, dyspepsia, and insomnia, of which he suffered more or less during his subsequent life.[2]

While he avoided the noisy excitements and dissipations of student life, he devoted his leisure to the duties and

---

[1] "*Doctor potius quam auditor*," says Beza, who studied in the same universities a few years later, and lodged at Orleans in the house or pension of Duchemin, a friend of Calvin.

[2] Beza (XXI. 122): "*Quibus continuatis vigiliis ille quidem solidam eruditionem et excellentissiman memoriam est consequutus, sed etiam vicissim, ut verisimile est, ventriculi imbecillitatem contraxit, quæ varios ipsi morbos et tandem etiam intempestivam mortem attulit.*"

enjoyments of friendship with like-minded fellow-students. Among them were three young lawyers, Duchemin, Connan, and François Daniel, who felt the need of a reformation and favored progress, but remained in the old Church. His letters from that period are brief and terse; they reveal a love of order and punctuality, and a conscientious regard for little as well as great things, but not a trace of opposition to the traditional faith.

His principal teacher in Greek and Hebrew was Melchior Volmar (Wolmar), a German humanist of Rottweil, a pupil of Lefèvre, and successively professor in the universities of Orleans and Bourges, and, at last, at Tübingen, where he died in 1561. He openly sympathized with the Lutheran Reformation, and may have exerted some influence upon his pupil in this direction, but we have no authentic information about it.[1] Calvin was very intimate with him, and could hardly avoid discussing with him the religious question which was then shaking all Europe. In grateful remembrance of his services he dedicated to him his Commentary on the Second Epistle to the Corinthians (Aug. 1, 1546).[2]

His teachers in law were the two greatest jurists of the age, Pierre d'Estoile (Petrus Stella) at Orleans, who was conservative, and became President of the Parliament of Paris, and Andrea Alciati at Bourges, a native of Milan, who was progressive and continued his academic career in Bologna and Padua. Calvin took an interest in the controversy of these rivals, and wrote a little preface to the

---

[1] Florimond de Ræmond (who shows a tendency to discredit the French Reformation by tracing it to a foreign, German source) asserts that Volmar first instilled the poison of heresy into the mind of Calvin, and advised him to exchange the Code of Justinian for the Gospel of Christ. But Calvin and Beza (*Op.* XXI. 122), while speaking highly of Volmar as a teacher and friend, say nothing about his religious influence.

[2] *Opera*, XII. no. 814. He apologizes for his long silence. The correspondence with Volmar is lost, but may yet be found.

Antapologia of his friend, Nicholas Duchemin, in favor of d'Estoile.[1] He acquired the degree of Licentiate or Bachelor of Laws at Orleans, Feb. 14, 1531 (1532).[2] On leaving the university he was offered the degree of Doctor of Laws without the usual fees, by the unanimous consent of the professors.[3] He was consulted about the divorce question of Henry VIII., when it was proposed to the universities and scholars of the Continent; and he gave his opinion against the lawfulness of marriage with a brother's widow.[4]

The study of jurisprudence sharpened his judgment, enlarged his knowledge of human nature, and was of great practical benefit to him in the organization and administration of the Church in Geneva, but may have also increased his legalism and over-estimate of logical demonstration.

In the summer of 1531, after a visit to Noyon, where he attended his father in his last sickness, Calvin removed a second time to Paris, accompanied by his younger brother, Antoine. He found there several of his fellow-students of Orleans and Bourges; one of them offered him the home of his parents, but he declined, and took up his abode in the College Fortet, where we find him again in 1533. A part of the year he spent in Orleans.

Left master of his fortune, he now turned his attention again chiefly to classical studies. He attended the lectures

---

[1] March 6, 1531. Herminjard, II. 314 sq. no. 328; Lefranc, 79 sq.

[2] In *Op.* XXI. 190, the degree is dated from the year 1532. "*Dans un act de se jour* [*Febr. 14*] *est nommé maistre Jean* CAUVIN *licencié es lois.*" In a document relating to the settlement of the estate of the deceased Gérard Cauvin, which Lefranc (p. 202) quotes from Le Vasseur (*Annal.*, p. 1169), and assigns to Feb. 14, 1531, Calvin is mentioned as "*licentié ès loix.*"

[3] "*Absque ullo precio, summo docentium omnium consensu,*" says Beza (*Op.* XXI. 122). Colladon (f. 54) adds that Calvin refused the offer ("*ce que toutesfois il refusa*"); but it is not clear whether he meant the gratuity or the degree itself, probably the former.

[4] Gerdes, IV. 201; M'Crie, 63; Dyer, *Life of Calvin*, p. 8. Burnet, in his *Hist. of the Ref. of the Ch. of England* (Part I. Bk. II.), refers to a letter of Calvin on the subject, which I cannot find in Herminjard.

of Pierre Danès, a Hellenist and encyclopædic scholar of great reputation.[1]

He showed as yet no trace of opposition to the Catholic Church. His correspondence refers to matters of friendship and business, but avoids religious questions. When Daniel asked him to introduce his sister to the superior of a nunnery in Paris which she wished to enter, he complied with the request, and made no effort to change her purpose. He only admonished her not to confide in her own strength, but to put her whole trust in God. This shows, at least, that he had lost faith in the meritoriousness of vows and good works, and was approaching the heart of the evangelical system.[2]

He associated much with a rich and worthy merchant, Estienne de la Forge, who afterwards was burned for the sake of the Gospel (1535).

He seems to have occasionally suffered in Paris of pecuniary embarrassment. The income from his benefices was irregular, and he had to pay for the printing of his first book. At the close of 1531 he borrowed two crowns from his friend, Duchemin. He expressed a hope soon to discharge his debt, but would none the less remain a debtor in gratitude for the services of friendship.

It is worthy of remark that even those of his friends who refused to follow him in his religious change, remained true to him. This is an effective refutation of the charge of coldness so often made against him. François Daniel of Orleans renewed the correspondence in 1559, and entrusted to him

---

[1] Lefranc (p. 89) calls him "*l'un des esprits les plus profonds et les plus puissants de cette Renaissance qui compta tant de génies universels*," and quotes the distich : —

> "*Magnus Budæus, major Danesius ille,*
> *Argivos norat, iste etiam reliquos.*"

[2] "*Nolui eam deducere a sententia . . . sed paucis admonui, ne suis se viribus efferret, ne quid sibi de se temere promitteret, sed omnia reponeret in Dei virtute, in quo sumus et vivimus.*" Herminjard, II. 347.

the education of his son Pierre, who afterwards became an advocate and bailiff of Saint-Benoît near Orleans.[1]

§ 71. *Calvin as a Humanist. Commentary on Seneca.*

"*L. Annei Se* | *necæ, Romani Senato* | *ris, ac philosophi clarissi* | *mi, libri duo de Clementia, ad Ne* | *ronem Cæsarem:* | *Joannis Caluini Nouiodunæi commentariis illustrati . . .* | *Parisiis. . . .* 1532." 4°. Reprinted 1576, 1597, 1612, and, from the *ed. princeps,* in *Opera,* vol. V. (1866) pp. 5–162. The commentary is preceded by a dedicatory epistle, a sketch of the life of Seneca.

H. Lecoultre: *Calvin d'après son commentaire sur le "De Clementia" de Sénèque* (1532). Lausanne, 1891 (pp. 29).

In April, 1532, Calvin, in his twenty-third year, ventured before the public with his first work, which was printed at his own expense, and gave ample proof of his literary taste and culture. It is a commentary on Seneca's book *On Mercy.* He announced its appearance to Daniel with the words, "*Tandem jacta est alea.*" He sent a copy to Erasmus, who had published the works of Seneca in 1515 and 1529. He calls him "the honor and delight of the world of letters."[2] It is dedicated to Claude de Hangest, his former schoolmate of the Mommor family, at that time abbot of St. Eloy (Eligius) at Noyon.

This book moves in the circle of classical philology and moral philosophy, and reveals a characteristic love for the best type of Stoicism, great familiarity with Greek and Roman literature,[3] masterly Latinity, rare exegetical skill,

---

[1] See the last three letters of Calvin to Daniel (1559 and 1560) in *Opera,* vol. XVII. 584, 680, and XVIII. 16. Lefranc says (p. 77): "*Rien de touchant comme cette correspondance où le grave réformateur montre une indulgence et une souriante bonhomie qui ne lui sont pas habituelles. . . . Cet échange de lettres révèle veritablement un Calvin affectueux et délicat qu'on a trop souvent méconnu, sur la foi des Bolsec et des Audin.*" There is a German monograph on *Pierre Daniel d'Orleans* by Hagen of Bern, translated into French by Paul de Felice, Orleans, 1876.

[2] "*Litterarum alterum decus ac primæ deliciæ.*" In his dedicatory letter to Claude de Hangest, April 4, 1532, which is also printed in Herminjard, II. p. 411.

[3] He freely quotes Aristotle, Plutarch, Virgil, Livy, Ovid, Horace, Pliny,

clear and sound judgment, and a keen insight into the evils of despotism and the defects of the courts of justice, but makes no allusion to Christianity. It is remarkable that his first book was a commentary on a moral philosopher who came nearer to the apostle Paul than any heathen writer.

It is purely the work of a humanist, not of an apologist or a reformer. There is no evidence that it was intended to be an indirect plea for toleration and clemency in behalf of the persecuted Protestants. It is not addressed to the king of France, and the implied comparison of Francis with Nero in the incidental reference to the Neronian persecution would have defeated such a purpose.[1]

Calvin, like Melanchthon and Zwingli, started as a humanist, and, like them, made the linguistic and literary culture of the Renaissance tributary to the Reformation. They all admired Erasmus until he opposed the Reformation, for which he had done so much to prepare the way. They went boldly forward, when he timidly retreated. They loved religion more than letters. They admired the heathen classics, but they followed the apostles and evangelists as guides to the higher wisdom of God.

§ 72. *Calvin's Conversion.* 1532.

Preface to his Commentary on the Psalms (*Opera*, XXXI. 21, 22, Latin and French in parallel columns), and his Reply to Sadolet (*Opera*, V. 389). See above, p. 296.

HENRY, I. ch. II. STÄHELIN, I. 16–28. KAMPSCHULTE, I. 230. LEFRANC, 96 sqq.

A brilliant career — as a humanist, or a lawyer, or a churchman — opened before Calvin, when he suddenly embraced the

Quintilian, Curtius, Macrobius, Terence, Diogenes Laërtius, and especially his favorite Cicero, whom he was for some time in the habit of reading through once a year. Lecoultre gives in an appendix a list of the works quoted by Calvin. He thinks that he was already then at heart a Protestant.

[1] "*Quum Nero diris suppliciis impotenter sæviret in Christianos.*" *Op.* V. 10. Henry, Herzog, Dorner, and Guizot assume an apologetic aim; while Stähelin and Kampschulte deny it.

cause of the Reformation, and cast in his lot with a poor persecuted sect.

Reformation was in the air. The educated classes could not escape its influence. The seed sown by Lefèvre had sprung up in France. The influence from Germany and Switzerland made itself felt more and more. The clergy opposed the new opinions, the men of letters favored them. Even the court was divided: King Francis I. persecuted the Protestants; his sister, Marguerite d'Angoulème, queen of Navarre, protected them. How could a young scholar of such precocious mind and intense studiousness as Calvin be indifferent to the religious question which agitated the universities of Orleans, Bourges, and Paris? He must have searched the Scriptures long and carefully before he could acquire such familiarity as he shows already in his first theological writings.

He speaks of his conversion as a sudden one (*subita conversio*), but this does not exclude previous preparation any more than in the case of Paul.[1] A city may be taken by a single assault, yet after a long siege. Calvin was not an unbeliever, nor an immoral youth; on the contrary, he was a devout Catholic of unblemished character. His conversion, therefore, was a change from Romanism to Protestantism, from papal superstition to evangelical faith, from scholastic traditionalism to biblical simplicity. He mentions no human agency, not even Volmar or Olivetan or Lefèvre. "God himself," he says, "produced the change. He instantly subdued my heart to obedience." Absolute obedience of his intellect to the word of God, and obedience of his will to the will of God: this was the soul of his religion. He strove in vain to attain peace of conscience by the mechanical methods

---

[1] "*Quum superstitionibus papatus magis pertinaciter addictus essem, quam ut facile esset e tam profundo luto me extrahi, animum meum, qui pro œtate nimis obduruerat, subita conversione (par une conversion subite) ad docilitatem subegit.*" *Opera*, XXXI. 21. Lefranc (p. 40) weakens the sense of this decisive passage.

of Romanism, and was driven to a deeper sense of sin and guilt. "Only one haven of salvation," he says, "is left open for our souls, and that is the mercy of God in Christ. We are saved by grace — not by our merits, not by our works." Reverence for the Church kept him back for some time till he learned to distinguish the true, invisible, divine essence of the Church from its outward, human form and organization. Then the knowledge of the truth, like a bright light from heaven, burst upon his mind with such force, that there was nothing left for him but to obey the voice from heaven. He consulted not with flesh and blood, and burned the bridge behind him.

The precise time and place and circumstances of this great change are not accurately known. He was very reticent about himself. It probably occurred at Orleans or Paris in the latter part of the year 1532.[1] In a letter of October, 1533, to Francis Daniel, he first speaks of the Reformation in Paris, the rage of the Sorbonne, and the satirical comedy against the queen of Navarre.[2] In November of the same year he publicly attacked the Sorbonne. In a familiar letter to Bucer in Strassburg, which is dated from Noyon, Sept. 4 (probably in 1534), he recommends a French refugee, falsely accused of holding the opinions of the Anabaptists, and says, "I entreat of you, master Bucer, if my prayers, if my tears are of any avail, that you would compassionate and help him in his wretchedness. The poor are left in a special manner to your care; you are the helper of the orphan. . . . Most learned Sir, farewell; thine from my heart."[3]

[1] So Kampschulte (I. 242), Lefranc (p. 98, "*dans la seconde moitié de l'année 1532*"), and, apparently, also the Strassburg editors, vol. XXI. 191. Beza seems to date the conversion further back (to 1528 or 1527) and traces it to the influence of Olivetan, and so also Henry and Merle d'Aubigné (I. 535). Stähelin (I. 21) puts it forward to the beginning of 1533. Calvin spent the greater part of the year 1532 to 1533 at Orleans. *Op.* XXI. 191.

[2] Ep. 19 in *Op.* X. Part II. 27. Bonnet, I. 12. Herminjard, III. 106. Lefranc, 109 sqq.

[3] "*Tuus ex animo.*" *Op.* X. Part II. 24. Bonnet, *Letters,* I. 9–11. Hermin-

There never was a change of conviction purer in motive, more radical in character, more fruitful and permanent in result. It bears a striking resemblance to that still greater event near Damascus, which transformed a fanatical Pharisee into an apostle of Jesus Christ. And, indeed, Calvin was not unlike St. Paul in his intellectual and moral constitution; and the apostle of sovereign grace and evangelical freedom had not a more sympathetic expounder than Luther and Calvin.[1]

Without any intention or effort on his part, Calvin became the head of the evangelical party in less than a year after his conversion. Seekers of the truth came to him from all directions. He tried in vain to escape them. Every quiet retreat was turned into a school. He comforted and strengthened the timid brethren in their secret meetings of devotion. He avoided all show of learning, but, as the old Chronicle of the French Reformed Church reports, he showed such depth of knowledge and such earnestness of speech that no one could hear him without being forcibly impressed. He usually began and closed his exhortations with the word of Paul, "If God is for us, who can be against us?" This is the keynote of his theology and piety.

He remained for the present in the Catholic Church. His aim was to reform it from within rather than from without, until circumstances compelled him to leave.

jard, III. 201, locates this letter in 1534, which is more likely than 1532. The letter presupposes a previous acquaintance with Bucer. This might be dated back with Kampschulte (I. 231) to the year 1528, if Calvin were that unnamed "*Noviodunensis juvenis*" whom Bucer, in a letter to Farel, dated May 1, 1528, mentions as having fled from persecution at Orleans to Strassburg to study Greek and Hebrew; but Bucer probably referred to Pierre Robert Olivetan, who was likewise from Noyon, and a relative and friend of Calvin, and perhaps brought Calvin into contact with Bucer. Herminjard, II. 132 (note 5), conjectures that the young man was Froment. But Froment was a native of Dauphiné, not of Noyon. Comp. *Op.* X. Part II. 1; XXI. 191.

[1] Audin, following in the track of Bolsec, traces Calvin's conversion to wounded ambition, and thereby exposes, as Kampschulte justly observes (I. 242), his utter ignorance and misconception of Calvin's character, whose only ambition was to serve God.

§ 73. *Calvin's Call.*

As in the case of Paul, Calvin's call to his life-work coincided with his conversion, and he proved it by his labors. "By their fruits ye shall know them."

We must distinguish between an ordinary and an extraordinary call, or the call to the ministry of the gospel, and the call to reform the Church. The ordinary ministry is necessary for the being, the extraordinary for the well-being, of the Church. The former corresponds to the priesthood in the Jewish dispensation, and continues in unbroken succession; the latter resembles the mission of the prophets, and appears sporadically in great emergencies. The office of a reformer comes nearest the office of an apostle. There are founders of the Church universal, as Peter and Paul; so there are founders of particular churches, as Luther, Zwingli, Calvin, Knox, Zinzendorf, Wesley; but none of the Reformers was infallible.

1. All the Reformers were born, baptized, confirmed, and educated in the historic Catholic Church, which cast them out; as the Apostles were circumcised and trained in the Synagogue, which cast them out. They never doubted the validity of the Catholic ordinances, and rejected the idea of re-baptism. Distinguishing between the divine substance and the human addition, Calvin said of his baptism, "I renounce the chrism, but retain the baptism." [1]

The Reformers were also ordained priests in the Roman Church, except Melanchthon and Calvin, — the greatest theologians among them. A remarkable exception. Melanchthon remained a layman all his life; yet his authority to teach is undoubted. Calvin became a regular minister; but how?

He was, as we have seen, intended and educated for the Roman priesthood, and early received the clerical tonsure.[2]

[1] "*Je renonce le cresme, et retient mon Baptesme.*" Colladon, in *Op.* XXI. 53.
[2] The value of the tonsure was differently estimated, but it was generally

He also held two benefices, and preached sometimes in Pont l'Evêque, and also in Lignières, a little town near Bourges, where he made the impression that "he preached better than the monks." [1]

But he never read mass, and never entered the higher orders, properly so called.

After he left the Roman Church, there was no Evangelical bishop in France to ordain him; the bishops, so far, all remained in the old Church, except two or three in East Prussia and Sweden. If the validity of the Christian ministry depended on an unbroken succession of diocesan bishops, which again depends on historical proof, it would be difficult to defend the Reformation and to resist the claims of Rome. But the Reformers planted themselves on the promise of Christ, the ever-present head of the Church, who is equally near to his people in any age. They rejected the Roman Catholic idea of ordination as a divinely instituted sacrament, which can only be performed by bishops, and which confers priestly powers of offering sacrifice and dispensing absolution. They taught the general priesthood of believers, and fell back upon the internal call of the Holy Spirit and the external call of the Christian people. Luther, in his earlier writings, lodged the power of the keys in the con-

excluded from the lower orders. Calvin says (*Inst.* IV. ch. 19, § 22): "Some represent the clerical tonsure to be the first order of all, and episcopacy the last; others exclude the tonsure, and place the archiepiscopal office among the orders." Peter the Lombard distinguishes seven orders, corresponding to the seven gifts of the Holy Spirit (Isa. 11 : 2, 3), — beadles, readers, exorcists, acolytes, subdeacons, deacons, priests. He regards the episcopate, not as a separate *ordo*, but only as a dignity with four grades, — patriarch, archbishop, metropolitan, bishop. Several schoolmen and canonists reckon eight or nine *ordines*, including bishops and archbishops. The Council of Trent defined the three *ordines majores*, — bishops, priests (presbyters), and deacons.

[1] Colladon, *Op.* XXI. 55 : "*Il prescha* (while he studied at Bourges) *quelquefois en une petite ville du pays de Berry, nommée Lignières, et eut entrée en la maison du seigneur du lieu qui estoit pour lors: lequel . . . disait . . . qu'il lui semblait que M. Jean Calvin preshoit mieux que les moines.*" His preaching at Pont l'Evêque is mentioned by Colladon, *ibid.* fol. 54, and by Beza, fol. 121. See above, p. 301.

gregation, and identified ordination with vocation. "Whoever is called," he says, "is ordained, and must preach: this is our Lord's consecration and true chrism." He even consecrated, by a bold irregularity, his friend Amsdorf as superintendent of Naumburg, to show that he could make a bishop as well as the pope, and could do it without the use of consecrated oil.

Calvin was regularly elected pastor and teacher of theology at Geneva in 1536 by the presbyters and the council, with the consent of the whole people.[1]

This popular election was a revival of the primitive custom. The greatest bishops of the early Church — such as Cyprian, Ambrose, and Augustin — were elected by the voice of the people, which they obeyed as the voice of God.

We are not informed whether Calvin was solemnly introduced into his office by prayer and the laying on of the hands of presbyters (such as Farel and Viret), after the apostolic custom (1 Tim. 4:14), which is observed in the Reformed Churches. He did not regard ordination as absolutely indispensable, but as a venerable rite sanctioned by the practice of the Apostles which has the force of a precept.[2] He even ascribed to it a semi-sacramental character. "The imposition of hands," he says, "which is used at the introduction of the true presbyters and ministers of the Church into their office, I have no objection to consider as a sacrament; for, in the first place, that sacrament is taken from the Scripture, and, in the next place, it is declared by Paul to be not unnecessary or useless, but a faithful symbol of spiritual grace (1 Tim. 4:14). I have not enumerated it as a third among the sacraments, because it is not ordinary

---

[1] Beza, *Vita C.* (XXI. 125 sq.): "*Suffragiis presbyterii et magistratus, accedente plebis consensu, delectus non concionator tantum (hoc autem primum recuserat), sed etiam sacrarum literarum doctor, quod unum admittebat, est designatus anno Domini MDXXXVI mense Augusto.*" Comp. Colladon, *ibid.* fol. 58 sq.: "*declaré Pasteur et Docteur en ceste Eglise [de Genève] avec légitime élection et approbation.*" [2] *Inst.* IV. ch. III. § 16.

or common to all the faithful, but a special rite for a particular office. The ascription of this honor to the Christian ministry, however, furnishes no reason of pride in Roman priests; for Christ has commanded the ordination of ministers to dispense his Gospel and his mysteries, not the inauguration of priests to offer sacrifices. He has commissioned them to preach the Gospel and to feed his flock, and not to immolate victims."[1]

The evangelical ministry in the non-episcopal Churches was of necessity presbyterial, that is, descended from the presbyterate, which was originally identical with the episcopate. Even the Church of England, during her formative period under the reigns of Edward VI. and Elizabeth, recognized the validity of presbyterial ordination, not only in the Lutheran and Reformed Churches of the Continent, but within her own jurisdiction, as in the cases of Peter Martyr, professor of theology at Oxford; Bucer, Fagius, and Cartwright, professors at Cambridge; John à Lasco, pastor in London; Dean Whittingham of Durham, and many others.[2]

2. But whence did Calvin and the other Reformers derive their authority to reform the old Catholic Church and to found new Churches? Here we must resort to a special divine call and outfit. The Reformers belong not to the regular order of priests, but to the irregular order of prophets whom God calls directly by his Spirit from the plough or the shepherd's staff or the workshop or the study. So he raises and endows men with rare genius for poetry or art or science or invention or discovery. All good gifts come from God; but the gift of genius is exceptional, and cannot be derived or propagated by ordinary descent. There are divine irregularities as well as divine regularities. God writes on a

---

[1] *Institutes*, IV. ch. XIX. § 28. (In Tholuck's ed. II. 470.)

[2] Keble says in his Introduction to Hooker's *Ecclesiastical Polity:* "Nearly up to the time when Hooker wrote (1594), numbers had been admitted to the ministry of the Church of England with no better than presbyterial ordination."

crooked as well as on a straight line. Even Paul was called out of due time, and did not seek ordination from Peter or any other apostle, but derived his authority directly from Christ, and proved his ministry by the abundance of his labors.

In the apostolic age there were apostles, prophets, and evangelists for the Church at large, and presbyter-bishops and deacons for particular congregations. The former are considered extraordinary officers. But their race is not yet extinct, any more than the race of men of genius in any other sphere of life. They arise whenever and wherever they are needed.

We are bound to the ordinary means of grace, but God is free, and his Spirit works when, where, and how he pleases. God calls ordinary men for ordinary work in the ordinary way; and he calls extraordinary men for extraordinary work in an extraordinary way. He has done so in times past, and will do so to the end of time.[1]

Hooker, the most "judicious" of Anglican divines, says: "Though thousands were debtors to Calvin, as touching divine knowledge, yet he was to none, only to God."

§ 74. *The Open Rupture. An Academic Oration.* 1533.

CALV. *Opera*, X. P. I. 30; XXI. 123, 129, 192. A very graphic account by Merle d'Aubigné, Bk. II. ch. xxx. (vol. II. 264-284).

For a little while matters seemed to take a favorable turn at the court for reform. The reactionary conduct of the Sorbonne and the insult offered to Queen Marguerite by the condemnation of her "Mirror of a Sinful Soul," — a tender and monotonous mystic reverie,[2] — offended her brother and

---

[1] Our own age is witness to this fact. I may refer to Dwight Lyman Moody, who is a plain, unordained layman, but a genuine, God-taught evangelist. He has probably converted more people to a Christian life than any clergyman or learned professor of theology of this age, and has made his home at Northfield a Jerusalem for Bible students from all parts of the country, and even from across the sea.

[2] *Le miroir de l'âme pécheresse* (1533). The book was condemned on purely

the liberal members of the University. Several preachers who sympathized with a moderate reformation, Gérard Roussel, and the Augustinians, Bertault and Courault, were permitted to ascend the pulpit in Paris.[1] The king himself, by his opposition to the German emperor, and his friendship with Henry VIII., incurred the suspicion of aiding the cause of heresy and schism. He tried, from political motives and regard for his sister, to conciliate between the conservative and progressive parties. He even authorized the invitation of Melanchthon to Paris as counsellor, but Melanchthon wisely declined.

Nicolas Cop, the son of a distinguished royal physician (William Cop of Basel), and a friend of Calvin, was elected Rector of the University, Oct. 10, 1533, and delivered the usual inaugural oration on All Saint's Day, Nov. 1, before a large assembly in the Church of the Mathurins.[2]

This oration, at the request of the new Rector, had been prepared by Calvin. It was a plea for a reformation on the basis of the New Testament, and a bold attack on the scholastic theologians of the day, who were represented as a set of sophists, ignorant of the Gospel. " They teach nothing," says Calvin, "of faith, nothing of the love of God, nothing of the remission of sins, nothing of grace, nothing of justification; or if they do so, they pervert and undermine it all by their laws and sophistries. I beg you, who are here present, not to tolerate any longer these heresies and abuses." [3]

---

negative evidence. The silence about purgatory and the intercession of saints was construed as a denial.

[1] Elie Courault (Coraud, Couraud, Coraldus) afterwards fled to Basel in 1534, and became a colleague of Farel and Calvin at Geneva in 1536. See Herminjard, IV. 114, note 9.

[2] Bulæus, *Historia Universitatis Parisiensis*, VI. 238, and in the " *Catalogus illustrium Academicorum Univ. Parisiensis* " at the end of the same volume. A notice of Cop in Herminjard, III. 129 sq. note 3.

[3] The incomplete draft of this address has been discovered by J. Bonnet among the MSS. of the Geneva Library, and the whole of it by Reuss and Cunitz in the library of St. Thomas in Strassburg. It is printed in *Opera,*

The Sorbonne and the Parliament regarded this academic oration as a manifesto of war upon the Catholic Church, and condemned it to the flames. Cop was warned and fled to his relatives in Basel.[1] Calvin, the real author of the mischief, is said to have descended from a window by means of sheets, and escaped from Paris in the garb of a vine-dresser with a hoe upon his shoulder. His rooms were searched and his books and papers were seized by the police.[2]

§ 75. *Persecution of the Protestants in Paris.* 1534.

BEZA in *Vita Calv.*, vol. XXI. 124. — JEAN CRESPIN: *Livre des Martyrs*, Genève, 1570. — The report of the *Bourgeois de Paris.* — GERDESIUS, IV. Mon. 11. — HENRY, I. 74; II. 333. — DYER, I. 29. — POLENZ, I. 282. — KAMPSCHULTE, I. 243. — "Bulletin de la Soc. de l'hist. du Prot. franç.," X. 34; XI. 253.

This storm might have blown over without doing much harm. But in the following year the reaction was greatly strengthened by the famous placards, which gave it the name of "the year of placards." An over-zealous, fanatical Protestant by the name of Feret, a servant of the king's apothecary, placarded a tract "on the horrible, great, intolerable abuses of the popish mass," throughout Paris and even at the door of the royal chamber at Fontainebleau, where the king was then residing, in the night of Oct. 18, 1534. In this placard the mass is described as a blasphemous denial of the one and all-sufficient sacrifice of Christ; while the pope, with all his brood (*toute sa vermine*) of cardinals, bishops, priests, and

X. Pars II. 30–36 (and the shorter draft, IX. 873–876). Comp. Herminjard, III. 117, note, and 418 sqq.

[1] Three hundred crowns were offered for his capture dead or alive. So Bucer wrote to Blaurer, Jan. 13, 1534, in Herminjard, III. 130. Cop informed Bucer, April 5, 1534, that a German was burned in Paris, for denying transubstantiation. *Ibid.* III. 159.

[2] According to Beza (XXI. 123), Queen Marguerite protected Calvin and honorably received him at the court; but he certainly left Paris very soon. Colladon says nothing of an interference of Marguerite. The story of the escape of Calvin is told by Papyrius Masson, and Desmay. See M'Crie, p. 100, note 59. It has been compared to Paul's escape at Damascus, Acts 9:25.

monks, are denounced as hypocrites and servants of Antichrist.[1]

All moderate Protestants deplored this untimely outburst of radicalism. It retarded and almost ruined the prospects of the Reformation in France. The best cause may be undone by being overdone.

The king was highly and justly incensed, and ordered the imprisonment of all suspected persons. The prisons were soon filled. To purge the city from the defilement caused by this insult to the holy mass and the hierarchy, a most imposing procession was held from the Louvre to Notre Dame, on Jan. 29, 1535. The image of St. Geneviève, the patroness of Paris, was carried through the streets: the archbishop, with the host under a magnificent däis, and the king with his three sons, bare-headed, on foot, a burning taper in their hands, headed the procession, and were followed by the princes, cardinals, bishops, priests, ambassadors, and the great officers of the State and of the University, walking two and two abreast, in profound silence, with lighted torches. Solemn mass was performed in the cathedral. Then the king dined with the prelates and dignitaries, and declared that he would not hesitate to behead any one of his own children if found guilty of these new, accursed heresies, and to offer them as a sacrifice to divine justice.

The gorgeous solemnities of the day wound up with a horrible *autodafé* of six Protestants: they were suspended by a rope to a machine, let down into burning flames, again drawn up, and at last precipitated into the fire. They died like

---

[1] They are indiscriminately called "*faux prophètes, damnables trompeurs, apostats, loups, faux pasteurs, menteurs, blasphémateurs, meurtriers des âmes, renonceurs de Jésus Christ, ravisseurs de l'honneur de Dieu, et plus détestables que les diables.*" Farel, then in Switzerland, was suspected of having some share in this incendiary publication, but without any evidence. Courault, who was then in confinement, advised not to publish the paper, "as it would excite great commotion in the minds of the people, and bring odium on the whole body of the faithful." *Hist. Martyr.*, fol. 64, quoted by M'Crie, p. 102.

heroes. The more educated among them had their tongues slit. Twenty-four innocent Protestants were burned alive in public places of the city from Nov. 10, 1534, till May 5, 1535. Among them was Etienne de la Forge (Stephanus Forgeus), an intimate friend of Calvin. Many more were fined, imprisoned, and tortured, and a considerable number, among them Calvin and Du Tillet, fled to Strassburg.[1]

These cruelties were justified or excused by charges of heresy, immorality, and disloyalty, and by a reference to the excesses of a fanatical wing of the Anabaptists in Münster, which took place in the same year.[2] But the Huguenots were then, as their descendants have always been, and are now, among the most intelligent, moral, and orderly citizens of France.[3]

The Sorbonne urged the king to put a stop to the printing-press (Jan. 13, 1535). He agreed to a temporary suspension (Feb. 26). Afterwards censors were appointed, first by Parliament, then by the clergy (1542). The press stimulated free thought and was stimulated by it in turn. Before 1500, four millions of volumes (mostly in folio) were printed; from 1500 to 1536, seventeen millions; after that time the number

---

[1] Beza (XXI. 124) gives a brief account of the persecution: "*Eousque inflammata fascinati Francisci Regis ira ob schedas quasdam adversus missam per urbem sparsas ipsiusque regii cubiculi foribus adfixas, ut publica decreta supplicatione, cui una cum liberis suis tribus nudo capite ardentem facem quasi expiationis causa gestans interfuit, quatuor urbis celebrioribus locis octonos martyres vivos ustulari juberet, atque adeo solemni jure jurando testaretur, se ne liberis quidem suis parsurum, si forte teterrimis illis, ut vocabat, hæresibus essent infecti.*" The Protestant reports are verified by that of a Roman Catholic, "*Bourgeois de Paris,*" who witnessed the burnings with satisfaction, as a spectacle well pleasing to God, and mentions the dates and places of execution (namely, Nov. 10, 1534, Nov. 18, Nov. 19, Dec. 4; Jan. 21, 1535, Jan. 22, Feb. 16, 19, 26, March 3, May 5), as well as the occupations of the victims, most of whom were workingmen, one a rich merchant. This report was published in 1854 and is reprinted in Michelet's *Histoire de France* (vol. X. 340 sq.).

[2] "*Pour excuser envers les princes protestants les persécutions qu'on faisait contre l'Evangile.*" Colladon (XXI. 57).

[3] Michelet (X. 339) says: "*Rien de plus saint, de plus pur, que les origines du protestantisme français. Rien de plus éloigné de la sanglante orgie de Munster.*"

is beyond calculation.[1] The printing-press is as necessary for liberty as respiration for health. Some air is good, some bad; but whether good or bad, it is the condition of life.

This persecution was the immediate occasion of Calvin's *Institutes*, and the forerunner of a series of persecutions which culminated under the reign of Louis XIV., and have made the Reformed Church of France a Church of martyrs.

§ 76. *Calvin as a Wandering Evangelist.* 1533–1536.

For nearly three years Calvin wandered as a fugitive evangelist under assumed names [2] from place to place in Southern France, Switzerland, Italy, till he reached Geneva as his final destination. It is impossible accurately to determine all the facts and dates in this period.

He resigned his ecclesiastical benefices at Noyon and Pont l'Evêque, May 4, 1534, and thus closed all connection with the Roman Church.[3] That year was remarkable for the founding of the order of the Jesuits at Montmartre (Aug. 15), which took the lead in the Counter-Reformation; by the election of Pope Paul III. (Alexander Farnese, Oct. 13), who confirmed the order, excommunicated Henry VIII., and established the Inquisition in Italy; and by the bloody persecution of the Protestants in Paris, which has been described in the preceding section.[4]

The Roman Counter-Reformation now began in earnest, and called for a consolidation of the Protestant forces.

Calvin spent the greater part of the year 1533 to 1534, under the protection of Queen Marguerite of Navarre, in her

---

[1] Michelet, *l.c.* 342 sq.

[2] Such as Charles d'Espeville, Martianus Lucanius, Carolus Passelius, Alcuin, Deperçan, Calpurnius. There is a monograph on these assumed names, *Diatribe de Pseudonymia Calvini,* by Liebe, Amsterdam, 1723, which includes several letters of importance. So says Kampschulte, I. 245.

[3] Le Vasseur, 1161. Herminjard, V. 104. *Op.* XXI. 193.

[4] Beza calls the year 1534 "*horrenda in multos pios sœvitia insignis*" (Calv. *Op.* XXI. 124).

native city of Angoulême. This highly gifted lady (1492–1549), the sister of King Francis I., grandmother of Henry IV., and a voluminous writer in verse and prose, was a strange mixture of piety and liberalism, of idealism and sensualism. She patronized both the Reformation and the Renaissance, Calvin and Rabelais; she wrote the *Mirror of a Sinful Soul*, and also the *Heptameron* in professed imitation of Boccaccio's *Decamerone;* yet she was pure, and began and closed the day with religious meditation and devotion. After the death of her royal brother (1547), she retired to a convent as abbess, and declared on her death-bed that, after receiving extreme unction, she had protected the Reformers out of pure compassion, and not from any wish to depart from the faith of her ancestors.[1]

Calvin lived at Angoulême with a wealthy friend, Louis du Tillet, who was canon of the cathedral and curé of Claix, and had acquired on his journeys a rare library of three or four thousand volumes.[2] He taught him Greek, and prosecuted his theological studies. He associated with honorable men of letters, and was highly esteemed by them.[3] He began there the preparation of his *Institutes*.[4] He also aided Olivetan in the revision and completion of the French translation of the Bible, which appeared at Neuchâtel in June, 1535, with a preface of Calvin.[5]

---

[1] Dyer (*Life of Calvin*, p. 18) says of her: "Plato's divine and earthly love never met more conspicuously in a human being," and quotes the remark of M. Génin, the editor of her correspondence: "*Le trait saillant du caractère de Marguerite c'est d'avoir allié toute sa vie les idées religieuses et les idées d'amour mondain.*"

[2] Ep. 20, *Op.* X. Pt. I. 37. Florimond de Ræmond (p. 883) extends Calvin's sojourn at Angoulême to three years, which is evidently an error.

[3] Florimond de Ræmond: "*Il estoit en bonne estimé et réputation, aimé de tous ceux qui aimoient les lettres.*"

[4] According to the same Roman Catholic historian.

[5] Ep. 29 in *Op.* X. Pars I. 51; the preface in vol. IX. 787–790. Beza (followed by Stähelin, I. 88) makes him take part also in the first edition, which appeared in 1534, and contained only the New Testament. But this seems to be an error. See Reuss, "Révue de Theologie," 1866, No. III. 318, and Kampschulte, I. 247; also Herminjard, III. 349, note 8.

From Angoulême Calvin made excursions to Nérac, Poitiers, Orleans, and Paris. At Nérac in Béarn, the little capital of Queen Marguerite, he became personally acquainted with Le Fèvre d'Étaples (Faber Stapulensis), the octogenarian patriarch of French Humanism and Protestantism. Le Fèvre, with prophetic vision, recognized in the young scholar the future restorer of the Church of France.[1] Perhaps he also suggested to him to take Melanchthon for his model.[2] Roussel, the chaplain and confessor of Marguerite, advised him to purify the house of God, but not to destroy it.

At Poitiers, Calvin gained several eminent persons for the Reformation. According to an uncertain tradition he celebrated with a few friends, for the first time, the Lord's Supper after the Reformed fashion, in a cave (*grotte de Croutelles*) near the town, which long afterwards was called "Calvin's Cave." [3]

Towards the close of the year 1534, he ventured on a visit to Paris. There he met, for the first time, the Spanish physician, Michael Servetus, who had recently published his heretical book *On the Errors of the Trinity*, and challenged him to a disputation. Calvin accepted the challenge at the risk of his safety, and waited for him in a house in the Rue Saint Antoine; but Servetus did not appear. Twenty years afterwards he reminded Servetus of this interview: "You know that at that time I was ready to do everything for you, and did not even count my life too dear that I might convert you from your errors." Would that he had succeeded at that time, or never seen the unfortunate heretic again.

---

[1] Beza (XXI. 123) : "*Excepit juvenem [Calvinum] bonus senex et libenter vidit, futurum augurans insigne cœlestis in Gallia instaurandi regni instrumentum.*"

[2] According to Florimond de Ræmond.

[3] Bayle, Art. *Calvin* and *La Place.* Crottet, *Petite Chronique Protestante de France,* 96 sqq. Stähelin, I. 32. Lefranc, 120. Herminjard, III. 202, note 4.

§ 77. *The Sleep of the Soul.* 1534.

Psychopannychia. Aureliæ, 1534; 2d and revised ed. Basel, 1536; 3d ed. Strassburg, 1542; French trans. Paris, 1558; republished in *Opera*, vol. V. 165–232. — Comp. the analysis of Stähelin, I. 36–40, and *La France Prot.* III. 549. English translation in *Calvin's Tracts*, III. 413–490.

Before Calvin left France, he wrote, at Orleans, 1534, his first theological book, entitled *Psychopannychia*, or the *Sleep of the Soul*. He refutes in it the hypothesis entertained by some Anabaptists, of the sleep of the soul between death and resurrection, and proves the unbroken and conscious communion of believers with Christ, their living Head. He appeals no more to philosophy and the classics, as in his earlier book on Seneca, but solely to the Scriptures, as the only rule of faith. Reason can give us no light on the future world, which lies beyond our experience.

He wished to protect, by this book, the evangelical Protestants against the charge of heresy and vagary. They were often confounded with the Anabaptists who roused in the same year the wrath of all the German princes by the excesses of a radical and fanatical faction at Münster.

§ 78. *Calvin at Basel.* 1535 to 1536.

The outbreak of the bloody persecution, in October, 1534, induced Calvin to leave his native land and to seek safety in free Switzerland. He was accompanied by his friend and pupil, Louis du Tillet, who followed him as far as Geneva, and remained with him till the end of August, 1537, when he returned to France and to the Roman Church.[1]

The travellers passed through Lorraine. On the frontier of Germany, near Metz, they were robbed by an unfaithful servant. They arrived utterly destitute at Strassburg, then a city of refuge for French Protestants. They were kindly received and aided by Bucer.

[1] M. Crottet, *Correspondance de Calvin avec L. du Tillet*, 1850.

After a few days' rest they proceeded to Basel, their proper destination. There Farel had found a hospitable home in 1524, and Cop and Courault ten years later. Calvin wished a quiet place for study where he could promote the cause of the Gospel by his pen. He lodged with his friend in the house of Catharina Klein (Petita), who thirty years afterwards was the hostess of another famous refugee, the philosopher, Petrus Ramus, and spoke to him with enthusiasm of the young Calvin, "the light of France." [1]

He was kindly welcomed by Simon Grynæus and Wolfgang Capito, the heads of the university. He prosecuted with Grynæus his study of the Hebrew. He dedicated to him in gratitude his commentary on the Epistle to the Romans (1539). He became acquainted also with Bullinger of Zürich, who attended the conference of Reformed Swiss divines for the preparation of the first Helvetic Confession (1536). [2]

According to a Roman Catholic report, Calvin, in company with Bucer, had a personal interview with Erasmus, to whom three years before he had sent a copy of his commentary on Seneca with a high compliment to his scholarship. The veteran scholar is reported to have said to Bucer on that occasion that "a great pestilence was arising in the Church against the Church." [3] But Erasmus was too polite, thus to insult a stranger. Moreover, he was then living at Freiburg in Germany and had broken off all intercourse with Protestants. When he returned to Basel in July, 1536, on his way to the Netherlands, he took sick and died; and at that time Calvin was in Italy. The report therefore is an idle fiction. [4]

---

[1] "*Lumen Galliæ.*" See the *Reminiscences of Basel*, by Petrus Ramus (1572), quoted in *Op.* XXI. 194. Ch. Waddington, *Ramus, sa vie, ses écrits et ses opinions*, Paris, 1855. Stähelin, I. 41 sqq. Kampschulte, I. 250.

[2] See above, p. 219. Ep. 2634, referred to in *Op.* XXI. 196.

[3] "*Video magnam pestem oriri in Ecclesia contra Ecclesiam.*"

[4] It rests on the sole authority of Florimond de Ræmond, p. 890. He puts the visit in the year 1534, when Calvin was yet in France, and could not

Calvin avoided publicity and lived in scholarly seclusion. He spent in Basel a year and a few months, from January, 1535, till about March, 1536.

§ 79. *Calvin's Institutes of the Christian Religion.*

1. The full title of the first edition is "CHRISTIA | NAE RELIGIONIS INSTI | *tutio totam fere pietatis summam et quic* | *quid est in doctrina salutis cognitu* ne- | *cessarium, complectens : omnibus pie* | *tatis studiosis lectu dignissi* | *mum opus, ac re-* | *cens edi-* | *tum.* | PRÆFATIO | AD CHRI | STIANISSIMUM REGEM FRANCIÆ, *qua* | *hic ei liber pro confessione fidei* | *offertur.* | JOANNE CAL- VINO | *Nouiodunensi authore.* | BASILEÆ, | *M.D. XXXVI.*" The dedica- tory Preface is dated '*X. Calendas Septembres*' (*i.e.* August 23), without the year; but at the close of the book the month of March, 1536, is given as the date of publication. The first two French editions (1541 and 1545) supplement the date of the Preface correctly : "*De Basle le vingt-troysiesme d'Aoust mil cinq cent trente cinq.*" The manuscript, then, was completed in August, 1535, but it took nearly a year to print it.

2. The last improved edition from the pen of the author (the fifth Latin) is a thorough reconstruction, and bears the title : "INSTITUTIO CHRI | STIANÆ RELIGIONIS, *in libros qua* | *tuor nunc primum digesta, certisque distincta cap- itibus, ad aptissimam* | *methodum : aucta etiam tam magna accessione ut pro- pemodum opus* | *novum haberi possit.* | JOANNE CALVINO AUTHORE. | OLIVA ROBERTI STEPHANI. | *Genevæ.* | M.D. LIX." The subsequent Latin edi- tions are reprints of the ed. of 1559, with an index by Nic. Colladon, another by Marlorat. The Elzevir ed. Leyden, 1654, fol., was especially esteemed for its beauty and accuracy. A convenient modern ed. by Tholuck (Berlin, 1834, 2d ed. 1846).

3. The first French edition appeared without the name and place of the printer (probably Michel du Bois at Geneva), under the title : "*Institution de la religion chrestienne en laquelle est comprinse une somme de piété. . . . composée en latin par J. Calvin et translatée par luy mesme. Avec la préface addressée au tres chrestien Roy de France, François premier de ce nom : par laquelle ce présent livre luy est offert pour confession de Foy.* M.D. XLI." 822 pp. 8°, 2d ed. Genève, Jean Girard, 1545; 3d ed. 15, 1; 4th ed. 1553; 5th ed. 1554; 6th ed. 1557; 7th ed. 1560, in fol.; 8th ed. 1561, in 8°; 9th ed. 1561, in 4°; 10th ed. 1562, etc.; 15th ed. Geneva, 1564. Elzevir ed. Leyden, 1654.

4. The Strassburg editors devote the first four volumes to the different editions of the *Institutes* in both languages. Vol. I. contains the *editio princeps Latina* of Basel, 1536 (pp. 10–247), and the variations of six editions inter-

accompany Bucer. Beza and Colladon know nothing of such an interview. Bayle doubted it. Merle d'Aubigné, III. 203–204 (Engl. trans. III. 183–185), however, accepts and embellishes it as if he had been present and heard the colloquy of the three scholars.

vening between the first and the last, viz., the Strassburg editions of 1539, 1543, 1545, and the Geneva editions of 1550, 1553, 1554 (pp. 253–1152); vol. II., the *editio postrema* of 1559 (pp. 1–1118); vols. III. and IV., the last edition of the French translation, or free reproduction rather (1560), with the variations of former editions.

5. The question of the priority of the Latin or French text is now settled in favor of the former. See JULES BONNET, in the *Bulletin de la Société de l'histoire du protestantisme français* for 1858, vol. VI. p. 137 sqq., Stähelin, vol. I. p. 55, and the Strassburg editors of the *Opera*, in the ample *Prolegomena* to vols. I. and III. Calvin himself says expressly (in the Preface to his French ed. 1541), that he first wrote the *Institutes* in Latin (*"première-ment l'ay mis en latin"*), for readers of all nations, and that he translated or reproduced them afterwards for the special benefit of Frenchmen (*"l'ay aussi translaté en notre langage"*). In a letter to his friend, François Daniel, dated Lausanne, Oct. 13, 1536, he writes that he began the French translation soon after the publication of the Latin (*Letters*, ed. Bonnet, vol. I. p. 21), but it did not appear till 1541, under the title given above. The erroneous assertion of a French original, so often repeated (by Bayle, Maimbourg, Basnage, and more recently by Henry, vol. I. p. 104; III. p. 177; Dorner, *Gesch. der protest. Theol.* p. 375; also by Guizot, H. B. Smith, and Dyer), arose from confounding the date of the Preface as given in the French editions (23 Aug., 1535), with the later date of publication (March, 1536). It is quite possible, however, that the dedication to Francis I. was first written in French, and this would most naturally account for the earlier date in the French editions.

6. On the differences of the several editions, comp. J. THOMAS: *Histoire de l'instit. chrétienne de J. Calv.* Strasbourg, 1859. ALEX. SCHWEIZER: *Central-dogmen,* I. 150 sqq. (Zürich, 1854). KÖSTLIN: *Calvin's Institutio nach Form und Inhalt,* in the "Studien und Kritiken" for 1868.

7. On the numerous translations, see above, pp. 225, 265; HENRY, vol. III. *Beilagen,* 178–189; and *La France Prot.* III. 553.

In the ancient and venerable city of Basel, on the borders of Switzerland, France, and Germany — the residence of Erasmus and Œcolampadius, the place where a reformatory council had met in 1430, and where the first Greek Testament was printed in 1516 from manuscripts of the university library — John Calvin, then a mere youth of twenty-six years, and an exile from his native land, finished and published, twenty years after the first print of the Greek Testament, his *Institutes of the Christian Religion*, by which he astonished the world and took at once the front rank among the literary champions of the evangelical faith.

This book is the masterpiece of a precocious genius of commanding intellectual and spiritual depth and power. It is one of the few truly classical productions in the history of theology, and has given its author the double title of the Aristotle and Thomas Aquinas of the Reformed Church.[1]

The Roman Catholics at once perceived the significance of the *Institutio*, and called it the Koran and Talmud of heresy.[2] It was burned by order of the Sorbonne at Paris and other places, and more fiercely and persistently persecuted than any book of the sixteenth century; but, we must add, it has found also great admirers among Catholics who, while totally dissenting from its theological system and antipopish temper, freely admit its great merits in the non-polemical parts.[3]

The Evangelicals greeted the *Institutio* at once with enthusiastic praise as the clearest, strongest, most logical, and most convincing defence of Christian doctrines since the days of the apostles. A few weeks after its publication Bucer wrote to the author: "It is evident that the Lord has elected you as his organ for the bestowment of the richest fulness of blessing to his Church." [4]

Nor is this admiration confined to orthodox Protestants. Dr. Baur, the founder of the Tübingen school of historical critics, declares this book of Calvin to be "in every respect a truly classical work, distinguished in a high degree by originality and acuteness of conception, systematic consistency, and clear, luminous method." [5]   And Dr. Hase pointedly calls it "the grandest scientific justification of Augustinian-

----

[1] Kampschulte, a Roman Catholic historian, and others, call him "the Aristotle;" Martin, a liberal French historian, and others, call him — more appropriately — "the Thomas Aquinas," of Protestantism.

[2] Florimond de Ræmond: "*l'Alcoran ou plutôt le Talmud de l'hérésie.*"

[3] See the testimonies of Bossuet, and especially of Kampschulte, quoted in § 68, p. 285 sq.

[4] "*Videmur nobis agnoscere, Dominum instituisse tui usum ecclesiis suis uberrimum concedere, eisque tuo ministerio latissime commodare.*"   Herminjard, IV. 118.

[5] *Dogmengeschichte*, vol. III. 27.

ism, full of religious depth with inexorable consistency of thought." [1]

The *Institutio* is not a book for the people, and has not the rousing power which Luther's Appeal to the German Nobility, and his tract on Christian Freedom exerted upon the Germans; but it is a book for scholars of all nations, and had a deeper and more lasting effect upon them than any work of the Reformers. Edition followed edition, and translations were made into nearly all the languages of Europe. [2]

Calvin gives a systematic exposition of the Christian religion in general, and a vindication of the evangelical faith in particular, with the apologetic and practical aim of defending the Protestant believers against calumny and persecution to which they were then exposed, especially in France. He writes under the inspiration of a heroic faith that is ready for the stake, and with a glowing enthusiasm for the pure Gospel of Christ, which had been obscured and deprived of its effect by human traditions, but had now risen from this rubbish to new life and power. He combines dogmatics and ethics in organic unity.

He plants himself firmly on the immovable rock of the Word of God, as the only safe guide in matters of faith and duty. He exhibits on every page a thorough, well-digested knowledge of Scripture which is truly astonishing. He does not simply quote from it as a body of proof texts, in a mechanical way, like the scholastic dogmaticians of the seventeenth century, but he views it as an organic whole, and weaves it into his system. He bases the authority of Scripture on its intrinsic excellency and the testimony of the Holy Spirit speaking through it to the believer. He makes also judicious and discriminating use of the fathers, especially St. Augustin,

---

[1] *Kirchengeschichte*, p. 405 (11th edition).

[2] Many editors print, as a motto, the distich of the Hungarian, Paul Thurius:

> " *Præter apostolicas post Christi tempora chartas,*
> *Huic peperere libro sæcula nulla parem.*"

not as judges but as witnesses of the truth, and abstains from those depreciatory remarks in which Luther occasionally indulged when, instead of his favorite dogma of justification by faith, he found in them much ascetic monkery and exaltation of human merit. " They overwhelm us," says Calvin, in the dedicatory Preface, " with senseless clamors, as despisers and enemies of the fathers. But if it were consistent with my present design, I could easily support by their suffrages most of the sentiments that we now maintain. Yet while we make use of their writings, we always remember that ' all things are ours,' to serve us, not to have dominion over us, and that 'we are Christ's alone' (1 Cor. 3 : 21–23), and owe him universal obedience. He who neglects this distinction will have nothing certain in religion; since those holy men were ignorant of many things, frequently at variance with each other, and sometimes even inconsistent with themselves." He also fully recognizes the indispensable use of reason in the apprehension and defence of truth and the refutation of error, and excels in the power of severe logical argumentation; while he is free from scholastic dryness and pedantry. But he subordinates reason and tradition to the supreme authority of Scripture as he understands it.

The style is luminous and forcible. Calvin had full command of the majesty, dignity, and elegance of the Latin language. The discussion flows on continuously and melodiously like a river of fresh water through green meadows and sublime mountain scenery. The whole work is well proportioned. It is pervaded by intense earnestness and fearless consistency which commands respect even where his arguments fail to carry conviction, or where we feel offended by the contemptuous tone of his polemics, or feel a shudder at his *decretum horribile*.

Calvin's system of doctrine agrees with the œcumenical creeds in theology and Christology; with Augustinianism in anthropology and soteriology, but dissents from the mediæval tradition in ecclesiology, sacramentology, and eschatology. We shall discuss the prominent features of this system in the chapter on Calvin's Theology.

The *Institutio* was dedicated to King Francis I. of France (1494–1547), who at that time cruelly persecuted his Protestant subjects. As Justin Martyr and other early Apologists addressed the Roman emperors in behalf of the despised and persecuted sect of the Christians, vindicating them against the foul charges of atheism, immorality, and hostility to Cæsar, and pleading for toleration, so Calvin appealed to the French monarch in defence of his Protestant countrymen, then a small sect, as much despised, calumniated, and persecuted, and as moral and innocent as the Christians in the old Roman empire, with a manly dignity, frankness, and pathos never surpassed before or since. He followed the example set by Zwingli who addressed his dying confession of faith to the same sovereign (1531). These appeals, like the apologies of the ante-Nicene age, failed to reach or to affect the throne, but they moulded public opinion which is mightier than thrones, and they are a living force to-day.

The preface to the *Institutio* is reckoned among the three immortal prefaces in literature. The other two are President De Thou's preface to his History of France, and Casaubon's preface to *Polybius*. Calvin's preface is superior to them in importance and interest. Take the beginning and the close as specimens.[1]

"When I began this work, Sire, nothing was farther from my thoughts than writing a book which would afterwards be presented to your Majesty. My intention was only to lay down some elementary principles, by which inquirers on the subject of religion might be instructed in the nature of true piety. And this labor I undertook chiefly for my countrymen, the French, of whom I apprehend multitudes to be hungering and thirsting after Christ, but saw very few possessing any real knowledge of him. That this was my design the book itself proves by its simple method and unadorned composition. But

[1] I have made use of the faithful translation of John Allen, compared with the Latin original.

when I perceived that the fury of certain wicked men in your kingdom had grown to such a height, as to have no room in the land for sound doctrine, I thought I should be usefully employed, if in the same work I delivered my instructions to them, and exhibited my confession to you, that you may know the nature of that doctrine, which is the object of such unbounded rage to those madmen who are now disturbing the country with fire and sword. For I shall not be afraid to acknowledge, that this treatise contains a summary of that very doctrine, which, according to their clamors, deserves to be punished with imprisonment, banishment, proscription, and flames, and to be exterminated from the face of the earth.   I well know with what atrocious insinuations your ears have been filled by them, in order to render our cause most odious in your esteem; but your clemency should lead you to consider that if accusation be accounted a sufficient evidence of guilt, there will be an end of all innocence in words and actions."

*   *   *   *   *   *   *   *   *

"But I return to you, Sire. Let not your Majesty be at all moved by those groundless accusations with which our adversaries endeavor to terrify you; as that the sole tendency and design of this new gospel, for so they call it, is to furnish a pretext for seditions, and to gain impunity for all crimes. 'For God is not the author of confusion, but of peace;' nor is 'the Son of God,' who came to destroy 'the works of the devil, the minister of sin.' And it is unjust to charge us with such motives and designs of which we have never given cause for the least suspicion. Is it probable that we are meditating the subversion of kingdoms? We, who were never heard to utter a factious word, whose lives were ever known to be peaceable and honest while we lived under your government, and who, even now in our exile, cease not to pray for all prosperity to attend yourself and your kingdom! Is it probable that we are seeking an unlimited license to commit crimes with impunity, in whose conduct, though many things may be blamed, yet there is nothing worthy of such severe reproach? Nor have we, by divine grace, profited so little in the gospel, but that our life may be to our detractors an example of chastity, liberality, mercy, temperance, patience, modesty, and every other virtue. It is an undeniable fact, that we sincerely fear and worship God, whose name we desire to be sanctified both by our life and by our death; and envy itself is constrained to bear testimony to the innocence and civil integrity of some of us, who have suffered the punishment of death, for that very thing which ought to be accounted their highest praise. But if the gospel be made a pretext for tumults, which has not yet happened in your kingdom; if any persons make the liberty of divine grace an excuse for the licentiousness of their vices, of whom I have known many; there are laws and legal penalties, by which they may be punished according to their deserts: only let not the gospel of God be reproached for the crimes of wicked men. You have now, Sire, the virulent iniquity of our calumniators laid before you in a sufficient number of instances, that you may not receive their accusations with too credulous an ear.

"I fear I have gone too much into the detail, as this preface already approaches the size of a full apology; whereas, I intended it not to contain our defence, but only to prepare your mind to attend to the pleading of our cause ; for though you are now averse and alienated from us, and even inflamed against us, we despair not of regaining your favor, if you will only once read with calmness and composure this our confession, which we intend as our defence before your Majesty. But, on the contrary, if your ears are so preoccupied with the whispers of the malevolent, as to leave no opportunity for the accused to speak for themselves, and if those outrageous furies, with your connivance, continue to persecute with imprisonments, scourges, tortures, confiscations, and flames, we shall indeed, like sheep destined to the slaughter, be reduced to the greatest extremities. Yet shall we in patience possess our souls, and wait for the mighty hand of the Lord, which undoubtedly will in time appear, and show itself armed for the deliverance of the poor from their affliction, and for the punishment of their despisers, who now exult in such perfect security.

"May the Lord, the King of kings, establish your throne in righteousness, and your kingdom with equity."

The first edition of the *Institutes* was a brief manual containing, in six chapters, an exposition 1) of the Decalogue; 2) of the Apostles' Creed; 3) of the Lord's Prayer; 4) of baptism and the Lord's Supper; 5) of the other so-called Sacraments; 6) of Christian liberty, Church government, and discipline. The second edition has seventeen, the third, twenty-one chapters. In the author's last edition of 1559, it grew to four or five times its original size, and was divided into four books, each book into a number of chapters (from seventeen to twenty-five), and each chapter into sections. It follows in the main, like every good catechism, the order of the Apostles' Creed, which is the order of God's revelation as Father, Son, and Holy Spirit. The first book discusses the knowledge of God the Creator (theology proper); the second, the knowledge of God the Redeemer (Christology); the third, of the Holy Spirit and the application of the saving work of Christ (soteriology); the fourth, the means of grace, namely, the Church and the sacraments.[1]

---

[1] He himself gives in the preface to the last edition the following account of the successive improvements of the work: "In the first edition of this work, not expecting that success which the Lord in his infinite goodness hath given, I handled the subject for the most part in a superficial manner, as is usual in small treatises. But when I understood that it had obtained from almost all

Although the work has been vastly improved under the revising hand of the author, in size and fulness of statement, the first edition contains all the essential features of his system. "*Ex ungue leonem.*" His doctrine of predestination, however, is stated in a more simple and less objectionable form. He dwells on the bright and comforting side of that doctrine, namely, the eternal election by the free grace of God in Christ, and leaves out the dark mystery of reprobation and preterition.[1] He gives the light without the shade, the truth without the error. He avoids the paradoxes of Luther and Zwingli, and keeps within the limits of a wise moderation. The fuller logical development of his views on predestination and on the Church, dates from his sojourn in Strassburg, where he wrote the second edition of the *Institutes*, and his Commentary on the Epistle to the Romans.

The following sections on some of his leading doctrines from the last edition give a fair idea of the spirit and method of the work:

pious persons such a favorable acceptance as I never could have presumed to wish, much less to hope, while I was conscious of receiving far more attention than I had deserved, I thought it would evince great ingratitude, if I did not endeavor at least, according to my humble ability, to make some suitable return for the attentions paid to me; — attentions of themselves calculated to stimulate my industry. Nor did I attempt this only in the second edition, but in every succeeding one the work has been improved by some farther enlargements. But though I repented not the labor then devoted to it, yet I never satisfied myself till it was arranged in the order in which it is now published. And I trust I have here presented to my readers what their judgments will unite in approving. Of my diligent application to the accomplishment of this service for the Church of God, I can produce abundant proof. For, last winter, when I thought that a quartan ague would speedily terminate in my death, the more my disorder increased, the less I spared myself till I had finished this book, to leave it behind me as some grateful return to such kind solicitations of the religious public. Indeed, I would rather it had been done sooner, but it is soon enough, if well enough. I shall think it has appeared at the proper time, when I shall find it to have been more beneficial than before to the Church of God. This is my only wish."

[1] See the quotations of the several passages bearing upon this doctrine in Schweizer's *Centraldogmen*, I. 150–152, and in Stähelin, I. 66–68.

The Connection between the Knowledge of God and the Knowledge of Ourselves.

(Book I. ch. 1, §§ 1, 2.)

1 "True and substantial wisdom principally consists of two parts, the knowledge of God and the knowledge of ourselves. But while these two branches of knowledge are so intimately connected, which of them precedes and produces the other, is not easy to discover. For, in the first place, no man can take a survey of himself but he must immediately turn to the contemplation of God, in whom he 'lives and moves' (Acts 17 : 28); since it is evident that the talents which we possess are not from ourselves, and that our very existence is nothing but a subsistence in God alone. These bounties, distilling to us by drops from heaven, form, as it were, so many streams conducting us to the fountain-head. Our poverty conduces to a clearer display of the infinite fulness of God. Especially the miserable ruin, into which we have been plunged by the defection of the first man, compels us to raise our eyes towards heaven not only as hungry and famished, to seek thence a supply for our wants, but, aroused with fear, to learn humility.

"For since man is subject to a world of miseries, and has been spoiled of his divine array, this melancholy exposure discovers an immense mass of deformity. Every one, therefore, must be so impressed with a consciousness of his own infelicity, as to arrive at some knowledge of God. Thus a sense of our ignorance, vanity, poverty, infirmity, depravity, and corruption, leads us to perceive and acknowledge that in the Lord alone are to be found true wisdom, solid strength, perfect goodness, and unspotted righteousness; and so, by our imperfections, we are excited to a consideration of the perfections of God. Nor can we really aspire toward him, till we have begun to be displeased with ourselves. For who would not gladly rest satisfied with himself? Where is the man not actually absorbed in self-complacency, while he remains unacquainted with his true situation, or content with his own endowments, and ignorant or forgetful of his own misery? The knowledge of ourselves, therefore, is not only an incitement to seek after God, but likewise a considerable assistance towards finding him.

2. "On the other hand, it is plain that no man can arrive at the true knowledge of himself, without having first contemplated the divine character, and then descended to the consideration of his own. For such is the native pride of us all, that we invariably esteem ourselves righteous, innocent, wise, and holy, till we are convinced by clear proofs of our unrighteousness, turpitude, folly, and impurity. But we are never thus convinced, while we confine our attention to ourselves and regard not the Lord, who is the only standard by which this judgment ought to be formed." . . .

Rational Proofs to Establish the Belief in the Scripture.

(Book I. ch. 8, §§ 1, 2.)

1. "Without this certainty [that is, the testimony of the Holy Spirit], better and stronger than any human judgment, in vain will the authority of

the Scripture be either defended by arguments, or established by the consent of the Church, or confirmed by any other supports ; since, unless the founda-tion be laid, it remains in perpetual suspense. Whilst, on the contrary, when regarding it in a different point of view from common things, we have once religiously received it in a manner worthy of its excellence, we shall then derive great assistance from things which before were not sufficient to estab-lish the certainty of it in our minds. For it is admirable to observe how much it conduces to our confirmation, attentively to study the order and disposition of the divine wisdom dispensed in it, the heavenly nature of its doctrine, which never savors of anything terrestrial, the beautiful agreement of all the parts with each other, and other similar characters adapted to conciliate respect to any writings. But our hearts are more strongly confirmed, when we reflect that we are constrained to admire it more by the dignity of the subjects than by the beauties of the language. For even this did not happen without the particular providence of God, that the sublime mysteries of the kingdom of heaven should be communicated, for the most part, in an humble and con-temptible style : lest if they had been illustrated with more of the splendor of eloquence, the impious might cavil that their triumph is only the triumph of eloquence. Now, since that uncultivated and almost rude simplicity procures itself more reverence than all the graces of rhetoric, what opinion can we form, but that the force of truth in the sacred Scripture is too powerful to need the assistance of verbal art ? Justly, therefore, does the apostle argue that the faith of the Corinthians was founded 'not in the wisdom of men, but in the power of God,' because his preaching among them was ' not with entic-ing words of man's wisdom, but in demonstration of the Spirit of power' (1 Cor. 2 : 4). For the truth is vindicated from every doubt, when, unassisted by foreign aid, it is sufficient for its own support. But that this is the peculiar property of the Scripture, appears from the insufficiency of any human com-positions, however artificially polished, to make an equal impression on our minds. Read Demosthenes or Cicero ; read Plato, Aristotle, or any others of that class ; I grant that you will be attracted, delighted, moved, and enrap-tured by them in a surprising manner ; but if, after reading them, you turn to the perusal of the sacred volume, whether you are willing or unwilling, it will affect you so powerfully, it will so penetrate your heart, and impress itself so strongly on your mind, that, compared with its energetic influence, the beauties of rhetoricians and philosophers will almost entirely disappear ; so that it is easy to perceive something divine in the sacred Scriptures, which far surpass the highest attainments and ornaments of human industry.

2. "I grant, indeed, that the diction of some of the prophets is neat and ele-gant, and even splendid ; so that they are not inferior in eloquence to the heathen writers. And by such examples the Holy Spirit hath been pleased to show that he was not deficient in eloquence, though elsewhere he hath used a rude and homely style. But whether we read David, Isaiah, and others that resemble them, who have a sweet and pleasant flow of words, or Amos, the herdsman, Jeremiah, and Zechariah, whose rougher language savors of rusticity ; that majesty of the Spirit which I have mentioned is everywhere conspicuous. . . . With respect to the sacred Scripture, though presumptuous

men try to cavil at various passages, yet it is evidently replete with sentences which are beyond the powers of human conception. Let all the prophets be examined, not one will be found who has not far surpassed the ability of men; so that those to whom their doctrine is insipid must be accounted utterly destitute of all true taste. . . .

11. "If we proceed to the New Testament, by what solid foundations is its truth supported? Three evangelists recite their history in a low and mean style. Many proud men are disgusted with that simplicity because they attend not to the principal points of doctrine; whence it were easy to infer, that they treat of heavenly mysteries which are above human capacity. They who have a spark of ingenuous modesty will certainly be ashamed, if they peruse the first chapter of Luke. Now the discourses of Christ, a concise summary of which is comprised in these three evangelists, easily exempt their writings from contempt. But John, thundering from his sublimity, more powerfully than any thunderbolt, levels to the dust the obstinacy of those whom he does not compel to the obedience of faith. Let all those censorious critics, whose supreme pleasure consists in banishing all reverence for the Scripture out of their own hearts and the hearts of others, come forth to public view. Let them read the Gospel of John: whether they wish it or not, they will there find numerous passages, which, at least, arouse their indolence and which will even imprint a horrible brand on their consciences to restrain their ridicule. Similar is the method of Paul and of Peter, in whose writings, though the greater part be obscure, yet their heavenly majesty attracts universal attention. But this one circumstance raises their doctrine sufficiently above the world, that Matthew, who had before been confined to the profit of his table, and Peter and John, who had been employed in fishing-boats, all plain, unlettered men, had learned nothing in any human school which they could communicate to others. And Paul, from not only a professed but a cruel and sanguinary enemy, being converted to a new man, proves by his sudden and unhoped-for change, that he was constrained, by a command from heaven, to vindicate that doctrine which he had before opposed. Let these deny that the Holy Spirit descended on the apostles; or, at least, let them dispute the credibility of the history: yet the fact itself loudly proclaims that they were taught by the Spirit, who, though before despised as some of the meanest of the people, suddenly began to discourse in such a magnificent manner on the mysteries of heaven. . . .

13. "Wherefore, the Scripture will then only be effectual to produce the saving knowledge of God, when the certainty of it shall be founded on the internal persuasion of the Holy Spirit. Thus those human testimonies, which contribute to its confirmation, will not be useless, if they follow that first and principal proof, as secondary aids to our imbecility. But those persons betray great folly, who wish it to be demonstrated to infidels that the Scripture is the Word of God, which cannot be known without faith. Augustin, therefore, justly observes, that piety and peace of mind ought to precede in order that a man may understand somewhat of such great subjects."

MEDITATION ON THE FUTURE LIFE.

(Book III. ch. 9, §§ 1, 3, 6.)

1. "With whatever kind of tribulation we may be afflicted, we should always keep the end in view; to habituate ourselves to a contempt of the present life, that we may thereby be excited to meditation on that which is to come. For the Lord, well knowing our strong natural inclination to a brutish love of the world, adopts a most excellent method to reclaim us and rouse us from one insensibility that we may not be too tenaciously attached to that foolish affection. There is not one of us who is not desirous of appearing through the whole course of his life, to aspire and strive after celestial immortality. For we are ashamed of excelling in no respect the brutal herds, whose condition would not be at all inferior to ours, unless there remained to us a hope of eternity after death. But if you examine the designs, pursuits, and actions of every individual, you will find nothing in them but what is terrestrial. Hence that stupidity, that the mental eyes, dazzled with the vain splendor of riches, powers, and honors, cannot see to any considerable distance. The heart also, occupied and oppressed with avarice, ambition, and other inordinate desires, cannot rise to any eminence. In a word, the whole soul, fascinated by carnal allurements, seeks its felicity on earth.

"To oppose this evil, the Lord, by continual lessons of miseries, teaches his children the vanity of the present life. That they may not promise themselves profound and secure peace in it, therefore he permits them to be frequently disquieted and infested with wars or tumults, with robberies or other injuries. That they may not aspire with too much avidity after transient and uncertain riches, or depend on those which they possess, sometimes by exile, sometimes by the sterility of the land, sometimes by a conflagration, sometimes by other means, he reduces them to indigence, or at least confines them within the limits of mediocrity. That they may not be too complacently delighted with conjugal blessings, he either causes them to be distressed with the wickedness of their wives, or humbles them with a wicked offspring, or afflicts them with want or loss of children. But if in all these things he is more indulgent to them, yet that they may not be inflated with vainglory, or improper confidence, he shows them by diseases and dangers the unstable and transitory nature of all mortal blessings. We therefore truly derive advantages from the discipline of the cross, only when we learn that this life, considered in itself, is unquiet, turbulent, miserable in numberless instances, and in no respect altogether happy; and that all its reputed blessings are uncertain, transient, vain, and adulterated with a mixture of many evils; and in consequence of this at once conclude that nothing can be sought or expected on earth but conflict, and that when we think of a crown we must raise our eyes toward heaven. For it must be admitted that the mind is never seriously excited to desire and meditate on the future life, without having previously imbibed a contempt of the present. . . .

3. "But the faithful should accustom themselves to such a contempt of the present life, as may not generate either hatred of life or ingratitude towards God himself. For this life, though it is replete with innumerable

miseries, is yet deservedly reckoned among the divine blessings which must not be despised. Wherefore if we discover nothing of the divine beneficence in it, we are already guilty of no small ingratitude towards God himself. But to the faithful especially it should be a testimony of the divine benevolence, since the whole of it is destined to the advancement of their salvation. For before he openly discovers to us the inheritance of eternal glory, he intends to reveal himself as our Father in inferior instances; and those are the benefits which he daily confers on us. Since this life, then, is subservient to a knowledge of the divine goodness, shall we fastidiously scorn it as though it contained no particle of goodness in it? We must, therefore, have this sense and affection, to class it among the bounties of the divine benignity which are not to be rejected. For if Scripture testimonies were wanting, which are very numerous and clear, even nature itself exhorts us to give thanks to the Lord for having introduced us to the light of life, for granting us the use of it, and giving us all the helps necessary to its preservation. And it is a far superior reason for gratitude, if we consider that here we are in some measure prepared for the glory of the heavenly kingdom. For the Lord has ordained that they who are to be hereafter crowned in heaven, must first engage in conflicts on earth, that they may not triumph without having surmounted the difficulties of warfare and obtained the victory. Another reason is, that here we begin in various blessings to taste the sweetness of the divine benignity, that our hope and desire may be excited after the full revelation of it. When we have come to this conclusion, that our life in this world is a gift of the divine clemency, which as we owe it to him, we ought to remember with gratitude, it will then be time for us to descend to a consideration of its most miserable condition, that we may be delivered from excessive cupidity, to which, as has been observed, we are naturally inclined. . . .

6. "It is certainly true that the whole family of the faithful, as long as they dwell on earth, must be accounted as 'sheep for the slaughter' (Rom. 8: 36), that they may be conformed to Christ their Head. Their state, therefore, would be extremely deplorable, if they did not elevate their thoughts towards heaven, to rise above all sublunary things, and look beyond present appearances (1 Cor. 15 : 19). On the contrary, when they have once raised their heads above this world, although they see the impious flourishing in riches and honors, and enjoying the most profound tranquillity; though they see them boasting of their splendor and luxury, and behold them abounding in every delight; though they may also be harassed by their wickedness, insulted by their pride, defrauded by their avarice, and may receive from them any other lawless provocations; yet they will find no difficulty in supporting themselves even under such calamities as these. For they will keep in view that day when the Lord will receive his faithful servants into his peaceful kingdom; will wipe every tear from their eyes (Isa. 25: 8; Rev. 7: 17), invest them with robes of joy, adorn them with crowns of glory, entertain them with his ineffable delights, exalt them to fellowship with His Majesty, and, in a word, honor them with a participation of his happiness. But the impious, who have been great in this world, he will precipitate down to the lowest ignominy; he will change their delights into torments, and their laughter

and mirth into weeping and gnashing of teeth; he will disturb their tranquillity with dreadful agonies of conscience, and will punish their delicacy with inextinguishable fire, and even put them in subjection to the pious, whose patience they have abused. For, according to Paul, it is a righteous thing with God, to recompense tribulation to those that trouble the saints, and rest to those who are troubled, when the Lord Jesus shall be revealed from heaven (2 Thess. 1 : 6, 7). This is our only consolation, and deprived of this, we must of necessity either sink into despondency of mind, or solace ourselves to our own destruction with the vain pleasures of the world. For even the psalmist confesses that he staggered, when he was too much engaged in contemplating the present prosperity of the impious; and that he could no otherwise establish himself, till he entered the sanctuary of God, and directed his views to the last end of the godly and of the wicked (Ps. 73 : 2, etc.).

"To conclude in one word, the cross of Christ triumphs in the hearts of believers over the devil and the flesh, over sin and impious men, only when their eyes are directed to the power of the resurrection."

CHRISTIAN LIBERTY.

(Book 3, ch. 19, § 9.)

1. "It must be carefully observed, that Christian liberty is in all its branches a spiritual thing; all the virtue of which consists in appeasing terrified consciences before God, whether they are disquieted and solicitous concerning the remission of their sins, or are anxious to know if their works, which are imperfect and contaminated by the defilements of the flesh, be acceptable to God, or are tormented concerning the use of things that are indifferent. Wherefore those are guilty of perverting its meaning, who either make it the pretext of their irregular appetites, that they may abuse the divine blessings to the purposes of sensuality, or who suppose that there is no liberty but what is used before men, and therefore in the exercise of it totally disregard their weak brethren.

2. "The former of these sins is the more common in the present age. There is scarcely any one whom his wealth permits to be sumptuous, who is not delighted with luxurious splendor in his entertainments, in his dress, and in his buildings; who does not desire a pre-eminence in every species of luxury; who does not strangely flatter himself on his elegance. And all these things are defended under the pretext of Christian liberty. They allege that they are things indifferent. This, I admit, provided they be indifferently used. But where they are too ardently coveted, proudly boasted, or luxuriously lavished, these things, of themselves otherwise indifferent, are completely polluted by such vices. This passage of Paul makes an excellent distinction respecting things which are indifferent: 'Unto the pure, all things are pure: but unto them that are defiled and unbelieving, is nothing pure; but even their mind and conscience is defiled' (Titus 1 : 15). For why are curses denounced on rich men, who 'receive their consolation,' who are 'satiated,' who 'now laugh,' who 'lie on beds of ivory,' who 'join field to field,' who 'have the harp and lyre, and the tabret, and wine in their feasts?' (Luke 6 : 24, 25; Amos 6 : 1;

Isa. 5 : 8).   Ivory and gold and riches of all kinds are certainly blessings of divine providence, not only permitted, but expressly designed for the use of men; nor are we anywhere prohibited to laugh, or to be satiated with food, or to annex new possessions to those already enjoyed by ourselves or by our ancestors, or to be delighted with musical harmony, or to drink wine.   This, indeed, is true; but amidst an abundance of all things, to be immersed in sensual delights, to inebriate the heart and mind with present pleasures, and perpetually to grasp at new ones, these things are very remote from a legitimate use of the divine blessings.   Let them banish, therefore, immoderate cupidity, excessive profusion, vanity, and arrogance; that with a pure conscience they may make a proper use of the gifts of God.   When their hearts shall be formed to this sobriety, they will have a rule for the legitimate enjoyment of them.   On the contrary, without this moderation, even the common pleasures of the vulgar are chargeable with excess.   For it is truly observed, that a proud heart frequently dwells under coarse and ragged garments, and that simplicity and humility are sometimes concealed under purple and fine linen.

3.   "Let all men in their respective stations, whether of poverty, of competence, or of splendor, live in the remembrance of this truth, that God confers his blessings on them for the support of life, not of luxury; and let them consider this as the law of Christian liberty, that they learn the lesson which Paul had learned, when he said: ' I have learned, in whatsoever state I am, therewith to be content.   I know both how to be abased, and I know how to abound: everywhere and in all things I am intrusted, both to be full and to be hungry, both to abound and to suffer need ' (Phil. 4 : 11, 12)."

The Doctrine of Election.

(Book 3, ch. 21, § 1.)

1.   " Nothing else [than election by free grace] will be sufficient to produce in us suitable humility, or to impress us with a due sense of our great obligations to God.   Nor is there any other basis for solid confidence, even according to the authority of Christ, who, to deliver us from all fear and render us invincible amidst so many dangers, snares, and deadly conflicts, promises to preserve in safety all whom the Father has committed to his care. . . . The discussion of predestination, a subject of itself rather intricate, is made very perplexed and therefore dangerous by human curiosity, which no barriers can restrain from wandering into forbidden labyrinths, and soaring beyond its sphere, as if determined to leave none of the divine secrets unscrutinized or unexplored. . . . The secrets of God's will which he determined to reveal to us, he discovers in his Word; and these are all that he foresaw would concern us, or conduce to our advantage. . . .

2.   " Let us bear in mind, that to desire any other knowledge of predestination than what is unfolded in the Word of God, indicates as great folly, as a wish to walk through impassable roads, or to see in the dark.   Nor let us be ashamed to be ignorant of some things relative to a subject in which there is a kind of learned ignorance (*aliqua docta ignorantia*). . . .

3. "Others desirous of remedying this evil, will leave all mention of predestination to be as it were buried. . . . Though their moderation is to be
commended in judging that mysteries ought to be handled with such great
sobriety, yet as they descend too low, they leave little influence on the mind
of man which refuses to submit to unreasonable restraints. . . . The Scripture is the school of the Holy Spirit, in which as nothing necessary and useful to be known is omitted, so nothing is taught which it is not beneficial to
know. . . . Let us permit the Christian man to open his heart and his ears to
all the discourses addressed to him by God, only with this moderation, that as
soon as the Lord closes his sacred mouth, he shall also desist from further
inquiry. . . . 'The secret things,' says Moses (Deut. 29: 29), 'belong unto
the Lord our God: but those things which are revealed belong unto us, and
to our children for ever, that we may do all the words of his law.'

5. "Predestination, by which God adopts some to the hope of life, and
adjudges others to eternal death, no one, desirous of the credit of piety, dares
absolutely to deny. . . . Predestination we call the eternal decree of God, by
which he has determined in himself, what he would have to become of every
individual of mankind. For they are not all created with a similar destiny;
but eternal life is fore-ordained for some, and eternal damnation for others.
Every man, therefore, being created for one or the other of these ends, we
say, he is predestinated either to life or to death. This God has not only testified in particular persons, but has given as specimen of it in the whole posterity of Abraham, which should evidently show the future condition of every
nation to depend upon his decision (Deut. 32: 8, 9)."

§ 80. *From Basel to Ferrara. The Duchess Renée.*

Shortly after, if not before, the publication of his great
work, in March, 1536, Calvin, in company with Louis Du
Tillet, crossed the Alps to Italy, the classical soil of the literary and artistic Renaissance. He hoped to aid the cause of
the religious Renaissance. He went to Italy as an evangelist,
not as a monk, like Luther, who learned at Rome a practical
lesson of the working of the papacy.

He spent a few months in Ferrara at the brilliant court
of the Duchess Renée or Renata (1511–1575), the second
daughter of Louis XII., of France, and made a deep and
permanent impression on her. She had probably heard of him
through Queen Marguerite and invited him to a visit. She
was a small and deformed, but noble, pious, and highly accomplished lady, like her friends, Queen Marguerite and Vittoria
Colonna. She gathered around her the brightest wits of the

Renaissance, from Italy and France, but she sympathized still more with the spirit of the Reformation, and was fairly captivated by Calvin. She chose him as the guide of her conscience, and consulted him hereafter as a spiritual father as long as he lived.[1] He discharged this duty with the frankness and fidelity of a Christian pastor. Nothing can be more manly and honorable than his letters to her. Guizot affirms, from competent knowledge, that "the great Catholic bishops, who in the seventeenth century directed the consciences of the mightiest men in France, did not fulfil the difficult task with more Christian firmness, intelligent justice and knowledge of the world than Calvin displayed in his intercourse with the Duchess of Ferrara."[2]

Renan wonders that such a stern moralist should have exercised a lasting influence over such a lady, and attributes it to the force of conviction. But the bond of union was deeper. She recognized in Calvin the man who could satisfy her spiritual nature and give her strength and comfort to fight the battle of life, to face the danger of the Inquisition, to suffer imprisonment, and after the death of her husband and her return to France (1559) openly to confess and to maintain the evangelical faith under most trying circumstances when her own son-in-law, the Duke of Guise, carried on a war of extermination against the Reformation. She continued to correspond with Calvin very freely, and his last letter in French, twenty-three days before his death, was

---

[1] Beza (xxi. 123): "*Illam [Ferrariensem Ducissam] in vero pietatis studio confirmavit, ut eum postea vivum semper dilexerit, ac nunc quoque superstes gratœ in defunctum memoriae specimen edat luculentum.*" Colladon (53) speaks likewise of the high esteem in which the Duchess, then still living, held Calvin before and after his death. Bolsec in his libel (Ch. v. 30), mentions the visit to Ferrara, but suggests a mercenary motive. "*Calvin,*" he says, "*s'en alla vers Allemaigne et Itallie: cherchant son adventure, et passa par la ville de Ferrare, ou il receut quelque aumone de Madame la Duchesse.*"

[2] St. Louis and Calvin, p. 207. He adds: "And the duchess was not the only person towards whom he fulfilled this duty of a Christian pastor. His correspondence shows that he exercised a similar influence, in a spirit equally lofty and judicious, over the consciences of many Protestants."

directed to her. She was in Paris during the dreadful massacre of St. Bartholomew, and succeeded in saving the lives
of some prominent Huguenots.[1]

Threatened by the Inquisition which then began its work
of crushing out both the Renaissance and the Reformation,
as two kindred serpents, Calvin bent his way, probably through
Aosta (the birthplace of Anselm of Canterbury) and over
the Great St. Bernard, to Switzerland.

An uncertain tradition connects with this journey a persecution and flight of Calvin in the valley of Aosta, which was
commemorated five years later (1541) by a memorial cross
with the inscription " *Calvini Fuga.*"[2]

---

[1] See the correspondence in the Letters by Bonnet, and in the Strassburg-
Braunschweig edition. On Renée and her relation to Calvin see Henry, I.
159, 450–454; III. Beilage 142–153; in his smaller work, 62–69; 478–483;
Stähelin, I. 94–108; Sophia W. Weitzel, *Renée of France, Duchess of Ferrara,*
New York, 1883; and Theod. Schott, in Herzog[2], XII. 693–701.

[2] In the city of Aosta, near the Croix-de-Ville, stands a column eight feet
high, surmounted by a cross of stone, with the following inscription:

HANC
CALVINI FUGA
EREXIT
ANNO MDXLI
RELIGIONIS CONSTANTIA
REPARAVIT
ANNO MDCCXLI.

The inscription was renewed again in 1841, with the following addition
(according to Merle d'Aubigné, who saw it himself, vol. V. 531):

CIVIUM MUNIFICENTIA
RENOVAVIT ET ADORNAVIT.
ANNO MDCCCXLI.

" *Religionis constantia* " must refer to the Roman faith which drove Calvin
and his heresy away. Dr. Merle d'Aubigné accepts Calvin's flight on the
ground of this monumental testimony as a historical fact, but the silence
of Calvin, Beza, and Colladon throws doubt on it. See J. Bonnet, *Calvin au
Val d'Aosta,* 1861; A. Rilliet, *Lettre à Mr. Merle d'Aubigné sur deux points
obscure de la vie de Calvin,* 1864; Stähelin, I. 110; Kampschulte, I. 280
(note); *La France Prot.,* III. 520; Thomas M'Crie, *The Early Years of Calvin,* pp. 95 and 104.

FONTANA: *Documenti del archivio vaticano e dell' Estenso circa soggiorno di
Calvino a Ferrara,* 1885. COMBA in " Rivista christiana," 1885; SANDOVINI in
" Rivista stor. italiana," 1887.

At Basel he parted from Du Tillet and paid a last visit to his native town to make a final settlement of family affairs.[1]

Then he left France, with his younger brother Antoine and his sister Marie, forever, hoping to settle down in Basel or Strassburg and to lead there the quiet life of a scholar and author. Owing to the disturbances of war between Charles V. and Francis I., which closed the direct route through Lorraine, he had to take a circuitous journey through Geneva.

[1] This visit to Noyon is mentioned by Beza in the Latin *Vita*, who adds that he then brought his only surviving brother Antoine, with him to Geneva (XXI. 125). Colladon (58) agrees, and informs us that Calvin left Du Tillet at Basel, who from there went to Neuchâtel. In his French *Life of C.*, Beza omits the journey to France: *"A son retour d'Italie . . . il passa à la bonne heure par ceste ville de Genève."*

CHAPTER X.

CALVIN'S FIRST SOJOURN AND LABORS IN GENEVA.
1536–1538.

From 1536, and especially from 1541, we have, besides the works and letters of Calvin and his correspondents and other contemporaries, important sources of authentic information in the following documents: —

1. *Registres du Conseil de Genève*, from 1536–1564. Tomes 29–58.
2. *Registres des actes de baptême et de marriage*, preserved in the archives of the city of Geneva.
3. *Registres des actes du Consistoire de Genève*, of which Calvin was a permanent member.
4. *Registres de la Vénérable Compagnie*, or the Ministerium of Geneva.
5. The Archives of Bern, Zürich, and Basel, of that period, especially those of Bern, which stood in close connection with Geneva and exercised a sort of protectorate over Church and State.

From these sources the Strassburg editors of Calvin's *Works* have carefully compiled the *Annales Calviniani*, in vol. XXI. (or vol. XII. of *Thesaurus Epistolicus Calvinianus*), 185–818 (published 1879). The same volume contains also the biographies of Calvin by Beza (French and Latin) and Colladon (French), the epitaphia, and a *Notice littéraire*, 1–178.

J. H. ALBERT RILLIET: *Le prémier séjour de Calvin à Genève*. In his and Dufour's ed. of Calvin's French Catechism. Geneva, 1878. — HENRY, vol. I. chs. VIII. and IX. — DYER, ch. III. — STÄHELIN, I. 122 sqq. — KAMPSCHULTE, I. 278–320. — MERLE D'AUBIGNÉ, Bk. XI. chs. I.–XIV.

§ 81. *Calvin's Arrival and Settlement at Geneva.*

CALVIN arrived at Geneva in the later part of July, 1536,[1] two months after the Reformation had been publicly introduced (May 21).

He intended to stop only a night, as he says, but Providence had decreed otherwise. It was the decisive hour of his life which turned the quiet scholar into an active reformer.

---

[1] Not in August (as stated by Beza, *Annal.* 126, 203, and most biographers). He went to Basel for two weeks (August 4–19), and returned to Geneva, according to promise, about the middle of August, for settlement. See his letter to Daniel, Oct. 13, 1536, in Herminjard, IV. 87; comp. 77 note; also Rilliet and Roget.

His presence was made known to Farel through the imprudent zeal of Du Tillet, who had come from Basel via Neuchâtel, and remained in Geneva for more than a year. Farel instinctively felt that the providential man had come who was to complete and to save the Reformation of Geneva. He at once called on Calvin and held him fast, as by divine command. Calvin protested, pleading his youth, his inexperience, his need of further study, his natural timidity and bashfulness, which unfitted him for public action. But all in vain. Farel, "who burned of a marvellous zeal to advance the Gospel," threatened him with the curse of Almighty God if he preferred his studies to the work of the Lord, and his own interest to the cause of Christ. Calvin was terrified and shaken by these words of the fearless evangelist, and felt "as if God from on high had stretched out his hand." He submitted, and accepted the call to the ministry, as teacher and pastor of the evangelical Church of Geneva.[1]

It was an act of obedience, a sacrifice of his desires to a sense of duty, of his will to the will of God.

Farel gave the Reformation to Geneva, and gave Calvin to Geneva — two gifts by which he crowned his own work and immortalized his name, as one of the greatest benefactors of that city and of Reformed Christendom.

Calvin was foreordained for Geneva, and Geneva for Calvin. Both have made "their calling and election sure."

He found in the city on Lake Leman "a tottering republic,

---

[1] Beza (*Vita*, XXI. 125): "*At ego tibi, inquit [Farellus], studia tua prætexenti denuncio omnipotentis Dei nomine futurum ut, nisi in opus istud Domini nobiscum incumbas, tibi non tam Christum quam te ipsum quærenti Dominus maledicat. Hac terribili denunciatione territus, Calvinus sese presbyterii et magistratus voluntati permisit, quorum suffragiis, accedente plebis consensu, delectus non concionator tantum (hoc autem primum recusarat), sed etiam sacrarum literarum doctor, quod unum admittebat, est designatus anno Domini MDXXXVI. mense Augusto.*" With this should be compared Calvin's own account in the Preface to his commentary on the Psalms, and *Ann. Calv.* 203 sq. Merle d'Aubigné, at the close of vol. V. 534–550, gives a dramatic description of Calvin's first arrival and interview with Farel at Geneva, with some embellishments of his imagination.

a wavering faith, a nascent Church." He left it a Gibraltar of Protestantism, a school of nations and churches.[1]

The city had then only about twelve thousand inhabitants, but by her situation on the borders of France and Switzerland, her recent deliverance from political and ecclesiastical despotism, and her raw experiments in republican self-government, she offered rare advantages for the solution of the great social and religious problems which agitated Europe.

Calvin's first labors in that city were an apparent failure. The Genevese were not ready yet and expelled him, but after a few years they recalled him. They might have expelled him again and forever: for he was poor, feeble, and unprotected. But they gradually yielded to the moulding force of his genius and character. Those who call him " the pope of Geneva " involuntarily pay him the highest compliment. His success was achieved by moral and spiritual means, and stands almost alone in history.

§ 82. *First Labors and Trials.*

Calvin began his labors, Sept. 5, 1536, by a course of expository lectures on the Epistles of Paul and other books of the New Testament, which he delivered in the Church of St. Peter in the afternoon. They were heard with increasing attention. He had a rare gift of teaching, and the people were hungry for religious instruction.

After a short time he assumed also the office of pastor which he had at first declined.

The Council was asked by Farel to provide a suitable support for their new minister, but they were slow to do it, not dreaming that he would become the most distinguished citi-

---

[1] Michelet has an eloquent chapter on the transformation of Geneva by Calvin, who made it from a city of pleasure and commerce "a fabric of saints and martyrs," a " *ville étonnante où tout était flamme et prière, lecture, travail, austerité* " (**XI.** 96).

zen, and calling him simply "that Frenchman." [1]   He received little or no salary till Feb. 13, 1537, when the Council voted him six gold crowns. [2]

Calvin accompanied Farel in October to the disputation at Lausanne, which decided the Reformation in the Canton de Vaud, but took little part in it, speaking only twice.   Farel was the senior pastor, twenty years older, and took the lead. But with rare humility and simplicity he yielded very soon to the superior genius of his young friend.   He was contented to have conquered the territory for the renewed Gospel, and left it to him to cultivate the same and to bring order out of the political and ecclesiastical chaos.   He was willing to decrease, that Calvin might increase.   Calvin, on his part, treated him always with affectionate regard and gratitude. There was not a shadow of envy or jealousy between them.

The third Reformed preacher was Courault, formerly an Augustinian monk, who, like Calvin, had fled from France to Basel, in 1534, and was called to Geneva to replace Viret. Though very old and nearly blind, he showed as much zeal and energy as his younger colleagues.   Saunier, the rector of the school, was an active sympathizer, and soon afterwards Cordier, Calvin's beloved teacher, assumed the government of the school and effectively aided the ministers in their arduous work.   Viret came occasionally from the neighboring Lausanne.   Calvin's brother, and his relative Olivetan, who joined them at Geneva, increased his influence.

The infant Church of Geneva had the usual trouble with the Anabaptists.   Two of their preachers came from Holland and gained some influence.   But after an unfruitful disputa-

[1] "*Ille Gallus.*" *Annal. Calv.* XXI. 204. The Registers were then kept in Latin, but after 1537, in French. The native languages superseded the Latin with the progress of the Reformation.

[2] Under that date the *Registres du Cons.* report : "*Icy est parlé de* CALVINUS *qu'il na encore guère reçeu et esté arresté que l'on luy délivre ung six escus soleil*" (*Annal.* 208).

tion they were banished by the large Council from the territory of the city as early as March, 1537.[1]

A more serious trouble was created by Peter Caroli, a doctor of the Sorbonne, an unprincipled, vain, and quarrelsome theological adventurer and turncoat, who changed his religion several times, led a disorderly life, and was ultimately reconciled to the pope and released from his concubine, as he called his wife. He had fled from Paris to Geneva in 1535, became pastor at Neuchâtel, where he married, and then at Lausanne. He raised the charge of Arianism against Farel and Calvin at a synod in Lausanne, May, 1537,[2] because they avoided in the Confession the metaphysical terms *Trinity* and *Person*, (though Calvin did use them in his *Institutio* and his Catechism,) and because they refused, at Caroli's dictation, to sign the Athanasian Creed with its damnatory clauses, which are unjust and uncharitable. Calvin was incensed at his arrogant and boisterous conduct and charged him with atheism. "Caroli," he said, "quarrels with us about the nature of God and the distinction of the persons; but I carry the matter further and ask him, whether he believes in the Deity at all? For I protest before God and man that he has no more faith in the Divine Word than a dog or a pig that tramples under foot holy things" (Matt. 7 : 6). This is the first manifestation of his angry temper and of that contemptuous tone which characterizes his polemical writings. He handed in with his colleagues a confession on the Trinity.[3]

---

[1] *Ann.* 208–210. " *Conseil des Deux-cents (Lundi* 19 *Mars). Fuit propositum negotium illorum Katabaptistarum sur lesquelz a esté advisé que iceulx et tous aultres de leur secte soyent perpetuellement bannys de ceste cité et terres dicelle sus poenne de la vye.*" They were asked to recant, but answered that their conscience did not allow it, whereupon they were "perpetually banished."

[2] The troubles with Caroli began in January, 1537; the synod convened May 13. *Opera*, X. 82, sqq.; letter of Farel, p. 102, of Calvin, 107; *Annal.* 207 and 211. Kampschulte (I. 296) gives a wrong date (March).

[3] *Confessio de Trinitate propter calumnias P. Caroli*, signed by Farel, Calvin, and Viret, and approved by Capito, Bucer, Myconius, and Grynæus, in *Opera*, IX. 703–710.

The synod after due consideration was satisfied with their orthodoxy, and declared Caroli convicted of calumny and unworthy of the ministry. He died in a hospital at Rome.[1]

§ 83. *The Reformers introduce Order and Discipline.*

Confession de la Foy laquelle tous les bourgeois et habitans de Genève et subjectz du pays doyvent jurer de garder et tenir; extraicte de l'instruction dont on use en l'église de la dicte ville, 1537. *Confessio Fidei in quam jurare cives omnes Genevenses et qui sub civitatis ejus ditione agunt, jussi sunt.* The French in *Opera,* vol. IX. 693–700 (and by Rilliet-Dufour, see below); the Latin in vol. V. 355–362. See also vol. XXII. 5 sqq. (publ. 1880).

Le Catéchisme de l'Eglise de Genève, c'est à dire le Formulaire d'instruire les enfans la Chrétienté fait en manière de dialogue ou le ministre interrogue et l'enfant respond. The first edition of 1537 is not divided into questions and answers, and bears the title *Instruction et Confession de Foy dont on use en l'Eglise de Genève.* A copy of it was discovered by H. BORDIER in Paris and published by TH. DUFOUR, together with the first ed. of the *Confession de la Foy,* at Geneva, 1878 (see below). A copy of a Latin ed. of 1545 had been previously found in the Ducal library at Gotha.

Catechismus sive Christianæ religionis institutio, communibus renatæ nuper in evangelio Genevensis ecclesiæ suffragiis recepta et vulgari quidem prius idiomate, nunc vero Latine etiam in lucem edita, JOANNE CALVINO *auctore.* The first draft, or *Catechismus prior,* was printed at Basel, 1538 (with a Latin translation of the Confession of 1537). Reprinted in *Opera* in both languages, vol. V. 313–364. The second or larger Catechism appeared in French, 1541, in Latin, 1545, etc.; both reprinted in parallel columns, *Opera,* vol. VI. 1–160.

(NIEMEYER in his *Coll. Conf.* gives the Latin text of the larger Cat. together with the prayers and liturgical forms; comp. his Proleg. XXXVII.– XLI. BÖCKEL in his *Bekenntniss-Schriften der evang. Reform. Kirche* gives a German version of the larger Cat., 127–172. An English translation was prepared by the Marian exiles, Geneva, 1556, and reprinted in DUN-LOP'S *Confessions,* II. 139–272).

Calvin had a hand in nearly all the French and Helvetic confessions of his age. See *Opera,* IX. 693–772.

* ALBERT RILLIET and THÉOPHILE DUFOUR: *Le Catéchisme français de Calvin publié en 1537, réimprimé pour la première fois d'après un exemplaire nouvellement retrouvé, et suivi de la plus ancienne Confession de Foi de l'Église de Genève (avec un notice sur le premier séjour de Calvin à Genève, par*

---

[1] On the controversies with Caroli, see Beza, *Vita,* in *Op.* XXI. 126 sq.; Letters, Nos. 638, 640, 644, 645, 665, in the 4th. vol. of Herminjard; Ruchat, vol. v.; Henry, I. 253; II. 37, 182; III. Beil., 209; and Merle d'Aubigné, VI. 362 sqq.

ALBERT RILLIET, *et une notice bibliographique sur le Catéchisme et la Confession de Foi de Calvin, par* THÉOPHILE DUFOUR), Genève (H. Georg.), and Paris (Fischbacher), 1878, 16°. pp. CCLXXXVIII. and 146; reprinted in *Opera*, XXII.

SCHAFF: *Creeds of Christendom*, I. 467 sqq.   STÄHELIN, I. 124 sqq. KAMPSCHULTE, I. 284 sqq.   MERLE D'AUBIGNÉ, VI. 328–357.

Geneva needed first of all a strong moral government on the doctrinal basis of the evangelical Reformation.   The Genevese were a light-hearted, joyous people, fond of public amusements, dancing, singing, masquerades, and revelries. Reckless gambling, drunkenness, adultery, blasphemy, and all sorts of vice abounded.   Prostitution was sanctioned by the authority of the State and superintended by a woman called the *Reine du bordel*.   The people were ignorant.   The priests had taken no pains to instruct them and had set them a bad example.   To remedy these evils, a Confession of Faith and Discipline, and a popular Catechism were prepared, the first by Farel as the senior pastor, with the aid of Calvin;[1] the second by Calvin.   Both were accepted and approved by the Council in November, 1536.[2]

The Confession of Faith consists of twenty-one articles in which the chief doctrines of the evangelical faith are briefly and clearly stated for the comprehension of the people.   It begins with the Word of God, as the rule of faith and practice, and ends with the duty to the civil magistracy.   The

---

[1] Beza treats the Confession as a work of Calvin, but the Strassburg editors defend the authorship of Farel.   *Opera*, XXII. Suppl. col. 11–18.   Beza says (XXI. 126): "*Tunc* [*i.e.* after the disputation at Lausanne, 1536] *edita est a Calvino Christianæ doctrinæ quædam veluti formula, vixdum emergenti e papatus sordibus Genevensi ecclesiæ accomodata.   Addidit etiam Catechismum, non illum in quæstiones et responsiones distributum, quem nunc habemus, sed alium multo breviorem præcipua religionis capita complexum.*"   But the Catechism appeared two months before the Confession.   "*Iam vero confessionem non sine ratione adjungendam curavimus.*"   Calv., *Opera*, V. 319.   Rilliet, *l.c.* p. IX.: "*La Conf. de Foy n'a paru que quelques mois plus tard.*"   The Confession is an extract from the Catechism, as the title says.   Merle d'Aubigné (VI. 337) regards the confession as the joint work of Calvin and Farel.

[2] *Annal.*, 206, "Nov. 10.   *La confession acceptée.   Vers la même époque première édition du catéchisme.*"

doctrine of predestination and reprobation is omitted, but it is clearly taught that man is saved by the free grace of God without any merit (Art. 10). The necessity of discipline by admonition and excommunication for the conversion of the sinner is asserted (Art. 19). This subject gave much trouble in Geneva and other Swiss churches. The Confession prepared the way for fuller Reformed Confessions, as the Gallican, the Belgic, and the Second Helvetic. It was printed and distributed in April, 1537, and read every Sunday from the pulpits, to prepare the citizens for its adoption.[1]

Calvin's Catechism, which preceded the Confession, is an extract from his *Institutes*, but passed through several transformations. On his return from Strassburg he re-wrote it on a larger scale, and arranged it in questions and answers, or in the form of a dialogue between the teacher and the pupil. It was used for a long time in Reformed Churches and schools, and served a good purpose in promoting an intelligent piety and virtue by systematic biblical instruction. It includes an exposition of the Creed, the Decalogue, and the Lord's Prayer. It is much fuller than Luther's, but less adapted for children. Beza says that it was translated into German, English, Scotch, Belgic, Spanish, into Hebrew by E. Tremellius, and "most elegantly" into Greek by H. Stephanus. It furnished the basis and material for a number of similar works, especially the Anglican (Nowell's), the Palatinate (Heidelberg), and the Westminster Catechisms, which gradually superseded it.

Calvin has been called "the father of popular education and the inventor of free schools."[2] But he must share this honor with Luther and Zwingli.

---

[1] *Reg. du Cons.* 17 and 27 avril, 1537. It had been previously examined and adopted in manuscript.

[2] Among others by George Bancroft, in his *Lit. and Hist. Miscellanies*, p. 406: "Calvin was the father of popular education, the inventor of the system of free schools."

Besides the Confession and Catechism, the Reformed pastors (*i.e.* Farel, Calvin, and Courault) presented to the Council a memorial concerning the future organization and discipline of the Church of Geneva, recommending frequent and solemn celebration of the Lord's Supper, at least once a month, alternately in the three principal churches, singing of Psalms, regular instruction of the youth, abolition of the papal marriage laws, the maintenance of public order, and the exclusion of unworthy communicants.[1] They regarded the apostolic custom of excommunication as necessary for the protection of the purity of the Church, but as it had been fearfully abused by the papal bishops, they requested the Council to elect a number of reliable, godly, and irreproachable citizens for the moral supervision of the different districts, and the exercise of discipline, in connection with the ministers, by private and public admonition, and, in case of stubborn disobedience, by excommunication from the privileges of church membership.

On Jan. 16, 1537, the Great Council of Two Hundred issued a series of orders forbidding immoral habits, foolish songs, gambling, the desecration of the Lord's Day, baptism by midwives, and directing that the remaining idolatrous images should be burned; but nothing was said about excommunication.[2] This subject became a bone of contention between the pastors and citizens and the cause of the expulsion of the Reformers. The election of syndics, Feb. 5, was favorable to them.

The ministers were incessantly active in preaching, catechising, and visiting all classes of the people. Five sermons

---

[1] *Mémoire de Calvin et Farel sur l'organisation de l'église de Genève.* In the Registers of the Council, it is called "*les articles donnés par M⁶ G. Farel et les aultres predicans.*" The document was recently brought to light by Gaberel (*Histoire de l'église de Genève*, 1858, Tom. I. 102), reprinted in *Opera*, vol. X. Part I. 5–14. A summary is given by Merle d'Aubigné, VI. 340 sqq.

[2] *Annal. Calv.* 206 sq.

were preached every Sunday, two every week day, and were well attended. The schools were flourishing, and public morality was steadily rising. Saunier, in a school oration, praised the goodly city of Geneva which now added to her natural advantages of a magnificent site, a fertile country, a lovely lake, fine streets and squares, the crowning glory of the pure doctrine of the gospel. The magistrates showed a willingness to assist in the maintenance of discipline. A gambler was placed in the pillory with a chain around his neck. Three women were imprisoned for an improper head-dress. Even François Bonivard, the famous patriot and prisoner of Chillon, was frequently warned on account of his licentiousness. Every open manifestation of sympathy with popery by carrying a rosary, or cherishing a sacred relic, or observing a saint's day, was liable to punishment. The fame of Geneva went abroad and began to attract students and refugees. Before the close of 1537 English Protestants came to Geneva to "see Calvin and Farel." [1]

On July 29, 1537, the Council of the Two Hundred ordered all the citizens, male and female, to assent to the Confession of Faith in the Church of St. Peter.[2] It was done by a large number. On Nov. 12, the Council even passed a measure to banish all who would not take the oath.[3]

---

[1] Bullinger's letter to Farel and Calvin, Nov. 1, 1537 (in the Simler collection of Zürich), and in *Op.* X., Pt. I. 128, also in Herminjard, IV. 309. Bullinger recommends three worthy English students of the Bible, "Eliott, Buttler, and Partridge," who had spent some time in Zürich. Bullinger had made the acquaintance of Farel at the disputation in Bern, January, 1528, and of Calvin in Basel, February, 1536.

[2] *Annal.* 213: "*De la confession: que l'on donne ordre faire que tous les dizenniers ameneront leurs gens dizenne par dizzenne en l'église S. Pierre et la leur seront leuz les articles touchant la confession en dieu et seront interrogués s'ils veulent cela tenir; aussi sera faict le serment de fidelité à la ville.*" A *dizennier* is a tithingman, or headborough.

[3] *Annal.* 216 from *Reg. du Cons.* Tom. 31, fol. 90. But the order could not be executed. Not one from the rue des Allemands would subscribe to the Confession. Even Saunier was opposed to the imposition of a personal pledge.

The Confession was thus to be made the law of Church and State. This is the first instance of a formal pledge to a symbolical book by a whole people.

It was a glaring inconsistency that those who had just shaken off the yoke of popery as an intolerable burden, should subject their conscience and intellect to a human creed; in other words, substitute for the old Roman popery a modern Protestant popery. Of course, they sincerely believed that they had the infallible Word of God on their side; but they could not claim infallibility in its interpretation. The same inconsistency and intolerance was repeated a hundred years later on a much larger scale in the "Solemn League and Covenant" of the Scotch Presbyterians and English Puritans against popery and prelacy, and sanctioned in 1643 by the Westminster Assembly of Divines which vainly attempted to prescribe a creed, a Church polity, and a directory of worship for three nations. But in those days neither Protestants nor Catholics had any proper conception of religious toleration, much less of religious liberty, as an inalienable right of man. "The power of the magistrates ends where that of conscience begins." God alone is the Lord of conscience.

The Calvinistic churches of modern times still require subscription to the Westminster standards, but only from the officers, and only in a qualified sense, as to substance of doctrine; while the members are admitted simply on profession of faith in Christ as their Lord and Saviour.[1]

---

[1] The Congregational or Independent and Baptist churches, however, while they disown the authority of general confessions, and hold to the voluntary principle, usually have local or congregational creeds and covenants which must be assented to by all applicants for membership. In this respect the Presbyterian churches are more liberal.

§ 84. *Expulsion of the Reformers.* 1538.

CALVIN'S correspondence from 1537 to 1538, in *Op.* vol. X., Pt. II. 137 sqq.
HERMINJARD, vols. IV. and V. — *Annal. Calv., Op.* XXI., fol. 215–235.

HENRY, I. ch. IX. — DYER, 78 sqq. — STÄHELIN, I. 151 sqq. — KAMPSCHULTE, I.
296–319. MERLE D'AUBIGNÉ, Bk. XI. chs. XI.–XIV. (vol. VI. 469 sqq.).

C. A. CORNELIUS: *Die Verbannung Calvins aus Genf. i.J. 1538.* München,
1886.

The submission of the people of Geneva to such a severe
system of discipline was only temporary. Many had never
sworn to the Confession, notwithstanding the threat of punishment, and among them were the most influential citizens of
the republic; [1] others declared that they had been compelled
to perjure themselves. The impossibility of enforcing the law
brought the Council into contempt. Ami Porral, the leader
of the clerical party in the Council, was charged with arbitrary conduct and disregard of the rights of the people. The
Patriots and Libertines who had hailed the Reformation in the
interest of political independence from the yoke of Savoy
and of the bishop, had no idea of becoming slaves of Farel,
and were jealous of the influence of foreigners. An intrigue
to annex Geneva to the kingdom of France increased the
suspicion. The Patriots organized themselves as a political
party and labored to overthrow the clerical *régime*. They
were aided in part by Bern, which was opposed to the tenet
of excommunication and to the radicalism of the Reformers.

There was another cause of dissatisfaction even among
the more moderate, which brought on the crisis. Farel in his
iconoclastic zeal had, before the arrival of Calvin, abolished
all holidays except Sunday, the baptismal fonts, and the
unleavened bread in the communion, all of which were
retained by the Reformed Church in Bern. [2] A synod of
Lausanne, under the influence of Bern, recommended the

---

[1] According to the testimony of Claude Rozet, the secretary of state.
He himself had not sworn the Confession, although he had read it publicly
and taken the oath of the citizens in St. Peter's, July 29, 1537.

[2] Beza, in Calvin's *Opera*, XXI. 128.

restoration of the old Bernese customs, as they were called. The Council enforced this decision. Calvin himself regarded such matters as in themselves indifferent, but would not forsake his colleagues.

Stormy scenes took place in the general assembly of citizens, Nov. 15, 1537. In the popular elections on Feb. 3, 1538, the anti-clerical party succeeded in the election of four syndics and a majority of the Council.[1]

The new rulers proceeded with caution. They appointed new preachers for the country, which was much needed. They prohibited indecent songs and broils in the streets, and going out at night after nine. They took Bern for their model. They enforced the decision of the Council of Lausanne concerning the Church festivals and baptismal fonts.

But the preachers were determined to die rather than to yield an inch. They continued to thunder against the popular vices, and censured the Council for want of energy in suppressing them. The result was that they were warned not to meddle in politics (March 12).[2] Courauld, who surpassed even Farel in vehemence, was forbidden to preach, but ascended the pulpit again, April 7, denounced Geneva and its citizens in a rude and insulting manner,[3] was imprisoned, and six days afterwards banished in spite of the energetic protests of Calvin and Farel. The old man retired to Thonon, on the lake of Geneva, was elected minister at Orbe, and died there Oct. 4 in the same year.

Calvin and Farel were emboldened by this harsh treatment of their colleague. They attacked the Council from the pulpit.

---

[1] The new syndics, Claude Richardet, Jean Philippe, Jean Lullin, and Ami de Chapeaurouge, were pronounced enemies of Farel and Viret. Ami Porral was not re-elected. Grynæus of Basel wrote several letters of comfort and encouragement to Farel and Calvin, Feb. 13, March 4, March 12, 1538. In Herminjard, IV. 361, 379, 401.

[2] *Ann. 222, " de point se mesler du magistrat."*

[3] He compared the state of Geneva with the kingdom of frogs, and the Genevese with rats. Merle d'Aubigné, VI. 455.

Even Calvin went so far as to denounce it as the Devil's Council. Libels were circulated against the preachers. They often heard the cry late in the evening, "To the Rhone with the traitors," and in the night they were disturbed by violent knocks at the door of their dwelling.

They were ordered to celebrate the approaching Easter communion after the Bernese rite, but they refused to do so in the prevailing state of debauchery and insubordination. The Council could find no supplies. On Easter Sunday, April 21, Calvin, after all, ascended the pulpit of St. Peter's; Farel, the pulpit of St. Gervais. They preached before large audiences, but declared that they could not administer the communion to the rebellious city, lest the sacrament be desecrated. And indeed, under existing circumstances, the celebration of the love-feast of the Saviour would have been a solemn mockery. Many hearers were armed, drew their swords, and drowned the voice of the preachers, who left the church and went home under the protection of their friends. Calvin preached also in the evening in the Church of St. Francis at Rive in the lower part of the city, and was threatened with violence.

The small Council met after the morning service in great commotion and summoned the general Council. On the next two days, April 22 and 23, the great Council of the Two Hundred assembled in the cloisters of St. Peter's, deposed Farel and Calvin, without a trial, and ordered them to leave the city within three days.[1]

They received the news with great composure. "Very well," said Calvin, "it is better to serve God than man. If we had sought to please men, we should have been badly rewarded, but we serve a higher Master, who will not with-

---

[1] The same Council deposed Claude Rozet, the secretary of state, who, in his official capacity, had recorded the oath of the people to the Confession of Faith, July 29, 1537. *Registers* of April 23, 1538. Rozet, *Chron. MS. de Genève*, Bk. IV. ch. 18 (quoted by Merle d'Aubigné, VI. 485).

hold from us his reward."[1] Calvin even rejoiced at the result
more than seemed proper.

The people celebrated the downfall of the clerical *régime*
with public rejoicings. The decrees of the synod of Lausanne
were published by sound of trumpets. The baptismal fonts
were re-erected, and the communion administered on the following Sunday with unleavened bread.

The deposed ministers went to Bern, but found little sympathy. They proceeded to Zürich, where a general synod was
held, and were kindly received. They admitted that they
had been too rigid, and consented to the restoration of the
baptismal fonts, the unleavened bread (provided the bread
was broken), and the four Church festivals observed in Bern;
but they insisted on the introduction of discipline, the division of the Church into parishes, the more frequent administration of the communion, the singing of Psalms in public
worship, and the exercise of discipline by joint committees of
laymen and ministers.[2]

Bullinger undertook to advocate this compromise before
Bern and Geneva. But the Genevese confirmed in general
assembly the sentence of banishment, May 26.

With gloomy prospects for the future, yet trusting in God,
who orders all things well, the exiled ministers travelled on
horseback in stormy weather to Basel. In crossing a torrent
swollen by the rains they were nearly swept away. In Basel
they were warmly received by sympathizing friends, especially
by Grynæus. Here they determined to wait for the call of
Providence. Farel, after a few weeks, in July, received and
accepted a call to Neuchâtel, his former seat of labor, on condition that he should have freedom to introduce his system of

---

[1] Beza, Rozet, and the *Registers* all report this answer with slight variations. Farel's answer to the messenger was: "Well and good; it is from
God."

[2] See the 14 Articles drawn up by Calvin and Farel, in Henry, I. Beilage, 8;
in *Op.* X., Part II. 190–192, and in Herminjard, V. 3–6.

discipline.   Calvin was induced, two months later, to leave Basel for Strassburg.

It was during this crisis that Calvin's friend and travelling companion, Louis du Tillet, who seems to have been of a mild and peaceable disposition, lost faith in the success of the Reformation.   He left Geneva in August, 1537, for Strassburg and Paris, and returned to the Roman Church.   He had relations in high standing who influenced him.   His brother, Jean du Tillet, was the famous registrar of the Parliament of Paris; another brother became bishop of Sainte-Brieux, afterwards of Meaux.[1]   He explained to Calvin his conscientious scruples and reasons for the change.   Calvin regarded them as insufficient, and warned him earnestly, but kindly and courteously.   The separation was very painful to both, but was relieved by mutual regard.   Du Tillet even offered to aid Calvin in his distressed condition after his expulsion, but Calvin gratefully declined, writing from Strassburg, Oct. 20, 1538 : " You have made me an offer for which I cannot sufficiently thank you; neither am I so rude and unmannerly as not to feel the unmerited kindness so deeply, that even in declining to accept it, I can never adequately express the obligation that I owe to you."   As to their difference of opinion, he appeals to the judgment of God to decide who are the true schismatics, and concludes the letter with the prayer: " May our Lord uphold and keep you in his holy protection, so directing you that you decline not from his way."[2]

---

[1] Herminjard, V. 107 (note 1¹); and p. 163.

[2] See the correspondence in Herminjard, IV. 354–359 and 384–400; V. 103–109; 161, 162; 186–200.   Du Tillet writes under his *nom seigneurial* De Haultmont to Charles d'Espeville (Calvin).   His last letter is dated Paris, Dec. 1, 1538, and closes with the desire to remain "always his friend and brother in Christ."   There is also an answer of Bucer to Du Tillet from Strassburg, Oct. 8, 1539 (in Herminjard, VI. 61–70), in which he refutes four objections which Du Tillet had made against the Protestants, viz.: 1) that they seceded from the Church of Christ; 2) that they rejected good customs and observances of the Church; 3) that they spoiled the goods of the Church; 4) that they denied many true dogmas and introduced false dogmas.

CHAPTER XI.

CALVIN IN GERMANY. FROM 1538–1541.

§ 85. *Calvin in Strassburg.*

I. CALVIN's correspondence from 1538–1541 in *Opera*, vols. X. and XI.;
HERMINJARD, vols. V. and VI.; BONNET-CONSTABLE, vol. I. 53 sqq.—
BEZA: *Vita Calv.*, in *Op.* XXI. 128 sq.—*Ann. Calv.*, *Op.* XXI. 226–285.
Contains extracts from the *Archives du chapitre de St. Thomas de Stras-
bourg.*

II. ALF. ERICHSON: *L'Église française de Strasbourg au XVIᵉ siècle, d'après
des documents inédits.* Strasb. 1885. Comp. also his other works on the
History of the Reformation in the Alsace.—C. A. CORNELIUS: *Die Rückkehr Calvin's nach Genf.* München, 1889. — E. DOUMERGUE (Prof. of the
Prot. Faculty of Montauban): *Essai sur l'histoire du Culte Réformé principalement au XIXᵉ Siècle.* Paris, 1890. Ch. I., *Calvin à Strasbourg*, treats of
the worship in the first French Reformed Church, the model of the
churches of France.—EDUARD STRICKER: *Johannes Calvin als erster
Pfarrer der reformirten Gemeinde zu Strassburg. Nach urkundlichen Quellen.*
Strassburg (Heitz & Mündel), 1890 (65 pp.). In commemoration of the
centenary of the church edifice of the French Reformed congregation
(built in 1790) by its present pastor.

III. HENRY, I. ch. X. — STÄHELIN, I. 168–283. — KAMPSCHULTE, I. 320–368. —
MERLE D'AUBIGNÉ, Bk. XI. chs. XV.–XVII. (vol. VI. 543–609).

CALVIN felt so discouraged by his recent experience that
he was disinclined to assume another public office, and Courault approved of this purpose. He therefore refused the first
invitation of Bucer to come to Strassburg, the more so as his
friend Farel was not included. But he yielded at last to
repeated solicitations, mindful of the example of the prophet
Jonah. Farel gave his hearty assent.

Strassburg [1] was since 1254 a free imperial city of Germany, famous for one of the finest Gothic cathedrals, large

---

[1] Or Strasbourg in French. *Argentoratum* was a Roman military station
in the time of Augustus.

commerce, and literary enterprise. Some of the first editions of the Bible were printed there. By its geographical situation, a few miles west of the Upper Rhine, it formed a connecting link between Germany, France, and Switzerland, as also between Lutheranism and Zwinglianism. It offered a hospitable home to a steady flow of persecuted Protestants from France, who called Strassburg the New Jerusalem. The citizens had accepted the Reformation in 1523 in the spirit of evangelical union between the two leading types of Protestantism. Bucer, Capito, Hedio, Niger, Matthias Zell, Sturm, and others, labored there harmoniously together. Strassburg was the Wittenberg of South-western Germany, and in friendly alliance with Zürich and Geneva.

Martin Bucer, the chief Reformer of the city, was the embodiment of a generous and comprehensive catholicity, and gave it expression in the Tetrapolitan Confession, which was presented at the diet of Augsburg in 1530.[1] He afterwards brought about, in the same irenic spirit, the Wittenberg Concordia (1536), which was to harmonize the Lutheran and Zwinglian theories on the Lord's Supper, but conceded too much to Luther (even the participation of the body and blood of Christ by unworthy communicants), and therefore was rejected by Bullinger and the Swiss Churches. He wrote to Bern in June, 1540, that next to Wittenberg no city in Germany was so friendly to the gospel and so large-hearted in spirit as Strassburg. He ended his labors in the Anglican Church as professor of theology in the University of Cambridge in 1551. Six years after his death his body was dug up, chained upright to a stake and burned, under Queen Mary; but his tomb was rebuilt and his memory honorably restored under Queen Elizabeth. His colleague Fagius shared the same fate.

The Zürichers, in a letter to Calvin, call Strassburg "the

---

[1] See vol. VI. 571 and 718.

Antioch of the Reformation"; Capito, "the refuge of exiled brethren"; the Roman Catholic historian, Florimond de Ræmond, "the retreat and rendez-vous of Lutherans and Zwinglians under the control of Bucer, and the receptacle of those that were banished from France."[1] Among the distinguished early refugees from France were Francis Lambert, Farel, Le Fèvre, Roussel, and Michel d'Arande. Unfortunately, Strassburg did not long occupy this noble position, but became a battlefield of bitter sectarian strife and, for some time, the home of a narrow Lutheran orthodoxy. The city was conquered by Louis XIV. and annexed to Roman Catholic France in 1681, to the detriment of her Protestant character, but was reconquered by Emperor William I. and incorporated with united Germany as the capital of Alsace and Lorraine in 1870. The university was newly organized and better equipped than ever before.[2]

Calvin arrived at Strassburg in the first days of September, 1538.[3] He spent there three years in useful labors. He was received with open arms by Bucer, Capito, Hedio, Sturm, and Niger, the leading men in the Church, and appointed by the Council professor of theology, with a moderate salary. He soon felt at home, and in the next summer bought the citizenship, and joined the guild of the tailors.[4]

---

[1] " *C'était le réceptacle des bannis de la France.*" *Hist. de la naissance de l'hérésie*, p. 838.

[2] It will take some time before the irritating question of language and nationality can be settled. When last in Strassburg, I asked, first, a shopkeeper whether the people speak more French or German, and received the prompt and emphatic answer: " *On parle toujours français à Strasbourg.*" The next person, in answer to the same question, replied: " *Man spricht mehr deutsch.*" At last, a market-woman told the truth: " *Man spricht dietsch.*" The Alsatian dialect prevails at home, the French in society, the high German in the university, among the government officials and soldiers.

[3] Not at the end of September, as Stähelin has it. See Stricker, p. 11, note, where he shows that Calvin preached his first sermon at Strassburg on the 8th of September.

[4] July 30, 1539. Some historians err in stating that the citizenship was presented to him. See Stricker, 44, and *Annal.* XXI. fol. 250: " *Uff den*

The sojourn of Calvin in this city was a fruitful episode in his life, and an education for more successful work in Geneva. His views were enlarged and deepened. He gained valuable experience. He came in contact with the Lutheran Church and its leaders. He learned to understand and appreciate them, but was unfavorably impressed with the want of discipline and the slavish dependence of the clergy upon the secular rulers. He labored indefatigably and successfully as professor, pastor, and author. He informed Farel (April 20, 1539) that, when the messenger called for copy of his book (the second edition of the *Institutes*), he had to read fifty pages, then to teach and to preach, to write four letters, to adjust some quarrels, and was interrupted by visitors more than ten times.[1]

It is in the fitness of things that three learned professors of the University of Strassburg, who lived during the French and German *régime*, and were equally at home in the language and theology of both nations, should give to the world the last and best edition of Calvin's works.

Calvin's economic condition during these three years was very humble. It is a shame for the congregation and the city government that they allowed such a man to struggle for his daily bread. For the first five months he received no pay at all, only free board in the house of a liberal friend. His countrymen were poor, but might have done something. He informed Farel, in April, 1539, that of his many friends in France, not one had offered him a copper, except Louis Du Tillet, who hoped to induce him to return. Hence he declined.[2] The city paid him a very meagre salary of fifty-

30 *tag Julij Anno 39 ist Johannes Calvinus uff unser Herren der statt Strassburg Saal erschinnen, und sich angeben lut der Ordnung und will dienen mit den schnydern.*"

[1] Herminjard, V. 286 sq.; *Opera*, X., Pars II. 337.

[2] " *Cum innumeros aliquando amicos in Gallia habuerim, nemo fuit qui assem mihi obtulerit; èt tamen si fecissent, poterant frui gratuita beneficentiæ jactantia : nihil enim illis constitisset offerre quod acceptassem. Exciderat mihi Ludovicus*

two guilders (about two hundred marks) for his professorial
duties from May, 1539.[1] His books were not profitable.
When the Swiss heard of his embarrassment, they wished to
come to his aid, and Fabri sent ten ducats to Farel for
Calvin.[2] But he preferred to sell his greatest treasure — the
library — which he had left in Geneva, and to take students
as boarders (*pensionnaires*). He trusted to God for the
future.[3]

With all his poverty he was happy in his independence, the
society of congenial friends, and his large field of usefulness.

§ 86. *The Church of the Strangers in Strassburg.*

Calvin combined the offices of pastor and professor of
theology in Strassburg, as he had done in Geneva. The
former activity kept him in contact with his French countrymen; the latter extended his influence among the scholars
in Germany.

[Du Tillet]; *ille unus fuit qui obtulit; sed ipse quoque suam largitionem nimis
magno venditabat : siquidem me tantum non ad recantandum hortabatur.*" Herminjard, V. 291 sq. See the letter of Du Tillet from Paris, Oct. 20, 1538, in
which he offers him to furnish "*assez à toute vostre necessité*" (*ibid.* p. 107).

[1] May 1, 1539: "*Joannes Calvinus so ein gelährter frommer Gesell sein soll und
zu Zeiten auch in Theologia lese, zudem auch zu den Reuwern französisch predige,
haben die Herren . . . ist beschlossen dasz man demselben nuhn fürter ein Jar
lang die 52 fl. alsz ein zuhelffer geben und soll prima Maij angehen.*" From the
Thomas-Archiv, in *Annal.* fol. 246.

[2] "*Decem coronatos.*" Libertet (Christophe Fabri) to Farel, May 8, 1539,
in Herminjard, V. 307.

[3] "It is very agreeable to me," he wrote to Farel, who had communicated
to his colleagues Calvin's wants, "I confess, that my brethren entertain such
a regard for me, that they are ready to supply my wants from their own
means. It could not be otherwise than that I must be greatly delighted with
such a testimony of their love (*quin tali amoris testimonio delecter*). Nevertheless, I have determined to abstain from putting both your kindness and theirs
in requisition, unless a greater necessity shall compel me. Wendelin [Wende-
lin Rihel], the printer, to whom I intrusted my book [the second edition of
the *Institutio*] to be printed, will provide me with as much as will be sufficient
for any extraordinary expenses. From my books which yet remain at Geneva,
there will be enough to satisfy my landlord till next winter. As to the future,
the Lord will provide." (Herminjard, *l.c.*)

He organized the first Protestant congregation of French refugees, which served as a model for the Reformed Churches of Geneva and France.

The number of refugees amounted at that time to about four hundred.[1] Most of them belonged to the "little French Church."[2] His first sermon was delivered in the Church of St. Nicholas, and attracted a large crowd of Frenchmen and Germans.[3] He preached four times a week (twice on Sunday), and held Bible classes. He trained deacons to assist him, especially in the care of the poor, whom he had much at heart. The names of the first two were Nicholas Parent, who afterwards became pastor at Neuchâtel, and Claude de Fer or Féray (Claudius Feræus), a French Hellenist, who had fled to Strassburg, taught Greek, and died of the pestilence in 1541, to the great grief of Calvin.

He introduced his favorite discipline, and as he was not interfered with by the magistracy he had better success than at Geneva during his first sojourn. "No house," he says, "no society, can exist without order and discipline, much less the Church." He laid as much stress upon it as Luther did upon doctrine, and he regarded it as the best safeguard of sound doctrine and Christian life. He excluded a student who had neglected public worship for a month and fallen into gross immorality, from the communion table, and would not admit him till he professed repentance.[4]

---

[1] A census of Strassburg, taken Oct. 18, 1553, enumerates one hundred Frenchmen who were citizens, thirty-five who were not citizens, and sixteen soldiers (in all 151 men), without including wives, children, and servants. From this Stricker (p. 5) infers that the foreign population numbered four hundred souls. Doumergue (*l.c.* p. 3) counts from five hundred to six hundred. Specklin (1536–1589), the author of a chronicle of Strassburg (edited by Rud. Reuss, Strassb. 1890), gives a much larger number, namely, fifteen hundred; but he is not very accurate, and must be corrected by the official census.

[2] "*Ecclesiola Gallicana,*" as Calvin calls it.

[3] Afterwards he preached in the *Klosterkirche der Reuerinnen,* now called the *Magdalenen Kirche.*

[4] Calvin to Farel, in Herminjard, V. 291.

Not a few of the younger members, however, objected to excommunication as a popish institution. But he distinguished between the yoke of Christ and the tyranny of the pope. He persevered and succeeded. " I have conflicts," he wrote to Farel, " severe conflicts, but they are a good school for me."

He converted many Anabaptists, who were wisely tolerated in the territory of Strassburg, and brought to him from the city and country their children for baptism. He was consulted by the magistrates on all important questions touching religion. He conscientiously attended to pastoral care, and took a kindly interest in every member of his flock. In this way he built up in a short time a prosperous church, which commanded the respect and admiration of the community of Strassburg.[1]

Unfortunately, this Church of the Strangers lasted only about twenty-five years, and was extinguished by the flames of sectarian bigotry, though not till after many copies had been made from it as a model. An exclusive Lutheranism, under the lead of Marbach, obtained the ascendency in Strassburg, and treated the Calvinistic Christians as dangerous heretics. When Calvin passed through the city on his way to Frankfort, in August, 1556, he was indeed honorably received by John Sturm and the students, who respectfully rose to their feet in his presence, but he was not allowed to preach to his own congregation, because he did not believe in the dogma of consubstantiation. A few years later the Reformed worship was altogether forbidden by order of the Council, Aug. 19, 1563.[2]

[1] Kampschulte, I. 324, thus sums up Calvin's pastoral labors in Strassburg: " *Strassburg hatte in Kurzem eine blühende wohlgeordnete französische Flüchtlingsgemeinde mit Predigt und Bibelstunden, mit regelmässiger Abendmahlsfeier und Psalmengesang, insbesondere aber mit einer strenge gehandhabten Disciplin, und nicht ohne Staunen erzählten die deutschen Pastoren bald einander von den Einrichtungen und dem merkwürdigen Eifer der neuen Emigrantenkirche in Strassburg.*"

[2] Stricker, pp. 11, 12, 64; Erichson, p. 65; Doumergue, p. 4; Calvin's letter to Bullinger, Sept. 12, 1563 (*Opera*, X. 151). Under the French rule the Reformed Church was reorganized in Strassburg.

§ 87. *The Liturgy of Calvin.*

I. *La forme des prieres et chantz ecclesiastiques, avec la maniere d'administrer les sacremens et consacrer le marriage, selon la coutume de l'Eglise ancienne,* A.D. 1542. In *Opera,* VI. 161–210 (from a copy at Stuttgart; the title is given in the old spelling without accents). Later editions (1543, 1545, 1562, etc.) add : *"la visitation des malades,"* and *" comme on l'observe à Genève."* An earlier edition of eighteen Psalms appeared at Strassburg, 1539. (See DOUEN, *Clément Marot,* I. 300 sqq.) An edition of the liturgy with the Psalms was printed at Strassburg, Feb. 15, 1542. (See DOUEN, *l.c.* 305, and 342 sqq.) A copy of an enlarged Strassburg ed. of 1545, entitled *La forme des prieres et chantz ecclesiastiques,* was preserved in the Public Library at Strassburg till Aug. 24, 1870, when it was burnt at the siege of the city in the Franco-German War (DOUEN, I. 451 sq.).

II. CH. D'HÉRICAULT : *Ouvres de Marot.* Paris, 1867. — FELIX BOVET : *Histoire du psautier des églises réformées.* Neuchâtel, 1872. — O. DOUEN : *Clément Marot et le Psautier Huguenot. Étude historique, littéraire, musicale et bibliographique; contenant les mélodies primitives des Psaumes,* etc. Paris (*à l'imprimerie national*), 1878 sq. 2 vols. royal 8vo. A magnificent work published at the expense of the French Republic on the recommendation of the Institute. The second volume contains the harmonies of Goudimel.

Farel published at Neuchâtel in 1533, and introduced at Geneva in 1537, the first French Reformed liturgy, which includes, in the regular Sunday service, a general prayer, the Lord's Prayer (before sermon), the Decalogue, confession of sins, repetition of the Lord's Prayer, the Apostles' Creed, a final exhortation and benediction.[1] It resembled the German liturgy of Bern, which was published in 1529, and which Calvin caused to be translated into French by his friend Morelet.[2] Of Farel's liturgy only the form of marriage survived. The rest was reconstructed and improved by Calvin

[1] Republished by Baum at Strassburg, 1859. Douen, *l.c.* I. 346.

[2] In a letter to Gaspard Megander, an influential minister at Bern (probably from Feb. 20, 1537), Calvin writes: *"Libellum tuum ceremonialem a Mauro* [Maurus Musæus, Morelet de Museau], *rogatu nostro, versum, cum nostro contulimus, a quo nihil penitus nisi brevitate differt."* Herminjard (vol. IV. 191) adds the following note: *"La liturgie usitée dans l'église genevoise était, selon toutes les vraisemblances, celle de Farel, publiée à Neuchâtel, le 29 août 1533, sous le titre suivant : 'La Manière et Fasson qu'on tient en baillant le sainct baptesme . . . ès lieux que Dieu de sa grâce a visités.' Nous avons constaté que la liturgie bernoise offre les plus grands rapports avec 'La Manière et Fasson,' et qu'elle en diffère seulement par la brièveté."*

in the liturgy which he first introduced in Strassburg, and with some modifications in Geneva after his return.

Calvin's liturgy was published twice in 1542. It was introduced at Lausanne in the same year, and gradually passed into other Reformed Churches.

Calvin built his form of worship on the foundation of Zwingli and Farel, and the services already in use in the Swiss Reformed Churches. Like his predecessors, he had no sympathy whatever with the Roman Catholic ceremonialism, which was overloaded with unscriptural traditions and superstitions. We may add that he had no taste for the artistic, symbolical, and ornamental features in worship. He rejected the mass, all the sacraments, except two, the saints' days, nearly all church festivals, except Sunday, images, relics, processions, and the whole pomp and circumstance of a gaudy worship which appeals to the senses and imagination rather than the intellect and the conscience, and tends to distract the mind with the outward show instead of concentrating it upon the contemplation of the saving truth of the gospel.

He substituted in its place that simple and spiritual mode of worship which is well adapted for intelligent devotion, if it be animated by the quickening presence and power of the Spirit of God, but becomes jejune, barren, cold, and chilly if that power is wanting. He made the sermon the central part of worship, and substituted instruction and edification in the vernacular for the reading of the mass in Latin. He magnified the pulpit, as the throne of the preacher, above the altar of the sacrificing priest. He opened the inexhaustible fountain of free prayer in public worship, with its endless possibilities of application to varying circumstances and wants; he restored to the Church, like Luther, the inestimable blessing of congregational singing, which is the true popular liturgy, and more effective than the reading of written forms of prayer.

The order of public worship in Calvin's congregation at Strassburg was as follows: —

The service began with an invocation,[1] a confession of sin and a brief absolution.[2] Then followed reading of the Scriptures, singing, and a free prayer. The whole congregation, male and female, joined in chanting the Psalms, and thus took an active part in public worship, while formerly they were but passive listeners or spectators. This was in accordance with the Protestant doctrine of the general priesthood of believers.[3] The sermon came next, and after it a

[1] "Nostre aide soit au nom de Dieu, qui a faict le Ciel et la terre. Amen." Opera, VI. 173.

[2] This confession is still in use and may be favorably compared with the confession in the Anglican liturgy. It is as follows (in modern spelling) : —

"Mes frères, qu'un chacun de nous se présente devant la face du Seigneur, avec confession de ses fautes et péchés, suivant de son cœur mes paroles.

"Seigneur Dieu, Père éternal et tout-puissant, nous confessons [et reconnaissons] sans feintise, devant ta Sainte Majesté, que nous sommes pauvres pécheurs, conçus et nés en iniquité et corruption, enclins à mal faire, inutiles à tout bien, et que par notre vice, nous transgressons sans fin et sans cesse tes saints commandements. En quoi faisant, nous acquérons, par ton juste jugement, ruine et perdition sur nous.

"Toutefois, Seigneur, nous avons déplaisir en nous-mêmes, de t'avoir offensé, et condamnons nous et nos vices, avec vraie repentance, désirant que ta grâce [et aide] subviennent à notre calamité.

"Veuille donc avoir pitié de nous, Dieu et Père très bénin, et plein de miséricorde, au nom de ton Fils Jésus-Christ, notre Seigneur ; effaçant donc nos vices et macules, élargis nous et augmente de jour en jour les grâces de ton Saint-Esprit, afin que, reconnaissant de tout notre cœur notre injustice, nous soyons touchés de déplaisir, qui engendre droite pénitence en nous : laquelle nous mortifiant à tous péchés produise en nous fruits de justice et innocence qui te soient agréables par ice-lui Jésus-Christ. Amen."

After this confession the Strassburg Liturgy adds a form of absolution, which was afterwards omitted : —

"Ici, dit le ministre quelques paroles de l'Écriture pour consoler les consciences, et fait l'absolution en cette manière :

"Un chacun de vous se reconnaisse vraiment pécheur, s'humiliant devant Dieu, et croie que le Père céleste lui veut être propice en Jésus-Christ. A tous ceux qui, en cette manière se repentent, et cherchent Jésus-Christ pour leur salut, je dénonce l'absolution au nom du Père, du Fils, et du Saint-Esprit. Amen."

[3] In this respect Calvin followed the example of the Lutheran churches. Gérard Roussel, who was one of the earliest refugees at Strassburg, reported to Briçonnet, bishop of Meaux, that the singing of Psalms, translated from the Hebrew, was there a prominent feature of worship, and that " le chant des

long general prayer and the Lord's Prayer. The service closed with singing and the benediction.[1]

The same order is substantially observed in the French Reformed Churches. Calvin prepared also liturgical forms for baptism and the holy communion. A form for marriage and the visitation of the sick had been previously composed by Farel. The combination of the liturgical and extemporaneous features continue in the Reformed Churches of the Continent. In the Presbyterian churches of Scotland and most of the Dissenting churches of England, and their descendants in America, the liturgical element was gradually ruled out by free prayer; while the Anglican Church pursued the opposite course.

Baptism was always performed before the congregation at the close of the public service, and in the simplest manner, according to the institution of Christ; without the traditional ceremony of exorcism, and the use of salt, spittle, and burning candles, because these are not commanded in the Scriptures, nourish superstition, and divert the attention from the spiritual substance of the ordinance to outward forms. Calvin regarded immersion as the primitive form of baptism, but pouring and sprinkling as equally valid.[2]

The communion was celebrated once a month in a simple

---

femmes, se mêlant à celui des hommes, produit un effet ravissant." Herminjard, I. 404–408. In another letter, he speaks also of the congregational chanting of the Apostles' Creed and the *Kyrie Eleison* at the communion. *Ibid.* I. 411–413. Doumergue, pp. 8, 9.

[1] An interesting description of the Reformed worship at Strassburg, by a French student in 1545, was first published in 1885 by Erichson, p. 7, and is given by Doumergue, *l.c.* p. 15 sq. He speaks of daily preaching and chanting of Psalms by the whole congregation (*"tant homme que femme avec un bel accord"*) from a tune book (*un livre de musique*), which each member had in his hand.

[2] He says, *Instit.* IV. ch. XV. § 19: " Whether the person who is baptized be wholly immersed, and whether thrice or once, or whether water be only poured or sprinkled upon him, is of no importance; churches ought to be left at liberty in this respect, to act according to the difference of countries. The very word *baptize*, however, signifies *to immerse;* and it is certain that immersion was the practice of the ancient Church."

but very solemn manner by the whole congregation. Calvin required the communicants to give him previous notice of their intention, that they might receive instruction, warning, or comfort, according to their need. Unworthy applicants were excluded.

The introduction of the Psalter in the vernacular was a most important feature, and the beginning of a long and heroic chapter in the history of worship and Christian life. The Psalter occupies the same important place in the Reformed Church as the hymnal in the Lutheran. It was the source of comfort and strength to the Huguenot Church of the Desert, and to the Presbyterian Covenanters of Scotland, in the days of bitter trial and persecution. Calvin himself prepared metrical versions of Psalms 25, 36, 43, 46,[1] 91, 113, 120, 138, 142, together with a metrical version of the Song of Simeon and the Ten Commandments.[2] He afterwards used the superior version of Clément Marot, the greatest French poet of that age, who was the poet of the court, and the psalmist of the Church (1497–1544). Calvin met him first at the court of the Duchess of Ferrara (1536), whither he had fled, and afterwards at Geneva (1542), where he encouraged him to continue his metrical translation of the Psalms. Marot's Psalter first appeared at Paris, 1541, and contained thirty Psalms, together with metrical versions of the Lord's Prayer, the Angelic Salutation, the Creed, and the Decalogue. Several editions, with fifty Psalms, were printed at Geneva in 1543, one at Strassburg in 1545. Later editions were enlarged with the translations of Beza. The popularity

---

[1] The same Psalm furnished the key-note to Luther's immortal hymn, "*Ein feste Burg ist unser Gott.*" Calvin's version begins: —

> " *Nostre Dieu est ferme appuy,*
> *Vertue, fortresse et seur confort,*
> *Auquel aurons en notre ennuy,*
> *Présent réfuge et très bon port.*"

[2] They were printed at Strassburg, 1539, and republished, together with an original hymn (*Salutation à Jésus-Christ*), from an edition of 1545, in *Opera,* VI. 212–224.

and usefulness of his and Beza's Psalter were greatly enhanced by the rich melodies of Claude Goudimel (1510–
1572), who joined the Reformed Church in 1562, and died
a martyr at Lyons in the night of the Massacre of St. Bartholomew. He devoted his musical genius to the Reformation. His tunes are based in part on popular songs, and
breathe the simple and earnest spirit of the Reformed cultus.
Some of them have found a place among the chorals of the
Lutheran Church.

§ 88. *Calvin as Theological Teacher and Author.*

The Reformers of Strassburg, aided by leading laymen, as
Jacob Sturm and John Sturm, provided for better elementary and higher education, and founded schools which
attracted pupils from France as early as 1525. Gérard
Roussel, one of the earliest of the refugees, speaks very
highly of them in a letter to the bishop of Meaux.[1] A
Protestant college (gymnasium), with a theological department, was established March 22, 1538, and placed under the
direction of John Sturm, one of the ablest pedagogues of his
times. It was the nucleus of a university which continued
German down to the French Revolution, was then half French-
ified, and is now again German in language and methods of
teaching. The first teachers in that college were Bucer for
the New Testament, Capito for the Old, Hedio for history
and theology, Herlin for mathematics, and Jacob Bedrot or
Pedrotus for Greek.[2] A converted Jew taught Hebrew.

---

[1] Herminjard, I. 407 ; also Farel in a letter of June 4, 1526, to Myconius,
ibid. 433 sq. On the schools in Strassburg see Roehrich, *Geschichte der
Reformation im Elsass,* I. 253, 261–264; A. G. Strobel, *Histoire du Gymnase
protestant de Strasbourg,* Strasb. 1838; Charles Schmidt, *La vie et les travaux de
Jean Sturm,* Strasb. 1855 (quoted by Herminjard); and R. Zöpffel, *Johann
Sturm, der erste Rektor der Strassburger Akademie,* Strassburg, 1887.

[2] Pedrotus (Padrut), whose name often occurs in Calvin's letters, was a
native of Pludenz in Vorarlberg, and famous as editor and expounder of
ancient classics, hence also called *Jacobus Græcus.* Capito recommended

Calvin was appointed assistant professor of theology in January, 1539.[1] He lectured on the Gospel of John, the Epistle to the Romans, and other books of the Bible. Many students came from Switzerland and France to hear him, who afterwards returned as evangelists. He speaks of several students in his correspondence with satisfaction. In some cases he was disappointed. He presided over public disputations. He refuted in 1539 a certain Robertus Moshamus, dean of Passau, in a disputation on the merits of good works, and achieved a signal victory to the great delight of the scholars of the city.[2]

But he had also an unpleasant dispute with that worthless theological turncoat, Peter Caroli, who appeared at Strassburg in October, 1539, as a troubler in Israel, as he had done before at Lausanne, and sought to prejudice even Bucer and Capito against Calvin on the subject of the Trinity.[3]

With all his professional duties he found leisure for important literary work, which had been interrupted at Geneva. He prepared a thorough revision of his *Institutes*, which superseded the first, and a commentary on the Epistle to the Romans, which opened the series of his invaluable exegetical works. Both were published at Strassburg by the famous printer Wendelin Rihel in 1539. He had been preceded, in the commentary on Romans, by Melanchthon, Bucer, Bullinger, but he easily surpassed them all. He also wrote, in French, a popular treatise on the Lord's Supper, in which he

him very highly in a letter to Blaarer, Nov. 26, 1525, in Herminjard, I. 440, note 16. He died of the pestilence at Strassburg, 1541.

[1] Calvin to Farel, January, 1539 (Herminjard, V. 230): "*Nuper ad publicam professionem invitus a Capitone protractus sum. Ita quotidie aut lego aut concionor.*" He preached four times, and lectured three times. The salary of 52 guilders for one year was to commence the first of May. It is mentioned in *Annal.* 246, by Herminjard, V. 231, note 19, and by Stricker, 22.

[2] He defeated him again at Worms in the presence of Melanchthon. Jacob Sturm, *Antipappi*, as quoted in Herminjard, VII. 26, note 6.

[3] "*Ter desertor, ter transfuga, ter proditor utriusque partis,*" ne is called by Calvin. See on this unimportant episode Stricker, pp. 30–39.

pointed out a *via media* between the realism of Luther and the spiritualism of Zwingli. Both parties, he says towards the close, have failed and departed from the truth in their passionate zeal, but this should not blind us to the great benefits which God through Luther and Zwingli has bestowed upon mankind. If we are not ungrateful and forgetful of what we owe to them, we shall be well able to pardon that and much more, without blaming them. We must hope for a reconciliation of the two parties.

At the Diet of Regensburg in 1541 he had, with the other Protestant delegates, to subscribe the Augsburg Confession. He could do so honestly, understanding it, as he said expressly, in the sense of the author who, in the year before, had published a revised edition with an important change in the 10th Article (on the doctrine of the Lord's Supper).[1]

Of his masterly answer to Sadolet we shall speak separately.

His many letters from that period prove his constant and faithful attention to the duties of friendship. In his letters to Farel he pours out his heart, and makes him partaker of his troubles and joys, and familiar with public events and private affairs even to little details. Farel could not stand a long separation and paid him two brief visits in 1539 and 1540.

§ 89. *Calvin at the Colloquies of Frankfurt, Worms, and Regensburg.*

CALVIN: *Letters* from Worms, Regensburg, and Strassburg, in *Opera*, XI., and Herminjard, vols. VI. and VII. His report on the Diet at Regensburg (*Les Actes de la journée impériale en la cité de Regenspourg*), in *Opera*, V. 509–684. — MELANCHTHON: Report on the Colloquy at Worms, in Latin, and the Acts of the Colloquy at Regensburg, in German, 1542.

---

[1] Calvin's letter to Martin Schalling, a minister at Regensburg, March, 1557, in *Opera*, XVI. 430: "*Nec vero Augustanam Confessionem repudio, cui pridem volens ac libens subscripsi sicut eam autor ipse interpretatus est.*" His colleagues, Bucer and Capito, understood the Augsburg Confession in the same irenic spirit.

See his *Epistolæ*, ed. Bretschneider, IV. 33–78, and pp. 728 sqq. — STURM: *Antipappus.* — SLEIDAN : *De Statu Eccles. et Reipublicæ Carolo V. Caesare,* Lib. XIII.

HENRY, vol. I. ch. XVII. — DYER, pp. 105 sqq. — STÄHELIN, I. 229–254. — KAMPSCHULTE, I. 328–342. — STRICKER, pp. 27 sqq. — LUDWIG PASTOR (Rom. Cath.) : *Die kirchlichen Reunionsbestrebungen während der Regierung Karls V. Aus den Quellen dargestellt.* Freiburg-i.-B., 1879 (507 pp.). He notices Calvin's influence, pp. 194, 196, 212, 230, 245, 258, 266, 484, but apparently without having read his correspondence, which is one of the chief sources ; he only refers to Kampschulte.

Calvin was employed, with Bucer, Capito, and Sturm, as one of the commissioners of the city and Church of Strassburg, on several public colloquies, which were held during his sojourn in Germany for the healing of the split caused by the Reformation. The emperor Charles V. was anxious, from political motives, to reconcile the Protestant princes to the Roman Church, and to secure their aid against the Turks. The leading theological spirits in these conferences were Melanchthon on the Lutheran, and Julius Pflug on the Roman Catholic side. They aimed to secure the reunion of the Church by mutual concessions on minor differences of doctrine and discipline. But the conferences shared the fate of all compromises. Luther and Calvin would not yield an inch to the pope, while the extreme men of the papal party, like Eck, were as unwilling to make any concession to Protestantism. A fuller account belongs to the ecclesiastical history of Germany.

Calvin, being a foreigner and a Frenchman, ignorant of the German language, acted a subordinate part, though he commanded the respect of both parties for his ability and learning, in which he was not inferior to any. Having no faith in compromises, or in the sincerity of the emperor, he helped to defeat rather than to promote the pacific object of these conferences. He favored an alliance between the Lutheran princes of the Smalkaldian League with Francis I., who, as the rival of Charles V., was inclined to such an alliance. He was encouraged in this line of policy by Queen

Marguerite, who corresponded with him at that time through his friend Sleidan, the statesman and historian.[1] He did succeed in securing, after repeated efforts, a petition of the Lutheran princes assembled at Regensburg to the French king in behalf of the persecuted Protestants in France (May 23, 1541).[2] But he had no more confidence in Francis I. than in Charles V. "The king," he wrote to Farel (September, 1540), "and the emperor, while contending in cruel persecution of the godly, both endeavor to gain the favor of the Roman idol."[3] He placed his trust in God, and in a close alliance of the Lutheran princes among themselves and with the Protestants in France and Switzerland.

He was a shrewd observer of the religious and political movements, and judged correctly of the situation and the principal actors. Nothing escaped his attention. He kept Farel at Neuchâtel informed even about minor incidents.

Calvin attended the first Colloquy at Frankfurt in February, 1539, in a private capacity, for the purpose of making the personal acquaintance of Melanchthon and pleading the cause of his persecuted brethren in France, whom he had more at heart than German politics.

The Colloquy was prorogued to Hagenau in June, 1540, but did not get over the preliminaries.

A more important Colloquy was held at Worms in November of the same year. In that ancient city Luther had made his ever memorable declaration in favor of the liberty of conscience, which in spite of the pope's protest had become an irrepressible power. Calvin appeared at this time in the

---

[1] Herminjard, VII. 198 sqq.; *Opera*, XI. 62 sqq.

[2] Herminjard, VII. 126–128; *Opera*, XI. Ep. 311, p. 220. Comp. Epp. 302, 307, 309. Calvin was not satisfied with the success. "*Quantum ad fratres attinet*," he wrote to Farel (July 6, 1541), "*qui ob evangelium laborant, non feci quod volui.*" Melanchthon incurred the displeasure of the emperor for favoring the French Protestants. Herminjard, VII. 179, note 16.

[3] "*Nihil hic novi audimus, nisi quod Rex et Cæsar, certatim in pios sæviendo, idolum Romanum sibi demereri student.*" Herminjard, VI. 315, comp. note 8.

capacity of a commissioner both of Strassburg and the dukes
of Lüneburg. He went reluctantly, being just then in ill
health and feeling unequal to the task. But he gathered
strength on the spot, and braced up the courage of Melanchthon who, as the spokesman of the Lutheran theologians,
showed less disposition to yield than on former occasions.
He took a prominent part in the discussion. He defeated
Dean Robert Mosham of Passau in a second disputation, and
earned on that occasion from Melanchthon, and the Lutheran
theologians who were present, the distinctive title "the
Theologian" by eminence.[1]

He also wrote at Worms, for his private solace, not for
publication, an epic poem in sixty-one distichs (one hundred
and twenty-two lines), which celebrates the triumph of Christ
and the defeat of his enemies (Eck, Cochlæus, Nausea, Pelar-
gus) after their apparent and temporary victory.[2] He was not
a poetic genius, but by study he made up the defects of nature.[3]

---

[1] Beza (*Opera*, vol. XXI. 130) : " *Calvinus . . . Domino Philippo Melanch-
thoni et Gaspari Crucigero beatæ memoriæ imprimis gratus, adeo ut eum ille sæpe
' Theologum' cognominaverit, hic vero privatum de cœna cum eo colloquium habuerit
eiusque cognitam sententiam diserte comprobarit.*" The Report of the *Strassburger Kirchenordnung*, II. 140, as quoted by Stricker (p. 28, note), says :
" *Auff welchem Colloquio auch Philippus [Melanchthon], Cruciger und andere fur-
neme Theologi Kundtschafft mit Calvino gemacht, dass sie ihn, per Excellentiam,
' den Theologum' genannt.*" Papire Masson (in *Vita Calv.*, as quoted by
Herminjard, VII. 26) : " *Wormatiam missus a civibus excercuit excellentis ingenii
vires tanto applausu theologorum Germaniæ, ut judicio Melanchthonis et reliquorum
singulari privilegio* Theologi *cognomen adeptus sit.*" A theologian in that eminently theological age meant a great deal more than a doctor of divinity nowadays.

[2] *Epinicion ad Christum*, in *Opera*, V. 423–428. Dyer (p. 106), Kampschulte
(I. 333), Henry (I. ch. XVIII), and even Merle d'Aubigné (VII. 23), were
mistaken in calling this *Song of Victory* the only poem of Calvin (I. 333).
He wrote also metrical versions of a number of Psalms, and a lyric hymn to
Christ. See *Opera*, VI. 212–224.

[3] As he says himself in the concluding lines : —

    " *Quod natura negat, studii pius efficit ardor,
        Ut coner laudes, Christe, sonare tuas.*"

He gave the manuscript to a few friends, but did not permit it to be printed
till the court of Toulouse, four years afterwards, put the poem in the list of

The Colloquy of Worms, after having hardly begun, was broken off in January, 1541, to be resumed at the approaching Diet of Regensburg (Ratisbon) in presence of the emperor on his return.

The Diet at Regensburg was opened April 5, 1541. Calvin appeared again as a delegate of Strassburg and at the special request of Melanchthon, but reluctantly and with little hope of success. He felt that he was ill suited for such work, and would only waste time.[1] After long and vexatious delays in the arrival of the deputies, the theological Colloquy was opened and conducted on the Roman Catholic side by Dr. John Eck, professor at Ingolstadt (who had disputed with Luther at Leipzig and promulgated the papal bull of excommunication), Julius Pflug, canon of Mainz (afterwards bishop of Naumburg), and John Gropper, canon and professor of canon law at Cologne; on the Protestant side by Melanchthon of Wittenberg, Bucer of Strassburg, and Pistorius of Nidda in Hesse. Granvella presided in the name of the emperor; Cardinal Contarini, an enlightened and well-disposed prelate, who was inclined to evangelical views and favored a moderate reformation, acted as legate of Pope Paul III., who sent, however, at the same time the intolerant Bishop Morone as a special nuncio. Calvin could see no difference between the two legates, except that Morone would like to subdue the Protestants with bloodshed, Contarini without bloodshed. He was urged to seek an interview with Contarini, but refused. He speaks favorably of Pflug and Gropper, but contemptuously of Eck, the sten-

---

forbidden books, and caused many inquiries after it. Otherwise he would have allowed it to be forgotten. See his preface in *Opera*, V. 422.

[1] "*Invitissimus*," he wrote to Farel (Feb. 19, 1541, in Herminjard, VII. 26), "*Ratisponam trahor: tum quia ipsam profectionem mihi molestissimam prospicio fore: tum quod valde timeo ne diuturna mora futura sit, ut solent sæpe numero comitia ad decimum mensem producere: tum quod minime idoneus mihi ad tales actiones videor, quidquid alii judicent. Sed Deum sequar, qui novit cur mihi hanc necessitatem imponat.*"

torian mouthpiece of the papal party, whom he regarded as an impudent babbler and vain sophist.[1] The French king was represented by Du Veil, whom Calvin calls a "busy blockhead." There were present also a good many bishops, the princes of the German States, and delegates of the imperial cities. The emperor, in an earnest speech, exhorted the divines, through an interpreter, to lay aside private feelings and to study only the truth, the glory of God, the good of the Church, and the peace of the empire.

The Colloquy passed slightly over the doctrines of original sin and the slavery of the will, where the Protestants were protected by the authority of St. Augustin. The Catholics agreed to the evangelical view of justification by faith (without the Lutheran *sola*), and conceded the eucharistic cup to the laity, but the parties split on the doctrine of the power of the Church and the real presence. Calvin was especially consulted on the last point, and gave a decided judgment in Latin against transubstantiation, which he rejected as a scholastic fiction, and against the adoration of the wafer which he declared to be idolatrous.[2] He was displeased with the submissiveness of Melanchthon and Bucer, although he did not doubt the sincerity of their motives. He loved truth and consistency more than peace and unity. "Philip," he wrote to

---

[1] See his judgment of these persons in the letter to Farel, April 24, 1541, in Herminjard, VII. 89. Of Eck he says: "*Nemini dubium est quin Davus ille* [referring to the impudent slave in the ancient drama] *sua importunitate sit omnia turbaturus.*" In a letter of May 12 he reports that Eck was struck by apoplexy (May 10), but recovered, adding: "*Nondum meretur mundus ista bestia liberari.*" (Herminjard, VII. 115 sq.) Eck died Feb. 16, 1543. Franz Burckhard, the Saxon Chancellor, gave, in a letter to Pontanus, April 22, 1541, a similar estimate of Pflug, Gropper, and Eck, and calls the last an "*ebrius sophista, qui pluris facit Bacchum quam ullam religionem*" (Mel. *Epist.* IV. 185). Mosellanus described Eck, as he appeared at the disputation in Leipzig, as "a big-bodied, broad-shouldered, stout-hearted, and impudent man, who looked more like a town-crier than a theologian." Melanchthon thought that "no pious person could listen without disgust to the sophisms and vain subtleties of that talking mountebank."

[2] Calvin to Farel, May 11, 1541, in Herminjard, VII. 111 sq.

Farel (May 12, 1541),[1] "and Bucer have drawn up ambiguous and varnished formulas concerning transubstantiation, to try whether they could satisfy the opposite party by giving them nothing.[2] I cannot agree to this device, although they have reasonable grounds for doing so; for they hope that in a short time they would begin to see more clearly if the matter of doctrine be left open; therefore they rather wish to skip over it, and do not dread that equivocation (flexiloquation) than which nothing can be more hurtful. I can assure you, however, that both are animated with the best intentions, and have no other object in view than to promote the kingdom of Christ; only in their method of proceeding they accommodate themselves too much to the times. . . . These things I deplore in private to yourself, my dear Farel; see, therefore, that they are not made public. One thing I am thankful for, that there is no one who is fighting now more earnestly against the wafer-god,[3] as he calls it, than Brentz."[4]

All the negotiations failed at last by the combined opposition of the extreme men of both parties.[5]

The emperor closed the Diet on the 28th of July, and promised to use his influence with the pope to convene a General Council for the settlement of the theological questions.[6]

Calvin had left Regensburg as soon as he found a chance,

[1] Herminjard, VII. 115.

[2] These formulas are printed in Melanchthon's *Epistolæ*, IV. 262–264.

[3] Or, in-breaded God, *impanatus Deus*.

[4] The leading Lutheran divine of Württemberg, who attended the Colloquy.

[5] The popular wit described the failure of the Colloquy in the line: "*Sie pflügen* (Pflug, Plough), *eggen* (Eck), *graben* (Grobber), *putzen* (Bucer or Butzer), *und backen* (Pistorius, whose German name was Becker), *und richten nichts aus.*" *Corp. Reform.* IV. 335.

[6] Calvin wrote to Viret from Strassburg, Aug. 13, 1541 (Herminjard, VII. 218): "*Finis comitiorum talis fuit qualem ego fore semper divinavi. Tota enim pacificationis actio in fumum abiit, cum ad concilium universale rejecta est, vel saltem nationale, si illud brevi obtineri nequeat. Quid enim hoc aliud est quam frustrari?*"

about the middle of June, much to the regret of Bucer and Melanchthon, who wished to retain him.[1]

His sojourn there was embittered by the ravages of the pestilence in Strassburg, which carried away his beloved deacon, Claude Féray (Feræus), his friends Bedrotus and Capito, one of his boarders, Louis de Richebourg (Claude's pupil), and the sons of Œcolampadius, Zwingli, and Hedio. He was thrown into a state of extreme anxiety and depression, which he revealed to Farel in a melancholy letter of March 29, 1541.[2] "My dear friend Claude, whom I singularly esteemed," he writes, "has been carried off by the plague. Louis (de Richebourg) followed three days afterwards. My house was in a state of sad desolation. My brother (Antoine) had gone with Charles (de Richebourg) to a neighboring village; my wife had betaken herself to my brother's; and the youngest of Claude's scholars [probably Malherbe of Normandy] is lying sick in bed. To the bitterness of grief there was added a very anxious concern for those who survived. Day and night my wife is constantly present to my thoughts, in need of advice, seeing that she is deprived of her husband.[3] . . . These events have produced in me so much sadness that it seems as if they would utterly upset the mind and depress the spirit. You cannot believe the grief which consumes me on account of the death of my dear friend Claude." Then he pays a touching tribute to Féray, who had lived in his house and stuck closer to him than a brother. But the most precious fruit of this sore affliction is his letter of comfort to the distressed father of Louis de Richebourg, which we shall quote in another connection.[4]

---

[1] Letter to Farel from Strassburg, early in July, 1541, in Herminjard, VII. 176. He gives in this letter an account of the later disputes at Regensburg on confession and absolution, the invocation of saints, and the primacy of the pope.

[2] Herminjard, VII. 55 sqq.; *Opera*, XI. 174 sqq.

[3] "*Mihi dies ac noctes animo obversatur uxor, consilii inops, quia capite suo caret.*"

[4] See below, § 92, p. 421.

§ 90. *Calvin and Melanchthon.*

The correspondence between CALVIN (14 letters) and Melanchthon (8 letters), and several letters of CALVIN to FAREL from Strassburg and Regensburg. HENRY, vol. I. chs. XII. and XVII.— STÄHELIN, I. 237–254.— MERLE D'AUBIGNÉ, bk. XI. ch. XIX. (vol. VII. 18–22, in Cates' translation).

One of the important advantages which his sojourn at Strassburg brought to Calvin and to the evangelical Church was his friendship with Melanchthon. It has a typical significance for the relationship of the Lutheran and Reformed Confessions, and therefore deserves special consideration.

They became first acquainted by correspondence through Bucer in October, 1538. Melanchthon brought Calvin at once into a friendly contact with Luther, who read with great pleasure Calvin's answer to Sadolet (perhaps also his *Institutes*), and sent his salutations to him at Strassburg.[1]

Luther never saw Calvin, and probably knew little or nothing of the Reformation in Geneva. His own work was then nearly finished, and he was longing for rest. It is very fortunate, however, that while his mind was incurably poisoned against Zwingli and Zürich, he never came into hostile conflict with Calvin and Geneva, but sent him before his departure a fraternal greeting from a respectful distance. His conduct foreshadows the attitude of the Lutheran Church and theology towards Calvin, who had the highest regard for Luther, and enjoyed in turn the esteem of Lutheran divines in proportion as he was known.

---

[1] In a letter to Bucer, Oct. 14, 1539: "*Salutabis Dn. Joannem Sturmium et Joannem Calvinum reverenter, quorum libellos cum singulari voluptate legi. Sadoleto optarem ut crederet Deum esse creatorem hominum extra Italiam.*" De Wette, V. 211; and Herminjard, VI. 73 (comp. note 6). Calvin refers to this compliment in a letter to Farel, Nov. 20, 1539 (in Herminjard, VI. 130). He also quotes, from a lost letter of Melanchthon, the words: "*Lutherus et Pomeranus [Bugenhagen] Calvinum et Sturmium jusserunt salutari. Calvinus magnam gratiam iniit.*" (*Ibid.* p. 131.) Luther is reported to have expressed also a favorable judgment on Calvin's tract on the Lord's Supper, published at Strassburg, 1541, in French. See vol. VI. 660.

Melanchthon was twelve years older than Calvin, as Luther was thirteen years older than Melanchthon. Calvin, therefore, might have sustained to Melanchthon the relation of a pupil to a teacher. He sought his friendship, and he always treated him with reverential affection.[1] In the dedication of his commentary on Daniel, he describes Melanchthon as "a man who, on account of his incomparable skill in the most excellent branches of knowledge, his piety, and other virtues, is worthy of the admiration of all ages." But while Melanchthon was under the overawing influence of the personality of Luther, the Reformer of Geneva was quite independent of Melanchthon, and so far could meet him on equal terms. Melanchthon, in sincere humility and utter freedom from jealousy, even acknowledged the superiority of his younger friend as a theologian and disciplinarian, and called him emphatically "the theologian."

They had many points of contact. Both were men of uncommon precocity; both excelled, above their contemporaries, in humanistic culture and polished style; both devoted all their learning to the renovation of the Church; they were equally conscientious and unselfish; they agreed in the root of their piety, and in all essential doctrines; they deplored the divisions in the Protestant ranks, and heartily desired unity and harmony consistent with truth.

But they were differently constituted. Melanchthon was modest, gentle, sensitive, feminine, irenic, elastic, temporizing, always open to new light; Calvin, though by nature as modest, bashful, and irritable, was in principle and conviction firm, unyielding, fearless of consequences, and opposed to all compromises. They differed also on minor points of doctrine and discipline. Melanchthon, from a conscientious love of truth and peace, and from regard for the demands of

---

[1] In a letter of 11 Cal. Maii, 1544 (*Opera*, XI. 698), he addresses him as "*ornatissime vir, fidelissime Christi minister, et amice mihi semper honorande. Dominus te semper spiritu suo regat, diuque nobis et ecclesiæ suæ incolumem conservet.*"

practical common sense, had independently changed his views on two important doctrines. He abandoned the Lutheran dogma of a corporal and ubiquitous presence in the eucharist, and approached the theory of Calvin; and he substituted for his earlier fatalistic view of a divine foreordination of evil as well as good the synergistic scheme which ascribes conversion to the co-operation of three causes: the Spirit of God, the Word of God, and the will of man. He conceded to man the freedom of either accepting or rejecting the Gospel salvation, yet without giving any merit to him for accepting the free gift; and on this point he dissented from Calvin's more rigorous and logical system.[1]

The sincere and lasting friendship of these two great and good men is therefore all the more remarkable and valuable as a testimony that a deep spiritual union and harmony may co-exist with theological differences.[2]

Calvin and Melanchthon met at Frankfurt, Worms, and Regensburg under trying circumstances. Melanchthon felt discouraged about the prospects of Protestantism. He deplored the confusion which followed the abolition of the episcopal supervision, the want of discipline, the rapacity of the princes, the bigotry of the theologians. He had allowed himself, with Luther and Bucer, to give his conditional assent to the scandalous bigamy of Philip of Hesse (May, 1540), which was the darkest blot in the history of the German Reformation, and worse than the successive polygamy of Henry VIII. His conscience was so much troubled about his own weakness that, at Weimar, on his way to the Colloquies at Hagenau and Worms, he was brought to the brink

---

[1] On these changes see the biographies of Melanchthon by Galle, Carl Schmidt, and Herrlinger; Gieseler's *Church History;* and Schaff's *Creeds of Christendom*, I. 261 sqq.

[2] Merle d'Aubigné (VII. 19) thinks that "esteem was uppermost in Melanchthon, and affection in Calvin"; that "on the one side the friendship was founded more on reflection (*réfléchi*), on the other it was more spontaneous"; but "on both sides it was the product of their noble and beautiful qualities."

of the grave, and would have died if Luther had not prayed him out of the jaws of the king of terrors. What a contrast between Melanchthon at Worms in 1540, and Luther at Worms in 1521! At the Diet of Regensburg, in 1541, he felt no better. His son was sick, and he dreamed that he had died. He read disaster and war in the stars. His letters to intimate friends are full of grief and anxious forebodings. "I am devoured by a desire for a better life," he wrote to one of them. He was oppressed by a sense of the responsibility that rested upon him as the spokesman and leader of the Reformation in the declining years of Luther, who had been formerly his inspiration and strength. It is natural that in this condition of mind he looked for a new support, and this he found in Calvin. We can thus easily understand his wish to die in his arms. But Calvin himself, though more calm and composed in regard to public affairs, was, as we have seen, deeply distressed at Regensburg by news of the ravages of the pestilence among his friends at Strassburg, besides being harassed by multiplying petitions to return to Geneva. These troubles and afflictions brought their hearts nearer to each other.

In their first personal interview at Frankfurt on the Main, in February, 1539, they at once became intimate, and freely discussed the burning questions of the day, relating to doctrine, discipline, and worship.[1]

As to doctrine, Calvin had previously sent to Melanchthon a summary, in twelve articles, on the crucial topic of the real presence. To these Melanchthon assented without dispute,[2] but confessed that he had no hope of satisfying those

---

[1] Calvin wrote to Farel, after his return to Strassburg, at the end of March, 1539: " *Cum Philippo fuit mihi multis de rebus colloquium.*"

[2] "*Sine controversia ipse assentitur.*" Calvin adds: " *de ipso (Mel.) nihil dubita, quin penitus nobiscum sentiat.*" Herminjard, V. 269. In a previous letter to Farel, October, 1538 (in Herminjard, V. 146 and note 24), he informed Farel that he had sent twelve articles of agreement with a letter to Melanchthon from Strassburg. The articles are lost, but may yet be recovered.

who obstinately insisted on a more gross and palpable presence.[1] Yet he was anxious that the present agreement, such
as it was, might be cherished until at length the Lord shall lead
both sides into the unity of his own truth. This is no doubt
the reason why he himself refrained from such a full and
unequivocal public expression of his own view as might lead
to a rupture in the Lutheran Church. He went as far as he
deemed it prudent by modifying the tenth article of the
Augsburg Confession, and omitting the anti-Zwinglian clause
(1540).

As to ecclesiastical discipline, Melanchthon deplored the
want of it in Germany, but could see no prospect of improvement, till the people would learn to distinguish the yoke of
Christ from the papal tyranny.

As to worship, Calvin frankly expressed his objection to
many ceremonies, which seemed to him to border too closely
on Judaism.[2] He was opposed to chanting in Latin, to
pictures and candles in churches, to exorcism in baptism,
and the like. Melanchthon was reluctant to discuss this
point, but admitted that there was an excess of trifling or
unnecessary Roman Catholic rites retained in deference to
the judgment of the Canonists, and expressed the hope that
some of them would be abandoned by degrees.

After the Colloquy at Regensburg the two Reformers saw
each other no more, but continued to correspond as far as

---

[1] " *Sed fatetur, esse in illa parte nonnullos qui crassius aliquid requirant:
atque id tanta pervicacia, ne dicam tyrannide, ut diu in periculo fuerit, quod eum
videbant a suo sensu nonnihil alienum.*" Herminjard, V. 269. Those men who
outluthered Luther, were not satisfied with the words of institution, *simpliciter*,
but demanded such scholastic terms as *substantialiter, essentialiter, corporaliter,
quantitative, ubiquitaliter, carnaliter*. When Matthæus Zell, preacher in the
Minster at Strassburg, told Melanchthon (in 1536) that he abhorred these
terms as diabolical additions, Melanchthon assented. See Röhrich *Mittheilungen aus der Geschichte der evang. Kirche des Elsasses*, III. 133, as quoted by
Stähelin, I. 169.

[2] Letter to Farel, April, 1539 (Herminjard, V. 292): " *Nuper Philippo in
faciem non dissimulavi, quin mihi admodum illa ceremoniarum copia displiceret.
Videri enim mihi formam quam tenent non procul esse a Judaismo.*"

their time and multiplicity of duties would permit. The correspondence of friendship is apt to diminish with the increase of age and cares. Several letters are preserved, and are most creditable to both parties.[1]

The first letter of Calvin after that Colloquy, is dated Feb. 16, 1543, and is a lengthy answer to a message from Melanchthon.[2]

"You see," he writes, "to what a lazy fellow you have intrusted your letter. It was full four months before he delivered it to me, and then crushed and rumpled with much rough usage. But although it has reached me somewhat late, I set a great value upon the acquisition. . . . Would, indeed, as you observe, that we could oftener converse together were it only by letters. To you that would be no advantage; but to me, nothing in this world could be more desirable than to take solace in the mild and gentle spirit of your correspondence. You can scarce believe with what a load of business I am here burdened and incessantly hurried along; but in the midst of these distractions there are two things which most of all annoy me. My chief regret is, that there does not appear to be the amount of fruit that one may reasonably expect from the labor bestowed; the other is, because I am so far removed from yourself and a few others, and therefore am deprived of that sort of comfort and consolation which would prove a special help to me.

"But since we cannot have even so much at our own choice, that each at his own discretion might pick out the corner of the vineyard where he might serve Christ, we must remain at that post which He Himself has allotted to each. This comfort we have at least, of which no far distant separation can deprive us, — I mean, that resting content with this fellowship which Christ has consecrated with his own blood, and has also confirmed and sealed by his blessed Spirit in our hearts, — while we live on the earth, we may cheer each other with that blessed hope to which your letter calls us that in heaven above we shall dwell forever where we shall rejoice in love and in continuance of our friendship."[8]

There can be no nobler expression of Christian friendship. In the same letter Calvin informs Melanchthon that he had dedicated to him his "Defence of the Orthodox Doctrine

---

[1] In Calvin's *Opera* there are fourteen letters of his to Melanchthon.

[2] Letters of John Calvin by Dr. Jules Bonnet, translated from the original Latin and French by Constable, vol. I. 349. In Calvin's *Opera*, XI. 515. The original copy is in Simler's Collection in the City Library of Zürich.

[8] "*Hoc saltem nobis nulla regionum longinquitas eripiet, quin hac conjunctione, quam Christus sanguine suo consecratam Spiritu quoque suo in cordibus nostris sanxit, contenti, dum vivimus in terra sustineamur beata illa spe, ad quam nos literæ tuæ revocant: in cœlis nos simul perpetuo victuros, ubi amore amicitiaque nostra fruemur.*"

on the Slavery and Deliverance of the Human Will against the Calumnies of Albert Pighius," which he had urged Calvin to write, and which appeared in February, 1543.[1] After some modest account of his labors in Geneva, and judicious reflections on the condition of the Church in Germany, he thus concludes : —

"Adieu, O man of most eminent accomplishments, and ever to be remembered by me and honored in the Lord ! May the Lord long preserve you in safety to the glory of his name and the edification of the Church. I wonder what can be the reason why you keep your *Daniel* a sealed book at home.[2] Neither can I suffer myself quietly, without remonstrance, to be deprived of the benefit of its perusal. I beg you to salute Dr. Martin reverently in my name. We have here with us at present Bernardino of Siena, an eminent and excellent man, who has occasioned no little stir in Italy by his secession. He has requested me that I would greet you in his name. Once more adieu, along with your family, whom may the Lord continually preserve."

On the 11th of May following, Melanchthon thanked Calvin for the dedication, saying :[3] " I am much affected by your kindness, and I thank you that you have been pleased to give evidence of your love for me to all the world, by placing my name at the beginning of your remarkable book, where all the world will see it." He gives due praise to the force and eloquence with which he refuted Pighius, and, confessing his own inferiority as a writer, encourages him to continue to exercise his splendid talents for the edification and encouragement of the Church. Yet, while inferior as a logician and polemic, he, after all, had a deeper insight into the mystery of predestination and free will, although unable to solve it. He gently hints to his friend that he looked too much to one side of the problem of divine sovereignty and human liberty, and says in substance : —

"As regards the question treated in your book, the question of predestination, I had in Tübingen a learned friend, Franciscus Stadianus, who used to

---

[1] " *Defensio sanæ et orthodoxæ doctrinæ de servitute et liberatione humani arbitrii adversus calumnias Alberti Pighii Campensis. Opera,* VI. 225–404.

[2] Melanchthon's Commentary on Daniel appeared in the same year at Wittenberg and Leipzig.

[3] *Opera,* vol. XI. 539–542. Also in *Corp. Reform.* V. 107.

say, I hold both to be true that all things happen according to divine fore-ordination, and yet according to their own laws, although he could not harmonize the two. I maintain the proposition that God is not the author of sin, and therefore cannot will it. David was by his own will carried into transgression.[1] He might have retained the Holy Spirit. In this conflict there is some margin for free will. . . . Let us accuse our own will if we fall, and not find the cause in God. He will help and aid those who fight in earnest. Μόνον θέλησον, says Basilius, καὶ θεὸς προαπαντᾷ. God promises and gives help to those who are willing to receive it. So says the Word of God, and in this let us abide. I am far from prescribing to you, the most learned and experienced man in all things that belong to piety. I know that in general you agree with my view. I only suggest that this mode of expression is better adapted for practical use." [2]

In a letter to Camerarius, 1552, Melanchthon expresses his dissatisfaction with the manner in which Calvin emphasized the doctrine of predestination, and attempted to force the Swiss churches to accept it in the *Consensus Genevensis*.[3]

Calvin made another attempt in 1554 to gain him to his view, but in vain.[4] On one point, however, he could agree to a certain modification; for he laid stress on the spontaneity of the will, and rejected Luther's paradoxes, and his comparison of the natural man to a dead statue.

It is greatly to the credit of Calvin that, notwithstanding his sensitiveness and intolerance against the opponents of his favorite dogma, he respected the judgment of the most eminent Lutheran divine, and gave signal proof of it by publishing a French translation of the improved edition of Melanchthon's *Theological Commonplaces* in 1546, with a commendatory preface of his own,[5] in which he says that the

---

[1] This is a direct contradiction to the assertion in the first edition of his *Loci* (1521), and his commentary on the Romans (1524), that God does all things not *permissive*, but *potenter*, and that he foreordained and wrought the adultery of David, and the treason of Judas, as well as the vocation of Paul. He so understood the Epistle to the Romans. In December, 1525, Luther expressed the same views in his book against Erasmus, which he never recalled, but pronounced one of his best books (1537).

[2] "*Ad usum accommodata.*"

[3] Mel. *Opera*, in the *Corpus Reformatorum*, VII. 390.

[4] *Opera*, XV. 215–217. Dated 6 Calendas Septembris.

[5] The preface is reprinted in his *Opera*, vol. IX. 847–850.

book was a brief summary of all things necessary for a Christian to know on the way of salvation, stated in the simplest manner by the profoundly learned author. He does not conceal the difference of views on the subject of free will, and says that Melanchthon seems to concede to man some share in his salvation; yet in such a manner that God's grace is not in any way diminished, and no ground is left to us for boasting.

This is the only example of a Reformer republishing and recommending the work of another Reformer, which was the only formidable rival of his own chief work on the same subject (the *Institutes*), and differed from it in several points.[1]

The revival of the unfortunate eucharistic controversy by Luther in 1545, and the equally unfortunate controversy caused by the imperial *Interim* in 1548, tried the friendship of the Reformers to the uttermost. Calvin respectfully, yet frankly, expressed his regret at the indecision and want of courage displayed by Melanchthon from fear of Luther and love of peace.

When Luther came out a year before his death with his most violent and abusive book against the "Sacramentarians,"[2] which deeply grieved Melanchthon and roused the just indignation of the Zwinglians, Calvin wrote to Melanchthon (June 28, 1545) : [3] —

"Would that the fellow-feeling which enables me to condole with you, and to sympathize in your heaviness, might also impart the power in some degree at least to lighten your sorrow. If the matter stands as the Zürichers say it does, then they have just occasion for their writing. ... Your Pericles allows himself to be carried beyond all bounds with his love of thunder, especially

[1] Henry justly remarks (I. 376) : "So free were these rare men of ambition, love of glory, and littleness of spirit, that they thought of nothing but the salvation of the world. Calvin wanted France to love Melanchthon as much as he did, and to be converted to Christ through him." Comp. Stähelin, I. 244.

[2] His "Short Confession on the Lord's Supper." See this *History*, vol. VI. 654 sqq.

[3] Bonnet-Constable, I. 442–444; *Opera*, XII. 98–100.

seeing that his own cause is by no means the better of the two. . . . We all of us acknowledge that we are much indebted to him. But in the Church we always must be upon our guard, lest we pay too great a deference to men. It is all over with her when a single individual has more authority than all the rest. . . . Where there is so much division and separation as we now see, it is indeed no easy matter to still the troubled waters, and bring about composure. . . . You will say he [Luther] has a vehement disposition and ungovernable impetuosity; as if that very vehemence did not break forth with all the greater violence when all show themselves alike indulgent to him, and allow him to have his way unquestioned. If this specimen of over-bearing tyranny has sprung forth already as the early blossom in the spring-tide of a reviving Church, what must we expect in a short time, when affairs have fallen into a far worse condition? Let us, therefore, bewail the calamity of the Church and not devour our grief in silence, but venture boldly to groan for freedom. . . . You have studiously endeavored, by your kindly method of instruction, to recall the minds of men from strife and contention. I applaud your prudence and moderation. But while you dread, as you would some hidden rock, to meddle with this question from fear of giving offence, you are leaving in perplexity and suspense very many persons who require from you somewhat of a more certain sound, on which they can repose. . . . Perhaps it is now the will of God to open the way for a full and satisfactory declaration of your own mind, that those who look up to your authority may not be brought to a stand, and kept in a state of perpetual doubt and hesitation. . . .

"In the mean time let us run the race set before us with deliberate courage. I return you very many thanks for your reply, and for the extraordinary kindness which Claude assures me had been shown to him by you.[1] I can form a conjecture what you would have been to myself, from your having given so kind and courteous a reception to my friend. I do not cease to offer my chief thanks to God, who has vouchsafed to us that agreement in opinion upon the whole of that question [on the real presence]; for although there is a slight difference in certain particulars, we are very well agreed upon the general question itself."

When after the defeat of the Protestants in the Smalkaldian War, Melanchthon accepted the Leipzig *Interim* with the humiliating condition of conformity to the Roman ritual, which the German emperor imposed upon them, Calvin was still more dissatisfied with his old friend. He sided, in this case, with the Lutheran non-conformists who, under the lead of Matthias Flacius, resisted the *Interim*, and were put under

---

[1] Claude de Senarcleus, a friend of Calvin, returned from Wittenberg with an album full of pious inscriptions of leading Lutheran divines, which is preserved in the Town Library of Geneva. Bonnet, *l.c.* I. 444.

the ban of the empire.   He wrote to Melanchthon, June 18, 1550, the following letter of remonstrance : [1] —

"The ancient satirist [Juvenal, I. 79] once said, —

'*Si natura negat, facit indignatio versum.*'

"It is at present far otherwise with me.   So little does my present grief aid me in speaking, that it rather renders me almost entirely speechless. . . . I would have you suppose me to be groaning rather than speaking.   It is too well known, from their mocking and jests, how much the enemies of Christ were rejoicing over your contests with the theologians of Magdeburg.[2] . . . If no blame attaches to you in this matter, my dear Philip, it would be but the dictate of prudence and justice to devise means of curing, or at least mitigating, the evil.   Yet, forgive me if I do not consider you altogether free from blame. . . .   In openly admonishing you, I am discharging the duty of a true friend; and if I employ a little more severity than usual, do not think that it is owing to any diminution of my old affection and esteem for you. . . .   I know that nothing gives you greater pleasure than open candor. . . . This is the sum of your defence : that, provided purity of doctrine be retained, externals should not be pertinaciously contended for. . . .   But you extend the distinction of non-essentials too far.   You are aware that the Papists have corrupted the worship of God in a thousand ways.   Several of those things which you consider indifferent are obviously repugnant to the Word of God. . . .   You ought not to have made such large concessions to the Papists. . . . At the time when circumcision was yet lawful, do you not see that Paul, because crafty and malicious fowlers were laying snares for the liberty of believers, pertinaciously refused to concede to them a ceremony at the first instituted by God?   He boasts that he did not yield to them, — no, not for an hour, — that the truth of God might remain intact among the Gentiles (Gal. 2 : 5). . . .   I remind you of what I once said to you, that we consider our ink too precious if we hesitate to bear testimony in writing to those things which so many of the flock are daily sealing with their blood. . . .   The trepidation of a general is more dishonorable than the flight of a whole herd of private soldiers. . . .   You alone, by only giving way a little, will cause more complaints and sighs than would a hundred ordinary individuals by open desertion.   And, although I am fully persuaded that the fear of death never compelled you in the very least to swerve from the right path, yet I am apprehensive that it is just possible that another species of fear may have proved too much for your courage.   For I know how much you are horrified at the charge of rude severity.   But we should remember that reputation must not be accounted by the servants of Christ as of more value than life.   We are no better than Paul was, who remained fearlessly on his way through ' evil and good report.' . . .   You know why I am so vehement.   I had rather die

[1] *Opera*, XIII. 593 sqq.

[2] The zealous Lutherans at Magdeburg which stood out a long siege by the army of the Elector Maurice.

with you a hundred times than see you survive the doctrines surrendered by you. . . .

"Pardon me for loading your breast with these miserable though ineffectual groans. Adieu, most illustrious sir, and ever worthy of my hearty regard. May the Lord continue to guide you by his Spirit, and sustain you by his might. May his protection guard you. Amen."

We have here a repetition of the scene between Paul and Peter at Antioch, concerning the rite of circumcision; and while we admire the frankness and boldness of Paul and Calvin in rebuking an elder brother, and standing up for principle, we must also admire the meekness and humility of Peter and Melanchthon in bearing the censure.

Melanchthon himself, after a brief interruption, reopened the correspondence in the old friendly spirit, during the disturbances of war between Elector Maurice and the Emperor Charles, which made an end of the controversy about the *Adiaphora.*

"How often," wrote Melanchthon, Oct. 1, 1552,[1] "would I have written to you, reverend sir and dearest brother, if I could find more trustworthy letter-carriers. For I would like to converse with you about many most important matters, because I esteem your judgment very highly and know the candor and purity of your soul.[2] I am now living as in a wasp's nest;[3] but perhaps I shall soon be called from this mortal life to a brighter companionship in heaven. If I live longer, I have to expect new exiles; if so, I am determined to turn to you. The studies are now broken up by pestilence and war. How often do I mourn and sigh over the causes of this fury among princes."

In a lengthy and interesting answer Calvin says:[4] —

"Nothing could have come to me more seasonably at this time than your letter, which I received two months after its despatch."[5] He assures him that it was no little consolation to him in his sore trials at Geneva to be assured of the continuance of his affection, which, he was told, had been inter-

---

[1] *Opera,* XIV. 368; *Corp. Ref.,* VII. 1085.

[2] "*Quia et judicium tuum magni facio, et scio integritatem animi et candorem in te summum esse.*"

[3] ὥσπερ ὄνος ἐν σφηκίαις.

[4] Bonnet-Constable, II. 360–366; *Opera,* XIV. 415–418.

[5] Nowadays a letter from Wittenberg will reach Geneva in less than two days.

rupted by the letter of remonstrance above referred to. "I have learned the more gladly that our friendship remains safe, which assuredly, as it grew out of a heartfelt love of piety, ought to remain forever sacred and inviolable."

In the unfortunate affair of Servetus, Melanchthon fully approved Calvin's conduct (1554).[1] But during the eucharistic controversy excited by Westphal, he kept an ominous silence, which produced a coolness between them. In a letter of Aug. 3, 1557, Calvin complains that for three years he had not heard from him, but expresses satisfaction that he still entertained the same affection, and closes with the wish that he may be permitted "to enjoy on earth a most delightful interview with you, and feel some alleviation of my grief by deploring along with you the evils which we cannot remedy."[2]

That wish was not granted. In a letter of Nov. 19, 1558,[3] he gives him, while still suffering from a quartan ague, a minute account of his malady, of the remedies of the doctors, of the formidable coalition of the kings of France and Spain against Geneva, and concludes with these words: —

"Let us cultivate with sincerity a fraternal affection towards each other, the ties of which no wiles of the devil shall ever burst asunder. . . . By no slight shall my mind ever be alienated from that holy friendship and respect which I have vowed to you. . . . Farewell, most illustrious light and distinguished doctor of the Church. May the Lord always govern you by his Spirit, preserve you long in safety, increase your store of blessings. In your turn, diligently commend us to the protection of God, as you see us exposed to the jaws of the wolf. My colleagues and an innumerable crowd of pious men salute you."

On the 19th of April, 1560, Melanchthon was delivered from "the fury of the theologians" and all his troubles. A year after his death Calvin, who had to fight the battle of faith four years longer, during the renewed fury of the eucharistic controversy with the fanatical Heshusius, addressed this touching appeal to his sainted friend in heaven: —

[1] See below, § 139, pp. 706 sqq.　　[2] *Opera*, XVI. 556–558.
[3] *Opera*, XVII. 384–386.

"O Philip Melanchthon! I appeal to thee who now livest with Christ in the bosom of God, and there art waiting for us till we shall be gathered with thee to that blessed rest. A hundred times, when worn out with labors and oppressed with so many troubles, didst thou repose thy head familiarly on my breast and say, 'Would that I could die in this bosom!' Since then I have a thousand times wished that it had been granted to us to live together; for certainly thou wouldst thus have had more courage for the inevitable contest, and been stronger to despise envy, and to count as nothing all accusations. In this manner, also, the malice of many would have been restrained who, from thy gentleness which they call weakness, gathered audacity for their attacks."[1]

Who, in view of this friendship which was stronger than death, can charge Calvin with want of heart and tender affection?

§ 91. *Calvin and Sadolet. The Vindication of the Reformation.*

SADOLETI: *Epistola ad Genevenses* (*Cal. Apr., i.e.* March 18, 1539). — CALVINI: *Responsio ad Sadoletum* (Sept. 1, 1539), *Argentorati ap. Wendelinum Richelium excusa.* In CALV. *Opera*, vol. V. 385–416. Calvin translated it into French, 1540 (republished at Geneva, 1860). English translation of both by HENRY BEVERIDGE in JOHN CALVIN'S *Tracts relating to the Reformation,* Edinburgh (Calvin Translation Society), 1844, pp. 3–68. — BEZA, *Vita C., Opera*, XXI. 129.

HENRY, vol. I. ch. XI. — DYER, 102 sq. — STÄHELIN, I. 291–304. — KAMPSCHULTE, I. 354 sq. (only a brief but important notice). — MERLE D'AUBIGNÉ, bk. XI. ch. XVI., and vol. VI. 570–594.

"Another evil, of a more dangerous kind, arose in the year 1539, and was at once extinguished by the diligence of Calvin. The bishop of Carpentras, at that time, was James Sadolet, a man of great eloquence, but he perverted it chiefly in suppressing the light of truth. He had been appointed a cardinal for no other reason than in order that his moral respectability might serve to put a kind of gloss on false religion. Observing his opportunity in the circumstances which had occurred, and thinking that he would easily ensnare the flock when deprived of its distinguished pastors, he sent, under the pretext of neighborhood (for the

[1] *Opera*, IX. 461.

city of Carpentras is in Dauphiny, which again bounds on
Savoy), a letter to his so-styled 'most Beloved Senate, Council,
and People of Geneva,' omitting nothing which might tend to
bring them both into the lap of the Romish Harlot.[1] There
was nobody at that time in Geneva capable of writing an
answer, and it is, therefore, not unlikely, that, had the letter
not been written in a foreign tongue (Latin), it would, in
the existing state of affairs, have done great mischief to the
city. But Calvin, having read it at Strasbourg, forgot all
his injuries, and forthwith answered it with so much truth
and eloquence, that Sadolet immediately gave up the whole
affair as desperate."

This is Beza's account of that important and interesting
controversy which occurred in the German period of Calvin's
life, and left a permanent impression on history.

The interregnum in Geneva furnished an excellent opportunity for Pierre de la Baume, who had been made a cardinal, to recover his lost bishopric. In this respect he only
followed the example of dispossessed princes. He brought
about, with the help of the pope, a consultation of the bishops
of the neighboring dioceses of Lyons, Vienne, Lausanne,
Besançon, Turin, Langres, and Carpentras. The meeting
was held at Lyons under the presidency of the cardinal of
Tournon, then archbishop of Lyons, and known as a bigoted
persecutor of the Waldenses. Jean Philippe, the chief author
of the banishment of Calvin, aided in the scheme. The
bishop of Carpentras, a town on the borders of Savoy, was
selected for the execution. A better choice could not have
been made.

Jacopo Sadoleto (born at Modena, 1477, died at Rome,
1547) was one of the secretaries of Pope Leo X., bishop of
Carpentras in Dauphiny since 1517, secretary of Clement

---

[1] "In Romanæ illius meretricis gremium," a frequent polemical designation
of the Roman Church, derived from a misinterpretation of the apocalyptic
harlot which means heathen Rome (Rev. 17 : 5).

VII. in 1523, a cardinal since 1536. He was frequently employed in diplomatic peace negotiations between the pope, the king of France, and the emperor of Germany. He had a high reputation as a scholar, a poet, and a gentleman of irreproachable character and devout piety. He best represents the Italian Renaissance in its leaning towards a moderate semi-evangelical reform within the Catholic Church. He was an admirer of Erasmus and Melanchthon, and one of the founders of the *Oratory* at Rome for purposes of mutual edification. He acted, like Contarini, as a mediator between the Roman and Protestant parties, but did not please either. In his commentary on the Epistle to the Romans, he expressed opinions on divine grace and free-will which gave offence in Rome and in Spain. His colleague, Cardinal Bembo, warned him against the study of St. Paul, lest it might spoil his classical style. Sadolet prevented the spread of Calvinism in his diocese, but was opposed to violent persecution. He kindly received the fugitive Waldenses after the terrible massacre of Mérindol and Cabrières, in 1545, and besought the clemency of Francis I. in their behalf. He was grieved and disgusted with the nepotism of Pope Paul III., and declined the appointment to preside over the Council of Trent as papal delegate, on the score of extreme poverty.

This highly respectable dignitary of the papal hierarchy made a very able and earnest effort to win back the orphan Church of Geneva to the sheepfold of Rome. He thereby came involuntarily into a literary conflict with Calvin, in which he was utterly defeated. Fresh from a visit to the pope, he addressed a letter of some twenty or more octavo pages "to his dearly beloved Brethren, the Magistrates, Senate, and Citizens of Geneva." It is written in elegant Latin, and with persuasive eloquence, of which he was a consummate master.

He assumes the air of authority as a cardinal and papal

legate, and begins with an apostolic greeting: "Very dear Brethren in Christ, — Peace to you and with us, that is, with the Catholic Church, the mother of all, both of us and you, love and concord from God, the Father Almighty, and from his Son Jesus Christ, our Lord, together with the Holy Spirit, perfect Unity in Trinity; to whom be praise and dominion for ever and ever." He flatters the Genevese by praising their noble city, the order and form of their republic, the worth of their citizens, and especially their "hospitality to strangers and foreigners," but he casts suspicion on the character and motives of the Reformers. This uncharitable and ungentlemanly reflection mars the beauty and dignity of his address, and weakened its effect upon the citizens of Geneva who, whatever were their religious views, had no doubt about the honesty and earnestness of Farel, Viret, and Calvin.

After this introduction Sadolet gives a very plausible exposition of the principle of the Catholic doctrines, but ignores the Bible. He admits that man is saved by faith alone, but adds the necessity of good works. He then asks the Genevese to decide, "Whether it be more expedient for their salvation to believe and follow what the Catholic Church has approved with general consent for more than fifteen hundred years, or innovations introduced within these twenty-five years by crafty men." He then adduces the stock arguments of antiquity, universality, unity, and inerrancy, while the Protestants were already broken up into warring sects — a manifest indication of falsehood. For "truth," he says, "is always one, while error is varied and multiform; that which is straight is simple, that which is crooked has many turns. Can any one who confesses Christ, fail to perceive that such teaching of the holy Church is the proper work of Satan, and not of God? What does God demand of us? What does Christ enjoin? That we be all one in him."

He closes with an earnest exhortation, and assures the Genevese: "Whatever I possibly can do, although it is very

little, still if I have in me any talent, skill, authority, industry, I offer them all to you and your interests, and will
regard it as a great favor to myself should you be able to
reap any fruit and advantage from my labor and assistance
in things human and divine."

The Council of Geneva politely acknowledged the receipt
of the cardinal's letter with thanks for the compliments
paid to the Genevese, and promised a full reply in due time.
This was March 27. On the next day a number of citizens,
under the lead of François Chamois, entered a protest against
the ordinance by which the Confession of Faith had been
adopted, July 29, 1537, and asked to be released from the
oath. The Romanists took courage. No one could be found
in Geneva who was able to answer the cardinal's letter, and
silence might be construed into consent.

Calvin received a copy of the appeal through Sulzer, a
minister of Bern, wrote an answer of more than twice its
length in six days, and despatched it to Geneva in time to
neutralize the mischief (Sept. 1). Though not mentioned
by name, he was indirectly assailed by the cardinal as the
chief among those who had been denounced as misleaders and
disturbers of the peace of Geneva. He therefore felt it his
duty to take up the pen in defence of the Reformation.

He begins by paying a just tribute to the cardinal for his
"excellent learning and admirable eloquence," which raised
him to a place among the first scholars of the age. Nor did
he impeach his motives. "I will give you credit," he says,
"for having written to the Genevese with the purest intention as becomes one of your learning, prudence, and gravity,
and for having in good faith advised them to the course
which you believed to be to their interest and safety." He
was, therefore, reluctant to oppose him, and he did so only
under an imperative sense of duty. We let him speak for
himself.[1]

---

[1] In the following extracts I make use of the translation of Henry Beveridge, with a few slight changes.

"I profess to be one of those whom, with so much enmity, you assail and stigmatize. For though religion was already established, and the form of the Church corrected, before I was invited to Geneva, yet having not only approved by my suffrage, but studied as much as in me lay to preserve and confirm what had been done by Viret and Farel, I cannot separate my case from theirs. Still, if you had attacked me in my private character, I could easily have forgiven the attack in consideration of your learning, and in honor of letters. But when I see that my ministry, which I feel assured is supported and sanctioned by a call from God, is wounded through my side, it would be perfidy, not patience, were I here to be silent and connive.

"In that Church I have held the office, first of Doctor, and then of Pastor. In my own right I maintain that, in undertaking these offices, I had a legitimate vocation. How faithfully and religiously I have performed them, there is no occasion for now showing at length. Perspicuity, erudition, prudence, ability, or even industry, I will not claim for myself, but that I certainly labored with the sincerity which became me in the work of the Lord, I can in conscience appeal to Christ, my Judge, and all his angels, while all good men bear clear testimony in my favor. This ministry, therefore, when it shall appear to have been of God (as it certainly shall appear after the cause has been heard), were I in silence to allow you to tear and defame, who would not condemn such silence as treachery ? Every person, therefore, now sees that the strongest obligations of duty — obligations which I cannot evade — constrain me to meet your accusations, if I would not with manifest perfidy desert and betray a cause with which the Lord has intrusted me. For though I am for the present relieved of the charge of the Church of Geneva, that circumstance ought not to prevent me from embracing it with paternal affection — God, when he gave it to me in charge, having bound me to be faithful forever."

He repels with modest dignity the frivolous charge of having embraced the cause of the Reformation from disappointed ambition.

"I am unwilling to speak of myself, but since you do not permit me to be altogether silent, I will say what I can consistently with modesty. Had I wished to consult my own interest, I would never have left your party. I will not, indeed, boast that there the road to preferment had been easy to me. I never desired it, and I could never bring my mind to catch at it; although I certainly know not a few of my own age who have crept up to some eminence — among them some whom I might have equalled, and others outstripped. This only I will be contented to say, it would not have been difficult for me to reach the summit of my wishes, viz., the enjoyment of literary ease with something of a free and honorable station. Therefore, I have no fear that any one not possessed of shameless effrontery will object to me, that out of the kingdom of the pope I sought for any personal advantage which was not there ready to my hand."

The Reformer follows the cardinal's letter step by step, and defeats him at every point. He answers his assertions with facts and arguments. He destroys, like a cobweb, his beautiful picture of an ideal Catholicism by a description of the actual papacy of those days, with its abuses and corruptions, which were the real cause of the Reformation. He gives a very dark account, indeed, but it is fully confirmed by what is authentically known of the lives of such popes as Alexander VI. and Leo X., by the invectives of Savonarola, by the observations of Erasmus and Luther on their experience in Rome, by such impartial witnesses as Machiavelli, wʰᵒ says that religion was almost destroyed in Italy owing ᵗᵒ the bad example set by the popes, and even by the testimony of an exceptionally good and pious pope, Adrian VI., who, with all his abhorrence of the Lutheran heresy, officially confessed the absolute necessity of a moral reform in the head and members of the hierarchy.

"We deny not," says Calvin, "that those over whom you preside are churches of Christ, but we maintain that the Roman pontiff, with his whole herd of pseudo-bishops, who have seized upon the pastor's office, are ravening wolves, whose only study has hitherto been to scatter and trample upon the kingdom of Christ, filling it with ruin and devastation. Nor are we the first to make the complaint. With what vehemence does Bernard thunder against Eugenius and all the bishops of his own age? Yet how much more tolerable was its condition than now?

"For iniquity has reached its height, and now those shadowy prelates, by whom you think the Church stands or perishes, and by whom we say that she has been cruelly torn and mutilated, and brought to the very brink of destruction, can bear neither their vices nor the cure of them. Destroyed the Church would have been, had not God, with singular goodness, prevented. For in all places where the tyranny of the Roman pontiff prevails, you scarcely see as many stray and tattered vestiges as will enable you to perceive that these Churches lie half buried. Nor should you think this absurd, since Paul tells you that Antichrist would have his seat in no other place than in the midst of God's sanctuary (2 Thess. 2:4). . . .

"But whatever the character of the men, still, you say, it is written, 'What they tell you, do.' No doubt, if they sit in the chair of Moses. But when, from the chair of verity, they intoxicate the people with folly, it is written, 'Beware of the leaven of the Pharisees' (Matt. 12:6). . . .

"Let your pontiff boast as he may of the succession of Peter: even if he should make good his title to it, he will establish nothing more than that obedience is due to him from the Christian people so long as he himself maintains his fidelity to Christ, and does not deviate from the purity of the gospel. . . . A prophet should be judged by the congregation (1 Cor. 14:29). Whoever exempts himself from this must first expunge his name from the list of the prophets. . . .

"As to your assertion, that our only aim in shaking off this tyrannial yoke was to set ourselves free for unbridled licentiousness after (so help us!) casting away all thoughts of future life, let judgment be given after comparing our conduct with yours. We abound, indeed, in numerous faults; too often do we sin and fall. Still, though truth would, modesty will not, permit me to boast how far we excel you in every respect, unless, perchance, you except Rome, that famous abode of sanctity, which having burst asunder the cords of pure discipline, and trodden all honor under foot, has so overflowed with all kinds of iniquity, that scarcely anything so abominable has ever been before."

At the close of his letter, Sadolet had cited the Reformers as criminals before the judgment-seat of God, in an imaginary confession to the effect that they had been actuated by base motives of pride and disappointed ambition in their assaults upon the holy Church and the vicegerent of Christ, and become guilty of "great seditions and schisms."

Calvin takes up the challenge by a counter-confession, which introduces us into the very heart of the great religious struggle of the sixteenth century, and is perhaps the ablest vindication of the Reformation to be found in the controversial literature of that time. He puts that movement on the ground of the Word of God against the commandments of men, and justifies it by the protests of the Hebrew prophets against the corruptions of the Levitical priesthood, and Christ's fearful denunciations of the Pharisees and Sadducees, who nailed the Saviour to the cross. The same confession contains also an incidental account of the spiritual experience and conversion of the author, who speaks for himself as well as his colleagues. We give it in full.

"Consider now what serious answer you are to make for yourself and your party. Our cause, as it is supported by the truth of God, will be at no loss for a complete defence. I am not speaking of our persons; their safety will be found not in defence, but in humble confession and suppliant deprecation. But in so far as our ministry is concerned, there is none of us who will not be able thus to speak: —

" ' O Lord, I have, indeed, experienced how difficult and grievous it was to bear the invidious accusations with which I was harassed on the earth; but with the same confidence with which I then appealed to Thy tribunal, I now appear before Thee, because I know that in Thy judgment truth always reigns — that truth by whose assurance supported I first ventured to attempt — with whose assistance provided I was able to accomplish whatever I have achieved in Thy Church.

" ' They charged me with two of the worst of crimes — heresy and schism. And the heresy was, that I dared to protest against dogmas which they received. But what could I have done ? I heard from Thy mouth that there was no other light of truth which could direct our souls into the way of life, than that which was kindled by Thy Word. I heard that whatever human minds of themselves conceive concerning Thy Majesty, the worship of Thy Deity, and the mysteries of Thy religion, was vanity. I heard that their introducing into the Church instead of Thy Word, doctrines sprung from the human brain, was sacrilegious presumption.

" ' But when I turned my eyes towards men, I saw very different principles prevailing. Those who were regarded as the leaders of faith, neither understood Thy Word, nor greatly cared for it. They only drove unhappy people to and fro with strange doctrines, and deluded them with I know not what follies. Among the people themselves, the highest veneration paid to Thy Word was to revere it at a distance, as a thing inaccessible, and abstain from all investigation of it.

" ' Owing to this supine state of the pastors, and this stupidity of the people, every place was filled with pernicious errors, falsehoods, and superstition. They, indeed, called Thee the only God, but it was while transferring to others the glory which thou hast claimed for Thy Majesty. They figured and had for themselves as many gods as they had saints, whom they chose to worship. Thy Christ was indeed worshipped as God, and retained the name of Saviour; but where He ought to have been honored, He was left almost without honor. For, spoiled of His own virtue, He passed unnoticed among the crowd of saints, like one of the meanest of them. There was none who duly considered that one sacrifice which He offered on the cross, and by which He reconciled us to Thyself — none who ever dreamed of thinking of His eternal priesthood, and the intercession depending upon it — none who trusted in His righteousness only. That confident hope of salvation which is both enjoined by Thy Word, and founded upon it, had almost vanished. Nay, it was received as a kind of oracle, that it was foolish arrogance, and, as they termed it, presumption for any one trusting to Thy goodness, and the righteousness of Thy Son, to entertain a sure and unfaltering hope of salvation.

" ' Not a few profane opinions plucked up by the roots the first principles of that doctrine which Thou hast delivered to us in Thy Word. The true meaning of Baptism and the Lord's Supper, also, was corrupted by numerous falsehoods. And then, when all, with no small insult to Thy mercy, put confidence in good works, when by good works they strove to merit Thy favor, to procure justification, to expiate their sins, and make satisfaction to Thee (each of these things obliterating and making void the virtue of Christ's cross), they were yet altogether ignorant wherein good works consisted. For, just as if they were not at all instructed in righteousness by Thy law, they had fabricated for themselves many useless frivolities, as a means of procuring Thy favor, and on these they so plumed themselves, that, in comparison of them, they almost contemned the standard of true righteousness which Thy law recommended, — to such a degree had human desires, after usurping the ascendancy, derogated, if not from the belief, at least from the authority, of Thy precepts therein contained.

"'That I might perceive these things, Thou, O Lord, didst shine upon me with the brightness of Thy Spirit; that I might comprehend how impious and noxious they were, Thou didst bear before me the torch of Thy Word; that I might abominate them as they deserved, Thou didst stimulate my soul.

"'But in rendering an account of my doctrine, Thou seest (what my own conscience declares) that it was not my intention to stray beyond those limits which I saw had been fixed by all Thy servants. Whatever I felt assured that I had learned from Thy mouth, I desired to dispense faithfully to the Church. Assuredly, the thing at which I chiefly aimed, and for which I most diligently labored, was, that the glory of Thy goodness and justice, after dispersing the mists by which it was formerly obscured, might shine forth conspicuous, that the virtue and blessings of Thy Christ (all glosses being wiped away) might be fully displayed. For I thought it impious to leave in obscurity things which we were born to ponder and meditate. Nor did I think that truths, whose magnitude no language can express, were to be maliciously or falsely declared.

"'I hesitated not to dwell at greater length on topics on which the salvation of my hearers depended. For the oracle could never deceive which declares (John 17:3): "This is eternal life to know Thee the only true God, and Jesus Christ, whom Thou hast sent."

"'As to the charge of forsaking the Church, which they were wont to bring against me, there is nothing of which my conscience accuses me, unless, indeed, he is to be considered a deserter, who, seeing the soldiers routed and scattered, and abandoning the ranks, raises the leader's standard, and recalls them to their posts. For thus, O Lord, were all thy servants dispersed, so that they could not, by any possibility, hear the command, but had almost forgotten their leader, and their service, and their military oath. In order to bring them together, when thus scattered, I raised not a foreign standard, but that noble banner of Thine which we must follow, if we would be classed among Thy people. Then I was assailed by those who, when they ought to have kept others in their ranks, had led them astray, and when I determined not to desist, opposed me with violence. On this grievous tumults arose, and the contest blazed and issued in disruption.

"'With whom the blame rests it is for Thee, O Lord, to decide. Always, both by word and deed, have I protested how eager I was for unity. Mine, however, was a unity of the Church, which should begin with Thee and end in Thee. For as oft as Thou didst recommend to us peace and concord, Thou, at the same time, didst show that Thou wert the only bond for preserving it.

"'But if I desired to be at peace with those who boasted of being the heads of the Church and pillars of faith, I behoved to purchase it with the denial of Thy truth. I thought that anything was to be endured sooner than stoop to such a nefarious compact. For Thy Anointed Himself hath declared, that though heaven and earth should be confounded, yet Thy Word must endure forever (Matt. 24 : 35).

"'Nor did I think that I dissented from Thy Church because I was at war with those leaders; for Thou hast forewarned me, both by Thy Son, and by the apostles, that that place would be occupied by persons to whom I ought by no means to consent. Christ had predicted not of strangers, but of men who should give themselves out for pastors, that they would be ravenous wolves and false prophets, and had, at the same time, cautioned me to beware of them. Where Christ ordered me to beware, was I to lend my aid? And the apostles declared that there would be no enemies of Thy Church more pestilential than those from within who should conceal themselves under the title of pastors (Matt. 7 : 15; Acts 20 : 29; 2 Pet. 2 : 1; 1 John 2 : 18).

"'Why should I have hesitated to separate myself from persons whom they forewarned me to hold as enemies? I had before my eyes the examples of Thy prophets, who I saw had a similar contest with the priests and false prophets of their day, though these were undoubtedly the rulers of the Church among the Israelitish people. But Thy prophets are not regarded as schismatics, because, when they wished to revive religion, which had fallen into decay, they desisted not, although opposed with the utmost violence. They still remained in the unity of the Church, though they were doomed to perdition by wicked priests, and deemed unworthy of a place among men, not to say saints.

"'Confirmed by their example, I, too, persisted. Though denounced as a deserter of the Church, and threatened, I was in no respect deterred or induced to proceed less firmly and boldly in opposing those, who, in the character of pastors, wasted Thy Church with a more than impious tyranny. My conscience told me how strong the zeal was with which I burned for the unity of Thy Church, provided Thy truth were made the bond of concord. As the commotions which followed were not excited by me, so there is no ground for imputing them to me. Thou, O Lord, knowest, and the fact itself has testified to men, that the only thing I asked was, that all controversies should be decided by Thy Word, that thus both parties might unite with one mind to establish Thy kingdom; and I declined not to restore peace to the Church at the expense of my head, if I were found to have been unnecessarily the cause of tumult.

"'But what did our opponents? Did they not instantly, and like madmen fly to fires, swords, and gibbets? Did they not decide that their only security was in arms and cruelty? Did they not instigate all ranks to the same fury? Did they not spurn at all methods of pacification? To this it is owing that a matter, which might at one time have been settled amicably, has blazed into such a contest. But although, amidst the great confusion, the judgments of men were various, I am freed from all fear, now that we stand at Thy tribunal, where equity, combined with truth, cannot but decide in favor of innocence.'

"Such, Sadolet, is our pleading, not the fictitious one which you, in order to aggravate our case, were pleased to devise, but that the perfect truth of which is known to the good even now, and will be made manifest to all creatures on that day. Nor will those who, instructed by our preaching, have adhered to our cause, be at loss what to say for themselves, since each will be ready with this defence: —

"'I, O Lord, as I had been educated from a boy, always professed the Christian faith. But at first I had no other reason for my faith than that which then everywhere prevailed. Thy Word, which ought to have shone on all Thy people like a lamp, was taken away, or at least suppressed as to us. And lest any one should long for greater light, an idea had been instilled into the minds of all, that the investigation of that hidden celestial philosophy was better delegated to a few, whom the others might consult as oracles — that the highest knowledge befitting plebeian minds was to subdue themselves into obedience to the Church. Then, the rudiments in which I had been instructed were of a kind which could neither properly train me to the legitimate worship of Thy Deity, nor pave the way for me to a sure hope of salvation, nor train me aright for the duties of the Christian life. I had learned, indeed, to worship Thee only as my God, but as the true method of worshipping was altogether unknown to me, I stumbled at the very threshold. I believed, as I had been taught, that I was redeemed by the death of Thy Son from the liability to eternal death, but the redemption I thought of was one whose virtue could never reach me. I anticipated a future resurrection, but hated to think of it, as being an event most dreadful. And this feeling not only had dominion over me in private, but was derived from the doctrine which was then uniformly delivered to the people by their Christian teachers.

"'They, indeed, preached of Thy clemency towards men, but confined it to those who should show themselves deserving of it. They, moreover, placed this desert in the righteousness of works, so that he only was received into Thy favor who reconciled himself to Thee by works. Nor, meanwhile, did they disguise the fact that we are miserable sinners, that we often fall through infirmity of the flesh, and that to all, therefore, Thy mercy behoved to be the common haven of salvation; but the method of obtaining it, which they pointed out, was by making satisfaction to Thee for offences. Then the satisfaction enjoined was, first, after confessing all our sins to a priest, suppliantly to ask pardon and absolution; and, secondly, by good to efface from Thy remembrance our bad actions. Lastly, in order to supply what was still wanting, we were to add sacrifices and solemn expiations. Then, because Thou wert a stern judge and strict avenger of iniquity, they showed how dreadful Thy presence must be. Hence they bade us flee first to the saints, that by their intercession Thou mightest be rendered exorable and propitious to us.

"'When, however, I had performed all these things, though I had some intervals of quiet, I was still far off from true peace of conscience; for, whenever I descended into myself, or raised my mind to Thee, extreme terror seized me — terror which no expiations or satisfactions could cure. And the more closely I examined myself, the sharper the stings with which my conscience was pricked, so that the only solace which remained to me was to delude myself by obliviousness. Still, as nothing better offered, I continued the course which I had begun, when, lo! a very different form of doctrine started up, not one which led us away from the Christian profession, but one which brought it back to its fountain-head, and, as it were, clearing away the dross, restored it to its original purity.

"'Offended by the novelty, I lent an unwilling ear, and at first, I confess, strenuously and passionately resisted; for (such is the firmness or effrontery with which it is natural to men to persist in the course which they have once undertaken) it was with the greatest difficulty I was induced to confess that I had all my life long been in ignorance and error. One thing, in particular, made me averse to those new teachers, viz. reverence for the Church.

"'But when once I opened my ears, and allowed myself to be taught, I perceived that this fear of derogating from the majesty of the Church was groundless. For they reminded me how great the difference is between schism from the Church, and studying to correct the faults by which the Church herself was contaminated. They spoke nobly of the Church, and showed the greatest desire to cultivate unity. And lest it should seem they quibbled on the term Church, they showed it was no new thing for Antichrists to preside there in place of pastors. Of this they produced not a few examples, from which it appeared they aimed at nothing but the edification of the Church, and in that respect were similarly circumstanced with many of Christ's servants whom we ourselves included in the catalogue of saints.

"'For inveighing more freely against the Roman Pontiff, who was reverenced as the Vicegerent of Christ, the Successor of Peter, and the Head of the Church, they excused themselves thus: Such titles as those are empty bugbears, by which the eyes of the pious ought not to be so blinded as not to venture to look at them and sift the reality. It was when the world was plunged in ignorance and sloth, as in a deep sleep, that the pope had risen to such an eminence; certainly neither appointed head of the Church by the Word of God, nor ordained by a legitimate act of the Church, but of his own accord, self-elected. Moreover, the tyranny which he let loose against the people of God was not to be endured, if we wished to have the kingdom of Christ amongst us in safety.

"'And they wanted not most powerful arguments to confirm all their positions. First, they clearly disposed of everything that was then commonly adduced to establish the primacy of the pope. When they had taken away all these props, they also, by the Word of God, tumbled him from his lofty height. On the whole, they make it clear and palpable, to learned and unlearned, that the true order of the Church had then perished, — that the keys under which the discipline of the Church is comprehended had been altered very much for the worse; that Christian liberty had fallen, — in short, that the kingdom of Christ was prostrated when this primacy was reared up. They told me, moreover, as a means of pricking my conscience, that I could not safely connive at these things as if they concerned me not; that so far art Thou from patronizing any voluntary error, that even he who is led astray by mere ignorance does not err with impunity. This they proved by the testimony of Thy Son (Matt. 15:14) : "If the blind lead the blind, both shall fall into the ditch."

" ' My mind being now prepared for serious attention, I at length perceived, as if light had broken in upon me, in what a stye of error I had wallowed, and how much pollution and impurity I had thereby contracted. Being exceedingly alarmed at the misery into which I had fallen, and much more at that which threatened me in the view of eternal death, I, as in duty bound, made it my first business to betake myself to Thy way, condemning my past life, not without groans and tears.

" ' And now, O Lord, what remains to a wretch like me, but, instead of defence, earnestly to supplicate Thee not to judge according to its deserts that fearful abandonment of Thy Word, from which, in Thy wondrous goodness, Thou hast at last delivered me.'

" Now, Sadolet, if you please, compare this pleading with that which you have put into the mouth of your plebeian. It will be strange if you hesitate which of the two you ought to prefer. For the safety of that man hangs by a thread whose defence turns wholly on this — that he has constantly adhered to the religion handed down to him from his forefathers. At this rate, Jews and Turks and Saracens would escape the judgment of God.

" Away, then, with this vain quibbling at a tribunal which will be erected, not to approve the authority of man, but to condemn all flesh of vanity and falsehood, and vindicate the truth of God only."

Calvin descends to repel with just indignation the groundless charge of avarice and greed which Sadolet was not ashamed to cast upon the Reformers, who might have easily reached the dignity and wealth of bishops and cardinals, but who preferred to live and die in poverty for the sake of their sacred convictions.

" Would not," he asked, " the shortest road to riches and honors have been to accept the terms which were offered at the very first ? How much would your pontiff then have paid to many for their silence ? How much would he pay for it even at the present day ? If they were actuated in the least degree by avarice, why do they cut off all hope of improving their fortune, and prefer to be thus perpetually wretched, rather than enrich themselves without difficulty and in a moment ?

" But ambition, forsooth, withholds them ! What ground you had for this other insinuation I see not, since those who first engaged in this cause could expect nothing else than to be spurned by the whole world, and those who afterwards adhered to it, exposed themselves knowingly and willingly to endless insults and revilings from every quarter."

He then answers to " the most serious charge of all " : that the Reformers had " dismembered the Spouse of Christ," while in fact they attempted " to present her as a chaste virgin of Christ," and, "seeing her polluted by base seducers, to recall her to conjugal fidelity," after having been defiled by the idolatry of image-worship and numberless superstitions. Peace and unity can only be found in Christ and his truth. He concludes with the wish: —

"May the Lord grant, Sadolet, that you and all your party may at length perceive that the only true bond of Church unity is Christ the Lord, who has reconciled us to God the Father, and will gather us out of our present dispersion into the fellowship of His body, that so, through His one Word and Spirit, we may grow together into one heart and one soul."

Such is a summary of that remarkable Answer — a masterpiece of dignified and gentlemanly theological controversy. There is scarcely a parallel to it in the literature of that age, which teems with uncharitable abuse and coarse invective. Melanchthon might have equalled it in courtesy and good taste, but not in adroitness and force. No wonder that the old lion of Wittenberg was delighted with this triumphant vindication of the evangelical Reformation by a young Frenchman, who was to carry on the conflict which he himself had begun twenty years before by his Theses and his heroic stand at the Diet of Worms. "This answer," said Luther to Cruciger, who had met Calvin at the Colloquies in Worms and Regensburg, "has hand and foot, and I rejoice that God raises up men who will give the last blow to popery, and finish the war against Antichrist which I began."[1]

---

[1] See vol. VI. 659. Kampschulte's impartial judgment on the Answer to Sadolet is worth quoting (I. 354): "*Es ist in Wahrheit eine der glänzendsten Streitschriften, die je aus seiner Feder geflossen, und auch wer seine Anschauungen nicht theilt, wird ihm in diesem Streite die Palme zuerkennen müssen. . . . Er entwickelt in der Vertheidigung des neuen Glaubenssystems eine Kraft der Rede, eine Gewandtheit der Beweisführung und eine Fülle der Gedanken, welche die rhetorischen, sentimentalen, oft auch inhaltsarmen Phrasen des Gegners um so mehr in ihrer Schwäche zeigen. Den Glanzpunkt der Schrift Calvin's bildet aber vielleicht seine eigene Vertheidigung. Mit Recht durfte er den versteckten Angriffen des Cardinals gegenüber auf sein vergangenes Leben hinweisen, um den Beweis zu liefern, dass nicht die Aussicht auf irdischen Gewinn oder äussere Ehren, sondern seine ernste Ueberzeugung seine Schritte geleitet, dass er erst nach schweren Kämpfen von der katholischen Kirche sich losgesagt. Diese Schrift war es, welche auch Luther's*

The Answer made a deep and lasting impression. It was widely circulated, with Sadolet's Letter, in manuscript, printed in Latin, first at Strassburg, translated into French, and published in both languages by the Council of Geneva at the expense of the city (1540). The prelates who had met at Lyons lost courage; the papal party in Geneva gave up all hope of restoring the mass. Three years afterwards Cardinal Pierre de la Baume died — the last bishop of Genèva.

§ 92. *Calvin's Marriage and Home Life.*

CALVIN's *Letters* to Farel and Viret quoted below.

JULES BONNET: *Idelette de Bure, femme de Calvin.* In the "Bulletin de la Société de l'histoire du protestantisme français." Quatrième année. Paris, 1856. pp. 636–646. — D. LENOIR, *ibid.* 1860. p. 26. (A brief note.)

HENRY, I. 407 sqq. — DYER, 99 sqq. — STÄHELIN, I. 272 sqq. — MERLE D'AUBIGNÉ, bk. XI. ch. XVII. (vol. VI. 601–608). — STRICKER, *l.c.* 42–50. — (KAMPSCHULTE is silent on this topic.)

The most important event in Calvin's private life during his sojourn in Germany was his marriage, which took place early in August, 1540.[1] He expresses his views on marriage in his comments on Ephesians 5 : 28–33. " It is a thing against nature," he remarks, " that any one should not love his wife, for God has ordained marriage in order that two may be made one person — a result which, certainly, no other alliance can bring about. When Moses says that a man shall leave father and mother and cleave unto his wife, he shows that a man ought to prefer marriage to every other union, as being the holiest of all. It reflects our union with Christ, who infuses his very life unto us; for we are flesh of his

Herz für den wälschen Rivalen erwärmte. Damals konnte Melanchthon nach Strassburg melden, dass Calvin in Wittenberg 'hoch in Gnaden stehe.'"

[1] The precise day is not known. Before Aug. 17 he was a married man, and received congratulations and greetings to his wife from Libertet (*Opera*, XI. Ep. 234, fol. 77). Merle d'Aubigné wrongly puts his marriage at the *end* of August; Bonnet and Stähelin, in September.

flesh, and bone of his bone. This is a great mystery, the dignity of which cannot be expressed in words."

He himself was in no hurry to get married, and put it off till he was over thirty. He rather boasted that people could not charge him with having assailed Rome, as the Greeks besieged Troy, for the sake of a woman. What led him first to think of it, was the sense of loneliness and the need of proper care, that he might be able the better to serve the Church. He had a housekeeper, with her son, a woman of violent temper who sorely tried his patience. At one time she abused his brother so violently that he left the house, and then she ran away, leaving her son behind. The disturbance made him sick.[1]

He was often urged by his friend Farel (who himself found no time to think of marrying till his old age), and by Bucer, to take a wife, that he might enjoy the comforts of a well-ordered home. He first mentions the subject in a letter to Farel, from Strassburg, May 19, 1539, in which he says: "I am none of those insane lovers who, when once smitten with the fine figure of a woman, embrace also her faults. This only is the beauty which allures me, if she be chaste, obliging, not fastidious, economical, patient, and careful for my health.[2] Therefore, if you think well of it, set out immediately, lest some one else [Bucer?] gets the start of you. But if you think otherwise we will let it pass." It seems Farel could not find a person that combined all these qualities, and the matter was dropped for several months.

In Feb. 6, 1540, Calvin, in a letter to the same friend, touched again upon the subject of matrimony, but only incidentally, as if it were a subordinate matter. After informing

---

[1] He tells the story to Farel, September, 1540, shortly after his marriage. *Opera*, XI. Ep. 238 (fol. 83 sq.), and Herminjard, VI. 313.

[2] "*Hæc sola est quæ me illectat pulchritudo, si pudica est, si morigera, si non fastuosa, si parca, si patiens, si spes est de mea valetudine fore solicitam.*" Herminjard, V. 314.

him about his trouble with Caroli, his discussion with Hermann, an Anabaptist, the good understanding of Charles V. and Francis I., and the alarm of the Protestant princes of Germany, he goes on to say: " Nevertheless, in the midst of such commotions as these, I am so much at my ease as to have the audacity to think of taking a wife. A certain damsel of noble rank has been proposed to me,[1] and with a fortune above my condition. Two considerations deterred me from that connection — because she did not understand our language, and because I feared she might be too mindful of her family and education." [2]

He sent his brother for another lady, who was highly recommended to him. He expected to get married March 10, and invited Farel to celebrate the wedding. But this project also failed, and he thought of abandoning all further attempts.

At last he married a member of his congregation, Idelette de Bure, the widow of Jean Stordeur (or Storder) of Liège,[3] a prominent Anabaptist whom he had converted to the orthodox faith,[4] and who had died of the pestilence in the previous February. She was probably the daughter of Lambert de Bure who, with six of his fellow-citizens, had been deprived of his property and banished forever, after having been legally convicted of heresy in 1533.[5] She was the mother of several children, poor, and in feeble health. She lived in retirement, devoted to the education of her children, and enjoyed the esteem of her friends for her good qualities of

[1] Probably by Bucer. She was of a patrician family of Strassburg, and her brother a great admirer of Calvin and anxious for the match.

[2] Herminjard, VI. 167 sq. It seems that the lady had no disposition to learn French, and asked time for consideration.

[3] Not of "une petite ville de la Gueldre," as Bonnet states (l.c., p. 639). Beza calls him "Storder Leodinensis."

[4] Florimond de Ræmond: " Calvin épousa la veuve de Jean Lestordeur, natif de Liège, de religion anabaptiste ; il l'a changée à son opinion : elle était appelée Idelette de Bure."

[5] According to Lenoir of Liège, in " Bulletin," etc., 1860, p. 26.

head and heart. Calvin visited her frequently as pastor, and was attracted by her quiet, modest, gentle character. He found in her what he desired — firm faith, devoted love, and domestic helpfulness. He calls her "the excellent companion of my life," "the ever-faithful assistant of my ministry," and a "rare woman."[1] Beza speaks of her as "a grave and honorable lady."[2]

Calvin lived in happy wedlock, but only for nine years. His wife was taken from him at Geneva, after a protracted illness, early in April, 1549. He felt the loss very deeply, and found comfort only in his work. He turned from the coffin to his study table, and resumed the duties of his office with quiet resignation and conscientious fidelity as if nothing had happened. He remained a widower the remaining fifteen years of his life. "My wife, a woman of rare qualities," he wrote, "died a year and a half ago, and I have now willingly chosen to lead a solitary life."

We know much less of Calvin's domestic life than of Luther's. He was always reticent concerning himself and his private affairs, while Luther was very frank and demonstrative. In selecting their wives neither of the Reformers had any regard to the charms of beauty and wealth which attract most lovers, nor even to intellectual endowment; they looked only to moral worth and domestic virtue. Luther married at the age of forty-one, Calvin at the age of thirty-one. Luther married a Catholic ex-nun, after having vainly recommended her to his friend Amsdorf, whom she proudly refused, looking to higher distinction. He married her under a sudden impulse, to the consternation of his friends, in the midst of the disturbances of the Peasants' War, that he might please his father, tease the pope, and vex the

---

[1] "*Optima socia vitæ*"; "*fida ministerii me iadjutrix*" (letter to Viret, April 7, 1549); "*singularis exempli femina*," etc.

[2] *Vita Calv.* (*Opera*, XXI. 130): "*Viduam Idelletam nomine, gravem honestumque feminam, Calvinus ex Buceri consilio uxorem duxit.*"

devil.   Calvin married, like Zwingli, a Protestant widow with several children; he married from esteem rather than affection, after due reflection and the solicitation of friends.

Katherine Luther cut a prominent figure in her husband's personal history and correspondence, and survived him several years, which she spent in poverty and affliction. Idelette de Bure lived in modest retirement, and died in peace fifteen years before Calvin.   Luther submitted as "a willing servant" to the rule of his "Lord Kathe," but he loved her dearly, played with his children in childlike simplicity, addressed to her his last letters, and expressed his estimate of domestic happiness in the beautiful sentence: "The greatest gift of God to man is a pious, kindly, God-fearing, domestic wife." [1]

Luther's home life was enlivened and cheered by humor, poetry, and song; Calvin's was sober, quiet, controlled by the fear of God, and regulated by a sense of duty, but none the less happy.   Nothing can be more unjust than the charge that Calvin was cold and unsympathetic.[2]

His whole correspondence proves the reverse.   His letters on the death of his wife to his dearest friends reveal a deep fountain of tenderness and affection.   To Farel he wrote, April 2, 1549: — [3]

---

[1] "*Die Welt hat nach Gottes Wort keinen lieblicheren Schatz auf Erden, denn den heiligen Ehestand.   Gottes höchste Gabe ist ein fromm, freundlich, gottesfürchtig und häuslich Gemahl haben, mit der du friedlich lebest, der du darfst alle dein Gut, ja dein Leib und Leben vertrauen, mit der du Kinderlein zeugest.*"   See Köstlin, *Luther's Leben*, p. 578, and Schaff, *History of the Chr. Church*, VI. §§ 77 and 78, pp. 454 sqq.

[2] "*Calvin*," says J. Bonnet, in his sketch of Idelette de Bure (*l.c.*, p. 637) "*fut grand sans cesser d'être bon ; il unit les qualités du cœur aux dons du génie ; il ressentit et il inspira les plus pures amitiés; il connut, enfin, les félicités domestiques dans une union trop courte, dont le mystère, à demi révélé par sa correspondance, répand un jour mélancolique et doux sur sa vie.*" — "There was in Calvin," says Merle d'Aubigné (VI. 602), "a lofty intellect, a sublime genius, but also that love of kindred, those affections of the heart, which complete the great man."

[3] *Opera*, Ep. 1171 (fol. 228).   The letter is wrongly dated April 11 by Henry and Bonnet (II. 203), who mistook 11 for Roman figures.

"Intelligence of my wife's death has perhaps reached you before now. I do what I can to keep myself from being overwhelmed with grief. My friends also leave nothing undone that may administer relief to my mental suffering. When your brother left, her life was all but despaired of. When the brethren were assembled on Tuesday, they thought it best that we should join together in prayer. This was done. When Abel, in the name of the rest, exhorted her to faith and patience, she briefly (for she was now greatly worn) stated her frame of mind. I afterwards added an exhortation, which seemed to me appropriate to the occasion. And then, as she had made no allusion to her children, I, fearing that, restrained by modesty, she might be feeling an anxiety concerning them, which would cause her greater suffering than the disease itself, declared in the presence of the brethren, that I should henceforth care for them as if they were my own. She replied, 'I have already committed them to the Lord.' When I replied, that that was not to hinder me from doing my duty, she immediately answered, 'If the Lord shall care for them, I know they will be commended to you.' Her magnanimity was so great, that she seemed to have already left the world. About the sixth hour of the day, on which she yielded up her soul to the Lord, our brother Bourgouin addressed some pious words to her, and while he was doing so, she spoke aloud, so that all saw that her heart was raised far above the world. For these were her words: 'O glorious resurrection! O God of Abraham, and of all our fathers, in thee have the faithful trusted during so many past ages, and none of them have trusted in vain. I also will hope.' These short sentences were rather ejaculated than distinctly spoken. This did not come from the suggestion of others, but from her own reflections, so that she made it obvious in few words what were her own meditations. I had to go out at six o'clock. Having been removed to another apartment after seven, she immediately began to decline. When she felt her voice suddenly failing her she said: 'Let us pray; let us pray. All pray for me.' I had now returned. She was unable to speak, and her mind seemed to be troubled. I, having spoken a few words about the love of Christ, the hope of eternal life, concerning our married life, and her departure, engaged in prayer. In full possession of her mind, she both heard the prayer, and attended to it. Before eight she expired, so calmly, that those present could scarcely distinguish between her life and her death. I at present control my sorrow so that my duties may not be interfered with. But in the meanwhile the Lord has sent other trials upon me. Adieu, brother, and very excellent friend. May the Lord Jesus strengthen you by His Spirit; and may He support me also under this heavy affliction, which would certainly have overcome me, had not He, who raises up the prostrate, strengthens the weak, and refreshes the weary, stretched forth His hand from heaven to me. Salute all the brethren and your whole family.

To Viret he wrote a few days later, April 7, 1549, as follows: —

"Although the death of my wife has been exceedingly painful to me, yet I subdue my grief as well as I can. Friends, also, are earnest in their duty to me. It might be wished, indeed, that they could profit me and themselves more; yet one can scarcely say how much I am supported by their attentions. But you know well enough how tender, or rather soft, my mind is. Had not a powerful self-control, therefore, been vouchsafed to me, I could not have borne up so long. And truly mine is no common source of grief. I have been bereaved of *the best companion of my life*, of one who, had it been so ordered, would not only have been the willing sharer of my exile and poverty, but even of my death.[1] During her life she was *the faithful helper of my ministry*.

"From her I never experienced the slightest hindrance. She was never troublesome to me throughout the entire course of her illness; she was more anxious about her children than about herself. As I feared these private cares might annoy her to no purpose, I took occasion, on the third day before her death, to mention that I would not fail in discharging my duty to her children. Taking up the matter immediately, she said, 'I have already committed them to God.' When I said that that was not to prevent me from caring for them, she replied, 'I know you will not neglect what you know has been committed to God.' Lately, also, when a certain woman insisted that she should talk with me regarding these matters, I, for the first time, heard her give the following brief answer: 'Assuredly the principal thing is that they live a pious and holy life. My husband is not to be urged to instruct them in religious knowledge and in the fear of God. If they be pious, I am sure he will gladly be a father to them; but if not, they do not deserve that I should ask for aught in their behalf.' This nobleness of mind will weigh more with me than a hundred recommendations. Many thanks for your friendly consolation.

"Adieu, most excellent and honest brother. May the Lord Jesus watch over and direct yourself and your wife. Present my best wishes to her and to the brethren."

In reply to this letter, Viret wrote to Calvin, April 10, 1549: —

"Wonderfully and incredibly have I been refreshed, not by empty rumors alone, but especially by numerous messengers who have informed me how you, with a heart so broken and lacerated, have attended to all your duties even better than hitherto, . . . and that, above all, at a time when grief was so fresh, and on that account all the more severe, might have prostrated your mind. Go on then as you have begun, . . . and I pray God most earnestly, that you may be enabled to do so, and that you may receive daily greater comfort and be strengthened more and more."

Calvin's character shines in the same favorable light at the loss of his only son who died in infancy (1542). He thanked Viret and his wife (he always sends greetings to Viret's wife

---

[1] "*Quæ si quid accidisset durius, non exilii tantum ac inopiæ voluntaria comes, sed mortis quoque futura erat.*" *Opera*, VIII. Ep. 1173 (fol. 230).

and daughter) for their tender sympathy with him in this bereavement, stating that Idelette would write herself also but for her grief. "The Lord," he says, "has dealt us a severe blow in taking from us our infant son; but it is our Father who knows what is best for his children."[1] He found compensation for his want of offspring in the multitude of his spiritual children. "God has given me a little son, and taken him away; but I have myriads of children in the whole Christian world."[2]

Of Calvin's deep sympathy with his friends in domestic affliction we have a most striking testimony in a private letter which was never intended for publication. It is the best proof of his extraordinary fidelity as a pastor. While he was in attendance at Ratisbon, the pestilence carried away, among other friends, Louis de Richebourg, who together with his older brother, Charles, lived in his house at Strassburg as a student and *pensionnaire*, under the tutorship of Claude Féray, Calvin's dearly beloved assistant. On hearing the sad intelligence, early in April, 1541, he wrote to his father—a gentleman from Normandy, probably the lord of the village de Richebourg between Rouen and Beauvais, but otherwise unknown to us—a long letter of condolence and comfort, from which we give the following extracts:[3]—

[1] Aug. 19, 1542, at the close. *Opera*, XI. 430.

[2] "*Dederat mihi Deus filiolum, abstulit; hoc quoque recenset* [Balduin or Baudouin, a jurisconsult] *inter probra liberis me carere. Atqui mihi filiorum sunt myriades in toto orbe Christiano.*" (*Responsio ad Balduini Convitia*, Geneva, 1561.) Roman writers speak of the sterility of his marriage as a reproach and judgment. Audin corrects them, but adds (ch. XIX.) that Calvin "shed no tears" over the loss of his son, and that "God did not permit him to become a father a second time!" Bonnet asserts (*l.c.* 643) that Calvin had two other children, a daughter and a son, who died likewise in infancy, and refers to a letter of Calvin to Viret of 1544; but this is a mistake, for Calvin, long after the death of his wife, speaks only of one infant son (*filiolus*), and Colladon, in his biography, says (*Opera*, XXI. 61) that Idelette de Bure had one son from him (*elle eut un fils de lui*).

[3] The letter was written in French and translated into Latin by Beza in his edition of *Calvini Epistolæ*, Genevæ, 1575, p. 280 (under the wrong date of

"RATISBON (Month of April), 1541.

"When I first received the intelligence of the death of Claude and of your son Louis, I was so utterly overpowered (*tout esperdu et confus en mon esprit*) that for many days I was fit for nothing but to weep; and although I was somehow upheld before the Lord by those aids wherewith He sustains our souls in affliction, yet among men I was almost a nonentity; so far at least as regards my discharge of duty, I appeared to myself quite as unfit for it as if I had been half dead (*un homme demi-mort*). On the one hand, I was sadly grieved that a most excellent and faithful friend [Claude Féray] had been snatched away from me — a friend with whom I was so familiar, that none could be more closely united than we were; on the other hand, there arose another cause of grief, when I saw the young man, your son, taken away in the very flower of his age, a youth of most excellent promise, whom I loved as a son, because, on his part, he showed that respectful affection toward me as he would to another father.

"To this grievous sorrow was still added the heavy and distressing anxiety we experienced about those whom the Lord had spared to us. I heard that the whole household were scattered here and there. The danger of Malherbe [1] caused me very great misery, as well as the cause of it, and warned me also as to the rest. I considered that it could not be otherwise but that my wife must be very much dismayed. Your Charles,[2] I assure you, was continually recurring to my thoughts; for in proportion as he was endowed with that goodness of disposition which had always appeared in him towards his brother as well as his preceptor, it never occurred to me to doubt but that he would be steeped in sorrow and soaked in tears. One single consideration somewhat relieved me, that he had my brother along with him, who, I hoped, would prove no small comfort in this calamity; even that, however, I could not reckon upon, when at the same time I recollected that both were in jeopardy, and neither of them were yet beyond the reach of danger. Thus, until the letter arrived which informed me that Malherbe was out of danger, and that Charles and my brother, together with my wife and the others, were safe,[3] I would have been all but utterly cast down, unless, as I have already mentioned, my heart was refreshed in prayer and private meditations, which are suggested by His Word. . . .

"The son whom the Lord had lent you for a season, He has taken away. There is no ground, therefore, for those silly and wicked complaints of foolish men: O blind death! O hard fate! O implacable daughters of Destiny!

1540). See *Opera*, XI. 188 sqq.; Herminjard, VII. 66–73; Bonnet-Constable, I. 222–229. I have used Constable's translation after comparing it with the French original. The concluding part, however, is only extant in Beza's Latin version.

[1] Probably the youngest of Féray's pupils, a native of Normandy. Herminjard, VII. 55, note 6.

[2] The older son of M. de Richebourg.

[3] "*Charles et mon frèrè, avec ma femme et les autres se portoyent bien.*" This explains why Calvin did not hurry back to Strassburg earlier than he did.

O cruel fortune! The Lord who had lodged him here for a season, at this stage of his career has called him away. What the Lord has done, we must, at the same time, consider has not been done rashly, nor by chance, neither from having been impelled from without, but by that determinate counsel, whereby He not only foresees, decrees, and executes nothing but what is just and upright in itself, but also nothing but what is good and wholesome for us. Where justice and good judgment reign paramount, there it is impious to remonstrate. When, however, our advantage is bound up with that goodness, how great would be the degree of ingratitude not to acquiesce, with a calm and well-ordered temper of mind, in whatever is the wish of our Father. . . .

"It is God who has sought back from you your son, whom He had committed to you to be educated, on the condition that he might always be His own. And, therefore, He took him away, because it was both of advantage to him to leave this world, and by this bereavement to humble you, or to make trial of your patience. If you do not understand the advantage of this, without delay, first of all, setting aside every other object of consideration, ask of God that He may show you. Should it be His will to exercise you still farther, by concealing it from you, submit to that will, that you may become wiser than the weakness of thine own understanding can ever attain to.

"In what regards your son, if you bethink yourself how difficult it is, in this most deplorable age to maintain an upright course through life, you will judge him to be blessed, who, before encountering so many coming dangers which already were hovering over him, and to be encountered in his day and generation, was so early delivered from them all. He is like one who has set sail upon a stormy and tempestuous sea, and before he has been carried out into the deeps, gets in safety to the secure haven. Nor, indeed, is long life to be reckoned so great a benefit of God, that we can lose anything, when separated only for the space of a few years, we are introduced to a life which is far better. Now, certainly, because the Lord Himself, who is the Father of us all, had willed that Louis should be put among the children as a son of His adoption, He bestowed this benefit upon you, out of the multitude of His mercies, that you might reap the excellent fruit of your careful education before his death; whence also you might know your interest in the blessings that belonged to you, 'I will be thy God, and the God of thy seed.'

"From his earliest boyhood, so far as his years allowed, Louis was grounded in the best studies, and had already made such a competent proficiency and progress, that we entertained great hope of him for the future. His manners and behavior had met with the approval of all good men. If at any time he fell into error, he not only patiently suffered the word of admonition, but also that of reproof, and proved himself teachable and obedient, and willing to hearken to advice. . . . That, however, which we rate most highly in him was, that he had imbibed so largely the principles of piety, that he had not merely a correct and true understanding of religion, but had also been faithfully imbued with the unfeigned fear and reverence of God.

"This exceeding kindness of God toward your offspring ought with good reason to prevail more effectually with you in soothing the bitterness of death, than death itself have power to inflict grief upon you.

" With reference to my own feelings, if your sons had never come hither at all, I should never have been grieved on account of the death of Claude and Louis. Never, however, shall this most crushing sorrow, which I suffer on account of both, so overcome me, as to reflect with grief upon that day on which they were driven hither by the hand of God to us, rather than led by any settled purpose of their own, when that friendship commenced which has not only continued undiminished to the last, but which, from day to day, was rather increased and confirmed. Whatever, therefore, may have been the kind or model of education they were in search of, I rejoice that they lived under the same roof with me. And since it was appointed them to die, I rejoice also that they died under my roof, where they rendered back their souls to God more composedly, and in greater circumstances of quiet, than if they had happened to die in those places where they would have experienced greater annoyance from the importunity of those by whom they ought to have been assisted, than from death itself. On the contrary, it was in the midst of pious exhortations, and while calling upon the name of the Lord, that these sainted spirits fled from the communion of their brethren here to the bosom of Christ. Nor would I desire now to be free from all sorrow at the cost of never having known them. Their memory will ever be sacred to me to the end of my days, and I am persuaded that it will also be sweet and comforting.

" But what advantage, you will say, is it to me to have had a son of so much promise, since he has been torn away from me in the first flower of his youth ? As if, forsooth, Christ had not merited, by His death, the supreme dominion over the living and the dead! And if we belong to Him (as we ought), why may He not exercise over us the power of life and of death ? However brief, therefore, either in your opinion or in mine, the life of your son may have been, it ought to satisfy us that he has finished the course which the Lord had marked out for him.

" Moreover, we may not reckon him to have perished in the flower of his age, who had grown ripe in the sight of the Lord. For I consider all to have arrived at maturity who are summoned away by death ; unless, perhaps, one would contend with Him, as if He can snatch away any one before his time. This, indeed, holds true of every one; but in regard to Louis, it is yet more certain on another and more peculiar ground. For he had arrived at that age, when, by true evidences, he could prove himself a member of the body of Christ: having put forth this fruit, he was taken from us and transplanted. Yes, instead of this transient and vanishing shadow of life, he has regained the real immortality of being.

" Nor can you consider yourself to have lost him, whom you will recover in the blessed resurrection in the kingdom of God. For they had both so lived and so died, that I cannot doubt but they are now with the Lord. Let us, therefore, press forward toward this goal which they have reached. There can be no doubt but that Christ will bind together both them and us in the same inseparable society, in that incomparable participation of His own glory. Beware, therefore, that you do not lament your son as lost, whom you acknowledge to be preserved by the Lord, that he may remain yours forever, who, at the pleasure of His own will, lent him to you only for a season. . . .

"Neither do I insist upon your laying aside all grief. Nor, in the school of Christ, do we learn any such philosophy as requires us to put off that common humanity with which God has endowed us, that, being men, we should be turned into stones.[1] These considerations reach only so far as this, that you do set bounds, and, as it were, temper even your most reasonable sadness, that, having shed those tears which were due to nature and to fatherly affection, you by no means give way to senseless wailing. Nor do I by any means interfere because I am distrustful of your prudence, firmness, or high-mindedness; but only lest I might here be wanting, and come short in my duty to you.

"Moreover, I have requested Melanchthon and Bucer that they would also add their letters to mine, because I entertained the hope that it would not be unacceptable that they too should afford some evidence of their good-will toward you.

"Adieu, most distinguished sir, and my much-respected in the Lord. May Christ the Lord keep you and your family, and direct you all with His own Spirit, until you may arrive where Louis and Claude have gone before."

[1] *"Neque hanc philosophiam discimus in schola Christi, ut eam quam nobis indidit humanitatem exuendo, ex hominibus lapides fiamus."* This shows how far Calvin was from heathen stoicism.

CHAPTER XII.

CALVIN'S SECOND SOJOURN AND LABORS AT GENEVA.
1541–1564.

The sources on this and the following chapters in § 81, p. 347.

§ 93. *The State of Geneva after the expulsion of the Reformers.*

I. The correspondence in *Opera*, vols. X. and XI., and HERMINJARD, vols. V., VI., and VII. — *Annal. Calv.*, XXI. 235–282. — The Chronicles of ROSET and BONIVARD; the histories of SPON, GABEREL, ROGET, etc.

II. HENRY, I. ch. XIX. — STÄHELIN, I. 283–299. — DYER, 113–123. — KAMP-SCHULTE, I. 342 sqq. — MERLE D'AUBIGNÉ, bk. XI. chs. XVIII. (vol. VI. 610 sqq.) and XIX. (vol. VII. 1 sqq.).

C. A. CORNELIUS (Cath.): *Die Rückkehr Calvins nach Genf.* München, 1889. Continuation of his essay, *Die Verbannung Calvins aus Genf.* München, 1886. Both in the Transactions of the Bavarian Academy of Sciences.

THE answer to Sadolet was one of the means of saving Geneva from the grasp of popery, and endearing Calvin to the friends of freedom. But there were other causes which demanded his recall. Internal disturbances followed his expulsion, and brought the little republic to the brink of ruin.

Calvin was right in predicting a short *régime* to his enemies. In less than a year they were demoralized and split up into factions. In the place of the expelled Reformers, two native preachers and two from Bern were elected on the basis of the Bernese customs, but they were below mediocrity, and not fit for the crisis. The supremacy of the State was guarded. Foreigners who could not show a good practical reason for their residence were banished; among them, even Saunier and Cordier, the rectors of the schools who faithfully adhered to the Reformers.

There were three main parties in Geneva, with subdivisions.

1. The government party was controlled by the syndics of 1538 and other enemies of the Reformers. They were called *Articulants* or, by a popular nickname, *Artichauds*,[1] from the twenty-one articles of a treaty with Bern, which had been negotiated and signed by three counsellors and deputies of the city — Ami de Chapeaurouge, Jean Lullin, and Monathon. The government subjected the Church to the State, and was protected by Bern, but unable to maintain order. Tumults and riots multiplied in the streets; the schools were ruined by the expulsion of the best teachers; the pulpit lost its power; the new preachers became objects of contempt or pity; pastoral care was neglected; vice and immorality increased; the old licentiousness and frivolities, dancing, gambling, drunkenness, masquerades, indecent songs, adulteries, reappeared; persons went naked through the streets to the sound of drums and fifes.

Moreover, the treaty with Bern, when it became known, was very unpopular because it conceded to Bern the rights of sovereignty. The Council of Two Hundred would not submit to it because it sacrificed their liberties and good customs. But the judges of Bern decided that the Genevese must sign the treaty and pay the costs. This created a great commotion. The people cried "treason," and demanded the arrest of the three deputies who had been outwitted by the diplomacy of Bern, but they made their escape; whereupon they were condemned to death as forgers and rebels. The discontent extended to the pastors who had been elected in the place of Farel and Calvin.

Within two years after the banishment of the Reformers, the four syndics who had decreed it came to grief. Jean Philippe, the captain-general of the city and most influential

---

[1] Dyer, p. 113, miscalls them *Artichokes*, because, as he fancies, they took "this plant for their device."

leader of the Artichauds, but a man of violent passions, was beheaded for homicide, and as a mover of sedition, June 10, 1540. Two others, Chapeaurouge and Lullin, were condemned to death as forgers and rebels; the fourth, Richardet, died in consequence of an injury which he received in the attempt to escape justice. Such a series of misfortunes was considered a nemesis of Providence, and gave the death-blow to the anti-reform party.

2. The party of the Roman Catholics raised its head after the expulsion of the Reformers, and received for a short time great encouragement from the banished bishop Pierre de la Baume, whom Paul III. had made a cardinal, and from the Letter of Cardinal Sadolet. A number of priests and monks returned from France and Savoy, but the Answer of Calvin destroyed all the hopes and prospects of the Romanists, and the government showed them no favor.

3. The third party was friendly to the Reformers. It reaped all the benefit of the blunders and misfortunes of the other two parties, and turned them to the best account. Its members were called by their opponents *Guillermains*, after Master Guillaume (Farel). They were led by Perrin, Porral, Pertemps, and Sept. They were united, most active, and had a definite end in view —the restoration of the Reformation. They kept up a correspondence with the banished Reformers, especially with Farel in Neuchâtel, who counselled and encouraged them. They were suspected of French sympathies and want of patriotism, but retorted by charging the government with subserviency to Bern. They were inclined to extreme measures. Calvin exhorted them to be patient, moderate, and forgiving.

As the Artichauds declined, the Guillermains increased in power over the people. The vacant posts of the late syndics were filled from their ranks. The new magistrates assumed a bold tone of independence towards Bern, and insisted on the old franchises of Geneva. It is curious that they were encouraged by a letter of the Emperor Charles V., who thus unwittingly aided the cause of Calvin.[1]

The way was now prepared for the recall of Calvin. The best people of Geneva looked to him as the saviour of their city. His name meant order, peace, reform in Church and State.

Even the Artichauds, overpowered by public opinion, proposed in a general assembly of citizens, June 17, 1540, the resolution to restore the former status, and spoke loudly against popery. Two of the new preachers, Marcourt and Morland, resigned Aug. 10, and returned to Bern. The other two, Henri de la Mare and Jacques Bernard, humbly besought the favor of Calvin, and begged him to return. A remarkable tribute from his rivals and enemies.[2]

§ 94. *Calvin's Recall to Geneva.*

Literature in § 93, especially the Correspondence and Registers.

Calvin did not forget Geneva. He proved his interest in her welfare by his Answer to Sadolet. But he had no inclination to return, and could only be induced to do so by unmistakable indications of the will of Providence.

He had found a place of great usefulness in a city where he could act as mediator between Germany and France, and benefit both countries; his Sunday services were crowded; his theological lectures attracted students from France and other countries; he had married a faithful wife, and enjoyed

---

[1] "*Es macht einen eigenthümlichen Eindruck,*" says Kampschulte (I. 365), "*Karl V. hier für den Sieg eines Mannes mitthätig zu sehen, dessen Wirksamkeit, wie kaum eine andere, dazu beigetragen hat, die Grundlagen seiner Macht zu untergraben.*"

[2] Bernard wrote a letter to Calvin, Feb. 6, 1541 (Herminjard, VII. 23), in which he says: "*Veni ergo, venerande mi pater in Christo: noster es perfecto. Te enim nobis donavit Dominus Deus. Suspirant etiam post te omnes. . . . Faxit Dominus Jesus, ut velox adventus tuus sit ad nos! Vale, ecclesiœque digneris succurrere nostrœ. Alioqui requiret de manu tua sanguinem nostrum Dominus Deus. Dedit enim te speculatorem domui Israel quœ apud nos est.*" Calvin answered, March 1, 1541, that he was very reluctant to return to Geneva, but would obey the voice of the Church. Herminjard, VII. 38–40.

a peaceful home. The government of Strassburg appreciated him more and more, and his colleagues wished to retain him. Melanchthon thought he could spare him less at the Colloquies of Worms and Ratisbon than anybody else. Looking to Geneva he could, from past experience, expect nothing but severe and hard trials. " There is no place in the world," he wrote to Viret, "which I fear more; not because I hate it, but because I feel unequal to the difficulties which await me there." [1] He called it an abyss from which he shrank back much more now than he had done in 1536. Indeed, he was not mistaken in his fears, for his subsequent life was an unbroken struggle. We need not wonder then that he refused call upon call, and requested Farel and Viret to desist from their efforts to allure him away.[2]

At the same time, he was determined to obey the will of God as soon as it would be made clear to him by unmistakable indications of Providence. "When I remember," he wrote to Farel, "that in this matter I am not my own master, I present my heart as a sacrifice and offer it up to the Lord." [3] A very characteristic sentence, which reveals the soul of his piety. A seal of Calvin bears this motto, and the emblem is a hand presenting a heart to God. Seven-

---

[1] March 1, 1541 (from Ulm on his journey to Ratisbon): "*Non aliter respondeo quam quod semper solitus sum: Nullum esse locum sub cœlo quem magis reformidem, non quia oderim, sed quoniam tot difficultates illic mihi propositas video, quibus superandis sentio me longe esse imparem. Quoties superiorum temporum subit recordatio, facere nequeo quin toto pectore exhorrescam, si cogar me iterum antiquis illis certaminibus objicere. Si mihi cum ecclesia illa tantum esset negocium, animo essem quietiore; certe minus terrerer. Sed vicinos* [allusion to Bern] *cogito, qui mihi olim tantum molestiæ exhibuerunt.*" Opera, XI. 167; Herminjard, VII. 43.

[2] Dyer (p. 121) and Kampschulte (I. 370) suspect, without any reason, that Calvin, in his repeated refusals, was influenced by the unworthy motive to humble the pride of the Genevese. What more could they do than bombard him with petitions and deputations? And this they did months before he accepted the call.

[3] " *Cor meum velut mactatum Domino in sacrificium offero.*" Oct. 24, 1540. Opera, XI. 100; Herminjard, VI. 339. Henry has appropriately chosen this sentence as the motto for his biography.

teen years later, when he looked back upon that critical
period of his life, he expressed the same view. "Although
the welfare of that Church," he says, "was so dear to me,
that I could without difficulty sacrifice my life for it; yet
my timidity presented to me many reasons of excuse for
declining to take such a heavy burden on my shoulders.
But the sense of duty prevailed, and led me to return to the
flock from which I had been snatched away. I did this with
sadness, tears, and great anxiety and distress of mind, the
Lord being my witness, and many pious persons who would
gladly have spared me that pain, if not the same fear had
shut their mouth." [1] He mentions especially Martin Bucer,
"that excellent servant of Christ," who threatened him with
the example of Jonah; as Farel, on Calvin's first visit to
Geneva, had threatened him with the wrath of God.

His friends in Geneva, the Council and the people, were
convinced that Calvin alone could save the city from anarchy,
and they made every effort to secure his return. His recall
was first seriously discussed in the Council early in 1539,
again in February, 1540, and decided upon Sept. 21, 1540.
Preparatory steps were taken to secure the co-operation of
Bern, Basel, Zürich, and Strassburg. On the 13th of October, Michel du Bois, an old friend of Calvin, was sent by
the Large Council with a letter to him, and directed to
press the invitation by oral representation. Without waiting for an answer, other petitions and deputations were
forwarded. On the 19th of October the Council of Two
Hundred resolved to use every effort for the attainment of
that object. Ami Perrin and Louis Dufour were sent (Oct.
21 and 22) as deputies, with a herald, to Strassburg " to fetch
Master Calvin." Twenty dollars gold (*écus au soleil*) were
voted, on the 27th, for expenses.[2] The *Registres* of that
month are full of actions concerning the recall of "the

---

[1] Preface to his Commentary on the Psalms (written in 1557), *Opera*,
XXXI. 27.   [2] *Annal.* 266 sqq.; Herminjard, VI. 331–335.

learned and pious Mr. Calvin." No more complete vindication of the cause of the Reformers could be imagined.

Farel's aid was also solicited. With incomparable self-denial he pardoned the ingratitude of the Genevese in not recalling him, and made every exertion to secure the return of his younger friend, whom he had first compelled by moral force to stop at Geneva. He bombarded him with letters. He even travelled from Neuchâtel to Strassburg, and spent two days there, pressing him in person and trying to persuade him, as well as Capito and Bucer, of the absolute necessity of his return to Geneva, which, in his opinion, was the most important spot in the world.

Dufour arrived at Strassburg in November, called upon the senate, followed Calvin to Worms, where he was in attendance on the Colloquy, and delivered the formal letter of invitation, dated Oct. 22, and signed by the syndics and Council of Geneva. It concludes thus: "On behalf of our Little, Great, and General Councils (all of which have strongly urged us to take this step), we pray you very affectionately that you will be pleased to come over to us, and to return to your former post and ministry; and we hope that by God's help this course will be a great advantage for the furtherance of the holy gospel, seeing that our people very much desire you, and we will so deal with you that you shall have reason to be satisfied." The letter was fastened with a seal bearing the motto: "*Post tenebras spero lucem.*"

Calvin was thus most urgently and most honorably recalled by the united voice of the Council, the ministers, and the people of that city which had unjustly banished him three years before.

He was moved to tears by these manifestations of regard and confidence, and began to waver. But the deputies of Strassburg at Worms, under secret instruction from their government, entered a strong protest against his leaving. Bucer, Capito, Sturm, and Grynæus, when asked for advice, decided

that Calvin was indispensable to Strassburg as the head of
the French Church which represented Protestant France;
as a theological teacher who attracted students from Germany, France, and Italy, to send them back to their own
countries as evangelists; and as a helper in making the
Church of Strassburg a seminary of ministers of the gospel.
No one besides Melanchthon could be compared with him.
Geneva was indeed an important post, and the gate to France
and Italy, but uncertain, and liable to be involved again in
political complications which might destroy the evangelical
labors of Calvin. The pastors and senators of Strassburg,
urged by the churches of Zürich and Basel, came at last to
the conclusion to consent to Calvin's return after the Colloquy of Worms, but only for a season, hoping that he may
soon make their city his final home for the benefit of the
whole Church.[1]

Thus two cities, we might almost say, two nations, were
contending for the possession of "the Theologian." His
whole future life, and a considerable chapter of Church history, depended on the decision. Under these circumstances
he could make no definite promise, except that he would pay
a visit to Geneva after the close of the Colloquy, on
condition of getting the consent of Strassburg and Bern.
He also prescribed, like a victorious general, the terms of
surrender, namely, the restoration of Church discipline.

He had previously advised that Viret be called from Lausanne. This was done in Dec. 31, 1540, with the permission
of Bern, but only for half a year. Viret arrived in Geneva
Jan. 17, 1541. His persuasive sermons were well attended,
and the magistrates showed great reverence for the Word of
God; but he found so much and such difficult work in church

---

[1] See the letters signed by Capito, Hedio, Bucer, Sturm, Bedrotus,
Grynæus (probably written by Bucer), October and November, 1540, in Herminjard, VI. 335 and 356 sqq., and the letter of the Council of Strassburg to
the Council of Geneva, Sept. 1, 1541, vol. VII. 227.

and school, in the hospital and the poorhouse, that he urged Calvin to come soon, else he must withdraw or perish.

On the 1st of May, 1541, the General Council recalled, in due form, the sentence of banishment of April 23, 1538, and solemnly declared that every citizen considered Calvin, Farel, and Saunier to be honorable men, and true servants of God.[1] On the 26th of May the senate sent another pressing request to Strassburg, Zürich, and Basel to aid Geneva in securing the return of Calvin.[2]

It is astonishing what an amount of interest this question of Calvin's return excited throughout Switzerland and Germany. It was generally felt that the fate of Geneva depended on Calvin, and that the fate of evangelical religion in France and Italy depended on Geneva. Letters arrived from individuals and corporations. Farel continued to thunder, and reproached the Strassburgers for keeping Calvin back. He was indignant at Calvin's delay. " Will you wait," he wrote him, "till the stones call thee?"

§ 95. Calvin's Return to Geneva. 1541.

In the middle of June, Calvin left Regensburg, before the close of the Colloquy, much to the regret of Melanchthon; and after attending to his affairs in Strassburg, he set out for Switzerland. The Genevese sent Eustace Vincent, a mounted herald, to escort him, and voted thirty-six écus for expenses (Aug. 26).

The Strassburgers requested him to retain his right of citizenship, and the annual revenues of a prebend, which they had assigned him as the salary of his theological professorship. "He gladly accepted," says Beza, "the former mark of respect, but could never be induced to accept the latter,

---

[1] " Pour gens de bien et de Dieu." Annal. 278.

[2] See the letters of the Council of Geneva to the Pastors of Zürich in Opera, XI. 220 sqq., and in Herminjard, VII. 129 sqq.

since the care of riches occupied his mind the least of anything."

Bucer, in the name of the pastors of Strassburg, gave him a letter to the Syndics and Council of Geneva, Sept. 1, 1541, in which he says: "Now he comes at last, Calvin, that elect and incomparable instrument of God, to whom no other in our age may be compared, if at all there can be the question of another alongside of him." He added that such a highly favored man Strassburg could only spare for a season, on condition of his certain return.[1] The Council of Strassburg wrote to the Council of Geneva on the same day, expressing the hope that Calvin may soon return to them for the benefit of the Church universal.[2] The Senate of Geneva, in a letter of thanks (Sept. 17, 1541), expressed the determination to keep Calvin permanently in their city, where he could be as useful to the Church universal as at Strassburg.[3]

Calvin visited his friends in Basel, who affectionately commended him to Bern and Geneva (Sept. 4).[4] Bern was not very favorable to Calvin and the clerical ascendency in Geneva, but gave him a safe-conduct through her territory.

At Soleure (Solothurn) he learned that Farel was deposed, without a trial, by the magistracy of Neuchâtel, because he had attacked a person of rank from the pulpit for scandalous conduct. He, therefore, turned from the direct route, and spent some days with his friend, trying to relieve him of the difficulty. He did not succeed at once, but his efforts were supported by Zürich, Strassburg, Basel, and

---

[1] The letter is in Latin with a French translation by Viret, *Opera*, X. 271; Herminjard, VII. 231–233. "*Venit tandem ad vos Calvinus, eximium profecto et rarissimum, cui vix secundum, si tamen secundum ullum, organum Christi hodie extat. . . . Venit ergo, dimissus ratione ea quam noster senatus perscribit, ut nimirum redeat.*"

[2] Herminjard, VII. 227–230, in Latin and French.

[3] Herminjard, VII. 253–255; *Opera*, XI. 268.

[4] *Opera*, XI. 274.

Bern; and the seignory of Neuchâtel resolved to keep Farel, who continued to labor there till his death.[1]

Calvin wrote to the Council of Geneva from Neuchâtel on Sept. 7, explaining the reason of his delay.[2] The next day he proceeded to Bern and delivered letters from Strassburg and Basel.

He was expected at Geneva on the 9th of September, but did not arrive, it seems, before the 13th. He wished to avoid a noisy reception, for which he had no taste.[3] But there is no doubt that his arrival caused general rejoicing among the people.[4]

The Council provided for the Reformer a house and garden in the Rue des Chanoines near St. Peter's Church,[5] and

---

[1] See the correspondence in Herminjard, VII. 242 sqq.

[2] Herminjard, VII. 239. The letter was received at Geneva, Sept. 12. See Herminjard's note 6 on p. 240.

[3] He says, in the Preface to his Commentary on the Psalms: "I have no intention of showing myself, and making a noise in the world." Kampschulte goes beyond the record when he asserts (I. 380, 381): "*Für den Empfang eines Fürsten hätte nicht mehr Theilnahme bewiesen werden können. . . . Am 13ten Sept. hielt er unter dem Jubel der Bevölkerung seinen feierlichen Einzug in Genf.*" Perhaps he followed here Stähelin, who says (I. 316) : "*Mit unglaublicher Begeisterung, wie im Triumphe, wurde er von dem Volk und dem Magistrate empfangen.*" There is no record of such a triumphant public entrance. See Beza and Colladon in the next note. Roget and Merle d'Aubigné (VII. 62 sq.) deny the fact of a popular ovation.

[4] Beza (XXI. 131): "*Calvinus XIII. Septembris anno Domini MDXLI Genevam regressus est, summa cum universi populi ac senatus inprimis singulare Dei erga se beneficium serio tum agnoscentis congratulatione.*" Colladon (XXI. 64): "*Calvin fut tellement receu de singulière affection par ce povre peuple recognoissant sa faute, et qui estoit affamé d'ouir son fidele Pasteur, qu'on ne cessa point qu'il ne fut arresté pour tousiours.*"

[5] It was the house of Sieur de Fresneville, between the house of Bonivard, on the west, and that of Abbé de Bonmont, on the east, where Calvin lived from 1543 till his death. But as this house was not ready on his arrival, he lodged for a while in an adjoining house of the abbot of Bonmont, which was rebuilt in 1708 (No. 13 Rue des Chanoines, now called Rue de Calvin) and passed into the possession of Adrien Naville, president of the Société Évangélique. The second house (No. 11) remained a Reformed parsonage till 1700; in 1834 it was acquired by the Roman Catholic clergy, who assigned it to the Sisters of Mercy of Vincent de Paul, but it is now owned by the State. See Th. Heyer, *De la maison de Calvin*, in the "Mémoires d'Archéologie," IX. 391–408. I have consulted Mr. Ed. Naville and Mr. Ed. Favre of Geneva, who confirmed the above statements.

promised him (Oct. 4), in consideration of his great learning and hospitality to strangers, a fixed salary of fifty gold dollars, or five hundred florins, besides twelve measures of wheat and two casks of wine.[1] It also voted him a new suit of broadcloth, with furs for the winter. This provision was liberal for those days, yet barely sufficient for the necessary expenses of the Reformer and the claims on his hospitality. Hence the Council made him occasional presents for extra services; but he declined them whenever he could do without them. He lived in the greatest simplicity compatible with his position. A pulpit in St. Peter's was prepared for him upon a broad, low pillar, that the whole congregation might more easily hear him.

The Council sent three horses and a carriage to bring Calvin's wife and furniture. It took twenty-two days for the escort from Geneva to Strassburg and back (from Sept. 17 to Oct. 8).[2]

On the 13th of September Calvin appeared before the Syndics and the Council in the Town Hall, delivered the letters from the senators and pastors of Strassburg and Basel, and apologized for his long delay. He made no complaint and demanded no punishment of his enemies, but asked for the appointment of a commission to prepare a written order of church government and discipline. The Council complied with this request, and resolved to retain him permanently, and to inform the Senate of Strassburg of this intention. Six prominent laymen, four members of the Little Council,

---

[1] "*Cinq cens florins, douze coppes de froment et deux bossot de vin.*" *Annal.* 284. Five hundred florins of Geneva were equivalent to about four thousand francs at the present standard of value. This is the estimate of Franklin and of Merle d'Aubigné, VII. 69. Galiffe (*Quelq. pages d'hist.* p. 89, as quoted by Kampschulte, I. 388, note 3) estimates Calvin's annual income at 9 to 10,000 francs of our money ($2000). A syndic at that time received only 100, a counsellor 25 francs, according to the same authority.

[2] Herminjard, VII. 289, note: "*On paya au voiturier, Emoz Daiz, pour 22 journées 7 florins, 4 sols.*"

two members of the Large Council, — Pertemps, Perrin, Roset, Lambert, Goulaz, and Porral, — were appointed to draw up the ecclesiastical ordinances in conference with the ministers.[1]

On Sept. 16, Calvin wrote to Farel: " Thy wish is granted, I am held fast here. May God give his blessing." [2]

He desired to retain Viret and to secure Farel as permanent co-laborers; but in this he was disappointed — Viret being needed at Lausanne, and Farel at Neuchâtel. By special permission of Bern, however, Viret was allowed to remain with him till July of the next year. His other colleagues were rather a hindrance than a help to him, as " they had no zeal and very little learning, and could not be trusted." Nearly the whole burden of reconstructing the Church of Geneva rested on his shoulders. It was a formidable task.

Never was a man more loudly called by government and people, never did a man more reluctantly accept the call, never did a man more faithfully and effectively fulfil the duties of the call than John Calvin when, in obedience to the voice of God, he settled a second time at Geneva to live and to die at this post of duty.

" Of all men in the world," says one of his best biographers and greatest admirers,[3] " Calvin is the one who most worked, wrote, acted, and prayed for the cause which he had embraced. The coexistence of the sovereignty of God and the freedom of man is assuredly a mystery ; but Calvin never supposed that because God did all, he personally had nothing to do. He points out clearly the twofold action, that of God and that of man. 'God,' said he, 'after freely bestowing his

---

[1] *Reg. du Conseil*, vol. XXXV. 324, quoted in *Annal.* 282, and by Hermin jard; Calvin's letter to Farel, Sept. 16, 1541, in *Opera*, XI. 281, and Hermin jard, VII. 249–250.

[2] " *Quod bene vertat Deus, hic retentus sum, ut volebas. Superest ut Viretun quoque mecum retineam, quem a me avelli nullo modo patiar. Tuæ quoque omni umque fratrum partes me hic adjuvare, nisi vultis me frustra excruciari, ac sine commodo esse miserrimum.*" Herminjard, VII. 249.

[3] Merle d'Aubigné, VII. 70.

grace on us, forthwith demands of us a reciprocal acknowledgment. When he said to Abraham, "I am thy God," it
was an offer of his free goodness; but he adds at the same
time what he required of him: "Walk before me, and be
thou perfect." This condition is tacitly annexed to all the
promises. They are to be to us as spurs, inciting us to promote the glory of God.' And elsewhere he says, 'This
doctrine ought to create new vigor in all your members,
so that you may be fit and alert, with might and main, to
follow the call of God.' "[1]

§ 96. *The First Years after the Return.*

Calvin entered at once upon his labors, and continued
them without interruption for twenty-three years — till his
death, May 27, 1564.

The first years were full of care and trial, as he had anticipated. His duties were more numerous and responsible
than during his first sojourn. Then he was supported by
the older Farel; now he stood at the head of the Church at
Geneva, though yet a young man of thirty-two. He had
to reorganize the Church, to introduce a constitution and
order of worship, to preach, to teach, to settle controversies,
to conciliate contending parties, to provide for the instruction of youth, to give advice even in purely secular affairs.
No wonder that he often felt discouraged and exhausted, but
trust in God, and a sense of duty kept him up.

Viret was of great service to him, but he was called back
to Lausanne in July, 1542. His other colleagues — Jacques
Bernard, Henri de la Mare, and Aimé Champereau — were
men of inferior ability, and not reliable. In 1542 four
new pastors were appointed, — Pierre Blanchet, Matthias de
Geneston, Louis Trappereau, and Philippe Ozias (or Ozeas).
In 1544 Geneva had twelve pastors, six of them for the
county Churches. Calvin gradually trained a corps of enthu-

[1] Comments on 2 Cor. 7 : 1 ; Gen. 17 : 1.

siastic evangelists. Farel and Viret visited Geneva on important occasions. For his last years, he had a most able and learned colleague in his friend Theodore Beza.

He pursued a wise and conciliatory course, which is all the more creditable to him when we consider the stern severity of his character and system. He showed a truly Christian forbearance to his former enemies, and patience with the weakness of his colleagues.[1]

"I will endeavor," he wrote to Bucer, in a long letter, Oct. 15, 1541, "to cultivate a good understanding and harmony with my neighbors, and also brotherly kindness (if they will allow me), with as much fidelity and diligence as I possibly can. So far as it depends on me, I shall give no ground of offence to any one. . . . If in any way I do not answer your expectation, you know that I am in your power, and subject to your authority. Admonish me, chastise me, exercise towards me all the authority of a father over his son. Pardon my haste. . . . I am entangled in so many employments that I am almost beside myself."[2]

To Myconius of Basel he wrote, March 14, 1542: —

"I value the public peace and concord so highly, that I lay restraint upon myself; and this praise even the adversaries are compelled to award to me.[3] This feeling prevails to such an extent, that, from day to day, those who were once open enemies have become friends; others I conciliate by courtesy, and I feel that I have been in some measure successful, although not everywhere and on all occasions.

"On my arrival it was in my power to have disconcerted our enemies most triumphantly, entering with full sail among the whole of that tribe who had done the mischief. I have abstained; if I had liked, I could daily, not merely with impunity, but with the approval of very many, have used sharp reproof. I forbear; even with the most scrupulous care do I avoid everything of the kind, lest even by some slight word I should appear to persecute any individual, much less all of them at once. May the Lord confirm me in this disposition of mind."[4]

[1] "Diese milde, versöhnliche Haltung nach seiner Rückkehr bildet eines der schönsten Blätter in der Geschichte Calvin's." So says Kampschulte (I. 390), but he unjustly diminishes the praise by adding: "Noch höher würde die Nachwelt sein Verdienst anschlagen, wenn er sich selbst desselben weniger bewusst gewesen wäre." How could he be unconscious of his intention? And he spoke of it not boastingly, but modestly, like Paul.

[2] Herminjard, VII. 293; Opera, XI. 299; Bonnet-Constable, I. 269.

[3] "Tanti enim mihi est publica pax et concordia, ut manum mihi injiciam: atque hanc laudem mihi adversarii ipsi tribuere coguntur."

[4] Herminjard, VII. 439; Bonnet-Constable, I. 291.

He met at first with no opposition, but hearty co-operation among the people. About a fortnight after his arrival he presented a formula of the ecclesiastical order to the Small Council. Objection was made to the monthly celebration of the Lord's Supper, instead of the custom of celebrating it only four times a year. Calvin, who strongly favored even a more frequent celebration, yielded his better judgment "in consideration of the weakness of the times," and for the sake of harmony. With this modification, the Small Council adopted the constitution Oct. 27; the Large Council confirmed it Nov. 9; and the general assembly of the citizens ratified it, by a very large majority, in St. Peter's Church, the 20th of November, 1541. The small minority, however, included some of the leading citizens who were opposed to ecclesiastical discipline. The Articles, after the insertion of some trifling amendments and additions, were definitely adopted by the three councils, Jan. 2, 1542.[1]

This was a great victory; for the ecclesiastical ordinances, which we shall consider afterwards, laid a solid foundation for a strong and well-regulated evangelical church.

Calvin preached at St. Peter's, Viret at St. Gervais. The first services were of a penitential character, and their solemnity was enhanced by the fearful ravages of the pestilence in the neighboring cities. An extraordinary celebration of the holy communion on the first Sunday in November, and a weekly day of humiliation and prayer were appointed to invoke the mercy of God upon Geneva and the whole Church.

The second year after his return was very trying. The pestilence, which in 1541 had been raging in Strassburg and

---

[1] *Registers*, Oct. 25 and 27, Nov. 9 and 20, 1541; and Jan. 2, 1542. *Opera*, X. 15; XI. 379; XXI. 287, 289, 290. The *Régisters du Conseil* of Jan. 2, 1542 (vol. XXXV. f. 449), record as follows: " *Ordonnances sus léglise : lesquelles hont esté passé par petit grand et général conseyl touteffoys hont estes corrigés, et avant quil soyent mys à limprymerie Resoluz que en ung conseyl extraordinaïre lesdictes ordonnances soyent vehues* [*vues*] *affin que telle quest passe par le général ne soyt changé.*" *Annal.*, XXI. 289 sq.

all along the Rhine, crept into Switzerland, diminishing the population of Basel and Zürich, and reached Geneva in the autumn, 1542. To the pestilence was added the scourge of famine, as is often the case. The evil was aggravated by the great influx of strangers who were attracted by Calvin's fame and sought refuge from persecution under his shelter. The pest-house outside of the city was crowded. Calvin and Pierre Blanchet offered their services to the sick, while the rest of the ministers shrank back.[1] The Council refused to let Calvin go, because the Church could not spare him.[2] Blanchet risked his life, and fell a victim to his philanthrophy in eight or nine months. Calvin, in a letter dated October, 1542, gives the following account to Viret, who, in July, had left for Lausanne :[3] —

"The pestilence also begins to rage here with greater violence, and few who are at all affected by it escape its ravages. One of our colleagues was to be set apart for attendance upon the sick. Because Peter [Blanchet] offered himself all readily acquiesced. If anything happens to him, I fear that I must take the risk upon myself, for, as you observe, because we are debtors to one another, we must not be wanting to those who, more than any others, stand in need of our ministry. And yet it is not my opinion, that while we wish to provide for one portion we are at liberty to neglect the body of the Church itself. But so long as we are in this ministry, I do not see that any pretext will avail us, if, through fear of infection, we are found wanting in the discharge of our duty when there is most need of our assistance."

Farel, on a like occasion, visited the sick daily, rich and poor, friend and foe, without distinction.[4] We must judge Calvin by his spirit and motive. He had undoubtedly the spirit of a martyr, but felt it his duty to obey the magistrates, and to spare his life till the hour of necessity. We may refer to the example of Cyprian, who fled during the

[1] They said that they would rather go "au diable" than to the pest-house.
[2] That Calvin offered himself is asserted not only by Beza (XXXI. 134), but also by Roset and Savion. See Bonnet, I. 334, note. Castellio, who was not a minister, though he wished to become one, also offered his services, but changed his mind when the lot fell on him.
[3] Bonnet-Constable, I. 334.
[4] Kirchhofer, *Leben Farels*, II. 33.

Decian persecution, but died heroically as a martyr in the Valerian persecution.

In 1545 Geneva was again visited by a pestilence, which some Swiss soldiers brought from France. The horrors were aggravated by a diabolical conspiracy of wicked persons, including some women, connected with the pest-house, for spreading the plague by artificial means, to gain spoils from the dead. The conspirators used the infected linen of those who had died of the disease, and smeared the locks of the houses with poison. A woman confessed, under torture, that she had killed eighteen men by her infernal arts. The ravages were fearful; Geneva was decimated; two thousand died out of a population of less than twenty thousand. Seven men and twenty-one women were burned alive for this offence. The physician of the lazaretto and two assistants were quartered.

Calvin formed a modest estimate of his labors during the first years, as may be seen from his letters. He wrote to Myconius, the first minister of Basel, March 14, 1542:[1] —

"The present state of our affairs I can give you in a few words. For the first month after resuming the ministry, I had so much to attend to, and so many annoyances, that I was almost worn out; such a work of labor and difficulty has it been to upbuild once more a fallen edifice (*collapsum edificium instaurare*). Although certainly Viret had already begun successfully to restore, yet, nevertheless, because he had deferred the complete form of order and discipline until my arrival, it had, as it were, to be commenced anew. When, having overcome this labor, I believed that there would be breathing-time allowed me, lo! new cares presented themselves, and those of a kind not much lighter than the former. This, however, somewhat consoles and refreshes me, that we do not labor altogether in vain, without some fruit appearing; which, although it is not so plentiful as we could wish, yet neither is it so scanty but that there does appear some change for the better. There is a brighter prospect for the future if Viret can be left here with me; on which account I am all the more desirous to express to you my most thankful acknowledgment, because you share with me in my anxiety that the Bernese may not call him away; and I earnestly pray, for the sake of Christ, that you would do your utmost to bring that about; for whenever the thought of his going away presents itself, I faint and lose courage entirely. . . . Our

[1] Herminjard, VII. 437 sq.; *Opera*, XI. 376 sq.; Bonnet-Constable, I. 289 sq.

other colleagues are rather a hindrance than a help to us; they are rude and self-conceited, have no zeal and less learning. But what is worst of all, I cannot trust them, even although I very much wish that I could; for by many evidences they show their estrangement from us, and give scarcely any indication of a sincere and trustworthy disposition. I bear with them, however, or rather I humor them, with the utmost lenity; a course from which I shall not be induced to depart, even by their bad conduct. But if, in the long run, the sore need a severer remedy, I shall do my utmost, and shall see to it by every method I can think of, to avoid disturbing the peace of the Church with our quarrels; for I dread the factions which must always necessarily arise from the dissensions of ministers. On my first arrival I might have driven them away had I wished to do so, and that is also even now in my power. I shall never, however, repent the degree of moderation which I have observed, since no one can justly complain that I have been too severe. These things I mention to you in a cursory way, that you may the more clearly perceive how wretched I shall be if Viret is taken away from me."

A month later (April 17, 1542), he wrote to Myconius:[1]—

"In what concerns the private condition of this Church, I somehow, along with Viret, sustain the burden of it. If he is taken away from me, my situation will be more deplorable than I can describe to you, and even should he remain, there is some hazard that very much may not be obtained in the midst of so much secret animosity [between Geneva and Bern]. But that I may not torment myself beforehand, the Lord will see to it, and provide some one on whom I am compelled to cast this care."

In February, 1543, he wrote to Melanchthon:—

"As to our own affairs, there is much that I might write, but the sole cause which imposes silence upon me is, that I could find no end. I labor here and do my utmost, but succeed indifferently. Nevertheless, all are astonished that my progress is so great in the midst of so many impediments, the greater part of which arise from the ministers themselves. This, however, is a great alleviation of my troubles, that not only this Church, but also the whole neighborhood, derive some benefit from my presence. Besides that, somewhat overflows from hence upon France, and even spreads as far as Italy."[2]

§ 97. *Survey of Calvin's Activity.*

Calvin combined the offices of theological professor, preacher, pastor, church-ruler, superintendent of schools, with the extra labors of equal, yea, greater, importance, as

---

[1] Herminjard, VII. 453; *Opera,* XI. 384; Bonnet-Constable, I. 297.

[2] Bonnet-Constable, I. 351; *Opera,* XI. 516. The last sentence, "as far as Italy," is confirmed by a most grateful letter of evangelical believers in Venice, Vicenza, and Treviso, "to the saints of the Church of God in Geneva," dated Venice, 8 Id. December, 1542. See *Opera,* XI. 472–474.

author, correspondent, and leader of the expanding movement of the Reformation in Western Europe. He was involved in serious disciplinary and theological controversies
with the Libertines, Romanists, Pelagians, Antitrinitarians,
and Lutherans. He had no help except from one or more
young men, whom he kept in his house and employed as
clerks. When unwell he dictated from his bed. He had
an amazing power for work notwithstanding his feeble
health. When interrupted in dictation, he could at once
resume work at the point where he left off.[1] He indulged
in no recreation except a quarter or half an hour's walk in
his room or garden after meals, and an occasional game of
quoits or *la clef* with intimate friends. He allowed himself
very little sleep, and for at least ten years he took but one
meal a day, alleging his bad digestion.[2] No wonder that he
undermined his health, and suffered of headache, ague, dyspepsia, and other bodily infirmities which terminated in a
premature death.

Luther and Zwingli were as indefatigable workers as
Calvin, but they had an abundance of flesh and blood, and
enjoyed better health. Luther liked to play with his
children, and to entertain his friends with his humorous
table-talk. Zwingli also found recreation in poetry and
music, and played on several instruments.

A few years before his death, Calvin was compelled to speak
of his work in self-defence against the calumnies of an ungrateful student and amanuensis, François Baudouin, a
native of Arras, who ran away with some of Calvin's papers,

---

[1] Beza (XXI. 169) : " *Ut . . . inter dictandum sæpe aliquot horas interturba-
tus statim ad dictata nullo commonefaciente rediret.*"

[2] Beza (XXI. 160) : " *Per decem minimum annos prandio abstinuit, ut nullum
omnino cibum extra statam cœnæ horam sumeret, ut eum mirum sit phthisim effugere
tam diu potuisse.*" Farther on (fol. 169) Beza says of Calvin : " *Victu sic
temperato, ut a sordibus et ab omni luxu longissime abesset : cibi parcissimi, ut per
multos annos semel quotidie cibum sumpserit, ventriculi imbecillitatem causatus.*"
Sometimes he abstained for thirty-six hours from all food. At the advice of
his physician, he ate an egg and drank a glass of wine at noon.

turned a Romanist, and publicly abused his benefactor. "I will not," he says, "enumerate the pleasures, conveniences, and riches I have renounced for Christ. I will only say that, had I the disposition of Baudouin, it would not have been very difficult for me to procure those things which he has always sought in vain, and which he now but too greedily gloats upon. But let that pass. Content with my humble fortune, my attention to frugality has prevented me from being a burden to anybody. I remain tranquil in my station, and have even given up a part of the moderate salary assigned to me, instead of asking for any increase. I devote all my care, labor, and study not only to the service of this Church, to which I am peculiarly bound, but to the assistance of all the Churches by every means in my power. I so discharge my office of a teacher, that no ambition may appear in my extreme faithfulness and diligence. I devour numerous griefs, and endure the rudeness of many; but my liberty is uncontrolled by the power of any man. I do not indulge the great by flattery; I fear not to give offence. No prosperity has hitherto inflated me; whilst I have intrepidly borne the many severe storms by which I have been tossed, till by the singular mercy of God I emerged from them. I live affably with my equals, and endeavor faithfully to preserve my friendships." [1]

Beza, his daily companion, thus describes "the ordinary labors" of Calvin, as he calls them: "During the week he preached every alternate, and lectured every third day; on Thursday he presided in the meetings of Presbytery (Consistory); and on Friday he expounded the Scripture in the assembly which we call ' the Congregation.' He illustrated

---

[1] *Responsio ad Balduini Convicia* (Geneva, 1562), in *Opera*, vol. IX. 561–580. Baudouin was an able lawyer, but a turncoat in religion. He died in 1573. On this personal controversy see *Responsio*, etc., *Opera*, VIII. 321 A, and Henry, vol. III. 549 sqq. Luther had a similar experience with John Agricola (Eisleben), his pupil and trusted friend, who publicly attacked him, and stirred up the Antinomian controversy.

several sacred books with most learned commentaries, besides answering the enemies of religion, and maintaining an extensive correspondence on matters of great importance. Any one who reads these attentively, will be astonished how one little man (*unicus homunculus*) could be fit for labors so numerous and great. He availed himself much of the aid of Farel and Viret,[1] while, at the same time, he conferred greater benefits on them. Their friendship and intimacy was not less hateful to the wicked than delightful to all the pious; and, in truth, it was a most pleasing spectacle to see and hear those three distinguished men carrying on the work of God in the Church so harmoniously, with such a variety of gifts. Farel excelled in a certain sublimity of mind, so that nobody could either hear his thunders without trembling, or listen to his most fervent prayers without being almost carried up to heaven. Viret possessed such suavity of eloquence, that his hearers were compelled to hang upon his lips. Calvin filled the mind of the hearers with as many weighty sentiments as he uttered words. I have often thought that a preacher compounded of the three would be absolutely perfect. In addition to these employments, Calvin had many others, arising out of circumstances domestic and foreign. The Lord so blessed his ministry that persons flocked to him from all parts of the Christian world; some to take his advice in matters of religion, and others to hear him. Hence, we have seen an Italian, an English, and, finally, a Spanish Church at Geneva, one city seeming scarcely sufficient to entertain so many guests. But though at home he was courted by the good and feared by the bad, and matters had been admirably arranged, yet there were not wanting individuals who gave him great annoyance. We will unfold these contests separately, that posterity may

---

[1] Who came to Geneva occasionally, the former from Neuchâtel, the latter from Lausanne.

be presented with a singular example of fortitude, which each may imitate according to his ability." [1]

We shall now consider this astounding activity of the Reformer in detail: his Church polity, his theological system, his controversies, and his relation to, and influence on, foreign churches.

[1] *Vita Calv.* in *Opera*, XXI. 132.

CHAPTER XIII.

CONSTITUTION AND DISCIPLINE OF THE CHURCH OF GENEVA.

§ 98. *Literature.*

I. CALVIN's *Institutio Christ. Religionis*, the fourth book, which treats of the Church and the Sacraments. — *Les | ordinances | ecclésiastiques de | l'église de Genève. | Item | l'ordre des escoles | de la dite cité.* | Gen., 1541. 92 pp. 4°; another ed., 1562, 110 pp. Reprinted in *Opera*, X. fol. 15–30. (*Projet d'ordinances ecclésiastiques*, 1541). The same vol. contains also *L'ordre du College de Genève; Leges academicæ* (1559), fol. 65–90; and *Les ordinances ecclésiastiques de* 1561, fol. 91–124. Comp. the *Prolegomena*, IX. sq., and also the earliest document on the organization and worship of the Church of Geneva, 1537, fol. 5–14.

II. Dr. GEORG WEBER: *Geschichtliche Darstellung des Calvinismus im Verhältniss zum Staat in Genf und Frankreich bis zur Aufhebung des Edikts von Nantes*, Heidelberg, 1836 (pp. 372). The first two chapters only (pp. 1–32) treat of Calvin and Geneva; the greater part of the book is a history of the French Reformation till 1685. — C. B. HUNDESHAGEN: *Ueber den Einfluss des Calvinismus auf die Ideen von Staat, und staats-bürgerlicher Freiheit*, Bern, 1842. — *AMÉDÉE ROGET: *L'église et l'état à Genève du vivant de Calvin. Étude d'histoire politico-ecclésiastique*, Genève, 1867 (pp. 92). Comp. also his *Histoire du peuple de Genève depuis la réforme jusqu'à l'escalade* (1536–1602), 1870–1883, 7 vols.

III. HENRY, Part II. chs. III.–VI. Comp. his small biography, pp. 165–196. — DYER, ch. III. — STÄHELIN, bk. IV. (vol. I. 319 sqq.). — KAMPSCHULTE, I. 385–480. This is the end of his work; vols. II. and III. were prevented by his premature death (Dec. 3, 1872), and intrusted to Professor Cornelius of Munich (a friend and colleague of the late Dr. Döllinger), but he has so far only published a few papers on special points, in the Transactions of the Munich Academy. See p. 230. — MERLE D'AUBIGNÉ, bk. XI. chs. XXII.–XXIV. (vol. VII. 73 sqq.). These are his last chapters on Calvin, coming down to February, 1542; the continuation was prevented by his death in 1872.

§ 99. *Calvin's Idea of the Holy Catholic Church.*

DURING his sojourn at Strassburg, Calvin matured his views on the Church and the Sacraments, and embodied them in the fourth book of the second edition of his *Institutes*, which appeared in the same year as his Commentary on the Epistle to the Romans (1539). His ideal was high and comprehensive, far beyond what he was able to realize in the little district of Geneva. "In no respect, perhaps," says a distinguished Scotch Presbyterian scholar,[1] "are the *Institutes* more remarkable than in a certain comprehensiveness and *catholicity* of tone, which to many will appear strangely associated with his name. But Calvin was far too enlightened not to recognize the grandeur of the Catholic idea which had descended through so many ages; this idea had, in truth, for such a mind as his, special attractions, and his own system mainly sought to give to the same idea a new and higher form. The narrowness and intolerance of his ecclesiastical rule did not so much spring out of the general principles laid down in the *Institutes*, as from his special interpretation and application of these principles."

When Paul was a prisoner in Rome, chained to a heathen soldier, and when Christianity was confined to a small band of humble believers scattered through a hostile world, he described to the Ephesians his sublime conception of the Church as the mystical "body of Christ, the fulness of Him who filleth all in all." Yet in the same and other epistles he finds it necessary to warn the members of this holy brotherhood even against such vulgar vices as theft, intemperance, and fornication. The contradiction is only apparent, and disappears in the distinction between the ideal and the real, the essential and the phenomenal, the Church as it is in the mind of Christ and the Church as it is in the masses of nominal Christians.

The same apparent contradiction we find in Calvin, in Luther, and other Reformers. They cherished the deepest respect for the holy Catholic Church of Christ, and yet felt

---

[1] Principal Tulloch of the University of St. Andrews, in *Luther and other Leaders of the Reformation*, p. 203 (3d ed. 1883).

it their duty to protest with all their might against the abuses and corruptions of the actual Church of their age, and especially against the papal hierarchy which ruled it with despotic power. We may go further back to the protest of the Hebrew Prophets against the corrupt priesthood. Christ himself, who recognized the divine economy of the history of Israel, and came to fulfil the Law and the Prophets, attacked with withering severity the self-righteousness and hypocrisy of the Scribes and Pharisees who sat in Moses' seat, and was condemned by the high priest and the Jewish hierarchy to the death of the cross. These scriptural antecedents help very much to understand and to justify the course of the Reformers.

Nothing can be more truly Catholic than Calvin's description of the historic Church. It reminds one of the finest passages in St. Cyprian and St. Augustin. After explaining the meaning of the article of the Apostles' Creed on the holy Catholic Church, as embracing not only the visible Church, but all God's elect, living and departed, he thus speaks of the visible or historic Catholic Church: [1]—

"As our present design is to treat of the visible Church, we may learn even from the title of *mother*, how useful and even necessary it is for us to know her; since there is no other way of entrance into life, unless we are conceived by her, born of her, nourished at her breast, and continually preserved under her care and government till we are divested of this mortal flesh and become 'like the angels' (Matt. 22:30). For our infirmity will not admit of our dismission from her school; we must continue under her instruction and discipline to the end of our lives. It is also to be remarked that out of her bosom there can be no hope of remission of sins, or any salvation, according to the testimony of Isaiah (37:32) and Joel (2:32); which is confirmed by Ezekiel (13:9), when he denounces that those whom God excludes from the heavenly life shall not be enrolled among his people. So, on the contrary, those who devote themselves to the service of God are said to inscribe their names among the citizens of Jerusalem. For which reason the Psalmist says, ' Remember me, O Lord, with the favor that thou bearest unto thy people: O visit me with thy salvation, that I may see the prosperity of thy chosen, that I may rejoice in the gladness of thy nation, that I may glory with thine inheritance' (Ps. 106:4, 5). In these words the paternal

[1] *Inst.* IV. ch. I. § 4; comp. §§ 2 and 3.

favor of God, and the peculiar testimony of the spiritual life, are restricted to his flock, to teach us that it is always fatally dangerous to be separated from the Church."[1]

So strong are the claims of the visible Church upon us that even abounding corruptions cannot justify a secession. Reasoning against the Anabaptists and other radicals who endeavored to build up a new Church of converts directly from the Bible, without any regard to the intervening historical Church, he says :[2]—

"Dreadful are those descriptions in which Isaiah, Jeremiah, Joel, Habakkuk, and others, deplore the disorders of the Church at Jerusalem. There was such general and extreme corruption in the people, in the magistrates, and in the priests that Isaiah does not hesitate to compare Jerusalem to Sodom and Gomorrah. Religion was partly despised, partly corrupted. Their manners were generally disgraced by thefts, robberies, treacheries, murders, and similar crimes.

"Nevertheless, the Prophets on this account neither raised themselves new churches, nor built new altars for the oblation of separate sacrifices ; but whatever were the characters of the people, yet because they considered that God had deposited his word among that nation, and instituted the ceremonies in which he was there worshipped, they lifted up pure hands to him even in the congregation of the impious. If they had thought that they contracted any contagion from these services, surely they would have suffered a hundred deaths rather than have permitted themselves to be dragged to them. There was nothing, therefore, to prevent their departure from them, but the desire of preserving the unity of the Church.

"But if the holy Prophets were restrained by a sense of duty from forsaking the Church on account of the numerous and enormous crimes which were practiced, not by a few individuals, but almost by the whole nation, it is extreme arrogance in us, if we presume immediately to withdraw from the communion of a Church, where the conduct of all the members is not compatible either with our judgment or even with the Christian profession.

"Now what kind of an age was that of Christ and his Apostles ? Yet the desperate impiety of the Pharisees, and the dissolute lives everywhere led by the people, could not prevent them from using the same sacrifices, and assembling in the same temple with others, for the public exercises of religion. How did this happen, but from a knowledge that the society of the wicked could not contaminate those who, with pure consciences, united with them in the same solemnities.

"If any one pay no deference to the Prophets and the Apostles, let him at least acquiesce in the authority of Christ. Cyprian has excellently remarked:

[1] "*Ut semper exitialis sit ab ecclesia discessio.*"
[2] *Ibid.* IV. ch. 1, §§ 18, 19.

'Although tares, or impure vessels, are found in the Church, yet this is not a reason why we should withdraw from it. It only behooves us to labor that we may be the wheat, and to use our utmost endeavors and exertions that we may be vessels of gold or of silver. But to break in pieces the vessels of earth belongs to the Lord alone, to whom a rod of iron is also given. Nor let any one arrogate to himself what is the exclusive province of the Son of God, by pretending to fan the floor, clear away the chaff, and separate all the tares by the judgment of man. This is proud obstinacy, and sacrilegious presumption, originating in a corrupt frenzy.'

"Let these two points, then, be considered as decided: first, that he who voluntarily deserts the external communion of the Church where the Word of God is preached, and the sacraments are administered, is without any excuse; secondly, that the faults either of few persons or of many form no obstacles to a due profession of our faith in the use of the ceremonies instituted by God; because the pious conscience is not wounded by the unworthiness of any other individual, whether he be a pastor or a private person; nor are the mysteries less pure and salutary to a holy and upright man, because they are received at the same time by the impure."

How, then, with such high churchly views, could Calvin justify his separation from the Roman Church in which he was born and trained? He vindicated his position in the Answer to Sadolet, from which we have given large extracts.[1] He did it more fully in his masterly work, " On the Necessity of Reforming the Church," which, "in the name of all who wish Christ to reign," he addressed to the Emperor Charles V. and the Diet to be assembled at Speier in February, 1544. It is replete with weighty arguments and accurate learning, and by far one of the ablest controversial books of that age.[2] The following is a passage bearing upon this point: [3] —

---

[1] See § 91, pp. 404 sqq.

[2] *Supplex exhortatio ad Cæsarem Carolum V. de necessitate reformandæ Ecclesiæ*, 1543, in *Opera*, VI. 453–534. English Version by Henry Beveridge, *Calvin's Tracts*, I. 123–237. The Strassburg editors call it a "*libellus et ab argumenti gravitate et a stili elegantia præ cæteris commendandus, hodieque lectu dignissimus.*" *Proleg.*, p. xxviii. Calvin wrote this book at the request of Bucer, who urged him to do so in a letter of Oct. 25, 1543. It appeared also in French.

[3] *Opera*, VI. 518 sqq.; Beveridge, *l.c.*, 211 sqq. Compare the *Institutes*, IV. ch. II. §§ 6–12.

"The last and principal charge which they bring against us is, that we have made a schism in the Church. And here they fiercely maintain against us, that for no reason is it lawful to break the unity of the Church. How far they do us injustice the books of our authors bear witness. Now, however, let them take this brief reply — that we neither dissent from the Church, nor are aliens from her communion. But, as by this specious name of Church, they are wont to cast dust in the eyes even of persons otherwise pious and right-hearted, I beseech your Imperial Majesty, and you, Most Illustrious Princes, first, to divest yourselves of all prejudice, that you may give an impartial ear to our defence; secondly, not to be instantly terrified on hearing the name of Church, but to remember that the Prophets and Apostles had, with the pretended Church of their days, a contest similar to that which you see us have in the present day with the Roman pontiff and his whole train. When they, by the command of God, inveighed freely against idolatry, superstition, and the profanation of the temple, and its sacred rites, against the carelessness and lethargy of priests, and against the general avarice, cruelty, and licentiousness, they were constantly met with the objection which our opponents have ever in their mouths — that by dissenting from the common opinion, they violated the unity of the Church. The ordinary government of the Church was then vested in the priests. They had not presumptuously arrogated it to themselves, but God had conferred it upon them by his law. It would occupy too much time to point out all the instances. Let us, therefore, be contented with a single instance, in the case of Jeremiah.

"He had to do with the whole college of priests, and the arms with which they attacked him were these: 'Come, and let us devise devices against Jeremiah; for the law shall not perish from the priest, nor counsel from the wise, nor the word from the prophet' (Jer. 18:18). They had among them a high priest, to reject whose judgment was a capital crime, and they had the whole order to which God himself had committed the government of the Jewish Church concurring with them. If the unity of the Church is violated by him, who, instructed solely by Divine truth, opposes himself to ordinary authority, the Prophet must be a schismatic; because, not at all deterred by such menaces from warring with the impiety of the priests, he steadily persevered.

"That the eternal truth of God preached by the Prophets and Apostles, is on our side, we are prepared to show, and it is indeed easy for any man to perceive. But all that is done is to assail us with this battering-ram, 'Nothing can excuse withdrawal from the Church.' We deny out and out that we do so. With what, then, do they urge us? With nothing more than this, that to them belongs the ordinary government of the Church. But how much better right had the enemies of Jeremiah to use this argument? To them, at all events, there still remained a legal priesthood, instituted by God; so that their vocation was unquestionable. Those who in the present day have the name of prelates, cannot prove their vocation by any laws, human or divine. Be it, however, that in this respect both are on a footing, still, unless they previously convict the holy Prophet of schism, they will prove nothing against us by that specious title of Church.

"I have thus mentioned one Prophet as an example. But all the others declare that they had the same battle to fight — wicked priests endeavoring to overwhelm them by a perversion of this term Church. And how did the Apostles act? Was it not necessary for them, in professing themselves the servants of Christ, to declare war upon the synagogue? And yet the office and dignity of the priesthood were not then lost. But it will be said that, though the Prophets and Apostles dissented from wicked priests in doctrine, they still cultivated communion with them in sacrifices and prayers. I admit they did, provided they were not forced into idolatry. But which of the Prophets do we read of as having ever sacrificed in Bethel? Which of the faithful, do we suppose, communicated in impure sacrifices, when the temple was polluted by Antiochus, and profane rites were introduced into it?

"On the whole, we conclude that the servants of God never felt themselves obstructed by this empty title of Church, when it was put forward to support the reign of impiety. It is not enough, therefore, simply to throw out the name of Church, but judgment must be used to ascertain which is the true Church, and what is the nature of its unity. And the thing necessary to be attended to, first of all, is, to beware of separating the Church from Christ, its Head. When I say Christ, I include the doctrine of his gospel which he sealed with his blood. Our adversaries, therefore, if they would persuade us that they are the true Church must, first of all, show that the true doctrine of God is among them; and this is the meaning of what we often repeat, viz. that the uniform characteristics of a well-ordered Church are the preaching of sound doctrine, and the pure administration of the Sacraments. For, since Paul declares (Eph. 2:20) that the Church is 'built upon the foundation of the Apostles and Prophets,' it necessarily follows that any church not resting on this foundation must immediately fall.

"I come now to our opponents.

"They, no doubt, boast in lofty terms that Christ is on their side. As soon as they exhibit him in their word we will believe it, but not sooner. They, in the same way, insist on the term Church. But where, we ask, is that doctrine which Paul declares to be the only foundation of the Church? Doubtless, your Imperial Majesty now sees that there is a vast difference between assailing us with the reality and assailing us only with the name of Church. We are as ready to confess as they are that those who abandon the Church, the common mother of the faithful, the 'pillar and ground of the truth,' revolt from Christ also; but we mean a Church which, from incorruptible seed, begets children for immortality, and, when begotten, nourishes them with spiritual food (that seed and food being the Word of God), and which, by its ministry, preserves entire the truth which God deposited in its bosom. This mark is in no degree doubtful, in no degree fallacious, and it is the mark which God himself impressed upon his Church, that she might be discerned thereby. Do we seem unjust in demanding to see this mark? Wherever it exists not, no face of a Church is seen. If the name, merely, is put forward, we have only to quote the well-known passage of Jeremiah, 'Trust ye not in lying words, saying, the temple of the Lord, the temple of the Lord, the temple of the Lord, are these' (Jer. 7 : 4). 'Is this house, which is called by my name, become a den of robbers in your eyes ?' (Jer. 7 : 11).

"In like manner, the unity of the Church, such as Paul describes it, we protest we hold sacred, and we denounce anathema against all who in any way violate it. The principle from which Paul derives unity is, that there is 'one Lord, one faith, one baptism, one God and Father of all,' who hath called us into one hope (Eph. 4 : 4–6). Therefore, we are one body and one spirit, as is here enjoined, if we adhere to God only, *i.e.* be bound to each other by the tie of faith. We ought, moreover, to remember what is said in another passage, 'that faith cometh by the word of God.' Let it, therefore, be a fixed point, that a holy unity exists amongst us, when, consenting in pure doctrine, we are united in Christ alone. And, indeed, if concurrence in any kind of doctrine were sufficient, in what possible way could the Church of God be distinguished from the impious factions of the wicked ? Wherefore, the Apostle shortly after adds, that the ministry was instituted 'for the edifying of the body of Christ : till we all come in the unity of the faith, and of the knowledge of the Son of God : that we be no more children, tossed to and fro, and carried about with every wind of doctrine, but speaking the truth in love, may grow up into him in all things, who is the Head, even Christ' (Eph. 4 : 12–15). Could he more plainly comprise the whole unity of the Church in a holy agreement in true doctrine, than when he calls us back to Christ and to faith, which is included in the knowledge of him, and to obedience to the truth ? Nor is any lengthened demonstration of this needed by those who believe the Church to be that sheepfold of which Christ alone is the Shepherd, and where his voice only is heard, and distinguished from the voice of strangers. And this is confirmed by Paul, when he prays for the Romans, 'The God of patience and consolation grant you to be of the same mind one with another, according to Christ Jesus ; that ye may with one accord and one mouth glorify God, even the Father of our Lord Jesus Christ' (Rom. 15 : 5, 6).

"Let our opponents, then, in the first instance, draw near to Christ, and then let them convict us of schism, in daring to dissent from them in doctrine. But, since I have made it plain that Christ is banished from their society, and the doctrine of his gospel exterminated, their charge against us simply amounts to this, that we adhere to Christ in preference to them. For what man, pray, will believe that those who refuse to be led away from Christ and his truth, in order to deliver themselves into the power of men, are thereby schismatics, and deserters from the communion of the Church ?

"I certainly admit that respect is to be shown to priests, and that there is great danger in despising ordinary authority. If, then, they were to say, that we are not at our own hand to resist ordinary authority, we should have no difficulty in subscribing to the sentiment. For we are not so rude as not to see what confusion must arise when the authority of rulers is not respected. Let pastors, then, have their due honor — an honor, however, not derogatory in any degree to the supreme authority of Christ, to whom it behooves them and every man to be subject. For God declares, by Malachi, that the government of the Israelitish Church was committed to the priests, under the condition that they should faithfully fulfil the covenant made with them, viz. that 'their lips should keep knowledge,' and expound the law to the people (Mal. 2:7). When the priests altogether failed in this condition, he declares, that, by their perfidy, the covenant was abrogated and made null. Pastors are mistaken if they imagine that they are invested with the government of the Church on any other terms than that of being ministers and witnesses of the truth of God. As long, therefore, as, in opposition to the law and to the nature of their office, they eagerly wage war with the truth of God, let them not arrogate to themselves a power which God never bestowed, either formerly on priests, or now on bishops, on any other terms than those which have been mentioned."

When the Romanists demanded miracles from the Reformers as a test of their innovations, Calvin replied that this was "unreasonable; for we forge no new gospel, but retain the very same, whose truth was confirmed by all the miracles ever wrought by Christ and the Apostles. The opponents have this advantage over us, that they confirm their faith by continual miracles even to this day. But they allege miracles which are calculated to unsettle a mind otherwise well established; for they are frivolous and ridiculous, or vain and false. Nor, if they were ever so preternatural, ought they to have any weight in opposition to the truth of God, since the name of God ought to be sanctified in all places and at all times, whether by miraculous events or by the common order of nature." [1]

Luther had the same Catholic Church feeling, and gave strong expression to it in his writings against the radicals, and in a letter to the Margrave of Brandenburg and Duke of Prussia (1532), in which he says: "It is dangerous and terrible to hear or believe anything against the unanimous testimony of the entire holy Christian Church as held from the beginning for now over fifteen hundred years in all the world." [2] And yet he asserted the right of conscience and

---

[1] Dedication of his *Institutes* to Francis I.

[2] *Briefe*, De Wett's ed. IV. 354. Still more striking is Luther's judgment on the Roman Church (in his book against the Anabaptists): *"Ich sage, dass unter dem Papst die wahre Christenheit ist; ja der rechte Ausbund der Christen-*

private judgment at Worms against popes and councils, because he deemed it "unsafe and dangerous to do anything against the conscience bound in the Word of God."

§ 100. *The Visible and Invisible Church.*

Comp. vol. VI. § 85, and the literature there quoted.

A distinction between real and nominal Christianity is as old as the Church, and has never been denied. "Many are called, but few are chosen." We can know all that are actually called, but God only knows those who are truly chosen. The kindred parables of the tares and of the net illustrate the fact that the kingdom of heaven in this world includes good and bad men, and that a final separation will not take place before the judgment day.[1] Paul distinguishes between an outward circumcision of the flesh and an inward circumcision of the heart; between a carnal Israel and a spiritual Israel; and he speaks of Gentiles who are ignorant of the written law, yet "do by nature the things of the law," and will judge those who, "with the letter and circumcision, are transgressors of the law." He thereby intimates that God's mercy is not bounded by the limits of the visible Church.[2]

Augustin makes a distinction between the true body of Christ, which consists of the elect children of God from the beginning, and the mixed body of Christ, which comprehends all the baptized.[3] In the Middle Ages the Church was identified with the dominion of the papacy, and the Cyprianic

---

heit, und viel frommer grosser Heiligen." Werke, XXVI. 257, Erlangen ed. Möhler (in his *Symbolik*, pp. 421, 437) sees in such expressions so many self-refutations of the Reformers in separating from the Catholic Church, and forgets that they were cast out with curses and anathemas.

[1] Matt. 13 : 24–30; 47–49.

[2] Rom. 2 : 14, 15, 28, 29; Col. 2 : 11.

[3] *Corpus Christi merum*, and *corpus Christi mixtum. De Doctr. Christ.* III. 32; *De Baptismo contra Donatistas*, IV. 5. The Donatist Tichonius used the less suitable designation of a twofold body of Christ (*corpus Christi bipartitum*).

maxim, " *Extra ecclesiam nulla salus*," was narrowed into
" *Extra ecclesiam Romanam nulla salus*," to the exclusion not
only of heretical sects, but also of the Oriental Church. Wiclif
and Hus, in opposition to the corruptions of the papal Church,
renewed the distinction of Augustin, under a different and
less happy designation of the congregation of the predestinated or the elect, and the congregation of those who are
only foreknown.[1]

The Reformers introduced the terminology " visible " and
"invisible " Church. By this they did not mean two distinct
and separate Churches, but rather two classes of Christians
within the same outward communion. The invisible Church
is in the visible Church, as the soul is in the body, or the
kernel in the shell, but God only knows with certainty who
belong to the invisible Church and will ultimately be saved;
and in this sense his true children are invisible, that is, not
certainly recognizable and known to men. We may object
to the terminology, but the distinction is real and important.

Luther, who openly adopted the view of Hus at the disputation of Leipzig, first applied the term "invisible " to the
true Church, which is meant in the Apostles' Creed.[2] The
Augsburg Confession defines the Church to be "the congregation of saints (or believers), in which the Gospel is purely
taught, and the sacraments are rightly administered." This
definition is too narrow for the invisible Church, and would
exclude the Baptists and Quakers.[3]

The Reformed system of doctrine extends the domain of
the invisible or true Church and the possibility of salvation

[1] See Wiclif's tract *De Ecclesia*, published by Loserth, 1886. Hus, in his
tract on the same subject, literally adopted Wiclif's view.

[2] He speaks of the *ecclesia invisibilis* in his second Commentary on the
Galatians, vol. III. 38. Erlangen ed. The Lutheran symbolical books do
not use the term, but teach the thing.

[3] The Ninth Article of the Augsburg Confession expressly condemns the
Anabaptists for rejecting infant baptism and maintaining the salvation of
unbaptized infants.

beyond the boundaries of the visible Church, and holds that
the Spirit of God is not bound to the ordinary means of
grace, but may work and save "when, where, and how he
pleases."[1] Zwingli first introduced both terms. He meant
by the "visible" Church the community of all who bear the
Christian name, by the "invisible" Church the totality of
true believers of all ages.[2] And he included in the invisible
Church all the pious heathen, and all infants dying in infancy, whether baptized or not. In this liberal view, however, he stood almost alone in his age and anticipated modern
opinions.[3]

Calvin defines the distinction more clearly and fully than
any of the Reformers, and his view passed into the Second
Helvetic, the Scotch, the Westminster, and other Reformed
Confessions.

"The Church," he says,[4] "is used in the sacred Scriptures in two senses.
Sometimes when they mention 'the Church' they intend that which is really
such in the sight of God (*quæ revera est coram Deo*), into which none are received but those who by adoption and grace are the children of God, and by
the sanctification of the Spirit are the true members of Christ. And then it

---

[1] See Westminster Confession of Faith, ch. X. 3.

[2] *Expos. Christ. Fidei* (written in 1531, and published by Bullinger, 1536) :
"*Credimus et unam sanctam esse, h.e. universalem ecclesiam. Eam autem esse
aut visibilem aut invisibilem. Invisibilis est, juxta Pauli verbum, quæ cœlo descen-
dit, hoc est, quæ Spiritu Sancto illustrante Deum cognoscit et amplectitur. De ista
ecclesia sunt quotquot per universum orbem credunt. Vocatur autem invisibilis non
quasi qui credunt sint invisibiles, sed quod humanis oculis non patet quinam credant;
sunt enim fideles soli Deo et sibi perspecti. Visibilis autem ecclesia non est Ponti-
fex Romanus cum reliquis cidarim gestantibus, sed quotquot per universum orbem
Christo nomen dederunt.*" *Opera,* IV. 58. Niemeyer, *Coll. Confess.,* p. 53. Zwingli
teaches the same distinction, but without the terms, in his earlier Confession
to Charles V. See Niemeyer, p. 22.

[3] See above, pp. 95, 177, 211. Bullinger probably agreed with the liberal
view of his revered teacher and friend, as we may infer from his unqualified
commendation of the last Confession of Zwingli, in which he most emphatically teaches the salvation of the pious heathen. Bullinger published it five
years after Zwingli's death, and said in the preface that in this book Zwingli
surpassed himself ("*hoc libello sese superans de vera fide nescio quid cygneum
vicina morte cantavit*").

[4] *Inst.* bk. IV. ch. I. § 7.

comprehends not only the saints at any one time resident on earth, but all the elect who have lived from the beginning of the world.

"But the word 'Church' is frequently used in the Scriptures to designate the whole multitude dispersed all over the world, who profess to worship one God and Jesus Christ, who are initiated into his faith by baptism, who testify their unity in true doctrine and charity by a participation of the sacred supper, who consent to the word of the Lord, and preserve the ministry which Christ has instituted for the purpose of preaching it. In this Church are included many hypocrites, who have nothing of Christ but the name and appearance; many persons, ambitious, avaricious, envious, slanderous, and dissolute in their lives, who are tolerated for a time, either because they cannot be convicted by a legitimate process, or because discipline is not always maintained with sufficient vigor.

"As it is necessary therefore to believe that Church which is invisible to us, and known to God alone, so this Church, which is visible to men, we are commanded to honor, and to maintain communion with it."

Calvin does not go as far as Zwingli in extending the number of the elect, but there is nothing in his principles to forbid such extension. He makes salvation dependent upon God's sovereign grace, and not upon the visible means of grace. He expressly includes in the invisible Church "all the elect who have lived from the beginning of the world," and even those who had no historical knowledge of Christ. He says, in agreement with Augustin : "According to the secret predestination of God, there are *many sheep without the pale of the Church*, and many wolves within it. For God knows and seals those who know not either him or themselves. Of those who externally bear his seal, his eyes alone can discern who are unfeignedly holy, and will persevere to the end, which is the completion of salvation." But in the judgment of charity, he continues, we must acknowledge as members of the Church "all those who, by a confession of faith, an exemplary life, and a participation in the sacraments, profess the same God and Christ with ourselves." [1]

[1] *Inst.* IV. ch. I. § 10.

§ 101. *The Civil Government.*

On civil government see *Institutes*, IV. ch. XX., *De politica administratione* (in Tholuck's ed. II. 475–496).

Calvin discusses the nature and function of Civil Government at length, and with the ability and wisdom of a statesman, in the last chapter of his *Institutes.*

He holds that the Church is consistent with all forms of government and social conditions, even with civil servitude (1 Cor. 7 : 21). But some kind of government is as necessary to mankind in this world as bread and water, light and air; and it is far more excellent, since it protects life and property, maintains law and order, and enables men to live peaceably together, and to pursue their several avocations.

As to the different forms of government, Calvin discusses the merits of monarchy, aristocracy, and democracy. All are compatible with Christianity and command our obedience. All have their advantages and dangers. Monarchy easily degenerates into despotism, aristocracy into oligarchy or the faction of a few, democracy into mobocracy and sedition. He gives the preference to a mixture of aristocracy and democracy. He infused a more aristocratic spirit into the democratic Republic of Geneva, and saw a precedent in the government of Moses with seventy elders elected from the wisest and best of the people. It is safer, he thinks, for the government to be in the hands of many than of one, for they may afford each other assistance, and restrain arrogance and ambition.

Civil government is of divine origin. "All power is ordained of God" (Rom. 13 : 1). "By me kings reign, and princes decree justice" (Prov. 8 : 15). The magistrates are called "gods" (Ps. 82 : 1, 6; a passage indorsed by Christ, John 10 : 35), because they are invested with God's authority and act as his vicegerents. "Civil magistracy is not only holy and legitimate, but far the most sacred and honorable in human life." Submission to lawful government is the duty of every citizen. To resist it, is to set at naught the ordinance of God (Rom. 13:3, 4; comp. Tit. 3:1; 1 Pet. 2:13, 14). Paul admonishes Timothy that in the public congregation "supplication, prayers, intercessions, thanksgivings be made for kings and for all that are in high places; that we may lead a tranquil and quiet life in all godliness and gravity" (1 Tim. 2:1, 2). We must obey and pray even for bad rulers, and endure in patience and humility till God exercises his judgment. The punishment of evildoers belongs only to God and to the magistrates. Sometimes God punishes the people by wicked rulers, and punishes these by other bad rulers. We, as individuals, must suffer rather than rebel. Only in one case are we required to disobey, — when the civil ruler commands us to do anything against the will of God and against our conscience. Then "we must obey God rather than men" (Acts 5:29).[1]

Calvin was thus a strong upholder of authority in the State. He did not advise or encourage the active resistance of the Huguenots at the beginning of the civil wars in France, although he gave a tacit consent.

Calvin extended the authority and duty of civil government to both Tables of the Law. He assigns to it, in Christian society, the office, — "to cherish and support the external worship of God, to preserve the true doctrine of religion, to defend the constitution of the Church, and to regulate our lives in a manner requisite for the social welfare." He proves this view from the Old Testament, and quotes the passage in Isaiah 49:23, that "kings shall be nursing-fathers

---

[1] He concludes his *Institutes* with this sentence: "Since this edict has been proclaimed by that celestial herald, Peter, 'we must obey God rather than men,' let us console ourselves with this thought, that we truly perform the obedience which God requires of us, when we suffer anything rather than deviate from piety. And that our hearts may not fail us, Paul stimulates us with another consideration: that Christ has redeemed us at the immense price which our redemption cost him, that we may not be submissive to the corrupt desires of men, much less be slaves to their impiety" (1 Cor. 7:23).

and queens nursing-mothers" to the Church. He refers to the examples of Moses, Joshua and the Judges, David, Josiah, and Hezekiah.

Here is the critical point where religious persecution by the State comes in as an inevitable consequence. Offences against the Church are offences against the State, and *vice versa*, and deserve punishment by fines, imprisonment, exile, and, if necessary, by death. On this ground the execution of Servetus and other heretics was justified by all who held the same theory; fortunately, it has no support whatever in the New Testament, but is directly contrary to the spirit of the gospel.

Geneva, after the emancipation from the power of the bishop and the duke of Savoy, was a self-governing Republic under the protection of Bern and the Swiss Confederacy. The civil government assumed the episcopal power, and exercised it first in favor, then against, and at last permanently for the Reformation.

The Republic was composed of all citizens of age, who met annually in general assembly (*conseil général*), usually in St. Peter's, under the sounding of bells and trumpets, for the ratification of laws and the election of officers. The administrative power was lodged in four Syndics; the legislative power in two councils, the Council of Sixty, and the Council of Two Hundred. The former existed since 1457; the latter was instituted in 1526, after the alliance with Freiburg and Bern, in imitation of the Constitution of these and other Swiss cities. The Sixty were by right members of the Council of Two Hundred. In 1530 the Two Hundred assumed the right to elect the ordinary or little Council of Twenty-Five, who were a part of the two other councils and had previously been elected by the Syndics. The real power lay in the hands of the Syndics and the little Council of Twenty-five, which formed an oligarchy with legislative, executive, and judicial functions.

Calvin did not change these fundamental institutions of the Republic, but he infused into them a Christian and disciplinary spirit, and improved the legislation. He was appointed, together with the Syndics Roset, Porral, and Balard, to draw up a new code of laws, as early as Nov. 1, 1541.[1] He devoted much time to this work, and paid attention even to the minutest details concerning the administration of justice, the city police, the military, the firemen, the watchmen on the towers, and the like.[2]

The city showed her gratitude by presenting him with "a cask of old wine" for these extra services.[3]

Many of his regulations continued in legal force down to the eighteenth century.

Calvin was consulted in all important affairs of the State, and his advice was usually followed; but he never occupied a political or civil office. He was not even a citizen of Geneva till 1559 (eighteen years after his second arrival), and never appeared before the councils except when some ecclesiastical question was debated, or when his advice was asked. It is a mistake, therefore, to call him the head of the Republic, except in a purely intellectual and moral sense.

The code of laws was revised with the aid of Calvin by his friend, Germain Colladon (1510–1594), an eminent jurisconsult and member of a distinguished family of French

---

[1] *Reg. du Conseil*, in *Annal.* vol. XXI. 287. Comp. vol. X. Pars I. 125.

[2] In the Grand Ducal Library of Gotha are preserved several drafts of Calvin, in his own handwriting, on the various departments of civil government, especially the reform of judicial proceedings. They are published in *Opera*, X. Pars I. 125–146. "*Nicht ohne Bewunderung*," says Kampschulte (I. 416), "*sehen wir in ihnen den gelehrten Verfasser der Institution selbst den untergeordneten Fragen der städtischen Verwaltung und Polizei seine Aufmerksamkeit zuwenden. Da finden wir ausführliche Instructionen für den Bauaufseher, Anordnungen für den Fall einer Feuersbrunst, Anweisungen für den Aufseher des städtischen Geschützwesens, Verhaltungsregeln sogar für den Nachtwächter, für die Ketten-, Thor-, und Thurmhüter.*"

[3] "*Resoluz quil luy soyt donné ung bossot de vin vieulx de celluy de l'hospital.*" *Registre du Conseil*, Nov. 17, 1542, quoted in *Annal.* vol. XXI. 305, and in *Opera*, X. P. I. 125.

refugees who settled at Geneva. The revised code was begun in 1560, and published in 1568.[1]

Among the laws of Geneva we mention a press law, the oldest in Switzerland, dated Feb. 15, 1560. Laws against the freedom of the press existed before, especially in Spain. Alexander VI., a Spaniard, issued a bull in 1501, instructing the German prelates to exercise a close supervision over printers. Ferdinand and Isabella the Catholic established a censorship which prohibited, under severe penalties, the printing, importation, and sale of any book that had not previously passed an examination and obtained a license. Rome adopted the same policy. Other countries, Protestant as well as Roman Catholic, followed the example. In Russia, the severest restrictions of the press are still in force.

The press law of Geneva was comparatively moderate. It put the press under the supervision of three prudent and experienced men, to be appointed by the government. These men have authority to appoint able and trustworthy printers, to examine every book before it is printed, to prevent popish, heretical, and infidel publications, to protect the publisher against piracy; but Bibles, catechisms, prayers, and psalms may be printed by all publishers; new translations of the Scriptures are privileged in the first edition.[2]

The censorship of the press continued in Geneva till the eighteenth century. In 1600 the Council forbade the printing of the essays of Montaigne; in 1763 Rousseau's *Emile* was condemned to be burned.

---

[1] On the Colladon family see *La France Protestante*, IV. 510 sqq. (second ed. by Bordier). Another distinguished member was Nicolas Colladon, who published a Life of Calvin in 1565, and succeeded him in the chair of theology in 1566.

[2] The Spanish censorship was applied to the vernacular versions of the Bible, the works of Erasmus, all Protestant books, the Mystics and Illuminati, the Molinists and Quietists. The natural consequence of this tyranny was the decadence of intellectual and literary activity. See H. C. Lea, *Chapters from the Religious History of Spain connected with the Inquisition*, Philadelphia, 1890.

It should be noted, however, that under the influence of Calvin Geneva became one of the most important places of publication. The famous Robert Stephen (Étienne, 1503–1559), being censured by the Sorbonne of Paris, settled in Geneva after the death of his father, Henri, as a professed Protestant, and printed there two editions of the Hebrew Bible, and an edition of the Greek Testament, with the Vulgate and Erasmian versions, in 1551, which for the first time contains the versicular division of the text according to our present usage. To him we owe the *Thesaurus Linguæ Latinæ* (third ed. 1543, in 4 vols.), and to his son, Henri, the *Thesaurus Linguæ Græcæ* (1572, 4 vols.). Beza published several editions of his Greek Testament in Geneva (1565–1598), which were chiefly used by King James' translators. In the same city appeared the English version of the New Testament by Whittingham, 1557; then of the whole Bible, 1560. This is the so-called " Geneva Bible," or " Breeches Bible " (from the rendering of Gen. 3 : 7), which was for a long time the most popular English version, and passed through about two hundred editions from 1560 to 1630.[1] Geneva has well maintained its literary reputation to this day.

§ 102. *Distinctive Principles of Calvin's Church Polity.*

Calvin was a legislator and the founder of a new system of church polity and discipline. He had a legal training, which was of much use to him in organizing the Reformed Church at Geneva. If he had lived in the Middle Ages, he might have been a Hildebrand or an Innocent III. But the spirit of the Reformation required a reconstruction of church government on an evangelical and popular basis.

Calvin laid great stress on the outward organization and order of the Church, but in subordination to sound doctrine and the inner spiritual life. He compares the former to the

---

[1] *The Bibles in the Caxton Exhibition*, London, 1878, p. 95.

body, while the doctrine which regulates the worship of God, and points out the way of salvation, is the soul which animates the body and renders it lively and active.[1]

The Calvinistic system of church polity is based upon the following principles, which have exerted great influence in the development of Protestantism: —

1. The autonomy of the Church, or its right of self-government under the sole headship of Christ.

The Roman Catholic Church likewise claims autonomy, but in a hierarchical sense, and under the supreme control of the pope, who, as the visible vicar of Christ, demands passive obedience from priests and people. Calvin vests the self-government in the Christian congregation, and regards all the ministers of the gospel, in their official character, as ambassadors and representatives of Christ. "Christ alone," he says, "ought to rule and reign in the Church, and to have all preeminence in it, and this government ought to be exercised and administered solely by his word; yet as he dwells not among us by a visible presence, so as to make an audible declaration of his will to us, he uses for this purpose the ministry of men whom he employs as his delegates, not to transfer his right and honor to them, but only that he may himself do his work by their lips; just as an artificer makes use of an instrument in the performance of his work." [2]

In practice, however, the autonomy both of the Roman Catholic hierarchy and of the Protestant Churches is more or less curtailed and checked by the civil government wherever Church and State are united, and where the State supports the Church. For self-government requires self-support. Calvin intended to institute synods, and to make the clergy

---

[1] *" De necessitate reformandæ Ecclesiæ "* (*Opera*, VI. 459 sq.): *" Regimen in ecclesia, munus pastorale, et reliquus ordo, una cum sacramentis, instar corporis sunt ; doctrina autem illa, quæ rite colendi Dei regulam præscribit, et ubi salutis fiduciam debeant hominum conscientiæ ostendit, anima est, quæ corpus ipsum inspirat, vividum et actuosum reddit ; facit denique, ne sit mortuum et inutile cadaver."*

[2] *Inst.* IV. ch. III. § 1.

independent of State patronage, but in this he did not succeed.

The Lutheran Reformers subjected the Church to the secular rulers, and made her an obedient handmaid of the State; but they complained bitterly of the selfish and arbitrary misgovernment of the princes. The congregations in most Lutheran countries of Europe have no voice in the election of their own pastors. The Reformers of German Switzerland conceded more power to the people in a democratic republic, and introduced synods, but they likewise put the supreme power into the hands of the civil government of the several cantons. In monarchical England the governorship of the Church was usurped and exercised by Henry VIII. and, in a milder form, by Queen Elizabeth and her successors, and acquiesced in by the bishops. The churches under Calvin's influence always maintained, at least in theory, the independence of the Church in all spiritual affairs, and the right of individual congregations in the election of their own pastors. Calvin derives this right from the Greek verb used in the passage which says that Paul and Barnabas ordained presbyters by the suffrages or votes of the people.[1] "Those two apostles," he says, "ordained the presbyters; but the whole multitude, according to the custom observed among the Greeks, declared by the elevation of their hands who was the object of their choice. . . . It is not credible that Paul granted to Timothy and Titus more power (1 Tim. 5 : 22; Tit. 1 : 5) than he assumed to himself." After quoting with approval two passages from Cyprian, he concludes that the apostolic and best mode of electing pastors is by the consent of the whole people; yet other pastors ought to preside over the election, "to guard the multitude from falling into improprieties through inconstancy, intrigue, and confusion."[2]

---

[1] Acts 14 : 23, χειροτονήσαντες, voting by uplifting the hand.

[2] *Inst.* IV. ch. III. § 15; comp. ch. IV. § 11 sqq., where he quotes the old rule : "Let him who is to preside over all, be chosen by all."

The Presbyterian Church of Scotland has labored and suffered more than any Protestant Church for the principle of the sole headship of Christ; first against popery, then against prelacy, and last against patronage. In North America this principle is almost universally acknowledged.

2. The parity of the clergy as distinct from a *jure divino* hierarchy whether papal or prelatical.

Calvin maintained, with Jerome, the original identity of bishops (overseers) and presbyters (elders); and in this he has the support of the best modern exegetes and historians.[1]

But he did not on this account reject all distinctions among ministers, which rest on human right and historical development, nor deny the right of adapting the Church order to varying conditions and circumstances. He was not an exclusive or bigoted Presbyterian. He had no objection to episcopacy in large countries, like Poland and England, provided the evangelical doctrines be preached.[2]   In his

---

[1] In his Commentary on Phil. 1:1, he correctly infers from the plural ἐπίσκοποι, that "*nomen episcopi omnibus Verbi ministris esse commune, quum plures uni ecclesiæ Episcopos attribuat. Sunt igitur synonyma Episcopus et Pastor. Atque hic locus ex iis unus est, quos Hieronymus ad illud probandum citat, in Epistola ad Evagrium, et in expositione Epistolæ ad Titum.*" In his Commentary on Acts 20:28 (comp. with verse 17), he says: "*Omnes Ephesinos Presbyteros indifferentur a Paulo sic [episcopi] vocantur, unde colligimus secundum Scripturæ usum nihil a Presbyteris differre Episcopos, sed vitio et corruptela factum esse, ut qui primas tenebant in singulis civitatibus Episcopi vocari coeperint.*" Comp. also his commentaries on the relevant passages in the Pastoral Epistles, and his *Inst.* IV. ch. III. § 8, and ch. IV. § 2 (where he quotes Jerome in full). The Lutheran symbols likewise teach the identity of the episcopate and presbyterate (see the second Appendix to the Smalcaldian Articles, p. 341, ed. J. T. Müller); but the Lutheran Churches in Germany have Superintendents and General Superintendents (called "Bishops" in Prussia, "Prelates" in Württemberg). Sweden, Norway, and Denmark retained or reintroduced episcopacy (*jure humano*, not *jure divino*). The church government of the Lutheran Churches in America is a compromise between the Presbyterian and synodical system and congregational independency.

[2] Melanchthon in this respect went much further and was willing to submit to a papacy, provided the pope would tolerate the free preaching of the gospel. He subscribed the Smalcaldian Articles with the restriction: "*De pontifice statuo, si evangelium admitteret, posse ei propter pacem et communem tranquillitatem Christianorum . . . superioritatem in episcopos . . . jure humano etiam a nobis permitti.*"

correspondence with Archbishop Cranmer and Protector Somerset, he suggests various improvements, but does not oppose episcopacy. In a long letter to King Sigismund Augustus of Poland, he even approves of it in that kingdom.[1]

But Presbyterianism and Congregationalism are more congenial to the spirit of Calvinism than prelacy. In the conflict with Anglican prelacy during the seventeenth century, the Calvinistic Churches became exclusively Presbyterian in Scotland, or Independent in England and New England. During the same period, in opposition to the enforced introduction of the Anglican liturgy, the Presbyterians and Congregationalists abandoned liturgical worship; while Calvin and the Reformed Churches on the Continent approved of forms of devotion in connection with free prayer in public worship.

3. The participation of the Christian laity in Church government and discipline. This is a very important feature.

In the Roman Church the laity are passive, and have no share whatever in legislation. Theirs is simply to obey the priesthood. Luther first effectively proclaimed the doc-

---

[1] He says in this letter, dated Geneva, 5th Dec., 1554: "The ancient Church indeed instituted patriarchates, and to different provinces assigned certain primacies, that by this bond of concord the bishops might remain more closely united among themselves. Exactly as if, at the present day, one archbishop should have a certain pre-eminence in the illustrious kingdom of Poland, not to lord it over the others, nor arrogate to himself a right of which they were forcibly deprived; but for the sake of order to occupy the first place in synods, and cherish a holy unity between his colleagues and brethren. Then there might be either provincial or urban bishops, whose functions should be particularly directed to the preservation of order. As nature dictates, one of these should be chosen from each college, to whom this care should be specially confided. But it is one thing to hold a moderate dignity such as is not imcompatible with the abilities of a man, and another to comprise the whole world under one overgrown government. What the Romanists keep prating about one single head is then altogether nugatory, because neither the sacred commandment of God, nor the established usage of the Church sanctions a second head to be joined with Christ, whom alone the Heavenly Father has set over all." Bonnet-Constable, III. 104. Comp. *Inst.* IV. ch. IV. §§ 1-4; Henry II. 68, 375; III. 427 sqq.; Dyer, 283 sqq.; 456 sq.

trine of the general priesthood of the laity, but Calvin put it into an organized form, and made the laity a regular agency in the local congregation, and in the synods and councils of the Church. His views are gaining ground in other denominations, and are almost generally adopted in the United States. Even the Protestant Episcopal Church gives, in the lower house of her diocesan and general conventions, to the laity an equal representation with the clergy.

4. Strict discipline to be exercised jointly by ministers and lay-elders, with the consent of the whole congregation.

In this point Calvin went far beyond the older Reformers, and achieved greater success, as we shall see hereafter.

5. Union of Church and State on a theocratic basis, if possible, or separation, if necessary to secure the purity and self-government of the Church. This requires fuller exposition.

§ 103. *Church and State.*

Calvin's Church polity is usually styled a theocracy, by friends in praise, by foes in censure.[1] This is true, but in a qualified sense. He aimed at the sole rule of Christ and his Word both in Church and State, but without mixture and interference. The two powers were almost equally balanced in Geneva. The early Puritan colonies in New England were an imitation of the Geneva model.

In theory, Calvin made a clearer distinction between the spiritual and secular powers than was usual in his age, when both were inextricably interwoven and confused. He compares the Church to the soul, the State to the body. The

---

[1] By Weber, Henry, and Stähelin, and many others; also by Kampschulte, who remarks (I. 471): "*Der Grundgedanke, von dem der Gesetzgeber Genfs ausgeht, ist die Theokratie. Er will in Genf den Gottesstaat herstellen.*" But Amédée Roget (*L'église et l'état à Genève du vivant de Calvin*) and Merle d'Aubigné (vol. VII. 120) dissent from this view and point to the limitations of the ecclesiastical power in Geneva. Merle d'Aubigné says: "Calvin was not a theocrat, unless the term be taken in the most spiritual sense."

one has to do with the spiritual and eternal welfare of man, the other with the affairs of this present, transitory life.[1] Each is independent and sovereign in its own sphere. He was opposed to any interference of the civil government with the internal affairs and discipline of the Church. He was displeased with the servile condition of the clergy in Germany and in Bern, and often complained (even on his deathbed) of the interference of Bern with the Church in Geneva. But he was equally opposed to a clerical control of civil and political affairs, and confined the Church to the spiritual sword. He never held a civil office. The ministers were not eligible to the magistracy and the councils.

Yet he did not go so far as to separate the two powers; on the contrary, he united them as closely as their different functions would admit. His fundamental idea was, that God alone is Lord on earth as well as in heaven, and should rule supreme in Church and State. In this sense he was theocratic or christocratic. God uses Church and State as two distinct but co-operative arms for the upbuilding of Christ's kingdom. The law for both is the revealed will of God in the Holy Scriptures. The Church gives moral support to the State, while the State gives temporal support to the Church.

Calvin's ideal of Christian society resembles that of Hildebrand, but differs from it on the following important points: —

1. Calvin's theory professed to be based upon the Scriptures, as the only rule of faith and practice; the papal theocracy drew its support chiefly from tradition and the canon law.

Calvin's arguments, however, are exclusively taken from the Old Testament. The Calvinistic as well as the papal theocracy is Mosaic and legalistic rather than Christian and evangelical. The Apostolic Church had no connection what-

---

[1] *Inst.* IV. ch. XX. § 1. " *Volui,*" he wrote to a friend, " *sicut æquum est, spiritualem potestatem a civili judicio distingui.*" *Epp. et Resp.* 263.

ever with the State except to obey its legitimate demands. Christ's rule is expressed in that wisest word ever uttered on this subject: "Render unto Cæsar the things that are Cæsar's; and unto God the things that are God's " (Matt. 22: 21).

2. Calvin recognized only the invisible headship of Christ, and rejected the papal claim to world-dominion as an antichristian usurpation.

3. He had a much higher view of the State than the popes. He considered it equally divine in origin and authority as the Church, and fully independent in all temporal matters; while the papal hierarchy in the Middle Ages often overruled the State by ecclesiastical authority. Hildebrand compared the Church to the sun, the State to the moon which borrows her light from the sun, and claimed and exercised the right of deposing kings and absolving subjects from their oaths of allegiance. Boniface VIII. formulated this claim in the well-known theory of the two swords.

4. Calvin's theocracy was based upon the sovereignty of the Christian people and the general priesthood of believers; the papal theocracy was an exclusive rule of the priesthood.

In practice, the two powers were not as clearly distinct at Geneva as in theory. They often intermeddled with each other. The ministers criticised the acts of the magistrates from the pulpit; and the magistrates called the ministers to account for their sermons. Discipline was a common territory for both, and the Consistory was a mixed body of clergymen and laymen. The government fixed and paid the salaries of the pastors, and approved their nomination and transfer from one parish to another. None could even absent himself for a length of time without leave by the Council. The Large Council voted on the Confession of Faith and Discipline, and gave them the power of law.

The Reformed Church of Geneva, in one word, was an established Church or State Church, and continues so to this day, though no more in an exclusive sense, but with liberty to Dissenters, whether Catholic or Protestant, who have of late been increasing by immigration.

The union of Church and State is tacitly assumed or directly asserted in nearly all the Protestant Confessions of Faith, which make it the duty of the civil government to support religion, to protect orthodoxy, and to punish heresy.[1]

In modern times the character of the State and its attitude towards the Church has undergone a material change in Switzerland as well as in other countries. The State is no longer identified with a particular Church, and has become either indifferent, or hostile, or tolerant. It is composed of members of all creeds, and should, in the name of justice, support all, or none; in either case allowing to all full liberty as far as is consistent with the public peace.

Under these circumstances the Church has to choose between liberty with self-support, and dependence with government support. If Calvin lived at this day, he would undoubtedly prefer the former. Calvinists and Presbyterians have taken the lead in the struggle for Church independence against the Erastian and rationalistic encroachments of the civil power. Free Churches have been organized in French Switzerland (Geneva, Vaud, Neuchâtel), in France, Holland, and especially in Presbyterian Scotland. The heroic sacrifices of the Free Church of Scotland in seceding from the Established Church, and making full provision for all her wants by voluntary contributions, form one of the brightest chapters in the history of Protestantism. The Dissenters in England have always maintained and exercised the voluntary principle since their legal recognition by the Toleration Act of 1689. In the British Provinces and in North America,

---

[1] Conf. Helvetica II. ch. XXX.; Conf. Gallicana, ch. XXXIX. ("God has put the sword into the hands of magistrates to suppress crimes against *the first as well as* the second table of his Commandments"); Conf. Belgica, ch. XXXVI.; Conf. Scotica, Art. XXIV.; Thirty-nine Articles, Art. XXXVII. (changed in the American recension); Westminster Conf. ch. XXIII. (changed in the American recension).

all denominations are on a basis of equality before the law, and enjoy, under the protection of the government, full liberty of self-government with the corresponding duty of self-support. The condition of modern society demands a peaceful separation of Church and State, or a Free Church in a Free State.

§ 104. *The Ecclesiastical Ordinances.*

Comp. § 83 (352 sqq.) and § 86 (367 sqq.). Calvin discusses the ministerial office in the third chapter of the fourth book of his *Institutes.*

Having considered Calvin's general principles on Church government, we proceed to their introduction and application in the little Republic of Geneva.

We have seen that in his first interview with the Syndics and Council after his return, Sept. 13, 1541, he insisted on the introduction of an ecclesiastical constitution and discipline in accordance with the Word of God and the primitive Church.[1] The Council complied with his wishes, and intrusted the work to the five pastors (Calvin, Viret, Jacques Bernard, Henry de la Mare, and Aymé Champereau) and six councillors (decided Guillermins), to whom was added Jean Balard as advisory member. The document was prepared under his directing influence, submitted to the councils, slightly altered, and solemnly ratified by a general assembly of citizens (the *Conseil général*), Jan. 2, 1542, as the fundamental church law of the Republic of Geneva.[2] Its essential features have passed into the constitution and discipline of most of the Reformed and Presbyterian Churches of Europe and America.

The official text of the " Ordinances " is preserved in the

---

[1] He wrote to Farel, Sept. 16, 1541 (in *Opera,* XI. 281; Herminjard, VII. 249) : "*Exposui (Senatui), non posse consistere ecclesiam, nisi certum regimen constitueretur, quale ex Verbo Dei nobis præscriptum est, et in veteri Ecclesia fuit observatum.*"

[2] See above, p. 440.

Registers of the Venerable Company, and opens with the following introduction: —

> "In the name of God Almighty, we, the Syndics, Small and Great Councils with our people assembled at the sound of the trumpet and the great clock, according to our ancient customs, have considered that the matter above all others worthy of recommendation is to preserve the doctrine of the holy gospel of our Lord in its purity, to protect the Christian Church, to instruct faithfully the youth, and to provide a hospital for the proper support of the poor, — all of which cannot be done without a definite order and rule of life, from which every estate may learn the duty of its office. For this reason we have deemed it wise to reduce the spiritual government, such as our Lord has shown us and instituted by his Word, to a good form to be introduced and observed among us. Therefore we have ordered and established to follow and to guard in our city and territory the following ecclesiastical polity, taken from the gospel of Jesus Christ." [1]

The document is inspired by a high view of the dignity and responsibility of the ministry of the gospel, such as we find in the Epistles of Paul to the Corinthians and Ephesians. " It may be confidently asserted," says a Catholic historian,[2] " that in no religious society of Christian Europe the clergy was assigned a position so dignified, prominent, and influential as in the Church which Calvin built up in Geneva."

In his *Institutes* Calvin distinguishes three *extraordinary* officers of the Church, — Apostles, Prophets, and Evangelists, — and four *ordinary* officers — Pastors (Bishops), Teachers, Ancients (Lay-elders), and Deacons.[3]

Extraordinary officers were raised up by the Lord at the beginning of his kingdom, and are raised up on special occasions when required "by the necessity of the times." The Reformers must be regarded as a secondary class of Apostles, Prophets, and Evangelists. Calvin himself intimates the parallel when he says: [4] "I do not deny that ever since that period [of the Apostles] God has sometimes raised up Apostles or Evangelists in their stead, *as he has done in our own*

---

[1] The French text in *Opera*, X. 16. note a.
[2] Kampschulte I. 396.
[3] In the " Ordinances " they are called *Pasteurs, Docteurs, Anciens, Diacres.*
[4] *Inst.* IV. ch. III. § 4.

time. For there was a necessity for such persons to recover
the Church from the defection of Antichrist. Nevertheless,
I call this an extraordinary office, because it has no place in
well-constituted Churches." [1]

The extraordinary offices cannot be regulated by law.
The Ordinances, therefore, give directions only for the ordinary offices of the Church.

1. The PASTORS,[2] or ministers of the gospel, as Calvin
likes to call them, have "to preach the Word of God, to
instruct, to admonish, to exhort and reprove in public and
private, to administer the sacraments, and, jointly with the
elders, to exercise discipline." [3]

No one can be a pastor who is not called, examined, ordained, or installed. In the examination, the candidate must
give satisfactory evidence of his knowledge of the Scriptures,
his soundness in doctrine, purity of motives, and integrity of
character. If he proves worthy of the office, he receives
a testimony to that effect from the Council to be presented
to the congregation. If he fails in the examination, he must
wait for another call and submit to another examination.
The best mode of installation is by prayer and laying on
of hands, according to the practice of the Apostles and the
early Church; but it should be done without superstition.

All the ministers are to hold weekly conferences for
mutual instruction, edification, correction, and encourage-

---

[1] This confirms the view I have taken of Calvin's extraordinary calling
(§ 73, pp. 313 sqq.). In his letter to Sadolet he expresses his firm conviction
that his ministry was from God. (See § 91, pp. 398 sqq.) Luther had the
same conviction concerning his own mission. On his return from the Wartburg to Wittenberg, he wrote to the Elector Frederick of Saxony that he had
his gospel not from men, but from heaven, and that he was Christ's evangelist.

[2] ποιμένες, *pastores*, Eph. 4:11. They are the same with Bishops and
Presbyters. "In calling those who preside over Churches by the appellations
of 'Bishops,' 'Presbyters,' and 'Pastors,' without any distinction, I have followed the usage of the Scripture." *Inst.* IV. ch. III. § 8. Then he quotes
Phil. 1:1; Tit. 1:5, 7; Acts 20:17, 28. See above, p. 469.

[3] " *Faire les corrections fraternelles.*"

ment in their official duties. No one should absent himself without a good excuse. This duty devolves also on the pastors of the country districts. If doctrinal controversies arise, the ministers settle them by discussion; and if they cannot agree, the matter is referred to the magistracy.

Discipline is to be strictly exercised over the ministers, and a number of sins and vices are specified which cannot be tolerated among them, such as heresy, schism, rebellion against ecclesiastical order, blasphemy, impurity, falsehood, perjury, usury, avarice, dancing, negligence in the study of the Scriptures.

The Ordinances prescribe for Sunday a service in the morning, catechism — that is, instruction of little children — at noon, a second sermon in the afternoon at three o'clock. Three sermons are to be preached during the week — Monday, Tuesday, and Friday. For these services are required, in the city, five regular ministers and three assistant ministers.

In the *Institutes*, Calvin describes the office of Pastors to be the same as that of the Apostles, except in the extent of their field and authority. They are all ambassadors of Christ and stewards of the mysteries of God (1 Cor. 4 : 1). What Paul says of himself applies to them all: "Woe is to me, if I preach not the gospel" (1 Cor. 9 : 16).

2. The office of the TEACHERS [1] is to instruct the believers in sound doctrine, in order that the purity of the gospel be not corrupted by ignorance or false opinions.

Calvin derived the distinction between Teachers and Pastors from Eph. 4 : 11, and states the difference to consist in this, "that Teachers have no official concern with discipline, nor the administration of the sacraments, nor admonitions and exhortations, but only with the interpretation of the Scripture; whereas the pastoral office includes all these duties." [2] He also says that the Teachers sustain the same

---

[1] διδάσκαλοι, *doctores*, Eph. 4 : 11.
[2] *Inst*. IV. ch. III. § 4.

resemblance to the ancient Prophets as the Pastors to the Apostles. He himself had the prophetic gift of luminous and convincing teaching in a rare degree. Theological Professors occupy the highest rank among Teachers.

3. The ANCIENTS or Lay-Elders watch over the good conduct of the people. They must be God-fearing and wise men, without and above suspicion. Twelve were to be selected — two from the Little Council, four from the Council of the Sixty, and six from the Council of the Two Hundred. Each was to be assigned a special district of the city.

This is a very important office in the Presbyterian Churches. In the *Institutes*, Calvin quotes in support of it the gifts of government.[1] "From the beginning," he says,[2] "every Church has had its senate or council, composed of pious, grave, and holy men, who were invested with that jurisdiction in the correction of vices. . . . This office of government is necessary in every age." He makes a distinction between two classes of Elders, — Ruling Elders and Teaching Elders, — on the basis of 1 Tim. 5:17: "Let the elders that rule well be counted worthy of double honor, *especially* those who labor in the word and in teaching."[3] The exegetical foundation for such a distinction is weak, but the ruling Lay-Eldership has proved a very useful institution and great help to the teaching ministry.

4. The DEACONS have the care of the poor and the sick, and of the hospitals. They must prevent mendicancy which is contrary to good order.[4] Two classes of Deacons are dis-

---

[1] κυβερνήσεις, 1 Cor. 12:28; comp. Rom. 12:8.

[2] *Inst.* IV. ch. III. § 8.

[3] In his Commentary on the passage. Comp. *Inst.* IV. ch. III. § 8: " *Gubernatores fuisse existimo seniores ex plebe delectos qui censuræ morum et exercendæ disciplinæ una cum episcopis præessent.*" The distinction was first made by Calvin and followed by many Presbyterian and some Lutheran divines, but it is denied by some of the best modern exegetes. Paul requires all presbyters to be apt to teach, 1 Tim. 3:2; 2 Tim. 2:2; 2:24. See Schaff's *History of the Apostolic Church,* p. 529 sq.

[4] Acts 6:1–3; Phil. 1:1; 1 Tim. 3:8 sqq.; 5:9, 10.

tinguished, those who administer alms, and those who devote themselves to the poor and sick.[1]

5. Baptism is to be performed in the Church, and only by ministers and their assistants. The names of the children and their parents must be entered in the Church registers.

6. The Lord's Supper is to be administered every month in one of the Churches, and at Easter, Pentecost, and Christmas. The elements must be distributed reverently by the ministers and deacons. None is to be admitted before having been instructed in the catechism and made a profession of his faith.

The remainder of the Ordinances contains regulations about marriage, burial, the visitation of the sick, and prisons.

The Ministers and Ancients are to meet once a week on Thursday, to discuss together the state of the Church and to exercise discipline. The object of discipline is to bring the sinner back to the Lord.[2]

The *Ecclesiastical Ordinances* of 1541 were revised and enlarged by Calvin, and adopted by the Little and Large Councils, Nov. 13, 1561. This edition contains also the oaths of allegiance of the Ministers, Pastors, Doctors, Elders, Deacons, and the members of the Consistory, and fuller directions concerning the administration of the sacraments, marriage, the visitation of the sick and prisoners, the election of members of the Consistory, and excommunication.[3]

A new revision of the *Ordinances* was made and adopted by the General Council, June 3, 1576.

§ 105. *The Venerable Company and the Consistory.*

The Church of Geneva consisted of all baptized and professing Christians subject to discipline. It had, at the time of Calvin, a uniform creed; Romanists and sectarians

---

[1] Comp. the *Inst.* IV. ch. III. 9.

[2] "*Les corrections ne soient sinon medicines pour reduyre les pecheurs a nostre Seigneur.*"   [3] *Opera*, X. Pars I. 91–124.

being excluded. It was represented and governed by the
Venerable Company and the Consistory.

1. The VENERABLE COMPANY was a purely clerical body,
consisting of all the pastors of the city and district of Geneva.
It had no political power. It was intrusted with the general
supervision of all strictly ecclesiastical affairs, especially the
education, qualification, ordination, and installation of the
ministers of the gospel. But the consent of the civil government and the congregation was necessary for the final induc-
tion to the ministry. Thus the pastors and the people were
to co-operate.

2. The CONSISTORY or PRESBYTERY was a mixed body
of clergymen and laymen, and larger and more influential
than the Venerable Company. It represented the union
of Church and State. It embraced, at the time of Calvin,
five city Pastors and twelve Seniors or Lay-Elders, two
of whom were selected from the Council of Sixty and ten
from the Council of Two Hundred. The laymen, therefore, had the majority; but the clerical element was comparatively fixed, while the Elders were elected annually
under the influence of the clergy. A Syndic was the
constitutional head.[1] Calvin never presided in form, but
ruled the proceedings in fact by his superior intelligence
and weighty judgment.[2]

The Consistory went into operation immediately after the
adoption of the *Ordinances*, and met every Thursday. The

---

[1] The revised *Eccles. Ordinances* of 1561 provide (*Opera*, X. P. I. 121) that
"one of the four Syndics preside over the Consistory with the marshal's staff
(*avec son bâton*) which signifies civil jurisdiction rather than spiritual regime,
*afin de mieux garder la distinction qui nous est monstrée en l'Escriture saincte entre
le glaive et authorité du Magistrat, et la superintendence qui doit estre en Eglise.*"
This regulation of Calvin refutes the assertion of Dyer (p. 142), that
"Calvin usurped the perpetual presidency of the Consistory," and that "he
wished Beza to succeed him in this presidency."

[2] "While he was not president of this body, it may be truly said that he
was its soul." Merle d'Aubigné (VII. 120). So also Cramer, Roget, and
others.

reports begin from the tenth meeting, which was held on Thursday, Feb. 16, 1542.[1]

The duty of the Consistory was the maintenance and exercise of discipline. Every house was to be visited annually by a Minister and Elder. To facilitate the working of this system the city was divided into three parishes — St. Peter's, the Magdalen, and St. Gervais. Calvin officiated in St. Peter's.

The Consistorial Court was the controlling power in the Church of Geneva. It has often been misrepresented as a sort of tribunal of Inquisition or Star Chamber. But it could only use the spiritual sword, and had nothing to do with civil and temporal punishments, which belonged exclusively to the Council. The names of Gruet, Bolsec, and Servetus do not even appear in its records.[2] Calvin wrote to the ministers of Zürich, Nov. 26, 1553: "The Consistory has no civil jurisdiction, but only the right to reprove according to the Word of God, and its severest punishment is excommunication." [3] He wisely provided for the preponderance of the lay-element.

At first the Council, following the example of Basel and Bern, denied to the Consistory the right of excommunication.[4] The persons excluded from the Lord's Table usually

---

[1] *Annal.,* XXI. 291, sub Février 16, 1542: "*Dixième séance du Consistoire, première dont il existe un procès verbal, lequel mentionne entre autres la présence de Calvin et de Viret. Les autres ministres membres du C., sont Bernard, Henri, et Champeraux. Viret est mentionné pour la dernière fois le 18 juillet. Calvin assiste régulièrement aux séances pendant tout l'exercice 1542–43, excepté cinq fois.*"

[2] A. Roget, *l.c.,* p. 31: "*Le Consistoire ne pouvait infliger aucune peine, et, chose remarquable, il n'avait aucune attribution doctrinale. L'ancien syndic Cramer, dans l'excellente préface qu'il a placée en tête des extraits des Registres du Consistoire, a fait observer que Gruet, Bolsec et Servet ne sont pas même nommés dans les documents qu'il a analysés; toutes les fois qu'un procès de doctrine est instruit, c'est le Conseil qui prononce, sur le préavis des pasteurs.*"

[3] *Opera,* XIV. 675: "*Nulla in Consistorio civilis jurisdictio, sed tantum reprehensiones ex Verbo Domini: ultima vero pœna, excommunicatio.*"

[4] On March 19, 1543, the Council of the Sixty resolved "*que le Consistoire n'ait ni jurisdiction ni puissance de défendre la cène, sinon seulement d'admonester*"

appealed to the Council, which often interceded in their behalf or directed them to make an apology to the Consistory. There was also a difference of opinion as regards the consequences of excommunication. The Consistory demanded that persons cut off from the Church for grievous offenses and scandalous lives should be banished from the State for a year, or until they repent; but the Council did not agree. Calvin could not always carry out his views, and acted on the principle to tolerate what he could not abolish.[1] It was only after his final victory over the Libertines in 1555 that the Council conceded to the Consistory the undisputed power of excommunication.[2]

From these facts we may judge with what right Calvin has so often been called "the Pope of Geneva," mostly by way of reproach.[3] As far as the designation is true, it is an involuntary tribute to his genius and character. For he had no material support, and he never used his influence for

---

et puis faire relation en Conseil, afin que la Seigneurie avise de juger sur les délinquants suivant leur démérites." Reg., quoted by Roget, p. 37. A month before, the government of Bern had categorically refused the right of excommunication to the ministers of Lausanne. Ruchat, V. 211.

[1] " Tolero quod tollere non licet," as he says in one of his letters.

[2] Roget (p. 67) : " Le point de vue soutenu par Calvin dans la question de la cène avait enfin triomphé irrévocablement et, dès 1555, nous trouvons le Consistoire en possession, d'une manière incontestée, du droit d'accorder ou de refuser la participation aux sacrements. Toutefois, le Conseil et les ministres ne sont pas complètement d'accord sur les conséquences que doit entrainer l'excommunication."

[3] Roget (p. 83 sq.) has collected such exaggerated judgments from several French writers and contradicts them. Florimond de Ræmond says : " Calvin se rendit le maistre, l'évesque, le seigneur, disposant de la religion, de l'estat, de la ville, du gouvernement, de la police, comme bon luy sembloit." Duruy : " Calvin eut dès 1541 et exerça jusqu'à sa mort un pouvoir absolu. Il organisa le gouvernement de Genève au profit presque exclusif des ministres du culte réformé." Capefigue : " Calvin réunissait tous les fils du pouvoir suprême en sa personne." Paul Janet : " Calvin a été le magistrat suprême d'une démocratie." Rosseuw St. Hilaire : " Tout excès appelle une réaction en sens contraire, Calvin subordonne l'Etat à l'Eglise." Saisset : " L'Etat devenait une théocratie et les citoyens de Genève n'étaient plus que les sujets d'un petit nombre de ministres, sujets eux-mêmes de Calvin, lequel dominait les trois Conseils du sein du Consistoire et paraissait à la fois le ROI et le PONTIFE souverain de la cité."

gain or personal ends. The Genevese knew him well and obeyed him freely.

§ 106. *Calvin's Theory of Discipline.*

Discipline is so important an element in Calvin's Church polity, that it must be more fully considered. Discipline was the cause of his expulsion from Geneva, the basis of his flourishing French congregation at Strassburg, the chief reason for his recall, the condition of his acceptance, the struggle and triumph of his life, and the secret of his moral influence to this day. His rigorous discipline, based on his rigorous creed, educated the heroic French, Dutch, English, Scotch, and American Puritans (using this word in a wider sense for strict Calvinists). It fortified them for their trials and persecutions, and made them promoters of civil and religious liberty.

The severity of the system has passed away, even in Geneva, Scotland, and New England, but the result remains in the power of self-government, the capacity for organization, the order and practical efficiency which characterizes the Reformed Churches in Europe and America.

Calvin's great aim was to realize the purity and holiness of the Church as far as human weakness will permit. He kept constantly in view the ideal of "a Church without spot or wrinkle or blemish," which Paul describes in the Epistle to the Ephesians (5:27). He wanted every Christian to be consistent with his profession, to show his faith by good works, and to strive to be perfect as our Father in heaven is perfect. He was the only one among the Reformers who attempted and who measurably carried out this sublime idea in a whole community.

Luther thought the preaching of the gospel would bring about all the necessary changes, but he had to complain bitterly, at the end of his life, of the dissolute manners of the students and citizens at Wittenberg, and seriously thought of leaving the city in disgust.[1]

Calvin knew well enough that the ideal could only be imperfectly realized in this world, but that it was none the less our duty to strive after perfection. He often quotes Augustin against the Donatists who dreamed of an imaginary purity of the Church, like the Anabaptists who, he observes, "acknowledge no congregation to belong to Christ, unless it be in all respects conspicuous for angelic perfection, and who, under pretext of zeal, destroy all edification." He consents to Augustin's remark that "schemes of separation are pernicious and sacrilegious, because they proceed from pride and impiety, and disturb the good who are weak, more than they correct the wicked who are bold." In commenting on the parable of the net which gathered of every kind (Matt. 13 : 47), he says: "The Church while on earth is mixed with good and bad and will never be free of all impurity. . . . Although God, who is a God of order, commands us to exercise discipline, he allows for a time to hypocrites a place among believers until he shall set up his kingdom in its perfection on the last day. As far as we are concerned, we must strive to correct vices and to purge the Church of impurity, although she will not be free from all stain and blemish till Christ shall separate the goats from the sheep."[2]

Calvin discusses the subject of discipline in the twelfth chapter of the fourth book of his *Institutes*. His views are sound and scriptural. "No society," he says at the outset,

[1] Friederich Julius Stahl, a convert from Judaism, a very able lawyer and statesman, and one of the chief champions of modern high-church Lutheranism, whose motto was, "Authority, not Majority" (although his wife was Reformed and he himself attributed his conversion to the Reformed Professor Krafft in Erlangen), says in his book, *Die Lutherische Kirche und die Union* (1860), that Calvin introduced a new principle into Protestantism; namely, the glorification of God by the full dominion of his Word in the life of Christendom ("*die Verherrlichung Gottes durch die wirkliche volle Herrschaft seines Wortes im Leben der Christenheit*").

[2] In Tholuck's ed. of Calvin's *Harmony of the Gospels*, I. P. II. 21.

"no house can be preserved in proper condition without discipline. The Church ought to be the most orderly society of all. As the saving doctrine of Christ is the soul of the Church, so discipline forms the nerves and ligaments which connect the members and keep each in its proper place. It serves as a bridle to curb and restrain the refractory who resist the doctrine of Christ; or as a spur to stimulate the inactive; and sometimes as a father's rod to chastise, in mercy and with the gentleness of the spirit of Christ, those who have grievously fallen away. It is the only remedy against a dreadful desolation in the Church."

One of the greatest objections which he had against the Roman Church of his day was the utter want of discipline in constant violation of the canons. He asserts, without fear of contradiction, that "there was scarcely one of the (Roman) bishops, and not one in a hundred of the parochial clergy, who, if sentence were to be passed upon his conduct according to the ancient canons, would not be excommunicated, or, to say the very least, deposed from his office."[1]

He distinguished between the discipline of the people and the discipline of the clergy.[2]

1. The discipline of members has three degrees: private admonition; a second admonition in the presence of witnesses or before the Church; and, in case of persistent disobedience, exclusion from the Lord's Table. This is in accordance with the rule of Christ (Matt. 18 : 15–17).

---

[1] *Inst.* IV. ch. V. § 14. In the same chapter (§ 1) he says of the bishops of his day that most of them were ignorant of the Scriptures, and either drunkards or fornicators or gamblers or hunters. "The greatest absurdity is that even boys, scarcely ten years of age, have, by the permission of the pope, been made bishops." Pope Leo X. himself was made archbishop in his eighth and cardinal-deacon in his thirteenth year. The Roman Church at that time tolerated almost anything but heresy and disobedience to the pope, which in her eyes is worse than the greatest moral crime.

[2] He objects to the word *clergy* as originating in a mistake, since Peter (1 Pet. 5 : 3) calls the whole Church God's κλῆροι or possessions; but he uses it for the sake of convenience.

The object of discipline is threefold: to protect the body
of the Church against contamination and profanation; to
guard the individual members against the corrupting influence
of constant association with the wicked; and to bring the
offender to repentance that he may be saved and restored to
the fellowship of the faithful. Excommunication and subsequent restoration were exercised by Paul in the case of the
Corinthian offender, and by the Church in her purer days.
Even the Emperor Theodosius was excluded from communion
by Bishop Ambrose of Milan on account of the massacre per-
petrated in Thessalonica at his order.[1]

Excommunication should be exercised only against flagi-
tious crimes which disgrace the Christian profession; such as
adultery, fornication, theft, robbery, sedition, perjury, contempt of God and his authority. Nor should it be exercised
by the bishop or pastor alone, but by the body of elders, and,
as is pointed out by Paul, "with the knowledge and approbation of the congregation; in such a manner, however, that
the multitude of the people may not direct the proceeding,
but may watch over it as witnesses and guardians, that nothing be done by a few persons from any improper motive."
Moreover, "the severity of the Church must be tempered
by a spirit of gentleness. For there is constant need of
the greatest caution, according to the injunction of Paul concerning a person who may have been censured, ' lest by any
means such a one should be swallowed up with his overmuch
sorrow' (2 Cor. 2 : 7); for thus a remedy would become a
poison."

When the sinner gives reasonable evidence of repentance

---

[1] Calvin quotes also Chrysostom's famous warning against the profanation of the sacrament by the connivance of unfaithful priests: " Blood shall
be required at your hands. Let us not be afraid of sceptres or diadems or
imperial robes; we have here a greater power. As for myself, I will rather
give up my body to death and suffer my blood to be shed, than I will be a
partaker of this pollution." There is a strong resemblance between Calvin
and Chrysostom, both as commentators and as fearless disciplinarians.

he is to be restored. Calvin objects to "the excessive austerity of the ancients," who refused to readmit the lapsed. He approves of the course of Cyprian, who says: "Our patience and kindness and tenderness is ready for all who come; I wish all to return into the Church; I wish all our fellow-soldiers to be assembled in the camp of Christ, and all our brethren to be received into the house of God our Father. I forgive everything; I conceal much. With ready and sincere affection I embrace those who return with penitence." Calvin adds: "Such as are expelled from the Church, it is not for us to expunge from the number of the elect, or to despair of them as already lost. It is proper to consider them as strangers to the Church, and consequently to Christ, but this only as long as they remain in a state of exclusion. And even then let us hope better things of them for the future, and not cease to pray to God on their behalf. Let us not condemn to eternal death the offender, nor prescribe laws to the mercy of God who can change the worst of men into the best." He makes a distinction between excommunication and anathema; the former censures and punishes with a view to reformation and restoration; the latter precludes all pardon, and devotes a person to eternal perdition. Anathema ought never to be resorted to, or at least very rarely. Church members ought to exert all means in their power to promote the reformation of an excommunicated person, and admonish him not as an enemy, but as a brother (2 Cor. 2 : 8). "Unless this tenderness be observed by the individual members as well as by the Church collectively, our discipline will be in danger of speedily degenerating into cruelty."

2. As regards the discipline of the clergy, Calvin objects to the exemption of ministers from civil jurisdiction, and wants them to be subject to the same punishments as laymen. They are more guilty, as they ought to set a good example. He quotes with approval the ancient canons, so shamefully

neglected in the Roman Church of his day, against hunting, gambling, feasting, usury, commerce, and secular amusements. He recommends annual visitations and synods for the correction and examination of delinquent clergymen.

But he rejects the prohibition of clerical marriage as an "act of impious tyranny contrary to the Word of God and to every principle of justice. With what impunity fornication rages among them [the papal clergy] it is unnecessary to remark; emboldened by their polluted celibacy, they have become hardened to every crime. . . . Paul places marriage among the virtues of a bishop; these men teach that it is a vice not to be tolerated in the clergy. . . . Christ has been pleased to put such honor upon marriage as to make it an image of his sacred union with the Church. What could be said more in commendation of the dignity of marriage? With what face can that be called impure and polluted, which exhibits a similitude of the spiritual grace of Christ? . . . Marriage is honorable in all; but whoremongers and adulterers God will judge (Heb. 13:4). The Apostles themselves have proved by their own example that marriage is not unbecoming the sanctity of any office, however excellent: for Paul testifies that they not only retained their wives, but took them about with them (1 Cor. 9:5)."

§ 107. *The Exercise of Discipline in Geneva.*

Calvin succeeded after a fierce struggle in infusing the Church of Geneva with his views on discipline. The Consistory and the Council rivalled with each other, under his inspiration, in puritanic zeal for the correction of immorality; but their zeal sometimes transgressed the dictates of wisdom and moderation. The union of Church and State rests on the false assumption that all citizens are members of the Church and subject to discipline.

Dancing, gambling, drunkenness, the frequentation of taverns, profanity, luxury, excesses at public entertainments, extravagance and immodesty in dress, licentious or irreligious songs were forbidden, and punished by censure or fine or imprisonment. Even the number of dishes at meals was regulated. Drunkards were fined three *sols* for each offence. Habitual gamblers were exposed in the pillory with cords around their neck. Reading of bad books and immoral novels was also prohibited, and the popular "Amadis de Gaul" was ordered to be destroyed (1559). A morality play on "the Acts of the Apostles," after it had been performed several times, and been attended even by the Council, was forbidden. Parents were warned against naming their children after Roman Catholic saints who nourished certain superstitions; instead of them the names of Abraham, Moses, David, Daniel, Zechariah, Jeremiah, Nehemiah became common. (This preference for Old Testament names was carried even further by the Puritans of England and New England.) The death penalty against heresy, idolatry, and blasphemy, and the barbarous custom of the torture were retained. Adultery, after a second offence, was likewise punished by death.

These were prohibitive and protective laws intended to prevent and punish irreligion and immorality.

But the Council introduced also coercive laws, which are contrary to the nature of religion, and apt to breed hypocrisy or infidelity. Attendance on public worship was commanded on penalty of three *sols*.[1] When a refugee from Lyons once gratefully exclaimed, "How glorious is the liberty we enjoy here," a woman bitterly replied: "Free indeed we formerly were to attend mass, but now we are compelled to hear a sermon." Watchmen were appointed to see that people went

---

[1] "*Les ministres ont prié que lon advise de fere venyr les gens aut sermon et specialement les dimanches et le iour des prieres affin de prier Dieu qui nous assiste, voyeant le trouble quest en leglise de Dieu et la machination dressé contre les fidelles.* ARRÊTÉ QUI IMPOSE UNE AMENDE DE 3 SOLZ À CEUX QUI NE VIENDRAIENT PAS." (*Rég. du Conseil.*) In *Annal.*, 394 sub Jan. 17, 1547.

to church. The members of the Consistory visited every house once a year to examine into the faith and morals of the family. Every unseemly word and act on the street was reported, and the offenders were cited before the Consistory to be either censured and warned, or to be handed over to the Council for severer punishment. No respect was paid to person, rank, or sex. The strictest impartiality was maintained, and members of the oldest and most distinguished families, ladies as well as gentlemen, were treated with the same severity as poor and obscure people.

Let us give a summary of the most striking cases of discipline. Several women, among them the wife of Ami Perrin, the captain-general, were imprisoned for dancing (which was usually connected with excesses). Bonivard, the hero of political liberty, and a friend of Calvin, was cited before the Consistory because he had played at dice with Clement Marot, the poet, for a quart of wine.[1] A man was banished from the city for three months because, on hearing an ass bray, he said jestingly: "He prays a beautiful psalm."[2] A young man was punished because he gave his bride a book on housekeeping with the remark: "This is the best Psalter." A lady of Ferrara was expelled from the city for expressing sympathy with the Libertines, and abusing Calvin and the Consistory. Three men who had laughed during the sermon were imprisoned for three days. Another had to do public penance for neglecting to commune on Whitsunday. Three children were punished because they remained outside of the church during the sermon to eat cakes. A man who swore by the "body and blood of Christ" was fined and condemned to stand for an hour in the pillory on the public square. A child was whipped for calling his mother a thief and a she-devil (*diabless*). A girl was beheaded for striking her parents, to vindicate the dignity of the fifth commandment.

[1] Roget, *Peuple de Genève*, II. 29, quoted by Merle d'Aubigné, VII. 124.
[2] "*Il chante un beau psaume.*"

A banker was executed for repeated adultery, but he died penitent and praised God for the triumph of justice. A person named Chapuis was imprisoned for four days because he persisted in calling his child Claude (a Roman Catholic saint) instead of Abraham, as the minister wished, and saying that he would sooner keep his son unbaptized for fifteen years.[1] Bolsec, Gentilis, and Castellio were expelled from the Republic for heretical opinions. Men and women were burnt for witchcraft. Gruet was beheaded for sedition and atheism. Servetus was burnt for heresy and blasphemy. The last is the most flagrant case which, more than all others combined, has exposed the name of Calvin to abuse and execration; but it should be remembered that he wished to substitute the milder punishment of the sword for the stake, and in this point at least he was in advance of the public opinion and usual practice of his age.[2]

The official acts of the Council from 1541 to 1559 exhibit a dark chapter of censures, fines, imprisonments, and executions. During the ravages of the pestilence in 1545 more than twenty men and women were burnt alive for witchcraft, and a wicked conspiracy to spread the horrible disease.[3] From 1542 to 1546 fifty-eight judgments of death and seventy-six decrees of banishments were passed.[4] During the years 1558 and 1559 the cases of various punishments for

[1] Régisters for April 27, 1546. Henry II. 429.

[2] For a fuller statement see chap. XVI.

[3] Calvin himself states this fact in a letter to Myconius of Basel, March 27, 1545 (*Opera*, XII. 55; Bonnet, I. 428), where he says: "A conspiracy of men and women has lately been discovered, who, for the space of three years, had spread the plague through the city by what mischievous device I know not. After fifteen women have been burnt, some men have even been punished more severely, some have committed suicide in prison, and while twenty-five are still kept prisoners, — the conspirators do not cease, notwithstanding, to smear the door-locks of the dwelling-houses with their poisonous ointment. You see in the midst of what perils we are tossed about. The Lord hath hitherto preserved our dwelling, though it has more than once been attempted. It is well that we know ourselves to be under His care."

[4] According to Galiffe, as quoted by Kampschulte, I. 425.

all sorts of offences amounted to four hundred and fourteen — a very large proportion for a population of 20,000.

The enemies of Calvin — Bolsec, Audin, Galiffe (father and son) — make the most of these facts, and, ignoring all the good he has done, condemn the great Reformer as a heartless and cruel tyrant.[1]

It is impossible to deny that this kind of legislation savors more of the austerity of old heathen Rome and the Levitical code than of the gospel of Christ, and that the actual exercise of discipline was often petty, pedantic, and unnecessarily severe. Calvin was, as he himself confessed, not free from impatience, passion, and anger, which were increased by his physical infirmities; but he was influenced by an honest zeal for the purity of the Church, and not by personal malice. When he was threatened by Perrin and the Favre family with a second expulsion, he wrote to Perrin: "Such threats make no impression upon me. I did not return to Geneva to obtain leisure and profit, nor will it be to my sorrow if I should have to leave it again. It was the welfare and safety of the Church and State that induced me to return."[2] He must be judged by the standard of his own, and not of our, age. The most cruel of those laws — against witchcraft, heresy, and blasphemy — were inherited from the Catholic Middle Ages, and continued in force in all countries of Europe,

---

[1] Take the following rhetorical caricature of Calvin's and Colladon's politico-religious code of laws from Audin (*Life of Calvin*, ch. XXXVI. 354, Am. ed.): "There is but one word heard or read: *Death*. Death to every one guilty of high treason against God; death to every one guilty of high treason against the State; death to the son that strikes or curses his father; death to the adulterer; death to heretics. . . . During the space of twenty years, commencing from the date of Calvin's recall, the history of Geneva is a bloody drama, in which pity, dread, terror, indignation, and tears, by turns, appear to seize upon the soul. At each step we encounter chains, thongs, a stake, pincers, melted pitch, fire, and sulphur. And throughout the whole there is blood. One imagines himself in Dante's *Hell*, where sighs, groans, and lamentations continually resound."

[2] This letter to Perrin is undated, but is probably from April, 1546. See *Opera*, XII. 338 sq. and Bonnet, II. 42 sq.

Protestant as well as Roman Catholic, down to the end of the seventeenth century. Tolerance is a modern virtue. We shall return to this subject again in the chapter on Servetus.

§ 108. *Calvin's Struggle with the Patriots and Libertines.*

Contre la secte phantastique et furieuse des Libertins qui se nomment Spirituelz. Geneva, 1545; 2d ed. 1547. Reprinted in *Opera*, vol. VII. 145–252. Latin version by Nic. des Gallars, 1546. FAREL also wrote a French book against the Libertines, Geneva, 1550.

The works of J. A. GALIFFE and J. B. G. GALIFFE on the Genevese families and the criminal processes of Perrin, Ameaux, Berthelier, etc., quoted above, p. 224. Hostile to Calvin. — AUDIN, chs. XXXV., XXXVI., and XLIII. Likewise hostile.

F. TRECHSEL: *Libertiner*, in the first ed. of Herzog's *Encykl.*, VIII. 375–380 (omitted in the second ed.), and his *Antitrinitarier*, I. 177 sqq. — HENRY II. 402 sqq. — HUNDESHAGEN in the "Studien und Kritiken," 1845, pp. 866 sqq. — DYER, 177, 198, 368, 390 sqq. — STÄHELIN, I. 382 sqq.; 457 sqq. On the side of Calvin.

CHARLES SCHMIDT: *Les Libertins spirituels*, Bâle, 1876 (pp. xiv. and 251). From a manuscript autograph of one J. F., an adept of the sect, written between 1547 and 1550. An extract in *La France Protest.* III. 590 sq.

It required a ten years' conflict till Calvin succeeded in carrying out his system of discipline. The opposition began to manifest itself in 1545, during the raging of the pestilence; it culminated at the trial of Servetus in 1553, and it finally broke down in 1555.

Calvin compares himself in this controversy with David fighting against the Philistines. "If I should describe," he says in the Preface to his Commentary on the Psalms (1557),[1] "the course of my struggles by which the Lord has exercised me from this period, it would make a long story, but a brief reference may suffice. It affords me no slight consolation that David preceded me in these conflicts. For as the Philistines and other foreign foes vexed this holy king by continual wars, and as the wickedness and treachery of the faithless of his own house grieved him still more, so was I on all sides assailed, and had scarcely a moment's rest from out-

[1] *Opera*, vol. XXXI. 27.

ward or inward struggles. But when Satan had made so
many efforts to destroy our Church, it came at length to this,
that I, unwarlike and timid as I am,[1] found myself compelled
to oppose my own body to the murderous assault, and so to
ward it off. Five years long had we to struggle without
ceasing for the upholding of discipline; for these evil-doers
were endowed with too great a degree of power to be easily
overcome; and a portion of the people, perverted by their
means, wished only for an unbridled freedom. To such
worthless men, despisers of the holy law, the ruin of the
Church was a matter of utter indifference, could they but
obtain the liberty to do whatever they desired. Many were
induced by necessity and hunger, some by ambition or by a
shameful desire of gain, to attempt a general overthrow, and
to risk their own ruin as well as ours, rather than be subject
to the laws. Scarcely a single thing, I believe, was left unattempted by them during this long period which we might
not suppose to have been prepared in the workshop of Satan.
Their wretched designs could only be attended with a shameful disappointment. A melancholy drama was thus presented to me; for much as they deserved all possible punishment, I should have been rejoiced to see them passing their
lives in peace and respectability: which might have been the
case, had they not wholly rejected every kind of prudent
admonition."

At one time he almost despaired of success. He wrote to
Farel, Dec. 14, 1547: " Affairs are in such a state of confusion that I despair of being able longer to retain the Church,
at least by my own endeavors. May the Lord hear your
incessant prayers in our behalf." And to Viret he wrote, on
Dec. 17, 1547: " Wickedness has now reached such a pitch
here that I hardly hope that the Church can be upheld much

---

[1] " *Qui imbellis sum et meticulosus* "; in the French ed., " *tout foible et crain-
tif que je suis.*" He more than once refers to his natural timidity; but he
risked his life on several occasions.

longer, at least by means of my ministry. Believe me, my power is broken, unless God stretch forth his hand."[1]

The adversaries of Calvin were, with a few exceptions, the same who had driven him away in 1538. They never cordially consented to his recall. They yielded for a time to the pressure of public opinion and political necessity; but when he carried out the scheme of discipline much more rigorously than they had expected, they showed their old hostility, and took advantage of every censurable act of the Consistory or Council. They hated him worse than the pope.[2] They abhorred the very word "discipline." They resorted to personal indignities and every device of intimidation; they nicknamed him "Cain," and gave his name to the dogs of the street; they insulted him on his way to the lecture-room; they fired one night fifty shots before his bedchamber; they threatened him in the pulpit; they approached the communion table to wrest the sacred elements from his hands, but he refused to profane the sacrament and overawed them. On another occasion he walked into the midst of an excited crowd and offered his breast to their daggers. As late as October 15, 1554, he wrote to an old friend : " Dogs bark at me on all sides. Everywhere I am saluted with the name of 'heretic,' and all the calumnies that can possibly be invented are heaped upon me; in a word, the enemies among my own flock attack me with greater bitterness than my declared enemies among the papists."[3]

And yet in the midst of these troubles he continued to discharge all his duties, and found time to write some of his most important works.

---

[1] Bonnet, II. 133 sq. and 135; *Opera*, XII. 632 sqq. The date of the letter to Viret is Dec. 17, not 14, as given by Bonnet.

[2] To them must be traced the saying: "They would rather be with Beza in hell than with Calvin in heaven." But Beza was in full accord with Calvin in discipline as well as doctrine. The saying is reported by Papyrius Masso: "*Genevenses inter jocos dicebant, malle se apud inferos cum Beza quam apud superos esse cum Calvino.*" Audin, p. 487.   [3] *Opera*, XV. 271.

It seems incredible that a man of feeble constitution and physical timidity should have been able to triumph over such determined and ferocious opposition. The explanation is in the justice of his cause, and the moral purity and " majesty " of his character, which so strongly impressed the Genevese.

We must distinguish two parties among Calvin's enemies — the Patriots, who opposed him on political grounds, and the Libertines, who hated his religion. It would be unjust to charge all the Patriots with the irreligious sentiments of the Libertines. But they made common cause for the overthrow of Calvin and his detested system of discipline. They had many followers among the discontented and dissolute rabble which abounds in every large city, and is always ready for a revolution, having nothing to lose and everything to gain.

1. The PATRIOTS or CHILDREN OF GENEVA (*Enfants de Genève*), as they called themselves, belonged to some of the oldest and most influential families of Geneva, — Favre (or Fabri), Perrin, Vandel, Berthelier, Ameaux.[1] They or their fathers had taken an active part in the achievement of political independence, and even in the introduction of the Reformation, as a means of protecting that independence. But they did not care for the positive doctrines of the Reformation. They wanted liberty without law. They resisted every encroachment on their personal freedom and love of amusements. They hated the evangelical discipline more than the yoke of Savoy.

They also disliked Calvin as a foreigner, who was not even naturalized before 1559. In the pride and prejudice of nativism, they denounced the refugees, who had sacrificed home and fortune to religion, as a set of adventurers, soldiers of fortune, bankrupts, and spies of the Reformer. " These

---

[1] The Galiffes fairly represent the animosity of these old families to Calvin, but far surpass their ancestors in literary and moral culture and respectability, which they owe to the effects of his reformation.

dogs of Frenchmen," they said, "are the cause that we are slaves, and must bow before Calvin and confess our sins. Let the preachers and their gang go to the ——." They deprived the refugees of the right to carry arms, and opposed their admission to the rights of citizenship, as there was danger that they might outnumber and outvote the native citizens. Calvin secured, in 1559, through a majority of the Council, at one time, the admission of three hundred of these refugees, mostly Frenchmen.

The Patriots disliked also the protectorate of Bern, although Bern never favored the strict theology and discipline of Calvin.

2. The LIBERTINES[1] or SPIRITUELS, as they called themselves, were far worse than the Patriots. They formed the opposite extreme to the severe discipline of Calvin. He declares that they were the most pernicious of all the sects that appeared since the time of the ancient Gnostics and Manichæans, and that they answer the prophetic description in the Second Epistle of Peter and the Epistle of Jude. He traces their immediate origin to Coppin of Yssel and Quintin of Hennegau, in the Netherlands, and to an ex-priest, Pocquet or Pocques, who spent some time in Geneva, and wanted to get a certificate from Calvin; but Calvin saw through the man and refused it. They revived the antinomian doctrines of the mediæval sect of the "Brethren and Sisters of the Free Spirit," a branch of the Beghards, who had their headquarters at Cologne and the Lower Rhine, and emancipated themselves not only from the Church, but also from the laws of morality.[2]

The Libertines described by Calvin were antinomian pantheists. They confounded the boundaries of truth and error,

[1] The synagogue of the Libertines in Jerusalem opposed Stephen, the forerunner of Paul, Acts 6:9.

[2] Gieseler connects both sects, vol. III. Part I. 385; comp. II. Part III. 266. Strype notices the existence of a similar sect in England at a later period, *Annals*, vol. II. Part II. 287 sqq. (quoted by Dyer, p. 177).

of right and wrong. Under the pretext of the freedom of the spirit, they advocated the unbridled license of the flesh. Their spiritualism ended in carnal materialism. They taught that there is but one spirit, the Spirit of God, who lives in all creatures, which are nothing without him. "What I or you do," said Quintin, "is done by God, and what God does, we do; for he is in us." Sin is a mere negation or privation, yea, an idle illusion which disappears as soon as it is known and disregarded. Salvation consists in the deliverance from the phantom of sin. There is no Satan, and no angels, good or bad. They denied the truth of the gospel history. The crucifixion and resurrection of Christ have only a symbolical meaning to show us that sin does not exist for us.

The Libertines taught the community of goods and of women, and elevated spiritual marriage above legal marriage, which is merely carnal and not binding. The wife of Ameaux justified her wild licentiousness by the doctrine of the communion of saints, and by the first commandment of God given to man: "Be fruitful and multiply and replenish the earth" (Gen. 1 : 28).

The Libertines rejected the Scriptures as a dead letter, or they resorted to wild allegorical interpretations to suit their fancies. They gave to each of the Apostles a ridiculous nickname.[1] Some carried their system to downright atheism and blasphemous anti-Christianity.

They used a peculiar jargon, like the Gypsies, and distorted common words into a mysterious meaning. They were experts in the art of simulation and justified pious fraud by the parables of Christ. They accommodated themselves to Catholics or Protestants according to circumstances, and concealed their real opinions from the uninitiated.

The sect made progress among the higher classes of France,

---

[1] They called St. Matthew, the publican, *usurier* (a usurer); St. Paul, *pot-cassé* (a broken vessel); St. Peter, on account of his denial of Christ, *renonceur de Dieu;* St. John, *jouvenceau et follet* (a childish youth), etc.

where they converted about four thousand persons. Quintin and Pocquet insinuated themselves into the favor of Queen Marguerite of Navarrè, who protected and supported them at her little court at Nérac, yet without adopting their opinions and practices.[1] She took offence at Calvin's severe attack upon them. He justified his course in a reply of April 28, 1545, which is a fine specimen of courtesy, frankness, and manly dignity. Calvin assured the queen, whose protection he had himself enjoyed while a fugitive from persecution, that he intended no reflection on her honor, or disrespect to her royal majesty, and that he wrote simply in obedience to his duty as a minister. "Even a dog barks if he sees any one assault his master. How could I be silent if God's truth is assailed?[2] . . . As for your saying that you would not like to have such a servant as myself, I confess that I am not qualified to render you any great service, nor have you need of it. . . . Nevertheless, the disposition is not wanting, and your disdain shall not prevent my being at heart your humble servant. For the rest, those who know me are well aware that I have never studied to enter into the courts of princes, for I was never tempted to court worldly honors.[3] For I have good reason to be contented with the service of that good Master, who has accepted me and retained me in the honorable office which I hold, however contemptible in the eyes of the world. I should, indeed, be ungrateful

---

[1] Bonnet, in a note on Calvin's letter to the queen (I. 429), says of her: "In the later years of her life [she died in 1549] her piety gradually degenerated into a kind of contemplative mysticism, whose chief characteristic was indifference towards outward forms, uniting the external ordinances of the Roman Church with the inward cherishing of a purer faith." See above, p. 323.

[2] "Un chien abaye, sil voyt quon assaille son maistre; ie serois bien lasche, si en voyant la verite de dieu ainsi assallye, ie faisois du muet sans sonner mot."

[3] "Au reste, ceulx qui me cognoissent, savent bien que nay iamais aspire davoir entree aux courtz des princes, dautant que ie nestois pas tenté de parvenir aux estatz" (honorum studio titillatus).

beyond measure if I did not prefer this condition to all the riches and honors of the world." [1]

Beza says: " It was owing to Calvin that this horrid sect, in which all the most monstrous heresies of ancient times were renewed, was kept within the confines of Holland and the adjacent provinces."

During the trial of Servetus the political and religious Libertines combined in an organized effort for the overthrow of Calvin at Geneva, but were finally defeated by a failure of an attempted rebellion in May, 1555.

§ 109. *The Leaders of the Libertines and their punishment:*
— *Gruet, Perrin, Ameaux, Vandel, Berthelier.*

We shall now give sketches of the chief Patriots and Libertines, and their quarrels with Calvin and his system of discipline. The heretical opponents — Bolsec, Castellio, Servetus — will be considered in a separate chapter on the Doctrinal Controversies.

1. JACQUES GRÜET was the first victim of Calvin's discipline who suffered death for sedition and blasphemy. His case is the most famous next to that of Servetus. Gruet[2] was a Libertine of the worst type, both politically and religiously, and would have been condemned to death in any other country at that time. He was a Patriot descended from an old and respectable family, and formerly a canon. He lay under suspicion of having attempted to poison Viret in 1535. He wrote verses against Calvin and the refugees which (as Audin says) were "more malignant than poetic." He was a regular frequenter of taverns, and opposed to any rules

---

[1] The French original in Henry, II. Beilage, 14, p. 112 sqq.; also in Bonnet and in *Opera*, XII. 64–68. The Latin editions date the letter April 20 instead of 28.

[2] A son of Humbert Gruet, notary public of Geneva; not to be confounded with Canon Claude Gruet. See *Opera*, XII. 546, note 9; Bonnet, *Letters fr.* I. 212, and Henry, II. 440.

in Church and State which interfered with personal liberty. When in church, he looked boldly and defiantly into the face of the preacher. He first adopted the Bernese fashion of wearing breeches with plaits at the knees, and openly defied the discipline of the Consistory which forbade it. Calvin called him a scurvy fellow, and gives an unfavorable account of his moral and religious character, which the facts fully justified.

On the 27th of June, 1547, a few days after the wife of Perrin had defied the Consistory,[1] the following libel, written in the Savoyard patois, was attached to Calvin's pulpit in St. Peter's Church: —

"Gross hypocrite (*Gros panfar*), thou and thy companions will gain little by your pains. If you do not save yourselves by flight, nobody shall prevent your overthrow, and you will curse the hour when you left your monkery. Warning has been already given that the devil and his renegade priests were come hither to ruin every thing. But after people have suffered long they avenge themselves. Take care that you are not served like Mons. Verle of Fribourg.[2] We will not have so many masters. Mark well what I say."[3]

The Council arrested Jacques Gruet, who had been heard uttering threats against Calvin a few days previously, and had written obscene and impious verses and letters. In his house were found a copy of Calvin's work against the Libertines with a marginal note, *Toutes folies*, and several papers and letters filled with abuse of Calvin as a haughty, ambitious, and obstinate hypocrite who wished to be adored, and to rob the pope of his honor. There were also found two Latin pages in Gruet's handwriting, in which the Scriptures

---

[1] On the date see *Opera*, XII. 546, note 7, and *Annal.* XXI. 407, sub Lundi Juin 27: "*Un écrit violent contre Calvin et ses collègues est trouvé dans la chaire d'un des temples.*" Calvin's letter to Viret, July 2, 1547: "*Postridie reperitur charta in suggestu qua mortem nobis minantur.*"

[2] Peter Wernly, a canon of St. Peter's, was killed in a fight with the Protestants, while endeavoring to save himself by flight, May 4, 1533.

[3] "*Nota bin mon dire.*" See the original of the placard in *Opera*, XII. 546, note 8. Gaberel and Ruchat give it in modern French. The editors of the *Opera* refer *panfar* to Abel Poupin ("*Panfar ventrosum dicit Poupinum*").

were ridiculed, Christ blasphemed, and the immortality of
the soul called a dream and a fable.

Gruet was tortured every day for a month, after the inhuman fashion of that age.[1] He confessed that he had affixed
the libel, and that the papers found in his house belonged to
him; but he refused to name any accomplices. He was condemned for religious, moral, and political offences; being
found guilty of expressing contempt for religion; of declaring that laws, both human and divine, were but the work of
man's caprice; and that fornication was not criminal when
both parties were consenting; and of threatening the clergy
and the Council itself.[2]

He was beheaded on the 26th of July, 1547. The execution instead of terrifying the Libertines made them more
furious than ever. Three days afterwards the Council was
informed that more than twenty young men had entered into
a conspiracy to throw Calvin and his colleagues into the
Rhone. He could not walk the streets without being insulted
and threatened.

Two or three years after the death of Gruet, a treatise of
his was discovered full of horrible blasphemies against Christ,
the Virgin Mary, the Prophets and Apostles, against the
Scriptures, and all religion. He aimed to show that the
founders of Judaism and Christianity were criminals, and
that Christ was justly crucified. Some have confounded
this treatise with the book "*De tribus Impostoribus*," which
dates from the age of Emperor Frederick II., and puts

---

[1] In the case of Gentilis and Servet, however, no mention is made of the
torture.

[2] The sentence of condemnation (*Opera*, XII. 567) reads: "*Par jceste
nostre diffinitive sentence, laquelle donnons icy par escript, toy Jaque Gruet con-
dampnons a debvoyr estre mene au lieu de Champel et illect debvoyer avoyer tranche
la teste de dessus les espaules, et ton corps attache aut gibet et la teste cloye en jcelluy
et ainsy finiras tes jours pour donner exemple aux aultres qui tel cas vouldroyent
commestre.*" The charges assigned are blasphemy against God, offence against
the civil magistracy, threats to the ministers of God, and "*crime de leze majeste
meritant pugnition corporelle.*"

Moses, Christ, and Mohammed on a level as religious impostors.

Gruet's book was, at Calvin's advice, publicly burnt by the hangman before Gruet's house, May 22, 1550.[1]

2. AMI PERRIN (Amy Pierre), the military chief (captain-general) of the Republic, was the most popular and influential leader of the Patriotic party. He had been one of the earliest promoters of the Reformation, though from political rather than religious motives; he had protected Farel against the violence of the priests, and had been appointed deputy to Strassburg to bring Calvin back to Geneva.[2] He was one of the six lay-members who, with the ministers, drew up the Ecclesiastical Ordinances of 1542, and for some time he supported Calvin in his reforms. He could wield the sword, but not the pen. He was vain, ambitious, pretentious, and theatrical. Calvin called him, in derision, the stage-emperor, who played now the " *Cæsar comicus*," and now the " *Cæsar tragicus*." [3]

---

[1] The sources for the case of Gruet are the acts of the criminal process and sentence, printed in *Opera*, XII. 563–568 (in French); letters of Calvin to Viret, July 2, 24, 1547 (in *Opera*, XII. 545, 559, in Bonnet II. 108 and 114); Calvin's report on the blasphemous book of Gruet, in *Opera*, XIII. 568–572 (in French, also printed in Henry, II. 120, and in Letters by Jules Bonnet, French ed., I. 311; English ed., II. 254); *Reg. du Conseil*, July 25, 1547, and May 22, 1550, noticed in *Annal.* 409, 465. — Of modern writers, see Henry (II. 410, 439, 441 sqq.; abridged in Stebbing's translation, II. 64 sqq., without the Beilage); Audin, ch. XXXVI. (pp. 396 sqq. of the English translation); Dyer, 213 sqq.; and Stähelin, I. 399 sqq.

[2] Oct. 21, 1540. A day afterwards, Dufour was appointed by the Council, and went in his place. *Annal.* 267. See above, p. 430.

[3] Beza calls him "*vanissimus, sed audax et ambitiosus*" (XXI. 138). Audin, the patron of all the enemies of Calvin, describes Perrin as "a man of noble nature, who wore the sword with great grace, dressed in good taste, and conversed with much facility; but a boaster at table and at the Council, where he deafened every one with his boastful loquacity, his fits of self-love, and his theatrical airs. . . . As to the rest, like all men of this stamp, he had an excellent heart, was devoted as a friend, with cool blood, and patriotic even to extremes. At table it was his delight to imitate the Reformer, elongating his visage, winking his eyes, and assuming the air of an anchorite of the Thebaid " (p. 390). Perrin's chief defender is the younger Galiffe.

Perrin's wife, Francesca, was a daughter of François Favre, who had taken a prominent part in the political struggle against Savoy, but mistook freedom for license, and hated Calvin as a tyrant and a hypocrite. His whole family shared in this hatred. Francesca had an excessive fondness for dancing and revelry, a violent temper, and an abusive tongue. Calvin called her "Penthesilea" (the queen of the Amazons who fought a battle against the Greeks, and was slain by Achilles), and "a prodigious fury."[1]

He found out too late that it is foolish and dangerous to quarrel with a woman. He forgot Christ's conduct towards the adulteress, and Mary Magdalene.

A disgraceful scene which took place at a wedding in the house of the widow Balthazar at Belle Rive, brought upon the family of Favre, who were present, the censure of the Consistory and the punishment of the Council. Perrin, his wife and her father were imprisoned for a few weeks in April, 1546. Favre refused to make any confession, and went to prison, shouting: "Liberty! Liberty! I would give a thousand crowns to have a general council."[2] Perrin made an humble apology to the Consistory. Calvin plainly told the Favre family that as long as they lived in Geneva they

---

[1] "*Prodigiosa furia.*" Letter to Farel, Sept. 1, 1546 (in *Opera*, XII. 377 sq., and Bonnet, II. 56). In the same letter he says: "She shamelessly undertakes the defence of all crimes." She did not spare Calvin's wife, and calumniously asserted among her own friends that Idelette must have been a harlot because Calvin confessed, at the baptism of his infant, that she and her former husband had been Anabaptists. So Calvin reports to Farel, Aug. 21, 1547 (in *Opera*, XII. 580 sq.; Bonnet, II. 124). Audin apologizes for Francesca, as "one of those women whom our old Corneille would have taken for heroines; excitable, choleric, fond of pleasure, enamoured of dancing, and hating Calvin as Luther hated a monk" (p. 390).

[2] Calvin reminded Francesca on that occasion that "her father had been already convicted of one adultery [in 1531], that the proof of another was at hand, and that there was a strong rumor of a third. I stated that her brother had openly contemned and derided both the Council and the ministers." Letter to Farel, April, 1546. She told him in reply: "*Méchant homme, vous voulez boire le sang de notre famille, mais vous sortirez de Genève avant nous.*" See the notes in *Opera*, XII. 334.

must obey the laws of Geneva, though every one of them wore a diadem.[1]

From this time on Perrin stood at the head of the opposition to Calvin. He loudly denounced the Consistory as a popish tribunal. He secured so much influence over the Council that a majority voted, in March, 1547, to take the control of Church discipline into their own hands. But Calvin made such a vigorous resistance that it was determined eventually to abide by the established Ordinances.[2]

Perrin was sent as ambassador to Paris (April 26, 1547), and was received there with much distinction. The Cardinal du Bellay sounded him as to whether some French troops under his command could be stationed at Geneva to frustrate the hostile designs of the German emperor against Switzerland. He gave a conditional consent. This created a suspicion against his loyalty.

During his absence, Madame Perrin and her father were again summoned before the Consistory for bacchanalian conduct (June 23, 1547). Favre refused to appear. Francesca denied the right of the court to take cognizance of her private life. When remonstrated with, she flew into a passion, and abused the preacher, Abel Poupin, as "a reviler, a slanderer of her father, a coarse swine-herd, and a malicious liar." She was again imprisoned, but escaped with one of her sons. Meeting Abel Poupin at the gate of the city she insulted him afresh and "even more shamefully than before."[3]

---

[1] See Calvin's letters to Farel, April, 1546, and Sept. 1, 1546 (in Opera, XII. 334 sqq., 377 sq., and Bonnet II. 38, 56), and extracts from the Registers of the Consistory and the Council in Annal. 377 sqq. Comp. Dyer, 208 sq.; Audin, 391 sq. Audin gives a lively description of the wedding and dancing at Belle Rive, and the examination before the Consistory.

[2] See the extracts from the Rég. du Conseil March and April, 1547, in Annal. 399–406.

[3] Calvin to Viret, July 2, 1547 (Opera, XII. 545, Bonnet, II. 108). Comp. Annal. 407 sq.; Gaberel, I. 387; Roget, II. 284. Bonivard and after him Gaberel report that Francesca rushed with her horse against Abel, who barely escaped serious injury. See note 6 in Opera, XII. 546.

On the 27th of June, 1547, Gruet's threatening libel was published.[1] Calvin was reported to have been killed. He received letters from Burgogne and Lyons that the Children of Geneva had offered five hundred crowns for his head.[2]

On his return from Paris, Perrin was capitally indicted on a charge of treason, and of intending to quarter two hundred French cavalry, under his own command, at Geneva. His excuse was that he had accepted the command of these troops with the reservation of the approval of the government of Geneva. Bonivard, the old soldier of liberty and prisoner of Chillon, took part against Perrin. The ambassadors of Bern endeavored to divert the storm from the head of Perrin to the French ambassador Maigret the Magnifique. Perrin was expelled from the Council, and the office of captain-general was suppressed, but he was released from prison, together with his wife and father-in-law, Nov. 29, 1547.[3]

The Libertines summoned all their forces for a reaction. They called a meeting of the Council of Two Hundred, where they expected most support. A violent scene took place on Dec. 16, 1547, in the Senate house, when Calvin, unarmed and at the risk of his life, appeared in the midst of the armed crowd and called upon them, if they designed to shed blood, to begin with him. He succeeded, by his courage and eloquence, in calming the wild storm and preventing a disgraceful carnage. It was a sublime victory of reason over passion, of moral over physical force.[4]

---

[1] See above, p. 502.

[2] Calvin to Farel, Aug. 21, 1547 (*Opera*, XII. 580; Bonnet, II. 123 and note); *Reg. of the Consistory*, Sept. 1, 1547.

[3] *Rég. du Conseil :* "*Perrin est relâché vu sa long détention et crie merci.*" *Annal.* 417. François Favre had been previously deprived of the rights of citizenship (Oct. 5) on the charge of exciting an émeute against the French refugees, and calling Calvin "*le grand diable.*" *Ibid.* 413 sq.

[4] Dec. 16 (not Sept. 16) is the date given in the Reg. of the Venerable Company, quoted in *Annal.* 418. Beza briefly alludes to the scene; Calvin gives an account of it in a letter to Viret, dated Dec. 17, 1547, a day after the occurrence (in *Opera*, XII. 632 sq.). This letter is misdated, Dec. 14, by Bonnet (II. 134, apparently a typographical error), and Sept. 17 by

The ablest of the detractors of Calvin cannot help paying here an involuntary tribute to him and to the truth of history. This is his dramatic account.

" The Council of the Two Hundred was assembled. Never had any session been more tumultuous; the parties, weary of speaking, began to appeal to arms. The people heard the appeal. Calvin appears, unattended; he is received at the lower part of the hall with cries of death. He folds his arms, and looks the agitators fixedly in the face. Not one of them dares strike him. Then, advancing through the midst of the groups, with his breast uncovered: 'If you want blood,' says he, 'there are still a few drops here; strike, then!' Not an arm is raised. Calvin then slowly ascends the stairway to the Council of the Two Hundred. The hall was on the point of being drenched with blood; swords were flashing. On beholding the Reformer, the weapons were lowered, and a few words sufficed to calm the agitation. Calvin, taking the arm of one of the councillors, again descends the stairs, and cries out to the people that he wishes to address them. He does speak, and with such energy and feeling, that tears flow from their eyes. They embrace each other, and the crowd retires in silence. The patriots had lost the day. From that moment, it was easy to foretell that victory would remain with the Reformer. The Libertines, who had shown themselves so bold when it was a question of destroying some front of a Catholic edifice, overturning some saint's niche, or throwing down an old wooden cross weakened by age, trembled like women before this man, who, in fact, on this occasion, exhibited something of the Homeric heroism." [1]

Notwithstanding this triumph, Calvin did not trust his enemies, and expressed in letters to Farel and Viret even the

Henry (II. 434) and Dyer (p. 219). The last error crept into the Latin editions, against the manuscripts, which give Dec. 17. The letter is defective at the beginning and was first published by Beza. Galiffe overlooked it. See the notes of the Strassburg editors, XII. 633.

[1] Audin, *Life of Calvin*, p. 394.

fear that he could no longer maintain his position unless
God stretch forth his hand for his protection.[1]

A sort of truce was patched up between the contending
parties. "Our çi-devant Cæsar (*hesternus noster Cæsar*),"
Calvin wrote to Farel, Dec. 28, 1547, "denied that he had
any grudge against me, and I immediately met him half-way
and pressed out the matter from the sore. In a grave and
moderate speech, I used, indeed, some sharp reproofs (*punc-
tiones acutas*), but not of a nature to wound; yet though he
grasped my hand whilst promising to reform, I still fear that
I have spoken to deaf ears."[2]

In the next year, Calvin was censured by the Council for
saying, in a private letter to Viret which had been inter-
cepted, that the Genevese "under pretence of Christ wanted
to rule without Christ," and that he had to combat their
"hypocrisy." He called to his aid Viret and Farel to make
a sort of apology.[3]

Perrin behaved quietly, and gained an advantage from
this incident. He was restored to his councillorship and the
office of captain-general (which had been abolished). He
was even elected First Syndic, in February, 1549. He held
that position also during the trial of Servetus, and opposed
the sentence of death in the Council (1553).

Shortly after the execution of Servetus, the Libertines
raised a demonstration against Farel, who had come to
Geneva and preached a very severe sermon against them
(Nov. 1, 1553).[4] Philibert Berthelier and his brother Fran-

---

[1] See the extracts quoted on p. 495.

[2] *Opera*, XII. 642 sq.: "*Tametsi resipiscentiam manu in manum implicita
promisit, vereor, ne frustra surdo cecinerim fabulam.*" Dyer (p. 221) misdates
this letter Dec. 2 (probably a typographical error).

[3] Registers of Council for October, 1548, in *Annal.* 436–438. About the
same time the wife of Calvin's brother, Antoine, was imprisoned on the
charge of adultery. *Ibid.* 441.

[4] He was charged with saying that "*la jeunesse de cette cité sont pires que les
brigands, meurtriers, larrons, luxurieux, athéists.*" Reg. of Nov. 3, 1553, in
Annal. 559.

çois Daniel, who had charge of the mint, stirred up the laborers to throw Farel into the Rhone. But his friends formed a guard around him, and his defence before the Council convinced the audience of his innocence. It was resolved that all enmity should be forgotten and buried at a banquet. Perrin, the chief Syndic, in a sense of weakness, or under the impulse of his better feelings, begged Farel's pardon, and declared that he would ever regard him as his spiritual father and pastor.[1]

After this time Calvin's friends gained the ascendency in the Council. A large number of religious refugees were admitted to the rights of citizenship.

Perrin, then a member of the Little Council, and his friends, Peter Vandel and Philibert Berthelier, determined on rule or ruin, now concocted a desperate and execrable conspiracy, which proved their overthrow. They proposed to kill all foreigners who had fled to Geneva for the sake of religion, together with their Genevese sympathizers, on a Sunday while people were at church. But, fortunately, the plot was discovered before it was ripe for execution. When the rioters were to be tried before the Council of the Two Hundred, Perrin and several other ringleaders had the audacity to take their places as judges; but when he saw that matters were taking a serious turn in favor of law and order, he fled from Geneva, together with Vandel and Berthelier. They were summoned by the public herald, but refused to appear. On the day appointed for the trial five of the fugitives were condemned to death; Perrin, moreover, to have his right hand cut off, with which he had seized the bâton of the Syndic at the riot. The sentence was executed in effigy in June, 1555.[2]

---

[1] Comp. the action of the Council, Nov. 13, in *Annal.* 561 and 562.

[2] *Rég. du Conseil*, June 3, 1555, in *Annal.* 608: "*Perrin est condamné par contumace quil ayt le poing du bras droit duquel il a attenté aux bastons sindicalz copé: et tous tans ledit Perrin que Belthesard, Chabod, Verna, et Michalet la teste copé: les testes et ledit poing cloués au gibet et les corps mis en quartier iouxte la coustume et condamnez a tous despens damps et interestz.*"

Their estates were confiscated, and their wives banished from Geneva. The office of captain-general was again abolished to avoid the danger of a military dictatorship.

But the government of Bern protected the fugitives, and allowed them to commit outrages on Genevese citizens within their reach, and to attack Calvin and Geneva with all sorts of reproaches and calumnies.

Thus the "comic Cæsar" ended as the "tragic Cæsar." An impartial biographer of Calvin calls the last chapter in Perrin's career "a caricature of the Catilinarian conspiracy."[1]

3. The case of PIERRE AMEAUX shows a close connection between the political and religious Libertines. He was a member of the Council of Two Hundred. He sought and obtained a divorce from his wife, who was condemned to perpetual imprisonment for the theory and practice of free-lovism of the worst kind. But he hated Calvin's theology and discipline. At a supper party in his own house he freely indulged in drink, and roundly abused Calvin as a teacher of false doctrine, as a very bad man, and nothing but a Picard.[2]

For this offence he was imprisoned by the Council for two months and condemned to a fine of sixty dollars. He made an apology and retracted his words. But Calvin was not satisfied, and demanded a second trial. The Council condemned him to a degrading punishment called the *amende honorable*, namely, to parade through the streets in his shirt, with bare head, and a lighted torch in his hand, and to ask on bended knees the pardon of God, of the Council, and of Calvin. This harsh judgment provoked a popular outbreak in the quarter of St. Gervais, but the Council proceeded in a body to the

---

[1] Dyer, p. 397.

[2] He said, according to the Registers of the Council, Jan. 27, 1546, "*que M. Calvin estoyt meschant homme et nestoyt que un picard et preschoyt faulce doctrine,*" etc. Comp. on his case *Annal.* 368, 370, 371. Audin calls Ameaux "a man of the bar-room with a wicked tongue and a soul destitute of energy" (p. 386). He gives quite an amusing account of the drinking party.

spot and ordered the wine-shops to be closed and a gibbet to
be erected to frighten the mob. The sentence on Ameaux
was executed April 5, 1546. Two preachers, Henri de la
Mare and Aimé Maigret, who had taken part in the drinking
scene, were deposed. The former had said before the Council that Calvin was "a good and virtuous man, and of great
intellect, but sometimes governed by his passions, impatient,
full of hatred, and vindictive." The latter had committed
more serious offences.[1]

4. PIERRE VANDEL was a handsome, brilliant, and frivolous cavalier, and loved to exhibit himself with a retinue of
valets and courtesans, with rings on his fingers and golden
chains on his breast. He had been active in the expulsion
of Calvin, and opposed him after his recall. He was imprisoned for his debaucheries and insolent conduct before the Consistory. He was Syndic in 1548. He took a leading part in the
conspiracy of Perrin and shared his condemnation and exile.[2]

5. PHILIBERT BERTHELIER (or Bertelier, Bertellier), an
unworthy son of the distinguished patriot who, in 1519, had
been beheaded for his part in the war of independence,
belonged to the most malignant enemies of Calvin. He had
gone to Noyon, if we are to believe the assertion of Bolsec, to
bring back scandalous reports concerning the early life of the
Reformer, which the same Bolsec published thirteen years
after Calvin's death, but without any evidence.[3] If the
Libertines had been in possession of such information, they
would have made use of it. Berthelier is characterized by
Beza as "a man of the most consummate impudence" and
"guilty of many iniquities." He was excommunicated by

---

[1] *Annal.* 378 and 380. The ministers interceded in behalf of De la Mare,
and the Council gave him six dollars (*écus*). Maigret was found guilty of
neglecting his duties and visiting houses of ill fame.

[2] *Annal.* 411, 611 sq. ; *Opera*, XII. 547, note 14, with references to Galiffe,
Bonivard, and Roget.

[3] See above, p. 302 sq. That abominable slander about sodomy, which
even Galiffe rejects. Audin and Spalding are not ashamed to repeat.

the Consistory in 1551 for abusing Calvin, for not going to church, and other offences, and for refusing to make any apology.   Calvin was absent during these sessions, owing to sickness.   Berthelier appealed to the Council, of which he was the secretary.   The Council at first confirmed the decision of the Consistory, but afterwards released him, during the syndicate of Perrin and the trial of Servetus, and gave him letters of absolution signed with the seal of the Republic (1553).[1]

Calvin was thus brought into direct conflict with the Council, and forced to the alternative of submission or disobedience; in the latter case he ran the risk of a second and final expulsion.   But he was not the man to yield in such a crisis.   He resolved to oppose to the Council his inflexible *non possumus*.

On the Sunday which followed the absolution of Berthelier, the September communion was to be celebrated.   Calvin preached as usual in St. Peter's, and declared at the close of the sermon that he would never profane the sacrament by administering it to an excommunicated person.   Then raising his voice and lifting up his hands, he exclaimed in the words of St. Chrysostom: " I will lay down my life ere these hands shall reach forth the sacred things of God to those who have been branded as his despisers."

This was another moment of sublime Christian heroism.

Perrin, who had some decent feeling of respect for religion and for Calvin's character, was so much impressed by this solemn warning that he secretly gave orders to Berthelier not to approach the communion table.   The communion was celebrated, as Beza reports, " in profound silence, and under a solemn awe, as if the Deity himself had been visibly present among them." [2]

---

[1] See extracts from the Registers, March and April, 1551, and in September, 1553, *Annal.* XXI. 475–479, 551 sq.

[2] Comp. the Reg. of the Council, and of the Venerable Company, Sept. 2, 1553, in *Annal.* 551.

In the afternoon, Calvin, as for the last time, preached on Paul's farewell address to the Ephesian Elders (Acts 20: 31); he exhorted the congregation to abide in the doctrine of Christ, and declared his willingness to serve the Church and each of its members, but added in conclusion: "Such is the state of things here that this may be my last sermon to you; for they who are in power would force me to do what God does not permit. I must, therefore, dearly beloved, like Paul, commend you to God, and to the Word of his grace."[1]

These words made a deep impression even upon his worst foes. The next day Calvin, with his colleagues and the Presbytery, demanded of the Council to grant them an audience before the people, as a law was attacked which had been sanctioned by the General Assembly. The Council refused the request, but resolved to suspend the decree by which the power of excommunication was declared to belong to the Council.

In the midst of this agitation the trial of Servetus was going on, and was brought to a close by his death at the stake, Oct. 27. A few days afterwards (Nov. 3), Berthelier renewed his request to be admitted to the Lord's Table — he who despised religion. The Council which had condemned the heretic, was not quite willing to obey Calvin as a legislator, and wished to retain the power of excommunication in their own hands. Yet, in order to avoid a rupture with the ministers, who would not yield to any compromise, the Council resolved to solicit the opinions of four Swiss cantons on the subject.[2]

Bullinger, in behalf of the Church and magistracy of Zürich, replied in December, substantially approving of Calvin's view, though he admonished him privately against undue severity. The magistrates of Bern replied that they

---

[1] The sermon was taken down by a stenographer, and translated into Latin by Beza.

[2] *Rég. du Conseil*, Nov. 7, 9, 23, 28, 1553, in *Annal.* 559–562.

had no excommunication in their Church. The answers of the two other cantons are lost, but seem to have been rather favorable to Calvin's cause.

In the meantime matters assumed a more promising aspect. On Jan. 1, 1554, at a grand dinner given by the Council and judges, Calvin being present, a desire for peace was universally expressed. On the second of February the Council of Two Hundred swore, with uplifted hands, to conform to the doctrines of the Reformation, to forget the past, to renounce all hatred and animosity, and to live together in unity.

Calvin regarded this merely as a truce, and looked for further troubles. He declared before the Council that he readily forgave all his enemies, but could not sacrifice the rights of the Consistory, and would rather leave Geneva. The irritation continued in 1554. The opposition broke out again in the conspiracy against the foreigners and the council, which has been already described. The plot failed. Berthelier was, with Perrin, condemned to death, but escaped with him the execution of justice by flight.[1]

This was the end of Libertinism in Geneva.

§ 110. *Geneva Regenerated. Testimonies Old and New.*

The final result of this long conflict with Libertinism is the best vindication of Calvin. Geneva came out of it a new city, and with a degree of moral and spiritual prosperity which distinguished her above any other Christian city for several generations. What a startling contrast she presents, for instance, to Rome, the city of the vicar of Christ and his cardinals, as described by Roman Catholic writers of the sixteenth century! If ever in this wicked world the ideal of Christian society can be realized in a civil community

---

[1] *Rég. du Conseil*, Aug. 6, 1555 (in *Annal.* 611 sq.) : " *Philibert Bertellier*, *P. Vandel, et J. B.* Sept *condamnés à mort par contumace*, Michael *Sept au banissement perpétuel, sans peine de mort ; six autres à la même peine ; deux à dix ans de banissement, et tous aux dépens.*"

with a mixed population, it was in Geneva from the middle of the sixteenth to the middle of the eighteenth century, when the revolutionary and infidel genius of Rousseau (a native of Geneva) and of Voltaire (who resided twenty years in the neighborhood, on his estate at Ferney) began to destroy the influence of the Reformer.

After the final collapse of the Libertine party in 1555, the peace was not seriously disturbed, and Calvin's work progressed without interruption. The authorities of the State were as zealous for the honor of the Church and the glory of Christ as the ministers of the gospel. The churches were well filled; the Word of God was preached daily; family worship was the rule; prayer and singing of Psalms never ceased; the whole city seemed to present the aspect of a community of sincere, earnest Christians who practised what they believed. Every Friday a spiritual conference and experience meeting, called the "Congregation," was held in St. Peter's, after the model of the meetings of "prophesying," which had been introduced in Zürich and Bern. Peter Paul Vergerius, the former papal nuncio, who spent a short time in Geneva, was especially struck with these conferences. "All the ministers," he says,[1] "and many citizens attend. One of the preachers reads and briefly explains a text from the Scriptures. Another expresses his views on the subject, and then any member may make a contribution if so disposed. You see, it is an imitation of that custom in the Corinthian Church of which Paul speaks, and I have received much edification from these public colloquies."

The material prosperity of the city was not neglected. Greater cleanliness was introduced, which is next to godliness, and promotes it. Calvin insisted on the removal of all filth from the houses and the narrow and crooked streets. He induced the magistracy to superintend the markets, and

---

[1] Letter in the Zürich library, quoted by Gaberel, I. 512, and Stähelin, I. 364.

to prevent the sale of unhealthy food, which was to be cast into the Rhone. Low taverns and drinking shops were abolished, and intemperance diminished. Mendicancy on the streets was prohibited. A hospital and poor-house was provided and well conducted. Efforts were made to give useful employment to every man that could work. Calvin urged the Council in a long speech, Dec. 29, 1544, to introduce the cloth and silk industry, and two months afterwards he presented a detailed plan, in which he recommended to lend to the Syndic, Jean Ami Curtet, a sufficient sum from the public treasury for starting the enterprise. The factories were forthwith established and soon reached the highest degree of prosperity. The cloth and silk of Geneva were highly prized in Switzerland and France, and laid the foundation for the temporal wealth of the city. When Lyons, by the patronage of the French crown, surpassed the little Republic in the manufacture of silk, Geneva had already begun to make up for the loss by the manufacture of watches, and retained the mastery in this useful industry until 1885, when American machinery produced a successful rivalry.[1]

Altogether, Geneva owes her moral and temporal prosperity, her intellectual and literary activity, her social refinement, and her world-wide fame very largely to the reformation and discipline of Calvin. He set a high and noble example of a model community. It is impossible, indeed, to realize his church ideal in a large country, even with all the help of the civil government. The Puritans attempted it in England and in New England, but succeeded only in part, and only for a short period. But nothing should prevent a pastor from making an effort in his own congregation on the voluntary principle. Occasionally we find parallel cases in small communities under the guidance of pastors of exceptional

---

[1] Gaberel, I. 524; Stähelin, I. 372. Even now the Swiss watches (of Geneva and Neuchâtel) are considered the best of those made wholly or mainly by hand labor.

genius and consecration, such as Oberlin in the Steinthal, Harms in Hermannsburg, and Löhe in Neudettelsau, who exerted an inspiring influence far beyond their fields of labor.

Let us listen to some testimonies of visitors who saw with their own eyes the changes wrought in Geneva through Calvin's influence.

William Farel, who knew better than any other man the state of Geneva under Roman Catholic rule, and during the early stages of reform before the arrival of Calvin, visited the city again in 1557, and wrote to Ambrosius Blaurer that he would gladly listen and learn there with the humblest of the people, and that "he would rather be the last in Geneva than the first anywhere else." [1]

John Knox, the Reformer of Scotland, who studied several years in Geneva as a pupil of Calvin (though five years his senior), and as pastor of the English congregation, wrote to his friend Locke, in 1556: "In my heart I could have wished, yea, I cannot cease to wish, that it might please God to guide and conduct yourself to this place where, I neither fear nor am ashamed to say, is *the most perfect school of Christ that ever was in the earth since the days of the Apostles.* In other places I confess Christ to be truly preached; but manners and religion to be so seriously reformed, I have not yet seen in any other place besides." [2]

Dr. Valentine Andreæ (1586–1654), a bright and shining light of the Lutheran Church of Würtemberg (a grandson of Jacob Andreæ, the chief author of the Lutheran *Formula of Concord*), a man full of glowing love to Christ, visited Geneva in 1610, nearly fifty years after Calvin's death, with the prejudices of an orthodox Lutheran against Calvinism, and was astonished to find in that city a state of religion

---

[1] Kirchhofer, *Farel's Leben*, II. 125.
[2] Thomas M'Crie, *Life of John Knox*, p. 129 (Philadelphia ed. 1845). I quoted a sentence from this letter by anticipation on p. 263, but cannot omit it at this place.

which came nearer to his ideal of a Christocracy than any community he had seen in his extensive travels, and even in his German fatherland.

"When I was in Geneva," he writes, "I observed something great which I shall remember and desire as long as I live. There is in that place not only the perfect institute of a perfect republic, but, as a special ornament, a moral discipline, which makes weekly investigations into the conduct, and even the smallest transgressions of the citizens, first through the district inspectors, then through the Seniors, and finally through the magistrates, as the nature of the offence and the hardened state of the offender may require. All cursing and swearing, gambling, luxury, strife, hatred, fraud, etc., are forbidden; while greater sins are hardly heard of. What a glorious ornament of the Christian religion is such a purity of morals! We must lament with tears that it is wanting with us, and almost totally neglected. If it were not for the difference of religion, I would have forever been chained to that place by the agreement in morals, and I have ever since tried to introduce something like it into our churches. No less distinguished than the public discipline was the domestic discipline of my landlord, Scarron, with its daily devotions, reading of the Scriptures, the fear of God in word and in deed, temperance in meat and drink and dress. I have not found greater purity of morals even in my father's home." [1]

A stronger and more impartial testimony of the deep and lasting effect of Calvin's discipline so long after his death could hardly be imagined.

[1] See his autobiography, written in 1642, and his " *Respublica Christianopolitana*," or " *Christianopolis*," 1619, — a description of a Christian model commonwealth, dedicated to John Arndt, the author of "True Christianity." Comp. Hossbach, *Das Leben Val. Andreæ*, p. 10; Henry, p. 196 (small biography); Tholuck's article in Herzog, I. 388 sqq.; Schaff, *Creeds*, I. 460 (which gives the German original). Andreæ's memory was revived by the great Herder. Spener said: "If I could raise any one from the dead for the welfare of the Church, it would be Andreæ."

NOTES. MODERN TESTIMONIES.

The condemnation of Calvin's discipline and his conduct toward the Libertines has been transplanted to America by two dignitaries of the Roman Church — Dr. John McGill, bishop of Richmond, the translator of Audin's *Life of Calvin* (Louisville, n. d.), and Dr. M. S. Spalding, archbishop of Baltimore (between 1864 and 1872), in his *History of the Protestant Reformation* (Louisville, 1860), 8th ed., Baltimore, 1875. This book is not a history, but a *chronique scandaleuse* of the Reformation, and unworthy of a Christian scholar. Dr. Spalding devotes twenty-two pages to Calvin (vol. I. 370–392), besides an appendix on Rome and Geneva, and a letter addressed to Merle d'Aubigné and Bungener (pp. 495–530). He ignores his Commentaries and Institutes, which have commanded the admiration even of eminent Roman Catholic divines, and simply repeats, with some original mistakes and misspellings, the slanders of Bolsec and Audin, which have long since been refuted.

"Calvin," he says, "crushed the liberties of the people in the name of liberty. A foreigner, he insinuated himself into Geneva and, serpent-like, coiled himself around the very heart of the Republic which had given him hospitable shelter. He thus stung the very bosom which had warmed him. He was as watchful as a tiger preparing to pounce on its prey, and as treacherous. . . . His reign in Geneva was truly a reign of terror. He combined the cruelty of Danton and Robespierre with the eloquence of Marat and Mirabeau. . . . He was worse than 'the Chalif of Geneva,' as Audin calls him — he was a very Nero ! . . . He was a monster of impurity and iniquity. The story of his having been guilty of a crime of nameless turpitude at Noyon, though denied by his friends, yet rests upon very respectable authority. Bolsec, a contemporary writer, relates it as certain. . . . He ended his life in despair, and died of a most shameful and disgusting disease which God has threatened to rebellious and accursed reprobates." The early Calvinists were hypocrites, and "their boasted austerity was little better than a sham, if it was not even a cloak to cover enormous wickedness. They exhibit their own favorite doctrine of total depravity in its fullest practical development !" The archbishop, however, is kind enough to add in conclusion (p. 391), that he "would not be understood as wishing to reflect upon the character or conduct of the present professors of Calvinistic doctrines, many of whom are men estimable for their civic virtues."

The best answer to such a caricature, which turns the very truth into a lie, is presented in the facts of this chapter. With ignorance and prejudice even the gods contend in vain. But it is proper, at this place, to record the judgments of impartial historians who have studied the sources, and cannot be charged with any doctrinal bias in favor of Calvinism. Comp. other testimonies in § 68, pp. 270 sqq.

GIESELER, one of the coolest and least dogmatic of church historians, says (K. G. III. P. I. p. 389) : "*Durch Calvin's eiserne Festigkeit wurden Genf's Sitten ganz umgewandelt: so dankte die Stadt der Reformation ihre Freiheit, ihre Ordnung, und ihren aufblühenden Wohlstand.*"

From the Article "Calvin" in *La France Protestante* (III. 530) : "*Une telle organisation, un pareil pouvoir sur les individus, une autorité aussi parfaite-*

ment inquisitoriale nous indignent aujourd'hui ; c'était chose toute simple avec' l'ardeur religieuse du XVIᵉ siècle. Le consistoire atteignit le but que Calvin s'était proposé. En moins de trois générations, les moeurs de Genève subirent une métamorphose complète. A la mondanité naturelle succéda cette austérité un peu raide, cette gravité un peu étudiée qui caractérisèrent, dans les siècles passés, les disciples du réformateur. L'histoire ne nous offre que deux hommes qui aient su imprimer à tout un peuple le cachet particulier de leur génie : Lycurgue et Calvin, deux grands caractères qui offrent plus d'une analogie. Que de fades plaisanteries ne s'est-on pas permises sur l'esprit genevois ! et Genève est devenue un foyer de lumières et d'émancipation intellectuelle, même pour ses détracteurs."

MARC-MONNIER.

Marc-Monnier was born in Florence of French parents, 1829, distinguished as a poet and historian, professor of literature in the University of Geneva, and died 1885. His " *La Renaissance de Dante à Luther* " (1884) was crowned by the French Academy.

From " *La Réforme, de Luther à Shakespeare* " (Paris, 1885), pp. 70–72.

" *Calvin fut donc de son temps comme les papes, les empereurs et tous les rois, même François 1ᵉʳ, qui brûlèrent des hérétiques, mais ceux qui ne voient dans Calvin que le meurtrier de Servet ne le connaissent pas. Ce fut une conviction, une intelligence, une des forces les plus étonnantes de ce grand siècle : pour le peser selon son mérite, il faut jeter dans la balance autre chose que nos tendresses et nos pitiés. Il faut voir tout l'homme, et le voir tel qu'il fut : ' un corps frêle et débile, sobre jusqu'à l'excès,' rongé par des maladies et des infirmités qui devaient l'emporter avant le temps, mais acharné à sa tâche, ' ne vivant que pour le travail et ne travaillant que pour établir le royaume de Dieu sur la terre ; devoué à cette cause jusqu'à lui tout sacrifier :' le repos, la santé, la vie, plus encore : les études favorites, et avec une infatigable activité qui épouvantait ses adversaires, menant de front, à brides abattues, religion, morale, politique, législation, littérature, enseignement, prédication, pamphlets, œuvres de longue haleine, correspondance énorme avec le roi et la reine de Navarre, la duchesse de Ferrare, le roi François 1ᵉʳ, avec d'autres princes encore, avec les réformateurs, les théologiens, les humanistes, les âmes travaillées et chargées, les pauvres prisonnières de Paris. Il écrivait dans l'Europe entière ; deux mille Églises s'organisaient selon ses idées ou celles de ses amis ; des missionnaires, animés de son souffle, partaient pour l'Angleterre, l'Écosse, les Pays-Bas, ' en remerciant Dieu et lui chantant des psaumes.' En même temps cet homme seul, ce malade surmené s'emparait à Genève d'un peuple allègre, raisonneur, indiscipliné, le tenait dans sa main et le forçait d'obéir. Sans être magistrat ni même citoyen (il ne le devint qu'aux dernières années de sa vie), sans mandat officiel ni titre reconnu, sans autre autorité que celle de son nom et d'une volonté inflexible, il commandait aux consciences, il gouvernait les maisons, il s'imposait, avec une foule de réfugiés venus de toute part, à une population qui n'a jamais aimé les étrangers ni les maîtres ; il heurtait enfin de parti pris les coutumes, les traditions, les susceptibilités nationales et il les brisait. Non seulement il pesait sur les consciences et les opinions, mais aussi sur les mœurs, proscrivait la luxure et même le luxe, la bijouterie, la soie et le velours, les cheveux longs, les coiffures frisées, la bonne chère : toute espèce de plaisir et de distraction ; cependant, malgré les haines et les colères suscitées par cette compression morale, ' le corps brisé, mais la tête haute,' il gouverna longtemps les Genevois par l'autorité de son caractère et fut accompagné à sa tombe par le peuple tout entier.   Voilà l'homme dont il est facile de rire, mais qu'il importe avant tout de connaître.*

" *Calvin détruisit Genève pour la refaire à son image et, en dépit de toutes les révolutions, cette reconstitution improvisée dure encore: il existe aux portes de la France une ville de strictes croyances, de bonnes études et de bonnes mœurs: une ' cité de Calvin.' *"

A remarkable tribute from a scholar who was no theologian, and no clergy-man, but thoroughly at home in the history, literature, manners, and society of Geneva.   Marc-Monnier speaks also very highly of Calvin's merits as a French classic, and quotes with approval the judgment of Paul Lacroix (in his ed. of select *Œuvres françoises de J. Calvin*): " *Le style de Calvin est un des plus grands styles du seizième siècle: simple, correct, élégant, clair, ingénieux, animé, varié de formes et de tons, il a commencé à fixer la langue française pour la prose, comme celui de Clement Marot l'avait fait pour les vers.*"

GEORGE BANCROFT.

George Bancroft, the American historian and statesman, born at Worcester, Mass., 1800, died at Washington, 1891, served his country as secretary of the Navy, and ambassador at London and Berlin, with the greatest credit.

" A word on Calvin, the Reformer."   From his *Literary and Historical Miscellanies* (New York, 1855), pp. 405 sqq.

" It is intolerance only, which would limit the praise of Calvin to a single sect, or refuse to reverence his virtues and regret his failings.   He lived in the time when nations were shaken to their centre by the excitement of the Reformation; when the fields of Holland and France were wet with the car-nage of persecution; when vindictive monarchs on the one side threatened all Protestants with outlawry and death, and the Vatican, on the other, sent forth its anathemas and its cry for blood.   In that day, it is too true, the influence of an ancient, long-established, hardly disputed error, the constant danger of his position, the intense desire to secure union among the antago-nists of popery, the engrossing consciousness that his struggle was for the emancipation of the Christian world, induced the great Reformer to defend the use of the sword for the extirpation of heresy.   Reprobating and lament-ing his adhesion to the cruel doctrine, which all Christendom had for centu-ries implicitly received, we may, as republicans, remember that Calvin was not only the founder of a sect, but foremost among the most efficient of mod-ern republican legislators.   More truly benevolent to the human race than Solon, more self-denying than Lycurgus, the genius of Calvin infused endur-ing elements into the institutions of Geneva, and made it for the modern world the impregnable fortress of popular liberty, the fertile seed-plot of democracy.

" We boast of our common schools; Calvin was the father of popular edu-cation, the inventor of the system of free schools.   We are proud of the free States that fringe the Atlantic.   The pilgrims of Plymouth were Calvinists;

the best influence in South Carolina came from the Calvinists of France. William Penn was the disciple of the Huguenots; the ships from Holland that first brought colonists to Manhattan were filled with Calvinists. He that will not honor the memory, and respect the influence of Calvin, knows but little of the origin of American liberty.

"If personal considerations chiefly win applause, then no one merits our sympathy and our admiration more than Calvin; the young exile from France, who achieved an immortality of fame before he was twenty-eight years of age; now boldly reasoning with the king of France for religious liberty; now venturing as the apostle of truth to carry the new doctrines into the heart of Italy, and hardly escaping from the fury of papal persecution; the purest writer, the keenest dialectician of his century; pushing free inquiry to its utmost verge, and yet valuing inquiry solely as the means of arriving at fixed conclusions. The light of his genius scattered the mask of darkness which superstition had held for centuries before the brow of religion. His probity was unquestioned, his morals spotless. His only happiness consisted in his 'task of glory and of good'; for sorrow found its way into all his private relations. He was an exile from his country; he became for a season an exile from his place of exile. As a husband he was doomed to mourn the premature loss of his wife; as a father he felt the bitter pang of burying his only child. Alone in the world, alone in a strange land, he went forward in his career with serene resignation and inflexible firmness; no love of ease turned him aside from his vigils; no fear of danger relaxed the nerve of his eloquence; no bodily infirmities checked the incredible activity of his mind; and so he continued, year after year, solitary and feeble, yet toiling for humanity, till after a life of glory, he bequeathed to his personal heirs, a fortune, in books and furniture, stocks and money, not exceeding two hundred dollars, and to the world, a purer reformation, a republican spirit in religion, with the kindred principles of republican liberty."

CHAPTER XIV.

CALVIN'S THEOLOGY.

§ 111. *Calvin's Commentaries.*

I. CALVIN's *Commentaries* on the Old Test. in *Opera*, vols. XXIII.–XLIV., on the New Test., vols. XLV. sqq. (not yet completed). Separate Latin ed. of the Commentaries on the New Test. by Tholuck, Berlin, and Halle, 1831, 1836, etc., 7 vols.; also on Genesis (by Hengstenberg, Berlin, 1838) and on the Psalms (by Tholuck, 1836, 2 vols.). Translations in French (by J. Girard, 1550, and others), English (by various writers, 1570 sqq.), and other languages. Best English ed. by the "Calvin Translation Soc.," Edinburgh, 1843–55 (30 vols. for the O. T., 13 for the N. T.). See list in Darling's *Cyclopædia Bibliographica*, sub "Calvin."

II. A. THOLUCK: *Die Verdienste Calvin's als Schriftausleger*, in his "Lit. Anzeiger," 1831, reprinted in his "Vermischte Schriften" (Hamburg, 1839), vol. II. 330–360, and translated by Wm. Pringle (added to Com.. on Joshua in the Edinb. ed. 1854, pp. 345–375). — G. W. MEYER: *Geschichte der Schrifterklärung*, II. 448–475. — D. G. ESCHER: *De Calvino interprete*, Traj., 1840. — ED. REUSS: *Calvin considéré comme exégète*, in "Revue," VI. 223. — A. VESSON: *Calvin exégète*, Montaub, 1855. — E. STÄHELIN: *Calvin*, I. 182–198. — SCHAFF: *Creeds of Christendom*, I. 457–460. — MERX: *Joel*, Halle, 1879, pp. 428–444. — FRED. W. FARRAR: *History of Interpretation* (London, 1886), pp. 342–354.

CALVIN was an exegetical genius of the first order. His commentaries are unsurpassed for originality, depth, perspicuity, soundness, and permanent value. The Reformation period was fruitful beyond any other in translations and expositions of the Scripture. If Luther was the king of translators, Calvin was the king of commentators. Poole, in the preface to his *Synopsis*, apologizes for not referring more frequently to Calvin, because others had so largely borrowed from him that to quote them was to quote him. Reuss, the chief editor of his works and himself an eminent biblical scholar, says that Calvin was " beyond all question the greatest exegete of the sixteenth century."[1] Archdeacon Farrar literally echoes this judgment.[2] Diestel, the best historian of Old Testament exegesis, calls him "the creator of genuine exegesis."[3] Few exegetical works outlive their generation; those of Calvin are not likely to be superseded any more than Chrysostom's *Homilies* for patristic eloquence, or Bengel's *Gnomon* for pregnant and stimulating hints, or Matthew Henry's *Exposition* for devotional purposes and epigrammatic suggestions to preachers.[4]

Calvin began his series of Commentaries at Strassburg with the Epistle to the Romans, on which his system of theology is chiefly built. In the dedication to his friend and Hebrew teacher Grynæus, at Basel (Oct. 18, 1539), he already lays down his views of the best method of interpretation, namely, comprehensive brevity, transparent clearness, and strict adherence to the spirit and letter of the author. He gradually

---

[1] "*Ohne alle Frage der grösste Exeget des (sechszehnten) Jahrhunderts.*" *Geschichte der heil. Schriften des Neuen Test.* p. 618 (6th ed. 1887).

[2] "The greatest exegete and theologian of the Reformation was undoubtedly Calvin." *History of Interpretation,* London, 1886, p. 342. Farrar quotes from Keble a manuscript note of Hooker, who says that "the sense of Scripture which Calvin alloweth" was held (in the Anglican Church) to be of more force than if "ten thousand Augustins, Jeromes, Chrysostoms, Cyprians were brought forth."

[3] "*Der Schöpfer der ächten Exegese.*" Diestel adds: "*Johannes Calvin ragt ebensowohl durch den Umfang seiner exegetischen Arbeiten wie durch eine seltene Genialitat in der Auslegung hervor; unübertroffen in seinem Jahrhundert, bieten seine Exegesen für alle folgenden Zeiten noch bis heute einen reichen Stoff der Schriftkenntniss dar.*" *Geschichte des Alten Testaments in der christl. Kirche,* Jena, 1869, p. 267. Dr. A. Merx of Heidelberg, another master in biblical philology, fully agrees: "*Calvin ist der grösste Exeget seiner Zeit . . . der Schöpfer der ächten Exegese*" (on *Joel,* p. 428), and he ascribes to him, besides the necessary learning, including Hebrew, the sagacity of understanding and explaining the whole from the parts, and the parts from the whole.

[4] G. Wohlenberg, a Lutheran divine, begins a notice of the new edition of Calvin's Commentaries on the New Test. (in Luthardt's "Theol. Lit.-blatt," Oct. 9, 1891) with this remark: "*Calvin's Commentare zum N. T. gehören zu den nie veraltenden Werken. Und so gut wie Bengel's 'Gnomon' immer wieder gedruckt und gelesen werden wird, so lange es eine gesunde und fromme Schrifterklärung giebt, so werden auch Calvin's Commentare nie vergessen werden.*"

expounded the most important books of the Old Testament, the Pentateuch, the Psalms, and the Prophets, and all the books of the New Testament, with the exception of the Apocalypse, which he wisely left alone. Some of his expositions, as the Commentary on the Minor Prophets, were published from notes of his free, extempore lectures and sermons. His last literary work was a Commentary on Joshua, which he began in great bodily infirmity and finished shortly before his death and entrance into the promised land.

It was his delight to expound the Word of God from the chair and from the pulpit. Hence his theology is biblical rather than scholastic. The Commentaries on the Psalms and the Epistles of Paul are regarded as his best. He was in profound sympathy with David and Paul, and read in their history his own spiritual biography. He calls the Psalms (in the Preface) "an anatomy of all the parts of the soul; for there is not an emotion of which any one can be conscious that is not here represented as in a mirror. Or, rather, the Holy Spirit has here drawn to the life the griefs, the sorrows, the fears, the doubts, the hopes, the cares, the perplexities, in short, all the distracting emotions with which the minds of men are wont to be agitated." He adds that his own trials and conflicts helped him much to a clearer understanding of these divine compositions.

He combined in a very rare degree all the essential qualifications of an exegete — grammatical knowledge, spiritual insight, acute perception, sound judgment, and practical tact. He thoroughly sympathized with the spirit of the Bible; he put himself into the situation of the writers, and reproduced and adapted their thoughts for the benefit of his age.

Tholuck mentions as the most prominent qualities of Calvin's commentaries these four: doctrinal impartiality, exegetical tact, various learning, and deep Christian piety. Winer praises his "truly wonderful sagacity in perceiving, and perspicuity in expounding, the meaning of the Apostle." [1]

1. Let us first look at his philological outfit. Melanchthon well says: "The Scripture cannot be understood theologically unless it be first understood grammatically." [2] He had passed through the school of the Renaissance; he had a rare knowledge of Greek; he thought in Greek, and could not help inserting rare Greek words into his letters to learned friends. He was an invaluable help to Luther in his translation of the Bible, but his commentaries are dogmatical rather than grammatical, and very meagre, as compared with those of Luther and Calvin in depth and force. [3]

Luther surpassed all other Reformers in originality, freshness, spiritual insight, bold conjectures, and occasional flashes of genius. His commentary on the Epistle to the Galatians, which he called "his wife," is a masterpiece of sympathetic exposition and forceful application of the leading idea of evangelical freedom to the question of his age. But Luther was no exegete in the proper sense of the term. He had no method and discipline. He condemned allegorizing as a mere "monkey-game" (*Affenspiel*), and yet he often resorted to it in Job, the Psalms, and the Canticles. He was eminently spiritual, and yet, as against Zwingli, slavishly literal in his interpretation. He seldom sticks to the text, but uses it only as a starting-point for popular sermons, or polemical excursions against papists and sectarians. He cared nothing for the consensus of the fathers. He applied private judgment to the interpretation with the utmost freedom, and judged the canonicity and authority of the several books of the Bible

---

[1] "*Calvinus miram in pervidenda apostoli mente subtilitatem, in exponenda prespicuitatem probavit.*" In the third ed. of his Com. on the Ep. to the Galatians.

[2] "*Ignavus in grammatica est ignavus in theologia.*" *Postill.* IV. 428.

[3] Calvin himself fully acknowledged the exegetical merits of Melanchthon, Bullinger, and Bucer, in their commentaries on Romans, but modestly hints at their defects to justify his own commentary, which is far superior. See his interesting dedication to Grynæus, written in 1539.

by a dogmatic and subjective rule — his favorite doctrine of
solifidian justification; and as he could not find it in James,
he irreverently called his epistle "an epistle of straw." He
anticipated modern criticism, but his criticism proceeded
from faith in Christ and God's Word, and not from scepticism. His best work is a translation, and next to it, his little
catechism for children.

Zwingli studied the Greek at Glarus and Einsiedeln that
he might be able "to draw the teaching of Christ from the
fountain." [1] He learnt Hebrew after he was called to Zürich.
He also studied the fathers, and, like Erasmus, took more to
Jerome than to Augustin. His expositions of Scripture are
clear, easy, and natural, but somewhat superficial. The other
Swiss Reformers and exegetes — Œcolampadius, Grynæus,
Bullinger, Pellican, and Bibliander — had a good philological preparation. Pellican, a self-taught scholar (d. 1556),
who was called to Zürich by Zwingli in 1525, wrote a little
Hebrew grammar even before Reuchlin,[2] and published at
Zürich comments on the whole Bible.[3] Bibliander (d. 1564)
was likewise professor of Hebrew in Zürich, and had some
acquaintance with other Semitic languages; he was, however, an Erasmian rather than a Calvinist, and opposed the
doctrine of the absolute decrees.

For the Hebrew Bible these scholars used the editions
of Daniel Bomberg (Venice, 1518-45); the Complutensian
Polyglot, which gives, besides the Hebrew text, also the
Septuagint and Vulgate and a Hebrew vocabulary (Alcala,
printed 1514-17; published 1520 sqq.); also the editions of

---

[1] He wrote in 1523 that, ten years before (when priest at Glarus), "operam
dedi Grœcianis literis, ut ex fontibus doctrinam Christi haurire possem."

[2] De Modo legendi et intelligendi Hebrœum, written at Tübingen or Basel in
1501, first printed in the Margarita philosophica, at Strassburg in 1504 (one or
two years before Reuchlin's Rudimenta Linguæ Hebr.), recently discovered
and republished by Nestle, Tübingen, 1877.

[3] Commentaria Bibliorum, Zürich, 1532-39, 7 vols. See Diestel, l.c., 272
sq., and Strack in Herzog [2] XI. 432 sqq.

Sabastian Münster (Basel, 1536), and of Robert Stephens (Etienne, Paris, 1539–46). For the Greek Testament they had the editions of Erasmus (Basel, five ed. 1516–35), the Complutensian Polyglot (1520), Colinæus (Paris, 1534), Stephens (Paris and Geneva, 1546–51). A year after Calvin's death, Beza began to publish his popular editions of the Greek Testament, with a Latin version (Geneva, 1565–1604).

Textual criticism was not yet born, and could not begin its operations before a collection of the textual material from manuscripts, ancient versions, and patristic quotations. In this respect, therefore, all the commentaries of the Reformation period are barren and useless. Literary criticism was stimulated by the Protestant spirit of inquiry with regard to the Jewish Apocrypha and some Antilegomena of the New Testament, but was soon repressed by dogmatism.

Calvin, besides being a master of Latin and French, had a very good knowledge of the languages of the Bible. He had learned the Greek from Volmar at Bourges, the Hebrew from Grynæus during his sojourn at Basel, and he industriously continued the study of both.[1] He was at home in classical antiquity; his first book was a Commentary on Seneca, *De Clementia*, and he refers occasionally to Plato, Aristotle, Plutarch, Polybius, Cicero, Seneca, Virgil, Horace, Ovid, Terence, Livy, Pliny, Quintilian, Diogenes Laërtius, Aulus Gellius, etc. He inferred from Paul's quotation of Epimenides, Tit. 1:12, "that those are superstitious who never venture to quote anything from profane authors.

---

[1] His knowledge of Hebrew was unjustly depreciated by the Roman Catholic Richard Simon. But Dr. Diestel, a most competent judge, ascribes to Calvin "a very solid knowledge of Hebrew." See above, p. 276, and p. 525. Tholuck, also, in his essay above quoted, asserts that "every glance at Calvin's Commentary on the Old Testament assures us not only that he understood Hebrew, but that he had a very thorough knowledge of this language." He mentions, by way of illustration, a number of difficult Hebrew and Greek words which Calvin correctly explains. He denies that he was dependent on Pellican's notes, as Semler had gratuitously suggested.

Since all truth is from God, if anything has been said aptly and truly even by impious men, it ought not to be rejected, because it proceeded from God. And since all things are of God, why is it not lawful to turn to his glory whatever may be aptly applied to this use?" On 1 Cor. 8 : 1, he observes: "Science is no more to be blamed when it puffs up than a sword when it falls into the hands of a madman." But he never makes a display of learning, and uses it only as a means to get at the sense of the Scripture. He wrote for educated laymen as well as for scholars, and abstained from minute investigations and criticisms; but he encouraged Beza to publish his Commentary on the New Testament in which philological scholarship is more conspicuous.

Calvin was also familiar with the patristic commentators, and had much more respect for them than Luther. He fully appreciated the philological knowledge and tact of Jerome, the spiritual depth of Augustin, and the homiletical wealth of Chrysostom; but he used them with independent judgment and critical discrimination.[1]

---

[1] He expresses his estimate of the Fathers in the Preface to his *Institutes* as follows: "Another calumny is their charging us with opposition to the fathers; I mean the writers of the earlier and purer ages, as if those writers were abettors of their impiety; whereas if the contest were to be terminated by this authority, the victory in most parts of the controversy, to speak in the most modest terms, would be on our side. But though the writings of those fathers contain many wise and excellent things, yet, in some respects, they have suffered the common fate of mankind; these very dutiful children reverence only their errors and mistakes, but their excellencies they either overlook, or conceal, or corrupt; so that it may be truly said to be their only study to collect dross from the midst of gold. Then they overwhelm us with senseless clamors, as despisers and enemies of the fathers. But we do not hold them in such contempt, but that if it were consistent with my present design, I could easily support by their suffrages most of the sentiments that we now maintain. Yet, while we make use of their writings, we always remember that ' All things are ours ' to serve us, not to have dominion over us, and that ' we are Christ's ' alone, and owe him universal obedience. He who neglects this distinction will have nothing decided in religion, since those holy men were ignorant of many things, frequently at variance with each other and sometimes even inconsistent with themselves." In the preface to his commentary on the Romans he praises the Fathers for their *pietas, eruditio,*

2. Calvin kept constantly in view the primary and fundamental aim of the interpreter, namely, to bring to light the true meaning of the biblical authors according to the laws of thought and speech.[1] He transferred himself into their mental state and environment so as to become identified with them, and let them explain what they actually did say, and not what they might or should have said, according to our notions or wishes. In this genuine exegetical method he has admirably succeeded, except in a few cases where his judgment was biassed by his favorite dogma of a double predestination, or his antagonism to Rome; though even there he is more moderate and fair than his contemporaries, who indulge in diffuse and irrelevant declamations against popery and monkery. Thus he correctly refers the "Rock" in Matt. 16 : 18 to the person of Peter, as the representative of all believers.[2] He stuck to the text. He detested irrelevant twaddle and diffuseness. He was free from pedantry. He never evades difficulties, but frankly meets and tries to solve them. He carefully studies the connection. His judgment is always clear, strong, and sound. Commentaries are usually dry, broken, and indifferently written. His exposition is an easy, continuous flow of reproduction and adaptation in elegant Erasmian Latinity. He could truly assert on his death-bed that he never knowingly twisted or misinterpreted a single passage of the Scriptures; that he always

and *sanctimonia*, and adds that their antiquity lent them such authority, "*ut nihil quod ab ipsis profectum sit, contemnere debeamus.*" Compare with this judgment Luther's bolder and cruder opinions on the Fathers, quoted in vol. VI. 534 sqq.

[1] In the dedicatory preface to his Com. on Romans he reminds his friend Grynæus of a conversation they had three years previously, on the best method of interpretation, when they agreed that the chief virtue of an interpreter was "*perspicua brevitas,*" and adds: "*Et sane quum hoc sit prope unicum illius officium, mentem scriptoris, quem explicandum sumpsit, patefacere: quantum ab ea lectores abducit, tantundem a scopo suo aberrat, vel certe a suis finibus quodammodo evagatur.*"

[2] *Harmon.* II. 107.

aimed at simplicity, and restrained the temptation to display acuteness and ingenuity.

He made no complete translation of the Bible, but gave a Latin and a French version of those parts on which he commented in either or both languages, and he revised the French version of his cousin, Pierre Robert Olivetan, which appeared first in 1535, for the editions of 1545 and 1551.[1]

3. Calvin is the founder of modern grammatico-historical exegesis. He affirmed and carried out the sound and fundamental hermeneutical principle that the biblical authors, like all sensible writers, wished to convey to their readers one definite thought in words which they could understand. A passage may have a literal or a figurative sense, but cannot have two senses at once. The word of God is inexhaustible and applicable to all times; but there is a difference between explanation and application, and application must be consistent with explanation.

Calvin departed from the allegorical method of the Middle Ages, which discovered no less than four senses in the Bible,[2] turned it into a nose of wax, and substituted pious imposition for honest exposition. He speaks of "puerile" and "far-fetched" allegories, and says that he abstains from them because there is nothing "solid and firm" in them. It is an almost sacrilegious audacity to twist the Scriptures this way and that way, to suit our fancy.[3] In commenting on the allegory of Sarah and Hagar, Gal. 4 : 22–26, he censures Origen for his arbitrary allegorizing, as if the plain historical e of the Bible were too mean and too poor. " I acknowledge," he says, "that Scripture is a most rich and inexhausti-

---

[1] See Reuss, *Gesch. des N. T.* § 474 (p. 539, 6th ed.). Reuss prepared from Calvin's French Commentaries a French version for his ed. of the *Opera.*

[2] Expressed in the memorial lines : —

> " *Litera gesta docet ; quid credas, Allegoria ;*
> *Moralis, quid agas ; quo tendas, Anagogia.*"

[3] *Pref. ad Romanos : " Affinis sacrilegio audacia est Scripturas temere huc illuc versare et quasi in re lusoria lascivire : quod a multis jam olim factitatum est.*"

ble fountain of all wisdom, but I deny that its fertility consists in the various meanings which any man at his pleasure
may put into it. Let us know, then, that the true meaning
of Scripture is the natural and obvious meaning; and let us
embrace and abide by it resolutely. Let us not only neglect as doubtful, but boldly set aside as deadly corruptions,
those pretended expositions which lead us away from the
natural meaning." He approvingly quotes Chrysostom, who
says that the word "allegory" in this passage is used in an improper sense.[1] He was averse to all forced attempts to harmonize difficulties. He constructed his Harmony of the Gospels
from the three Synoptists alone, and explained John separately.

4. Calvin emancipated exegesis from the bondage of dogmatism. He was remarkably free from traditional orthodox
prepossessions and prejudices, being convinced that the truths
of Christianity do not depend upon the number of *dicta pro-
bantia*. He could see no proof of the doctrine of the Trinity
in the plural *Elohim*,[2] nor in the three angel visitors of Abraham, 18 : 2, nor in the Trisagion, Ps. 6 : 3,[3] nor of the divinity
of the Holy Spirit in Ps. 33 : 6.[4]

---

[1] "*Et certe Chrysostomus in vocabulo Allegoriæ fatetur esse catechresin (κατά-
χρησις) : quod verissimum est.*"

[2] *Ad. Gen.* 1 : 1 (*Opera*, XXIII. 15) : "*Habetur apud Moses* אלהים, *nomen
pluralis numeri. Unde colligere solent, hic in Deo notari tres personas ; sed quia
parum solida mihi videtur tantæ rei probatio, ego in voce non insistam. Quin potius
monendi sunt lectores ut sibi a violentis ejusmodi glossis caveant. Putant illi se
testimonium habere adversus Arianos ad probandam Filii et Spiritus divinitatem,
interea se involvunt in errorem Sabellii.*" But in the words, "Let us make
man," Gen. 1 : 26, he admits, after rejecting the Rabbinical fancies, the intimation of a plurality in God : "*Christiani apposite plures subesse in Deo personas
ex hoc testimonio contendunt. Neminem extraneum advocat Deus : hinc colligimus,
intus eum aliquid distinctum invenire : ut certe æterna eius sapientia et virtus in
ipso resident.*" (*Ib.* 25.)

[3] On this passage he remarks : "*Veteres hoc testimonio usi sunt, quum vellent
adversus Arianos tres personas in una Dei essentia probare. Quorum ego sententiam
non improbo ; sed si mihi res cum hæreticis esset, mallem firmioribus testimoniis uti.*"

[4] Older Lutheran divines (even Walch, *Biblioth. theol.* IV. 413) charged
him with Judaizing and Socinian misinterpretation of the O. T. proof texts
for the Trinity and the divinity of the Messiah. Aegidius Hunnius, in his
Calvinus Judaizans (Wittenberg, 1593), thought that Calvin ought to have

5. He prepared the way for a proper historical understanding of prophecy. He fully believed in the Messianic prophecies, which are the very soul of the faith and hope of Israel; but he first perceived that they had a primary bearing and practical application to their own times, and an ulterior fulfilment in Christ, thus serving a present as well as a future use. He thus explained Psalms 2, 8, 16, 22, 40, 45, 68, 110, as typically and indirectly Messianic. On the other hand, he made excessive use of typology, especially in his Sermons, and saw not only in David but in every king of Jerusalem a "figure of Christ." In his explanation of the protevangelium, Gen. 3:15, he correctly understands the "seed of the woman," collectively of the human race, in its perpetual conflict with Satan, which will culminate ultimately in the victory of Christ, the head of the race.[1] He widens the sense of the formula "that it might be fulfilled" ($\H{\iota}\nu\alpha\ \pi\lambda\eta\rho\omega\theta\hat{\eta}$), so as to express sometimes simply an analogy or correspondence between an Old Testament and a New Testament event. The prophecy, Hos. 11:1, quoted by Matthew as referring to the return of the Christ-child from Egypt, must, accordingly, "not be restricted to Christ," but is "skilfully adapted to the present occasion."[2] In like manner, Paul, in Rom. 10:6, gives only an embellishment and adaptation of a word of Moses to the case in hand.[3]

been burnt for his abominable perversion of the Scriptures. D. Pareus of Heidelberg defended him against this charge in his *Orthodoxus Calvinus*. Modern Lutheran exegesis fully sustains him.

[1] *Ad Gen.* 3:15 (*Opera*, XXIII. 71): "*Generaliter semen interpretor de posteris. Sed quum experientia doceat, multum abesse quin supra diabolum victores emergant omnes filii Adæ, ad caput unum venire necesse est, ut reperiamus ad quem pertineat victoria. Sic Paulus a semine Abrahæ ad Christum nos deducit. . . . Quare sensus est (meo judicio), humanum genus, quod opprimere conatus erat Satan, fore tandem superius.*"

[2] *Harm.* I. 80. Tholuck's ed. On ver. 23 in the same chapter, Calvin says (p. 83): "*Non deducit Matthæus Nazaræum a Nazareth: quasi sit hæc propria et certa etymologia, sed tantum est allusio,*" etc.

[3] Comp. his notes on Gen. 3:15; Isa. 4:2; 6:3; Ps. 33:6; Matt. 2:15; 8:17; 11:11; John 1:51; 2:17; 5:31 sq.; 2 Cor. 12:7; 1 Pet. 3:19; Heb. 2:6–8; 4:3; 11:21.

6. He had the profoundest reverence for the Scriptures, as containing the Word of the living God and as the only infallible and sufficient rule of faith and duty; but he was not swayed by a particular theory of inspiration. It is true, he never would have approved the unguarded judgments of Luther on James, Jude, Hebrews, and the Apocalypse;[1] but he had no hesitancy in admitting incidental errors which do not touch the vitals of faith. He remarks on Matt. 27:9: "How the name of Jeremiah crept in, I confess I know not, *nor am I seriously troubled about it.* That the name of Jeremiah has been put for Zechariah by an error, the fact itself shows, because there is no such statement in Jeremiah."[2] Concerning the discrepancies between the speech of Stephen in Acts 7 and the account of Genesis, he suggests that Stephen or Luke drew upon ancient traditions rather than upon Moses, and made "a mistake in the name of Abraham."[3]

He was far from the pedantry of the Purists in the seventeenth century, who asserted the classical purity of the New Testament Greek, on the ground that the Holy Spirit could not be guilty of any solecism or barbarism, or the slightest violation of grammar; not remembering that the Apostles and Evangelists carried the heavenly treasure of truth in earthen vessels, that the power and grace of God might become more manifest, and that Paul himself confesses his rudeness "in speech," though not "in knowledge." Calvin justly remarks, with special reference to Paul, that by a singular providence of God the highest mysteries were committed to us "*sub contemptibili verborum humilitate,*" that our faith may not rest on the power of human eloquence,

---

[1] See Luther's judgments in vol. VI. 35 sq.

[2] *Harm.* II. 349 (Tholuck's ed.): "*Quomodo Jeremiæ nomen obrepserit, me nescire fateor, nec anxie laboro : certe Jeremiæ nomen errore positum esse pro Zacharia* (13:7), *res ipsa ostendit: quia nihil tale apud Jeremiam legitur, vel etiam quod accedat.*"

[3] *Ad Acta* 7:16: "*In nomine Abrahæ erratum esse palam est. . . . Quare hic locus corrigendus est.*" According to Gen. 50:13, Abraham bought the cave of Machpelah at Hebron, and Jacob was buried there, and not at Shechem.

but solely on the efficacy of the divine Spirit; and yet he fully recognized the force and fire, the majesty and weight of Paul's style, which he compares to flashes of lightning.[1]

The scholastic Calvinists, like the scholastic Lutherans of the seventeenth century, departed from the liberal views of the Reformers, and adopted a mechanical theory which confounds inspiration with dictation, ignores the human element in the Bible, and reduces the sacred writers to mere penmen of the Holy Spirit. This theory is destructive of scientific exegesis. It found symbolical expression, but only for a brief period, in the Helvetic Consensus Formula of 1675, which, in defiance of historical facts, asserts even the inspiration of the Masoretic vowel points. But notwithstanding this restraint, the Calvinistic exegetes adhered more closely to the natural grammatical and historical sense of the Scriptures than their Lutheran and Roman Catholic contemporaries.[2]

7. Calvin accepted the traditional canon of the New Testament, but exercised the freedom of the ante-Nicene Church concerning the origin of some of the books. He denied the Pauline authorship of the Epistle to the Hebrews on account of the differences of style and mode of teaching (*ratio*

---

[1] See his admirable comments on 1 Cor. 1 : 17 sqq., and 2 Cor. 11 : 6, where he mentions the *majestas, altitudo, pondus,* and *vis* of Paul's words, and says: "*Fulmina sunt, non verba. An non dilucidius Spiritus Sancti efficacia apparet in nuda verborum rusticitate (ut ita loquar) quam in elegantiæ et nitoris larva?*"

[2] Fr. Turretin, a strict scholastic Calvinist, and one of the authors of the Helvetic Consensus Formula, opposed the allegorical method and defended the sound, one-sense principle (in his *Inst. Theol. Elencticæ,* quæst. XIX., vol. I. 135): "*Nos ita sentimus, Scripturæ S. unicum tantum competere verum et genuinum sensum, sed sensum illum duplicem posse esse, vel* SIMPLICEM, *vel* COMPOSITUM. SIMPLEX *et historicus est, qui unius rei declarationem continet, absque ullius alterius significatione, qui vel præcepta, vel dogmata, vel historias spectat. Et hic rursus duplex, vel* PROPRIUS *et* GRAMMATICALIS, *vel* FIGURATUS *et* TROPICUS. PROPRIUS *qui ex verbis propriis oritur;* TROPICUS *qui ex verbis figuratis.* SENSUS COMPOSITUS *seu mixtus est in oraculis typi rationem habentibus, cujus pars est in typo, pars in antitypo; quæ non constituunt duos sensus, sed duas partes unius ejusdemque sensus intenti a Spiritu Sancto, qui cum litera mysterium respexit, ut in isto Oraculo, ' Os non confringetis ei,' Exo. 12 : 46, plenus non potest haberi sensus, nisi cum veritate typi, seu Agni Paschalis, conjungatur veritas Antitypi seu Christi ex Jo. 19 : 36.*"

docendi), but admitted its apostolic spirit and value. He doubted the genuineness of the Second Epistle of Peter, and was disposed to ascribe it to a pupil of the Apostle, but he saw nothing in it which is unworthy of Peter. He prepared the way for a distinction between authorship and editorship as to the Pentateuch and the Psalter.

He departed from the traditional view that the Scripture rests on the authority of the Church. He based it on internal rather than external evidence, on the authority of God rather than the authority of men. He discusses the subject in his *Institutes*,[1] and states the case as follows : —

"There has very generally prevailed a most pernicious error that the Scriptures have only so much weight as is conceded to them by the suffrages of the Church, as though the eternal and inviolable truth of God depended on the arbitrary will of men.[2] . . . For, as God alone is a sufficient witness of Himself in His own Word, so also the Word will never gain credit in the hearts of men till it be confirmed by the internal testimony of the Spirit. It is necessary, therefore, that the same Spirit, who spake by the mouths of the prophets, should penetrate into our hearts, to convince us that they faithfully delivered the oracles which were divinely intrusted to them. . . . Let it be considered, then, as an undeniable truth, that they who have been inwardly taught by the Spirit, feel an entire acquiescence in the Scripture, and that it is self-authenticated, carrying with it its own evidence, and ought not to be made the subject of demonstrations and arguments from reason; but it obtains the credit which it deserves with us by the testimony of the Spirit. For though it commands our reverence by its internal majesty, it never seriously affects us till it is confirmed by the Spirit in our hearts. Therefore, being illuminated by him, we now believe the divine original of the Scripture, not from our own judgment or that of others, but we esteem the certainty that we have received it from God's own mouth, by the ministry of men, to be superior to that of any human judgment, and equal to that of an intuitive perception of God himself in it. . . . Without this certainty, better and stronger than any human judgment, in vain will the authority of the Scripture be either defended by arguments, or established by the authority of the Church, or confirmed by any other support, since, unless the foundation be laid, it remains in perpetual suspense."[3]

[1] Bk. I. ch. VII. and VIII.

[2] Luther said substantially the same thing in his controversy with Eck : "The Church cannot give any more authority or power to the Scripture than it has of itself. A Council cannot make that to be Scripture which is not Scripture by its own nature."

[3] Selected from *Inst.* I. VII. §§ 1, 4, 5, and VIII. § 1.

This doctrine of the intrinsic merit and self-evidencing character of the Scripture, to all who are enlightened by the Holy Spirit, passed into the Gallican, Belgic, Second Helvetic, Westminster, and other Reformed Confessions. They present a fuller statement of the objective or formal principle of Protestantism, — namely, the absolute supremacy of the Word of God as the infallible rule of faith and practice, — than the Lutheran symbols which give prominence to the subjective or material principle of justification by faith.[1]

At the same time, the ecclesiastical tradition is of great value, as a witness to the human authorship and canonicity of the several books, and is more fully recognized by modern biblical scholarship, in its conflict with destructive criticism, than it was in the days of controversy with Romanism. The internal testimony of the Holy Spirit and the external testimony of the Church join in establishing the divine authority of the Scriptures.

§ 112. *The Calvinistic System.*

Comp. § 78, pp. 327–343, and the exposition of the Augustinian System and the Pelagian controversy in vol. III. §§ 146–158, pp. 783–856. — Dorner: *Geschichte der protestantischen Theologie*, pp. 374–404. — Loofs: *Dogmengeschichte*, 2d ed., pp. 390–401.

Calvin is still a living force in theology as much as Augustin and Thomas Aquinas. No dogmatician can ignore his *Institutes* any more than an exegete can ignore his *Commentaries*. Calvinism is embedded in several confessions of the Reformed Church, and dominates, with more or less rigor, the spirit of a large section of Protestant Christendom, especially in Great Britain and North America. Calvinism is not the name of a Church, but it is the name of a theological school in the Reformed Churches. Luther is the only one among the Reformers whose name was given to the Church which he founded. The Reformed Churches are indepen-

---

[1] Comp. vol. VI. 36 sqq.

dent of personal authority, but all the more bound to the teaching of the Bible.

Calvinism is usually identified with Augustinianism, as to anthropology and soteriology, in opposition to Pelagianism and Semi-Pelagianism. Augustin and Calvin were intensely religious, controlled by a sense of absolute dependence on God, and wholly absorbed in the contemplation of his majesty and glory. To them God was everything; man a mere shadow. Blessed are the elect upon whom God bestows all his amazing mercy; but woe to the reprobate from whom he withholds it. They lay equal emphasis on the doctrines of sin and grace, the impotence of man and the omnipotence of God, the sinfulness of sin and the sovereignty of regenerating grace. In Christology they made no progress. Their theology is Pauline rather than Johannean. They passed through the same conflict with sin, and achieved the same victory, by the power of divine grace, as the great Apostle of the Gentiles. Their spiritual experience is reflected in their theology. But Calvin left us no such thrilling record of his experience as Augustin in his *Confessions*. He barely alludes to his conversion, in the preface to his Commentary on the Psalms and in his Answer to Sadolet.

The profound sympathy of Calvin with Augustin is shown in the interesting fact that he quotes him far more frequently than all the Greek and Latin fathers combined, and quotes him nearly always with full approbation.[1]

But in some respects Augustin and Calvin were widely different. Augustin wandered for nine years in the laby-

[1] According to the Index of the List of Authors quoted in Calvin's *Institutes*, which is appended to Beveridge's translation, Edinburgh, 1856, vol. III. 626–663, the number of his quotations from the principal fathers is as follows: 228 from Augustin; 39 from Pope Gregory I.; 27 from Chrysostom; 23 from Bernard; 18 from Ambrose; 14 from Cyprian; 12 from Jerome; 11 from Hilary; 7 from Tertullian. Of classical authors there are, in the *Institutes*, 7 quotations from Plato; 5 from Aristotle; 9 from Cicero; 3 from Seneca; 2 from Plutarch, etc. The Index theologicus in *Opera*, XXII. 136–143, gives 7 columns of quotations from Augustin. This does not include the commentaries.

rinth of the Manichæan heresy, and found at last rest and peace in the orthodox Catholic Church of his day, which was far better than any philosophical school or heretical sect, though not much purer than in the sixteenth century. He became the chief architect of scholastic and mystic theology, which ruled in the Middle Ages, and he still carries more weight in the Roman communion than any of the ancient fathers. Calvin was brought up in the Roman Catholic Church, but fled from its prevailing corruptions to the citadel of the Holy Scripture, and became the most formidable enemy of the papacy. If Augustin had lived in the sixteenth century, he might, perhaps, have gone half way with the Reformers; but, judging from his high estimate of visible church unity and his conduct towards the schismatic Donatists, it is more probable that he would have become the leader of an evangelical school of Catholicism within the Roman Church.

The difference between the two great teachers may be briefly stated in two sentences which are antagonistic on the surface, though reconcilable at bottom. Augustin says: "I would not believe the gospel if it were not for the Church."[1] Calvin teaches (in substance, though not in these words): "I would not believe the Church if it were not for the gospel." The reconciliation must be found in the higher principle: I believe in Christ, and therefore I believe in the gospel and the Church, which jointly bear witness of him.

As to the doctrines of the fall, of total depravity, the slavery of the human will, the sovereignty of saving grace, the bishop of Hippo and the pastor of Geneva are essentially agreed; the former has the merit of priority and originality;

---

[1] *Contra Ep. Manichæi quam vocant Fundamenti*, c. 5: "*Ego evangelio non crederem nisi me moveret ecclesiæ auctoritas.*" This famous anti-Manichæan passage is often quoted by Roman Catholics against Protestants. Calvin discusses it at length in his *Inst.* (Bk. I. ch. VII. § 3), and tries to deprive it of its anti-Protestant force, but he admits it in the sense that "the authority of the Church is an introduction to prepare us for the faith of the gospel."

the latter is clearer, stronger, more logical and rigorous, and far superior as an exegete.

Their views are chiefly derived from the Epistle to the Romans as they understood it, and may be summed up in the following propositions: God has from eternity foreordained all things that should come to pass, with a view to the manifestation of his glory; he created man pure and holy, and with freedom of choice; Adam was tried, disobeyed, lost his freedom, and became a slave of sin; the whole human race fell with him, and is justly condemned in Adam to everlasting death; but God in his sovereign mercy elects a part of this mass of corruption to everlasting life, without any regard to moral merit, converts the elect by irresistible grace, justifies, sanctifies, and perfects them, and thus displays in them the riches of his grace; while in his inscrutable, yet just and adorable counsel he leaves the rest of mankind in their inherited state of condemnation, and reveals in the everlasting punishment of the wicked the glory of his awful justice.

The Lutheran system is a compromise between Augustinianism and Semi-Pelagianism. Luther himself was fully agreed with Augustin on total depravity and predestination, and stated the doctrine of the slavery of the human will even more forcibly and paradoxically than Augustin or Calvin.[1] But the Lutheran Church followed him only half way. The Formula of Concord (1577) adopted his doctrine of total depravity in the strongest possible terms, but disclaimed the doctrine of reprobation; it represents the natural man as spiritually dead like "a stone" or "a block," and teaches a

---

[1] *De Servo Arbitrio*, against Erasmus (1525). He never retracted this book, but declared it many years afterwards to be one of his best. He was followed by Amsdorf, Flacius, Wigand, and Brenz. See *Church History*, vol. VI. 430 sqq.; Köstlin, *Luther's Theologie*, I. 773 sqq.; Luthardt, *Dogmatik*, p. 120 (6th ed.), and his *Lehre vom freien Willen;* Harnack, *Dogmengeschichte*, III. 714 sq.; and Loofs, *Leitfaden zum Studium der Dogmengeschichte*, 2d ed. Halle, 1890, pp. 322–324, and 317–350.

particular and unconditional election, but also an universal vocation.[1]

The Augustinian system was unknown in the ante-Nicene age, and was never accepted in the Eastern Church. This is a strong historical argument against it. Augustin himself developed it only during the Pelagian controversy; while in his earlier writings he taught the freedom of the human will against the fatalism of the Manichæans.[2] It triumphed in the Latin Church over Pelagianism and Semi-Pelagianism, which were mildly condemned by the Synod of Orange (529). But his doctrine of an absolute predestination, which is only a legitimate inference from his anthropological premises, was indirectly condemned by the Catholic Church in the Gott-schalk controversy (853), and in the Jansenist controversy (1653), although the name and authority of the great doctor and saint were not touched.

The Calvinistic system was adopted by a large portion of the Reformed Church, and has still able and earnest advocates. Calvin himself is now better understood, and more highly respected by scholars (French and German) than ever before; but his predestinarian system has been effectively opposed by the Arminians, the Quakers, and the Methodists, and is undergoing a serious revision in the Presbyterian and Calvinistic Churches of Europe and America.

The Augustinian, Lutheran, and Calvinistic systems rest on the same anthropology, and must stand or fall together with the doctrine of the universal damnation of the whole human race on the sole ground of Adam's sin, including

---

[1] See Schaff, *Creeds of Christendom*, I. 313 sqq.; and the works on the *Formula Concordiæ*.

[2] Calvin was well aware of Augustin's change on this point. "Origen, Ambrose, and Jerome," he says, "believed that God dispenses his grace among men, according to his foreknowledge of the good use which every individual will make of it. Augustin also was once of the same sentiment, but when he had made a greater proficiency in scriptural knowledge, he not only retracted, but powerfully confuted it." Then he quotes in proof a number of passages. *Inst.* III. ch. XXII. § 8.

infants and entire nations and generations which never heard of Adam, and which cannot possibly have been in him as self-conscious and responsible beings.[1] They have alike to answer the question how such a doctrine is reconcilable with the justice and mercy of God. They are alike dualistic and particularistic. They are constructed on the ruins of the fallen race, instead of the rock of the redeemed race; they destroy the foundation of moral responsibility by teaching the slavery of the human will; they turn the sovereignty of God into an arbitrary power, and his justice into partiality; they confine the saving grace of God to a particular class. Within that favorite and holy circle all is as bright as sunshine, but outside of it all is as dark as midnight. These systems have served, and still serve, a great purpose, and satisfy the practical wants of serious Christians who are not troubled with theological and philosophical problems; but they can never satisfy the vast majority of Christendom.

We are, indeed, born into a world of sin and death, and we cannot have too deep a sense of the guilt of sin, especially our own; and, as members of the human family, we should feel the overwhelming weight of the sin and guilt of the whole race, as our Saviour did when he died on the cross. But we are also born into an economy of righteousness and life, and we cannot have too high a sense of God's saving grace which passeth knowledge. As soon as we enter into the world we are met with the invitation, "Suffer little children to come unto me." The redemption of the race is as much an accomplished fact as the fall of the race, and it alone can answer the question, why God permitted or caused the fall. Where

---

[1] Augustin based his view of a quasi pre-existence of all men in the loins of Adam on a false exegesis of Rom. 5 : 12, ἐν ᾧ, by following the Vulgate rendering *in quo* (*in whom*), and referring it back to Adam; while it has the meaning *because* (ἐπὶ τούτῳ ὅτι = διότι), or *on condition that* (ἐπὶ τούτῳ ὥστε, *ea ratione ut, inasmuch as*). It is neuter, not masculine. On the exegesis of that famous passage, and the doctrinal discussions on it, see my extensive notes in Lange's *Comm. on Romans*, pp. 172 sqq.

sin has abounded, grace has abounded not less, but much more.

Calvinism has the advantage of logical compactness, consistency, and completeness. Admitting its premises, it is difficult to escape its conclusions. A system can only be overthrown by a system. It requires a theological genius of the order of Augustin and Calvin, who shall rise above the antagonism of divine sovereignty and human freedom, and shall lead us to a system built upon the rock of the historic Christ, and inspired from beginning to end with the love of God to all mankind.

NOTES ON AMERICAN CALVINISM.

1. Calvinism was imported and naturalized in America, by the Puritans, since 1620, and dominated the theology and church life of New England during the colonial period. It found its ablest defender in Jonathan Edwards, — the great theological metaphysician and revival preacher, — who may be called the American Calvin. It still controls the orthodox Congregational and Baptist churches. But it has provoked Unitarianism in New England (as it did in England), and has undergone various modifications. It is now gradually giving way to a more liberal and catholic type of Calvinism. The new Congregational Creed of 1883 is thoroughly evangelical, but avoids all the sharp angles of Calvinism.

2. The Presbyterian Calvinism is best represented by the theological systems of Charles Hodge, W. G. T. Shedd, and Henry B. Smith. The first is the mildest, the second the severest, the third the broadest, champion of modern American Calvinism; they alike illustrate the compatibility of logical Calvinism with a sweet and lovely Christian temper, but they dissent from Calvin's views by their infralapsarianism, their belief in the salvation of all infants dying in infancy, and of the large number of the saved.

Henry B. Smith, under the influence of modern German theology, took a step in advance, and marks the transition from old Calvinism to Christological divinity, but died before he could elaborate it. "The central idea," he says, in his posthumous *System cf Christian Theology* (New York, p. 341, 4th ed., 1890), "to which all the parts of theology are to be referred, and by which the system is to be made a system, or to be constructed, is what we have termed the Christological or Mediatorial idea, viz., that God was in Christ reconciling the world unto himself. This idea is central, not in the sense that all the other parts of theology are logically deduced from it, but rather that they centre in it. The idea is that of an *Incarnation in order to Redemption*. This is the central idea of Christianity, as distinguished, or distinguishable, from all other religions, and from all forms of philosophy; and by this, and this alone, are we able to construct the whole system of the Christian faith on its proper grounds. This idea is the proper centre of unity to the whole Christian system, as the soul is the centre of unity to the body, as the North Pole is to all the magnetic needles. It is so really the centre of unity that when we analyze and grasp and apply it, we find that the whole of Christian theology is in it." To this remarkable passage should be added a note which Dr. George L. Prentiss, his most intimate friend, found among the last papers of Dr. Smith, which may be called his theological will and testament. "What Reformed theology has got to do is to *christologize* predestination and decrees, regeneration and sanctification, the doctrine of the Church, and *the whole of eschatology.*"

3. The movement for the revision of the Westminster Confession of Faith has seized, by an irresistible force within the last few years, the Presbyterian Churches of England, Scotland, and North America, and is inspired by the cardinal truth of God's love to all mankind (John 3 : 16), and the consequent duty of the Church to preach the gospel to every creature, in obedience to Christ's command (Mark 16 : 15; Matt. 28 : 19, 20). The United Presbyterian Church (1879) and the Free Church (1891) of Scotland express their dissent from the Westminster Standards in an explanatory statement, setting forth their belief in the general love of God, in the moral responsibility of man, and in religious liberty, — all of which are irreconcilable with a strict construction of those standards. The English Presbyterian Church has adopted a new creed, together with a declaratory statement (1890). The General Assembly of the Presbyterian Church in the United States ordered, in 1889, a revision of the Westminster Confession, which is now going on; and, at the same time, the preparation of a new, short, and popular creed that will give expression to the living faith of the present Church, and serve, not as a sign of division and promoter of sectarian strife, but as a bond of harmony with other evangelical churches, and help rather than hinder the ultimate reunion of Christendom. See Schaff, *Creed Revision in the Presbyterian Churches,* 1890.

§ 113. *Predestination.*

1. *Inst.* Bk. III. chs. XXI.–XXIV. *Articuli de Prædestinatione,* first published from an autograph of Calvin by the Strassburg editors, in *Opera,* IX. 713. The *Consensus Genevensis* (1552), *Opera,* VIII. 249–366. Calvin's polemical writings against Pighius (1543), vol. VI. 224–404; Bolsec (1551), vol. VIII. 85–140; and Castellio (1557–58), vol. IX. 253–318. He treats the subject also in several of his sermons, *e.g.* on First and Second Timothy.

2. ALEX. SCHWEIZER: *Die Protestantischen Centraldogmen* (Zürich, 1854), vol. I. 150–179. — STÄHELIN, I. 271 sqq. — DORNER: *Geschichte der protest. Theol.,* 386–395. — PHILIP SCHAFF: *Creeds of Christendom,* I. 451–455.

LUTHER AND CALVIN.

The dogma of a double predestination is the corner-stone of the Calvinistic system, and demands special consideration.

Calvin made the eternal election of God, Luther made the temporal justification by faith, the article of the standing or falling Church, and the source of strength and peace in the battle of life. They agreed in teaching salvation by free grace, and personal assurance of salvation by a living faith in Christ and his gospel. But the former went back to the ultimate root in a pre-mundane unchangeable decree of God; the latter looked at the practical effect of saving grace upon the individual conscience. Both gave undue prominence to their favorite dogma, in opposition to Romanism, which weakened the power of divine grace, magnified human merit, and denied the personal certainty of salvation. They wished to destroy all basis for human pride and boasting, to pluck up Phariseeism by the root, and to lay a firm foundation for humility, gratitude, and comfort. This was a great progress over the mediæval soteriology.

But there is a higher position, which modern evangelical theology has reached. The predestinarian scheme of Calvin and the solifidian scheme of Luther must give way or be subordinated to the Christocentric scheme. We must go back to Peter's confession, which has only one article, but it is the most important article, and the oldest in Christendom. The central place in the Christian system belongs to the divine-human person and work of Christ: this is the immovable rock of the Church, against which the gates of Hades shall never prevail, and on which the creeds of Christendom will have to unite (Matt. 16:16–18; comp. 1 Cor. 2:2; 3:11; Rom. 4:25; 1 John 4:2, 3). The Apostles' Creed and the Nicene Creed are Christocentric and Trinitarian.

The Reformers All Predestinarians.

All the Reformers of the sixteenth century, following the lead of Augustin and of the Apostle Paul, — as they understood him, — adopted, under a controlling sense of human depravity and saving grace, and in antagonism to self-righteous legalism, the doctrine of a double predestination which decides the eternal destiny of all men.[1] Nor does it seem possible, logically, to evade this conclusion if we admit the two premises of Roman Catholic and Evangelical orthodoxy — namely, the wholesale condemnation of all men in Adam, and the limitation of saving grace to the present life. All orthodox Confessions reject Universalism, and teach that some men are saved, and some are lost, and that there is no possibility of salvation beyond the grave. The predestinarians maintain that this double result is the outcome of a double decree, that history must harmonize with the divine will and cannot defeat it. They reason from the effect to the cause, from the end to the beginning.

Yet there were some characteristic differences in the views of the leading Reformers on this subject. Luther, like Augustin, started from total moral inability or the *servum arbitrium;* Zwingli, from the idea of an all-ruling *providentia;* Calvin, from the eternal *decretum absolutum.*

The Augustinian and Lutheran predestinarianism is moderated by the churchly and sacramental principle of baptismal regeneration. The Calvinistic predestinarianism confines the sacramental efficacy to the elect, and turns the baptism of the non-elect into an empty form; but, on the other hand, it opens a door for an extension of electing grace beyond the limits of the visible Church. Zwingli's position was peculiar: on the one hand, he went so far in his supralapsarianism as to make God the sinless author of sin (as the magistrate in inflicting capital punishment, or the soldier in the battle,

---

[1] The essential agreement of the Reformers on the doctrine of free-will and predestination has been proven by scholars of different schools, as Jul. Müller (*Lutheri doctrina de prædestinatione et libero arbitrio,* and in his *Dogmatische Abhandlungen,* pp. 169–179), Hundeshagen (*Conflicte des Zwinglianismus, Lutherthums, und Calvinismus in der Bernischen Landeskirche von 1532–1558*), Baur (*Der Gegensatz des Katholicismus und Protestantismus,* and in his *Dogmengeschichte*), Schweizer (*Centraldogmen*), Gieseler, Hagenbach, Dorner, Luthardt, Loofs, and others.

are innocently guilty of murder); but, on the other hand, he undermined the very foundation of the Augustinian system — namely, the wholesale condemnation of the race for the single transgression of one; he admitted hereditary sin, but denied hereditary guilt; and he included all infants and pious heathen in the kingdom of heaven.   Such a view was then universally abhorred, as dangerous and heretical.[1]

Melanchthon, on further study and reflection, retreated in the Semi-Pelagian direction, and prepared the way for Arminianism, which arose, independently, in the heart of Calvinism at the beginning of the seventeenth century.   He abandoned his earlier view, which he characterized as Stoic fatalism, and proposed the Synergistic scheme, which is a compromise between Augustinianism and Semi-Pelagianism, and makes the human will co-operate with preceding divine grace, but disowns human merit.[2]

The Formula of Concord (1577) rejected both Calvinism and Synergism, yet taught, by a logical inconsistency, total disability and unconditional election, as well as universal vocation.

CALVIN'S THEORY.

Calvin elaborated the doctrine of predestination with greater care and precision than his predecessors, and avoided their "paradoxes," as he called some extravagant and unguarded expressions of Luther and Zwingli.   On the other

---

[1] Calvin expressed to Bullinger, in a confidential letter, January, 1552, his dissatisfaction with the paradoxical expressions of Zwingli's tract *De Providentia*. "*Zwinglii libellus,*" he writes, "*ut familiariter inter nos loquamur, tam duris paradoxis refertus est, ut longissime ab ea quam adhibui moderatione distet.*" Bullinger, however, never contradicted the liberal sentiments of his teacher and friend, and believed in extraordinary modes of salvation, "*sine externo ministerio, quo et quando velit (Deus): et quod ejus potentiæ est.*"   Second Helv. Conf. I. 7.

[2] For a fuller exposition of Melanchthon's Synergism see Herrlinger's monograph; Frank, *Theologie der Concordienformel;* Dorner, *Geschichte der protest. Theologie,* pp. 361–374, and his *System der christl. Glaubenslehre,* II. 706 sq. and 716 sq.; Schweizer, *Centraldogmen,* I. 380 sqq.; Schaff, *Creeds of Christendom,* I. 262 sq.; Loofs, *Dogmengeschichte,* pp. 403 sq. (2d ed.).

hand, he laid greater emphasis on the dogma itself, and assigned it a higher position in his theological system. He was, by his Stoic temper and as an admirer of Seneca, predisposed to predestinarianism, and found it in the teaching of Paul, his favorite apostle. But his chief interest in the doctrine was religious rather than metaphysical. He found in it the strongest support for his faith. He combined with it the certainty of salvation, which is the privilege and comfort of every believer. In this important feature he differed from Augustin, who taught the Catholic view of the subjective uncertainty of salvation.[1] Calvin made the certainty, Augustin the uncertainty, a stimulus to zeal and holiness.

Calvin was fully aware of the unpopularity of the doctrine. "Many," he says, "consider nothing more unreasonable than that some of the common mass of mankind should be foreordained to salvation, and others to destruction. . . . When the human mind hears these things, its petulance breaks all restraint, and it discovers a serious and violent agitation as if alarmed by the sound of a martial trumpet." But he thought it impossible to "come to a clear conviction of our salvation, till we are acquainted with God's eternal election, which illustrates his grace by this comparison, that he adopts not all promiscuously to the hope of salvation, but gives to some what he refuses to others." It is, therefore, not from the general love of God to all mankind, but from his particular favor to the elect that they, and they alone, are to derive their assurance of salvation and their only solid comfort. The reason of this preference can only be found in the inscrutable will of God, which is the supreme law of the universe. As to others, we must charitably assume that they are among the elect; for there is no certain sign of reprobation except perseverance in impenitence until death.

Predestination, according to Calvin, is the eternal and

---

[1] *De Dono Persev.*, ch. XXXIII.

unchangeable decree of God by which he foreordained, for his own glory and the display of his attributes of mercy and justice, a part of the human race, without any merit of their own, to eternal salvation, and another part, in just punishment of their sin, to eternal damnation. "Predestination," he says, "we call the eternal decree of God, by which he has determined in himself the destiny of every man. For they are not all created in the same condition, but eternal life is foreordained for some, and eternal damnation for others. Every man, therefore, being created for one or the other of these ends, we say, he is predestinated either to life or to death." [1]

This applies not only to individuals, but to whole nations. God has chosen the people of Israel as his own inheritance, and rejected the heathen; he has loved Jacob with his posterity, and hated Esau with his posterity. "The counsel of God, as far as concerns the elect, is founded on his gratuitous mercy, totally irrespective of human merit; but to those whom he devotes to condemnation the gate of life is closed by a just and irreprehensible, though incomprehensible judgment." [2] God's will is the supreme rule of justice,[3] so that "what he wills must be considered just for the very reason that he wills it. When you ask, therefore, why the Lord did so, the answer must be, Because he would. But if you go further and ask why he so determined, you are in search of something higher and greater than the will of God, which can never be found. Let human temerity, therefore, desist from seeking that which is not, lest it should fail of finding that which is. This will be a sufficient restraint to

---

[1] "*Prædestinationem vocamus æternum Dei decretum, quo apud se constitutum habuit, quid de unoquoque homine fieri vellet. Non enim pari conditione creantur omnes; sed aliis vita æterna, aliis damnatio æterna præordinatur. Itaque, prout in alterutrum finem quisque conditus est, ita vel ad vitam, vel ad mortem prædestinatum dicimus.*" *Inst.* III. ch. XXI. § 5 (*Opera*, vol. II. pp. 682, 683).

[2] *Ibid.* III. ch. XXI. § 7.

[3] "*Summa justitiæ regula est Dei voluntas.*"

any one disposed to reason with reverence concerning the secrets of his God." [1] Calvin infers from the passage, " God hath mercy on whom he will have mercy, and whom he will, he hardeneth" (Rom. 9:13), that Paul attributes both equally " to the mere will of God. If, therefore, we can assign no reason why God grants mercy to his people but because such is his pleasure, neither shall we find any other cause but his will for the reprobation of others. For when God is said to harden or show mercy to whom he pleases, men are taught by this declaration to seek no cause behind his will." [2]

Predestination, therefore, implies a twofold decree — a decree of *election* unto holiness and salvation, and a decree of *reprobation* unto death on account of sin and guilt. Calvin deems them inseparable. " Many indeed," he says, " as if they wished to avert odium from God, admit election in such a way as to deny that any one is reprobated. But this is puerile and absurd, because election itself could not exist without being opposed to reprobation. . . . Whom God passes by, he reprobates (*Quos Deus præterit, reprobat*), and from no other cause than his determination to exclude them from the inheritance which he predestines for his children." [3]

[1] *Inst.* III. ch. XXII. § 1.

[2] *Ibid.* III. ch. XXII. 11. Calvin's definition of divine justice is contrary to the general conception of human justice, which must be a reflection of divine justice.

[3] *Ibid.* III. ch. XXIII. § 1. The scholastic Calvinists distinguished in reprobation a negative element, namely, *præteritio* or *indebitæ gratiæ negatio*, and a positive element of predamnation, *prædamnatio* or *debitæ pœnæ destinatio*. See the definitions of Wolleb, Keckermann, Heidegger, etc., in Heppe's *Dogmatik der evang. reform. Kirche* (1861), p. 132. The Westminster Confession (ch. III. 7) uses the term " passing by," which is equivalent to preterition or omission; the Gallican Conf. (ch. XII.) and the Belgic Conf. (ch. XVI.) use the milder term *laisser, relinquere, to leave*, namely, in the natural state of condemnation and ruin. Shedd (*Syst. Theol.* I. 433) says : " Reprobation comprises preterition and condemnation or damnation," and he makes these distinctions: 1) Preterition is a sovereign act; condemnation is a judicial act. 2) The reason of preterition is unknown; the reason of damnation is sin. 3) In preterition God's action is permissive (inaction rather than action); in condemnation, God's action is efficient and positive. His proof text is Luke 17 : 34 : " The one shall be taken, and the other shall be left."

God bestows upon the reprobate all the common mercies of daily life as freely as upon the elect, but he withholds from them his saving mercy. The gospel also is offered to them, but it will only increase their responsibility and enhance their damnation, like the preaching of Christ to the unbelieving Jews (Isa. 6 : 9, 10 ; Matt. 13 : 13–15). But how shall we reconcile this with the sincerity of such an offer?

INFRALAPSARIANISM AND SUPRALAPSARIANISM.

Within the Calvinistic system there arose two schools in Holland during the Arminian controversy, the Infralapsarians (also called Sublapsarians) and the Supralapsarians, who held different views on the order of the divine decrees and their relation to the fall (*lapsus*). The Infralapsarians adjust, as it were, the eternal counsel of God to the temporal fall of man, and assume that God decreed, first to create man in holiness; then to permit him to fall by the self-determination of his free will; next, to save a definite number out of the guilty mass; and last, to leave the rest in sin, and to ordain them to eternal punishment.[1] The Supralapsarians reverse the order, so that the decree of election and reprobation precedes the decree of creation; they make uncreated and unfallen man (that is, a *non-ens*) the object of God's double decree. The Infralapsarians, moreover, distinguish between an efficient or active and a permissive or passive decree of God, and exclude the fall of Adam from the efficient decree; in other words, they maintain that God is not in any sense the author of the fall, but that he simply

---

[1] This is the order given in the *Formula Consensus Helvetica*, canon IV. (in Niemeyer, p. 731): "*Ita Deus gloriam suam illustrare constituit, ut decreverit, primo quidem hominem integrum* CREARE, *tum ejusdem lapsum* PERMITTERE, *ac demum ex lapsis quorundam misereri, adeoque eosdem* ELIGERE, *alios vero in corrupta massa* RELINQUERE, *æternoque tandem exitio devovere.*" This does not go beyond the limits of Augustinianism. Van Oosterzee errs when he says (*Christian Dogmatics*, vol. I. p. 452) that the Form. Cons. Helv. asserts the supralapsarian view.

allowed it to come to pass for higher ends. He did not cause it, but neither did he prevent it. The Supralapsarians, more logically, include the fall itself in the efficient and positive decree; yet they deny as fully as the Infralapsarians, though less logically, that God is the author of sin. The Infralapsarians attribute to Adam before the fall the gift of free choice, which was lost by the fall; some Supralapsarians deny it. The doctrine of probation (except in the one case of Adam) has no place in the Calvinistic system, and is essentially Arminian. It is entirely inapplicable to infants dying in infancy. The difference between the two schools is practically worthless, and only exposes the folly of man's daring to search the secrets of God's eternal counsel. They proceed on a pure metaphysical abstraction, for in the eternal God there is no succession of time, no before nor after.[1]

Calvin was claimed by both schools. He must be classed rather with the Supralapsarians, like Beza, Gomarus, Twysse, and Emmons. He saw the inconsistency of exempting from the divine foreordination the most important event in history, which involved the whole race in ruin. "It is not absurd," he says, "to assert that God not only foresaw, but also foreordained the fall of Adam and the ruin of his posterity." He expressly rejects the distinction between permission (*permissio*) and volition (*voluntas*) in God, who cannot permit what he does not will. "What reason," he asks, "shall we assign for God's permitting the destruction of the impious, but because it is his will? It is not probable that man procured his own destruction by the mere permission, and with-

---

[1] On the distinction, see Beza, *Summa totius Christianismi* (*Opera*, I. 170); Limborch, *Theol. Christ.* IV. 2; Heppe, *Dogmatik der evang. reform. Kirche*, pp. 108 sqq., and the curious order of Beza there printed, as if the order of the divine counsels were a mathematical problem. The infralapsarian view is milder and passed into most of the Calvinistic Confessions. The Westminster Confession is a compromise between the two schools, and puts the fall of Adam under a *permissive* decree (ch. V. 4), and yet not under a *bare* permission, but including it in the *purpose* of God, who *ordered* it for his own glory (VI. 1).

out any appointment of God. As though God had not determined what he would choose to be the condition of the chief of his creatures. I shall not hesitate, therefore, to confess with Augustin, ' that the will of God is the necessity of things, and what he has willed will necessarily come to pass ; as those things are really about to happen which he has foreseen.' "[1]

But while his inexorable logic pointed to this abyss, his moral and religious sense shrunk from the last logical inference of making God the author of sin ; for this would be blasphemous, and involve the absurdity that God abhors and justly punishes what he himself decreed. He attributes to Adam the freedom of choice, by which he might have obtained eternal life, but he wilfully disobeyed.[2] Hence his signifi-

---

[1] *Inst.* III. XXIII. 7 and 8. The passage quoted from Augustin is *De Gen. ad lit.*, l. VI. c. 15. In *Inst.* III. ch. XXIV. 12, Calvin uses strong supralapsarian language : " Those whom God has created to a life of shame and death (*quos in vitæ contumeliam et mortis exitium creavit*), that they might be instruments of his wrath, and examples of his severity, he causes to reach their appointed end ; sometimes depriving them of the opportunity of hearing the Word, sometimes by the preaching of it increasing their blindness and stupidity." Then he illustrates this by examples, especially that of Pharaoh, and the aim of the parables of Christ (Matt. 13 : 11 ; John 12 : 39, 40). In the *Consensus Genevensis* (Niemeyer, p. 251), he says that the fall was ordained by the admirable counsel of God (*admirabili Dei consilio fuisse ordinatum*). Beza understood Calvin correctly.

[2] He gives his view of the primitive state in *Inst.* I. ch. XV. § 8 : " God has furnished the soul of man with a mind capable of discerning good from evil, and just from unjust; and of discovering, by the light of reason, what ought to be pursued or avoided : whence the philosophers called this directing faculty τὸ ἡγεμονικόν, the principal or governing part. To this he hath annexed the will, on which depends the choice. The primitive condition of man was ennobled with those eminent faculties; he possessed reason, understanding, prudence, and judgment, not only for the government of his life on earth, but to enable him to ascend even to God and eternal felicity. To these were added choice, to direct the appetites, and regulate all the organic motions, so that the will was entirely conformed to the government of reason. In this integrity man was endued with free will, by which, if he had chosen, he might have obtained eternal life. For here it would be unreasonable to introduce the question respecting the secret predestination of God, because we are not discussing what might possibly have happened or not, but what was the real nature of man. *Adam, therefore, could have stood if he would, since he fell merely by his own will;* but because his will was flexible to either side, and he

cant phrase: "Man falls, God's providence so ordaining it; yet he falls by his own guilt."[1] Here we have supralapsarian logic combined with ethical logic. He adds, however, that we do not know the reason why Providence so ordained it, and that it is better for us to contemplate the guilt of man than to search after the hidden predestination of God. "There is," he says, "a learned ignorance of things which it is neither permitted nor lawful to know, and avidity of knowledge is a species of madness."

Here is, notwithstanding this wholesome caution, the crucial point where the rigorous logic of Calvin and Augustin breaks down, or where the moral logic triumphs over intellectual logic. To admit that God is the author of sin would destroy his holiness, and overthrow the foundation of morality and religion. This would not be Calvinism, but fatalism and pantheism. The most rigorous predestinarian is driven to the alternative of choosing between logic and morality. Augustin and Calvin could not hesitate for a moment. Again and again, Calvin calls it blasphemy to make God the author of sin, and he abhorred sin as much as any man ever did. It is an established fact that the severest Calvinists have always been the strictest moralists.[2]

---

was not endued with constancy to persevere, therefore he so easily fell. Yet his choice of good and evil was free; and not only so, but his mind and will were possessed of consummate rectitude, and all his organic parts were rightly disposed to obedience, till destroying himself he corrupted all his excellencies."

[1] "*Lapsus est enim primus homo, quia Dominus ita expedire censuerat; cur censuerit, nos latet. Certum tamen est non aliter censuisse, nisi quia videbat, nominis sui gloriam inde merito illustrari. Unde mentionem gloriæ Dei audis, illic justitiam cogita. Justum enim esse oportet quod laudem meretur.* CADIT IGITUR HOMO, DEI PROVIDENTIA SIC ORDINANTE, SED SUO VITIO CADIT. . . . *Propria ergo malitia, quam acceperat a Domino puram naturam corrupit; sua ruina totam posteritatem in exitium secum attraxit.*" *Inst.* III. ch. XXIII. § 8 (vol. II. p. 705). In his reply to Castellio (*Opera*, IX. 294) he says: "*Prævidit Deus lapsum Adæ: penes ipsum facultas erat prohibendi: noluit. Cur noluerit, alia non potest afferri ratio nisi quia alio tendebat ejus voluntas.*"

[2] Comp. here the powerful sections against the abuse of the doctrine of election, in III. ch. XXIII. 12 sqq.

INFANT SALVATION AND DAMNATION.

Are infants dying in infancy included in the decree of reprobation? This is another crucial point in the Augustinian system, and the rock on which it splits.

St. Augustin expressly assigns all unbaptized children dying in infancy to eternal damnation, because of original sin inherited from Adam's transgression. It is true, he mitigates their punishment and reduces it to a negative state of privation of bliss, as distinct from positive suffering.[1] This does credit to his heart, but does not relieve the matter; for " *damnatio*," though " *levissima*" and " *mitissima*," is still *damnatio*.

The scholastic divines made a distinction between *pœna damni*, which involves no active suffering, and *pœna sensus*, and assigned to infants dying unbaptized the former but not the latter. They invented the fiction of a special department for infants in the future world, namely, the *Limbus Infantum*, on the border region of hell at some distance from fire and brimstone. Dante describes their condition as one of "sorrow without torment."[2] Roman divines usually describe their condition as a deprivation of the vision of God. The Roman Church maintains the necessity of baptism for salvation, but admits the baptism of blood (martyrdom) and the baptism of intention, as equivalent to actual baptism. These exceptions, however, are not applicable to infants, unless the vicarious desire of Christian parents be accepted as sufficient.

Calvin offers an escape from the horrible dogma of infant damnation by denying the necessity of water baptism for salvation, and by making salvation dependent on sovereign

---

[1] See the passages in vol. III. 835 sq. Augustin was called *durus infantum pater*. But his view was only the logical inference from the doctrine of the necessity of baptism for salvation, which was taught long before him on the ground of John 3 : 8 and Mark 16 : 16. Even Pelagius excluded unbaptized infants from the kingdom of heaven, though not from eternal life. He assigned them to a middle state of half-blessedness.

[2] *Inferno*, IV. 28, *duol senza martiri, i.e.* mental, not physical pain.

election alone, which may work regeneration without baptism, as in the case of the Old Testament saints and the thief on the cross. We are made children of God by faith and not by baptism, which only recognizes the fact. Calvin makes sure the salvation of all *elect* children, whether baptized or not. This is a great gain. In order to extend election beyond the limits of the visible means of grace, he departed from the patristic and scholastic interpretation of John 3 : 5, that "water" means the sacrament of baptism, as a necessary condition of entrance into the kingdom of God. He thinks that a reference to Christian baptism before it was instituted would have been untimely and unintelligible to Nicodemus. He, therefore, connects water and Spirit into one idea of purification and regeneration by the Spirit.[1]

Whatever be the meaning of "water," Christ cannot here refer to infants, nor to such adults as are beyond the reach of the baptismal ordinance. He said of children, as a class, without any reference to baptism or circumcision : "Of such is the kingdom of God." A word of unspeakable comfort to bereaved parents. And to make it still stronger, he said: "It is not the will of your Father, who is in heaven, that *one* of these little ones should perish" (Matt. 18 : 14). These declarations of our Saviour, which must decide the whole question, seem to justify the inference that *all* children who die before having committed any actual transgression, are included in the decree of election. They are born into an economy of salvation, and their early death may be considered as a sign of gracious election.

But Calvin did not go so far. On the contrary, he inti-

---

[1] "*Aqua nihil aliud est quam interior Spiritus Sancti purgatio et vegetatio.*" Com. *in loco.* He takes καί epexegetically and lays the stress on πνεῦμα, which alone is mentioned in the following verses, 6 and 8. Similarly Grotius : "*Spiritus aquæus, i.e. aquæ instar emundans.*" But the natural reference is to *baptismal* water, as the symbol of purification and remission of sins. Comp. John 1 : 33; Tit. 3 : 5; Eph. 5 : 26. The different interpretations are discussed at length in Schaff's ed. of Lange's *Comm. on John,* pp. 126 sqq.

mates very clearly that there are *reprobate* or non-elect children as well as reprobate adults. He says that "*some* infants," having been previously regenerated by the Holy Spirit, "are certainly saved," but he nowhere says that *all* infants are saved.[1] In his comments on Rom. 5 : 17, he confines salvation to the infants of *pious* (elect) parents, but leaves the fate of the rest more than doubtful.[2] Arguing with Catholic advocates of free-will, who yet admitted the damnation of unbaptized infants, he asks them to explain in any other way but by the mysterious will of God, the terrible fact "that the fall of Adam, independent of any remedy, should involve *so many nations with their infant children* in eternal death. Their tongues so loquacious on every other point must here be struck dumb."[3]

---

[1] *Inst.* bk. IV. ch. XVI. 17 : "*Infantes, qui servandi sint* — UT CERTE EX EA ÆTATE OMNINO ALIQUI SERVANTUR — *antea a Domino regenerari minime obscurum est.*" This was the doctrine of the Westminster divines, and is expressed in the Westminster Confession, ch. X. 3 : "*Elect* infants, dying in infancy, are regenerated and saved by Christ through the Spirit, who worketh when, and where, and how he pleaseth." Although this passage admits of a liberal construction, yet the natural sense, as interpreted by the private opinions of the framers of the Confession, makes it almost certain that the existence and damnation of non-elect infants is implied. The Presbyterian Revisionists, therefore, wishing to avoid this logical implication, propose to strike out *elect*, or to substitute *all* for it (as the Cumberland Presbyterians have done in their Confession). The change will be acted upon by the General Assembly in May, 1892.

[2] "*De piorum liberis loquor, ad quos promissio gratiæ dirigitur; nam alii a communi sorte nequaquam eximuntur.*"

[3] "*Tot gentes una cum liberis eorum infantibus.*" *Inst.* III. ch. XXIII. § 7. To this should be added the challenge to Castellio : "Put forth now thy virulence against God, who hurls innocent babes even from their mothers' breast into eternal death." Calvin here argues *e concessis*. The passage has been often distorted. We give it in Latin with the connection (*Opera*, IX. 289) : "*Negas Deo licere nisi propter facinus damnare quenquam mortalium. Tolluntur e vita innumeri adhuc infantes. Exsere nunc tuam virulentiam contra Deum, qui innoxios fœtus a matrum uberibus avulsos in æternam mortem præcipitat. Hanc blasphemiam, ubi palam detecta est, quisquis non detestabitur, mihi pro sua libidine maledicat.*" In the same way he challenges Castellio (fol. 289), to explain the admitted fact, that God allows innocent infants to be devoured by tigers or lions or bears or wolves ("*qui fit ut Deus parvulos infantes a tigribus vel ursis vel leonibus vel lupis laniari vorarique sineat*"). The attempt of Dr. Shields of

And in this connection he adds the significant words: "It is an *awful* (*horrible*) *decree*, I confess, but no one can deny that God foreknew the future, final fate of man before he created him, and that he did foreknow it, because it was appointed by his own decree." [1]

Our best feelings, which God himself has planted in our hearts, instinctively revolt against the thought that a God of infinite love and justice should create millions of immortal beings in his own image — probably more than half of the human race — in order to hurry them from the womb to the tomb, and from the tomb to everlasting doom! And this not for any actual sin of their own, but simply for the transgression of Adam of which they never heard, and which God himself not only permitted, but somehow foreordained. This, if true, would indeed be a "*decretum horribile*."

Calvin, by using this expression, virtually condemned his own doctrine. The expression so often repeated against him, does great credit to his head and heart, and this has not been sufficiently appreciated in the estimate of his character. He ventured thus to utter his humane sentiments far more strongly than St. Augustin dared to do. If he, nevertheless, accepted this horrible decree, he sacrificed his reason and heart to the rigid laws of logic and to the letter of the Scripture as he understood it. We must honor him for his obedience, but as he claimed no infallibility, as an interpreter, we must be allowed to challenge his interpretation.

Zwingli, as already remarked, was the first and the only

Princeton to prove that Calvin believed in the salvation of *all* infants, is an entire failure ("The Presbyt. and Ref. Review" for October, 1890).

[1] "*Decretum quidem horribile fateor.*" This famous expression is often ignorantly applied to the whole doctrine of predestination, while Calvin only uses it of the decree of reprobation. The decree of election is glorious and most comforting. There is no need, therefore, of moderating the term *horribile*, which means *horrible, terrible, dreadful*. In French he calls it "*ce décret qui nous doit espouvanter*," a decree which should terrify us. Hase (*Kirchengeschichte*, III. I. 196) says: "*Calvin ist ein dogmatischer Dante: dieselbe grauenvolle Lust, die Majestät Gottes auch in der Hölle anzuerkennen und zu preisen, diese grauenvolle Macht, welche fühlende Wesen geschaffen hat zu ewiger Qual.*"

Reformer who entertained and dared to express the charitable hope and belief in universal infant salvation by the atonement of Christ, who died for all. The Anabaptists held the same view, but they were persecuted as heretics by Protestants and Catholics alike, and were condemned in the ninth article of the Augsburg Confession.[1] The Second Scotch Confession of 1590 was the first and the only Protestant Confession of the Reformation period which uttered a testimony of abhorrence and detestation of the cruel popish doctrine of infant damnation.[2]

But gradually the doctrine of universal infant salvation gained ground among Arminians, Quakers, Baptists, Wesleyans, Presbyterians, and is now adopted by almost all Protestant divines, especially by Calvinists, who are not hampered by the theory of baptismal regeneration.[3]

Zwingli, as we have previously shown, was equally in advance of his age in regard to the salvation of pious heathens, who die in a state of readiness for the reception of the gospel; and this view has likewise penetrated the modern Protestant consciousness.[4]

---

[1] "They condemn the Anabaptists, who disapprove the baptism of children, and affirm that *children are saved without baptism.*" The edition of 1540 adds after "baptism" "*et extra ecclesiam Christi,*" which must refer to heathen infants. The German text omits the clause and condemns the Anabaptists simply for rejecting infant baptism. This shows that Melanchthon was in doubt on the subject of infant damnation.

[2] "*Abhorremus et detestamur . . . crudele judicium contra infantes sine baptismo morientes.*"

[3] Among English Calvinists, who teach universal infant salvation, are Doddridge, Thomas Scott, John Newton, Toplady, Robert S. Candlish; among American Calvinists, Drs. Charles Hodge, A. A. Hodge, and B. B. Warfield, of Princeton, and Drs. H. B. Smith, G. L. Prentiss, and Shedd, of Union Seminary, New York. Comp. on this subject Schaff, *Creeds of Christendom,* I. 378, 381, 794, 898; Dr. Prentiss, who brings out the theological bearings, in the "Presbyterian Review" for 1883; Benjamin B. Warfield, *The Development of the Doctrine of Infant Salvation,* New York (Christ. Lit. Co.), 1891, pp. 61; also Chas. P. Krauth (Lutheran), *Infant Baptism and Infant Salvation,* Philadelphia (Lutheran Book Store), 1874, pp. 83.

[4] See above, pp. 95 sqq.

DEFENCE OF THE DOCTRINE OF PREDESTINATION.

Calvin defended the doctrine of predestination in his *Institutes*, and his polemical writings against Pighius, Bolsec, and Castellio, with consummate skill against all objections, and may be said to have exhausted the subject on his side of the question. His arguments were chiefly drawn from the Scriptures, especially the ninth chapter of the Epistle to the Romans; but he unduly stretched passages which refer to the historical destiny of individuals and nations in this world, into declarations of their eternal fate in the other world; and he undervalued the proper force of opposite passages (such as Ezek. 33 : 11; 18 : 23, 32; John 1 : 29; 3 : 16; 1 John 2 : 2; 4 : 14; 1 Tim. 2 : 4; 2 Pet. 3 : 9) by a distinction between the secret and revealed will of God (*voluntas arcani* and *voluntas beneplaciti*), which carries an intolerable dualism and contradiction into the divine will.

He closes the whole discussion with this sentence : "Now while many arguments are advanced on both sides, let our conclusion be to stand astonished with Paul at so great a mystery; and amidst the clamor of petulant tongues let us not be ashamed to exclaim with him, 'O man, who art thou that repliest against God?' For, as Augustin justly contends, it is acting a most perverse part to set up the measure of human justice as the standard by which to measure the justice of God."

Very true; but how can we judge of God's justice at all without our own sense of justice, which comes from God? And how can that be justice in God which is injustice in man, and which God himself condemns as injustice? A fundamental element in justice is impartiality and equity.

PRACTICAL EFFECT.

The motive and aim of this doctrine was not speculative but practical. It served as a bulwark of free grace, an antidote to Pelagianism and human pride, a stimulus to humility and gratitude, a source of comfort and peace in trial and despondency. The charge of favoring license and carnal security was always indignantly repelled as a slander by the Pauline " God forbid! " and refuted in practice. He who believes in Christ as his Lord and Saviour may have a reasonable assurance of being among the elect, and this faith will constrain him to follow Christ and to persevere to the end lest he be cast away. Those who believe in the perseverance of saints are likely to practice it. Present unbelief is no sure sign of reprobation as long as the way is open for repentance and conversion.

Calvin sets the absolute sovereignty of God and the infallibility of the Bible over against the pretended sovereignty and infallibility of the pope. Fearing God, he was fearless of man. The sense of God's sovereignty fortified his followers against the tyranny of temporal sovereigns, and made them champions and promoters of civil and political liberty in France, Holland, England, and Scotland.

CONFESSIONAL APPROVAL.

The doctrine of predestination received the official sanction of the pastors of Geneva, who signed the Consensus Genevensis prepared by Calvin (1552).[1] It was incorporated, in its milder, infralapsarian form, in the French Confession (1559), the Belgic Confession (1561), and the Scotch Confession (1560). It was more logically formulated in the Lambeth Articles (1595), the Irish Articles (1615), the Canons of Dort (1619), the Westminster Confession and Larger Catechism (1647), and the Helvetic Consensus Formula (1675). On the other hand, the First Helvetic Confession (1536), the Heidelberg Catechism (1563), the Second

---

[1] The Consensus Genevensis was occasioned by the controversy with Pighius and Bolsec, but received no authority outside of Geneva. The attempt to enlist Zürich, Bern, and Basel in favor of this dogma created disturbance and opposition. See Schaff, *Creeds*, etc., 1. 474 sqq.

Helvetic Confession (1566), and the Anglican Articles (1571, Art. XVII.) indorse merely the positive part of the free election of believers, and are wisely silent concerning the decree of reprobation and preterition; leaving this to theological science and private opinion.[1] It is noteworthy that Calvin himself omitted the doctrine of predestination in his own catechism. Some minor Reformed Confessions, as that of Brandenburg, expressly declare that God sincerely wishes the salvation of *all* men, and is not the author of sin and damnation.

NOTES.

AUTHORITATIVE STATEMENTS OF THE CALVINISTIC DOCTRINE OF A DOUBLE PREDESTINATION.

I. Calvin's Articuli de Prædestinatione.

Calvin gave a condensed statement of his system in the following articles, which were first published by the Strassburg editors, in 1870, from his autograph in the University library of Geneva: —

[*Ex autographo Calvini Bibl. Genev., Cod. 145, fol. 100.*]

"*Ante creatum primum hominem statuerat Deus æterno consilio quid de toto genere humano fieri vellet.*

"*Hoc arcano Dei consilio factum est ut Adam ab integro naturæ suæ statu deficeret ac sua defectione traheret omnes suos posteros in reatum æternæ mortis.*

"*Ab hoc eodem decreto pendet discrimen inter electos et reprobos: quia alios sibi adoptavit in salutem, alios æterno exitio destinavit.*

"*Tametsi justæ Dei vindictæ vasa sunt reprobi, rursum electi vasa misericordiæ, causa tamen discriminis non alia in Deo quærenda est quam mera eius voluntas, quæ summa est justitiæ regula.*

"*Tametsi electi fide percipiunt adoptionis gratiam, non tamen pendet electio a fide, sed tempore et ordine prior est.*

---

[1] The Second Helvetic Confession (chs. VIII. and IX.) uses the term *reprobate* (ἀδόκιμος, *reprobus*), but says nothing of a decree of reprobation. *Reprobate* is descriptive of moral character, and means *not approved*, *unfit*, Rom. 1:28; 1 Cor. 9:27; 2 Cor. 13:5–7; 2 Tim. 3:8; Tit. 1:16. The plural *reprobates* is an inaccurate rendering of the A. V. in 2 Cor. 13:6, 7, and 2 Tim. 3:8, and suggests the idea of a class of persons. The R. V. correctly has *reprobate*, since the Greek word is an adjective, not a noun.

"*Sicut initium et perseverantia fidei a gratuita Dei electione fluit, ita non alii vere illuminantur in fidem, nec alii spiritu regenerationis donantur, nisi quos Deus elegit: reprobos vero vel in sua cœcitate manere necesse est, vel excidere a parte fidei, si qua in illis fuerit.*

"*Tametsi in Christo eligimur, ordine tamen illud prius est ut nos Dominus in suis censeat, quam ut faciat Christi membra.*

"*Tametsi Dei voluntas summa et prima est rerum omnium causa, et Deus diabolum et impios omnes suo arbitrio subiectos habet, Deus tamen neque peccati causa vocari potest, neque mali autor, neque ulli culpœ obnoxius est.*

"*Tametsi Deus peccato vere infensus est et damnat quidquid est iniustitiæ in hominibus, quia illi displicet, non tamen nuda eius permissione tantum, sed nutu quoque et arcano decreto gubernantur omnia hominum facta.*

"*Tametsi diabolus et reprobi Dei ministri sunt et organa, et arcana eius judicia exsequuntur, Deus tamen incomprehensibili modo sic in illis et per illos operatur ut nihil ex eorum vitio labis contrahat, quia illorum malitia iuste recteque utitur in bonum finem, licet modus sœpe nobis sit absconditus.*

"*Inscite vel calumniose faciunt qui Deum fieri dicunt autorem peccati, si omnia eo volente et ordinante fiant: quia inter manifestam hominum pravitatem et arcana Dei iudicia non distinguunt.*"

II. The Lambeth Articles.

In full agreement with Calvin are the LAMBETH ARTICLES, 1595. They were intended to be an obligatory appendix to the Thirty-nine Articles which, in Art. XVII., present only the positive side of the doctrine of predestination, and ignore reprobation. They were prepared by Dr. Whitaker, Professor of Divinity in Cambridge, and approved by Dr. Whitgift, Archbishop of Canterbury, Dr. Hutton, Archbishop of York, and a number of prelates convened at Lambeth Palace, London; also by Hooker (with a slight modification; see Hooker's *Works*, ed. by Keble, II. 752 sq.). But they were not sanctioned by Queen Elizabeth, who was displeased that a Lambeth Synod was called without her authority, nor by James I., and gradually lost their power during the Arminian reaction under the Stuarts. They are as follows:—

"1. God from eternity hath predestinated certain men unto life; certain men he hath reprobated.

"2. The moving or efficient cause of predestination unto life is not the foresight of faith, or of perseverance, or of good works, or of anything that is in the person predestinated, but only the good will and pleasure of God.

"3. There is predetermined a certain number of the predestinate, which can neither be augmented nor diminished.

"4. Those who are not predestinated to salvation shall be necessarily damned for their sins.

"5. A true, living, and justifying faith, and the Spirit of God justifying [sanctifying] is not extinguished, falleth not away; it vanisheth not away in the elect, either finally or totally.

"6. A man truly faithful, that is, such a one who is endued with a justifying faith, is certain, with the full assurance of faith, of the remission of his sins and of his everlasting salvation by Christ.

"7. Saving grace is not given, is not granted, is not communicated to all men, by which they may be saved if they will.

"8. No man can come unto Christ unless it shall be given unto him, and unless the Father shall draw him; and all men are not drawn by the Father that they may come to the Son.

"9. It is not in the will or power of every one to be saved."

The Lambeth Articles were accepted by the Convocation at Dublin, 1615, and engrafted on the IRISH ARTICLES OF RELIGION, which were probably composed by the learned Archbishop Ussher (at that time Professor of Divinity in Trinity College, Dublin), and form the connecting link between the Thirty-Nine Articles and the Westminster Confession. Some of the strongest statements of the Irish Articles passed literally (without any acknowledgment) into the Westminster Confession. The Irish Articles are printed in Schaff's *Creeds of Christendom*, III. 526–544.

III. THE WESTMINSTER CONFESSION.

CHAP. III. *Of God's Eternal Decree.*

The WESTMINSTER CONFESSION OF FAITH, prepared by the Westminster Assembly in 1647, adopted by the Long Parliament, by the Kirk of Scotland, and the Presbyterian Churches of America, gives the clearest and strongest symbolic statement of this doctrine. It assigns to it more space than to the holy Trinity, or the Person of Christ, or the atonement.

"1. God from all eternity did, by the most wise and holy counsel of his own will, freely and unchangeably ordain whatsoever comes to pass; yet so as thereby neither is God the author of sin, nor is violence offered to the will of the creatures, nor is the liberty or contingency of second causes taken away, but rather established.

"2. Although God knows whatsoever may or can come to pass upon all supposed conditions, yet hath he not decreed anything because he foresaw it as future, or as that which would come to pass upon such conditions.

"3. By the decree of God, for the manifestation of his glory, some men and angels are predestinated unto everlasting life, and others foreordained to everlasting death.

"4. These angels and men, thus predestinated and foreordained, are particularly and unchangeably designed; and their number is so certain and definite that it cannot be either increased or diminished.

"5. Those of mankind that are predestinated unto life, God, before the foundation of the world was laid, according to his eternal and immutable purpose, and the secret counsel and good pleasure of his will, hath chosen in Christ, unto everlasting glory, out of his mere free grace and love, without any foresight of faith or good works, or perseverance in either of them, or any other thing in the creature, as conditions, or causes moving him thereunto; and all to the praise of his glorious grace.

"6. As God hath appointed the elect unto glory, so hath he, by the eternal and most free purpose of his will, foreordained all the means thereunto. Wherefore they who are elected, being fallen in Adam, are redeemed by Christ, are effectually called unto faith in Christ by his Spirit working in due season; are justified, adopted, sanctified, and kept by his power through faith unto salvation. Neither are any other redeemed by Christ, effectually called, justified, adopted, sanctified, and saved, but the elect only.

"7. The rest of mankind God was pleased, according to the unsearchable counsel of his own will, whereby he extendeth or withholdeth mercy as he pleaseth, for the glory of his sovereign power over his creatures, to pass by, and to ordain them to dishonor and wrath for their sin, to the praise of his glorious justice.

"8. The doctrine of this high mystery of predestination is to be handled with special prudence and care, that men attending the will of God revealed in his Word, and yielding obedience thereunto, may, from the certainty of their effectual vocation, be assured of their eternal election. So shall this doctrine afford matter of praise, reverence, and admiration of God; and of humility, diligence, and abundant consolation to all that sincerely obey the gospel."

IV. METHODISM AND CALVINISM.

The severest condemnation of the Westminster Calvinism came from JOHN WESLEY, the most apostolic man that the Anglo-Saxon race has produced. He adopted the Arminian creed and made it a converting agency; he magnified the free grace of God, like the Calvinists, but extended it to all men. In a sermon on *Free Grace*, preached at Bristol (*Sermons*, vol. I. 482 sqq.), he charges the doctrine of predestination with "making vain all preaching, and tending to destroy holiness, the comfort of religion and zeal for good works, yea, the whole Christian revelation by involving it in fatal contradictions." He goes so far as to call it "a doctrine full of blasphemy," because "it represents our blessed Lord as a hypocrite, a deceiver of the people, a man void of common sincerity, as mocking his helpless creatures by offering what he never intends to give, by saying one thing and meaning another." It destroys "all the attributes of God, his justice, mercy, and truth, yea, it represents the most holy God as worse than the devil, as both more false, more cruel, and more unjust." This is as hard and unjust as anything that Pighius, Bolsec, Castellio, and Servetus said against Calvin. And yet Wesley coöperated for some time with George Whitefield, the great Calvinistic revival preacher, and delivered his funeral sermon in Tottenham-Court-Road, Nov. 18, 1770, on the text, Num. 23: 10, in which he spoke in the highest terms of Whitefield's personal piety and great usefulness (*Sermons*, I. 470–480). "Have we read or heard," he asked, "of any person since the apostles, who testified the gospel of the grace of God through so widely extended a space, through so large a part of the habitable world? Have we read or heard of any person, who called so many thousands, so many myriads of sinners to repentance? Above all, have we read or heard of any, who has been a blessed instrument in his hand of bringing so many sinners from 'darkness to light, and from the power of Satan unto God?'" — This is a striking illustration how widely great and good men may differ in theology, and yet how nearly they may agree in religion.

Charles Wesley fully sided with the Arminianism of his brother John, and abused his poetic gift by writing poor doggerel against Calvinism.[1] He had a bitter controversy on the subject with Toplady, who was a devout Calvinist. But their theological controversy is dead and buried, while their devotional hymns still live, and Calvinists and Methodists heartily join in singing Wesley's " Jesus, Lover of my Soul," and Toplady's " Rock of Ages, cleft for me."

V. MODERN CALVINISM.

Modern Calvinism retains the doctrine of an all-ruling providence and saving grace, but denies reprobation and preterition, or leaves them to the sphere of metaphysical theology. It lays also great stress on the moral responsibility of the human will, and on the duty of offering the gospel sincerely to every creature, in accordance with the modern missionary spirit. This, at least, is the prevailing and growing tendency among Presbyterian Churches in Europe and America, as appears from the recent agitation on the revision of the Westminster Confession. The new creed of the Presbyterian Church of England, which was adopted in 1890, avoids all the objectionable features of old Calvinism, and substitutes for the eight sections of the third chapter of the Westminster Confession the following two articles, which contain all that is necessary in a public confession : —

ART. IV. *Of Providence.*

" We believe that God the Creator upholds all things by the word of his power, preserving and providing for all his creatures, according to the laws of their being; and that he, through the presence and energy of his Spirit in nature and history, disposes and governs all events for his own high design; yet is he not in any wise the author or approver of sin, neither are the freedom and responsibility of man taken away, nor have any bounds been set to the sovereign liberty of him who worketh when and where and how he pleaseth."

ART. XII. *Of Election and Regeneration.*

" We humbly own and believe that God the Father, before the foundation of the world, was pleased of his sovereign grace to choose unto himself in Christ a people, whom he gave to the Son, and to whom the Holy Spirit imparts spiritual life by a secret and wonderful operation of his power, using as his ordinary means, where years of understanding have been reached, the truths of his Word in ways agreeable to the nature of man; so that, being born from above, they are the children of God, created in Christ Jesus unto good works."

---

[1] This is a specimen : —

> " O Horrible Decree,
>   Worthy of whence it came!
> Forgive their hellish blasphemy,
>   Who charge it on the Lamb!"

§ 114. *Calvinism examined.*

We cannot dismiss this important subject without examining the Calvinistic system of predestination in the light of Christian experience, of reason, and the teaching of the Bible.

Calvinism, as we have seen, starts from a double decree of absolute predestination, which antedates creation, and is the divine program of human history. This program includes the successive stages of the creation of man, an universal fall and condemnation of the race, a partial redemption and salvation, and a partial reprobation and perdition: all for the glory of God and the display of his attributes of mercy and justice. History is only the execution of the original design. There can be no failure. The beginning and the end, God's immutable plan and the issue of the world's history, must correspond.

We should remember at the outset that we have to deal here with nothing less than a solution of the world-problem, and should approach it with reverence and an humble sense of the limitation of our mental capacities. We stand, as it were, before a mountain whose top is lost in the clouds. Many who dared to climb to the summit have lost their vision in the blinding snow-drifts. Dante, the deepest thinker among poets, deems the mystery of predestination too far removed from mortals who cannot see "the first cause in its wholeness," and too deep even for the comprehension of the saints in Paradise, who enjoy the beatific vision, yet "do not know all the elect," and are content "to will whatsoever God wills."[1] Calvin himself confesses that "the pre-

---

[1] *Paradiso*, XX. 130–138 : —

> " *O predestinazion, quanto rimota*
> *È la radice tua da quegli aspetti*
> *Che la prima cagion non veggion tota !*

> " *E voi, mortali, tenetevi stretti*
> *A giudicar; chè noi, che Dio vedemo,*
> *Non conosciamo ancor tutti gli eletti :*

destination of God is a labyrinth, from which the mind of man can by no means extricate itself." [1]

The only way out of the labyrinth is the Ariadne thread of the love of God in Christ, and this is a still greater, but more blessed mystery, which we can adore rather than comprehend.

The Facts of Experience.

We find everywhere in this world the traces of a revealed God and of a hidden God; revealed enough to strengthen our faith, concealed enough to try our faith.

We are surrounded by mysteries. In the realm of nature we see the contrasts of light and darkness, day and night, heat and cold, summer and winter, life and death, blooming valleys and barren deserts, singing birds and poisonous snakes, useful animals and ravenous beasts, the struggle for existence and the survival of the fittest. Turning to human life, we find that one man is born to prosperity, the other to misery; one a king, the other a beggar; one strong and healthy, the other a helpless cripple; one a genius, the other an idiot; one inclined to virtue, another to vice; one the son of a saint, the other of a criminal; one in the darkness of heathenism, another in the light of Christianity. The best men as well as the worst are exposed to fatal accidents, and whole nations with their innocent offspring are ravaged and decimated by war, pestilence, and famine.

Who can account for all these and a thousand other differences and perplexing problems? They are beyond the control of man's will, and must be traced to the inscrutable will of God, whose ways are past finding out.

> " Ed ènne dolce così fatto scemo,
> Perchè il ben nostro in questo ben s'affina,
> Che quel che vuole Dio, e noi volemo."

[1] Com. on Rom. 9 : 14 : " Est prædestinatio Dei vere labyrinthus, unde hominis ingenium nullo modo se explicare queat."

Here, then, is predestination, and, apparently, a double predestination to good or evil, to happiness or misery.

Sin and death are universal facts which no sane man can deny. They constitute the problem of problems. And the only practical solution of the problem is the fact of redemption. "Where sin has abounded, grace did abound more exceedingly; that as sin reigned in death, even so might grace reign through righteousness unto eternal life, through Jesus Christ our Lord" (Rom. 5 : 20, 21).

If redemption were as universal in its operation as sin, the solution would be most satisfactory and most glorious. But redemption is only partially revealed in this world, and the great question remains: What will become of the immense majority of human beings who live and die without God and without hope in this world? Is this terrible fact to be traced to the eternal counsel of God, or to the free agency of man? Here is the point where Augustinianism and Calvinism take issue with Pelagianism, Semi-Pelagianism, Synergism, and Arminianism.

The Calvinistic system involves a positive truth: the election to eternal life by free grace, and the negative inference: the reprobation to eternal death by arbitrary justice. The former is the strength, the latter is the weakness of the system. The former is practically accepted by all true believers; the latter always has been, and always will be, repelled by the great majority of Christians.

The doctrine of a gracious election is as clearly taught in the New Testament as any other doctrine. Consult such passages as Matt. 25 : 34; John 6 : 37, 44, 65; 10 : 28; 15 : 16; 17 : 12; 18 : 9; Acts 13 : 48; Rom. 8 : 28–39; Gal. 1 : 4; Eph. 1 : 4–11; 2 : 8–10; 1 Thess. 1 : 4; 2 Thess. 2 : 13, 14; 2 Tim. 1 : 9; 1 Pet. 1 : 2. The doctrine is confirmed by experience. Christians trace all their temporal and spiritual blessings, their life, health, and strength, their regeneration and conversion, every good thought and deed to the undeserved mercy of God, and hope to be saved solely by the merits of Christ, "by grace through faith," not by works of their own. The more they advance in spiritual life, the more grateful they feel to God, and the less inclined to claim any merit. The greatest saints are also the humblest. Their theology reflects the spirit and attitude of prayer, which rests on the conviction that God is the free giver of every good and perfect gift, and that, without God, we are nothing. Before the throne of grace all Christians may be called Augustinians and Calvinists.

It is the great merit of Calvin to have brought out this doctrine of salvation by free grace more forcibly and clearly than any divine since the days of Augustin. It has been the effective theme of the great Calvinistic preachers and writers in Europe and America to this day. Howe, Owen, Baxter, Bunyan, South, Whitefield, Jonathan Edwards, Robert Hall, Chalmers, Spurgeon, were Calvinists in their creed, though belonging to different denominations, — Congregational, Presbyterian, Episcopal, Baptist, — and had no superiors in pulpit power and influence. Spurgeon was the most popular and effective preacher of the nineteenth century, who addressed from week to week five thousand hearers in his Tabernacle, and millions of readers through his printed sermons in many tongues. Nor should we forget that some of the most devout Roman Catholics were Augustinians or Jansenists.

On the other hand, no man is saved mechanically or by force, but through faith, freely, by accepting the gift of God. This implies the contrary power of rejecting the gift. To accept is no merit, to reject is ingratitude and guilt. All Calvinistic preachers appeal to man's responsibility. They pray as if everything depended on God; and yet they preach and work as if everything depended on man. And the Church is directed to send the gospel to every creature. We pray for the salvation of all men, but not for the loss of a single human being. Christ interceded even for his murderers on the cross.

Here, then, is a practical difficulty. The decree of reprobation cannot be made an object of prayer or preaching, and this is an argument against it. Experience confirms election, but repudiates reprobation.

The Logical Argument.

The logical argument for reprobation is that there can be no positive without a negative; no election of some without a reprobation of others. This is true by deductive logic, but not by inductive logic. There are degrees and stages of election. There must be a chronological order in the history of salvation. All are called sooner or later; some in the sixth, others in the ninth, others in the eleventh, hour, according to God's providence. Those who accept the call and persevere in faith are among the elect (1 Pet. 1:1; 2:9). Those who reject it, become reprobate by their own unbelief, and against God's wish and will. There is no antecedent decree of reprobation, but only a *judicial* act of reprobation in consequence of man's sin.

Logic is a two-edged sword. It may lead from predestinarian premises to the conclusion that God is the author of sin, which Calvin himself rejects and abhors as a blasphemy. It may also lead to fatalism, pantheism, or universalism. We must stop somewhere in our process of reasoning, or sacrifice a part of the truth. Logic, it should be remembered, deals only with finite categories, and cannot grasp infinite truth. Christianity is not a logical or mathematical problem, and cannot be reduced to the limitations of a human system. It is above any particular system and comprehends the truths of all systems. It is above logic, yet not illogical; as revelation is above reason, yet not against reason.

We cannot conceive of God except as an omniscient and omnipotent being, who from eternity foreknew and, in some way, also foreordained all things that should come to pass in his universe. He foreknew what he foreordained, and he foreordained what he foreknew; his foreknowledge and fore-ordination, his intelligence and will are coeternal, and must harmonize. There is no succession of time, no before nor after in the eternal God. The fall of the first man, with its effects upon all future generations, cannot have been an accident which God, as a passive or neutral spectator, simply permitted to take place when he might so easily have pre-vented it. He must in some way have foreordained it, as a means for a higher end, as a negative condition for the greatest good. So far the force of reasoning, on the basis of belief in a personal God, goes to the full length of Calvin-istic supralapsarianism, and even beyond it, to the very verge of universalism. If we give up the idea of a self-conscious, personal God, reason would force us into fatalism or pantheism.

But there is a logic of ethics as well as of metaphysics. God is holy as well as almighty and omniscient, and there-fore cannot be the author of sin. Man is a moral as well as an intellectual being, and the claims of his moral constitution are equal to the claims of his intellectual constitution. Con-science is as powerful a factor as reason. The most rigid believer in divine sovereignty, if he be a Christian, cannot get rid of the sense of personal accountability, though he may be unable to reconcile the two. The harmony lies in God and in the moral constitution of man. They are the two complementary sides of one truth. Paul unites them in one sentence: "Work out your own salvation with fear and trembling; for it is God who worketh in you both to will and to work, for his good pleasure" (Phil. 2 : 13). The problem, however, comes within the reach of possible solution, if we distinguish between sovereignty as an inherent power, and the exercise of sovereignty. God may limit the exercise of his sovereignty to make room for the free action of his creatures. It is by his sovereign decree that man is free. Without such self-limitation he could not admonish men to repent and believe. Here, again, the Calvinistic logic must either bend or break. Strictly carried out, it would turn the exhortations of God to the sinner into a solemn mockery and cruel irony.

THE SCRIPTURE ARGUMENT.

Calvin, though one of the ablest logicians, cared less for logic than for the Bible, and it is his obedience to the Word of God that induced him to accept the *decretum horribile* against his wish and will. His judgment is of the greatest weight, for he had no superior, and scarcely an equal, in thorough and systematic Bible knowledge and exegetical insight.

And here we must freely admit that not a few passages, especially in the Old Testament, favor a double decree to the extent of supreme supralapsarianism; yea, they go beyond the Calvinistic system, and seem to make God himself the author of sin and evil. See Ex. 4 : 21; 7 : 13 (repeatedly said of God's hardening Pharaoh's heart); Isa. 6 : 9, 10; 44 : 18; Jer. 6 : 21; Amos 3 : 6 ("Shall there be evil in a city, and the Lord hath not done it?"); Prov. 16 : 4; Matt. 11 : 25; 13 : 14, 15; John 12 : 40; Rom. 9 : 10–23; 11 : 7, 8; 1 Cor. 14 : 3; 2 Thess. 2 : 11; 1 Pet. 2 : 8; Jude 4 ("who were of old set forth unto this condemnation ").[1]

The rock of reprobation is the ninth chapter of Romans. It is not accidental that Calvin elaborated and published the second edition of his *Institutes* simultaneously with his Commentary on the Romans, at Strassburg, in 1539.

There are especially three passages in the ninth chapter, which in their strict literal sense favor extreme Calvinism,

---

[1] The last passage is often quoted for a decree of reprobation; but the verb προγεγραμμένοι is wrongly translated "ordained" in the E. V. Προγράφω means to *write before,* and refers to previous writings, namely, the Scriptures of the O. T. Calvin correctly translates "*præscripti in hoc judicium,*" but refers it, metaphorically, to the book of the divine counsel: "*æternum Dei consilium liber vocatur.*"

and are so explained by some of the severest grammatical commentators of modern times (as Meyer and Weiss).

(*a*) 9 : 13: "Jacob I loved, but Esau I hated," quoted from Mal. 1: 2, 3. This passage, whether we take it in a literal or anthropopathic sense, has no reference to the eternal destiny of Jacob and Esau, but to their representative position in the history of the theocracy. This removes the chief difficulty. Esau received a temporal blessing from his father (Gen. 27 : 39, 40), and behaved kindly and generously to his brother (33 : 4); he probably repented of the folly of his youth in selling his birthright,[1] and may be among the saved, as well as Adam and Eve — the first among the lost and the first among the saved.

Moreover, the strict meaning of a positive hatred seems impossible in the nature of the case, since it would contradict all we know from the Bible of the attributes of God. A God of love, who commands us to love all men, even our enemies, cannot hate a child before his birth, or any of his creatures made in his own image. "Can a woman forget her sucking child," says the Lord, "that she should not have compassion on the son of her womb? Yea, these may forget, yet will I not forget thee" (Isa. 49 : 15). This is the prophet's conception of the tender mercies of God. How much more must it be the conception of the New Testament? The word *hate* must, therefore, be understood as a strong Hebraistic expression for loving less or putting back; as in Gen. 29 : 31, where the original text says, " Leah was hated " by Jacob, *i.e.* loved less than Rachel (comp. ver. 30). When our Saviour says, Luke 14 : 26: " If any man *hateth* not his own father and mother and wife and children and brothers and sisters, yea, and his own life also, he cannot be my disciple," he does not mean that his disciples should break the

---

[1] This is implied in the passage, Heb. 12 : 17, whether we refer μετάνοια to Esau's late repentance (Calvin, Bleek), or to a change of mind in Isaac (Beza, Weiss).

fifth commandment, and act contrary to his direction: "Love your enemies, pray for them that persecute you" (Matt. 5:44), but simply that we should prefer him above everything, even life itself, and should sacrifice whatever comes in conflict with him. This meaning is confirmed by the parallel passage, Matt. 10:37: "He that *loveth* father and mother *more than me* is not worthy of me."

(*b*) 9:17. Paul traces the hardening of Pharaoh's heart to the agency of God, and so far makes God responsible for sin. But this was a judicial act of punishing sin with sin; for Pharaoh had first hardened his own heart (Ex. 8:15, 32; 9:34). Moreover, this passage has no reference to Pharaoh's future fate any more than the passage about Esau, but both refer to their place in the history of Israel.

(*c*) In 9:22 and 23, the Apostle speaks of "vessels of wrath *fitted unto destruction*" (κατηρτισμένα εἰς ἀπώλειαν), and "vessels of mercy which *he* (God) *prepared unto glory*" (ἅ προητοίμασεν εἰς δόξαν). But the difference of the verbs, and the difference between the passive (or middle) in the first clause and the active in the second is most significant, and shows that God has no direct agency in the destruction of the vessels of wrath, which is due to their self-destruction; the participle perfect denotes the result of a gradual process and a state of maturity for destruction, but not a divine purpose. Calvin is too good an exegete to overlook this difference, and virtually admits its force, although he tries to weaken it.

"They observe," he says of his opponents, "that it is not said without meaning, that the vessels of wrath are fitted for destruction, but that God prepared the vessels of mercy; since by this mode of expression, Paul ascribes and challenges to God the praise of salvation, and throws the blame of perdition on those who by their choice procure it to themselves. But though I concede to them that *Paul softens the asperity of the former clause by the difference of phraseology;* yet it is not at all consistent to transfer the preparation for destruction to any other than the secret counsel of God, which is also asserted just before in the context, 'that God raised up Pharaoh, and whom he will he hardeneth.' Whence it follows, that the cause of hardening is the secret counsel of God. This, however, I maintain, which is observed by Augustin, that when God turns wolves into sheep, he renovates them by more powerful grace to conquer their obstinacy; and therefore the obstinate are not converted, because God exerts not that mightier grace, of which he is not destitute if he chose to display it." [1]

PAUL'S TEACHING OF THE EXTENT OF REDEMPTION.

Whatever view we may take of these hard passages, we should remember that the ninth chapter of Romans is only a part of Paul's philosophy of history, unfolded in chapters 9–11. While the ninth chapter sets forth the divine sovereignty, the tenth chapter asserts the human responsibility, and the eleventh looks forward to the future solution of the dark problem, namely, the conversion of the fulness of the Gentiles and the salvation of all Israel (11 : 25). And he winds up the whole discussion with the glorious sentence: "God hath shut up *all* unto disobedience, that he might have mercy upon *all*" (32). This is the key for the understanding, not only of this section, but of the whole Epistle to the Romans.[2]

---

[1] *Inst.* III. ch. XXII. 1. In his Com. on Rom. 9 . 22, 23, he ignores this distinction and explains κατηρτισμένα, "given up and appointed to destruction, made and formed for this end" (*devota et destinata exitio : sunt enim vasa iræ, id est in hoc facta et formata, ut documenta sint vindictæ et furoris Dei*). This is the extreme supralapsarian exposition. But other Reformed exegetes fully acknowledge the difference of phraseology. It was pressed by those members of the Westminster Assembly who sympathized with the hypothetical universalism of the Saumur school of Cameron and Amyrauld. "The non-elect," said Dr. Arrowsmith, "are said to be fitted to that destruction which their sins bring upon them, but not by God." See Mitchell, *Minutes of the Westminster Assembly,* pp. 152 sqq.; Schaff, *Creeds,* I. 770 sq.

[2] "*Das ganze Summarium und der herrliche Schlussstein des ganzen bisherigen Brieftheils.*" Weiss in the 6th ed. of Meyer on Romans (p. 555). Godet:

And this is in harmony with the whole spirit and aim of this Epistle. It is easier to make it prove a system of conditional universalism than a system of dualistic particularism. The very theme, 1 : 16, declares that the gospel is a power of God for the salvation, not of a particular class, but of "every one" that believeth. In drawing a parallel between the first and the second Adam (5 : 12–21), he represents the effect of the latter as equal in extent, and greater in intensity than the effect of the former; while in the Calvinistic system it would be less. We have no right to limit "the many" (οἱ πολλοί) and the "all" (πάντες) in one clause, and to take it literally in the other. "If, by the trespass of the one [Adam], death reigned through the one, much more shall they that receive the abundance of grace and of the gift of righteousness reign in life through the one, even Jesus Christ. So, then, as through one trespass the judgment came unto *all men* to condemnation; even so through one act of righteousness the free gift came unto *all men* to justification of life. For as through the one man's disobedience *the many* [i.e. *all*] were made sinners, even so through the obedience of the one shall *the many* [*all*] be made righteous" (5 : 17–19).[1] The same parallel, without any restriction, is more briefly expressed in the passage (1 Cor. 15 : 21): "As in Adam *all* die, so also in Christ shall *all* be made alive"; and in a different form in Rom. 11 : 32 and Gal. 3 : 22, already quoted.

"*C'est ici comme le point final apposé à tout ce qui précede; ce dernier mot rend compte de tout le plan de Dieu, dont les phases principales viennent d'être esquissées.*" The ἵνα τοὺς πάντας (Jews and Gentiles) teaches not, indeed, the forced acceptance of mercy by all, but, at all events, the universality of the divine purpose and intention. Meyer sees in this passage a conclusive exegetical argument against a *decretum reprobationis*.

[1] Unfortunately the A. V. obliterates the force of the parallel in the fifth chapter of Romans by neglecting the definite article before πολλοί. "The many" of the original is opposed to "the one," and is equivalent to "all"; while "many" would be opposed to "few." The Revised Version of 1881 corrects these mistakes.

These passages contain, as in a nutshell, the theodicy of Paul. They dispel the darkness of the ninth chapter of Romans. They exclude all limitations of God's plan and intention to a particular class; they teach not, indeed, that all men will be actually saved — for many reject the divine offer, and die in impenitence, — but that God sincerely *desires* and actually *provides* salvation for all. Whosoever is saved, is saved by grace; whosoever is lost, is lost by his own guilt of unbelief.

THE OFFER OF SALVATION.

There remains, it is true, the great difficulty that the offer of salvation is limited in this world, as far as we know, to a part of the human race, and that the great majority pass into the other world without any knowledge of the historical Christ.

But God gave to every man the light of reason and conscience (Rom. 1:19; 2:14, 15). The Divine Logos "lighteth every man" that cometh into the world (John 1:9). God never left himself "without witness" (Acts 14:17). He deals with his creatures according to the measure of their ability and opportunity, whether they have one or five or ten talents (Matt. 25:15 sqq.). He is "no respecter of persons, but in every nation he that feareth him and worketh righteousness, is acceptable to him" (Acts 10:35).

May we not then cherish at least a charitable hope, if not a certain belief, that a God of infinite love and justice will receive into his heavenly kingdom all those who die innocently ignorant of the Christian revelation, but in a state of preparedness or disposition for the gospel, so that they would thankfully accept it if offered to them? Cornelius was in such a condition before Peter entered his house, and he represents a multitude which no man can number. We cannot know and measure the secret operations of the Spirit of God, who works "when, where, and how he pleases."

Surely, here is a point where the rigor of the old orthodoxy, whether Roman Catholic, or Lutheran, or Calvinistic,
must be moderated. And the Calvinistic system admits more
readily of an expansion than the churchly and sacramental
type of orthodoxy.

The General Love of God to all Men.

This doctrine of a divine will and divine provision of a
universal salvation, on the sole condition of faith, is taught
in many passages which admit of no other interpretation,
and which must, therefore, decide this whole question. For
it is a settled rule in hermeneutics that dark passages must
be explained by clear passages, and not *vice versa*. Such
passages are the following: —

"I have no pleasure in the death of him that dieth, saith
the Lord our God: wherefore turn yourselves, and live"
(Ezek. 18 : 32, 23; 33 : 11). "And I, if I be lifted up from
the earth, will draw *all men* unto myself" (John 12 : 32).
"God so loved the *world*" (that is, all mankind) "that he
gave his only begotten Son, that *whosoever* believeth on him
should not perish, but have eternal life" (John 3 : 16).
"God our Saviour *willeth* that *all men* should be saved and
come to the knowledge of the truth" (1 Tim. 2 : 4).[1] "The
grace of God hath appeared, bringing salvation to *all men*"
(Tit. 2 : 11). "The Lord is long-suffering to you-ward, *not
wishing* that *any* should perish, but that *all* should come to
repentance" (2 Pet. 3 : 9).[2] "Jesus Christ is the propitia-
tion for our sins; and not for ours only, but *also for* (the

---

[1] Calvin explains "all men" to mean men of all classes and conditions
("*de hominum generibus, non singulis personis*"). See his Comm. on 1 Tim.
2 : 4, and his sermon on the passage. But the Apostle emphasizes "all
men" with reference to prayer "for all men," which he commands in ver. 1,
and which cannot be limited.

[2] Calvin arbitrarily explains this passage of the "*voluntas Dei quæ nobis
in evangelio patefit,*" but not "*de arcano Dei consilio quo destinati sunt reprobi
in suum exitium.*"

sins of) *the whole world*" (1 John 2 : 2). It is impossible to state the doctrine of a universal atonement more clearly in so few words.[1]

To these passages should be added the divine exhortations to repentance, and the lament of Christ over the inhabitants of Jerusalem who "would not" come to him (Matt. 23 : 37). These exhortations are insincere or unmeaning, if God does not want all men to be saved, and if men have not the ability to obey or disobey the voice. The same is implied in the command of Christ to preach the gospel to the whole creation (Mark 16 : 15), and to disciple all nations (Matt. 28 : 19).

It is impossible to restrict these passages to a particular class without doing violence to the grammar and the context.

The only way of escape is by the distinction between a *revealed* will of God, which declares his willingness to save *all* men, and a *secret* will of God which means to save only *some* men.[2] Augustin and Luther made this distinction. Calvin uses it in explaining 2 Pet. 3 : 9, and those passages of the Old Testament which ascribe repentance and changes to the immutable God.

But this distinction overthrows the system which it is intended to support. A contradiction between intention and expression is fatal to veracity, which is the foundation of human morality, and must be an essential attribute of the Deity. A man who says the reverse of what he means is called, in plain English, a hypocrite and a liar. It does not help the matter when Calvin says, repeatedly, that there are not two wills in God, but only two ways of speaking adapted

---

[1] Calvin understands "*totus mundus*" in this passage to mean "*tota ecclesia!*" This is as impossible as the confinement of "the world," John 3 : 16, to "the elect." He mentions, however, also a better explanation, that Christ died "*sufficienter pro toto mundo, sed pro electis tantum efficaciter.*"

[2] Various terms for the distinction: *voluntas revelata* and *voluntas arcana ; voluntas signi* and *voluntas beneplaciti* (εὐδοκίας) ; *voluntas universalis* and *voluntas specialis; verbum externum et verbum internum.* The oft-quoted proof text, Deut. 29 : 29, teaches a distinction, but not a contradiction, between the secret things and the revealed things of God.

to our weakness. Nor does it remove the difficulty when he warns us to rely on the revealed will of God rather than brood over his secret will.

The greatest, the deepest, the most comforting word in the Bible is the word, "God is love," and the greatest fact in the world's history is the manifestation of that love in the person and the work of Christ. That word and this fact are the sum and substance of the gospel, and the only solid foundation of Christian theology. The sovereignty of God is acknowledged by Jews and Mohammedans as well as by Christians, but the love of God is revealed only in the Christian religion. It is the inmost essence of God, and the key to all his ways and works. It is the central truth which sheds light upon all other truths.

§ 115. *Calvin's Theory of the Sacraments.*

Inst. bk. IV. chs. XIV.–XIX.

Next to the doctrine of predestination, Calvin paid most attention to the doctrine of the sacraments. And here he was original, and occupied a mediating position between Luther and Zwingli. His sacramental theory passed into all the Reformed Confessions more than his view of predestination.

Calvin accepts Augustin's definition that a sacrament (corresponding to the Greek "mystery") is "a visible sign of an invisible grace," but he improves it by emphasizing the sealing character of the sacrament, according to Rom. 4 : 11, and the necessity of faith as the condition of receiving the benefit of the ordinance. "It is," he says, "an outward sign by which the Lord seals in our consciences the promises of his good-will towards us, to support the weakness of our faith, or a testimony of his grace towards us, with a reciprocal attestation of our piety towards him." It is even more expressive than the word. It is a divine seal of authentication, which sustains and strengthens our faith. "Lord, I believe, help thou mine unbelief" (Mark 9 : 24). To be efficacious, the sacraments must be accompanied by the Spirit, that internal Teacher, by whose energy alone our hearts are penetrated, and our affections moved. Without the influence of the Spirit, the sacraments can produce no more effect upon our minds, than the splendor of the sun on blind eyes, or the sound of a voice upon deaf ears. If the seed falls on a desert spot, it will die; but if it be cast upon a cultivated field, it will bring forth abundant increase.

Calvin vigorously opposes, as superstitious and mischievous, the scholastic *opus operatum* theory that the sacraments justify and confer grace by an intrinsic virtue, provided we do not obstruct their operation by a mortal sin. A sacrament without faith misleads the mind to rest in the exhibition of a sensuous object rather than in God himself, and is ruinous to true piety.

He agrees with Augustin in the opinion that the sign and the matter of the sacrament are not inseparably connected, and that it produces its intended effect only in the elect. He quotes from him the sentence: "The morsel of bread given by the Lord to Judas was poison; not because Judas received an evil thing, but because, being a wicked man, he received a good thing in a sinful manner." But this must not be understood to mean that the virtue and truth of the sacrament depend on the condition or choice of him who receives it. The symbol consecrated by the word of the Lord is in reality what it is declared to be, and preserves its virtue, although it confers no benefit on a wicked and impious person. Augustin happily solves this question in a few words: "If thou receive it carnally, still it ceases not to be spiritual; but it is not so to thee." The office of the sacrament is the same as that of the word of God; both offer Christ and his heavenly grace to us, but they confer no benefit without the medium of faith.

Calvin discusses at length the seven sacraments of the Roman Church, the doctrine of transubstantiation, and the mass. But it is sufficient here to state his views on baptism and the Lord's Supper, the only sacraments which Christ directly instituted for perpetual observance in the Church.

§ 116. *Baptism.*

Inst. IV. chs. XV. and XVI.   Also his *Brieve instruction, pour armer tous bons fideles contre les erreurs de la secte commune des Anabaptistes,* Geneva, 1544, 2d ed. 1545; Latin version by Nicolas des Gallars. In *Opera,* VII. 45 sqq. This tract was written against the fanatical wing of the Anabaptists at the request of the pastors of Neuchâtel. His youthful treatise *On the Sleep of the Soul* was also directed against the Anabaptists. See above, § 77, pp. 325 sqq. Calvin's wife was the widow of a converted Anabaptist.

Baptism, Calvin says, is the sacrament of ablution and regeneration; the Eucharist is the sacrament of redemption and sanctification.   Christ "came by water and by blood" (1 John 5:6); that is, to purify and to redeem.   The Spirit, as the third and chief witness, confirms and secures the witness of water and blood; that is, of baptism and the eucharist (1 John 5:8).[1]   "This sublime mystery was strikingly exhibited on the cross, when blood and water issued from Christ's side, which on this account Augustin justly called 'the fountain of our sacraments.'"

I. Calvin defines baptism as "a sign of initiation, by which we are admitted into the society of the Church, in order that, being incorporated into Christ, we may be numbered among the children of God."

II. Faith derives three benefits from this sacrament.

1. It assures us, like a legal instrument properly attested, that all our sins are cancelled, and will never be imputed unto us (Eph. 5:26; Tit. 3:5; 1 Pet. 3:21).   It is far

---

[1] Calvin confines himself (IV. ch. XIV. § 22) to the genuine words of the three witnesses in this passage, and justly ignores the interpolation of the *textus receptus,* which is omitted in the Revised Version.

more than a mark or sign by which we profess our religion before men, as soldiers wear the insignia of their sovereign. It is "for the remission of sins," past and future. No new sacrament is necessary for sins committed after baptism. At whatever time we are baptized, we are washed and purified for the whole life. "Whenever we have fallen, we must recur to the remembrance of baptism, and arm our minds with the consideration of it, that we may be always certified and assured of the remission of our sins."

2. Baptism shows us our mortification in Christ, and our new life in him. All who receive baptism with faith experience the efficacy of Christ's death and the power of his resurrection, and should therefore walk in newness of life (Rom. 6 : 3, 4, 11).

3. Baptism affords us "the certain testimony that we are not only engrafted into the life and death of Christ, but are so united to him as to be partakers of all his benefits" (Gal. 3 : 26, 27).

But while baptism removes the guilt and punishment of hereditary and actual sin, it does not destroy our natural depravity, which is perpetually producing works of the flesh, and will not be wholly abolished till the close of this mortal life. In the mean time we must hold fast to the promise of God in baptism, fight manfully against sin and temptation, and press forward to complete victory.

III. On the question of the validity of baptism by unworthy ministers, Calvin fully agrees with Augustin against the view of the Donatists, who measured the virtue of the sacrament by the moral character of the minister. He applies the argument to the Anabaptists of his day, who denied the validity of Catholic baptism on account of the idolatry and corruption of the papal Church. "Against these follies we shall be sufficiently fortified, if we consider that we are baptized not in the name of any man, but in the name of the Father, the Son, and the Holy Spirit, and consequently that it is not the

baptism of man, but of God, by whomsoever administered."
The papal priests "did not baptize us into the fellowship of
their own ignorance or sacrilege, but into the faith of Jesus
Christ, because they invoked, not their own name, but the
name of God, and baptized in no name but his. As it was
the baptism of God, it certainly contained the promise of
remission of sins, mortification of the flesh, spiritual vivifica-
tion, and participation of Christ. Thus it was no injury to
the Jews to have been circumcised by impure and apostate
priests; nor was the sign on that account useless, so as to
render it necessary to be repeated, but it was sufficient
to recur to the genuine original. . . . When Hezekiah and
Josiah assembled together out of all Israel, those who had
revolted from God, they did not call any of them to a second
circumcision."

He argues against the Anabaptists from the fact also, that
the apostles who had received the baptism of John, were not
rebaptized. "And among us, what rivers would be sufficient
for the repetition of ablutions as numerous as the errors
which are daily corrected among us by the mercy of the
Lord." [1]

---

[1] These passages (IV. ch. XV. §§ 16 and 17) furnish arguments against the
decision of the Old-School-Presbyterian General Assembly held at Cincinnati,
1845, which, with an overwhelming majority, declared Roman Catholic baptism to be invalid, and thus virtually unchurched and unbaptized the greater
part of Christendom, including the founders of the Protestant churches, who
were baptized in the Roman communion, as the apostles were circumcised in
the synagogue. But Drs. Charles Hodge of Princeton and Henry B. Smith
of New York — the two leading Presbyterian divines of that day — vigorously
protested against that anomalous decision; and when, in the United Assembly,
held likewise at Cincinnati, in the year 1885, an attempt was made to
re-enact that decision, it failed by a very large majority. Calvin did not
unchurch the Church of Rome. "While we refuse," he says (*Inst.* IV. ch.
II. § 12), "to allow to the papists the [exclusive] title of the Church, without
any qualification or restriction, we do not deny that there are churches among
them. . . . I affirm that there are churches, in as much as God has wonderfully preserved among them a remnant of his people, and as there still
remain some marks of the Church, especially those, the efficacy of which
neither the craft of the devil, nor the malice of men can ever destroy."

IV. He pleads for the simplicity of the ordinance against the adventitious medley of incantation, wax-taper, spittle, salt, and "other fooleries," which from an early age were publicly introduced. "Such theatrical pomps dazzle the eye and stupify the minds of the ignorant." The simple ceremony as instituted by Christ, accompanied by a confession of faith, prayers, and thanksgivings, shines with the greater lustre, unencumbered with extraneous corruptions. He disapproves the ancient custom of baptism by laymen in cases of danger of death. God can regenerate a child without baptism.

V. The mode of baptism was not a subject of controversy at that time. Calvin recognized the force of the philological and historical argument in favor of immersion, but regarded pouring and sprinkling as equally valid, and left room for Christian liberty according to the custom in different countries.[1] Immersion was then still the prevailing mode in England, and continued till the reign of Elizabeth, who was herself baptized by immersion.

VI. But while meeting the Baptists half-way on the question of the mode, he strenuously defends pædobaptism, and devotes a whole chapter to it.[2] He urges, as arguments, circumcision, which was a type of baptism; the nature of the covenant, which comprehends the offspring of pious parents; Christ's treatment of children, as belonging to the kingdom of heaven, and therefore entitled to the sign and seal of membership; the word of Peter addressed to the converts on the day of Pentecost, who were accustomed to infant circumcision, that "the promise is to you and your children" (Acts 2 : 39); Paul's declaration that the children are sanc-

---

[1] IV. ch. XV. 19: " *Cæterum mergaturne totus qui tingitur, idque ter an semel, an infusa tantum aqua aspergatur, minimum refert : sed id pro regionum diversitate ecclesiis liberum esse debet. Quanquam et ipsum* BAPTIZANDI *verbum* MERGERE *significat, et mergendi ritum veteri ecclesiæ observatum fuisse constat.*" See above, p. 373, note. Luther held substantially the same view, with a stronger leaning to immersion or dipping, which he prescribes in his *Taufbüchlein*, 1523. See vol. VI. 218 and 607 sq. [2] Ch. XVI. 1–32.

tified by their parents (1 Cor. 7 : 14), etc. He refutes at
length the objections of the Anabaptists, with special reference to Servetus, who agreed with them on that point.

He assigns to infant baptism a double benefit: it ratifies to
pious parents the promise of God's mercy to their children,
and increases their sense of responsibility as to their education; it engrafts the children into the body of the Church,
and afterwards acts as a powerful stimulus upon them to be
true to the baptismal vow.

§ 117. *The Lord's Supper.   The Consensus of Zürich.*

I. *Inst.* IV. chs. XVII. and XVIII.   Comp. the first ed., cap. IV., in *Opera*,
I. 118 sqq. — *Petit traicté de la sainte cène de nostre Seigneur Jésus-Christ.
Auquel est demontré la vraye institution, profit et utilité d'icelle*, Genève, 1541,
1542, 1549.   *Opera*, V. 429–460.   Latin version by Nicholas des Gallars:
*Libellus de Cœna Domini, a Ioanne Calvino pridem Gallica lingua scriptus,
nunc vero in Latinum sermonem conversus*, Gen., 1545.   Also translated into
English.   Remarkably moderate. — The two catechisms of Calvin. —
*Consensio mutua in re sacramentaria Tigurinæ Ecclesiæ et D. Calvini minis-
tri Genevensis Ecclesiæ jam nunc ab ipsis authoribus edita* (usually called
Consensus Tigurinus), simultaneously published at Geneva and Zürich,
1551; French ed. *L'accord passé*, etc., Gen., 1551.   In *Opera*, VII. 689–748.
The Latin text also in Niemeyer's *Collectio Conf.*, pp. 191–217.   A German
translation (*Die Züricher Uebereinkunft*) in Bickel's *Bekenntnissschriften
der evang. reform. Kirche*, pp. 173–181.   Comp. the correspondence of
Calvin with Bullinger, Farel, etc., concerning the Consensus. — Calvin's
polemical writings against *Joachim Westphal*, namely, *Defensio sanæ et
orthodoxæ doctrinæ de sacramentis*, Geneva, 1554, Zürich, 1555; *Secunda
Defensio . . . contra Westphali calumnias*, Gen., 1556; and *Ultima Admonitio ad Westphalum*, Gen., 1557.   In *Opera*, IX. 1–120, 137–252.   Lastly,
his book against *Tilemann Hesshus* (Hesshusen), *Dilucida Explicatio sanæ
doctrinæ de vera participatione carnis et sanguinis Christi in sacra Cœna, ad
discutiendas Heshusii nebulas*, Gen., 1561.   In *Opera*, IX. 457–524.   (In the
Amsterdam ed., Tom. IX. 648–723.)   Klebiz of Heidelberg, Beza, and
Pierre Boquin also took part in the controversy with Hesshus.

II. For a comparative statement of the eucharistic views of Luther, Zwingli,
and Calvin, see this *History*, vol. VI. 669–682; and *Creeds of Christendom*,
I. 455 sqq.; 471 sqq.   Calvin's doctrine has been fully set forth by
EBRARD in his *Dogma v. heil. Abendmahl*, II. 402–525, and by NEVIN in
his *Mystical Presence*, Philad., 1846, pp. 54–67; and in the "Mercersburg
Review" for September, 1850, pp. 421–548 (against Dr. Hodge in the
"Princeton Review" for 1848).   Comp. also §§ 132–134 below; HENRY,
P. I. ch. XIII.; and STÄHELIN, II. 189 sqq.

In the eucharistic controversy, which raged with such fury in the age of the Reformation, and was the chief cause of separation in its ranks, Calvin consistently occupied from the beginning to the end the position of a mediator and peacemaker between the Lutherans and Zwinglians, between Wittenberg and Zürich.

The way for a middle theory was prepared by the Tetrapolitan or Swabian Confession, drawn up by Martin Bucer, a born compromiser, during the Diet of Augsburg, 1530,[1] and by the Wittenberg Concordia, 1536, which for a while satisfied the Lutherans, but was justly rejected by the Swiss.

Calvin published his theory in its essential features in the first edition of the *Institutes* (1536), more fully in the second edition (1539), then in a special tract written at Strassburg. He defended it in various publications, and adhered to it with his usual firmness. It was accepted by the Reformed Churches, and never rejected by Luther; on the contrary, he is reported to have spoken highly of Calvin's tract, *De Cœna Domini*, when he got hold of a Latin copy in 1545, a year before his death.[2]

Calvin approached the subject with a strong sense of the mystery of the vital union of Christ with the believer, which is celebrated in the eucharist. "I exhort my readers," he says, in the last edition of his *Institutes*, " to rise much higher than I am able to conduct them; for as to myself, whenever I handle this subject, after having endeavored to say everything, I am conscious of having said but very little in comparison with its excellence. And though the conceptions of the mind can far exceed the expressions of the tongue; yet, with the magnitude of the subject, the mind itself is

[1] Ch. XVIII. See vol. VI. 720.

[2] See vol. VI. 660. But Luther never gave up his dislike of Zwingli; and in one of his last letters, in which he describes himself as " *infelicissimus omnium hominum,*" he wrote: " Blessed is the man that walketh not in the counsel of the *Sacramentarians*, nor standeth in the way of the *Zwinglians*, nor sitteth in the seat of the *Zürichers.*" De Wette, V. 778.

oppressed and overwhelmed. Nothing remains for me, therefore, but to break forth in admiration of that mystery, which
the mind is unable clearly to understand, or the tongue to
express." [1]

He aimed to combine the spiritualism of Zwingli with the
realism of Luther, and to avoid the errors of both. And he
succeeded as well as the case will admit. He agreed with
Zwingli in the figurative interpretation of the words of institution, which is now approved by the best Protestant exegetes, and rejected the idea of a corporal presence and oral
participation in the way of transubstantiation or consubstantiation, which implies either a miracle or an omnipresence of
the body of Christ. But he was not satisfied with a purely
commemorative or symbolical theory, and laid the chief
stress on the positive side of an actual communion with the
ever-living Christ. He expressed in private letters the opinion that Zwingli had been so much absorbed with overturning the superstition of a carnal presence that he denied or
obscured the true efficacy of the sacrament.[2] He acknowledged the mystery of the real presence and real participation,

[1] *Inst.* IV. ch. XVII. 7.

[2] He wrote from Strassburg, May 19, 1539, to André Zébédée, a minister
at Orbe: "*Nihil fuisse asperitatis in Zwinglii doctrina, tibi minime concedo.
Siquidem videre promptum est, ut nimium occupatus in evertenda carnalis præsentiæ superstitione, veram communicationis vim ut simul disjecerit, aut certe obscura-
rit.*" Herminjard, V. 318. In the same letter he characterizes Zwingli's
view as *falsa et perniciosa.* In a letter to Farel, Feb. 27, 1540, he disapproves
Zébédée's extravagant eulogy of Zwingli, and expresses his preference for
Luther: "*Nam si inter se comparantur, scis ipse, quanto intervallo Lutherus
excellat.*" But he disowns any intention to dishonor his memory. Herminjard, V. 191. In a letter to Richard du Bois, from Strassburg, 1540 (*ibid.*
VI. 425), he says, with evident allusion to Zwingli and Œcolampadius, that he
never liked the view of those who in "*evertenda localis præsentiæ superstitione
nimis occupati, veræ præsentiæ virtutem vel elevabant extenuando, vel subticendo ex
hominum memoria quodammodo delebant. Sed est aliquid medium,*" etc. In a
letter to Viret (Sept. 3, 1542, in *Opera*, XI. 438) he remarks that he never
read all of Zwingli's works, and hoped that towards the end of his life
he retracted and corrected what first had escaped him carelessly, but "I
remember, in his earlier writings how profane his doctrine of the sacraments
is (*quam profana sit ejus de sacramentis doctrina*)."

but understood them spiritually and dynamically. He confined the participation of the body and blood of Christ to believers, since faith is the only means of communion with Christ; while Luther extended it to all communicants, only with opposite effects.

The following is a brief summary of his view from the last edition of the *Institutes* (1559) : —

After receiving us into his family by baptism, God undertakes to sustain and to nourish us as long as we live, and gives us a pledge of his gracious intention in the sacrament of the holy communion. This is a spiritual banquet, in which Christ testifies himself to be the bread of life, to feed our souls for a true and blessed immortality. The signs of bread and wine represent to us the invisible nourishment which we receive from the body and blood of Christ. They are exhibited in a figure and image, adapted to our feeble capacity, and rendered certain by visible tokens and pledges, which the dullest minds can understand. This mystical benediction, then, is designed to assure us that the body of the Lord was once offered as a sacrifice for us upon which we may now feed, and that his blood was once shed for us and is our perpetual drink. " His flesh is true meat, and his blood is true drink " (John 6 : 55). " We are members of his body, of his flesh, and of his bones " (Eph. 5 : 30). " This is a great mystery " (ver. 32), which can be admired rather than expressed. Our souls are fed by the flesh and blood of Christ, just as our corporal life is preserved and sustained by bread and wine. Otherwise there would be no propriety in the analogy of the sign. The breaking of the bread is indeed symbolical, yet significant; for God is not a deceiver who sets before us an empty sign. The symbol of the body assures us of the donation of the invisible substance, so that in receiving the sign we receive the thing itself. The thing signified is exhibited and offered to all who come to that spiritual banquet, but it is advantageously enjoyed only by those who receive it with true faith and gratitude.

Calvin lays great stress on the supernatural agency of the Holy Spirit in the communion. This was ignored by Luther and Zwingli. The Spirit raises our hearts from earth to heaven, as he does in every act of devotion (*sursum corda*), and he brings down the life-giving power of the exalted Redeemer in heaven, and thus unites what is, according to our imperfect notions, separated by local distance.[1] The medium of communication is faith. Calvin might have sustained his view by the old liturgies of the Oriental Church, which have a special prayer invoking the Holy Spirit at the consecration of the eucharistic elements.[2]

He quotes several passages from Augustin in favor of the spiritual real presence. Ratramnus in the ninth, and Berengar in the eleventh, century had likewise appealed to Augustin against the advocates of a carnal presence and participation.[3]

When Luther reopened the eucharistic controversy by a fierce attack upon the Zwinglians (1545), who defended their martyred Reformer in a sharp reply, Calvin was displeased with both parties, and labored to bring about a reconciliation.[4] He corresponded with Bullinger (the Melanchthon of the Swiss Church), and, on his invitation, he went to Zürich with Farel (May, 1549). The delicate negotiations were carried on by both parties with admirable frankness, moderation, wisdom, and patience. The result was the "Consensus Tigurinus," in which Calvin states his doctrine as nearly as possible in agreement with Zwingli. This document was published in 1551, and adopted by all the Reformed Cantons, except Bern, which cherished a strong dislike to Calvin's rigorism. It was also favorably received in France, England, and in parts of Germany. Melanchthon declared

---

[1] See the passages quoted in vol. VI. 679, note 1.

[2] The ἐπίκλησις πνεύματος ἁγίου. The Latin liturgies ascribe the power of consecration to Christ's words of institution. See vol. III. 513.

[3] See vol. IV. 549 sqq. and 564 sqq. Calvin refers to the Berengar controversy.

[4] See his letter to Bullinger, quoted in vol. VI. 661.

to Lavater (Bullinger's son-in-law) that he then for the first time understood the Swiss, and would never again oppose them; but he struck out the clause of the "Consensus" which confined the efficacy of the sacrament to the elect.

But while the "Consensus" brought peace to the Swiss Churches, and satisfied the Melanchthonians, it was assailed by Westphal and Hesshus, who out-luthered Luther in zeal and violence, and disturbed the last years of Melanchthon and Calvin. We shall discuss this controversy in the next chapter.

The Calvinistic theory of the Eucharist passed into all the Reformed Confessions, and is very strongly stated in the Heidelberg Catechism (1563), the chief symbol of the German and Dutch Reformed Churches.[1] In practice, however, it has, among Presbyterians, Congregationalists, and Baptists, largely given way to the Zwinglian view, which is more plain and intelligible, but ignores the mystical element in the holy communion.

[1] Questions 76, 78, 79. Comp. Westminster Confession, ch. XXIX. 7, and Westminster Larger Catechism, qu. 170.

CHAPTER XV.

THEOLOGICAL CONTROVERSIES.

§ 118. *Calvin as a Controversialist.*

CALVIN was involved in several controversies, chiefly on account of his doctrine of predestination. He displayed a decided superiority over all his opponents, as a scholar and a reasoner. He was never at a loss for an argument. He had also the dangerous gift of wit, irony, and sarcasm, but not the more desirable gift of harmless humor, which sweetens the bitterness of controversy, and lightens the burden of daily toil. Like David, in the imprecatory Psalms, he looked upon the enemies of his doctrine as enemies of God. "Even a dog barks," he wrote to the queen of Navarre, "when his master is attacked; how could I be silent when the honor of my Lord is assailed?"[1] He treated his opponents — Pighius, Bolsec, Castellio, and Servetus — with sovereign contempt, and called them "*nebulones,*[2] *nugatores, canes, porci, bestiæ.* Such epithets are like weeds in the garden of his chaste and elegant style. But they were freely used by the ancient fathers, with the exception of Chrysostom and Augustin, in dealing with heretics, and occur even

[1] This characteristic expression he uses repeatedly; for instance, in the work on the Necessity of Reforming the Church, in *Opera,* VI. 503 : " *Canis, si quam suo domino violentiam inferri viderit, protinus latrabit : nos tot sacrilegiis violari sacrum Dei nomen taciti aspiceremus ? Et ubi esset illud : Opprobria exprobantium tibi ceciderunt super me* (Ps. 69 : 9)? " And, again in the same book (fol. 507), with the addition, that a dog would rather risk his life than be silent.

[2] In applying the epithet *nebulo* to Castellio, he translates it by the French *un brouillon,* which means a confused and turbulent fellow (not a scamp). Schweizer renders it *Wirrkopf* (I. 212).

in the Scriptures, but impersonally.[1] His age saw nothing improper in them. Beza says that "no expression unworthy of a good man ever fell from the lips of Calvin." The taste of the sixteenth century differed widely from that of the nineteenth. The polemical writings of Protestants and Romanists alike abound in the most violent personalities and coarse abuse. Luther wielded the club of Hercules against Tetzel, Eck, Emser, Cochlæus, Henry VIII., Duke Henry of Brunswick, and the Sacramentarians. Yet there were honorable exceptions even then, as Melanchthon and Bullinger. A fiery temper is a propelling force in history; nothing great can be done without enthusiasm; moral indignation against wrong is inseparable from devotion to what is right; hatred is the negative side of love. But temper must be controlled by reason, and truth should be spoken in love, "with malice to none, with charity for all." Opprobrious and abusive terms always hurt a good cause; self-restraint and moderation strengthen it. Understatement commands assent; overstatement provokes opposition.

§ 119. *Calvin and Pighius.*

I. ALBERTUS PIGHIUS: *De libero hominis arbitrio et divina gratia libri decem.* Coloniæ, 1542, mense Augusto. Dedicated to Cardinal Sadolet. He wrote also *Assertio hierarchiæ ecclesiasticæ*, a complete defence of the Roman Church, dedicated to Pope Paul III., 1538.

CALVIN: *Defensio sanæ et orthodoxæ doctrinæ de servitute et liberatione humani arbitrii adversus calumnias Alberti Pighii Campensis.* With a preface to Melanchthon. Geneva, 1543. In *Opera*, VI. 225–404. (Amsterdam ed. t. VIII. 116 sqq.) The same in French, Geneva, 1560.

II. BAYLE: Art. *Pighius*, in his "Dict. hist." — HENRY, II. 285 sqq. (English trans. I. 492 sqq.). — DYER (1850), pp. 158–165. — SCHWEIZER: *Die protest. Centraldogmen* (1854), I. 180–200. Very satisfactory. — WERNER (R. Cath.): *Geschichte der apologetischen und polemischen Literatur der christl. Theologie* (1865), IV. 272 sq. and 298. Superficial. — STÄHELIN, II. 281–287. — Prolegomena to Calvin's *Opera*, VI. pp. XXIII.–XXV.

As Erasmus had attacked Luther's doctrine on the slavery of the human will, and provoked Luther's crushing reply,

---

[1] Isa. 56 : 10; Matt. 7 : 6; Phil. 3 : 2; Rev. 22 : 15.

Albert Pighius attacked Luther and chiefly Calvin on the same vulnerable point.

Pighius (or Pigghe) of Campen in Holland, educated at Louvain and Cologne, and a pupil of Pope Adrian VI., whom he followed to Rome, was a learned and eloquent divine and deputed on various missions by Clement VII. and Paul III. He may have seen Calvin at the Colloquies in Worms and Ratisbon. He died as canon and archdeacon of Utrecht, Dec. 26, 1542, a few months after the publication of his book against Calvin and the other Reformers. Beza calls him the first sophist of the age, who, by gaining a victory over Calvin, hoped to attain to a cardinal's hat. But it is wrong to judge of motives without evidence. His retirement to Utrecht could not promote such ambition.[1]

Pighius represents the dogma of the slavery of the human will, and of the absolute necessity of all that happens, as the cardinal error of the Reformation, and charges it with leading to complete moral indifference. He wrote ten books against it. In the first six books, he defends the doctrine of free-will; in the last four books, he discusses divine grace, foreknowledge, predestination, and providence, and, last, the Scripture passages on these subjects. He teaches the Semi-Pelagian theory with some Pelagian features, and declares that "our works are meritorious before God." After the Synod of Trent had more carefully guarded the doctrine of justification against Semi-Pelagianism, the Spanish Inquisition placed his book, *De libero arbitrio*, and his tract, *De peccato originali*, on the Index, and Cardinal Bona recommended caution in reading them, since he did not always present the reliable

---

[1] Henry says (II. 289) that Pighius was converted by Calvin's argument, but he died (December, 1542) before Calvin's reply was published (February, 1543). The story rests on the authority of Crakanthorpe, who asserts, in his *Defensio Ecclesiæ Anglicanæ*, that Pighius by reading Calvin's *Institutes* for the purpose of refuting them, became himself a Calvinist in one of the chief articles of faith (he does not say which). The story has been long ago rejected by Gerdesius, *Hist. Evang. Renovati*, III. § 50. Comp. Dyer, p. 160.

orthodox doctrine. Pighius was not ashamed to copy, without acknowledgment, whole pages from Calvin's *Institutes*, where it suited his purpose. Calvin calls him a plagiarist, and says, " With what right he publishes such sections as his own, I cannot see, unless he claims, as enemy, the privilege of plunder."

The arguments of Pighius against the doctrine of the slavery of the human will are these: It contradicts common sense; it is inconsistent with the admitted freedom of will in civil and secular matters; it destroys all morality and discipline, turns men into animals and monsters, makes God the author of sin, and perverts his justice into cruelty, and his wisdom into folly. He derives these heresies from the ancient Gnostics and Simon Magus, except that Luther surpassed them all in impiety.

Calvin's answer was written in about two months, and amidst many interruptions. He felt the weight of the objections, but he always marched up to the cannon's mouth. He admits, incidentally, that Luther often used hyperbolical expressions in order to rouse attention. He also allows the *liberum arbitrium* in the sense that man acts voluntarily and of his inner impulse.[1] But he denies that man, without the assistance of the Holy Spirit, has the power to choose what is spiritually good, and quotes Rom. 6:17; 7:14, 23. "Man has *arbitrium spontaneum*, so that he willingly and by choice does evil, without compulsion from without, and, therefore, he incurs guilt. But, owing to native depravity, his will is so given to sin that it always chooses evil. Hence spontaneity and enslavement may exist together. The *voluntas* is *spontanea*, but not *libera;* it is not *coacta*, yet *serva*." This is an anticipation of the artificial distinction between natural ability and moral inability — a distinction which is practically useless. As regards the teaching of the early Church, he could not deny that the Fathers, especially Origen, exalt the free-

---

[1] *Sponte et libenter, interiore electionis motu.*

dom of the will; but he could claim Augustin in his later writings, in which he retracted his earlier advocacy of freedom. The objection that the slavery of the will nullifies the exhortations to repent, would be valid, if God did not make them effective by his Spirit.

The reply of Calvin to Pighius is more cautious and guarded than Luther's reply to Erasmus, and more churchly than Zwingli's tract on Providence. In defending himself, he defended what was then the common Protestant doctrine, in opposition to the then prevailing Pelagianism in the Roman Church. It had a good effect upon the Council of Trent, which distinctly disowned the Pelagian and Semi-Pelagian heresy.[1]

Calvin dedicated his book to Melanchthon, as a friend who had agreed with him and had advised him to write against Pighius, if he should attack the Reformation. But Melanchthon, who had taught the same doctrine, was at that time undergoing a change in his views on the freedom of the will, chiefly because he felt that the denial of it would make God the author of sin, and destroy man's moral accountability.[2] He was as competent to appreciate the logical argument in favor of necessity, but he was more open to the force of ethical and practical considerations. In his reply to Calvin's dedication, May 11, 1543, he acknowledged the compliment paid to him, but modestly and delicately intimated his dissent and his desire that Protestants should unite in the defence of those more important doctrines, which commended themselves by their simplicity and practical usefulness. "I wish," he says, "you would transfer your eloquence to the adorning of these momentous subjects, by which our friends would be strengthened, our enemies terrified, and the weak encouraged; for who in these days possesses a more forcible

---

[1] See the remarks of Schweizer on the value of this controversy, *l.c.*, I. 198.

[2] The successive changes are marked in the editions of his *Loci Theologici*, 1525, 1535, 1544, 1548. See above, p. 548.

or splendid style of disputation? . . . I do not write this letter to dictate to you who are so learned a man, and so well versed in all the exercises of piety. I am persuaded, indeed, that it agrees with your sentiments, though less subtle and more adapted for use." [1]

Calvin intended to answer the second part of the work of Pighius, but as he learned that he had died shortly before, he did not wish "to insult a dead dog" (!), and applied himself "to other pursuits." [2] But nine years afterwards he virtually answered it in the *Consensus Genevensis* (1552), which may be considered as the second part of his refutation of Pighius, although it was occasioned by the controversy with Bolsec.

§ 120. *The Anti-Papal Writings. Criticism of the Council of Trent. 1547.*

I. Most of Calvin's anti-papal writings are printed in *Opera*, Tom. VI. (In the Amsterdam ed., Tom. IX. 37–90; 99–335 and 409–485.) An English translation in vols. I. and III. of *Tracts relating to the Reformation by John Calvin, translated from the original Latin by Henry Beveridge, Esq.* Edinburgh (Calvin Translation Society), 1844 and 1851.

II. *Acta Synodi Tridentinæ cum antidoto.* In *Opera*, VII. 365–506. Comp. Schweizer, I. 239–249; Dyer, p. 229 sq.; Stähelin, II. 255 sqq.

Calvin's anti-papal writings are numerous. Among them his Answer to Cardinal Sadolet (1540), and his Plea for the Necessity of the Reformation, addressed to Emperor Charles V.

---

[1] " *Et quidem scio, hæc cum tuis congruere, sed sunt* παχύτερα, *et ad usum accommodata.*" He also refers to Basil's saying: μόνον θέλησον, καὶ θεὸς προαπαντᾷ. Calvin's *Opera*, XI. 539–542. Melanchthon's letters are usually interspersed with Greek words and sentences.

[2] *Cons. Genev.:* "*Paulo post librum editum, moritur Pighius. Ergo ne cani mortuo insultarem, ad alias lucubrationes me converti.*" He characterizes Pighius as a "*homo phrenetica plane audacia præditus,*" because he attempted to establish the freedom of man, and to overthrow the secret counsel of God, by which he elects some to salvation and others to eternal ruin (*alios æterno exitio destinat*). It is no excuse for Calvin's insulting language on a dead enemy that St. Jerome said of his former friend Rufinus: "The scorpion now lies under ground!" Among polemic theologians charity is a great rarity.

(1544), deserve the first place. They are superior in ability and force to any similar works of the sixteenth century. They have been sufficiently noticed in previous sections.[1] I will only add the manly conclusion of the Plea to the Emperor: —

"But be the issue what it may, we will never repent of having begun, and of having proceeded thus far. The Holy Spirit is a faithful and unerring witness to our doctrine. We know, I say, that it is the eternal truth of God that we preach. We are, indeed, desirous, as we ought to be, that our ministry may prove salutary to the world; but to give it this effect belongs to God, not to us. If, to punish, partly the ingratitude, and partly the stubbornness of those to whom we desire to do good, success must prove desperate, and all things go to worse, I will say what it befits a Christian man to say, and what all who are true to this holy profession will subscribe: We will die, but in death even be conquerors, not only because through it we shall have a sure passage to a better life, but because we know that our blood will be as seed to propagate the Divine truth, which men now despise."

Next to these books in importance is his criticism of the Council of Trent, published in November, 1547.

The Council of Trent, which was to heal the divisions of Western Christendom, convened after long delay, Dec. 13, 1545; then adjourned, convened again, and finally closed, Dec. 4, 1563, a few months before Calvin's death. In the fourth, fifth, and sixth sessions (1546), it settled the burning questions of the rule of faith, original sin, and justification, in favor of the present Roman system and against the views of the Reformers. The Council avoided the ill-disguised Pelagianism and Semi-Pelagianism of Eck, Pighius, and other early champions of Rome, and worded its decrees with great caution and circumspection; but it decidedly condemned the Protestant doctrines of the supremacy of the Bible, the slavery of the natural will, and justification by faith alone.

Calvin was the first to take up the pen against these decisions. He subjected them to a searching criticism. He admits, in the introduction, that a Council might be of great use and restore the peace of Christendom, provided it be

[1] See pp. 398–413; 452–466.

truly œcumenical, impartial, and free. But he denies that
the Council of Trent had these essential characteristics.
The Greek and the Evangelical Churches were not represented at all. It was a purely Roman Council, and under
the control of the pope, who was himself the chief offender,
and far more disposed to perpetuate abuses than to abolish
them. The members, only about forty, mostly Italians, were
not distinguished for learning or piety, but were a set of wran-
gling monks and canonists and minions of the pope. They
gave merely a nod of assent to the living oracle of the
Vatican, and then issued the decrees as responses of the Holy
Spirit. "As soon as a decree is framed," he says, "couriers
flee off to Rome, and beg pardon and peace at the feet of
their idol. The holy father hands over what the couriers
have brought to his private advisers for examination. They
curtail, add, and change as they please. The couriers return,
and a *sederunt* is appointed. The notary reads over what
no one dares to disapprove, and the asses shake their ears in
assent. Behold the oracle which imposes religious obligations
on the whole world. . . . The proclamation of the Council
is entitled to no more weight than the cry of an auctioneer."

Calvin dissects the decrees with his usual polemic skill.
He first states them in the words of the Council, and then
gives the antidote. He exposes the errors of the Vulgate,
which the Council put on a par with the original Hebrew
and Greek originals, and defends the supremacy of the Scriptures and the doctrine of justification by faith.

He wrote this work in two or three months, under constant
interruption, while Chemnitz took ten years to complete his.
He submitted the manuscript to Farel, who was delighted
with it. He published also a French edition in a more popular form.

Cochlæus prepared, with much personal bitterness, a refutation of Calvin (1548), and was answered by Des Gallars,[1]

[1] *Apologia Calvini contra Cochlæum.*

and Beza, who numbers Cochlæus among the monsters of the animal kingdom.[1]

After the close of the Council of Trent, Martin Chemnitz, the leading divine of the Lutheran Church after the death of Melanchthon, wrote his more elaborate *Examen Concilii Tridentini* (1565–1573; second ed. 1585), which was for a long time a standard work in the Roman controversy.

§ 121. *Against the German Interim.* 1549.

Interim Adultero-Germanum: Cui adjecta est vera Christianæ pacificationis et ecclesiæ reformandæ ratio, per JOANNEM CALVINUM. *Cavete a fermento Pharisæorum,* 1549. *Opera,* VII. 541–674. — It was reprinted in Germany, and translated into French (1549) and Italian (1561). See HENRY, II. 369 sqq.; III. Beilage, 211 sq.; DYER, 232 sq.

On the Interim, comp. the German Histories of RANKE (V. 25 sqq.) and JANSSEN (III. 625 sqq.), and the monograph of LUDWIG PASTOR (Rom. Cath.): *Die kirchlichen Reunionsbestrebungen während der Regierung Karls V.* Freiburg, 1879, pp. 357 sqq.

Calvin's tract on the false German Interim is closely connected with his criticism of the Council of Trent. After defeating the Smalkaldian League, the Emperor imposed on the Protestants in Germany a compromise confession of faith to be used till the final decision of the General Council. It was drawn up by two Roman Catholic bishops, Pflug (an Erasmian) and Helding, with the aid of John Agricola, the chaplain of Elector Joachim II. of Brandenburg. Agricola was a vain, ambitious, and unreliable man, who had once been a secretary and table companion of Luther, but fell out with him and Melanchthon in the Antinomian controversy. He was suspected of having been bribed by the Catholics.[2]

The agreement was laid before the Diet of Augsburg, and

---

[1] *Brevis et utilis zoographia Joh. Cochlæi,* 1549. Reprinted in Baum's *Beza,* I. 357–363.

[2] The Emperor presented him with fifty crowns; King Ferdinand, with five hundred thaler. Janssen, III. 625. Comp. G. Kawerau (a specialist in the history of the Lutheran Reformation), *Johann Agricola von Eisleben,* Berlin, 1881.

is called the AUGSBURG INTERIM. It was proclaimed, with an earnest exhortation, by the Emperor, May 15, 1548. It comprehended the whole Roman Catholic system of doctrine and discipline, but in a mild and conciliatory form, and without an express condemnation of the Protestant views. The doctrine of justification was stated in substantial agreement with that of the Council of Trent. The seven sacraments, transubstantiation, the mass, the invocation of the saints, the authority of the pope, and all the important ceremonies, were to be retained. The only concession made to the Protestants was the use of the cup by the laity in the holy communion, and the permission for married priests to retain their wives. The arrangement suited the views of the Emperor, who, as Ranke remarks, wished to uphold the Catholic hierarchy as the basis of his power, and yet to make it possible for Protestants to be reconciled to him. It is very evident that the adoption of such a confession was a virtual surrender of the cause of the Reformation and would have ended in a triumph of the papacy.

The Interim was received with great indignation by the Protestants, and was rejected in Hesse, ducal Saxony, and the Northern cities, especially in Madgeburg, which became the headquarters of the irreconcilable Lutherans under the lead of Flacius. In Southern Germany it was enforced with great rigor by Spanish soldiers. More than four hundred pastors in Swabia and on the Rhine were expelled from their benefices for refusing the Interim, and wandered about with their families in poverty and misery. Among them was Brenz, the Reformer of Würtemburg, who fled to Basel, where he received a consolitary letter from Calvin (Nov. 5, 1548). Martin Bucer, with all his zeal for Christian union, was unwilling to make a compromise at the expense of his conscience, and fled from Strassburg to England, where he was appointed professor of divinity in the University of Cambridge.

It was forbidden under pain of death to write against the Interim. Nevertheless, over thirty attacks appeared from the "Chancellery of God" at Magdeburg. Bullinger and Calvin wrote against it.

Calvin published the imperial proclamation and the text of the Interim in full, and then gave his reasons why it could never bring peace to the Church. He begins with a quotation from Hilary in the Arian controversy: "Specious indeed is the name of peace, and fair the idea of unity; but who doubts that the only peace of the Church is that which is of Christ?" This is the key-note of his own exposition on the true method of the pacification of Christendom.

Elector Maurice of Saxony, who stood between two fires, — his Lutheran subjects and the Emperor, — modified the Augsburg Interim, with the aid of Melanchthon and the other theologians of Wittenberg, and substituted for it the LEIPZIG INTERIM, Dec. 22, 1548. In this document the chief articles of faith are more cautiously worded so as to admit of an evangelical interpretation, but the Roman ceremonies are retained, as *adiaphora*, or things indifferent, which do not compromise the conscience nor endanger salvation. It gave rise to the Adiaphoristic Controversy between the strict and the moderate Lutherans. Melanchthon was placed in a most trying position in the midst of the contest. In the sincere wish to save Protestantism from utter overthrow and Saxony from invasion and desolation by imperial troops, he yielded to the pressure of the courtiers and accepted the Leipzig Interim in the hope of better times. For this conduct he was severely attacked by Flacius, his former pupil, and denounced as a traitor. When Calvin heard the news, he wrote an earnest letter of fraternal rebuke to Melanchthon, and reminded him of Paul's unyielding firmness at the Synod of Jerusalem on the question of circumcision.[1]

---

[1] Letter of July 18, 1550, quoted in § 90, pp. 395 sq. Dyer decidedly defends Melanchthon in this adiaphoristic controversy, and makes the follow-

Protestantism in Germany was brought to the brink of ruin, but was delivered from it by the treason of the Elector Maurice. This shrewd, selfish politician and master in the art of dissimulation, had first betrayed the Protestants, by aiding the Emperor in the defeat of the Smalkaldian League, whereby he gained the electorate; and then he rose in rebellion against the Emperor and drove him and the Fathers of Trent out of Tyrol (1551). He died in 1553 of a deadly wound which he received in a victorious battle against his old friend Albrecht of Brandenburg.[1]

The final result of the defeat of the Emperor was the Augsburg Treaty of Peace, 1555, which for the first time gave to the Lutherans a legal status in the empire, though with certain restrictions. This closes the period of the Lutheran Reformation.

§ 122. *Against the Worship of Relics.* 1543.

Advertissement tres-utile du grand proffit qui reviendroit à la Chrestienté, s'il se faisoit inventoire de tous les corps sainctz et reliques, qui sont tant en Italie qu'en France Allemaigne, Hespaigne, et autres Royaumes et Pays. Gen., 1543, 1544, 1551, 1563, 1579, 1599. Reprinted in *Opera*, VI. 405–452. A Latin edition by Nicolaus Gallasius (des Gallars) was published at Geneva, 1548. It appeared also in English (*A very profitable treatise*, etc.), London, 1561, and in two German translations (by Jakob Eysenberg of Wittenberg, 1557, etc., and by J. Fischart, 1584, or 1583, under the title *Der heilig Brotkorb der h. Römischen Reliquien*). See Henry, II. 333 and III., Appendix, 204–206. A new English translation by Beveridge in *Calvin's Tracts relating to the Reformation*, Edinb., 1844, pp. 289–341.

In the same year in which Calvin answered Pighius, he published a French tract on Relics, which was repeatedly

---

ing remark (p. 240) : " What a prospect do these squabbles hold out for the future union of the Protestant Church! A silly and scandalous, we had almost said, a childish, quarrel about a surplice and a few minor ceremonies divides the Protestants into hostile factions at the moment of their most eminent peril! With such feelings, how should they hope in quieter times to arrange those more serious questions, which turned on really important points of doctrine ? "

[1] For a description of the character of Moritz, see Ranke, *Deutsche Geschichte im Zeitalter der Reformation*, vol. V. 160 sqq. (6th ed. 1881).

printed and translated. It was the most popular and effective of his anti-papal writings. He indulged here very freely in his power of ridicule and sarcasm, which reminds one almost of Voltaire, but the spirit is altogether different. He begins with the following judicious remarks, which best characterize the book : —

"Augustin, in his work, entitled *On the Labor of Monks*, complaining of certain itinerant impostors, who, as early as his day, plied a vile and sordid traffic, by carrying the relics of martyrs about from place to place, adds, ' If, indeed, they are relics of martyrs.' By this expression he intimates the prevalence, even in his day, of abuses and impostures, by which the ignorant populace were cheated into the belief that bones gathered here and there were those of saints. While the origin of the imposture is thus ancient, there cannot be a doubt that in the long period which has since elapsed, it has exceedingly increased, considering, especially, that the world has since been strangely corrupted, and has never ceased to become worse, till it has reached the extreme wherein we now behold it.

"But the first abuse and, as it were, beginning of the evil was, that when Christ ought to have been sought in his Word, sacraments, and spiritual influences, the world, after its wont, clung to his garments, vests, and swaddling-clothes; and thus overlooking the principal matter, followed only its accessory. The same course was pursued in regard to apostles, martyrs, and other saints. For when the duty was to meditate diligently on their lives, and engage in imitating them, men made it their whole study to contemplate and lay up, as it were in a treasury, their bones, shirts, girdles, caps, and similar trifles.

"I am not unaware that in this there is a semblance of pious zeal, the allegation being, that the relics of Christ are kept on account of the reverence which is felt for himself, and in order that the remembrance of him may take a firmer hold of the mind. And the same thing is alleged with regard to the saints. But attention should be paid to what Paul says, viz., that all divine worship of man's devising, having no better and surer foundation than his own opinion, be its semblance of wisdom what it may, is mere vanity and folly.

"Besides, any advantage, supposed to be derived from it, ought to be contrasted with the danger. In this way it would be discovered that the possession of such relics was of little use, or was altogether superfluous and frivolous, whereas, on the other hand, it was most difficult, or rather impossible, that men should not thereby degenerate into idolatry. For they cannot look upon them, or handle them, without veneration; and there being no limit to this, the honor due to Christ is forthwith paid to them. In short, a longing for relics is never free from superstition, nay, what is worse, it is the parent of idolatry, with which it is very generally conjoined.

"All admit, without dispute, that God carried away the body of Moses from human sight, lest the Jewish nation should fall into the abuse of worshipping it. What was done in the case of one ought to be extended to all, since the reason equally applies. But not to speak of saints, let us see what Paul says of Christ himself. He declares, that after the resurrection of Christ he knew him no more after the flesh, intimating by these words that everything carnal which belonged to Christ should be consigned to oblivion and be discarded, in order that we may make it our whole study and endeavor to seek and possess him in spirit. Now, therefore, when men talk of it as a grand thing to possess some memorial of Christ and his saints, what else is it than to seek an empty cloak with which to hide some foolish desire that has no foundation in reason ? But even should there seem to be a sufficient reason for it, yet, seeing it is so clearly repugnant to the mind of the Holy Spirit, as declared by the mouth of Paul, what more do we require ? "

The following is a summary of this tract: —

What was at first a foolish curiosity for preserving relics has degenerated into abominable idolatry. The great majority of the relics are spurious. It could be shown by comparison that every apostle has more than four bodies and every saint two or three. The arm of St. Anthony, which was worshipped in Geneva, when brought out from the case, turned out to be a part of a stag. The body of Christ could not be obtained, but the monks of Charroux pretend to have, besides teeth and hair, the prepuce or pellicle cut off in his circumcision. But it is shown also in the Lateran church at Rome. The blood of Christ which Nicodemus is said to have received in a handkerchief or a bowl, is exhibited in Rochelle, in Mantua, in Rome, and many other places. The manger in which he laid at his birth, his cradle, together with the shirt which his mother made, the pillar on which he leaned when disputing in the Temple, the water-pots in which he turned water into wine, the nails, and pieces of the cross, are shown in Rome, Ravenna, Pisa, Cluny, Angers, and elsewhere.

The table of the last Supper is at Rome, in the church of St. John in the Lateran; some of the bread at St. Salvador in Spain; the knife with which the Paschal Lamb was cut up, is at Treves.[1] What semblance of possibility is there that

[1] The holy coat is still at Treves, and was worshipped by many thousands of devout pilgrims in the year of our Lord 1891!

that table was found seven or eight hundred years after? Besides, tables were in those days different in shape from ours, for people used to recline at meals. Fragments of the cross found by St. Helena are scattered over many churches in Italy, France, Spain, etc., and would form a good ship-load, which it would take three hundred men to carry instead of one. But they say that this wood never grows less! Some affirm that their fragments were carried by angels, others that they dropped down from heaven. Those of Poitiers say that their piece was stolen by a maid-servant of Helena and carried off to France. There is still a greater controversy as to the three nails of the cross: one of them was fixed in the crown of Constantine, the other two were fitted to his horse's bridle, according to Theodoret, or one was kept by Helena herself, according to Ambrose. But now there are two nails at Rome, one at Siena, one at Milan, one at Carpentras, one at Venice, one at Cologne, one at Treves, two at Paris, one at Bourges, etc. All the claims are equally good, for the nails are all spurious. There is also more than one soldier's spear, crown of thorns, purple robe, the seamless coat, and Veronica's napkin (which at least six cities boast of having). A piece of broiled fish, which Peter offered to the risen Saviour on the seashore, must have been wondrously well salted if it has kept for these fifteen centuries! But, jesting apart, is it supposable that the apostles made relics of what they had actually prepared for dinner?

Calvin exposes with equal effect the absurdities and impieties of the wonder-working pictures of Christ; the relics of the hair and milk of the Virgin Mary, preserved in so many places, her combs, her wardrobe and baggage, and her house carried by angels across the sea to Loreto; the shoes of St. Joseph; the slippers of St. James; the head of John the Baptist, of which Rhodes, Malta, Lucca, Nevers, Amiens, Besançon, and Noyon claim to have portions; and his fingers, one of which is shown at Besançon, another at Toulouse, another at Lyons, another at Bourges, another at Florence. At Avignon they have the sword with which John was beheaded, at Aix-la-Chapelle the linen cloth placed under him by the kindness of the executioner, in Rome his girdle and the altar at which he said prayers in the desert. It is strange, adds Calvin, that they do not also make him perform mass.

The tract concludes with this remark: "So completely are the relics mixed up and huddled together, that it is impossible to have the bones of any martyr without running the risk of worshipping the bones of some thief or robber, or, it may be, the bones of a dog, or a horse, or an ass, or — Let every one, therefore, guard against this risk. Henceforth no man will be able to excuse himself by pretending ignorance."

§ 123. *The Articles of the Sorbonne with an Antidote.* 1544.

Articuli a facultate s. theol. Parisiensi determinati super materiis fidei nostræ hodie controversis. Cum Antidoto (1543), 1544. *Opera*, VII. 1–44. A French edition appeared in the same year. English translation by Beveridge, in *Calvin's Tracts*, I. 72–122.

The theological faculty of the University of Paris published, March 10, 1542, a summary of the most obnoxious doctrines of the Roman Church, in twenty-five articles, which were sanctioned by an edict of the king of France, and were to be subscribed by all candidates of the priesthood.[1]

Calvin republished these articles, and accompanied each, first with an ironical defence, and then with a scriptural antidote. This *reductio ad absurdum* had probably more effect in Paris than a serious and sober mode of refutation. The following is a specimen: —

"ARTICLE VI. OF THE SACRIFICE OF THE MASS.

" *The sacrifice of the Mass is, according to the institution of Christ, available for the living and the dead.*"

"Proof, — Because Christ says, 'This do.' But to do is to sacrifice, according to the passage in Vergil: 'When I will do (make an offering) with

---

[1] Bulæus, *Historia Univ. Paris.*, VI. 384, and the French text in *Opera*, vol. VII., Proleg., pp. ix–xii.

a calf in place of produce, do you yourself come.'[1] As to which signification, see Macrobius. But when the Lutherans deride that subtlety, because Christ spoke with the Apostles in the common Hebrew or Syriac tongue, and the Evangelists wrote in Greek, answer that the common Latin translation outweighs them. And it is well known that the sense of Scripture must be sought from the determination of the Church. But of the value of sacrifice for the living and the dead we have proof from experience. For many visions have appeared to certain holy monks when asleep, telling them that by means of masses souls had been delivered from Purgatory. Nay, St. Gregory redeemed the soul of Trajan from the infernal regions."[2]

"ANTIDOTE TO ARTICLE VI.

"The institution of Christ is, 'Take and eat' (Matt. 26 : 26; Mark 14 : 22; 1 Cor. 11 : 24), but not, *offer*. Therefore, sacrifice is not conformable to the institution of Christ, but is plainly repugnant to it. Besides, it is evident from Scripture that it is the peculiar and proper office of Christ to offer himself; as an apostle says, that by one offering he has forever perfected those that are sanctified (Heb. 10 : 14). Also, that 'once, in the end of the world, hath he appeared to put away sin by the sacrifice of himself' (9 : 26). Also, that after this sanctification, 'there remains no more a sacrifice for sins' (10 : 26). For to this end also was he consecrated a priest after the order of Melchisdec, without successor or colleague (Heb. 5 : 6; 7 : 21).

"Christ, therefore, is robbed of the honor of the priesthood, when the right of offering is transferred to others. Lastly, no man ought to assume this honor unless called by God, as an apostle testifies. But we read of none having been called but Christ. On the other hand, since the promise is destined for those only who communicate in the sacrament, by what right can it belong to the dead?"

§ 124. *Calvin and the Nicodemites.* 1544.

CALVIN : *Petit traicté monstrant que c'est que doit faire un homme fidele, coynoissant la verité de l'Evangile quand il est entre les papistes*, 1543. *Excuse de* IEHAN CALVIN *à Messieurs les Nicodémites, sur la complaincte qu'il font de sa trop grand rigueur.* (*Excusatio ad Pseudo-Nicodemitas.*) 1544. Embodied in the tracts *De vitandis superstitionibus quæ cum sincera fidei confessione pugnant.* Genevæ, 1549, 1550, and 1551. This collection contains also

---

[1] "' Hoc facite.' Facere autem est sacrificare, justa illud Vergilii : ' Quum faciam vitulâ pro frugibus, ipse venito.'" (Verg. E. III. 77.)

[2] This refers to the mediæval legend which has found its way into Dante's *Divina Comedia* (*Purg.* X. 75; *Par.* XX. 109–111), that the Emperor Trajan, nearly five hundred years after his death, was disinterred, and his soul translated from hell to heaven by the prayers of Pope Gregory I., who had learned that he was a just emperor, although he persecuted the Christians. But the pope was punished for his interest in a heathen, and warned by an angel never to make a similar request. Trajan is the only pagan in Dante's Paradise.

the opinions of Melanchthon, Bucer, and Peter Martyr on the question raised by the Nicodemites. Reprinted in *Opera*, VI. 537–644. A German translation appeared at Herborn, 1588; an English translation by R. Golding, London, 1548. See the bibliographical notes in HENRY, III.; Beilage, 208 sq.; Proleg. to *Opera*, VI. pp. xxx–xxxiv; and *La France Protest.*, III. 584 sq. DYER, 187 sqq. STÄHELIN, I. 542 sqq.

A great practical difficulty presented itself to the Protestants in France, where they were in constant danger of persecution. They could not emigrate *en masse*, nor live in peace at home, without concealing or denying their convictions. A large number were Protestants at heart, but outwardly conformed to the Roman Church. They excused their conduct by the example of Nicodemus, the Jewish Rabbi, who came to Jesus by night.

Calvin, therefore, called them "Nicodemites," but with this difference, that Nicodemus only buried the body of Christ, after anointing it with precious aromatics; while they bury both his soul and body, his divinity and humanity, and that, too, without honor. Nicodemus interred Christ when dead, but the Nicodemites thrust him into the earth after he has risen. Nicodemus displayed a hundred times more courage at the death of Christ than all the Nicodemites after his resurrection. Calvin confronted them with the alternative of Elijah: "How long halt ye between two opinions? If the Lord be God, follow him: if Baal, then follow him" (1 Kings 18:21). He advised them either to leave their country for some place of liberty, or to absent themselves from idolatrous worship, even at the risk of their lives. The glory of God should be much dearer to us than this transitory life, which is only a shadow.

He distinguished several classes of Nicodemites: first, false preachers of the gospel, who adopt some evangelical doctrines (meaning probably Gérard le Roux or Roussel, for whom Margaret of Navarre had procured the bishopric of Oléron); next, worldly people, courtiers, and refined ladies, who are used to flattery and hate austerity; then, scholars and literary men, who love their ease and hope for gradual improvement with the spread of education and intelligence; lastly, merchants and citizens, who do not wish to be interrupted in their avocations. Yet he was far from disowning them as brethren because of their weakness. Owing to their great danger they could better expect pardon if they should fall, than he himself who lived in comparative security.

The Nicodemites charged Calvin with immoderate austerity. "Away with this Calvin! he is too impolite. He would reduce us to beggary, and lead us directly to the stake. Let him content himself with his own lot, and leave us in peace; or, let him come to us and show us how to behave. He resembles the leader of an army who incites the common soldiers to the attack, but himself keeps out of the reach of danger." To this charge he replied (in substance): "If you compare me with a captain, you should not blame me for doing my duty. The question is not, what I would do in your condition, but what is our present duty — yours and mine. If my life differs from my teaching, then woe to me. God is my witness that my heart bleeds when I think of your temptations and dangers, and that I cease not to pray with tears that you may be delivered. Nor do I condemn always the persons when I condemn the thing. I will not boast of superior courage, but it is not my fault, if I am not more frequently in danger. I am not far from the shot of the enemy. Secure to-day, I do not know what shall be to-morrow. I am prepared for every event, and I hope that God will give me grace to glorify him with my blood as well as with my tongue and pen. I shall lay down my life with no more sadness than I now write down these words."

The French Protestants were under the impression that Luther and Melanchthon had milder and more practicable views on this subject, and requested Calvin to proceed to Saxony for a personal conference. This he declined from

want of time, since it would take at least forty days for the
journey from Geneva to Wittenberg and back. Nor had he
the means. "Even in favorable seasons," he wrote to an
unknown friend in France,[1] "my income barely suffices
to meet expenses, and from the scarcity with which we had
to struggle during the last two years, I was compelled to run
into debt." He added that "the season was unfavorable for
consulting Luther, who has hardly had time to cool from the
heat of controversy." He thus missed the only opportunity
of a personal interview with Luther, who died a year later.
It is doubtful whether it would have been satisfactory. The
old hero was then discontented with the state of the world
and the Church, and longing for departure.

But Calvin prevailed on a young gentleman of tolerable
learning to undertake the journey for him. He gave him
a literal Latin translation of his tracts against the Nicodemites, together with letters to Luther and Melanchthon (Jan.
20, 1545). He asked the latter to act as mediator according
to his best judgment. The letter to Luther is very respectful and modest. After explaining the case, and requesting
him to give it a cursory examination and to return his opinion in a few words, Calvin thus concludes this, his only,
letter to the great German Reformer: —

"I am unwilling to give you this trouble in the midst of so many weighty
and various employments; but such is your sense of justice that you cannot
suppose me to have done this unless compelled by the necessity of the case;
I therefore trust that you will pardon me. Would that I could fly to you,
that I might even for a few hours enjoy the happiness of your society; for
I would prefer, and it would be far better, not only upon this question, but
also about others, to converse personally with yourself; but seeing that it
is not granted to us on earth, I hope that shortly it will come to pass in the
kingdom of God. Adieu, most renowned sir, most distinguished minister
of Christ, and my ever-honored father. The Lord himself rule and direct
you by His own Spirit, that you may persevere even unto the end, for the
common benefit and good of His own Church."

[1] Bonnet (I. 418, note) conjectures that it was Louis du Chemin, or François
Daniel.

Luther was still so excited by his last eucharistic controversy with the Swiss, and so suspicious, that Melanchthon deemed it inexpedient to lay the documents before him.[1]

"I have not shown your letter to Dr. Martin," he replied to Calvin, April 17, 1545, "for he takes many things suspiciously, and does not like his answers to questions of the kind you have proposed to him, to be carried round and handed from one to another. . . . At present I am looking forward to exile and other sorrows. Farewell! On the day on which, thirty-eight hundred and forty-six years ago, Noah entered into the ark, by which God gave testimony of his purpose never to forsake his Church, even when she quivers under the shock of the billows of the great sea."

He gave, however, his own opinion; and this, as well as the opinions of Bucer and Peter Martyr, and Calvin's conclusion, were published, as an appendix to the tracts on avoiding superstition, at Geneva in 1549.[2] Melanchthon substantially agreed with Calvin; he asserts the duty of the Christian to worship God alone (Matt. 4 : 10), to flee from idols (1 John 5 : 21), and to profess Christ openly before men (Matt. 10 : 33); but he took a somewhat milder view as regards compliance with mere ceremonies and non-essentials. Bucer and Peter Martyr agreed with this opinion. The latter refers to the conduct of the early disciples, who, while holding worship in private houses, still continued to visit the temple until they were driven out.

We now proceed to Calvin's controversies with Protestant opponents.

§ 125. *Calvin and Bolsec.*

I. *Actes du procès intenté par Calvin et les autres ministres de Genève à Jérôme Bolsec de Paris* (1551). Printed from the Register of the Venerable Company and the Archives of Geneva, in *Opera*, VIII. 141–248. — CALVIN: *De æterna Dei Prædestinatione*, etc., usually called *Consensus Genevensis* (1552) — chiefly an extract from the respective sections of his *Institutes;* reprinted in *Opera*, VIII. 249–366. It is the second part of his answer to Pighius ("the dead dog," as he calls him), but occasioned by the process of Bolsec, whose name he ignores in contempt. — CALVIN'S letter to Libertetus (Fabri of Neuchâtel), January, 1552, in *Opera*, XIV. 278 sq. — The Letters of the Swiss Churches on the Bolsec affair, reprinted in vol. VIII. 229 sqq. — BEZA: *Vita Calv.* ad ann. 1551.

---

[1] *Opera*, XII. 61.   [2] *Opera*, VI. 617–644.

II. Hierosme Hermes Bolsec, *docteur Médecin à Lyon: Histoire de la vie, mœurs, actes, doctrine, constance et mort de Jean Calvin, jadis ministre de Genève,* Lyon, 1577; *Rééditée avec une introduction, des extraits de la vie de Th. de Bèze, par le même, et des notes à l'appui par* M. Louis-François Chastel, *magistrat.* Lyon, 1875 (xxxi and 328). On the character and different editions of this book, see *La France Protest.,* II. 755 sqq.

III. Bayle: "Bolsec" in his "Diction. historique et critique." — F. Trechsel: *Die Protest. Antitrinitarier* (Heidelberg, 1844), Bd. I. 185–189 and 276–284. — Henry, III. 44 sqq., and the second *Beilage* to vol. III., which gives the documents (namely, the charges of the ministers of Geneva, Bolsec's defence, his poem written in prison, the judgments of the Churches of Bern and Zürich — all of which are omitted in the English version, II. 130 sqq.). — Audin (favorable to Bolsec), ch. XXXIX. — Dyer, 265–283. — * Schweizer: *Centraldogmen,* I. 205–238. — Stähelin, I. 411–414; II. 287–292. — * *La France Prot.,* sub "Bolsec," tom. II. 745–776 (second ed.). Against this article: *Lettre d'un protestant Genevois aux lecteurs de la France Protestante,* Genève, 1880. In defence of that article, Henri L. Bordier: *L'école historique de Jérôme Bolsec, pour servir de supplément à l'article Bolsec de la France Protestante,* Paris (Fischbacher), 1880.

Hieronymus (Hierosme) Hermes Bolsec, a native of Paris, was a Carmelite monk, but left the Roman Church, about 1545, and fled for protection to the Duchess of Ferrara, who admitted him to her house under the title of an almoner. There he married, and adopted the medical profession as a means of livelihood. Ever afterwards he called himself "Doctor of Medicine." He made himself odious by his turbulent character and conduct, and was expelled by the Duchess for some deception (as Beza reports).

In 1550 he settled at Geneva with his wife and a servant, and practised his profession. But he meddled in theology, and began to question Calvin's doctrine of predestination. He denounced Calvin's God as a hypocrite and liar, as a patron of criminals, and as worse than Satan. He was admonished, March 8, 1551, by the Venerable Company, and privately instructed by Calvin in that mystery, but without success. On a second offence he was summoned before the Consistory, and openly reprehended in the presence of fifteen ministers and other competent persons. He acknowledged that a certain number were elected by God to salvation, but he denied predestination to destruction; and, on closer examination, he extended election to all mankind, maintaining that grace efficacious to salvation is equally offered to all, and that the cause, why some receive and others reject it, lies in the free-will, with which all men were endowed. At the same time he abhorred the name of merits. This, in the eyes of Calvin, was a logical contradiction and an absurdity; for, he says, "if some were elected, it surely follows that others are not elected and left to perish. Unless we confess that those who come to Christ are drawn by the Father through the peculiar operation of the Holy Spirit on the elect, it follows either that all must be promiscuously elected, or that the cause of election lies in each man's merit."

On the 16th of October, 1551, Bolsec attended the religious conference, which was held every Friday at St. Peter's. John de St. André preached from John 8 : 47 on predestination, and inferred from the text that those who are not of God, oppose him to the last, because God grants the grace of obedience only to the elect. Bolsec suddenly interrupted the speaker, and argued that men are not saved because they are elected, but that they are elected because they have faith. He denounced, as false and godless, the notion that God decides the fate of man before his birth, consigning some to sin and punishment, others to virtue and eternal happiness. He loaded the clergy with abuse, and warned the congregation not to be led astray.

After he had finished this harangue, Calvin, who had entered the church unobserved, stepped up to him and so overwhelmed him, as Beza says, with arguments and with quotations from Scripture and Augustin, that "all felt exceedingly ashamed for the brazen-faced monk, except the monk himself." Farel also, who happened to be present, addressed the assembly. The lieutenant of police apprehended Bolsec for abusing the ministers and disturbing the public peace.

On the same afternoon the ministers drew up seventeen articles against Bolsec and presented them to the Council, with the request to call him to account. Bolsec, in his turn, proposed several questions to Calvin and asked a categorical answer (October 25). He asserted that Melanchthon, Bullinger, and Brenz shared his opinion.

The Consistory asked the Council to consult the Swiss Churches before passing judgment. Accordingly, the Council sent a list of Bolsec's errors to Zürich, Bern, and Basel. They were five, as follows: —

1. That faith depends not on election, but election on faith.

2. That it is an insult to God to say that he abandons some to blindness, because it is his pleasure to do so.

3. That God leads to himself all rational creatures, and abandons only those who have often resisted him.

4. That God's grace is universal, and some are not more predestinated to salvation than others.

5. That when St. Paul says (Eph. 1:5), that God has elected us through Christ, he does not mean election to salvation, but election to discipleship and apostleship.

At the same time Calvin and his colleagues addressed a circular letter to the Swiss Churches, which speaks in offensive and contemptuous terms of Bolsec, and charges him with cheating, deception, and impudence. Beza also wrote from Lausanne to Bullinger.

The replies of the Swiss Churches were very unsatisfactory to Calvin, although the verdict was, on the whole, in his favor. They reveal the difference between the German and the French Swiss on the subject of divine decrees and free-will. They assent to the doctrine of free election to salvation, but evade the impenetrable mystery of absolute and eternal reprobation, which was the most material point in the controversy.

The ministers of Zürich defended Zwingli against Bolsec's

charge, that in his work on Providence he made God the author of sin, and they referred to other works in which Zwingli traced sin to the corruption of the human will. Bullinger, in a private letter to Calvin, impressed upon him the necessity of moderation and mildness. "Believe me," he said, "many are displeased with what you say in your *Institutes* about predestination, and draw the same conclusions from it as Bolsec has drawn from Zwingli's book on Providence." This affair caused a temporary alienation between Calvin and Bullinger. It was not till ten years afterwards that Bullinger decidedly embraced the Calvinistic dogma, and even then he laid no stress on reprobation.[1]

Myconius, in the name of the Church of Basel, answered evasively, and dwelt on what Calvin and Bolsec believed in common.

The reply of the ministers of Bern anticipates the modern spirit of toleration. They applaud the zeal for truth and unity, but emphasize the equally important duty of charity and forbearance. The good Shepherd, they say, cares for the sheep that has gone astray. It is much easier to win a man back by gentleness than to compel him by severity. As to the awful mystery of divine predestination, they remind Calvin of the perplexity felt by many good men who cling to the Scripture texts of God's universal grace and goodness.

The effect of these letters was a milder judgment on Bolsec. He was banished for life from the territory of Geneva for exciting sedition and for Pelagianism, under pain of being whipped if he should ever return. The judgment was announced Dec. 23, 1551, with the sound of the trumpet.[2]

Bolsec retired to Thonon, in Bern, but as he created new disturbances he was banished (1555). He left for France,

---

[1] On Bullinger's views see above, pp. 210 sq., and Schweizer, I. 225, 255 sqq.

[2] Beza: "*Senatus . . . illum tum ut seditiosum, tum ut mere Pelagianum XXIII. Dec. publice damnatum urbe expulit, fustuariam pœnam minatus, si vel in urbe vel in urbis territorio esset deprehensus.*" Reg. of the Ven. Comp. in *Annal.* 498: "*MᵉIerosme fut banni à son de trompe des terres de Genève.*"

and sought admission into the ministry of the Reformed Church, but returned at last to the Roman communion.[1] He was classed by the national synod of Lyon among deposed ministers, and characterized as "an infamous liar" and "apostate" (1563). He lived near Lyon and at Autun, and died at Annecy about 1584. Thirteen years after Calvin's death he took mean and cowardly revenge by the publication of a libellous "Life of Calvin," which injured him much more than Calvin; and this was followed by a slanderous "Life of Beza," 1582. These books would long since have been forgotten, had not partisan zeal kept them alive.[2]

The dispute with Bolsec occasioned Calvin's tract, "On the Eternal Predestination of God," which he dedicated to the Syndics and Council of Geneva, under the name of *Consensus Genevensis*, or Agreement of the Genevese Pastors, Jan. 1, 1552. But it was not approved by the other Swiss Churches.

Beza remarks of the result of this controversy: "All that Satan gained by these discussions was, that this article of the Christian religion, which was formerly most obscure, became clear and transparent to all not disposed to be contentious."

The quarrel with Bolsec caused the dissolution of the friendship between Calvin and Jacques de Bourgogne, Sieur de Falais et Bredam, a descendant of the dukes of Burgundy, who with his wife, Jolunde de Brederode, a descendant of the old counts of Holland, settled in Geneva, 1548, and lived for some time in Calvin's house at his invitation, when the

---

[1] According to Beza, Bolsec forsook his wife and allowed her to become a prostitute to the canons of Autun.

[2] Bayle said in his day: "*Bolsec seroit un homme tout-à-fait plongé dans les ténèbres de l'oubli, s'il ne s'était rendu fameux par certains ouvrages satiriques* [meaning his attacks on Calvin and Beza], *que les moines et les missionnaires citent encore.*" In recent times Galiffe and Audin have come up to the defence of Bolsec, but have been refuted by Henri L. Bordier in *La France Protestante,* II. 766 sqq., and in *L'ecole historique de Jérôme Bolsec*, Paris, 1880. Schweizer (I. 207) calls those libels "*ersonnene Verleumdungen, wie rechtschaffene Katholiken längst zugeben, anderen aber gut genug zum Wiederabdrucken.*"

wife of the latter was still living. His cook, Nicolas, served Calvin as clerk. Calvin took the greatest interest in De Falais, comforted him over the confiscation of his goods by Charles V., at whose court he had been educated, and wrote a defence for him against the calumnies before the emperor.[1] He also dedicated to him his Commentary on the First Epistle to the Corinthians. His friendly correspondence from 1543 to 1852 is still extant, and does great credit to him.[2] But De Falais could not penetrate the mysteries of theology, nor sympathize with the severity of discipline in Geneva. He was shocked at the treatment of Bolsec; he felt indebted to him as a physician who had cured one of his maid-servants of a cancer. He interceded for him with the magistrates of Geneva and of Bern. He wrote to Bullinger: "Not without tears am I forced to see and hear this tragedy of Calvin." He begged him to unite with Calvin for the restoration of peace in the Church.

He left Geneva after the banishment of Bolsec and moved to Bern, where he lost his wife (1557) and married again. Bayle asserts, without authority, that in disgust at the Protestant dissensions he returned to the Roman Church.[3]

Even Melanchthon was displeased with Calvin's conduct in this unfortunate affair; but the alienation was only superficial and temporary. Judging from the imperfect information of Lælius Socinus, he was disposed to censure the Genevese for an excess of zeal in behalf of the "Stoic doctrine of necessity," as he called it, while he applauded the Zürichers for greater moderation. He expressed himself to

---

[1] *Apologia illustris D. Jacobi a Burgundia Fallesii Bredanique domini, qua apud Imperatoriam Majestatem inustas sibi criminationes diluit fideique suæ confessionem edit.* In *Opera*, X. Pt. I. 269–294.

[2] It was published at Amsterdam in a separate volume, 1774, and is reprinted in the *Opera* and in the collection of Bonnet. Comp. on Calvin's friendship with De Falais, Henry, III. 64–69; Stähelin, II. 293–302.

[3] Bolsec, in his life of Calvin, invented, among other slanders, the story that the real cause of De Falais' leaving Geneva was an attempt of Calvin on the chastity of his wife!

this effect in private letters.[1] Socinus appealed to the judgment of Melanchthon in a letter to Calvin, and Calvin, in
his reply, could not entirely deny it. Yet, upon the whole,
Melanchthon, like Bullinger, was more on the side of Calvin,
and in the more important affair of Servetus, both unequivo-
cally justified his conduct, which is now generally condemned
by Protestants.

§ 126. *Calvin and Castellio.*

I. CASTELLIO's chief work is his *Biblia sacra latina* (Basil., 1551, 1554, 1555,
1556, 1572; the N. T. also at Amst., 1683, Leipz., 1760, Halle, 1776).
His French version is less important. He defended both against the
attacks of Beza (*Defensio suarum translationum Bibliorum*, Basil., 1562).
After the execution of Servetus, 1553, Castellio wrote several anonymous
or pseudonymous booklets against Calvin, and against the persecution of
heretics, which provoked the replies of Calvin and Beza (see below).
His views against predestination and the slavery of the will are best set
forth in his four *Dialogi de prœdestinatione, de electione, de libero arbitrio,
de fide*, which were published after his death at Basel, 1578, 1613, 1619,
and in English, 1679. See a chronological list of his numerous works in
La France Protestante, vol. IV. 126–141. I have before me (from the
Union Seminary Library) a rare volume: *Sebastiani Castellionis Dialogi
IV.*, printed at Gouda in Holland anno 1613, which contains the four
Dialogues above mentioned (pp. 1–225)', Castellio's Defence against
Calvin's *Adv. Nebulonem*, his Annotations on the ninth ch. of Romans,
and several other tracts.

CALVIN: *Brevis Responsio ad diluendas nebulonis cuiusdam calumnias quibus doctrinam de œterna Dei prœdestinatione fœdare conatus est*, Gen. (1554), 1557.
In *Opera*, IX. 253–266. The unnamed *nebulo* (in the French ed. *le broul-
lion*) is Castellio. *Calumniœ nebulonis cujusdam adversus doctrinam Joh.
Calvini de occulta Dei providentia. Johannis Calvini ad easdem responsio*,
Gen., 1558. In *Opera*, IX. 269–318. In this book Castellio's objections
to Calvin's predestinarian system are set forth in twenty-four theses, with

---

[1] He wrote to Caspar Peucer, his son-in-law, Feb. 1, 1552: "*Lelius mihi
scribit, tanta esse Genevœ certamina de Stoica necessitate, ut carceri inclusus sit
quidam [Bolsec] a Zenone [Calvino] dissentiens. O rem miseram! Doctrina
salutaris obscuratur peregrinis disputationibus.*" Mel.'s *Opera* (*Corp. Ref.*), vol.
VII. 932. To his friend Camerarius he wrote, under the same date, Feb. 1,
1552 (VII. 930): "*Hic Polonus a Lelio accepit literas. . . . Ac vide seculi
furores, certamina Allobrogica [Genevensia] de Stoica necessitate tanta sunt, ut
carceri inclusus sit quidam, qui a Zenone dissentit. Lelius narrat, se κορυφαίῳ
cuidam [Calvino] scripsisse, ne tam vehementer pugnet. Et mitiores sunt Tigurini.*"

a defence, and then answered by Calvin. The first thesis charges Calvin with teaching: " *Deus maximam mundi partem nudo puroque voluntatis suce arbitric creavit ad perditionem.*" Thes. V.: " *Nullum adulterium, furtum, homicidium committitur, quin Dei voluntas intercedat.*"

BEZA: *Ad Seb. Castellionis calumnias, quibus unicum salutis nostræ fundamentum, i.e. æternam Dei prædestinationem evertere nititur, responsio,* Gen., 1558. In his *Tractat. theol.* I. 337–423 (second ed. Geneva, 1582).

II. BAYLE: *Castalion* in his " Dict. hist. et crit."— JOH. C. FÜSSLIN: *Lebensgeschichte Seb. Castellio's.* Frankf. and Leipzig, 1776.— F. TRECHSEL: *Die protest. Antitrinitarier,* vol. I. (1839), pp. 208–214.— C. RICH. BRENNER: *Essai sur la vie et les écrits de Séb. Chatillon,* 1853.— HENRY: II. 383 sqq.; III. 88 sqq.; and Beilage, 28–42.— *ALEX. SCHWEIZER: *Centraldogmen,* I. 310–356; and *Sebastian Castellio als Bekämpfer der Calvinischen Prädestinationslehre,* in Baur's " Theol. Jahrbücher" for 1851.— STÄHELIN, I. 377–381; II. 302–308. — JACOB MAEHLY: *Seb. Castellio, ein biographischer Versuch,* Basel, 1862.— JULES BONNET: *Séb. Chatillion ou la tolérance au XVIe siècle,* in the " Bulletin de la Société de l'hist. du protest. français," Nos. XVI. and XVII., 1867 and 1868. — EM. BROSSOUX: *Séb. Chasteillon,* Strasbourg, 1867.— B. RIGGENBACH, in Herzog[2], III. 160 sqq. — LUTTEROTH: *Castallion* in Lichtenberger, II. 672–677. — *LA FRANCE PROTESTANTE (2d ed.): *Chateillon,* tom. IV. 122–142. — *FERD. BUISSON: *Sébastien Castellion,* Paris, 1892, 2 vols.

Castellio was far superior to Bolsec as a scholar and a man, and lived in peace with Calvin until differences of opinion on predestination, free-will, the Canticles, the descent into Hades, and religious toleration made them bitter enemies. In the heat of the controversy both forgot the dignity and moderation of a Christian scholar.

Sebastian Castellio or Castalio was born at Chatillon in Savoy, in 1515, six years after Calvin, of poor and bigoted parents.[1] He acquired a classical and biblical education by hard study. He had a rare genius for languages, and mastered Latin, Greek, and Hebrew. In 1540 he taught Greek at Lyons, and conducted the studies of three noblemen. He published there a manual of biblical history under the

---

[1] His French name is *Bastien de Chatillon* or *Chateillon.* He assumed, not without vanity, the classical name *Castalio* with allusion to the Castalian fountain at the foot of Parnassus. The usual spelling is *Castellio.* His precise origin is uncertain. He was either a Frenchman or a Savoyard. He was numbered with the liberal anti-calvinistic Italians, and charged with using a corrupt French dialect. See Bayle, *l.c.,* and Schweizer, I. 311.

title *Dialogi sacri*, which passed through several editions
in Latin and French from 1540 to 1731. He wrote a Latin
epic on the prophecies of Jonah; a Greek epic on John the
Baptist, which greatly delighted Melanchthon; two versions
of the Pentateuch, with a view to exhibit Moses as a master
in all the arts and sciences; a translation of the Psalms, and
other poetic portions of the Old Testament.

These works were preparatory to a complete Latin translation of the Bible, which he begun at Geneva, 1542, and finished at Basel, 1551. It was dedicated to King Edward VI.
of England, and often republished with various improvements. He showed some specimens in manuscript to Calvin,
who disapproved of the style. His object was to present
the Bible in classical Latinity according to the taste of the
later humanists and the pedantic Ciceronianism of Cardinal
Bembo. He substituted classical for biblical terms; as *lotio*
for *baptismus, genius* for *angelus, respublica* for *ecclesia, collegium* for *synagoge, senatus* for *presbyterium, furiosi* for *dœmo-
niaci*. He sacrificed the contents to style, obliterated the
Hebraisms, and weakened the realistic force, the simplicity
and grandeur of the biblical writers. His translation was
severely criticised by Calvin and Beza as tending to secu-
larize and profane the sacred book, but it was commended as
a meritorious work by such competent judges as Melanchthon and Richard Simon. Castellio published also a French
version of the Bible with notes (1555), but his French was
not nearly as pure and elegant as his Latin, and was severely
criticised by Beza. He translated portions of Homer, Xenophon, the Dialogues of Ochino, and also two mystical books,
the *Theologia Germanica* (1557), and, in the last year of
his life, the *Imitatio Christi* of Thomas à Kempis, — "*e latino
in latinum*," that is, from monkish into classical Latin, —
omitting, however, the fourth book.

Castellio was a philologist and critic, an orator and poet,
but not a theologian, and unable to rise to the lofty height

of Calvin's views and mission. His controversial tracts are full
of bitterness. He combined a mystical with a sceptical tendency.[1] He was an anachronism; a rationalist before Rationalism, an advocate of religious toleration in an age of intolerance.

Castellio became acquainted with Calvin at Strassburg, and
lived with him in the same house (1540). Calvin appreciated his genius, scholarship, and literary industry, and, on
his return to Geneva, he secured for him a call as rector of
the Latin school at a salary of four hundred and fifty florins
(November, 1541), in the place of his old teacher, Maturin
Cordier. He treated him at first with marked kindness and
forbearance. In 1542, when the pestilence raged, Castellio
offered to go to the hospital, but he was either rejected as
not qualified, not being a minister, or he changed his mind
when the lot fell on him.[2]

Early in the year 1544, Castellio took offence at some of
Calvin's theological opinions, especially his doctrine of predestination. He disliked his severe discipline and the one-
man-power. He anticipated the rationalistic opinion on the
Song of Solomon, and described it as an obscene, erotic poem,
which should be stricken out of the canon.[3] He also objected
to the clause of Christ's descent into Hades in the Apostles'
Creed, or rather to Calvin's figurative explanation of it, as
being a vicarious foretaste of eternal pain by Christ on the
cross.[4] For these reasons Calvin opposed his ordination,

---

[1] Stähelin (II. 303) calls him "*ein rationalistischer Gefühlstheologe mit ausge-
prägt æsthetischem Anstrich.*"

[2] The latter is Beza's explanation, *Vita Calv.* in *Annal., Opera,* XXI. 134.

[3] "*Carmen obscœnum et lascivum, quo Salomo impudicos suos amores descrip-
serit.*" Comp. *Reg. du Conseil,* Jan. 28, 1544, in *Annal.* 329.

[4] Calvin, in his catechism, explains the *descensus ad inferos* to mean the
suffering of the "*dolores mortis*" (Acts 2 : 24) or "*horribiles angustias*" on the
cross in behalf of the elect. This unhistorical exposition passed into the Heidelberg Catechism, Quæst. 44: "Christ, my Lord, by his inexpressible anguish,
pains, and terrors, which he suffered in his soul on the cross and before, has
redeemed me from the anguish and torment of hell." The true meaning of
the clause is, that the descent was an event which took place between the
death and the resurrection of Christ. Comp. 1 Pet. 3: 19; 4: 6; Eph. 4: 9.

but recommended an increase of his salary, which the Council refused, with the direction that he should keep better discipline in the school.[1] He also gave him an honorable public testimony when he wished to leave Geneva, and added private letters of recommendation to friends. Castellio went to Lausanne, but soon returned to Geneva. In April, 1544, he asked the Council to continue him in his position for April, May, and June, which was agreed to.[2]

In a public discussion on some Scripture text in the weekly congregation at which about sixty persons were present, May 30, 1544, he eulogized St. Paul and drew an unfavorable contrast between him and the ministers of Geneva, charging them with drunkenness, impurity, and intolerance. Calvin listened in silence, but complained to the Syndics of this conduct.[3] Castellio was summoned before the Council, which, after a patient hearing, found him guilty of calumny, and banished him from the city.[4]

He went to Basel, where the liberal spirit of Erasmus had not yet died out. He lived there several years in great poverty till 1553, when he obtained a Greek professorship in the University. That University was the headquarters of opposition to Calvinism. Several sceptical Italians gathered there. Fr. Hotoman wrote to Bullinger: " Calvin is no better spoken of here than in Paris. If one wishes to scold another, he calls him a Calvinist. He is most unjustly and immoderately assailed from all quarters." [5]

In the summer of 1554, an anonymous letter was addressed to the Genevese with atrocious charges against Calvin, who suspected that it was written by Castellio, and complained

---

[1] See *Reg. du Conseil*, Jan. 14, 1544, quoted in *Annal.* 328.

[2] Extract from *Reg. du Conseil*, April 12, 1544, in *Annal.* 333.

[3] May 31, *Annal.* 336.

[4] This is the report of Beza: "*ex urbe excedere jussus est*"; but Castellio seems to have remained in Geneva till July 14. See *Reg. du Conseil*, in *Annal.* 340.

[5] Trechsel, *Antitrinitarier*, I. 219; Stähelin, II. 304.

of it to Antistes Sulzer of Basel; but Castellio denied the authorship before the Council of Basel. About the same time appeared from the same anonymous source a malignant tract against Calvin, which collected his most obnoxious utterances on predestination, and was sent to Paris for publication to fill the French Protestants, then struggling for existence, with distrust of the Reformer (1555). Calvin and Beza replied with much indignation and bitterness, and heaped upon the author such epithets as dog, slanderer, corrupter of Scripture, vagabond, blasphemer. Calvin, upon insufficient information, even charged him with theft. Castellio, in self-defence, informs us that, with a large family dependent on him, he was in the habit of gathering driftwood on the banks of the Rhine to keep himself warm, and to cook his food, while working at the completion of his translation of the Scriptures till midnight. He effectively replied to Calvin's reproachful epithets: "It ill becomes so learned a man as yourself, the teacher of so many others, to degrade so excellent an intellect by such foul and sordid abuse."

Castellio incurred the suspicion of the Council of Basel by his translation of Ochino's *Dialogues*, which contained opinions favorable to Unitarianism and polygamy (1563). He defended himself by alleging that he acted not as judge, but only as translator, for the support of his family. He was warned to cease meddling with theology and to stick to philology.

He died in poverty, Dec. 29, 1563, only forty-eight years old, leaving four sons and four daughters from two wives. Calvin saw in his death a judgment of God, but a few months afterwards he died himself. Even the mild Bullinger expressed satisfaction that the translator of Ochino's dangerous books had left this world.[1] Three Polish Socinians, who

---

[1] He wrote to Zanchi at Chiavenna, March 17, 1564: "*Optime factum, quod Basileæ mortuus est Castellio.*" Quoted by Trechsel, I. 214, from the Simler Collection in Zürich.

happened to pass through Basel, were more merciful than the orthodox, and erected to Castellio a monument in the cloister adjoining the minster. Faustus Socinus edited his posthumous works. The youngest of his children, Frederic Castellio, acquired some distinction as a philologist, orator, musician, and poet, and was appointed professor of Greek, and afterwards of rhetoric, in Basel.

Castellio left no school behind him, but his writings exerted considerable influence on the development of Socinian and Arminian opinions. He opposed Calvinism with the same arguments as Pighius and Bolsec, and charged it with destroying the foundations of morality and turning God into a tyrant and hypocrite. He essentially agreed with Pelagianism, and prepared the way for Socinianism.

He differed also from Calvin on the subject of persecution. Being himself persecuted, he was one of the very few advocates of religious toleration in opposition to the prevailing doctrine and practice of his age. In this point also he sympathized with the Unitarians. After the execution of Servetus and Calvin's defence of the same, there appeared, under the false name of Martinus Bellius, a book against the theory of religious persecution, which was ascribed to Castellio.[1] He denied the authorship. He had, however, contributed to it a part under the name of Basilius (Sebastian) Montfortius (Castellio). The pseudo-name of Martinus Bellius, the editor who wrote the dedicatory preface to Duke Christopher of Württemberg (the protector of Vergerius), has never been unmasked. The book is a collection of judgments of different writers against the capital punishment of heretics.

---

[1] *De hæreticis an sint persequendi, et omnino quomodo sit cum eis agendum, doctorum virorum tum veterum tum recentiorum sententiæ. Liber hoc tam turbulento tempore pernecessarius. Magdeburgi, per Georg. Rausch,* 1554, *mense martio,* 173 pp. 8°. I copy the title of the book (which I have not seen) from *La France Prot.,* IV. 130. The writer of this article and Baum attribute the book to Castellio, but Schweizer, I. 315 sq., shows that he wrote only a part of it. Comp. Buisson, *l.c.,* I. 358 sqq., and II. 1 sqq.

Calvin and Beza were indignant, and correctly ascribed the book to a secret company of Italian "Academici," — Lælius Socinus, Curio, and Castellio. They also suspected that Magdeburg, the alleged place of publication, was Basel, and the printer an Italian refugee, Pietro Perna.

Castellio wrote also a tract, during the Huguenot wars in France, 1562, in which he defended religious liberty as the only remedy against religious wars.[1]

§ 127. *Calvinism and Unitarianism. The Italian Refugees.*

Comp. §§ 38–40 (pp. 144–163).

I. CALVIN: *Ad questiones Georgii Blandatræ responsum* (1558); *Responsum ad Fratres Polonos quomodo mediator sit Christus ad refutandum Stancari errorem* (1560); *Impietas Valentini Gentilis detecta et palam traducta qui Christum non sine sacrilega blasphemia Deum essentiatum esse fingit* (1561); *Brevis admonitio ad Fratres Polonos ne triplicem in Deo essentiam pro tribus personis imaginando tres sibi Deos fabricent* (1563); *Epistola Jo. Calv. quo fidem Admonitionis ab eo nuper editæ apud Polonos confirmat* (1563). All in *Opera*, Tom. IX. 321 sqq. The correspondence of Calvin with Lelio Sozini and other Italians, see below. On the controversy with Servetus, see next chapter.

The Socinian writings are collected in the *Bibliotheca fratrum Polonorum quos Unitarios vocant*, Irenopoli (Amsterdam), 1656 sqq., 8 vols in 11 tomes fol. It contains the writings of the younger Socinus and his successors (Schlichting, Crell, etc.).

II. TRECHSEL: *Die Protestantischen Antitrinitarier*, Heidelberg, 1839 and 1844, 2 vols. The first volume treats chiefly of Servetus; the second, of the Italian Antitrinitarians. — OTTO FOCK: *Der Socinianismus*, Kiel, 1847. (The first part contains the history, the second and more valuable part the system, of Socinianism.) — SCHWEIZER: *Die Protest. Centraldogmen* (Zürich, 1854), vol. I. 293 sqq. — HENRY, III. 276 sqq. — DYER, 446 sqq. — STÄHELIN, II. 319 sqq. — L. COLIGNY: *L'Antitrinitarianism à Genève au temps de Calvin.* Genève, 1873. — HARNACK: *Dogmengeschichte*, III. (1890) 653–691. Comp. SAND: *Bibliotheca Antitrinitariorum*, 1684.

The Italian Protestants who were compelled to flee from the Inquisition, sought refuge in Switzerland, and organized congregations under native pastors in the Grisons, in Zürich,

---

[1] "*Conseil à la France désolée, auquel est montrée la cause de la guerre présente et le remède qui y pourroit être mis, et principalement est avisé si on doit forcer les consciences.*" The writer in *La France Prot.*, IV. 135–138, gives large extracts from this exceedingly rare tract. See also Buisson, II. 225 sqq.

and Geneva. A few of them gathered also in Basel, and associated there with Castellio and the admirers of Erasmus.[1]

An Italian Church was organized at Geneva in 1542, and reorganized in 1551, under Galeazzo Caraccioli, Marquis of Vico. Its chief pastors were Ragnione, Count Martinengo (who died 1557), and Balbani.

Among the 279 fugitives who received the rights of citizenship in that city on one day of the year 1558, there were 200 Frenchmen, 50 Englishmen, 25 Italians, and 4 Spaniards.

The descendants of the refugees gradually merged into the native population. Some of the best families in Geneva, Zürich, and Basel still bear the names and cherish the memories of their foreign ancestors. In the valleys of Poschiavo and Bregaglia of the Grisons, several Protestant Italian congregations survive to this day.[2]

The Italian Protestants were mostly educated men, who had passed through the door of the Renaissance to the Reformation, or who had received the first impulse from the writings of Luther, Zwingli, and Calvin. We must distinguish among them two classes, as they were chiefly influenced either by religious or intellectual motives. Those who had experienced a severe moral struggle for peace of conscience, became strict Calvinists ; those who were moved by a desire for freedom of thought from the bondage of an exclusive creed, sympathized more with Erasmus than with Luther and Calvin, and had a tendency to Unitarianism and Pelagianism. Zanchi warned Bullinger against recommending Italians for sound doctrine until he had ascertained their views on God and on original sin. The same national characteristics continue to this day among the Romanic races. If Italians, Frenchmen, or Spaniards cease to be Romanists, they are apt to become sceptics and agnostics. They rarely stop midway.

---

[1] Henry, II. 422; Schweizer, I. 293.

[2] On the Italian refugees in the Grisons, and in Zürich, see above, §§ 38, 39, and 40; and Trechsel, *l.c.*, II. 64 sqq.

The ablest, most learned, and most worthy representatives of orthodox Calvinism among the converted Italians were Peter Martyr Vermigli of Florence (1500–1562), who became, successively, professor at Strassburg (1543), at Oxford (1547), and last at Zürich (1555), and his younger friend, Jerome Zanchi (1516–1590), who labored first in the Grisons, and then as professor at Strassburg (1553) and at Heidelberg (1568). Calvin made several ineffectual attempts to secure both for the Italian congregation in Geneva.[1]

The sceptical and antitrinitarian Italians were more numerous among the scholars. Calvin aptly called them "sceptical Academicians." They assembled chiefly at Basel, where they breathed the atmosphere of Erasmian humanism. They gave the Swiss Churches a great deal of trouble. They took offence at the Catholic doctrine of the Trinity, which they misconstrued into tritheism, or Sabellianism, at the orthodox Christology of two natures in one person, and at the Calvinistic doctrines of total depravity and divine predestination, which they charged with tending to immorality. They doubted the right of infant baptism, and denied the real presence in the Eucharist. They hated ecclesiastical discipline. They admired Servetus, and disapproved of his burning. They advocated religious toleration, which threatened to throw everything into confusion.

To this class belong the two Sozini, — uncle and nephew, — Curio, Ochino (in his latter years), Renato, Gribaldo, Biandrata, Alciati, and Gentile. Castellio is also counted with these Italian sceptics. He thoroughly sided with their anti-Calvinism, and translated from the Italian manuscripts into Latin the last books of Ochino.

---

[1] See above, pp. 156 and 162, and C. Schmidt, *Peter Martyr Vermigli. Leben und ausgewählte Schriften,* Elberfeld, 1858 (p. 296). Vergerio, the former bishop of Capo d'Istria and papal nuncio, is also numbered among the orthodox Italians, but he had no settled opinions, and was no theologian in the proper sense. See above, § 38, pp. 144 sqq. E. Tremellio, a converted Jew of Ferrara (1510–1580), one of the most learned Orientalists, was a Calvinist.

Thus the seeds for a new and heretical type of Protestantism were abundantly sown by these Italian refugees in the soil of the Swiss Churches, which had received them with open-hearted hospitality.

Fausto Sozini (1539–1604) formulated the loose heterodox opinions of this school of sceptics into a theological system, and organized an ecclesiastical society in Poland, where they enjoyed toleration till the Jesuitical reaction drove them away.   Poland was the Northern home of the Italian Renaissance.   Italian architects built the great churches and palaces in Cracow, Warsaw, and other cities, and gave them an Italian aspect.   Fausto Sozini spent some time in Lyons, Zürich (where he collected the papers of his uncle), and Basel, but labored chiefly in Poland, and acquired great influence with the upper classes by his polished manners, amiability, and marriage with the daughter of a nobleman.   Yet he was once mobbed by fanatical students and priests at Cracow, who dragged him through the streets and destroyed his library. He bore the persecution like a philosopher.   His writings were published by his nephew, Wiszowaty, in the first two volumes of the *Bibliotheca fratrum Polonorum*, 1656.

This is not the place for a full history of Socinianism. We have only to do with its initiatory movements in Switzerland, and its connection with Calvin.   But a few general remarks will facilitate an understanding.

Socinianism, as a system of theology, has largely affected the theology of orthodox Protestantism on the Continent during the seventeenth and eighteenth centuries, and was succeeded by modern Unitarianism, which has exerted considerable influence on the thought and literature of England and America in the nineteenth century.   It forms the extreme left wing of Protestantism, and the antipode to Calvinism. The Socinians admitted that Calvinism is the only logical system on the basis of universal depravity and absolute foreknowledge and foreordination ; but they denied these premises, and taught moral ability, free-will, and, strange to say, a limitation of divine foreknowledge. God foreknows and foreordains only the necessary future, but not the contingent future, which depends on the free-will of man. The two systems are therefore directly opposed in their theology and anthropology.

And yet there is a certain intellectual and moral affinity between them; as there is between Lutheranism and Rationalism. It is a remarkable fact that modern Unitarianism has grown up in the Calvinistic (Presbyterian and Independent) Churches of Geneva, France, Holland, England, and New England, while Rationalism has been chiefly developed in Lutheran Germany. But the reaction is also found in those countries.

The Italian and Polish Socinians took substantially the same ground as the English and American Unitarians. They were opposed alike to Romanism and Calvinism; they claimed intellectual freedom of dissent and investigation as a right; they elevated the ethical spirit of Christianity above the dogmas, and they had much zeal for higher liberal education. But they differ on an important point. The Socinians had a theological system, and a catechism; the modern Unitarians refuse to be bound by a fixed creed, and are independent in church polity. They allow more liberty for new departures, either in the direction of rationalism and humanitarianism, or in the opposite direction of supernaturalism and trinitarianism.

Calvin was in his early ministry charged with Arianism by a theological quack (Caroli), because he objected to the damnatory clauses of the pseudo-Athanasian creed, and expressed once an unfavorable opinion on the Nicene Creed.[1] But his difficulty was only with the scholastic or metaphysical terminology,[2] not with the doctrine itself; and as to the

---

[1] As a "*carmen cantillando magis aptum, quam confessionis formula.*" In his tract *De vera Ecclesiæ reformatione.* Comp. § 82, pp. 351 sq.

[2] οὐσία, ὑπόστασις, πρόσωπον, essentia, substantia, persona, etc., and other terms of the Nicene age.

divinity of Christ and of the Holy Spirit, he was most emphatic.

It is chiefly due to Calvin's and Bullinger's influence that Unitarianism, which began to undermine orthodoxy, and to unsettle the Churches, was banished from Switzerland. It received its death-blow in the execution of Servetus, who was a Spaniard, but the ablest and most dangerous antitrinitarian. His case will be discussed in a special chapter.

§ 128. *Calvin and Lælius Socinus.*

F. TRECHSEL (pastor at Vechingen, near Bern): *Die protest. Antitrinitarier vor Faustus Socinus nach den Quellen und Urkunden geschichtlich dargestellt.* Heidelberg, 1839, 1844. The first part of this learned work, drawn in part from manuscript sources, is devoted to Michael Servetus and his predecessors; the second part to Lelio Sozini and his sympathizing contemporaries. The third section of vol. II. 137–201, with documents in the Appendix, pp. 431–459, treats of Lelio Sozini. — HENRY, II. 484 sqq.; III. 440, Beilage, 128. — DYER, 251 (very brief).

Lælius Socinus, or Lelio Sozini, of Siena (1525–1562), son of an eminent professor of law, was well educated, and carried away by the reform movement in his early youth. He voluntarily separated from the Roman Church, in 1546, at the sacrifice of home and fortune. He removed to Chiavenna in 1547, travelled in Switzerland, France, England, Germany, and Poland, leading an independent life as a student, without public office, supported by the ample means of his father. He studied Greek, Hebrew, and Arabic with Pellican and Bibliander at Zürich and with Foster at Wittenberg, that he might reach "the fountain of the divine law" in the Bible. He made Zürich his second home, and died there in the prime of early manhood, leaving his unripe doubts and crude opinions as a legacy to his more gifted and famous nephew, who gave them definite shape and form.

Lælius was learned, acute, polite, amiable, and prepossessing. He was a man of affairs, better fitted for law or diplomacy than for theology. He was constitutionally a sceptic, of the type of Thomas: an honest seeker after truth; too independent to submit blindly to authority, and yet too religious to run into infidelity. His scepticism stumbled first at the Roman Catholic, than at the Protestant orthodoxy, and gradually spread over the doctrines of the resurrection, predestination, original sin, the trinity, the atonement, and the sacraments. Yet he remained in respectful connection with the Reformers, and communed with the congregation at Zürich, although he thought that the Consensus Tigurinus attributed too much power to the sacrament. He enjoyed the confidence of Bullinger and Melanchthon, who treated him with fatherly kindness, but regarded him better fitted for a secular calling than for the service of the Church. Calvin also was favorably impressed with his talents and personal character, but displeased with his excessive "inquisitiveness." [1]

L. Socinus came to Geneva in 1548 or 1549, seeking instruction from the greatest divine of the age. He opened his doubts to Calvin with the modesty of a disciple. Soon afterwards he addressed to him a letter from Zürich, asking for advice on the questions, whether it was lawful for a Protestant to marry a Roman Catholic; whether popish baptism was efficacious; and how the doctrine of the resurrection of the body could be explained.

Calvin answered in an elaborate letter (June 26, 1549),[2] to the effect that marriage with Romanists was to be condemned; that popish baptism was valid and efficacious, and should be resorted to when no other can be had, since the Roman communion, though corrupt, still retained marks of the true Church as well as a scattered number of elect individuals, and since baptism was not a popish invention but

---

[1] "*Inexplicabilis curiositas*," as he called it, adding: "*Utinam non simul accederet phrenetica quædam protervia.*" Letter to Bullinger, Aug. 7, 1554 (*Opera*, XV. 208).

[2] *Ep.* 1212 in *Opera*, VIII. 307–311. We have in all four letters of Calvin to the elder Socinus, and one from Socinus to Calvin.

a divine institution and gift of God who fulfils his promises; that the question on the mode of the resurrection, and its relation to the changing states of our mortal body, was one of curiosity rather than utility.

Before receiving this answer, Socinus wrote to Calvin again from Basel (July 25, 1549) on the same subjects, especially the resurrection, which troubled his mind very much.[1] To this Calvin returned another answer (December, 1549), and warned him against the dangers of his sceptical bent of mind.[2]

Socinus was not discouraged by the earnest rebuke, nor shaken in his veneration for Calvin. During the Bolsec troubles, when at Wittenberg, he laid before him his scruples about predestination and free-will, and appealed to the testimony of Melanchthon, whom he had informed about the harsh treatment of Bolsec. Calvin answered briefly and not without some degree of bitterness.[3]

Socinus visited Geneva a second time in 1554, after his return from a journey to Italy, and before making Zürich his final home. He was then, apparently, still in friendly relations to Calvin and Caraccioli.[4] Soon afterwards he opened to Calvin, in four questions, his objections to the doctrine of the vicarious atonement. Calvin went to the trouble to answer them at length, with solid arguments, June, 1555.[5]

But Socinus was not satisfied. His scepticism extended further to the doctrine of the sacraments and of the Trinity.

[1] *Opera*, XIII. 337 sq.

[2] Ep. 1323 in *Opera*, XIII. 484–487.

[3] *Opera*, XIV. 228. The answer of Calvin in the Geneva library is without date. Bonnet, who first published it (II. 315), puts it at the end of 1551; but it probably belongs to the beginning of 1552. See Melanchthon's letters of Feb. 1, 1552, in which he mentions Lælio's reports about Bolsec's treatment, quoted p. 621, note.

[4] As may be inferred from a postscript to his letter to Bullinger, dated Geneva, April 19, 1554, in Trechsel, II. 437.

[5] *Responsio ad aliquot Lælii Socini Senensis quæstiones*, printed among the *Consilia theologica*, in *Opera*, vol. X. 160–165. Comp. vol. XV. 642.

He doubted first the personality of the Holy Spirit, and then the eternal divinity of Christ. He disapproved the execution of Servetus, and advocated toleration.

Various complaints against Socinus reached Bullinger. Calvin requested him to restrain the restless curiosity of the sceptic. Vergerio, then at Tübingen, Saluz of Coire, and other ministers, sent warnings. Bullinger instituted a private inquiry in a kindly spirit, and was satisfied with a verbal and written declaration of Socinus (July 15, 1555) to the effect that he fully agreed with the Scriptures and the Apostles' Creed, that he disapproved the doctrines of the Anabaptists and Servetus, and that he would not teach any errors, but live in quiet retirement. Bullinger protected him against further attacks.

Socinus ceased to trouble the Reformers with questions. He devoted himself to the congregation of refugees from Locarno, and secured for them Ochino as pastor, but exerted a bad influence upon him. Fortified with letters of recommendation he made another journey to Italy, via Germany and Poland, to recover his property from the Inquisition. Calvin gave him a letter to Prince Radziwill of Poland, dated June, 1558, to further his object.[1] But Socinus was bitterly disappointed in his wishes, and returned to Zürich in August, 1559. The last few years of his short life he spent in quiet retirement. His nephew visited him several times, and revered him as a divinely illuminated man to whom he owed his most fruitful ideas.

The personal relation of Calvin and the elder Socinus is one of curious mutual attraction and repulsion, like the two systems which they represent.[2]

[1] Ep. 2876 in *Opera*, XVII. 181 sq. Henry, III. Beilage, 128 sq., first published this letter of recommendation, but misdated it, June, 1553. Lælius did not start on his last journey to Italy before 1558.

[2] Trechsel, II. 166, thus describes the personal relationship: "*So manche Erfahrung von Calvin's Schroffheit Lelio sowohl an sich selbst als an andern gemacht hatte, so war doch nichts im Stande, sein achtungsvolles Zutrauen zu dem*

The younger Socinus, the real founder of the system called after him, did not come into personal contact with Calvin, and labored among the scattered Unitarians and Anabaptists in Poland.

Calvin took a deep interest in the progress of the Reformation in Poland, and wrote several letters to the king, to Prince Radziwill, and some of the Polish nobility. But when the writings of Servetus and antitrinitarian opinions spread in that kingdom, he warned the Polish brethren, in one of his last writings, against the danger of this heresy.

§ 129. *Bernardino Ochino*. 1487–1565.

Comp. § 40, p. 162. OCHINO's *Sermons, Tragedy, Catechism, Labyrinths*, and *Dialogues*. His works are very rare; one of the best collections is in the library of Wolfenbüttel; copious extracts in Schelhorn, Trechsel, Schweizer, and Benrath. A full list in Benrath's monograph, Appendix II. 374–382. His letters (Italian and Latin), *ibid*. Appendix I. 337–373. Ochino is often mentioned in Calvin's and Bullinger's correspondence.

ZACCARIA BOVERIO (Rom. Cath.) in the Chronicle of the Order of the Capuchins, 1630 (inaccurate and hostile). BAYLE's "Dict." — SCHELHORN: *Ergötzlichkeiten aus der Kirchenhistorie*, Ulm and Leipzig, 1764, vol. III. (with several documents in Latin and Italian). — TRECHSEL: *Antitrinitarier*, II. 202–270. — SCHWEIZER: *Centraldogmen*, I. 297–309. — CESARE CANTÙ (Rom. Cath.): *Gli Eretici d' Italia*, Turin, 1565–1567, 3 vols. — BÜCHSENSCHÜTZ: *Vie et écrits de B. O.*, Strasbourg, 1872. — * KARL BENRATH: *Bernardino Ochino von Siena. Ein Beitrag zur Geschichte der Reformation*, Leipzig, 1875 (384 pp.; 2d ed. 1892; transl. by HELEN ZIMMERN, with preface by William Arthur, London, 1876, 304 pp.; the letters of Ochino are omitted). — Comp. C. SCHMIDT in his *Peter Martyr Vermigli* (1858), pp. 21 sqq., and art. in Herzog² X. 680–683. (This article is unsatisfactory and shows no knowledge of Benrath, although he is mentioned in the lit.)

ausserordentlichen Manne zu schwächen. Gerade wie ein Pol den entgegensetzten anzieht, so wurde Lelio's negative Natur von der positiven Calvin's unaufhörlich angezogen, so konnte der Mann des Zweifels aus einer Art von Instinkt nicht umhin, bei dem Felsenmann des Glaubens, der mit beispielloser Kühnheit und Consequenz die Tiefen der Gottheit erforschte, gleichsam seine Ergänzung zu suchen, ohne dass die totale Divergenz beider Naturen eine Uebereinstimmung des Denkens und der Ansichten jemals erwarten liess."

MI SARA FACILE TUTTO IN CHRISTO PER EL QUAL VIVO ET SPERO DI MORIRE.

(From Ochino's letter to the Council of Siena, Sept. 5, 1540; reproduced
from Benrath's monograph.)

THE CAPUCHIN MONK.

Bernardino Ochino[1] is one of the most striking and picturesque characters among the Italian Protestants of the Reformation period.   He was an oratorical genius and monkish
saint who shone with meteoric brilliancy on the sky of Italy,

[1] Also spelled *Occhino*, in Latin *Ocellus*.

but disappeared at last under a cloud of scepticism in the far North.

He reminds one of three other eloquent monks: Savonarola, who was burnt in Florence at the stake; Father Gavazzi, who became a Calvinist and died peacefully in Rome; and Père Hyacinthe, who left the Carmelite order and the pulpit of Notre Dame in Paris without joining any Protestant Church.

Ochino was born in the fair Tuscan city of Siena, which is adorned by a Gothic marble dome and gave birth to six popes, fifty cardinals, and a number of canonized saints, among them the famous Caterina of Siena; but also to Protestant heretics, like Lelio and Fausto Sozini. He joined the Franciscans, and afterwards the severe order of the Capuchins, which had recently been founded by Fra Matteo Bassi in 1525. He hoped to gain heaven by self-denial and good works. He far surpassed his brethren in ability and learning,[1] although his education was defective (he did not know the original languages of the Bible). He was twice elected Vicar-General of the Order. He was revered by many as a saint for his severe asceticism and mortification of the flesh. Vittoria Colonna, the most gifted woman of Italy, and the Duchess Renata of Ferrara were among his ardent admirers. Pope Paul III. intended to create him a cardinal.[2]

OCHINO AS AN ORATOR.

Ochino was the most popular preacher of Italy in his time. No such orator had appeared since the death of Savonarola in 1498. He was in general demand for the course of sermons during Lent, and everywhere — in Siena, Naples, Rome, Florence, Venice — he attracted crowds of people who listened to him as to a prophet sent from God.

[1] Boverius (ad ann. 1535): "*Bernardinus divinis et humanis literis non mediocriter imbutus.*"

[2] Sand, Seckendorf, C. Schmidt (in Herzog), and others, state that the pope made Ochino his confessor; but this is without support, and intrinsically improbable. See Benrath, 33 sq. (German ed.).

We can hardly understand from his printed sermons the extravagant laudations of his contemporaries. But good preachers were rare in Italy, and the effect of popular oratory depends upon action as much as on diction. We must take into account the magnetism of his personality, the force of dramatic delivery, the lively gestures, the fame of his monastic sanctity, his emaciated face, his gleaming eyes, his tall stature and imposing figure. The portrait prefixed to his "Nine Sermons," published at Venice, 1539, shows him to us as he was at the time: a typical Capuchin monk, with the head bent, the gaze upturned, the eyes deeply sunk under the brows, the nose aquiline, the mouth half open, the head shaved on top, the beard reaching down to his breast.

Cardinal Sadolet compared him to the orators of antiquity. One of his hearers in Naples said, This man could make the very stones weep.[1]

Cardinal Bembo[2] secured him for Lent at Venice through Vittoria Colonna, and wrote to her (Feb. 23, 1539): "I have heard him all through Lent with such pleasure that I cannot praise him enough. I have never heard more useful and edifying sermons than his, and I no longer wonder that you esteem him so highly. He preaches in a far more Christian manner than other preachers, with more real sympathy and love, and utters more soothing and elevating thoughts. Every one is delighted with him." A few months later (April 4, 1539) he wrote to the same lady: "Our Fra Bernardino is literally adored here. There is no one who does not praise him to the skies. How deeply his words penetrate, how elevating and comforting his discourses!" He begged him to eat meat and to restrain from excessive abstinence lest he should break down.

---

[1] "*Predicava con ispirito grande che faceva piagnere i sassi.*" Some wrongly attribute this saying of Rosso to the Emperor Charles V., who heard Ochino at Naples. Benrath, 24, note.

[2] He was then the historiographer of Venice, but was soon afterwards created cardinal by Paul III., March 24, 1539.

Even Pietro Aretino, the most frivolous and immoral poet of that time, was superficially converted for a brief season by Ochino's preaching, and wrote to Paul III. (April 21, 1539): "Bembo has won a thousand souls for Paradise by bringing to Venice Fra Bernardino, whose modesty is equal to his virtue. I have myself begun to believe in the exhortations trumpeted forth from the mouth of this apostolic monk."

Cardinal Commendone, afterwards Bishop of Amelia, an enemy of Ochino, gives this description of him: "Every thing about Ochino contributed to make the admiration of the multitude almost overstep all human bounds, — the fame of his eloquence; his prepossessing, ingratiating manner; his advancing years; his mode of life; the rough Capuchin garb; the long beard reaching to his breast; the gray hair; the pale, thin face; the artificial aspect of bodily weakness; finally, the reputation of a holy life. Wherever he was to speak the citizens might be seen in crowds; no church was large enough to contain the multitude of listeners. Men flocked as numerously as women. When he went elsewhere the crowd followed after to hear him. He was honored not only by the common people, but also by princes and kings. Wherever he came he was offered hospitality; he was met at his arrival, and escorted at his departure, by the dignitaries of the place. He himself knew how to increase the desire to hear him, and the reverence shown him. Obedient to the rule of his order, he only travelled on foot; he was never seen to ride, although his health was delicate and his age advanced. Even when Ochino was the guest of nobles — an honor he could not always refuse — he could never be induced, by the splendor of palaces, dress, and ornament, to forsake his mode of life. When invited to table, he ate of only one very simple dish, and he drank little wine; if a soft bed had been prepared for him, he begged permission to rest on a more comfortable pallet, spread his cloak on the ground, and laid down to rest. These practices gain him incredible honor throughout all Italy."

CONVERSION TO PROTESTANTISM.

Ochino was already past fifty when he began to lose faith in the Roman Church. The first traces of the change are found in his "Nine Sermons" and "Seven Dialogues," which were published at Venice in 1539 and 1541. He seems to have passed through an experience similar to that of Luther in the convent at Erfurt, only less deep and lasting. The vain monastic struggle after righteousness led him to despair of himself, and to find peace in the assurance of justification by faith in the merits of Christ. As long as he was a monk, so he informs us, he went even beyond the requirements of his order in reading masses, praying the Pater Noster and Ave Maria, reciting Psalms and prayers, confessing trifling sins once or twice a day, fasting and mortifying his body. But he came gradually to the conviction that Christ has fully satisfied for his elect, and conquered Paradise for them; that monastic vows were not obligatory, and were even immoral; and that the Roman Church, though brilliant in outward appearance, was thoroughly corrupt and an abomination in the eyes of God.

In this transition state he was much influenced by his personal intercourse with Jean de Valdés and Peter Martyr. Valdés, a Spanish nobleman who lived at Rome and Naples, was an evangelical mystic, and the real author of that remarkable book, "On the Benefit of Christ's Death" (published at Venice, 1540). It was formerly attributed to Aonio Paleario (a friend of Ochino), and had a wide circulation in Italy till it was suppressed and publicly burnt at Naples in 1553.

During the Lent season of 1542, Ochino preached his last course of sermons at Venice. The papal agents watched him closely and reported some expressions as heretical. He was forbidden to preach, and cited to Rome.

Caraffa had persuaded Pope Paul III. to use violent measures for the suppression of the Protestant heresy. In Rome,

Peter had conquered Simon Magus, the patriarch of all heretics; in Rome. the successor of Peter must conquer all successors of the arch-heretic. The Roman Inquisition was established by the bull *Licet ab initio*, July 21, 1542, under the direction of six cardinals. with plenary power to arrest and imprison persons suspected of heresy, and to confiscate their property. The famous General of the Capuchins was to be the first victim of the " Holy Office."

Ochino departed for Rome in August. Passing through Bologna, he called on the noble Cardinal Contarini, who in the previous year had met Melanchthon and Calvin at the Colloquy of Ratisbon, and was suspected of having a leaning to the Lutheran doctrine of justification, and to a moderate reformation. The cardinal was sick, and died soon after (August 24). The interview was brief, but left upon Ochino the impression that there was no chance for him in Rome. He continued his journey to Florence, met Peter Martyr in a similar condition, and was warned of the danger awaiting both. He felt that he must choose between Rome or Christ, between silence or death, and that flight was the only escape from this alternative. He resolved to save his life for future usefulness, though he was already fifty-six years old, gray-haired, and enfeebled by his ascetic life. If I remain in Italy, he said, my mouth is sealed; if I leave, I may by my writings continue to labor for the truth with some prospect of success.

He proved by his conduct the sincerity of his conversion to Protestantism. He risked every thing by secession from the papacy. An orator has no chance in a foreign land with a foreign tongue.[1]

---

[1] Caraffa, the restorer of the Inquisition, ascribed his conversion to impure motives, but without evidence. On these calumnies see Benrath, pp. 170 sq. Audin (ch. XLV.), drawing on his imagination, says that Ochino, tempted by the demon of doubt and pride, fled to Geneva with a young girl whom he had seduced!

OCHINO IN SWITZERLAND.

In August, 1542, he left Florence; Peter Martyr followed two days later. He was provided with a servant and a horse by Ascanio Colonna, a brother of Vittoria, his friend.[1] At Ferrara, the Duchess Renata furnished him with clothing and other necessaries, and probably also with a letter to her friend Calvin. According to Boverius, the annalist of the Capuchins, who deplores his apostasy as a great calamity for the order, he was accompanied by three lay brethren from Florence.

He proceeded through the Grisons to Zürich, and stopped there two days. He was kindly received by Bullinger, who speaks of him in a letter to Vadian (Dec. 19, 1542) as a venerable man, famous for sanctity of life and eloquence.

He arrived at Geneva about September, 1542, and remained there three years. He preached to the small Italian congregation, but devoted himself chiefly to literary work by which he hoped to reach a larger public in his native land. He was deeply impressed with the moral and religious prosperity of Geneva, the like of which he had never seen before, and gave a favorable description of it in one of his Italian sermons.[2]

"In Geneva, where I am now residing," he wrote in October, 1542, "excellent Christians are daily preaching the pure word of God. The Holy Scriptures are constantly read and openly discussed, and every one is at liberty to propound what the Holy Spirit suggests to him, just as, according to the testimony of Paul, was the case in the primitive Church. Every day there is a public service of devotion. Every Sunday there is catechetical instruction of the young, the simple, and the ignorant. Cursing and swearing, unchastity, sacrilege, adultery, and impure living, such as prevail in many places

[1] Colonna sent him afterwards through a messenger some means of support to Switzerland, as we learn from a letter of Bullinger.

[2] Quoted in Italian by Trechsel, II. 203, in German by Benrath, p. 169.

where I have lived, are unknown here. There are no pimps and harlots. The people do not know what rouge is, and they are all clad in a seemly fashion. Games of chance are not customary. Benevolence is so great that the poor need not beg. The people admonish each other in brotherly fashion, as Christ prescribes. Lawsuits are banished from the city; nor is there any simony, murder, or party spirit, but only peace and charity. On the other hand, there are no organs here, no noise of bells, no showy songs, no burning candles and lamps, no relics, pictures, statues, canopies, or splendid robes, no farces, or cold ceremonies. The churches are quite free from all idolatry." [1]

Ochino wrote at Geneva a justification of his flight, in a letter to Girolamo Muzio (April 7, 1543). In a letter to the magistrates of Siena, he gave a full confession of his faith based chiefly on the eighth chapter of the Epistle to the Romans (Nov. 3, 1543). He published, in rapid succession, seven volumes of Italian sermons or theological essays.[2]

He says in the Preface to these sermons: "Now, my dear Italy, I can no more speak to you from mouth to mouth; but I will write to you in thine own language, that everybody may understand me. My comfort is that Christ so willed it, that, laying aside all earthly considerations, I may regard only the truth. And as the justification of the sinner by Christ is the beginning of the Christian life, let us begin with it in the name of our Lord Jesus Christ." His sermons are evangelical, and show a mystical tendency, as we might expect from a disciple of Valdes. He lays much stress on the vital union of the soul with Christ by faith and love. He teaches a free salvation by the sole merits of Christ, and the Calvinistic doctrine of sovereign election, but with-

---

[1] "*Le chiese sono purgatissime da ogni idolatria.*" This testimony is confirmed by Vergerio, Farel, Knox, and others. See § 110, pp. 516 sqq.

[2] *Prediche*, Geneva, 1542–1544, several editions; also in Latin, French, German, and English. See Benrath, pp. 374 sq., and his summary of the contents, pp. 175 sqq.

out the negative inference of reprobation. He wrote also a popular, paraphrastic commentary on his favorite Epistle to the Romans (1545), which was translated into Latin and German. Afterwards, he published sermons on the Epistle to the Galatians, which were printed at Augsburg, 1546.

He lived on good terms with Calvin, who distrusted the Italians, but after careful inquiry was favorably impressed with Ochino's "eminent learning and exemplary life."[1] He mentions him first in a letter to Viret (September, 1542) as a venerable refugee, who lived in Geneva at his own expense, and promised to be of great service if he could learn French.[2] In a letter to Melanchthon (Feb. 14, 1543), he calls him an "eminent and excellent man, who has occasioned no little stir in Italy by his departure."[3] Two years afterwards (Aug. 15, 1545), he recommended him to Myconius of Basel as "deserving of high esteem everywhere."[4]

Ochino associated at Basel with Castellio, and employed him in the translation of his works from the Italian. This connection may have shaken his confidence in the Calvinistic doctrine of predestination and free-will.

OCHINO IN GERMANY.

He labored for some time as preacher and author in Strassburg, where he met his old friend Peter Martyr, and in Augsburg, where he received from the city council a regular

---

[1] He wrote to Pellican, April 19, 1543 : "*Quoniam Italicis plerisque ingeniis non multum fido . . . , contuli cum eo diligenter. . . . Hoc testimonium pio et sancto viro visum est. . . . Est enim præstanti et ingenio et doctrina et sanctitate.*" *Opera*, XI. 528.

[2] *Opera*, XI. 447 sq. Comp. letter to Viret, October, 1542, *ibid*. 458 : "*Bernardus noster miris machinis impetitus est, ut nobis abduceretur : constanter tamen perstat.*"

[3] "*Magnum et præclarum virum, qui suo discessu non parum Italiam commovit.*" *Opera*, XI. 517.

[4] "*Bern. Senensis, vir nuper in Italia magni nominis, dignus certe qui habeatur ubique in pretio.*" *Opera*, XII. 135. Benrath (192) gives the wrong date of this letter, viz. 1542, — probably a typographical error.

salary of two hundred guilders as preacher among the foreigners. This was his first regular settlement after he had left Italy. At Augsburg he lived with his brother-in-law and sister. He seems to have married at that time, if not earlier.[1]

OCHINO IN ENGLAND.

After his victory over the Smalkaldian League, the Emperor Charles V. held a triumphant entry in Augsburg, Jan. 23, 1547, and demanded the surrender of the apostate monk, whose powerful voice he had heard from the pulpit at Naples eleven years before. The magistrates enabled Ochino to escape in the night. He fled to Zürich, where he accidentally met Calvin, who arrived there on the same day. From Zürich he went to Basel.

Here he received, in 1547, a call to England from Archbishop Cranmer, who needed foreign aid in the work of the Reformation under the favorable auspices of the young King Edward VI. At the same time he called Peter Martyr, then professor at Strassburg, to a theological professorship at Oxford, and two years afterwards he invited Bucer and Fagius of Strassburg, who refused to sign the Augsburg Interim, to professorial chairs in the University of Cambridge (1549). Ochino and Peter Martyr made the journey together in company with an English knight, who provided the outfit and the travelling expenses.

Ochino labored six years in London, from 1547 to 1554, — probably the happiest of his troubled life, — as evangelist among the Italian merchants and refugees, and as a writer in aid of the Reformation. His family followed him. He enjoyed the confidence of Cranmer, who appointed him canon of Canterbury (though he never resided there), and received a competent salary from the private purse of the king.

---

[1] Benrath, p. 194. We know nothing of his wife and children, not even their names. An old monk is not well fitted for a happy family life.

His chief work of that period is a theological drama against the papacy under the title "A Tragedy or a Dialogue of the unjust, usurped primacy of the Bishop of Rome," with a flat-tering dedication to Edward VI. He takes the ground of all the Reformers, that the pope is the predicted Antichrist, seated in the temple of God; and traces, in a series of nine conversations, with considerable dramatic skill but imperfect historical information, the gradual growth of the papacy from Boniface III. and Emperor Phocas (607) to its downfall in England under Henry VIII. and Edward VI.[1]

Ochino again in Switzerland.

After the accession of Queen Mary, Ochino had to flee, and went a second time to Geneva. He arrived there a day after the burning of Servetus (Oct. 28, 1553), which he dis-approved, but he did not lose his respect for Calvin, whom he called, in a letter of Dec. 4, 1555, the first divine and the ornament of the century.[2]

He accepted a call as pastor of the Italian congregation at Zürich. Here he associated freely with Peter Martyr, but more, it would seem, with Lælius Socinus, who was also a native of Siena, and who by his sceptical opinions exerted an unsettling influence on his mind.

He wrote a catechism for his congregation (published at Basel, 1561) in the form of a dialogue between "Illuminato" (the catechumen) and "Ministro." He explains the usual five parts — the Decalogue (which fills one-half of the book), the Apostles' Creed, the Lord's Prayer, Baptism, and the Lord's Supper, with an appendix of prayers.

His last works were his "Labyrinths" (1561) and "Thirty Dialogues" (1563), translated by Castellio into Latin, and

---

[1] The book was translated from Latin into English by Dr. John Ponnet, afterwards bishop of Winchester, and published in London, 1549. Benrath gives a good summary, pp. 215 sqq.

[2] " *Seculi nostri decus.*" Benrath, 364 sq.

published by an Italian printer at Basel. In these books Ochino discusses the doctrines of predestination, free-will, the Trinity, and monogamy, in a latitudinarian and sceptical way, which made the heretical view appear stronger in the argument than the orthodox.

The most objectionable is the dialogue on polygamy (Dial. XXI.), which he seemed to shield by the example of the patriarchs and kings of the Old Testament; while monogamy was not sufficiently defended, although it is declared to be the only moral form of marriage.[1] The subject was much ventilated in that age, especially in connection with the bigamy of Philip of Hesse and the deplorable connivance of the Lutheran Reformers. A dialogue in favor of polygamy appeared in 1541, under the fictitious name of " Huldericus Neobulus," in the interest of Philip of Hesse. From this dialogue Ochino borrowed some of his strongest arguments.[2] This accounts for his theoretical error. He certainly could have had no personal motive, for he was then in his seventy-seventh year, a widower with four children.[3] His moral life had always been unblemished, as his congregation and Bullinger testified.

The End.

The dialogue on polygamy caused the unceremonious deposition and expulsion of the old man from Zürich by the Council, in December, 1563. In vain did he protest against misinterpretation, and beg to be allowed to remain during the cold winter with his four children. He was ordered to quit the city within three weeks. Even the mild Bullinger

---

[1] I learn from Schelhorn (III. 2152), that this dialogue appeared in an English translation, " by a Person of Quality," in London, 1657.

[2] The correspondence of the two books has been proven by Schelhorn, *l.c.*, III. 2140 sqq., and I. 631 sqq. Bucer was suspected of being concealed under the Neobulus, but he denied it. See Schelhorn, I. 634.

[3] His wife died in consequence of an accident shortly before the Dialogues were published. Benrath, p. 307.

did not protect him. He went to Basel, but the magistrates of that city were even more intolerant than the clergy, and would not permit him to remain during the winter. Castellio, the translator of the obnoxious books, was also called to account, but was soon summoned to a higher judgment (December 23). The printer, Perna, who had sold all the copies, was threatened with punishment, but seems to have escaped it.

Ochino found a temporary hiding-place in Nürnberg, and sent from there in self-defence an ill-tempered attack upon Zürich, to which the ministers of that city replied.[1]

Being obliged to leave Nürnberg, he turned his weary steps to Poland, and was allowed to preach to his country-men at Cracow. But Cardinal Hosius and the papal nuncio denounced him as an atheist, and induced the king to issue an edict by which all non-Catholic foreigners were expelled from Poland (Aug. 6, 1564).

Ochino entered upon his last weary journey. At Pinczow he was seized by the pestilence and lost three of his children; nothing is known of the fourth. He himself survived, but a few weeks afterwards he took sick again and ended his lonely life at the end of December, 1564, at Schlackau in Moravia: a victim of his sceptical speculations and the intol-erance of his age. A veil is thrown over his last days: no monument, no inscription marks his grave. What a sad contrast between the bright morning and noon-day, and the gloomy evening, of his public life!

A false rumor was spread that before his journey to Poland he met at Schaffhausen the cardinal of Lorraine on his return from the Council of Trent, and offered to prove twenty-four errors against the Reformed Church. The offer was declined with the remark: "Four errors are enough." The rumor was investigated, but could not be verified. He himself denied

---

[1] *Spongia adversus aspergines Bernardini Ochini*, etc., printed in Hottinger's *Historia Eccles. N. Ti.*, and in Schelhorn, III. 2157–2194.

it, and one of his last known utterances was: " I wish to be neither a Bullingerite, nor a Calvinist, nor a Papist, but simply a Christian."[1]

His sceptical views on the person of Christ and the atonement disturbed and nearly broke up the Italian congregation in Zürich. No new pastor was elected; the members coalesced with the German population, and the antitrinitarian influences disappeared.

§ 130. *Cælius Secundus Curio.* 1503-1569.

CURIO's works and correspondence. — TRECHSEL, I. 215 sqq., and WAGEMANN in Herzog,[2] III. 396-400 (where the literature is given).

Celio Secundo Curione or Curio was the youngest of twenty-three children of a Piedmontese nobleman, studied history and law at Turin, became acquainted with the writings of Luther, Zwingli, and Melanchthon through an Augustinian monk, and labored zealously for the spread of Protestant doctrines in Pavia, Padua, Venice, Ferrara, and Lucca. He barely escaped death at the stake, and fled to Switzerland with letters of recommendation by the Duchess Renata, the friend of Calvin. He received an appointment as professor of eloquence in Lausanne (1543-1547) and afterwards in Basel. He was the father-in-law of Zanchius. He attracted students from abroad, declined several calls, kept up a lively correspondence with his countrymen and with the Reformers, and wrote a number of theological and literary works. He sided with the latitudinarians, and thereby lost the confidence of Calvin and Bullinger; but he maintained his ground in Basel, and became the ancestor of several famous theological families of that city (Buxtorf, Zwinger, Werenfels, Frey).

Curio sympathized with Zwingli's favorable judgment of the noble heathen, and thought that they were as acceptable

---

[1] From a letter of Knibb to Bullinger, Easter, 1564, in the Simler Collection in Zürich. Trechsel, II. 265; Benrath, 315.

to God as the pious Israelites. Vergerio, formerly a friend of Curio, charged him with the Pelagian heresy and with teaching that men may be saved without the knowledge of Christ, though not without Christ.[1]

Curio advanced also the hopeful view that the kingdom of heaven is much larger than the kingdom of Satan, and that the saved will far outnumber the lost.[2]

Such opinions were disapproved by Peter Martyr, Zanchi, Bullinger, Brenz, John a Lasco, and all orthodox Protestants of that age, as paradoxical and tending to Universalism. But modern Calvinists go further than Curio, at least in regard to the large majority of the saved.[3]

§ 131. *The Italian Antitrinitarians in Geneva. Gribaldo, Biandrata, Alciati, Gentile.*

See lit. in § 127, and SANDIUS: *Bibliotheca antitrinitaria.* TRECHSEL (I. 277–390) is still the best authority on the early Antitrinitarians in Switzerland, and gives large extracts from the sources. FOCK (I. 134) has only a few words on them. — Comp. in addition, HEBERLE: *G. Blandrata*, in the "Tübinger Zeitschrift für Theologie," for 1840, No. IV. DORNER: *Hist. of Christology*, German ed., II. 656 sqq.

The antitrinitarian leaven entered the Italian congregation at Geneva during and after the trial of Servetus, but was suppressed by the combined action of the Swiss Churches. This constitutes the last chapter of Antitrinitarianism in Switzerland.

---

[1] *"Absque Christi cognitione, licet non sine Christo, aliquos salutem adipisci."* Letter of Vergerio to Bullinger (Tübingen, Sept. 6, 1554), quoted by Trechsel, I. 217. Vergerio denounced Curio to the Swiss Churches. See his letters to Amerbach, in Trechsel, II. 463–465.

[2] *De amplitudine beati regni Dei dialogi II.* Printed at Poschiavo in the Grisons, 1554.

[3] Dr. Charles Hodge (*Syst. Theol.* III. 879 sq.) says: "We have reason to believe, as urged in the first volume of this work, and as often urged elsewhere, that the number of the finally lost in comparison with the whole number of the saved will be very inconsiderable."

Several Italian refugees denounced the execution of Servetus, adopted his views and tried to improve them, but were far inferior to him in genius and originality.

They circulated libels on Calvin, and ventilated their opinions in the weekly conference meetings of the Italian congregation, which were open to questions and free discussions.

1. MATTEO GRIBALDO, a noted professor of jurisprudence at Padua, bought the estate of Farges in the territory of Bern, near Geneva, and spent there a part of each year. He attended the Italian meetings on his visits to the town. During the trial of Servetus he openly expressed his disapproval of civil punishment for religious opinions, and maintained that everybody should be allowed to believe what he pleased. He at first concealed his views on the doctrine of Servetus, except among intimate friends. After an examination before the Council, he was ordered to leave the city on suspicion of heretical opinions on the Trinity (1559). These opinions were crude and undigested. He vacillated between dyotheism or tritheism and Arianism. He could not conceive of Father and Son except as two distinct beings or substances: the one begetting, the other begotten; the one sending, the other sent. He compared their relation to that between Paul and Apollos, who were two individuals, yet one in the abstract idea of the apostolate.

Before his dismission from Geneva he had, through the influence of Vergerio, received an appointment as professor of law in the University of Tübingen. Passing through Zürich he called on Bullinger, and complained bitterly of the conduct of Calvin. He gained the applause of the students in Tübingen, and was often consulted by Duke Christopher of Würtemberg on important matters.

But rumors of his heresies reached Tübingen, and inquiries were sent to Geneva. Calvin warned his old teacher, Melchior Volmar, against him, and Beza alarmed Vergerio by unfavorable reports. Vergerio informed the Duke of the charges.

Gribaldo was subjected to an examination before the academic senate in the presence of the Duke, and was pressed for a decided answer to the question, whether he agreed with the Athanasian Creed and the edict of Theodosius I. respecting the Trinity and the Catholic faith. He asked three weeks' time for consideration, but escaped to his villa at Farges, where his family still resided.

There he was apprehended by the magistrates of Bern at the instance of the Duke of Würtemberg, in September, 1557. His papers were seized and found to contain antitrinitarian and other heresies. He was ordered to renounce his errors by a confession drawn up with his own hand, and banished from the territory of Bern; but on his promise to keep quiet, he was allowed to return the following year for the sake of his seven children. He died of the plague which visited Switzerland in 1564, and swept away thirty-eight thousand persons in the territory of Bern, besides seven thousand in Basel, and fourteen hundred at Coire. It was a fatal time for the Reformed Church, for between 1564 and 1566 several of the leaders died; as Calvin, Farel, Bibliander, Borrhaus, Blaurer, Fabricius, and Saluz.[1]

2. GIORGIO BIANDRATA (or BLANDRATA), an educated physician of a noble family of Saluzzo in Piedmont (born about 1515), escaped the inquisition by flight to Geneva in 1557. He agreed substantially with Gribaldo, but was more subtle and cautious. He called Calvin his reverend father, and consulted him on theological questions. He seemed to be satisfied, but returned again and again with new doubts. Calvin, overburdened with labor and care, patiently listened and spent whole hours with the sceptic. He also answered his objections in writing.[2] At last he refused further discussion as useless. "He tried," wrote Calvin to Lismann, "to circumvent me like a serpent, but God gave me strength to withstand his cunning."

[1] Trechsel, II. 356.
[2] *Ad questiones Blandratæ responsum*, 1558. See lit. in § 127.

The spirit of doubt spread more and more in the Italian congregation. One of the principal sympathizers of Biandrata was GIANPAOLO ALCIATI, a Piedmontese who had served in the army, and was not used to reverent language.

Martinengo, the worthy Italian pastor, shortly before his death, begged Calvin to take care of the little flock and to extirpate the dangerous heresy. Accordingly, a public meeting of the Italian congregation was held May 18, 1558, in the presence of Calvin and two members of the Council. Calvin, in the name of the Council, invited the malcontents to utter themselves freely, and assured them that they should not be punished. Biandrata appealed to certain expressions of Calvin, but was easily convicted of mistake. Alciati went so far as to declare that the orthodox party "worshipped three devils worse than all the idols of popery." After a three hours' discussion, it was resolved that all the members of the congregation should subscribe a confession of faith, which asserted the divinity of Christ and the Holy Spirit, as being consistent with the essential unity of the Godhead.

Six members at first refused to subscribe, but yielded afterwards with the exception, it seems, of Biandrata and Alciati. They felt unsafe in Geneva, and went to Bern. There they found a sympathizer in Zurkinden, the secretary of the city, who engaged in an angry controversy with Calvin.

Biandrata left for Poland, gained the confidence of Prince Radziwill, propagated his Unitarian opinions, and justified himself before a synod at Pinczow (1561). In 1563 he accepted a call of Prince John Sigismund of Transylvania as his physician, and converted him and many others to his views, but was charged by Faustus Socinus to have in his last years favored the Jesuits from mercenary motives. It is possible that the old man, weary of theological strife, lost himself in the maze of scepticism, like Ochino. Tradition reports that he was robbed and murdered by his own nephew after 1585.

3. The peace of the Italian congregation was again disturbed by GIOVANNE VALENTI GENTILE of Calabria, a schoolmaster of some learning and acuteness, who was attracted to Geneva by Calvin's reputation, but soon imbibed the sentiments of Gribaldo and Biandrata. He was one of the six members who had at first refused to sign the Italian confession of faith. Soon after the departure of Biandrata and Alciati he openly professed their views, urged, as he said, by his conscience. He charged the orthodox doctrine of the Trinity with quaternity, — adding a general divine essence to the three divine essences of Father, Son, and Spirit, — and maintained that the Father was the only divine essence, the " essentiator." Both these ideas he borrowed from Servetus. The Son is only an image and reflection of the Father.

Gentile was thrown into prison, July, 1557, by order of the Council, on the charge of violating the confession he had signed. He repeated his views and appealed to the ministers and the Council for protection against the tyranny of Calvin, but he was refuted by the ministers. At last he apologized for his severe language against Calvin, whom he had always revered as a great man, but he refused to recant his views. The Council asked the judgment of five lawyers, who decided that, according to the imperial laws (*De summa Trinitate et fide catholica et de hereticis*), Gentile deserved death by fire. The Council, instead, pronounced the milder sentence of death by the sword (Aug. 15). It seems that Calvin's advice, which had been disregarded in the case of Servetus, now prevailed in the case of Gentile.

The fear of death induced Gentile to withdraw his charges against the orthodox doctrine, and to sign a brief confession of faith in three divine Persons in one Essence, and in the unity, coequality, and coeternity of the Son and Holy Spirit with the Father. He was released of the sentence of death; yet in view of his perjury, his heresies, and false accusations against the Church of Geneva, he was condemned by the magistrates to make an *amende honorable*, that is, in his shirt, bareheaded, and barefooted, with a lighted torch in his hand, to beg on his knees the judge's pardon, to burn his writings with his own hand, and to walk through the principal streets under the sound of the trumpet. The sentence was carried out on the second of September. He submitted to it with surprising readiness, happy to escape death at such a cheap price. He also promised on oath not to leave the city without permission.

But he was hardly set at liberty when he escaped and joined his friends Gribaldo and Alciati at Farges. Soon afterwards he spent some time at Lyons. He studied the ante-Nicene Fathers, who confirmed his subordinationism, and wrote a book (*Antidota*) in defence of his views and against the chapter on the Trinity in Calvin's *Institutes*. He declared that the orthodox terms of *homoousia, person, substance, trinity, unity*, were profane and monstrous, and obscured the true doctrine of the one God. He also attacked the doctrine of the two natures in Christ and the communication of attributes as idle speculations, which should be banished from the Church. He borrowed from Origen the distinction between the original God ($a\grave{v}\tau o\theta\epsilon\acute{o}\varsigma$), that is, the Father and the derived or secondary God ($\theta\epsilon\acute{o}\varsigma$, $\delta\epsilon\upsilon\tau\epsilon\rho\acute{\iota}$-$\theta\epsilon o\varsigma$, $\dot{\epsilon}\tau\epsilon\rho\acute{o}\theta\epsilon o\varsigma$) — that is, the Son. The Father alone is God in the strict sense of the term — the *essentiator ;* the Son is *essentiatus* and subordinate. He spoke most disrespectfully and passionately of the orthodox views. Calvin refuted his opinions in a special book (1561).

Gentile roused the suspicion of the Catholic authorities in Lyons and was imprisoned, but was set free after fifty days on his declaration that his writings were only opposed to Calvinism, not to orthodoxy.

But he felt unsafe in France, and accepted, with Alciati, an invitation of Biandrata to Poland in the summer of 1563.

After the royal edict, which expelled all the Antitrinitarians, he returned to Switzerland, was apprehended by the authorities of Bern, convicted of heresies, deceits, and evasions, and beheaded on the tenth of September, 1566. On the way to the place of execution, he declared that he died a martyr for the honor of the supreme God, and charged the ministers who accompanied him with Sabellianism. He received the death-stroke with firmness, amid the exhortations of the clergy and the prayers of the multitude for God's mercy. Benedict Aretius, a theologian of Bern, published in the following year the acts of the process with a refutation of Gentile's objections to the orthodox doctrine.

The fate of Gentile was generally approved. No voice of complaint or protest was heard, except a feeble one from Basel. Calvin had died more than two years before, and now the city of Bern, which had opposed his doctrinal and disciplinary rigor, condemned to death a heretic less gifted and dangerous than Servetus. Gentile himself indirectly admitted that a teacher of false religion was deserving of death, but he considered his own views as true and scriptural.[1]

The death of Gentile ends the history of Antitrinitarianism in Switzerland. In the same year the strictly orthodox Second Helvetic Confession of Bullinger was published and adopted in the Reformed Cantons.

§ 132. *The Eucharistic Controversies. Calvin and Westphal.*

I. The Sources are given in § 117. See especially Calvin's *Opera*, vol. IX. 1–252, and the Prolegomena, pp. i–xxiv. The correspondence between Bullinger, à Lasco, Farel, Viret, and Calvin, on the controversy, in his *Opera*, vols. XV. and XVI. The letters of Melanchthon from this period in the *Corpus Reform.* vols. VII.–IX. The works of Westphal are quoted below.

II. PLANCK (neutral): *Geschichte des Protest. Lehrbegriff's* (Leipzig, 1799), vol. V. Part II. 1–137. — EBRARD (Reformed): *Das Dogma vom heil. Abendmahl*, II. 525–744. — NEVIN (Reformed), in the "Mercersburg Review" for 1850, pp. 486–510. — MÖNCKEBERG (Lutheran): *Joachim Westphal und Joh. Calvin*, 1865. — WAGENMANN in Herzog[2], XVII. 1–6.

[1] See on this last chapter in the history of Gentile, Trechsel, II. 355–380.

HENRY, III. 298–357. — DYER, 401–412. — STÄHELIN, II. 112 sqq., 189 sqq. — GIESELER, III. Part II. 280 sqq. — DORNER: *Geschichte der protest. Theol.*, 400 sqq. — SCHAFF, *Creeds*, I. 279 sqq.

The sacramental controversy between Luther and Zwingli was apparently solved by the middle theory of Calvin, Bullinger, and Melanchthon, and had found a symbolical expression in the Zürich Consensus of 1549, for Switzerland, and even before that, in the Wittenberg Concordia of 1536 and in Melanchthon's irenical restatement of the 10th article of the Altered Augsburg Confession of 1540, for Germany. Luther's renewed attack upon the Swiss in 1544 was isolated, and not supported by any of his followers; while Calvin, from respect for Luther, kept silent.

But in 1552 a second sacramental war was opened by Westphal in the interest of the high Lutheran theory, and gradually spread over all Germany and Switzerland.

We may well "lament," with Calvin in his letter to Schalling (March, 1557), that those who professed the same gospel of Christ were distracted on the subject of his Last Supper, which should have been the chief bond of union among them.[1]

The Westphal-Calvin controversy did not concern the *fact* of the real presence, which was conceded by Calvin in all his previous writings on the subject, but the subordinate questions of the *mode* of the presence, of the *ubiquity* of Christ's body, and the effect of the sacrament on *unworthy* communicants, whether they received the very body and blood of Christ, or only bread and wine, to their condemnation. Calvin clearly states the points of difference in the preface to his "Second Defence" : —

---

[1] "*Dolendum est quum nos pauci numero idem profiteamur evangelium, sacræ cœnæ occasione, quam præcipuum inter nos unitatis vinculum esse decebat, in varias sententias distrahi. Sed hoc longe atrocius, non minus hostiliter confligere quam si nihil esset nobis cum Christo commune.*" *Opera*, XVI. 429. Planck, the impartial Lutheran historian, calls the sacramental controversy "*die ärgerlichste aller Streitigkeiten*" (*l.c.*, V. I. p. 1).

" That I have written reverently of the legitimate use, dignity, and efficacy of the sacraments, even he himself [Westphal] does not deny. How skilfully or learnedly in his judgment, I care not, since it is enough to be commended for piety by an enemy. The contest remaining with him embraces three articles:
"First, he insists that the bread of the Supper is substantially (*substantiali-ter*) the body of Christ. Secondly, in order that Christ may exhibit himself present to believers, he insists that his body is immense (*immensum*), and exists everywhere, though without place (*ubique esse, extra locum*). Thirdly, he insists that no figure is to be admitted in the words of Christ, whatever agreement there may be as to the thing. Of such importance does he deem it to stick doggedly to the words, that he would sooner see the whole globe convulsed than admit any exposition.
" We maintain that the body and blood of Christ are truly offered (*vere offerri*) to us in the Supper in order to give life to our souls; and we explain, without ambiguity, that our souls are invigorated by this spiritual aliment (*spirituali alimento*), which is offered to us in the Supper, just as our bodies are nourished by daily bread. Therefore we hold, that in the Supper there is a true partaking (*vera participatio*) of the flesh and blood of Christ. Should any one raise a dispute as to the word 'substance,' we assert that Christ, from the substance of his flesh, breathes life into our souls; nay, infuses his own life into us (*propriam in nos vitam diffundere*), provided always that no transfusion of substance be imagined."[1]

The Swiss had in this controversy the best of the argument and showed a more Christian spirit. The result was disastrous to Lutheranism. The Palatinate, in part also Hesse, Bremen, Anhalt, and, at a later period, the reigning dynasty of Prussia, passed over into the Reformed Church. Hereafter there were two distinct and separate Confessions in Protestant Germany, the Lutheran and the Reformed, which in the Westphalia Treaty were formally recognized on a basis of legal equality. The Lutheran Church might have sustained still greater loss if Melanchthon had openly professed his essential agreement with Calvin. But the magnetic power of Luther's name and personality, and of his great work saved his doctrine of the Eucharist and the ubiquity of Christ's body, which was finally formulated and fixed in the Formula of Concord (1577).

Joachim Westphal (1510–1574), a rigid Lutheran minister and afterwards superintendent at Hamburg, who inherited

[1] *Opera*, IX. 47.

the intolerance and violent temper, but none of the genius
and generosity of Luther, wrote, without provocation, a tract
against the "Zürich Consensus," and against Calvin and
Peter Martyr, in 1552. He aimed indirectly at the Philip-
pists (Melanchthonians), who agreed with the Calvinistic
theory of the Eucharist without openly confessing it, and
who for this reason were afterwards called Crypto-Calvinists.
He had previously attacked Melanchthon, his teacher and
benefactor, and compared his conduct in the Interim controversy with Aaron's worship of the golden calf.[1] He taught
that the very body of Christ was in the bread substantially,
that it was ubiquitous, though illocal (*extra locum*), and that
it was partaken by Judas no less than by Peter. He made
no distinction between Calvin and Zwingli. He treats as
"sacramentarians" and heretics all those who denied the
corporal presence, the *oral* manducation, and the *literal* eating
of Christ's body with the teeth, even by unbelievers. He
charges them with holding no less than twenty-eight conflicting opinions on the words of institution, quoting extracts
from Carlstadt, Zwingli, Œcolampadius, Bucer, à Lasco,
Bullinger, Peter Martyr, Schwenkfeld, and chiefly from
Calvin. But nearly all these opinions are essentially the
same, and that of Carlstadt was never adopted by any Church
or any Reformed theologian.[2] He speaks of their godless
perversion of the Scriptures, and even their "satanic blasphemies." He declared that they ought to be refuted by the
rod of the magistrates rather than by the pen.[3]

[1] *Historia vituli aurei Aaronis Exod. 32 ad nostra tempora et controversias
accommodata*, Magdeburg, 1549.

[2] See the remarks of the Strassburg editors in vol. IX. Proleg. p. x. There
are really only two Reformed theories on the Eucharist — the Zwinglian and
the Calvinistic, and the latter was embodied in all the Reformed Confessions.
A Lutheran polemic of the seventeenth century conclusively proved to his
own satisfaction that "the cursed Calvinistic heretics hold six hundred and
sixty-six theses in common with the Turks ! "

[3] *Farrago confusanearum et inter se dissidentium opinionum de Cœna Domini
ex Sacramentariorum libris congesta.* Magdeburg, 1552 (a small pamphlet, with
a preface).

As his first attack was ignored by the Swiss, he wrote another and larger tract in 1553, in which he proved the Lutheran view chiefly from 1 Cor. 11 : 29, 30, and urged the Lutherans to resist the progress of the Zwinglian or, as it was now called, Calvinistic heresy.[1]

The style and taste of his polemic may be inferred from his calling Bullinger "the bull of Zürich," Calvin "the calf of Geneva," and à Lasco "the Polish bear."

About the same time, in the autumn and winter of 1553, John à Lasco, a Polish nobleman, a friend of Calvin, and minister of a foreign Reformed congregation in London, fled with one hundred and seventy-five Protestants from persecution under the bloody Mary, and sought shelter on Danish and German shores; but was refused even a temporary refuge in cold winter at Helsingör, Copenhagen, Rostock, Lübeck, and Hamburg (though they found it at last in East Friesland). Westphal denounced these noble men as martyrs of the devil, enraged the people against them, and gloried in the inhuman cruelty as an act of faith.[2]

This conduct roused the Swiss to self-defence. Bullinger vindicated the orthodoxy of the Zürich ministry with his usual moderation. Calvin heard of the treatment of the refugees through a letter of Peter Martyr, then at Strassburg,

---

[1] *Recta fides de Cœna Domini*, Magdeburg, 1553. This was followed by *Collectanea sententiarum Aurelii Augustini de Cœna Domini*, Ratisbon, 1555 (the preface is dated September, 1554), and *Fides Cyrilli de præsentia corporis et sanguinis Christi*, Frankfort, 1555.

[2] A full account in Joh. Utenhoven (who accompanied à Lasco), *Simplex et fidelis narratio*, etc. Basil., 1560. The spirit of this rare book may be judged from the concluding sentence (quoted by Dalton who examined a copy in Cracow) : " In conclusion let us pray all the pious for Christ's sake not to harbor any hatred against those who have thus persecuted us in our affliction, and not to call fire from heaven as James and John did for the refusal of hospitality, but rather to pray for them that they may repent and be saved." See extracts in Planck, *l.c.*, 36 sqq., and H. Dalton, *Johannes à Lasco* (Gotha, 1881), 427 sqq. Mönckeberg attempts to apologize for Westphal, but without effect. Dorner says (*l.c.*, 401, note) : " *Westphal wird zum Selbstankläger in der Vorrede zu der Collectanea aus Augustin, rühmt die That der Unbarmherzigkeit als eine gute That, und stellt Nebuchadnezzar als Vorbild für solche Fälle auf.*"

in May, 1554, and took up his sharp and racy pen in three successive pamphlets. He at first wished to issue a joint remonstrance of the Swiss Churches, and sent a hasty draft to Bullinger. But Zürich, Basel, and Bern found it too severe, and refused to sign it. He corrected the draft, and published it in his own name under the title "Defence of the Sound and Orthodox Doctrine on the Sacraments," as laid down in the Consensus Tigurinus (Geneva, 1555). He treated Westphal with sovereign contempt, without naming him. Westphal replied in a tract thrice as large, complaining of the unworthy treatment, denying the intention of disturbing the peace of the Church, but repeating his charges against the Sacramentarians.[1] Calvin, after some hesitation, prepared a "Second Defence," now openly directed "*contra Westphali calumnias*," and published it, with a preface to the Churches of Germany, in January, 1556. Westphal replied in two writings, one against Calvin and one against à Lasco, and sent letters to the leading cities of North Germany, urging them to unite in an orthodox Lutheran Confession against the Zürich Consensus. He received twenty-five responses, and issued them at Magdeburg, 1557. He also reprinted Melanchthon's former opinions on the real presence (Hamburg, 1557). To meet these different assaults Calvin issued his "Last Admonition to Westphal" (1557). Westphal continued the controversy, but Calvin kept silent and handed him over to Beza.

Besides these main contestants several others took part in the fight: on the Lutheran side, Timan, Schnepf, Alberus, Gallus, Judex, Brenz, Andreæ, etc.; on the Reformed side, à Lasco, Ochino, Polanus, Bibliander, and Beza.

Calvin indignantly rebuked the "rude and barbarous insults" to persecuted members of Christ, and characterized the ultra-Lutherans as men who would rather have peace

---

[1] *Adversus cujusdam Sacramentarii falsam criminationem justa defensio,* Frankfort, 1555.

with the Turks and Papists than with Swiss Christians. He called them "apes of Luther." He triumphantly vindicated against misrepresentations and objections his doctrine of the spiritual real presence of Christ, and the sealing communication of the life-giving virtue of his body in heaven to the believer through the power of the Holy Spirit.

He might have defended his doctrine even more effectually if he had restrained his wrath and followed the brotherly advice of Bullinger, and even Farel, who exhorted him not to imitate the violence of his opponent, to confine himself to the thing, and to spare the person. But he wrote to Farel (August, 1557): "With regard to Westphal and the rest it was difficult for me to control my temper and to follow your advice. You call those 'brethren' who, if that name be offered to them by us, do not only reject, but execrate it. And how ridiculous should we appear in bandying the name of brother with those who look upon us as the worst of heretics." [1]

§ 133. *Calvin and the Augsburg Confession. Melanchthon's Position in the Second Eucharistic Controversy.*

Comp. HENRY, III. 335–339 and Beilage, pp. 102–110; the works on the Augsburg Confession, and the biographies of Melanchthon.

During the progress of this controversy both parties frequently appealed to the Augsburg Confession and to Melanchthon. They were both right and both wrong; for there are two editions of the Confession, representing the earlier and the later theories of its author on the Lord's Supper. The original Augsburg Confession of 1530, in the tenth article, teaches Luther's doctrine of the real presence so clearly and strongly that even the Roman opponents did not object to it.[2]   But from the time of the Wittenberg Con-

---

[1] *Opera*, XVI. 552.

[2] The *Catholica Refutatio Augustanæ Confessionis* of Drs. Eck, Faber, and Cochlæus says: "*Decimus articulus* [of the Augsburg Confession] *in verbis nihil offendit si modo credant* [the Lutheran signers], *sub qualibet specie integrum Christum esse.*"

cordia in 1536, or even earlier,[1] Melanchthon began to change
his view on the real presence as well as his view on predestination and free-will; in the former he approached Calvin,
in the latter he departed from him. He embodied the former
change in the Altered Confession of 1540, without official
authority, yet in good faith, as the author of the document,
and in the conviction that he represented public sentiment,
since Luther himself had moderated his opposition to the
Swiss by assenting to the Wittenberg Concordia.[2] The
altered edition was made the basis of negotiations with
the Romanists at the Colloquies of Worms and Ratisbon in
1541, and at the later Colloquies in 1546 and 1557. It was
printed (with the title and preface of the *Invariata*) in the
first collection of the symbolical books of the Lutheran Church
(*Corpus Doctrinæ Philippicum*) in 1559; it was expressly
approved by the Lutheran princes at the Convention of
Naumburg in 1561, after Melanchthon's death, as an improved
modification and authentic interpretation of the Confession,
and was adhered to by the Melanchthonians and the Reformed
even after the adoption of the Book of Concord (1580).

The text in the two editions is as follows: —

ED. 1530.	ED. 1540.
"*De Cœna Domini docent, quod cor-pus et sanguis Christi* VERE ADSINT [the German text adds: *unter der Gestalt des Brots und Weins*], *et* DISTRIB-UANTUR *vescentibus in Cœna Domini*, ET IMPROBANT SECUS DOCENTES." [In the German text: "*Derhalben wird auch die Gegenlehre verworfen.*"]	"*De Cœna Domini docent, quod* CUM PANE ET VINO *vere* EXHIBEANTUR *corpus et sanguis Christi vescentibus in Cœna Domini.*"

[1] Comp. his letters to Schnepf, Agricola, and Brenz, from the years 1534
and 1535; Matthes, *Leben Melanchthons*, p. 349; C. Schmidt, *Philipp Melanchthon*, pp. 580 sqq.

[2] Luther did not object to the change. When he broke out more fiercely
than ever against the Swiss, in his "Short Confession on the Holy Sacrament"
(1544), Melanchthon, in a letter to Bullinger, called this book not unjustly
"*atrocissimum scriptum.*" See vol. VI. 654 sq.

Ed. 1530.	Ed. 1540.
"Concerning the Lord's Supper, they teach that the body and blood of Christ *are truly present* [under the form of bread and wine], and are *distributed* to those that eat in the Lord's Supper. *And they disapprove of those who teach otherwise.*" [In the German text: "*Wherefore also the opposite doctrine is rejected.*"]	"Concerning the Lord's Supper, they teach that *with bread and wine* are truly *exhibited* the body and blood of Christ to those who eat in the Lord's Supper." [Disapproval of dissenting views is omitted.]

It is to this revised edition of the document, and to its still living author, that Calvin confidently appealed.

"In regard to the Confession of Augsburg," he says in his *Last Admonition to Westphal*, "my answer is, that, as it was published at Ratisbon (1541), it does not contain a word contrary to our doctrine.[1] If there is any ambiguity in its meaning, there cannot be a more competent interpreter than its author, to whom, as his due, all pious and learned men will readily pay this honor. To him I boldly appeal; and thus Westphal with his vile garrulity lies prostrate. . . . If Joachim wishes once for all to rid himself of all trouble and put an end to controversy, let him extract one word in his favor from Philip's lips. The means of access are open, and the journey is not so very laborious, to visit one of whose consent he boasts so loftily, and with whom he may thus have familiar intercourse. If I shall be found to have used Philip's name rashly, there is no stamp of ignominy to which I am not willing to submit.

"The passage which Westphal quotes, it is not mine to refute, nor do I regard what, during the first conflict, before the matter was clearly and lucidly explained, the importunity of some may have extorted from one who was then too backward in giving a denial. It were too harsh to lay it down as a law on literary men, that after they have given a specimen of their talent and learning, they are never after to go beyond it in the course of their lives. Assuredly, whosoever shall say that Philip has added nothing by the labor of forty years, does great wrong to him individually, and to the whole Church.

"The only thing I said, and, if need be, a hundred times repeat, is, that in this matter Philip can no more be torn from me than he can from his own bowels.[2] But although fearing the thunder which threatened to burst from violent men (those who know the boisterous blasts of Luther understand what

---

[1] "*De Confessione Augustana sic respondeo, verbulum in ea, qualis Ratisponæ edita fuit, non exstare doctrinæ nostræ contrarium.*" *Opera*, IX. 148. Comp. his letter to Schalling at Ratisbon, March, 1557, quoted on p. 377, note (*Opera*, XVI. 430).

[2] "*Solum quod dixi et quidem centies si opus sit, confirmo, non magis a me Philippum quam a propriis visceribus in hac causa posse divelli.*" *Opera*, IX. 149.

I mean), he did not always speak out openly as I could have wished, there is no reason why Westphal, while pretending differently, should indirectly charge him with having begun to incline to us only after Luther was dead. For when more than seventeen years ago we conferred together on this point of doctrine, at our first meeting, not a syllable required to be changed.[1] Nor should I omit to mention Gaspar Cruciger, who, from his excellent talents and learning, stood, next after Philip, highest in Luther's estimation, and far beyond all others. He so cordially embraced what Westphal now impugns, that nothing can be imagined more perfectly accordant than our opinions.

"But if there is still any doubt as to Philip, do I not make a sufficient offer when I wait silent and confident for his answer, assured that it will make manifest the dishonesty which has falsely sheltered itself under the venerable name of that most excellent man?"

Calvin urged Melanchthon repeatedly to declare openly his view on the points in controversy. In a letter of March 5, 1555, after thanking him for his approval of the condemnation of Servetus, he says: "About 'the bread-worship' (περὶ τῆς ἀρτολατρείας), your most intimate opinion has long since been known to me, which you do not even dissemble in your letter. But your too great slowness displeases me, by which the madness of those whom you see rushing on to the destruction of the Church, is not only kept up, but from day to day increased." Melanchthon answered, May 12, 1555: "I have determined to reply simply and without ambiguity, and I judge that I owe that work to God and the Church, nor at the age to which I have arrived, do I fear either exile or other dangers." On August 23 of the same year, Calvin expressed his gratification with this answer and wrote: "I entreat you to discharge, as soon as you can, the debt which you acknowledge you owe to God and the Church." He adds with undue severity: "If this warning, like a cock crowing rather late and out of season, do not awaken you, all will cry out with justice that you are a sluggard. Farewell, most distinguished sir, whom I venerate from the heart." In another letter of Aug. 3, 1557, he complains of

---

[1] He refers to their meeting at Frankfurt, which took place in 1539, seven years before Luther's death and five years before his last book against the Sacramentarians. See above, § 90, pp. 388 sq.

the silence of three years and apologizes for the severity of his last letter, but urges him again to come out, like a man, and to refute the charge of slavish timidity. "I do not think," he says, "you need to be reminded by many words, how necessary it is for you to hasten to wipe out this blot from your character." He proposes that Melanchthon should induce the Lutheran princes to convene a peaceful conference of both parties at Strassburg, or Tübingen, or Heidelberg, or Frankfurt, and attend the conference in person with some pious, upright, and moderate men. "If you class me," he concludes, "in the number of such men, no necessity, however pressing, will prevent me from putting up this as my chief vow, that before the Lord gather us into his heavenly kingdom I may yet be permitted to enjoy on earth, a most delightful interview with you, and feel some alleviation of my grief by deploring along with you the evils which we cannot remedy." In his last extant letter to Melanchthon, dated Nov. 19, 1558, Calvin alludes once more to the eucharistic controversy, but in a very gentle spirit, assuring him that he will never allow anything to alienate his mind " from that holy friendship and respect which I have vowed to you. . . . Whatever may happen, let us cultivate with sincerity a fraternal affection towards each other, the ties of which no wiles of Satan shall ever burst asunder."

Melanchthon would have done better for his own fame if, instead of approving the execution of Servetus, he had openly supported Calvin in the conflict with Westphal. But he was weary of the *rabies theologorum*, and declined to take an active part in the bitter strife on "bread-worship," as he called the notion of those who were not contented with the presence of the body of Christ in the sacramental *use*, but insisted upon its presence in and under the *bread*. He knew what kind of men he had to deal with. He knew that the court of Saxony, from a sense of honor, would not allow an open departure from Luther's doctrine. Prudence, timidity, and respect for the memory of Luther were the mingled motives of his silence. He was aware of his natural weakness, and confessed in a letter to Christopher von Carlowitz, in 1548: "I am, perhaps, by nature of a somewhat servile disposition, and I have before endured an altogether unseemly servitude; as Luther more frequently obeyed his temperament, in which was no little contentiousness, than he regarded his own dignity and the common good."

But in his private correspondence he did not conceal his real sentiments, his disapproval of "bread-worship" and of the doctrine of the ubiquity of Christ's body. His last utterance on the subject was in answer to the request of Elector Frederick III. of the Palatinate, who tried to conciliate the parties in the fierce eucharistic controversy at Heidelberg. Melanchthon warned against scholastic subtleties and commended moderation, peace, biblical simplicity, and the use of Paul's words that "the bread which we break is *the communion of the body* of Christ" (1 Cor. 10 : 16), not "changed into," nor the "substantial," nor the "true" body. He gave this counsel on the first of November, 1559. A few months afterwards he died (April 17, 1560).

The result was that the Elector deposed the leaders of both parties, Heshusius and Klebitz, called distinguished foreign divines to the University, and entrusted Zacharias Ursinus (a pupil of Melanchthon) and Caspar Olevianus (a pupil of Calvin) with the task of composing the Heidelberg or Palatinate Catechism, which was published Jan. 19, 1563. It became the principal symbolical book of the German and Dutch branches of the Reformed Church. It gives clear and strong expression to the Calvinistic-Melanchthonian theory of the spiritual real presence, and teaches the doctrine of election, but without a word on reprobation and preterition. In both respects it is the best expression of the genius and final doctrinal position of Melanchthon, who was himself a native of the Palatinate.

NOTES. MELANCHTHON'S LAST WORDS ON THE EUCHARIST.

Letter to Calvin, Oct. 14, 1554. Melanchthon approves of the execution of Servetus and continues: "*Quod in proximis literis me hortaris, ut reprimam ineruditos clamores illorum, qui renovant certamen περὶ ἀρτολατρείας, scito, quosdam præcipue odio mei eam disputationem movere, ut habeant plausibilem causam ad me opprimendum.*" He expresses the hope to discuss this subject with him once more before his death. (Mel's *Opera* in the *Corp. Reform.* VIII. 362 sq.)

To Hardenberg, pastor in Bremen, who was persecuted for resisting the doctrine of ubiquity, he wrote, May 9, 1557 (*ibid.* IX. 154): "*Crescit, ut vides, non modo certamen, sed etiam rabies in scriptoribus, qui ἀρτολατρείαν stabiliunt.*"

Letter to Mordeisen, counsellor of the Elector of Saxony, Nov. 15, 1557 (*ibid.* IX. 374): "*Si mihi concedetis, ut in alio loco vivam, respondebo illis indoctis sycophantis et vere et graviter, et dicam utilia ecclesiæ.*"

One of his last utterances is reported by Peucer, his son-in-law, "*ex arcanis sermonibus Dom. Philippi,*" in an autograph of Jan. 3, 1561 (vol. IX. 1088–1090). Here Melanchthon asserts the real presence, but declines to describe the mode, and rejects the ubiquity of Christ's body. He also admits the figurative sense of the words of institution, which Luther so persistently denied. "*Consideranda est,*" he says, "*interpretatio verborum Christi, quæ ab aliis κατὰ τὸ ῥητόν, ab aliis κατὰ τρόπον accipiuntur. Nec sunt plures interpretationes quam duæ. Posterior Pauli est sine omni dubio, qui vocat κοινωνίαν corporis panem, et aperte testatur, οὐκ ἐξιστάναι τῆς φύσεως τὰ ὁρώμενα σύμβολα.* ERGO NECESSE EST ADMITTI *τρόπον. Cum hac consentit vetustas Græca et Latina. Græci σύμβολα ἀντίτυπα, Latini 'signa' et 'figuras' vocant res externas et in usu corpus et sanguinem, ut discernant hunc sacrum et mysticum cibum a profano, et admoneant Ecclesiam de re signata, quæ vere exhibetur et applicatur credentibus, et dicunt esse symbola τοῦ ὄντως σώματος, contra Entychem, ut sciat Ecclesia, non esse inania symbola aut notas tantum professionis, sed symbola rerum præsentium Christi vere præsentis et efficacis et impertientis atque applicantis credentibus promissa beneficia.*"

From Melanchthon's *Judicium de controversia cœnæ Domini ad illustr. Principem ac D. D. Fridericum, Comitem Palatinum Rheni, Electorem,* dated Nov. 1, 1559 (IX. 960 sqq.): "*Non difficile, sed periculosum est respondere. Dicam tamen, quæ nunc de controversia illius loci monere possum : et oro Filium Dei, ut et consilia et eventus gubernet. Non dubium est de controversia Cœnæ ingentia certamina et bella in toto orbe terrarum secutura esse : quia mundus dat pœnas idololatriæ, et aliorum peccatorum. Ideo petamus, ut Filius Dei nos doceat et gubernet. Cum autem ubique multi sint infirmi, et nondum instituti in doctrina Ecclesiæ, imo confirmati in erroribus : necesse est initio habere rationem infirmorum.*

"*Probo igitur consilium Illustrissimi Electoris, quod rixantibus utrinque mandavit silentium ne distractio fiat in tenera Ecclesia, et infirmi turbentur in illo loco, et vicinia : et optarim rixatores in utraque parte abesse. Secundo, remotis contentiosis, prodest reliquos de una forma verborum convenire. Et in hac controversia optimum esset retinere verba Pauli: 'Panis quem frangimus, κοινωνία ἐστὶ τοῦ σώματος.' Et copiose de fructu cœnæ dicendum est, ut invitentur homines ad amorem hujus pignoris, et crebrum usum. Et vocabulum κοινωνία declarandum est.*

" *Non dicit* [Paulus], *mutari naturam panis, ut Papistæ dicunt : non dicit, ut* BREMENSES, *panem esse substantiale corpus Christi. Non dicit, ut* HESHUSIUS, *panem esse verum corpus Christi : sed esse* κοινωνίαν, *id est, hoc, quo fit consociatio cum corpore Christi : quæ fit in usu, et quidem non sine cogitatione, ut cum mures panem rodunt.* . . .

" *Sed hanc veram et simplicem doctrinam de fructu, nominant quidam cothurnos : et postulant dici, an sit corpus in pane, aut speciebus panis? Quasi vero Sacramentum propter panem et illam Papisticam adorationem institutum sit. Postea fingunt, quomodo includant pani : alii conversionem, alii transubstantiationem, alii ubiquitatem excogitarunt. Hæc portentosa omnia ignota sunt eruditæ vetustati.* . . .

" *Ac maneo in hac sententia : Contentiones utrinque prohibendas esse, et forma verborum una et simili utendum esse. Si quibus hæc non placent, nec volunt ad communionem accedere, his permittatur, ut suo judicio utantur, modo non fiant distractiones in populo.*

" *Oro autem filium Dei, Dominum nostrum Jesum Christum sedentem ad dextram æterni patris, et colligentem æternam Ecclesiam voce Evangelii, ut nos doceat, gubernet, et protegat. Opto etiam, ut aliquando in pia Synodo de omnibus controversiis horum temporum deliberetur.*"

§ 134. *Calvin and Heshusius.*

I. HESHUSIUS: *De Præsentia Corporis Christi in Cœna Domini contra Sacramentarios.* Written in 1559, first published at Jena, 1560 (and also at Magdeburg and Nürnberg, 1561). *Defensio veræ et sacræ confessionis de vera Præsentia Corporis Christi in Cœna Domini adversus calumnias Calvini, Boquini, Bezæ, et Clebitii.* Magdeburg, 1562.

II. CALVINUS: *Dilucida Explicatio sanæ Doctrinæ de vera Participatione Carnis et Sanguinis Christi in Sacra Cœna ad discutiendas Heshusii nebulas.* Genevæ, 1561. Also in French. *Opera*, IX. 457–524. Comp. Proleg. xli–xliii.
— BEZA wrote two tracts against Heshusius : Κρεωφαγία *sive Cyclops*, etc., and *Abstersio calumniarum quibus Calvinus aspersus est ab Heshusio.* Gen., 1561. BOQUIN and KLEBITZ likewise opposed him.

III. J. G. LEUCKFELD: *Historia Heshusiana.* Quedlinburg, 1716. — T. H. WILKENS: *Tilemann Hesshusen, ein Streittheologe der Lutherskirche.* Leipzig, 1860. — C. SCHMIDT: *Philipp Melanchthon.* Elberfeld, 1861, pp. 639 sqq. — HACKENSCHMIDT, Art. "Hesshusen" in Herzog[2], VI. 75–79. — HENRY, III. 339–344, and Beilage, 221. Comp. also PLANCK, HEPPE, G. FRANK, and the extensive literature on the Reformation in the Palatinate and the history of the Heidelberg Catechism (noticed in SCHAFF'S *Creeds of Christendom*, I. 529–531).

Tilemann Heshusius (in German Hesshus or Hesshusen) was born in 1527 at Niederwesel in the duchy of Cleves, and died at Helmstädt in 1588. He was one of the most energetic and pugnacious champions of scholastic orthodoxy who outluthered Luther and outpoped the pope.[1] He identified piety with orthodoxy, and orthodoxy with illocal con-insubstantiation,[2] or "bread-worship," to use Melanchthon's expression. He occupied influential positions at Gosslar, Rostock, Heidelberg, Bremen, Magdeburg, Zweibrücken, Jena, and Prussia; but with his turbulent disposition he stirred up strife everywhere, used the power of excommunication very freely, and was himself no less than seven times deposed from office and expelled. He quarrelled also with his friends Flacius, Wigand, and Chemnitz. But while he tenaciously defended the literal eating of Christ's body by unbelievers as well as believers, he dissented from Westphal's coarse and revolting notion of a chewing of Christ's body with the teeth, and confined himself to the *manducatio oralis*. He rejected also the doctrine of ubiquity, and found fault with its introduction into the Formula of Concord.[3]

Heshusius was originally a pupil and table-companion of Melanchthon, and agreed with his moderate opinions, but, like Westphal and Flacius, he became an ungrateful enemy

[1] The other leaders of the anti-Melanchthonian ultra-Lutheranism were Amsdorf (d. 1565), Westphal (d. 1574), Flacius (d. 1575), Judex (d. 1574), Jimann (d. 1557), Gallus (d. 1570), and Wigand (d. 1587). The chief pupils of Melanchthon were Eber (d. 1569), Cruciger (d. 1548) and his son (d. 1575), Camerarius (d. 1574), Peucer, Krell, Pezel, Pfeffinger, Hardenberg, Major, Menius. One of the noblest traits of Luther was his hearty appreciation of Melanchthon to the end of his life, notwithstanding the marked difference. His narrow followers entirely lacked this element of liberality and generosity. Comp. Dorner, *Geschichte der protest. Theologie*, pp. 330 sqq.

[2] I coin this word from the Lutheran formula *cum, in,* and *sub pane et vino.* The usual designation "consubstantiation" is repudiated by Lutherans in the sense of impanation or local inclusion.

[3] Planck and Heppe give him a bad character, and charge him with inordinate ambition and avarice. According to Heppe he was "*einer der widerwärtigsten lutherischen Pfaffen seiner Zeit.*" Hackenschmidt judges him more mildly as a consistent advocate of the tendency which makes no distinction between religion and theology, church authority and police force. The Strassburg editors (*Opera*, IX. Prol. p. xli.) call him a "*vir imperiosus et φιλονεικότατος.*" Bullinger compared him to the Homeric Thersites, who was despised for scurrility.

of his benefactor.   He was recommended by him to a professorship at Heidelberg and the general superintendency of
the Lutheran Church in the Palatinate on the Rhine (1558).
Here he first appeared as a champion of the strict Lutheran
theory of the substantial presence, and attacked "the Sacramentarians" in a book "On the Presence of the Body of
Christ in the Lord's Supper." He quarrelled with his colleagues, especially with Deacon Klebitz, who was a Melanchthonian, but no less violent and pugnacious.   He even tried
to wrest the eucharistic cup from him at the altar.   He
excommunicated him because he would not admit the *in* and
sub, but only the *cum* (*pane et vino*), in the scholastic formula
of the Lutheran doctrine of the real presence.   Elector
Frederick III., called the Pious, restored peace by dismissing
both Heshusius and Klebitz (Sept. 16, 1559), with the
approval of Melanchthon.   He afterwards ordered the preparation of the Heidelberg Catechism, and introduced the
Reformed Church into the Palatinate, 1563.[1]

On the other hand, the Lutheran clergy of Würtemberg,
under the lead of Brenz, in a synod at Stuttgart, gave the
doctrine of the ubiquity of Christ's body, which Luther had
taught, but which Melanchthon had rejected, symbolical
authority for Würtemberg (Dec. 19, 1559).[2]

Calvin received the book of Heshusius from Bullinger,
who advised him to answer the arguments, but to avoid
personalities.[3]   He hesitated for a while, and wrote to
Olevianus (November, 1560) : "The loquacity of that brawler
is too absurd to excite my anger, and I have not yet decided
whether I shall answer him, I am weary of so many pamphlets, and shall certainly not think his follies worthy of
many days' labor.   But I have composed a brief analysis of
this controversy, which will, perhaps, be shortly published."

---

[1] See § 133, p. 669.   [2] Planck, vol. V. Part II. 383 sqq.

[3] He wrote to him: "*Oro, si statuisti respondere, respondeas ad argumenta,
diligenter preterita persona illa Thersitis homerici.*"

It was one of his last controversial pamphlets and appeared in 1561.

In the beginning of his response he made that most touching allusion to his departed friend Melanchthon, which we have noticed in another connection.[1] What a contrast between this noble tribute of unbroken friendship and the mean ingratitude of Heshusius, who most violently attacked Melanchthon's memory immediately after his death.[2]

Calvin reiterates and vindicates the several points brought out in the controversy with Westphal, and refutes the arguments of Heshusius from the Scripture and the Fathers with his wonted intellectual vigor and learning, seasoned with pepper and salt. He compares him to an ape clothed in purple, and to an ass in a lion's skin. The following are the chief passages: —

"Heshusius bewails the vast barbarism which appears to be impending, as if any greater or worse barbarism were to be feared than that from him and his fellows. To go no further for proof, let the reader consider how fiercely he sneers and tears at his master, Philip Melanchthon, whose memory he ought sacredly to revere. . . . Such is the pious gratitude of the scholar, not only towards the teacher to whom he owes whatever little learning he may possess, but towards a man who has deserved so highly of the whole Church. . . .

"Though there is some show about him, he does nothing more by his magniloquence than vend the old follies and frivolities of Westphal and his fellows. He harangues loftily on the omnipotence of God, on putting implicit faith in his word, and subduing human reason, in terms he may have learned from other sources, of which I believe myself also to be one. I have no doubt, from his childish stolidity of glorying, that he imagines himself to combine the qualities of Melanchthon and Luther. From the one he ineptly borrows flowers, and having no better way of rivalling the vehemence of the other, he substitutes bombast and sound. . . .

"Westphal boldly affirms that the body of Christ is chewed by the teeth, and confirms it by quoting with approbation the recantation of Berengar, as given by Gratian. This does not please Heshusius, who insists that it is eaten by the mouth but not touched by the teeth, and greatly disproves those gross modes of eating. . . .

"Heshusius argues that if the body of Christ is in heaven, it is not in the Supper, and that instead of him we have only a symbol. As if, forsooth,

[1] See § 90, p. 398.
[2] *Responsio ad præjudicium Philippi Melanchthonis*, 1560.

the Supper were not, to the true worshippers of God, a heavenly action, or, as it were, a vehicle which carries them above the world. But what is this to Heshusius, who not only halts on the earth, but drives his nose as far as he can into the mud? Paul teaches that in baptism we put on Christ (Gal. 3 : 27). How acutely will Heshusius argue that this cannot be if Christ remain in heaven? When Paul spoke thus it never occurred to him that Christ must be brought down from heaven, because he knew that he is united to us in a different manner, and that his blood is not less present to cleanse our souls than water to cleanse our bodies. . . . Of a similar nature is his objection that the body is not received truly if it is received symbolically; as if by a true symbol we excluded the exhibition of the reality.

"Some are suspicious of the term *faith*, as if it overthrew the reality and the effect. But we ought to view it far otherwise, viz. that the only way in which we are conjoined to Christ is by raising our minds above the world. Accordingly, the bond of our union with Christ is faith, which raises us upwards, and casts its anchor in heaven, so that instead of subjecting Christ to the figments of our reason, we seek him above in his glory.

"This furnishes the best method of settling a dispute to which I adverted, viz. whether believers alone receive Christ, or all, without exception, to whom the symbols of bread and wine are distributed, receive him? Correct and clear is the solution which I have given: Christ offers his body and blood to all in general; but as unbelievers bar the entrance of his liberality, they do not receive what is offered. It must not, however, be inferred from this that when they reject what is given, they either make void the grace of Christ, or detract in any respect from the efficacy of the sacrament. The Supper does not, through their ingratitude, change its nature, nor does the bread, considered as an earnest or pledge given by Christ, become profane, so as not to differ at all from common bread, but it still truly testifies communion with THE FLESH AND BLOOD OF CHRIST."

This is the conclusion of Calvin's last deliverance on the vexed subject of the sacrament. For the rest he handed his opponent over to Beza, who answered the "Defence" of Heshusius with two sharp and learned tracts.

The eucharistic controversy kindled by Westphal and Klebitz was conducted in different parts of Germany with incredible bigotry, passion, and superstition. In Bremen, John Timann fought for the carnal presence, and insisted upon the ubiquity of Christ's body as a settled dogma (1555); while Albert Hardenberg, a friend of Melanchthon, opposed it, and was banished (1560); but a reaction took place afterwards, and Bremen became a stronghold of the Reformed Confession in Northern Germany.

§ 135.   *Calvin and the Astrologers.*

CALVIN: *Advertissement contre l'astrologie qu'on appelle justiciaire : et autres curi-osités qui régnent aujourdhuis dans le monde.* Genève, 1549 (55 pp.). The French text is reprinted in *Opera*, vol. VII. 509–542. *Admonitio adversus astrologiam quam judiciariam vocant ; aliasque præterea curiositates nonnullas, quæ hodie in universam fere orbem grassantur,* 1549. The Latin translation is by Fr. Hottman, sieur de Villiers, at that time secretary of Calvin, who dictated to him the work in French. The Latin text is reprinted in the Amsterdam ed., vol. IX. 500–509. An English translation: *An Admonition against Astrology, Judiciall and other curiosities that reigne now in the world*, by Goddred Gylby, appeared in London without date, and is mentioned by HENRY, III. Beil. 212. Comp. HENRY, II. 391 sq.

Calvin's clear, acute, and independent intellect was in advance of the crude superstitions of his age. He wrote a warning against judicial astrology[1] or divination, which presumes to pronounce judgment upon a man's character or destiny as written in the stars. This spurious science, which had wandered from Babylon[2] to ancient Rome and from heathen Rome to the Christian Church, flourished especially in Italy and France at the very time when other superstitions were shaken to the base. Several popes of the Renaissance — Sixtus IV., Julius II., Leo X., Paul III. — were addicted to it, but Pico della Mirandola wrote a book against it. King Francis I. dismissed his physician because he was not sufficiently skilled in this science. The Duchess Renata of Ferrara consulted, even in her later years, the astrologer Luc Guaric. The court of Catherine de Medici made extensive use of this and other black arts, so that the Church and the State had to interfere.

But more remarkable is the fact that such an enlightened scholar as Melanchthon should have anxiously watched the constellations for their supposed bearing upon human events. Lelio Sozini was at a loss to know whether Melanchthon

---

[1] *Astrologia judiciaria* as distinct from *astrologia naturalis*, or simply *astrologia*.

[2] Hence " *Chaldæi*," " *mathematici*," " *astrologi*," were identical terms.

depended most on the stars, or on their Maker and Ruler.[1] In this respect Luther, notwithstanding his strong belief in witchcraft and personal encounters with the devil, was in advance of his more learned friend, and refuted his astrological calculation of the nativity of Cicero with the Scripture fact of Esau's and Jacob's birth in the same hour. Yet he regarded the comets, or "harlot stars," as he called them, as tokens of God's wrath, or as works of the devil. Zwingli saw in Halley's comet, which appeared a few weeks before the disaster of Cappel, a sign of war and of his own death. The independent and heretical Servetus believed and practised astrology and wrote a defence of it (*Apologetica Disceptatio pro Astrologia*).

Nothing of this kind is found in Calvin. He denounced the attempt to reveal what God has hidden, and to seek him outside of his revealed will, as an impious presumption and a satanic delusion. It is right and proper, he maintains, to study the laws and motions of the heavenly bodies.[2] True astronomy leads to the praise of God's wisdom and majesty; but astrology upsets the moral order. God is sovereign in his gifts and not bound to any necessity of nature. He has foreordained all things by his eternal decree. Sometimes sixty thousand men fall in one battle; are they therefore born under the same star? It is true the sun works upon the earth, and heat and dearth, rain and storm come down from the skies, but the wickedness of man proceeds from his will. The astrologers appealed to the first chapter of Genesis and to the prophet Jeremiah, who calls the stars *signs*, but Calvin met them by quoting Isa. 44 : 25 : "who frustrateth the *tokens* of the liars and maketh diviners mad." In conclusion

---

[1] He wrote to Bullinger from Wittenberg, Aug. 20, 1550: "*Omnes ab uno Melanchthone [pendent], qui Astrologiæ judiciariæ fuit addictus, et unus ille ab astrisne magis, an ab astrorum conditore ac domino pendeat, ignoro.*" Quoted by Trechsel, *Antitrin.* II. 154, note 4.

[2] Comp. *Inst.* I. ch. V. §§ 2 and 5, where he speaks highly of astronomy.

he rejects the whole theory and practice of astrology as not only superfluous and useless, but even pernicious.[1]

In the same tract he ridicules the alchemists, and incidentally exhibits a considerable amount of secular learning.

Calvin discredited also the ingenious speculations of Pseudo-Dionysius on the Celestial Hierarchy, as "mere babbling," adding that the author of that book, which was sanctioned by Thomas Aquinas and Dante, spoke like a man descended from heaven and giving an account of things he had seen with his own eyes; while Paul, who was caught up to the third heaven, did not deem it lawful for man to utter the secret things he had seen and heard.[2]

Calvin might have made his task easier if he had accepted the heliocentric theory of Copernicus, which was known in his time, though only as a hypothesis.[3]

But in this matter Calvin was no more in advance of his age than any other divine. He believed that "the whole heaven moves around the earth," and declared it preposterous to set the conjecture of a man against the authority of God, who in the first chapter of Genesis had pointed out the relation of the sun and moon to the earth. Luther speaks with contempt of that upstart astronomer who wishes to reverse

[1] " *Curiositas non modo supervacanea et ad nullam rem utilis, verum etiam exitiosa.*"

[2] *Inst.* Bk. I. ch. XIV. § 4.

[3] Copernicus finished his work *De Orbium cœlestium Revolutionibus* in 1530, and dedicated it to the pope; but it was not published till 1543, by Osiander of Nürnberg, to whom he had given the manuscript, and who announced the discovery in the preface as a mere hypothesis. He received a copy on his death-bed at Frauenburg on the borders of Prussia and Poland. He was probably a devout man, and is often credited with the prayer graven on his tombstone: "I ask not the grace accorded to Paul; not that given to Peter; give me only the favor which thou didst show to the thief on the cross" ("*non parem Pauli gratiam requiro,*" etc.); but this inscription is taken from a poem of Æneas Sylvius *De Passione Domini,* and was put upon the monument of Copernicus at Thorn by Dr. Melchior Pyrnesius (1589). Copernicus is there represented with folded hands before a crucifix. See Prowe's work on Copernicus, and Luthardt in the "Theol. Literaturblatt" for April 22, 1892 (p. 188).

the entire science of astronomy and the sacred Scripture, which tells us that Joshua commanded the sun to stand still, and not the earth. Melanchthon condemned the system in his treatise on the "Elements of Physics," published six years after the death of Copernicus, and cited against it the witness of the eyes, which inform us that the heavens revolve in the space of twenty-four hours; and passages from the Psalms and Ecclesiastes, which assert that the earth stands fast and that the sun moves around it. He suggests severe measures to restrain such impious teaching as that of Copernicus.

But we must remember that the Copernican theory was opposed by philosophers as well as theologians of all creeds for nearly a hundred years, under the notion that it contradicts the testimony of the senses and the geocentric teaching of the Bible. When towards the close of the sixteenth century Galileo Galilei (1564–1642) became a convert to the Copernican theory, and with his rude telescope discovered the satellites of Jupiter and the phases of Venus, he was denounced as a heretic, summoned before the Inquisition at Rome and commanded by Bellarmin, the standard theologian of the papacy, to abandon his error, and to teach that the earth is the immovable centre of the universe (Feb. 26, 1616). The Congregation of the Index, moved by Pope Paul V., rendered the decree that "the doctrine of the double motion of the earth about its axis and about the sun is false, and entirely contrary to the Holy Scripture," and condemned the works of Copernicus, Kepler, and Galileo, which affirm the motion of the earth. They remained on the Index Purgatorius till the time of Benedict XIV. Even after the triumph of the Copernican system in the scientific world, there were respectable theologians, like John Owen and John Wesley, who found it inconsistent with their theory of inspiration, and rejected it as a delusive and arbitrary hypothesis tending towards infidelity. "*E pur si muove*," the earth does move for all that!

There can be no contradiction between the Bible and science; for the Bible is not a book of astronomy or geology or science; but a book of religion, teaching the relation of the world and man to God; and when it touches upon the heavenly bodies, it uses the phenomenal popular language without pronouncing judgment for or against any scientific theory.

CHAPTER XVI.

SERVETUS: HIS LIFE, OPINIONS, TRIAL, AND EXECUTION.

§ 136. *The Servetus Literature.*

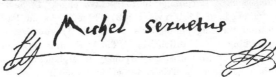

I. THEOLOGICAL WORKS OF MICHAEL SERVETUS.

DE TRINI-
TATIS ERRORIBUS
LIBRI SEPTEM.
PER MICHAELEM SERUETO, ALIÀS
REUES AB ARAGONIA
HISPANUM
ANNO MDXXXI.

This book was printed at Hagenau in the Alsace, but without the name of the place, or of the publisher or printer. It contains 120 pages.

Dialogo | rum de Trinitate | Libri duo. | De justicia regni Chri | sti, Capitula quatuor. | Per Michaelem Serveto, | aliâs Reves, ab Aragonia | Hispanum. | Anno MDXXXII. Likewise printed at Hagenau. It concludes with the words: "*Perdat Dominus omnes ecclesiæ tyrannos. Amen. Finis.*"

These two works (bound in one volume in the copy before me) were incorporated in revised shape in the *Restitutio.*

CHRISTIANI=
SMI RESTITV=
T I O.

Totius ecclesiæ apostolicæ est ad sua limina vocatio, in integrum restituta cognitione Dei, fidei Christi, iustificationis nostræ, regenerationis baptismi, et cæ næ domini manducationis. Restituto denique nobis re gno, cælesti, Babylonis impiæ captiuitate soluta, et An tichristo cum suis penitus destructo.

בפרת ההיא יעסוד מיכאר־ השר

καὶ ἐγένετο πόλεμος ἐν τῷ οὐρανῷ.

M. D. LIIL.
[Facsimile of title page.]

734   A P O L O G I A.

nima quædam, omnia in se contemplans, et lucide continens: mortalibus olim velata, et per Christum reuelata: quam et plerique dixerunt, fuisse ipsammet animam Christi. Sapientiam nos vere dicimus, instar animæ Christi, rationem diuinam de Christo, personalem Christi substantiam in Deo relucentem, et omnia continentem. In ea primaria luce esse reliqua omnia secundario relucentia, vt in anima tua relucent res aliæ, quæ sunt in ipsa. Vnde est anima nostra vera imago illius sapientiæ Dei, et ab ea vere reformatur. Nec solum dicimus, in sapientia Dei omnia relucere, sed et inde habere suum esse, ex inuisibilibus visibilia facta. Dicimus item, eam a Christo sapientiæ lucem, et in angelos, et in animas nostras se diffundentem, velut speculum lucidum, varias nobis et angelis rerum cognitiones dare. Atque ita quicquid angeli vnquam cognouerunt, a Christo acceperunt, sicut et nos. Benedictus ille sit in secula seculorum, qui sapientiam suam infundens, hanc de se nobis cognitionem dedit. Benedicti sint in ipso, qui ipsum vere credent esse filium Dei, ab æterno in Deo relucentem, et in æternum regnantem. Amen. Amen.

M. S. V.
1 5 5 3.

[Facsimile of last page.]

This work was printed at Vienne in Dauphiné, at the expense of the author, who is indicated on the last page by the initial letters M. S. V.; i.e. *Michael Servetus Villanovanus.* It contains in 734 octavo pages: 1) Seven books on the Trinity (the ed. of 1531 revised); 2) Three books on Faith and the Righteousness of the kingdom of Christ (revised); 3) Four books on Regeneration and the kingdom of Antichrist; 4) Thirty Epistles to Calvin; 5) Sixty Signs of the reign of Antichrist; 6) Apology to Melanchthon and his colleagues on the mystery of the Trinity and ancient discipline.

One thousand (some say eight hundred) copies were printed and nearly all burnt or otherwise destroyed. Four or five were saved: namely, one sent by Servetus through Frelon to Calvin; one taken from the five bales seized at Lyons for the use of the Inquisitor Ory; a third transmitted for inspection to the Swiss Churches and Councils; a fourth sent by Calvin to Bullinger; a fifth given by Calvin to Colladon, one of the judges of Servetus, in which the objectionable passages are marked, and which was, perhaps, the same with the fourth copy. Castellio (1554) complained that he could not get a copy.

At present only two copies of the original edition are known to exist; one in the National Library of Paris (the Colladon copy), the other in the Imperial Library of Vienna. Willis gives the curious history of these copies, pp. 535–541; comp. his note on p. 196. Audin says that he used the annotated copy which bears the name of Colladon on the title-page, and the marks of the flames on the margins; how it was rescued, he does not know. It is this copy which passed into the hands of Dr. Richard Mead, a distinguished physician in London, who put a Latin note at the head of the work: " *Fuit hic liber D. Colladon qui ipse nomen suum adscripsit. Ille vero simul cum Calvino inter judices sedebat qui auctorem Servetum flammis damnarunt. Ipse indicem in fine confecit. Et porro in ipso opere lineis ductis hic et illic notavit verba quibus ejus blasphemias et errores coargueret. Hoc exemplar unicum quantum scire licet flammis servatum restat : omnia enim quæ reperire poterat auctoritate sua ut comburerentur curavit Calvinus.*" (Quoted from Audin.) This must be the copy now in Paris. Dr. Mead began to republish a handsome edition in 1723, but it was suppressed and burnt by order of Gibson, the bishop of London.

In 1790, the book rose like a phœnix from its ashes in the shape of an exact reprint, page for page, and line for line, so that it can only be distinguished from the first edition by the date of publication at the bottom of the last page in extremely small figures — 1790 (not 1791, as Trechsel, Stähelin, Willis, and others, say). The reprint was made from the original copy in the Vienna Library by direction of Chr. Th. Murr, M.D. (See his *Adnotationes ad Bibliothecas Hallerianas, cum variis ad scripta Michaelis Serveti pertinentibus*, Erlangen, 1805, quoted by Willis.) The edition must have been small, for copies are rare. My friend, the Rev. Samuel M. Jackson, is in possession of a copy which I have used, and of which two pages, the first and the last, are given in facsimile.

A German translation of the *Restitutio* by Dr. BERNHARD SPIESS: *Michael Servets Wiederherstellung des Christenthums zum ersten Mal übersetzt.* Erster Bd., Wiesbaden (Limbarth), 1892 (323 pp.). The second vol. has not yet appeared. He says in the preface: "*An Begeisterung für Christus und an biblischem Purismus ist Servet den meisten Theologen unserer Tage weit überlegen [?] ; von eigentlichen Lästerungen ist nichts bei ihm zu entdecken.*" Dr. Spiess, like Dr. Tollin, is both a defender of Servetus and an admirer of Calvin. He translated the first ed. of his *Institutes* (1536) into German (Wiesbaden, 1887).

The geographical and medical works of Servetus will be noticed in the next sections.

II. CALVINISTIC SOURCES.

CALVIN : *Defensio orthodoxæ fidei de sacra trinitate contra prodigiosos errores Michaelis Serveti Hispani, ubi ostenditur hæreticos jure gladii coërcendos esse*, etc., written in 1554, in *Opera*, VIII. (Brunsw., 1870), 453–644. The same volume contains thirty letters of Servetus to Calvin, 645–720, and the *Actes du procès de Mich. Servet.*, 721–872. See also the correspondence of Calvin from the year 1553 in vol. XIV. 58 sqq. (The *Defensio* is in the Amsterdam ed., vol. IX. 510–567.) Calvin refers to Servetus after his death several times in the last ed. of the *Institutes* (I. III. § 10, 22; II. IX. § 3, 10; IV. XVI. 29, 31), in his *Responsio ad Balduini Con-*

vitia (1562), *Opera*, IX. 575, and in his Commentary on John 1 : 1 (written in 1554) : " *Servetus, superbissimus ex gente Hispanica nebulo.*"

BEZA gives a brief account in his *Calvini Vita*, ad a. 1553 and 1554, where he says that " Servetus was justly punished at Geneva, not as a sectary, but as a monster made up of nothing but impiety and horrid blasphemies, with which, by his speeches and writings, for the space of thirty years, he had infected both heaven and earth." He thinks that Servetus uttered a satanic prediction on the title-page of his book : " Great war took place in heaven, *Michael* and his angels fighting with [not against] the dragon." He also wrote an elaborate defence of the death-penalty for heresy in his tract *De hæreticis a civili magistratu puniendis, adversus Martini Bellii* [pseudonym] *farraginem et novorum academicorum sectam.* Geneva (Oliva Rob. Stephani), 1554; second ed. 1592; French translation, 1560. See Heppe's *Beza*, p. 38 sq.

III. ANTI-CALVINISTIC.

BOLSEC, in his *Histoire de la vie . . . de Jean Calvin* (1577), chs. III. and IV., discusses the trial of Servetus in a spirit hostile alike to Calvin and Servetus. He represents the Roman Catholic view. He calls Servetus "a very arrogant and insolent man," and a " monstrous heretic," who deserved to be exterminated. " *Desireroy,*" he says, p. 25, "*que tous semblables fussent exterminez : et l'église de nostre Seigneur fut bien purgée de telle vermine.*" His more tolerant editor, L. F. Chastel, protests against this wish by an appeal to Luke 9 : 55.

IV. DOCUMENTARY SOURCES.

The Acts of the process of Servetus at Vienne were published by the Abbé D'ARTIGNY, Paris, 1749 (Tom. II. *des Nouveaux Mémoires*). — *The Acts of the process at Geneva,* first published by J. H. ALBERT RILLIET : *Relation du procès criminel intenté à Genève en 1553 contre Michel Servet, rédigée d'après les documents originaux.* Genève, 1844. Reprinted in *Opera,* vol. VIII. — English translation, with notes and additions, by W. K. TWEEDIE : *Calvin and Servetus.* Edinburgh, 1846. German translation by BRUNNEMANN (see below).

V. MODERN WORKS.

* L. MOSHEIM, the famous Lutheran Church historian (1694–1755), made the first impartial investigation of the Servetus controversy, and marks a reaction of judgment in favor of Servetus, in two monographs, *Geschichte des berühmten Spanischen Arztes Michael Serveto,* Helmstædt, 1748, 4° (second vol. of his *Ketzergeschichte*) ; and *Neue Nachrichten von Serveto,* 1750. He had first intrusted his materials to a pupil, HENR. AB. ALLWOERDEN, who published a *Historia Michaelis Serveti,* Helmstadii, 1727 (238 pp., with a fine portrait of Servetus and the scene of his execution) ; but as this book was severely criticised by Armand de la Chapelle, the pastor of the French congregation at the Hague, Mosheim wrote his first work chiefly from copies of the acts of the trial of Servetus at Geneva (which are verified by the publication of the original documents in 1844), and his second work from the trial at Vienne, which were fur-

nished to him by a French ecclesiastic. Comp. HENRY, III. 102 sq.; DYER, 540 sq.

In the nineteenth century Servetus has been thoroughly discussed by the biographers of Calvin: HENRY (vol. III. 107 sqq., abridged in Stebbing's transl., vol. II.); AUDIN (chs. XL. and XLI.); DYER (chs. IX. and X., pp. 296–367); STÄHELIN (I. 422 sqq.; II. 309 sqq.); and by AMÉDÉE ROGET, in his *Histoire du peuple de Genève* (vol. IV., 1877, which gives the history of 1553–1555). Henry, Stähelin, and Roget vindicate Calvin, but dissent from his intolerance; Dyer aims to be impartial; Audin, like Bolsec, condemns both Calvin and Servetus.

* F. TRECHSEL: *Michael Servet und seine Vorgänger*, Heidelberg, 1839 (the first part of his *Die protest. Antitrinitarier*). He draws chiefly from Servetus's works and from the proceedings of the trial in the archives of Bern, which agree with those of Geneva, published afterwards by Rilliet. His work is learned and impartial, but with great respect for Calvin. Comp. his valuable article in the first ed. of Herzog, vol. XIV. 286–301.

* W. K. TWEEDIE: *Calvin and Servetus*, London, 1846.

EMILE SAISSET: *Michael Servet*, I. *Doctrine philosophique et religieuse de M. S.;* II. *Le procès et la mort de M. S.* In the "Revue des deux Mondes" for 1848, and in his "Mélanges d'histoire," 1859, pp. 117–227. Saisset was the first to assign Servetus his proper place among scientists and pantheists. He calls him "*le théologien philosophe panthéiste précurseur inattendu de Malebranche et de Spinoza, de Schleiermacher et de Strauss.*"

J. S. PORTER (Unitarian): *Servetus and Calvin*, 1854.

KARL BRUNNEMANN: *M. Serv., eine aktenmässige Darstellung des 1553 in Genf gegen ihn geführten Kriminal-processes*, Berlin, 1865. (From Rilliet.)

* HENRI TOLLIN (Lic. Theol., Dr. Med., and minister of the French Reformed Church at Magdeburg): I. *Charakterbild Michael Servets*. Berlin, 1876, 48 pp. 8° (transl. into French by Mme. Picheral-Dardier, Paris, 1879); II. *Das Lehrsystem Michael Servets, genetisch dargestellt*, Gütersloh, 1876–1878, 3 vols. (besides many smaller tracts; see below).

* R. WILLIS (M.D.): *Servetus and Calvin*. London, 1877 (541 pp.), with a fine portrait of Servetus and an ugly one of Calvin. More favorable to the former.

MARCELINO MENENDEZ PELAYO (R. Cath.): *Historia de las Heterodoxos Espanjoles*. Madrid, 1877. Tom. II. 249–313.

DON PEDRO GONZALES DE VELASCO: *Miguel Serveto*. Madrid, 1880 (23 pp.). He has placed a statue of Serveto in the portico of the Instituto antropologico at Madrid.

* Prof. Dr. A. v. D. LINDE: *Michael Servet, een Brandoffer der Gereformeerde Inquisitie*. Groningen, 1891 (326 pp.). Hostile to Calvin, as the title indicates, and severe also against Tollin, but valuable for the literary references, distributed among the chapters.

(Articles in Encyclop., by CHARLES DARDIER, in Lichtenberger's "Encycl. des Sciences religieuses," vol. XI., pp. 570–582 (Paris, 1881); in LAROUSSE's "Grand Dictionnaire universel," vol. XIV. 621–623; ALEX.

Gordon, in "Encycl. Brit." XXI. 684–686; by Bernh. Riggenbach, in Herzog [2], XIV. 153–161.)

The theology of Servetus is analyzed and criticised by Heberle: *M. Servets Trinitätslehre und Christologie* in the "Tübinger Zeitschrift" for 1840; Baur: *Die christl. Lehre v. d. Dreieinigkeit und Menschwerdung Gottes* (Tübingen, 1843), III. 54–103; Dorner: *Lehre v. d. Person Christi* (Berlin, 1853), II. 613, 629, 649–660; Punjer: *De M. Serveti doctrina*, Jena, 1876.

The tragedy of Servetus has been dramatized by Max Ring (*Die Genfer*, 1850), José Echegaray (1880), and Albert Hamann (1881).

Servetus has been more thoroughly discussed and defended in recent times than any man connected with the Reformation.

The greatest Servetus scholar and vindicator is Dr. Tollin, pastor of a Huguenot Church in Germany, who calls himself "a Calvinist by birth and a decided friend of toleration by nature." He was led to the study of Servetus by his interest in Calvin, and has written a Serveto-centric library of about forty books and tracts, bearing upon every aspect of Servetus: his *Theology, Anthropology, Soteriology, Eschatology, Diabology, Antichristology*, his relations to the Reformers (Luther, Bucer, Melanchthon), and to Thomas Aquinas, and also his medical and geographical writings. He has kindly furnished me with a complete list, and I will mention the most important below in their proper places.

Dr. Tollin assumes that Servetus was radically misunderstood by all his opponents — Catholic, Calvinistic, and Lutheran, and even by his Socinian and other Unitarian sympathizers. He thinks that even Calvin misunderstood him, though he understood him better than his other contemporaries. He makes Servetus a real hero, the peer of Calvin in genius, the discoverer of the circulation of the blood, the founder of comparative geography (the forerunner of Ritter), and the pioneer of modern Christology, which, instead of beginning with the pre-existent Logos, rises from the contemplation of the man Jesus to the recognition of Jesus Christ as the Messiah, then as the Son of God, and last as God. But he has overdone the subject, and put some of his own ideas into the brain of Servetus, who, like Calvin, must be studied and judged in the light of the sixteenth, and not of the nineteenth, century.

Next to Tollin, Professor Harnack, Neander's successor in Berlin, has formed a most favorable idea of Servetus. Without entering into an analysis of his views, he thinks that in him "the best of all that came to maturity in the sixteenth century was united, if we except the evangelical Reformation," and thus characterizes him: "*Servede ist gleich bedeutend als empirischer Forscher, als kritischer Denker, als speculativer Philosoph und als christlicher Reformer im besten Sinn des Worts. Es ist eine Paradoxie der Geschichte, dass Spanien — das Land, welches von den Ideen der neuen Zeit im 16 Jahrhundert am wenigsten berührt gewesen ist — diesen einzigen Mann hervorgebracht hat.*" (*Dogmengeschichte*, Bd. III. 661.)

§ 137. *Calvin and Servetus.*

We now come to the dark chapter in the history of Calvin which has cast a gloom over his fair name, and exposed him, not unjustly, to the charge of intolerance and persecution, which he shares with his whole age.

The burning of Servetus and the *decretum horribile* are sufficient in the judgment of a large part of the Christian world to condemn him and his theology, but cannot destroy the rocky foundation of his rare virtues and lasting merits. History knows only of one spotless being — the Saviour of sinners. Human greatness and purity are spotted by marks of infirmity, which forbid idolatry. Large bodies cast large shadows, and great virtues are often coupled with great vices.

Calvin and Servetus — what a contrast! The best abused men of the sixteenth century, and yet direct antipodes of each other in spirit, doctrine, and aim: the reformer and the deformer; the champion of orthodoxy and the archheretic; the master architect of construction and the master architect of ruin, brought together in deadly conflict for rule or ruin. Both were men of brilliant genius and learning; both deadly foes of the Roman Antichrist; both enthusiasts for a restoration of primitive Christianity, but with opposite views of what Christianity is.

They were of the same age, equally precocious, equally bold and independent, and relied on purely intellectual and spiritual forces. The one, while a youth of twenty-seven, wrote one of the best systems of theology and vindications of the Christian faith; the other, when scarcely above the age of twenty, ventured on the attempt to uproot the fundamental doctrine of orthodox Christendom. Both died in the prime of manhood, the one a natural, the other a violent, death.

Calvin's works are in every theological library; the books

of Servetus are among the greatest rareties. Calvin left
behind him flourishing churches, and his influence is felt
to this day in the whole Protestant world; Servetus passed
away like a meteor, without a sect, without a pupil; yet he
still eloquently denounces from his funeral pile the crime
and folly of religious persecution, and has recently been
idealized by a Protestant divine as a prophetic forerunner of
modern christo-centric theology.

Calvin felt himself called by Divine Providence to purify
the Church of all corruptions, and to bring her back to the
Christianity of Christ, and regarded Servetus as a servant of
Antichrist, who aimed at the destruction of Christianity.
Servetus was equally confident of a divine call, and even
identified himself with the archangel Michael in his apoca-
lyptic fight against the dragon of Rome and "the Simon
Magus of Geneva."

A mysterious force of attraction and repulsion brought
these intellectual giants together in the drama of the Reformation. Servetus, as if inspired by a demoniac force, urged
himself upon the attention of Calvin, regarding him as the
pope of orthodox Protestantism, whom he was determined
to convert or to dethrone. He challenged Calvin in Paris
to a disputation on the Trinity when the latter had scarcely
left the Roman Church, but failed to appear at the appointed place and hour.[1] He bombarded him with letters
from Vienne; and at last he heedlessly rushed into his power

---

[1] See above, p. 324. Beza thus reports this incident: "Not long after
Calvin returned [from Angoulême, in 1534] to Paris, as if called there by
the hand of God himself; for the impious Servetus was even then disseminat-
ing his heretical poison against the sacred Trinity in that city. He professed
to desire nothing more earnestly than to have an opportunity for entering
into discussion with Calvin, who waited long for Servetus, the time and place
for an interview having been appointed, with great danger to his own life,
since he was at that time under the necessity of being concealed on account
of the incensed rage of his adversaries. Calvin was disappointed in his
expectations of meeting Servetus, who wanted courage to endure even the
sight of his opponent."

at Geneva, and into the flames which have immortalized his name.[1]

The judgment of historians on these remarkable men has undergone a great change. Calvin's course in the tragedy of Servetus was fully approved by the best men in the sixteenth and seventeenth centuries.[2] It is as fully condemned in the nineteenth century. Bishop Bossuet was able to affirm that all Christians were happily agreed in maintaining the rightfulness of the death penalty for obstinate heretics, as murderers of souls. A hundred years later the great historian Gibbon echoed the opposite public sentiment when he said: "I am more deeply scandalized at the single execution of Servetus than at the hecatombs which have blazed at auto-da-fés of Spain and Portugal." [3]

It would be preposterous to compare Calvin with Torquemada.[4] But it must be admitted that the burning of Servetus is a typical case of Protestant persecution, and makes Calvin responsible for a principle which may be made to justify an indefinite number of applications. Persecution deserves much severer condemnation in a Protestant than in a Roman

---

[1] "If ever a poor fanatic thrust himself into the fire, it was Michael Servetus." Coleridge, in his *Table-Talk.*

[2] See the judgments below in § 139.

[3] In a footnote in ch. LIV. of his work on the *Decline and Fall of the R. E.* (Smith's ed. V. 552). He assigns three reasons for this judgment: (1) the zeal of Calvin was envenomed by personal malice and perhaps envy [?]; (2) the deed of cruelty was not varnished by the pretence of danger to the Church or State; (3) Calvin violated the golden rule of doing as he would be done by. Gibbon's prejudice against Calvinism is expressed in the sentence (p. 551) that "many a sober Christian would rather admit that a wafer is God than that God is a cruel and capricious tyrant."

[4] James Martineau states that "in his eighteen years of office, Cardinal Thomas de Torquemada had burned alive, it is computed, eighty-eight hundred victims, and punished ninety thousand in various ways, not for offences against the moral law, or crimes against society, but for thoughts of their own about religion, which only God, and not the pope, had allowed; or for being Jews that would not be apostates; or for refusing on the rack to confess what they had never done." *The Seat of Authority in Religion,* 1890, p. 156; comp. Llorente's *Histoire Critique de l'Inquisition,* IV. 251 sq.

Catholic, because it is inconsistent. Protestantism must stand or fall with freedom of conscience and freedom of worship.

From the standpoint of modern Christianity and civilization, the burning of Servetus admits of no justification. Even the most admiring biographers of Calvin lament and disapprove his conduct in this tragedy, which has spotted his fame and given to Servetus the glory of martyrdom.

But if we consider Calvin's course in the light of the sixteenth century, we must come to the conclusion that he acted his part from a strict sense of duty and in harmony with the public law and dominant sentiment of his age, which justified the death penalty for heresy and blasphemy, and abhorred toleration as involving indifference to truth. Even Servetus admitted the principle under which he suffered; for he said, that incorrigible obstinacy and malice deserved death before God and men.[1]

Calvin's prominence for intolerance was his misfortune. It was an error of judgment, but not of the heart, and must be excused, though it cannot be justified, by the spirit of his age.[2]

Calvin never changed his views or regretted his conduct towards Servetus. Nine years after his execution he justified it in self-defence against the reproaches of Baudouin (1562), saying: "Servetus suffered the penalty due to his heresies, but was it by my will? Certainly his arrogance destroyed him not less than his impiety. And what crime was it of mine if our Council, at my exhortation, indeed, but in conformity with the opinion of several Churches, took

---

[1] "*Hoc crimen est morte simpliciter dignum, et apud Deum et apud homines.*" In the twenty-seventh letter to Calvin (*Christianismi Restitutio*, p. 656). He speaks there of the punishment of Ananias and Sapphira, who were "*incorrigibiles, in malitia obstinati.*" Calvin refers to this admission of Servetus, and charges him with inconsistency. *Opera*, VIII. 462.

[2] This is admitted now by all impartial historians. Michelet (XI. 96) calls this blot in Calvin's life "*crime du temps plus que de l'homme même.*"

vengeance on his execrable blasphemies? Let Baudouin abuse me as long as he will, provided that, by the judgment of Melanchthon, posterity owes me a debt of gratitude for having purged the Church of so pernicious a monster."[1]

In one respect he was in advance of his times, by recommending to the Council of Geneva, though in vain, a mitigation of punishment and the substitution of the sword for the stake.

Let us give him credit for this comparative moderation in a semi-barbarous age when not only hosts of heretics, but even innocent women, as witches, were cruelly tortured and roasted to death. Let us remember also that it was not simply a case of fundamental heresy, but of horrid blasphemy, with which he had to deal. If he was mistaken, if he misunderstood the real opinions of Servetus, that was an error of judgment, and an error which all the Catholics and Protestants of that age shared. Nor should it be overlooked that Servetus was convicted of falsehood, that he overwhelmed Calvin with abuse,[2] and that he made common cause with the Libertines, the bitter enemies of Calvin, who had a controlling influence in the Council of Geneva at that time, and hoped to overthrow him.

It is objected that there was no law in Geneva to justify the punishment of Servetus, since the canon law had been abolished by the Reformation in 1535; but the Mosaic law was not abolished, it was even more strictly enforced; and it is

---

[1] *Responsio ad Balduini Convicia, Opera,* IX. 575 : " *Iustas quidem ille pœnas dedit : sed an meo arbitrio ? Certe arrogantia non minus quam impietas perdidit hominem. Sed quodnam meum crimen, si Senatus noster meo hortatu, ex plurium tamen ecclesiarum sententia, exsecrabiles blasphemias ultus est ? Vituperet me sane hac in parte Franciscus Balduinus, modo Philippi Melanchthonis iudicio posteritas mihi gratitudinem debeat, quia tam exitiali monstro ecclesiam purgaverim. Senatum etiam nostrum, sub cuius ditione aliquando vixit, perstringat ingratus hospes : modo idem Philippus scripto publice edito testetur dignum esse exemplum quod imitentur omnes christiani principes."*

[2] He called him at the trial *Simon Magus, impostor, sycophanta, nebulo, perfidus, impudens, ridiculus mus, cacodæmon, homicida,* etc.

from the Mosaic law against blasphemy that Calvin drew his chief argument.

On the other hand, however, we must frankly admit that there were some aggravating circumstances which make it difficult to reconcile Calvin's conduct with the principles of justice and humanity. Seven years before the death of Servetus he had expressed his determination not to spare his life if he should come to Geneva. He wrote to Farel (Feb. 13, 1546): "Servetus lately wrote to me, and coupled with his letter a long volume of his delirious fancies, with the Thrasonic boast, that I should see something astonishing and unheard of. He offers to come hither, if it be agreeable to me. But I am unwilling to pledge my word for his safety; for if he does come, and my authority be of any avail, I shall never suffer him to depart alive."[1] It was not inconsistent with this design, if he aided, as it would seem, in bringing the book of Servetus to the notice of the Roman inquisition in Lyons. He procured his arrest on his arrival in Geneva. He showed personal bitterness towards him during the trial. Servetus was a stranger in Geneva, and had committed no offence in that city. Calvin should have permitted him quietly to depart, or simply caused his expulsion from the territory of Geneva, as in the case of Bolsec. This would have been sufficient punishment. If he had recommended expulsion instead of decapitation, he would have saved himself the reproaches of posterity, which will never forget and never forgive the burning of Servetus.

In the interest of impartial history we must condemn the intolerance of the victor as well as the error of the victim,

---

[1] "*Servetus nuper ad me scripsit ac litteris adjunxit longum volumen suorum deliriorum, cum Thrasonica jactantia, me stupenda et hactemus inaudita visurum. Si mihi placeat, huc se venturum recipit. Sed nolo fidem meam interponere.* NAM SI VENERIT, MODO VALEAT MEA AUCTORITAS, VIVUM EXIRE NUNQUAM PATIAR." *Opera*, VIII. 283; Henry, III. Beil. 65–67; Bonnet-Constable, II. 17. Grotius discovered this damaging letter in Paris, which was controverted, but is now generally admitted as genuine. There is an exact copy of it in Geneva.

and admire in both the loyalty to conscientious conviction. Heresy is an error; intolerance, a sin; persecution, a crime.

§ 138. *Catholic Intolerance.*

Comp. vol. VI. §§ 11 and 12 (pp. 50–86), and SCHAFF: *The Progress of Religious Liberty as shown in the History of Toleration Acts.* New York, 1889.

This is the place to present the chief facts on the subject of religious toleration and intolerance, which gives to the case of Servetus its chief interest and importance in history. His theological opinions are of far less consequence than his connection with the theory of persecution which caused his death.

Persecution and war constitute the devil's chapter in history; but it is overruled by Providence for the development of heroism, and for the progress of civil and religious freedom. Without persecutors, there could be no martyrs. Every church, yea, every truth and every good cause, has its martyrs, who stood the fiery trial and sacrificed comfort and life itself to their sacred convictions. The blood of martyrs is the seed of toleration; toleration is the seed of liberty; and liberty is the most precious gift of God to every man who has been made in his image and redeemed by Christ.

Of all forms of persecution, religious persecution is the worst because it is enacted in the name of God. It violates the sacred rights of conscience, and it rouses the strongest and deepest passions. Persecution by word and pen, which springs from the hatred, envy, and malice of the human heart, or from narrowness and mistaken zeal for truth, will continue to the end of time; but persecution by fire and sword contradicts the spirit of humanity and Christianity, and is inconsistent with modern civilization. Civil offences against the State deserve civil punishment, by fine, imprisonment, confiscation, exile, and death, according to the degree of guilt. Spiritual offences against the Church should be spiritually judged, and punished by admonition, deposition, and excommunication, with a view to the reformation and restoration of the offender. This is the law of Christ. The temporal punishment of heresy is the legitimate result of a union of Church and State, and diminishes in rigor as this union is relaxed. A religion established by law must be protected by law. Hence the Constitution of the United States in securing full liberty of religion, forbids Congress to establish by law any religion or church.[1] The two were regarded as inseparable. An established church must in self-defence persecute dissenters, or abridge their liberties; a free church cannot persecute. And yet there may be as much individual Christian kindness and charity in an established church, and as much intolerance and bigotry in a free church. The ante-Nicene Fathers had the same zeal for orthodoxy and the same abhorrence of heresy as the Nicene and post-Nicene Fathers, the mediæval popes and schoolmen, and the Reformers; but they were confined to the spiritual punishment of heresy. In the United States of America persecution is made impossible, not because the zeal for truth or the passions of hatred and intolerance have ceased, but because the union between Church and State has ceased.

The theory of religious persecution was borrowed from the Mosaic law, which punished idolatry and blasphemy by death. "He that sacrificeth unto any god, save unto Jehovah only, shall be utterly destroyed."[2] "He that blasphemeth the name of Jehovah, he shall surely be put to death; all the congregation shall certainly stone him: as

---

[1] In the First Amendment of the Constitution: "Congress shall make no law respecting an establishment of religion, or prohibiting the free exercise thereof."

[2] Ex. 22:20; comp. Deut. 13:5–15; 17:2–5, etc.

well the stranger, as the home-born, when he blasphemeth the name of Jehovah, shall be put to death."[1]

The Mosaic theocracy was superseded in its national and temporal provisions by the kingdom of Christ, which is "not of this world." The confounding of the Old and New Testaments, of the law of Moses and the gospel of Christ, was the source of a great many evils in the Church.

The New Testament furnishes not a shadow of support for the doctrine of persecution. The whole teaching and example of Christ and the Apostles are directly opposed to it. They suffered persecution, but they persecuted no one. Their weapons were spiritual, not carnal. They rendered to God the things that are God's, and to Cæsar the things that are Cæsar's. The only passage which St. Augustin could quote in favor of coercion, was the parabolic "Constrain them to come in" (Luke 14 : 23), which in its literal acceptation would teach just the reverse, namely, a forced salvation. St. Thomas Aquinas does not quote any passage from the New Testament in favor of intolerance, but tries to explain away those passages which commend toleration (Matt. 13 : 29, 30; 1 Cor. 11 : 19; 2 Tim. 2 : 24). The Church has never entirely forgotten this teaching of Christ and always, even in the darkest ages of persecution, avowed the principle, " *Ecclesia non sitit sanguinem*"; but she made the State her executor.

In the first three centuries the Church had neither the power nor the wish to persecute. Justin Martyr, Tertullian, and Lactantius were the earliest advocates of the liberty of conscience. The Toleration Edict of Constantine (313) anticipated the modern theory of the right of every man to choose his religion and to worship according to his conviction. But this was only a step towards the union of the empire with the Church, when the Church assumed the position and power of the heathen state religion.

[1] Lev. 24 : 16; comp. 1 Kings 21 : 10, 13.

The era of persecution within the Church began with the first Œcumenical Council, which was called and enforced by Constantine. This Council presents the first instance of a subscription to a creed, and the first instance of banishment for refusing to subscribe. Arius and two Egyptian bishops, who agreed with him, were banished to Illyria. During the violent Arian controversies, which shook the empire between the first and second Œcumenical Councils (325–381), both parties when in power freely exercised persecution by imprisonment, deposition, and exile. The Arians were as intolerant as the orthodox. The practice furnished the basis for a theory and public law.

The penal legislation against heresy was inaugurated by Theodosius the Great after the final triumph of the Nicene Creed in the second Œcumenical Council. He promulgated during his reign (379–395) no less than fifteen severe edicts against heretics, especially those who dissented from the doctrine of the Trinity. They were deprived of the right of public worship, excluded from public offices, and exposed, in some cases, to capital punishment.[1] His rival and colleague, Maximus, put the theory into full practice, and shed the first blood of heretics by causing Priscillian, a Spanish bishop of Manichæan tendency, with six adherents, to be tortured, condemned, and executed by the sword.

The better feeling of the Church raised in Ambrose of Milan and Martin of Tours a protest against this act of inhumanity. But public sentiment soon approved of it. Jerome seems to favor the death penalty for heresy on the ground of Deut. 13:6–10. The great Augustin, who had

---

[1] See the Theodosian and Justinian Codes under the titles: *De summa Trinitate, De Catholica Fide, De Hæreticis, De Apostatis*. For a summary compare Gibbon, ch. XXVII. (vol. III. 197 sqq.), and Milman, *Latin Christianity*, bk. III. ch. V. (I. 512 sqq.). Gibbon says: "Theodosius considered every heretic as a rebel against the supreme powers of heaven and of earth; and each of these powers might exercise their peculiar jurisdiction over the soul and body of the guilty."

himself been a Manichæan heretic for nine years, justified forcible measures against the Donatists, in contradiction to his noble sentiment: "Nothing conquers but truth, the victory of truth is love."[1] The same Christian Father who ruled the thinking of the Church for many centuries, and moulded the theology of the Reformers, excluded all unbaptized infants from salvation, though Christ emphatically included them in the kingdom of heaven. Leo I., the greatest of the early popes, advocated the death penalty for heresy and approved of the execution of the Priscillianists. Thomas Aquinas, the master theologian of the Middle Ages, lent the weight of his authority to the doctrine of persecution, and demonstrated from the Old Testament and from reason that heretics are worse criminals than debasers of money, and ought to be put to death by the civil magistrate.[2] Heresy was regarded as the greatest sin, and worse than murder, because it destroyed the soul. It took the place of idolatry in the Mosaic law.

The Theodosian Code was completed in the Justinian Code (527–534); the Justinian Code passed into the Holy Roman Empire, and became the basis of the legislation of Christian Europe. Rome ruled the world longer by law and by the cross than she had ruled it by the sword. The canon law likewise condemns to the flames persons convicted of heresy.[3] This law was generally accepted on the Continent in the thirteenth century.[4] England in her isolation was more independent, and built society on the foundation

---

[1] Comp. vol. III. 144 sq.

[2] *Summa Theol. Secunda Secundæ*, Quest. XI. (*de hæresi*), Art. 3. In Migne's ed. Tom. III. 107.

[3] See Boehmer, *Inst. Juris Canonici*, 1747, lib. V. tit. 7, § 10.

[4] Friedberg, *Lehrbuch des katholischen und evangelischen Kirchenrechts*, 2d ed. 1884, p. 221: "*Im XIII. Jahrhundert erfolgt überall die rechtliche staatliche Feststellung der Todesstrafe und Vermögensconfiscation für Ketzerei, und die Kirche hat diese staatlichen Strafen nicht nur gebilligt, sondern auch verlangt, und die weltliche Obrigkeit, die sie nicht verhänge, selbst mit der Strafe der Ketzerei bedroht.*"

of the common law; but Henry IV. and his Parliament devised the sanguinary statute *de hæretico comburendo*, by which William Sawtre, a parish priest, was publicly burnt at Smithfield (Feb. 26, 1401) for denying the doctrine of transubstantiation, and the bones of Wiclif were burnt by Bishop Fleming of Lincoln (in 1428). The statute continued in force till 1677, when it was formally abolished.

On this legal and theological foundation the mediæval Church has soiled her annals with the blood of an army of heretics which is much larger than the army of Christian martyrs under heathen Rome. We need only refer to the crusades against the Albigenses and Waldenses, which were sanctioned by Innocent III., one of the best and greatest of popes ; the tortures and autos-da-fé of the Spanish Inquisition, which were celebrated with religious festivities; the fifty thousand or more Protestants who were executed during the reign of the Duke of Alva in the Netherlands (1567–1573) ; the several hundred martyrs who were burned in Smithfield under the reign of the bloody Mary; and the repeated wholesale persecutions of the innocent Waldenses in France and Piedmont, which cried to heaven for vengeance.

It is vain to shift the responsibility upon the civil government. Pope Gregory XIII. commemorated the massacre of St. Bartholomew not only by a *Te Deum* in the churches of Rome, but more deliberately and permanently by a medal which represents " The Slaughter of the Huguenots " by an angel of wrath. The French bishops, under the lead of the great Bossuet, lauded Louis XIV. as a new Constantine, a new Theodosius, a new Charlemagne, a new exterminator of heretics, for his revocation of the Edict of Nantes and the infamous dragoonades against the Huguenots.

Among the more prominent individual cases of persecution, we may mention the burning of Hus (1415) and Jerome of Prague (1416) by order of the Council of Constance, the burning of Savonarola in Florence (1498), the burning of the three English Reformers at Oxford (1556), of Aonio Paleario at Rome (1570), and of Giordano Bruno (1600) in the same city and on the same spot where (1889) the liberals of Italy have erected a statue to his memory. Servetus was condemned to death at the stake, and burnt in effigy, by a Roman Catholic tribunal before he fell into the hands of Calvin.

The Roman Church has lost the power, and to a large extent also the disposition, to persecute by fire and sword. Some of her highest dignitaries frankly disown the principle of persecution, especially in America, where they enjoy the full benefit of religious freedom.[1] But the Roman curia has never officially disowned the theory on which the practice of persecution is based. On the contrary, several popes since the Reformation have indorsed it. Pope Clement VIII. denounced the Toleration Edict of Nantes as "the most accursed that can be imagined, whereby liberty of conscience is granted to everybody; which is the worst thing in the world." Pope Innocent X. "condemned, rejected, and annulled" the toleration articles of the West-phalian Treaty of 1648, and his successors have ever protested against it, though in vain. Pope Pius IX., in the Syllabus of 1864, expressly condemned, among the errors of this age, the doctrine of religious toleration and liberty.[2]

---

[1] Among these is Cardinal Gibbons of Baltimore, who says (*The Faith of our Fathers*, Balto., 1890, 36th ed., p. 284 sq.): "I am not the apologist of the Spanish Inquisition, and I have no desire to palliate or excuse the excesses into which that tribunal may at times have fallen. From my heart I abhor and denounce every species of violence, and injustice, and persecution, of which the Spanish Inquisition may have been guilty. And in raising my voice against coercion for conscience's sake, I am expressing not only my own sentiments, but those of every Catholic priest and layman in the land.

"Our Catholic ancestors, for the last three hundred years, have suffered so much for freedom of conscience, that they would rise up in judgment against us, were we to become the advocates and defenders of religious persecution. We would be a disgrace to our sires were we to trample on the principle of liberty which they held dearer than life."

[2] *Syllabus Errorum*, § III. 15; VI. 55; X. 78.

And this pope has been declared to be officially infallible by the Vatican decree of 1870, which embraces all his predecessors (notwithstanding the stubborn case of Honorius I.) and all his successors in the chair of St. Peter. Leo XIII. has moderately and cautiously indorsed the doctrine of the Syllabus.[1]

§ 139. *Protestant Intolerance. Judgments of the Reformers on Servetus.*

The Reformers inherited the doctrine of persecution from their mother Church, and practised it as far as they had the power. They fought intolerance with intolerance. They differed favorably from their opponents in the degree and extent, but not in the principle, of intolerance. They broke down the tyranny of popery, and thus opened the way for the development of religious freedom; but they denied to others the liberty which they exercised themselves. The Protestant governments in Germany and Switzerland excluded, within the limits of their jurisdiction, the Roman Catholics from all religious and civil rights, and took exclusive possession of their churches, convents, and other property. They banished, imprisoned, drowned, beheaded, hanged, and burned Anabaptists, Antitrinitarians, Schwenkfeldians, and other dissenters. In Saxony, Sweden, Norway, and Denmark no religion and public worship was allowed but the Lutheran. The Synod of Dort deposed and expatriated all Arminian ministers and school-teachers. The penal code of Queen Elizabeth and the successive acts of Uniformity aimed at the complete extermination of all dissent, whether papal or protestant, and made it a crime for an Englishman to be anything else than an Episcopalian. The Puritans when in power ejected two thousand ministers

---

[1] See his Encyclicals of Nov. 1, 1885 (*Immortale Dei*), and of June 20, 1888 (*Libertas præstantissimum naturæ donum*). They are printed in the latest ed. of Schaff's *Creeds of Christendom*, II. 555–602.

from their benefices for non-conformity; and the Episcopalians paid them back in the same coin when they returned to power. " The Reformers," says Gibbon, with sarcastic severity, " were ambitious of succeeding the tyrants whom they had dethroned. They imposed with equal rigor their creeds and confessions; they asserted the right of the magistrate to punish heretics with death. The nature of the tiger was the same, but he was gradually deprived of his teeth and fangs." [1]

Protestant persecution violates the fundamental principle of the Reformation. Protestantism has no right to exist except on the basis of freedom of conscience.

How, then, can we account for this glaring inconsistency? There is a reason for everything. Protestant persecution was necessary in self-defence and in the struggle for existence. The times were not ripe for toleration. The infant Churches could not have stood it. These Churches had first to be consolidated and fortified against surrounding foes. Universal toleration at that time would have resulted in universal confusion and upset the order of society. From anarchy to absolute despotism is but one step. The division of Protestantism into two rival camps, the Lutheran and the Reformed, weakened it; further divisions within these camps would have ruined it and prepared an easy triumph for united Romanism, which would have become more despotic than ever before. This does not justify the principle, but it explains the practice, of intolerance.

The Reformers and the Protestant princes and magistrates were essentially agreed on this intolerant attitude, 'both towards the Romanists and the heretical Protestants, at least to the extent of imprisonment, deposition, and expatriation. They differed only as to the degree of

---

[1] *Decline and Fall*, ch. LIV. It should be remembered, however, that the most intolerant form of intolerance is the intolerance of infidelity as manifested in the French Revolution during " the reign of terror."

severity.   They all believed that the papacy is anti-Christian
and the mass idolatrous; that heresy is a sin against God
and society; that the denial of the Trinity and the divinity
of Christ is the greatest of heresies, which deserves death
according to the laws of the empire, and eternal punishment
according to the Athanasian Creed (with its three damnatory
clauses); and that the civil government is as much bound
to protect the first as the second table of the Decalogue,
and to vindicate the honor of God against blasphemy.   They
were anxious to show their zeal for orthodoxy by severity
against heresy.   They had no doubt that they themselves
were orthodox according to the only true standard of
orthodoxy — the Word of God in the Holy Scriptures.
And as regards the dogmas of the Trinity and Incarnation,
they were fully agreed with their Catholic opponents, and
equally opposed to the errors of Servetus, who denied those
dogmas with a boldness and contempt unknown before.

Let us ascertain the sentiments of the leading Reformers
with special reference to the case of Servetus.   They form
a complete justification of Calvin as far as such a justification is possible.

LUTHER.

Luther, the hero of Worms, the champion of the sacred
rights of conscience, was, in words, the most violent, but
in practice, the least intolerant, among the Reformers.   He
was nearest to Romanism in the condemnation of heresy, but
nearest to the genius of Protestantism in the advocacy of
religious freedom.   He was deeply rooted in mediæval piety,
and yet a mighty prophet of modern times.   In his earlier
years, till 1529, he gave utterance to some of the noblest
sentiments in favor of religious liberty.   "Belief is a free
thing," he said, "which cannot be enforced."   "If heretics
were to be punished by death, the hangman would be the
most orthodox theologian."   "Heresy is a spiritual thing

which no iron can hew down, no fire burn, no water drown."[1] "To burn heretics is contrary to the will of the Holy Spirit."[2] "False teachers should not be put to death; it is enough to banish them."[3]

But with advancing years he became less liberal and more intolerant against Catholics, heretics, and Jews. He exhorted the magistrates to forbid all preaching of Anabaptists, whom he denounced without discrimination as false prophets and messengers of the devil, and he urged their expulsion.[4] He raised no protest when the Diet of Speier, in 1529, passed the cruel decree that the Anabaptists be executed by fire and sword without distinction of sex, and

---

[1] In his book *Von weltlicher Obrigkeit wie weit man ihr Gehorsam schuldig sei* (1523), in *Werke* XXII. 90: "*Ketzerei kann man nimmermehr mit Gewalt wehren, es gehört ein ander Griff dazu, und ist hie ein ander Streit und Handel, denn mit dem Schwert. Gottes Wort soll hie streiten; wenn das nicht ausreicht, so wird's wohl unausgerichtet bleiben von weltlicher Gewalt, ob sie gleich die Welt mit Blut füllet. Ketzerei ist ein geistlich Ding, das kann man mit keinem Eisen hauen, mit keinem Feuer verbrennen, mit keinem Wasser ertränken. Es ist aber allein das Wort Gottes da, das thut's, wie Paulus sagt 2 Cor. 10 : 4, 5 : 'Unsere Waffen sind nicht fleischlich, sondern mächtig in Gott.'*"

[2] Conclus. LXXX. in the *Resol. de Indulgentiis*, 1518. This is one of the theses which the Sorbonne of Paris condemned in 1521.

[3] His last liberal utterance on the subject is in his letter to Link, 1528: "*Nullo modo possum admittere, falsos doctores occidi: satis est eos relegari.*" *Briefe*, III. 347 sq. (De Wette's ed.). In the same year he wrote his book *Von der Wiedertaufe an zwei Pfarrherrn* (Erl. ed. vol. XXVI) in which he treats the doctrines of the Baptists without mercy, but at the same time expresses sincere regret at the cruel treatment of them, saying: "*Es ist nicht recht und mir wahrlich leid, dass man solche elende Leute so jämmerlich ermordet, verbrennet und gräulich umbringt; man sollte ja einen jeglichen lassen glauben, was er wollt; glaubt er unrecht, so hat er genug Strafen an dem ewigen Feuer in der Höllen. Warum will man sie denn auch noch zeitlich martern, so ferne sie allein im Glauben irren und nicht auch daneben aufrührerisch sind oder sonst der Obrigkeit widerstreben! Lieber Gott, wie bald ist's geschehen, dass einer irre wird und dem Teufel in Stricke fällt? Mit der Schrift und Gottes Wort sollt man ihnen wehren und widerstehen, mit Feuer wird man wenig ausrichten.*" I have quoted this and other passages in vol. VI. 59 sq., but could not well omit them here on account of the connection.

[4] *Von den Schleichern und Winkelpredigern*, addressed to Eberhard von der Tannen on the Wartburg, 1531. *Werke*, XXXI. 214 sqq.

even without a previous hearing before the spiritual judges.[1] The Elector of Saxony considered it his duty to execute this decree, and put a number of Anabaptists to death in his dominions. His neighbor, Philip of Hesse, who had more liberal instincts than the contemporary princes of Germany, could not find it in his conscience to use the sword against differences of belief.[2] But the theologians of Wittenberg, on being consulted by the Elector John Frederick about 1540 or 1541, gave their judgment in favor of putting the Anabaptists to death, according to the laws of the empire. Luther approved of this judgment under his own name, adding that it was cruel to punish them by the sword, but more cruel that they should damn the ministry of the Word and suppress the true doctrine, and attempt to destroy the kingdoms of the world.[3]

---

[1] "*Dass alle und jede Widertäuffer und Widergetaufte, Mann und Weibspersonen verständigs Alters vom natürlichen Leben zum Tode mit Feuer, Schwert oder dergleichen nach Gelegenheit der Personen ohne vorgehende der geistlichen Richter Inquisition gerichtet oder gebracht werden.*" This was the same Diet in which the Lutheran Protestants entered their protest against the decision of the majority (hence their name); but they assented to the cruel decree against the Anabaptists, and also to the exclusion of the Zwinglians from toleration, with the exception of the Landgrave of Hesse, who protested also against this intolerance.

[2] In 1540 he boasted that no Anabaptist had been executed for opinion's sake by him, whereas in other German lands the number of such martyrdoms was, up to 1530, hard upon two thousand. "*Wir können in unserem Gewissen nicht finden,*" he said to the elector, "*jemanden des Glaubens halben, wo wir nicht sonst genugsam Ursache der Verwirkung haben mögen, mit dem Schwert richten zu lassen. Denn so es die Meinung haben sollte, müssten wir keinen Juden noch Papisten, die Christum am höchsten blasphemiren, bei uns dulden und sie dergestalt richten lassen.*" G. L. Schmidt, *Justus Menius, der Reformator Thüringens* (Gotha, 1867), vol. I. 144. Comp. *Corpus Reform.* IX. 757.

[3] He wrote beneath the judgment of the Wittenberg theologians: "PLACET MIHI MARTINO LUTHERO. *Wiewol es crudele anzusehen, dass man sie mit dem Schwert straft, so ists doch crudelius, dass sie ministerium verbi damniren und keine gewisse Lehre treiben, und rechte Lehre unterdrücken, und dazu regna mundi zerstören wollen.*" The last sentence refers to the chiliastic views held by many of the Anabaptists, for which they are condemned in the Augsburg Confession. Seidemann, in the sixth vol. of De Wette's "Correspondence of Luther," p. 291. He assigns this document to the year 1541. Comp. *Corp. Ref.* IV. 737-740.

If we put a strict construction on this sentence, Luther must be counted with the advocates of the death-penalty for heresy. But he made a distinction between two classes of Anabaptists — those who were seditious or revolutionary, and those who were mere fanatics. The former should be put to death, the latter should be banished.[1] In a letter to Philip of Hesse, dated November 20, 1538, he urgently requested him to expel from his territory the Anabaptists, whom he characterizes as children of the devil, but says nothing of using the sword.[2] We should give him, therefore, the benefit of a liberal construction.[3]

At the same time, the distinction was not always strictly observed, and fanatics were easily turned into criminals, especially after the excesses of Münster, in 1535, which were greatly exaggerated and made the pretext for punishing innocent men and women.[4] The whole history of the Ana-

---

[1] "*Anabaptistæ occidendi. D. dixit: Duplices sunt. Quidam aperte sediotiose docent contra magistratus; eos jure occidit elector. Reliqui habent fanaticas opiniones, ii plerumque relegantur.*" G. Loesche, *Analecta Lutherana et Melanchthoniana. Tischreden Luthers und Aussprüche Melanchthons*, Gotha, 1892, p. 137.

[2] "*Es ist nicht allein mein Bedenken, sondern auch demüthiges Bitten, E. F. G. wollten sie [die Wiedertäufer] ernstlich des Landes verweisen, denn est ist gleichwol des Teufels Samen,*" etc. Luther's *Briefe, Sendschreiben und Bedenken*, vol. VI. by Joh. Karl Seidemann (Berlin, 1856), p. 216.

[3] This is the conclusion of my friend, Dr. Köstlin, of Halle, the distinguished biographer of Luther. In reply to a letter, March 12, 1892, he communicated to me his careful opinion as follows: "*Nirgends, auch nicht in seiner späteren Zeit, that Luther Aeusserungen, in welchen er den Grundsatz des damaligen allgemeinen Rechts (auch der Carolina), dass z. B. Bestreitung der Trinitätslehre oder andere bloss dogmatische Irrlehre schon als solche mit dem Tod bestraft werden sollte, sich angeeignet hatte. So weit wir sehen, hat er darin doch immer sehr von Calvin und auch von Melanchthon, ja von allen anderen Hauptlehrern der Reformation sich unterschieden. Insbesondere beschränkt er sich, z. B. einem Antitrinitarier wie Joh. Campan gegenüber ('filium Satanæ, adversarium Dei, quem plus etiam quam Arius blasphemat'), doch auf den Wunsch, dass die Obrigkeit 'tales furias non vocatas' nicht zulassen möge. Briefe v. De Wette IV. 321. Auch die schärfsten Ausserungen der Tischreden (cf. auch die Colloquien ed. Bindseil) gehen nie weiter, soweit sie dogmatische Irrlehren betreffen.*"

[4] See L. Keller: *Geschichte der Wiedertäufer und ihres Reichs zu Münster*, Münster, 1880, and his *Die Reformation*, p. 451, where he speaks of new sources discovered since 1880.

baptist movement in the sixteenth century has to be rewritten and disentangled from the *odium theologicum*.

As regards Servetus, Luther knew only his first work against the Trinity, and pronounced it, in his *Table Talk* (1532), an "awfully bad book."[1] Fortunately for his fame, he did not live to pronounce a judgment in favor of his execution, and we must give him the benefit of silence.

His opinions on the treatment of the Jews changed for the worse. In 1523 he had vigorously protested against the cruel persecution of the Jews, but in 1543 he counselled their expulsion from Christian lands, and the burning of their books, synagogues, and private houses in which they blaspheme our Saviour and the Holy Virgin. He repeated this advice in his last sermon, preached at Eisleben a few days before his death.[2]

MELANCHTHON.

Melanchthon's record on this painful subject is unfortunately worse than Luther's. This is all the more significant because he was the mildest and gentlest among the Reformers. But we should remember that his utterances on the subject are of a later date, several years after Luther's death. He thought that the Mosaic law against idolatry and blasphemy was as binding upon Christian states as the Decalogue, and was applicable to heresies as well.[3] He therefore

---

[1] *"Ein gräulich bös Buch."* When Melanchthon informed him that the opinions of Servetus found much applause in Italy, he remarked that "Italy was full of pestilential opinions, and that if such errors as those of Servetus should get there, horrible abominations would arise" (*horribiles abominationes ibi orituras*). Bindseil, *Martini Lutheri Colloquia*, Tom. I. 376. Comp. Tollin, *M. Luther und M. Servet*, Berlin, 1875, and *M. Servet und Martin Butzer* (or *Servet und die oberländischen Reformatoren*, Berlin, 1880, vol. I. 105 sq.). Tollin tries to prove in both these books, on the strength of an obscure passage in a letter of Servetus to Œcolampadius, that Servetus accompanied Butzer as amanuensis in September, 1530, from Augsburg to Coburg to see Luther. But neither Bucer nor Luther say a word about it.

[2] Erlangen ed., vol. XXII. 558 sq.

[3] *Corpus Reformatorum*, vol. VIII. 520. He mentions among the heresies worthy of death the *deliramenta Samosateni* and *Manichæi*.

fully and repeatedly justified the course of Calvin and the
Council of Geneva, and even held them up as models for
imitation! In a letter to Calvin, dated Oct. 14, 1554, nearly
one year after the burning of Servetus, he wrote : —

"Reverend and dear Brother: I have read your book, in which you have
clearly refuted the horrid blasphemies of Servetus; and I give thanks to the
Son of God, who was the βραβευτής [*the awarder of your crown of victory*] in
this your combat. To you also the Church owes gratitude at the present
moment, and will owe it to the latest posterity. I perfectly assent to your
opinion. I affirm also that your magistrates did right in punishing, after
a regular trial, this blasphemous man."[1]

A year later, Melanchthon wrote to Bullinger, Aug. 20,
1555 : —

"Reverend and dear Brother: I have read your answer to the blasphemies
of Servetus, and I approve of your piety and opinions. I judge also that
the Genevese senate did perfectly right, to put an end to this obstinate man,
who could never cease blaspheming. And I wonder at those who disapprove
of this severity."[2]

Three years later, April 10, 1557, Melanchthon incidentally
(in the admonition in the case of Theobald Thamer, who
had returned to the Roman Church) adverted again to the

---

[1] *Corpus Reformat.* vol. VIII. 362 (also in Calvin's *Opera,* XV. 268 sq.):
"*Reverende vir et carissime frater: Legi scriptum tuum, in quo refutasti luculenter
horrendas Serveti blasphemias: ac Filio Dei gratias ago, qui fuit βραβευτής huius
tui agonis. Tibi quoque ecclesia et nunc et ad posteros gratitudinem debet et debebit.*
Tuo judicio prorsus assentior. Affirmo etiam vestros magistratus
juste fecisse, quod hominem blasphemum, re ordine judicata, inter-
fecerunt."
(The rest of this letter is an answer to Calvin's request that he should
define his views on the predestinarian and eucharistic controversies. Melanchthon declined to do this for prudential reasons, but intimated his dissent from
the carnal theory of the real presence by calling it ἀρτολατρία, and expresses
the hope of conversing with him once more, " *antequam ex hoc mortali carcere
mens discedat.*")

[2] *Corpus Reform.* VIII. 523. After thanking Bullinger for a number of
books, he adds: "*Legi etiam quæ de Serveti blasphemiis respondistis, et pietatem
ac judicia vestra probo. Judico etiam Senatum Genevensem recte fecisse quod
hominem pertinacem et non omissurum blasphemias sustulit. Ac miratus sum, esse
[aliquos], qui severitatem illam improbent. Mitto de ea quæstione breves pagellas,
sed tamen sententiæ nostræ testes.*" This refers to his consilium on the rightful
ness of the punishment of heretics by the civil magistrate (1555).

execution of Servetus, and called it "a pious and memorable example to all posterity."[1] It is an example, indeed, but certainly not for imitation.

This unqualified approval of the death penalty for heresy and the connivance at the bigamy of Philip of Hesse are the two dark spots on the fair name of this great and good man. But they were errors of judgment. Calvin took great comfort from the indorsement of the theological head of the Lutheran Church.[2]

MARTIN BUCER.

Bucer, who stands third in rank among the Reformers of Germany, was of a gentle and conciliatory disposition, and abstained from persecuting the Anabaptists in Strassburg. He knew Servetus personally, and treated him at first with kindness, but after the publication of his work on the Trinity, he refuted it in his lectures as a "most pestilential book."[3] He even declared in the pulpit or in the lecture-room that Servetus deserved to be disembowelled and torn to pieces.[4] From this we may infer how fully he would have approved his execution, had he lived till 1553.

---

[1] *Commonefactio de Thammero,* vol. IX. 133: "*Dedit vero et Genevensis Reipublicæ Magistratas ante annos quatuor punitæ insanabilis blasphemiæ adversus Filium Dei, sublato Serveto Arragone pium et memorabile ad omnem posteritatem exemplum.*"

[2] He wrote to Melanchthon, March 5, 1555: "Your letter, most reverend sir, was grateful to me, not only because whatever comes from you is dear to me, and because it has assured me that the affection, which you entertained for me in the commencement of our intercourse, still remains unaltered; but above all because in it I find a magnificent eulogy, in which you commend my zeal in crushing the impiety of Servetus. Whence also I conjecture that you have not been offended with the honest freedom of my admonitions." He referred to Melanchthon again in his reply to the Reproaches of Baudouin, 1562. See above, § 137.

[3] So he wrote to Ambrosius Blaurer, Dec. 29, 1531: "*Pestilentissimum illum de Trinitate librum novi, proh dolor, et hic in publicis prælectionibus nostris confutavi.*"

[4] *Dignum esse, qui avulsis visceribus discerperetur.*" So reports Calvin Sept. 8, 1553. This is confirmed by a letter of Professor Frecht of Tübingen to Capito, dated Nov. 25, 1538. See Tollin, *Michael Servet und Martin Butzer,*

THE SWISS CHURCHES.

The Swiss Reformers ought to have been in advance of those of Germany on this subject, but they were not. They advised or approved the exclusion of Roman Catholics from the Reformed Cantons, and violent measures against Anabaptists and Antitrinitarians. Six Anabaptists were, by a cruel irony, drowned in the river Limmat at Zürich by order of the government (between 1527 and 1532).[1] Other Cantons took the same severe measures against the Anabaptists. Zwingli, the most liberal among the Reformers, did not object to their punishment, and counselled the forcible introduction of Protestantism into the neutral territories and the Forest Cantons. Ochino was expelled from Zürich and Basel (1563).

As regards the case of Servetus, the churches and magistrates of Zürich, Schaffhausen, Basel, and Bern, on being consulted during his trial, unanimously condemned his errors, and advised his punishment, but without committing themselves to the mode of punishment.[2]

Bullinger wrote to Calvin that God had given the Council of Geneva a most favorable opportunity to vindicate the truth against the pollution of heresy, and the honor of God against blasphemy. In his Second Helvetic Confession (ch. XXX.) he teaches that it is the duty of the magistrate to use the sword against blasphemers. Schaffhausen fully agreed with Zürich. Even the authorities of Basel, which was the headquarters of the sceptical Italians and enemies

in the "Magazin für die Lit. des Auslandes," Berlin, 1876, and *Servet und die oberländischen Reformatoren*, Bd. I. (*Michael Servet und Martin Butzer*), Berlin, 1880, pp. 232 sqq. Tollin thinks that Bucer meant the book, not the person of Servetus; but books have no *viscera*.

[1] See above, § 26, pp. 87 sqq.

[2] The judgments of the magistrates and ministers of Zürich, Schaffhausen, Basel, and Bern are printed in Calvin's *Opera*, VIII. 808–823 (in German and Latin). The judgment of the pastors of Zürich, dated Oct. 2, 1553, is also inserted in Calvin's *Defensio, ibid.* fol. 555–558.

of Calvin, gave the advice that Servetus, whom their own Œcolampadius had declared a most dangerous man, be deprived of the power to harm the Church, if all efforts to convert him should fail. Six years afterwards the Council of Basel, with the consent of the clergy and the University, ordered the body of David Joris, a chiliastic Anabaptist who had lived there under a false name (and died Aug. 25, 1556), to be dug from the grave and burned, with his likeness and books, by the hangman before a large multitude (1559).[1]

Bern, which had advised moderation in the affair of Bolsec two years earlier, judged more severely in the case of Servetus, because he " had reckoned himself free to call in question all the essential points of our religion," and expressed the wish that the Council of Geneva might have prudence and strength to deliver the Churches from "this pest." Thirteen years after the death of Servetus, the Council of Bern executed Valentino Gentile by the sword (Sept. 10, 1566) for an error similar to but less obnoxious than that of Servetus, and scarcely a voice was raised in disapproval of the sentence.[2]

The Reformers of French Switzerland went further than those of German Switzerland. Farel defended death by fire, and feared that Calvin in advising a milder punishment was guided by the feelings of a friend against his bitterest foe. Beza wrote a special work in defence of the execution of Servetus, whom he characterized as " a monstrous compound of mere impiety and horrid blasphemy."[3] Peter Martyr called him " a genuine son of the devil," whose "pestiferous and detestable doctrines" and "intolerable blasphemies" justified the severe sentence of the magistracy.[4]

[1] See Nippold, *Ueber Leben, Lehre und Sekte des David Joris*, in the "Zeitschrift für historische Theologie," 1863, No. I., and 1864, No. IV.

[2] See above, § 131, p. 658.

[3] "*Monstrum ex mera impietate horrendisque blasphemiis conflatum.*" *Vita Calv.* (*Annal.* XXI. 148).

[4] See the whole passage in Trechsel's *Zusätze* to vol. I.

CRANMER.

The English Reformers were not behind those of the Continent in the matter of intolerance. Several years before the execution of Servetus, Archbishop Cranmer had persuaded the reluctant young King Edward VI. to sign the death-warrant of two Anabaptists — one a woman, called Joan Bocher of Kent, and the other a foreigner from Holland, George van Pare; the former was burnt May 2, 1550, the latter, April 6, 1551.

The only advocates of toleration in the sixteenth century were Anabaptists and Antitrinitarians, who were themselves sufferers from persecution. Let us give them credit for their humanity.

GRADUAL TRIUMPH OF TOLERATION AND LIBERTY.

The reign of intolerance continued to the end of the seventeenth century. It was gradually undermined during the eighteenth century, and demolished by the combined influences of Protestant Dissenters, as the Anabaptists, Socinians, Arminians, Quakers, Presbyterians, Independents, of Anglican Latitudinarians, and of philosophers, like Bayle, Grotius, Locke, Leibnitz; nor should we forget Voltaire and Frederick the Great, who were unbelievers, but sincere and most influential advocates of religious toleration; nor Franklin, Jefferson, and Madison in America. Protestant Holland and Protestant England took the lead in the legal recognition of the principles of civil and religious liberty, and the Constitution of the United States completed the theory by putting all Christian denominations on a parity before the law and guaranteeing them the full enjoyment of equal rights.

Hand in hand with the growth of tolerance went the zeal for prison reform, the abolition of torture and cruel punishments, the abrogation of the slave trade, serfdom, and slavery, the improvement of the condition of the poor and miserable, and similar movements of philanthropy, which are the late but genuine outgrowth of the spirit of Christianity.

§ 140. *The Early Life of Servetus.*

For our knowledge of the origin and youth of Servetus we have to depend on the statements which he made at his trials before the Roman Catholic court at Vienne in April, 1553, and before the Calvinistic court at Geneva in August of the same year. These depositions are meagre and inconsistent, either from defect of memory or want of honesty. In Geneva he could not deceive the judges, as Calvin was well acquainted with his antecedents. I give, therefore, the preference to his later testimony.[1]

MICHAEL SERVETO, better known in the Latinized form SERVETUS, also called REVES,[2] was born at Villa-nueva or Villanova in Aragon (hence "Villanovanus"), in 1509, the year of the nativity of Calvin, his great antagonist.[3] He informed the court of Geneva that he was of an ancient and noble Spanish family, and that his father was a lawyer and notary by profession.

---

[1] A. v. d. Linde, p. 3 sq., presents the contradictory statements of Servetus in parallel columns.

[2] In the title of his first book. "Reves" is an abridged anagram of Serveto. Others derive it from the maiden name of his mother. But we know nothing of his family. The form "Servede" never occurs among his contemporaries, and not before 1597, but is used by several modern writers, as Herzog, Guericke, Hase, Dorner, Harnack.

[3] Place and date are disputed. In the trial at Vienne he stated that he was born at Tudela in the old Spanish kingdom of Navarre, that he was then forty-two years old, which would put his birth in 1511. In the trial at Geneva he declared himself to be "Espagnol Arragonese de Villeneufve," and to be forty-four years old. This is confirmed by the author's name on the title-page of his first book: "Per Michaelem Serveto, aliàs Reves ab *Aragonia Hispanum*," by the subscription at the end of his *Restitutio* "M. S. V." [Villanovanus] and by the name "Villeneuve," under which he was known in France. So also Willis and v. d. Linde. But Tollin decides for Tudela and for the year 1511. See his *Servet's Kindheit und Jugend*, in Kahnis' "Zeitschrift für hist. Theol.," 1875.

The hypothesis that he was of Jewish or Moorish extraction is an unwarranted inference from his knowledge of Hebrew and the Koran.

He was slender and delicate in body, but precocious, inquisitive, imaginative, acute, independent, and inclined to mysticism and fanaticism. He seems to have received his early education in a Dominican convent and in the University of Saragossa, with a view at first to the clerical vocation.

He was sent by his father to the celebrated law-school of Toulouse, where he studied jurisprudence for two or three years. The University of Toulouse was strictly orthodox, and kept a close watch against the Lutheran heresy. But it was there that he first saw a complete copy of the Bible, as Luther did after he entered the University of Erfurt.

The Bible now became his guide. He fully adopted the Protestant principle of the supremacy and sufficiency of the Bible, but subjected it to his speculative fancy, and carried opposition to Catholic tradition much farther than the Reformers did. He rejected the œcumenical orthodoxy, while they rejected only the mediæval scholastic orthodoxy. It is characteristic of his mystical turn of mind that he made the Apocalypse the basis of his speculations, while the sober and judicious Calvin never commented on this book.

Servetus declared, in his first work, that the Bible was the source of all his philosophy and science, and to be read a thousand times.[1] He called it a gift of God descended from heaven.[2] Next to the Bible, he esteemed the ante-Nicene Fathers, because of their simpler and less definite teaching. He quotes them freely in his first book.

We do not know whether, and how far, he was influenced

---

[1] *Omnem philosophiam et scientiam ego in Biblia reperio.* . . . *Lege obsecro millies Bibliam.*" (*De Trinitatis Erroribus*, fol. 78b and 79.)

[2] " *Datus est de cœlo liber ut in eo Deum investigemus, adjuvante ad hoc fide quæ non est ille crudus sophistarum assensus, sed motus cordis, sicut dicit Scriptura, corde creditur.*" (*Ibid.* f. 107b.) " *Figmenta sunt imaginaria quæ Scripturæ limites transgrediuntur.*" (*Ibid.* f. 81b.)

by the writings of the Reformers. He may have read some
tracts of Luther, which were early translated into Spanish,
but he does not quote from them.[1]

We next find Servetus in the employ of Juan Quintana,
a Franciscan friar and confessor to the Emperor Charles V.
He seems to have attended his court at the coronation by
Pope Clement VII. in Bologna (1529), and on the journey
to the Diet of Augsburg in 1530, which forms an epoch in
the history of the Lutheran Reformation.[2] At Augsburg
he may have seen Melanchthon and other leading Lutherans,
but he was too young and unknown to attract much
attention.

In the autumn of 1530 he was dismissed from the service
of Quintana; we do not know for what reason, probably on
suspicion of heresy.

We have no account of a conversion or moral struggle in
any period of his life, such as the Reformers passed through.
He never was a Protestant, either Lutheran or Reformed,
but a radical at war with all orthodoxy. A mere youth of
twenty-one or two, he boldly or impudently struck out an
independent path as a Reformer of the Reformation. The
Socinian society did not yet exist; and even there he would
not have felt at home, nor would he have long been tolerated. Nominally, he remained in the Roman Church, and
felt no scruple about conforming to its rites. As he stood
alone, so he died alone, leaving an influence, but no school
nor sect.

From Germany Servetus went to Switzerland and spent
some time at Basel. There he first ventilated his heresies
on the trinity and the divinity of Christ.

---

[1] Tollin conjectures that he had read the writings of Luther, Melanchthon,
and Bucer, and was especially influenced by Erasmus.

[2] See Tollin, *Die Beichtväter Kaiser Karls V.*, three short papers in the
" Magazin für die Lit. des Auslandes," 1874, and *Servet auf dem Reichstag zu
Augsburg*, in Thelemann's " Evang. Reform. Kirchenzeitung," 1876, No. 17-
24.

He importuned Œcolampadius with interviews and letters, hoping to convert him. But Œcolampadius was startled and horrified. He informed his friends, Bucer, Zwingli, and Bullinger, who happened to be at Basel in October, 1530, that he had been troubled of late by a hot-headed Spaniard, who denied the divine trinity and the eternal divinity of our Saviour. Zwingli advised him to try to convince Servetus of his error, and by good and wholesome arguments to win him over to the truth. Œcolampadius said that he could make no impression upon the haughty, daring, and contentious man. Zwingli replied: "This is indeed a thing insufferable in the Church of God. Therefore do everything possible to prevent the spread of such dreadful blasphemy." Zwingli never saw the objectionable book in print.

Servetus sought to satisfy Œcolampadius by a misleading confession of faith, but the latter was not deceived by the explanations and exhorted him to "confess the Son of God to be coequal and coeternal with the Father"; otherwise he could not acknowledge him as a Christian.

§ 141. *The Book against the Holy Trinity.*

Servetus was too vain and obstinate to take advice. In the beginning of 1531, he secured a publisher for his book on the "Errors of the Trinity," Conrad Koenig, who had shops at Basel and Strassburg, and who sent the manuscript to Secerius, a printer at Hagenau in Alsace. Servetus went to that place to read the proof. He also visited Bucer and Capito at Strassburg, who received him with courtesy and kindness and tried to convert him, but in vain.

In July, 1531, the book appeared under the name of the author, and was furnished to the trade at Strassburg, Frankfort, and Basel, but nobody knew where and by whom it was published. Suspicion fell upon Basel.

This book is a very original and, for so young a man, very remarkable treatise on the Trinity and Incarnation in opposition to the traditional and œcumenical faith. The style is crude and obscure, and not to be compared with Calvin's, who at the same age and in his earliest writings showed himself a master of lucid, methodical, and convincing statement in elegant and forcible Latin. Servetus was familiar with the Bible, the ante-Nicene Fathers (Tertullian and Irenæus), and scholastic theology, and teemed with new, but ill-digested ideas which he threw out like firebrands. He afterwards embodied his first work in his last, but in revised shape. The following is a summary of the Seven Books on the Trinity: —

In the first book he proceeds from the historical Jesus of Nazareth, and proves, first, that this man is Jesus the Christ; secondly, that he is the Son of God; and thirdly, that he is God.[1] He begins with the humanity in opposition to those who begin with the Logos and, in his opinion, lose the true Christ. In this respect he anticipates the Socinian and modern humanitarian Christology, but not in a rationalistic sense; for he asserts a special indwelling of God in Christ (somewhat resembling Schleiermacher), and a deification of Christ after his exaltation (like the Socinians).[2] He rejects the identity of the Logos with the Son of God and the doctrine of the communication of attributes. He distinguishes between the Hebrew names of God: *Jehovah* means exclusively the one and eternal God; *Elohim* or *El* or *Adonai* are names of God and also of angels, prophets,

---

[1] "*Primo, hic est Jesus Christus.   Secundo, hic est filius Dei.   Tertio, hic est Deus.*" (p. 1a.)

[2] "*Secundum carnem homo est, et spiritu est Deus, quia quod natum est de spiritu, spiritus est, et spiritus est deus.   Et ita Esaiæ 9. Puer natus est nobis, vocabitur nomen eius deus fortis.   Vide clare et dei nomen et fortitudinem nato puero attributam, cui data est omnis potestas in cœlo et in terra.   Et Thomas Iohannis 20. eum appellat, Deus meus, Dominus meus.   Et Rom. nono* CHRISTUS *dicitur in omnibus laudandus et benedicendus.   Multisque aliis locis eius divinitas ostenditur, quia exaltatus est, ut acciperet divinitatem, et nomen super omne nomen.*" 10a.

and kings (John 10 : 34–36).[1] The prologue of John speaks of things that were, not of things that are. Everywhere else the Bible speaks of the *man* Christ. The Holy Spirit means, according to the Hebrew *ruach* and the Greek *pneuma*, wind or breath, and denotes in the Bible now God himself, now an angel, now the spirit of man, now a divine impulse.

He then explains away the proof texts for the doctrine of the Trinity, 1 John 5 : 7 (which he accepts as genuine, though Erasmus omitted it from his first edition); John 10 : 30; 14 : 11; Rom. 11 : 36. The chief passages, the baptismal formula (Matt. 28 : 19) and the apostolic benediction (2 Cor. 13 : 14) where the Father, the Son, and the Spirit are co-ordinated, he understands not of three persons, but of three dispositions of God.

In the second book he treats of the Logos, the person of Christ, and the Spirit of God, and chiefly explains the prologue to the fourth Gospel. The Logos is not a metaphysical being, but an oracle; the voice of God and the light of the world.[2] The Logos is a disposition or dispensation in God, so understood by Tertullian and Irenæus.[3] Before the incarnation the Logos was God himself speaking; after the incarnation the Logos is Jesus Christ, who makes God known to us.[4]

---

[1] "*Notes differentiam inter* יהוה *proprium Dei nomen, et* אלהים אדני אל *et alia similia Deo attributa. Et quod Thomas Iohannis 20. non Iehovah, sed Elohim et Adonai de* CHRISTO *dixerit, infra probabo.*" 14a. "*Similiter et* אלים *de angelis et hominibus fortibus dicitur, Psal. 88 et Iob 41.*" 14b. He identifies Christ with the Elohim instead of Jehovah.

[2] "Λόγος *non philosophicam illam rem, sed oraculum, vocem, sermonem, eloquium Dei sonat. Usurpatur enim a verbo* λέγω, *quod est dico.*" 47a.

[3] "*Per sacramentum Verbi intelligit quandam in Deo dispositionem seu dispensationem, qua placitum est ei arcanum voluntatis suæ nobis revelare. Et hoc Tertullianus* οἰκονομίαν, *et Irenæus dispositionem sæpissime appellant.*" 48a.

[4] "*Verbum in Deo proferente, est ipsemet Deus loquens. Post prolationem est ipsa caro, seu Verbum Dei, antequam sermo ille caro fieret, intelligebatur ipsum Dei oraculum intra nubis caliginem nondum manifestatum, quia Deus erat ille sermo. Et postquam Verbum homo factum est, per Verbum intelligimus ipsum* CHRISTUM, *qui est Verbum Dei, et vox Dei, nam, quasi vox, est ex ore Dei prolatus.*" 48a and b. He refers for proof to Rev. 19 : 13: τὸ ὄνομα αὐτοῦ 'Ο λόγος τοῦ Θεοῦ.

All that God before did through the Word, Christ does in the flesh. To him God has given the kingdom and the power to atone and to gather all things in him.

The third book is an exposition of the relation of Christ to the divine Logos.

The fourth book discusses the divine dispositions or manifestations. God appeared in the Son and in the Spirit. Two divine manifestations are substituted for the orthodox tripersonality. The position of the Father is not clear; he is now represented as the divinity itself, now as a disposition and person. The orthodox christology of two natures in one person is entirely rejected. God has no nature (from *nasci*), and a person is not a compound of two natures or things, but a unit.

The fifth book is a worthless speculative exposition of the Hebrew names of God. The Lutheran doctrine of justification is incidentally attacked as calculated to make man lazy and indifferent to good works.

The sixth book shows that Christ is the only fountain of all true knowledge of God, who is incomprehensible in himself, but revealed himself in the person of his Son. He who sees the Son sees the Father.

The seventh and last book is an answer to objections, and contains a new attack on the doctrine of the Trinity, which was introduced at the same time with the secular power of the pope. Servetus probably believed in the fable of the donation of Constantine.

It is not surprising that this book gave great offence to Catholics and Protestants alike, and appeared to them blasphemous. Servetus calls the Trinitarians tritheists and atheists.[1] He frivolously asked such questions as whether God had a spiritual wife or was without sex.[2] He calls the

---

[1] "*Tritheitæ . . . Athei, hoc est sine Deo.*"   21b.

[2] "*Debuissent dicere quod habebat [Deus] uxorem quandam spiritualem, vel quod solus ipse masculo-fœmineus aut Hermaphroditus, simul erat pater et mater.*"

three gods of the Trinitarians a deception of the devil, yea (in his later writings), a three-headed monster.[1]

Zwingli and Œcolampadius died a few months after the publication of the book, but condemned its contents beforehand. Luther's and Bucer's views on it have already been noticed. Melanchthon felt the difficulties of the trinitarian and christological problems and foresaw future controversies. He gave his judgment in a letter to his learned friend Camerarius (dated 5 Id. Febr. 1533) : —

"You ask me what I think of Servetus? I see him indeed sufficiently sharp and subtle in disputation, but I do not give him credit for much depth. He is possessed, as it seems to me, of confused imaginations, and his thoughts are not well matured on the subjects he discusses. He manifestly talks foolishness when he speaks of justification. περὶ τῆς τριάδος [on the subject of the Trinity] you know, I have always feared that serious difficulties would one day arise. Good God! to what tragedies will not these questions give occasion in times to come : εἰ ἐστιν ὑπόστασις ὁ λόγος [is the Logos an hypostasis]? εἰ ἐστιν ὑπόστασις τὸ πνεῦμα [is the Holy Spirit an hypostasis]? For my own part I refer to those passages of Scripture that bid us call on Christ, which is to ascribe divine honors to him, and find them full of consolation."[2]

39b. This reminds one of the reasoning of the Mohammedans that God has no wife, therefore he can have no son. He approves of the objection of the Turks : "Nec mirum, si Turci nos asinarios vocant, postquam nos Deum vocare asinum non erubescimus." 12a.

[1] The last expression I could not find in the work De Trinitatis Erroribus, but it occurs in his letters to Calvin, and in a lettter to Poupin, where he says : "Pro uno Deo habetis tricipitem cerberum." Calvin's Opera, VIII. 750. It was made the chief ground of the charge of blasphemy at the trial in Geneva. "Un Dieu party en trois . . . est un diable à trois testes comme le Cerberus que les Poetes anciens ont appellé le chien d'enfer, un monstre." Ibid. 728, Art. IX. Tollin, in his article Der Verfasser de Trinitatis Erroribus ("Jahrbücher für protest. Theologie," 1891, p. 414), derives these offensive phrases from the papal controversialist Cochlæus, who in his Lutherus septiceps, 1529, says : "Quid ad hæc Janus Bifrons? Quid Geryon Triceps? Quid Cerberus trifaux? fabulæ sunt poetarum et jocosa figmenta." Cochlæus compared these fables with the seven-capped Luther, who surpassed them all in monstrosity.

[2] He adds in Greek that it is not profitable to inquire curiously into the ideas and differences of the divine persons. Opera, ed. Bretschneider, II. 630, and his letter to Brenz, July, 1533, II. 660. Also Tollin, Ph. Melanchthon und M. Servet, Berlin, 1876.

Cochlæus directed the attention of Quintana, at the Diet of Regensburg, in 1532, to the book of Servetus which was sold there, and Quintana at once took measures to suppress it. The Emperor prohibited it, and the book soon disappeared.

Servetus published in 1532 two dialogues on the Trinity, and a treatise on Justification. He retracted, in the preface, all he had said in his former work, not, however, as false, but as childish.[1] He rejected the Lutheran doctrine of justification, and also both the Lutheran and Zwinglian views of the sacrament. He concluded the book by invoking a malediction on "all tyrants of the Church." [2]

§ 142. *Servetus as a Geographer.*

As Servetus was repulsed by the Reformers of Switzerland and Germany, he left for France and assumed the name of MICHEL DE VILLENEUVE. His real name and his obnoxious books disappeared from the sight of the world till they emerged twenty years later at Vienne and at Geneva. He devoted himself to the study of mathematics, geography, astrology, and medicine.

In 1534 he was in Paris, and challenged the young Calvin to a disputation, but failed to appear at the appointed hour.

He spent some time at Lyons as proof-reader and publisher of the famous printers, Melchior and Caspar Trechsel. He issued through them, in 1535, under the name of " Villanovanus," a magnificent edition of Ptolemy's Geography, with a self-laudatory preface, which concludes with the hope that "no one will underestimate the labor, though pleasant

---

[1] " *Quæ nuper contra receptam de Trinitate sententiam, septem libris, scripsi, omnia nunc, candide lector, retracto. Non quia falsa sint, sed quia imperfecta, et tamquam a parvulo parvulis scripta. . . . Quod autem ita barbarus, confusus et incorrectus, prior liber prodierit, imperitiæ meæ et typographi incuriæ adscribendus est.*"

[2] " *Perdat Dominus omnes ecclesiæ tyrannos. Amen.*"

in itself, that is implied in the collation of our text with that
of earlier editions, unless it be some Zoilus of contracted
brow, who cannot look without envy upon the zealous labors
of others." A second and improved edition appeared in
1541.[1]

The discoveries of Columbus and his successors gave
a strong impulse to geographical studies, and called forth
several editions of the work of Ptolemy the famous Alexandrian geographer and astronomer of the second century.[2]
The edition of Villeneuve is based upon that of Pirkheimer
of Nürnberg, which appeared at Strassburg, 1525, with fifty
charts, but contains considerable improvements, and gave to
the author great reputation.   It is a very remarkable work,
considering that Servetus was then only twenty-six years of
age. A year later Calvin astonished the world with an
equally precocious and far more important and enduring
work — the *Institutes of the Christian Religion.*

The most interesting features in the edition of Villeneuve

[1] The following is the full title of the second edition which I found (together with a copy of the first) in the library of the American Geographical
Society at New York : —
    " Claudii | PTOLEMÆI | ALEXAN | drini | *Geographicæ Enarrationis,* | *Libri
Octo.* | *Ex Bilibaldi Pircke* | ymheri tralatione, sed ad Græca e't prisca exem-
plaria à Michaele Villanouano | secundò recogniti, et locis innumeris denuò
castigati. Adiecta insuper ab eodem scho | lia, quibus et difficilis ille Primus
Liber nunc primum explicatur, et exoleta Urbium | nomina ad nostri seculi
morem exponuntur. Quinquaginta illæ quoque cum ueterum tum | recentium
Tabulæ adnectuntur, variisque incolentium ritus et mores explicantur. . . .
Prostant Lugduni apud Hugonem à Porta. | MDXLI." fol. Dedicated " *Am-
plissimō illustrissimoque ac reverendissimo D. Dno Petro Palmerio, Archiepiscopo
et Comiti Viennensi Michael Villanouanus Medicus G. D.*" Dated "Viennæ
pridie Cal. Martii, MDXLI." The last page has the imprimatur of Caspar
Trechsel, Viennæ, 1541. The work is illustrated with fifty maps. Willis
(pp. 86 sqq.) gives condensed translations of some passages, which I have
used, and compared with the original. Tollin represents Servetus as a forerunner of Karl Ritter in comparative geography, *Michael Servet als Geograph,*
1875 (pp. 182).
    [2] Editions were published at Rome, Bologna, Strassburg (1523 and 1525),
Basel (1533, with a preface of Erasmus; 1546), Venice (1558). The last and
best Græco-Latin edition of Ptolemy is by Carl Müller, Paris, 1883 sqq.

are his descriptions of countries and nations. The following extracts give a fair idea, and have some bearing on the church history of the times :—

" The SPANIARD is of a restless disposition, apt enough of understanding, but learning imperfectly or amiss, so that you shall find a learned Spaniard almost anywhere sooner than in Spain.[1] Half-informed, he thinks himself brimful of information, and always pretends to more knowledge than he has in fact. He is much given to vast projects never realized; and in conversation he delights in subtleties and sophistry. Teachers commonly prefer to speak Spanish rather than Latin in the schools and colleges of the country; but the people in general have little taste for letters, and produce few books themselves, mostly procuring those they want, from France. . . . The people have many barbarous notions and usages, derived by implication from their old Moorish conquerors and fellow-denizens. . . . The women have a custom, that would be held barbarous in France, of piercing their ears and hanging gold rings in them, often set with precious stones. They besmirch their faces, too, with minium and ecruse — red and white lead — and walk about on clogs a foot or a foot and a half high, so that they seem to walk above rather than on the earth. The people are extremely temperate, and the women never drink wine. . . . Spaniards are notably the most superstitious people in the world in their religious notions; but they are brave in the field, of signal endurance under privation and difficulty, and by their voyages of discovery have spread their name over the face of the globe."

" ENGLAND is wonderfully well-peopled, and the inhabitants are long-lived. Tall in stature, they are fair in complexion, and have blue eyes. They are brave in war, and admirable bowmen. . . ."

" The people of SCOTLAND are hot-tempered, prone to revenge, and fierce in their anger; but valiant in war, and patient beyond belief of cold, hunger, and fatigue. They are handsome in person, and their clothing and language are the same as those of the Irish; their tunics being dyed yellow, their legs bare, and their feet protected by sandals of undressed hide. They live mainly on fish and flesh. They are not a particularly religious people. . . ."

" The ITALIANS make use in their everyday talk of the most horrid oaths and imprecations. Holding all the rest of the world in contempt, and calling them barbarians, they themselves have nevertheless been alternately the prey of the French, the Spaniards, and the Germans. . . ."[2]

" GERMANY is overgrown by vast forests, and defaced by frightful swamps. Its climate is as insufferably hot in summer as it is bitterly cold in winter. . . .

---

[1] " Ut alibi potius quam in ipsa Hispania Hispanum doctum invenias."

[2] " Irrident Neapolitani Calabros, Calabri Appulos, hos autem omnes Romani, Romanos Hetrusci, quos et alii vicissim irrident: quin et mortales cæteros omnes irrident Itali, contemnunt et barbaros appellant: cum sint ipsi tamen nunc Hispanis, nunc Gallis, nunc Germanis prædæ expositi. . . . Italia in universum magis adhuc superstitiosa gens quam pugnat. Superba Roma, gentium imperio viduata, sedes facta summi pontificis."

Hungary is commonly said to produce oxen; Bavaria, swine; Franconia, onions, turnips, and licorice; Swabia, harlots; Bohemia, heretics; Switzerland, butchers; Westphalia, cheats; and the whole country gluttons and drunkards. . . . The Germans, however, are a religious people; not easily turned from opinions they have once espoused, and not readily persuaded to concord in matters of schism; every one valiantly and obstinately defending the heresy he has himself adopted."[1]

This unfavorable account of Germany, borrowed in part from Tacitus, was much modified and abridged in the second edition, in which it appears as "a pleasant country with a temperate climate." Of the Swabians he speaks as a singularly gifted people.[2] The fling at the ignorance and superstition of the Spaniards, his own countrymen, was also omitted.

The most interesting part of this geographical work on account of its theological bearing, is the description of Palestine. He declared in the first edition that "it is mere boasting and untruth when so much of excellence is ascribed to this land; the experience of merchants and travellers who have visited it, proving it to be inhospitable, barren, and altogether without amenity. Wherefore you may say that the land was promised indeed, but is of little promise when spoken of in everyday terms." He omitted this passage in the second edition in deference to Archbishop Palmier. Nevertheless, it was made a ground of accusation at the trial of Servetus, for its apparent contradiction with the Mosaic account of the land "flowing with milk and honey."

§ 143. *Servetus as a Physician, Scientist, and Astrologer.*

Being supplied with the necessary funds, Servetus returned to Paris in 1536 and took his degrees as magister and doctor of medicine. He acquired great fame as a physician.

[1] "*Sunt enim Germani in Dei cultum propensi, semel tamen imbutas opiniones non facile deserunt, nec in schismate queunt ad concordiam reduci, sed hæresim quisque suam valide tuetur.*"

[2] "*Suabia, ingenio singulari prædita, præstantissima Germaniæ a Plutarcho dicta.*"

The medical world was then divided into two schools, — the Galenists, who followed Hippocrates and Galen, and the Averrhoists, who followed Averrhoes and Avicenna. Servetus was a pupil of Champier, and joined the Greek school, but had an open eye to the truth of the Arabians.

He published in 1537 a learned treatise on Syrups and their use in medicine. It is his most popular book, and passed through four editions in ten years.[1]

He discovered the pulmonary circulation of the blood or the passage of the blood from the right to the left chamber of the heart through the lungs by the pulmonary artery and vein. He published it, not separately, but in his work on the Restitution of Christianity, as a part of his theological speculation on the vital spirits. The discovery was burnt and buried with this book; but nearly a hundred years later William Harvey (1578–1658), independently, made the same discovery.[2]

Servetus lectured in the University on geography and astrology, and gained much applause, but excited also the envy and ill-will of his colleagues, whom he treated with overbearing pride and contempt.

He wrote an "Apologetic Dissertation on Astrology,"[3] and severely attacked the physicians as ignoramuses, who in return denounced him as an impostor and wind-bag. The

---

[1] *Syroporum universa Ratio ad Galeni censuram diligenter exposita*, etc. Parisiis ex officina Simonis Colinæi, 1537 ; Venetiis, 1545 and 1548, and Lugduni, 1546 and 1547. Comp. Willis, ch. XI. 111 sq.; v. d. Linde, pp. 53 sqq. (with the full title on p. 54).

[2] *Restit. Christ.*, bk. V. p. 170. See G. Sismond, *The unnoticed Theories of Servetus*, London, 1826; Flourens, *Histoire de la découverte de la circulation du sang*, Paris, 1854; sec. ed. 1857; Tollin, *Die Entdeckung des Blutkreislaufs durch Michael Servet*, Jena, 1876 (comp. his *Kritische Bemerkungen über Harvey und seine Vorgänger*, 1882) ; Willis (who is a doctor of medicine), pp. 210 sqq.; and v. d. Linde, pp. 123 sqq. Harvey probably never saw the *Restitutio*, and is therefore as much entitled to the merit of an original discovery as Columbus, who was ignorant of the expeditions of the Norsemen to North America.

[3] Reprinted in Berlin, 1880.

senate of the University sided with the physicians, and the Parliament of Paris forbade him to lecture on astrology and to prophesy from the stars (1538).[1]

He left Paris for Charlieu, a small town near Lyons, and practised medicine for two or three years.

At his thirtieth year he thought that, after the example of Christ, he should be rebaptized, since his former baptism was of no value. He denied the analogy of circumcision. The Jews, he says, circumcised infants, but baptized only adults. This was the practice of John the Baptist; and Christ, who had been circumcised on the eighth day, was baptized when he entered the public ministry. The promise is given to believers only, and infants have no faith. Baptism is the beginning of regeneration, and the entrance into the kingdom of heaven. He wrote two letters to Calvin on the subject, and exhorted him to follow his example.[2]

His arrogance made him so unpopular that he had to leave Charlieu.[3]

§ 144. *Servetus at Vienne. His Annotations to the Bible.*

Villeneuve now repaired to Vienne in Dauphiné and settled down as a physician under the patronage of Pierre Palmier, one of his former hearers in Paris, and a patron of learning, who had been appointed archbishop of that see. He was provided with lodgings in the archiepiscopal palace, and made a comfortable living by his medical practice. He spent thirteen years at Vienne, from 1540 to 1553, which were probably the happiest of his fitful life. He conformed to the Catholic religion, and was on good terms with the higher

---

[1] V. d. Linde, pp. 65 sqq. In this respect Servetus was behind Calvin, who boldly attacked the superstition of astrology (see above, § 135, pp. 676 sqq.); but, strange to say, even in our days the "*Vox Stellarum*" is regularly printed in England and finds thousands of readers. Willis, p. 125.

[2] Ep. XV. and XVI. *ad Calv.*, in *Christianismi Restitutio*, pp. 613–619.

[3] Bolsec (p. 18 sq.) reports that Servetus was "*constrainct de se partir de Charlieu pour les folies lesquelles il faisoit.*"

clergy. Nobody suspected his heresy, or knew anything of his connection with the work on the " Errors of the Trinity."

He devoted his leisure to his favorite literary and theological studies, and kept the publishers of Lyons busy. We have already mentioned the second edition of his " Ptolemy," which he dedicated to Palmier with a complimentary preface.

A year afterwards (1542) he published a new and elegant edition of the Latin Bible of Santes Pagnini, a learned Dominican monk and pupil of Savonarola, but an enemy of the Reformed religion.[1] He accompanied it with explanatory notes, aiming to give "the old historical but hitherto neglected sense of the Scriptures." He anticipated modern exegesis in substituting the typical for the allegorical method and giving to the Old Testament prophecies an immediate bearing on their times, and a remote bearing on Christ. Thus he refers Psalms II., VIII., XXII., and CX. to David, as the type of Christ. It is not likely that he learned this method from Calvin, and it is certain that Calvin did not learn it from him. But Servetus goes further than Calvin, and anticipates the rationalistic explanation of Deutero-Isaiah by referring " the servant of Jehovah" to Cyrus as the anointed of the Lord. Rome put his comments on the Index (1559). Calvin brought them up against him at the trial, and, without knowing that the text of the book was literally taken from another edition without acknowledgment, said that he dexterously filched five hundred livres from the publisher in payment for the vain trifles and impious follies with which he had encumbered almost every page of the book.[2]

---

[1] The first edition of Pagnini had appeared at Lyons, 1528. The translation of the Old Testament rests on a good knowledge of Hebrew, and was much used by Protestants, *e.g.* Robert Olivetan in his French version.

[2] Willis (p. 142) charges Servetus with gross plagiarism, since his edition is a literal reprint of the edition of Melchior Novesianus of Cologne, 1541, while he declared in the preface that his text was corrected in numberless places by himself.

§ 145. *Correspondence of Servetus with Calvin and Poupin.*

While engaged in the preparation of his last work at
Vienne, Servetus opened a correspondence with Calvin
through Jean Frellon, a learned publisher at Lyons and
a personal friend of both.[1] He sent him a copy of his book
as far as then finished, and told him that he would find in it
"stupendous things never heard of before."[2] He also proposed
to him three questions: 1) Is the man Jesus Christ the Son
of God, and how? 2) Is the kingdom of God in man, when
does man enter into it, and when is he born again? 3) Must
Christian baptism presuppose faith, like the Lord's Supper,
and to what end are both sacraments instituted in the New
Testament?[3]

Calvin seems to have had no time to read the whole manuscript, but courteously answered the questions to the effect,
1) that Christ is the Son of God both according to his divine
nature eternally begotten, and according to his human nature
as the Wisdom of God made flesh; 2) that the kingdom of
God begins in man when he is born again, but that the
process of regeneration is not completed in a moment, but
goes on till death; 3) that faith is necessary for baptism,
but not in the same personal way as in the Lord's Supper;
for according to the type of circumcision the promise was
given also to the children of the faithful. Baptism and the
Lord's Supper are related to each other as circumcision and
the passover. He referred to his books for details, but
was ready to give further explanation if desired.[4]

---

[1] Frellon employed Servetus as an editor and translator, and was probably a Protestant, as we may infer from his friendly relation to Calvin. But
Henry (III. 129) supposes that he was a Catholic. Henry (III. 129) thinks
that the correspondence began as early as 1540.

[2] See the letter of Calvin to Farel, quoted on p. 692.

[3] Calvin gives the questions and answers in his *Refutatio Errorum Mich.
Serveti, Opera,* VIII. 482–484. Servetus omits them in the *Restitutio.*

[4] " *Sed quia mihi videor omnibus objectis alibi satisfecisse, fusiorem explica-
tionem inde peti melim. Si quid deest, paratus sum adjicere, si fuero admonitus.*"
Opera, VIII. 484.

Servetus was by no means satisfied with the answer, and wrote back that Calvin made two or three Sons of God; that the Wisdom of God spoken of by Solomon was allegorical and impersonal; that regeneration took place in the moment of baptism by water and the spirit, but never in infant baptism. He denied that circumcision corresponded to baptism. He put five new theological questions to Calvin, and asked him to read the fourth chapter on baptism in the manuscript of the *Restitutio* which he had sent him.[1]

To these objections Calvin sent another and more lengthy response.[2] He again offered further explanation, though he had no time to write whole books for him, and had discussed all these topics in his *Institutes*.[3]

So far there is nothing to indicate any disposition in Calvin to injure Servetus. On the contrary we must admire his patience and moderation in giving so much of his precious time to the questions of a troublesome stranger and pronounced opponent. Servetus continued to press Calvin with letters, and returned the copy of the *Institutes* with copious critical objections. " There is hardly a page," says Calvin, " that is not defiled by his vomit." [4]

[1] " *Rogo te per Deum, postquam pollicitus es te paratum reliqua adjicere, si fueris admonitus, doce me primo quæ est vera fides, et qualiter illa a spiritu regenerationis vivificetur. Secundo, an sine promissione possit quis justificari. Tertio, qualis sit internus homo, non ex sanguinibus genitus, sed ex Deo. Quarto, quis est homo ille qui a Christo alitur in cœna, an vere, an imaginarie. Quinto, quæ sit gratia adventus Christi. Annon eousque regnavit mors? annon patres omnes fuerunt antea in inferno? Demum te precor, ne graveris iterum legere quartum librum de Baptismo* [in the printed *Restitutio* it is entitled *De Regeneratione superna, et de regno Antichristi*, pp. 355–576]. *Nam videris eum nondum legisse. Deus misereatur nostri. Amen.*" *Opera*, VIII. 486.

[2] VIII. 487–495.

[3] " *Quod me rogas tibi de aliis quoque capitibus respondeam, id facerem, si possem breviter. Neque enim satis divino quid proprie desideres. Magis autem sum occupatus quam ut tibi uni vacet libros integros scribere. Deinde nihil quæris quod non reperias in mea Institutione, si illinc petere libeat. Quanquam labori non parcerem, si mihi notus esset scopus quo tendis.*" P. 494.

[4] " *Quoscunque meos libros nancisci potuit, non destitit insulsis conviciis farcire, ut nullam paginam a suo vomitu puram relinqueret.*" P. 481. Comp. the French in the fifth footnote.

Calvin sent a final answer to the questions of Servetus, which is lost, together with a French letter to Frellon, which is preserved.[1] This letter is dated Feb. 13, 1546, under his well-known pseudonym of Charles Despeville, and is as follows: —

" Seigneur Jehan, As your last letter was brought to me on my departure, I had no leisure to reply to the enclosure it contained. After my return I use the first moment of my leisure to comply with your desire; not indeed that I have any great hope of proving serviceable to such a man, seeing him disposed as I do. But I will try once more, if there be any means left of bringing him to reason, and this will happen when God shall have so wrought in him that he has become altogether another man. Since he has written to me in so proud a spirit, I have been led to write to him more sharply than is my wont, being minded to take him down a little in his presumption.[2] But I could not do otherwise. For I assure you there is no lesson he needs so much to learn as humility. This must come to him through the grace of God, not otherwise. But we, too, ought to lend a helping hand. If God give such grace to him and to us that the present answer will turn to his profit, I shall have cause to rejoice. If he persists, however, in the style he has hitherto seen fit to use, you will only lose your time in soliciting me further in his behalf; for I have other affairs that concern me more nearly, and I shall make it a matter of conscience not to busy myself further, not doubting that he is a Satan who would divert me from more profitable studies. Let me beg of you, therefore, to be content with what I have already done, unless you see occasion for acting differently."

Frellon sent this letter to Villeneuve by a special messenger, together with a note in which he addresses him as his "dear brother and friend." [3]

On the same day Calvin wrote the famous letter to Farel already quoted. He had arrived at the settled conviction

[1] Calvin's letter to Jean Frellon and Frellon's letter to Servetus, both in French, found their way into the judicial archives of the archbishop of Vienne, and were first published by the Abbé d'Artigny, Paris, 1749 (in *Nouveaux Mémoires d'histoire*, tom. II. 70), and independently from a copy of the original, by Mosheim, Helmstadt, 1750 (in his *Neue Nachrichten von Mich. Serveto*, pp. 89, 90). They are reprinted in Henry, III. 132, and in Calvin's *Opera*, VIII. 833 sq.

[2] "*Je luy ay bien voulu rabbatre un petit de son orgueil, parlant à luy plus durement que ma coustume ne porte.*"

[3] On the envelope is written: "*A mon bon frere et amy maistre Michel Villanovanus Docteur en Medicine soyt donnée ceste presente à Vienne.*"

that Servetus was an incorrigible and dangerous heretic, who deserved to die.[1] But he did nothing to induce him to come to Geneva, as he wished, and left him severely alone.. In 1548 he wrote to Viret that he would have nothing more to do with this desperately obstinate heretic, who shall force no more letters from him.[2]

Servetus continued to trouble Calvin, and published in his *Restitutio* no less than thirty letters to him, but without dates and without replies from Calvin.[3] They are conceived in a haughty and self-sufficient spirit. He writes to the greatest divine of the age, not as a learner, or even an equal, but as a superior. In the first of these printed letters he charges Calvin with holding absurd, confused, and contra-dictory opinions on the sonship of Christ, on the Logos, and on the Trinity. In the second letter he tells him: "You make three Sons of God: the human nature is a son to you, the divine nature is a son, and the whole Christ is a son. . . . All such tritheistic notions are a three-headed illusion of the Dragon, which easily crept in among the sophists in the present reign of Antichrist. Or have you not read of the spirit of the dragon, the spirit of the beast, the spirit of the false prophets, three spirits? Those who acknowledge the trinity of the beast are possessed by three spirits of demons. These three spirits incite war against the immacu-

---

[1] See p. 692. Bolsec speaks of a similar letter to Viret, from which he quotes this passage: "*Servetus cupit huc venire, sed a me accessitus. Ego autem nunquam committam, ut fidem meam eotenus obstrictam habeat. Iam enim constitu-tum habeo, si veniat, nunquam pati, ut salvus exeat.*" But no such letter has been found. Perhaps it was the same as the letter to Farel, which may have been sent first to Viret, as Farel was at that time in Metz (Henry, III. 133). Bolsec asserts also (p. 21) that Calvin informed the Cardinal de Tournon of the heresy of Servetus, but that the Cardinal laughed at the idea of one heretic accusing another.

[2] "*A me nihil posthac extorquebit.*" See Henry, II. 460; III. 134.

[3] *Restit.* pp. 577–664; reprinted in Calvin's *Opera*, VIII. 645–714, from Chr. Theoph. de Murr's ed., with marginal variations of the Paris copy. The manuscripts are not extant.

late Lamb, Jesus Christ (Apoc. 16).   False are all the invisible gods of the Trinitarians, as false as the gods of the Babylonians.   Farewell." [1]   He begins the third letter with the oft-repeated warning (*sœpius te monui*) not to admit that impossible monster of three things in God.   In another letter he calls him a reprobate and blasphemer (*improbus et blasphemus*) for calumniating good works.   He charges him with ignorance of the true nature of faith, justification, regeneration, baptism, and the kingdom of heaven.

These are fair specimens of the arrogant, irritating, and even insulting tone of his letters.   At last Servetus himself broke off his correspondence with Calvin, who, it seems, had long ceased to answer them, but he now addressed his colleagues. He wrote three letters to Abel Poupin, who was minister at Geneva from 1543 to 1556, when he died.   The last is preserved, and was used in evidence at the trial.[2]   It is not dated, but must have been written in 1548 or later.   Servetus charges the Reformed Christians of Geneva that they had a gospel without a God, without true faith, without good works ; and that instead of the true God they worshipped a three-headed Cerberus.   " Your faith in Christ," he continues, " is a mere pretence and without effect; your man is an inert trunk, and your God a fabulous monster of the enslaved will.   You reject baptismal regeneration and

---

[1] "*Draconis fuit hæc triceps illusio, quæ in sophistas facile irrepsit, instante regno Antichristi.   An non legisti ibi spiritum draconis, spiritum bestiæ, et spiritum pseudoprophetæ tres spiritus ?   Tres sunt vere dæmoniorum spiritus, a quibus occupati tenentur, qui bestiæ trinitatem agnoscunt.   Orbem hi tres spiritus concitant contra agnum immaculatum Iesum Christum, filium Dei, apo. 16.   Falsi ergo sunt trinitariorum invisibiles dii, adeo falsi, sicut dii Babyloniorum: cum præsertim dii illi in Babylone colantur.   Vale.*"   Restit. pp. 580, 581.

[2] It was not signed, but written very legibly by his own hand, and was acknowledged as his.   Henry gives a facsimile of it at the end of his third volume, from the archives of Geneva.   It is reprinted in *Opera*, VIII. 750 sq. " Every line of this letter," as Dyer (p. 309) well says, " betrays the heated and fanatical imagination of the writer, and his hatred of Calvin and the Genevese Church."

shut the kingdom of heaven against men. Woe unto you, woe, woe!"[1]

He concludes this remarkable letter with the prediction that he would die for this cause and become like unto his Master.[2]

§ 146. "*The Restitution of Christianity.*"

During his sojourn at Vienne, Servetus prepared his chief theological work under the title, "The Restitution of Christianity." He must have finished the greater part of it in manuscript as early as 1546, seven years before its publication in print; for in that year, as we have seen, he sent a copy to Calvin, which he tried to get back to make some corrections, but Calvin had sent it to Viret at Lausanne, where it was detained. It was afterwards used at the trial and ordered by the Council of Geneva to be burnt at the stake, together with the printed volume.[3]

[1] "*Evangelium vestrum est sine uno Deo, sine fide vera, sine bonis operibus. Pro uno Deo habetis tricipitem cerberum, pro fide vera habetis fatale somnium, et opera bona dicitis esse inanes picturas. Christi fides est vobis merus fucus, nihil efficiens; homo est vobis iners truncus, et Deus est vobis servi arbitrii chimæra. Regenerationem ex aqua cælestem non agnoscitis, sed velut fabulam habetis. Regnum cælorum clauditis ante homines, ut rem imaginariam a nobis excludendo. Væ vobis, væ, væ!*"

[2] "*Mihi ob eam rem moriendum esse certo scio, sed non propterea animo deficior, ut fiam discipulus similis præceptori. Hoc doleo, quod per vos non licuit mihi emendare locos aliquot in scriptis meis, quæ sunt apud Calvinum. Vale, et a me non amplius literas exspecta. Super custodiam meam stabo, contemplabor, et videbo quid sit dicturus. Nam veniet, certe veniet, et non tardabit.*"

[3] He declared at the trial in Geneva, Aug. 17, 1553, that he sent a copy to Calvin about six years before, in order to get his judgment ("*il y a environ six ans, pour en avoir son jugement*"). *Opera*, VIII. 734. Calvin informed Farel, Feb. 13, 1546, that Servetus had sent him a large volume of ravings, which must be the *Restitutio*.

Baron F. de Schickler, President of the "Société de l'Histoire du Protestantism français," informs me (June 3, 1892) that the library of this society (52 rue des Saint Pères, Paris) possesses a manuscript copy of the *Restitutio*, which was made with great accuracy, as he thinks, in 1613, from a copy that existed at that time in the library of Cassel. But it seems that it was transcribed from a *printed* copy, for on the first page of the MS. is written: "*Hic liber erat in octavo (ut loquuntur) impressus, et paginas continebat* 734 [the

The proud title indicates the pretentious and radical character of the book. It was chosen, probably, with reference to Calvin's "Institution of the Christian Religion." In opposition to the great Reformer he claimed to be a Restorer. The Hebrew motto on the title-page was taken from Dan. 12:1: "And at that time shall Michael stand up, the great prince"; the Greek motto from Rev. 12:7: "And there was war in heaven," which is followed by the words, "Michael and his angels going forth to war with the dragon; and the dragon warred, and his angels; and they prevailed not, neither was their place found any more in heaven. And the great dragon was cast down, the old serpent, he that is called the Devil and Satan, the deceiver of the whole world."

The identity of the Christian name of the author with the name of the archangel is significant. Servetus fancied that the great battle with Antichrist was near at hand or had already begun, and that he was one of Michael's warriors, if not Michael himself.[1]

His "Restitution of Christianity" was a manifesto of war. The woman in the twelfth chapter of Revelation he understood to be the true Church; her child, whom God saves, is the Christian faith; the great red dragon with seven heads and horns is the pope of Rome, the Antichrist predicted by Daniel, Paul, and John. At the time of Constantine and the Council of Nicæa, which divided the one God into three parts, the dragon began to drive the true Church into the wilderness, and retained his power for twelve hundred and sixty prophetic days or years; but now his reign is approaching to a close.

number of the printed pages]. *Pertinebat ad Mauricii illustratissimi Hessiæ principis ac Dom. bibliothecam quæ Casellis est, urbe illius reaionis metropoli et principis sede.*

[1] In the first Dialogue on the Trinity between Peter and Michael. Peter says: "*En adest, Servetus est, quem ego quærebam.*" *Restit.* p. 199. This is a direct assertion of his authorship which he concealed on the title-page, and only intimated on the last page by the initials "M. S. V."

He was fully conscious of a divine mission to overthrow the tyranny of the papal and Protestant Antichrist, and to restore Christianity to its primitive purity. "The task we have undertaken," he says in the preface, "is sublime in majesty, easy in perspicuity, and certain in demonstration; for it is no less than to make God known in his substantial manifestation by the Word and his divine communication by the Spirit, both comprised in Christ alone, through whom alone do we plainly discern how the deity of the Word and the Spirit may be apprehended in man. . . . We shall now see God, unseen before, with his face revealed, and behold him shining in ourselves, if we open the door and enter in. It is high time to open this door and this way of the light, without which no one can read the sacred Scriptures, or know God, or become a Christian." Then he gives a brief summary of topics, and closes the preface with this prayer: —

"O Christ Jesus, Son of God, who hast been given to us from heaven, who in thyself makest the Deity visibly manifest, open thyself to thy servant that so great a manifestation may be truly understood. Grant unto me now, who entreats thee, thy good Spirit, and the efficacious word; direct my mind and my pen that I may declare the glory of thy divinity and give expression to the true faith concerning thee. The cause is thine, and it is by a certain divine impulse that I am led to treat of thy glory from the Father, and the glory of thy Spirit. I once began to treat of it, and now I am constrained to do so again; for the time is, in truth, completed, as I shall now show to all the pious, from the certainty of the thing itself and from the manifest signs of the times. Thou hast taught us that a lamp must not be hidden. Woe unto me if I do not preach the gospel. It concerns the common cause of all Christians, to which we are all bound."

He forwarded the manuscript to a publisher in Basel, Marrinus, who declined it in a letter, dated April 9, 1552, because it could not be safely published in that city at that time. He then made an arrangement with Balthasar Arnoullet, bookseller and publisher at Vienne, and Guillaume Guéroult, his brother-in-law and manager of his printing establishment, who had run away from Geneva for bad conduct. He assured them that there were no errors in the

book, and that, on the contrary, it was directed against the
doctrines of Luther, Calvin, Melanchthon, and other heretics.
He agreed to withhold his and their names and the name of
the place of publication from the title-page. He assumed
the whole of the expense of publication, and paid them in
advance the sum of one hundred gold dollars. No one
in France knew at that time that his real name was Servetus, and that he was the author of the work, " On the Errors
of the Trinity."

The " Restitution " was secretly printed in a small house,
away from the known establishment, within three or four
months, and finished on the third of January, 1553. He
corrected the proofs himself, but there are several typographical errors in it. The whole impression of óne thousand
copies was made up into bales of one hundred copies each;
five bales were sent as white paper to Pierre Martin, type-
founder of Lyons, to be forwarded by sea to Genoa and
Venice; another lot to Jacob Bestet, bookseller at Chatillon;
and a third to Frankfort. Calvin obtained one or more
copies, probably from his friend Frellon of Lyons.[1]

The first part of the " Restitution " is a revised and enlarged edition of the seven books " On the Errors of the
Trinity." The seven books are condensed into five; and
these are followed by two dialogues on the Trinity between
Michael and Peter, which take the place of the sixth and
seventh books of the older work. The other part of the
" Restitution," which covers nearly two-thirds of the volume
(pp. 287–734), is new, and embraces three books on Faith
and the Righteousness of the Kingdom of Christ (287–354),
four books on Regeneration and the Reign of Antichrist
(355–576), thirty letters to Calvin (577–664), Sixty Signs
of Antichrist (664–670), and the Apology to Melanchthon
on the Mystery of the Trinity and on Ancient Discipline

---

[1] These facts came out at the trial of Vienne. On the few remaining
copies of the original edition of the *Restitutio* see above, § 136, p. 682.

(671–734). Calvin and Melanchthon are the two surviving Reformers whom he confronts as the representatives of orthodox Protestantism.[1]

§ 147. *The Theological System of Servetus.*

CALVIN, in his *Refutatio Errorum Mich. Serveti, Opera*, vol. VIII. 501–644, presents the doctrines of Servetus from his writings, in thirty-eight articles, the response of Servetus, the refutation of the response, and then a full examination of his whole system. — H. TOLLIN: *Das Lehrsystem Michael Servet's genetisch dargestellt*. Gütersloh, 1878, 3 vols. 8°. The most complete exposition of the theological opinions of Servetus.

Calvin and Tollin represent two opposite extremes in the doctrinal and personal estimate of Servetus : Calvin is wholly polemical, and sees in the *Restitutio* a volume of ravings ("*volumen deliriorum*") and a chaos of blasphemies ("*prodigiosum blasphemiarum chaos*") ; Tollin is wholly apologetical and eulogistic, and admires it as an anticipation of reverent, Christocentric theology; neither of them is strictly historical.

TRECHSEL's account (I. 119–144) is short, but impartial. — BAUR, in his "History of the Doctrine of the Trinity and the Incarnation" (Tübingen, 1843, 3 vols.) devotes, with his usual critical grasp and speculative insight, fifty pages to Servet's views on God and Christ (I. 54–103). — DORNER, in his great "History of the Doctrine of the Person of Christ" (Berlin, 1853), discusses his Christology profoundly, but rather briefly (II. 649–656). Both recognize the force of his arguments against the dyophysitism of the Chalcedonian Christology, and compare his Christology with that of Apollinaris.

Before we proceed to the heresy trial, we must give a connected statement of the opinions of Servetus as expressed in his last and most elaborate work.

To his contemporaries the *Restitutio* appeared to be a confused compound of Sabellian, Samosatenic, Arian, Apollinarian, and Pelagian heresies, mixed with Anabaptist errors and Neo-platonic, pantheistic speculations. The best judges — Calvin, Saisset, Trechsel, Baur, Dorner, Harnack — find the root of his system in pantheism. Tollin denies his pantheism, although he admits the pantheistic coloring of some of his expressions; he distinguishes no less than five phases

---

[1] Zwingli, Œcolampadius, Capito, Luther, and Bucer had died (in this order) before 1552.

in his theology before it came to its full maturity, and characterizes it as an "intensive, extensive, and protensive Panchristism, or 'Christocentricism.'"[1]

Servetus was a mystic theosophist and Christopantheist. Far from being a sceptic or rationalist, he had very strong, positive convictions of the absolute truth of the Christian religion. He regarded the Bible as an infallible source of truth, and accepted the traditional canon without dispute. So far he agreed with evangelical Protestantism; but he differed from it, as well as from Romanism, in principle and aim. He claimed to stand above both parties as the restorer of primitive Christianity, which excludes the errors and combines the truths of the Catholic and Protestant creeds.

The evangelical Reformation, inspired by the teaching of St. Paul and Augustin, was primarily a practical movement, and proceeded from a deep sense of sin and grace in opposition to prevailing Pelagianism, and pointed the people directly to Christ as the sole and sufficient fountain of pardon and peace to the troubled conscience; but it retained all the articles of the Apostles' Creed, and especially the doctrines of the Trinity and Incarnation. It should be noticed, however, that Melanchthon, in the first edition of his *Loci* (1521), omitted these mysteries as objects of adoration rather than of speculation,[2] and that Calvin, in the controversy with Caroli, spoke lightly of the Nicene and Athanasian terminology, which was derived from Greek philosophy rather than from the Bible.

---

[1] He calls it "*Christocentrik*," III. Preface, xiii. "*Was den Servet zum Servet machte*," he says, "*ist seine Lehre von Christo.*" Comp. II. 151–159. He assumes that Servetus composed the seven books on the "Errors of the Trinity" at different times: books I. and II. at Toulouse in 1528, while yet a student of seventeen (!); books III. and IV. at Basel in 1531; the last three books at Strassburg; and that the two Dialogues on the Trinity represent the fourth, and the "Restitution" the fifth, phase of his theology.

[2] In the editions after 1543 he discussed the doctrine of the Trinity and of the person of Christ and opposed Servetus. See Baur, III. 19 sqq., and Dorner, II. 613 sqq.

Servetus, with the Bible as his guide, aimed at a more radical revolution than the Reformers. He started with a new doctrine of God and of Christ, and undermined the very foundations of the Catholic creed. The three most prominent *negative* features of his system are three denials: the denial of the orthodox dogma of the Trinity, as set forth in the Nicene Creed; the denial of the orthodox Christology, as determined by the Œcumenical Council of Chalcedon; and the denial of infant baptism, as practised everywhere except by the Anabaptists. From these three sources he derived all the evils and corruptions of the Church. The first two denials were the basis of the theoretical revolution, the third was the basis of the practical revolution which he felt himself providentially called to effect by his anonymous book.

Those three negations in connection with what appeared to be shocking blasphemy, though not intended as such, made him an object of horror to all orthodox Christians of his age, Protestants as well as Roman Catholic, and led to his double condemnation, first at Vienne, and then at Geneva. So far he was perfectly understood by his contemporaries, especially by Calvin and Melanchthon. But the *positive* features, which he substituted for the Nicene and Chalcedonian orthodoxy, were not appreciated in their originality, and seemed to be simply a repetition of old and long-condemned heresies.

There were Antitrinitarians before Servetus, not only in the ante-Nicene age, but also in the sixteenth century, especially among the Anabaptists — such as Hetzer, Denck, Campanus, Melchior Hoffmann, Reed, Martini, David Joris.[1] But he gathered their sporadic ideas into a coherent original system, and gave them a speculative foundation.[2]

---

[1] For an account of their opinions see Trechsel, I. 13–55, and the great works of Baur and Dorner, above quoted.

[2] Baur (*l.c.*, III. 54) says: "*Die in den genannten Irrlehrern oder Schwarmgeistern, wie Luther sie treffend nannte, gleich Feuerfunken ausgestreuten und bald*

1. CHRISTOLOGY.

Servetus begins the "Restitution," as well as his first book against the Trinity, with the doctrine of Christ. He rises from the humanity of the historical Jesus of Nazareth to his Messiahship and Divine Sonship, and from this to his divinity.[1] This is, we may say, the view of the Synoptical Gospels, as distinct from the usual orthodox method which, with the Prologue of the fourth Gospel, descends from his divinity to his humanity through the act of the incarnation of the second person of the Trinity. In this respect he anticipates the modern humanitarian Christology. Jesus is, according to Servetus, begotten, not of the first person of God, but of the essence of the one undivided and indivisible God. He is born, according to the flesh, of the Virgin Mary by the overshadowing cloud of the Spirit (Matt. 1:18, 20, 23; Luke 1:32, 35). The whole aim of the gospel is to lead men to believe that Jesus is the Christ, the Son of God (comp. John 20:31).[2] But the term "Son of God" is in the Scriptures always used of the man Jesus, and never of the Logos.[3] He is the one true and natural son of God, born of the substance of God; we are sons by adoption, by an act of grace. We are made sons of God by faith (John 1:12;

da bald dort an einen entzündbaren Stoff sich ansezenden Ideen erhielten erst in dem Spanier Michael Servet, welchen der Zug seines Geistes demselben Kreise zuführte, eine festere Consistenz und Haltung. Diess ist es, was Servet seine historische Bedeutung gibt. Er wurde der Mittelpunct, in welchem jene vereinzelten, noch formlosen Elemente sich zur Einheit zusammenschlossen und durch die Energie seines Geistes sich zu einer in sich zusammenhängenden Theorie ausbildeten."

[1] "Ipse homo Iesus est ostium et via, a quo et merito exordium sumam. . . . Pronomine ad sensum demonstrante ipsum hominem, verberibus cæsum et flagellatum, concedam hæc tria simpliciter vera esse. Primo, hic est Iesus Christus. Secundo, hic est filius Dei. Tertio, hic est Deus." Rest. p. 5.

[2] "Semper dixi, et dico, et dicam, esse omnia scripta, ut credamus, hunc Iesum esse filium Dei." Rest. 293.

[3] "Ne unus quidem dari potest in scripturis locus, in quo ponatur vox filius quæ non accipiatur pro homine filio." Rest. 689.

Gal. 3 : 26 ; Rom. 8 : 23 ; Eph. 1 : 5). He is, moreover, truly and veritably God. The whole essence of God is manifest in him; God dwells in him bodily.[1]

To his last breath Servetus worshipped Jesus as the Son of the eternal God. But he did not admit him to be the *eternal* Son of God except in an ideal and pantheistic sense, in which the whole world was in the mind of God from eternity, and comprehended in the Divine Wisdom (Sophia) and the Divine Word (Logos).

He opposed the Chalcedonian dualism and aimed (like Apollinaris) at an organic unity of Christ's person, but made him a full human personality (while Apollinaris substituted the divine Logos for the human spirit, and thus made Christ only a half man). He charges the scholastic and orthodox divines, whom he calls sophists and opponents of the truth, with making two Sons of God — one invisible and eternal, another visible and temporal. They deny, he says, that Jesus is truly man by teaching that he has two distinct natures with a communication of attributes.[2] Christ does not consist of, or in, two natures. He had no previous personal pre-existence as a second hypostasis : his personality dates from his conception and birth. But this man Jesus is, at the same time, consubstantial with God ($\acute{o}\mu oo\acute{v}\sigma\iota o\varsigma$). As man and wife are one in the flesh of their son, so God

---

[1] "*Christus est Deus. Dicitur vere Deus, substantialiter Deus, cum in eo sit deitas corporaliter*" (p. 14). He quotes in proof Isa. 9 : 6; 45 : 3; John 20 : 28; Rom. 9 : 5; Phil. 2 : 5–11.

[2] "*Negant, hominem esse hominem et concedunt, Deum esse asinum. . . . Ad eundem modum concedunt fieri posse, ut Deus sit asinus, et spiritus sanctus sit mulus, sustentans mulum*" (p. 15). The same profane and offensive comparisons occur in his first book, and among mediæval schoolmen, who illustrated the relations of the Trinity by the analogy of horse, ass, and mule (*in mulo equus et asinus; in spiritu pater et filius*). They also raised such foolish questions as, whether God might not have become an ass or a cucumber as well as a man, and what effect the sacrament would have upon a dog or a mouse. From reverence to profanity, as from the sublime to the ridiculous, there is only one step.

and man are one in Christ.[1] The flesh of Christ is heavenly
and born of the very substance of God.[2] By the deification
of the flesh of Christ he materialized God, destroyed the
real humanity of Christ, and lost himself in the maze of a
pantheistic mysticism.

2. THEOLOGY.

The fundamental doctrine of Servetus was the absolute
unity, simplicity, and indivisibility of the Divine being, in
opposition to the tripersonality or threefold hypostasis of
orthodoxy.[3] In this respect he makes common cause with
the Jews and Mohammedans, and approvingly quotes the
Koran. He violently assails Athanasius, Hilary, Augustin,
John of Damascus, Peter the Lombard, and other champions
of the dogma of the Trinity.[4] But he claims the ante-Nicene
Fathers, especially Justin, Clement of Alexandria, Irenæus,
and Tertullian, for his view. He calls all Trinitarians "tritheists" and "atheists."[5] They have not one absolute God,

---

[1] "*Deus et homo unum sunt in Christo, quo vir et uxor unum sunt in una filii
carne. . . . Magnum est mysterium, quod caro illa fit Deo homousios [homousios],
in unam hypostasim ei connexa. Ita Deus coaluit cum humana natura, ut illum
extolleret filium sibi hominem generando. . . . Deus et homo unum in ipso sunt.*"
Rest. 269.

[2] "*Caro ipsa Christi est cœlestis de substantia Dei genita.*" *Rest.* 74; comp.
48, 50, 72, 77.

[3] Tollin (*Thomas Aquinas, der Lehrer Servet's*, in Hilgenfeld's "Zeitschrift
für wissenschaftliche Theologie," 1892) tries to show that Servetus only
followed out consistently the view of Thomas Aquinas, who proved the simplicity of the divine essence from reason, but the Trinity only from the faith
of the Church.

[4] He calls Athanasius and Augustin worshippers of the beast and of
images ("*Athanasium imaginum cultorem cum charactere bestiœ,*" p. 702; comp.
p. 398). He probably confounded the first Council of Nicæa (325), where
Athanasius was present, with the second Council of Nicæa (787), which sanctioned the worship of images. For this historical blunder Calvin takes
Servetus, who set himself up as "*temporum omnium censor,*" severely to task
(*Opera*, VIII. 591 sq.).

[5] "*Veri ergo hi sunt tritoitœ [for tritheitœ], et veri sunt athei, qui Deum unum
non habent, nisi tripartitum et aggregativum.*" *Rest.* 30; comp. 34.

but a three-parted, collective, composite God — that is, an unthinkable, impossible God, which is no God at all. They worship three idols of the demons, — a three-headed monster, like the Cerberus of the Greek mythology.[1] One of their gods is unbegotten, the second is begotten, the third proceeding. One died, the other two did not die. Why is not the Spirit begotten, and the Son proceeding? By distinguishing the Trinity in the abstract from the three persons separately considered, they have even four gods. The Talmud and the Koran, he thinks, are right in opposing such nonsense and blasphemy.

He examines in detail the various patristic and scholastic proof texts for the Trinity, as Gen. 18:2; Ex. 3:6; Ps. 2:7; 110:1; Isa. 7:14; John 1:1; 3:13; 8:58; 10:18; 14:10; Col. 1:15; 2:9; 1 Pet. 3:19; Heb. 1:2.

Yet, after all, he taught himself a sort of trinity, but substitutes the terms "dispositions," "dispensations," "economies," for hypostases and persons. In other words, he believed, like Sabellius, in a trinity of revelation or manifestation, but not in a trinity of essence or substance. He even avowed, during the trial at Geneva, a trinity of persons and the eternal personality of Christ; but he understood the term "person" in the original sense of a mask used by players on the stage, not in the orthodox sense of a distinct hypostasis or real personality that had its own proper life in the Divine essence from eternity, and was manifested in time in the man Jesus.[2]

---

[1] *Rest.* 59, 119, etc. On these expressions, which shocked the pious feelings of all Christendom, see above, § 141, p. 719.

[2] In his last reply to Calvin (*Opera*, VIII. 536), he tells him: "*Mentiris. Trinitatem ego voco, et doceo, verissimam trinitatem. . . . Reale discrimen tollo, non personale. . . . Realem in Deo distinctionem ego repudio.*" Calvin, in his *Institutes* (I. ch. XIII. § 22) gives the following account of the trinity of Servetus: "The word *Trinity* was so odious and even detestable to Servetus, that he asserted all Trinitarians, as he called them, to be atheists. I omit his impertinent and scurrilous language, but this was the substance of his speculations: That it is representing God as consisting of three parts, when three persons are said to subsist in his essence, and that this triad is merely

Servetus distinguished — with Plato, Philo, the Neo-Platonists, and several of the Greek Fathers — between an ideal, invisible, uncreated, eternal world and the real, visible, created, temporal world. In God, he says, are from eternity the ideas or forms of all things : these are called "Wisdom" or "Logos," "the Word" (John 1:1). He identifies this ideal world with "the Book of God," wherein are recorded all things that happen (Deut. 32:32; Ps. 139:16; Rev. 5:1), and with the living creatures and four whirling wheels full of eyes, in the vision of Ezekiel (1:5; 10:12). The eyes of God are living fountains in which are reflected all things, great and small, even the hairs of our head (Matt. 10:30), but particularly the elect, whose names are recorded in a special book.

The Word or Wisdom of God, he says, was the seed out of which Christ was born, and the birth of Christ is the model of all births.[1] The Word may be called also the soul of Christ, which comprehends the ideas of all things. In Christ was the life, and the life was the light of the world (John 1:4 sqq.). He goes here into speculations about the nature of light and of the heavenly bodies, and ventilates his Hebrew learning. He distinguishes three heavens — the two material heavens of water and air, spoken of by Moses in

imaginary, being repugnant to the divine unity. At the same time he maintained the persons to be certain external ideas, which have no real subsistence in the divine essence, but give us a figurative representation of God under this or the other form; and, that in the beginning there was no distinction in God, because the Word was once the same as the Spirit; but that after Christ appeared God of God, there emanated from him another God, even the Spirit. Though he sometimes glosses over his impertinencies with allegories, as when he says that the eternal Word of God was the Spirit of Christ with God, and the reflection of his image, and that the Spirit was a shadow of the Deity; yet he afterwards destroys the deity of both, asserting that according to the mode of dispensation there is a part of God in both the Son and the Spirit; just as the same Spirit substantially diffused in us, and even on wood and stones, is a portion of the Deity."

[1] " *Verbum ipsum Dei quod erat semen generationis Christi. . . . Ipsa Christi generatio sit aliorum generationum omnium specimen et prototypus. . . . Vere fuit in Deo substantiale semen Christi, et in eo rerum omnium seminales rationes, et exemplares formæ.*" *Rest.* p. 146.

the account of creation,[1] and a third, spiritual heaven of fire, the heaven of˜ heavens, to which Paul was elevated (2 Cor. 12 : 2), in which God and Christ dwell, and which gives splendor to the angels. Christ has revealed the true heaven to us, which was unknown to the Jews.

All things are one in God, in whom they consist.[2] There is one fundamental ground or principle and head of all things, and this is Jesus Christ our Lord.[3]

In the fifth book, Servetus discusses the doctrine of the Holy Spirit. He identifies him with the Word, from which he differs only in the form of existence. God is, figuratively speaking, the Father of the Spirit, as he is the Father of Wisdom and the Word. The Spirit is not a third metaphysical being, but the Spirit of God himself. To receive the Holy Spirit means to receive the anointing of God. The indwelling of the Spirit in us is the indwelling of God (1 Cor. 3 : 16; 6 : 19; 2 Cor. 6 : 16; Eph. 2 : 22). He who lies to the Holy Spirit lies to God (Acts 5 : 4). The Spirit is a modus, a form of divine existence. He is also called the Spirit of Christ and the Spirit of the Son (Gal. 4 : 6; Rom. 8 : 9; 1 Pet. 1 : 11). The human spirit is a spark of the Divine Spirit, an image of the Wisdom of God, created, yet similar. God breathes his Spirit into man in his birth, and again in regeneration.

In connection with this subject, Servetus goes into an investigation of the vital spirits in man, and gives a minute description of the lesser circulation of the blood, which, as we have seen, he first discovered.[4] He studied theology

---

[1] שׁמים, the dual. "*Duos cœlos ad literam accipimus aërium et aqueum*," p. 157. He regards the Hebrew word as a contraction of שׁם and מים, and equivalent to "waters" (p. 155); while it is derived from שׁמח, *to be high*.

[2] "*Omnia sunt unum in Deo, in quo uno consistunt.*" *Rest.* 161.

[3] "*Unicum est principium, unica verbi lux, lux omniformis, et caput omnium, Iesus Christus dominus noster, principium creaturarum Dei.*" *Rest.* 162.

[4] *Rest.* 169 : "*Ut vero totam animæ et spiritus rationem habeas, lector, divinam hic philosophiam adjungam, quam facile intelligis, si in anatome fueris exercitatus,*" etc. See above, § 143, p. 724.

as a physician and surgeon, and studied medicine as a theologian.

He discusses also the procession of the Spirit, which he regards not as a metaphysical and eternal process, but as a historical manifestation, identical with the mission. Herein he differs from both the Greek and the Latin theories, but unjustly charges the Greeks (who distinguish the procession from the Father alone, and the mission from the Father and the Son) with error in denying the *Filioque*. The Spirit, he says, proceeds from the Father and the Son, and he proceeds from the Father through the Son, who is the proper fountain of the Spirit. But he dates this procession from the day of Pentecost. In the Old Testament the Holy Spirit was unknown, which he proves from John 7:39 and Acts 19:2 (but contrary to such passages as Ps. 51:13; 1 Sam. 10:6; 16:13; Isa. 11:2; 61:1; 1 Pet. 1:11). The spirit in the Old Testament was only a spirit of servitude and fear, not of adoption and love (Rom. 8:15; Gal. 4:6). Christ calls us friends and brethren (John 15:15; 20:17). The Jews knew only a sanctification of the flesh and external things, not of the spirit. The anointing we receive from Christ is the anointing of the Spirit (2 Cor. 1:21; 1 John 2:20, 27). The Holy Spirit becomes ours in regeneration. We are deified or made partakers of the divine nature by Christ.

3. CHRISTOPANTHEISM.

The premises and conclusions of the speculations of Servetus are pantheistic. He adopts the conception of God as the all-embracing substance. "All is one and one is all, because all things are one in God, and God is the substance of all things." [1] "As the Word of God is essentially man, so the Spirit of God is essentially the spirit of man.

---

[1] "*Ultimo ex præmissis comprobatur vetus illa sententia, omnia esse unum, quia omnia sunt unum in Deo, in quo uno consistunt.*" *Rest.* 161.

By the power of the resurrection all the primitive elements of the body and spirit have been renewed, glorified, and immortalized, and all these are communicated to us by Christ in baptism and the Lord's Supper. The Holy Spirit is the breath from the mouth of Christ (John 20 : 22). As God breathes into man the soul with the air, so Christ breathes into his disciples the Holy Spirit with the air. . . . The deity in the stone is stone, in gold it is gold, in the wood it is wood, according to the proper ideas of things. In a more excellent way the deity in man is man, in the spirit it is spirit."[1] "God dwells in the Spirit, and God is Spirit. God dwells in the fire, and God is fire; God dwells in the light, and God is light; God dwells in the mind, and he is the mind itself." In one of his letters to Calvin he says: "Containing the essence of the universe in himself, God is everywhere, and in everything, and in such wise that he shows himself to us as fire, as a flower, as a stone." God is always in the process of becoming.[2] Evil as well as good is comprised in his essence. He quotes Isa. 45 : 7: "I form the light, and create darkness; I make peace, and create evil; I am the LORD, that doeth all these things." The evil differs from the good only in the direction.

When Calvin charged him with pantheism, Servetus restated his view in these words: "God is in all things by essence, presence, and power, and himself sustains all things."[3] Calvin admitted this, but denied the inference that the substantial Deity is in all creatures, and, as the latter confessed before the judges, even in the pavement on which they stand, and in the devils.[4] In his last reply to

[1] " Deitas in lapide est lapis, in auro est aurum, in ligno lignum, secundum proprias ideas. Excellentiore iterum modo, deitas in homine est homo, in spiritu est spiritus : sicut adjectio hominis in Deo est Deus, et adjectio spiritus hominis in eo est spiritus sanctus." Rest. 182.

[2] " Semper est Deus in fieri."   [3] Calv. Opera, VIII. 518, art. XXXIV.

[4] Ibid. 550 : " Sed hinc non sequitur in omnibus creaturis substantialem esse deitatem. Multo minus, quod ipse coram judicibus confessus est, pavimentum, quod

Calvin he tells him: "With Simon Magus you shut up God in a corner; I say, that he is all in all things; all beings are sustained in God."[1]

He frequently refers with approval to Plato and the Neo-Platonists (Plotin, Jamblichus, Proclus, Porphyry).[2]

But his views differ from the ordinary pantheism. He substitutes for a cosmopantheism a *Christopantheism*. Instead of saying, The *world* is the great God, he says, *Christ* is the great God.[3] By Christ, however, he means only the ideal Christ; for he denied the eternity of the real Christ.

4. ANTHROPOLOGY AND SOTERIOLOGY.[4]

Servetus was called a Pelagian by Calvin. This is true only with some qualifications. He denied absolute predestination and the slavery of the human will, as taught first by all the Reformers. He admitted the fall of Adam in consequence of the temptation by the devil, and he admitted also hereditary sin (which Pelagius denied), but not hereditary guilt. Hereditary sin is only a disease for which the child is not responsible. (This was also the view of Zwingli.)

---

pedibus calcamus, deitatis esse particeps, et in diabolis omnia deorum esse plena." In his *Institutes* (l. I. ch. 13, § 22), Calvin calls the promiscuous confusion of the Son of God, and the Spirit with all the creatures, "the most execrable" (*omnium maxime execrandum*) of the opinions of Servetus.

[1] "*Cum Simone Mago tu Deum in angulo recludis: ego eum dico esse omnia in omnibus. Entia omnia dico in Deo sustineri.*" In his abusive notes on Calvin's articles, written in prison. *Opera*, VIII. 548.

[2] He also quotes for the same purpose Philo, Plutarch, Parmenides, Hermes Trismegistus, Zoroaster, and the Jewish rabbis, Aben-Ezra and Moses Egyptius.

[3] "*Mundum Zoroaster et Trismegistus dixerunt, esse magnum Deum. Nos Christum dicimus esse magnum-Deum, mundi dominum, et omnipotentem. . . . Iesus Christus, factor mundi, fuit et est in Deo substantialiter, verius quam mundus, et per ipsum mundus secundario in Deo consistit.*" *Rest.* 213. "*Unicum est principium, unica verbi lux, lux omniformis, et caput omnium, Iesus Christus dominus noster, principium creaturarum Dei.*" P. 162.

[4] See here the book *De Regeneratione superna, et de regno Antichristi*, in the *Restit.*, pp. 355 sqq.

There is no guilt without knowledge of good and evil.[1]
Actual transgression is not possible before the time of age
and responsibility, that is, about the twentieth year.[2] He
infers this from such passages as Ex. 30:14; 38:26; Num.
14:29; 32:11; Deut. 1:39.

The serpent has entered human flesh and taken possession of it. There is a thorn in the flesh, a law of the
members antagonistic to the law of God; but this does
not condemn infants, nor is it taken away in baptism (as
the Catholics hold), for it dwells even in saints, and the
conflict between the spirit and the serpent goes on through
life.[3] But Christ offers his help to all, even to infants and
their angels.[4]

In the fallen state man has still a free-will, reason, and
conscience, which connect him with the divine grace. Man
is still the image of God. Hence the punishment of murder,
which is an attack upon the divine majesty in man (Gen.
9:6). Every man is enlightened by the Logos (John 1:17).
We are of divine origin (Acts 17:29). The doctrine of the
slavery of the human will is a great fallacy (*magna fallacia*),
and turns divine grace into a pure machine. It makes men
idle, and neglect prayer, fasting, and almsgiving. God is free

---

[1] " *Nullum est penitus nec in cœlesti, nec in terrestri justitia, crimen, sine scientia
boni et mali : quanquam sine ea sint nunc infantium animœ sub tenebras in infernum
deductœ.*" *Rest.* 387.

[2] " *Circa vicesimum annum incipit vera peccatorum remissio, sicut tunc incipi-
unt vera, et actualia secundœ mortis peccata.*" . . . 363. " *Peccatum mortale non
committitur ante vicesimum annum, sicut nec crimen corporali justitia capitale.*"
363 sq.

[3] *Rest.* 366: " *Quamvis autem universœ carni intrusus nunc sit serpens, et
originalem habeat etiam in carne infantum nidum : hoc tamen nec infantes illos
damnat, nec tollitur per baptismum, cum sanctis etiam insit. Nec abjiciuntur
carnis sordes in baptismo, nec tollitur lex membrorum, nec angelus Satanœ. Perpetuo in nobis ipsis duos habemus pugnantes principes, Deum in spiritu et serpentem
in carne.*" He calls original sin " *serpentis occupatio, inhabitatio et potestas, ab
ipso Adam ducens originem.*"

[4] *Rest.* 369: " *Adventus Christi omnia innovavit, et omnibus opem tulit, etiam
parvulis, et eorum angelis. Cœlestia, terrestria, et infernalia, adventum Christi
senserunt, et per eum sunt immutata.*"

himself and gives freedom to every man, and his grace works freely in man. It is our impiety which turns the gift of freedom into slavery.[1] The Reformers blaspheme God by their doctrine of total depravity and their depreciation of good works. All true philosophers and theologians teach that divinity is implanted in man, and that the soul is of the same essence with God.[2]

As to predestination, there is, strictly speaking, no before nor after in God, as he is not subject to time. But he is just and merciful to all his creatures, especially to the little flock of the elect.[3] He condemns no one who does not condemn himself.

Servetus rejected also the doctrine of forensic justification by faith alone, as injurious to sanctification. He held that man is justified by faith and good works, and appealed to the second chapter of James and the obedience of Abraham. On this point he sympathized more with the Roman theory. Justification is not a declaratory act of imputation, but an efficacious act by which man is changed and made righteous. Love is greater than faith and knowledge, because God is love. It embraces all good works which clothe, preserve, and strengthen faith and increase the reward of future glory. He who loves is better than he who believes.[4]

---

[1] *Rest.* 568: "*Impietas nostra facit arbitrium ex libero servum.*"

[2] 634 sq.: "*Philosophi veri, ac etiam theologi affirmant, esse menti hominis insitam divinitatem esseque animam Deo ὁμοούσιον, consubstantialem.*"

[3] *Rest.* 321: "*Concludendum est igitur, veram Dei in omnes suas creaturas esse justitiam et misericordiam: at in pusillum gregem suum, solum sibi peculiariter prædestinatum, insignem gratiæ sublimitatem.*" Melanchthon wrote to Camerarius that Servetus "*de justificatione manifeste delirat,*" but Tollin (III. 194) maintains that he supplements the one-sided forensic view of the Reformers. Comp. also Henry, III. 267–272.

[4] See the chapter *De Charitate, quid fides efficiat, quid charitas, et opera,* pp. 342 sqq., and the letters to Calvin, where he gives ten reasons for the utility of good works, and the letter to Poupin, where he charges the Church of Geneva that it had a gospel without good works.

5. THE SACRAMENTS.[1]

Servetus admitted only two sacraments, therein agreeing with the Protestants, but held original views on both.

(a) As to the sacrament of BAPTISM, he taught, with the Catholic Church, baptismal regeneration, but rejected, with the Anabaptists, infant baptism.

Baptism is a saving ordinance by which we receive the remission of sins, are made Christians, and enter the kingdom of heaven as priests and kings, through the power of the Holy Spirit who sanctifies the water.[2]   It is the death of the old man and the birth of the new man.   By baptism we put on Christ and live a new life in him.[3]

But baptism must be preceded by the preaching of the gospel, the illumination of the Spirit, and repentance, which, according to the preaching of John the Baptist and of Christ, is the necessary condition of entering the kingdom of God. Therefore, Servetus infers, no one is a fit subject for baptism before he has reached manhood.   By the law of Moses priests were not anointed before the thirtieth year (Num. 4 : 3). Joseph was thirty years old when he was raised from the prison to the throne (Gen. 41 : 46).   According to the rabbinical tradition Adam was born or created in his thirtieth year.   Christ was baptized in the Jordan when he was thirty years (Luke 3 : 21–23), and that is the model of all true Christian baptism.[4]   He was circumcised in infancy, but the carnal circumcision is the type of the spiritual circumcision

---

[1] *De Circumcisione vera, cum reliquis Christi et Antichristi mysteriis,* in *Rest.* 411 sqq., and *De Baptismi efficacia,* 483 sqq.

[2] *" Baptismo vere adest spiritus. . . . Per operationem spiritus habet baptismus eam efficaciam, ut vere dicamus, baptismum nos salvare, ad Tit. 3 et I. Pet. 3. Per solam enim fidem sine baptismo non complentur omnia salutis Christi mysteria. Baptismus nos salvat et lavat, sicut panis cœnœ corpore Christi nos cibat, interno mysterio."   Rest.* 497.

[3] *Rest.* 484 sq.

[4] *" Mysterium magnum est.   Triginta annorum Christus baptismum accepit, exemplum nobis dans, ac nos ita docens, ante eam œtatem non esse quem satis aptum ad mysteria regni cœlorum "* (p. 412).

of the heart, not of water baptism.[1] Circumcision was adapted to real infants who have not yet committed actual transgression; baptism is intended for spiritual infants — that is, for responsible persons who have a childlike spirit and begin a new life.

(*b*) Servetus rejected INFANT BAPTISM as irreconcilable with these views, and as absurd. He called it a doctrine of the devil, an invention of popery, and a total subversion of Christianity.[2] He saw in it the second root of all the corruptions of the Church, as the dogma of the Trinity was the first root.

By his passionate opposition to infant baptism he gave as much offence to Catholics and Protestants as by his opposition to the dogma of the Trinity. But while on this point he went further than the most fanatical Anabaptists, he did not belong to their society, and rejected the revolutionary opinions concerning obedience to government, and holding civil and military offices.

Children are unfit to perform the office of priests which is given to us in baptism. They have no faith, they cannot repent, and cannot enter into a covenant. Moreover, they do not need the bath of regeneration for the remission of sins, as they have not yet committed actual transgression.

But children are not lost if they die without baptism. Adam's sin is remitted to all by the merits of Christ. They are excluded from the Church on earth; they must die and go to Sheol; but Christ will raise them up on the resurrection day and save them in heaven. The Scripture does not

---

[1] " *Circumcisio illa carnalis fuit typus secundæ circumcisionis spiritualis, quæ per Christum fit, Roma. 2. et Colossen. 2.*" *Rest.* 411.

[2] "*Pædobaptismum esse dico detestandam abominationem, spiritus sancti extinctionem, ecclesiæ Dei desolationem, totius professionis Christianæ confusionem, innovationis, per Christum factæ, abolitionem, ac totius ejus regni conculcationem.*" *Rest.* 576. Tollin (III. 136) is certainly mistaken when he asserts that Servet's view of infant baptism was an exotic plant, foreign to his system. It is inseparable from it, and one of his fundamental doctrines.

condemn the Ismaelites or the Ninevites or other barbarians. Christ gives his blessing to unbaptized children. How could the most merciful Lord, who bore the sins of a guilty world, condemn those who have not committed an impiety?[1]

Servetus agreed with Zwingli, the Anabaptists, and the Second Scotch Confession, in rejecting the cruel Roman dogma, which excludes all unbaptized infants, even of Christian parents, from the kingdom of heaven.

(c) In the doctrine of the LORD'S SUPPER, Servetus differs from the Roman Catholic, the Lutheran, and the Zwinglian theories, and approaches, strange to say, the doctrine of his great antagonist, Calvin.[2] Baptism and the Lord's Supper represent the birth and the nourishment of the new man. By the former we receive the spirit of Christ; by the latter we receive the body of Christ, but in a spiritual and mystical manner. Baptism kindles and strengthens faith; the eucharist strengthens love and unites us more and more to Christ. By neglecting this ordinance the spiritual man famishes and dies away. The heavenly man needs heavenly food, which nourishes him to life eternal (John 6:53).[3]

---

[1] "Parvulis, non baptizatis, data est a Christo benedictio. Clementissimus ille et misericors dominus, qui impiorum peccata gratis sustulit, quomodo eos, qui impietatem non commiserunt, tam rigide damnaret?" P. 357. A noble and truly Christian sentiment, which puts to shame his orthodox opponents. Calvin, however, did not make water baptism a necessary condition of salvation, and left the way open for the doctrine of universal infant salvation by sovereign election.

[2] De Cœna Domini, Rest. 502 sqq. Tollin (III. 136): "In keiner Lehre Servet's zeigt sich so sehr als in der Abendmahlslehre sein vermittelnder Standpunkt. Tritt er doch wieder als Schiedsrichter auf zwischen dem magisch-materialistischen Katholicismus und dem quäkerischen Spiritismus, zwischen Realismus und Idealismus, zwischen lutherischer Mystik und zwingli'scher Rationalistik." He thinks that Servetus anticipated the eucharistic doctrine of Bucer and Calvin; but Bucer laid it down in the Tetrapolitan Confession in 1530, before he knew Servetus, and Calvin in his tract De Cœna in 1540.

[3] "Baptismus et cœna Domini sunt vita et fomentum ipsius fidei: sunt vita, fomentum, et nutrimentum interni hominis, per fidem ex Deo geniti. Per prædicationem evangelii plantatur fides, quod nec sine operatione spiritus fieri potest. . . . Per cœnam Domini, quœ baptismum consequitur, nutritur, adolescit et incrementa

Servetus distinguishes three false theories on the Lord's Supper, and calls their advocates *transubstantiatores* (Romanists), *impanatores* (Lutherans), and *tropistæ* (Zwinglians).[1] Against the first two theories, which agree in teaching a carnal presence and manducation of Christ's body and blood by all communicants, he urges that spiritual food cannot be received by the mouth and stomach, but only by the spiritual organs of faith and love. He refers, like Zwingli, to the passage in John 6:63, as the key for understanding the words of institution and the mysterious discourse on eating the flesh and drinking the blood of Christ.

He is most severe against the papal doctrine of transubstantiation or transelementation; because it turns bread into no-bread, and would make us believe that the body of Christ is eaten even by wild beasts, dogs, and mice. He calls this dogma a Satanic monstrosity and an invention of demons.[2]

To the Tropists he concedes that bread and wine are symbols, but he objects to the idea of the absence of Christ in heaven. They are symbols of a really present, not of an absent Christ.[3] He is the living head and vitally connected with all his members. A head cut off from the body would be a monster. To deny the real presence of Christ is to destroy his reign.[4] He came to us to abide with us forever.

---

vitæ suscipit, ille in baptismo genitus novus homo. Magis et magis tunc in dies in nobis Christus formatur, et nos magis et magis in unum Christi corpus cum aliis membris ædificamur per charitatem. . . . Charitatis symbolum est cœna. . . . Ita se habet cœna ad charitatem, sicut baptismus ad fidem. Cœna igitur et charitate neglectis, recedit a nobis Christus, arescit fides, evanescit spiritus, fame contabescit et moritur homo Christianus." Rest. 501 sq.

[1] Transubstantiationists, Consubstantiationists, and Tropists. Tollin invents three corresponding German terms: *Umsubstanzler, Einbroter, Figürler.*

[2] He says in this connection (p. 510): *" Papistica omnia dogmata esse doctrinas dæmoniorum et meras illusiones, 2 Thess. 2 et 1 Tim. 4."*

[3] *" Non enim absentis rei sunt hæc symbola, ut in umbris legis, sed est visibile signum rei invisibilis, et externum symbolum rei internæ."* Rest. 507 sq.

[4] *" An non monstrum erit, Christum vocari caput, si suis membris non jungitur? Res mortua est corpus totum, si ab eo caput separes. Pernitiosus admodum est error, et ipsissima regni Christi destructio, negare præsentiam ejus in nobis."* Rest. 508.

He withdrew only his visible presence till the day of judgment, but promised to be with us invisibly, but none the less really, to the end of the world.[1]

6. The Kingdom of Christ, and the Reign of Antichrist.[2]

We have already noticed the apocalyptic fancies of Servetus. He could not find the kingdom of God or the kingdom of heaven, so often spoken of in the Gospels (while Christ speaks only twice of the "Church"), in any visible church organization of his day. The true Church flourished in the first three centuries, but then fled into the wilderness, pursued by the dragon; there she has a place prepared by God, and will remain "a thousand two hundred and three-score prophetic days" or years (Rev. 12 : 6) — that is, from 325 till 1585.

The reign of Antichrist, with its corruptions and abominations, began with three contemporaneous events : the first Œcumenical Council of Nicæa (325), which split the one Godhead into three idols; the union of Church and State under Constantine, when the king became a monk; and the establishment of the papacy under Sylvester, when the bishop became a king.[3] From the same period he dates the general practice of infant baptism with its destructive consequences. Since that time the true Christians were everywhere persecuted and not allowed to assemble. They were scattered as sheep in the wilderness.

Servetus fully agreed with the Reformers in opposition to

---

[1] "*Non dixit, non ero vobiscum ; sed, non videbitis me, et ego vobiscum sum.*" *Rest.* 509.

[2] *De fide et justitia regni Christi. Rest.* 287 sqq. *Signa sexaginta Regni Christi et Antichristi et revelatio eius jam nunc præsens,* 664–670. Comp. above, § 146.

[3] "*Quamvis post Christum mox cœpit Antichristi mysterium : vere tamen emicuit et stabilitum est regnum tempore Sylvestri et Constantini. Quo tempore est mox œcumenico concilio a nobis ereptus filius Dei, fugata ecclesia, et abominationes omnes legibus decretæ. Hinc transierunt tempus et tempora et dimidium temporis, anni mille ducenti sexaginta.*" *Rest.* 666.

the papacy as an antichristian power, but went much further, and had no better opinion of the Protestant churches. He called the Roman Church "the most beastly of beasts and the most impudent of harlots." [1]

He finds no less than sixty signs or marks of the reign of Antichrist in the eschatological discourses of Christ, in Daniel (chs. 7 and 12), in Paul (2 Thess. 2:3, 4; 1 Tim. 4:1), and especially in the Apocalypse (chs. 13–18).

But this reign is now drawing to a close. The battle of Michael with Antichrist has already begun in heaven and on earth, and the author of the "Restitution" has sounded the trumpet of war, which will end in the victory of Christ and the true Church. Servetus might have lived to see the millennium (in 1585), but he expected to fall in the battle, and to share in the first resurrection.

He concludes his eschatological chapter on the reign of Antichrist with these words: "Whosoever truly believes that the pope is Antichrist, will also truly believe that the papistical trinity, pædobaptism, and the other sacraments of popery are doctrines of the dæmons. O Christ Jesus, thou Son of God, most merciful deliverer, who so often didst deliver thy people from distresses, deliver us poor sinners from this Babylonian captivity of Antichrist, from his hypocrisy, his tyranny, and his idolatry. Amen." [2]

7. Eschatology.

Servetus was charged by Calvin and the Council of Geneva with denying the immortality of the soul. This was a heresy punishable by death. Etienne Dolet was executed

---

[1] *Rest.* 462 sq. : " *O bestiam bestiarum sceleratissimam, meretricum impudentissimam. . . . Papa est Deus, in papatu est trinitas, draconis bestiæ et pseudoprophetæ. Trinitatem papisticam faciunt tres realiter distincti spiritus, qui Ioanni dicuntur tres immundi spiritus ranarum, multis rationibus. Quia sunt de abyssi aquis immundis, sicut ranæ,*" etc. Comp. his exposition of prophetic passages, pp. 393 sqq. and 666 sqq.

[2] " *Libera nos miseros ab hac Babylonica Antichristi captivitate, ab hypocrisi ejus, tyrannide, et idololatria. Amen.*" *Rest.* 670.

on the place Maubert at Paris, Aug. 2, 1546, for this denial.[1] But Servetus denied the charge. He taught that the soul was mortal, that it deserved to die on account of sin, but that Christ communicates to it new life by grace.[2] Christ has brought immortality to light (2 Tim. 1:10; 1 Pet. 1:21–25). This seems to be the doctrine of conditional immortality of believers. But he held that all the souls of the departed go to the gloomy abode of Sheol to undergo a certain purification before judgment. This is the baptism of blood and fire, as distinct from the baptism of water and spirit (1 Cor. 3:11–15). The good and the bad are separated in death. Those who die without being regenerated by Christ have no hope. The righteous progress in sanctification. They pray for us (for which he gives six reasons, and quotes Zach. 1:12, 13; Luke 15:10; 16:27, 28; 1 Cor. 13:18); but we ought not to pray for them, for they do not need our prayers, and there is no Scripture precept on the subject.[3]

The reign of the pope or Antichrist will be followed by the millennial reign of Christ on earth (Rev. 20:4–7). Then will take place the first resurrection.

Servetus was a chiliast, but not in the carnal Jewish sense. He blames Melanchthon for deriding, with the papal crowd, all those as chiliasts who believe in the glorious reign of Christ on earth, according to the book of Revelation and the teaching of the school of St. John.[4]

---

[1] He had translated the words of Plato: Σὺ γὰρ οὐκ ἔσῃ: "*Après la mort tu ne seras plus rien du tout,*" instead of "*Car tu ne seras plus,*" as the Sorbonne wanted. Tollin, III. 288, mentions this fact and refers to *Reg. fac. theol. Paris.* MM. 248 in the Paris state archives.

[2] "*Christus reparator animas nostras reddidit immortales, et vitalem earum spiritum incorruptibilem.*" *Rest.* 551. He distinguished between the soul and the spirit, according to the Platonic trichotomy. After the death of the body, the soul is a mere shadow.

[3] *Rest.* 718.

[4] "*Quamquam tu cum vulgo papistico seniores illos omnes, et apostolicos viros, ut chiliastas rideas.*" *Rest.* 719.

The general resurrection and judgment follow after the millennium. Men will be raised in the flower of manhood, the thirtieth year — the year of baptismal regeneration, the year in which Christ was baptized and entered upon his public ministry.[1] "Then wilt thou," so he addresses Philip Melanchthon, who, next to Calvin, was his greatest enemy, "with all thy senses, see, feel, taste, and hear God himself. If thou dost not believe this, thou dost not believe in a resurrection of the flesh and a bodily transformation of thy organs."[2]

After the general judgment, Christ will surrender his mediatorial reign with its glories to the Father, and God will be all in all (Acts 3 : 21 ; 1 Cor. 15 : 24–28).

§ 148. *The Trial and Condemnation of Servetus at Vienne.*

See D'ARTIGNY in *Nouveaux Mémoires d'histoire*, etc.; MOSHEIM'S *Neue Nachrichten*, etc.; and CALVIN'S *Opera*, VIII. 833–856.

Shortly after the publication of the " Restitution," the fact was made known to the Roman Catholic authorities at Lyons through Guillaume Trie, a native of Lyons and a convert from Romanism, residing at that time in Geneva. He corresponded with a cousin at Lyons, by the name of Arneys, a zealous Romanist, who tried to reconvert him to his religion, and reproached the Church of Geneva with the want of discipline. On the 26th of February, 1553, he wrote to Arneys that in Geneva vice and blasphemy were punished, while in France a dangerous heretic was tolerated, who deserved to be burned by Roman Catholics as well as Protestants, who blasphemed the holy Trinity, called Jesus Christ an idol, and the baptism of infants a diabolic invention. He gave his name as Michael Servetus, who called

---

[1] " *Dies baptismi assimilatur diei resurrectionis.*" *Rest.* 413.

[2] " *Deum ipsum tu beatus corporeis his omnibus tuis sensibus videbis, tanges, gustabis, olfacies et audies. Si hoc non credis, non credis carnis resurrectionem et corporeum tuorum organorum futuram glorificationem.*" *Rest.* 718.

himself at present Villeneuve, a practising physician at Vienne. In confirmation he sent the first leaf of the "Restitution," and named the printer Balthasar Arnoullet at Vienne.[1]

This letter, and two others of Trie which followed, look very much as if they had been dictated or inspired by Calvin. Servetus held him responsible.[2] But Calvin denied the imputation as a calumny.[3] At the same time he speaks rather lightly of it, and thinks that it would not have been dishonorable to denounce so dangerous a heretic to the proper authorities. He also frankly acknowledges that he caused his arrest at Geneva.[4] He could see no material difference in principle between doing the same thing, indirectly, at Vienne and, directly, at Geneva. He simply denies that he was the originator of the papal trial and of the letter of Trie; but he does not deny that he furnished material for evidence, which was quite well known and publicly made use of in the trial where Servetus's letters to Calvin are mentioned as *pieces justificatives.* There can be no doubt that Trie, who describes

---

[1] " *C'est un Espagnol Portugallois nommé Michael Servetus de son propre nom, mais il se nomme Villeneuve à présent, faisant le Médecin. Il a demeuré quelque temps à Lyon, maintenant il se tient à Vienne, où le livre dont je parle a été imprimé par un quidam qui a là dressé imprimerie, nommé Balthazard Arnoullet. Et afin que vous ne pensiez que je en parle à crédit, je vous envoye la première feuille pour enseigne.*" The specimens seemed to have been the title-page, the index, and, perhaps, a few pages, which did not prove the authorship of Villeneuve, nor his identity with Servetus. The three letters of Trie are published in French by D'Artigny (p. 79 sq.) and Mosheim (p. 90), and in Calvin's *Opera,* VIII. 835–838, 840–844.

[2] This was also the opinion of Bolsec and the pseudonymous Martinus Bellius, and is repeated by the Abbé d'Artigny, Wallace, Willis, and v. d. Linde, who charge Calvin with having deliberately and dishonorably betrayed Servetus. But this cannot be proven, and would involve a downright falsehood, of which Calvin was incapable.

[3] He calls it a "*futilis calumnia,*" and thinks it preposterous to suppose that he was in friendly correspondence with the popish authorities. " *Unde mihi tanta cum papæ satellitio repente familiaritas? unde etiam tanta gratia?*" *Refut. error. Mich. Serv.,* in *Opera,* VIII. 479.

[4] " *Nec sane dissimulo, mea opera consilioque jure in carcerem fuisse conjectum.*" *Ibid.* VIII. 461.

himself as a comparatively unlettered man, got his information about Servetus and his book from Calvin, or his colleagues, either directly from conversation, or from pulpit denunciations. We must acquit Calvin of *direct* agency, but we cannot free him of indirect agency in this denunciation.[1]

Calvin's indirect agency in the first, and his direct agency in the second arrest of Servetus admit of no proper justification, and are due to an excess of zeal for orthodoxy.

Arneys conveyed this information to the Roman Catholic authorities. The matter was brought to the knowledge of Cardinal Tournon, at that time archbishop of Lyons, a cruel persecutor of the Protestants, and Matthias Ory, a regularly trained inquisitor of the Roman see for the kingdom of France. They at once instituted judicial proceedings.

Villeneuve was summoned before the civil court of Vienne on the 16th of March. He kept the judges waiting for two hours (during which he probably destroyed all suspicious papers), and appeared without any show of embarrassment. He affirmed that he had lived long at Vienne, in frequent company with ecclesiastics, without incurring any suspicion

---

[1] Trechsel thinks that it can by no means be proven that Calvin caused the letter of Trie, but that he probably gave occasion to it by incidental and unintentional expressions. "*Wenn auch Calvin,*" he says, I. 144, "*wahrscheinlich durch gelegentliche und unabsichtliche Aeusserungen zur Entdeckung Servets Anlass gab, so ist es doch durchaus unerwiesen, dass er Trie's Brief provocirt oder gar dictirt habe.*" Dyer, who is not friendly to Calvin, gives as the result of his examination of the case, this judgment (p. 314): "The Abbé d'Artigny goes further than the evidence warrants, in positively asserting that Trie's letter was written at Calvin's dictation, and in calling it Calvin's letter in the name of Trie. It is just possible that Trie may have written the letter without Calvin's knowledge, and the latter is therefore entitled to the benefit of the doubt. He cannot absolutely be proved to have taken the first step in delivering Servetus into the fangs of the Roman Catholic inquisition; but what we shall now have to relate will show that he at least aided and abetted it." Principal Cunningham (*The Reformers,* pp. 323 sqq.) goes into an elaborate argument to vindicate Calvin from the charge of complicity, in opposition to Principal Tulloch, who denounces the conduct of Calvin, if it could be proven (he leaves it undecided), as "one of the blackest pictures of treachery." An evident rhetorical exaggeration.

for heresy, and had always avoided all cause of offence. His apartments were searched, but nothing was found to incriminate him. On the following day the printing establishment of Arnoullet was searched with no better result. On the return of Arnoullet from a journey he was summoned before the tribunal, but he professed ignorance.

Inquisitor Ory now requested Arneys to secure additional proof from his cousin at Geneva. Trie forwarded on the 26th of March several autograph letters of Servetus which, he said, he had great difficulty in obtaining from Calvin (who ought to have absolutely refused). He added some pages from Calvin's *Institutes* with the marginal objections of Servetus to infant baptism in his handwriting. Ory, not yet satisfied, despatched a special messenger to Geneva to secure the manuscript of the *Restitutio*, and proof that Villeneuve was Servetus and Arnoullet his printer. Trie answered at once, on the last of March, that the manuscript of the *Restitutio* had been at Lausanne for a couple of years (with Viret), that Servetus had been banished from the churches of Germany (Basel and Strassburg) twenty-four years ago, and that Arnoullet and Guéroult were his printers, as he knew from a good source which he would not mention (perhaps Frellon of Lyons).

The cardinal of Lyons and the archbishop of Vienne, after consultation with Inquisitor Ory and other ecclesiastics, now gave orders on the 4th of April for the arrest of Villeneuve and Arnoullet. They were confined in separate rooms in the Palais Delphinal. Villeneuve was allowed to keep a servant, and to see his friends. Ory was sent forth, hastened to Vienne, and arrived there the next morning.

After dinner Villeneuve, having been sworn on the Holy Gospels, was interrogated as to his name, age, and course of life. In his answers he told some palpable falsehoods to mislead the judges, and to prevent his being identified with Servetus, the heretic. He omitted to mention his residence in Toulouse, where he had been known under his real name, as the books of the University would show. He denied that he had written any other books than those on medicine and geography, although he had corrected many.   On being shown some notes he had written on Calvin's *Institutes* about infant baptism, he acknowledged at last the authorship of the notes, but added that he must have written them inconsiderately for the purpose of discussion, and he submitted himself entirely to his holy Mother, the Church, from whose teachings he had never wished to differ.

At the second examination, on the sixth day of April, he was shown some of his epistles to Calvin. He declared, with tears in his eyes, that those letters were written when he was in Germany some twenty-five years ago, when there was printed in that country a book by a certain Servetus, a Spaniard, but from what part of Spain he did not know! At Paris he had heard Mons. Calvin spoken of as a learned man, and had entered into correspondence with him from curiosity, but begged him to keep his letters as confidential and as brotherly corrections.[1] Calvin suspected, he continued, that I was Servetus, to which I replied, I was not Servetus, but would continue to personate Servetus in order to continue the discussion. Finally we fell out, got angry, abused each other, and broke off the correspondence about ten years ago. He protested before God and his judges that he had no intention to dogmatize or to teach anything against the Church or the Christian religion. He told similar lies when other letters were laid before him.

Servetus now resolved to escape, perhaps with the aid of some friends, after he had secured through his servant a debt of three hundred crowns from the Grand Prior of the monastery of St. Pierre. On the 7th of April, at four o'clock in

---

[1] "*Sub sigillo secreti et comme fraternelles* [*sic*] *corrections.*" He himself, however, published in the *Restitutio*, as we have seen, thirty letters of his to Calvin without Calvin's permission.

the morning, he dressed himself, threw a night-gown over his clothes, and put a velvet cap upon his head, and, pretending a call of nature, he secured from the unsuspecting jailer the key to the garden. He leaped from the roof of the outhouse and made his escape through the court and over the bridge across the Rhone. He carried with him his golden chain around his neck, valued at twenty crowns, six gold rings on his fingers, and plenty of money in his pockets.

Two hours elapsed before his escape became known. An alarm was given, the gates were closed, and the neighboring houses searched; but all in vain.

Nevertheless the prosecution went on. Sufficient evidence was found that the "Restitution" had been printed in Vienne; extracts were made from it to prove the heresies contained therein. The civil court, without waiting for the judgment of the spiritual tribunal (which was not given until six months afterwards), sentenced Servetus on the 17th of June, for heretical doctrines, for violation of the royal ordinances, and for escape from the royal prison, to pay a fine of one thousand *livres tournois* to the Dauphin, to be carried in a cart, together with his books, on a market-day through the principal streets to the place of execution, and to be burnt alive by a slow fire.[1]

On the same day he was burnt in effigy, together with the five bales of his book, which had been consigned to Merrin at Lyons and brought back to Vienne.

The goods and chattels of the fugitive were seized and confiscated. The property he had acquired from his medical practice and literary labors amounted to four thousand crowns. The king bestowed them on the son of Monsieur

---

[1] "*Estre bruslé tout vif à petit-feu, tellement que son corps soit mis en cendre.*" The whole sentence of the tribunal is printed in Calvin's *Opera*, VIII. 784–787. It was communicated to the Council of Geneva, as a ground for demanding the prisoner.

de Montgiron, lieutenant-general of Dauphiné and presiding judge of the court.[1]

Arnoullet was discharged on proving that he had been deceived by Guéroult, who seems to have escaped by flight. He took care that the remaining copies of the heretical book in France should be destroyed. Stephens, the famous publisher, who had come to Geneva in 1552, sacrificed the copies in his hands. Those that had been sent to Frankfort were burnt at the instance of Calvin.

On the 23d of December, two months after the execution of Servetus, the ecclesiastical tribunal of Vienne pronounced a sentence of condemnation on him.[2]

§ 149. *Servetus flees to Geneva and is arrested.*

RILLIET: *Relation du procès*, etc., quoted above, p. 684. (Tweedie's translation in his *Calvin and Servetus*, pp. 62 sqq.) *Opera*, VIII. 725–856.

Escaped from one danger of death, Servetus, as by "a fatal madness," as Calvin says, rushed into another.[3] Did he aspire to the glory of martyrdom in Geneva, as he seemed to intimate in his letter to Poupin? But he had just escaped martyrdom in France. Or did he wish to have a personal interview with Calvin, which he had sought in Paris in 1534, and again in Vienne in 1546? But after publishing his abusive letters and suspecting him for denunciation, he could hardly entertain such a wish. Or did he merely intend to pass through the place on his way to Italy? But in this case he need not tarry there for weeks, and he might have taken another route through Savoy, or by the sea. Or did

---

[1] See Montgiron's letter to the Council of Geneva in *Opera*, VIII. 791, and in Rilliet-Tweedie, p. 156.

[2] Calvin's *Opera*, VIII. 851–856 (copied from d'Artigny, II. 123, and Mosheim, *Neue Nachrichten*, etc., p. 100 sq.). Villanovanus is therein condemned as "*maximus hæreticus*," and his *scripta* as "*erronea, nefanda, impia, sacrilega, et plusquam hæretica.*"

[3] "*Nescio quid dicam, nisi fatali vesania fuisse correptum ut se præcipitem jaceret.*" Calvin. See Henry, III. 151.

he hope to dethrone "the pope of Geneva" with the aid of his enemies, who had just then the political control of the Republic?[1]

He lingered in France for about three months. He intended, first, as he declared at the trial, to proceed to Spain, but finding the journey unsafe, he turned his eye to Naples, where he hoped to make a living as physician among the numerous Spanish residents. This he could easily have done under a new name.

He took his way through Geneva. He arrived there after the middle of July, 1553, alone and on foot, having left his horse on the French border. He took up his lodging in the Auberge de la Rose, a small inn on the banks of the lake. His dress and manner, his gold chain and gold rings, excited attention. On being asked by his host whether he was married, he answered, like a light-hearted cavalier, that women enough could be found without marrying.[2] This frivolous reply provoked suspicion of immorality, and was made use of at the trial, but unjustly, for a fracture disabled him for marriage and prevented libertinage.[3]

He remained about a month, and then intended to leave for Zürich. He asked his host to hire a boat to convey him over the lake some distance eastward.

But before his departure he attended church, on Sunday, the 13th of August. He was recognized and arrested by an officer of the police in the name of the Council.[4]

---

[1] Willis (p. 284) thinks that the enemies of Calvin detained him with the view to make political capital out of him. He infers this from the fact that the windows of his room were nailed up. As if he could not have passed out through the door! Moreover, it was not the windows of his room in the tavern, as Willis says, but the windows of the prison that were nailed up, as Servetus stated at the trial, to prove that he had no intercourse with outsiders. See Rilliet-Tweedie, p. 154.

[2] "On trouve bien assez de femmes sans se marrier." Comp. Trechsel, I. 306.

[3] He declared, Aug. 23, that he was impotent on account of a rupture. Opera, VIII. 769.

[4] The following is an extract from the Registers of the Company of Pastors sub. Aug. 13 (in Opera, VIII. 725): "M. Servetus having been recognized

Calvin was responsible for this arrest, as he frankly and repeatedly acknowledged.[1] It was a fatal mistake. Servetus was a stranger and had committed no offence in Geneva. Calvin ought to have allowed him quietly to proceed on his intended journey. Why then did he act otherwise? Certainly not from personal malice, nor other selfish reasons; for he only increased the difficulty of his critical situation, and ran the risk of his defeat by the Libertine party then in power. It was an error of judgment. He was under the false impression that Servetus had just come from Venice, the headquarters of Italian humanists and sceptics, to propagate his errors in Geneva, and he considered it his duty to make so dangerous a man harmless, by bringing him either to conviction and recantation, or to deserved punishment. He was determined to stand or fall with the principle of purity of doctrine and discipline. Rilliet justifies the arrest as a necessary measure of self-defence. "Under pain of abdication," he says, " Calvin must do everything rather than suffer by his side in Geneva a man whom he considered the greatest enemy of the Reformation; and the critical position in which he saw it in the bosom of the Republic, was one

by some brethren (*par quelques frères*), it was found good to cause him to be imprisoned, that he might no longer infect the world with his blasphemies and heresies; for he is known to be wholly incorrigible and desperate (*du tout incorrigible et desesperé*)."

[1] In the *Refutatio, Opera*, VIII. 461, 725, and in letters to Farel (Aug. 20) and Sulzer (Sept. 8, 1553). " Servetus," he wrote to Sulzer in Basel, during the trial, " escaped from prison some way or other, and wandered in Italy for nearly four months. At length, in an evil hour, he came to this place, when, at my instigation, one of the Syndics ordered him to be conducted to prison; for I do not disguise it that I considered it my duty to put a check, so far as I could, upon this most obstinate and ungovernable man, that his contagion might not spread farther. We see with what wantonness impiety is making progress everywhere, so that new errors are ever and anon breaking forth; we see how very inactive those are whom God has armed with the sword for the vindication of the glory of his name." The reference to a four months' wandering in Italy (*per Italiam erravit fere quatuor menses*, that is, from April 7th to the end of July) is an error. Servetus at the trial denied that he had been in Italy at that time or at Venice at any time.

motive more to remove, if it was possible, the new element of dissolution which the free sojourn of Servetus would have created. . . . To tolerate Servetus with impunity at Geneva would have been for Calvin to exile himself. . . . He had no alternative. The man whom a Calvinist accusation had caused to be arrested, tried, and condemned to the flames in France, could not find an asylum in the city from which that accusation had issued." [1]

§ 150. State of Political Parties at Geneva in 1553.

Calvin's position in Geneva at that time was very critical. For in the year 1553 he was in the fever-heat of the struggle for church discipline with the Patriots and Libertines, who had gained a temporary ascendency in the government. Amy Perrin, the leader of the patriotic party, was then captain-general and chief syndic, and several of his kinsmen and friends were members of the Little Council of Twenty-five.[2] During the trial of Servetus the Council sustained Philibert Berthelier against the act of excommunication by the Consistory, and took church discipline into its own hands. The foreign refugees were made harmless by being deprived of their arms. Violence was threatened to the Reformer. He was everywhere saluted as "a heretic," and insulted on the streets. Beza says: "In the year 1553, the wickedness of the seditions, hastening to a close, was so turbulent that both Church and State were brought into extreme danger. . . . Everything seemed to be in a state of preparation for accomplishing the plans of the seditious, since all was subject to their power." And Calvin, at the close of that year, wrote to a friend: "For four years the factions have done all to lead by degrees to the overthrow of this Church, already very weak. . . . Behold two years

---

[1] Translated by Tweedie, p. 87.
[2] Pernet de Fosses, Gaspard Favre, Claude Vandel, Pierre Vandel, and Baptiste Sept. See *Opera*, VIII. 737, note 6.

of our life have passed as if we lived among the avowed enemies of the gospel."

The hostility of the Council to Calvin and his discipline continued even after the execution of Servetus for nearly two more years. He asked the assistance of Bullinger and the Church of Zürich to come to his aid again in this struggle.[1] He wrote to Ambrose Blaurer, Feb. 6, 1554: "These last few years evil disposed persons have not ceased on every occasion to create for us new subjects of vexation. At length in their endeavors to render null our excommunication, there is no excess of folly they have left unattempted. Everywhere the contest was long maintained with much violence, because in the senate and among the people the passions of the contending parties had been so much inflamed that there was some risk of a tumult."[2]

We do not know whether Servetus was aware of this state of things. But he could not have come at a time more favorable to him and more unfavorable to Calvin. Among the Libertines and Patriots, who hated the yoke of Calvin even more than the yoke of the pope, Servetus found natural supporters who, in turn, would gladly use him for political purposes. This fact emboldened him to take such a defiant attitude in the trial and to overwhelm Calvin with abuse.

The final responsibility of the condemnation, therefore, rests with the Council of Geneva, which would probably have acted otherwise, if it had not been strongly influenced by the judgment of the Swiss Churches and the government of Bern. Calvin conducted the theological part of the examination of the trial, but had no direct influence upon the result. His theory was that the Church may convict and denounce the heretic theologically, but that his condemnation and punishment is the exclusive function of the State,

---

[1] Letters of Nov. 26 and Dec. 30, 1553, in Bonnet-Constable, II. 422-430.

[2] *Ibid.* III. 17. Comp. also his letter of Oct. 15, 1554, quoted in § 108, p. 496, and his letter to John Wolf of Zürich, Dec. 26, 1554.

and that it is one of its most sacred duties to punish attacks made on the Divine majesty.

"From the time Servetus was convicted of his heresy," says Calvin, "I have not uttered a word about his punishment, as all honest men will bear witness; and I challenge even the malignant to deny it if they can."[1] One thing only he did: he expressed the wish for a mitigation of his punishment.[2] And this humane sentiment is almost the only good thing that can be recorded to his honor in this painful trial.

§ 151. *The First Act of the Trial at Geneva.*

Servetus was confined near the Church of St. Pierre, in the ancient residence of the bishops of Geneva, which had been turned into a prison. His personal property consisted of ninety-seven crowns, a chain of gold weighing about twenty crowns, and six gold rings (a large turquoise, a white sapphire, a diamond, a ruby, a large emerald of Peru, and a signet ring of coralline). These valuables were surrendered to Pierre Tissot, and after the process given to the hospital. The prisoner was allowed to have paper and ink, and such books as could be procured at Geneva or Lyons at his own expense. Calvin lent him Ignatius, Polycarp, Tertullian, and Irenæus. But he was denied the benefit of counsel, according to the ordinances of 1543. This is contrary to the law of equity and is one of the worst features of the trial. He was not subjected to the usual torture.

The laws of Geneva demanded that the accuser should become a prisoner with the accused, in order that in the event of the charge proving false, the former might undergo

---

[1] *Opera*, VIII. 461: "*Ex quo convictus est, me nullum de pœna verbum fecisse, non solum boni omnes viri mihi testes erunt sed malis etiam concedo ut proferant si quid habent.*" Servetus complained of hard treatment in prison, but for this the Council and the jailer alone were responsible.

[2] In his letter to Farel, Aug. 20, 1553: "*Spero capitale saltem judicium fore; pœnæ vero atrocitatem remitti cupio.*"

punishment in the place of the accused. The person employed for this purpose was Nicolas de la Fontaine, a Frenchman, a theological student, and Calvin's private secretary. The accused as well as the accuser were foreigners. Another law obliged the Little Council to examine every prisoner within twenty-four hours after his arrest. The advocate or "Speaker" of Nicolas de la Fontaine in the trial was Germain Colladon, likewise a Frenchman and an able lawyer, who had fled for his religion, and aided Calvin in framing a new constitution for Geneva.

The trial began on the 15th of August and continued, with interruptions, for more than two months. It was conducted in French and took place in the Bishop's Palace, according to the forms prescribed by law, in the presence of the Little Council, the herald of the city, the Lord-Lieutenant, and several citizens, who had a right to sit in criminal processes, but did not take part in the judgment. Among these was Berthelier, the bitter enemy of Calvin.

Servetus answered the preliminary questions as to his name, age, and previous history more truthfully than he had done before the Catholic tribunal, and incidentally accused Calvin of having caused the prosecution at Vienne. It is not owing to Calvin, he said, that he was not burnt alive there.

The deed of accusation, as lodged by Nicholas de la Fontaine, consisted of thirty-eight articles which were drawn up by Calvin (as he himself informs us), and were fortified by references to the books of Servetus, which were produced in evidence, especially the "Restitution of Christianity," both the manuscript copy, which Servetus had sent to Calvin in advance, and a printed copy.[1]

The principal charges were, that he had published heretical opinions and blasphemies concerning the Trinity, the person

---

[1] The articles are given in full by Rilliet, and in *Opera*, VIII. 727–731. Calvin mentions forty articles in a letter to Farel (Aug. 20), but they are reduced to thirty-eight by the notation.

of Christ, and infant baptism. He gave evasive or orthodox-sounding answers. He confessed to believe in the trinity of persons, but understood the word "person" in a different sense from that used by modern writers, and appealed to the first teachers of the Church and the disciples of the apostles.[1] He denied at first that he had called the Trinity three devils and Cerberus;[2] but he had done so repeatedly and confessed it afterwards. He professed to believe that Jesus Christ was the Son of God according to his divinity and humanity; that the flesh of Christ came from heaven and of the substance of God; but as to the matter it came from the Virgin Mary. He denied the view imputed to him that the soul was mortal. He admitted that he had called infant baptism "a diabolical invention and infernal falsehood destructive of Christianity." This was a dangerous admission; for the Anabaptists were suspected of seditious and revolutionary opinions.

He was also charged with having, "in the person of M. Calvin, defamed the doctrines of the gospel and of the Church of Geneva." To this he replied that in what he had formerly written against Calvin, in his own defence, he had not intended to injure him, but to show him his errors and faults, which he was ready to prove by Scripture and good reasons before a full congregation.

This was a bold challenge. Calvin was willing to accept it, but the Council declined, fearing to lose the control of the affair by submitting it to the tribunal of public opinion. The friends of Servetus would have run the risk of seeing

---

[1] "*Respond quil croit en lessence divine en troys personnes et quil na point dog-matise en celle sorte. Vray est quil prent le nom de personne aultrement que les modernes ne le prennent et quil le prent comment les premiers docteurs de leglise et disciples des apotres lont prys.*" *Opera,* VIII. 738. I retain the ancient spelling.

[2] "*Interrogé sil entend que la Trinité soit troys diables et soit troys [un] Cerberus, respond que non, et quil ne la point dict en ceste sorte et quil ne le veult point mainte-nir.*" Comp. with this the passage in his letter to Poupin which was after-wards produced in evidence and acknowledged by him: "*Pro uno Deo habetis tricipitem Cerberum.*"

him defeated in public debate. That charge, however, which seemed to betray personal ill-feeling of Calvin, was afterwards very properly omitted.

On the following day, the 16th of August, Berthelier, then smarting under the sentence of excommunication by the Consistory, openly came to the defence of Servetus, and had a stormy encounter with Colladon, which is omitted in the official record, but indicated by blanks and the abrupt termination: "Here they proceeded no further, but adjourned till to-morrow at mid-day."

On Thursday, the 17th of August, Calvin himself appeared before the Council as the real accuser, and again on the 21st of August.[1] He also conferred with his antagonist in writing. Servetus was not a match for Calvin either in learning or argument; but he showed great skill and some force.

He contemptuously repelled the frivolous charge that, in his Ptolemy, he had contradicted the authority of Moses, by describing Palestine as an unfruitful country (which it was then, and is now). He wiped his mouth and said, "Let us go on; there is nothing wrong there."

The charge of having, in his notes on the Latin Bible, explained the servant of God in the fifty-third chapter of Isaiah, as meaning King Cyrus, instead of the Saviour, he disposed of by distinguishing two senses of prophecy — the literal and historical sense which referred to Cyrus, and the mystical and principal sense which referred to Christ. He quoted Nicolaus de Lyra; but Calvin showed him the error, and asserts that he audaciously quoted books which he had never examined.

As to his calling the Trinity "a Cerberus" and "a dream of Augustin," and the Trinitarians "atheists," he said that he did not mean the true Trinity, which he believed himself,

---

[1] On this and the subsequent encounter we have also an account from Calvin in his "Defence," which is more minute than the official report. *Opera,* VIII. 743 sqq.

but the false trinity of his opponents; and that the oldest teachers before the Council of Nicæa did not teach that trinity, and did not use the word. Among them he quoted Ignatius, Polycarp, Clement of Rome, Irenæus, Tertullian, and Clement of Alexandria. Calvin refuted his assertion by quotations from Justin Martyr, Tertullian, and Origen. On this occasion he charges him, unjustly, with total ignorance of Greek, because he was embarrassed by a Greek quotation from Justin Martyr, and called for a Latin version.[1]

In discussing the relation of the divine substance to that of the creatures, Servetus declared that "all creatures are of the substance of God, and that God is in all things." Calvin asked him: "How, unhappy man, if any one strike the pavement with his foot and say that he tramples on thy God, wouldst thou not be horrified at having the Majesty of heaven subjected to such indignity?" To this Servet replied: "I have no doubt that this bench, and this buffet, and all you can show me, are of the substance of God." When it was objected that in his view God must be substantially even in the devil, he burst out into a laugh, and rejoined: "Can you doubt this? I hold this for a general maxim, that all things are part and parcel of God, and that the nature of things is his substantial Spirit."[2]

The result of this first act of the trial was unfavorable to the prisoner, but not decisive.

Calvin used the freedom of the pulpit to counteract the efforts of the Libertine party in favor of Servetus.

§ 152. *The Second Act of the Trial at Geneva.*

The original prosecution being discharged, the case was handed over to the attorney-general, Claude Rigot, in com-

---

[1] "He could no more read Greek," says Calvin, in the *Refutatio*, "than a boy learning his A B C." *Opera*, VIII. 498.

[2] *Opera*, VIII. 496: "*ex traduce Dei orta* (or, *une partie et portion de Dieu*) *esse omnia, et rerum naturam esse substantialem Dei spiritum.*"

pliance with the criminal ordinance of 1543. Thus the second act of the trial began. The prisoner was examined again, and a new indictment of thirty articles was prepared, which bore less on the actual heresies of the accused than on their dangerous practical tendency and his persistency in spreading them.[1]

The Council wrote also to the judges of Vienne to procure particulars of the charges which had been brought against him there.

Servetus defended himself before the Council on the 23d of August, with ingenuity and apparent frankness against the new charges of quarrelsomeness and immorality. As to the latter, he pleaded his physical infirmity which protected him against the temptation of licentiousness. He had always studied the Scripture and tried to lead a Christian life. He did not think that his book would disturb the peace of Christendom, but would promote the truth. He denied that he had come to Geneva for any sinister purpose; he merely wished to pass through on his way to Zürich and Naples.

At the same time he prepared a written petition to the Council, which was received on the 24th of August. He demanded his release from the criminal charge for several reasons, which ought to have had considerable weight: that it was unknown in the Christian Church before the time of Constantine to try cases of heresy before a civil tribunal; that he had not offended against the laws either in Geneva or elsewhere; that he was not seditious nor turbulent; that his books treated of abstruse questions, and were addressed to the learned; that he had not spoken of these subjects to anybody but Œcolampadius, Bucer, and Capito; that he had ever refuted the Anabaptists, who rebelled against the magistrates and wished to have all things in common. In case he was not released, he demanded the aid of an advocate

---

[1] *Articles du procureur-général* in *Opera*, VIII. 763–766.

acquainted with the laws and customs of the country. Certainly a very reasonable request.[1]

The attorney-general prepared a second indictment in refutation of the arguments of Servetus, who had studied law at Toulouse. He showed that the first Christian emperors claimed for themselves the cognizance and trial of heresies, and that their laws and constitutions condemned antitrinitarian heretics and blasphemers to death. He charged him with falsehood in declaring that he had written against the Anabaptists, and that he had not communicated his doctrine to any person during the last thirty years. The counsel asked for was refused because it was forbidden by the criminal statutes (1543), and because there was "not one jot of apparent innocence which requires an attorney." The very thing to be proved!

A new examination followed which elicited some points of interest. Servetus stated his belief that the Reformation would progress much further than Luther and Calvin intended, and that new things were always first rejected, but afterwards received. To the absurd charge of making use of the Koran, he replied that he had quoted it for the glory of Christ, that the Koran abounds in what is good, and that even in a wicked book one may find some good things.

On the last day of August the Little Council received answer from Vienne. The commandant of the royal palace in that city arrived in Geneva, communicated to them a copy of the sentence of death pronounced against Villeneuve, and begged them to send him back to France that the sentence might be executed on the living man as it had been already executed on his effigy and books. The Council refused to surrender Servetus, in accordance with analogous cases, but promised to do full justice. The prisoner himself, who could see only a burning funeral pile for him in Vienne, preferred

1 *Opera*, VIII. 797.

to be tried in Geneva, where he had some chance of acquittal or lighter punishment. He incidentally justified his habit of attending mass at Vienne by the example of Paul, who went to the temple, like the Jews; yet he confessed that in doing so he had sinned through fear of death.[1]

The communication from Vienne had probably the influence of stimulating the zeal of the Council for orthodoxy. They wished not to be behind the Roman Church in that respect. But the issue was still uncertain.

The Council again confronted Servetus with Calvin on the first day of September. On the same day it granted, in spite of the strong protest of Calvin, permission to Philibert Berthelier to approach the communion table. It thus annulled the act of excommunication by the Consistory, and arrogated to itself the power of ecclesiastical discipline.

A few hours afterwards the investigation was resumed in the prison. Perrin and Berthelier were present as judges, and came to the aid of Servetus in the oral debate with Calvin, but, it seems, without success; for they resorted to a written discussion in which Servetus could better defend himself, and in which Calvin might complicate his already critical position. They wished, moreover, to refer the affair to the Churches of Switzerland which, in the case of Bolsec, had shown themselves much more tolerant than Calvin. Servetus demanded such reference. Calvin did not like it, but did not openly oppose it.

The Council, without entering on the discussion, decided that Calvin should extract in Latin, from the books of Servetus, the objectionable articles, word for word, contained therein; that Servetus should write his answers and vindications, also in Latin; that Calvin should in his turn furnish his replies; and that these documents be forwarded to the

---

[1] *Opera*, VIII. 789: "*Et puys après a confessé quil avait peché en ce, mais que cestoit par crainte de la mort.*"

Swiss Churches as a basis of judgment. All this was fair and impartial.[1]

On the same day Calvin extracted thirty-eight propositions from the books of Servetus with references, but without comments.

Then, turning with astonishing energy from one enemy to the other, he appeared before the Little Council on the 2d of September to protest most earnestly against their protection of Berthelier, who intended to present himself on the following day as a guest at the Lord's table, and by the strength of the civil power to force Calvin to give him the tokens of the body and blood of Christ. He declared before the Council that he would rather die than act against his conscience. The Council did not yield, but resolved secretly to advise Berthelier to abstain from receiving the sacrament for the present. Calvin, ignorant of this secret advice, and resolved to conquer or to die, thundered from the pulpit of St. Peter on the 3d of September his determination to refuse, at the risk of his life, the sacred elements to an excommunicated person. Berthelier did not dare to approach the table. Calvin had achieved a moral victory over the Council.[2]

In the mean time Servetus had, within the space of twenty-four hours, prepared a written defence, as directed by the Council, against the thirty-eight articles of Calvin. It was both apologetic and boldly aggressive, clear, keen, violent, and bitter. He contemptuously repelled Calvin's interference in the trial, and charged him with presumption in framing articles of faith after the fashion of the doctors of the Sorbonne, without Scripture proof.[3] He affirmed that

---

[1] *Opera*, VIII. 796. The Latin text of the three documents is embodied in Calvin's *Refutatio Errorum*, *ibid.* 501–553.

[2] See above, § 109, p. 513 sq.

[3] VIII. 507: " *Eam sibi jam autoritatem arrogat Calvinus, ut instar magistrorum Sorbonicorum articulos scribat, et quidvis pro sua libidine damnet, nullam penitus ex sacris [de l'écriture sainte] addu̧cens rationem.*"

he either misunderstood him or craftily perverted his meaning. He quotes from Tertullian, Irenæus, and pseudo-Clement in support of his views. He calls him a disciple of Simon Magus, a criminal accuser, and a homicide.[1] He ridiculed the idea that such a man should call himself an orthodox minister of the Church.

Calvin replied within two days in a document of twenty-three folio pages, which were signed by all the fourteen ministers of Geneva.[2] He meets the patristic quotations of Servetus with counter-quotations, with Scripture passages and solid arguments, and charges him in conclusion with the intention " to subvert all religion." [3]

These three documents, which contained the essence of the doctrinal discussion, were presented to the Little Council on Tuesday the 5th of September.

On the 15th of September Servetus addressed a petition to the Council in which he attacked Calvin as his persecutor, complained of his miserable condition in prison and want of the necessary clothing, and demanded an advocate and the transfer of his trial to the Large Council of Two Hundred, where he had reason to expect a majority in his favor.[4] This course had probably been suggested to him (as Rilliet conjectures) by Perrin and Berthelier through the jailer, Claude de Genève, who was a member of the Libertine party.

On the same day the Little Council ordered an improvement of the prisoner's wardrobe (which, however, was delayed by culpable neglect), and sent him the three documents, with permission to make a last reply to Calvin, but took no action on his appeal to the Large Council, having no disposition to renounce its own authority.

---

[1] VIII. 515 : " *Simonis Magi discipulus . . . accusator criminalis, et homicida.*"

[2] Calvinus, Poupinus, Gallasius, Bernardus, Bourgoinus, Malisianus, Calvetus, Pyrerius, Copus, Baldinus, J. a Sancto Andrea, Faber, Macarius, Colladonus.

[3] " *Ut luce sanæ doctrinæ exstincta totam religionem everteret.*"

[4] *Opera*, VIII. 797, and Rilliet-Tweedie, p. 182.

Servetus at once prepared a reply by way of explanatory annotations on the margin and between the lines of the memorial of Calvin and the ministers. These annotations are full of the coarsest abuse, and read like the production of a madman. He calls Calvin again and again a liar,[1] an impostor, a miserable wretch (*nebulo pessimus*), a hypocrite, a disciple of Simon Magus, etc. Take these specimens: "Do you deny that you are a man-slayer? I will prove it by your acts. You dare not deny that you are Simon Magus. As for me, I am firm in so good a cause, and do not fear death. . . . You deal with sophistical arguments without Scripture. . . . You do not understand what you say. You howl like a blind man in the desert. . . . You lie, you lie, you lie, you ignorant calumniator. . . . Madness is in you when you persecute to death. . . . I wish that all your magic were still in the belly of your mother. . . . I wish I were free to make a catalogue of your errors. Whoever is not a Simon Magus is considered a Pelagian by Calvin. All, therefore, who have been in Christendom are damned by Calvin; even the apostles, their disciples, the ancient doctors of the Church and all the rest. For no one ever entirely abolished free-will except that Simon Magus. Thou liest, thou liest, thou liest, thou liest, thou miserable wretch."

He concludes with the remark that "his doctrine was met merely by clamors, not by argument or any authority," and he subscribed his name as one who had Christ for his certain protector.[2]

He sent these notes to the Council on the 18th of September. It was shown to Calvin, but he did not deem it

[1] "*Mentiris*" occurs in almost every sentence. He naively apologizes for writing on Calvin's own paper, because there were many little words, such as "*mentiris*," which would not be otherwise understood; and he hopes that Calvin would not be offended, as there would have been inextricable confusion had he not adopted this method.

[2] "*Michael Servetus subscribit solus hic quidem, sed qui Christum habet protectorem certissimum*." From the MS., in *Opera*, VIII. 553, note.

expedient to make a reply. Silence in this case was better than speech.

The debate, therefore, between the two divines was closed, and the trial became an affair of Protestant Switzerland, which should act as a jury.

§ 153. *Consultation of the Swiss Churches. The Defiant Attitude of Servetus.*

On the 19th of September the Little Council, in accordance with a resolution adopted on the 4th, referred the case of Servetus to the magistrates and pastors of the Reformed Churches of Bern, Zürich, Schaffhausen, and Basel for their judgment.

Two days afterwards Jaquemoz Jernoz, as the official messenger, was despatched on his mission with a circular letter and the documents, — namely the theological debate between Calvin and Servetus, — a copy of the "Restitution of Christianity," and the works of Tertullian and Irenæus, who were the chief patristic authorities quoted by both parties.

On the result of this mission the case of Servetus was made to depend. Servetus himself had expressed a wish that this course should be adopted, hoping, it seems, to gain a victory, or at least an escape from capital punishment. On the 22d of August he was willing to be banished from Geneva; but on the 22d of September he asked the Council to put Calvin on trial, and handed in a list of articles on which he should be interrogated. He thus admitted the civil jurisdiction in matters of religious opinions which he had formerly denied, and was willing to stake his life on the decision, provided that his antagonist should be exposed to the same fate.[1] Among the four "great and infallible"

---

[1] "*Ie demand que mon faulx accusateur soyt puni pœna talionis; et que soyt detenu prisonier comme moy, jusques à ce que la cause soyt definie pour mort de luy ou de moy ou aultre poine.*" The petition concludes: "*Ie vous demande justice, messeigneurs, justice, justice, justice.*" *Opera*, VIII. 805.

reasons why Calvin should be condemned, he assigned the fact that he wished to "repress the truth of Jesus Christ, and follow the doctrines of Simon Magus, against all the doctors that ever were in the Church." He declared in his petition that Calvin, like a magician, ought to be exterminated, and his goods be confiscated and given to Servetus, in compensation for the loss he had sustained through Calvin. "To dislodge Calvin from his position," says Rilliet, "to expel him from Geneva, to satisfy a just vengeance — these were the objects toward which Servetus rushed."

But the Council took no notice of his petition.

On the 10th of October he sent another letter to the Council, imploring them, for the love of Christ, to grant him such justice as they would not refuse to a Turk, and complaining that nothing had been done for his comfort as promised, but that he was more wretched than ever. The petition had some effect. The Lord Syndic, Darlod, and the Secretary of State, Claude Roset, were directed to visit his prison and to provide some articles of dress for his relief.

On the 18th of October the messenger of the State returned with the answers from the four foreign churches. They were forthwith translated into French, and examined by the magistrates. We already know the contents.[1] The churches were unanimous in condemning the theological doctrines of Servetus, and in the testimony of respect and affection for Calvin and his colleagues. Even Bern, which was not on good terms with Calvin, and had two years earlier counselled toleration in the case of Bolsec, regarded Servetus a much more dangerous heretic and advised to remove this "pest." Yet none of the Churches consulted expressly suggested the death penalty. They left the mode of punishment with the discretion of a sovereign State. Haller, the pastor of Bern, however, wrote to Bullinger of Zürich that, if Servetus had

---

[1] See above, pp. 708 sqq., and Calvin's *Opera*, VIII. 806 sq.

fallen into the hands of Bernese justice, he would undoubtedly have been condemned to the flames.

§ 154. *Condemnation of Servetus.*

On the 23d of October the Council met for a careful examination of the replies of the churches, but could not come
to a decision on account of the absence of several members, especially Perrin, the Chief Syndic, who feigned sickness. Servetus had failed to excite any sympathy among the
people, and had injured his cause by his obstinate and defiant
conduct. The Libertines, who wished to use him as a tool
for political purposes, were discouraged and intimidated by
the counsel of Bern, to which they looked for protection
against the hated régime of Calvin.

The full session of the Council on the 26th, to which all
counsellors were summoned on the faith of their oath,
decided the fate of the unfortunate prisoner, but not without
a stormy discussion. Amy Perrin presided and made a last
effort in favor of Servetus. He at first insisted upon his
acquittal, which would have been equivalent to the expulsion
of Calvin and a permanent triumph of the party opposed to
him. Being baffled, he proposed, as another alternative, that
Servetus, in accordance with his own wishes, be transferred
to the Council of the Two Hundred. But this proposal was
also rejected. He was influenced by political passion rather
than by sympathy with heresy or love of toleration, which
had very few advocates at that time. When he perceived
that the majority of the Council was inclined to a sentence
of death, he quitted the Senate House with a few others.

The Council had no doubt of its jurisdiction in the case;
it had to respect the unanimous judgment of the Churches,
the public horror of heresy and blasphemy, and the imperial
laws of Christendom, which were appealed to by the attorney-
general. The decision was unanimous. Even the wish of

Calvin to substitute the sword for the fire was overruled, and the papal practice of the *auto-da-fé* followed, though without the solemn mockery of a religious festival.

The judges, after enumerating the crimes of Servetus, in calling the holy Trinity a monster with three heads, blaspheming the Son of God, denying infant-baptism as an invention of the devil and of witchcraft, assailing the Christian faith, and after mentioning that he had been condemned and burned in effigy at Vienne, and had during his residence in Geneva persisted in his vile and detestable errors, and called all true Christians tritheists, atheists, sorcerers, putting aside all remonstrances and corrections with a malicious and perverse obstinacy, pronounced the fearful sentence: —

" We condemn thee, Michael Servetus, to be bound, and led to the place of Champel, there to be fastened to a stake and burnt alive, together with thy book, as well the one written by thy hand as the printed one, even till thy body be reduced to ashes; and thus shalt thou finish thy days to furnish an example to others who might wish to commit the like.

"And we command our Lieutenant to see that this our present sentence be executed." [1]

Rilliet, who published the official report of the trial in the interest of history, without special sympathy with Calvin, says that the sentence of condemnation is " odious before our consciences, but was just according to the law." Let us thank God that those unchristian and barbarous laws are abolished forever.

Calvin communicated to Farel on the 26th of October a brief summary of the result, in which he says: " The messenger has returned from the Swiss Churches. They are unanimous in pronouncing [2] that Servetus has now renewed those impious errors with which Satan formerly disturbed the Church, and that he is a monster not to be borne.   Those

[1] *Opera*, VIII. 827–830. See also Rilliet, and Henry (III., Beilage, pp. 75 sqq.).   The sentence was in the usual legal form, like that of Vienne.

[2] " *Uno consensu pronunciant omnes,*" etc.   *Opera*, XIV. 657.

of Basel are judicious. The Zürichers are the most vehement of all. . . . They of Schaffhausen agree. To an appropriate letter from the Bernese is added one from the Senate in which they stimulate ours not a little. Cæsar, the comedian [so he sarcastically called Perrin], after feigning illness for three days, at length went up to the assembly in order to free that wretch [Servetus] from punishment. Nor was he ashamed to ask that the case be referred to the Council of the Two Hundred. However, Servetus was without dissent condemned. He will be led forth to punishment to-morrow. We endeavored to alter the mode of his death, but in vain. Why we did not succeed, I defer for narration until I see you."

This letter reached Farel on his way to Geneva, where he arrived on the same day, in time to hear the sentence of condemnation. He had come at the request of Calvin, to perform the last pastoral duties to the prisoner, which could not so well be done by any of the pastors of Geneva.

§ 155. *Execution of Servetus.* Oct. 27, 1553.

FAREL, in a letter to Ambrosius Blaarer, December, 1553, preserved in the library of St. Gall, and copied in the *Thesaurus Hottingerianus* of the city library of Zürich, gives an account of the last moments and execution of Servetus. See HENRY, vol. III. Beilage, pp. 72–75. CALVIN, at the beginning of his "Defence," *Opera*, VIII. 460, relates his own last interview with Servetus in prison on the day of his death.

When Servetus, on the following morning, heard of the unexpected sentence of death, he was horror-struck and behaved like a madman. He uttered groans, and cried aloud in Spanish, "Mercy, mercy!"

The venerable old Farel visited him in the prison at seven in the morning, and remained with him till the hour of his death. He tried to convince him of his error. Servetus asked him to quote a single Scripture passage where Christ was called "Son of God" *before* his incarnation. Farel could not satisfy him. He brought about an interview with

Calvin, of which the latter gives us an account. Servetus, proud as he was, humbly asked his pardon. Calvin protested that he had never pursued any personal quarrel against him. "Sixteen years ago," he said, "I spared no pains at Paris to gain you to our Lord. You then shunned the light. I did not cease to exhort you by letters, but all in vain. You have heaped upon me I know not how much fury rather than anger. But as to the rest, I pass by what concerns myself. Think rather of crying for mercy to God whom you have blasphemed." This address had no more effect than the exhortation of Farel, and Calvin left the room in obedience, as he says, to St. Paul's order (Tit. 3:10, 11), to withdraw from a self-condemned heretic. Servetus appeared as mild and humble as he had been bold and arrogant, but did not change his conviction.

At eleven o'clock on the 27th of October, Servetus was led from the prison to the gates of the City Hall, to hear the sentence read from the balcony by the Lord Syndic Darlod. When he heard the last words, he fell on his knees and exclaimed: "The sword! in mercy! and not fire! Or I may lose my soul in despair." He protested that if he had sinned, it was through ignorance. Farel raised him up and said: "Confess thy crime, and God will have mercy on your soul." Servetus replied: "I am not guilty; I have not merited death." Then he smote his breast, invoked God for pardon, confessed Christ as his Saviour, and besought God to pardon his accusers.[1]

On the short journey to the place of execution, Farel again attempted to obtain a confession, but Servetus was silent. He showed the courage and consistency of a martyr in these last awful moments.

Champel is a little hill south of Geneva with a fine view

---

[1] "*Ut Deus accusatoribus esset propitius.*" Farel. This is certainly a Christian act. Henry (III. 191) admits that Servetus in his last moments showed some noble traits towards his enemies.

on one of the loveliest paradises of nature.[1] There was
prepared a funeral pile hidden in part by the autumnal leaves
of the oak trees. The Lord Lieutenant and the herald on
horseback, both arrayed in the insignia of their office, arrive
with the doomed man and the old pastor, followed by a
small procession of spectators. Farel invites Servetus to
solicit the prayers of the people and to unite his prayers
with theirs. Servetus obeys in silence. The executioner
fastens him by iron chains to the stake amidst the fagots,
puts a crown of leaves covered with sulphur on his head,
and binds his book by his side. The sight of the flaming
torch extorts from him a piercing shriek of "misericordias"
in his native tongue. The spectators fall back with a
shudder. The flames soon reach him and consume his
mortal frame in the forty-fourth year of his fitful life. In
the last moment he is heard to pray, in smoke and agony,
with a loud voice: "Jesus Christ, thou Son of the eternal
God, have mercy upon me!"[2]

This was at once a confession of his faith and of his error.
He could not be induced, says Farel, to confess that Christ
was the *eternal* Son of God.

The tragedy ended when the clock of St. Peter's struck
twelve. The people quietly dispersed to their homes.
Farel returned at once to Neuchâtel, even without calling
on Calvin. The subject was too painful to be discussed.

---

[1] It is now covered by a beautiful villa, gardens, and vineyards. The
pleasant road of half an hour from the city to Champel is called "the
Philosophers' Way," on which Arminius, when a student of Beza, is said to
have begun his meditations on the mysteries of predestination and free-will,
which immortalized his name. So Henry reports in his small biography of
Calvin, p. 346, and in his large work, III. 198, note 1.

[2] Farel does not mention this, nor some other circumstances which are
more or less apocryphal (and omitted by Rilliet): for instance, that the executioner did not understand his business, and piled up green oak-wood; that
many threw dry bundles into the slow-burning fire, and that Servetus suffered
nearly half an hour. See the anonymous *Historia de Morte Serveti*, ascribed
to a Genevese, who was an enemy of Calvin. Henry, III. 200 sq.

The conscience and piety of that age approved of the execution, and left little room for the emotions of compassion. But two hundred years afterwards a distinguished scholar and minister of Geneva echoed the sentiments of his fellow-citizens when he said: " Would to God that we could extinguish this funeral pile with our tears." [1] Dr. Henry, the admiring biographer of Calvin, imagines an impartial Christian jury of the nineteenth century assembled on Champel, which would pronounce the judgment on Calvin, "Not guilty"; on Servetus, "Guilty, with extenuating circumstances." [2]

The flames of Champel have consumed the intolerance of Calvin as well as the heresy of Servetus.

§ 156. *The Character of Servetus.*

Servetus — theologian, philosopher, geographer, physician, scientist, and astrologer — was one of the most remarkable men in the history of heresy. He was of medium size, thin and pale, like Calvin, his eyes beaming with intelligence, and an expression of melancholy and fanaticism. Owing to a physical rupture he was never married. He seems never to have had any particular friends, and stood isolated and alone.

His mental endowments and acquirements were of a high order, and placed him far above the heretics of his age and almost on an equality with the Reformers. [3] His discoveries

---

[1] Jean Senebier (b. at Geneva, 1742; d. 1809), *Hist. litter. de Genève* (Gen. 1786, 3 vols.), I. 215: "*Il seroit à souhaiter que nos larmes eussent pu éteindre le bûcher de cet infortuné.*" Quoted by Henry, III. 207.

[2] *Leben Joh. Calvin's,* III. 209 sq.

[3] Mosheim compares him with Calvin in genius, yet calls his method "a model of confusion." Stähelin (I. 428) likewise thinks that in intellectual endowment he was equal (*ebenbürtig*) to the greatest men of his great century, even to Calvin, but that he lacked the chief qualification of a reformer — moral character. Tollin puts him on a par with Calvin and Luther. But such exaggeration is refuted by history. The fruits are the test of a man's true greatness.

have immortalized his name in the history of science. He knew Latin, Hebrew, and Greek (though Calvin depreciates his knowledge of Greek), as well as Spanish, French, and Italian, and was well read in the Bible, the early fathers, and the schoolmen. He had an original, speculative, and acute mind, a tenacious memory, ready wit, a fiery imagination, ardent love of learning, and untiring industry. He anticipated the leading doctrines of Socinianism and Unitarianism, but in connection with mystic and pantheistic speculations, which his contemporaries did not understand. He had much uncommon sense, but little practical common sense. He lacked balance and soundness. There was a streak of fanaticism in his brain. His eccentric genius bordered closely on the line of insanity. For

> "Great wits are sure to madness near allied,
> And thin partitions do their bounds divide."

His style is frequently obscure, inelegant, abrupt, diffuse, and repetitious. He accumulates arguments to an extent that destroys their effect. He gives eight arguments to prove that the saints in heaven pray for us; ten arguments to show that Melanchthon and his friends were sorcerers, blinded by the devil; twenty arguments against infant baptism; twenty-five reasons for the necessity of faith before baptism; and sixty signs of the apocalyptic beast and the reign of Antichrist.[1]

In thought and style he was the opposite of the clear-headed, well-balanced, methodical, logical, and thoroughly sound Calvin, who never leaves the reader in doubt as to his meaning.

The moral character of Servetus was free from immorality of which his enemies at first suspected him in the common opinion of the close connection of heresy with vice. But he was vain, proud, defiant, quarrelsome, revengeful, irreverent

[1] *Restit.* pp. 564, 570, 586, 664, 700, 718.

in the use of language, deceitful, and mendacious. He abused popery and the Reformers with unreasonable violence. He conformed for years to the Catholic ritual which he despised as idolatrous. He defended his attendance upon mass by Paul's example in visiting the temple (Acts 21 : 26), but afterwards confessed at Geneva that he had acted under compulsion and sinned from fear of death. He concealed or denied on oath facts which he had afterwards to admit.[1] At Vienne he tried to lie himself out of danger, and escaped; in Geneva he defied his antagonist and did his best, with the aid of the Libertines in the Council, to ruin him.

The severest charge against him is blasphemy. Bullinger remarked to a Pole that if Satan himself should come out of hell, he could use no more blasphemous language against the Trinity than this Spaniard; and Peter Martyr, who was present, assented and said that such a living son of the devil ought not to be tolerated anywhere. We cannot even now read some of his sentences against the doctrine of the Trinity without a shudder. Servetus lacked reverence and a decent regard for the most sacred feelings and convictions of those who differed from him. But there was a misunderstanding on both sides. He did not mean to blaspheme the true God in whom he believed himself, but only the three false and imaginary gods, as he wrongly conceived them to be, while to all orthodox Christians they were the Father, the Son, and the Holy Spirit of the one true, eternal, blessed Godhead.

He labored under the fanatical delusion that he was called by Providence to reform the Church and to restore the Christian religion. He deemed himself wiser than all the fathers, schoolmen, and reformers. He supported his delusion by a fanciful interpretation of the last and darkest book of the Bible.

---

[1] Tollin (*Charakterbild*, p. 38) defends Servetus's veracity by resolving his contradictory statements into innocent errors of memory and comparing them to the variations in the four Gospel narratives!

Calvin and Farel saw, in his refusal to recant, only the obstinacy of an incorrigible heretic and blasphemer. We must recognize in it the strength of his conviction. He forgave his enemies; he asked the pardon even of Calvin. Why should we not forgive him? He had a deeply religious nature. We must honor his enthusiastic devotion to the Scriptures and to the person of Christ. From the prayers and ejaculations inserted in his book, and from his dying cry for mercy, it is evident that he worshipped Jesus Christ as his Lord and Saviour.[1]

§ 157. *Calvin's Defence of the Death Penalty for Heretics.*

The public sentiment, Catholic and Protestant, as we have seen, approved of the traditional doctrine, that obstinate heretics should be made harmless by death, and continued unchanged down to the close of the seventeenth century.

But there were exceptions. As in the case of the execution of the Spanish Priscillianists in the fourth century, the genuine spirit of Christianity and humanity raised a cry of indignation and horror through the mouths of St. Ambrose of Milan, and St. Martin of Tours; so there were not a few in the sixteenth century who protested against the burning of Servetus. Most of these — Lelio Socino, Renato, Curio, Biandrata, Alciati, Gribaldo, Gentile, Ochino, and Castellio — were Italian refugees and free-thinkers who sympathized more or less with his heretical opinions. It was especially three professors in the University of Basel — Borrhaus (Cellarius), Curio, and Castellio — who were sus-

---

[1] *Rest.* p. 356: " *O Christe Jesu, domine Deus noster, adesto, veni, vide, et pugna pro nobis.*" P. 576: " *O pater omnipotens, pater misericordiæ, eripe nos miseros ab his tenebris mortis, per nomen filii tui Jesu Christi domini nostri. O fili Dei, Jesu Christe, qui pro nobis mortuus es, ne moreremur, succurre, ne moriamur,*" etc. Comp. also the prayer at the beginning of his book, quoted above in § 146.

pected at Geneva of being followers of Servetus. For the same reason some Anabaptists, like David Joris, who lived at that time in Basel under the assumed name of John von Bruck, took his part. Anonymous libels in prose and verse appeared against Calvin. He was denounced as a new pope and inquisitor, and Geneva, heretofore an asylum of religious liberty, as a new Rome.[1] A hundred Servetuses seemed to arise from the ashes at Champel; but they were all inferior men, and did not understand the speculative views of Servetus, who had exhausted the productive powers of antitrinitarianism.[2]

Not only dissenters and personal enemies, but also, as Beza admits, some orthodox and pious people and friends of Calvin were dissatisfied with the *severity* of the punishment, and feared, not without reason, that it would justify and encourage the Romanists in their cruel persecution of Protestants in France and elsewhere.

Under these circumstances Calvin felt it to be his disagreeable duty to defend his conduct, and to refute the errors of Servetus. He was urged by Bullinger to do it. He completed the work in a few months and published it in Latin and French in the beginning of 1554.[3] It had an

---

[1] The Sicilian, Camillo Renato wrote a long poem, *De injusto Serveti incendio*, which is copied by Trechsel, I. 321–28, from the Simler collection in Zürich. Several poems came from Italian refugees in the Grisons.

[2] On these later Antitrinitarians, see the preceding chapter. They were deistic; Servetus pantheistic. Trechsel says (I. 269): "*In Servet schien sich die produktive Kraft des Antitrinitarianismus erschöpft zu haben. Von der Höhe der Genialität und speculativer Weltbetrachtung sank er zu der Stufe des trivialen ohnmächtigen Zweifels hinunter, und die jugendliche Frische und Fülle, die sich in den Ideen des spanischen Arztes offenbarte, wich einem altklugen, verständelnden, halbaufgeklärten Wesen, das sich in einer Fluth von subjektiven Meinungen ohne Halt und innere Bedeutung zu erkennen gab. Nicht wenig wurde der kirchlichen Parthei und Calvin an ihrer Spitze durch die geistige Bedeutungslosigkeit ihrer Gegner der Kampf und Widerstand erleichtert, und doch dauerte er noch dreizehn Jahre und endigte mit einer ähnlichen gewaltsamen Katastrophe, wie diejenige, mit welcher er begonnen hatte.*" He means the execution of Gentile at Bern, 1566.

[3] Zurkinden in Bern received a copy Feb. 10, 1554; Sulzer in Basel, Feb. 26.

official character and was signed by all the fifteen ministers of Geneva.[1]

Beza aided him in this controversy and undertook to refute the pamphlet of Bellius, and did so with great ability and eloquence.[2]

Calvin's work against Servetus gave complete satisfaction to Melanchthon. It is the strongest refutation of the errors of his opponent which his age produced, but it is not free from bitterness against one who, at last, had humbly asked his pardon, and who had been sent to the judgment seat of God by a violent death. It is impossible to read without pain the following passage: " Whoever shall now contend that it is unjust to put heretics and blasphemers to death will knowingly and willingly incur their very guilt. This is not laid down on human authority; it is God who speaks and prescribes a perpetual rule for his Church. It is not in vain that he banishes all those human affections which soften our hearts; that he commands paternal love and all the benevolent feelings between brothers, relations, and friends to cease; in a word, that he almost deprives men of their nature in order that nothing may hinder their holy zeal. Why is so implacable a severity exacted but that we may know that God is defrauded of his honor, unless the piety that is due to him be preferred to all human duties, and that when his

---

[1] *Defensio orthodoxæ fidei de sacra Trinitate, contra prodigiosos errores Michaelis Serveti Hispani : ubi ostenditur hæreticos jure gladii coërcendos esse, et nominatim de homine hoc tam impio juste et merito sumptum Genevæ fuisse supplicium.* Per JOHANNEM CALVINUM. Oliva Roberti Stephani (261 pages). It is also quoted under the sub-title: *Fidelis Expositio errorum Mich. Serveti et brevis eorundem Refutatio,* etc., or simply as *Refutatio Errorum M. S.* The French version is entitled: *Declaration pour maintenir la vraye foy que tiennent tous Chréstiens de la Trinité des personnes en un seul Dieu. Par* JEAN CALVIN. *Contre les erreurs détestables de Michel Servet, Espaignol. Où il est aussi monstré, qu'il est licite de punir les heretiques ; et qu'à bon droict ce meschant a esté executé par justice en la ville de Genève* (356 pages). The work is accordingly cited under different titles — *Defensio, Refutatio, Declaration.* See the bibliographical notices in Calvin's *Opera,* VIII. Proleg. xxix-xxxiii.

[2] See succeeding section.

glory is to be asserted, humanity must be almost obliterated from our memories?"

Calvin's plea for the right and duty of the Christian magistrate to punish heresy by death, stands or falls with his theocratic theory and the binding authority of the Mosaic code. His arguments are chiefly drawn from the Jewish laws against idolatry and blasphemy, and from the examples of the pious kings of Israel. But his arguments from the New Testament are failures. He agrees with Augustin in the interpretation of the parabolic words: "Constrain them to come in" (Luke 14:23).[1] But this can only refer to moral and not to physical force, and would imply a forcible salvation, not destruction. The same parable was afterwards abused by the French bishops to justify the abominable dragoonades of Louis XIV. against the Huguenots. Calvin quotes the passages on the duty of the civil magistrate to use the sword against evil-doers (Rom. 13:4); the expulsion of the profane traffickers from the temple (Matt. 21:12); the judgment on Ananias and Sapphira (Acts 5:1 sqq.); the striking of Elymas with blindness (13:11); and the delivery of Hymenæus and Alexander to Satan (1 Tim. 1:20). He answers the objections from the parables of the tares and of the net (Matt. 13:30, 49), and from the wise counsel of Gamaliel (Acts 5:34). But he cannot get over those passages which contradict his theory, as Christ's rebuke to John and James for wishing to call down fire from heaven (Luke 9:54), and to Peter for drawing the sword (Matt. 26:52), his declaration that his kingdom is not of this world (John 18:36), and his whole spirit and aim, which is to save and not to destroy.

---

[1] In his commentary on that passage (*Harm. Evang.*, Pars. II. 43, Tholuck's edition), Calvin says: "*Non improbo, quod Augustinus hoc testimonio sœpius contra Donatistas usus est, ut probaret, piorum principum edictis ad veri Dei cultum et fidei unitatem licite cogi prœfractos et rebelles: quia, etsi voluntaria est fides, videmus tamen, iis mediis utiliter domari eorum pervicaciam, qui non nisi coacti parent.*"

In his juvenile work on Seneca and in earlier editions of his *Institutes*, Calvin had expressed noble sentiments on toleration;[1] even as Augustin did in his writings against the Manichæans, among whom he himself had lived for nine years; but both changed their views for the worse in their zeal for orthodoxy.

Calvin's "Defence" did not altogether satisfy even some of his best friends. Zurkinden, the State Secretary of Bern, wrote him Feb. 10, 1554: "I wish the former part of your book, respecting the right which the magistrates may have to use the sword in coercing heretics, had not appeared in your name, but in that of your council, which might have been left to defend its own act. I do not see how you can find any favor with men of sedate mind in being the first formally to treat this subject, which is a hateful one to almost all."[2] Bullinger intimated his objections more mildly in a letter of March 26, 1554, in which he says: "I only fear that your book will not be so acceptable to many of the more simple-minded persons, who, nevertheless, are attached both to yourself and to the truth, by reason of its brevity and consequent obscurity, and the weightiness of the subject. And, indeed, your style appears somewhat perplexed, especially in this work." Calvin wrote in reply, April 29, 1554: "I am aware that I have been more concise than usual in this treatise. However, if I should appear to have faithfully and honestly defended the true doctrine, it will more than recompense me for my trouble. But though the candor and justice which are natural to you, as well as your love towards me, lead you to judge of me favorably, there are others who assail me harshly as a master in cruelty and atrocity, for attacking with my pen not only a

---

[1] See Henry, II. 121–124; III. 224.

[2] "*Ego non video gratiam aliquam te inire posse apud sedati animi homines, quod primus omnium ex professo fere hoc argumentum tractandum susceperis, omnibus ferme invisum.*" Bibl. Gen. cod. 114. Trechsel, I. 269; *Opera*, XV. 22.

dead man, but one who perished by my hands. Some, even not self-disposed towards me, wish that I had never entered on the subject of the punishment of heretics, and say that others in the like situation have held their tongues as the best way of avoiding hatred. It is well, however, that I have you to share my fault, if fault it be; for you it was who advised and persuaded me to it. Prepare yourself, therefore, for the combat." [1]

§ 158. *A Plea for Religious Liberty.*   *Castellio and Beza.*

Cf. § 126, p. 627, and especially FERD. BUISSON, *Sébastien Castellion.* Paris (Hachette et Cie), 1892. 2 vols. 8vo (I. 358–413; II. 1–28).

A month after Calvin's defence of the death penalty of heretics, there appeared at Basel a pseudonymous book in defence of religious liberty, dedicated to Duke Christopher of Würtemberg.[2] It was edited and prefaced professedly by MARTINUS BELLIUS, whose real name has never been discovered with certainty. Perhaps it was Martin Borrhaus of Stuttgart (1499–1564), professor of Hebrew learning in the University of Basel, and known under the name of "Cellarius," in honor of his first protector, Simon Cellarius (not to be confounded with Michael Cellarius of Augsburg). He

---

[1] "*Alii me durius exagitant, quod sævitiæ et atrocitatis sim magister, quod mortum hominem, qui manibus meis periit, calamo proscindam. Sunt etiam quidam non malevoli, qui argumentum illud nunquam me attigisse cuperent, de hæreticis puniendis. Dicunt enim alios omnes, ut invidiam fugerent, data opera tacuisse. Sed bene se habet, quod te habes culpæ socium, si quæ tamen culpa est, quia mihi auctor et hortator fuisti. Vide igitur, ut te ad certamen compares.*" Henry, III. 236 and Beilage, p. 87; *Opera*, XV. 124.

[2] *De hæreticis, an sint persequendi, et omnino quomodo sit cum eis agendum multorum tum veterum tum recentiorum sententiæ. Liber hoc tam turbulento tempore pernecessarius. Magdeburgi* [false name for Basel] *per Georgium Rausch, anno Domini 1554, mense Martio* (173 pp., 8vo). The name of the editor who wrote the dedicatory preface is given as MARTINUS BELLIUS (in French, MARTIN BELLIE), which was explained by the contemporaries as "*Guerre à la guerre, guerre à ceux qui usent du glaive.*" Buisson, I. 358. A copy which belonged to Boniface Amerbach, is in the University Library of Basel (II. 15).

studied at Heidelberg and Wittenberg, appeared first among the Zwickau Prophets, and then in connection with Carlstadt (who ended his days likewise as a professor at Basel).[1] The book was misdated from Magdeburg, the stronghold of the orthodox Lutherans, in opposition to the tyranny of the Imperial Interim. A French edition appeared, nominally at Rouen, but was probably printed at Lyons, where Castellio had a brother in the printing business.[2]

Calvin at once suspected the true authors, and wrote to Bullinger, March 28, 1554: "A book has just been clandestinely printed at Basel under false names, in which Castellio and Curio pretend to prove that heretics should not be repressed by the sword. Would that the pastors of that church at length, though late, aroused themselves to prevent the evil from spreading wider."[3] A few days afterwards Beza wrote to Bullinger about the same book, and gave it as his opinion that the feigned Magdeburg was a city on the Rhine [Basel], and that Castellio was the real author, who treated the most important articles of faith as useless or indifferent, and put the Bible on a par with the Ethics of Aristotle.[4]

Castellio wrote, however, only a part of the book. He adopted the pseudonym of *Basilius* (*i.e.* Sebastian) *Montfortius* (*i.e.* Castellio).[5]

---

[1] See Riggenbach in Herzog,[2] III. 166, and Buisson, II. 10 sq.

[2] *Traicté des hérétiques, à savoir si on les doit persécuter, et comme on se doit conduire avec eux, selon l'advis, opinion, et sentence de pleusieurs auteurs tant anciens que modernes: grandement nécessaire en ce temps plein de troubles, et très utile à tous, et principalement aux Princes et Magistrats, pour cognoistre quel est leur office en une chose tant difficile et périlleuse.* Rouen, Pierre Freneau, 1554 (139 pp., 8vo). I copy the title from Buisson, I. 358. He gives a full analysis and extracts (pp. 360 sqq.). The book is exceedingly rare.

[3] *Opera*, XV. 96.

[4] *Opera*, XV. 97.

[5] As Schweizer has shown, see above, p. 627. Buisson ignores Schweizer, but comes to the same conclusion (I. 404): "BASILE *est un équivalent très plausible de* SÉBASTIEN, *et* MONTFORT *éveille une idée toute voisine de celle de* CASTELLUM *ou de* CHATILLON."

The body of this work consists of a collection of testimonies in favor of religious toleration, extracted from the writings of Luther (his book, *Von weltlicher Obrigkeit*, 1523), Brenz (who maintain that heresy as long as it keeps in the intellectual sphere should be punished only by the Word of God), Erasmus, Sebastian Frank, several Church Fathers (Lactantius, Chrysostom, Jerome, and Augustin, in his anti-Manichæan writings), Otto Brunsfeld (d. at Bern, 1534), Urbanus Rhegius (Lutheran theologian, d. 1541), Conrad Pellican (Hebrew professor at Zürich, d. 1556), Caspar Hedio, Christoph Hoffmann, Georg Kleinberg (a pseudonym) and even Calvin (in the first edition of his *Institutes*). This collection was probably made by Curio.

The epilogue is written by Castellio, and is the most important part of the book. He examines the different biblical and patristic passages quoted for and against intolerance. He argues against his opponents from the multiplicity of sects which disagree on the interpretation of Scripture, and concludes that, on their principles, they should all be exterminated except one. He justly charges St. Augustin with inconsistency in his treatment of the Donatists, for which, he says, he was punished by the invasion of the Arian Vandals. The lions turned against those who had unchained them. Persecution breeds Christian hypocrites in place of open heretics. It provokes counter-persecution, as was just then seen in England after the accession of Queen Mary, which caused the flight of English Protestants to Switzerland. In conclusion he gives an allegorical picture of a journey through the centuries showing the results of the two conflicting principles of force and liberty, of intolerance and charity, and leaves the reader to decide which of the two armies is the army of Jesus Christ.

Castellio anticipated Bayle and Voltaire, or rather the Baptists and Quakers. He was the champion of religious liberty in the sixteenth century. He claimed it in the name of the gospel and the Reformation. It was appropriate that this testimony should come from the Swiss city of Basel, the home of Erasmus.[1]

But the leaders of the Swiss Reformation in Geneva and Zürich could see in this advocacy of religious freedom only a most dangerous heresy, which would open the door to all kinds of errors and throw the Church of Christ into inextricable confusion.

Theodore Beza, the faithful aid of Calvin, took up his pen against the anonymous sceptics of Basel, and defended the right and duty of the Christian magistrate to punish heresy. His work appeared in September, 1554; that is, five months after the book of Martinus Bellius. It was Beza's first published theological treatise (he was then thirty-five years of age).[2]

The book has a polemic and an apologetic part. In the former, Beza tries to refute the principle of toleration; in the latter, to defend the conduct of Geneva. He contends that the toleration of error is indifference to truth, and that it destroys all order and discipline in the Church. Even the enforced unity of the papacy is much better than anarchy. Heresy is much worse than murder, because it destroys the soul. The spiritual power has nothing to do with temporal punishments; but it is the right and duty of the civil government, which is God's servant, to see to it that he receives his full honor in the community. Beza appeals to the laws of Moses and the acts of kings Asa and Josiah against blasphemers and false prophets. All Christian rulers have

---

[1] Michelet (*Renaissance*) says: "*Un pauvre prote d'imprimerie, Sébastien Chateillon, posa pour tout l'avenir la grande loi de la tolérance.*" Buisson has chosen this sentence as the motto of his work. He calls Castellio (II. 268) "*dans le protestantisme français, le premier des modernes.*"

[2] It was entitled: *De hæreticis a civili magistratu puniendis libellus, adversus Martini Bellii farraginem et novorum Academicorum sectam*, THEODORO BEZA VEZELIO *auctore*. Oliva Roberti Stephani, MDLIIII (271 pp., 8vo). Reprinted in his *Tractationes Theologicæ*, 2d ed., 1582, pp. 85-169. Nicolas Colladon published a French translation: *Traitté de l'authorité du magistrat en la punition des hérétiques*, etc., 1560. Buisson, II. 19.

punished obstinate heretics. The œcumenical synods (from 325 to 787) were called and confirmed by emperors who punished the offenders. Whoever denies to the civil authority the right to restrain and punish pernicious errors against public worship undermines the authority of the Bible. He cites in confirmation passages from Luther, Melanchthon, Urbanus Rhegius, Brenz, Bucer, Capito, Bullinger, Musculus, and the Church of Geneva. He closes the argument as follows: " The duty of the civil authority in this matter is hedged about by these three regulations: (1) It must strictly confine itself to its own sphere, and not presume to define heresy; that belongs to the Church alone. (2) It must not pass judgment with regard to persons, advantages, and circumstances, but with pure regard to the honor of God. (3) It must proceed after quiet, regular examination of the heresy and mature consideration of all the circumstances, and inflict such punishment as will best secure the honor due to the divine Majesty and the peace and unity of the Church."

This theory, which differs little from the papal theory of intolerance, except in regard to the definition of heresy and the mode and degree of punishment, was accepted for a long time in the Reformed Churches with few dissenting voices; but, fortunately, there was no occasion for another capital punishment of heresy in the Church of Geneva after the burning of Servetus.

The evil which Calvin and Beza did was buried with their bones; the greater good which they did will live on forever. Dr. Willis, though a decided apologist of Servetus, makes the admission: " Calvin must nevertheless be thought of as the real herald of modern freedom. Holding ignorance to be incompatible with the existence of a people at once religious and free, Calvin had the schoolhouse built beside the Church, and brought education within the reach of all. Nor did he overlook the higher culture." [1]

[1] *Servetus and Calvin*, p. 514. See below, § 161.

CHAPTER XVII.

CALVIN ABROAD.

CALVIN'S Correspondence in his *Opera*, vols. X.-XX. — HENRY, III. 395-549 (*Calvin's Wirksamkeit nach aussen*). — STÄHELIN, I. 505-588; II. 5 sqq.

§ 159. *Calvin's Catholicity of Spirit.*

CALVIN was a Frenchman by birth and education, a Swiss by adoption and life-work, a cosmopolitan in spirit and aim.

The Church of God was his home, and that Church knows no boundaries of nationality and language. The world was his parish. Having left the papacy, he still remained a Catholic in the best sense of that word, and prayed and labored for the unity of all believers. Like his friend Melanchthon, he deeply deplored the divisions of Protestantism. To heal them he was willing to cross ten oceans. Thus he wrote, in reply to Archbishop Cranmer, who had invited him (March 20, 1552), with Melanchthon and Bullinger, to a meeting in Lambeth Palace for the purpose of drawing up a consensus creed for the Reformed Churches.[1] After expressing his zeal for the Church universal, he continues (Oct. 14, 1552) : —

"I wish, indeed, it could be brought about that men of learning and authority from the different churches should meet somewhere, and after thoroughly discussing the different articles of faith, should, by a unanimous decision, deliver down to posterity some certain rule of doctrine. But amongst the chief evils of the age must be reckoned the marked division between the different churches, insomuch that human society can hardly be said to be established among us, much less a holy communion of the members of Christ, which, though all profess it, few indeed really observe with

---

[1] See Cranmer's letter of invitation in Calvin's *Opera*, XIV. 306.

sincerity. But if the clergy are more lukewarm than they should be, the fault lies chiefly with their sovereigns, who are either so involved in their secular affairs, as to neglect altogether the welfare of the Church, and indeed religion itself, or so well content to see their own countries at peace as to care little about others; and thus the members being divided, the body of the Church lies lacerated.

"As to myself, if I should be thought of any use, I would not, if need be, object to cross ten seas for such a purpose. If the assisting of England were alone concerned, that would be motive enough with me. Much more, therefore, am I of opinion, that I ought to grudge no labor or trouble, seeing that the object in view is an agreement among the learned, to be drawn up by the weight of their authority according to Scripture, in order to unite Churches seated far apart. But my insignificance makes me hope that I may be spared. I shall have discharged my part by offering up my prayers for what may have been done by others. Melanchthon is so far off that it takes some time to exchange letters. Bullinger has, perhaps, already answered you. I only wish that I had the power, as I have the inclination, to serve the cause." [1]

This noble project was defeated or indefinitely postponed by the death of Edward VI. and the martyrdom of Cranmer, but it continues to live as a *pium desiderium*. In opposition to a mechanical and enforced uniformity, Calvin suggested the idea of a spiritual unity with denominational variety, or of one flock in many folds under one shepherd.[2] This idea was taken up in our age by the Evangelical Alliance, the Pan-Anglican Council, the Pan-Presbyterian Alliance, the Pan-Methodist Conference, the Young Men's Christian Associations, the Christian Endeavor Societies, and similar volun-

---

[1] "*Quantum ad me attinet, si quis mei usus fore videbitur, ne decem quidem maria, si opus sit, ob eam rem trajicere pigeat. Si de juvando tantum Angliæ regno ageretur, jam mihi ea satis legitima ratio foret. Nunc cum quæratur gravis et ad Scripturæ normam probe compositus doctorum hominum consensus, quo ecclesiæ procul alioqui dissitæ inter se coalescant, nullis vel laboribus vel molestiis parcere fas mihi esse arbitror. Verum tenuitatem meam facturam spero, ut mihi parcatur. Si votis prosequar, quod ab aliis susceptum erit, partibus meis defunctus ero.* D. PHILIPPUS *longius abest, quam ut ultro citroque commeare brevi tempore literæ queant.* D. BULLINGERUS *tibi forte jam rescripsit. Mihi utinam par studii ardori suppeteret facultas!*" See *Opera*, XIV. 312 sqq.; Cranmer's *Works* (Parker Soc. ed.), vol. II. pp. 430–433.

[2] John 10: 16, μία ποίμνη (not αὐλή), εἷς ποιμήν. The E. V., following the Latin Vulgate, wrongly translates, "one *fold*," which suggests the Roman idea of one external organization, like the papacy.

tary associations, which bring Christians of different churches and nationalities together for mutual conference and co-operation, without interfering with their separate organization and denominational preferences.

A lasting monument of Calvin's catholicity is his immense correspondence, which fills ten quarto volumes of the last edition of his works, and embraces in all no less than forty-two hundred and seventy-one letters. He left to Beza a collection of manuscripts with discretionary power to publish from it what he deemed might promote the edification of the Church of God. Accordingly, Beza edited the first collection of Calvin's letters eleven years after his death, at Geneva, 1575. This edition was several times republished, and gradually enriched by letters discovered in various libraries by Liebe, Mosheim, Bretschneider, Crottet, Jules Bonnet, Henry, Reuss, and Herminjard.

No theologian has left behind him a correspondence equal in extent, ability, and interest. In these letters Calvin discusses the profoundest topics of religion; he gives advice as a faithful pastor; administers comfort to suffering brethren; pours out his heart to his friends; solves difficult political questions, as a wise statesman, in the complications of the little Republic with Bern, Savoy, and France. Among his correspondents are all the surviving Reformers — Melanchthon, Bucer, Bullinger, Farel, Viret, Cranmer, Knox, Beza, Peter Martyr, John à Lasco; crowned heads — Queen Marguerite of Navarre, the Duchess Renée of Ferrara, King Sigismund Augustus of Poland, the Elector Otto Heinrich of the Palatinate, Duke Christopher of Würtemberg; statesmen and high officers, like Duke Somerset, the Protector of England, Prince Radziwil of Poland, Admiral Coligny of France, the magistrates of Zürich, Bern, Basel, St. Gall, and Frankfort; and humble confessors and martyrs to whom he sent letters of comfort in prison.

§ 160. *Geneva an Asylum for Protestants from all Countries.*

Calvin gave to Geneva a cosmopolitan character which it retains to this day. It became, through him, as already stated, the capital of the Reformed Churches, and was called the Protestant Rome. Philip II. of Spain wrote to the French king: "Geneva is the source of all misfortune to France, the refuge of all heretics, the most terrible enemy of Rome. I am ready at any time, with all the power of my kingdom, to aid in its destruction." That city was, indeed, in the sixteenth century what North America has become, on a much larger scale, since the seventeenth century. It was an asylum for persecuted confessors of the evangelical faith without distinction of nationality, an impregnable moral fortress built upon the rock of the Bible.[1]

Zürich, Basel, and Strassburg were the only places in that age which can be compared with Geneva in generous hospitality to strangers.

At the beginning of the sixteenth century the city of Geneva numbered 12,000 souls, in 1543 not more than 13,000; but in the seven years from 1543 to 1550 it increased to 20,000, or at the rate of 1000 a year. This increase was chiefly due to the continuous influx of persecuted Protestants from France, Italy, and England. Some came also from Spain and Holland.[2] Most of them were educated men and not a few of them distinguished for learning and social position, as Cordier, Colladon, Etienne (Stephens), Marot, Ochino, Carraccioli, Knox, Whittingham. They had made sacrifices for the sake of religion, and thereby acquired the

---

[1] Michelet (*Histoire de France*, vol. X. 414) calls Calvinistic Geneva "*la cité de l'esprit bâtie de stoicisme sur le roc de la prédestination,*" and (in vol. XI. 93) "*la fabrique des saints et des martyrs, la sombre forge où se forgeaissent les élus de la mort.*"

[2] Fourteen hundred French families settled in Geneva in eight years, during the reign of Henri II. Gaberel, *Histoire de l'Église de Genève*, I. 346; Michelet, X. 414.

honor of confessors with the spirit of martyrs. There were special congregations for Italians and Englishmen, who were provided by the city with suitable places of worship. Calvin treated the refugees with great hospitality. He secured to them as far as possible the rights of citizenship. Some of them were even elected to the Large Council. An insult to a refugee from religious persecution was as punishable as an insult to a minister of the gospel. The favor and privileges accorded to these foreigners excited the envy and jealousy of the native Genevese, who opposed their admission to citizenship and their right to carry arms. This exclusive nativism gave Calvin a great deal of trouble.

The little Republic of Geneva was continually exposed to the danger of absorption by Savoy, France, and Spain, which hated her as the stronghold of heresy. It was in a large measure due to the wisdom and firmness of Calvin that in those critical times she preserved her liberty and independence. He also resisted the repeated attempts of Bern to interfere with the doctrine and discipline of the Church.

Geneva offers a wonderful aspect in modern history. "Embracing the *élite* of three nations, melted into one whole by the spirit of one man, it continues in the midst of mighty and bitter foes, without any external support, simply through its moral force. It has no territory, no army, no treasures, no temporal, no material resources. There it stands, a city of the spirit, built of Christian stoicism on the rock of predestination."

§ 161. *The Academy of Geneva. The High School of Reformed Theology.*

I. Calvin: *Leges Academiæ Genevensis*, or *L'Ordre du Collège de Genève*, first published in Latin and French. Geneva, 1559. Republished by Charles Le Fort, professor of law at Geneva, on the third centennial of the founding of the Academy, June 5, 1859, and in *Opera*, X. 65–90.

II. Berthault: *Mathurin Cordier. L'enseignement chez les premiers Calvinistes.* Paris, 1876 (85 pp.). — Massebieau: *Les colloques scolaires du seizième siècle et leurs auteurs.* Paris, 1878. — AMIEL et BOUVIER: *L'enseignement superieur à Genève depuis la fondation de l'académie jusqu'à 1876.* Gen., 1878. Comp. HENRY, III. 386 sqq.; STÄHELIN, II. 487–498; GABEREL, II. 109 sqq.; BUISSON: *Séb. Castellion* (Paris, 1892), I. 121–151.

One of the most important institutions of Geneva which strengthened the Reformed religion at home, and extended it abroad, is the Academy founded by Calvin. Knowing that the ignorance of the Roman priesthood was a source of much superstition and corruption, he labored zealously for the education of the ministry and the whole people, and secured the best teachers, as Cordier, Saunier, Castellio, and Beza.

There was a college in Geneva, since 1428, called after its founder "College Versonnex," for the training of the clergy; but it had fallen into decay, and was reorganized after Calvin's return in 1541. Tuition was free. To avoid overcrowding and to bring the facilities of education within the reach of every youth, four elementary schools were established for each of the four quarters of the city. At first a small fee was charged, but it was abolished by the council after 1571, at the request of Beza. A much larger attendance was the effect. Calvin is sometimes called the founder of the common school system.

He wished to establish a full university with four faculties, but the limited means of the little Republic would not permit that; so he confined himself to an Academy. He himself collected for it from house to house 10,024 gold guilders, a very large sum for that time. Several foreign residents contributed liberally: Carraccioli, 2954; Pierre Orsières, 312; Matthieu de la Roche, 260 guilders. Of the native Genevese, Bonivard, the old champion of liberty, bequeathed his whole fortune to the institution.[1] The Council put up a commodious building. Calvin drew up the programme of studies and the academic statutes, which, after careful examination, were unanimously approved.

---

[1] Senebier, *Hist. lit.* I. 48 sq.; Henry, III. 386.

The Academy was solemnly dedicated on June 5, 1559, in the church of St. Peter, in the presence of the whole Council, the ministers, and six hundred students. Calvin invoked the blessing of God upon the institution, which was to be forever dedicated to science and religion, and made some short and weighty remarks in French. Michael Roset, the Secretary of State, read the Confession of Faith and the statutes by which the institution was to be guided. Theodore Beza was proclaimed rector and delivered an inaugural address in Latin. Calvin closed with prayer. Ten able and experienced professors were associated with him for the different departments of grammar, logic, mathematics, physics, music, and the ancient languages. Calvin himself was to continue his theological lectures in connection with Beza.

The statutes which were read on this occasion lay great stress on French and Latin composition. The Latin authors to be studied are: Cæsar, Livy, Cicero, Virgil, and Ovid; the Greek authors: Herodotus, Xenophon, Homer, Demosthenes, Plutarch, and Plato. There was also a special chair of Hebrew which was assigned to Chevalier, a pupil of Vatable and formerly tutor of Queen Elizabeth. Teachers and pupils had to sign the Apostles' Creed and a confession of faith, which, however, wisely omitted the favorite dogma of predestination, and was abolished in 1576 in order to admit "Papists and Lutherans." Religious exercises opened and closed the daily instructions.

The success of the school was extraordinary. No less than nine hundred young men from almost all the nations of Europe were matriculated in the first year as regular scholars, and almost as many, mostly refugees from France and England, prepared themselves by the theological lectures of Calvin for the work of evangelists and teachers in their native land. Among these was John Knox, the great Reformer of Scotland.

The Academy continued to flourish with some interruptions. It attracted students from all parts of Protestant Europe, and numbered among its teachers such men as Casaubon, Spangenheim, Hotoman, Francis and Alphonse Turretin, Leclerc, Pictet de Saussure, and Charles Bonnet. It was the chief nursery of Protestant ministers and teachers for France, and the principle school of reformed theology and literary culture for more than two hundred years. A degree from that Academy was equivalent in Holland to a degree of any University. Arminius was sent there by the city of Amsterdam to be educated under Beza (1582), who gave him a good testimonial, not knowing that he would become the leader of a mighty reaction against Calvinism.

In 1859 the third centennial of the Academy was celebrated in Geneva.

The evangelistic work of that Academy was resumed and is successfully carried on in the spirit of Calvin by the Evangelical Society and the Free Theological Seminary of Geneva, which numbered among its first teachers Merle d'Aubigné, the distinguished historian of the Reformation.

§ 162. *Calvin's Influence upon the Reformed Churches of the Continent.*

Calvin's moral power extended over all the Reformed Churches, and over several nationalities — Swiss, French, German, Polish, Bohemian, Hungarian, Dutch, English, Scotch, and American. His religious influence upon the Anglo-Saxon race in both continents is greater than that of any native Englishman, and continues to this day.[1]

---

[1] It is interesting to read the judgment on Calvin's influence by a highly accomplished lady, who moved in the best society of England and the Continent. The Baroness Bunsen, whose husband was successively Prussian Ambassador in Italy, Switzerland, and England, writes in one of her letters (Aug. 19, 1865) : "I read in the winter a life of Calvin by Bungener, and a very painful book it is, but the subject is of grand effect from the display of moral

CALVIN AND FRANCE.

Calvin never entered French soil after his settlement in Geneva, and was not even a citizen of the Republic till 1559; but his heart was still in France. From the time he wrote that eloquent letter to Francis the First, in dedicating to him his *Institutes*, he followed the Protestant movement with the liveliest interest. He was the head of the French Reformation and consulted at every step. He was called as pastor to the first Protestant church in Paris, but declined. He gave to the Huguenots their creed and form of government. The Gallican Confession of 1559, also called the Confession of Rochelle, was, in its first draft, his work, and his pupil Antoine de la Roche Chandieu (also called Sadeel) brought it into its present enlarged shape, in which it was presented by Beza to Charles IX. at the Colloquy at Poissy, 1561, and signed at the Synod of La Rochelle, 1571, by the Queen Jeanne d'Albret of Navarre; her son, Prince Henry of Navarre (Henry IV.); Prince Condé; Prince Louis, Count of Nassau; Admiral Coligny; Chatillon; several nobles, and all the preachers present.[1]

The history of French Protestantism down to 1564 is largely identified with Calvin's name. He induced the Swiss Cantons and the princes of the Smalkaldian League to intercede for the persecuted Huguenots. He sent messengers and letters of comfort to the prisoners. "The reverence," says one of his biographers, "with which his name was mentioned, the boundless confidence reposed in his person, the enthusiasm of the disciples who hastened to him, or came from him, surpasses all the usual experience of men. Congrega-

power almost unequalled. . . . The merit of Calvin is his own, and he has been the creative instrument of the strength of England, of Scotland, of the United States of America, not to speak of the Protestants of France, who have been scattered abroad to sow good seed in every country into which they fled, as not being suffered to build up their own."

[1] Schaff, *Creeds of Christendom*, vol. I. 490–501.

tions appealed to him for preachers; princes and noblemen for decisive counsel in political complications; those in doubt for instruction; the persecuted for protection; the martyrs for exhortation and encouragement in cheerful suffering and dying. And as the eye of a father watches over his children, Calvin watched with untiring care of love over all these relations in their manifold ramifications, and sought to be the same to the great community of his brethren in France what he was to the little Republic at home."[1]

Roman Catholic writers have made Calvin responsible for the civil wars in France, as they have made Luther responsible for the Peasants' War and the Thirty Years' War. But the Reformers preached reformation by the word and the spirit, not revolution by the sword. The chief cause of the religious wars in the sixteenth and seventeenth centuries was the intolerance of the papacy. Bossuet charges Calvin with complicity in the conspiracy of Amboise, which was a political *coup d'état* to check the power of the Guises (1560). Calvin was indeed informed of the plot, but warned against it, first privately, then publicly, and predicted its disastrous failure. He constantly upheld the principle of obedience to the rightful magistrate, and opposed violent measures. "The first drop of blood," he said, "which we shed will cause streams of blood to flow. Let us rather a hundred times perish than bring such disgrace upon the name of Christianity and the cause of the gospel."[2] Afterwards when a war in self-defence was inevitable, he reluctantly gave his consent, but protested against all excesses.[3]

Calvin did not live to weep over the terrible massacre of St. Bartholomew's day, nor to rejoice over the Edict of Nantes; but his spirit accompanied "the Church of the

---

[1] Stähelin, I. 507.

[2] See Letters in Bonnet, II. 382–391; his letter to Bullinger, May 11, 1560; Basnage, *Hist. de la Religion des Égl. réf.* II. 192–200; Henry, III. 545 sqq.; Dyer, 478 sqq.; Stähelin, I. 615–619.

[3] Stähelin, I. 626 sqq.

Desert," whose motto was the burning bush (Ex. 3 : 2) ; and
every Huguenot who left France for the sake of his faith,
carried to his new home in Switzerland, or Brandenburg, or
Holland, or England, or America, a profound reverence for
the name of John Calvin.

CALVIN AND THE WALDENSES.

The Waldenses are the only mediæval sect which survives
to this day, because they progressed with the Reformation
and adhered to the Bible as their rule of faith.[1] They sent a
deputation of two of their pastors, in 1530, to Œcolampadius
at Basel, Bucer and Capito at Strassburg, and Berthold Haller
at Bern, for information concerning the principles of the
Reformation, and made common cause with the Protestants.[2]
They were distinguished for industry, virtue, and simple,
practical piety, but their heresy attracted the attention of the
authorities.   They were cited before the Parliament at Aix,
and the heads of their families were condemned to death in
November, 1540.   The execution of the atrocious sentence
was delayed till the king's wishes should be ascertained.   In
February, 1541, Francis granted them pardon for the past,
but required them to recant within three months.   They
adhered to their faith.   On the 28th of April, 1545, a fiendish
scheme of butchery — under the direction of Baron d'Oppède,
military governor of Provence, and Cardinal Tournon, the
bigoted and bloodthirsty archbishop of Lyons — was carried
out against these innocent people.   Their chief towns of
Merindol and Cabrières, together with twenty-eight villages,

[1] The cognate Bohemian Brethren continued under a new name in the
Moravian Brotherhood (*Unitas Fratrum, Brüdergemeinde*).

[2] *Creeds of Christendom*, I. 565 sqq. See also a report of conversations
which Calvin had at Strassburg with Matthias Czervenka, a Bohemian, about
the Bohemian Brethren in Gindely, *Quellen zur Gesch. der böhmischen Brüder*,
Wien, 1859, p. 68, quoted in *Annal. Calv.* XXI. 260 sqq. Calvin objected to
the Waldenses at that time, that they claimed merit and did not leave room
for the doctrine of justification by faith in Christ.

were destroyed, the women outraged, and about four thousand persons slaughtered.

Great numbers of the Waldenses sought refuge in flight. The noble and humane Bishop Sadolet of Carpentras, received them kindly, and interceded for them with the King. Four thousand went to Geneva. Calvin started a subscription for them, provided them with lodging and employment at the fortifications, and made every effort to get the Swiss Cantons to intercede with King Francis in behalf of those Waldenses who remained in France. He travelled to Bern, Zürich, and Aarau for this purpose. He even intended to go to Paris, but was prevented by sickness. The Cantons actually wrote to the king in the strongest terms, but he rebuked them for meddling with his affairs. Viret visited the French court with letters of recommendation from the Swiss Cantons and the Smalkaldian League, but likewise without result.[1]

Since that time there has been a fraternal intercourse between the Waldenses and the French Swiss, and many of their most useful pastors were educated at Geneva and Lausanne. The Waldensian Confession of 1655 is Calvinistic and based upon the Gallican Confession of 1559.[2] After many persecutions in their mountain homes in Piedmont, the Waldenses obtained freedom in 1848, and since that time, and especially since 1870, they have become zealous evangelists in the united kingdom of Italy, with a church even in Rome and a flourishing theological college in Florence.

CALVIN IN GERMANY.

Calvin labored three years in Germany; he felt closely allied to the Lutheran Church; he had the profoundest regard for Luther, in spite of his infirmities; he was the intimate friend of Melanchthon; he attended three colloquies

---

[1] Baum, *Beza*, I. 240 sqq.; Stähelin, I. 509–512; Dyer, 193–198.
[2] *Creeds of Christendom*, III. 757–770 (French and English).

between Lutheran and Roman Catholic divines; he once
signed the Augsburg Confession (1541), as understood, explained, and improved by its author. He followed the
progress of the Reformation in Germany step by step with
the warmest interest, as is shown in his correspondence and
various writings.

He did not labor for a separate Reformed Church in Germany, but for a free confederation of the Swiss and Lutheran
Churches. But the fanatical bigotry of such men as Flacius,
Westphal, and Heshusius produced a reaction and drove a
large part of the moderate or Melanchthonian Lutherans into
the Reformed communion.

The Reformed Church in the Electoral Palatinate was the
result of a co-operation of Melanchthonian and Calvinistic
influences under the pious Elector, Frederick III. The Heidelberg Catechism is the joint work of Ursinus, a pupil of
Melanchthon, and Olevianus, a pupil of Calvin. It appeared
in 1563, three years after Melanchthon's death, one year
before Calvin's death, and became the leading symbol of the
Palatinate and the Reformed Churches in Germany and
Holland.[1] It gives the best expression to Calvin's views on
the Lord's Supper, and on Election, but wisely omits all
reference to an eternal decree of reprobation and preterition;
following in this respect Calvin's own catechism. The well-
known first question is a gem and presents the bright and
comforting side of the doctrine of Election: —

" What is thy only comfort in life and in death ? "

" That I, with body and soul, both in life and in death, am not my own, but
belong to my faithful Saviour Jesus Christ, who with His precious blood has
fully satisfied for all my sins, and redeemed me from all the power of the
devil; and so preserves me, that without the will of my Father in heaven not
a hair can fall from my head; yea, that all things must work together for
my salvation. Wherefore, by His Holy Spirit, He also assures me of eternal life, and makes me heartily willing and ready henceforth to live unto
Him."

[1] See Schaff, *Creeds of Christendom*, vol. I. pp. 529 sqq.

The influence of Calvinism and Presbyterian Church government extended, indirectly, also over the Lutheran Church and was modified in turn by Lutheranism.

John Sigismund, Elector of Brandenburg, and ancestor of the Kings of Prussia and Emperors of Germany, adopted the Calvinistic faith in a moderate form (1613).[1] Frederick William, "the great Elector," the proper founder of the Prussian Monarchy, secured the legal recognition of the Reformed Church in the Treaty of Westphalia (1648), and answered the Revocation of the Edict of Nantes (1685) by a hospitable invitation of the persecuted Huguenots to his country, where they settled in large numbers. King Frederick William III. introduced, at the third centenary of the Reformation (1817), the Evangelical Union of the Lutheran and Reformed Churches of Prussia; and among the chief advocates of the union was Schleiermacher, the son of a Calvinistic minister, the pupil of the Moravians, and the renovator of German theology, which itself is the result of a commingling of Lutheran and Reformed elements with a decided advance upon narrow confessionalism.

We may add that, while Calvin's rigorous doctrine of predestination in its dualistic form will never satisfy the German mind, his doctrine of the sacraments has made great progress in the Lutheran Church and seems to offer a solid basis for a satisfactory theory on the mystery of the spiritual real presence and fruition of Christ in the Holy Supper.

CALVIN AND HOLLAND.

The Netherlands derived the Reformation first from Germany, and soon afterwards from Switzerland and France. The Calvinists outnumbered the Lutherans and Anabaptists, and the Reformed Church became the State religion in Holland.

---

[1] *Creeds of Christendom,* I. 555 sqq.

Two Augustinian monks were burned for heresy in Brussels in 1523, and were celebrated by Luther in a stirring hymn as the first evangelical martyrs. This was the fiery signal of a fearful persecution, which raged during the reigns of Charles V. and Philip II., and resulted at last in the establishment of national independence and civil and religious liberty. During that memorable struggle of eighty years, more Protestants were put to death for their conscientious belief by the Spaniards than Christians suffered martyrdom under the Roman Emperors in the first three centuries. William of Orange, the hero of the war and a liberal Calvinist, was assassinated by an obscure fanatic (1584).[1] His second son, Maurice, a strict Calvinist (d. 1625), carried on and completed the conflict (1609). The horrible barbarities practised upon men, women, and unborn children, especially during the governorship of that bloodhound, the Duke of Alva, from 1567–1573, are almost beyond belief. We quote from the classical history of Motley: "The number of Netherlanders who were burned, strangled, beheaded, or buried alive, in obedience to the edicts of Charles V., and for the offences of reading the Scriptures, of looking askance at a graven image, or of ridiculing the actual presence of the body and blood of Christ in a wafer, have been placed as high as one hundred thousand by distinguished authorities, and have never been put at a lower mark than fifty thousand. The Venetian envoy Navigero placed the number of victims

---

[1] Motley (*The Rise of the Dutch Republic*, III. 617) thus characterizes William of Orange, the Washington of Holland: "He was more than anything else a religious man. From his trust in God, he ever derived support and consolation in the darkest hours. Implicitly relying upon Almighty wisdom and goodness, he looked danger in the face with a constant smile, and endured incessant labors and trials with a serenity which seemed more than human. While, however, his soul was full of piety, it was tolerant of error. Sincerely and deliberately himself a convert to the Reformed Church, he was ready to extend freedom of worship to Catholics on the one hand, and to Anabaptists on the other, for no man ever felt more keenly than he that the Reformer who becomes in his turn a bigot is doubly odious."

in the provinces of Holland and Friesland alone at thirty thousand, and this in 1546, ten years before the abdication, and five before the promulgation of the hideous edict of 1550." [1] Of the administration of the Duke of Alva, Motley says: "On his journey from the Netherlands, he is said to have boasted that he had caused eighteen thousand six hundred inhabitants of the provinces to be executed during the period of his government. The number of those who had perished by battle, siege, starvation, and massacre, defied computation. . . . After having accomplished the military enterprise [in Portugal] entrusted to him, he fell into a lingering fever, at the termination of which he was so much reduced that he was only kept alive by milk which he drank from a woman's breast. Such was the gentle second childhood of the man who had almost literally been drinking blood for seventy years. He died on the 12th of December, 1582." [2]

The Bible, with the Belgic Confession and the Heidelberg Catechism, was the spiritual guide of the Protestants, and inspired them with that heroic courage which triumphed over the despotism of Spain, and raised Holland to an extraordinary degree of political, commercial, and literary eminence. [3]

[1] J. L. Motley, *The Rise of the Dutch Republic*, vol. I. p. 114.

[2] *Ibid.* vol. II. 497.   Comp. the description of Alva's cruelties and the sufferings of the Protestants under his reign of terror on pp. 503 sq., and B. ter Haar's *History of the Reformation* (German translation from the Dutch), II. 86 sqq. and 127 sqq.

[3] Motley, who was a Unitarian, does at least this justice to the practical effects of Calvinism in Holland and elsewhere: "The doctrine of predestination, the consciousness of being chosen soldiers of Christ, inspired those Puritans who founded the commonwealths of England, of Holland, and of America with a contempt of toil, danger, and death which enabled them to accomplish things almost supernatural. No uncouthness of phraseology, no unlovely austerity of deportment, could, except to vulgar minds, make that sublime enthusiasm ridiculous, which on either side the ocean ever confronted tyranny with dauntless front, and welcomed death on battlefield, scaffold, or rack with perfect composure. The early Puritan at least believed. The very intensity of his belief made him — all unconsciously to himself, and narrowed

The Belgic Confession of 1561 was prepared by Guido de Brès, and revised by Francis Junius, a student of Calvin. It became the recognized symbol of the Reformed Churches of Holland and Belgium.

In the beginning of the seventeenth century, Arminianism rose as a necessary and wholesome reaction against scholastic Calvinism, but was defeated in the Synod of Dort, 1619, which adopted the five knotty canons of unconditional predestination, limited atonement, total depravity, irresistible grace, and the perseverance of saints. The Dutch Reformed Church in the United States still holds to the Canons of Dort. But Arminianism, although temporarily expelled, was allowed to return to Holland after the death of Maurice, and gradually pervaded the national Church. It largely entered the Church of England under the Stuarts. It assumed new vigor through the great Methodist Revival, which made it a converting and missionary agency in both hemispheres, and the most formidable rival of Calvinism in the Anglo-American Churches. A greater man and more abundant in self-denying and fruitful apostolic labors has not risen in the Protestant churches since the death of Calvin than John Wesley, whose "parish was the world." But he was aided in the great Anglo-American Revival by George Whitefield, who was both a Calvinist and a true evangelist.

Calvinism emphasizes divine sovereignty and free grace; Arminianism emphasizes human responsibility. The one restricts the saving grace to the elect: the other extends it to all men on the condition of faith. Both are right in what they assert; both are wrong in what they deny. If one important truth is pressed to the exclusion of another truth of equal importance, it becomes an error, and loses its hold upon the conscience.

as was his view of his position — the great instrument by which the widest human liberty was to be gained for all mankind." *History of the United Netherlands*, vol. IV. 548.

The Bible gives us a theology which is more human than Calvinism, and more divine than Arminianism, and more Christian than either of them.[1]

§ 163. *Calvin's Influence upon Great Britain.*

CALVIN AND THE CHURCH OF ENGLAND.

Calvin first alludes to the English Reformation in a letter to Farel, dated March 15, 1539, where he gives the following judgment of Henry VIII.: "The King is only half wise. He prohibits, under severe penalties, besides depriving them of the ministry, the priests and bishops who enter upon matrimony; he retains the daily masses; he wishes the seven sacraments to remain as they are. In this way he has a mutilated and torn gospel, and a church stuffed full as yet with many toys and trifles. Then he does not suffer the Scripture to circulate in the language of the common people throughout the kingdom, and he has lately put forth a new verdict by which he warns the people against the reading of the Bible. He lately burned a worthy and learned man [John Lambert] for denying the carnal presence of Christ in the bread. Our friends, however, though sorely hurt by atrocities of this kind, will not cease to have an eye to the condition of his kingdom."

With the accession of Edward VI. he began to exercise a direct influence upon the Anglican Reformation. He addressed a long letter to the Protector Somerset, Oct. 22, 1548, and advised the introduction of instructive preaching and strict discipline, the abolition of crying abuses, and the drawing up of a summary of articles of faith, and a catechism for children. Most of his suggestions were adopted. It is remarkable that in this letter, as well as that to the king of Poland, he makes no objection to the Episcopal form of gov-

---

[1] See *Creeds of Christendom*, I. 502 sqq. and 508 sqq.

ernment, nor to a liturgy. At the request of Archbishop Cranmer, he wrote also letters to Edward VI., and dedicated to him his Commentary on Isaiah. He sent them by a private messenger who was introduced to the King by the Duke of Somerset. His correspondence with Cranmer has been already alluded to.[1] As a consensus creed of Reformed Churches was found to be impracticable, he encouraged the archbishop to draw up the articles of religion for the Church of England.

These articles which appeared first in 1553, and were afterwards reduced from forty-one to thirty-nine under Queen Elizabeth, in 1563, show the influence of the Augsburg Confession in the doctrines of the Trinity, justification and the Church, and the influence of Calvin in the doctrines of the Eucharist, and of predestination, which, however, is stated with wisdom and moderation (Art. XVII.), without reprobation and preterition.[2]

During the reign of Queen Mary, many leading Protestants fled to Geneva, and afterwards obtained high positions in the Church under Queen Elizabeth. Among them were the translators of the Geneva version of the Bible, which owes much to Calvin and Beza, and continued to be the most popular English version till the middle of the seventeenth century, when it was superseded by the version of 1611.

During the reign of Queen Elizabeth Calvin's theological influence was supreme, and continued down to the time of Archbishop Laud. His *Institutes* were translated soon after the appearance of the last edition, and passed through six editions in the life of the translator. They were the textbook in the universities, and had as great an authority as the *Sentences* of Peter the Lombard, or the *Summa* of Thomas Aquinas, in the Middle Ages. We have previously quoted the high tributes of the "judicious" Hooker and Bishop

[1] § 159, pp. 799 sq.
[2] See *Creeds of Christendom*, vol. I. 613 sqq.; 633 sqq.

Sanderson to Calvin.[1] Heylyn, the admirer and biographer of Archbishop Laud, says that "Calvin's book of *Institutes* was for the most part the foundation on which the young divines of those times did build their studies." Hardwick, speaking of the latter part of the Elizabethan period, asserts that "during an interval of nearly thirty years, the more extreme opinions of the school of Calvin, not excluding his theory of irrespective reprobation, were predominant in almost every town and parish." [2]

The nine Lambeth Articles of 1595, and the Irish Articles of Archbishop Ussher of 1615, give the strongest symbolical expression to the Calvinistic doctrine of unconditional election and reprobation, but lost their authority under the later Stuarts.[3]

Calvin, however, always maintained his commanding position as a commentator among the scholars of the Anglican Church. His influence revived in the evangelical party, and his sense of the absolute dependence on divine grace for comfort and strength found classical expression in some of the best hymns of the English language, notably in Toplady's

"Rock of Ages cleft for me."

CALVIN AND THE CHURCH OF SCOTLAND.

Still greater and more lasting was Calvin's influence upon Scotland. It extended over discipline and church polity as well as doctrine.

The Presbyterian Church of Scotland, under the sole headship of Christ, is a daughter of the Reformed Church of Geneva, but has far outgrown her mother in size and importance, and is, upon the whole, the most flourishing of the Reformed Churches in Europe, and not surpassed by any

---

[1] See above, p. 286 sq.
[2] *A History of the Articles of Religion* (1859), p. 167.
[3] See above, p. 564, and *Creeds of Christendom*, I. 658 sqq.

denomination in general intelligence, liberality, and zeal for the spread of Christianity at home and abroad.

The hero of the Scotch Reformation, though four years older than Calvin, sat humbly at his feet and became more Calvinistic than Calvin. John Knox, the Scot of the Scots, as Luther was the German of the Germans, spent the five years of his exile (1554–1559), during the reign of the Bloody Mary, mostly at Geneva, and found there "the most perfect school of Christ that ever was since the days of the Apostles."[1] After that model he led the Scotch people, with dauntless courage and energy, and the *perfervidum ingenium Scotorum*, from mediæval semi-barbarism into the light of modern civilization, and acquired a name which, next to those of Luther, Zwingli, and Calvin, is the greatest in the history of the Protestant Reformation.[2]

In the seventeenth century Scotch Presbyterianism and English Puritanism combined to produce a second and more radical reformation, and formulated the rigorous principles of Puritanic Calvinism in doctrine, discipline, and worship. The Westminster standards of 1647 have since governed the Presbyterian, and, in part, also the Congregational or Independent, and the regular Baptist Churches of the British Empire and the United States, with such modifications and adaptations as the progress of theology and church life demands.[3]

[1] See above, § 110, p. 518.
[2] *Creeds of Christendom*, I. 669–685, and the literature there given.
[3] *Ibid.* I. 685–813.

CHAPTER XVIII.

THE CLOSING SCENES IN CALVIN'S LIFE.

§ 164. *Calvin's Last Days and Death.*

CALVIN had labored in Geneva twenty-three years after his second arrival, — that is, from September, 1541, till May 27, 1564,[1] — when he was called to his rest in the prime of manhood and usefulness, and in full possession of his mental powers; leaving behind him an able and worthy successor, a model Reformed Church based on the law of Moses and the gospel of Christ; a flourishing Academy, which was a nursery of evangelical preachers for Switzerland and France, and survives to this day; and a library of works from his pen, which after more than three centuries are still a living and moulding power.[2]

He continued his labors till the last year, writing, preaching, lecturing, attending the sessions of the Consistory and the Venerable Company of pastors, entertaining and counselling strangers from all parts of the Protestant world, and corresponding in every direction. He did all this notwithstanding his accumulating physical maladies, as headaches, asthma, dyspepsia, fever, gravel, and gout, which wore out his delicate body, but could not break his mighty spirit.

When he was unable to walk he had himself transported to church in a chair. On the 6th of February, 1564, he preached his last sermon. On Easter day, the 2d of April,

---

[1] In the same year (1564) Michelangelo died, and Shakespeare and Galileo were born. Adding the two years of his first sojourn, from 1536 to 1538, Calvin spent twenty-five years in Geneva.

[2] He lived, says a Scotch divine, "somewhat less than fifty-five years, but into that period the work of centuries was compressed." Tweedie, *l.c.*, p. 57.

he was for the last time carried to church and received the sacrament from the hands of Beza.

On the 25th of April, he made his last will and testament. It is a characteristic document, full of humility and gratitude to God, acknowledging his own unworthiness, placing his whole confidence in the free election of grace, and the abounding merits of Christ, laying aside all controversy, and looking forward to the unity and peace in heaven.[1]

Luther, defying all forms of law, begins his last will with the words: "I am well known in heaven, on earth, and in hell," and closes: "This wrote the notary of God and the witness of his gospel, Dr. Martin Luther."

On the 26th of April, Calvin wished to see once more the four Syndics and all the members of the Little Council in the Council Hall, but the Senators in consideration of his health offered to come to him. They proceeded to his house on the 27th in solemn silence. As they were assembled round him he gathered all his strength and addressed them without interruption, like a patriarch, thanking them for their kindness and devotion, asking their pardon for his occasional outbreaks of violence and wrath, and exhorting them to persevere in the pure doctrine and discipline of Christ. He moved them to tears.[2] In like manner, on the 28th of April, he addressed all the ministers of Geneva whom he had invited to his house, in words of solemn exhortation and affectionate regard. He asked their pardon for any failings, and thanked them for their faithful assistance. He grasped the hands of every one. "They parted," says Beza, "with heavy hearts and tearful eyes."[3]

[1] Beza's *Vita*, in *Opera*, XXI. pp. 162 sqq. (in Latin); Henry, III. p. 171 (in French); translation in the next section.

[2] See, besides the account of Beza, the entry in the *Rég. du Conseil*, April 27, *Annal.* XXI. 815.

[3] See the *Discours d'adieu aux membres du Petit Conseil*, and the *Discours d'adieu aux ministres*, in his *Opera*, Tom. IX. 887–890, in Beza's *Vita*, and in the appendix to Bonnet's *French Letters*, Tom. II. 573. Comp. also Henry, III. 582 sqq.; Stähelin, II. 462–468. Translation in the next section.

These were sublime scenes worthily described by an eye-witness, and represented by the art of a painter.[1]

On the 19th of May, two days before the pentecostal communion, Calvin invited the ministers of Geneva to his house and caused himself to be carried from his bed-chamber into the adjoining dining-room. Here he said to the company: "This is the last time I shall meet you at table," — words that made a sad impression on them. He then offered up a prayer, took a little food, and conversed as cheerfully as was possible under the circumstances. Before the repast was quite finished he had himself carried back to his bed-room, and on taking leave said, with a smiling countenance: "This wall will not hinder my being present with you in spirit, though absent in body."

From that time he never rose from his bed, but he continued to dictate to his secretary.

Farel, then in his eightieth year, came all the way from Neuchâtel to bid him farewell, although Calvin had written to him not to put himself to that trouble. He desired to die in his place. Ten days after Calvin's death, he wrote to Fabri (June 6, 1564): "Oh, why was not I taken away in his place, while he might have been spared for many years of health to the service of the Church of our Lord Jesus Christ! Thanks be to Him who gave me the exceeding grace to meet this man and to hold him against his will in Geneva, where he has labored and accomplished more than tongue can tell. In the name of God, I then pressed him and pressed him again to take upon himself a burden which appeared to him harder than death, so that he at times asked me for God's sake to have pity on him and to allow him to serve God in a manner which suited his nature. But when he recognized the will of God, he sacrificed his own will and accomplished more than was expected from him, and surpassed not only others, but even himself. Oh, what a glorious course has he happily finished!"

[1] Hornung's picture of Calvin on his death-bed, addressing the senators.

Calvin spent his last days in almost continual prayer, and in ejaculating comforting sentences of Scripture, mostly from the Psalms. He suffered at times excruciating pains. He was often heard to exclaim: "I mourn as a dove " (Isa. 38:14); "I was dumb, I opened not my mouth; because thou didst it" (Ps. 39:9); "Thou bruisest me, O Lord, but it is enough for me that it is thy hand." His voice was broken by asthma, but his eyes remained bright, and his mind clear and strong to the last. He admitted all who wished to see him, but requested that they should rather pray for him than speak to him.

On the day of his death he spoke with less difficulty. He fell peacefully asleep with the setting sun towards eight o'clock, and entered into the rest of his Lord. "I had just left him," says Beza, "a little before, and on receiving intimation from the servants, immediately hastened to him with one of the brethren. We found that he had already died, and so very calmly, without any convulsion of his feet or hands, that he did not even fetch a deeper sigh. He had remained perfectly sensible, and was not entirely deprived of utterance to his very last breath. Indeed, he looked much more like one sleeping than dead." [1]

He had lived fifty-four years, ten months, and seventeen days.

"Thus," continues Beza, his pupil and friend, "withdrew into heaven, at the same time with the setting sun, that most brilliant luminary, which was the lamp of the Church. On the following night and day there was immense grief

---

[1] The original entry in the Register of the Council of Geneva under date "*Samedi, Mai 27, 1564*," relative to the death of Calvin, is this: "*Ce iourd'huy environ huit heures du soir le sp. Ian Calvin est allé a Dieu, sain et entier, graces a Dieu, de sens et entendement.*" Under date of "*Lundi, Mai 29*," the succession of Beza to the place of Calvin is thus announced in the same Register: "*De Bèze succède à la place de Calvin. Il aura la charge quil avoit oultre ce quil a faire les leçons. Arreste quon luy baille le gage quavoit M. Calvin. Et au reste quand se viendra ceans quon se contente quil soit assis au banc dabas et quon luy presente la maison dudit Sr. Calvin sil y veult aller.*" Calvin's Opera, XXI. 815.

and lamentation in the whole city; for the Republic had lost its wisest citizen, the Church its faithful shepherd, the Academy an incomparable teacher — all lamented the departure of their common father and best comforter, next to God. A multitude of citizens streamed to the death-chamber and could scarcely be separated from the corpse. Among them were several foreigners, as the distinguished Ambassador of the Queen of England to France, who had come to Geneva to make the acquaintance of the celebrated man, and now wished to see his remains. At first all were admitted; but as the curiosity became excessive and might have given occasion to calumnies of the enemies,[1] his friends deemed it best on the following morning, which was the Lord's Day, to wrap his body in linen and to enclose it in a wooden coffin, according to custom. At two o'clock in the afternoon the remains were carried to the common cemetery on Plain Palais (*Planum Palatium*), followed by all the patricians, pastors, professors, and teachers, and nearly the whole city in sincere mourning."[2]

Calvin had expressly forbidden all pomp at his funeral and the erection of any monument over his grave. He wished to be buried, like Moses, out of the reach of idolatry. This was consistent with his theology, which humbles man and exalts God.

---

[1] What these calumnies were, is not stated; they were first made public by Bolsec fifteen years later (see Note below). Francis Junius, in his animadversions upon Bellarmin, says that he was at Geneva when Calvin closed his life, but that he never saw, heard, knew, thought, or even dreamed of the blasphemies and curses which the papists said he uttered at his death.

[2] "*Pomeridiana vero secunda, sequentibus funus patriciis, una cum pastoribus professoribusque scholæ omnibus totaque pœne civitate non sine uberibus lacrymis prosequente elatus est, communique cœmiterio, quod Planum Palatium vocant, nulla penitus extraordinaria pompa nulloque addito cippo (sic enim mandarat) conditus, cui propterea, his versiculis parentavi.*" Then follow the *Parentalia* and a description of Calvin's character and habits. In his French biography, which is dated Aug. 19, 1564, Beza says that Calvin was buried "*comme il l'avait ordonné, au cemetiere commun appelé Plein palais sans pompe ni appareil quelconques-là où il gist auiourd'huy attendant la resurrection qu'il nous a enseignée et a si constamment esperée,*" etc. He closes both biographies with a list of Calvin's works. *Opera*, XXI. 47–50.

Beza, however, wrote a suitable epitaph in Latin and French, which he calls "Parentalia" (*i.e.* offering at the funeral of a father) : —

> " Shall honored Calvin to the dust return,
> From whom e'en Virtue's self might learn ;
> Shall he — of falling Rome the greatest dread,
> By all the good bewailed, and now (tho' dead)
> The terror of the vile — lie in so mean,
> So small a tomb, where not his name is seen ?
>   Sweet Modesty, who still by Calvin's side
> Walked while he lived, here laid him when he died.
> O happy tomb with such a tenant graced !
> O envied marble o'er his ashes placed ! "[1]

On the third centennial of the Reformation of Geneva, in 1835, a splendid memorial medal was struck, which on the one side shows Calvin's likeness, with his name and dates of birth and death ; on the other, Calvin's pulpit with the verse : "He held fast to the invisible as if he saw Him" (Heb. 11 : 27), and the circular inscription : "Broken in body ; Mighty in spirit ; Victor by faith ; the Reformer of the Church ; the Pastor and Protector of Geneva." [2]

At the third centenary of his death (1864), his friends in Geneva, aided by gifts from foreign lands, erected to his

---

[1] In his Latin *Vita :* —

> " *Romæ ruentis terror ille maximus,*
> *Quem mortuum lugent boni, horrescunt mali,*
> *Ipsa a quo potuit virtutem discere virtus,*
> *Cur adeo exiguo ignotoque in cespite clausus*
>   *Calvinus lateat, rogas?*
> *Calvinum adsidue comitata modestia vivum,*
> *Hoc tumulo manibus condidit ipsa suis.*
> *O te beatum cespitem tanto hospite !*
> *O cui invidere cuncta possint marmora !* "

There are besides one Hebrew, ten Greek, two Latin, and three French "*Epitaphia in Calvinum scripta,*" in Beza's *Poemata,* 1597, and in Calvin's *Opera,* vol. XXI. 169, 173–178. The three French sonnets are from Chandieu, a pupil of Calvin.

[2] On the obverse : *Johannes Calvinus Natus Novioduni, 1509. Mortuus Genevæ, 1564.* On the reverse : "*Il tint ferme comme s'il eust veu celuy qui est invisible*" (*Heb. 1*Γ*: 27*). *Genev. Jubil Ann., 1835.* And the inscription : "*Corpore fractus : Animo potens : Fide victor : Ecclesiæ Reformator : Genevæ Pastor et Tutamen.*" See Henry, III. 592.

memory the "Salle de la Reformation," a noble building, founded on the principles of the Evangelical Alliance, and dedicated to the preaching of the pure gospel and the advocacy of every good cause.

The Reformed Churches of both hemispheres are the monument of Calvin, more enduring than marble.

Zwingli, of all the Reformers, died first (1531), in the prime of life, on the battlefield, with the words trembling on his lips: "They can destroy the body, but not the soul." The star of the Swiss Reformation went down with him, but only to rise again.

Next followed Luther (1546). He, too, died away from home, at Eisleben, his birthplace, disgusted with the disorders of the times, weary of the world and of life, but holding fast to the faith of the gospel, repeating the precious words: "God so loved the world as to give His only begotten Son," and, in the language of the 31st Psalm, committing his spirit into the hands of his faithful God, who had redeemed him.

Melanchthon left this world at his own home (1560), like Calvin; his last and greatest sorrow was the dissensions in the Church for which he could shed tears as copious as the waters of the Elbe. He desired to die that he might be delivered first of all from sin, and also from "the fury of theologians." He found great comfort in the fifty-third chapter of Isaiah, and the first, and seventeenth chapters of John; and when asked by his son-in-law (Peucer), whether he desired anything, he replied: "Nothing but heaven."

John Knox, the Calvin of Scotland, "who never feared the face of man," survived his friend eight years (till 1572), and found his last comfort likewise in the Psalms, the fifty-third chapter of Isaiah, and the sacerdotal prayer of our Saviour.

The providence of God, which rules and overrules the movements of history, raised up worthy successors for the Reformers, who faithfully preserved and carried forward their work : Bullinger for Zwingli, Melanchthon for Luther, Beza for Calvin, Melville for Knox.

The extraordinary episcopal power which Calvin, owing to his extraordinary talents and commanding character, had exercised without interruption, ceased with his death. Beza was elected his successor on the 29th of May, 1564, as "*modérateur*" of the ecclesiastical affairs of Geneva, only for one year.[1] But he was annually re-elected till 1580, when he felt unequal to carrying any longer the heavy burden of duty. He was willing, however, to continue the correspondence with foreign Churches. He divided his untiring activity between Switzerland and France, and exercised a controlling influence on the progress of the Reformation in those two countries. He saw a Huguenot prince, Henry IV., ascend the throne of France; he lamented his abjuration of the evangelical faith, but rejoiced over the Edict of Nantes which gave legal existence to Protestantism; and he carried, as the last survivor of the noble race of the Reformers, the ideas of the Reformation to the beginning of the seventeenth century. His theology marks the transition from the broad Calvinism of Calvin to the narrow, scholastic, and supralapsarian Calvinism of the next generation, which produced the reaction of Arminianism not only in Holland and England, but also in France and Geneva.

NOTE. A CALUMNY.

It is painful to notice that sectarian hatred and malice followed the Reformers to their death-beds. Fanatical Romanists represented Zwingli's heroic death as a judgment of God, and invented the myths that Œcolampadius committed suicide and was carried off by the devil; that Luther hung himself by his handkerchief on the bed-post and emitted a horrible stench; and that Calvin died in despair.

The myth of Luther's suicide was soberly and malignantly repeated by an ultramontane priest (Majunke, editor of the "Germania" in Berlin), and gave

---

[1] He himself suggested a similar change in an address before the Venerable Company of Pastors and Professors, June 2, 1564. *Annales*, in *Opera*, XXI. 816.

rise to a lively controversy in 1890. It must be added, however, that learned and honest Catholics indignantly protested against the calumny. (*Cf.* my article, *Did Luther commit Suicide?* in "Magazine of Christian Literature," New York, for December, 1890.)

As to Calvin, it is quite probable that his body, broken by so many diseases, soon showed signs of decay, which put a stop to the reception of strangers, and may have given rise to some "calumnies," of which Beza vaguely speaks. But it was not till fifteen years after his death, that Bolsec, the apostate monk, fastened upon Calvin's youth an odious vice (see above, p. 302), and spread the report that he died of a terrible malady,—that of being eaten by worms, — with which the just judgment of God destroys His enemies. He adds that Calvin even invoked the devils and cursed his studies and writings. ("*Il mourut invoquant les diables. . . . Même il maudissait l'heure qu'il avait jamais étudié et écrit.*") But he gives no authority, living or dead.

Audin (*Life of Calvin*, p. 532, Engl. transl.) repeats this infamous fabrication with some variations and dramatic embellishments, on the alleged testimony of an unknown student, who, as he says, sneaked into the death-chamber, lifted the black cloth from the face of Calvin and reported: "*Calvinus in desperatione furiens vitam obiit turpissimo et fœdissimo morbo quem Deus rebellibus et maledictis comminatus est, prius excruciatus et consumptus, quod ego verissime attestari audeo, qui funestum et tragicum illius exitum et exitium his meis oculis præsens aspexi. Joann. Harennius, apud Pet. Cutzenum!*"

We regret to say that a Roman Catholic archbishop, Dr. Spalding, whose work on the Reformation gives no evidence of any acquaintance with the writings of Calvin or Beza, retails the slanders of Bolsec and Audin, and informs American readers that Calvin was "a very Nero" and "a monster of impurity and iniquity!" (See above, § 110, p. 520.)

Calvin's whole life and writings, his testament, and dying words to the senators and ministers of Geneva, and the minute account of his death by his friend Beza, who was with him till his last moments, ought to be sufficient to convince even the most incredulous who is not incurably blinded by bigotry.

§ 165. *Calvin's Last Will, and Farewells.*

CALVIN'S LAST WILL AND TESTAMENT, April 25, 1564.

In BEZA's *Vita Calv.*, French and Latin; in *Opera*, XX. 298 and XXI. 162. Henry gives the French text, III., Beilage, 171 sqq. The English translation is by Henry Beveridge, Edinburgh, 1844.

"In the name of God, Amen. On the 25th day of April, in the year of our Lord 1564, I, Peter Chenalat, citizen and notary of Geneva, witness and declare that I was called upon by that admirable man, John Calvin, minister of the Word of God in this Church of Geneva, and a citizen of the same State, who, being sick in body, but of sound mind, told me that it was his intention to execute his testament, and explain the nature of his last will, and begged me to receive it, and to write it down as he should rehearse and dictate it with his tongue. This I declare that I immediately did, writing down word for word as he was pleased to dictate and rehearse; and that I have in no respect added to or subtracted from his words, but have followed the form dictated by himself.

"'In the name of the Lord, Amen. I, John Calvin, minister of the Word of God in this Church of Geneva, being afflicted and oppressed with various diseases, which easily induce me to believe that the Lord God has determined shortly to call me away out of this world, have resolved to make my testament, and commit my last will to writing in the manner following: First of all, I give thanks to God, that taking mercy on me, whom He had created and placed in this world, He not only delivered me out of the deep darkness of idolatry in which I was plunged, that He might bring me into the light of His gospel, and make me a partaker in the doctrine of salvation, of which I was most unworthy; and not only, with the same mercy and benignity, kindly and graciously bore with my faults and my sins, for which, however, I deserved to be rejected by Him and exterminated, but also vouchsafed me such clemency and kindness that He has deigned to use my assistance in preaching and promulgating the truth of His gospel. And I testify and declare, that it is my intention to spend what yet remains of my life in the same faith and religion which He has delivered to me by His gospel; and that I have no other defence or refuge for salvation than His gratuitous adoption, on which alone my salvation depends. With my whole soul I embrace the mercy which He has exercised towards me through Jesus Christ, atoning for my sins with the merits of His death and passion, that in this way He might satisfy for all my crimes and faults, and blot them from His remembrance. I testify also and declare, that I suppliantly beg of Him, that He may be pleased so to wash and purify me in the blood which my Sovereign Redeemer has shed for the sins of the human race, that under His shadow I may be able to stand at the judgment-seat. I likewise declare, that, according to the measure of grace and goodness which the Lord hath employed towards me, I have endeavored, both in my sermons and also in my writings and commentaries, to preach His Word purely and chastely, and faithfully to interpret His sacred Scriptures. I also testify and declare, that, in all the contentions and disputations in which I have been engaged with the enemies of the gospel, I have used no impostures, no wicked and sophistical devices, but have acted candidly and sincerely in defending the truth. But, woe is me! my ardor and zeal (if indeed worthy of the name) have been so careless and languid, that I confess I have failed innumerable times to execute my office properly, and had not He, of His boundless goodness, assisted me, all that zeal had been fleeting and vain. Nay, I even acknowledge, that if the same goodness had not assisted me, those mental endowments which the Lord bestowed upon me would, at His judgment-seat, prove me more and more guilty of sin and sloth. For all these reasons, I testify and declare that I trust to no other security for my salvation than this, and this only, viz. that as God is the Father of mercy, He will show Himself such a Father to me, who acknowledge myself to be a miserable sinner. As to what remains, I wish that, after my departure out of this life, my body be committed to the earth (after the form and manner which is used in this Church and city), till the day of a happy resurrection arrive. As to the slender patrimony which God has bestowed upon me, and of which I have determined to dispose in this will and testament, I appoint Anthony Calvin, my very dear brother, my heir, but in the way of honor only, giving to him for his own the silver cup which I received as a present from Varanius, and with which I desire he will be contented. Everything else belonging to my succession I give him in trust, begging he will at his death leave it to his children. To the Boys' School I bequeath out of my succession ten gold pieces; as many to poor strangers; and as many to Joanna, the daughter of Charles Constans, and myself by affinity. To Samuel and John, the sons of my brother, I bequeath, to be paid by him at his death, each four hundred gold pieces; and to Anna, and Susanna, and Dorothy, his daughters, each three hundred gold pieces; to David, their brother, in reprehension of his juvenile levity and petulance, I leave only twenty-five gold pieces. This is the amount of the whole patrimony and goods which the Lord has bestowed on me, as far as I can estimate, setting a value both on my library and movables, and all my domestic utensils, and, generally, my whole means and effects; but should they produce a larger sum, I wish the surplus to be divided proportionally among all the sons and daughters of my brother, not excluding David, if, through the goodness of God, he shall have returned to good behavior. But should the whole exceed the above-mentioned sum, I believe it will be no great matter, especially after my debts are paid, the doing of which I have carefully committed to my said brother, having confidence in his faith and good-will; for which reason I will and appoint him executor of this my testament, and along with him my distinguished friend, Lawrence Normand, giving power to them to make out an inventory of my effects, without being obliged to comply with the strict forms of law. I empower them also to sell my movables, that they may turn them into money, and execute my will above written, and explained and dictated by me, John Calvin, on this 25th day of April, in the year 1564.' [1]

"After I, the aforesaid notary, had written the above testament, the aforesaid John Calvin immediately confirmed it with his usual subscription and handwriting. On the following day, which was the 26th day of April of same year, the same distinguished man, Calvin, ordered me to be sent for, and along with me, Theodore Beza, Raymond Chauvet, Michael Cop, Lewis Enoch, Nicholas Colladon, and James Bordese, ministers and preachers of the Word of God in this Church of Geneva, and likewise the distinguished Henry Scrimger, Professor of Arts, all citizens of Geneva, and in presence of them all, testified and declared that he had dictated to me this his instrument in the form above written; and, at the same time, he ordered me to read it in their hearing, as having been called for that purpose. This I declare I did articulately, and with clear voice. And after it was so read, he testified and declared that it was his last will, which he desired to be rati-

---

[1] A part of Calvin's furniture belonged to the Republic of Geneva, as is proved by the inventory preserved in the archives. His books were purchased after his death by the Council. In spite of his poverty he could not escape the charge of avarice. See below, p. 838.

fied. In testimony and confirmation whereof, he requested them all to
subscribe said testament with their own hands. This was immediately done
by them, month and year above written, at Geneva, in the street commonly
called Canon Street, and at the dwelling-place of said testator. In faith and
testimony of which I have written the foresaid testament, and subscribed it
with my own hand, and sealed it with the common seal of our supreme
magistracy.

" PETER CHENALAT."

CALVIN'S FAREWELL TO THE SYNDICS AND SENATORS OF GENEVA,
April 27, 1564.

From BEZA'S *Vita Calvini*. The Latin text in *Opera*, XXI. 164 sqq. The French
    text in vol. IX. 887–890. Comp. *Rég. du Conseil*, fol. 38, in *Annales*, XXI.
    815. Translated by Henry Beveridge, Esq., for "The Calvin Translation
    Society," 1844 (Calvin's *Tracts*, vol. I. lxxxix–xciii).

"This testament being executed, Calvin sent an intimation to the four
syndics, and all the senators, that, before his departure out of life, he was
desirous once more to address them all in the Senate house, to which he
hoped he might be carried on the following day. The senators replied that
they would rather come to him, and begged that he would consider the state
of his health. On the following day, when the whole Senate had come to him
in a body, after mutual salutations, and he had begged pardon for their
having come to him when he ought rather to have gone to them, first premis-
ing that he had long desired this interview with them, but had put it off until
he should have a surer presentiment of his decease, he proceeded thus : —
  "'Honored Lords, — I thank you exceedingly for having conferred so
many honors on one who plainly deserved nothing of the kind, and for having
so often borne patiently with my very numerous infirmities. This I have
always regarded as the strongest proof of your singular good-will toward me.
And though in the discharge of my duty I have had various battles to fight,
and various insults to endure, because to these every man, even the most
excellent, must be subjected, I know and acknowledge that none of these
things happened through your fault; and I earnestly entreat you that if, in
anything, I have not done as I ought, you will attribute it to the want of
ability rather than of will; for I can truly declare that I have sincerely
studied the interest of your Republic. Though I have not discharged my
duty fully, I have always, to the best of my ability, consulted for the public
good; and did I not acknowledge that the Lord, on His part, hath sometimes
made my labors profitable, I should lay myself open to a charge of dissimulation. But this I beg of you, again and again, that you will be pleased to
excuse me for having performed so little in public and in private, compared
with what I ought to have done. I also certainly acknowledge, that on
another account also I am highly indebted to you, viz. your having borne
patiently with my vehemence, which was sometimes carried to excess; my
sins, in this respect, I trust, have been pardoned by God also. But in regard

to the doctrine which I have delivered in your hearing, I declare that the Word of God, intrusted to me, I have taught, not rashly nor uncertainly, but purely and sincerely; as well knowing that His wrath was otherwise impending on my head, as I am certain that my labors in teaching were not displeasing to Him.   And this I testify the more willingly before God, and before you all, because I have no doubt whatever that Satan, according to his wont, will stir up wicked, fickle, and giddy men, to corrupt the pure doctrine which you have heard of me.'

"Then referring to the great blessings with which the Lord had favored them, 'I,' says he, 'am the best witness from how many and how great dangers the hand of Almighty God hath delivered you.   You see, moreover, what your present situation is.   Therefore, whether in prosperity or adversity, have this, I pray you, always present before your eyes, that it is He alone who establishes kings and states, and on that account wishes men to worship Him. Remember how David declared that he had fallen when he was in the enjoyment of profound peace, and assuredly would never have risen again, had not God, in His singular goodness, stretched out His hand to help him.   What, then, will be the case with such diminutive mortals as we are, if it was so with him who was so strong and powerful?   You have need of great humbleness of mind, that you may walk carefully, setting God always before you, and leaning only on His protection; assured, as you have often already experienced, that, by His assistance, you will stand strong, although your safety and security hang, as it were, by a slender thread.   Therefore, if prosperity is given you, beware, I pray you, of being puffed up as the wicked are, and rather humbly give thanks to God.   But if adversity befalls you, and death surrounds you on every side, still hope in Him who even raises the dead. Nay, consider that you are then especially tried by God, that you may learn more and more to have respect to Him only.   But if you are desirous that this republic may be preserved in its strength, be particularly on your guard against allowing the sacred throne on which He hath placed you to be polluted. For He alone is the supreme God, the King of kings, and Lord of lords, who will give honor to those by whom He is honored, but will cast down the despisers.   Worship Him, therefore, according to His precepts; and study this more and more, for we are always very far from doing what it is our duty to do.   I know the disposition and character of each of you, and I know that you need exhortation.   Even among those who excel, there is not one who is not deficient in many things.   Let every one examine himself, and wherein he sees himself to be defective, let him ask of the Lord.   We see how much iniquity prevails in the counsels of this world.   Some are cold; others, negligent of the public good, give their whole attention to their own affairs; others indulge their own private affections; others use not the excellent gifts of God as is meet; others ostentatiously display themselves, and, from overweening confidence, insist that all their opinions shall be approved of by others.   I admonish the old not to envy their younger brethren, whom they may see adorned, by God's goodness, with some superior gifts.   The younger, again, I admonish to conduct themselves with modesty, keeping far aloof from all haughtiness of mind.   Let no one give disturbance to his neighbor, but let every one shun deceit and all that bitterness of feeling which, in the administration of the Republic, has led many away from the right path. These things you will avoid if each keeps within his own sphere, and all conduct themselves with good faith in the department which has been intrusted to them. In the decision of civil causes let there be no place for partiality or hatred; let no one pervert justice by oblique artifices; let no one, by his recommendations, prevent the laws from having full effect; let no one depart from what is just and good. Should any one feel tempted by some sinister affection, let him firmly resist it, having respect to Him from whom he received his station, and supplicating the assistance of His Holy Spirit.

"'Finally, I again entreat you to pardon my infirmities, which I acknowledge and confess before God and His angels, and also before you, my much respected lords.'

"Having thus spoken, and prayed to Almighty God that He would crown them more and more with His gifts, and guide them by His Holy Spirit, for the safety of the whole Republic, giving his right hand to each, he left them in sorrow and tears, all feeling as if they were taking a last farewell of their common parent."

CALVIN'S FAREWELL TO THE MINISTERS OF GENEVA, April 28, 1564.

From BEZA'S *Vita Calvini.* The Latin text in *Opera,* XXI. 166 sq. Translation by Henry Beveridge for "The Calvin Translation Society," Edinburgh, 1844 (I. xciii), from the Latin text. There is another report, in French, by minister Jean Pinaut, dated May 1, which is fuller as regards Calvin's persecutions, and the confession of his infirmities, which always displeased him and for which he asks forgiveness. It also makes grateful mention of Farel, Viret, and Beza, and an unpleasant allusion to Bern, which always more feared than loved Calvin. It is printed in *Opera,* vol. IX. 891, 892, and in the *Letters of John Calvin* by JULES BONNET, transl. by Gilchrist, vol. IV. 372–377.

"On the 28th of April, when all of us in the ministry of Geneva had gone to him at his request, he said : —

"'Brethren, after I am dead, persist in this work, and be not dispirited; for the Lord will save this Republic and Church from the threats of the enemy. Let dissension be far away from you, and embrace each other with mutual love. Think again and again what you owe to this Church in which the Lord hath placed you, and let nothing induce you to quit it. It will, indeed, be easy for some who are weary of it to slink away, but they will find, to their experience, that the Lord cannot be deceived. When I first came to this city, the gospel was, indeed, preached, but matters were in the greatest confusion, as if Christianity had consisted in nothing else than the throwing down of images ; and there were not a few wicked men from whom I suffered the greatest indignities ; but the Lord our God so confirmed me, who am by no means naturally bold (I say what is true), that I succumbed to none of their attempts. I afterwards returned thither from Strassburg in obedience to my calling, but with an unwilling mind, because I thought I should prove unfruitful. For not knowing what the Lord had determined, I saw nothing before me but numbers of the greatest difficulties. But proceeding in this work, I at length perceived that the Lord had truly blessed my labors. Do you also persist in this vocation, and maintain the established order; at the same time, make it your endeavor to keep the people in obedience to the doctrine; for there are some wicked and contumacious persons. Matters, as you see, are tolerably settled. The more guilty, therefore, will you be before God, if they go to wreck through your indolence. But I declare, brethren, that I have lived with you in the closest bonds of true and sincere affection, and now, in like manner, part from you. But if, while under this disease, you have experienced any degree of peevishness from me, I beg your pardon, and heartily thank you, that when I was sick, you have borne the burden imposed upon you.'

"When he had thus spoken, he shook hands with each of us. We, with most sorrowful hearts, and certainly not unmoistened eyes, departed from him."

Beza modestly omits Calvin's reference to himself which is as follows : " Quant à nostre estat interieur, vous avez esleu Monsieur de Beze pour tenir ma place. Regardez de le soulager, car la charge est grande et a de la peine, en telle sorte qu'il faudroit qu'il fust accablé soubs le fardeau. Mais regardez à le supporter. De luy, ie sçay qu'il a bon vouloir et fera ce qu'il pourra." Pinaut's report, in Calv. Opera, IX. 894.

§ 166. Calvin's Personal Character and Habits.

Calvin is one of those characters that command respect and admiration rather than affection, and forbid familiar approach, but gain upon closer acquaintance. The better he is known, the more he is admired and esteemed. Those who judge of his character from his conduct in the case of Servetus, and of his theology from the " decretum horribile," see the spots on the sun, but not the sun itself. Taking into account all his failings, he must be reckoned as one of the greatest and best of men whom God raised up in the history of Christianity.

He has been called by competent judges of different creeds and schools, " the theologian " par excellence, " the Aristotle of the Reformation," " the Thomas Aquinas of the Reformed Church," " the Lycurgus of a Christian democracy," " the Pope of Geneva." He has been compared, as a church ruler, to Gregory VII. and to Innocent III. The sceptical Renan even, who entirely dissents from his theology, calls him "the most Christian man of his age." Such a combination of theoretic and practical pre-eminence is without a parallel in history. But he was also an intolerant inquisitor and persecutor, and his hands are stained with the blood of a heretic.[1] Take these characteristics together, and you have the whole Calvin; omit one or the other of them, and you do him injustice. He will ever command admiration and even reverence, but can never be popular among the masses. No pilgrimages will be made to his grave. The fourth centennial of his birth, in 1909, is not likely to be celebrated with such enthusiasm as Luther's was in 1883, and Zwingli's in 1884. But the impression he made on the Swiss, French, Dutch, and especially on the Anglo-Saxon race in Great Britain and America, can never be erased.[2]

Calvin's bodily presence, like that of St. Paul, was weak. His earthly tent scarcely covered his mighty spirit. He was of middle stature, dark complexion, thin, pale, emaciated, and in feeble health; but he had a finely chiseled face, a well-formed mouth, pointed beard, black hair, a prominent nose, a lofty forehead, and flaming eyes which kept their lustre to

[1] His enemies in Geneva even started the proverb, if we are to believe the untrustworthy Baudouin: "Better with Beza in hell than with Calvin in heaven."

[2] See the collection of remarkable tributes in § 68, pp. 270 sqq. I will only add two more from Dr. Baur and Dr. Möhler, the great historians who were colleagues and antagonists, the champions, indeed, of opposite creeds in one of the most important theological controversies of the nineteenth century. The Protestant Baur, in his *Kirchengeschichte* (IV. 374), calls Calvin a man "*von seltener Gelehrsamkeit, feiner, vielseitiger Bildung, scharfem, durchdringendem Geiste, kräftigem, aber strengem Charakter, vollkommen würdig, den übrigen Häuptern der Reformation zur Seite zu stehen, an Schärfe des Geistes zum Theil ihnen noch überlegen.*" The Roman Catholic Möhler, the author of the *Symbolik*, which caused a great sensation in its day, says in his posthumous *Kirchengeschichte* (III. 189): "*Calvin besass sehr viel Scharfsinn und eine ausnehmende Beredtsamkeit, und war weit gelehrter als alle übrigen Reformatoren, so dass Lehren, die bei einem andern abscheulich gewesen wären, aus seinem Munde wohl klingen;*" but he adds: "*Zu bedauern aber ist, dass eine so grosse geistige Kraft im Dienste des Irrthums war.*"

the last. He seemed to be all bone and nerve. He looked in death, Beza says, like one who was asleep. A commanding intellect and will shone through the frail body. There are several portraits of him; the best is the oil painting in the University Library of Geneva, which presents him in academic dress and in the attitude of teaching, with the mouth open, one hand laid upon the Bible, the other raised.[1]

He calls himself timid and pusillanimous by nature; but his courage rose with danger, and his strength was perfected in weakness. He belonged to that class of persons who dread danger from a distance, but are fearless in its presence. In his conflict with the Libertines he did not yield an inch, and more than once exposed his life. He was plain, orderly, and methodical in his habits and tastes, scrupulously neat in his dress, intemperately temperate, and unreasonably abstemious. For many years he took only one meal a day, and allowed himself too little sleep.

Calvin's intellectual endowments were of the highest order and thoroughly disciplined: a retentive memory, quick perception, acute understanding, penetrating reason, sound judgment, complete command of language. He had the classical culture of the Renaissance, without its pedantry and moral weakness. He made it tributary to theology and piety. He was not equal to Augustin and Luther as a creative genius and originator of new ideas, but he surpassed them both and all his contemporaries as a scholar, as a polished and eloquent writer, as a systematic and logical thinker, and as an organizer and disciplinarian. His talents, we may say, rose to the

---

[1] It is reproduced on p. 256. Mr. Theophile Dufour, the librarian, assured me in 1886 that it is the most authentic portrait. Professor Diodati, a former librarian, wrote to Dr. Henry (III. P. I. Preface, p. vii): "*Quant au portrait que l'on voit à notre bibliothèque, il a toujours passé pour authentique et fidèle. Nos peintres s'accordent à reconnaître qu'il est bien de l'époque de Calvin et qu'il est peint d'une manière remarquable. On l'a souvent attribué a Holbein; mais cette opinion n'est pas constatée. Ce que l'on peut dire c'est qu'on y retrouve sa manière. En l'étudiant attentivement on lui trouve un air de vérité frappant.*"

full height of genius. His mind was cast in the mould of
Paul, not in that of John. He had no mystic vein, and little
imagination. He never forgot anything pertaining to his
duty; he recognized persons whom he had but once seen
many years previously. He spoke very much as he wrote,
with clearness, precision, purity, and force, and equally well
in Latin and French. He never wrote a dull line. His
judgment was always clear and solid, and so exact, that, as
Beza remarks, it often appeared like prophecy. His advice
was always sound and useful. His eloquence was logic set
on fire. But he lacked the power of illustration, which is
often, before a popular audience, more effective in an orator
than the closest argument.

His moral and religious character was grounded in the fear
of God, which is "the beginning of wisdom." Severe against
others, he was most severe against himself. He resembled a
Hebrew prophet. He may be called a Christian Elijah. His
symbol was a hand offering the sacrifice of a burning heart
to God. The Council of Geneva were impressed with "the
great majesty" of his character.[1] This significant expression accounts for his overawing power over his many enemies in Geneva, who might easily have crushed him at any
time. His constant and sole aim was the glory of God, and
the reformation of the Church. In his eyes, God alone was
great, man but a fleeting shadow. Man, he said, must be
nothing, that God in Christ may be everything. He was
always guided by a strict sense of duty, even in the punishment of Servetus. In the preface to the last edition of his
Institutes (1559), he says: "I have the testimony of my own
conscience, of angels, and of God himself, that since I undertook the office of a teacher in the Church, I have had no other
object in view than to profit the Church by maintaining the

---

[1] "*Dieu lui avait imprimé un charactère d'une si grande majesté.*" *Registres,*
June 8, 1564. Grenus, *Fragments Biographiques.*

pure doctrine of godliness; yet I suppose there is no man more slandered or calumniated than myself." [1]

Riches and honors had no charms for him. He soared far above filthy lucre and worldly ambition. His only ambition was that pure and holy ambition to serve God to the best of his ability. He steadily refused an increase of salary, and

---

[1] He meets these calumnies in a letter to Christopher Piperin, Oct. 18, 1555 (*Opera*, XV. 825 sq.), from which I quote the following passage: "When I hear that I am everywhere so foully defamed, I have not such iron nerves as not to be stung with pain. But it is no slight consolation to me that yourself and many other servants of Christ and pious worshippers of God sympathize with me in my injuries. . . . Why should I worry honest people with my zeal for vindicating my own reputation? Did there exist a greater necessity for it, having entreated their indulgence, I might lay my defence before them. But the scurrilous calumnies with which malignant men bespatter me are too unfounded and too silly to require any labored refutation on my part. The authors of them would tax me with self-importance, and laugh at me as being too anxiously concerned for my character. One example of these falsehoods is that immense sum of money which you mention. Everybody knows how frugally I live in my own house. Every one sees that I am at no expense for the splendor of my dress. It is well known everywhere that my only brother is far from being rich, and that the little which he has, he acquired without any influence of mine. Where, then, was that hidden treasure dug up? But they openly give out that I have robbed the poor. Well, this charge also, these most slanderous of men will be compelled to confess, was falsely got up without any grounds. I have never had the handling of one farthing of the money which charitable people have bestowed on the poor. About eight years ago, a man of rank [David de Busanton, a refugee; see Calvin's letter to Viret, Aug. 17, 1545, *Opera*, XII. 139] died in my house who had deposited upwards of two thousand crowns with me, and without demanding one scrap of writing to prove the deposit. When I perceived that his life was in danger, though he wished to intrust that sum to my management, I refused to undertake so responsible a charge. I contrived, however, that eight hundred crowns should be sent to Strassburg to relieve the wants of the exiles. By my advice he chose men above suspicion to distribute the remainder of the sum. When he wished to appoint me one of their number, to which the others made no objections, I refused; but I see what nettles my enemies. As they form an estimate of my character from their own, they feel convinced that I must amass wherever I find a good opportunity. But if during my lifetime I do not escape the reputation of being rich, death will at last vindicate my character from this imputation." See his testament, p. 829. Nevertheless Bolsec (ch. XI.) unscrupulously repeated and exaggerated the calumny about the misappropriation of the legacy of two thousand crowns. Comp. the editorial notes in *Opera*, XV. 825 and 826.

frequently also presents of every description, except for the poor and the refugees, whom he always had at heart, and aided to the extent of his means. He left only two hundred and fifty gold crowns, or, if we include the value of his furniture and library, about three hundred crowns, which he bequeathed to his younger brother, Antoine, and his children, except ten crowns to the schools, ten to the hospital for poor refugees, and ten to the daughter of a cousin. When Cardinal Sadolet passed through Geneva in disguise (about 1547), he was surprised to find that the Reformer lived in a plain house instead of an episcopal palace with a retinue of servants, and himself opened the door.[1] When Pope Pius IV. heard of his death he paid him this tribute: "The strength of that heretic consisted in this, — that money never had the slightest charm for him. If I had such servants, my dominions would extend from sea to sea." In this respect all the Reformers were true successors of the Apostles. They were poor, but made many rich.

Calvin had defects which were partly the shadow of his virtues. He was passionate, prone to anger, censorious, impatient of contradiction, intolerant towards Romanists and heretics, somewhat austere and morose, and not without a trace of vindictiveness. He confessed in a letter to Bucer, and on his death-bed, that he found it difficult to tame "the wild beast of his wrath," and he humbly asked forgiveness for his weakness. He thanked the senators for their patience with his often "excessive vehemence." His intolerance sprang from the intensity of his convictions and his zeal for the truth. It unfortunately culminated in the tragedy of Servetus, which must be deplored and condemned, although justified by the laws and the public opinion in his age. Tolerance is a modern virtue.

Calvin used frequently contemptuous and uncharitable language against his opponents in his polemical writings,

---

[1] This incident is related by Drelincourt, Bungener, and others, and believed in Geneva.

which cannot be defended, but he never condescended to coarse and vulgar abuse, like so many of his contemporaries.[1]

He has often been charged with coldness and want of domestic and social affection, but very unjustly. The chapter on his marriage and home life, and his letters on the death of his wife and only child show the contrary.[2] The charge is a mistaken inference from his gloomy doctrine of eternal reprobation; but this was repulsive to his own feelings, else he would not have called it "a horrible decree." Experience teaches that even at this day the severest Calvinism is not seldom found connected with a sweet and amiable Christian temper. He was grave, dignified, and reserved, and kept strangers at a respectful distance; but he was, as Beza observes, cheerful in society and tolerant of those vices which spring from the natural infirmity of men. He treated his friends as his equals, with courtesy and manly frankness, but also with affectionate kindness. And they all bear testimony to this fact, and were as true and devoted to him as he was to them. The French martyrs wrote to him letters of gratitude for having fortified them to endure prison and torture with patience and resignation.[3] "He obtained," says Guizot, "the devoted affection of the best men and the esteem of all, without ever seeking to please them." "He possessed," says Tweedie, "the secret and inexplicable power of binding men to him by ties that nothing but sin or death could sever. They treasured up every word that dropped from his lips."

Among his most faithful friends were many of the best men and women of his age, of different character and disposition, such as Farel, Viret, Beza, Bucer, Grynæus, Bullinger, Knox, Melanchthon, Queen Marguerite, and the Duchess

---

[1] Comp. above, § 118, p. 595.

[2] See above, § 92, pp. 413–424.

[3] Michelet (XI. 95): "*Les martyrs, à leur dernier jour, se faisaient une consolation, un devoir d'écrire à Calvin. Ils n'auraient pas quitté la vie sans remercier celui dont la parole les avait menés à la mort. Leurs lettres, respectueuses, nobles et douces, arrachant les larmes.*"

Renée. His large correspondence is a noble monument to
his heart as well as his intellect, and is a sufficient refutation of all calumnies. How tender is his reference to his departed friend Melanchthon, notwithstanding their difference
of opinion on predestination and free-will : " It is to thee, I
appeal, who now livest with Christ in the bosom of God,
where thou waitest for us till we be gathered with thee to
a holy rest. A hundred times hast thou said, when, wearied
with thy labors and oppressed by thy troubles, thou reposedst
thy head familiarly on my breast, ' Would that I could die
in this bosom ! ' Since then I have a thousand times wished
that it had happened to us to be together." How noble is his
admonition to Bullinger, when Luther made his last furious
attack upon the Zwinglians and the Zürichers (1544), not to
forget " how great a man Luther is and by what extraordinary gifts he excels." And how touching is his farewell
letter to his old friend Farel (May 2, 1564) : " Farewell, my
best and truest brother ! And since it is God's will that you
should survive me in this world, live mindful of our friendship, of which, as it was useful to the Church of God, the
fruits await us in heaven. Pray, do not fatigue yourself on
my account. It is with difficulty that I draw my breath, and
I expect that every moment will be my last. It is enough
that I live and die for Christ, who is the reward of his followers both in life and in death. Again, farewell, with the
brethren."

Calvin has also unjustly been charged with insensibility to
the beauties of nature and art. It is true we seek in vain for
specific allusions to the earthly paradise in which he lived, —
the lovely shores of Lake Leman, the murmur of the Rhone,
the snowy grandeur of the monarch of mountains in Cha-
mounix. But the writings of the other Reformers are equally
bare of such allusions, and the beauties of Switzerland were
not properly appreciated till towards the close of the eighteenth century, when Haller, Goethe, and Schiller directed

attention to them. Calvin, however, had a lively sense of the wonders of creation and expressed it more than once. "Let us not disdain," he says, "to receive a pious delight from the works of God, which everywhere present themselves to view in this very beautiful theatre of the world"; and he points out that "God has wonderfully adorned heaven and earth with the utmost possible abundance, variety, and beauty, like a large and splendid mansion, most exquisitely and copiously furnished, and exhibited in man the master-piece of his works by distinguishing him with such splendid beauty and such numerous and great privileges." [1]

He had a taste for music and poetry, like Luther and Zwingli. He introduced, in Strassburg and Geneva, congregational singing, which he described as "an excellent method of kindling the heart and making it burn with great ardor in prayer," and which has ever since been a most important part of worship in the Reformed Churches. He composed also a few poetic versifications of Psalms, and a sweet hymn to the Saviour, to whose service and glory his whole life was consecrated.

NOTE.

Calvin's "*Salutation à Iésus Christ*" was discovered by Felix Bovet of Neuchâtel in an old Genevese prayer-book of 1545 (Calvin's Liturgy), and published, together with eleven other poems (mostly translations of Psalms), by the Strassburg editors of Calvin's works in 1867. (See vol. VI. 223 and Prolegg. XVIII. sq.) It reveals a poetic vein and a devotional fervor and tenderness which one could hardly expect from so severe a logician and polemic. A German translation was made by Dr. E. Stähelin of Basel, and an English translation by Mrs. Henry B. Smith of New York, and published in Schaff's *Christ in Song*, 1868. ("I greet Thee, who my sure

---

[1] *Institutes*, bk. I. ch. XIV. 20. This whole chapter on Creation is replete with admiration for the beauty and order of God's universe. "Were I desirous," he says (21), "of pursuing the subject to its full extent, there would be no end; since there are as many miracles of divine power, as many monuments of divine goodness, as many proofs of divine wisdom as there are species of things in the world, and even as there are individual things either great or small."

Redeemer art." New York ed. p. 678; London ed. p. 549.) We give it here in the original old French: —

> " *Ie te salue, mon certain Redempteur,*
>   *Ma vraye fianc' et mon seul Salvateur,*
>   *Qui tant de labeur,*
>   *D'ennuys et de douleur*
>   *As enduré pour moy :*
>   *Oste de noz cueurs*
>   *Toutes vaines langueurs,*
>   *Fol soucy et esmoy.*

> " *Tu es le Roy misericordieux;*
>   *Puissant par tout et regnant en tous lieux;*
>   *Vueille donc regner*
>   *En nous, et dominer*
>   *Sur nous entierement,*
>   *Nous illuminer,*
>   *Ravyr et nous mener*
>   *A ton haut Firmament.*

> " *Tu es la vie par laquelle vivons,*
>   *Toute sustanc' et toute forc' avons :*
>   *Donne nous confort*
>   *Contre la dure mort,*
>   *Que ne la craignons point,*
>   *Et sans desconfort*
>   *La passons d'un cueur fort*
>   *Quand ce viendra au point.*

> " *Tu es la vraye et parfaite douceur,*
>   *Sans amertume, despit ne rigueur :*
>   *Fay nous savourer,*
>   *Aymer et adorer,*
>   *Ta tresdouce bonté;*
>   *Fay nous desirer,*
>   *Et tousiours demeurer*
>   *En ta douce unité.*

> " *Nostre esperanc' en autre n'est qu'en toy,*
>   *Sur ta promesse est fondée nostre foy :*
>   *Vueilles augmenter,*
>   *Ayder et conforter*
>   *Nostre espoir tellement,*
>   *Que bien surmonter*
>   *Nous puissions, et porter*
>   *Tout mal patiemment.*

" *A toy cryons comme povres banys,*
 Enfans d'Eve pleins de maux infinis :
 A toy souspirons,
 Gemissons et plorons,
 En la vallée de plours ;
 Pardon requerons
 Et salut desirons,
 Nous confessans pecheurs.

" *Or avant donq, nostre Mediateur,*
 Nostre advocat et propiciateur,
 Tourne tes doux yeux
 Icy en ces bas lieux,
 Et nous vueille monstrer
 Le haut Dieu des Dieux,
 Et aveq toy 'és cieux
 Nous faire tous entrer.

" *O debonnair', o pitoyabl' et doux,*
 Des ames saintes amyabl' espoux,
 Seigneur Iesus Christ,
 Encontre L'antechrist
 Remply de cruauté,
 Donne nous L'esprit
 De suyvir ton escript
 En vraye verité."

CHAPTER XIX.

THEODORE BEZA.

Sources: BEZA's Correspondence, mostly unprinted, but many letters are given in the *Beilagen zu* BAUM's *Theodor Beza* (see below), and in HERMINJARD's *Correspondance des réformateurs dans les pays de langue française* (vols. VI. sqq.); and his published works (the list to the number of ninety is given in the article "Bèze, Théodore de," in HAAG, *La France Protestante*, 2d ed. by Bordier, vol. II., cols. 520–540). By far the most important· of them are, his *Vita J. Calvini*, best ed. in Calvin's *Opera*, XXI., and his *Tractationes theologicæ* (1582). He also had much to do with the *Histoire ecclésiastique des églises réformées au royaume de France*, best ed. by Baum, Cunitz, and Rodolphe Reuss (the son of Edward Reuss, the editor of Calvin), Paris, 1883–1889. 3 vols. small quarto.

ANTOINE DE LA FAYE: *De vita et obitu Th. Bezæ*, Geneva, 1606. — FRIEDRICH CHRISTOPH SCHLOSSER: *Leben des Theodor de Beza und des Peter Martyr Vermili*, Heidelberg, 1809. — *JOHANN WILHELM BAUM: *Theodor Beza nach handschriftlichen Quellen dargestellt*, Leipzig, I. Theil, 1843, with *Beilagen* to bks. I. and II. II. Theil, 1851, with *Anhang die Beilagen enthaltend*, 1852 (unfortunately this masterly book only extends to 1563). — *HEINRICH HEPPE: *Theodor Beza. Leben und ausgewählte Schriften*, Elberfeld, 1861 (contains the whole life, but is inferior in style to Baum). — Art. *Beza* by BORDIER in *La France Protestante*.

JÉROME BOLSEC: *Histoire de la vie, mœurs, doctrine, et déportements de Théodore de Bèze*, Paris, 1582; republished by an unnamed Roman Catholic in Geneva, 1835, along with Bolsec's "Life of Calvin," to counteract the effect of the celebration of the third centennial of the Reformation. It has no historical value, but is a malignant libel, like his so-called "Life of Calvin," as this specimen shows: "*Bèze, toute sa jeunesse, a été un très-débauché et dissolu, sodomite, adultère et suborneur de femmes mariées* [Bolsec elsewhere asserts that Claudine Denosse was married when Beza seduced her], *larron, trompeur, homicide de sa propre géniture, traître, vanteur, cause et instigateur d'infinis meurtres, guerres, invasions, brûlemens de villes, palais et maisons; de saccagemens de temples, et infinies autres ruines et malheurs*" (ed. 1835, p. 188).

Much use has been made of the allusions to Beza in HENRY M. BAIRD's *Rise of the Huguenots* (New York, 1879), and *Huguenots and Henry of Navarre* (1886), also of the article on "Bèze, Theodore de," in Haag, *La France*

Protestante, mentioned above. See also Principal CUNNINGHAM: *The Reformers*, Edinburgh, 1862; "Calvin and Beza," pp. 345–413 (theological and controversial).

§ 167. *Life of Beza to his Conversion.*

THE history of the Swiss Reformation would not be complete without an account of Calvin's faithful friend and successor, Theodore Beza, who carried on his work in Geneva and France to the beginning of the seventeenth century.

In the ancient duchy of Burgundy is the village of Vezelay. It was once the scene of a great gathering, for to it in 1146 came Louis VII. and his vassals, to whom Bernard preached the duty of rescuing the Holy Sepulchre from the infidels so convincingly, that the king and his knights then and there took the oath to become crusaders. Four and forty years later (1190), in the same place, Philip Augustus of France and Richard the Lionheart of England, under similar pleadings, made the same vow.

The village clusters around the castle in which, in 1519, lived the rich Pierre de Besze,[1] the bailiff of the county, a descendant of one of the proudest families of the duchy. His wife was Marie Bourdelot, beloved and renowned for her intelligence and her charities. They had already two sons and four daughters, when on the 24th of June in that year, 1519, another son was born who was destined to render the name illustrious to the end of time. This son was christened Theodore. Thus the future reformer was of gentle birth — a fact which was recognized when in after years he pleaded for the Protestant faith before kings, and princes, and members of the nobility and of the fashionable world.

But the providential preparation for the part he was destined to play extended far beyond the conditions of his birth.

---

[1] This was the old spelling as appears from Beza's signature. The modern French spell it *Bèze*, the English and Germans *Beza*, which is the Latin form.

Geneue, ce 12 de May, 1571

Th. de Beze

Gentle breeding followed. His mother died when he was not quite three years old, but already was he a stranger to his father's house; for one of his uncles, Nicolas de Besze, seigneur de Cette et de Chalonne, and a councillor in the Parliament of Paris, had taken him with him to Paris and adopted him, so great was the love he bore him, and when the time came he was put under the best masters whom money and influence could secure. The boy was precocious, and his uncle delighted in his progress. One day at table he entertained a guest from Orleans, who was a member of the royal council. The conversation turned upon the future of Theodore, whereupon the friend commended Melchior Wolmar, the famous Greek scholar at Orleans, who was also the teacher of Calvin, as the best person to educate the lad. The uncle listened attentively, and sent Theodore thither and secured him admission into Wolmar's family. This was in 1528, when Theodore was only nine years old. With Wolmar he lived till 1535, first at Orleans and then at Bourges, and doubtless learned much from him. Part of this learning was not at all to the mind of his father or his uncle Claudius, the Abbot of the Cistercian monastery of Froimont in the diocese of Beauvais, who, on the death of his brother Nicolas, on Nov. 29, 1532, had undertaken the pious duty of superintending the boy's education; for Wolmar, in common with many sober-minded scholars of that day, had broken with the Roman Church and taken up the new ideas inculcated by Luther, and which were beginning to make a stir in France. Indeed, it was his known adherence to these views which compelled his flight to Germany in the year 1535. Thus the future reformer, in his tenderest and most susceptible years, had impressed upon him the doctrine of justification by faith in the righteousness of Christ, heard much of the corrupt state of the dominant Church, and was witness to the efforts of that Church to put to death those who differed from her teaching.

Nothing was further from the mind of the father and

uncle, and also from that of Theodore himself, than that he
should be an advocate of the new views. The career marked
out for him was that of law, in which his uncle Nicolas
had been so distinguished. To this end he was sent to the
University of Orleans. Although very young, he attracted
attention. He joined the German nation — for the students
in universities then were divided into factions, according
to their ancestry, and Burgundy was accounted part of Germany — and rapidly became a favorite. But he did not give
himself up to mere good-fellowship. He studied hard, and
on Aug. 11, 1539, attained with honor the degree of licentiate
of the law.

His education being thus advanced, Beza, now twenty
years old, came to Paris, there, as his father desired, to
prosecute further law studies; but his reluctance to such
a course was pronounced and invincible, so much so that
at length he won his uncle to his side, and was allowed by
his father to pursue those literary studies which afterwards
accrued so richly to the Reformed Church; but at the time
he had no inkling of his subsequent career. By his uncle
Claudius' influence the possessor of two benefices which
yielded a handsome income, and enriched further by his
brother's death in 1541, well-introduced and well-connected,
a scholar, a wit, a poet, handsome, affable, amiable, he lived
on equal terms with the best Parisian society, and was one
of the acknowledged leaders.[1]

---

[1] The Jesuit Maimbourg, a declared enemy, in his *Histoire du Calvinisme*
(Paris,.1682, 18mo, p. 217), has thus described him at this time: *"Homme bien
fait, de belle taille, ayant le visage fort agréable, l'air fin et délicat, et toutes les
manières d'un homme du monde qui le faisoient estimer des Grands et surtout des
dames, ausquelles il prenoit grand soin de ne pas déplaire. Pour l'esprit, on ne
peut nier qu'il ne l'eust très-beau, vif, aisé, subtil, enjoûé et poli, ayant pris peine
de le cultiver par l'étude des belles lettres, et particulièrement de la poësie, où il excel-
loit en françois et en latin, sçachant avec cela un peu de philosophie et de droit qu'il
avoit appris aux écoles d'Orléans."* "He was well made, of good size, having
a very agreeable countenance, a refined and delicate air, and the carriage of
a man of the world, who had won the esteem of the great, and especially

That he did not escape contamination he has himself confessed, but that he sinned grossly he has as plainly denied.[1] In 1544 he made in the presence of two friends, Laurent de Normandie and Jean Crespin, eminent jurists, an irregular alliance with Claudine Denosse,[2] a burgher's daughter, and at the time declared that when circumstances favored he would publicly marry her.   His motive in making a secret marriage was his desire to hold on to his benefices. But he was really attached to the woman, and was faithful to her, as she was to him; and there was nothing in their relationship which would have seriously compromised him with the company in which he lived.   The fact that they lived together happily for forty years shows that they followed the leading of sincere affection, and not a passing fancy.   In 1548 he published his famous collection of poems — *Juvenilia*.   This gave him the rank of the first Latin poet of his day, and his ears were full of praises.   He dedicated his book to Wolmar. It did not occur to him that anybody would ever censure him for his poems, least of all on moral grounds; but this is precisely what happened.   Prurient minds have read between his lines what he never intended to put there, and imagined offences of which he was not guilty even in thought.[3]   And what made the case blacker against him was his subsequent Protestantism.   Because he became a leader of the Reformed Church, free-thinkers and livers and the adherents of the old faith have brought up against him the fact that in the days of his worldly and luxurious life he had used their language, and been as pagan and impure as they.

of the ladies, whom he took much pains not to displease. It cannot be denied that he was very attractive, lively, easy, subtle, playful, and polished, having cultivated his mind by reading literature, particularly poetry, wherein he himself excelled both in French and Latin, mingling with it a little philosophy and law which he had taken in at Orleans."

[1] Baum, I. 60–63.

[2] Anciently spelled Desnosze.

[3] Thus they have taken the characters mentioned in them as actual, whereas they are purely imaginary.

The book had scarcely begun its career, and the praises had scarcely begun to be received, ere Beza fell seriously sick. Sobered by his gaze into the eyes of death, his conscience rebuked him for his duplicity in receiving ecclesiastical benefices as if he was a faithful son of the Church, whereas he was at heart a Protestant; for his cowardice in cloaking his real opinions; for his negligence in not keeping the promise he had voluntarily made to the woman he had secretly married four years before; and for the general condition of his private and public life. The teachings of Wolmar came back to him. This world seemed very hollow; its praises and honors very cloying. The call to a higher, purer, nobler life was heard, and he obeyed; and, although only convalescent, leaving father and fatherland, riches and honors, he fled from the city of his triumphs and his trials, and, taking Claudine Denosse with him, crossed the border into Switzerland,[1] and on Oct. 23, 1548, entered the city of Geneva. He was doubtless attracted thither because his intimate friend Jean Crespin, one of the witnesses of his secret alliance, was living there, likewise a fugitive for religion's sake — and there lived John Calvin.

From being the poet of the Renaissance, bright, witty, free, Beza, from the hour he joined the Reformed Church, became a leader in all its affairs and one of the chiefs of Protestantism.[2]

*§ 168. *Beza at Lausanne and as a Delegate to the German Princes.*

Beza's earliest business after greeting Calvin was to marry in church Claudine Denosse. Then he looked around for

---

[1] He adopted the alias of Thibaud de May. So Heppe, p. 20.

[2] For having left France because he was a Protestant he was condemned by the Parliament of Paris to death, and all his property confiscated to the State (May 31, 1550). By special royal mandate his property was restored to him in 1564, although he was at the time at the head of the Reformed Church of France. *Cf.* Baum, I. 66 sq.

an occupation that would support him. He considered for a
time going into the printing business with Crespin, but on
his return from a visit to Wolmar at Tübingen he yielded to
the persuasions of Pierre Viret, who entertained him as he
was passing through Lausanne, and on Nov. 6, 1549, became
professor of Greek in the Academy there,[1] and entered upon
a course of great usefulness and influence. He showed his
zeal as well as biblical learning by giving public lectures on
the Epistle to the Romans and on the Epistles of Peter; and
that he still was a poet, and that, too, of the Renaissance,
only in the religious and not usual sense (of regeneration
and not renascence), by continuing the translation of the
Psalms begun by Clement Marot, and by publishing a drama,
classically constructed, on the Sacrifice of Abraham.[2] All
these performances were in the French language.

While at Lausanne, Beza was taken sick with the plague.
Calvin in writing of this to Farel, under date of June 15,
1551, thus pays his tribute to the character of Beza: "I would
not be a man if I did not return his love who loves me more
than a brother and reveres me as a father: but I am still
more concerned at the loss the church would suffer if in the
midst of his career he should be suddenly removed by death,
for I saw in him a man whose lovely spirit, noble, pure manners, and open-mindedness endeared him to all the righteous.
I hope, however, that he will be given back to us in answer
to our prayers."

Lausanne was then governed by Bern. It was therefore
particularly interested in Bern's alliance with Geneva, and
when this was renewed in 1557, after it had been suffered to
lapse a year, Beza considered it very providential. In the
spring of that year, 1557, persecution broke out against the
neighboring Waldenses, and on nomination of the German

---

[1] His colleague in the Latin chair was the distinguished François Hotman
(Latin, Hotomanus), who afterwards founded a law school at Geneva.

[2] It was performed by the students of the Lausanne academy and elsewhere
and translated into several languages.

clergy and with special permission of Bern, Beza, and Farel began a series of visits through Switzerland and upon the Protestant princes of Germany in the interest of the persecuted. The desire was to stir up the Protestants to unite in an appeal to the king of France. Beza was then thirty-eight years old and had been for eight years a successful teacher and preacher. He was therefore of mature years and established reputation. But what rendered the choice of him still more an ideal one was his aristocratic bearing and his familiarity with court life. He accepted his appointment with alacrity, as a man enters upon a course particularly suited to him. Thus Beza started out upon the first of the many journeys which furnished such unique and invaluable services to the cause of French Protestantism.

The two delegates made a favorable impression everywhere. The Lutherans especially were pleased with them, although at first inclined to look askance upon two such avowed admirers and followers of Calvin. But when they had returned full of rejoicing that they had accomplished their design and that the Protestant princes and cantons would unite in petitioning the French king on behalf of the persecuted Waldenses, albeit to small effect, alas! they were called to sharp account because at Göppingen on May 14, 1557, they had defined their doctrine of the Eucharist in terms which emphasized the points of agreement and passed by those of disagreement.[1] This was in the interest of peace. They rightly felt that it would be shameful to shipwreck their Christian attempt upon the shoals of barren controversy. But the *odium theologicum* compelled their home friends to charge them with disloyalty to the truth! Calvin, however, raised his voice in defence of Beza's conduct, and the strife of tongues quickly ceased.

How little Beza had suffered in general reputation, or at

---

[1] See the text in Baum, I. 405–409.

least in the eyes of the powerful Calvin, was almost immediately manifest.

On the evening of the 4th of September, 1557, three or four
hundred Protestants in Paris who had quietly assembled in
the Rue St. Jaques to celebrate the Lord's Supper were set
upon by a mob, and amid insults and injuries haled to prison.
Their fate deeply stirred the Protestants everywhere, and
Beza with some companions was again sent to the Protestant
cantons and princes to invoke their aid as before, and because
the princes were quicker at promising than performance he
went again the next year. But Henry II. paid small attention to the note of the Protestant powers.

§ 169. Beza at Geneva.

In 1558 the city of Geneva established a high school, and
Beza was called, at Calvin's suggestion, to the Greek professorship. Much to the regret of Viret and his colleagues, he
accepted. He was influenced by various considerations, the
chief of which were his desire to escape from the trouble
caused by Viret's establishment of the Genevan church discipline, which had led to a falling out with Bern, Lausanne's
ruler, and from the embarrassments still resulting from his
well-meant attempts at union among the Protestants, and
probably still more by his desire to labor at the side of Calvin,
whom he so greatly revered and whose doctrines he so vigorously and honestly defended. He was honorably dismissed
to Geneva and warmly commended to the confidence of the
brethren there. When on June 5, 1559, the Academy was
opened, he was installed as rector. Thus, in his fortieth year,
he entered upon his final place of residence and upon his
final labors. Henceforward he was inseparable from the
work of Calvin, and however far and frequently he might
go from Geneva, it was there that he left his heart.

On Calvin's nomination, Beza was admitted to citizenship
at Geneva, and shortly afterwards (March 17, 1559) he suc-

ceeded to the pastorate of one of the city churches.[1] But each new labor imposed upon him only demonstrated his capacity and zeal. The Academy and the congregation flourished under his assiduous care, and Calvin found his new ally simply invaluable. There was soon a fresh call upon his diplomacy. Anne du Bourg, president of the Parliament of Paris, boldly avowed his Protestantism before Henry II., and was arrested. When the news reached Calvin, he despatched Beza to the Elector Palatine, Frederick III., to interest this powerful prince. The result of his mission was a call on Du Bourg from the Elector to become professor of law in his university at Heidelberg. But the intervention availed nothing. Du Bourg was tried, and executed Dec. 23, 1559.

Shortly after his return, Beza was sent forth again, July 20, 1560. The occasion was, however, quite different. The Prince de Condé, shorn of his power by the Guises, had fled to Nérac. He desired to attach to the Protestant party his brother, Antoine de Bourbon-Vendôme, king of Navarre. Calvin had already, by letter, made some impression on the irresolute and fickle king, but Condé induced his brother to send for Beza, who, with his eloquence and his courtly bearing, quite captivated the king, who declared that he would never hear the mass again, but would do all he could to advance the Protestant cause. His zeal was, however, of very short duration; for no sooner did his brother, the cardinal of Bourbon, arrive, than he and his queen, Jeanne d'Albret, who afterwards was a sincere convert to Protestantism, heard mass in the convent of the Cordeliers at Nérac. Beza, seeing that Antoine would not hold out, but was certain to fall into the power of the Catholic party, quietly left him, Oct. 17, and after many dangers reached Geneva early in November. The journey had taken three weeks, and had, for the most part, to be performed at night.[2]

---

[1] Pierre Viret had followed him to Geneva, Jan. 13, 1559, and was one of his colleagues in ecclesiastical service.

[2] Baum, II. 122. Unfortunately Beza's account of it is lost.

§ 170.   *Beza at the Colloquy of Poissy.*[1]

Beza was now considered by all the French Reformed as their most distinguished orator, and next to Calvin their most celebrated theologian.   This commanding position he had attained by many able services.   When, therefore, the queen-mother Catherine determined to hold a discussion between the French prelates and the most learned Protestant ministers, the Parisian pastors, seconded by the Prince of Condé, the Admiral Coligny, and the king of Navarre, implored Beza to come, and to him was committed the leadership.   At first he declined.   But in answer to renewed and more urgent appeals he came, and on Aug. 22, 1561, he was again in Paris, for the first time since his precipitate flight, in October, 1548 — thirteen years before.   The preliminary meeting was in the famous château of St. Germain-en-Laye, on the Seine, a few miles below Paris.   There, on Aug. 23, he made his appearance.   On the evening of that day he was summoned to the apartments of the king of Navarre, and in the presence of the queen-mother and other persons of the highest rank, he had his first encounter in debate with Cardinal Lorraine. The subject was transubstantiation.   The Cardinal was no match for Beza, and after a weak defence, yielded the floor, saying that the doctrine should not stand in the way of a reconciliation.   On Tuesday, Sept. 9, 1561, the parties to the Colloquy assembled in the nuns' refectory at Poissy, some three miles away.   It was soon evident that there was not to be any real debate.   The Catholic party had all the advantages and acted as sole judges.[2]   It was a foregone

---

[1] Baum, II. 168–419, Heppe, 104–148, Baird (*Rise of the Huguenots*), I. 493–577, give full, accurate, and interesting accounts of the famous Colloquy of Poissy, to which the reader is referred.   Only the briefest mention can be made in this place.

[2] The entirely proper request of the Protestants that the bishops should not be at the same time parties and judges, that the questions in debate should be decided solely by the Word of God in the originals, and that the minutes

conclusion that the verdict was to be given to the Catholic party, whatever the arguments might be. Nevertheless, Beza and his associates went through the form of a debate, and courageously held their ground. In characteristic fashion they first knelt, and Beza prayed, commencing his prayer with the confession of sins used in the Genevan liturgy of Calvin. He then addressed the assembly upon the points of agreement and of disagreement between them, and was quietly listened to until he made the assertion that the Body of Christ was as far removed from the bread of the Eucharist as the heavens are from the earth. Then the prelates broke out with the cry "*Blasphemavit! blasphemavit!*" ("he has blasphemed"), and for a while there was much confusion. Beza had followed the obnoxious expression with a remark which was intended to break its force, affirming the spiritual presence of Christ in the Eucharist; but the noise had prevented its being heard. Instead, however, of yielding to the clamor the queen-mother insisted that Beza should be heard out, and he finished his speech. The Huguenots claimed the victory, but the Roman Catholics spread the story that they had been easily and decidedly beaten. The prelates requested the points in writing, and it was not till Sept. 16 that they made a reply. The Cardinal of Lorraine was the spokesman. No opportunity was given the Protestants to rejoin, as they were ready to do at once.

On Sept. 24 a third conference was held, but in the small chamber of the prioress, not in the large refectory, and a fourth in the same place on Sept. 26. But the Colloquy had degenerated into a rambling debate, and its utterly unprofitable character was manifest to all. The queen-mother did, it is

should not be accepted unless signed by the secretary on each side, had been refused. With studied indignity the Protestant ministers, who numbered twelve, all distinguished men, were required to appear as culprits brought to the bar, for they were separated by a railing from the prelates and courtiers.

true, flatter herself that there might be an agreement, and
zealously labored to produce it. But in vain. Her expectation really showed how shallow were her religious ideas.

Beza stayed at St. Germain until the beginning of November,[1] and then, worn out, and threatened with a serious illness, he sought rest in Paris. There he had a visit from his
oldest step-brother, and also a pressing and affectionate letter
from his father, who had learned to what honor his son had
come, forgave him for his persistence in heresy, and expressed
a great desire to see him. Beza started for Vezelay, but on
the way met a courier with the intelligence that the Protestants required his instant attendance to help them at a
crisis in their affairs, because acts of violence against them
had taken place in all parts of France. And Beza, ever sub-
ordinating private to public duties, turned back to Paris,
and no further opportunity of seeing his father ever came to
him.[2]

§ 171. *Beza as the Counsellor of the Huguenot Leaders.*

On the 20th of December an assembly of notables, including representatives from each of the parliaments, the princes
of the blood, and members of the Council, had been called
to suggest some decree of at least a provisional nature
upon the religious question. It was January, 1562, before
it convened. It enacted on Jan. 17 the famous law known
as the "Edict of January," whereby the Huguenots were
recognized as having certain rights, chief of which was
that of assembling for worship by day outside of the walled
cities.[3] The churches which they had seized were, however,
not restored to them, and they were forbidden to build
others.

---

[1] His leave of absence from Geneva had been much extended in answer to
the request of the king of Navarre, Condé, and Coligny. Heppe, 161.

[2] *Cf.* the touching account of these events in Heppe, 158–61.

[3] Baird, I. 576 sq.

Beza counselled the Protestants to accept the edict, although it gave them very much less than their rights; and they obeyed.

On Jan. 27, 1562, he was again at St. Germain by command of Catherine, to argue with Catholic theologians upon the use of images and the worship of saints. As before, the gulf between Protestants and Roman Catholics stood revealed, and the conference did no good except to show that the Protestants had some reason, at all events, for their opinions. Yet they did entertain hopes of maintaining the peace, when the news that on March 1 the Duke of Guise had massacred hundreds of defenceless Protestants, in a barn at Vassy, while engaged in peaceful worship, spread consternation far and wide. The court was then at Monceaux, and there Beza appeared as deputy of the Protestants of Paris to demand of the king of Navarre punishment for this odious violation of the Edict of January. The queen-mother received the demand graciously and promised compliance, but the king responded roughly and laid all the blame on the Protestants, who, he declared, had excited the attack by throwing stones at the Duke of Guise. "Well then," said Beza, "he should have punished only those who did the throwing." And then he added these memorable words: "Sire, it is in truth the lot of the Church of God, in whose name I am speaking, to endure blows, and not to strike them. But also may it please you to remember that it is an anvil that has worn out many hammers." [1]

Civil war now broke out, Condé on one side and the Guises on the other; and Beza, although so unwilling, was fairly involved in it.

In a lull in the strife the third national Synod of the

---

[1] "*Sire, c'est à la vérité à l'Église de Dieu, au nom de laquelle je parle, d'endurer les coups, et non pas d'en donner. Mais aussi vous plaira-t-il vous souvenir que c'est une enclume qui a usé beaucoup de marteaux.*" Quoted by Baird, II. 28; cf. Baum, II. 567.

Reformed Church was held at Orleans on April 25. Beza was present, and his translation of the Psalms was sung upon the streets.

On May 20, 1562, the Prince of Condé sent a memorable answer to the petition of the Guises that King Charles would take active measures to extirpate heresy in his domains. The reply was really the work of Beza, and is a masterpiece of argument and eloquence.[1]

The necessity of securing allies induced Condé to send Beza to Germany and Switzerland. He went first to Strassburg, then to Basel, and at length on Friday, Sept. 4, he arrived at Geneva. How earnest must have been the conversations between him and Calvin! How glad must his many friends have been to welcome back home the leader of French Protestantism!

Beza resumed his former mode of life. Two weeks passed and he had just begun to feel himself able in peace to carry out his plans for the Academy and the Genevan churches, when a messenger riding post haste from D'Andelot, a brother of Coligny, and his fellow-deputy to the German princes, announced the fresh outbreak of trouble in France. Beza was at first inclined to stay at home, mistrusting the necessity of his presence among the Huguenot troops, but Calvin urged him to go, and so he went, and for the next seven months Beza was with the Huguenot army. He acted as almoner and treasurer. He followed Condé to the battle of Dreux, Dec. 19, 1562, at which Condé was taken prisoner. It was made a matter of reproach that he took an active part in the battle. He did indeed ride in the front rank, but he denied that he struck a blow. He was in citizen's dress. He then retired to Normandy with Coligny. The expected help from England did not arrive, and it was determined to send him to

---

[1] Baum says (II. 642) that it may with confidence be placed by the side of the most eloquent passages in the French language. A judgment in which Baird (II. 61) concurs.

London. So utterly sick was Beza of the military life that he seriously meditated going directly back to Geneva from London. But the Pacification Edict of March 12, 1563, freed Condé and ended hostilities, and Beza did not make his contemplated English journey.

This unexpected turn in his affairs was brought about by an untoward event. On the 18th of February, 1563, the Duke of Guise was assassinated by a poor fanatical Huguenot wretch, who, under torture, accused Beza of having instigated him by promising him Paradise and a high place among the saints if he died for his deed.[1] The calumny was afterwards denied by the man who had made it, but Beza considered himself obligated to make a formal reply. He called upon all who had heard him to declare if he had ever favored any other than strictly legal measures against the late Duke. And as for his alleged promise, he said that he was too good a Bible student to declare that any one could win Paradise by works.[2]

Peace having come, Beza was at liberty to return home. But his heart was heavy because the affairs in France were in a very unsatisfactory condition. Still, there was nothing to be accomplished by staying, and so, loaded down with thanks and praises from the leading Huguenots for his invaluable services in the field, in the camp, at the council-board, and in the religious assembly, surrounded with the leaders of the Huguenot army and the preachers and nobles, amid shouts and sighs, Beza, on Tuesday, March 30, 1563, took his departure from Orleans. On the Sunday before, he had preached his farewell sermon, in which he expressed his disappointment that the Edict of Pacification had brought the Huguenots so little advantage.[3]

On his way back he passed through Vezelay. His father

---

[1] Baum, II. 711; Baird, II. 105.
[2] Baum, II. 714, 716.
[3] Baird, II. 118.

was dead, but there must have been many associations of childhood which endeared the place to him. Here he learned that his wife was safe at Strassburg with Condé's mother-in-law. Bending his steps thither, he rejoined her, and together they made the journey home, where they arrived May 5, 1563.[1]

As they journeyed they knew that they were in perpetual danger, but they did not know that some of their enemies were looking for them to turn towards the Netherlands. But so it was. In June of that year a rumor was circulated at Brussels that there had been a quarrel between him and Calvin, and that in consequence he would not return to Geneva. Margaret of Parma, then regent of the Netherlands, thought to do a splendid deed, and gave orders that if he entered her domains he was to be taken, dead or alive, and offered to his capturer or murderer a thousand florins. But there having been no such break, Beza, on the contrary, took the shortest practicable route for Geneva.[2]

§ 172. *Beza as the Successor of Calvin, down to* 1586.

Beza received his warmest welcome from Calvin, who was already under the shadow of death. There was no one else

---

[1] Referring to the entire length of service in France, Baum says: "He had been absent twenty-two months. They were the most wearing and the most perilous, but also the most fruitful months in his life. For during that period, with courage and dignity, with learning and acuteness, with penetrating force and charming eloquence, he had before princes and kings preached the gospel and exalted the name of Christ. As the representation in this work has abundantly shown, amid incessant struggles against unwise or faint-hearted friends, against cunning and powerful foes, many times and most daringly at the risk of his own life, he developed into one of the great leaders who procured for the Reformed Church of France its soul-liberty, which, though, it is true, less than it claimed should have been given, was still secured to it by law." With these words Baum (II. 731) closes his authoritative but, alas, unfinished work upon Beza.

[2] Baird, II. 388. In the regent's proclamation, Beza was described as "*homme de moïenne stature, ayant barbe à demy blanche, et le visage hault et large.*"

whom the great Reformer could so confidentially take into his counsels. And as the time of his departure drew near, he relied more and more upon him. Their friendship was based upon respect and affection and was never disturbed. The relation of the two men resembled that between Zwingli and Bullinger, and was most useful to the Church.

It was of course perfectly understood by Beza that he was to be Calvin's successor, so the year which passed before Calvin died was a year of preparation for the new duties. At last the time came, and Calvin passed away. Beza conducted the funeral, and shortly after wrote his classical life of his patron, friend, and predecessor. The city Council elected him Calvin's successor; the Venerable Company of Pastors, as the presbytery of Geneva called itself, elected him their moderator, and continued him in this office till 1580, when he compelled them to allow him to retire. So he continued Calvin's leadership in city and church affairs. He preached and lectured to the students. He received the fugitives from France, and the visitors from other lands. He gave his advice and opinion upon the innumerable things which turned up daily. He conducted an enormous correspondence. And every now and then he had to enter the field of controversy and repel "heretics," like Ochino and Castellio, or Lutherans like Andreä and Selnecker.

Nor could this leadership have fallen into better hands. For Beza, although inferior to Calvin in theological acquirements and acumen, was his superior in knowledge and experience of court life and in grace of manner. He was eminently fitted to be the host of the Protestant scholars and martyrs, who flocked or fled to Geneva from every quarter. And so the theological school became under him the most famous of its kind in the world, and the little republican city was the virtual capital of Continental Protestantism.

Incessantly occupied as he was by public affairs, but bearing his burdens with courage and faith, he was suddenly called upon to transact delicate business of a private nature. In 1568 the plague entered Geneva and carried off his step-brother Nicolas,[1] who had succeeded his father as bailiff of Vezelay, joined the Huguenots, and come as a fugitive to Geneva with his wife, Perrette Tribolé, when Vezelay fell into Roman Catholic hands. He had been only a few days in the city when he died. Beza felt it incumbent upon him to go to Burgundy to see whether he could not save at least a part of their inheritance for his two nephews; and this errand, after a great deal of trouble, he accomplished successfully.

In 1571, after an absence of some eight years, he was again summoned to France, this time by Coligny and the young Prince de Béarn, to attend the seventh national Synod of the Reformed Church of France convened in La Rochelle. The Venerable Company of Pastors would not part with him without a protest, but yielded to the express wish of the Syndics of the Republic. Beza himself was reluctant to go, and indeed had declined a previous summons; but the crisis demanded an authoritative expression of the views of the Swiss Churches upon the proposed reforms in the discipline of the Church, and so he went. The Synod lasted from the 2d to the 17th of April. He was elected its moderator. A revised Confession of Faith was drawn up, and a vigorous reply made to the demand for increased authority on the part of the temporal chiefs. On his way back to Geneva he took part in another Synod, held at Nismes, and was specially charged with the refutation of the opponents to the established discipline.

On St. Bartholomew's Day, Sunday, Aug. 24, 1572, very many Protestants were murdered in Paris, and for days thereafter the shocking scenes were repeated in different

---

[1] Also called by some *Pierre.*

parts of France.[1] On the 1st of September the first company of fugitives, many covered with wounds, made their appearance in Geneva. A day of fasting and prayer was ordered, and Beza exhorted his Swiss hearers to stand firm and to provide all needed help to their stricken brethren. Four thousand livres were collected in Geneva, and the wants of the crowd of sufferers attended to.[2]

In 1574 Beza met Henry of Condé by appointment at Strassburg, and successfully undertook the negotiations which resulted in enlisting John Casimir to come with an army to the succor of the Huguenots.

But Beza's advice was not always considered prudent by the city authorities, who were more alive than he to the great risk the city ran of reprisals in view of its connivance with the Huguenot schemes. Thus in December of this year, 1574, Beza countenanced a bootless military errand in the direction of Mâcon and Châlons, and the magistrates gently but firmly called him to account, and plainly told him that he should never act so imprudently.[3]

On Nov. 26, 1580, the Peace of Fleix brought rest to France for a little while. Beza showed his courage and fidelity on this occasion by writing to King Henry of Navarre, the Protestant leader, a letter in which he candidly informed the king that he himself and his court stood in great need of reformation. It is proof of the respect in which the Reformer was held that the king received the rebuke in good part, and of the king's light-mindedness that he did not attempt to reform.[4]

---

[1] The whole number of the massacred is reckoned at about thirty thousand. *Cf.* the monograph of Henri Bordier: *La Saint-Barthélemy et la critique moderne.* Genève et Paris, 1879.

[2] Heppe, 248. Baird (II. 554–557) gives a graphic description of the Genevese reception of the refugees, and shows how the city for so doing was exposed to the revenge of Charles IX.

[3] Baird, *The Huguenots and Henry of Navarre*, I. 50.

[4] Baird, *ibid.*, I. 213 sq.

§ 173. *Beza's Conferences with Lutherans.*

The bitter theological differences between Lutherans and
Reformed had long been a disgrace. Beza had in early life
brought trouble upon himself by minimizing them, as has
been already recorded, but in his old age he made one more
attempt in that direction. Count Frederick of Würtemberg,
a Lutheran, but a friend of reconciliation, called a conference
at Montbéliard (or Mömpelgard), a city in his domains in
which were many Huguenot refugees, with whom the Lutherans would not fraternize. The count hoped that a discussion
between the leaders on each side might mend matters.
Accordingly he summoned Beza, confessedly the ablest advocate of Calvinism. On March 21, 1586, the conference began.
It took a wide range, but it came to nothing. Beza showed
a beautiful spirit of reconciliation, but Andreä, the Lutheran
leader, in the very spirit of Luther at the famous Marburg
Conference with Zwingli (1529), refused to take Beza's hand
at parting (March 29).[1]

Undeterred by this churlish exhibition, Beza left Montbéliard for another round of visits at German courts to induce
them once more to plead with France to restore to the
Huguenots their rights of worship; for the Peace of Fleix
had not lasted long, and the country was again plunged in
the horrors of civil war.

The Montbéliard conference had an echo in the Bern
Colloquy of April 15th to 18th, 1588, in which Samuel
Huber, pastor at Burgdorf, near Bern, a notorious polemic,
and Beza represented the Lutheran and Calvinist parties,
respectively. It was Beza's last appearance as a public dis-
putant, and the hero of so many wordy battles once more

---

[1] Heppe, 287. Although he could not greet him as a brother, Andreä
kindly offered to give Beza his hand as a mark of his love toward him as a
fellow-man — a condescension which not unnaturally the Genevese reformer
at once declined. Baird, *ibid.*, I. 401.

carried off the palm. In fact, his victory was much more
decided than such contests were usually, as the Bernese
Council condemned Huber for misrepresenting Beza and
Calvinism generally.

Beza had left Geneva with a heavy heart because his faithful and beloved wife had just died, and when he returned,
found public matters in a critical condition. The magistrates
had felt themselves compelled by the condition of the city
treasury to economize as much as possible, and had dismissed
two of the professors in the Academy, and contemplated other
retrenchments. Beza knew that these extreme measures
would probably greatly cripple the institution, and so, old as
he was, and failing, he undertook to give a full course of
instruction in theology, and persisted with it for more than
two years, — until the crisis was passed, — and for these extra
duties he would not take any compensation.

§ 174. *Beza and Henry IV.*

In the course of his long life Beza had few joys, aside from
the abiding one of his religion, and many sorrows. His heart
was bound up with the fortunes of the Reformed Church in
France, and they were usually bad. Still he took courage
every time a little improvement was noticeable. Much hope
had he cherished in consequence of the accession of Henry of
Navarre (1589), because he was a Protestant. But early in
the summer of 1593, the news reached Geneva that the king,
upon whom religion and morality sat very lightly, in the
interests of peace and national prosperity, was determined to
abjure the Protestant faith. Alas for all their hopes! Beza
was greatly moved, and addressed the monarch a letter in
which he set forth the éternal consequences of the change
the king was about to make.[1] He felt assured, however, that
Henry would be delivered from the machinations of his and
their enemies, and not take the fatal step. But ere Beza's

[1] See the letter in Heppe, 294–299.

letter reached him the deed was done. In the ancient abbey church at St. Denis on the morning of Sunday, July 25, 1593, King Henry of Navarre, the son of Jeanne d'Albret, the only Huguenot who ever sat upon the throne of France, abjured his faith, and took a solemn oath to protect the Roman, Catholic, and Apostolic religion.

Beza was deeply grieved at this apostasy. But when he learned that the king favored his old co-religionists in many ways, and especially, when in 1598, he published the Edict of Nantes, which put the Protestants on a nearly common footing with the Roman Catholics in France, Beza took a more hopeful view of the king's condition. In 1599 the king, in the course of a war with Charles Emmanuel, approached near Geneva. The city saw in this a chance to obtain from the king the promise of his protection, especially against the Duke of Savoy, who had built a fort called St. Catherine, quite near Geneva. To effect this the city sent a delegation headed by Beza, and the interview between the monarch and the reformer was honorable to both. The king gladly gave his promise, and the next year the fort was destroyed. He also came to Geneva and received its hospitality.

§ 175. *Beza's Last Days.*

Beza's life was now drawing to its close. The weight of years had become a grievous burden. His bodily powers gradually deserted him. He partially lost his hearing. His memory became so enfeebled that the past only remained to him, while recent events made no lasting impression. It was the breaking up of an extraordinarily vigorous constitution, which had so supported him for sixty-five years that he had scarcely known what it was to be sick. Then he took the prudent course of giving up one by one the duties which he had so long discharged. In 1586 he was excused from preaching daily, and henceforth till 1600 preached only on Sunday. In 1598 he retired from active duty in the Acad-

emy, and sold his library, giving part of the proceeds, which
were considerable, to his wife, and part to the poor.   In 1600
he rendered his last public services in the Academy, and
preached his last sermon — the only one preached in the
seventeenth, by a reformer of the sixteenth, century.[1]

Occasionally something of the old wit flashed forth.   As
when he made his reply to the silly rumor that he had
yielded to the argumentation of François de Sales and had
gone over to Rome.   The facts are these : François came to
Geneva in 1597 with the express purpose of converting Beza.
He was then thirty years old, very zealous, very skilful, and
in many other cases had been successful.   But he met his
match in the old Reformer, who however listened to him
courteously.   What argument failed to accomplish, the priest
thought money might do, and so he offered Beza in the name
of the pope a yearly pension of four thousand gold crowns
and a sum equal to twice as much as the value of all his
personal effects !   This brought matters to a climax, and Beza
dismissed him with the polite but sarcastic and decisive
rebuke, " Go, sir ; I am too old and too deaf to be able to
hear such words." [2]

But from some quarter the report got abroad that Beza had
yielded.   This was added to as it passed along until it was
confidently asserted that Beza and many other former Genevan Protestants were on their way to Rome to enter the
papal fold.   Their very route was told, and on an evening in
the middle of September, 1597, the faithful people of Siena
waited by the gate of their city to receive the great leader !
But for some reason he did not come.   Then it was said that
he was dead ; but that ere he died he had made his peace
with the Church and had received extreme unction.

When the friends of Beza heard these idle tales, they merely
smiled.   But Beza concluded to give convincing proof of two
facts : first, that he was not dead, and second, that he was

---

[1] Heppe, 307.   [2] Ibid. 314.

still a Protestant of the straitest Calvinistic school; and so quite in the old manner he nailed the lie by a biting epigram.

When in 1600 François would hold a public discussion with the Genevans, Beza, knowing how unprofitable such discussions were, forbade it. Whereupon it was given out that the Reformers were afraid to meet their opponents!

Another flare of the old flame of poetry was occasioned by the visit from King Henry IV., already alluded to. It was a poem of six stanzas, *Ad inclytum Franciæ et Navarræ regem Henricum IV.* ("to the renowned King of France and Navarre, Henry IV.") "It was his last, his swan song." [1]

Wearied by the vigils of a perilous and exciting time, Beza had long anxiously looked for his final rest. He had fought a good fight and had kept the faith and was ready to receive his crown. On Sunday, Oct. 13, 1605, he died.

In his will [2] Beza ordered his burial to be in the common cemetery of Plain Palais, where Calvin was buried, and near the remains of his wife. But in consequence of a Savoyard threat to carry off his body to Rome, by order of the magistrates, he was buried in the cloister of the cathedral of St. Peter, in the city of Geneva.

Of the six great Continental Reformers, — Luther, Melanchthon, Zwingli, Bullinger, Calvin, and Beza, — Beza was the most finished gentleman, according to the highest standard of his time. He was not lacking in energy, nor was he always mild. But he was able to hold court with courtiers, be a wit with wits, and show classical learning equal to that of the best scholars of his age. Yet with him the means were only valued because they reached an end, and the great end he had ever in mind was the conservation of the Reformed Church of Geneva and France.

His public life was an extraordinary one. Like the Apostle Paul he could say that he had been "in journeyings often,

---

[1] Heppe, 310.
[2] Given at length in a German translation by Heppe, 304–306.

in perils of rivers, in perils of robbers, in perils from my own countrymen, in perils in the city, in perils in the wilderness, in perils among false brethren; in labor and travail, in watchings often, in hunger and thirst, in fastings often, in cold and nakedness. Besides those things that are without, there is that which presseth upon me daily, anxiety for all the churches" (2 Cor. 11:26-28). It was indeed a brilliant service which this versatile man rendered. Under his watchful care the city of Geneva enjoyed peace and prosperity, the Academy flourished and its students went everywhere preaching the Word, while the Reformed Church of France was built up by him. Calvin lived again and in some respects lived a bolder life in his pupil and friend.

It is pleasant to get glimpses of Beza's home life. Men like him are seldom able to enjoy their homes. But Beza had for forty years the love and devotion of the wife of his youth. They had no children, but his fatherly heart may have found some expression in adopting his wife's niece Genevieve Denosse, whom he educated with great care, and also in his parental solicitude for his brother's children. It is perhaps to be taken as indicative of the domestic character of the man that, on the advice of friends, within a year after his wife died (1589), he married Catherine del Piano, a widow of a Genevese. He also adopted her grand-daughter. It is probable that he always lived in some state; at all events his will proves that he had considerable property.

§ 176. *Beza's Writings.*

Beza's name will ever be most honorably associated with biblical learning. Indeed, to many students his services in this department will constitute his only claim to notice. Every one who knows anything of the uncial manuscripts of the Greek New Testament has heard of the Codex Bezæ, or of the history of the printed text of the New Testament has heard of Beza's editions and of his Latin translation with notes. The Codex Bezæ, known as D in the list of the uncials, also as Codex Cantabrigiensis, is a manuscript of the Gospels and Acts, originally also of the Catholic Epistles, dating from the sixth century.[1] Its transcriber would seem to have been a Gaul, ignorant of Greek. Beza procured it from the monastery of St. Irenæus, at Lyons, when the city was sacked by Des Adrets, in 1562, but did not use it in his edition of the Greek Testament, because it departed so widely from the other manuscripts, which departures are often supported by the ancient Latin and Syriac versions. He presented it to the University of Cambridge in 1581, and it is now shown in the library among the great treasures.

Beza was also the possessor of an uncial manuscript of the Pauline Epistles, also dating from the sixth century. How he got hold of it is unknown. He merely says (Preface to his 3d ed. of the N. T., 1582) that it had been found at Clermont, near Beauvais, France. It may have been another fortune of war. After his death it was sold, and ultimately came into the Royal (now the National) Library in Paris, and there it is preserved.[2] Beza made some use of it. Both these manuscripts were accompanied by a Latin version of extreme antiquity.

Among the eminent editors of the Greek New Testament, Beza deserves prominent mention. He put forth four folio editions of Stephen's Greek text; viz. 1565, 1582, 1589, with a Latin version, the Latin Vulgate, and Annotations. He issued also several octavo editions with his Latin version, and brief marginal notes (1565, 1567, 1580, 1590, 1604).[3]

What especially interests the English Bible student is the

---

[1] A very full description of it is given by Scrivener, *Introduction to the Criticism of the New Testament*, 3d ed. 120–127; *cf.* Gregory, *Prolegomena in N. T. Tischendorfianum ed. viii. maior*, 369–374; Schaff, *Companion to the Greek Testament*, 122–124.

[2] For full description, see Scrivener, *ibid.* 163–166; *cf.* Gregory, *ibid.* 419–422.

[3] Schaff, *ibid.* 237–238, and his tract on the *Revision of the N. T.*, p. 28 sq.

close connection he had with the Authorized Version. Not only were his editions in the hands of King James' revisers, but his Latin version with its notes was constantly used by them. He had already influenced the authors of the Genevan version (1557 and 1560), as was of course inevitable, and this version influenced the Authorized. As Beza was undoubtedly the best Continental exegete of the closing part of the sixteenth century, this influence of his Latin version and notes was on the whole beneficial. But then it must be confessed that he was also responsible for many errors of reading and rendering in the Authorized Version.[1]

Beza was the chief theologian of the Reformed Church after Calvin. Principal Cunningham has shown[2] the part Beza played in bringing about the transition from the original Calvinism to the scholastic form, hard and mechanical, and so unconsciously preparing the way for the great reaction from Calvinism, viz. Arminianism; for Arminius had been a student in the Genevan Academy under Beza. Beza drew up in the form of a chart a curious scheme of a system of theology, and he published it in his *Tractationes* (mentioned below) along with a commentary, *Summa totius Christianismi sive descriptio et distributio causarum salutis electorum et exitii reproborum, ex sacris literis collecta et explicata*, pp. 170 sqq. Heppe reprints the chart.

The chief work published by Beza, though not acknowledged by him, is the famous and invaluable *Histoire ecclésiastique des Églises Réformées au royaume de France*, originally issued at Antwerp in 1580, 3 vols. 8vo. The

---

[1] The late Ezra Abbot, the biblical textual critic, at Dr. Schaff's request, made a very careful collation of the different editions of Beza with the Authorized Version, and found that "the Authorized Version agrees with Beza's text of 1589 against Stephen's of 1550 in about ninety places; with Stephen's against Beza in about forty; and in from thirty to forty places, in most of which the variations are of a trivial character, it differs from both." Schaff: *The Revision of the English Version of the New Testament*, New York, 1873 (Introd. p. xxviii). *Cf.* Farrar, *History of Interpretation*, p. 342, note 3.

[2] See his *Reformers* (pp. 345–413) mentioned at the head of this chapter.

best edition of which is that by Baum (d. 1881), Cunitz (d. 1886), and Rodolphe Reuss, Paris, 1883–89, 3 vols. small quarto. It is well known to scholars that the first four books are in a great degree composed of extracts from contemporaneous works, especially the *Histoire des Martyrs* by Crespin, and the *Histoire de l'estat de France*, attributed to Regnier de la Plancée, but no indication is given whence the extracts are taken. This defect in modern eyes is removed in the edition spoken of. The genesis of the work seems to be this, that Beza received reports from all parts of France in reply to the Synod's recommendation that the churches write their histories for the benefit of posterity, that he arranged these, and inserted much autobiographical matter, but as he had to employ unknown persons to assist him, he modestly refused to put his name to the book.

Beza's "Life of Calvin" was written in French, and immediately translated by himself into Latin (Geneva, 1565). It is the invaluable, accurate, and sympathetic picture of the great Reformer by one who knew him intimately and revered him deeply. It has been constantly used in the former chapters of this volume. It is by far the best of the contemporary biographies of any of the Reformers.

Beza collected his miscellanies under the title *Tractationes theologicæ*, Geneva, 1570, 2d ed. 1582, 3 vols. folio. In these volumes will be found united his chief essays, including the *De hæreticis à civili magistratu puniendis, adversus M. Bellium* (I. 85–169), already analyzed. The first part was reprinted as late as 1658 under the new title *Opuscula, in quibus pleraque Christianæ religionis dogmata adversus hæreses nostris temporibus renovatas solide ex verbo Dei defenduntur.*

In 1573 he published a curious volume of correspondence on theological subjects, *Epistolarum Theologicarum.* The letters are written to different persons and are variously dated from 1556 to 1572. The volume is printed in small italics and was so popular that the third edition appeared at Hanover in 1597. But the number of his letters published is greatly exceeded by those still in manuscript.

In 1577 he published *Lex Dei, moralis, ceremonialis, et politica, ex libris Mosis excerpta, et in certas classes distributa.* This is simply the legal portions of the Pentateuch classified, without note or comment, apparently under the theory that the Mosaic law is still binding.

In 1581 Beza, in connection with Daneau and Salnar, issued the *Harmonia Confessionum Fidei*, designed to promote Christian union among the evangelical churches.[1]

Mention has already been made of Beza as a poet. His *Poëmata*, Paris, 1548, commonly called *Juvenilia*, consists of epigrams, epitaphs, elegies, and bucolics. They are classical in expression, and erotic in sentiment, though not so vicious as such a libeller as Bolsec would have us believe. His *Abraham's Sacrifice*, already alluded to, was written in French (Geneva, 1550), and translated into Italian (Florence, 1572), English (London, 1577), and Latin (Geneva, 1597). It was republished along with the *Poëmata*, Geneva, 1597. Of much more importance is his translation of the Psalms, completing that begun by Clément Marot. It was undertaken at Calvin's request, and published in sections, and finished at Geneva in 1560.

[1] See Schaff, *Creeds*, I. 354; II. 193 sqq.

JACOBUS FABER, Stapulensis.

Reformationis Gallicanæ Prodromus,
m. 1537.

APPENDIX.

LITERATURE ON THE REFORMATION IN FRANCE.

Comp. the literature in § 58, pp. 223–230; and Schaff's *Creeds of Christendom*, vol. I. 490 sq.

The best libraries on the history of Protestantism in France are in Paris (*Société de l'histoire du Protestantisme français*, 54 rue des Saint-Pères), Geneva, Zürich, Basel, and Strassburg. The most important works are in the library of the Union Theological Seminary at New York.

I. Ecclesiastical History of Protestantism in France.

* A. L. Herminjard: *Correspondance des Réformateurs dans les pays de langue française.* Genève and Paris, 1866–1886. 7 vols. From 1512 to 1542. To be continued.

* Calvin's Correspondence from 1528 to his death in 1564, in his *Opera*, vols. X.–XX.

[* Theodore Beza]: *Histoire ecclésiastique des églises réformées au royaume de France,* from the beginning of the Reformation to the first civil war (1521–1563). Anvers, 1580, 3 vols.; Toulouse, 1882, in 2 vols.; best ed. by Baum, Cunitz, and Rodolphe Reuss, with ample commentary and bibliographical notices. Paris (Fischbacher), 1883–1889, 3 vols. Part of *Les Classiques du Protestantisme français, XVIᵉ, XVIIᵉ, et XVIIIᵉ siècles,* published with the patronage of the *Société de l'histoire du Protestantisme français.*

This work was formerly ascribed to Beza, but is a compilation by several anonymous authors under the direction and with the co-operation of Beza. Some portions are literally borrowed from Crespin's "Martyrology." Senebier thinks that the first part was prepared by Beza, the other two under his direction. See Soldan, I. 88; Heppe, *Theod. Beza,* p. 382 sq.; *La France Prot.* (2d ed.), II. 535; and especially the *notice bibliographique,* etc., of R. Reuss in the third volume of Baum's edition.

* Jean Crespin (a friend of Beza and publisher in Geneva; d. 1572): *Livre des martyrs (Acta Martyrum), depuis le temps de Wiclif et de Jean Hus jusqu'à présent,* 1554. Latin ed.: *Acta Martyrum,* or *Actiones et Monimenta Martyrum,* etc. 1st ed. 1556. Enlarged edition, Genève, 1619, 2 vols. fol.; Amsterd., 1684. Several French, Latin, Dutch, English, and German editions. See Polenz, *Gesch. des franz. Calvinismus,* I. 723–735, and *La France Protest.,* IV. 885–910. Latest and best edition, under the title *Histoire des martyrs persecutez et mis à mort pour la vérité de l'Évangile depuis le temps des apostres jusqu'à présent* (1619), Toulouse, 1889. 3 large vols. 8vo. With notes, etc., by M. Lelièvre.

FLORIMOND DE RAEMOND (Rom. Cath.): *L'histoire de la naissance, progrès et décadence de l'hérésie de ce siècle.* Paris, 1610.

LOUIS MAIMBOURG (Jesuit historian and controversialist, 1620–1686): *Histoire du calvinisme.* Paris, 2d ed., 1682, 2 vols. 12mo. He presents Calvinism as the direct road to atheism. Calvin's doctrine of predestination, he says, (I. 110) "*détruit absolument toute l'idée qu'on doit avoir de Dieu, et ensuite conduit tout droit à l'Athéisme.*"

PETER JURIEU (Protestant historian and controversialist, 1637–1713): *Histoire du Calvinisme et celle du Papisme mises en parallèle, ou apologie pour les réformateurs, pour la réformation, et pour les réformez.* Rotterdam, 1683. 3 vols. An answer to Maimbourg. He wrote also against Bossuet.

PIERRE BAYLE (sceptic): *Critique générale de l'histoire du calvinisme.* Rotterdam, 1684.

Bishop BOSSUET: *Histoire des variations des églises protestantes.* Paris, 1688. 2 vols. Several editions and translations — not historical, but polemical and partial. The ablest French work against Protestantism, containing arguments derived from its divisions and changes.

* ELIE BENOÎT (1640–1728): *Histoire de l'Édit de Nantes.* Delft, 1693–1695. 5 vols. 4to. English and Dutch translations. The first volume goes to the death of Henri IV. in 1610; vols. II., III., and IV. to 1683; vol. V. to 1688.

SERRANUS (JEAN DE SERRES, historiographer of France, 1540–1598): *Commentarii de statu religionis et reipublicæ in regno Galliæ,* 1571–1580 (five parts).

THEOD. AGRIPPA D'AUBIGNÉ (ALBINÆUS), a Huguenot in the service of Henry IV.; d. at Geneva, 1630): *Histoire universelle* (from 1550 to the end of the sixteenth century). Maillé, 1616–1620. 3 vols. Amsterd. (Geneva), 1626, 2 vols. Also in his *Œuvres complètes,* Paris, 1873.

PHILIPPE DU PLESSIS-MORNAY: *Mémoires.* Paris, 1624–1625, 2 vols. 4to; Amsterd., 1651. *Mémoires et Lettres.* Paris, 1824. 12 vols. Mornay was the most accomplished and influential Protestant nobleman of his age, a fertile author, soldier, diplomatist, and statesman, who lived under six reigns from Henry II. to Louis XIII. — Mme. DU PLESSIS-MORNAY: *Mémoires et Correspondance.* Paris, 1868. 2 vols. On the life of her husband.

JEAN AYMON (d. 1712): *Tous les synodes nationaux des églises réformées de France.* La Haye, 1710. 2 vols. 4to.

* JOHN QUICK (a learned Non-conformist, d. 1706): *Synodicon in Gallia reformata; or the Acts, Decisions, and Canons of the National Councils of the Reformed Churches in France.* London, 1692. 2 vols. fol. (with a history of the Church till 1685). Much more accurate than Aymon.

E. A. LAVAL: *Compendious History of the Reformation in France . . . to the Repealing of the Edict of Nantes.* London, 1737–1741. 7 vols. 8vo.

W. S. BROWNING: *A History of the Huguenots.* 1829–1839. 3 vols. 8vo. Reprinted at Philadelphia (Lea & Blanchard), 1845.

EDWARD SMEDLEY (d. 1836): *History of the Reformed Religion in France.* London, 1832–1834. 3 vols. 12mo. Reprinted New York (Harper & Bros.).

CHARLES COQUEREL (1797–1851): *Histoire des églises du Désert chez les Protestants de France depuis la fin du règne de Louis XIV. jusqu'à la révolution française.* Paris, 1841. 2 vols. 8vo. New ed. 1857.

N. Peyrat: *Histoire des pasteurs du Désert.* Paris, 1842. 2 vols. 8vo.

Guill. de Félice (Prof. at Montauban, d. 1871): *Histoire des protestants de France.* Toulouse, 1851; with supplement by F. Bonifas, 1874. English translation by Lobdell, 1851. By the same: *Histoire des synodes nationaux des églises réformées de France.* Paris, 1864.

C. Drion: *Histoire chronologique de l'église protestante de France jusqu'à la Révocation.* Paris, 1855. 2 vols. 12mo.

*W. G. Soldan: *Geschichte des Protestantismus in Frankreich bis zum Tode Karl's IX.* Leipzig, 1855. 2 vols. *Frankreich und die Bartholomäusnacht,* 1854. The same, translated by Charles Schmidt: *La France et la St. Barthélemy.* Paris, 1855. 147 pp.

E. Stähelin: *Der Uebertritt Heinrich's IV.* Basel, 1856. (The change of Henry IV. was dictated by political and patriotic motives to secure himself on the throne, to give peace to France, and liberty to the Huguenots.)

*G. von Polenz: *Geschichte des französischen Calvinismus bis zur National-versammlung i. J. 1789, zum Theil aus handschriftl. Quellen.* Gotha, 1857–1869. 5 vols. 8vo.

*Eugène and Émile Haag (brothers): *La France protestante.* Paris, 1856 sqq. 10 vols.; 2d ed. revised, published under the auspices of the "Société de l'histoire du Protestantisme français," and under the direction of Henri Bordier, Paris (Sandoz et Fischbacher), 1877 sqq. Biographies of distinguished Huguenots in alphabetical order. Very important. So far (till 1888) 6 vols. (The sixth volume ends with *Gasparin.*)

E. Castel: *Les Huguenots et la Constitution de l'église réformée de France en 1559.* Paris and Geneva, 1859. 16mo.

J. M. Dargaud: *La Liberté religieuse en France.* Paris, 1859. 4 vols. 8vo.

H. de Triqueti: *Les premiers jours du Protestantisme en France depuis son origine jusqu'au premier synode national de 1559.* Paris, 1859. 16mo (302 pp.). Popular.

Henri Lutteroth: *La Réformation en France pendant sa première période.* Paris, 1859. 8vo (233 pp.).

*Merle d'Aubigné: *Histoire de la Réformation en Europe au temps de Calvin.* Paris, 1862–1878. English translation by William L. R. Cates. London (Longmans, Green, & Co.), 1863–1878. 8 vols. (Republished by the Carters in New York.) This great work comes down to 1542, and embraces the Reformation in French Switzerland, France, England, Scotland, and Spain. The author intended to carry it down to the death of Calvin, 1564, but died (1872) before he completed it.

H. White: *Massacre of St. Bartholomew.* London, 1868. 8vo. New York, 1868.

F. Puaux: *Histoire de la Réformation française.* Paris, 1868. 7 vols. 12mo.

W. M. Blackburn: *Admiral Coligny and the Rise of the Huguenots.* Philadelphia, 1869. 2 vols. 8vo.

Adolphe Schaeffer: *Les Huguenots du seizième siècle.* Paris, 1870. (331 pp.).

*W. Henley Jervis: *A History of the Church of France, from the Concordat of Bologna, A.D. 1516, to the Revolution.* London, 1872. 2 vols. 8vo. pp. xxiv, 476, xi, 452.

Felix Bovet: *Histoire du psautier des églises réformées.* Neuchâtel, 1872.

* O. Douen: *Clément-Marot et le Psautier Huguenot.* Paris, 1878 sq. 2 vols. (à l'imprimerie nationale). Very important for the history of worship in the French Reformed Church, with a history of Marot and his relation to Calvin. The second volume contains *les harmonistes du Psautier,* a discussion of the influence of the Reformation on music, the Psalms of Goudimel, and the French bibliography on the Psalter.

O. Douen: *Les premiers pasteurs du Désert* (1685–1700) *d'après des documents pour la plupart inédits.* Paris (Grassart), 1879. 2 vols. 8vo.

* Henri Bordier: *La Saint-Barthélemy et la critique moderne.* Genève and Paris, 1879 (116 pp., with illustrations).

Jules Delaborde: *Gaspar de Coligny, Amiral de France.* Paris (Fischbacher), 1879. 3 vols.

* Henry M. Baird (Professor in the University of the City of New York): *History of the Rise of the Huguenots of France* (1515–1574). New York, 1879. 2 vols. 8vo. *The Huguenots and Henry of Navarre* (1574–1610). New York, 1886. 2 vols. 8vo. *The Edict of Nantes and its Recall.* In the "Commemoration of the Bi-centenary of the Revocation of the Edict of Nantes" (Oct. 22, 1885), by the Huguenot Society of America. New York, 1886.

E. Muhlenbeck: *Claude Rouget. Une église Calviniste au XVIᵐᵉ siècle (1551–1581). Histoire de la communauté réformée de Ste-Marie-aux-Mines (Alsace).* Paris and Strasbourg, 1881 (515 pp.). 8vo.

H. Baumgarten: *Vor der Bartholomäusnacht.* Strassburg, 1882 (263 pp.).

Baron Kervyn de Lettenhove: *Les Huguenots et les Gueux* (1560–1585). Bruges, 1883–1885. 6 vols. Includes the contemporary history of the Netherlands. A very partial book.

Eugène Bersier (Reformed pastor in Paris, d. 1889): *Coligny avant les guerres de religion.* Paris, 1884.

Ernest Gaullieur (archiviste de la ville de Bordeaux): *Histoire de la réformation à Bordeaux et dans le ressort du parlement de Guyenne.* Bordeaux and Paris, 1884 sqq. The first vol. extends from 1523–1563.

Theo. Schott: *Die Aufhebung des Ediktes von Nantes im Oktober, 1685.* Halle, 1885. 8vo.

[Léon Pilatte]: *Édits, Déclarations et Arrests concernant la religion prétendue réformée, 1662–1751, précédés de l'Édit de Nantes.* Paris, 1885.

* L. Aguesse (d. 1862): *Histoire de l'établissement du Protestantisme en France contenant l'histoire politique et religieuse de la nation depuis François Iᵉʳ jusqu'à l'édit de Nantes.* Paris, 1886. 4 vols. A posthumous work of twenty years' labor, published by Charles Menetrier and Mme. Menetrier, *née* Aguesse.

* Edmond Hugues: *Antoine Court. Histoire de la restauration du Protestantisme en France,* Paris, 4th ed. revised, 1875, 2 vols. — *Les Synodes du Désert. Actes et règlements des synodes nationaux et provinciaux tenus au désert de France de l'an 1715 à l'an 1793.* Paris (Fischbacher), 1885–1886. 3 large vols. *Supplément au tome premier,* 1887.

N. Weiss (librarian and ed. of the Bulletin of the Soc. of the Hist. of French Prot.): *La chambre ardente, étude sur la liberté de conscience en France sous François Iᵉʳ et Henri II* (1540–1550) *suivie d'environ 500 arrêts inédits, rendus par le parlement de Paris de Mai 1547 à Mars 1550.* Paris, 1889 (432 pp.). 8vo.

PHILIP SCHAFF: *History of the Edict of Nantes.* An address delivered before the Huguenot Society of America, March 21, 1889. New York, 1890.

* CHARLES DARDIER: *Paul Rabaut: Ses lettres à Antoine Court* (1739–1755), Paris, 1884, 2 vols.; and *Ses Lettres à Divers* (1744–1794), *avec préface, notes et pièces justificatives.* Paris, 1892. 2 vols.

* *Bulletin historique et littéraire.* A monthly periodical published by the *Société de l'histoire du Protantisme français.* Paris (54 rue des Saints-Pères), 1853 sqq. (39e année, 1890). Contains historical studies and important documents of the sixteenth, seventeenth, and eighteenth centuries.

II. GENERAL HISTORIES OF FRANCE.

FRANCISCUS BELCARIUS PEGUILIO (BEAUCAIRE DE PEGUILLON, bishop of Metz): *Rerum Gallicarum Commentarii ab anno 1461 ad annum 1580.* Lugd. 1625 fol. 1026 pp. Strongly anti-Calvinistic.

Choix de chroniques et mémoires sur l'histoire de France, in the Pantheon littéraire of J. A. BUCHON. Paris, 1836–1838. 8 vols.

Nouvelle collection des mémoires pour servir à l'histoire de France, by PETITOT, MICHAUD, and POUJOULAT. 1re serie, tom. VI. Paris, 1839.

* THUANUS (JACQUES AUGUSTE DE THOU, 1553–1617): *Historiarum sui temporis libri 138,* from 1546–1607 (several editions in 5, 7, and 16 vols.). The author was a moderate Catholic, witnessed the massacre of St. Bartholomew, and helped to prepare the Edict of Nantes. His history was put in the Index Expurg. 1609, but survived the papal condemnation.

LACRETELLE: *Histoire de France pendant les guerres de religion.* Paris, 1814–1816. 4 vols.

SIMONDE DE SISMONDI: *Histoire des Français.* Par. 1821–1844. 31 vols. 8vo (from vol. XVI.).

* JULES MICHELET (1798–1876): *Histoire de France.* 1833–1862 (new ed. 1879). 14 vols. (Vols. IX. *La Renaissance;* X, *La Réforme;* XI. *Les Guerres de Religion.*)

Sir JAMES STEPHEN: *Lectures on the History of France.* 1857, 3d ed. 2 vols.

* LEOP. V. RANKE: *Französische Geschichte namentlich im 16. und 17. Jahrh.* Stuttgart and Tübingen, 1852–1868; 3d ed. 1877. 6 vols. (English translation in part, London, 1852. 2 vols.)

* HENRI MARTIN: *Histoire de France depuis les temps les plus reculés jusqu'en 1789.* Paris, 1837; 4th ed. 1854–1878. 17 vols. (vols. VIII.–X.)

* BORDIER and CHARTON: *Histoire de France.* Paris, 1858, 1872; nouvelle éd. 1881. 2 vols. with numerous illustrations. Gives very accurate information on the Protestant Reformation.

III. HISTORY OF THE HUGUENOT REFUGEES.

CHARLES WEISS (Prof. au lycée Bonaparte, d. 1881): *Histoire des réfugiés protestants de France depuis la révocation de l'édit de Nantes jusqu'à nos jours.*

Paris, 1853. 2 vols. English translation by W. H. Herbert. London and New York, 1854. 2 vols.

SAMUEL SMILES: *The Huguenots, their Settlements, Churches, and Industries in England and Ireland.* London, 1867 (Am. ed. with Appendix by G. P. Disosway, New York, 1867).

W. H. FOOTE (pastor of the Presbyterian Church, Romney, W. Va.): *The Huguenots; or, Reformed French Church; their principles delineated; their characters illustrated; their sufferings and successes recorded. In three parts. I. The Huguenot in France, at home. II. The Huguenot dispersed in Europe. III. The Huguenot at home in America.* With an Appendix. Richmond, 1870. pp. xx, 627.

DAVID C. A. AGNEW (of the Free Church of Scotland): *Protestant Exiles from France in the Reign of Louis XIV.; or, the Huguenot Refugees and their Descendants in Great Britain and Ireland.* 2d ed. (corrected and enlarged), 1871–1874. 3 vols. 3d ed. (remodelled and greatly enlarged), including the French-speaking refugees in former reigns. London and Edinburgh, 1886. 2 vols. pp. 457 and 548.

R. LANE POOLE: *A History of the Huguenots of the Dispersion at the Recall of the Edict of Nantes.* London, 1880.

CHARLES W. BAIRD (brother of Henry M. B.): *History of the Huguenot Emigration to America.* New York, 1885. 2 vols.

LE BARON F. DE SCHICKLER (President of the Soc. of the Hist. of French Protestantism): *Les églises du refuge en Angleterre.* Paris, 1892. 3 vols. (pp. 431, 536, 432).

HENRY TOLLIN (minister of the Huguenot Church in Magdeburg): *Geschichte des hugenottischen Refuges in Deutschland; Geschichte der französichen Colonieen der Provinz Sachsen,* Halle, 1892; *Geschichte der französichen Colonie von Magdeburg.* Magdeburg, 1893. 3 vols.

Geschichtsblätter des DEUTSCHEN HUGENOTTEN-VEREINS. Magdeburg, 1892 sq. (Ten numbers till 1893.) Historical sketches of Huguenot churches in Germany.

The *Proceedings* of the HUGUENOT SOCIETY OF LONDON of which three volumes, 8vo, have appeared (1885–1892) contain many historical papers of importance. Of the *Publications* of the same Society, six volumes, quarto, have appeared up to 1891. Vol. VI. contains the despatches of the Venetian ambassadors from France, 1560–1563.

Bulletin de la Commission de l'Histoire des Églises Wallonnes. The Hague. Five volumes, 8vo, have appeared (1885–1892). Contains many articles on French Protestant Church History.

The Publications of the HUGUENOT SOCIETY OF AMERICA. New York, 1886 sqq.

Lichtenberger's *Encyclopédie des Sciences Religieuses* (13 vols.) contains many good articles on French Protestantism, especially vol. V. 186–191.

ALPHABETICAL INDEX OF NAMES AND TOPICS.